Children's Thinking

Developmental Function and Individual Differences

Third Edition

David F. Bjorklund

Florida Atlantic University

Wadsworth
Thomson Learning™

Australia • Canada • Denmark • Japan • Mexico • New Zealand • Philippines • Puerto Rico
Singapore • South Africa • Spain • United Kingdom • United States

Psychology Editor: Stacey Purviance
Editorial Assistant: Amy Wood
Assistant Editor: Faith Stoddard
Project Editor: Trudy Brown
Print Buyer: Stacey Weinberger
Permissions Editor: Susan Walters
Publisher/Executive Editor: Vicki Knight
Production Service: Robin Gold / Forbes Mill Press

Copy Editor: Robin Gold
Cover Designer: Joan Greenfield
Cover Image: © TSM/Mug Shots; Tony Stone Images
Compositor: TBH Typecast
Cover and Text Printer/Binder:
    R. R. Donnelley & Sons, Crawfordsville

For permission to use material from this text,
contact us by
    Web: www.thomsonrights.com
    Fax: 1-800-730-2215
    Phone: 1-800-730-2214

Library of Congress Cataloging-in-Publication Data

Bjorklund, David F.
    Children's thinking : developmental function and individual
differences / David F. Bjorklund. — 3rd ed.
        p.   cm.
    Includes bibliographical references and index.
    ISBN 0-534-35660-5
    1. Cognition in children.   2. Individual differences in children.
I. Title.
BF723.C5B48   1999
1555.4'13—dc21   99-34362

This book is printed on acid-free recycled
paper.

For more information, contact
Wadsworth/Thomson Learning
10 Davis Drive
Belmont, CA 94002-3098
USA
www.wadsworth.com

International Headquarters
Thomson Learning
290 Harbor Drive, 2nd Floor
Stamford, CT 06902-7477
USA

UK/Europe/Middle East
Thomson Learning
Berkshire House
168-173 High Holborn
London WC1V 7AA
United Kingdom

Asia
Thomson Learning
60 Albert Street #15-01
Albert Complex
Singapore 189969

Canada
Nelson/Thomson Learning
1120 Birchmount Road
Scarborough, Ontario M1K 5G4
Canada

Contents

Preface

The field of cognitive development continues to be dynamic. Ideas and findings from a variety of areas combine to produce a picture of a developing child who is born prepared to make some sense of the world, but whose mind is also shaped by forces in the physical and social environment. This theme, of the continuous transaction between a child's biological constitution (including genetics) and his or her physical and social environment, continues to serve as a focus for the third edition. This book is still unique in that it deals with both developmental function and individual differences in children's thinking. But much is new and exciting in the field of cognitive development, and much of it is presented in the pages that follow.

The third edition, as did the first two, contains 14 chapters, but I have made some changes relative to the second edition. Both the second and third editions included chapters on Piaget's theory, information-processing approaches, perception, memory, language, representation, and social cognition; two chapters on intelligence; and an introductory chapter. One chapter omitted from the third edition is on emerging theories of cognitive development. The theories formerly presented in that chapter are now integrated in the chapter on Piaget (Chapter 4 "Piaget's Theory and the Neo-Piagetians) and in the chapter on information-processing approaches to cognitive development (Chapter 5). Most of the material from two former chapters, "Reading and Number Concepts" and "Culture, Schooling, and Cognition," have been combined into a single "new" chapter, "Schooling and Cognition" (Chapter 12).

There are two truly new chapters in this edition. Early in the book (Chapter 3), I introduce the sociocultural perspective of development. This perspective is rooted in the rediscovery of the work of the Soviet psychologist Lev Vygotsky, but it also appears in the developmental contextual approaches of such American psychologists as Richard Lerner and Barbara Rogoff. I tried to emphasize in the second edition the importance of taking a sociocultural perspective and that such a perspective is not at odds with the idea that children's cognitive development is strongly influenced by their biology. This point is made even clearer in this edition by the inclusion of this brief chapter, immediately following the Chapter 2, "Biological Bases of Cognitive Development."

The second new chapter is on problem solving and reasoning (Chapter 10). I added this chapter at the request of reviewers and people who have used the second edition. The omission of a chapter devoted to problem solving from the previous editions was obvious. I had never been overly enamored by the topic, so it was with some reluctance that I delved into the literature. What I found surprised me. There's much "new" and exciting in the well-worn area of children's problem solving, and I've tried to capture some of this excitement. I may even try an experiment or two in my own laboratory based on some of the ideas I gleaned while preparing this chapter.

I have also added a brief epilogue at the end of the book. In this epilogue, I identified seven "truths" about cognitive development, based on the research and theory presented in the preceding 14 chapters. These "truths" are actually themes introduced in Chapter 1, but themes can get easily lost while working one's way through the details of the subsequent 13 chapters. My goal with the epilogue was to show that the field of cognitive development does indeed tell a coherent story, even if it is sometimes difficult to follow when you are trying to master the intricacies of the specific topics within the field.

Much is also new in the "old" chapters. "Biological Bases of Cognitive Development" (Chapter 2) includes new research in the field of developmental cognitive neuroscience and evolutionary perspectives of cognitive development, including selectionist theories of development and cognition. As in the previous edition, the chapter is written for students who have no substantial background in biology. Although the book is written so that most of this chapter can be skipped without affecting readers' comprehension of the rest of the book, I strongly recommend that all students read at least the first section of Chapter 2, which introduces developmental models that deal seriously with the interaction of biological and environmental factors. Included are the developmental systems approach (or developmental contextualism) proposed by Gottlieb, Lerner, and others, and models from behavioral genetics, particularly Scarr and McCartney's genotype → environment theory. These perspectives provide models for thinking about how nature and nurture interact to produce the intellectually varied creatures that human infants and children become. I think even biophobic students will find these perspectives interesting (even if they don't fully agree with them).

Related to issues of biological influences on cognitive development are the ideas of neo-nativists and their detractors and what it means for something to be "innate." These ideas are introduced in the opening chapter, and the debate about just how much knowledge infants come into the world with is highlighted in several chapters, particularly those on perception (Chapter 6) and representation (Chapter 7). The past five years has seen an explosion of behavioral genetics research on intelligence, and this new work is discussed in Chapter 14, along with other fascinating research on the modifiability of the intelligence of seriously deprived children and of environmental factors that affect the development of cognition during childhood.

The chapter on language development (Chapter 9) has been reorganized, and a connectionist explanation of language development is presented along with the more traditional Chomskian perspective. The chapter on memory development (Chapter 8) has also been reorganized to give the reader a better feel for the importance of memory in children's everyday lives, as well as its significance on laboratory and school-type tasks. Neo-Piagetian theories have been included along with Piaget's theory (Chapter 4) to give the reader a better appreciation of underlying assumptions that many of these newer theories share with Piaget. Included in Chapter 4 is a discussion of the new "theory theories" of cognitive development, particularly as presented by Alison Gopnik and Andrew Meltzoff. Emergent literacy is discussed in Chapter 12, "Schooling and Cognition," as is a brief discussion of the "reading wars" between the phonics and whole-language perspectives.

I have included many examples of cultural differences and similarities in cognitive development. This is the focus of much of the chapter on the sociocultural perspective of cognitive development (Chapter 3), but cultural differences are also featured in the chapters on Piaget's theory, information processing, memory, language, and schooling and cognition. I have also included the often-controversial topic of gender differences in some chapters, notably in the chapters on perception, memory, language, social cognition, and schooling and cognition. Although always a politically "hot" topic, I think examining reliable gender differences can tell us something about development in general and about individual differences that are not gender related. I have tried to present these data and theories in a responsible and noninflammatory way; moreover, the dominant theme of this book is that biological and environmental effects interact in complex and dynamic ways, making any explanation of either biological or environmental determinism simply wrong.

In an effort to make the book a bit more readable for undergraduate students, I have reduced the number of citations. One result of this is that I fail to acknowledge many authors who made important contributions to the field, and I apologize for this. But on the plus side, I believe that this makes the text more readable and prevents the reference section from getting too large. There are about 100 fewer references in the third edition than there were in the second. Of the approximately 1600 references, about 550 of them (34%) are new, most of them presenting research and theory published in the past five years. Approximately 630 references that were in the second edition have been omitted from the third.

I have done my best to make this book readable. I have attempted to present complicated theory and data in an intellectually honest way and to be comprehensible (and, I hope, exciting) to advanced undergraduate and graduate students. I have provided examples of actual children whenever possible, although I have avoided making the book a list of cute stories devoid of theoretical concepts. I have also made liberal use of figures and tables (140 in total, 30% new to this edition) to support the text and to foster comprehension. I have sprinkled through the book several cartoons, which I find often make a point better than a couple of pages of text, and I have included about as many photographs, mainly to illustrate some procedure or apparatus.

I have kept several pedagogical features that I first introduced in the second edition. These include the "Key Terms and Concepts" and "Suggested Readings" sections at the end of each chapter, and a glossary at the end of the book. Key terms and their definitions are presented in the same order they were found in the chapter, and all terms are also presented alphabetically in the glossary. I provide a brief paragraph about each suggested reading to explain why each particular paper or book is worth perusing.

I've enjoyed writing this third edition and have learned a lot in the process. I hope that this book conveys the excitement I felt in discovering some of these new findings in the field of cognitive development. The book is not just about "what's new," however, but about the field as a whole, including classic studies from earlier decades. Although I have focused on the "new," I have attempted not to forget the "tried and true" research that still informs us about the nature of children's thinking today. And I have tried to make connections among different levels of analysis—macroprocesses and microprocesses, biology and environment, developmental function and individual differences—to provide a synthesis of the field of cognitive development. I have had great fun while doing this.

Acknowledgments

Anyone who writes a book such as this does so with much help from many people. My greatest gratitude goes to my wife, Barbara. Barbara provided constructive criticism on many chapters, while working on a textbook of her own—all in addition to being a supportive and understanding spouse. My deepest thanks and love go to Barbara, and I hope I can repay the debt.

I would like to thank my editors, Jim Brace-Thompson and Stacey Purviance, and the Wadsworth staff for all the work they did to keep this book on schedule. I also want to thank my students and colleagues for their comments on early versions of chapters, including Rhonda Douglas Brown, Susan Eagan, Cynthia Park, and Kristina Rosenblum. Finally, I would like to thank the conscientious professional reviewers for their consistently constructive comments:

Mark Alcorn, University of Northern Colorado
Phillip M. Clark, Ohio State University
John A. Dixon, Trinity University
Jane F. Gaultney, University of North Carolina–Charlotte
Rebecca J. Glover, University of North Texas
Catherine Harris, Boston University
Marian Heinrichs, University of Minnesota
Katherine Kipp, University of Georgia
John J. Rieser, Vanderbilt University

David F. Bjorklund
Fort Lauderdale, Florida

Children's Thinking

Developmental Function and Individual Differences

An Introduction to Cognitive Development

Basic Concepts in Cognitive Development
Cognition • *Development*

Some Issues in Cognitive Development
Stages of Development • *Domain-General versus Domain-Specific Abilities*
Nature and Nurture • *The Stability and Plasticity of Intelligence*

Changes That Occur in Cognitive Development
Changes in Representation • *Changes in Intentional Control*

Overview of the Remainder of the Book

Summary

Key Terms and Concepts

Suggested Readings

Intelligence is our species' most important tool for survival. Evolution has provided other species with greater speed, coats of fur, camouflage, or antlers to help them adapt to changing environments. Human evolution is different. It has provided us with powers of discovery and invention by which we change the environment or develop techniques for coping with environments we cannot change. Although we are not the only thinkers in the animal kingdom, no other species has our powers of intellect. How we think and the technological and cultural innovations afforded by our intellect separate us from all other species and, as a result, have altered the principles of natural selection that govern the evolution of life on this planet.

This remarkable intelligence does not arise fully formed in the infant, however. Because human intelligence is flexible, we require substantial experience to master the cognitive feats that typify adult thinking, and we spend the better part of two decades developing an adult nervous system. Little in the way of complex thought patterns is built into the human brain, ready to go at birth, although biology obviously predisposes us to develop the ability for complex thought. Our mental prowess develops gradually over childhood, changing in quality as it does.

I will examine two aspects of cognitive development in this book: **developmental function** and **individual differences.** In the present context, *developmental function* refers to the form that cognition takes over time—to age-related differences in thinking. What are the mental abilities of infants? What is a 2-year-old's understanding of numbers, words, and family relations? What about that of a 4- or 6-year-old? How do school-age children and adolescents conceptualize cause and effect? How do they evaluate the relative worth of two products in the grocery store? People concerned with developmental function are usually interested in universals — what is true about the course and causes of development for all members of the species. I should actually rephrase this to "what is generally true about the course of development for all members of the species," for clearly there is substantial variation. Assessments of developmental function, then, are

typically based on averages, with individual variations among children being seen as unimportant.

But we all know that at some level this variation *is* important. Our impressive intellectual skills are not uniform among members of the species. Some people at every age make decisions more quickly, perceive relations among events more keenly, or think more deeply than others. How can these differences best be described and conceptualized? What is the nature of these differences? Once differences have been established, to what extent can they be modified? Will differences observed in infancy and early childhood remain stable, or are some intellectual differences limited to a particular time during development? There is also substantial variability in cognitive functioning *within* any given child. A particular 4-year-old will often show a wide range of behaviors on very similar tasks, depending on the context that he or she is in. Increasingly, developmental psychologists have come to realize the significance of individual differences and variability in cognitive performance among and within people of a given age and to see these variations as providing interesting and important information about developmental outcomes.

Although the people who study individual differences in thinking have traditionally not been the same people who study developmental function (Cronbach, 1957), the picture is changing, and I will attempt, where possible, to integrate the two concepts. Individual differences, like thought itself, have developmental histories, making the relationship between developmental function and individual differences a dynamic one. That is, individual differences do not simply constitute genetic or "innate" characteristics of a child, but emerge as children develop, often showing different manifestations at different times in development. Several chapters in this book are devoted exclusively to examining individual differences. In other chapters, individual differences in intellectual abilities are discussed in conjunction with the developmental function of those same abilities. The concept of within-child variability appears throughout the book.

In this first chapter, I introduce the topic of cognitive development — how thinking changes over time. In addition to describing developmental and individual differences in cognition, scientists who study children's thinking are also concerned with the mechanisms that underlie cognition and its development. How do biological (genetic) factors interact with experiences in the physical and social world to yield a particular pattern of development? Do children develop all their intellectual skills uniformly, or do some skills develop at faster rates than others? Is development relatively continuous and gradual over childhood, or are there major disruptions in its course? These and other issues are introduced in this chapter. Before delving too deeply into these issues, however, I need to define some basic terms. These definitions are followed by a look at some issues that have dominated the field of cognitive development during the last century and other issues that concern the contemporary scientist.

Basic Concepts in Cognitive Development

Cognition

Cognition refers to the processes or faculties by which knowledge is acquired and manipulated. Cognition is usually thought of as being mental. That is, cognition is a reflection of a mind. It is not directly observable. We cannot see the process whereby an 8-month-old discovers that the Mickey Mouse doll hidden under the blanket continues to exist even though it is out of his sight; nor can we directly assess the steps a 7-year-old child takes to compute the answer to the problem $15 - 9 = ?$. Although we cannot see or directly measure what underlies children's performance on these and other tasks, we can infer what is going on in their heads by assessing certain aspects of their behavior. That is, cognition is never measured directly but is inferred from the behaviors we can observe.

What psychologists can observe and quantify are things such as the number of words children remember from a list of 20, the number of seconds it takes to identify well-known pictures or words, or the

amount of time 6-month-olds spend looking at a picture of a familiar face relative to an unfamiliar one. For the most part, cognitive developmentalists are not interested in these overt, countable behaviors. What they *are* interested in, however, are the processes or skills that underlie these behaviors. What mental operations does a 6-year-old engage in that are different from those performed by a 4-year-old or an 8-year-old? How does speed in identifying words reflect how information is stored in the minds of children of different ages? What kind of mental picture has the infant formed of the familiar face of his mother that allows him to tell her face apart from all other faces? How are such mental pictures created? How are they modified?

This is not to say that cognitive psychologists are unconcerned with societally important phenomena such as reading, adding numbers, or communicating effectively. Many are, and they have developed research programs aimed at fostering in children these and other intellectual skills critical for success in a technological society. But the behaviors themselves are seen as secondary. What is important and what needs to be understood are the mechanisms that underlie performance. By discovering the mental factors that mediate intelligent behavior, we can better understand that behavior and its development, which in turn can help us better understand children.

Cognition includes not only our conscious and deliberate attempts at solving problems but also the unconscious and nondeliberate processes that are involved in routine daily tasks. We are not aware of the mental activity that occurs when we recognize a familiar tune on the radio or even when we read the morning paper. Yet, much in the way of cognitive processing is happening. Reading for most of us has become nearly automatic. We can't drive by a billboard without reading it. It is something we just do without giving it any "thought." But the mechanisms involved in reading are complex, even in the well-practiced adult.

Cognition involves mental activity of all types, including activity that is geared toward acquiring, understanding, and modifying information. Cognition includes such activities as developing a plan for solving a problem, executing that plan, and evaluating the success of the plan, making modifications as needed. These can be thought of as higher-order processes, or macromechanisms of cognition, which are often available to consciousness (that is, we are aware that we're doing them). Cognition also involves the initial encoding of a stimulus (that is, deciding how to define a physical stimulus so it can be thought about) and classifying what kind of thing it is ("Is this a letter, a word, a picture of something familiar?"). These can be thought of as basic processes, or micromechanisms of cognition, that occur outside of consciousness (we experience the product but are unaware of the process).

Cognition, then, reflects knowledge and what one does with it, and the main point of this book is that cognition develops.

Development

Change over Time

Development refers to changes in structure or function over time. **Structure** refers to some substrate of the organism, such as nervous tissue, muscle, or limbs, or—in cognitive psychology—the mental knowledge that underlies intelligence. When speaking of cognitive development, we use structure to mean some hypothetical mental construct, faculty, or ability that changes with age. For example, children's knowledge of terms such as *dog*, *lion*, and *zebra* could be construed as existing in some sort of mental structure, with the meanings of these words changing over time. Or we could hypothesize some form of mental organization that permits children to place objects in serial arrays according to height.

In contrast to structure, **function** denotes actions related to a structure. These include actions external to the structure being studied, such as neurochemical or hormonal secretions, and other exogenous factors that can best be described as "experience"—that is, external sources of stimulation. Function can also be endogenous, or internal, to the structure itself—for example, the exercise of a muscle, the firing of a nerve cell, or the activation of a cognitive

process, such as retrieving from memory the name of your first-grade teacher or computing the answer to the problem $26 + 17 = ?$. With respect to cognitive development, function refers to some action by the child, such as retrieving the definition of a word from memory, making comparisons between two stimuli, or adding two numbers to arrive at a third.

Development is characteristic of the species and has its basis in biology. Its general course, therefore, is relatively predictable. By viewing development as a biological concept that is generally predictable across all members of the species, I do not mean to imply that experience and culture do not also play a role in development. During the last decade, developmental psychologists have become increasingly aware that a child's development cannot be described or understood outside of the context in which it occurs. Several "ecological" approaches to cognitive development have emerged recently (Ceci, 1996; Rogoff, 1990), stemming, in part, from the rediscovery of the work of the Soviet psychologist Lev Vygotsky (1978). Writing in the 1920s and 1930s, Vygotsky proposed a sociocultural view, emphasizing that development was guided by adults interacting with children, with the cultural context determining to a large extent how, where, and when these interactions would take place. There are many cultural universals, with children around the world being reared in socially structured, language-using groups, and thus some aspects of development are also universal. But many aspects of culture vary considerably among people, such as the available technology and how and when children are expected to learn the survival skills of their society (for example, formal schooling versus no formal schooling). Such differences can have considerable influence on how cognition develops.

Although not all cognitive developmental psychologists adhere to such a sociocultural perspective, nearly all recognize the importance of a child's culture in shaping his or her development. This does not contradict a belief that there are strong biological constraints on development. What it does is recognize that members of *Homo sapiens* are social animals and that it doesn't make sense to talk of human nature (or human development) independent of human culture.

Structure, Function, and Development

Development is usually conceived as a bidirectional relationship between structure and function, in which the activity of the structure itself and stimulation from the environment can contribute to changes in the structure, which in turn contribute to changes in how that structure operates. Function does more than just maintain a structure (that is, prevent atrophy); function is necessary for proper development to occur. Function is limited, of course, to the actions that structures are capable of performing. This bidirectional, or reciprocal, relationship between structure and function can be expressed as structure ↔ function.

The **bidirectionality of structure and function** can best be illustrated with work in embryology. Chick embryos, for example, display spontaneous movement before muscle and skeletal development is complete. Such movement obviously stems from the maturation of the underlying structures, in this case bones, muscle, and nervous tissue. When embryonic chicks are given a drug to temporarily paralyze them for as little as one to two days, deformations of the joints of the legs, toes, and neck develop, which in turn affect the subsequent movement of the limbs (Drachman & Coulombre, 1962). In other words, the spontaneous activity (function) of the skeletal structures is necessary for the proper development and functioning of the joints.

Let me provide an example of the bidirectional relationship between structure and function at the behavioral level. Individual differences in activity level are found in newborns and are believed to be biologically based (Phillips, King, & DuBois, 1978). A highly active toddler will make it difficult for her parents to confine her to a playpen, resulting in a child who has a greater number of experiences outside of her playpen than a less active child has. These experiences will presumably affect the child's developing intellect (structure), which in turn will affect that child's actions (function). Thus, inherent characteristics of the child (biological structures) influence her behavior, the experiences she has, the reactions of others to her—all of which influence the development of the child's underlying cognitive/behavioral structures, and so on.

The *functioning* of mental structures promote changes in the structures themselves. This view is most clearly reflected in the work of the Swiss psychologist Jean Piaget. He believed that the activity of the child (or of the child's cognitive structures) is a necessary condition for development to occur. That is, for structures to change, they must be active. It is the structures' making contact with the external world that is responsible, to a large extent, for their development. Such a viewpoint makes children important contributors to their own development. It is not simply the environment that is shaping children's intellects or a particular level of intellectual ability that has been dictated by genes, but an active interaction between thinking children and their world that is responsible for cognitive growth. (More will be said of Piaget's theory in Chapter 4.)

I think it is fair to say that all developmental psychologists agree there is a reciprocal, bidirectional influence between "structures" (be they physical, such as neurons, or hypothetical, such as cognitive structures) and the activity of those structures (that is, the child's behavior). There is still much room for debate concerning how various subsystems of the child (neuronal, behavioral, social) interact to produce development, but developmental psychologists agree that development must be viewed as a two-way street. Development is *not* simply the result of the unfolding of genetic sequences unperturbed by variations in environment (structure → function), nor the product of "experience" on a pliable child (function → structure). The concept of the bidirectionality of structure and function is central to developmental psychology and will be a theme throughout this book. A more in-depth discussion of bidirectional models of development, along with more examples, is provided in Chapter 2 in a discussion of the developmental systems approach.

The Adaptive Nature of Cognitive Immaturity

We usually think of development as something progressive—going from simple to more complex structures or behaviors, with children getting "better" or more "complete" over time. This is a wholly reasonable point of view, but such a perspective can cause us to interpret early or immature forms of cognition as merely less effective and incomplete versions of the adult model. Although this might be generally true, it is not always the case. Early or immature forms of development can serve some function of their own, adapting the infant or young child to his or her particular environment (Oppenheim, 1981). For example, young infants' relatively poor perceptual abilities might protect their nervous systems from sensory overload (Turkewitz & Kenny, 1982), preschool children's tendencies to overestimate their physical and cognitive skills might bolster their self-esteem (Bjorklund, Gaultney, & Green, 1993), and infants' slow information processing might prevent them from establishing intellectual habits early in life that will be detrimental later on when their life conditions are considerably different (Bjorklund & Green, 1992). The point I want to make here is that infants' and young children's cognitive and perceptual abilities might be well suited for their particular time in life rather than being just incomplete versions of the more sophisticated abilities they will one day posses (Bjorklund, 1997a). What we consider to be immature and ineffective styles of thought might sometimes have an adaptive value for the young child at that particular point in development and should not be viewed solely as "deficiencies."

Children's immature cognition can be seen as having an integrity and possibly a function of its own, rather than being seen only as something that must be overcome (Bjorklund, 1997a). Such a perspective can have important consequences not only for how we view development but also for education and remediation. Expecting children who are developmentally delayed or who have learning deficits to master "age-appropriate" skills might be counterproductive, even if possible. Young and delayed children's immature cognition might suit them for mastering certain skills; although attempting to "educate" them beyond their present cognitive abilities could result in advanced surface behavior, the general effectiveness of that behavior might be minimally or even detrimentally influenced, despite the considerable effort expended (Bjorklund & Schwartz, 1996; Goodman, 1992).

Some Issues in Cognitive Development

Most issues central to cognitive development are central to developmental psychology in general. For example, stages of development, the nature/nurture issue, and the stability of behavior over time are as significant to social and personality development as they are to cognitive development. Yet, each area of psychology has its own way of expressing these concerns and of defining the questions that stimulate research and theory. The following section introduces some of the issues key to cognitive development research.

Stages of Development

One issue that has been the source of great debate among cognitive developmentalists is the extent to which development is stagelike in nature. When speaking of children, we frequently refer to **stages.** The "terrible twos" is a stage reserved for 2-year-olds, and we speak of a stubborn child who refuses to wear anything but his "Godzilla" underwear as being in a stage—a stage we hope will be past by wash day. In everyday conversation, we use the term stage to refer to a period of time in which a child displays a certain type of thought or behavior. Stages during childhood are not permanent but are transitory times as a child makes his or her way to adulthood. Stages are related to age. When we see children engaging in behavior appropriate to a younger child, we often say that they have regressed to an earlier stage.

The epitome of stage theories in cognitive development belongs to Piaget. Piaget proposed four major stages of cognitive development. The earliest, which he called sensorimotor, typifies the hands-on problem solving of infants and toddlers. All later stages involve the use of mental symbols, permitting children to represent objects and ideas through symbols such as language. Differences between these later stages are somewhat more subtle than the drastic differences between the infant and the symbol user, but they reflect striking differences in the quality of thinking just the same. When an apple is divided into four pieces, for instance, a 4-year-old will probably think that the result is more apple. The 8-year-old knows that this notion is nonsense.

As will be seen in the remainder of this section and throughout this book, not all age-related changes reflect stages of development. In fact, some developmentalists would go as far as saying that no aspect of development is truly stagelike. But there is general agreement concerning what characteristics age-related changes must have for them to be considered indicative of stages. The disagreement lies not in what constitutes a stage but in whether or not development has these characteristics. John Flavell (1971) listed several attributes of stages, including these:

a. Stages entail qualitative rather than quantitative differences.
b. The change from one stage to another is relatively abrupt; in other words, development is discontinuous.
c. Children's thinking within a stage is relatively even, or *homogeneous*. That is, all stage-related skills are integrated with one another, resulting in homogeneity of cognitive function, or similar cognitive functioning across a wide range of tasks.

Let us briefly examine these characteristics of stages.

Qualitative versus Quantitative Differences

Stage theories are based on the belief that children's thinking in each stage is qualitatively different from that in earlier or later stages. **Qualitative differences** are those of type, or kind. These can be contrasted with **quantitative differences**, which are differences in things that can be counted. Contrast,

for example, the differences in how a 14-month-old and a 20-month-old play with a toy telephone. Most 14-month-olds play with the phone by seeing how it responds to them. They pull on the cord, pound indiscriminately on the buttons with their palms to hear the bell ring, and shake the receiver, swinging the rest of the toy around them. Most important to their play are the perceptual consequences of their actions on the toy. Within half a year, another approach to playing with this same toy can be observed. Most 20-month-old children recognize the phone as a toy that represents something else in the adult world, and they behave toward it accordingly. Although having few words, they pick up the receiver and "talk" into it, even though much of their talk is gibberish. They hold the phone to the ears of their parents, expecting them to play along and to say something into the phone. Even dogs and cats may be asked to play along with the phone game. The game can also be expanded to substitute other objects for the toy phone, such as a shoe or a banana. Underlying these differences in play are the ways in which children conceptualize objects and interact with them, and these differences seem to be qualitative in nature.

Problems arise when we try to define what constitutes a qualitative change. The difference between the perceptually based play of the 14-month-old and the symbolically based play of the 20-month-old certainly appears to be qualitative. The older child doesn't do more with the toy or do it faster than the younger child does; the entire nature of the play is different. The same can be said for the difference between the 4-year-old and the 8-year-old, who hold different beliefs about an apple as a function of how many pieces it is cut into. In other words, when one cannot see, on the surface, ways in which the different approaches to a problem vary quantitatively, they must vary qualitatively. Qualitative differences are subjective ("It certainly looks like a different type of behavior to me") and reflect our inability to describe the change in ways that can be easily quantified.

Yet, does the surface appearance of a qualitative change mean that the mechanisms underlying development also vary qualitatively in nature?

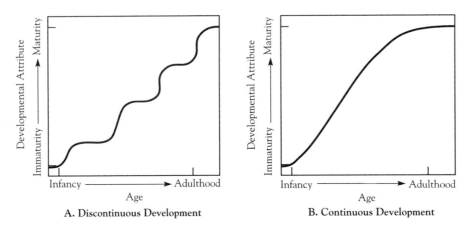

FIGURE 1-1   Stage, or discontinuity, theorists propose that development proceeds in a steplike fashion (a), with qualitative changes from one stage to the next occurring abruptly. Nonstage, or continuity, theorists propose that development proceeds in a continuous fashion (b), with quantitative changes occurring gradually over time.

Remember that cognition deals with unobservables. Behavior serves only as the outward manifestation of what we are really interested in. Perhaps, for instance, changes in the amount of information that children can consider at any one time are responsible for the drastically different behaviors observed in the 4-year-old and the 8-year-old described earlier. Four-year-olds know that 4 is greater than 2. They also know that any particular object can be divided into pieces and, in some cases, be put back together again. Yet, these are different pieces of knowledge, and coordinating them at one time requires greater memory capacity than they can muster. Or possibly it takes them so long to process one piece of information that by the time a second piece needs to be considered, it is too late. The first piece has been dealt with and is lost from their immediate memory. The 8-year-old, by comparison, can hold onto two thoughts at once and can think about things quickly enough that the first item of information is still available by the time the second piece comes into consciousness. Such changes in the amount of information that can be remembered and the speed with which that information can be processed are quantitative. It is possible that these or related quantitative changes, which can change gradually and in linear fashion, are responsible for

the apparent qualitative and nonlinear changes that are observed in overt behavior.

The issue of the extent to which cognitive development is qualitative or quantitative is much debated. Many argue that it is both (Flavell & Wohlwill, 1969). Surely many changes within a stage are quantitative in nature. A 30-month-old girl plays with the toy telephone in much the same way as the 20-month-old does, yet she uses more words and skills (such as knowing how to dial and to mimic real phone conversations) than does the younger child. The two children are doing the same type of thing, but the older child is doing it better. More controversial is whether the underlying causes of cognitive change are quantitative or qualitative.

Continuity versus Discontinuity

Stated simply, stage theories propose that changes from one stage to another are reasonably abrupt, representing **discontinuity** rather than **continuity.** According to these theories, there is not much transition period from one stage to the next, so the qualitatively different behaviors appear suddenly and function at maturity from their onset. Furthermore, all stage-related skills make the jump at once. Note that as defined here, discontinuity refers to a sudden

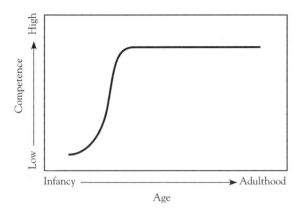

FIGURE 1-2 Some cognitive abilities mature early in life and are stable over the course of development, reflecting developmental invariance.

change in observed functioning and not necessarily to the changes that underlie the intelligent behavior. Figure 1-1 graphically illustrates the distinction between discontinuous (stagelike) development and continuous (nonstagelike) development.

The developmental patterns in Figure 1-1 reflect regular enhancements with age, regardless of whether such enhancements take the form of stagelike discontinuities or gradual and continuous changes. Children become more competent with age, reaching maturity in adolescence or early adulthood. Developmental function need not follow such a pattern, however, and some important aspects of cognitive development seem to take a very different course.

One alternative can be described as reflecting **developmental invariance** and is depicted in Figure 1-2. In this case, cognitive skill does not improve steadily over childhood, but reaches adult competence early in life and remains stable thereafter. Such a developmental function typifies many sensory capabilities that approach adult levels in infancy or early childhood. There has also been much speculation of late that some basic cognitive skills, such as the knowledge of the permanence of objects—for years believed to develop gradually during the first two years of life—have a much faster

onset. Some of these ideas and the research associated with them will be discussed in Chapter 7.

Other abilities can actually decline over childhood. For example, although infants can discriminate a wide range of language sounds, by adolescence this ability has declined and it becomes difficult for adolescents to hear many of the sounds produced in some foreign languages (see the discussion of infant phoneme discrimination ability and language acquisition in Chapter 9). And some aspects of development clearly do decline through adulthood and old age. For example, the speed with which people can process information shows a steady, age-related decline beginning in middle age (Kail & Salthouse, 1994). So there is no one developmental pattern; rather, different mental abilities show different patterns of change, depending on when during the life span they are observed.

Homogeneity of Cognitive Function

Stage theories propose that all stage-related functions are well integrated, so that how children solve one problem is similar to how they solve other problems. A 2-year-old acts like a 2-year-old in all she says and does, and an 8-year-old is every inch an 8-year-old in all of his activities. In other words, cognition is relatively uniform, or *homogeneous*, within an individual.

Many developmental psychologists would agree with the general statement that cognition is highly integrated within a given child at any one time. But development is not quite as even as some stage theories would have us believe. It is not unusual for a child to excel at one intellectual skill but be average or even below average at others. Some 6-year-olds, for example, seem to know all there is to know about dinosaurs: their eating habits, their approximate sizes, and the types of armament they had. These same children might find it difficult to remember their phone numbers or to brush their teeth every morning. Another child might do very well at reading and the language arts in general but have great difficulty in mastering the basics of mathematics. Motivation is certainly one reason for some discrepancies of these types. Yet, it is not uncommon to find less glaring differences in many children. Children, as well as adults, often have pockets of expertise that are seemingly inconsistent with the rest of their cognitive skills. Also, for any given skill, a single child can show great variability in the level at which that skill is displayed, depending on the specific context. Many stage theories have difficulty explaining these discrepancies. In general, there is substantial **homogeneity of cognitive function** but not quite as much as classic stage theorists propose. One task of cognitive development researchers is to explain how development can appear so even most of the time and for most tasks and yet so uneven at other times and for other tasks.

But how much homogeneity is necessary before one can comfortably declare that it's enough to warrant a stage? Unfortunately, psychologists do not agree on this point, and that's a problem. What one psychologist sees as evenness, and thus stagelike, another sees as uneven (or at least not even enough), thus violating one condition for "stageness." Also, how homogeneous a child's cognitive abilities are depends on where one looks (Flavell, 1982). First, a certain level of homogeneity is imposed by limits in children's information-processing capacity. Although a given child's cognitive skills can vary, there is a limit of cognitive sophistication beyond which he or she cannot function. This limit, presumably dictated by maturational factors, expands with age but, at any given point in development, restricts the range of cognitive competencies that a child can display (see Chapter 5 and a discussion of Fischer's theory in Chapter 4).

Second, the type of cognitive tasks psychologists tend to study are relatively demanding, and such challenging tasks might yield greater heterogeneity of function than would the more mundane tasks that constitute the vast majority of children's daily cognitive encounters. Children's cognition appears to be relatively even to an unobtrusive observer because most of the things children do are highly routinized. We see unevenness in their abilities primarily when children's cognitive competencies are pushed to their limits.

Third, there might be more homogeneity of function during the *initial* cognitive treatment of a

problem and more variability in how information is handled later in the task. For example, given a set of written problems to solve, most adults and older children begin by reading the problems, attempting to discern what the nature of the task will be. What happens after this "reading stage" is more likely to vary among individuals as a function of many factors. Similarly, when faced with a very difficult problem, children might adopt a "fall-back" strategy that they use consistently. For example, when given single-digit addition problems, children might resort to counting by ones on their fingers, even though they had solved the same problems just seconds earlier and could just "retrieve" the answer. In other words, how homogeneous cognitive function is seems to be a function of where one looks for it.

I do not want to give the impression, however, that stages are solely in the mind of the perceiver, although the concept is admittedly not well defined. To constitute a stage, the cognitive ability under study must go through discontinuous, qualitative changes, and related cognitive abilities must also be relatively even within a child at any single time. Based on this definition, some developmental changes seem clearly to be nonstagelike in nature, as we'll see throughout this book. However, other age-related changes come closer to fitting the bill for a stage. More important than labeling developmental change as being "stagelike" or not, is gaining an understanding of the nature of the change. Whether we choose to use the term "stage" to describe a pattern of change will influence how we think about development, but the pattern itself is important — not the name we give it.

Domain-General versus Domain-Specific Abilities

Stage theories assume that cognition is homogeneous, or even, for children within a stage. Implicit in such an assumption is that a general mechanism controls cognition across all domains. Thus, domain-general theories assume that at any point in time, a child's thinking is influenced by a single set of factors, with these factors affecting different aspects of cognition (that is, different domains of thought) equally. One does not need to be a stage theorist, however, to believe in **domain-general abilities.** Development can progress through quantitative mechanisms (for example, increased memory capacity, faster speed of processing), with such mechanisms affecting all aspects of cognition.

In contrast to domain-general accounts of cognitive development are theories that postulate **domain-specific abilities.** Knowing a child's ability for one aspect of cognition might tell us nothing about his or her level of cognitive ability for other aspects of thinking because different cognitive domains are controlled by different mind/brain functions. At the extreme, domain-specific theories propose that different areas of the brain affect different aspects of cognition, with these areas being unaffected by what goes on in other areas of the brain.

The idea of the independence of different cognitive functions is best reflected in the work of the philosopher Jerry Fodor (1983). Fodor proposed the concept of **modularity** in brain functions, meaning that certain areas of the brain are dedicated to performing specific cognitive tasks (such as processing language). These modules represent special-purpose systems that are "informationally encapsulated" (or "cognitively impenetrable," in the words of Pylyshyn, 1980), meaning that other parts of the mind/brain can neither influence nor access the workings of the module. Many modules are innate, part of the neural network an infant is born with and the result of millions of years of evolution; other modules can be developed as a result of experience and become encapsulated over time. Fodor proposed that the outputs of these modules become available to a central information processor (a domain-general mechanism) but the activity of this central processor does not affect the domain-specific modules.

Robbie Case (1992a) has put the controversy between domain-general and domain-specific theorists succinctly: "Is the mind better thought of as a general, all-purpose computing device, whose particular forte is general problem solving? Or is it better thought of as a modular device, each of whose modules has evolved to serve a unique biological function that it performs in its own unique and spe-

cialized way?" (p. 3). As we'll see in Chapters 4 and 5, the predominant theories of cognitive development throughout this century have been domain-general ones. Domain-specific theories have arisen primarily because of the failure of the domain-general theories to account for the heterogeneity of cognitive function that is frequently observed in development. Many of these will be discussed in Chapters 4, 5, and 7.

Some compromises between these two approaches are possible and likely necessary. For example, many researchers have shown that children think differently as a function of how much background knowledge they have in a particular domain. So, for example, chess experts show better memory spans for the positions of chess pieces than for sets of digits (Chi, 1978), and soccer experts show greater comprehension for soccer stories than for nonsoccer stories (Schneider, Körkel, & Weinert, 1989). Yet, such differences in cognitive performance as a function of background knowledge (that is, such domain-specificity) can be explained in terms of domain-general mechanisms. Children who are experts use less of their general information-processing resources in thinking about information from their domain of expertise than they do in thinking about information from other areas, accounting for their uneven performance without postulating innate, modular brain structures (Bjorklund, 1987a; see Chapter 5).

Modularity implies inflexibility, in that the individual is constrained by biology to process certain information in certain ways. This can be good, increasing the likelihood that complex information will be properly processed and understood. In discussing the benefits of constraints for infants, Annette Karmiloff-Smith (1992) states that "they enable the infant to accept as input only those data which it is initially able to compute in specific ways. The domain specificity of processing provides the infant with a limited yet organized (nonchaotic) system from the outset" (pp. 11–12). But the hallmark of human cognition is flexibility. Our species has come to dominate the globe, for better or worse, because we are able to solve problems that biology could not have imagined, and we have developed technological systems that expand our intellectual powers (such as writing, mathematics, and computers). Such cognition could not be achieved by a totally encapsulated mind/brain, and of course no domain-specific theorist proposes this degree of modularity. What we must keep in mind is the certainty that both domain-general and domain-specific abilities exist and be cautious of claims that postulate otherwise.

Nature and Nurture

Most modularity theorists hold that the infant is born with specific mind/brain modules, designed by evolution to perform specific cognitive tasks. This represents the philosophy of **nativism,** which holds, essentially, that human intellectual abilities are innate. The opposing philosophical position is **empiricism,** which holds that nature provides only species-general learning mechanisms, with cognition arising as a result of experience. As stated, each of these two extreme positions is clearly wrong. In fact, as far as developmental psychologists are concerned, there is no nature/nurture dichotomy. Biological factors are inseparable from experiential factors, with the two continuously interacting. This makes it impossible to identify any purely biological or experiential effects. But it is often convenient to speak of "biological" and "experiential" factors, and when psychologists do, there is always the implicit assumption of the bidirectional interaction of these factors, as discussed earlier in this chapter (that is, structure ↔ function).

At one level it is trivial to state that biology and experience interact. There is really no other alternative. It's *how* they interact to yield a particular pattern of development that is significant. For example, the currently popular transactional view holds that children's genetic constitutions influence how they experience the environment. A sickly and lethargic child seeks less stimulation and gets less cognitively facilitating attention from adults than does a more active, healthy child, resulting in slower or less advanced levels of cognitive development for the sickly child. A child who processes language easily might be more apt to take advantage of the reading material that surrounds him than will a child whose

genetically based talents lie in other areas, such as the ability to comprehend spatial relations. Environment is thus seen as very important from this perspective, but one's biology influences which environments are most likely to be experienced and, possibly, how those experiences will be interpreted. These issues will be discussed in greater detail in the chapters devoted to individual differences, particularly in Chapter 14, where the heritability of intelligence and the role of experience in individual differences in intelligence will be explored.

What Does "Innate" Mean?

The term "innate" can be contentious, and many psychologists would just as soon not see it used at all. What exactly does it mean for something to be "innate"? If we simply mean "based in genetics," then surely just about every human behavior can be deemed innate at some level and the term is meaningless. If, however, we mean a specific type of behavior or knowledge (of grammar, for example) is determined by genetics with little or no input needed from the environment, the term has a more specific meaning, but again, it is still not very useful. For, as we'll see more clearly in our discussions later in this chapter and in Chapter 2, all genetic effects are mediated by "environment," broadly defined.

Usually, when a developmental psychologist uses the term "innate," he or she means that there are some genetically based *constraints* on behavior or development. By constraints, we mean usually that the brain can only process a certain type of information in a certain way. Constraints here mean that the brain is not flexible enough to make sense of any information in any possible way. (More about such constraints in Chapter 2.) But even here there are different types of constraints. Jeffrey Elman and his colleagues (1996) have specified three general types of innate constraints: *representational, architectural,* and *chronotopic,* and I will discuss each of them briefly below.

Representational constraints (or **representational innateness**) refers to representations that are hardwired into the brain so that some types of "knowledge" are innate. For example, several theorists have proposed that infants come into the world (or develop very early in life) some basic ideas about the nature of objects (their solidity, for example), mathematics (simple concepts of addition and subtraction), or grammar (see Pinker, 1997; Spelke & Newport, 1998; Chapter 7 of this book). This type of innateness corresponds to what most people think of when they talk about innate concepts. This does not mean that there is no development. All abilities must develop. But, according to this perspective, children (or animals) come into the world able to make sense of certain aspects of their environments, given only minimal experience (basic notions of physics, how to build webs if you're a spider, for example).

Architectural constraints (or **architectural innateness**) refers to ways in which the architecture of the brain is organized at birth. For example, some neurons are excitatory and others inhibitory, or neurons can differ in the amount of activation that is required for them to fire. At a somewhat higher level, neurons in a particular area of the brain might be more or less densely packed or have many or few connections with other local neurons. And at a higher level yet, different areas of the brain are connected with other areas of the brain, affecting the global organization of the organ. Architectural constraints limit the type and manner in which information can be processed by the brain, not because the brain comes equipped with innate representations (for example, what a grammar is), but because certain neurons/areas of the brain can only process certain types of information and pass it along to certain other areas of the brain. Thus, architectural constraints imply limits on what is processed, as do representational constraints. Unlike representational constraints, however, architectural constraints permit (or require) a high degree of learning to occur. For example, the architecture of a particular area of the brain might be best suited for processing a certain type of information (language, for instance) but the architecture will change as a function of the quantity and quality of the information it receives. Structures in the brain are not preformed to "know" grammar, for instance but are biased toward processing information about language and develop a grammar as a result of interactions with the world. Variants of architectural innateness have been proposed by several theorists under a variety of names (see Chapter 7). In general, I will use the term architectural innateness (or architectural constraints) to refer to situations in which there are genetic limitations on how information can be processed.

Chronotopic constraints (or **chronotopic innateness**) refers to limitations on the developmental timing of events. For example, certain areas of the brain might develop before others. This would mean that early developing areas would likely come to have different processing responsibilities than would later developing areas. Similarly, some areas of the brain might be most receptive to certain types of experiences (to "learning") at specified times, making it imperative that certain experiences (exposure to patterned light or language, for example) occur during this "critical period" of development. For example, children around the world acquire language in about the same way and at about the same time. If, however, for some reason children are not exposed to language until later in life, their level of language proficiency is greatly reduced. The human brain appears to be prepared to make sense of language and makes it easy for children to acquire the language that they hear around them. But such neural readiness is constrained by time. Wait too long, and the ability to acquire a fully articulated language is lost. The issue of developmental timing will be discussed in greater detail in Chapter 2 and with relation to language in Chapter 9.

Nature/Nurture and Developmental Contextualism

I have noticed two shifts in emphasis in the cognitive development field during the past decades, which at first glance might seem contradictory. The first is a greater emphasis given to the role of context in development (including cultural context). The second is a greater acknowledgment of the role of biological factors in development. In a field where nature and nurture have traditionally occupied opposite scientific, philosophical, and often political poles, seeing an increasing emphasis on both seems a contradiction, perhaps reflecting a field composed of mutual antagonists, each taking an extreme perspective to counterbalance the other. This is not the case, however. Rather, the current perspective on the dynamic transaction of nature and nurture is one in which biological and environmental factors not only can peacefully coexist but also are intricately entwined.

Let me provide one brief illustration of how biology and environment are viewed as separate, interacting components of a larger system. Richard Lerner (1991) has been a proponent of the **developmental systems approach** (or **developmental contextual model**). The basic contention of this model is that all parts of the organism (such as genes, cells, tissues, and organs), as well as the whole organism itself, interact dynamically with "the contexts within which the organism is embedded" (Lerner, 1991, p. 27). This means that one must always consider the organism-context as a unit and that there are multiple levels of the organism and multiple levels of the context. Figure 1-3 graphically presents the developmental contextual model, showing the many bidirectional influences between children, who are born with biological propensities and dispositions, and the contexts in which they find themselves. Perhaps more than anything else, this figure demonstrates the complexity of development. But of equal importance, it demonstrates the interactions that occur between the many levels of life, from genes and hormones to family and culture, and the fact that cultural effects cannot be meaningfully separated from their biological influences, and vice versa. The dynamic nature of development, which results from the interaction of a child at many different levels (genetic, hormonal, physical environment, social environment, self-produced activity, and so on) is a theme that runs through most contemporary theories of development (Fischer & Bidell, 1998; Gottlieb, Wahlsten, & Lickliter, 1998; Magnusson & Cairns, 1996; Thelen & Smith, 1998). The developmental systems approach will be examined in greater detail in Chapter 2.

The Stability and Plasticity of Intelligence

Given that a particular level of intellectual competence has been established, to what extent will it remain constant over time? Will a precocious infant become a bright 3-year-old and later a talented adult? Or is it more likely that a slow-witted 5-year-old will become an above-average high-school student, and a sluggish infant a whiz-kid computer jock? Once patterns have been established, what does it take to change them? Can they be modified by later experience? How plastic, or pliable, is the human intellect?

The stability and plasticity of intelligence are related. **Stability** refers to the degree to which children maintain over time their same relative rank order in comparison with their peers in some aspect of cognition. Does the high-IQ 3-year-old maintain her position in the intellectual pecking order at age 8 or 18? **Plasticity** concerns the extent to which children can be shaped by experience. More specifically with respect to cognition, once a pattern of intellectual competence is established, to what extent can it be altered? Is our cognitive system highly flexible, capable of being bent and rebent, or, once an intellectual pattern has been forged, is it relatively resistant to subsequent manipulation?

For the better part of this century, psychologists believed that individual differences in intelligence are relatively stable over time and not likely to be strongly modified by subsequent environments. These views were held both by people who believed that such differences were mainly inherited and by those who believed that they were mainly a function of environment, but for different reasons. People on the "nature" side assumed that intelligence was primarily an expression of one's inheritance and that this expression would be constant over one's lifetime. People on the other side of the fence emphasized the role of early experience in shaping intelligence. Experience was the important component affecting levels of intelligence, with experiences during the early years of life being most critical.

Jerome Kagan (1976) referred to this latter view as *the tape recorder model* of development. Every experience was seen as being recorded for posterity, without the opportunity to rewrite or erase something once it has been recorded. Evidence for this view was found in studies of children reared in non-stimulating institutions (Spitz, 1945). Infants receiv-

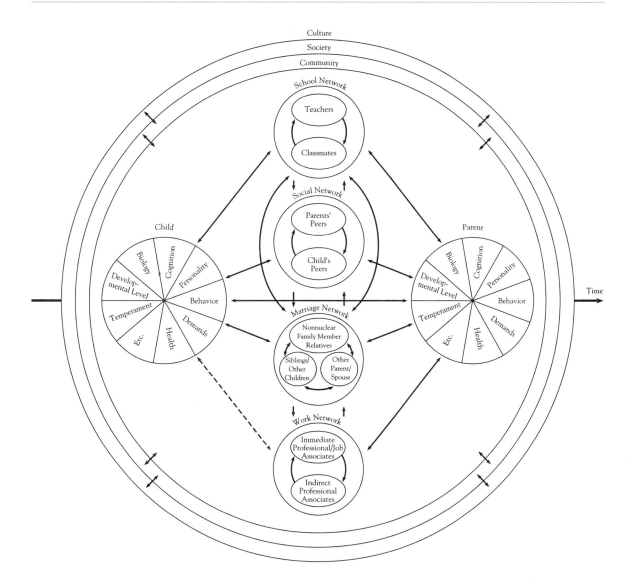

FIGURE 1-3   A developmental contextual model of person-context interaction. SOURCE: "Changing Organism-Context Relations as the Basic Process of Development: A Developmental Contextual Perspective," by R. M. Lerner, 1991, *Developmental Psychology*, 27, 27–32. Copyright © 1991 American Psychological Association. Reprinted with permission.

ing little in the way of social or physical stimulation showed signs of retardation as early as 3 or 4 months of age. These deleterious effects became exacerbated the longer children remained institutionalized, and they were maintained long after children left the in-stitutions (Dennis, 1973). The finding of long-term consequences of early experience was consistent with Freudian theory, which held that experiences during the oral and anal stages of development (from birth to about 2 years) have important effects on adult personality. This also seems to be the opinion shared by the media and general public ("Help them thrive from birth to five").

Evidence of the permanence of the effects of early experience was also found in the animal literature. For example, Harry Harlow and his colleagues demonstrated in a series of classic studies that isolating infant rhesus monkeys from their mothers (and other monkeys) adversely affected their later social and sexual behaviors (Harlow, Dodsworth, & Harlow, 1965). Without steady interaction with other monkeys during infancy, young monkeys grew up lacking many of the social skills that facilitate important adaptive exchanges such as mating, cooperation with others, and play. Furthermore, their maladaptive behaviors apparently remained stable over the life of the animals.

Exceptions were found, however, and many began to believe that these exceptions were actually the rule. In one classic study, for instance, mentally retarded infants were removed from their overcrowded and understaffed orphanage to an institution for the mentally retarded (Skeels, 1966; see discussion of this study in Chapter 14). There they received lavish attention by women inmates, and within the course of several years they were demonstrating normal levels of intelligence. In other work, isolated monkeys were placed in therapy sessions with younger, immature monkeys on a daily basis over a six-month period. By the end of therapy, these isolates were behaving in a reasonably normal fashion and could become integrated into a laboratory monkey troop (Suomi & Harlow, 1972). Each of these studies demonstrates plasticity by a young organism and resilience concerning the negative effects of early environments.

Kagan (1976) proposed that one reason to expect resilience is that development does not proceed as a tape recorder does. Rather, development is transformational, with relatively drastic changes occurring between adjacent stages. During these times the "tapes" are changed. Alternatively, methods of representing and interpreting the world change, so that the codes of the earlier tapes are "lost" to the child. The tapes of our infancy might still reside in our heads, but we've lost the ability to play them or, maybe, the ability to understand the code in which they were written. In this view, plasticity should be the rule rather than the exception, especially for the experiences of infancy and early childhood.

Note that from this perspective we would not predict that all forms of behavior or cognition are modifiable. If the cognitive ability in question does not go through transformations in its development, there is every reason to expect that early patterns will be maintained. That is, cognitive abilities that change quantitatively over time, and not qualitatively, should show relative stability. The level of performance might change, but, given regular, continuous changes in developmental function, there is every reason to expect children to maintain their same rank order. Similarly, if an environment responsible for establishing a particular pattern of behavior (for example, a nonstimulating institution) remains relatively constant over time, there is no reason to expect remarkable changes in children's relative mental functioning. (These issues will be examined in greater depth in Chapter 14.)

One important thing to remember here is that, yes, stimulation and experience are important in the early years of life, but so is later experience. Although early intellectual stimulation is important to get children off to a good start, later experiences are necessary to maintain that positive beginning. And although most children who start life in unstimulating circumstances remain there, enhancements in intellectual skills are apt to occur for such children if the environments take a change for the better. This does not mean that there is infinite plasticity in cognitive development, but merely that early experience (just as biology) is not necessarily destiny, and that change is as much a characteristic of human cognition as is stability.

Changes That Occur in Cognitive Development

As we'll see throughout this book, cognitive development is not a monolithic process. Many aspects of cognition change in the course of development. Some of these changes are in basic processes, such as speed of information processing. Others, however, are more large-scale or global, and these global changes have been the focus of major theories of cognitive development. I believe that global changes in cognitive development can be reduced to two primary areas: how objects and events in the world (and in the mind/brain) are represented, and the degree to which learning and problem solving can be intentionally controlled by the child.

Changes in Representation

One key issue that all theories of cognitive development must address concerns age differences in how children represent experience. There is more than one way to represent a thing, and children of different ages seem to use different ways of representing their world.

Adults, as well, use a variety of techniques to represent knowledge. While providing directions to my house to someone over the phone, for instance, I must convey some long-term **representation** of the route to my home verbally, through a language code. But how is it represented in my head? I might think of the route I take by generating visual images of the buildings and landmarks I pass and convert those into words. In fact, what I have done in the past is to sketch a map and then transform that map into words that can be understood by my listener. What the person on the other end of the phone must do is encode the information. At one level, my friend might attend only to the sounds of the words I speak, encoding the acoustic properties of the words. If he does, he will probably be late for dinner. More likely, he will attend to the semantic, or meaning, features of the words. Once a basic meaning has been derived, however, he might convert the message to a mental (or physical) map, realizing that he will be better able to find my house if the relevant information is in the form of a visual image.

How children represent knowledge and how they encode events in their world change developmentally. Traditional theories have proposed that infants and toddlers much younger than 18 months are limited to knowing the world only through raw perception and their actions on things, with little or no use

of symbols. This position has been questioned recently, with new research showing that even infants have access to some symbol systems (see Gelman & Williams, 1998; Spelke & Newport, 1998). Some researchers have even suggested that abstract, symbolic representation is innate, in that even newborns reveal behavior requiring seemingly symbolic representation, such as imitation of facial gestures (Meltzoff & Moore, 1985). Much of this research will be discussed in Chapter 7.

Most cognitive developmentalists agree that there are age differences in how children represent their world, and that these differences are central to age differences in thinking. These researchers disagree, however, about the nature of these differences and whether they are quantitative or qualitative in nature. Can all children use all types of symbols, and do they simply use them with different frequencies? Or does representation develop in a stagelike manner, with the more advanced forms of symbol use being unavailable to younger children? Research and theory pertinent to these and other issues related to changes in representation are central to the study of cognitive development, and they will be discussed in the pages ahead.

Changes in Intentional Control

Much cognitive development (and educational) research is concerned with how children solve particular problems. Much of what interests cognitive developmental psychologists is how children go about finding solutions to more complex problems that might have multiple paths to a solution. For example, how do children solve a puzzle, how do they go about remembering a grocery list, or how do they study for a history exam? Problem solving begins in infancy, but the problems children face and their solutions become more complicated with age.

One central concern of cognitive developmentalists has been the degree to which children of different ages can intentionally guide their problem solving. Much research on this topic has addressed the use of strategies. **Strategies** are usually defined as deliberate, goal-directed mental operations that are aimed at solving a problem (Harnishfeger &

Bjorklund, 1990a). We use strategies intentionally to help us achieve a specified goal. Strategies can be seen in the behavior of infants. Six-month-olds alter how hard they swing at mobiles over their cribs to yield slightly different movement from the inanimate object. Eighteen-month-old toddlers will deliberately stack boxes one on top of another so that they can reach the kitchen shelf and the chocolate-chip cookies. These are no less willful strategies than is the rhyming mnemonic the sixth-grader uses to remember how many days there are in each month or the plan the 15-year-old uses as she plays all her trump cards first in a game of bridge. Yet, strategies do change with development, and children seem increasingly able to carry out successful strategies as they grow older. One key research question in cognitive development concerns changes in the strategies children use and the situations in which they use them.

Although children around the world increasingly display goal-directed problem-solving behavior, this is especially evident for children from technologically advanced societies in which formal schooling is necessary to become a successful adult. Much of what children learn in school can only (or best) be acquired by deliberate study. This contrasts with how children in cultures without formal schooling often learn complicated tasks. Much of what children in all cultures learn about their world they acquire incidentally, without specific intention and sometimes without specific awareness. This type of learning and development is important also, and recent research, particularly in the area of memory development, has recognized this (see Chapter 8).

Although I said that there were two major issues that encompass almost all aspects of cognitive development (representation and intentionality), a third issue concerns all cognitive developmentalists, and that is the mechanisms responsible for change. Although we can observe changes in how children represent their world and see evidence of enhanced intentional, goal-directed behavior with age, as scientists, we very much want to know the causes of these changes. Thus, description of change is not enough, although it is a necessary start. Perhaps the

principal goal of cognitive developmentalists is to discover the underlying mechanisms of change, and much of the research in the remainder of this book addresses this issue.

Overview of the Remainder of the Book

As I mentioned earlier in this chapter, two themes have come to dominate cognitive developmental thinking over the past decade or so: (1) an increasing emphasis on the biological basis of development, and (2) an increasing emphasis on the sociocultural influence on development. These seemingly contradictory trends are actually quite compatible and are the focus of Chapters 2 and 3. In Chapter 2, I discuss the biological basis of cognitive development. This chapter was written for the beginning student, so a solid background in biology is not necessary to understand the material in the chapter. The chapter focuses on models of biology-environment interaction and on the development of the brain, as well as new ideas (evolutionary psychology) and new approaches (developmental cognitive neuroscience) to the study of cognitive development. Chapter 3 presents the sociocultural perspective of cognitive development, emphasizing the theorizing of Lev Vygotsky and his contemporary followers.

The next two chapters are devoted to major theoretical approaches to cognitive development research. In Chapter 4, I describe the theory of Jean Piaget. Piaget has unquestionably been the most influential person in the cognitive development field, and any appreciation of contemporary research requires an understanding of the theory that more than any other has stimulated interest in children's thinking. The chapter discusses the principles and assumptions of Piaget's theory and describes the four major stages of development he proposed. Because of the impact he has had on the field of cognitive development, his work and theory will surface continually in other chapters of the book. I also discuss major neo-Piagetian theories in this chapter, including the ideas of Kurt Fischer, Robbie Case, and "theory theories" of development.

Chapter 5 examines information-processing approaches to children's thinking. Information-processing accounts of cognition replaced Piaget's theory as the most popular approaches to the study of cognitive development and present an important alternative to Piagetian theory. However, information-processing theories have recently been challenged, and just as alternative theories to Piaget's were presented at the conclusion of Chapter 4, I present new theories and approaches that are extensions of the traditional information-processing perspective at the end of Chapter 5, including inhibition/resistance to interference models of development, fuzzy-trace theory, and, briefly, connectionist models of development.

The next six chapters examine specific topics in cognitive development. Chapter 6 deals with perception. Much of the information in this chapter relates to perceptual abilities in infancy, although perceptual abilities in childhood are also examined. Chapter 7 addresses developmental differences in representation, looking particularly at new research demonstrating greater representational knowledge and abilities in infants and young children than was previously believed. Included in this chapter are discussions of infants' object concepts and imitative abilities, and children's theories of mind. Chapter 8 looks at memory and includes topics ranging from parents' roles in "teaching" children how to remember, implicit memory, and memory strategies, to forgetting, infantile amnesia, and children as courtroom eyewitnesses. Chapter 9 is devoted to language, examining children's acquisition of a first and second language, communication, and the developmental relationship between language and thought. Children's problem solving, including rule acquisition, and analogical, formal, and scientific reasoning, are examined in Chapter 10. Chapter 11 examines certain aspects of social cognition. The term social cognition covers many diverse subjects, and I don't pretend to have examined most of them here. Among the topics included in this chapter are Bandura's social cognitive theory, Dodge's social

information-processing theory, the development of self-concept, perspective taking, children's humor, and the cognitive bases of gender identification.

Chapter 12 is a bridge between Chapters 2 through 10, which deal primarily with developmental function, and Chapters 13 and 14, which deal primarily with individual differences. Chapter 12 examines the development of and individual differences in two important technological skills, reading and arithmetic, along with other aspects of the role of schooling on cognitive development, including cross-cultural differences in cognition and academic performance, the role of schooling on intelligence, and the benefits and detriments of academic preschools and enrichment programs.

Chapters 13 and 14 each deal with individual differences in intelligence. Chapter 13 examines basic approaches to the study of intelligence, including the psychometric, information-processing, and Piagetian approaches. I also include some newer perspectives on intelligence, including Sternberg's triarchic theory, Gardner's theory of multiple intelligences, and Ceci's bioecological approach. Chapter 14 looks at the stability of intelligence over time and examines issues relating to the heritability of intelligence. Recent findings from behavioral genetics, as well as work that examines environmental influences on establishing, maintaining, and modifying intellectual functioning, are discussed in this chapter.

The book ends with a brief epilogue, which attempts to abstract several "truths," or generalizations, about cognitive development.

Summary

The study of cognitive development involves an examination of how children's thinking changes over time. *Cognition* refers to the acquisition and manipulation of knowledge. It includes conscious, effortful processes, such as those involved in making important decisions, and unconscious, automatic processes, such as those involved in recognizing a familiar face, word, or object. Cognition cannot be observed directly but must be inferred from behavior.

Development refers to changes in *structure* or *function* over time, with such a relationship being conceived as *bidirectional* in nature (*structure* ↔ *function*). Development has its roots in biology, and its course is relatively predictable. Yet, within any given age or stage, there are individual differences in children's thinking, with the organism-environment interaction being critical for an understanding of the course of development. Although development is often viewed as being progressive, children's immature cognitions might provide them with some adaptive advantages.

Changes between *stages* of development are said by stage theorists to be qualitative rather than quantitative in nature. *Qualitative differences* are those of type, or kind, whereas *quantitative differences* are those of amount or speed. Shifts from one stage to another are theorized to occur abruptly, reflecting *discontinuity* rather than *continuity* in development. Stage theorists posit that children's abilities are highly integrated within a stage. Many (but not all) cognitive developmentalists agree that there is substantial *homogeneity of cognitive function*, although not as much homogeneity as predicted by many stage theories. Cognitive development does not always increase gradually (or discontinuously) over time but in some domains might reach adult levels early, with a skill showing *developmental invariance*.

Most traditional approaches to cognitive development have posited *domain-general abilities*, although recent research has shown that many aspects of cognition and its development are *domain-specific* in nature, with some forms of cognition being *modular*.

The current perspective on the nature/nurture issue with respect to cognitive development and intelligence favors a transactional view that sees children playing a critical role in their own development. Three different type of innate constraints have been proposed: *representational*, referring to innate representations; *architectural*, referring to innate characteristics of neurons and their connections with other groups of neurons; and *chronotopic*, referring to maturational (timing) constraints. Biological and environmental factors are seen as interacting in bidirectional relationships, as reflected by the *developmental systems approach.*

Stability refers to the degree to which children maintain their same rank order relative to their peers over time. *Plasticity* refers to the extent to which individuals can be shaped by the environment. For most of this century, it was believed that intelligence is relatively stable over time and that experiences later in life cannot greatly affect patterns of intelligence established earlier. More recent research suggests that some characteristics—but not others—are stable and that human intelligence can be substantially modified under certain circumstances. It is important to consider the issues of stability and plasticity along with issues of developmental function.

Among several other important theoretical issues, the two most critical are developmental differences in *representation* and the extent to which children are able to intentionally control their problem solving through *strategies*.

Key Terms and Concepts

developmental function
individual differences
cognition
development
structure
function
bidirectionality of structure and function
    (structure ↔ function)
stages
qualitative versus quantitative differences
continuity versus discontinuity of development
developmental invariance
homogeneity of cognitive function
domain-general abilities
domain-specific abilities
modularity
nativism
empiricism
representational constraints (or representational
    innateness)
architectural constraints (or architectural innateness)
chronotopic constraints (or chronotopic innateness)
developmental systems approach (developmental
    contextual model)

stability
plasticity (of cognition and behavior)
representation
strategies

Suggested Readings

FLAVELL, J. H. (1992). Cognitive development: Past, present, and future. *Developmental Psychology, 28*, 988–1005. This article presents a brief history of thought in cognitive development, current issues, and predictions for research in the future.

BJORKLUND, D. F., & GREEN, B. L. (1992). The adaptive nature of cognitive immaturity. *American Psychologist, 47*, 46–54. This article presents the argument that some aspects of infants' and young children's immature thinking are adaptive and that attempts to accelerate development should be carefully thought out before being implemented.

ELMAN, J. L., BATES, E. A., JOHNSON, M. H., KARMILOFF-SMITH, A., PARISI, D., & PLUNKETT, K. (1996). *Rethinking innateness: A connectionist perspective on development*. Cambridge, MA: M.I.T. Press. This book discusses issues related to the concept of innateness as it relates to developmental psychology. Although numerous aspects of development are discussed, most discussion is related to brain development and language development. The authors present a connectionist (computer modeling) perspective, but the book is valuable even for those who want to avoid such approaches.

Biological Bases of Cognitive Development

Evolution and Cognitive Development

Evolutionary Psychology • *Selectionist Theories of Cognitive and Brain Development*

Models of Gene-Environment Interaction

The Developmental Systems Approach • *The Genotype → Environment Theory*

The Development of the Brain

Neuronal Development • *The Development of the Neocortex*
The Brain's Plasticity

Relevance of Developmental Cognitive Neuroscience to Understanding Cognitive Development and Implications for Education

Developmental Biology and Cognitive Development

Summary

Note

Key Terms and Concepts

Suggested Readings

In recent years, I've begun including a brief lecture on the biological basis of cognitive development in my undergraduate class, discussing brain development and the evolution of mental abilities. Invariably, one student will approach me after class and ask why we need to know anything about biology to understand children's thinking. The question, actually, is not a trivial one. For much of this century, social and behavioral scientists interested in cognition gave only lip service, at best, to biology. The mind might emanate from the brain, but understanding the brain was not seen as a prerequisite to understanding the mind. In fact, there existed in the social and behavioral sciences what can be called biophobia and an implicit belief that acknowledging biology was akin to rejecting the influence of environment or culture on behavior, something at odds with the central theme of the social sciences (see Tooby & Cosmides, 1992). The study of cognition was essentially isolated from the study of the brain.

Things have clearly changed. The new field of cognitive science takes as a given the close connection between mind and brain. As philosopher John Searle (1992) states: "Mental phenomena are caused by neurophysiological processes in the brain and are themselves features of the brain. . . . Mental events and processes are as much part of our biological natural history as digestion, mitosis, or enzyme secretion" (p. 1). Moreover, cognitive scientists are not only concerned with immediate biological causes (for example, how the brain affects behavior), but also with factors that influenced the evolution of human cognition.

Looking at the biological basis of cognition and its development does not mean that one ignores the psychological level. Biology and psychology provide different levels of analysis. Much as psychology and anthropology present different pictures of human behavior (one at the level of the individual and the other at the level of the culture), so too do biology and psychology. Moreover, just as concepts in biology must be consistent with the known facts of chemistry, so also must concepts in psychology be consistent with the known facts of biology. Thus, proposing theories of mind that are inconsistent with what we know about physiology or evolution cannot lead to a productive theory of cognition (see Cosmides, Tooby, & Barkow, 1992).

But psychology cannot be reduced to biology. Knowing how nerve cells function will not tell us all we need to know about how we think. The concepts of psychology, while being consistent with the concepts of biology, represent a different level of analysis. Developing a theory of the brain is important, of course, but it is not enough. Having a theory of the brain does not obviate having a theory of the mind. Cognitive psychology is not just something to do until the biologists get better at their trade. Developmental psychologists should not blindly accept all that biologists propose but should be mindful of the biological causes of cognitive development and formulate theories and design experiments accordingly (Bjorklund, 1997b).

In this chapter, I first provide a look at ideas from evolutionary theory and how such Darwinian ideas can contribute to an understanding of the developing modern child. In the next section, I examine a couple of developmental theories that take biology seriously, particularly the relation between genetic/ biologic factors and environmental/experiential factors. I then provide a brief overview of brain development. In this, and in later chapters, I will comment on the relation between brain and cognitive development. Although no one ever doubted that the brain was the seat of cognition, only recently, with the emergence of the field of **developmental cognitive neuroscience,** have brain-cognition relations in development been taken seriously (Byrnes & Fox, 1998; Johnson, 1998; Nelson & Bloom, 1997). Developmental cognitive neuroscience takes data from a variety of sources— molecular biology, cell biology, artificial intelligence, evolutionary theory, as well as conventional cognitive development—to create a picture of how the mind/brain develops. As will be made clear soon, contemporary biologically based theories of development do not hold that "biology is destiny," but rather deal with the classic nature/nurture controversy by explaining how genes and environments interact to produce a particular pattern of development.

Because most research in cognitive development over this century has essentially ignored biological causation, most of what is covered in the rest of the book is at the psychological rather than the biological level. However, I firmly believe that we will develop an understanding of cognitive development only by taking biology seriously, and reference to biological factors will be made throughout the remainder of the book.

Evolution and Cognitive Development

What is the adaptive value of certain cognitive abilities? How might cognitive abilities have a different adaptive value at different times in development? In what contexts should certain cognitive abilities develop? How do some evolved human characteristics, such as bipedality or prolonged immaturity, affect the ontogeny of cognition? These are the questions asked by developmentalists that relate to evolution.

When biologists speak of **evolution,** they mean the process of change in gene frequencies in populations over many generations that in time produces new species. Modern evolutionary theory had its beginnings in the ideas of Charles Darwin, whose 1859 book *On the Origin of Species* represents one of the grandest ideas of science. The book made an immediate impact on the scientific community and is considered by many today to be one of the most important books ever written. The crux of the theory is that many more members of a species are born in each generation than will survive. They all have different combinations of inherited traits; that is, there is substantial *variation* among members of a species. Conditions in the environment for that particular generation cause some members of that species to survive and reproduce while others do not, a process that Darwin referred to as **natural selection** (Mayr, 1982). The inherited traits of the survivors will be passed on to the next generation of that species, whereas the traits of the nonsurvivors will not. Over the course of many generations, the predominant traits of a species will change by this mechanism. The major principle of Darwin's theory is *reproductive fitness,* which basically refers to the

likelihood that an individual will become a parent and a grandparent.

Darwin's theory has gone through some substantial modifications during the last century or so, the most significant being the inclusion of modern genetic theory into formulations of evolution. Among scientists today, the *fact* of evolution is not questioned, although some lively debates center on the *mechanisms* of evolution. Despite controversies, evolutionary theory is the backbone of modern biology (see Mayr, 1982), and because human cognition and behavior are rooted in biology, evolutionary theory should also be the backbone of modern psychology.

Evolutionary theory has had an influence on developmental psychology since its beginnings. Some of the early giants of developmental psychology were greatly influenced by evolutionary theory, among them James Mark Baldwin, G. Stanley Hall, and Jean Piaget. From time to time during the last century, scientists have emphasized the importance of having a knowledge of evolutionary theory for developing a knowledge of children's thinking (for example, Fishbein, 1976). This is one of those times.

One thing that evolutionary theory provides is a framework for interpreting all aspects of behavior and development. It does this, in part, by providing an explanation for *how* a particular mechanism came about (through natural selection), but also a possible explanation of *why* this mechanism evolved. In my early training, I was taught not to ask "why" questions. Scientists ask "how" questions, for example, 'How do children come to appreciate that other people have perceptions and ideas other than their own?', not *why* do they develop this ability. Evolutionary theory provides answers to both the "how" and "why" questions. The "how" is through natural selection over evolutionary time, in that children who could not learn to see the perspectives of another person did not grow up to have children of their own. Of course, this is not a sufficient answer to "how" this ability develops in individual children (see Chapter 7 on the development of theory of mind), but it does provide a mechanism for how it developed in the species. The "why" suggests that this ability was likely important for survival, or that it was *adaptive*. Children who could understand the perspective of another were able to anticipate other people's actions and act accordingly. Such *adaptationist* reasoning must be used cautiously, of course. Not all aspects of present-day life were necessarily adaptive for our ancient ancestors. Some aspects might have been neutral, some associated with other characteristics, and others just not sufficiently maladaptive to result in extinction. But having a theory that provides a framework for asking why a particular behavior or pattern of development is present, can help us develop a better understanding of human nature and ask better "how" questions.

Evolutionary theory is currently influencing cognitive development in at least two ways. The first is through the newly developed field of evolutionary psychology (Barkow, Cosmides, & Tooby, 1992; Buss, 1995). This field explains human behavior through evolutionary theory; evolutionary theorists ask "why" questions and provide answers about adaptive fit to environments. It is important to understand that what might have been adaptive to our ancestors 100,000 or one million years ago might not be adaptive to us today. Our preference for sweets and fat is a good case in point. Although these foods would have been rare and much valued sources of energy to our ancient ancestors, they are easily available to people from post-industrial cultures today and are responsible in large part for our high incidence of heart disease (Nesse & Williams, 1994). Many cognitive mechanisms can be seen similarly, and, alternatively, many of the technological problems we must solve as modern humans are only centuries old at most and have no specific mechanisms that have evolved to solve them.

The second way evolutionary theory is influencing current research and theory in cognitive development is by applying selectionist explanations to current phenomenon (Cziko, 1995; Siegler, 1996). Rather than speculating about what environmental conditions might have been two million years ago or assuming what the adaptive value of a particular behavior might have been, these theorists use Darwin's idea of natural selection to explain how the brain or the mind develops. I will examine briefly each of these approaches in the following sections, and we

will encounter evolutionary interpretations of patterns of development throughout the remainder of the book.

Evolutionary Psychology

Recently it has been suggested that cognitive psychology is the missing link in the evolution of human behavior. Cosmides and Tooby (1987) proposed that information-processing mechanisms evolved and "these mechanisms in interaction with environmental input generate manifest behavior. The causal link between evolution and behavior is made through psychological mechanisms" (p. 277). According to Cosmides and Tooby, adaptive behavior is predicated on adaptive thought, at least in humans. Natural selection operates on the cognitive level—information-processing programs evolved to solve real-world problems. How do I tell friend from foe? When do I fight and when do I flee? From this viewpoint, it becomes fruitful to ask what kind of cognitive operations an organism must have "if it is to extract and process information about its environment in a way that will lead to adaptive behavior" (Cosmides & Tooby, 1987, p. 285). From an evolutionary perspective, we must ask: What is the purpose of a behavior and the cognitive operations that underlie that behavior? What problem was it designed to solve?

It is also important in the realm of cognitive development to remember that cognitive processes *develop* and that the problems infants and children face are different from those faced by adults. Researchers can fruitfully ask how children's cognitions are adapted to the cultural contexts in which they find themselves, rather than to the contexts experienced by adults (Bjorklund, 1997a; Turkewitz & Kenny, 1982). For example, what type of information should helpless infants be attentive to? Might some information that is of vital importance to them be less important to older children and adults, and vice versa?

Also, evolutionary theory suggests that most psychological mechanisms evolved to accomplish specific adaptive functions, what Cosmides and Tooby (1987) refer to as **Darwinian algorithms.** That is, rather than affecting general intelligence, for example, Darwinian algorithms affect very specific cognitive operations, such as face recognition or the processing of certain types of social relationships. This suggests that infants, children, and adults have evolved some cognitive abilities to deal with specific problems, and that such abilities will be independent of other intellectual skills (that is, they will be *modular,* as discussed in Chapter 1). This perspective, that evolution has shaped human cognition with a set of domain-specific brain modules, is captured by Steven Pinker's (1997) statement: "The mind is organized into modules or mental organs, each with a specialized design that makes it an expert in one area of interaction with the world. The modules' basic logic is specified by our genetic program. Their operation was shaped by natural selection to solve problems of the hunting and gathering life led by our ancestors in most of our evolutionary history" (p. 21). Although some theorists with an evolutionary psychological perspective have proposed that domain-general mechanisms can coexist with sets of domain-specific mechanisms (Bjorklund & Kipp, 1996; Mithen, 1996), most evolutionary psychological accounts dismiss the existence of any domain-general mechanisms.

Implicit in the idea that there are domain-specific mechanisms, is that there are *constraints* (representational, architectural, and chronotopic, see Chapter 1) on learning (Gelman & Williams, 1998). Constraints imply restrictions, and restrictions are usually thought of as being bad. Human cognition is exceptional for its flexibility, not for its restrictiveness. But constraints, from this perspective, *enable* learning, rather than hamper it. Children enter a world of sights, sounds, objects, language, and other people. If all types of learning were truly equiprobable, children would be overwhelmed by stimulation that bombards them from every direction. Instead, the argument goes, infants and young children are constrained to process certain information in "core domains" (such as the nature of objects, language) in certain ways. They come into the world with some idea of how the world is structured, and this leads to faster and more

efficient processing of information within specific domains. According to Gelman and Williams (1998), "From an evolutionary perspective, learning cannot be a process of arbitrary and completely flexible knowledge acquisition. In core domains, learning processes are the means to functionally defined ends: acquiring and storing the particular sorts of relevant information which are necessary for solving particular problems" (p. 600).

Another insight relevant to cognitive development and to education derived from evolutionary psychology is the idea that much of what we teach children in school is "unnatural" in that they involve tasks never encountered by our ancestors. For example, although our species has apparently been using language for tens of thousands of years, reading is a skill that goes back only a few thousand years and it is only in this century that a majority of people on the planet are literate. David Geary (1995) has referred to cognitive abilities that were selected for in evolution, such as language, as **biologically primary abilities,** and skills that build on these primary abilities but are principally cultural inventions, such as reading, as **biologically secondary abilities.** Biologically primary abilities are acquired universally and children typically have high motivation to perform tasks involving them. Biologically secondary abilities, on the other hand, are culturally determined, and often tedious repetition and external motivation are necessary for their mastery. It is little wonder that reading, a supposed "language art," and higher mathematics give many children substantial difficulty.

It is important to emphasize here that an evolutionary account of development is *not* one of biological determinism. That is, although evolution works through changing frequencies in genes within the population, natural selection requires a dynamic interaction between organisms and their environments. Organisms choose environments, the very act of which serves to modify those environments. Environments, in turn, affect the organism, by "selecting" some behaviors that "match" the environments over others. Because of this dynamic interaction between organisms and environments, we must evaluate organisms' interactions with their environments if we want to understand adaptation and cognitive development. Thus, this position rejects any simple notion of biological determinism (for example, "genes cause behavior") on cognitive development, intelligence, or the educability of children.

Selectionist Theories of Cognitive and Brain Development

The major tenets of Darwin's theory of natural selection are simple: Organisms produce more offspring than can survive (known as *superfecundity*), there is variability among offspring, and offspring that are better adapted to their environment survive, that is, organisms are "selected" by the environment. Actually, organisms that don't adapt well to their environments die, so there is both positive selection (survival) and negative selection (death). Other than explaining human evolution, how can such concepts be applied to human cognitive development?

The key here is *variability*, not so much between individuals (although this is obviously important), but *within* a single individual. **Selectionist theorists** propose that people possess a wide range of behaviors or cognitions (that is, there is substantial variability), and they emit these behaviors or thoughts in certain environments. Those behaviors or cognitions that are adaptive increase in frequency (that is, survive), and those that are not adaptive decrease in frequency (and may eventually "die"). From this perspective, cognitive development can be seen as a process of children trying out different behaviors or cognitive operations (the availability of which changes with age), and keeping those that work (that the environment "selects") and dropping those that don't work (that the environment does not "select" or "selects" against).

B. F. Skinner's (1974) theory of operant conditioning was essentially a selectionist theory. Animals (including human children) emit behaviors, some of which get reinforced (selected) by the environment. Those that get reinforced increase in frequency in those environments, and those that do not get rein-

forced decrease in frequency in those environments. Skinner's emphasis on overt behavior and his belief that cognitive mechanisms and explanations have no place in the study of human behavior, make his theory inappropriate for the study of cognitive development. But his adoption of selectionist thinking is a clear demonstration of the application of Darwin's ideas to changes, not over evolutionary time, but over the lifetime of an individual.

If Skinner's behaviorism is not the right model for cognitive development, how can a selectionist theory be applied to the understanding of children's thinking? Rather than positing that it is only overt *behaviors* that are variable, it is only a small step to propose that children possess many different *cognitive operations*, and that these are used to solve certain problems (Cziko, 1995; Siegler, 1996). New cognitive operations emerge during development, but these new operations coexist with older (and often simpler) cognitive operations and "compete" with one another for use to solve problems. Those that solve problems effectively increase in frequency, and those that do not decrease in frequency. Robert Siegler's (1996) *adaptive strategy choice model* is perhaps the best developed contemporary selectionist theory of cognitive development, and I will discuss it in some detail in Chapter 5.

Selectionist theories are also being applied in brain development. Here, it is not organisms, behaviors, or cognitive operations that are generated in great number and variability, but neurons (Changeux & Dehaene, 1989; Edelman, 1987). Neurons that "fit" well with their surrounding environment (in this case, other neurons) survive, and those that do not fit die. This approach to brain development will be discussed later in this chapter.

Evolutionary theory provides an overarching perspective of human psychological functioning, including development. Evolutionary thinking is part of the cognitive-science perspective that has influenced the study of human cognition and cognitive development over the past two decades. Understanding that our brain and mind evolved to solve specific problems, that the problems faced by infants and children were (and remain today) different than those faced by adults, and that the principles of natural selection can be applied not only to changes over evolutionary time but also to changes over a lifetime, can provide us with a better perspective on human nature and human development.

Models of Gene-Environment Interaction

All self-respecting developmentalists believe that development is the result of an interaction between genetic/biologic factors and environmental/experiential factors. There is really no other alternative. Some theorists are more explicit about the nature of the interaction than others, however, and in this section I will examine two approaches that examine gene-environment interactions and their consequences for development. Each approach posits that the child is an active agent in his or her own development, that development proceeds through the bidirectional effect of structure and function, and that the context in which development occurs is as important as the genes the individual inherits. The two approaches are the *developmental systems approach* (or *developmental contextualism*), as advocated by Gilbert Gottlieb (1991a; Gottlieb, Wahlsten, & Lickliter, 1998), Richard Lerner (1991), and others (see Turkewitz & Devenny, 1993), and a theory based on research in behavioral genetics, the *genotype → environment theory* as presented by Sandra Scarr and Kathleen McCartney (1983; Scarr, 1992, 1993). Although debate between theorists in these two camps can be vigorous (see Scarr, 1993), for our purposes, the difference between the two approaches can be seen as a matter of degree.

The Developmental Systems Approach

The Concept of Epigenesis

The **developmental systems approach** (so called because it views development as occurring within a system of interacting levels) is centered around the concept of **epigenesis,** defined by Gottlieb (1991a)

as "the emergence of new structures and functions during the course of development" (p. 7). Gottlieb (1991a; Gottlieb et al., 1998) states that epigenesis reflects a bidirectional relationship between all levels of biological and experiential variables, such that genetic activity both influences and is influenced by structural maturation, which is bidirectionally related to function and activity. This relationship can be expressed as follows:

genetic activity (DNA $\leftrightarrow$ RNA $\leftrightarrow$ proteins) $\leftrightarrow$ structural maturation $\leftrightarrow$ function, activity.

According to Gottlieb (1991a), "Individual development is characterized by an increase of complexity of organization (that is, the emergence of new structural and functional properties and competencies) at all levels of analysis (molecular, subcellular, cellular, organismic) as a consequence of horizontal and vertical coactions among the organism's parts, including organism-environment coactions" (p. 7).

The point here is that functioning at any level influences functioning at adjacent levels. For example, genes clearly direct the production of proteins, which in turn determine the formation of structures, such as muscle or nerve cells. But activity of these and surrounding cells can turn on or off a particular gene, causing the cessation or commencement of genetic activity. Moreover, experience in the form of self-produced activity or stimulation from external sources can alter the development of sets of cells. From this perspective, there are no simple genetic or experiential causes of behavior; all development is the product of epigenesis, with complex interactions occurring among multiple levels. This bidirectional approach to development is expressed in Figure 2-1. This figure suggests that we can never understand development merely by looking for genetic effects or for environmental effects; to understand development, we must look at the organism-context relationship (Lerner, 1991). Mark Johnson (1998), in his review of the neural basis of cognitive development, makes this point especially clear: "Since it has become evident that genes interact with their environment at all levels, including the molecular, there

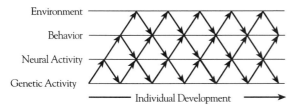

Environment

Behavior

Neural Activity

Genetic Activity

Individual Development

FIGURE 2-1 A simplified schematic of the developmental systems approach, showing a hierarchy of four mutually interacting components. SOURCE: Adapted from "Experiential Canalization of Behavioral Development: Theory," by G. Gottlieb, 1991, *Developmental Psychology, 27,* 4–13. Copyright © 1991 American Psychological Association. Reprinted with permission.

is no aspect of development that can be said to be strictly "genetic," that is, exclusively a product of information contained in the genes" (p. 4).

If the relations expressed in Figure 2-1 approximate reality, there should be substantial plasticity in development. Yet, it is undeniable that development is constrained by one's genes. Because our parents were humans, we develop in a way that a chimpanzee embryo can never develop (and vice versa). However, environments also constrain development. Genes will be expressed differently in different environments, yielding different patterns of development.

But if there is so much plasticity in development, why do almost all members of a species (human or otherwise) develop in a species-typical pattern? The answer is that a child (or a puppy or a chimp) inherits not only species-typical genes, but also a species-typical environment. For example, ducks begin life in eggs, usually surrounded by other eggs, with their mother staying close by them before they hatch. They are able to hear and vocalize before hatching, and it turns out that these abilities contribute to an important aspect of posthatching behavior. Under normal conditions, when baby ducks, shortly after hatching, are put into a large container and hear the maternal call of two species of birds—their own and another—they invariably approach the call from their own species. They seem instinctively to know what their own species sounds like and to

move toward that sound, something that makes good sense in the wild. However, when experimental procedures are performed so that the embryonic duck in the egg does not hear its mother or any of its siblings and its own vocal chords are temporarily prevented from functioning so that it can produce no sound itself, it fails after hatching to show the species-typical pattern of approaching the call of its own species (see Gottlieb, 1991b). In other words, prehatching experience, particularly hearing its own self-produced vocalizations, play a major role in posthatching species-typical behavior. The reason that nearly all ducks approach the species-typical call after hatching is that nearly all ducks inherit not only the genetic disposition to make such a selection but also the species-typical environment that provides the necessary experiences for such a pattern to develop.

This is fine for ducks, but how does this relate to human cognitive development? The idea is that human children develop in species-typical environments, both prenatal and postnatal, and that experiences in these environments serve to direct development in species-typical ways. Take, for example, a proposal by Gerald Turkewitz (1993) concerning the functioning of the two hemispheres of the brain. The brain comprises two sections, called *hemispheres,* which are connected by a large bundle of nerves called the corpus callosum. Although similar, the two hemispheres are not identical. Each hemisphere controls the opposite side of the body, with one hemisphere typically predominating over the other, resulting in a left- or right-side preference. For example, there are far more right-handed people in the world than left handers, which reflects a hemispheric asymmetry, with the left hemisphere (which controls the right side of the body) being dominant relative to the right (which controls the left side of the body). Such an asymmetry is found even in neonates, with newborns turning their heads to the right more often than to the left (see the discussion of brain lateralization later in this chapter). Also, newborns process speech sounds more effectively when the sounds are presented to the right ear (and thus left hemisphere) than when they are presented to the left ear, further demonstrating hemispheric asymmetries. The right hemisphere seems to be more involved in recognizing faces, another important ability for human infants to have.

What is the origin of these asymmetries? Turkewitz (1993) proposes that they have to do with the timing of brain development and the nature of prenatal auditory experiences. Turkewitz presents evidence that the right hemisphere begins developing before the left hemisphere, but that later in prenatal development, the left hemisphere catches up and surpasses the right in size and complexity. Early in development, when the right hemisphere is developing most rapidly, because of characteristics of the uterine environment and the relatively undeveloped state of the fetus's auditory system, the most salient auditory signals for a fetus are internally generated sounds, such as gastrointestinal gurglings and cardiovascular noises (that is, the heartbeat and the sound of pumping blood) produced by the mother. These are hardly important sounds for such a cognitively flexible and social species as *Homo sapiens*. As gestation proceeds and the fetus's auditory system improves, externally produced noises become more salient, particularly maternal speech. This is when the left hemisphere is developing most rapidly. Turkewitz suggests that it is the interaction of the timing of development (faster development for the right hemisphere early and for the left hemisphere late) with auditory experiences (clearer signals from external speech sources later in development) that causes hemispheric asymmetries. Because the left hemisphere is developing most rapidly when maternal speech is most salient, it develops a specialty for processing speech. This leaves the right hemisphere "unspecialized," so to speak. This means that after birth, when vision is possible, "the right hemisphere would be relatively unengaged and available for processing the facial information. In this way the right hemisphere could begin to develop a specialization for dealing with facial information" (Turkewitz, 1993, p. 136).

Turkewitz's proposal is intriguing. It suggests that asymmetries observed in infancy (and expressed later in visual and language processing in adults) have their origins in prenatal experiences, in interaction with genetically paced maturation. Turkewitz might be wrong, but the argument is logically sound and consistent with what we know about development, and aspects of his hypothesis are testable. Viewing development from this perspective provides a new meaning for the term *instinctive*. A behavior or function that is inborn in almost all members of the species might be instinctive, but if so, we must consider both the species-typical genes and the species-typical environment as factors contributing to that behavior.

Developmental Timing

As any comedian will tell you, timing is everything. In the developmental systems approach, the timing of a particular event in the course of development can influence substantially what effect that event will have on development. In the Turkewitz example just described, rapid development of the left hemisphere occurs when the acoustic characteristics of the uterine environment are most conducive to processing speech sounds. Were the timing of things different, a different pattern of development might result.

Perhaps the concept most central to the issue of the timing of development is that of a **critical period.** The critical period for a specific skill or ability is the time in development (usually early in life) when it is most easily acquired. If a requisite experience occurs outside of this critical period (either too early or too late in development), the target skill will not be readily acquired or possibly not acquired at all. (The term *sensitive period* is sometimes used rather than *critical period* to reflect the fact that although the organism is most sensitive to a particular event at a particular time, similar or perhaps more intense experiences later in development can still have considerable influence on development. For the sake of simplicity, I will use the term critical period throughout this chapter.) Figure 2-2 depicts the idea that a behavior is most easily acquired during a critical period. Researchers have suggested that many aspects of human cognitive development can be described as critical periods (see Bornstein, 1989;

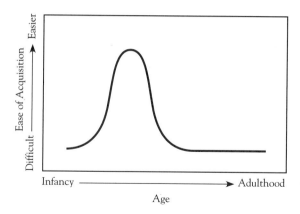

FIGURE 2-2   Some cognitive abilities, such as language, might be most easily acquired during a critical period in (usually early) development.

Ceci, 1996), with language being perhaps the clearest example (Lenneberg, 1967; Newport, 1991). Both a first and second language are acquired more easily when learned in early childhood. Although adolescents and adults can learn a second language, it is usually only with great difficulty, and they rarely attain the facility in that language observed when it is learned during childhood. (More will be said about a critical period for language acquisition in Chapter 9.)

Examples of the significance of timing of perceptual experience come from research by Robert Lickliter (1990), working with auditory and visual stimulation of bobwhite quails. Like ducks, bobwhite quails approach the maternal call of their own species shortly after hatching. As demonstrated earlier by Gottlieb, this phenomenon has been attributed to auditory experiences the birds have before hatching. But, Lickliter reasoned, it is due to more than just the presence of auditory experiences before hatching, but also the *absence* of other sensory experiences, following an argument originally made by Turkewitz and Kenny (1982). Turkewitz and Kenny argued that the sensory systems in infants of many species function poorly at birth. Such inefficient functioning is actually adaptive, however, in that it protects the infant from sensory overload, permit-

ting it to deal with small bits of simplified stimuli, making it easier for the immature being to make sense of its world. Also, poor functioning in one sense (vision, for example) might permit an earlier-developing sense (hearing, for example) to develop without undue competition for neural resources.

This is exactly the logic that Lickliter adopted for his study with bobwhite quails. As in all vertebrates, hearing develops before vision (Gottlieb, 1971). Lickliter argued that the slower development of vision in bobwhite quails allows the auditory system to develop without competition from the visual system. What would happen if quails were given extra visual experience before hatching? One possibility is that it might hinder important aspects of auditory development, such as showing a preference for the maternal call.

Lickliter (1990) developed a procedure whereby he removed part of the eggshell and provided visual experience to bobwhite quails two to three days before hatching. He then tested those birds in an auditory preference test in which the birds were placed in an oval container with speakers at opposite ends. From one speaker came the maternal call of a bobwhite quail, and from the other speaker came the maternal call of a chicken. The researchers observed which speaker, if either, the chicks approached.

The results of this experiment are shown in Figure 2-3. Control quails had the end of the egg opened but received no visual experience. This ensured that the behavior of the experimental birds would not be caused by removing part of the eggshell, per se, but by the additional visual experience the chicks received. As can be seen in the figure, the control birds demonstrated the species-typical pattern when tested, with nearly all of the birds showing a preference for the maternal call of their own species (that is, approaching the speaker from which the bobwhite quail call came). This was not the case for the birds who had the extra visual experience, however. A majority of these birds showed no preference or approached the speaker producing the maternal call of a chicken! I should note that these animals displayed greater visual discrimination abilities. That is, the prehatching visual experience resulted in enhanced visual abilities but

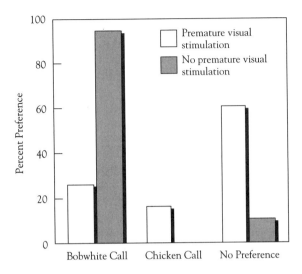

FIGURE 2-3　Percentage of bobwhite quail chicks that approached the bobwhite maternal call, the chicken maternal call, or showed no preference as a function of whether they received premature visual stimulation or not. SOURCE: Adapted from R. Lickliter (1990), Premature visual stimulation accelerates intersensory functioning in bobwhite quail neonates. *Developmental Psychobiology, 23,* 15–27.

at the expense of auditory abilities, which are important in their early development of attachment.

This and other studies (see Bjorklund, 1997a) clearly demonstrate that the timing of perceptual experience is critically important, and that earlier experience is not always better experience. This is worth remembering for human infants. Might their sensory limitations actually be adaptive, and might extra stimulation in one modality interfere with development in other modalities? Or consider a related question: Is early learning always beneficial? Might providing an infant with too much stimulation or "learning tasks" too soon in development have a negative effect?

There is little research on this issue. In one study conducted on infant monkeys, Harry Harlow (1959) began giving monkeys training on a discrimination-learning task at different ages ranging from 60 to 366 days. For example, monkeys were to choose which of several stimuli that varied in several dimensions (size, shape, color, and so on) was associ-

ated with a prize. Beginning at 120 days of age or older, monkeys were given a more complicated learning task. Monkeys' performance on these more complicated problems is shown in Figure 2-4 as a function of the age at which they began training. Chance performance for these problems was 50%. As can be seen, monkeys who began training early in life (at 60 and 90 days) never solved many more than 60% of the problems and soon fell behind the monkeys who began training later (at 120 and 150 days of age). That is, despite having more experience with the problems, the early-trained monkeys performed more poorly than the later trained monkeys. Harlow concluded,

> There is a tendency to think of learning or training as intrinsically good and necessarily valuable to the organism. It is entirely possible, however, that training can be either helpful or harmful, depending upon the nature of the training and the organism's stage of development. (p. 472)

In the only research with human infants that I am aware of related to this idea, Hanus Papousek (1977) conditioned infants to turn their heads to a buzzer or a bell. Training began either at birth or at 31 or 44 days of age. Infants who began training at birth took many more trials before they learned the task (814 trials) than infants who began later (278 and 224 trials for the 31- and 44-day-old infants, respectively). The age (in days) at which infants reached criterion on this conditioning problem as a function of when they began training is shown in Figure 2-5. Similar to Harlow's results with monkeys, infants who began at birth required more days to learn the task than did the infants who began at an older age.

Although there has been almost no research with human infants on the topic of "sensory overstimulation," researchers have speculated that some of the deficits experienced by premature infants are caused by exposure to too much sensory information too soon. Heidelise Als (1995) suggests that the early sensory stimulation that premature infants experience might adversely affect brain development by requiring them to process perceptual stimulation that the brain would not normally deal with for several more weeks. As in the research with

FIGURE 2-4   Discrimination learning set performance for monkeys as a function of age at which testing was begun. SOURCE: H. Harlow, (1959, December). The development of learning in the Rhesus monkey. *American Scientist,* 459–479.

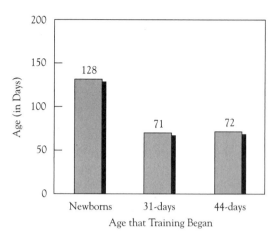

FIGURE 2-5   Age at which infants reached criterion as a function of when training was begun. SOURCE: Adapted from Papousek, H. (1977). The development of learning ability in infancy (Entwicklung der Lern-fähigkeit im Säuglingsalter). In G. Nissen (Ed.) *Intelligence, learning, and learning disabilities (Intelligenz, Lernen und Lernstörungen)* (pp. 75–93). Berlin: Springer-Verlag.

quail chicks, the result might be enhanced performance later in life in some domains, but at the expense of functioning in others, which often leads to forms of learning disabilities. This idea is provocative, although still speculative. But it is consistent with the idea that the timing of developmentally sensitive periods in the brain are correlated with the species-typical timing of perceptual experiences. When stimulation exceeds the species-typical schedule, patterns of development will be accordingly affected.

These findings do not mean that infants (or preemies) should not be given adequate stimulation, or that early learning is maladaptive. It's unlikely that learning experiences such as infants in the Papousek study had would have any long-term effects. Many more infants in the world are potentially subject to receiving too *little* rather than too much stimulation. However, the research does suggest that stimulation far in excess of the species norm can adversely affect later learning and that there might be no benefit to beginning a learning task very early in life (Bjorklund, 1997a).

More generally, the differential timing of maturation in various areas of the brain influences how the brain becomes organized. For example, Elman et al. (1996) proposed that early developing brain regions effectively serve as filters for later developing areas. The type and manner in which these early developing areas can process information determines in a very real sense the type and way later developing areas can process information. These can be potent constraints on brain development, what I referred to in Chapter 1 as *chronotopic constraints.* From this perspective, it is not content that is inherited (representational constraints) but, rather, the timing of events, and this timing is responsible, in large part, for the species-typical patterns of brain and cognitive development that we see.

The Genotype → Environment Theory

Related to the developmental systems approach are several theories that stem from the field of **behavioral genetics**, which studies genetic effects on behavior and complex psychological characteristics such as intelligence and personality (Plomin, DeFries, McClearn, & Rutter, 1997; Scarr, 1992). These theories have attracted much attention among mainstream developmentalists, partly because they use human behavioral outcomes such as personality or IQ scores as data rather than generalizing results from ducks, rats, or bobwhite quails to humans. This is also a reason for the substantial controversy the approach has produced.

Academic psychologists have long been reluctant to accept a strong influence of genetics on human behavior. The argument against a genetic influence on behavior goes something like this: If we are what our genes determine us to be, then there is little hope of modifying the human spirit or human behavior through environmental intervention. If genes affect not only blood type and eye color but also behavior, personality, and intelligence, biology truly is destiny.

Yet biology rarely dictates anything in an absolute way. As illustrated by Figure 2-1, all genetic effects are moderated by environmental ones. Even the genes for eye color must be expressed in a developing embryo, which is exposed to uncountable environmental factors as a result of its own development. The fact that genes influence behavior does not mean that environment plays only an inconsequential role.

The view that genetic causes do not necessarily seal our destiny is expressed by Richard Dawkins (1982), a sociobiologist who firmly believes that our social behavior (such as altruism) is greatly influenced by genetics:

> People seem to have little difficulty in appreciating the modifiability of "environmental" effects on human development. If a child has had bad teaching in mathematics, it is accepted that the resulting deficiency can be remedied by extra good teaching the following year. But any suggestion that the child's mathematical deficiency might have a genetic origin is likely to be greeted with something approaching despair: If it is in the genes, "it is written," it is "determined" and nothing can be done about it. This is pernicious rubbish on an almost astrological scale. Genetic causes and environmental causes are in principle no different from each other. Some influences of

both types may be hard to reverse; others may be easy to reverse. Some may be usually hard to reverse but easy if the right agent is applied. The important point is that there is no general reason for expecting genetic influences to be any more irreversible than environmental ones. (p. 13)

Thus, even a scientist whom others consider to be an extremist with respect to the influence of genetics on behavior does not believe that genes are destiny. To deny the significant role of genetics in behavior is to place one's head in the sand, but to proclaim that genetics determines our personalities, intellects, and behavior is to seriously misinterpret reality.

Genotype → Environment Effects

One of the most influential theories from behavioral genetics with respect to cognitive development is Sandra Scarr and Kathleen McCartney's genotype → environment theory. Basically, Scarr and McCartney's proposal is that one's genotype (genetic constitution) influences which environments one encounters and the type of experiences one has. Their basic contention is that *genes drive experience.* One's genetic makeup determines how one organizes one's world. Thus, environment does play a significant role in shaping intellect, but a person's inherited characteristics largely determine what those experiences are and how they are perceived.

Figure 2-6 presents a schematic of Scarr and McCartney's model of behavioral development. A child's phenotype (his or her observed characteristics) is influenced both by the child's genotype and by his or her rearing environment. The child's genotype is determined by the genotype of his or her parents. The parents' genotype also influences the environment. Parents' genetic characteristics affect the types of environments they feel most comfortable in. In this model, however, the child's genotype has an impact on the environment, which affects the child's development. Thus, characteristics of the child, as well as the rearing environment and genetic contributions of the parents, influence the course of development.

Scarr and McCartney posit three types of **genotype → environment effects** that vary in influence

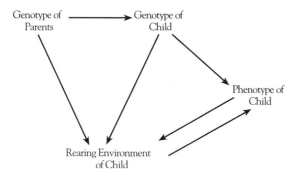

FIGURE 2-6   Scarr and McCartney's model of behavioral development. SOURCE: Adapted from "How People Make Their Own Environments: A Theory of Genotype-Environment Effects," by S. Scarr and K. McCartney, *Child Development, 54,* 424–435. Copyright © 1983 The Society for Research in Child Development, Inc. Adapted with permission

over the course of development. They are *passive, evocative,* and *active.* Passive effects occur when genetically related parents provide the rearing environment of the child. When biological parents rear a child, the effects of genetics and environment cannot be separated because the people who provide the genetic constitution for a child also provide the environment. The influence of passive effects is proposed to decline with age.

Evocative effects occur when the child elicits responses from others that are influenced by his or her genotype. For example, an irritable child is responded to differently than a well-tempered child, and the type of attention received by an infant who likes to cuddle is different from that received by an infant who does not want to be held. During early childhood, an attentive and cooperative child receives more positive interactions from parents and teachers than an uncooperative, distractible child does. Evocative effects presumably remain constant throughout development.

Active effects occur when one's genotype affects the type of environments one chooses to experience. A person actively selects an environment in which he or she feels comfortable. Accordingly, people with different genotypes choose to interact in different environments and thus have different experiences that influence their development. Active effects increase with age as children become increasingly independent of their parents and able to select their own environments.

How does Scarr and McCartney's model relate to cognitive development? For one thing, this model suggests that parents' environmental influence on children should be greatest during the early childhood years and decrease with age as active genotype → environment effects increase. Evidence for this position comes from an adoption study by Scarr and Weinberg (1978). They reported that the average correlations of the IQs of samples of adopted siblings (that is, genetically unrelated children living together) measured in early childhood ranged from .25 to .39. This means that there was a moderate level of similarity between the IQs of biologically unrelated children growing up together, a reflection of an environmental influence on IQ. However, the correlation of the IQs for adopted siblings measured late in adolescence was 0! This means that knowing the IQ of one child would not help you predict to any degree the IQ of his or her adopted sibling. The predictive power is zero. Taken together, the results reflect the fact that the longer these genetically unrelated siblings lived together, the less alike in terms of IQ scores they became. Similar findings of reduced correlations of IQs with age have been reported for dizygotic (nonidentical) twins. Correlations of the IQs of dizygotic twins computed during the preschool years ranged from .60 to .75 but were reduced to .55 when measured later in childhood (Matheny et al., 1981). In fact, siblings in general become less alike in most respects the older they get (McCartney, Harris, & Bernieri, 1990). Following Scarr and McCartney's model, passive genotype → environment effects, as reflected by the type of environments parents provide for their children, decrease with age, and active genotype → environment effects increase; as they get older, children are increasingly able to select environments that suit their particular needs, and such selection is determined primarily by one's genotype.

But then, do genes *cause* intelligence? Interestingly, Scarr and McCartney's theory ends up giving the environment a substantial role in directing development. Genotype causes a child to choose certain environments, environments that are compatible with the child's genetic constitution, and the experiences in these environments shape the child's cognition (and other important psychological characteristics). From this perspective, one's genes serve to select "appropriate" environments, but it is experience that actually is responsible for crafting the intellect (see also Bouchard et al., 1990). (The heritability of intelligence is discussed in greater detail in Chapter 14.)

Scarr and McCartney's model illustrates how genetic and environmental factors might interact to produce different patterns and levels of intelligence. What is particularly attractive about this model is its consideration of developmental effects. Genetic and environmental effects are not viewed as constants but as dynamic factors that have different effects on intelligence at different points in time. This theory, in effect, postulates a transaction between developmental function and individual differences. As children become more autonomous with age, the influence of genetic and environmental factors on individual differences changes.

"Good Enough" Parents

Scarr has expanded her initial position and proposed that "ordinary differences between families have little effect on children's development, unless the family is outside of a normal, developmental range. Good enough, ordinary parents probably have the same effects on their children's development as culturally defined super-parents" (1992, p. 15). In other words, because of the strong influence of genotype → environment effects, individual differences in parenting should have little consequence for children's development. Although this is a logical extension of the original theory, it takes the theory to an extreme that many contemporary developmental psychologists don't like; several psychologists have criticized the theory harshly (see Baumrind, 1993; Jackson, 1993).

As we'll see in Chapter 14, differences in how children are reared are related to individual differences in their level of intelligence and academic achievement. Scarr's point, reiterated and expanded

in a response to her critics (Scarr, 1993), is that children around the world grow up to be productive (and reproductive) members of their societies despite considerable differences in child-rearing practices. A behaviorally flexible species that required high-quality parenting for survival would likely be extinct before too long. Thus, the species evolved so that children could tolerate great flexibility in child-rearing practices and still grow up to be "normal."

But this is not the level of development that Scarr's critics are concerned with. They point out that differences in parenting style and opportunities make a tremendous difference in the eventual outcome of a child (Baumrind, 1993), and **"good enough" parents** are just not good enough for a sizable minority of children in our society. Scarr (1993) concurs. Children who lack opportunities and experiences associated with the dominant culture will show intellectual and social detriments relative to children in the majority culture. Scarr notes that these effects can often be ameliorated by education. The difference between Scarr and her critics seems primarily to be one of focus: Scarr is taking an evolutionary perspective, looking at how individual children become functioning members of the species; her critics are focusing instead on individual differences among children within a culture. Each level is important and each is legitimate, but it is easy for the two camps to argue right past one another, certain that the other camp is missing the point, when in reality they are each talking about different levels of human functioning.

In support of both Scarr and her critics is research on "resilient" children—children who develop social and intellectual competence despite growing up in impoverished and "high-risk" environments (Masten & Coatsworth, 1998). Why do some children from the worst environments "make it," while others flounder? Perhaps the single most important factor is competent parenting, starting early in life. This fact is consistent with Scarr's critics, who point out that individual differences in how parents interact with their children is essential to their eventual success. However, Masten and Coatsworth point out that, although many parents do fail to provide adequate warmth and support for their children, it does not take extraordinary efforts to raise a competent child, even in unfavorable environments. "Through the process of evolution, parenting has been shaped to protect development; nature has created in ordinary parents a powerful protective system for child development" (Masten & Coatsworth, 1998, p. 213).

Both the developmental systems approach and the genotype → environment model posit continuous, bidirectional interactions between biologic and environmental factors in development. There are some important distinctions between the two approaches, centering mainly around the degree to which experience modifies the organism versus the degree to which a biological organism shapes its own development. Much vigorous debate could and has been generated based on these distinctions. But the critical point for our purposes is that these two models take the transaction of biologic and environmental factors seriously, making it clear that we need to give more than lip service to the interaction of the multiple factors that produce development. This is more easily said than done, but these approaches demonstrate how biology and environment can be included in serious scientific models that help us put development in proper perspective.

The Development of the Brain

The human brain is perhaps the most marvelous invention in the universe. Unlike the brains of any other species, ours provides us with self-awareness and a behavioral flexibility that has allowed us to create culture and to adapt to a limitless diversity of environments. Other animal brains are quite impressive, but only the human brain has led to language, mathematics, physics, and art.

Differences in thinking between humans and other mammals are, of course, directly related to differences in their brains. But the human brain does not have any special structures that other mammals don't have. The major differences between human brains and those of other mammals is primarily in the greater amount of area that is devoted to the

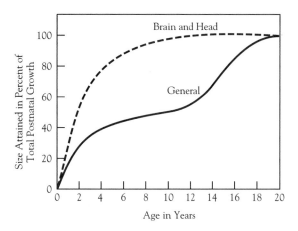

FIGURE 2-7 Growth curves for the brain and head and the body in general. SOURCE: Adapted from "The Measurement of the Body in Childhood," by R. E. Scammon. In J. A. Harris, C. M. Jackson, D. G. Paterson, R. E. Scammon, (Eds.), *The Measurement of Man*, The University of Minnesota Press, 1930.

cerebral cortex and the extended period of postnatal growth.

At birth, the human brain weighs about 350 grams—25% of its eventual adult weight of about 1400 grams. Compare this to overall body weight. At birth, an infant weighs only about 5% of what he or she will weigh as an adult. Stated another way, the brain accounts for about 10% of the overall body weight of a newborn, while accounting for only about 2% of the overall body weight of an adult. By 6 months the brain weighs 50% of what it will in adulthood; at 2 years about 75%; at 5 years, 90%; and at 10 years, 95% (Tanner, 1978). In contrast, total body weight is about 20% of eventual adult weight at 2 years and only 50% at 10 years. So the brain, which grows rapidly before birth, continues its rapid development postnatally. The rapid postnatal growth of the brain and head relative to the body in general is depicted in Figure 2-7.

From this perspective, babies are brainy creatures indeed. But from another point of view, the brain of a newborn is grossly underdeveloped. Although the brain works effectively enough to direct basic physiological functions (breathing, wake/sleep cycles), it cannot control coordinated movement and it cannot perform the mental operations so characteristic of our species. Despite its size, the infant brain is far from the organ it will become.

The human brain, directly or indirectly, is responsible for controlling all aspects of behavior, from respiration and digestion to learning and our most advanced forms of cognition. Our concern here is with the portion of the brain associated with thought, the neocortex, or cerebral cortex. The neocortex is the most recent structure to appear in evolutionary time, associated primarily with mammals, having its greatest manifestation in primates and especially humans (MacLean, 1990). Other areas of the brain—such as the limbic system, which is the seat of emotion—are also important and significantly influence human behavior, but the neocortex,—particularly the *frontal lobes* of the neocortex—provides the characteristics that we most associate with humanness. I will discuss briefly certain aspects of the neocortex and its development later in this section.

Our knowledge of brain development and its relation to cognition has increased substantially during the past decade, primarily because of new technologies that permit the imaging of brain activities (Johnson, 1998; Thatcher et al., 1996). These **neuroimaging techniques** include *high-density event-related potentials*, which are a form of EEG (electroencephalography) measurements that permits the detailed recording of brain activity when children solve cognitive tasks or are presented with specific stimuli; *positron emission tomography* (PET), in which radioactive materials are injected into participants and changes in radioactivity are used to reflect glucose consumption in specific areas of the brain; and *functional magnetic resonance imaging* (f MRI), which is a noninvasive technique that measures blood flow to the brain while children are performing cognitive tasks. There are, of course, limits to such methods, but these, and related, new technologies promise that a new understanding of the relation between brain and cognitive development will be soon upon us. But we must first examine the basic building block of the brain—the neuron.

Neuronal Development

The brain, and the nervous system in general, is a communication system. Electrical and chemical signals are transmitted from one **neuron,** or specialized nerve cell, to another. Estimates of the number of neurons in the mature human brain vary from 10 billion to more than 100 billion. Each neuron is connected to hundreds, and in many cases thousands, of other neurons via **synapses,** which are the small spaces between neurons through which messages are passed. The result is many trillions of connections among neurons.

Figure 2-8 presents a drawing of a neuron. The main part of the neuron is the cell body, which contains the nucleus. Extending from the cell body are many protractions, one of which is called the **axon,** a long fiber that carries messages away from the cell body to other cells. The other, more numerous fibers are called **dendrites,** which receive messages from other cells and transfer them to the cell body. Unlike most other cells in the human body, neurons are not compressed together but are separated. As mentioned earlier, the tiny spaces between the dendrites of one cell and the axon of another are called synapses. Electrical messages flowing down the axon of one cell cause the release of certain chemicals, called **neurotransmitters,** into the synapse. Neurotransmitters, which include dopamine, acetylcholine, and serotonin, move across the space between the cells and are "read" at the dendrites of the adjacent cell, which convert the message back to an electrical signal and pass it on to its cell body. So two neurons do not actually touch one another, but pass their information chemically through the small gaps that separate them. Conditions at the synapse (amount of and type of neurotransmitters available) affect the transmission of the messages among neurons.

Proliferation, Migration, and Differentiation

Neurons go through at least three stages of development (Nowakowski, 1987; Spreen et al., 1984). The first stage is referred to as **proliferation,** which is the

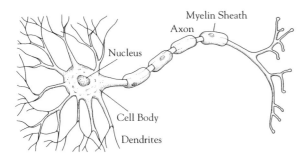

FIGURE 2-8 Primary structures of the neuron.
SOURCE: From *Looking at Children: An Introduction to Child Development,* by D. F. Bjorklund and B. R. Bjorklund, 1992. Belmont, CA: Wadsworth, p. 127.

process of cell division by mitosis. Proliferation occurs early in development, during the prenatal period. The seventh month after conception marks, essentially, the end of neuron production; with the exception of a few brain regions that produce neurons throughout life (for example, the olfactory bulbs), nearly all the neurons that one will ever have are present at birth and months before.

The second stage in neuronal development is **migration.** Once produced, the cells migrate, or move, to what will be their permanent position in the brain, where they collect together with other cells to form the major parts of the brain. Not all cells migrate at the same time, but most cells have arrived at the final position in the brain by 5 months after conception (Spreen et al., 1984). Obviously, it is important that cells destined to be in a certain part of the brain be where they are supposed to be. Mistakes do occasionally happen, however, and faulty neural migration has been found to be associated with a variety of human disorders, including some forms of dyslexia (reading disabilities), schizophrenia, fetal alcohol syndrome, and methylmercury poisoning, among others (Nowakowski, 1987).

The third stage in neuronal development is **differentiation.** Once at their final destination, neurons begin to grow in size, produce more and longer dendrites, and extend their axons farther and farther away from the cell body. Synapses are created during this stage. When an axon meets an appropriate dendrite from another neuron, a synapse is formed.

Synaptogenesis, Selective Cell Death, and the Role of Experience

The process of synapse formation, or **synaptogenesis,** is rapid during the early years of life when the brain is first becoming organized. Synaptogenesis continues throughout life, as the brain changes in response to new information, although the rate at which new synapses are formed is never as great as it is during those pre- and postnatal months when the brain is growing most rapidly. Synapse formation is perhaps more rapid in the months immediately following birth, but the peak of synapse formation varies for different parts of the brain. For example, there is a burst of synapse formation in the visual cortex beginning about 3 or 4 months that peaks between 4 and 12 months. At this time, the visual cortex has about 50% *more* synapses than there are in the adult brain. A similar pattern is found in the prefrontal cortex (the "thinking" part of the brain), but the peak number of synapses is not attained until about 24 months of age (Huttenlocher, 1994).

At this point, the infant brain has many more synapses and neurons than it needs, and a process of cell and synaptic pruning begins. Actually, the pruning had begun late during the prenatal period in a process known as **selective cell death.** Cell death and synaptic pruning occur at different rates for different parts of the brain. For example, the adult density of synapses for the visual cortex is attained between 2 and 4 years of age; in contrast, children continue to have more neurons and synapses than adults in the prefrontal areas into their teen years (Huttenlocher, 1994). Dendritic branching seems to follow a somewhat different pattern. The dendrites of many neurons increase in diversity from infancy to adulthood (Quartz & Sejnowski, 1997; see Figure 2-9).

What determines whether synapses will be formed and maintained and whether neurons will live or die? One apparently important component is sensory and motor *experience*. Greenough, Black,

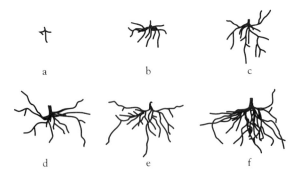

FIGURE 2-9   Drawings of basal dendrites of layer V human pyramidal cells: (a) newborn; (b) 3 months; (c) 6 months; (d) 15 months; (e) 24 months; (f) adult. SOURCE: Schade, J. P., & van Groenigen, W. B. (1961). Structural organization of the human cerebral cortex. I. Maturation of the middle frontal gyrus. *Acta Anatomica, 47* 72–111.

and Wallace (1987) proposed that specific experiences produce neural activity that in turn determines which of the excess synapses will survive (see also Johnson, 1998). The nervous system of animals (including humans) has been prepared by evolution to expect certain types of stimulation, such as a three-dimensional world consisting of moving objects. Greenough and his colleagues referred to the processes whereby synapses are formed and maintained when an organism has species-typical experiences as **experience-expectant processes** (or **experience-expectant synaptogenesis**); as a result, functions will develop for all members of a species, given a species-typical environment. Early experience of merely viewing a normal world, for example, is sufficient for the visual nervous system to develop properly. Those neurons and connections that receive the species-expected experience live and become organized with other activated neurons, and those that do not receive such activation die. Thus, although the infant comes into the world prepared and "prewired" for certain experiences and to develop certain abilities, these abilities are substantially influenced by experience. What is hardwired seems to be a susceptibility to certain environmental experiences and not the circuitry for

detailed behaviors themselves (a form of architectural constraints discussed in Chapter 1).

Examples of experience-expectant processes can be seen in research that restricts the species-typical perceptual experiences of an animal. For instance, cats or rats reared in total darkness or in the absence of patterned light, later have difficulty making simple visual discriminations. That is, because they were not exposed to visual stimulation early in life, when later provided with visual experience they act as if they cannot see or at least do not see normally (Crabtree & Riesen, 1979). In humans, cataract patients who suddenly gain sight via surgery have difficulty making simple visual discriminations. For example, for several weeks after surgery, they can tell the difference between a square and a triangle only by counting the corners (Senden, 1960). Visual abilities for both animals and humans improve with time, although the longer the period of deprivation, the less reversible are the effects (Crabtree & Riesen, 1979; Timney, Mitchell, & Cynader, 1980).

The behavioral effects of sensory deprivation are reflected in changes at the neuronal level. For example, when a kitten's eyes first open, about half of the neurons in the visual cortex respond selectively to direction of movement or orientation of a stimulus (that is, firing only when an object in their visual field moves in a certain direction or is in a particular orientation, such as diagonal lines or straight lines). Usually, after several weeks of normal visual experience, all the cells in the visual cortex become sensitive to the orientation of a stimulus or to direction of movement. Following the arguments of Greenough and his colleagues, this is what the cells are "expected" to do, given species-typical experiences. But when kittens are prevented from seeing any patterns (that is, when they experience only homogeneous light without any objects to see), the cells of the visual cortex make fewer connections with other cells and gradually lose their sensitivity to orientation. Experience (or lack of experience) changes the structure and organization of the young brain, even for something as basic as vision. As with behavior, recovery of normal neuronal structure and responsivity following exposure to pattern light occurs, although the amount or degree of recovery declines with longer periods of deprivation (Blakemore & Van Sluyters, 1975; Cynader, Berman, & Hein, 1976).

Greenough and his colleagues proposed a second process of synapse development, which they called **experience-dependent processes** (or **experience-dependent synaptogenesis**). In this case, connections among neurons are made that reflect the unique experiences of an individual, rather than the experiences that all members of a species can expect to have. In both cases, the overproduction of neurons enables an individual to make connections (and thus store information) that reflect his or her particular environment. When certain experiences are not had—when the world does not cause certain neurons to be activated and synapses to join—the neurons die.

Bertenthal and Campos (1987) relate the ideas of Greenough and his colleagues to the old nature/nurture issue and the question of whether infants come into the world fully prepared by biology or as blank slates. They write, "What determines the survival of synaptic connections is the principle of use: Those synapses activated by sensory or motor experience survive; the remainder are lost through disuse. For Greenough et al., then, experience does not create tracings on a blank tablet; rather experience erases some of them" (p. 560).

Related to the ideas of Greenough and his colleagues are *selectionist models* of neural development that propose, essentially, that many more neurons are produced than can ever survive, and that these neurons "compete" with one another for use (Changeaux & Dehaene, 1989; Edelman, 1987). For example, Gerald Edelman proposed the concept of **neural Darwinism,** in which groups of neurons are in constant competition with one another, each attempting to recruit adjacent neurons to their group and thus perform a particular function. Groups that receive the most stimulation develop strong synapses, are able to recruit more neurons to their group, and thus survive. What determines which groups flourish and which decline? One important factor is use. Neurons and groups of neurons are selected because they perform important tasks frequently, making them more likely to be used in the future. Because different groups are constantly competing for the same cells, changes in patterns of activation can result in changes in brain organization. Eventually, relatively stable patterns are achieved, but the process is an adaptive one, with the synaptic connections developing as a function of the types of information the young organism receives. Thus, through a process of activity-dependent competition, experience sculpts the brain into its final form.

Much research indicates that the activation of neurons is critical for their eventual function (and even their eventual survival). Stated another way, neurons (and the number of synapses and the degree of dendritic branches each one has) depends on experience. This set of facts led Quartz and Sejnowski (1997) to propose a model of **neural constructivism.** Basically, they contend that brain and cognitive development proceeds as a dynamic interaction between the development of the neural substrate and the environment. Although the number of neurons might decrease with age and many synapses might be pruned away, new synapses form and dendritic branching increases well into adulthood. Experience changes the brain, which results in different representations of the world (as reflected by number of synapses and changes in the complexity of axons and dendrites), which in turn affects what new information can be learned. The process is a constructive one (that is, an active interaction between specific brain structures and experience), similar to the process proposed by Piaget to describe cognitive development. (Piaget's ideas will be discussed in some detail in Chapter 4.) One interpretation that emanates from neural constructivism is that there are few areas in the brain that, at birth, are "implanted with knowledge," what I referred to as representational innateness in Chapter 1. There are surely processing constraints (architectural innateness), but for neural constructivism to be true, little in the brain can be pre-wired to afford the domain specificity that many nativists propose. Quartz and Sejnowski (1997) further believe that selectionist theories, discussed in the previous paragraph, minimize the role of experience in brain development. According to Quartz and Sejnowski, the role of early pruning and selective-cell death has been overemphasized in these popular accounts and the constructive role of experience has not been emphasized enough.

The message here is that early brain development is not exclusively under genetic control, consistent with the developmental systems approach discussed earlier. Certainly, genes determine what the basic structure of the brain will be. But experiences play an important role in shaping the precise circuitry of the brain. From electrical and chemical activities of the growing nerve cells before birth to the information obtained through the senses after birth, the brain becomes organized by information it receives and its own activation as much as or more than by the unfolding of a genetic blueprint.

Rises and Declines in Neural Development

The pattern just described for synaptogenesis was one of rapid development (that is, synapse creation) followed by a decline in the number of synapses (and neurons). Other aspects of brain development show a similar rise and decline over childhood. For example, evidence indicates that the basic metabolism of the brain (the rate at which it uses energy) increases sharply after the first year of life and peaks at about 150 percent of the adult rate between the ages of 4 and 5 years (Chugani, Phelps, & Mazziota, 1987). Evidence for this comes from studies using PET scans, which measure the amount of glucose uptake in the resting brain. After age 5 or so, the rate of glucose consumption slows down, reaching adult levels at about age 9 years. Thus, not only do infants and children have more neurons and synapses than adults, but their brains are also working harder (or at least using more calories) than those of adults.

In addition to changes in the actual structure of the neurons, developmental changes occur in the presence of various neurotransmitters. Neurotransmitters are chemicals that are found in the synapses (that is, the spaces between cell endings) that promote the electrical/chemical communication between cells. Several of these show increases followed by decreases over infancy and childhood, similar to the changes seen in synapses. These include glutamate, GABA, and serotonin (Johnson, 1998).

What function might there be in this rise and fall in several aspects of brain development? One proposal is that the hypermetabolism seen during the preschool years might be necessary for the rapid learning that occurs during this time (Elman et al., 1996). (Think of how children's language development proceeds from uttering only single words around 18 months to speaking in long paragraphs by age 3 or 4.) Preschool children also have more neurons and synapses than older children, and, I think it's fair to say, more to learn that is truly "new." These elevated levels of synapses and neurotransmitters also surely afford greater plasticity should brain damage occur.

Why the slowdown in later childhood into adulthood? I have no good answer for this other than to suggest that the tasks that must be solved by the older brain apparently require a different organization, needing less flexibility in number of neurons and perhaps synapses (much of what the brain will need to process "automatically" has already been established by 4 years of age) but greater differentiation in dendritic branching.

Myelination

Not all aspects of neuronal development show the "rise and decline" pattern, however. Some processes show only increases over early development, and one such important characteristic is **myelination. Myelin** is a fatty substance that surrounds the axons of neurons and promotes faster transmission of electrical signals. Compared with unmyelinated fibers, myelinated nerve fibers fire more rapidly, have lower thresholds of sensitivity to stimulation, and have greater functional specificity, meaning that there is less "leakage" of electrical impulse, so that only the target set of neurons are likely to get activated.

The process of myelination is a gradual one, beginning during the prenatal months and continuing into adolescence and beyond. Figure 2-10 shows the schedule of myelination for various parts of the human brain. The thin line on the left denotes when myelination for that brain structure begins, and the thicker line on the right denotes when myelination has reached adult levels. Note that myelination begins prenatally for the sensory system, with most sensory structures being completely myelinated within the first year. This corresponds to the well-developed sensory abilities of human infants and the adultlike sensory capacities they possess long before they can speak. Myelination of the motor areas follows closely, with most of these brain structures being completely myelinated before the second year. Again, this corresponds to the development of motor abilities in young children, most of whom are walking before their second birthdays. The final areas, which are labeled the integrative systems, correspond to the higher brain areas and are involved in complex cognition. Here a slower development of myelination is seen, continuing well into adolescence and adulthood (see Korner, 1991; Yakovlev & Lecours, 1967).

Although only relatively gross assessments can be made, changes in degree of myelination in the integrative brain areas over the course of childhood and adolescence are associated with changes in complex mental processes, such as language, planning, and attention (Lecours, 1975). One reason proposed for this relation is that faster transmission of nerve impulses is afforded by fully myelinated nerves. Speed of processing plays an important role in cognition and cognitive development (see Chapter 5), and it is likely that age-related changes in myelination contribute significantly to these cognitive changes. Also, because increased myelination results in less "leakage" of signals between neurons, there is less interference. This has also been suggested as an important component of cognitive development, with older children showing greater resistance to interference (Dempster, 1993) or greater abilities to inhibit irrelevant cognitive signals (Diamond, 1991; Harnishfeger & Bjorklund, 1993), resulting in broad changes in overall cognitive competencies. The correlation between cognitive development and levels of myelination is seen not only in humans, but also in monkeys (Gibson, 1991). Although the sequence of myelination provides a rough index of general brain development, it is an imperfect one. Neurological functioning begins before myelin appears on nerves, and specific loss of myelin does not always result in the expected loss of function in diseases such as multiple sclerosis (see Korner, 1991).

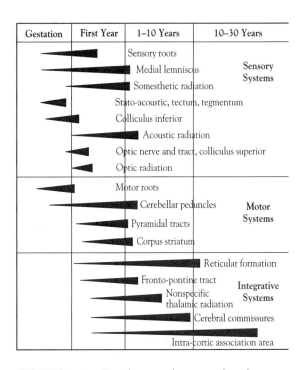

FIGURE 2-10 Developmental pattern of myelination for different areas of the human brain. SOURCE: "The Myelenogenetic Cycles of Regional Maturation of the Brain," by P. I. Yakovlev and A. R. Lecours. In A. Minkowski (ed.), *Regional Development of the Brain in Early Life*. Copyright © 1967 Blackwell Scientific Publications, Ltd. Reprinted with permission.

The amount of myelination is influenced, to some extent, by experience. Research has shown that animals given extra or atypical experience (for example, swimming for rats) or prevented from having species-typical experience (for example, raising kittens or mice in the dark) have corresponding increases or decreases in degree of myelination (see Korner, 1991). However, the amount of change in myelination resulting from these enriching or depriving experiences is relatively small (about 10 to 20%), suggesting that the developmental rate of myelination is largely under genetic control. Nevertheless, as Korner (1991) points out, the effect of experience on myelination, although small compared with that attributed to genetic control, is significant, and "mutual interaction of biology and experience must always be considered to be the rule" (p. 191).

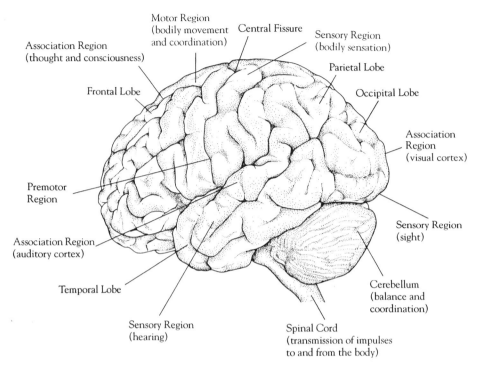

FIGURE 2-11   A lateral view of the left side of the human brain showing the major structures. All but the cerebellum and the spinal cord are part of the neocortex. SOURCE: D. F. Bjorklund and B. R. Bjorklund, 1992. *Looking at Children: An Introduction to Child Development.* Belmont, CA: Wadsworth, p. 129.

The Development of the Neocortex

When most people think of the brain, they think of what's on the surface, a convoluted series of lobes. This is the **neocortex,** or **cerebral cortex,** which is a multilayered, flat sheet of neurons, only 3 to 4 millimeters thick, that surrounds the rest of the brain. Figure 2-11 provides a lateral view of the brain; all structures shown except the cerebellum and the spinal cord are part of the neocortex. Of course, there is much more to the brain than the neocortex, but because the neocortex is the part of the brain primarily associated with thinking, it is the only major part of the brain that I will discuss in this chapter.

The neocortex consists of two approximately equal halves, or **hemispheres,** connected by a thick

mass of nerves called the **corpus callosum.** The neocortex can be further divided into regions. Primary areas such as the various sensory regions directly receive information from the senses. Other primary areas, such as the motor regions, send instructions directly to muscles. Secondary areas consist of regions that integrate information and have many connections with other areas of the brain. These are the association (or thought) regions and are responsible for our more complex mental functioning.

Let me provide a research example of the connection between development of the prefrontal lobes of the neocortex and cognitive development. Development of the prefrontal lobes in humans is rapid between birth and about 2 years of age. The prefrontal lobes are proposed to be involved in many acts of "higher" cognition, but one important function of the prefrontal lobes appears to be in the inhibition of responses (Fuster, 1989; see Chapter 5 for a more in-depth discussion of the role of the frontal lobes in inhibition). For example, there are some tasks in which children must *not* execute a previously acquired response (that is, they must inhibit that response) so that they can make a new response. One such task is the A-not-B object permanence task of Piaget (see Chapter 4 for a more in-depth discussion of object permanence). On this task, infants watch as a toy is hidden in one of two wells. The infants are distracted for a delay period, after which they are allowed to retrieve the toy. Over trials, the hiding place is changed to well B following a series of correct retrievals from well A. Piaget reported that infants younger than 12 months have great difficulty performing this task, and typically look for the hidden object at the A location, where they were successful previously.

Adele Diamond (1985) tested 25 infants in the A-not-B task, beginning at about 7 months and continuing until 12 months of age. She reported that the delay between hiding and searching that was necessary to produce the A-not-B error increased with age at a rate of about 2 seconds per month. That is, 7.5-month-old infants would search for the hidden object at the erroneous A position following only a 2-second delay. By 12 months of age infants made the error only if approximately 10 seconds transpired between the hiding of the object and the beginning of the search.

Although such research suggests that memory might be a factor in infants' performance, Diamond believes that the more important factor is infants' ability to *inhibit* prepotent responses in solving the A-not-B task. Diamond (1991) proposes that over the course of the first year, infants' prefrontal lobes develop gradually, which results in their becoming increasingly able to inhibit their behavioral responses. Despite "knowing" that the object was hidden at location B, young infants cannot stop themselves from executing a response that has been correct in the immediate past. They have learned a response, and before they can learn a new one, they must inhibit the old one. This ability develops over the first year, with girls showing faster progress than boys, suggesting more rapid maturational develop-

ment of the prefrontal cortex in girls than boys through this age period (Diamond, 1985). That maturation of the prefrontal cortex is involved in performing this task has received support from a study by Bell and Fox (1992). They recorded EEG activity from the frontal lobes of 7- to 12-month-old infants performing the A-not-B tasks and found changes in EEG patterns as a function of age and delay.

Cerebral Lateralization

Much attention has been devoted to the fact that the brain consists of two nearly identical hemispheres. The hemispheres are not perfectly alike, however, and researchers have demonstrated that each has its own specialization. Such specialization of the two hemispheres is referred to as **cerebral lateralization.** Certain mental skills or abilities have been hypothesized to be limited to (or better developed in) one hemisphere or the other. Evidence of this comes from studies of brain-damaged people and people whose right and left hemispheres have been surgically disconnected. These cerebral-lateralization studies revealed that in right-handed people, the left hemisphere is specialized for processing phonetic, syntactic, and certain semantic aspects of language, as well as other analytic, logical, or temporal information. In contrast, the right hemisphere is best suited for processing intonational and pragmatic aspects of language, as well as nonverbal, spatial, and visual information (Corballis, 1990; Hellige, 1993).

It is overly simplistic, of course, to propose that any particular type of information processing is limited to one side of the brain or the other. In neurologically intact people, both hemispheres are involved in most, if not all, cognitive tasks (remember that one hemisphere "knows" what the other is doing because they are connected by the corpus callosum), although for certain relatively simple tasks, one hemisphere or the other typically takes the lead (Hellige, 1993). Nevertheless, it has been clearly documented that the two hemispheres do process information differently and that the left hemisphere (in right-handed people and some left handers as well) is primarily responsible for the production and comprehension of language. What has long interested developmental psychologists is when such lateralization comes about and its relation to language development.

One of the first scientists to investigate the biological (that is, brain-based) basis of language development was Eric Lenneberg (1967). Lenneberg proposed the *equipotentiality hypothesis*, stating that lateralization is a gradual process that develops during childhood and is not complete until adolescence. Lenneberg based his ideas on the observation that people with specific injuries to language areas of the brain are more apt to recover their language ability if the injury happens in childhood rather than in adulthood. Basically, the right hemisphere of a young child can take over the responsibility of language if the left hemisphere is damaged. The best explanation for this, Lenneberg stated, is that the two halves of the brain have not yet divided up their responsibilities (that is, have not become fully lateralized), giving the right hemisphere the necessary flexibility to acquire a new role.

Despite Lenneberg's claim, the best evidence available today suggests that brain lateralization is present, to some degree, from birth (Corballis, 1990; Turkewitz, 1993; Witelson, 1987). The evidence for this comes from a variety of sources. For example, one test for lateralization is the dichotic-listening task, where people are presented with different audio signals simultaneously to their left and right ears and asked periodically to make decisions about information coming into the left ear (right hemisphere) or right ear (left hemisphere). Evidence of lateralization is demonstrated when people show a right-ear advantage — that is, when they show faster or more accurate performance based on information presented directly to the left hemisphere. Variants of this task have been used with children as young as 2 years of age (Hiscock & Kinsbourne, 1980), and the results consistently reveal a right-ear advantage for children (Witelson, 1987). In research using a similar paradigm, 8.5-month-old infants showed the same pattern of lateralization that adults do for listening to various types of melody changes in music (Balaban, Anderson, & Wisniewski, 1998). Other research has shown that 1- to 4-month-old infants change their sucking rate more to changes in language sounds presented to the right ear than to the same sounds presented to the left ear (Entus, 1977). Even newborns seem to be biased to process language with the left side of their brains. In research that measured the electrical reaction of newborns' brains to various sounds, the left hemisphere responded more to language sounds than did the right, with music and other nonlanguage sounds producing greater reactions from the right hemisphere (Molfese & Molfese, 1980). Other research using electrophysiological patterns in the brain (auditory evoked potentials) reports not only differences between the left and right hemispheres early in life, but also sex differences as early as 3 months of age (Shucard & Shucard, 1990). Shucard and Shucard (1990) have suggested that these findings might reflect a slower rate of brain maturation for boys for the left relative to the right hemisphere, whereas the reverse pattern is true for girls.

The results indicate that lateralization is a characteristic of the infant (even newborn) brain. Left-brain biases are found for motor behavior as well as language, with infants and young children showing a right-side bias for head turning, visually directed hand reaching, and manipulation of objects (Corballis, 1990). (Recall our earlier discussion of Turkewitz's [1993] theory that such early lateralization is based on prenatal experience.) This does not necessarily mean, however, that further changes in lateralization are not possible. For example, although young children show a distinct preference for using their left or right hands (that is, being left or right handed) (Ramsay & Weber, 1986), these preferences apparently increase over childhood (Merola & Liederman, 1985). Although such evidence does not necessarily imply that lateralization is increasing with age, it does suggest at least that with age and experience, children become increasingly reliant on one hemisphere over another to perform certain tasks (Witelson, 1987).

Although the two hemispheres are apparently specialized to perform different tasks, there seem to be individual differences in the extent to which people rely on the two hemispheres, a distinction important to educators. For example, several researchers and theorists have proposed individual styles of processing, with some individuals excelling more in the sequential, analytical processing characteristic of the left hemisphere and others excelling more in the simultaneous, holistic processing characteristic of the right hemisphere (Das, Kirby, & Jarman, 1975; Kaufman & Kaufman, 1983). Some general relationships between hemispheric cognitive style and measures of academic achievement have been reported. For example, Das and Molloy (1975) found that high levels of both successive and simultaneous processing were necessary to attain the higher reading comprehension scores in an average group of fourth-grade boys. Students who were significantly higher in either successive or simultaneous processing attained only moderate scores.

One particularly interesting study reported differences in hemispheric processing between children of different social classes (Waber et al., 1984). In this study, fifth- and seventh-grade children from both low socioeconomic status (low-SES) and high socioeconomic status (high-SES) backgrounds had sets of words or digits flashed either to their right visual fields (the right portion of their retinas) or to their left visual fields (the left portion of their retinas). The children were to determine whether consecutively presented items (words or digits) were the same. The high-SES children reported stimuli presented to the left visual field (and thus going to the left cerebral hemisphere) more accurately than stimuli presented to the right visual field (and thus going to the right cerebral hemisphere), reflecting a left-hemisphere advantage. In contrast, no systematic differences were found for the low-SES children, who performed equally well regardless of whether the stimuli were presented to the left or right visual fields. This pattern persisted even when IQ differences between the high- and low-SES groups were controlled for.

These findings indicate different patterns of brain lateralization for children from different socioeconomic levels. Moreover, they suggest that differences in cognitive and learning styles observed among children from different social backgrounds are related to differences in hemispheric organization. According to Waber and her colleagues, high-SES children, unlike their low-SES peers, seem to rely on the analytic processing associated with the left hemisphere more than on the global processing associated

with the right. The origin of these differences is not known, but it seems likely that the different experiences of low- and high-SES children play an important role in lateralization of cognitive function.

The findings and interpretation of Waber and her colleagues must, for now, be viewed cautiously. But research that considers possible individual differences in hemispheric specialization and their relationship to individual differences in cognitive functioning reflects the growing interdependence between the fields of cognitive development and developmental biology, and this should be applauded. We must avoid, however, jumping to conclusions and accepting anything as fact simply because it is based in biology or on biological theory. This, perhaps, is especially true for research dealing with hemispheric specialization. Individual differences in hemispheric specialization have been accepted by many educators and laypeople as fact. Seminars and popular books abound that attempt to teach people to make better use of one hemisphere or the other, or helping "right-brain" people cope in a "left-brain" world.

The left-brain/right-brain dichotomy is based on solid experimental and neuropsychological evidence. But the more subtle distinction of individual differences in people's hemispheric dominance is less well founded. It seems too early to jump on a bandwagon that proposes that individual differences in hemispheric specialization correspond to important differences in intellectual functioning. Nevertheless, differences in hemispheric specialization might be a fruitful source of data for responsible scientists and educators to further examine the connection between the developing brain and developing cognitive systems.

The Brain's Plasticity

Plasticity, discussed in Chapter 1, refers to the ability to change. With respect to the nervous system, to what extent can new synapses be formed and different parts of the brain take over a function intended for another part? Put another way, plasticity also refers to the potential outcomes that are possible for a single neuron, bundle of neurons, or larger brain structure. Given certain experiences at certain times during life, how might these cells become organized?

Neuronal Plasticity

Concerning the production of new neurons, there is virtually no plasticity. With a few exceptions, a newborn comes into the world with more neurons than he or she will ever need. From birth on, there is a loss of neurons (that is, cell degeneration)—a rapid loss over the first year of infancy and a gradual decline thereafter.

The picture is different for the formation of new synapses. Although it was believed not too many years ago that synapse production is limited to infancy, new research indicates that new synaptic connections can be formed throughout life (see Greenough et al., 1987). What causes new synapses to form? The answer is experience. Perhaps the most convincing evidence of the effects of experience on brain structures comes from studies providing environmental stimulation for laboratory animals, mostly rats and mice. In studies dating back to 1949 (Hebb, 1949), researchers have raised groups of laboratory animals in environments constructed to be enriched or stimulating and compared their brain development and learning ability to those raised in environments considered deprived (Hymovitch, 1952; Turner & Greenough, 1985). Enriched environments usually included animals raised together in large cages that were filled with a variety of objects with which they could interact. Various platforms, toys, and mazes filled some of the cages—not too dissimilar from the cages one might buy for the family gerbil.

These experiments have shown that rats and mice raised in enriched environments are superior at a wide range of complex tasks, such as maze learning. The differences in learning ability between enriched and nonenriched animals are of a general nature, with the most likely explanation for these effects being that "the groups differ in the amount of stored knowledge upon which they can draw in novel situations" (Greenough et al., 1987, p. 547). Concerning changes found in their brains, enriched animals have heavier and thicker neocortexes, larger neurons with more dendrites, and impor-

tantly, more synaptic connections. In one study, enriched rats had 20 to 25% more synapses per neuron in their visual cortexes than did rats raised in individual cages (Turner & Greenough, 1985). And these effects are not limited to infant animals; the behavioral and brain benefits of living in a stimulating environment are found even when experienced by older animals (Greenough et al., 1986).

Synaptic plasticity is greatest in infancy. With age and experience, neurons and synapses that were formed prenatally or in infancy die, and with their death connections that could have formed are now impossible. Thus, experience serves not only to create new connections, but also to make other ones impossible or less likely. Even though with age the plasticity to form new synapses decreases, it does not disappear; we retain substantial neural plasticity throughout life. What does change is the degree to which experience can change the brain and the intensity of the experience needed to produce change.

Let me make it clear that losing plasticity should not be viewed as a totally negative thing. As a result of genetic programming and experience, neurons become dedicated, or committed to certain functions, effectively eliminating plasticity. This commitment affords greater efficiency of processing, permitting sets of neurons to specialize. For a species such as humans, who have long life spans and must deal with a large diversity of social circumstances, retaining some plasticity into adulthood is necessary, but there is much about human life that does not change substantially over time and circumstances, and individuals are best served by a nervous system that early in life commits neurons to basic functions.

Recovery of Function from Brain Damage

Perhaps the best-known evidence for the plasticity of the nervous system comes from case studies of people who have experienced brain damage and exhibit deficits in physical or mental functioning. These studies document the process of readjustment these people go through and the differences their ages make to their readjustment.[1]

The most studied type of brain damage of this sort concerns the areas of the brain controlling language. Since the 19th century, there have been numerous reports indicating that children who experience brain damage to the language areas of their left hemispheres before they are able to speak are eventually able to attain more advanced levels of language than older children or adults who experience similar brain damage (Annett, 1973; Woods & Carey, 1979). Likewise, left-hemisphere brain injury for children who can already talk can produce an initial loss of language ability, but in many cases language is recovered and the child talks again at a normal or near-normal level. Studies conducted on adults have not found the same degree of recovery (see Witelson, 1985). Full recovery of language, even in young children, is rare, however, showing that the human brain is not completely plastic, even early in life (Witelson, 1987). Yet, the evidence clearly shows that "there is a remarkable functional plasticity for language functions following brain damage in childhood in that the eventual cognitive level reached is often far beyond that observed in cases of adult brain damage, even those having extensive remedial education. These results attest to the operation of marked neural plasticity at least in the immature brain" (Witelson, 1987, p. 676).

The picture is different, however, when brain damage influences more general cognitive functioning rather than a specific cognitive ability such as language (Levine, 1993; Witelson, 1987). Evidence reviewed by Kolb and Whishaw (1990) from both animal and human research demonstrates that younger children and animals show more permanent deficits than older children and animals do after brain damage to areas that control general processes, such as IQ, brain size, and some species-typical behaviors. For example, in one study, brain damage before the age of 1 resulted in lower IQs for children than did similar brain damage that occurred after a child's first birthday (Riva & Cazzaniga, 1986); another study reported greater reductions in IQ for children who suffered brain damage before the age of 5 than for those who suffered similar injury after 5 (Kornhuber et al., 1985). In research with rats, Kolb and Whishaw (1981) reported that brain lesions inflicted shortly after birth resulted in a smaller adult brain (about 25% smaller) than lesions inflicted on adult animals (about 12% smaller).

In general, although brain damage affecting some specific skill, such as language, can be better compensated for when it occurs earlier in life rather than later, the reverse appears to be true for brain damage that affects more general intellectual abilities. In some cases, early insults affect how large portions of a system will develop, making the consequences of early injury very severe. In other cases, early brain insults can be compensated for by a pliable system that is not yet set in its ways and can make adjustments to unexpected changes. The relationship between age at injury and degree of plasticity for specific and general skills is shown in Figure 2-12. As can be seen, the degree of plasticity observed is a function not only of age at injury but also of the nature of the brain injury.

Slow Growth and Plasticity

Earlier in this century, it was believed that if children suffered severe deprivation for much more than their first year of life, they were destined to a life of mental retardation and psychopathology. More recently, both human and animal work has clearly shown that this is not true (Clark & Hanisee, 1982; Suomi & Harlow, 1972). When the course of a young child's or young animal's life changes drastically, patterns of development can also be radically altered.

Let me provide one research example of the reversibility of the effects of negative early experience here (the topic is discussed in greater detail in Chapter 14). With the political turmoil in Southeast Asia during the 1970s, there were many abandoned and sickly children who were subsequently adopted by American families. Generally, follow-up interviews of adopted Asian children who were malnourished and socially deprived as infants revealed that their intellectual and social development was at or above normal by early childhood (Clark & Hanisee, 1982; Winick, Meyer, & Harris, 1975). In the 1982 study by Clark and Hanisee, for example, 25 adopted Asian children were given a test of verbal intelligence, the Peabody Picture Vocabulary Test (PPVT), and a test of social competence, the Vineland Social Maturity Scale (VSMS). The average age of the children at the time of testing was

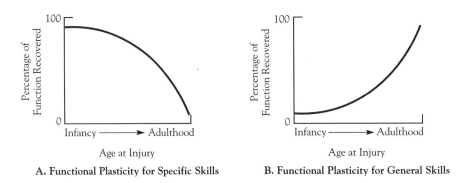

A. Functional Plasticity for Specific Skills   B. Functional Plasticity for General Skills

FIGURE 2-12   Theoretical relationship between age when brain damage is suffered and recovery of function depending on whether the brain injury affects a specific skill (such as language) or a more general skill (such as intelligence or planning). SOURCE: Adapted from "Neurobiological Aspects of Language in Children," by S. F. Witelson, 1987, *Child Development, 58*, 653–688. Copyright © 1987 The Society for Research in Child Development, Inc. Adapted with permission.

44 months, and all the children had been in their adoptive homes for at least 23 months before testing. Before being adopted, most of the children had experienced physical and psychological deprivation. Sixteen of them were reported to have been malnourished sometime during infancy, with many displaying dehydration and muscle weakness. Despite their inauspicious beginnings, the children fared exceptionally well on the tests of verbal and social competencies. The national average on both the PPVT and the VSMS is 100. The adopted children's average scores were 120 on the PPVT and 137 on the VSMS. These children, impoverished and malnourished as infants, showed no residual signs of their early deprivation within two years of having been placed in upper-middle-class homes.

This plasticity of behavior and intelligence is attributed, in part, to the slow growth of the brain. Although the human brain is large relative to the rest of the body at birth, it continues to grow well into early adulthood. In fact, not only does the human brain develop slowly, but so also does the rest of the body. Members of *Homo sapiens* require more years to attain adult status (about 15 years) than other primates, such as lemurs (about 2 years), macaque monkeys (about 4 years), and chimpanzees (about 8 years) (Poirier & Smith, 1974). This prolonged immaturity provides humans the time necessary to master the complexities of social life. But it also provides the opportunity to change behavior and to acquire novel patterns later in life. Seen in this light, the extended immaturity of the human nervous system provides opportunities for behavioral flexibility and plasticity unsurpassed by any other species.

An immature brain means a slow and inefficient brain. Partly because of the extent of myelination and partly because of a paucity of experience, young children process information more slowly than older children do (see Kail, 1991). This slower speed of processing translates directly into less-efficient processing (Case, 1985; Dempster, 1985). The overall slower speed of mental processing for younger relative to older children means that more of their processing is effortful in nature, in that it uses substantial portions of their limited mental resources (Hasher & Zacks, 1979). In contrast, more of older children's and adults' cognitive processing is automatic, in that it can be done quickly without conscious awareness and requires little or none of one's limited mental capacity. In other words, young children must work harder mentally to obtain the same results as older children.

This inefficiency has its drawbacks, of course. You can't teach much of a complex nature to young children, you can't expect them to gain as much from experiences as older children, and they can't be relied on to make many important decisions on their own. Despite the obvious disadvantages of a slow and inefficient brain, it also has its benefits. According to Bjorklund and Green (1992),

> Because little in the way of cognitive processing can be automatized early, presumably because of children's incomplete myelination, they are better prepared to adapt, cognitively, to later environments. If experiences early in life yielded automization, the child would lose the flexibility necessary for adult life. Processes automatized in response to the demands of early childhood may be useless and likely detrimental for coping with the very different cognitive demands faced by adults. Cognitive flexibility in the species is maintained by an immature nervous system that gradually permits the automization of more mental operations, increasing the likelihood that lessons learned as a young child will not interfere with the qualitatively different tasks required of the adult. (pp. 49–50)

This should not be seen as implying that the effects of early social or physical deprivation can always be reversed. As will be seen in later chapters, early experiences (or lack of them) can have relatively permanent, negative consequences. The experiences of infancy and toddlerhood establish patterns of behavior that can potentially influence the accomplishments of later years, particularly when those experiences are stable over childhood. But the inefficiency of the young brain does offer children some protection from the perils of an early damaging environment.

Relevance of Developmental Cognitive Neuroscience to Understanding Cognitive Development and Implications for Education

The new emphasis on neuroscience has caught the attention of many developmental and educational psychologists, as well as policy makers. For example, in 1997 each of the major weekly news magazines in the United States (*Newsweek*, *Time*, and *U.S. News*

and World Reports) had issues focusing on the new neuroscience research as it relates to young children. And the President of the United States held a special conference at the White House in the spring of 1997 to examine some of this new research.

How can these new findings, focusing on brain-based research into young children's cognitions, get translated into more practical information about cognitive development and education? James Byrnes and Nathan Fox (1998) recently asked this question. They reviewed some of the new neuroscience techniques and research findings from the developmental neurosciences and concluded that we are on the threshold of a new revolution, equivalent to the cognitive revolution 40 years ago that replaced behavioral perspectives of how children learn and think. Byrnes and Fox do not argue for a blind acceptance of everything that comes from modern neuroscience. We should have evidence from multiple neuropsychological sources before jumping to any conclusions. In their review, they discussed research in neuroscience that has direct implications for educational practice, including attention, memory, reading, and math. (See also accompanying commentaries by Berninger & Corina, 1998, and Brown & Bjorklund, 1998.) I will discuss some of this research later in the book, but here I would like to present some other research inspired by new discoveries and theories in the cognitive neurosciences that has direct implications for education, namely the connection between music education and spatial abilities.

Leng and Shaw (1991) proposed that areas of the brain that are involved in processing temporal-spatial information are also involved in the processing of music. Spatial-temporal reasoning involves the maintenance and transformation of mental images in memory and is likely involved in many higher-order forms of cognition, such as those used in mathematics and engineering. Moreover, according to the theory, patterns of neural activity associated with temporal-spatial cognition can be strengthened through experience. This led Frances Rauscher and her colleagues to postulate that listening to or receiving instruction in music may facilitate temporal-spatial abilities.

In an initial experiment, adults listened to selections from Mozart for 10-minute periods over three days (Rauscher, Shaw, & Ky, 1993). Control groups listened either to a variety of less-well structured music (such as Philip Glass's minimalist music) or to no music at all. Rauscher and her colleagues reported that the adults who listened to Mozart showed an immediate improvement on tasks of temporal-spatial abilities compared with people in the other groups. That is, listening to Mozart enhanced adults' spatial reasoning abilities, at least immediately after listening to the music. (Recent research has even found the effect on maze learning in rats who were exposed to Mozart in utero and for their first 60 days of life [Rauscher, Robinson, & Jens, 1998]). Rauscher and her colleagues reasoned, based on neuropsychological evidence, that the brains of young children should be more plastic than the brains of adults and that effects of music instruction on temporal-spatial reasoning might be even greater for children than for adults.

They tested this hypothesis in two experiments with preschool children (Rauscher et al., 1994; Rauscher et al., 1997). In their most recent study (Rauscher et al., 1997), preschool children were given either 10 months of piano keyboard lessons, singing lessons, computer lessons, or no lessons. Changes in their temporal-spatial reasoning were assessed, as measured by performance on the Object Assembly task from the Wechsler Preschool and Primary Scale of Intelligence-Revised (WPPSI-R). This test requires children to create a familiar object from scrambled pieces (for example, an image of a dog is broken up into pieces and children must put the pieces together to form the familiar image). Also tested was children's spatial-recognition memory. Here, children must simply match an image to one of several similar images. Rauscher and colleagues reported no improvements for any group of children for the spatial-recognition memory tasks over the 10-month period (adjusting for the improvements that are simply caused by being 10 months older). Similarly, no gains were observed on the Object Assembly task for children in the singing, computer, and "no lessons" groups. In contrast, children who received 10 months of keyboard

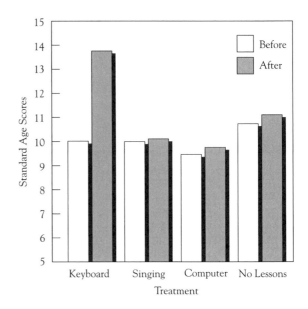

FIGURE 2-13   Standard scores on spatial-temporal task, before and after training, for preschool children in the keyboard, singing, computer, and "no lessons" groups. Only children who received keyboard lessons showed improvements in the spatial-temporal task over the 10-month period. SOURCE: "Music training causes long-term enhancement of preschool children's spatial-temporal reasoning," by F. H. Rauscher et al., 1997, *Neurological Research, 19,* 2–8. Used by permission.

instructions demonstrated significant improvement on the Object Assembly task. This effect is shown in Figure 2-13. Rauscher and her colleagues (1994) concluded that "success on the Object Assembly task is directed by cortical pattern development facilitated by the music lessons. As with musical performance, task performance requires forming an ideal mental representation of something which is eventually realized" (p. 20).

Based on the same neuropsychological evidence and the success of Rauscher et al.'s (1994) early research, Martin Gardiner and his colleagues (1996) evaluated the relation between music and arts training during the early elementary school years and mathematics performance. These researchers assigned first-grade children to a special music and arts program and compared their math performance with those of children who did not receive the special music education. Gardiner and colleagues evaluated the percentage of children who were at or above grade level (that is, the 50th percentile) on the mathematics section of the Metropolitan Achievement Test (MAT) at the end of kindergarten, before the music training began, and at the end of first grade, after seven months of music training. The percentage of children in the Music/Arts group and the control group who were at or above the 50th percentile in kindergarten and at the end of first grade are shown in Figure 2-14. As can be seen, children in the Music/Arts group were actually behind children in the control group at the end of kindergarten, before the special program began. However, by the end of first grade the situation had reversed. Now, children who had the Music/Arts training were more likely to be at or above grade level than control children. This is solid evidence that music education can enhance not only spatial abilities but also early mathematics, and this research was initiated based on ideas from the new field of developmental cognitive neuroscience.

It's worth noting that this research has caught the attention of some policy makers and as a result might have a more immediate impact on education than other less "glitzy" research. In 1997, Georgia Governor Zell Miller attended a child-development conference in which some of the research relating exposure to music and intellectual development was discussed. He later proposed that the State of Georgia spend $105,000 a year to give new parents tapes of Beethoven's *Ode to Joy* and other music to play for their babies (*Miami Herald*, January 17, 1998). And in 1998 Florida Governor Lawton Chiles signed a bill requiring toddlers attending state-run preschools to listen to classical music every day (*Sun Sentinel*, May 22, 1998). Will the musical experience really make a difference? Maybe, maybe not, given all the other countless influences on a child's life. But providing parents with "music to develop by" might foster some aspects of cognitive development directly, and, of equal or perhaps greater importance, might start parents thinking about their children's intellectual growth in general and what they can do to foster it.

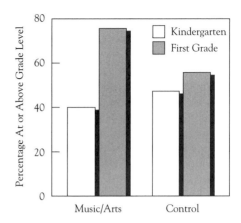

FIGURE 2-14 Percentage of children who were at or above grade level (50th percentile) on the mathematics portion of the Metropolitan Achievement Test at the end of kindergarten, before music/arts training began, and at the end of first grade, for children in the Music/Arts and Control groups. SOURCE: Adapted from "Learning improved by arts training," by M. F. Gardiner et al., 1996, *Nature, 381*, 284.

Developmental Biology and Cognitive Development

As the field of cognitive psychology evolved into cognitive science, people interested in mental functioning became increasingly aware of the need to coordinate the psychological level of explanation with the biological level. A similar realization is occurring now in the field of cognitive development. Admittedly, the presentation in this chapter is cursory, but I believe that it provides a foundation for the proper understanding of the ontogeny of human thought.

Many more topics could have been considered in this chapter. For example, hormones apparently play a major role in influencing cognition. Prenatal hormones are known to influence the brain and how later information is processed. More specifically, the class of male hormones called androgens are said to "masculinize" the brain, affecting certain sex differences in thinking (for example, spatial ability), as well as how sexual signals are processed (that is, sexual orientation) (see Money, 1988). Some recent research examining the role of prenatal exposure to male hormones in children's sex typing (specifically, toy preference) will be discussed in Chapter 11. The field of behavioral genetics has also blossomed in the past two decades, looking at the role of genetics in such diverse behaviors as alcoholism, religiosity, intelligence, learning disabilities, and amount of television viewing (see Plomin, DeFries et al., 1997). I will examine some of the data and claims of behavioral genetics in Chapter 14, when looking at individual differences in intelligence.

By acknowledging the importance of biological factors to cognitive development, I do not mean to suggest that the future of the field lies in biology. But having an idea of both the neural and evolutionary causes of behavior and development will help the psychologist ask better research questions and achieve a better understanding of development. For example, a knowledge of the developmental relationship between brain and behavior has important implications not only for theories of cognitive development but also for societal practices. How pliable is human intelligence? When, in development, can children most benefit from certain educational experiences? Is earlier always better, or are there certain sensitive periods for particular experiences distributed throughout the course of development?

The study of cognition, including its development, has gone through substantial changes since its beginnings in the 1950s. We cannot be certain what the future will hold, but it seems certain that a closer attention to the biological bases of cognition and cognitive development will be part of the new paradigm.

Summary

Developmental psychology has become increasingly concerned with the biological causes of cognition. Although psychology provides a different level of analysis than biology, concepts in psychology must be consistent with the known facts in biology. The new field of *developmental cognitive neuroscience* takes data from a variety of sources—molecular biology, cell biology, artificial intelligence, evolutionary theory, as well as conventional cognitive development—to create a picture of how the mind/brain develops

Darwin's idea of variation and *natural selection* remains the cornerstone of evolutionary theory. *Evolutionary psychologists* believe that information-processing mechanisms (*Darwinian algorithms*) have evolved in response to specific environmental pressures, equipping humans to solve specific problems. A distinction has been made between cognitive skills such as language that have been selected for in evolution (called *biologically primary abilities*) and those, such as reading, that are primarily determined by culture (called *biologically secondary abilities*). Other researchers have developed *selectionist theories*, based on Darwin's concept of natural selection, to account for cognitive and brain development.

The *developmental systems approach* centers around the concept of *epigenesis*, a bidirectional relationship between all levels of biological and experiential variables, such that genetic activity both influences and is influenced by structural maturation, which is bidirectionally related to function and activity. Organisms inherit not only a species-typical genotype but also a species-typical environment, and species-typical experiences early in life can greatly influence the course of development. Timing of experience can be crucial for development. Many early perceptual and cognitive abilities are governed by *critical periods*, those times in development when certain skills or abilities are most easily acquired.

Scarr and McCartney's *genotype → environment theory* proposes that genotype drives experience. They describe three kinds of genotype → environment effects: passive, which occur when biological parents rear the child; evocative, which occur when characteristics of the child elicit responses from others; and active, which occur when children select environments in which they choose to interact. Passive effects decrease in influence over time, whereas active effects increase. Data supporting this theory show that parents' environmental influence on their children's intelligence is greatest during the early years and wanes as the children approach adolescence.

The nervous systems consists of *neurons*, which transport chemical and electrical signals. Neurons go through at least three stages of development: *proliferation*, *migration*, and *differentiation*. The formation of *synapses* (*synaptogenesis*) occurs during this last stage. Synapse formation is rapid during prenatal development and continues to be rapid during the early months of life. A complementary process of *selective cell death* also occurs, with many neurons dying. Nearly all the neurons an individual will ever have are produced by early infancy, although synaptogenesis occurs throughout life. Some neural connections are made by all members of a species, given normal experiences (*experience-expectant processes*), whereas other connections are made as a result of the unique experiences of an individual (*experience-dependent processes*). Neurons live (and form synapses with other neurons) or die as a function of use, with groups of neurons apparently competing with one another to recruit other neurons, a process referred to as *neural Darwinism*. *Myelin* is a fatty substance that surrounds axons, promoting faster transmission of electrical signals. Different areas of the brain begin and end the process of myelination at different times, and degree of *myelination* is related to certain sensory, motor, and intellectual levels of development. Extent of myelination is also influenced by experience, but apparently less so than the structure and function of neurons.

The *neocortex* (or *cerebral cortex*) is divided into two *hemispheres* that are connected by the *corpus callosum*. *Lateralization* refers to the specialization of the two hemispheres, and recent evidence suggests that lateralization of the brain is present to some degree in young infants. Neuronal *plasticity* has been most clearly demonstrated in studies with animals, including rearing animals in deprived or enriched environments. With age, the plasticity needed to form new synapses declines, but it does not disappear. Examination of the recovery of function after brain damage shows that, at least for damage to areas of the brain that control specific abilities such as language, plasticity is greater the earlier the damage occurs. Humans' prolonged im-

maturity contributes to our behavioral plasticity and to children's abilities to overcome the effects of deleterious early environments.

Research and theory in *developmental cognitive neuroscience* is influencing research and theory in cognitive development and educational psychology. For example, based on neuropsychological theory, research has shown a connection between music instruction and spatial ability and mathematics performance in children.

Note

1. Before proceeding, I must mention some problems that are inevitable when using brain-damage research to understand brain function. These include the facts that (a) brain damage can rarely be narrowed to one area; (b) brain damage frequently involves complications beyond that of simple lesions; (c) disorders following brain damage might not reveal how the brain functions normally; and (d) lesions in one area of the brain can lead to changes in other areas of the brain (Fuster, 1989). Nevertheless, despite these, and other, reservations, much can be learned about brain functioning from studying brain damage, especially when viewed in combination with other sources of data.

Key Terms and Concepts

developmental cognitive neuroscience
evolution
natural selection
Darwinian algorithms
biologically primary abilities
biologically secondary abilities
selectionist theories
developmental systems approach (developmental contextual model)
epigenesis
hemispheres
critical (sensitive) period
behavioral genetics
genotype → environment effects
"good enough" parents
neuroimaging techniques
neuron
synapse
axon
dendrites
neurotransmitters
proliferation (of neurons)
migration (of neurons)

differentiation (of neurons)
synaptogenesis
selective cell death
experience-expectant processes (or experience-expectant
    synaptogenesis)
experience-dependent processes (or experience-
    dependent synaptogenesis)
neural Darwinism
neural constructivism
myelin
myelination
neocortex
corpus callosum
hemispheres
cerebral lateralization
plasticity (of the brain)

Suggested Readings

BARKOW, J. H., COSMIDES, L., & TOOBY, J. (Eds.). (1992).
*The adapted mind: Evolutionary psychology and the gener-
ation of culture.* New York: Oxford University Press.
This volume presents various review articles on evolu-
tionary psychology. The introduction by Cosmides,
Tooby, and Barkow ("Evolutionary Psychology and
Conceptual Integration") and the first chapter by
Tooby and Cosmides ("The Psychological Foundations
of Culture") provide an outstanding introduction to
the new field of evolutionary psychology.

CZIKO, G. (1995). *Without miracles: Universal selection theory and the second Darwinian revolution.* Cambridge,
MA: M.I.T. Press. This book presents an examination
of the historical, philosophical, and scientific basis of
selectionist theories, especially as applied to human
cognition.

GOTTLIEB, G. (1991). Experiential canalization of behavioral development: Theory. *Developmental Psychology,*
27, 4–13. This short article presents the basic ideas
of the developmental systems approach as argued by
Gottlieb and others. Associated articles in this special
edition of *Developmental Psychology* provide additional
theory and data pertinent to the developmental systems approach.

SCARR, S. (1993). Biological and cultural diversity: The
legacy of Darwin for development. *Child Development,*
64, 1333–1353. Scarr presents a relatively detailed account of her genotype → environment theory here,
emphasizing the importance of an evolutionary theory
to developmental psychologists. This paper is a response to critics of her theory (by Baumrind and by
Jackson, same issue), and Scarr is careful to be precise
about her theorizing.

JOHNSON, M. H. (1998). The neural basis of cognitive development. In D. Kuhn & R. S. Siegler (Vol. Eds.),
Cognition, perception, and language (Vol. 2) (pp. 1–49),
in W. Damon (Gen. Ed.), *Handbook of child psychology*
(5th ed.). New York: Wiley. This chapter represents
the most current review of contemporary research on
the neuronal basis of children's cognitive development.

3

The Social Construction of Mind:
Sociocultural Perspectives on Cognitive Development

The Role of Culture in Cognitive Development

Tools of Intellectual Adaptation • *The Social Origins of Early Cognitive Competencies*
The Zone of Proximal Development • *Apprenticeship in Thinking and Guided Participation*
Assessing Cognitive Development from a Sociocultural Perspective

Implications for Education

Sociocultural Theory and Cognitive Development

Summary

Note

Key Terms and Concepts

Suggested Readings

In the opening chapter, I stated that there were two obvious trends in cognitive development over the past decade or so. The first was an increased emphasis on the biological basis of development. The second was an increasing emphasis on the social construction of cognition—the perspective that how children learn to think is governed largely by the culture in which they grow up. I hope, after reading Chapter 2, you agree that the "new view" of how biology influences psychological development gives experience a substantial role to play. But this is not the same as believing that the social environment plays a critical role in shaping development. For example, most researchers who examine the biological basis of development rarely investigate the social environment in great detail, and rarely see cognitive development as "constructed" by the social environment.

This is exactly the view that proponents of the **sociocultural perspective** of development take. Sociocultural psychologists believe that how we develop, particularly how we learn to think, is primarily a function of the social and cultural environment in which we are reared. This viewpoint emphasizes what makes people different thinkers rather than what we all, as human beings, share in common. Traditional views of cognitive development, such as Piaget's (discussed in detail in the following chapter), emphasized *cognitive universals*—aspects of development that characterize all children in all parts of the world in essentially the same ways. For theorists like Piaget, and other contemporary theorists such as Sandra Scarr, whose ideas of "good enough" parenting were discussed in Chapter 2, individual differences in the environments children grow up in certainly affect their view of the world, but they do not affect much the "big picture" of cognitive development. Certainly, children growing up in an information-age society will have different things to think about than will children growing up in a hunter-gatherer society, but, according to theorists such as Piaget, each will solve problems relevant to their daily lives using species-typical cognitive mechanisms that develop according to a species-typical schedule. Sociocultural theorists see cognitive development very differently.

The overriding theme of this chapter is that cognitive development is inseparable from its cultural context. Culture is transmitted to children by their parents and other members of society. Within the adult-child interchanges of daily life, children's intellectual processes are developed to handle the tasks and problems pertinent to their particular surroundings. Parents might not be conscious of their instructional techniques, but cultural practices of child rearing are usually well suited for the type of life children can expect to face as adults. Sociocultural theory addresses how children come to understand and function in their social world. From the sociocultural perspective, how children understand their physical world "is embedded within knowledge of the sociocultural world . . . and it is the latter that enables and guides the former" (Nelson, 1996, p. 5).

The current interest in sociocultural perspectives in contemporary developmental psychology can be traced to the rediscovery of the ideas of the Russian psychologist Lev Vygotsky (1962, 1978) (see Blasi, 1996; Rogoff, 1990, 1998; Wertsch & Tulviste, 1992). Vygotsky, writing in the 1920s and 1930s, emphasized that development is guided by adults interacting with children, with the cultural context determining largely how, where, and when these interactions take place. Vygotsky proposed that cognitive development occurs in situations where a child's problem solving is guided by an adult. For Vygotsky and his contemporary followers, cognitive development progresses through the collaborations of members of one generation with another. Children's development is embedded within a culture and proceeds as they are guided through life in collaboration with others. Elaborating on this perspective, Barbara Rogoff (1998) views development as a process of *transformation of participation*. From this perspective:

> Evaluation of development focuses on how individuals participate in and contribute to ongoing activity rather than on "outcome" and individuals' possessions of concepts and skills. Evaluation of development examines the ways people transform their participation, analyzing how they coordinate with others in shared endeavors, with attention to

the purposes and dynamic nature of the activity itself and its meaning in the community. The investigation of people's actual involvement and changing goals in activities becomes the basis of understanding development rather than simply the surface to try to get past (p. 18).

From this perspective, it is clear why Vygotsky and modern sociocultural theorists propose that it is impossible to evaluate the individual without also taking into consideration other significant people and institutions in the community.

The Role of Culture in Cognitive Development

Vygotsky proposed that we should evaluate development from the perspective of four interrelated levels in interaction with children's environments—microgenetic, ontogenetic, phylogenetic, and sociohistorical. **Ontogenetic development,** development of the individual over his or her lifetime, is the topic of this book and the level of analysis for nearly all developmental psychologists. **Microgenetic development** refers to changes that occur over relatively brief periods of time, such as the changes that one may see in a child solving addition problems every week for 11 consecutive weeks (Siegler & Jenkins, 1989), or even the changes in the use of memory strategies that children use over five different trials in the course of a 20-minute session (Coyle & Bjorklund, 1997). This is obviously a finer-grained analysis than that afforded by the traditional ontogenetic level. **Phylogenetic development** refers to changes over evolutionary time, measured in thousands and even millions of years. Here, Vygotsky anticipated the current evolutionary psychology perspective, believing that an understanding of the species' history can provide insight into child development. Finally, **sociohistorical development** refers to the changes that have occurred in one's culture and the values, norms, and technologies such a history has generated. For example, children growing up in Western nations today have received a legacy of literacy, computers, and a legal and "human

rights" tradition that influences their development in ways that children growing up in other cultures without literacy, computers, or Western values can't even imagine (and vice versa).

Vygotsky's claim that multiple aspects of a child's endowment (genetic, cultural) must be viewed in interaction, makes his theory reminiscent of the developmental systems approach discussed in the previous chapter (see Tudge, Putnam, & Valsiner, 1996). Vygotsky stressed the need to understand how changing organisms develop in changing environments. Focusing only on the individual or only on the environment could not provide an adequate explanation of development (Blasi, 1996). However, what modern-day researchers have emphasized most about Vygotsky's ideas is his belief that development can only be meaningfully studied in the social and cultural context in which it occurs.

Tools of Intellectual Adaptation

Vygotsky claimed that infants are born with a few *elementary mental functions*—attention, sensation, perception and memory—that are eventually transformed by the culture into new and more sophisticated mental processes he called *higher mental functions*. Take memory, for example. Young children's early memorial capabilities are limited by biological constraints to the images and impressions they can produce. However, each culture provides its children with **tools of intellectual adaptation** that permit them to use their basic mental functions more adaptively. Thus, children in information-age societies might learn to remember more efficiently by taking notes on what to remember, whereas their agemates in preliterate societies might have learned other memory strategies, such as representing each object they must remember by tying a knot in a string or by tying a string around their finger to remind them to perform a chore. Such socially transmitted memory strategies and other cultural tools teach children how to use their minds—in short, *how* to think. And because each culture also transmits specific beliefs and values, it teaches children *what* to think as well.

A subtle difference in cultural tools of intellectual adaptation that can make a noticeable difference on children's cognitive task performance can be found in how a language names its numbers. For example, in all languages, the first ten digits must be learned by rote. However, after that, some languages take advantage of the base-ten number system and name numbers accordingly. English does this beginning at 20, (twenty-one, twenty-two, and so on). However, the teen numbers in English are not so easily represented. Rather, 11 and 12 also must be memorized. Not until 13 does a base-ten system begin (three + ten = "thirteen"), and even then, several of the number names do not correspond to the formula digit + ten. "Fourteen," "sixteen," "seventeen," "eighteen," and "nineteen" do, but the number names for "thirteen" and "fifteen" are not as straightforward (that is, they are not expressed as "threeteen" and "fiveteen"). Moreover, for the teen numbers, the digit unit is stated first ("fourteen," "sixteen"), whereas the decade unit is stated first for the numbers 20 through 99 ("twenty- one," "thirty-three"). Thus, the number system becomes very regular in English beginning with the 20s.

Other languages, such as Chinese, have a more systematic number-naming system. In Chinese, as in English, the first ten digits must be memorized, However, from this point, the Chinese number-naming system follows a base-ten logic, with the name for 11 translating as "ten one," the name for 12 translating as "ten two," and so on. The Chinese and English languages are similar beginning at 20, and both use the base-ten logic once the "hundreds" are reached.

Kevin Miller and his colleagues (1995) reasoned that differences in the number-naming systems between English and Chinese might be associated with early mathematical competence, specifically counting. They tested 3- through 5-year-old children in Champaign-Urbana, Illinois, and Bejing, China. They asked each child to count as high as possible. Differences between the Chinese and U. S. sample are shown by age in Figure 3-1. As can be seen, there were no cultural differences for the 3-year-olds, but the Chinese children began to show an advantage by age 4, and this advantage was even

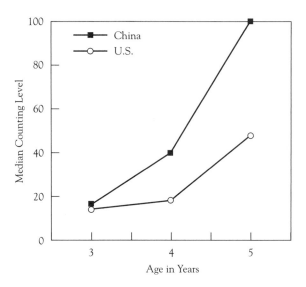

FIGURE 3-1   Median level of counting (highest number reached) by age for Chinese and U.S. preschoolers. SOURCE: Miller, K. F., Smith, C. M., Zhu, J., & Zhang, H. (1995). Preschool origins of cross-national differences in mathematical competence. *Psychological Science, 6,* 56–60.

larger at age 5. Further analyses indicated that cultural differences were limited to the teens decade. Although almost all children could count to 10 (94% of the American children and 92% of the Chinese children), only 48% of the American children could count to 20, compared with 74% of the Chinese children. Once children could count to 20, there were no cultural differences for counting to 100. These findings indicate how differences in the naming-number system of a language can contribute to early differences in a cognitive skill. This early difference in a *tool of intellectual adaptation* might contribute to later differences in mathematical abilities found between Chinese and American children (see Chapter 12).

In sum, Vygotsky claimed that human cognition, even when carried out in isolation, is inherently *sociocultural* because it is affected by the beliefs, values, and tools of intellectual adaptation transmitted to individuals by their culture. And because these values and intellectual tools can vary substantially from culture to culture, Vygotsky believed that neither the course nor the content of intellectual growth was as "universal" as Piaget and others had assumed.

The Social Origins of Early Cognitive Competencies

Vygotsky viewed young children as curious explorers who are actively involved in learning and discovering new principles. However, he placed little emphasis on *self*-initiated discovery, choosing instead to stress the importance of *social* contributions to cognitive growth.

For example, Vygotsky believed that higher psychological processes (those involving self-awareness) have a social origin, developing first on the social plane and only later becoming internalized and developing on the psychological plane (Wertsch & Tulviste, 1992). Vygotsky referred to this dual-nature of cognitive development in terms of the **general genetic law of cultural development.** According to Vygotsky (1981, p. 163), "Any function in the child's cultural development appears twice, or on two planes. First it appears on the social plan, and then on the psychological plane. First it appears between people as an interpsychological category, and then within the child as an intrapsychological category. This is equally true with regard to voluntary attention, logical memory, the formation of concepts, and the development of volition." According to Wertsch and Tulviste (1992), cognitive processes such as memory or cognition are not understood as characteristics of individuals, but rather as functions that can be carried out either between people or internally. Following this logic, Vygotsky believed that to understand cognition and cognitive development, psychologists should not focus on individuals as they execute some context-independent cognitive process (as Western psychologists have traditionally done) but should examine individuals as they participate in culturally valued activities.

According to Vygotsky, many of the truly important "discoveries" that children make occur within the context of cooperative, or collaborative *dialogues* between a skillful tutor, who might model the activity and transmit verbal instructions, and a novice pupil, who first seeks to understand the tutor's in-

struction and eventually internalizes this information, using it to regulate his or her own performance.

To illustrate collaborative (or guided) learning as Vygotsky viewed it, imagine Miguel, a 4-year-old, trying to put together a jigsaw puzzle. His early attempts get him no where. His mother notices his difficulties and sits down beside him and offers some assistance. She first suggests that Miguel should look for the corner pieces, selecting one and showing Miguel. Next, she suggests that Miguel should look for other edge pieces, starting with those that match the patterns and colors of one of the corner pieces. Miguel selects several pieces, attempts to put them together, and on his third attempt finds a piece that fits. Miguel continues to look for other pieces, but becomes frustrated. His mother then selects two pieces, places them close together and says, "See if these two fit." Miguel puts them together, smiles, and continues to look for other pieces. Miguel's mother gives him a few words of encouragement, and continues to help Miguel when he runs into trouble. But Miguel is getting the hang of it, and his mother's assistance is needed less and less. This kind of social interaction, claimed Vygotsky, fosters cognitive growth.

The Zone of Proximal Development

How? First, Miguel and his mother are operating in what Vygotsky called the **zone of proximal development** — defined as the difference between a child's "actual developmental level as determined by independent problem solving" and his or her level of "potential development as determined through problem solving under adult guidance or in collaboration with more capable peers" (Vygotsky, 1978, p. 86). It is in this zone in which sensitive instruction should be aimed and in which new cognitive growth can be expected to occur. Miguel obviously becomes a more competent puzzle-solver with his mother's help than without it. More important, he will internalize the problem-solving techniques that his mother uses in collaboration with him and will ultimately use them on his own, rising to a new level of independent mastery. In other words, children can best learn to solve problems at a level between their current ability and their ability when assisted by an adult. Within this zone adults can do the most effective teaching.

One important thing to remember here is that the skills of the child continue to develop, requiring modifications by the adults. Thus, the sociocultural approach is by necessity dynamic—ever changing—with both adults and children progressing as a result of their repeated transactions (Saxe, Guberman, & Gearhart, 1987).

Related to the concept of zone of proximal development is the concept of **scaffolding** (Wood, Bruner, & Ross, 1976). Scaffolding occurs when experts are sensitive to abilities of a novice and respond contingently to the novice's responses in a learning situation, so that the novice gradually increases his or her understanding of a problem. Scaffolding obviously will be most effective when done in the zone of proximal development, and occurs not just in formal educational settings, but any time a more expert person tailors his or her interactions to guide a child to a level near the limits of his or her performance. The behavior of Miguel's mother in the earlier example reflected scaffolding and working in the zone of proximal development.

Evidence of scaffolding can be seen in a study in which mothers were instructed to teach their 5-year-old children how to play a board game involving the use of dice to compute moves (Reubens et al., 1998). In this research, kindergarten children played a board game of "Chutes and Ladders" with their mothers, with the spinner being replaced by a pair of dice. Children had to compute their moves by adding the numbers on the two dice. To what extent did mothers help their children add or attempt to teach their children arithmetic strategies in the process of playing the game? Mothers' behavior varied with the competence of their children. For children who were using fact retrieval and mental arithmetic spontaneously (that is, who did not have to count out loud or on their fingers to arrive at an answer), mothers provided little support or advice, as little or none was needed. In contrast, mothers of less arithmetically competent children prompted their 5-year-olds to count the dice, modeled or instructed use of simple addition strategies (for exam-

ple, counting all the pips on the dice) and often re-represented the problem by holding up their fingers to correspond to the pips on the dice. Mothers tended to use these overt procedures more on the early trials and gradually declined their use of specific prompts and instructions as their children took more responsibility for solving the "problem" on their own. In other words, these mothers were "working in the zone of proximal development" to teach their children simple arithmetic strategies in the context of a social game.

There was variability in the degree of scaffolding shown by different mothers, of course. Let me provide one example from this research of a particularly effective mother. Five-year-old Yolanda and her mother were playing a game of "Chutes and Ladders," using dice to compute their moves. On her first move, Yolanda threw the dice and just stared at them, said nothing, and then looked at her mother. Her mother asked, "How many is that?" Yolanda shrugged her shoulders, and her mother said "Count them." Yolanda shrugged again, and her mother then pointed to the dots on the first die saying, "One, two, three," then to the dots on the second die, saying "four, five. You have five. Now you count them." Yolanda complied, pointing to each dot as she counted out loud, and then moved her piece on the board. The mother then threw the dice and asked Yolanda, "How many do I have?" Yolanda shrugged her shoulders, her mother counted the dots on the dice out loud and then said, "You count them," which Yolanda did. The next five turns that each took went very much the same as their first turns, with Yolanda professing not to know what to do and her mother modeling counting and then directing Yolanda to count the dots on the dice. On the sixth move, Yolanda counted the dots on the dice immediately after her mother's request (no shrug and no modeling of counting by mother), and did the same on her mother's turn. Her mother then hesitated on the next several turns before asking Yolanda how many dots she had. Eventually, Yolanda threw the dice and counted the dots herself spontaneously, without any prodding from her mother, and continued to do so, on both her and her mother's turns, throughout most of the game. The mother corrected Yolanda when she made a mistake counting, but she became less directive as Yolanda took more of the responsibility for the game herself.

Contrast the behavior of Yolanda's mother with that of Darrell's mother. Darrell would roll the dice and begin counting each pip on the dice, starting with the die closest to him ("one, two, three") and then continuing to count the pips on the second dice ("four, five, six, seven, eight"). While he was counting, his mother would interrupt him and instruct him to count from the larger number, a more sophisticated strategy. For example, when the child rolled a "6 and 5" and started counting the dots, the mother would interrupt his counting by saying, "No, Darrell, start counting from the six here" pointing at the six and saying, "you know this is six." The child would start over counting each pip on the dice, asking his mother to stop. This continued throughout the game with mom rolling the dice during her turn and modeling retrieval of arithmetic facts (for example, "3 plus 4 is 7") which was beyond this child's capability. Darrell usually ignored his mother's demonstrations and instructions and, as a result, showed no improvement in arithmetic strategy use over the course of the sessions.

All the responsibility for determining the extent of adult involvement is not on the adult. Both adults and children jointly determine the degree to which children can function independently. For example, children who are less able to solve problems on their own will elicit more support from adults than will more capable children. More skilled children need less adult support, or scaffolding, to solve a problem (Plumert & Nichols-Whitehead, 1996).

I have been careful not to use the word "competence" in describing children's problem-solving abilities. In Vygotsky's sociocultural perspective, learning and development are the result of interacting in specific culturally defined tasks that have specific rules. Unlike other theories of cognitive development (for example, Piaget's), "competence" is not an absolute level beyond which a child cannot exceed, but rather, is task specific (Fischer & Bidell, 1998; Laboratory of Comparative Human Cognition, 1983). A child can show a high level of ability on one highly practiced task but be much less adept on a very similar, perhaps even objectively less-demanding, task. A child's level of intellectual functioning is always evaluated by performance on specific tasks or in specific culturally determined situations.

Apprenticeship in Thinking and Guided Participation

Adults' interactions with children vary depending on their culture. Although child rearing in all cultures can take advantage of the zone of proximal development, what is taught will depend on what roles the child is expected to play eventually in society. Barbara Rogoff (1990; Rogoff et al., 1993) has viewed the transaction between children and adults as reflecting an "apprenticeship in thinking," with novice children improving their "skills and understanding through participation with more skilled partners in culturally organized activities" (1990, p. 39). All the responsibility for the apprenticeship is not placed on the adults, however. Children might actively place themselves in positions to learn, prompting adults to increase the level of instruction as they become increasingly competent.

Rogoff developed the concept of **guided participation** to extend Vygotsky's concept of the zone of proximal development. The zone of proximal development has typically been applied to situations where there is explicit instruction between an older, more skilled teacher, and a younger, less knowledgeable learner. Rogoff uses the term guided participation to refer to adult-child interactions, not only during explicit instruction, but also during the more routine activities and communication of everyday life. Guided participation is "the process and system of involvement of individuals with others, as they communicate and engage in shared activities" (Rogoff et al., 1993, p. 6). Guided participation focuses on day-to-day activities in children's lives, such as doing chores, watching television, and eavesdropping on parents. Rogoff believes that children's cognitions are shaped during such mundane activities, as much as or more so than in more formal educational settings.

The idea of an apprenticeship or guided participation might seem reasonable in cultures where children are integrated early into the daily activities of adult life, such as among the agrarian Mayans of Guatemala and Mexico, or the !Kung of Africa, whose hunting and gathering lifestyles have remained virtually unchanged for thousands of years. But this idea is not as easily grasped for a culture such as our own. Many school-age children do not even know what their parents do for a living and might not have seen their parents in action at their jobs. Moreover, children are generally excluded from adult activities, being segregated from adults much of the day. Other children around the world, for example, sleep in the same room or even the same bed as their parents throughout childhood, and babies never leave home unless they are strapped to their mothers' backs.

Many aspects of cognitive development in information-age cultures have been shifted from parents to professional educators, whose job it is to teach important cultural knowledge and skills to children. Yet, much learning certainly transpires between parent and child in postindustrial societies, particularly during the preschool years; in many ways, these transactions are designed to prepare children for the schooling that will follow. For example, formal education in the United States, Europe, and Japan involves children's responding to adults' questions when the adults already know the answers. It also involves learning and discussing things that have no immediate relevance—knowledge for knowledge's sake. Such context-independent learning, foreign to many cultures, is fostered in infancy and early childhood in our own culture. For example, as will be discussed in Chapter 8 on memory, parents of young children frequently prompt them to name objects or to recall recent events (Rogoff, 1990). Take, for instance, the following interchange between 19-month-old Brittany and her mother:

Mother: "Brittany, what's at the park?"
Brittany: "Babysing."
Mother: "That's right, the babyswing. And what else?"
Brittany: [Shrugs.]

Mother: "A slide?"
Brittany: [Smiling, nods yes.]
Mother: "And what else is at the park?"
Brittany: [Shrugs.]
Mother: "A see . . ."
Brittany: "See-saw!"
Mother: "That's right, a see-saw."

This type of interchange is not at all unusual for a mother and a child from mainstream America, and it is a good example of Vygotsky's zone of proximal development. Brittany, in this case, is learning to recall specific objects with her mother's help but also is learning the importance of remembering information out of context (mother and daughter are in their living room at the time, miles from the park). Brittany is learning that she can be called on to state facts to her mother that her mother already knows. She is also learning that she can depend on her mother to help provide answers when she is unable to generate them herself.

Another way parents in postindustrial cultures prepare their children for formal education is by talking to them. In the United States and most of the developed world, parents talk to their young children, including them as conversational partners. Although the type of language environment children are exposed to does influence their language development (Moerk, 1986), children around the world acquire language at about the same time, even in cultures where children are "seen and not heard." But children who are not included as conversational partners by adults might not be prepared for the type of language interaction used in school. These children might become proficient users of language in their own community, while being perceived as language deficient in school (Rogoff, 1990).

Another school-related skill that might be associated with parent-child conversations is reading. We know that reading to children is an important predictor of children's later reading ability (Stevenson & Fredman, 1990; see Chapter 12). There are substantial differences in how frequently preschool children are read to (see Adams, Treiman, & Pressley, 1998), and differences in how children are read to can have important implications for later language, and possibly reading, development. For example, Whitehurst and his colleagues (1988) trained parents of 2- and 3-year-old children in a technique of *interactive story reading*. Instead of just reading to the children, parents were told to stop every so often and to ask open-ended questions (such as "What is Eeyore doing?"), and were encouraged to expand on their children's responses, suggest alternative possibilities, and to make the questions progressively more challenging as children's understanding increased. A control group of parents was simply asked to read to their children. Analysis of tape recordings of the sessions indicated that the parents in the two groups did read to their children equally often, and that parents in the experimental group followed the interactive story reading instructions they were provided. After one month of such reading, children in the experimental group were 8.5 months more advanced than children in the control group on a measure of verbal expression, despite the fact that the two groups were equal at the beginning of the study. In later research, similar, though somewhat less dramatic, gains were observed for a group of low-income 2-year-olds attending a public day-care facility in Mexico (Valdez-Menchaca & Whitehurst, 1992). The effect, it seems, is quite robust and demonstrates that the way in which parents or teachers read to young children—ways that take into consideration children's understanding of the task and encourage their active participation—facilitates their subsequent language development and prepares them for life in a literate society. (For an example of interactive story reading, see the excerpt from Tudge, Putnam, & Valsiner (1996) in "Assessing Cognitive Development from a Sociocultural Perspective" later in this chapter.)

Is it just reading to children that prepares them for life in a literate society, or might talking to children also be related to later reading skills? Apparently so, but not all types of talking are equally effective at fostering later reading ability. Reese (1995) recorded conversations between mothers and their preschool children and related aspects of these conversations to children's understanding of print at 70 months of age. Most children were just beginning kindergarten, and so few were actually reading.

Children's understanding of print and prereading skills were assessed by their familiarity with letters and their ability to identify simple words (such as *cat* and *no*), a test of vocabulary, their knowledge about how books are read (front to back, with sentences running from left to right), and their ability both to comprehend and to produce coherent stories. Reese reported that mothers' conversations with their children about past events, especially when including elaborations of those events and associations with other events, was a good predictor of children's subsequent print skills. Reese proposed that mothers provide scaffolding by increasingly involving their children in collaborative conversations. According to Reese (1995), "a tentative conclusion that can be drawn from this study is that children who participate to a greater degree in early adult-child conversations may be honing different abilities from those children who allow the adult to direct the interaction" (p. 402)

Play is another area in which parents and older siblings guide children's development. One particularly important type of play for our purposes is **symbolic play.** Symbolic play is essentially pretending and can be solitary (for example, the child pretending that a chair is a car) or cooperative (for example, a child pretending that he's the driver of the car and his mother is a passenger). Symbolic play has been viewed by many as requiring mental representation and as an indication of children's general cognitive development (Piaget, 1962). According to Bornstein and his colleagues (1996), "In symbolic play, young children advance upon their cognitions about people, objects, and actions and in this way construct increasingly sophisticated representations of the world" (p. 2923).

But how do parents, or more expert siblings and peers, contribute to children's symbolic play development? It seems that young children are more likely to engage in symbolic play when they are playing with someone else, rather than alone, and that mothers in particular bring out high levels of symbolic play in their children (Bornstein et al., 1996; Youngblood & Dunn, 1995). Consistent with Vygotsky's idea of a zone of proximal development and Rogoff's idea of guided participation, young children who interact with a more skilled partner who structures the situation appropriately for them, advance in their skills faster than when such support is not provided. Evidence for this comes from a study in which mothers and their 21-month-old children were videotaped during play sessions (Damast, Tamis-LeMonda, & Bornstein, 1996). Many mothers adjusted their level of play to that of their children's or slightly above the level their child was displaying. And mothers who knew more about play development were more likely to increase the level of play with their children than were less knowledgeable mothers, and thus provided appropriately challenging play interactions.

Why might it be important to facilitate symbolic play? Children learn about "people, objects, and actions" through symbolic play, and research indicates that such play might be related to other aspects of cognitive development. Researchers have found a relationship between the amount of cooperative social play preschoolers engage in (often with a sibling or parent) and later understanding of other peoples' feelings and beliefs (Astington & Jenkins, 1995; Youngblood & Dunn, 1995). An understanding that other people have thoughts, feelings, and beliefs other than one's own reflects what has been called a *theory of mind*, and will be discussed in Chapter 7. Developing an advanced theory of mind is necessary if children are to succeed in any society, and it appears that the guided participation afforded by parents, siblings, and other more expert partners during symbolic play contributes to this development.

Although the process of guided participation may be universal, how it is carried out likely varies as a function of how children are perceived and treated in a culture. Rogoff and her colleagues (1993) proposed that different parent-child interactions (that is, differences in the nature of guided participation) occur in different cultures. They made contrasts between two general types of cultures: (1) cultures such as ours, where beginning in the preschool years children are often segregated from adults and receive much culturally important information and instruction outside of the context of skilled activity (that is, in school); and (2) cultures where children are in close contact most of the

day with adults and observe and interact with adults while they perform culturally important activities. Rogoff and her associates observed 14 families with toddlers in each of four communities, two where culturally important information is transmitted mainly out of context, through formal schooling (Salt Lake City, United States, and Keçiören, a middle-class community in Turkey), and two where culturally important information is transmitted mainly in context (the Guatemalan Mayan town of San Pedro, and Dhol-Ki-Patti, a tribal village in India). Rogoff and her colleagues observed toddlers and their caregivers doing routine activities (for example, feeding, dressing), while playing social games (for example, peek-a-boo, finger games) and while playing with novel objects (for example, a clear plastic jar with a small doll inside, an embroidery hoop, a jumping jack—a marionette that kicks its legs when its bottom string is pulled and the top string is held). Following are examples of guided participation in each of the four communities.[1]

Salt Lake City. A 21-month-old boy and his mother, exploring a glass jar that contains a peewee doll:

> Sandy's mother held the jar up and chirped excitedly, "What is it? What's inside?" and then pointed to the peewee doll inside. "Is that a little person?" When Sandy pulled down on the jar, she suggested, "Can you take the lid off?"
>
> Sandy inspected the round knob on top and said, "Da ball."
>
> "Da ball, yeah," his mother confirmed. "Pull the lid," she encouraged, and demonstrated pulling on the knob. "Can you pull?" Sandy put his hand on hers, and they pulled the lid off together triumphantly. "What's inside?" asked his mother, and took the peewee out. "Who is that?"
>
> Sandy reached for the lid, and his mother provided running commentary. "OK, you put the lid back on." And when Sandy exclaimed "Oh!" his mother repeated "Oh!" after him. When Sandy lost interest, his mother asked with mock disappointment, "Oh, you don't want to play anymore?" and suggested, "We could make him play peek-a-boo."
>
> When Sandy took the peewee out, she asked, "Where did she go?" and sang, "There, she's all

gone," as she covered the peewee with her hands, "Aaall gone." (p. 81)

Keçiören, Turkey.   A 14-month-old girl and her mother, playing with an embroidery hoop.

A mother introduced a game in which she and her 14-month-old daughter, Lamia, took turns putting the embroidery hoop on each other's head and then dropping it on the floor. The mother created a sense of pretend excitement by saying, "Ay ay ay . . . ," each time they dropped the hoop. This was followed by joint laughter. The game became explicitly pretend when the mother put the hoop on Lamia's head, making the girl look like a bug with the handles of the hoop sticking out like antennas. The older brother chipped in, saying, "Lamia is a bug, Lamia became a bug." "What kind of a bug?" asked the mother in a coquettish way. "A lady bug," the mother and brother said simultaneously. (p. 136)

Dhol-Ki-Patti, India.   An 18-month-old girl and her mother, playing with a jumping jack.

Roopa was not holding the top and bottom strings taut enough to cause the jumping jack to jump, so her mother took Roopa's hand in her own, grasped the bottom string with both hands, and pulled on the string twice, saying, "Pull here, pull here," as she demonstrated. She then released her hold of Roopa's hand to enable Roopa to do it on her own.

But the jumping jack fell to the ground because Roopa was not holding it tight. The mother, quick to help, lifted the jumping jack as Roopa reached for it. Twice again, she pulled on the bottom string with her left hand, repeating, "Pull it here." Then she released her hold, letting Roopa take the object. She held her hands close to (but not touching) Roopa's, ready to help if necessary. (p. 114)

San Pedro, Guatemala.   A 19-month-old boy and his mother, playing with a jumping jack.

The mother used a firm manner of placing the child's hands on the strings to mark the importance of holding firmly onto them, positioning the jumping-jack toy in a position that indicated to the child to hold the bottom string lower, and tapping the child gently on the arm, indicating not to pull the string so hard. (p. 71)

Although toddlers and caregivers in all communities interacted in ways permitting all participants to develop an understanding of the task at hand and their own participation in the task, there were important differences between the middle-class and more traditional communities. Parents in Salt Lake City and the Turkish town placed a greater emphasis on verbal than nonverbal instruction, with the adults providing a good deal of structure to foster children's involvement in learning, including praise and other techniques to motivate children. The middle-class parents also frequently instructed their children in specific tasks. In contrast, parents in the Mayan and Indian villages used more explicit nonverbal communication and rarely directly instructed their children in a particular task. In these communities, children are rarely segregated from adults; because children are around adults most of the day, they can observe competent adult behavior and interact with adults while they perform the important tasks of their society. Rogoff and her colleagues reported that observation skills are more important and better developed in the traditional than the middle-class communities, with children in traditional communities being better at attending to relevant adult behavior.

The findings of Rogoff and her colleagues make it clear that there is no single path to becoming an effective member of society, but that, depending on the demands of one's particular community, different forms of guided participation are apt to be used. One form is not necessarily better than another. It depends on how a competent adult in a society is supposed to behave.

It is easy to think of cognitive development as something that "just happens" exactly the same way for children worldwide. After all, evolution has provided humans with a unique nervous system, and the center of our flexible intelligence is the brain. Yet intelligence is also rooted in the environment, particularly in the culture. Understanding how cultural beliefs and technological tools influence cognitive development through child-rearing practices helps us better comprehend the process of development and our role as adults in fostering that process.

Assessing Cognitive Development from a Sociocultural Perspective

From the perspective of the researcher, how can one effectively measure how a child and a more experienced partner interact in a particular context? One must look at the characteristic of the context (some contexts might constrain the possible interactions more than others), the child, and the more experienced partner, all in interaction with one another. It is not enough (although it might be necessary) to assess what the child does and then independently assess what the experienced partner does. All factors must be evaluated together. Let me provide an example of such an interaction by examining what happens in a joint-reading activity between a 4-year old child, whom we'll call Rose, and her mother (adapted from Tudge, Putnam, and Valsiner, 1996, pp. 215–216). For her regular bedtime story, Rose chose *Mike Mulligan and the Steam Shovel* for her mother to read. (The text of the story is placed in quotation marks.)

Mother: "Mike Mulligan and the Steam Shovel." [She turns the page.]
Rose: "To Mike."
Mother: Good. "Mike Mulligan had a steam shovel. A beautiful red steam shovel. Her name was . . . ? [Mother pauses.]
Mother: What was her name?
Rose: "Marianne."
Mother: Marianne. "Mike Mulligan was very proud of Marianne."
Mother: "It was Mike Mulligan and Marianne and some others who cut through the high mountains so that trains could go through. It was Mike Mulligan and Marianne and some others who lowered the hills and straightened the curves to make the long highways for the automobiles."
Rose: [Pointing to the picture.] And the holes for um er for the er um cars.
Mother: Yep, there are some holes for the cars to go through. "It was Mike Mulligan and Marianne and some others who smoothed out the ground and filled the holes to make the landing fields for the airplanes."
Mother: Rose, look at this airport. What do you think is strange about that airport? [Rose looks at the picture.]

Mother: Have you ever been to an airport that looked like that? [Rose shakes her head, indicating No.] What's different about that airport? Why does it look different from the airports we've been to?
Rose: Got houses.
Mother: It's got houses, but that wasn't what I was thinking of. But that's true. I was thinking that the airports that we've been to, the airplane landing is a long rectangular-shaped road called a landing strip, a runway. Is that what this one looks like?
Rose: [Shakes head, No]
Mother: No. What's different about this one?
Rose: Don't know.
Mother: It's round! Have you ever seen . . . been to an airport where the airplane landed on a round road?
Rose: No.
Mother: [Laughs] Pretty strange. Oooh, look at that.
Mother: "Then along came new gasoline shovels, and the new electric shovels and the new diesel motor shovels and took all the jobs away from the steam shovels. Mike Mulligan and Marianne were . . ." [pauses and looks down at Rose]
Rose: ". . . very sad."
Mother: Why were they sad?
Rose: Because they um, because, because um all the um gasoline shovels and all the [looks at mother] . . . shovels and all the mo . . . the motor shovels took all the jobs away from her.
Mother: Aaaah [sad]. That's right.
Mother: "All the other steam shovels were sold for . . ." [pauses]
Rose: ". . . junk."
Mother: ". . . or just left out in old gravel pits just to rust away."

What would one look at in this interaction to describe it in terms of a social constructivist perspective? First, the two are working toward the same goal (joint reading of the story) and seem to be jointly attending to the task. The two partners are also generally responsive to one another. This is obviously a familiar routine for mother and child, and each knew what to expect of the other. The two are not sharing equally in the load, however. The mother takes the lead in most of the exchanges. Although we have a dyadic (two-way) interaction, the relations are not symmetrical. In this case, mother is doing most of the work, although that might change over time as Rose's reading improves. Note also that although the mother is contributing more to the interaction, Rose is not a passive participant. She selected the book, responded appropriately when her mother requested, and interjected her own comments at times. The mother seems to be providing adequate scaffolding for her daughter. When the context was clear, she requested that her daughter fill in parts of the text, but read most of the text for Rose.

Implications for Education

Vygotsky's theory has some rather obvious implications for education. He stressed active rather than passive learning and took great care to assess what the learner already knows, thereby estimating what he or she is now capable of learning. Teachers in Vygotsky's classroom would favor guided participations in which they structure the learning activity, provide helpful hints or instructions that are carefully tailored to the child's current abilities, and then monitor the learner's progress, gradually turning over more of the mental activity to their pupils. Teachers can also arrange **cooperative** (or **collaborative**) **learning** exercises in which students are encouraged to assist each other; the idea here is that the less competent members of the team are likely to benefit from the instruction they receive from their more skillful peers, who also benefit by playing the role of teacher (Palinscar, Brown, & Campione, 1993).

Is there any evidence that Vygotsky's guided-learning approach might be a particularly effective educational strategy? Consider a study by Freund (1990), in which she had 3- to 5-year-olds help a puppet decide which furnishings (for example, sofas, beds, bathtubs, and stoves) should be placed in each of six rooms of a dollhouse that the puppet was moving into. Children were first tested to determine what they already knew about proper furniture placement. Then each child worked at a similar task, either alone or with his or her mother (Vygotsky's guided learning). Then to assess what they had learned, children performed a final, rather complex, furniture-sorting task. The results were clear. Chil-

dren who had sorted furniture with help from their mothers showed dramatic improvements in sorting ability, whereas those who had practiced on their own showed little improvement at all, even though they had received some corrective feedback from the experimenter (see also Diaz, Neal, & Vachio, 1991; Rogoff, 1998).

Similar advances in problem-solving skills have been reported when children collaborate with peers rather than working alone (Azmitia, 1992; Manion & Alexander, 1997), and the youngsters who gain the most from these collaborations are those who were initially much less competent than their partners (Manion & Alexander, 1997; Tudge, 1992). Johnson and Johnson (1987) conducted a meta-analysis of 378 studies that compared achievement of people working alone versus cooperatively and found that cooperative learning resulted in superior performance in more than half of the studies; in contrast, working alone resulted in improved performance in fewer than 10% of the studies.

There appear to be several reasons why cooperative learning is effective:

1. Motivation seems to be enhanced when children work on problems together (Johnson & Johnson, 1989).
2. Cooperative learning requires that children explain their ideas to one another, persuade, and resolve conflicts. These all require children to examine their own ideas more closely and be able to articulate them so someone else can understand them. Related to this are the results of a study in which fourth-grade children were given scientific reasoning problems to solve, either in pairs or alone, with some asked to talk aloud while solving the problems and others given no special instructions about talking aloud (Teasley, 1995). Did working in pairs and/or talking aloud make any difference in children's performance? Children who worked in pairs and talked aloud generated better hypotheses than children who did not talk aloud. This result suggests that collaborative learning leads to improved problem solving not simply because of the collaboration per se, but because

collaboration increases "the likelihood that children would engage in the kinds of talk that support learning" (Teasley, 1995, p. 218).

3. Children are more likely to use high-quality cognitive strategies and metacognitive approaches during cooperative learning (Johnson & Johnson, 1989), which results in generating ideas that no one in the group would likely have generated alone.

Peer collaboration is not the cure-all, however, that the results of some of these studies might seem to imply. Performance is not always enhanced by collaborative learning (Pine & Messer, 1998). In fact, when older peers are compared with parents as partners in collaborative learning exercises, parents usually are the more effective collaborators (Ellis & Rogoff, 1986). Performance on collaborative learning tasks also varies as a function of the competency of the "expert" in the pair. When the more competent peer lacks confidence or does not modify his or her behavior appropriately for the less-skilled peer (that is, does a poor job at scaffolding), achievement is usually no better than when working alone (Levin & Druyan, 1993; Tudge, 1992).

As with other aspects of sociocultural theory, the effectiveness of collaborative learning will vary with culture. American children, accustomed to competitive and "do your own work" classrooms, seem to have particular difficulties adjusting to the shared-decision making found in cooperative learning (see Rogoff, 1998), although they get better at cooperative decision making with practice (for example, Socha & Socha, 1994). As the structure of schools change to support peer collaboration, with teachers' roles being that of active participants in the children's learning experiences and not simply directors of it, the benefits of cooperative learning correspondingly increase (see Rogoff, 1998).

One interesting finding about collaborative learning is that young children will sometimes remember the behaviors of others as their own, an error of **source monitoring**—the ability to determine the origins of one's knowledge, memory, or beliefs. For example, Mary Ann Foley and Hilary Ratner had children make a collage with an adult, with the

child and adult taking turns putting pieces on the collage (Foley & Ratner, 1998a; Foley, Ratner, & Passalacqua, 1993). After completing the collage, children were unexpectedly asked who had put each item on it, themselves or the adult. Foley and Ratner were interested in *attribution errors*—would children falsely attribute a piece to themselves that the adult had actually put on (an "I did it" error), or vice versa (a "You did it" error, when the child had actually placed the piece on the collage but said the adult had). Four-year-olds made a disproportionate number of "I did it errors," attributing actions to themselves that adults had actually performed. The children tended to re-code the actions of the adults as their own. Foley and Ratner suggested that this bias might lead to better learning of the actions of others, partly because misattributing the actions of others to oneself could cause children to link the actions to a common source (themselves) and thus produce a more integrated and easily retrievable memory. In support of this, Ratner and Foley (1997) reported that 5-year-old children who performed a collaborative task with adults (place furniture in a doll house, as in the study by Freund [1990] discussed earlier) later made many "I did errors"; however, these children later showed greater memory for the location of the furniture in each room than did children in a noncollaboration group. Thus, collaboration led to greater learning, but not in a way that might have been expected. Rather, young children's immature cognitive system resulted in a high number of source-monitoring errors, which actually resulted in better learning (Bjorklund 1997a).

Sociocultural Theory and Cognitive Development

I must admit that I was not much of a fan of Vygotsky's theory and the sociocultural perspective in general when it began to gain popularity in the 1980s. In fact, the first edition of this textbook (published in 1989) had no mention of Vygotsky's sociocultural theory. (The book did have a section on Vygotsky's views on the role of private speech on cognition, a topic that will be discussed in Chapter

9 on language development.) I had become more enlightened by the second edition (published in 1995), and I finally have an entire (if brief) chapter devoted to sociocultural theory in this edition.

Why was I so opposed to Vygotsky's ideas? I saw the popularization of his theory as an effort by latent behaviorists to resurrect a theory of development that focused entirely on the forces of the environment to shape behavior and that neglected any influence of biology. I saw it as a poorly camouflaged attempt to return developmental psychology to the strong behavioral perspective exemplified by B. F. Skinner and his followers decades earlier.

What changed my mind? It was the 1990 book by Barbara Rogoff, *Apprenticeship in Thinking*. Rogoff presented Vygotsky's theory, and her own provocative ideas, in a way that a researcher who believed that development is caused by a multitude of interacting factors, including biological ones, could comprehend. She presented data from studies conducted around the world, and I finally came to see sociocultural theory, not as the antithesis of a theory that believed that development is a biological concept, but rather as one that was quite consistent with contemporary accounts of psychological development.

The focus of sociocultural theory is unabashedly the social environment. But one need not reject any idea of looking at biological factors to adopt a sociocultural perspective. Contemporary sociocultural theorists clearly view development as occurring in a system of interacting levels (Rogoff, 1998). These levels don't include the genetic or neural activity levels found in Gottlieb's developmental systems model (see Figure 2-1), but rather include the child and his or her behavior, people interacting with the child, other people in the immediate environment, and the school, the family, and the community.

I think it is easy to espouse a belief in the idea that development is the result of multiple levels of causation, each interacting in a bidirectional way. It is more difficult to practice such a belief, however. I don't doubt that some researchers taking a sociocultural approach *do* view any mention of biological causation as unnecessary, as well as I believe some people who focus more on biological causation see the environment as nothing much more than a

place for the genes to express themselves. And, at times, it is certainly convenient to talk about a pattern of development or a characteristic of a child as being primarily "environmental" or "biological" in origin. I will do this in later chapters in the book. There are surely some spirited debates ahead for developmental scientists concerning *how* biological and sociocultural mechanisms interact to produce a developing child. But there should not be any debates concerning *if* they do. It took me several years to realize that the sociocultural perspective of development was indeed a modern one and one not necessarily at odds with other, more biologically oriented, models of development. I hope the readers of this book will learn faster than I did.

Summary

Sociocultural perspectives of cognitive development hold that a child's cognition is constructed by the social environment. Contemporary sociocultural theories are based on the ideas of Soviet psychologist Lev Vygotsky, who proposed that development should be evaluated from the perspective of four interrelated levels in interaction with children's environments—*microgenetic, ontogenetic, phylogenetic,* and *sociohistorical*. Each culture transmits beliefs, values, and preferred methods of thinking or problem solving—its *tools of intellectual adaptation*—to each successive generation. Thus, culture teaches children what to think and how to think about it.

According to Vygotsky's general *genetic law of cultural development*, cognitive function occurs on two planes, first on the social, between individuals, and only later is internalized by the child. Children acquire cultural beliefs and problem-solving strategies in the context of collaborative dialogues with more skillful partners as they gradually internalize their tutor's instructions to master tasks within their *zone of proximal development*. Related to the concept of the zone of proximal development is *scaffolding*, which occurs when experts are sensitive to abilities of a novice and respond contingently to the novice's responses in a learning situation, and *guided participation*, which refers to adult-child interactions, not only during explicit instruction, but also during the more routine activities and communication of everyday life.

Different cultures prepare their children for adult life differently. For example, in modern Western societies, parents talk to children extensively and prepare them for the type of tasks they will encounter in schools; in more traditional societies, adults are less likely to use language and more likely to demonstrate certain abilities to their children.

Sociocultural theory has been applied to educational settings, suggesting that *cooperative learning* results in improved learning relative to when children solve problems on their own. Research has found that cooperative learning often produces better performance than individual learning, but characteristics of the participants and the schools affect how beneficial cooperative learning is.

Note

1. From "Guided participation in cultural activity by toddlers and caregivers," by B. Rogoff, J. Mistry, A. Göncü, C. Mosier, 1993, *Monographs of the Society for Research in Child Development, 58* (Serial No. 236, No. 8). Copyright ©1993, The Society for Research in Child Development, Inc., Reprinted with permission.

Key Terms and Concepts

sociocultural perspective
ontogenetic development
microgenetic development
phylogenetic development
sociohistorical development
tools of intellectual adaptation
zone of proximal development
general genetic law of cultural development

scaffolding
guided participation
symbolic play
cooperative (collaborative) learning
source monitoring

Suggested Readings

ROGOFF, B. (1990). *Apprenticeship in thinking: Cognitive development in social context.* New York: Oxford University Press. I was a slow convert to the sociocultural perspective of development, but Rogoff's book made me see the light. Rogoff provides the right mix of theory and data to provide a convincing argument for taking seriously Vygotsky's concept of the zone of proximal development as well as her own important contribution of the idea of guided participation.

TUDGE, J., PUTNAM, S., & VALSINER, J. (1996). Culture and cognition in developmental perspective. In R. B. Cairns, G. H. Elder, Jr., & E. J. Costello (Eds.), *Developmental Science* (pp. 190–222). New York: Cambridge University Press. This chapter presents an excellent account of the sociocultural perspective as involving a dynamic relation between the culture and a child's developing cognition.

MILLER, K. F., SMITH, C. M., ZHU, J., & ZHANG, H. (1995). Preschool origins of cross-national differences in mathematical competence. *Psychological Science*, 6, 56–60. This paper presents a good example of a study examining how cultural differences in "tools of intellectual adaptation" (in this case, how different languages represent numbers) can influence children's cognitive performance. It demonstrates how subtle differences between two cultures can have unexpected intellectual differences.

WERTSCH, J. V., & TULVISTE, P. (1992). L. S. Vygotsky and contemporary developmental psychology. *Developmental Psychology*, 28, 548–557. This article, written as part of a series to commemorate the intellectual giants of developmental psychology, presents a brief overview of Vygotsky's ideas and how they have influenced contemporary developmental psychology.

Piaget's Theory and the Neo-Piagetians

Jean Piaget (1896–1980) has had a greater impact on the field of developmental psychology than any other theorist in the brief history of our science. The self-proclaimed experimental philosopher formulated a grand theory of intelligence that made children themselves, rather than their environment or their genetic constitution, the primary force in the development of thought. Piaget changed the way we look at children. Following Piaget, we no longer view the young child as an incomplete adult. Piaget taught us that children's thinking at any given age reflects a unique way of interpreting the world. Development is more than the simple acquisition of skills and knowledge. The 4-year-old is not just a smaller model of the 12-year-old who merely lacks the experience and knowledge of his older peer. Rather, in addition to quantitative differences in what these two children know (that is, differences in amount, degree, or speed), there are qualitative differences in how they know it (that is, differences in form, or type). As a result of Piaget's work, it is difficult for us today to conceive of the child as a passive organism, shaped and molded by environmental pressures. At any given developmental level, children are seekers of stimulation who act on their environment as much as their environment acts on them. Children determine to a large extent what experiences they will have and thus how their individual development will proceed.

Most contemporary theorists start with Piagetian theory (or at least phenomena brought to light by Piaget) and attempt to build on the edifice Piaget and his colleagues established in more than 50 years of work. Many cognitive developmentalists hold great reverence for Piaget's theory because of the impact it has had on the field of developmental psychology (see Brainerd, 1996). Although the number of active researchers today who are strict adherents of Piaget's theory is relatively small, a familiarity with Piaget's theory is essential for an understanding of cognitive development as it is studied today.

Piaget did not approach the task of understanding the development of knowledge as a traditional psychologist nor as a biologist (the field in which he received his formal training). Rather, he created an experimental philosophy that sought answers to philosophical questions through empiricism. He called this new approach **genetic epistemology**. Epistemology is the study of knowledge and its acquisition. *Genetic*, as used here, does not refer to genes, DNA, or inheritance but is used as it was commonly applied during the early part of this century, as a synonym for *developmental*. Thus, genetic epistemology is the experimental study of the development of knowledge.

Some Assumptions of Piaget's Theory

Piaget was a stage theorist. He believed that cognition develops in a series of discrete stages, with children's thinking at any particular stage being qualitatively different from that which preceded it or that which will follow it (see Chapter 1 for a discussion of what constitutes a developmental "stage"). In other words, Piaget did not view cognitive development as the gradual accretion of knowledge or skills. Rather, he viewed cognitive development as a series of transformations, with children's thinking going through abrupt changes over relatively brief periods of time. Despite his belief in the discontinuous nature of changes in children's thinking, Piaget believed that the functions underlying cognitive development are continuous. New abilities do not just pop up but emerge from earlier abilities. Given this continuity, Piaget hypothesized transition, or preparatory phases between stages—brief times when a child can have one foot in each of two qualitatively different cognitive worlds.

Piaget also believed that the mechanisms of cognitive development are domain general. Children come into the world with a general, species-typical nervous system, without being specially prepared to acquire any one type of information more than another. Thus, all intellectual accomplishments of infancy, for example, are governed by a general developmental function. Infants' mastery of early language, knowledge of objects, imitation abilities, and problem-solving skills are all interrelated and are the products of changes in a single cognitive system. Before describing Piaget's account of children's thinking at each stage of development, I must introduce several assumptions Piaget made concerning the nature of development. One concept central to Piaget's theory is that of structures.

Structures

According to Piaget, cognition develops through the refinement and transformation of mental structures (Piaget & Inhelder, 1969). **Structures** are unobservable mental systems that underlie intelligence and intelligent behavior. In a sense, all cognitive psychologists are concerned with unobservables and examine behavior only to achieve an understanding of what goes on in the head. Structuralism, however, is a specific orientation within cognitive psychology, and an appreciation of what Piaget meant by structures is essential for understanding Piagetian theory.

Unfortunately, it is easier to develop an appreciation of structures than it is to define them precisely in a way that is comprehensible to the uninitiated. Structures are most simply viewed as some enduring knowledge base by which children interpret their world. Structures, in effect, are representations of reality. Children know their world through their structures. Structures are the means by which experience is interpreted and organized. For Piaget, cognitive development is the development of structures. Children enter the world with some reflexes by which they interpret their surroundings, and what underlies these reflexes are structures (or more properly, schemes).[1] As development progresses, it is structures that change.

Intrinsic Activity

A second central thesis of Piagetian theory is the idea that the child is intrinsically active. Children are not passive creatures, waiting to be stimulated by their surroundings before they behave. Rather, they are active initiators and seekers of stimulation. Of course, when Piaget spoke of a child being intrinsically active, he was actually referring to a property of structures. Structures are intrinsically active and must be exercised so that they can be strengthened, consolidated, and developed. Structures are most active when they are newly acquired, as any parent of a young child who has just learned a new game

(such as rolling a ball back and forth with Daddy) can attest.

Intrinsic activity in children can be viewed as curiosity. Children are not content with what they already know but seek to know more. Although a child can be enticed to acquire certain information through external rewards, such exogenous reinforcements are not necessary to motivate learning and development. The motivation for development is within the child. From this perspective, children play an important role in their own development; they are the movers and shakers of their own experience and thus are primarily responsible for their own development. Piaget made the child not only the focus of development but also its major perpetrator. Environmental and genetic sources play a role in influencing development as well, of course, and Piaget most explicitly believed that development is the result of an interaction between a biologically prepared child and his or her environment. Nevertheless, unlike most of his contemporaries, Piaget placed his emphasis squarely on the child.

Consistent with his focus on the child him- or herself as the primary "cause" of development, Piaget emphasized that the role of teachers should not be to *instruct* children (that is, to transmit knowledge), but rather to provide opportunities for them to *discover* knowledge. According to Piaget, "Children should be able to do their own experimenting and their own research. Teachers, of course, can guide them by providing appropriate materials, but the essential thing is that in order for a child to understand something, he must construct it for himself; he must reinvent it" (Piaget, 1972, p. 27).

Piaget believed that the authority status of teachers actually hampered learning. "It is despite adult authority, and not because of it, that the child learns. And also it is to the extent that the intelligent teacher has known to efface him or herself, to become an equal and not a superior, to discuss and to examine, rather than to agree and constrain morally, that the traditional school has been able to render service" (Piaget, 1977, cited in Rogoff, 1998, p. 38).

As these quotes indicate, Piaget did not believe that children learn much from interacting with adults. This is quite different from the sociocultural perspective of Vygotsky. Piaget saw development as a process of discovery (as did Vygotsky), and, Piaget believed, discovery isn't possible if one is instructed by an authority figure. Piaget felt more kindly, however, to the role of peers in influencing cognitive change. Peers are of equal status, and the mind develops through the inevitable conflict that occurs when children interact with other children. Other children's ideas conflict with a child's own, causing disequilibration, which children seek to resolve. Because peers are equal in status, they must work together to resolve these conflicts, and cognitive development is the consequence.

The Constructive Nature of Cognition

Related to the concept of intrinsic activity is Piaget's belief that cognition is a constructive process. According to Piaget, when children act on their world, they interpret the objects and events that surround them in terms of what they already know. For Piaget, there is no such thing as objective reality. We interpret the world through our own personal perspective, and reality is a construction based on the information in the environment and in our heads. Piaget believed that our current state of knowledge guides our processing, substantially influencing how (and what) new information is acquired. In other words, the world is not out there for everyone to perceive in exactly the same manner. Knowing is an active, constructive process—an interaction between the environment and the active individual.

This position, known as **constructivism,** is not unique to Piaget. Constructivist viewpoints have been adopted by numerous psychologists dating back to Bartlett (1932) and can be found in the work of contemporary researchers describing the memories of both adults (Loftus, 1992) and children (Nelson, 1996). However, Piaget's constructivist position has a distinct developmental perspective. If reality is a construction, children at different developmental levels must surely construct different realities. The same event experienced by a 2-, 7-, and 14-year-old will be interpreted very differently by each. This is true not only because of differences in the amount of knowledge possessed by these children (that is, quantitative differences), but also because of differences in how each can process information (that is, qualitative differences). For a 6-month-old whose rattle is hidden by a blanket, reality is that the rattle no longer exists. A 3-year-old boy believes that wearing girls' clothes or playing girls' games transforms him temporarily into a girl; and a 6-year-old is convinced that a baloney-and-cheese sandwich cut into quarters provides more to eat than when it is cut into halves. An older child or adult believes none of this, but, for Piaget, reality is not an absolute but a construction based on our past experiences and our current cognitive structures.

Functional Invariants

Piaget used the term **functional invariants** to describe processes that characterize all biological systems (including intelligence) and operate throughout the life span. Piaget proposed two functional invariants: organization and adaptation.

Organization

Through the process of **organization**, every intellectual operation is related to all other acts of intelligence. Thus, one structure does not exist independently of other structures but is coordinated with them. Such a concept is consistent with Piaget's domain-general view of cognitive development. Similarly, organization is the tendency to integrate structures into higher-order systems or structures. For example, a week-old infant has one scheme for sucking and another for hand and arm movements. It doesn't take long, however, for these two schemes to become coordinated, resulting in a thumb-sucking scheme. Thumb sucking is not innate but represents the organization of two initially independent schemes into an integrated, higher-order scheme (even if these schemes become coordinated before birth).

Adaptation

The second functional invariant in Piaget's theory is **adaptation.** In its simplest form, adaptation is the organism's tendency to adjust its structures to environmental demands. Piaget defined two aspects of adaptation: assimilation and accommodation. Basically, **assimilation** is the incorporation of new information into already-existing schemes. Assimilation is not a passive process; it often requires that children modify or distort environmental input (hence, one source of cognitive errors) so that they can incorporate it into their current schemes. Assimilation is not the mere registration of a stimulus but the active construction of external data to fit the child's existing schemes.

Given Piaget's assumption of intrinsic activity, it is the nature of schemes to be active and sometimes used for no apparent reason. Piaget proposed that the application of a scheme for no apparent reason is an example of functional assimilation. If schemes are to develop they must be used, so schemes are applied to objects in the world merely for the sake of exercise. Functional assimilation is most easily observed in infancy, with infants applying inborn reflexes to objects. According to Piaget, the "reflex is consolidated and strengthened by virtue of its own functioning" (Piaget, 1952, p. 32).

Complementary to assimilation is the process of **accommodation,** in which a current scheme is changed to incorporate new information. Accommodation occurs when children are confronted with information that cannot be interpreted by current cognitive schemes. Accommodation is obviously an active process, resulting in the modification of existing schemes as a result of those schemes' interaction with the environment.

Piaget stressed that every act of intelligence involves both assimilation and accommodation. However, some actions involve a predominance of one over the other. For example, Piaget proposed that play is the purest form of assimilation, with children modifying the information in the environment to fit their make-believe actions. Conversely, Piaget proposed that there is a relative predominance of accommodation in imitation, with children adjusting their schemes to match those of a model.

Knowledge is constructed by these complementary processes of assimilation and accommodation. In fact, Piaget viewed knowledge as an activity and not a state, per se. Furth (1969) interpreted Piaget's position concerning the acquisition of knowledge by

suggesting that knowledge "can be viewed as a structuring of the environment according to underlying subjective structures [assimilation] or as a structuring of the subject in living interaction with the environment [accommodation]" (p. 20).

As a simple example of assimilation and accommodation, consider the grasp of an infant. Babies will reflexively grasp objects placed in the palms of their hands. This grasping scheme can be applied to a variety of objects that fit easily into the infant's hand. So grasping the handle of a rattle, daddy's finger, or the railing of a crib all involve (primarily) assimilation. The infant is incorporating information into an existing scheme. If the same infant is presented with a small ball, some small modifications in hand movements are required if the infant is to "know" this new object and successfully apply the grasping scheme to it. These modifications constitute (primarily) accommodation, permitting the infant to incorporate new data by slightly changing current schemes.

Assimilation and accommodation also describe the functioning of older children. The 2-year-old who calls all men "Daddy," for example, is using the verbal label she acquired to refer to her father to refer to all adult males (assimilation). She must learn to restrict her use of the term Daddy to her father and develop new terms for other men (accommodation), lest she cause her mother embarrassment. Likewise, many college students reading this chapter will need to alter their way of thinking about children and development to make sense of Piagetian theory. Piaget is not easily assimilated, and much accommodation is typically required before his theory is understood and appreciated.

Equilibration

Piaget stated that at least four major factors contribute to development: (1) maturation, the gradual unfolding of genetic plans; (2) the physical environment, the child's actions on objects in his or her world; (3) social transmission, the knowledge abstracted from people in the environment; and (4) equilibration, a concept unique to Piagetian theory. Piaget proposed that the first three factors are not sufficient to explain development, and that

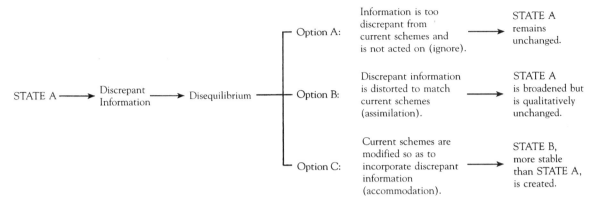

FIGURE 4-1   A schematic representation of the equilibration model. Although Piaget specified that equilibration involves accommodation (option C), options A and B reflect ways in which children may achieve temporary states of stability.

development can only be understood when maturation, the physical environment, and social transmission are integrated with the concept of equilibration.

Equilibration refers to the organism's attempt to keep its cognitive structures in balance. This concept of Piaget's explains the motivation for development; it is meant to answer the questions "Why should we develop at all?" and "Why do cognitive structures change?" When a child encounters some information that does not match his or her current schemes, an imbalance, or disequilibrium, results. The child experiences cognitive incongruity, with the new information not quite fitting his or her current state of knowledge. States of disequilibrium are intrinsically dissatisfying, and there is an attempt to reinstate equilibrium.

How is this equilibration achieved? According to Piaget, equilibration is achieved by altering one's cognitive structures. That is, given the disconfirming information, accommodation can occur, with the child slightly modifying current schemes to match the environmental data. As a result, a new and more stable structure develops. This new structure is more stable because fewer intrusions will set it into a state of disequilibrium than the immediately previous structure was vulnerable to.

Discrepant information is not always dealt with in such a way as to produce cognitive change (that

is, by accommodation). If new information is too discrepant from a child's current schemes, for example, accommodation becomes impossible and assimilation becomes unlikely. The alternative is to ignore (that is, not act on) the information, thus returning the structures to their original state. For instance, a first-grader given algebra problems to solve will likely remain in a state of disequilibrium only briefly, realizing very soon that he or she hasn't the foggiest idea what these symbols mean, and will go on to something else.

Another alternative is to distort the new information by assimilation, making it compatible with the old structures. In this case no qualitative change in the structures occurs, only a possible broadening of the original schemes. Nevertheless, the environmental intrusion is dealt with effectively, although it might not appear that way to an outsider. For example, the same algebra problem given to a 12-year old will likely be recognized as a math problem, and the child might apply his or her basic arithmetic schemes to derive an "answer." Such an answer will likely be wrong, but distorting an algebra problem to an arithmetic one can re-establish a temporary equilibrium. The equilibration process is schematically represented in Figure 4-1.

Let me provide one more example of how the equilibration process might work. A 3-year-old in the bathtub is confronted for the first time by a bar of soap that floats. The child has no scheme for floating soap. Toy boats float, but soap sinks. This new information produces cognitive incongruity, or a state of disequilibrium. The child can distort somewhat the characteristics of the soap in her mind and assimilate it into her "toy boat" scheme. She also has the option of hiding it under the wash-cloth and pretending it was never there. Her third option is to modify her current "soap" scheme by ac-commodating this new information and changing slightly her knowledge of soaps.

Accommodation, and thus the attainment of more stable structures, is most apt to occur when the new information is only slightly discrepant from current structures. Information that exactly matches current structures can be assimilated into those structures, and information that is too different from what a child already knows is likely to be either dis-torted or ignored. Regardless, children remain ac-tive operators on their environments throughout and following the re-establishment of equilibrium.

Stages of Development

Piaget divided cognitive development into four ma-jor stages, or periods: sensorimotor, preoperations, concrete operations, and formal operations. A brief description of the major characteristics of children's thinking during each of these stages is provided in Table 4-1. Piaget insisted that the order in which children progress through these stages is invariant and culturally universal; stages cannot be skipped. So, from a Piagetian perspective, a precocious 8-year-old who has mastered analytic geometry has ac-quired these skills by going through the same stage sequence as her adolescent peers; but she has gone through them at a faster rate.

This assumption of the invariant order of stages is a direct consequence of Piaget's belief that devel-opment is *epigenetic* in nature—that it proceeds gradually, with later developments being based on earlier developments (see discussion of epigenesis in Chapter 2). According to Piaget (1967), a new cog-nitive skill does not arise fully formed. Rather, it has

TABLE 4-1 Characteristics of major periods in Piaget's theory

Period and approximate age range	Major characteristics
Sensorimotor: birth to 2 years	Intelligence is limited to the infant's own actions on the environment. Cognition progresses from the exercise of reflexes (for example, sucking, visual orienting) to the beginning of symbolic functioning.
Preoperations: 2 to 7 years	Intelligence is symbolic, expressed via language, imagery, and other modes, permitting children to mentally represent and compare objects out of immediate perception. Thought is intuitive rather than logical and is egocentric, in that children have a difficult time taking the perspective of another.
Concrete operations: 7 to 11 years	Intelligence is symbolic and logical. (For example, if A is greater than B and B is greater than C, then A must be greater than C.) Thought is less egocentric. Children's thinking is limited to concrete phenomena and their own past experiences; that is, thinking is not abstract.
Formal operations: 11 to 16 years	Children are able to make and test hypotheses; possibility dominates reality. Children are able to introspect about their own thought processes and, generally, can think abstractly.

a history, in that the structure that underlies the new skill is a transformation of an earlier structure. Nothing starts out fully formed. Thus, the abstract reasoning of the adolescent, according to Piaget, can be traced back to the overt actions of the infant. A child cannot display reasoning at the concrete operational level until he or she has mastered the prerequisites at the preoperational level. In a sense, development at earlier stages is preparatory for de-velopment at later stages; "new" structures do not suddenly appear, nor do they lie dormant until the proper level of maturation has been achieved. Rather, in Piagetian psychology, "new" structures are new only in the particular form or organization that they take. Each current structure can be traced to earlier, more primitive structures, which were necessary for the attainment of the more advanced structure. Piaget referred to this characteristic of development as **hierarchization.**

The Sensorimotor Stage

The first major stage in Piaget's theory is the **sensorimotor stage,** or sensorimotor period, which lasts from birth to approximately 2 years of age (Piaget, 1952, 1954, 1962). During this period, children's intelligence is limited to their own actions. During their first 18 months or so, children develop some complex problem-solving skills, but they do this without the benefit of mental representation. They know the world only by their direct actions (both sensory and motoric) on it.

During the first two years, cognition is transformed in two major ways. First, there is a progression from an action-based to a symbol-based intelligence—from sensorimotor to representational thinking. Second, there is a related change in personal perspective. Young infants, asserted Piaget, are unable to differentiate themselves from the external world. All the universe is one for young infants, with themselves at the center. By the end of the sensorimotor stage, not only are infants able to distinguish themselves from the objects they act on, but they also realize that these objects have an existence independent of their actions on the objects. In general, during infancy, children increasingly move from cognition centered on their immediate actions to cognition that displaces them in time and space from the things they wish to think about.

Piaget divided the sensorimotor stage into six substages. As with Piaget's theory in general, infants progress through these increasingly complex substages in an invariant sequence, with the successful accomplishments of earlier substages being the basis for the accomplishments of later substages. Central to each substage is children's problem-solving skills,

particularly the extent to which they display intentionality, or **goal-directed behavior,** and this will be the focus of my description of Piaget's sensorimotor substages. A brief description of the major characteristics of children's intelligence at each sensorimotor substage is presented in Table 4-2.

There are many more specific cognitive accomplishments of the sensorimotor stage besides general problem solving. Two of the most studied, both by Piaget and others, have been children's acquisition of a sense of object permanence (the belief that objects exist independent of one's perceptions or actions) and imitation. I will outline Piaget's accounts of the development of object permanence and imitation following a general description of the substages of the sensorimotor stage. Contemporary research on these two topics, much of it questioning Piaget's interpretation if not his descriptions, will be presented in Chapter 7.

Substages of the Sensorimotor Stage

Substage 1: The use of reflexes (birth to 1 month). Infants enter the world with a set of inherited action patterns, or reflexes through which they interpret their experiences. Piaget used the term reflex broadly, so that infant reflexes include not only obvious behaviors such as sucking and grasping but also more subtle behaviors such as eye movements, orientation to sound, and vocalization. This is where intellectual development begins, for, according to Piaget, from these **basic reflexes** the child first makes contact with the world, acquiring knowledge of objects in the environment that later will serve as the basis for more complex accomplishments.

During this first substage, infants are primarily engaged in applying inherited reflexes to objects. If an object "fits" infants' reflexes (or, more appropriately, the schemes underlying these reflexes), they apply their reflexes to the object, assimilating it into their existing schemes. However, accommodation also occurs during the first weeks of life. For example, Piaget (1952) made careful observations of his son, Laurent, making adjustments to nursing. Piaget noted how Laurent would suck his hand or a quilt

TABLE 4-2 Characteristics of the sensorimotor substages in Piaget's theory

Substage and approximate age range	Major characteristics
Substage 1 (basic reflexes): birth to 1 month	Cognition is limited to inherited reflex patterns.
Substage 2 (primary circular reactions): 1 to 4 months	Infant acquires first adaptations, extends basic reflexes; reflex is activated by chance (for example, thumb comes in contact with lips, activating sucking reflex); infant attempts to reproduce reflex, resulting in acquisition of new, noninherited behavior (thumb sucking) that can be activated at the infant's discretion; initial occurrence of behavior is by chance, so need follows action.
Substage 3 (secondary circular reactions): 4 to 8 months	By chance, infant causes interesting event in environment to occur (for example, infant kicks mattress, causing mobile over crib to move) and tries to re-create event; beginning of control of objects and events external to infant; as in previous stage, initial occurrence of interesting event is by chance, so need follows action.
Substage 4 (coordination of secondary circular reactions): 8 to 12 months	Infant uses two previously acquired schemes in coordination with each other to achieve a goal; first sign of need preceding action, or goal-directed behavior, is exhibited.
Substage 5 (tertiary circular reactions): 12 to 18 months	Infant discovers new means through active experimentation, develops new techniques to solve problems; goal-directed behavior is exhibited, but entire problem-solving process is conducted by overt trial and error; intelligence is still limited to child's actions on objects.
Substage 6 (mental combinations): 18 to 24 months	Infant shows first signs of symbolic functioning; infant is able to represent events in environment in terms of symbols (for example, language, imagery); problem solving can now be covert.

even when not hungry, the reflex being released by almost anything that touched his lips. Piaget also observed that Laurent's ability to locate the nipple and nurse successfully improved gradually over the first three weeks of life, as he learned to apply his sucking reflex selectively to the nipple (rather than to the skin surrounding the nipple) when hungry.

Piaget's observations tell us a number of things about the cognitive abilities of infants during the first month of life. First, during this time infants are highly restricted in what they can know. Behaviors are elicited by environmental events over which they have little control, and the range of their schemes is highly limited. Second, although active, young infants do not act on their environment to obtain specific outcomes. In other words, according to Piaget, they cannot separate need from action and thus cannot be said to behave intentionally.

Third, Piaget's observations demonstrate adaptation by infants. This adaptation involves the assimilation of objects into inherited schemes and also the accommodation of those schemes.

Substage 2: Primary circular reactions (1 to 4 months). In this second substage of the sensorimotor period, reflexes are extended so that new patterns of behavior are acquired that were not part of the basic biological apparatus with which the child was born. However, these new acquisitions are still based on innate reflexes and so do not reflect new behaviors, per se. What they do reflect is the accommodation of reflex schemes to the environment, and, often, the coordination of such schemes. In other words, infants can modify their reflexes as a result of the environment, reflecting what can be easily recognized as learning.

The basic mechanism for this change in behavior is the *circular reaction*, a concept first introduced by the American psychologist James Mark Baldwin (1895). Most simply stated, circular reactions are acquired, repetitive behaviors. **Primary circular reactions** are the first class of these patterns to be observed in development and the only ones that are based on hereditary reflexes. Piaget discussed these first circular reactions primarily with regard to sucking, vision, hearing, vocalizations, and grasping. For example, Piaget detailed how Laurent, between 1 month 1 day and 1 month 21 days, acquired the ability to suck his thumb. The initial contact between Laurent's hand and his mouth was by chance. That is, babies don't start out by thinking, "Gee, I'd like to suck my thumb. I wonder how I should go about it?" Rather, in the process of random activity or activity directed toward a biological outcome (for example, nursing), reflexes are fortuitously activated. However, once his thumb or fingers were in his mouth, sucking occurred. Laurent repeatedly attempted to re-create the experience, gradually coordinating his arm, hand, and finger movements with his mouth until he had established the ability to suck his thumb whenever (presumably) he pleased.

What significance do such observations have concerning the development of intelligence? The significance is the advancement that this represents beyond the previous substage. In substage 1, infants are primarily victims of their environment. They actively assimilate objects to reflexive schemes, but the exercise of these reflexes depends on the chance occurrence of a stimulus that fits with a hereditary action pattern. In substage 2, infants show the first primitive signs of intentionality—of initiating a scheme that although composed of reflexes is itself not inherited. That is, once infants acquire the ability to suck their thumbs, that behavior is theirs to use whenever and wherever they please.

Substage 3: Secondary circular reactions (4 to 8 months).   As previously mentioned, a circular reaction is a repetitive behavior. Unlike primary circular reactions characteristic of substage 2, **secondary circular reactions** are not based on reflexes but represent the first acquired adaptations of new (that is, not reflexive) behaviors.

The establishment of secondary circular reactions is similar in form to the establishment of the earlier primary circular reactions. With no intention beforehand, babies cause something interesting to happen and attempt to re-create the interesting event. A major difference between primary and secondary circular reactions is that for the former, the interesting events are based on reflexes and thus necessarily centered on the infant's body. In contrast, for secondary circular reactions, interesting events are found in the external world. This is especially true of visual events, although Piaget discussed secondary circular reactions for other schemes, particularly grasping and hearing.

Let me provide an observation of my own. My daughter, Heidi, at 4 months of age, was lying in her playpen. She did not seem particularly interested in any of the toys that surrounded her, although she was awake, alert, and active. Strung over her head was a "crib gym," a complex mobile with parts that spin when they are hit. I had spun the objects for her on several occasions, and when I did, Heidi seemed to like it. But today was to be different. While flailing her arms and legs, she hit the mobile, causing it to spin. She happened to be looking at the mobile, and its movement caught her attention. She suddenly stopped and stared intently at the moving object over her head. It ceased moving, and she began to shake her arms and legs, to squirm, and finally to cry. Again she hit the mobile, and again she froze and quieted, staring straight ahead at the wonderful event she had caused.

My daughter did not start out to spin the mobile. Her hand made contact while, from the point of view of an adult observer, she was randomly moving her limbs. The result of her act was an interesting visual event. She had caused a change in an object she was looking at and tried to reproduce that outcome. Although she apparently realized, at some level, that she was responsible for the change, babies do not have a well-developed sense of cause and effect. As such, she presumably did not know whether it was the movement of her legs, the turn of her head, or her vocalizations that made the difference. (In fact, Piaget [1954] observed that infants at this stage will attempt to exert control over objects and events in their world without an awareness of the necessity of physical contact between agent and object.) However, through a trial-and-error process, she reduced her options concerning what exactly she did that made the interesting event occur, and she eventually gained control over the situation.

Substage 4: Coordination of secondary circular reactions (8 to 12 months).

The intentionality observed during substage 3 is limited in at least two respects. First, as mentioned previously, the initial relation between an infant's behavior and environmental outcome occurs by chance. The "need" of hitting a mobile to watch it move, for example, arises from the chance discovery of this phenomenon, and not vice versa. Second, the infant's need seems to be mainly that of repetition—that is, the need to activate a scheme. The goal of a secondary circular reaction appears to be its own exercise. A major change in intentionality is found in substage 4, in that the need now precedes the act. That is, we have for the first time goal-directed behavior and the beginning of the differentiation between means and ends (that is, cause and effect).

This means/ends separation is first accomplished by the coordination of two previously acquired secondary schemes to obtain a specific goal. Previously, a secondary circular reaction was executed only for its own sake; now, with the **coordination of secondary circular reactions,** one circular reaction can be used in the service of another.

Piaget suggested that one of the simplest coordinations is that of removing an obstacle to retrieve a visible object. Piaget (1952) provided a lengthy description of experiments in which he placed obstacles, such as his hand, between his son, Laurent, and some desired objects. Laurent acquired the ability to brush aside his father's hand to obtain a desired goal. Laurent was able to use one well-established scheme (striking) in order that another scheme be activated (reaching, grasping and retrieving an object).

Substage 5: Tertiary circular reactions (12 to 18 months).

As with coordination of secondary circular reactions, **tertiary circular reactions** are characterized by clear means/ends differentiation. Need precedes action. However, unlike infants in substage 4, infants during this substage are not restricted to applying previously acquired and consolidated schemes to achieve a goal. Rather, when faced with a problem, children can now make subtle alterations in their existing schemes that are directly related to obtaining a solution to their conundrum. This, Piaget stated, reflects a process of active experimentation.

Piaget (1952) provided the example of his daughter Jacqueline attempting to get a long stick through the bars of her playpen. The intent is there from the beginning, but it is only through a process of trial and error that the stick is successfully maneuvered between the bars and into the playpen. Piaget noted his daughter's surprise when some of her attempts failed, and the gradual accommodations she made before she mastered the problem successfully.

Along with their new intellectual tools come increasing locomotive abilities. By 12 months of age most babies can get around well, be it on two limbs or four, and this combination of increased locomotor and cognitive skills results in a child who is apt to be into everything. Children of this age often show a peak in curiosity. They want to know what makes things tick, and more importantly, how *they* can make them tick. They are explorers and adventurers. Is it possible to unravel the toilet paper, getting it all into the toilet without breaking the paper? How does one get into the bathroom sink? Isn't it interesting how by turning one knob the music becomes so much louder? Adults are often perplexed as to why 15-month-olds find dog food and kitty litter so fascinating, why they are so interested in electric sockets and wastebaskets, and why they insist on climbing out of their high chairs and manipulating and mouthing everything on the kitchen table.

Although children during this substage are wonderful problem solvers, their intelligence, according to Piaget, is still basically limited to physical actions on objects. They know objects by acting on them and cannot yet make mental comparisons or represent objects and events symbolically. These children solve problems by a trial-and-error process, with all their trials available for public examination. So, for example, if a 15-month-old wants to see if her brother's tricycle fits beneath the coffee table, she will have to do it by physically attempting to place it under the table. It makes no difference that the tricycle rises a foot above the table. She cannot simply examine the two objects and discern that one is too big to fit under the other. She can learn this, however, by attempting it, although it may take several such tries before she concludes what, to an adult, is obvious.

Substage 6: Invention of new means through mental combinations (18 to 24 months).   Until substage 6, development through the sensorimotor stage is relatively continuous, with behavior patterns acquired at one substage being superimposed on those of earlier substages. In contrast, the transition between substages 5 and 6 is more drastic and discontinuous. It is during this last sensorimotor substage that, according to Piaget, symbolic functioning is first seen. Children show the first glimmer of mental representation, of being able to think about objects without having to directly act on them. With the advent of mental representation, the process of children's problem solving is no longer totally in the open. Trial-and-error procedures can occur covertly in the head, producing what appears to be sudden comprehension or insight. New means can be invented through **mental combinations**.

Piaget proposed that the symbolic function is expressed by language, deferred imitation, gestures, symbolic play, and mental imagery. (Piaget made it clear that the most obvious demonstration of the symbolic function, language, was made possible by the advent of the symbolic function, and not vice versa.) These varied mental abilities arise alongside the more action-based forms of intelligence during the latter part of the second year. During this substage, the cognitions of the sensorimotor stage begin to be internalized as representational thought, setting the stage for a revolutionary change in the nature of human intelligence.

The Development of Object Permanence

If a tree falls in the middle of the forest and no one is there to hear it, is there any noise? This perennial philosophical question would be answered very easily by young infants, presuming, of course, that they could communicate their answer to us. Their answer would be no, for there can be no noise unless someone is there to perceive it. But the young infant would go on to say that there is also no tree and no forest. Nothing exists unless it is directly perceived, or, more precisely, unless it is personally perceived by them.

This hypothetical philosophical discussion illustrates Piaget's concept of object permanence or, more appropriately, the lack of object permanence. **Object permanence** refers to the knowledge that objects have an existence in time and space independent of one's perception or action on those objects. For infants who lack object permanence, out of sight is literally out of mind. Object permanence is obviously a cognitive skill necessary for normal intellectual functioning in all human cultures, and this has been the most investigated cognitive content of Piaget's infancy theory. Understandably, Piaget discussed the development of object permanence in the context of his broader theory of sensorimotor intelligence (Piaget, 1954).

Piaget stated that during the first two substages of the sensorimotor stage (from birth to approximately 4 months), objects are understood only as extensions of infants' actions. Objects have no reality for babies independent of their perceptions or actions upon them. For example, a 2- or 3-month-old follows his mother with his eyes, but when she leaves his visual field, he continues to gaze at the point where he lost sight of her, not anticipating her reappearance at another location.

The first semblance of object permanence appears during the third sensorimotor substage (approximately 4 to 8 months). Infants now attempt to retrieve an object that "disappears," although only if the object is still partially visible. For example, babies at this stage fetch a toy that has been partially covered by a cloth, apparently, realizing, that the entire toy exists under the cloth even though they can see only a portion of it. They do not search, however, for a toy that is completely hidden, even if the hiding occurred right before their eyes. An exception to this behavior seems to be that late in this substage, infants search for a completely hidden object if they are moving in that direction when the object is hidden. So, for example, a 6-month-old infant playing with a favorite toy does not attempt to retrieve that toy when her father places it under a blanket while she is watching. She does retrieve it, however, if she is reaching for the toy in front of her as Dad places the blanket over it.

By substage 4 (approximately 8 to 12 months), infants can retrieve a completely hidden object. To do this, they must be able to use one scheme (removing an obstacle) in the service of another (retrieving a desired object), which, according to Piaget, is the major cognitive accomplishment of this substage. However, object permanence is not yet complete, for if an object is hidden in one location and then later moved to a second, all while the child is watching, the infant searches at the first location and often acts quite surprised not to find the desired object.

Let me provide an observation for what has been termed the *A-not-B* object-permanence task. At approximately 10 months, my daughter Heidi was seated in her high chair, having just completed lunch. She was banging her spoon on the tray of the chair when it fell to the floor to her right. She leaned to the right, saw the spoon on the floor, and vocalized to me; I retrieved it for her. She began playing with the spoon again, and it fell to the right a second time. She again leaned to the right, saw the spoon on the floor, and vocalized until I returned it to her. Again, she played with the spoon, and again it fell to the floor, but this time to her left. After hearing the clang of the spoon hitting the floor, Heidi leaned to the right to search for the spoon, and she continued her search for several seconds before looking at me with a puzzled expression. Heidi had been watching the spoon at the time it fell. Thus, when it fell the third time, she had both visual and auditory cues to tell her where it must be. But she searched where she had found the vanished object before. She trusted her past experience with the fallen spoon more than her perceptions. At this age children still understand objects by their actions on them, in these cases by their prior actions.

In substage 5 (approximately 12 to 18 months), infants can solve problems like the one just described. What they cannot yet do, however, is solve

what Piaget called *invisible displacements*. In invisible displacements, an object is hidden in one container and then hidden under another container out of the vision of the observer. An example from Piaget (1954) will help clarify this task:

> Jacqueline is sitting on a green rug playing with a potato which interests her very much (it is a new object for her). She says "po-terre" [pomme de terre] and amuses herself by putting it into an empty box and taking it out again. . . . I then take the potato and put it in the box while Jacqueline watches. Then I place the box under the rug and turn it upside down, thus leaving the object hidden by the rug without letting the child see my maneuver, and I bring out the empty box. I say to Jacqueline, who has not stopped looking at the rug and who has realized that I was doing something under it: "Give papa the potato." She searches for the object in the box, looks at me, again looks at the box minutely, looks at the rug, etc., but it does not occur to her to raise the rug in order to find the potato underneath. During the five subsequent attempts the reaction is uniformly negative. . . . Each time Jacqueline looks in the box, then looks at everything around her including the rug, but does not search under it. (p. 68)

To solve invisible displacement problems, according to Piaget, children must be able to mentally represent objects, something that is not found until the last sensorimotor substage, beginning around 18 months.

Imitation during the Sensorimotor Stage

Imitation refers to matching one's behavior to that of a model. True imitation is not reflexive but is voluntary and selective, involving the modification of one's own behavior in accordance with that of a model. Piaget believed that imitation is the purest example of accommodation. Piaget (1962) did not view imitation as a unique cognitive phenomenon but, rather, proposed that imitation is primarily a function of the development of general intellectual abilities during the sensorimotor stage.

In substage 1 (birth to 1 month), infants are limited to interpreting the world through their inherited reflexes. During this first substage, some imitation-like behavior can be seen, but it is reflexive in nature and not true imitation. For example, a baby may begin crying when she hears the cries of other babies. Although this response could reflect merely an annoyance at being disturbed by the aversive wailing of nurserymates, Piaget suggested that infants may confuse the cries of others with their own, thus eliciting crying in a reflexive manner.

During substages 2 and 3 (1 to 8 months), sounds that infants can already make are repeated for their own sake (primary circular reactions), and such reactions can be prolonged by the presence of a model displaying the same behavior as the infant. In these cases, the baby initiates a behavior that is mimicked by the adult, which in turn activates the baby to continue that behavior. Piaget's (1962) description of such interaction with his daughter will help illustrate this phenomenon: "I noted a differentiation in the sounds of her laughter. I imitated them. She reacted by reproducing them quite clearly, but only when she had already uttered them immediately before" (p. 10). Piaget referred to this behavior as *mutual imitation*, with the infant imitating the adult who is imitating her. The imitation is exact, but only to the extent that the adult imitates the infant exactly. This, again, is not true imitation, for nothing new is acquired by the imitative-like behaviors observed here, with this pre-imitation representing primarily the assimilation of previously acquired circular reactions.

Piaget first observed true imitation in substage 4 (8 to 12 months). Children in this substage can imitate behaviors for which they receive no visual or auditory feedback, such as facial gestures. Infants can see the movements of their own fingers or hear their own voices when they attempt to imitate a hand gesture or a sound produced by another person, but they cannot see themselves imitate an adult's grimace or pout. Piaget referred to these unseen actions as *invisible gestures*. Infants in this substage are also now able to acquire new behaviors by imitation. Before this substage, infants' matching is limited to schemes they have previously acquired. During substage 4, infants can learn new patterns of responding by actively and intentionally imitating a model. Accommodation begins to predominate over

assimilation. Although new behaviors are learned through imitation, the model's behavior must be very similar to what a child can already produce if it is to give rise to imitation. Patterns that are too discrepant from a child's current schemes are not good candidates for imitation.

The process of true imitation begun during substage 4 continues in substage 5 (12 to 18 months). Piaget contended that imitation becomes more systematic and exact at this time. It becomes more deliberate and is more accommodative to the model than at previous substages. Nevertheless, the differences between imitation in substage 4 and in substage 5 are those of degree rather than kind.

In both substage 4 and substage 5, children are limited to imitating a model in the model's presence. They are unable to observe a model and delay imitation for any length of time. Delayed, or **deferred imitation** is the hallmark of Piaget's sixth sensorimotor substage (18 to 24 months). With the advent of mental representation, children can observe a model and mentally code the behavior as images or "suggestions of actions" (Piaget, 1962, p. 62). With mental representation, events can be coded symbolically and retrieved at a later time. An interesting example of deferred imitation is provided by Piaget (1962):

> [Jacqueline] had a visit from a little boy of [one year, six months], whom she used to see from time to time, and who, in the course of the afternoon, got into a terrible temper. He screamed as he tried to get out of a play-pen and pushed it backwards, stamping his feet. J. stood watching him in amazement, never having witnessed such a scene before. The next day, she herself screamed in her play-pen and tried to move it, stamping her foot lightly several times in succession. The imitation of the whole scene was most striking. Had it been immediate, it would naturally not have involved representation, but coming as it did after an interval of more than twelve hours, it must have involved some representative or pre-representative element. (p. 63)

In addition to being able to defer imitation, the substage 6 child can mentally practice a behavior before actually imitating it. The trial-and-error process involved in the substage 5 child's imitation of a model can now be accomplished covertly. Accordingly, a substage 6 child's first public attempt at imitation is likely to be more accurate than that of a substage 5 child, primarily because the trial-and-error process of the latter child is all overt.

Replications of Piaget's Sensorimotor Sequence

There has been no lack of research or alternate theories concerning the development of intelligence over the sensorimotor stage. One of the largest research projects to provide a test of Piaget's theory of infant development is that of Uzgiris and Hunt (1975). Based on the observations of Piaget (1952, 1954, 1962), Uzgiris and Hunt developed a test of sensorimotor intelligence that assessed the development of circular reactions, object permanence, imitation, space, and causality. One major contribution of this work was their demonstration of interobserver reliability. A major complaint with Piaget's observations was that they were highly subjective. Uzgiris and Hunt developed items that could be scored reliably by independent examiners. The average agreement between different examiners' evaluations of infants' performance on this scale was an impressive 96%.

In addition to demonstrating that Piagetian tasks could be standardized, the sequence of sensorimotor accomplishments that Uzgiris and Hunt found in their cross-sectional sample was much as Piaget described. A number of other, smaller-scale studies have investigated the sequential nature of sensorimotor accomplishments (including object permanence and imitation), and most of these studies confirm the basic Piagetian substage sequence (Kaye & Marcus, 1981; Kopp, Sigman, & Parmelee, 1974). Research using results from infant psychometric tests also has provided support for Piaget's developmental progression (McCall, Eichorn, & Hogarty, 1977). The consistency of the research findings led Uzgiris (1983) to claim that the "available literature on infant functioning during the sensorimotor period demonstrates that an orderly sequence of achievements is manifested in the formation of a number of competencies. The regularity of these se-

quences and their high correlation with chronological age are among the most consistently reported findings" (p. 182).

Despite the replicability of the substage sequence as presented by Piaget, much new research, using methodologies quite different from that of Piaget, has challenged the accuracy of Piaget's account of infant intelligence. Most of this work has proposed that infants have far more knowledge and abilities than Piaget attributed to them. For example, research by Willatts (1990) has shown that infants are better problem solvers and have a more developed sense of causality than Piaget proposed (see Chapter 10). Other research has shown that even very young infants have some relatively sophisticated ideas about the permanency of objects (Baillargeon, 1987; Spelke, 1991), infants can solve the A-not-B object permanence tasks at a much younger age than Piaget proposed (Reznick, Fueser, & Bosquet, 1998), are capable of imitating facial gestures shortly after birth (Meltzoff & Moore, 1985), and possess at least rudimentary symbolic abilities before their first birthdays (Gelman & Williams, 1998; Spelke & Newport, 1998). Piaget's observations were not wrong, he just did not take a close enough look at the phenomena under study. Much of this research will be discussed in Chapter 7. For now, it is important to understand the basic sequence of development described by Piaget and his belief that such development reflects domain-general changes in cognitive development.

The Development of Operations

With the advent of symbols, children's thinking becomes uniquely human. We might not be the only thinking species, and other species may occasionally use symbols (Savage-Rumbaugh et al., 1993), but the intellectual prowess that language, imagery, and deferred imitation provide us makes us different from any other creature on the planet. During the first year of life, human infants are actually less advanced in sensorimotor accomplishments than chimpanzees and gorillas are (see Antinucci, 1989). In comparing the intellectual abilities of a 12-month-old infant, a 3-year-old child, and a 21-year-old adult, most would agree that the 3-year-old and the 21-year-old are more alike, cognitively speaking, despite their vast age difference. But no one would mistake a 3-year-old and 21-year-old as intellectual equals. Despite the fact that both the young child and the adult possess and use symbols, there are many differences in their cognitions.

The three stages that follow the sensorimotor stage are all similar in that the child has symbolic (that is, mental representational) abilities, but they differ in how children are able to use these symbols for thought (Piaget & Inhelder, 1969). Piaget labeled these three stages **preoperations,** describing children's thinking between the ages of 2 and 7 years, **concrete operations,** occurring between the ages of 7 and 11 years, and **formal operations,** characterizing the advent of adult thinking beginning about 11 years of age (see Table 4-1). As the names denote, each stage is characterized by operations, or in the case of preoperations, the lack of them. Most of Piaget's work beyond the infancy period dealt, in one way or another, with the development of operations. **Operations** are particular types of cognitive schemes, and they describe general ways that children act on their world.

Piaget specified four characteristics of operations. First, they are mental, and thus require the use of symbols. Not all symbol users possess operations, however, as is apparent in Piaget's description of preschool children as preoperational.

Second, operations derive from action. Operations can be thought of as internalized actions. This should not be surprising given Piaget's belief that every form of cognition has its origins in earlier forms. With respect to operations, a child's overt actions for a particular cognitive function (counting, for example) serve as a necessary basis for the internalization of that process. Children will first count on their fingers or physically line up red checkers with an equal number of black checkers, discovering through action that the one-to-one correspondence between red and black checkers remains the same no matter where they start counting or how they arrange the pieces.

A third characteristic of operations is that they exist in an organized system. Piaget referred to this

concept of overall integration as *structures d'ensemble* or **structures of the whole**. Piaget believed that all cognitive operations are integrated with all other operations, so that a child's cognition at any particular time should be relatively even, or homogeneous. This assumption has provoked substantial controversy, and data pertinent to this issue will be presented in this and subsequent chapters.

A fourth aspect of operations is that they are logical in that they follow a system of rules, the most critical of which are those of **reversibility.** Reversibility comes in two types: **negation** (or **inversion**) and **compensation** (or **reciprocity**). The negation rule states that an operation can always be negated, or inverted. For example, in arithmetic, subtraction is the inverse of addition. If 5 plus 2 equals 7, then 7 minus 2 must equal 5. Such a rule would seem to be obviously critical in children's learning basic arithmetic. This brings to mind the 6-year-old who proudly announced to his mother that he learned that day at school that 3 plus 2 equals 5. After praising him for his new knowledge, his mother asked him how much 2 plus 3 equaled, and the child answered that he didn't know; he hadn't learned that one yet. The compensation rule states that for any operation there exists another operation that compensates for the effects of the first. For example, if water is poured from a short, fat glass into a tall, thin glass, the increased height of the water level in the second glass is compensated for by a decrease in the breadth of the water.

The following sections give a general account of Piaget's description of the thought of preoperational, concrete operational, and formal operational children. Some specific cognitive contents of these periods are also discussed, and both Piagetian and non-Piagetian research are examined. Many other topics relating to the development of operations in Piaget's theory will be discussed in later chapters.

The Transition from Preoperational to Concrete Operational Thought

Piaget described preoperational thought, although based on symbols, as lacking the logic characteristic of concrete operations. By this, Piaget meant that operations do not generate contradictions. In contrast to concrete operational children, preoperational children are greatly influenced by the appearance of things, and their thought is said to be intuitive. Thus, young children are less affected by what, according to logic, must be and more affected by what, according to appearance, seems to be.

The example of conservation. Perhaps giving an example is the easiest way to explain the distinction between preoperational and concrete operational thought. **Conservation,** the realization that an entity remains the same despite changes in its form, is the sine qua non of concrete operations. For Piaget, conservation is not just a convenient task to illustrate cognitive differences among children but represents the basis for all rational thinking (Piaget, 1965).

The concept of conservation can apply to any substance that can be quantified, and conservation has been studied with respect to length, number, mass, weight, area, and volume. In general, Piaget's conservation tasks take the following form:

A = B
B → B'
A ? B'

In words, the equivalence between A and B is first established (for example, two balls of clay). Object B is then transformed while children watch (for example, rolling one ball of clay into a sausage). The children are then asked to judge the equivalence of the transformed object with the initial, unchanged object, and to provide a justification for their decision. Basically, the children must realize that the quantitative relation between the two objects remains the same despite changes in appearance of one.

Piaget's conservation-of-liquid task is illustrated in Figure 4-2. A child is presented with two identical glasses containing equal amounts of water. A third glass is introduced that is taller and thinner than the original two containers. The water in one of the original glasses is then poured into the third, taller glass, all while the child watches. The water level in the new glass is, of course, higher than the

"Is there the same amount of water in the two glasses, or does one have more?"

Water is poured from one of the original glasses to a taller, thinner glass.

"Is there the same amount of water in the two glasses now, or does one have more? Why?"

FIGURE 4-2 Piaget's conservation-of-liquid problem

water level in the original glass because of its narrower width. The child is then asked if the two glasses have the same amount of water in them.

Most 5-year-old children answer by saying no, the amounts of liquid are not the same anymore—there is more water in the new, taller glass. Ask them why this is so, and they will point out the difference in the height of the water. They will ignore the fact that the shorter glass is wider, and if this is pointed out to them, they will either dismiss it as insignificant, or in some cases, actually change their minds and tell you that there is more water in the shorter glass because it is so fat. They will admit that the water in the two glasses was the same to begin with, and they do not believe that anyone is playing a trick on them. The difference in appearance between the water levels in the two glasses is too great for them to believe that the same amount of water is contained in both.

In contrast, most 8-year-olds given the same problem tell you that the two glasses still contain the same amount of water. When pressed to explain why, they say that all you did was pour the water from one glass to the other, and that you could just as easily pour it back to confirm equivalence. If you ask them "Why do they look so different then?" they will likely comment that although the water level is much higher in the tall, skinny glass, it is much wider in the short, fat glass, and that the difference in height is made up for by the difference in width. Children's responses to such questions are important, for in conservation problems, it is not sufficient just to provide the correct answer to demonstrate concrete operations; a justification that involves the concept of reversibility is also necessary.

This example demonstrates the intuitive thinking of the preoperational child. There really seems to be more water in the tall, skinny glass. In fact, most objective adults would probably concur, although we know that this cannot be so. The young child's intuitive approach to the problem leads to some contradictions. What happens when the water in the tall glass is returned to its original container? Most preoperational children will tell you that the water in the two glasses is now the same as it was to begin with. The contradiction, however, is one of objective fact; there is no apparent contradiction to the child. Some cognitive discrepancy (disequilibrium) can be experienced by slightly older and cognitively more advanced children, who realize that something is not quite right but can't figure out exactly what it is. For Piaget, these children are in a transition phase between preoperations and concrete operations. Their cognitive structures are thrown into states of disequilibrium, and within a short time they will make the accommodations necessary to achieve conservation. No such disequilibrium is experienced by younger children, as they assimilate the information to their preoperative schemes.

With a few mainly laboratory-based exceptions, conservation is not something that children are taught. The notion of conservation develops gradually, and once it is acquired, most children assume that they always thought that way. Ask most 8-year-old conservers if they ever in their lives thought the glass with the higher water level had more water, and they will answer "No" and often give you a funny look to think an adult would ask such a question.

An operational knowledge of conservation does not develop simultaneously for all properties of material; conservation of some properties develops before others. Piaget referred to this phenomena as *horizontal decalage*. When children acquire the concept of conservation for one property, they do not realize that the same general principle applies to other properties. Piaget claimed that the order in which conservation for different properties is acquired is constant across children. Thus, conservation of number is acquired before conservation of mass, and these are acquired before conservation of weight, which precedes the conservation of volume. This pattern of development has generally been confirmed by other researchers (for example, Brainerd & Brainerd, 1972; Uzgiris, 1964).

It's worth noting here that Piaget's concept of horizontal decalage implicitly acknowledges that there is variability in development and that a child's thinking will not always be at the same level for all related contents. But even here, he tried to show how there is regularity in this variability, with the order in which the various types of conservation are mastered being acquired in an invariant order. Thus, although Piaget did not ignore heterogeneity, or unevenness, in cognitive development, his emphasis was clearly on what was universal and invariant.

Conservation and cultural differences.   Although the developmental sequence of attaining conservation is apparently universal, there are individual differences in the rate at which conservation, and other concrete operational abilities, are achieved. Piaget acknowledged that the social environment plays a role in cognitive development, although admittedly the role was a relatively minor one. Piaget proposed that the course of cognitive development is universal—that children in all cultures around the world will progress through these stages in the same order. However, the rate at which these cognitive accomplishments are achieved can vary as a function of the social environment, and this was the main (though not exclusive) role Piaget gave to culture in influencing cognitive development.

Cultural differences in the rate of attaining conservation have been repeatedly observed, with most studies finding a slower rate of development for nonschooled children relative to schooled children (Dasen, 1977). Yet, these cultural differences in rate of development might be attributed less to differences in the actual competence of these children than to cultural differences in the nature of the tasks and how they are administered. For example, in many studies, children from traditional cultures were tested either through interpreters or in their second or third language (see Nyiti, 1982). This contrasts sharply with the way American or European children are tested and makes it difficult to interpret differences in performance found between these groups. In a study of conservation, Nyiti (1982) compared two cultural groups of Canadian children: Europeans (white and English speaking) and Micmac Indians. The Indian children attended school, where they learned English but spoke their native language (Micmac) at home. Both the European and Indian children were given a series of conservation tasks, following standard Piagetian procedures. The European children were all tested in English. The Indian children were divided into two groups, with half being tested in English by a European and the other half being tested in Micmac by a Micmac Indian. There was no difference in how the European and Indian children performed the tasks when tested in their "home" language — European children in English and Indian children in Micmac. When the Indian children were tested in English by a European examiner, however, they gave much shorter and less complete answers and were significantly less likely to be classified as conservers than their European counterparts were.

These results suggest that certain aspects of cognitive development as described by Piaget are universal and that concepts such as conservation develop on a predictable schedule in all cultures (Nyiti, 1982). This truism can be overlooked, however, if one is not mindful of the cultural context in which performance is assessed.

Reversibility. Piaget's description of children's performance on conservation tasks illustrates the importance of the concept of reversibility. Preoperational children, stated Piaget, are unable to apply the reversibility rules of negation or compensation to arrive at correct solutions to conservation prob-

lems. Preoperational and concrete operational children differ in ways other than reversibility, however. Generally, Piaget described preoperational children as being more influenced by their immediate perceptions, more egocentric, and less apt to identify transformational relations between events, all relative to concrete operational children. Each of these factors is discussed briefly in the following text.

Perceptual centration versus decentration. Preoperational children's perception is said to be centered, in that they attend to and make judgments based on the most salient aspect of their perceptual field. They are highly attentive to particular portions of a perceptual array and often are unable to integrate various parts into a whole. In the conservation-of-liquid problem just discussed, their attention is directed only to the difference in height of the water levels, and they are unable (according to Piaget) to coordinate the two dimensions of height and width simultaneously. In contrast, concrete operational children's perception is said to be decentered, in that they can divorce themselves from specific aspects of a perceptual array and attend to and make decisions based on the entire perceptual field. Unlike their younger peers, they can consider two dimensions at once, partly because they are not so highly focused on one dimension that differences in the other escape their awareness.

The role of perceptual **centration** and **decentration** in young children's performance on conservation-of-liquid tasks is illustrated nicely in an experiment cited by Bruner (1966). In this experiment, children were presented with different-sized clear beakers and asked to pour water from one beaker (for example, a skinny one) into a second beaker (for example, a fat one). However, the second beaker was shielded by a screen so that the children could not see the resulting water level. When asked whether there was still the same amount of water in the second beaker as was in the first, most children gave conservation responses. When the screen was removed revealing the difference in water level relative to the original beaker, almost all 4-year-olds who had given a conservation response when the beaker had been screened changed their minds when faced with the perceptual evidence. They could not ignore the discrepancy in the size of the beakers or of the height of the water level; they confessed to being in error previously and gave a nonconservation judgment.

Perceptual centration is not limited to young children's performance on laboratory tasks but is reflected in their everyday thinking. For example, Piaget (1969a) noted that preoperational children often use height as a means of estimating age. Take, for example, the 5-year-old who told her 35-year-old, 4-foot-11-inch mother that she was the "youngest mommy in the whole neighborhood." In actuality, she was the shortest mommy in the whole neighborhood, and, if truth be known, one of the oldest among her daughter's friends.

This age-height relation was illustrated in an experiment by Kratochwill and Goldman (1973). In their study, children between the ages of 3 and 9 years were shown realistic photographs of people from four age groups: infants, children, adolescents, and middle-aged adults. The size of the person's image in the photograph was varied, so that some photos were 3 inches tall and others $5^{1}/4$ inches tall. Children were given pairs of photos and asked to select the picture of the older person. Overall, the percentage of correct responses increased with age, but more interestingly, younger children were more apt than older children to choose incorrectly the taller, younger figure (for example, $5^{1}/4$ inch picture of an infant versus a 3-inch picture of an adolescent). This doesn't mean that preschool children cannot evaluate the age of a person based on other factors such as facial characteristics. In fact, when children are not distracted by size and height cues, they can (Montepare & McArthur, 1986). Yet, when height cues are present, young children have a difficult time ignoring them, despite often obvious age differences based on other characteristics.

Egocentricity.   In general, Piaget described preoperational children as being more egocentric than older, concrete operational children. Piaget used the term **egocentricity** to describe young children's intellectual perspective. Young children interpret the world through preoperative eyes and generally as-sume that others see the world as they do. Their cognition is centered around themselves, and they have a difficult time putting themselves in someone else's shoes. They, of course, are less egocentric than the sensorimotor child, who knows objects and events only by direct action on them. Yet, they are more self-centered in cognitive perspective than concrete operational children.

According to Piaget, this egocentric perspective permeates young children's entire cognitive life, influencing their perceptions, their language, and their social interactions. For example, 6-year-old Jamal assumes that all children in the first grade have older siblings and can never be the eldest child in their family. Jamal is in first grade and he has an older brother; therefore, all first-graders, if they have siblings at all, must have older siblings.

Don't be misled, however, into believing that preschool children are so self-centered as to be impervious to others in their environment. They can identify and empathize with the emotions of others (Hoffman, 1975) and realize that they possess knowledge that others do not share. In fact, research during the last three decades has indicated that Piaget underestimated the perspective-taking abilities of young children, and that egocentricity is far from an all-or-none matter.

The bulk of research on egocentricity has concentrated on two topics: (1) young children's abilities to take the visual perspective of others and (2) communication. The latter will be discussed in Chapter 9; for the former, Piaget and Inhelder's (1967) study of the three-mountain task served as the beginning of a long line of research. In this task, children were seated in front of a three-dimensional display of three mountains. The mountains differed in size, color, and form, with each having a different object on its peak (a red cross, a snow cap, or a small house). A doll was then moved to different locations around the display, and the children were to select from a set of pictures the one that corresponded to the doll's point of view. Piaget and Inhelder reported that most children younger than the age of 8 years were unable to determine how the doll viewed the array, but instead gave egocentric responses, choosing pictures that represented their *own* view of the mountains. That is, children stated that the doll saw what they saw.

Piaget and Inhelder's three-mountain task has been criticized as being unusually difficult, and later research showed that children will respond without egocentrism when provided with less complicated visual displays (Borke, 1975; Newcombe & Huttenlocher, 1992). Flavell and his colleagues (Flavell, Everett et al., 1981; Masangkay et al., 1974) refined Piaget's original conceptions concerning visual perspective taking and proposed two developmental levels of knowledge about visual perception. At level 1, children are able to determine that another person might see something that he or she does not. This is reflected in a task where children are familiarized with a card having a different picture on each side (for example, a dog and a cat). The card is held upright between the child and the experimenter and the child is asked what the experimenter sees. Children as young as 2.5 years can consistently provide nonegocentric responses to these types of questions, indicating that they realize that other people have perceptions different from their own. In fact, Rheingold, Hay, and West (1976) observed the pointing behavior of toddlers, and reported that 18-month-old children will point to objects in their surroundings to direct an adult's attention to the objects. These young children wish to share their visual experiences, realizing that their perceptions are not necessarily the same as those of another.

In contrast to level-1 perspective taking, level 2 involves the knowledge that an object that is simultaneously viewed by two people can give rise to different visual impressions. At level 2, children realize *how* another person might view the same object they are viewing and understand that the two views might differ. This is reflected by a task in which a picture is placed on a table so that it is right side up for the child but up side down for the experimenter seated on the opposite side of the table. The child is asked how the experimenter sees the picture. This is a more difficult task, and children typically do not solve level-2 tasks consistently until 4 or 5 years of age. Nevertheless, the level-2 tasks used by Flavell and his colleagues seem to be simplified versions of Piaget's three-mountain task and indicate that the

difficulty of the task greatly influences children's visual perspective-taking abilities.

Like most other aspects of preoperational thought, the young child's egocentricity is viewed as ineffective, which, in most situations, it is. However, there might be some adaptive advantage to a young child's egocentricity (Bjorklund, 1997a; Bjorklund & Green, 1992). From a global perspective, young children should be self-centered and less concerned with the thoughts, feelings, and behavior of others. They are universal novices and need to learn the complicated ways of their culture, making a self-centered perspective for young children likely beneficial from a Darwinian perspective. For instance, research with both adults and children has shown that when information is related to oneself (for example, when one is asked to determine how words on a list or events in a story relate to oneself) it is remembered better than when no self-referencing is done (Kail & Levine, 1976; Mood, 1979). Young children's tendencies to relate new information to themselves might thus give them a learning advantage, making egocentricity beneficial and not detrimental for the young child (Bjorklund & Green, 1992; Mood, 1979).

States versus transformations. According to Piaget, preoperational children center their attention on specific **states** and ignore the **transformations** between states. In the conservation-of-liquid example, young children fail to consider the transformation of the water from one glass to the next, despite the fact that they observe it and possibly even do the pouring. Each event is viewed as a separate entity, and relations between entities are not considered.

An example of this is a simple experiment in which children are asked to arrange (or draw) a series of sticks depicting "the successive movements of a bar that falls from a vertical, upright position to a horizontal one" (Flavell, 1963, p. 158). The correct depiction of this is shown in Figure 4-3. Although the task is easily accomplished by older children, preoperational children have considerable difficulty making (or sometimes even recognizing) the proper sequence. Each stick is treated independently of the others, making the notion of transformation from

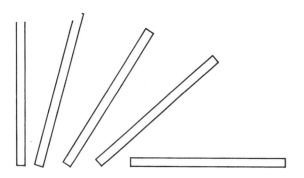

FIGURE 4-3   The falling-sticks task. Children are to arrange the sticks to depict the successive movements of a stick falling from an upright to a horizontal position.

vertical to horizontal difficult. The preoperational child has been described as viewing the world as a series of still pictures, whereas the older child and the adult see a movie.

The Development of Class Inclusion

Piaget examined many aspects of cognitive development, some of which have been discussed here and others will be discussed in other chapters. Perhaps the most studied Piagetian indicator of differences between the preschool and school-aged child, other than conservation, is **class inclusion**. Class inclusion involves the knowledge that a class must always be smaller than any more inclusive class in which it is contained. In a typical class-inclusion problem, children are given several examples from two subordinate categories of a single superordinate category (for example, seven pictures of dogs and three pictures of cats). They are then asked whether there are more dogs or more animals; in other words, they are asked to make a comparison between a subordinate set (dogs) and its superordinate set (animals). Although preschool children can easily make correct numerical judgments when comparing two subordinate sets (for example, dogs versus cats), correct responses on class-inclusion problems using Inhelder and Piaget's procedures are not found reliably

until late childhood or early adolescence (see Winer, 1980).

Inhelder and Piaget's description of the development of class inclusion has generally been replicated using variants of their original tasks (Winer, 1980). As with other aspects of Piaget's theory, however, there has been considerable controversy concerning the nature of the task itself and young children's class-inclusion abilities. For example, the questions posed to children in class-inclusion problems have been criticized as being a bit bizarre. Why would any well-meaning adult ask a child if there are more dogs or more animals? It is an unusual question and can easily be misinterpreted by children. Research by Brainerd and Kaszor (1974) indicated, however, that children who had failed class-inclusion problems rarely misinterpreted the questions. Moreover, there was no relation between children's abilities to recall the class-inclusion questions and their performance on the task.

Children's difficulty in dealing with subordinate and superordinate concepts can be seen in other situations in which potentially confusing questions are not a problem. For instance, my daughter Heidi at 6 years of age called me at work one day to talk.

"Is Julie visiting you today?" I asked.
"Which Julie?" Heidi asked. "Julie my friend or Julie my cousin?"
"Julie your friend," I said.
"No," she replied.
"Then your cousin's there?"
"No, she's not here either."

When I initially posed the question, she was not able to respond because I did not specify which Julie. She could field a question about Julie her friend or Julie her cousin, but I had to make up my mind which one I wanted to know about. She could not deal with the larger set of Julies, in general.

There has been much debate among psychologists concerning how children go about solving class-inclusion problems and when they can comprehend class-inclusion relations. One interesting study by McCabe and her colleagues found qualitative differences in how children of different ages solved these problems (McCabe et al., 1982). The researchers gave standard class-inclusion problems to children ranging in age from 3 to 8 years. They reported that the 7- and 8-year-olds performed the best, followed by the 3- and 4-year-olds, with the 5- and 6-year-old children performing the worst! This somewhat anomalous finding was explained by how children of different ages had approached the task. The 3- and 4-year-olds failed to discern any rule governing task performance and so responded randomly. As a result, they were correct on about 50% of the trials. In contrast, the 5- and 6-year-olds had figured out a rule for solving the task and followed the rule consistently. As it happened, however, the rule (pick the larger of the two subordinate sets) produced consistently wrong answers. The oldest children also had a rule for guiding their problem solving, and, for most of the children, the rule yielded correct solutions.

As is the case for much of Piaget's work, there is evidence that children much younger than hypothesized by Piaget can solve class-inclusion problems when they are trained or when the task is simplified. Even 3- and 4-year-olds have been shown to solve class-inclusion problems after being trained and to generalize this training to similar problems (Siegel et al., 1978; Waxman & Gelman, 1986). Other researchers have influenced children's performance by making the differences between the two subordinate categories more distinctive. For example, techniques that have increased children's likelihood of recognizing the difference in size between the superordinate and subordinate sets involve simply enumerating the items in each subclass (Brainerd & Kaszor, 1974), making the superordinate set visually salient (Wilkinson, 1976), requiring them to graphically represent hierarchies (through drawings or construction of graphs) (Greene, 1991), and making sure that children are highly familiar with the concepts used in the task. For example, several researchers have presented children with standard class-inclusion problems but have varied the typicality of the subordinate categories used (Carson & Abrahamson, 1976; Lane & Hodkin, 1985). Category typicality refers to differences in how representative various items are of their superordinate category (Rosch, 1975). Both adults (Rosch, 1975)

and children (Bjorklund, Thompson, & Ornstein, 1983) evaluate some members of natural language categories as being better examples of those categories than other members (see discussion of category typicality in Chapter 7). With respect to class inclusion, both Carson and Abrahamson (1976) and Lane and Hodkin (1985) reported better performance when category-typical items were used as exemplars. For example, children were more likely to answer class-inclusion problems correctly when presented with pictures of robins and blue jays (both typical examples of birds) than when presented with pictures of chickens and ducks (both atypical examples). In other words, the children's knowledge of category relations influenced their class-inclusion decisions, indicating that children's abilities to deal simultaneously with subordinate and superordinate relations is not absolute but varies as a function of their knowledge of the category relations used in the task.

The Transition from Concrete to Formal Operational Thought

Children in the concrete operational stage are impressive thinkers. Given a set of data, they can arrive at an answer (generally) free of contradictions. They can solve reasonably complex problems, as long as the general form of the problem and of the solution are previously known to them. Their thought is directed to the objects and events in their immediate experience, and "thinking about things" suffices to get most people through most of the routine tasks of everyday life. However, most of us also recognize that a change takes place in early adolescence. Children no longer are tied to thinking about concrete objects. Their thought can roam to discover or invent objects, events, and relations independent of their previous experiences. Their thinking is no longer restricted to things but can be applied to itself. As one Piagetian scholar has put it: "Concrete operations consist of thought thinking about the environment, but formal operations consist of thought thinking about itself" (Brainerd, 1978a, p. 215).

Hypothetico-deductive reasoning. The benchmark of formal operations is what Piaget referred to as **hypothetico-deductive reasoning** (Inhelder & Piaget, 1958). Deductive reasoning, which entails going from the general to the specific, is not, in itself, a formal operational process. Concrete operational children can arrive at a correct conclusion if they are provided with the proper evidence. However, their reasoning is confined to events and objects with which they are already familiar. "Concrete" operations are so named because children's thinking is limited to tangible facts and objects and not to hypotheses. Formal operational children, on the other hand, are not restricted to thinking about previously acquired facts but can generate hypotheses—what is possible is more important than what is real.

Thinking during the formal operational period can be done solely on the basis of symbols, with no need for referents in real life. Although this might bring to mind a person whose head is perpetually in the clouds and who cannot carry on a conversation without getting into metaphysics, this was not Piaget's intention. Rather, we have a person who is not tied to actual facts in his or her thinking but can postulate what might be as well as what is. The formal-operational thinker can generate ideas of things not yet experienced, accounting for the novel (to the child) and often grand ideas adolescents generate concerning morality, ethics, justice, government, and religion. Adolescents are entering, cognitively, the adult arena and ponder many of the weighty issues of the day without having had to experience directly the things they think about. The theories of most adolescents are naive because of their limited knowledge, but Piaget believed these children are flexing their mental muscles, using their newly acquired symbolic skills to deal with ideas rather than with things.

Hypothetical thinking is also critical for most forms of mathematics beyond arithmetic. If $2x + 5 = 15$, what does x equal? The problem does not deal with concrete entities such as apples or oranges but with numbers and letters. Mathematics in general is based on hypotheses and not necessarily in reality. Let y be 22; or let it be 7, or -12, or 45 degrees, or the cosine of angle AB. Once provided with a premise, formal operational thinkers can go on to solve the problem. They don't ask, "Is y *really* 22?" It is an arbitrary, hypothetical problem, and one that can be answered only if it is approached abstractly, using a symbol system that does not require concrete referents.

Thinking like a scientist. In addition to developing deductive reasoning abilities, Piaget theorized that formal operational children are able to think inductively, going from specific observations to broad generalizations. **Inductive reasoning** is the type of thinking that characterizes scientists, where hypotheses are generated and then systematically tested in experiments. By controlling for extraneous or potentially confounding factors, experiments lead to conclusions about nature. Inhelder and Piaget (1958) used a series of tasks to assess scientific reasoning, one of which, the pendulum problem, I will discuss briefly.

In the pendulum problem, children are given a rod from which strings of different lengths can be suspended. Objects of varying weight can be attached to the strings. The apparatus for this problem is shown in Figure 4-4. The children are shown how the pendulum operates (one places a weighted string on the rod and swings it) and are asked to determine the factors responsible for the speed with which the pendulum swings (the rate of oscillation). The children are told that in addition to varying the length of the string and the weight of the object attached to it, they can drop the object from varying heights (for example, high versus low) and alter the force of the push they give the object when initially propelling it. Thus, in attempting to solve the problem of the oscillating pendulum, the children can consider four possible factors (string length, weight of object, height of release, and force of push), with several levels within each factor (for example, three lengths of string; four weights of objects). The children are given the opportunity to experiment with the apparatus before providing an answer to the question of which factors are responsible for the pendulum's rate of oscillations. The correct answer is the length of the string—short strings swing faster than long strings, regardless of all other factors.

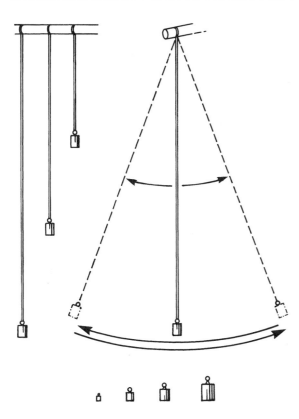

TABLE 4-3 Possible combinations and outcomes
of pendulum problem

Weight of object	Height of drop	Force of push	Length of string	
			Short	**Long**
Light	Low	Easy	Fast	Slow
		Hard	Fast	Slow
	High	Easy	Fast	Slow
		Hard	Fast	Slow
Heavy	Low	Easy	Fast	Slow
		Hard	Fast	Slow
	High	Easy	Fast	Slow
		Hard	Fast	Slow

FIGURE 4-4 The apparatus for the pendulum problem. Children are to determine what factors or combination of factors are responsible for the rate at which the pendulum oscillates. SOURCE: "The Pendulum Problem" from *The Growth of Logical Thinking from Childhood to Adolescence*, by B. Inhelder and Jean Piaget. Copyright © 1985 Basic Books. Reprinted with permission.

How might a scientist go about solving this problem? The first step is to generate a hypothesis. It doesn't matter if the hypothesis is correct or not, merely that it be testable and yield noncontradictory conclusions. This initial step is within the ability of concrete operational children. The next step is what separates the concrete from the formal operational thinkers—the testing of one's hypothesis. The trick is to vary a single factor while holding the others constant. For example, a child might examine the rate of oscillation for the 100-gram weight in combination with all the other factors (that is, short string, high release, easy push; short string, high re-

lease, hard push; short string, low release, short push, and so on). This can then be done for other weights, until the child has tested all of the various combinations. Table 4-3 presents the 16 possible combinations and their outcomes for a pendulum problem involving four factors and two levels for each factor (long versus short string; heavy versus light weight; low versus high release; easy versus hard push).

Concrete operational children often get off to a good start on this problem but rarely arrive at the correct answer. Their observations are generally accurate (which is not the case for preoperational children), but they usually fail to isolate relevant variables and will arrive at a conclusion before exhaustively testing their hypotheses. For example, children might observe that the pendulum swings fast with a short string and a heavy weight and conclude that both string length and weight are jointly responsible for rate of oscillation. According to Inhelder and Piaget (1958), it is not until formal operations that children can test their hypotheses correctly and arrive at the only possible, logical conclusion. More will be said about scientific reasoning in Chapter 10.

Thinking about Thinking.   A further formal operational characteristic involves the ability to examine the contents of one's thought. Concrete operational thinkers have available to them some powerful problem-solving skills. But, according to Piaget, they are not able to reflect on the content of their thinking to arrive at new insights. Concrete operational children gain knowledge from the outside world but cannot learn anything new by contemplating what they already know. In contrast, formal operational children can acquire new information as a result of internal reflection. Piaget (1971) used the term **reflective abstraction** to refer to "a rearrangement, by means of thought, of some matter previously presented to the subject in a rough or immediate form" (p. 320). In other words, formal operational children can reflect on knowledge they already possess and, without needing additional information from the external environment, arrive at a previously unknown truth. Reflective abstraction is thinking about thinking and might allow a child to apply more readily information that he or she knows to new situations, or to discover alternative cognitive routes to solving old problems.

Egocentricity in Adolescence.   One interesting observation Piaget made about adolescents that ties their cognition to that of much younger children concerns egocentricity. Egocentricity is usually associated with preoperational thought. Piaget defined egocentrism broadly as an inability to decenter, however, and proposed that adolescents demonstrate their own form of centration. Piaget stated that adolescents are concerned about their future in society and often with how they might transform society, but many of the grand social and political ideas of adolescents conflict with the beliefs or attitudes of others (particularly people in authority). Adolescents also might believe that these abstract ideas are unique to them, making them impatient

with the "stodgy and simple-minded" ideas of their elders. This view changes as the adolescent approaches adulthood, and many of us can identify with Mark Twain, who professed to be impressed by how much his father had learned between Twain's 14th and 21st birthdays.

Adolescence is a time when young people are trying to leave childhood behind and adopt adult roles, an attempt that often results in extreme self-consciousness. Adolescents' self-centered perspectives result in the mistaken belief that other people are as concerned with their feelings and behavior as they are, which only enhances their self-consciousness. David Elkind (1967; Elkind & Bowen, 1979) has hypothesized that adolescents feel that they are constantly "on stage" or playing to an **imaginary audience**. This hypothesis has been confirmed in several studies, where adolescents' responses to potentially embarrassing situations and their tendencies to reveal aspects of themselves to others were related to age and formal operational abilities (Adams & Jones, 1981; Elkind & Bowen, 1979; Gray & Hudson, 1984). Although there are some discrepancies in the results, the effect of the imaginary audience seems to peak in early adolescence and to decline as formal operational skills increase.

Elkind also proposed that the egocentrism of adolescence leads to what he called the **personal fable,** a belief in one's uniqueness and invulnerability. This is reflected in the often reckless behavior of adolescents and the belief that bad things happen only to other people (for example, "I won't get pregnant," or "I can get off the tracks before the train gets here") (Arnett, 1992).

The risk-taking behavior that springs from adolescents' personal fable clearly has its drawbacks, but it might also have some adaptive value, just as preschool children's egocentricity might. For example, teenage egocentricity ensures that adolescents will experiment with new ideas and generally behave more independently (Bjorklund & Green, 1992). Many of these experiences will be beneficial to adult functioning and might hasten the entry into adult life. Many parents do not welcome such independence, for the negative consequences of much adolescent risk taking are real, but the end result for most adolescents of their egocentricity might be adaptive in the long run.

The State of Piaget's Theory Today

Piaget is a giant in the field of human development. As one scholar quoted by Harry Beilin (1992) put it, "assessing the impact of Piaget on developmental psychology is like assessing the impact of Shakespeare on English literature or Aristotle on philosophy—impossible" (p. 191). What does Piaget's theory, initially formulated more than 70 years ago, tell us about development today? Piaget continues to influence contemporary developmentalists. His work is cited more frequently by developmental researchers than that of anyone else. But much of the interest Piaget has generated has been criticism rather than praise. Does this theory paint an accurate picture of cognitive development, or is it ready to be relegated to the historical archives? Obviously, I would not commit an entire chapter to this theory if I did not think it had substantial merit. But 25-some years of intense investigation (some would say 25 years of Piaget bashing) has shown that Piaget's theory is not the final word.

Before detailing the criticisms of Piaget's theory, however, I think it is appropriate to acknowledge some of the lasting contributions that the man and the theory made to developmental psychology.

Piaget's Contributions

Here is a list of the major contributions that Piaget made to the field of cognitive development. The list is based, in part, on an assessment of Piaget's contributions made by several prominent researchers, written in honor of the centennial of Piaget's birth (Brainerd, 1996; Flavell, 1996; Elkind, 1996; Fischer & Hencke, 1996; Kessen, 1996; Gopnik, 1996; Siegler & Ellis, 1996):

1. Piaget founded the field of cognitive development as we know it. The study of children's thinking has focused on high-level, cognitive tasks, very different from the emphasis on basic-level and mainly unconscious cognition that has characterized the study of adult cognition. Because of Piaget, cognitive development is a unique field to itself, and not simply the application of ideas and methods developed in the study of adult cognition to children.

2. The child is an active, self-motivated agent, playing an important role in his or her own development. This is reflected by Piaget's idea of constructivism, which might seem obvious to anyone today who has seriously considered the nature of cognitive development, but was an innovation of Piaget and counter to the dominant perspective of his time.

3. Piaget's equilibration model was one of the first attempts to explain, rather than just describe, the process of development. Despite the many years since Piaget originally formulated this model, it is only recently that psychologists have taken seriously the challenge to explain, and not just describe, developmental transitions (Case, 1992a; Fischer, 1980; Fischer & Bidell, 1998; Siegler, 1996).

4. Piaget introduced many interesting and useful concepts to cognitive development, including *scheme, object permanence, egocentrism, centration, decentration,* and *conservation,* among many others. Accompanying these concepts were many experimental tasks used to assess them, many of which are still used by psychologists today.

5. Piaget provided a highly memorable description of cognitive development that gave a relatively accurate picture of how children of different ages think. Piaget's description of development still captures much of the richness and uniqueness of children's thinking. Most preschool children do take a relatively egocentric perspective of the world and their attention is centered on the obvious physical characteristics of stimuli. Most concrete operational children cannot engage in introspection about their own thought processes, they don't think hypothetically, and they rarely approach problems in a scientific way. Children can, under certain circumstances, be trained or biased to think in a more advanced

way, but such training is usually limited and rarely transforms the child into a totally different type of thinker. In other words, Piaget's description of intellectual development has ecological validity in that it depicts well the day-to-day functioning of most children.

6. Piaget's influence extended beyond the field of cognitive development to other areas of development (social, emotional), and, importantly, to education.

7. Piaget made more important empirical discoveries, on a wide range of topics, than any other developmental psychologist, and he is not likely to be displaced from this lofty seat of honor soon.

8. Finally, Piaget asked important questions and drew literally thousands of researchers to the study of cognitive development. And as often happens when heuristic theories such as Piaget's are repeatedly scrutinized, some of his research led to new insights while pointing to problems with his original ideas. We now turn to some of these problems.

Competence or Performance?

Piaget's theory has stimulated more research than any other theory in cognitive development. However, there are considerable shortcomings in his theory. Piaget believed that he was assessing children's competencies—their actual abilities. Research cited earlier concerning young children's visual perspective taking (for example, Borke, 1975) clearly demonstrates that children often have greater mental skills than Piaget attributed to them. Other researchers have shown that children who do not spontaneously solve problems in a concrete operational way can be trained to do so. For example, although scientists have replicated the stages involved in the acquisition of conservation proposed by Piaget (Brainerd & Brainerd, 1972), many have demonstrated that nonconservers as young as 4 years of age can be trained to conserve by way of a variety of techniques (Brainerd & Allen, 1971; Gelman, 1969), and more recent research has reported success in training mentally retarded children to conserve (Hendler & Weisberg, 1992). The magnitude of training effects is greater for older than for younger children, with few studies revealing convincing evidence that 3-year-olds can be trained to conserve (Field, 1987). In a review of the conservation training literature, however, Field (1987) concluded that 76% of all studies successfully induced conservation in preschool children, with a smaller percentage of these studies demonstrating generalization to other materials and transfer over delayed (one week or longer) periods.

Despite the impressive training and transfer effects shown by numerous researchers for conservation, the training effects are confined to the laboratory. Will 4-year-old children who are taught to conserve in the lab be convinced that they have the same amount of sandwich regardless of whether it is cut into two pieces or four? Much recent work in cognitive development has been concerned with context specificity—the extent to which cognitive competence is limited to a specific context (Ceci, 1996)—and future research should investigate whether conservation training can be generalized beyond the laboratory and into the homes and schools of children.

Training studies have not been limited to teaching preoperational children conservation and other concrete operational tasks but also have been used to teach formal operational reasoning to concrete operational children. Many of the observations of adolescent thinking made by Inhelder and Piaget (1958) have been replicated by others using their original problems (Lovell, 1961) as well as modifications of their experimental tasks (Kuhn & Brannock, 1977). As is the case for Piaget's research on concrete operations, however, subsequent research has indicated that Piaget underestimated children's intellectual abilities in many ways. Children much younger than proposed by Inhelder and Piaget have been shown to display formal operational reasoning under some conditions. Subtle differences in how the instructions are given or in the task materials influence the likelihood that children will successfully perform formal operational tasks (Danner & Day, 1977; Slater & Kingston, 1981), and several researchers have demonstrated that concrete operational children can be trained to solve formal operational problems (Adey & Shayer, 1992; Stone & Day, 1978). In general, research has indicated that young children have greater competencies with respect to some formal operational abilities than Inhelder and Piaget originally proposed, although they will display these competencies only under limited conditions.

In other situations, however, research has shown that Piaget's account of formal operations greatly overestimates how adults actually think (Capon & Kuhn, 1979; Kuhn et al., 1977). For example, a study by Capon and Kuhn (1979) investigated whether adults tend to use formal operational abilities in a practical task. These researchers interviewed 50 women in a supermarket and asked them to judge which of two sizes of the same product was the better buy. For example, one task involved two bottles of garlic powder: a smaller bottle containing 1.25 ounces (35 grams) selling for 41 cents, and a larger bottle containing 2.37 ounces (67 grams) selling for 77 cents. The women were provided with pencil and paper that they were told they could use if they wished, and asked to justify their explanations. The most direct way to arrive at the correct answer is to compute the price per unit of weight for each product and to compare the two. This involves reasoning about proportions, which Inhelder and Piaget (1958) said was a scheme characteristic of formal operations. Fewer than 30% of the women used a proportional reasoning strategy, and at least 50% of the women used a strategy that yielded inconclusive evidence at best and was just as likely to be wrong as right. For instance, some women used a subtraction strategy, saying, for example, "With the bigger one you get 32 more grams for 36 more cents," concluding that the bigger one was thus the better buy. Others merely relied on their past experiences, making statements such as "The big one must be cheaper" without providing any justification for the statement. In general, formal operational reasoning was not observed for a majority of these women. This does not mean that these adults would not have displayed formal reasoning under some other conditions, but it does suggest that formal operations are not typical of adult thought in general.

As this research reflects, American adults do not often reason at the formal level, and apparently there are some cultures—particularly those where formal schooling is rare or nonexistent—in which no one solves Piaget's formal-operational problems (Cole, 1990; Dasen, 1977).

Why do some people fail to attain formal operations? Dasen's (1977) cross-cultural research provides one clue: They might not have had sufficient exposure to the kinds of schooling that stress logic, mathematics, and science—experiences that Piaget believed help the child to reason at the formal level (Cole, 1990). Indeed, Tulkin and Konner (1973) found that preliterate Bushman hunters who fail Piaget's problems do often reason at the formal level on at least one task—tracking prey. Clearly, this is an activity of great importance to them that requires the systematic testing of inferences and hypotheses.

Piaget's picture of adult intelligence is one of a reasonable, systematic, and logical thinker. This picture is shared by few psychologists who study adult cognition. We adults, in general, are not nearly as logical and systematic in our thinking as Piaget would have us be. We take shortcuts, make estimates, and arrive at conclusions before exhausting all possible combinations of elements or considering all the facts. Formal operations as described by Piaget might reflect the best adults can do, but they are not characteristic of how grown-ups deal with real-world problems on a daily basis.

Training studies not only demonstrate that children can perform at more advanced levels than Piaget proposed but have also suggested some very non-Piagetian mechanisms for developmental change. For example, in a pioneering conservation-training study by Gelman (1969), preschool children were required to ignore irrelevant dimensions of a problem (such as where two rows of dots begin or end) and focus instead on the relevant dimension (for example, the number of dots in a row). By learning to focus on the proper dimension, children were able to solve conservation problems and to generalize their acquired skill to other materials. Such research indicates that young children have the competence to solve conservation problems, but that limitations of memory prevent them from displaying this competence under some circumstances. This challenges Piaget's very notion of structures, stages, and operations.

Are Operations Reasonable?

What is implied by the concept of operations? First, Piaget claimed that operations represent mental and logical functioning. Operations are not available to the preschool-age child, and logical operations change in form between the concrete and formal operational periods. In other words, the development of operationality represents qualitative changes in thinking. Although the pattern of cognitive change Piaget observed between the ages of 2 and 15 years has been replicated by many researchers using Piaget's original tasks, others have reported that preoperational children can think logically (even hypothetically) under certain stimulus and instructional conditions. Are these children using primitive forms of operations, or are they circumventing the problem by using nonoperational techniques to arrive at logical answers? If the latter, might this not reflect an artificial solution to the problem and one that is not representative of the normal course of development? Or might it reflect the possibility that even operational children do not use operations to solve these problems but, like their younger counterparts, find alternative paths without the need for logic?

Second, the concept of operations implies substantial integration. Piaget's "structures of the whole" principle is concerned specifically with the organization of operations. Discrepancies in cognitive abilities are found both within a given child and between different children, indicating that cognitive functioning is not as homogeneous, or even, as Piaget proposed. A particular child can display a highly egocentric attitude in one situation yet show impressive perspective-taking skills in another.

Such contradictory findings challenge Piaget's notion of stages of development that represent qualitatively unique forms of thinking, with transitions between stages reflecting discontinuities in development. (See Brainerd, 1978b, and related commentaries for a thorough discussion of criticisms of

Piaget's stage theory.) As Flavell (1978) has written: "However much we may wish it otherwise, human cognitive growth may simply be too contingent, multiform, and heterogeneous—too variegated in developmental mechanisms, routes, and rates—to be accurately characterized by any single stage theory of the Piagetian kind" (p. 187). In response, several theorists have proposed that changes in children's thinking over time are primarily quantitative in nature, with transitions from simpler to more complex forms of thinking reflecting continuities in development (Carey, 1985; Klahr & Wallace, 1976). Others have maintained a belief that cognitive development proceeds by way of qualitative, stagelike change, but not in the lockstep way that Piaget proposed (Case, 1985; 1998; Fischer, 1980; see discussion of neo-Piagetian theories later in this chapter).

It seems clear that stages of development are not as discrete and clear-cut as Piaget hypothesized. Cognitive development is more variable, more heterogeneous, and involves many aspects of quantitative (as opposed to qualitative) changes than Piaget proposed. Yet, Piaget and many others working in the Piagetian tradition were not hallucinating when they observed children's thinking and described it in terms of stages. How stagelike cognitive development is seems to be a function of where one looks for it. For example, maturation apparently sets an upper limit on information-processing capacity (see Chapter 5) beyond which a child cannot exceed; cognition might be more homogeneous on the everyday tasks that children routinely perform rather than on the usually demanding tasks that psychologists favor; and there might be more homogeneity at certain points in problem solving routines (for example, when starting to solve a problem) than at other points (Flavell, 1982; see discussion of homogeneity versus heterogeneity of cognitive function in Chapter 1).

Despite the considerable merit of Piaget's theory, most developmental psychologists today believe that Piaget's account of operations attributes more stagelike properties to development than the data warrant. A fair statement concerning cognitive development is that average cognitive competencies increase with age, although there is a substantial range of cognitive abilities that children of any given age can display. Most of a child's cognitive functioning occurs within a relatively narrow range of competencies, and this range possibly broadens with age. However, a child can display cognitive abilities substantially above (or below) his or her average, but only under optimal (or restrictive) conditions.

In sum, Piaget's account of the development of operations does not fully capture what actually occurs in development. New theories are needed to account for some of the discrepancies researchers have found in Piaget's theory. Some of these theories, based on information-processing approaches, will be discussed in Chapter 5. Before looking at these approaches, however, I would like to examine briefly four contemporary neo-Piagetian approaches that adopt some of Piaget's ideas about the nature of development while addressing some discrepancies that have arisen between Piaget's theory and new data. These are the theories of Kurt Fischer and Robbie Case, the "theory theory" as presented by Alison Gopnik and Andrew Meltzoff, and Annette Karmiloff-Smith's representational redescription theory.

Neo-Piagetian Theories

"Traditional" Neo-Piagetian Theories of Case and Fischer

Early neo-Piagetian theories accepted many of the basic premises of Piaget's theory (for example, an intrinsically active child, constructivism, discontinuities in development), but interpreted them through contemporary information-processing perspectives, particularly the idea of limited mental resources (Case, 1974; Pascual-Leone, 1970). The theories of Kurt Fischer and Robbie Case are in this tradition. Their theories have gone through some substantial modifications since their first inceptions (Case, 1974; Fischer, 1980), but both still assume that a child's level of thinking is limited by information-

processing constraints. Each also acknowledges that there is much more heterogeneity of cognitive functioning than Piaget proposed. Case and Fischer each also use evidence from studies of brain development to support their ideas. Despite the similarities, there are many differences between the two accounts, and I will describe each briefly.

Fischer's Skill Theory

Kurt Fischer (1980; Fischer & Bidell, 1991, 1998) was perhaps the first major neo-Piagetian theorist to consider seriously the issue of heterogeneity and variability of cognitive function. Fischer's approach was to blend what would seem on the surface to be two incompatible theories: Piaget's cognitive development theory and B. F. Skinner's behaviorism (and more recently, Vygotsky's sociocultural approach). Fischer takes as his starting point the position that development is the result of a dynamic interaction between a child and the environment. Piaget, of course, made the same assumption, but Piaget gave the environment only a small role in affecting development. Piaget believed that the child in active interaction with the environment, and is the principal "cause" of development. Fischer takes the environment more seriously than did Piaget. The consequence is a theory that gives more equal weight to the contributions of the child and of the environment in influencing development and a theory that predicts greater heterogeneity of cognitive function than was proposed by Piaget.

Fischer theorizes that children develop *skills* (or *dynamic skills*). Fischer defines a skill as "a capacity to act in an organized way in a specific context (Fischer & Bidell, 1998, p. 478), making skills both action based and context specific. Consistent with sociocultural theory (see Chapter 3), skills are also culturally defined. An important aspect of Fischer's theory is that skills are seen as jointly defined by the organism and the environment. Thus, only skills that are exercised in the most supportive of environments will be developed to their highest level. To the extent that a child's environment encourages development of various skills equally, there will be homogeneity (or evenness) of cognitive function.

That is, if the environment is relatively homogeneous with respect to supporting all of a child's skills, development will proceed evenly. To the extent that one's environment is heterogeneous, however, with some skills being exercised more consistently or receiving more support than others, development will be relatively uneven. Because the world in which most children live is not homogeneous with respect to opportunities to develop different skills, Fischer assumes, quite contrary to Piaget, that heterogeneity of cognitive function is the rule rather than the exception.

Fischer proposes that skills show an invariant developmental progression (à la Piaget) with respect to optimal level of performance. **Optimal level** refers to the maximum level of complexity of a skill that the individual can control, or, in other words, the best performance that a child can show, working on his or her own. Children's level of performance can exceed this optimal level when they are supported by a more skilled partner through the process of scaffolding (see Chapter 3). In fact, Fischer states that it is inappropriate to think of a child as "possessing" a fixed level of a skill. Rather, one's dynamic skills are always changing as a people adjust and reorganize their skills in response to situations in the environment. Consistent with Fischer's position that skills are jointly defined by the environment and the child, he proposes that the optimal level of performance is realized only for those skills practiced in the most supportive of environments.

Skills are also self-organizing, in that they change as other skills change (a single skill can involve many different aspects of psychological functioning) and as a function of experience. Skills become coordinated with other skills and, as a result, produce qualitatively new systems.

Such change is not random, however. Although there is substantial variability in skills (and thus development) both between and within individuals, skills nonetheless develop in a step-by-step sequence of ten hierarchical levels, with these levels being grouped into three tiers (sensorimotor, representational, and abstract). Each tier reflects the general type of information that a child can control. In the

sensorimotor tier (approximately 3 to 24 months), children's skills are limited to their actions on and perceptions of objects in their environments. In the *representational tier* (approximately 2 to 12 years), children can represent concrete objects mentally, and in the *abstract tier* (approximately 12 to 26 years) they can combine representational sets so that objects can be thought of as general, intangible attributes. Each tier consists of four levels, with the highest skill level of one tier (for example, sensorimotor, level 4) corresponding to the first level of the next tier (for example, representational, level 1). A brief outline of Fischer's levels is presented in Table 4-4.

By stressing the role that the environment plays in the development of skills, Fischer's theory acknowledges the significance of experience far more than Piaget's does. Fischer's ten hierarchical levels and the cyclical, predictable nature of development are certainly reminiscent of Piaget, however, and Fischer's concept of optimal level is consistent with contemporary information-processing viewpoints (see Chapter 5). What, then, is the contribution of this theory, and how is it similar to or different from other formulations, particularly that of Piaget?

Contrasts between Fischer's and Piaget's theories can most readily be made with respect to the basic structures of their theories: *skills* and *schemes*. Schemes are structures by which the child knows the world. Schemes are based on action and, for Piaget, are the things that do the assimilating and accommodating. Schemes develop from earlier schemes and have a high degree of generality in that they are integrated with one another (structures of the whole) and thus result in a high degree of homogeneity of cognitive function. Skills are also structures by which a child knows the world, and, like schemes, they are based in action and develop from earlier acquired skills. Similarly, skills are relatively well integrated and are characterized by the type of representations a child can control (sensorimotor, representational, abstract). Unlike schemes, however, most or all of a child's skills are never at the same level at a given time. Development of skills is induced by the environment in dynamic

TABLE 4-4 Outline of stages in Fischer's skill theory

Hierarchical level	Tier	Cyclical level	Characteristic structure	Estimated age range of emergence
1		1	Single set	3 to 4 months
2		2	Mapping	7 to 8 months
3	Sensorimotor skills	3	System	11 to 13 months
4	————————	4 = 1	System of systems	20 to 24 months
5		2		4 to 5 years
6	Representational skills	3		6 to 7 years
7	————————	4 = 1		10 to 12 years
8		2		14 to 16 years
9	Abstract skills	3		18 to 20 years
10		4		24 to 26 years

SOURCE: Adapted from "Processes of Cognitive Development: Optimal Level and Skill Acquisition," by K. W. Fischer and S. L. Pipp. In R. J. Sternberg (Ed.), *Mechanisms of Cognitive Development*. Copyright © 1984 W. H. Freeman and Company. Adapted with permission of the author.

interaction with the child, and only skills that are induced most consistently operate at their optimal level in a child.

Both schemes and skills are viewed as developing from simpler to more complex states of organization. For Piaget, schemes are organized into stages, whereas for Fischer, skills are organized into levels and then tiers. The major difference between the two theorists is that Piaget's stages reflect a high degree of generality and characterize the child. A child *is* a concrete operational thinker or *is* in the sensorimotor period. In contrast, levels characterize skills that are specific to particular objects and tasks. In Fischer's theory, children are not described as being at level 4 or at level 7. One can specify the optimal level of performance that a child is able to achieve, but this does not reflect a classification of the child. Accordingly, the range of expected behaviors for a given child is very broad, especially in comparison with the high degree of generality predicted for children at a particular stage in Piaget's theory.

One further difference is that unlike Piaget, Fischer maintains that there are several different developmental routes to any particular outcome. That is, although all skills are based on earlier skills, it is not necessary for all children to progress through

the same sequence of skills in exactly the same order. This is due partly to the great variability that exists in cognitive functioning. For example, a child might have achieved a level-5 skill for conservation of length but have level-6 skills for the more-practiced conservation of number and solids. The child might coordinate these two level-6 skills to arrive at a level-7 skill and can then abstract the rule for level-7 conservation of length without ever having attained the level-6 skill for this particular content (Fischer, 1980).

Case's Theory

Perhaps the most influential neo-Piagetian theory has been that of Robbie Case (Case, 1985, 1992a, 1998; Case & Okamoto, 1996). Whereas Fischer's theory represents an integration of concepts from Piagetian theory and behaviorism, Case integrates Piagetian theory with ideas from information processing (see Chapter 5). Case proposes that domain-general changes in processing capacity (or processing efficiency) account for developmental changes in cognitive functioning. More will be said about this aspect of Case's theory in Chapter 5. Here, I want to focus on the aspect of Case's theory most similar to that of Piaget: the stage-like nature of cognitive development as reflected by the concept of central conceptual structure.

Case believes that children become increasingly efficient in their ability to process information, effectively increasing the capacity of their working memories. Through practice and maturation, children become faster (and thus more efficient) at processing information, meaning that they can execute an increasing number of mental processes. In a sense, Case replaces Piaget's concepts of assimilation, accommodation, and equilibration with developmental differences in processing efficiency.

Were Case to stop here, his model of cognitive development would not qualify as neo-Piagetian, but rather as one based on the assumptions of information-processing psychology. However, Case, like Piaget, also proposes that development consists of stages and that these stages build on one another (basically, Piaget's epigenetic principle). Yet, as most neo-Piagetians, Case acknowledges that development is more heterogeneous than proposed by Piaget and that there are important differences both between and within individuals in how cognitive structures are formed (that is, different development routes are possible).

Case proposes four major stages of development: *sensorimotor* (birth to 18 months), *interrelational* (18 months to 5 years), *dimensional* (5 to 11 years), and *vectorial* or *abstract dimensional* (11 to 19 years). Each major stage is proposed to have its own distinctive type of cognitive structure, just as in Piaget's theory. Each stage also consists of three substages, with progress from one substage to the next seen as a function of working-memory capacity (how many things a child can hold in mind at once, see Chapter 5).

Case's stages of cognitive development are similar in form to those proposed by Piaget. In the sensorimotor stage, infants represent objects in terms of their physical movements, much as proposed by Piaget. Such representations can be coordinated with one another, through the substage sequence. During the interrelational stage, children can detect and coordinate relations among objects, events, and people. During the dimensional stage, children can

form comparisons of two dimensions, such as height and width in conservation of liquid problems. During the vectorial stage, children can understand abstract systems. This permits them to solve verbal analogies, use proportional reasoning, and infer psychological traits in other people.

Case proposes that one major change in development is the extent to which children can assemble **executive control structures** for solving problems. Executive control structures involve a representation of the problem situation, a representation of the objectives of the task (that is, the desired outcome), and a representation of the particular strategy or procedures for solving the problem. There are developmental differences in how children represent the problem situation, objects, and strategies in executive control structures, primarily in the number of options that can be considered and coordinated by a child at any one time.

Executive control structures are limited by a child's optimal level of cognitive competence, which is strongly influenced by maturational factors. Much as in Fischer's theory, however, different children will encounter different tasks in their lives, and because of this, there will be much individual variation, both between and within children, in the sophistication of executive control structures. Nevertheless, Case believes that there is far more homogeneity of cognitive function than critics of stage theories propose, and he postulates that there is a cross-domain upper limit beyond which a child cannot function (compare this with Fischer's optimal level). Case and his colleagues have presented evidence from children over a broad age range demonstrating substantial consistency in cognitive performance over a wide range of tasks, supportive of the position that cognitive development is under the influence of domain-general mechanisms, à la Piaget (see Case, 1992a, 1998; Case & Okamoto, 1996). Nevertheless, Case acknowledges that cognitive performance is not nearly as even as proposed by Piaget.

How can one resolve these anomalous findings? Case's answer is that there must be some truth to both positions, that some aspects of human cognitive development are domain specific in nature whereas others are domain general. Despite recognizing that some aspects of cognitive development are domain specific, Case still finds too much homogeneity in children's cognition to ignore it. In summarizing his work, Case (1992a) stated that "at each successive developmental level, children possess a more complex general conceptual representation of their quantitative world, and . . . this general representation enables them to assemble a variety of more specific executive control structures to meet the requirements of particular tasks" (p. 352). Case coined the term **central conceptual structure** to refer to such a general representation and defined it as "a network of semantic nodes and relations that represent children's core knowledge in a domain and that can be applied to a full range of tasks that domain entails" (Case & Okamoto, 1996, p. v).

Case has provided a theory that acknowledges that some aspects of cognition are domain specific in nature, while retaining the stagelike progression and domain-general mechanisms that were central to Piaget's theory. Although not explicitly taking a constructivist position (the term constructivism is not included in the index of either of Case's [1985, 1992a] major books), Case, like Fischer, views development as occurring gradually, with later structures developing from earlier structures through a child's interaction with his or her environment.

Age-Related Changes in Brain and Cognitive Development

Like all modern theorists, both Fischer and Case believe that changes in brain development directly underlie changes in cognitive development. However, these theorists have done more than make this broad (and obviously true) statement, but have sought evidence from the new field of developmental cognitive neuroscience to support their positions (Case, 1992b, 1998; Fischer & Bidell, 1998; Fischer & Rose, 1996).

For example, Fischer examines data looking at changes in brain growth over childhood and notes that brain growth is not continuous but occurs in spurts that correspond quite nicely to the various

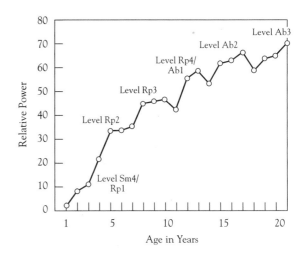

FIGURE 4-5   Development of relative power in alpha EEG in occipital-parietal area (see text). Labels in figure denote levels in Fischer's skill theory. Changes in relative power correspond to changes in levels in Fischer's theory. SOURCE: Fischer, K. W., & Rose, S. P. (1996). Dynamic growth cycles of brain and cognitive development. In R. W. Thatcher, G. R. Lyon, J. Rumsey, & N. Krasnegor (Eds.) *Developmental neuroimaging: Mapping the development of brain and behavior* (pp. 263–279). San Diego: Academic Press. Reprinted by permission.

levels of his theory. He also notes that developmental changes in EEG functioning (Thatcher, 1996), which measures the activity of the brain rather than simply its physical growth, correspond well with his levels of development. Figure 4-5 presents a summary of changes in the relative power of a certain type of EEG wave (alpha) in the occipital-parietal area of the brain. Relative power refers to the percentage of energy in one particular type of EEG wave (here, the alpha band) relative to energy in all EEG bands. The higher the value, the more powerful is the alpha band. As can be seen from the figure, the relative power of the alpha band increases with age, but not in a straight line. Rather, it increases in spurts, with those spurts corresponding to levels of cognitive development in Fischer's theory. The labels on the figure denote specific transitions between levels. (For example, "Level Sm4/Rp1" corresponds to the fourth sensorimotor level, which is the same

(A)   (B)

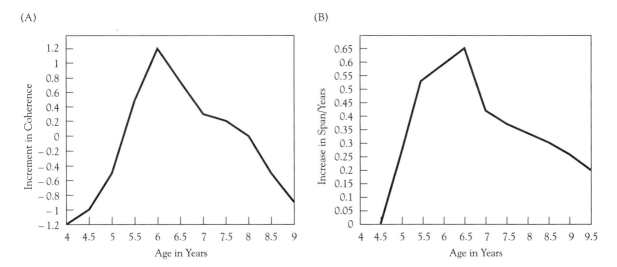

FIGURE 4-6   Age changes in EEG coherence (A) and increases in working memory (B). Changes in EEG coherence correspond to rate of increases in working memory over childhood. SOURCE: Case, R. (1998). The development of conceptual structures. In D. Kuhn & R. S. Siegler (Vol. Eds.), *Cognition, perception, and language* (Vol. 2) (pp. 745–800), in W. Damon (Gen. Editor), Handbook of child psychology (5th ed.). New York: Wiley.

as the first representational level, "Level Rp2" corresponds to the second level of the representational tier, and so on). Fischer believes that changes in EEG power, particularly in the frontal lobes, "plays a central role in cementing together skill systems to form a new unit at the beginning of a new tier" (Fischer & Rose, 1996, p. 271). Fischer observes other cyclical changes in brain development that are associated with cognitive development (for example, hemispheric changes and changes in EEG power from the front-to-back of the brain), but, for our purposes, it is sufficient to note that aspects of Fischer's theory can be tied to developmental changes in brain functioning.

Case (1992b, 1998) has used some of the same data as Fischer did to find support for this theory. Central to Case's theory is the idea of processing limitations on cognitive development. He and others have proposed that the frontal lobes play a central role in resource allocations that are so important to individual and developmental differences in working memory. Support for this comes from the relationship between age-related changes in working

memory and corresponding changes in the coherence patterns of EEG. EEG coherence refers to the similarity in electrical responses in different areas of the brain at a particular point in time, as measured by correlations of the frequencies of brain-wave patterns. Figure 4-6(A) presents changes in EEG coherence between the frontal and posterior lobes between the ages of 2 and 9 years (from Thatcher, 1992), and Figure 4-6(B) presents changes in increases in working-memory span between the ages of 4.5 and 9.5 years. Note that coherence between the frontal and posterior lobes of the brain increases between the ages of 4 and 6 years and then decreases (that is, the EEG frontal and posterior patterns become less coherent) from ages 6 through 9. A similar pattern is observed for changes in working memory, although changes in working memory seem to lag slightly behind changes in EEG coherence. Children show the greatest improvement in working memory between 4.5 and 5.5 years, and continue to increase in rate until 6.5 years. The amount of gain in working memory decreases steadily from this age onward (although absolute level of working memory is still increasing), corresponding to the changes in EEG coherence.

We must remember that these findings are correlational. Just because certain changes in brain-wave patterns correspond to certain changes in cognitive development does not mean that the two are causally related. But the findings are a step in the right direction. What is exciting about this research is that solid neuroscience research is supporting well-established theory in cognitive development. Findings like these will influence both theory and research in the decades to come, and produce, I am sure, a better picture of how brain and mind develop.

Theory Theories of Cognitive Development

A growing group of developmental psychologists view infants and children as having sets of innate theories that they modify over the course of childhood until their understanding of the world is like that of adults in their culture. In many respects, these theories are very different from Piaget's, particularly in their proposals that children posses substantial innate knowledge or processes and that there is no domain-general set of logical structures as Piaget believed. But in another way, many theory theorists see themselves as the inheritors of Piaget's tradition. This is because they see cognitive development as being a constructive process much as Piaget did, with mechanisms of change that are not so dissimilar from those proposed by Piaget.

First, I should state that there is no one "**theory theory**" of cognitive development. A variety of researchers have adopted the general framework to describe several aspects of cognitive development, including many of the accomplishments attained in infancy (Gopnik & Meltzoff, 1997; Baillargeon, 1994), children's acquisition of concepts (Carey, 1985; Keil, 1998; Wellman & Gelman, 1998), and children's understanding of how people's minds work (Perner, 1991; Wellman, 1990), some of which will be discussed in later chapters. Perhaps the best general description of the theory theory of cognitive development can be found in Alison Gopnik's and Andrew Meltzoff's (1997) book, *Words, Thoughts, and Theories*.

Gopnik's and Meltzoff's Theory Theory of Cognitive Development

Advocates of the theory theory propose that the process of cognitive development is similar, or perhaps identical to, the process of scientific discovery. An initial theory is tested (experimentation) and revised when the old theory can't explain the new data. Children use these theories to predict, interpret, and explain the world, just as scientists do. In fact, Gopnik and Meltzoff suggest that scientific reasoning is not a *late* invention (either in evolutionary time or over the course of childhood), but has long characterized our species and infants and children. The nature of theories and how they're tested might change in adulthood, but the basic processes of theory generation, theory testing, and theory change are characteristics not just of people in white lab coats, but of children from birth. According to Gopnik and Meltzoff, "It is not that children are little scientists but that scientists are big children. Scientific progress is possible because scientists employ cognitive processes that are first seen in very young children" (p. 32).

What is very different from Piaget's theory is that theory theorists believe that infants come into the world with knowledge or processing constraints for particular domains. This perspective, often referred to as a **neo-nativism** or **structural-constraint theory,** is at odds with Piaget's contention that cognitive development is a process of construction. How can the idea that the mind is specifically prepared to think—to have innate knowledge—be compatible with the idea that development is a process of constructing reality from previous cognitive structures in interaction with the world? Theory theorists attempt to integrate these two ideas, resulting in an approach that is simultaneously neo-Piagetian and neo-nativist.

Neo-nativists propose that changes that Piaget believed go through gradual, constructivist development, actually are innate and await only the requisite motor or sensory skills for their demonstration. Two good examples of such abilities are object permanence and imitation. As we saw earlier in this chapter, Piaget proposed that both knowledge of objects and imitation develop gradually during infancy, following the six-stage sequence of the sensorimotor period. From his epigenetic perspective, Piaget believed that the mature forms of these skills are acquired late in the second year of life (or later) and are the result of transformations from earlier skills. Recent research has shown, however, that very young infants can demonstrate reasonably sophisticated levels of object permanence and imitation when the tasks are modified to reflect their limited motor abilities. Such findings reflect to some researchers (Spelke & Newport, 1998) innate cognitive knowledge that does not develop through constructive processes (these lines of research are discussed more fully in Chapter 7).

Along these lines, many neo-nativists argue that little, if anything, develops—that development is not a constructive process but, rather, that infants are born with innate knowledge for interpreting the world (representational innateness as discussed in Chapter 1; see Spelke, 1991). Theory theorists rarely take this strong perspective. Rather, they advocate that the innate constraints will be very general in nature (architectural innateness as discussed in Chapter 1). Gopnik and Meltzoff propose a *"starting-state"* nativism, in contrast with a representational innateness (or, in their terms, modularity nativism). The representational innateness approach holds that infants come into the world with cognitive abilities that require little or no development. For example, this approach proposes that knowledge of objects (object permanence), language, and space are innate, requiring only the proper environmental stimuli for them to be demonstrated (see Mandler, 1998; Spelke & Newport, 1998). Such knowledge is proposed to be domain specific and to impose constraints on the child, in that the mind/brain is designed to process certain types of information in certain ways, meaning that there is not infinite flexibility in what is learned (thus the name *structural-constraint theory*). Stated more positively, these constraints make it easier for the child to learn certain things, such as language (Gelman & Williams, 1998).

In contrast, the starting-state perspective holds that children are born with sets of rules for operating on particular representations. However, the rules and the representations they generate are altered by experience. Thus, domain-specific mechanisms constrain what and how information can be processed, but development is still a constructive process with both the content (for example, knowledge of objects) and processes of operating on that content changing with experience.

How should development proceed from a theory-theory perspective? According to Gopnik and Meltzoff, "We will typically see a pattern in which the child holds to a particular set of predictions and interpretations for some time; the child has a particular theory. Then we may expect a period of disorganization, in which the theory is in crisis. And finally, we should see a new, equally coherent and stable theory emerge" (p. 63). This to me is reminiscent of Piaget's equilibration model, discussed earlier in this chapter. Gopnik and Meltzoff make no explicit comparison between the process of change they propose and Piaget's equilibration model (although they do make it clear that the mechanisms of their two theories are different), but the transition from one stable theory to another, following a period of disorganization, is similar to Piaget's idea of changes from one set of structures to another, following a period of disequilibration.

One question that is fair to ask of the theory-theory approach to cognitive development, is that if development is the process of testing and changing theories, why do children all over the globe end up with basically the same adult theories of the world? Experience plays an important role in this formulation, and experiences will surely vary considerably for children growing up in information-age societies from those growing up in traditional hunter-gatherer societies. And of course adults in these cultures do differ considerably in their thinking, but their understanding of the physical and social world are remarkably the same. How can a theory theory explain such similarity of cognitive functioning?

Gopnik and Meltzoff's theory theory proposes that powerful mechanisms revise current theories when children are faced with conflicting evidence. Children around the world are born with the same initial theories. That is, all infants start with the same ideas about how the world works and modify these theories as they grow. They also try to solve basically the same problems about how the physical and social world works, and they get similar information at about the same time in their lives. Remember that children not only inherit a species-typical genome, but they also inherit a species-typical environment. They are prepared by biology to make sense of their world, and human culture ensures that their evolved processing constraints have a chance to work by presenting them with an environment that humans and their ancestors have experienced for hundreds of thousands of years.

Karmiloff-Smith's Representational Redescription Theory

Annette Karmiloff-Smith (1991, 1992) has developed a theory of cognitive development that incorporates many of the assumptions of the theory theory approach just discussed. She believes that the human infant is biologically constrained to process certain classes of stimuli that are relevant to human existence, including knowledge of physical objects, space, cause and effect, and language, all topics studied by Piaget and proposed by him to develop through active constructivism. Karmiloff-Smith proposes, however, that nativism and constructivism need not be mutually incompatible concepts. Rather, nativism describes the initial state of human cognitive development but "does not preclude a constructivist approach with respect to subsequent development" (1991, p. 173). She also states that a constructivist approach need not require a domain-general, stagelike perspective as offered by Piaget.

The centerpiece of Karmiloff-Smith's theory is **representational redescription,** a process whereby the mind re-represents its own representations (see Mandler, 1992, for a similar account of redescription in infancy). This ability to make representations of representations makes the human mind distinct from the minds of all other species. Karmiloff-Smith believes that much special-purpose knowledge (for example, knowledge related to physical objects, language, and cause and effect) is modular in nature,

being activated by specific environmental stimuli and, as described by Fodor (1983) (see Chapter 1), inaccessible to other parts of the cognitive system. Such knowledge, proposes Karmiloff-Smith, is similar to the knowledge possessed by other species (for example, the knowledge spiders have about making webs); it is complex, procedural knowledge, which must reside somewhere in the brain but is not available to conscious evaluation and is not easily modified. Humans go beyond this level of representation by the process of representational redescription, making certain aspects of knowledge available to other parts of the cognitive system.

Karmiloff-Smith proposes that there are three ways that knowledge gets into a child's brain. Some knowledge is innately specified, other knowledge is gained through interaction with the environment, and yet other knowledge is arrived at by the process of representational redescription. Representational redescription involves the process whereby the mind uses knowledge it already possesses by re-representing its own internal representations. According to Karmiloff-Smith, "human development crucially involves the passage from representations that constitute knowledge in the mind to representations that acquire the status of knowledge to other parts of the mind" (1991, p. 175). From this perspective, representational redescription can be seen as similar to Piaget's concept of *reflective abstraction*, whereby children discover new information by examining the contents of their own mind (that is, introspecting). Whereas Piaget proposed that reflective abstraction is a characteristic of formal operational thinking, however, Karmiloff-Smith sees representational redescription as involving a series of levels, beginning at the implicit (I) level and progressing through levels of increasing explication (E1, E2, and possibly E3). Levels E1, E2, and E3 all involve representational redescription.

Knowledge represented at the implicit level is unavailable to other aspects of the cognitive system and unavailable to consciousness. In other words, it is modularlike, reflecting efficient, innate procedures for dealing with specific information. For example, neonates' knowledge of physical objects or infants' and young children's knowledge of linguistically relevant stimuli would be represented at the implicit level. There is no redescription here, and this knowledge, impressive as it may be, is similar to the knowledge a spider has about making a web, a blue jay has about building a nest, or a newborn goat has about avoiding falling off cliffs.

Related to this is the idea that implicit learning (acquiring new knowledge without explicit awareness) is an early developing ability. For example, recent research has shown that 6- and 10-year-old children learn serial sequences of responses (that is, learning which of several responses follows one another) as well as adults do, despite having no explicit (verbalizable) knowledge of what they have learned (Meulemans, Van der Linden, & Perruchet, 1998). Similarly, implicit memory (memory without awareness) has also been proposed to be an early developing ability that shows little improvement across childhood (see Chapter 8).

At the E1 level (first level of explication), knowledge can be redescribed so that it is made available to other cognitive systems. However, this knowledge is not yet conscious. For example, as young children master language, they are able to ignore aspects of the external stimuli and to focus on the internal meaning of language, which they use to formulate linguistic theories. Young children are very good, for example, at determining what is and is not a grammatical sentence—but they can rarely tell you why this is the case. The fact that this knowledge is unavailable to conscious awareness makes the E1 level similar to what others theorists might still call implicit (Clements & Perner, 1994). The important distinction here is that knowledge is made available to other cognitive systems, even if not to consciousness.

For knowledge to be conscious requires additional redescription (level E2), and for it to be verbalized so that the knowledge can be shared with others requires a further level of redescription (E3). For example, Karmiloff-Smith (1979) describes English-speaking children's correct usage of the articles *a* and *the* during the preschool years. Certainly by 5 years of age, children know the rules for using *a* and *the*, but not until 9 or 10 years of age do they

become consciously aware of the rules. According to Karmiloff-Smith, it is not until this time that children are able to redescribe their representations so that these representations are available not only to other cognitive systems but also to consciousness. Redescriptions can get much more complicated and abstract than a conscious knowledge of simple grammatical rules. The process of generating theories in science, philosophy, politics, or everyday social interaction requires going far beyond the data given and often involves re-representing information initially available to once insular, modularlike cognitive systems. (Although Karmiloff-Smith distinguishes between E2 and E3 levels of representation, she notes that no research has focused on the E2 level—conscious access without verbal report. Her writings thus concentrate on E3 representations, although she sometimes refers to a combination of E2 and E3 levels, E2/3.)

For Karmiloff-Smith as for Piaget, children are intrinsically active, spontaneously building theories about how the world works. Building these theories involves taking advantage of both acquired and innate knowledge. Theory building, then, accomplished by the process of representational redescription, is a constructive process. But stages of representation that are observed are more likely to be domain specific than domain general as in Piaget's theory. There is, for example, no such thing as a "stage E1 child." Rather, any given child will have knowledge represented at a variety of levels, both within and between domains. Nevertheless, because knowledge can be available to consciousness through the explication processes involved in representational redescription, some aspects of cognition and development can be domain general in nature.

Karmiloff-Smith retains many of Piaget's assumptions regarding the process of development (constructivism, intrinsic activity, levels of representation) while recognizing the significance of innate knowledge for early cognitive functioning and that neither cognition within an individual child nor the course of development for children as a group is as homogeneous as Piaget proposed.

Summary

Jean Piaget's theory of intellectual development has had a profound impact on how we view children, their thinking, and their development. Piaget believed that abstract *structures* or *schemes* within the child underlie intelligence and that cognitive development is the development of structures. Piaget viewed the child as being *intrinsically active* and thus responsible to a large extent for his or her own development. He believed that cognition is constructive (a belief known as *constructivism*) and that our current state of knowledge influences how we perceive and process new information. Piaget believed that cognitive development is domain general in nature and that all cognitive abilities develop together as a result of a single underlying set of mechanisms.

Piaget described the *functional invariants* of *organization* and *adaptation* as processes that are characteristic of all biological systems (including intelligence) and operate throughout the life span. Organization is an organism's tendency to integrate structures into higher-order systems or structures. Adaptation is the process of adjustment the organism goes through in response to the environment; this process has two complementary components. *Assimilation* is the structuring of environmental input to fit a child's current schemes, and *accommodation* is the structuring of the child's schemes to match environmental data.

Piaget proposed *equilibration* as a mechanism for development. When confronted with information that cannot be assimilated into existing structures, one enters a state of cognitive incongruity, or disequilibrium. When disequilibrium is resolved by accommodation, a new, more stable structure results. Piaget stressed that equilibration is an active process, even when structures are relatively stable.

Piaget postulated four major stages, or periods, of cognitive development. He hypothesized that stages are (1) qualitatively different in form from each preceding or following stage; (2) culturally universal, so that all children progress through them in a single, invariant order; and (3) based on earlier, more primitive cognitive structures (*hierarchization*).

During the *sensorimotor stage* (from birth to about 2 years), children's thinking is limited to their own actions on objects. Piaget described six substages during the sensorimotor period. During the earliest substages, cognition is limited to inherited reflexes (substage 1) and simple extensions of these reflexes (substage 2). Infants are capable of developing new (that is, not reflexive) behaviors during substages 3 through 5, with goal-directed behavior being seen first in substage 4. Infants become capable of mentally representing environmental events by substage 6. Piaget described the development of *object permanence* and *imitation* in the context of his broader theory of sensorimotor development.

Sometime between 18 and 24 months, children begin to use symbols, exemplified by language, imagery, pretend play, and deferred imitation. From this point on, development consists of the acquisition of operations. Piaget described three major periods between the ages of approximately 2 and 16 years: *preoperations* (between 2 and 7 years), *concrete operations* (between 7 and 11 years), and *formal operations* (between 11 and 16 years). Piaget proposed four characteristics of operations: operations are (1) mental, (2) derived from action, (3) integrated with one another (*structures of the whole*), and (4) reversible. Piaget specified two types of *reversibility: negation* (or *inversion*) and *compensation* (or *reciprocity*).

Piaget described the thought of preoperational children as being intuitive, in contrast with the logical thought of concrete operational children. He proposed that preoperational and concrete operational children differ on several factors. Most critically, the thought of preoperational children lacks *reversibility*, the benchmark of operations. Piaget described the perception of preoperational children as being *centered* on the most salient aspects of a perceptual array, in contrast with the *decentered* perception of concrete operational children. Preoperational children are said to be *egocentric*, in that they have a difficult time seeing the perspective (visual, communicative, or social) of another. Although he described concrete operational children as less egocentric, recent research has indicated that even preschool-age children can easily take the perspective of another in certain situations. Finally, Piaget claimed that preoperational children attend to specific states and ignore transformations between states.

Differences between preoperational and concrete operational children are displayed on many tasks, the most critical of which is *conservation*. Conservation represents the cognitive constancy of quantitative relations and refers to the knowledge that the quantity of a substance remains the same despite a perceptual transformation of that substance. *Class inclusion*, refers to the knowledge that any subordinate category (dogs, for example) can be no larger than its superordinate category (animals, for example). Piaget found that children typically do not solve class-inclusion problems until late in childhood, although non-Piagetian research has found that class-inclusion performance is influenced by a variety of factors and, under some circumstances, is displayed by preschool children.

The major factor in the transition from concrete to *formal operations* is the advent of *hypothetico-deductive reasoning*. With this type of reasoning, thinking can be done solely in terms of symbols, without need for referents in real life; the child can think in terms of what is possible as well as what is real. Piaget described the formal operational child as being able to think like a scientist, or to use *inductive reasoning*. Formal operational children are able to think about thinking, or to reflect upon the outcome of their own thought (*reflective abstraction*).

Although Piaget's account of the development of operations has generated tremendous interest for more than five decades, research investigating his account has generally been critical. Findings of contemporary research seriously question some aspects of operations. Non-Piagetian research indicates that Piaget often underestimated the cognitive competencies of children; children have typically been found to be more competent than Piaget proposed, and numerous studies have demonstrated that both concrete and formal operational abilities can be easily trained. Young children can display sophisticated cognitive processing in certain situations and, in general, are less homogeneous with respect to cognitive functioning than Piaget proposed.

Fischer's skills theory integrates aspects of Piagetian theory with aspects of behaviorism in an attempt to account for the unevenness of cognitive function within a stagelike framework. Fischer proposed that there is an optimal level of performance, and a child's skills will be at that level only for those skills that are most consistently supported by the environment. Case's neo-Piagetian theory integrates Piaget's ideas with those of information processing, proposing domain-general changes in processing efficiency as an important contributor to cognitive development. Case proposed age differences in how children assemble and use *executive control structures*. Like Fischer, Case proposed that there is substantial homogeneity of cognitive function, as reflected by the *central conceptual structure* underlying most of a child's cognitions at any one time. *Theory theories* combine ideas from *neo-nativism* and Piaget's constructivism, proposing that cognitive development progresses by children generating, testing, and changing theories about the physical and social world. Karmiloff-Smith adopts a neo-nativist perspective, arguing that much knowledge and many skills are present at birth or shortly thereafter and do not involve the constructive processes proposed by Piaget. Development beyond early infancy is constructive in nature, however, with the process of *representational redescription* being the principal mechanism of cognitive development. Karmiloff-Smith proposes four levels of representation: implicit (I) is unavailable to other cognitive systems and thus unavailable to consciousness; levels E1, E2, and E3 (explication levels 1, 2, and 3) all involve representational redescription, with the latter two reflecting conscious and verbalizable knowledge.

Note

1. At this point, some comment is appropriate concerning Piaget's use of the term *structure* and of the related term *scheme*. When discussing broad theoretical or philosophical issues, Piaget used the term structure to refer to any system within the child that underlies intelligence. However, when discussing a particular system reflecting some specific knowledge, Piaget used the term scheme. Schemes reflect children's knowledge at all stages of development. When referring to

some specific cognitive content, Piaget reserved the term cognitive structure to reflect a special type of scheme—those characterized by mental representation. By this definition, the organization that underlies sensorimotor intelligence is not in the form of cognitive structures but in the form of schemes. In the remainder of this chapter I will use the term scheme whenever referring to the abstract organization that underlies some specific knowledge. I will use the term structure when referring to general aspects of Piaget's theory or his philosophical positions. In either case, both terms are used to represent the abstract knowledge that underlies children's intelligence.

One further comment is in order here. Early translations and reviews of Piaget's work used the terms schema and schemata rather than scheme or schemes. Piaget had slightly different meanings for these terms and commented that the translations using schema were inaccurate (Piaget & Inhelder, 1969). To be consistent with Piaget's original intention, I will use the term scheme rather than schema throughout this and other chapters.

Key Terms and Concepts

genetic epistemology
structures (schemes)
intrinsic activity
constructivism
functional invariants
organization
adaptation
assimilation
accommodation
equilibration
hierarchization
sensorimotor stage
goal-directed behavior
basic reflexes
primary circular reactions
secondary circular reactions
coordination of secondary circular reactions
tertiary circular reactions
mental combinations
object permanence
deferred imitation
preoperations
concrete operations
formal operations
operations
structures of the whole (structures d'ensemble)

reversibility
negation (inversion)
compensation (reciprocity)
conservation
centration
decentration
egocentricity
states versus transformations
class inclusion
hypothetico-deductive reasoning
inductive reasoning
reflective abstraction
imaginary audience
personal fable
optimal level
executive control structures
central conceptual structure
theory theories
neo-nativism (structural-constraint theory)
representational redescription

Suggested Readings

BRAINERD, C. F. (1996). Piaget: A centennial celebration. *Psychological Science*, 7, 191–195. This is the introductory article to a special issue of *Psychological Science* devoted to commemorating the centennial of Piaget's birth. Piaget's many contributions are summarized in the articles in this issue, written by prominent cognitive developmental psychologists, documenting that, Piaget's influence and legacy lives on.

FLAVELL, J. H. (1982). On cognitive development. *Child Development*, 53, 1–10. This paper, based on the author's presidential address to the Society for Research in Child Development, addresses the important question "How stagelike is cognitive development?"

PIAGET, J., & INHELDER, B. (1969). *The psychology of the child*. New York: Basic Books. This book by Piaget and his long-time collaborator presents a brief overview of Piaget's theory in Piaget's own words. One word of caution: It is difficult to read works by Piaget before reading works written by others about Piaget.

PIAGET, J. (1952). *The origins of intelligence in children*. New York: Norton. This is Piaget's first book in his series of three on infant cognition and presents many of the central concepts of his theory of sensorimotor intelligence. It was the first book by Piaget I ever read, perhaps accounting for my fondness for it.

FISCHER, K. W., & BIDELL, T. (1998). Dynamic development of psychological structures in action and thought. In R. M. Lerner (Vol. Ed.), *Theoretical models of human development,* (Vol. 1) (pp. 467–561), in W. Damon (Gen. Ed.), *Handbook of child psychology* (5th ed.). New York: Wiley. This chapter presents an updated version of Fischer's skill theory. It emphasizes the dynamic aspect of cognitive development and reflects a greater awareness of sociocultural influences than earlier versions of the theory.

CASE, R. (1998). The development of conceptual structures. In D. Kuhn & R. S. Siegler (Vol. Eds.), *Cognition, perception, and language* (Vol. 2) (pp. 745–800), in W. Damon (Gen. Editor), *Handbook of child psychology* (5th ed.). New York: Wiley. This chapter presents the most recent summary of Case's neo-Piagetian theory and the perspective that important aspects of cognition develop in a stagelike manner.

GOPNIK, A., & MELTZOFF, A. N. (1997). *Words, thoughts, and theories.* Cambridge, MA: MIT Press. Gopnik and Meltzoff present their version of a theory theory of cognitive development, focusing primarily on development in infancy and young children. This is a clear presentation of the basic ideas behind theory theories of cognitive development.

KARMILOFF-SMITH, A. (1991). Beyond modularity: Innate constraints and developmental change. In S. Carey & R. Gelman (Eds.), *The epigenesis of mind: Essays on biology and cognition* (pp. 171–197). Hillsdale, NJ: Erlbaum. This is the abbreviated version of Karmiloff-Smith's theory, but one that should give the reader a good feel of the important concepts of her influential ideas.

Information-Processing Approaches

Assumptions of the Information-Processing Approaches
Limited Capacity • The Information-Processing System
Representation of Knowledge • Automatic and Effortful Processes

Information-Processing Perspectives on Development
The Short-Term Store • Speed of Processing
Developmental Differences in the Efficiency of Processing

The Role of Strategies in Cognitive Development
Mediational and Production Deficiencies • What Are Production-Deficient Children Doing?
Utilization Deficiencies • The Cost of Strategy Use
Siegler's Adaptive Strategy-Choice Model • Implicit Strategy Use

Children's Knowledge Base and Cognitive Development
Experts and Novices • Knowledge and Strategies

Attention
Sustaining Attention • Selective Attention
Attentional Strategies • What Do Children Know about Attention?

New Approaches to Developmental Differences in Information Processing
Inhibition and Resistance to Interference • Fuzzy-Trace Theory
Connectionist Perspective of Developmental Change

Summary • Notes
Key Terms and Concepts
Suggested Readings

Although Piaget's approach to cognitive development stands as the major theoretical contribution of the past century, the computer as a model for how children handle knowledge has also contributed substantially to our understanding. During the 1950s and 1960s, developmental psychologists began looking at changes in children's thinking in terms of a computer metaphor. Like computers, humans can be viewed as information-processing systems. From this perspective, cognitive development can be seen as reflecting changes in either *hardware* (the capacity of memory systems and the speed with which information is processed through the systems) or *software* (children's access to and ability to use strategies or other learning devices) or both. From their inception more than 40 years ago, information-processing approaches have strongly influenced theory and research in developmental psychology, challenging and eventually replacing Piagetian theory as the major perspective in cognitive development. Information-processing approaches continue to dominate research in cognitive development, although few today believe that the mind is perfectly analogous to a computer.

Assumptions of the Information-Processing Approaches

There is no single information-processing theory of cognition or cognitive development. Rather, information-processing theories are built on a set of assumptions concerning how humans acquire, store, and retrieve information.

Perhaps the most obvious assumption of information-processing approaches is that people process information. Processing refers to mentally acting on information in order to know it. We can act on an external stimulus to make sense of it (such as the writing on this page), or we can act on information that already resides in our heads. These mental actions can be referred to as operations, processes, procedures, strategies, information-processing components, or programs. Each of these terms refers to mental actions taken by the individual to make sense of "input," or, in other words, to think.

Limited Capacity

Central to the information-processing approaches is the idea of **limited capacity.** We can deal with only so much information at any single time. Theorists have used a variety of metaphors for capacity, including a space metaphor (one has only so much mental space in which to store or operate on information), an energy metaphor (one has only so much energy to allocate to the storage or execution of cognitive operations), and a time metaphor (one can only perform operations so fast). So, for example, most of us have enough mental space to walk and chew gum at the same time. Add to these operations a nontrivial arithmetic problem, however, and a change in our rate of gum chewing or walking will be discerned. We have added something else to do, and doing it will interfere with the execution of other operations.

Traditionally, the assumption of limited capacity has implied that cognition is domain general, so that all types of mental operations—chewing gum, walking, reading, and solving algebra word problems—use the same limited pool of mental resources. In this way, information-processing approaches are similar to Piaget's theory. As we'll see later in this chapter, however, this assumption has been challenged, and some information-processing theories have been modified to accommodate evidence of domain-specific cognitive abilities. I think it is fair to say that most capacity theorists today assume that there are multiple capacities or resources, although the number of such resources and the extent to which they influence many versus a limited number of cognitive tasks is much debated (Kail & Salthouse, 1994).

The Information-Processing System

Another assumption of information-processing approaches is that information moves through the system. The pathways between input and storage can be depicted schematically with a flowchart such as the one in Figure 5-1. Typically, processing is viewed as occurring serially, with the product of one stage of processing serving as the input for the next stage, and so on until some final response or decision is

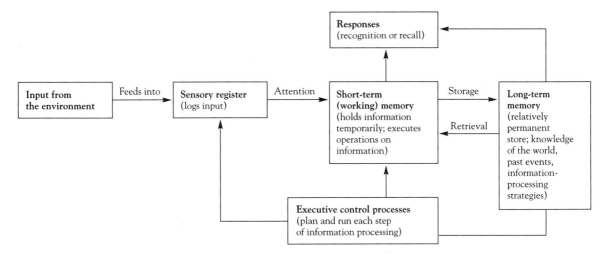

FIGURE 5-1 The flow of information through the memory system. SOURCE: Based on Shaffer, D. R. (1996). *Developmental Psychology: Childhood and adolescence* (4th ed.). Pacific Grove, CA: Brooks/Cole, as adapted from "Human Memory: A Proposed System and Its Control Processes," by R. C. Atkinson & R. M. Shiffrin, 1968, in K. W. Spence and J. T. Spence (Eds.), *The Psychology of Learning and Motivation: Advances in Research and Theory* (Vol. 2), Copyright © 1968 by Academic Press, Inc.

made. The initial **multistore models** of the sort shown in the figure were first suggested as theories of memory (Atkinson & Shiffrin, 1968). At the risk of oversimplification, it may be said that these theories assumed that information from the external world is initially represented, perceptually intact, in **sensory registers**. There is a separate sensory register, or *sensory store*, for each sense modality (for example, vision, audition), and presumably they can hold large quantities of information—but only for a matter of milliseconds. From this initial registration, information is passed through to the **short-term store**, where capacity is smaller but the representations are more durable, lasting for seconds. The short-term store has also been referred to as the *primary memory*, the *working memory*, or the *contents of consciousness*. It is our short-term store that makes contact with the world, holding information long enough for us to evaluate it. We apply strategies, or control processes, for remembering or solving problems in the short-term store. The short-term store is where we live, mentally. Its capacity is limited, however, and if something is not done to information once it is in the short-term store, it will be lost. If we apply some cognitive operation to the information in the

short-term store, that information is transferred to the **long-term store**, where presumably it is retained indefinitely.

Representation of Knowledge

How is information represented in long-term memory? Endel Tulving (1985) proposed that information in the long-term store can be represented in one of two general ways: declarative memory and nondeclarative memory (see also Parkin, 1997). **Declarative memory** refers to facts and events and comes in two types: episodic and semantic memory. **Episodic memory**—literally, memory for episodes—can be consciously retrieved, such as what you had for breakfast this morning, the gist of a conversation you had with your mother last night, and the Christmas visit to your grandparents when you were 5 years old. Such memory is sometimes called **explicit memory**, which refers to the fact that it is available to conscious awareness and can be directly (explicitly) assessed by tests of recall or recognition memory. **Semantic memory** refers to our knowledge of language, rules, and concepts. So, for instance, the meaning of the term "democracy" or the rules for multiplication are examples of semantic memory. You might remember learning the definition of "democracy" and the rules for multiplication in the fourth grade—an example of episodic memory—but your actual knowledge of these terms and rules are examples of semantic memory.

The second general type of memory has been termed **nondeclarative,** or **procedural memory**. Nondeclarative memory refers to knowledge of procedures that are unconscious. For example, some have argued that the learning and memory observed in classical and operant conditioning are unconscious, as are many familiar routines once they have become well practiced (such as tying one's shoe). Such memory is sometimes called **implicit memory**, which refers to the fact it is unavailable to conscious awareness ("memory without awareness") and can be assessed only indirectly (that is, you just can't ask someone to remember something they know only implicitly). (Implicit memory will be discussed in greater detail in Chapter 8.)

In addition to tapping different "types" of memories, there is also evidence that different areas of the brain are involved in declarative and nondeclarative memories (Schacter, 1992). This supports the argument that memory is not a single phenomenon (that is, domain-general), but rather a set of domain-specific mental operations that may show different patterns of developmental function. More will be said on this issue in Chapter 8.

Automatic and Effortful Processes

Cognitive theorists assume that mental processes can be placed on a continuum relative to how much of one's limited capacity each process requires for its execution (Hasher & Zacks, 1979; Shiffrin & Schneider, 1977). At one extreme are **automatic processes**, which require none of the short-term store's limited capacity; at the other extreme are **effortful processes**, which require the use of mental resources for their successful completion. In addition to not requiring any mental effort, truly automatic processes are hypothesized (1) to occur without intention and without conscious awareness, (2) not to interfere with the execution of other processes, (3) not to improve with practice, and (4) not to be

influenced by individual differences in intelligence, motivation, and education (Hasher & Zacks, 1979). In contrast, effortful processes, which have also been called strategies or control processes, are hypothesized (1) to be available to consciousness, (2) to interfere with the execution of other effortful processes, (3) to improve with practice, and (4) to be influenced by individual differences in intelligence, motivation, and education. The automatic-effortful continuum of mental processes is illustrated in Figure 5-2.

Although it is easy to conceive of effortful processes (after all, they are available to consciousness), it is less easy to appreciate automatic processes, precisely because we cannot reflect on them. One process that has been proposed to be automatic is *frequency of occurrence* judgments (Hasher & Zacks, 1979). When people perform some task—for example, determining whether they recognize pictures of familiar and unfamiliar faces—they are rarely consciously aware of how frequently different faces appear. Yet, when later asked to make decisions about frequency of occurrence (for instance, by being shown pairs of pictures and asked to select which member of a pair has been shown more frequently), people are amazingly accurate in their judgments, despite their lack of conscious awareness. What is interesting is that there are few age differences in frequency of occurrence judgments, with kindergarten children often being as accurate as adults (Hasher & Zacks, 1979).

Some interesting new research relates the degree of effortful processing to glucose consumption in the brain. For example, Haier and his colleagues (1992) used PET scans, which measure the amount of glucose areas of the brain use while performing cognitive tasks (see Chapter 2). The researchers reported that the amount of glucose consumption declined as adult participants became more effective at solving a problem. In other words, as processing became less effortful (as defined in cognitive terms) it required less energy (as defined by glucose consumption), illustrating a direct connection between changes in the efficiency of cognitive performance and efficiency in brain functioning. In other research, higher ability people have been shown to have lower glucose consumption when solving problems

Automatic Processes ⟶	*Effortful Processes*
Require no mental effort	Require mental effort
Are not available to consciousness	Are available to consciousness
Do not interfere with other processes	Interfere with other processes
Do not improve with practice	Improve with practice
Do not vary with individual differences in intelligence, motivation, and education	Vary with individual differences in intelligence, motivation, and education

FIGURE 5-2   A hypothetical continuum of cognitive processes.

than lower ability people do (Haier et al., 1988), suggesting that brighter people use less energy when executing a task than less-bright people do. This finding was supported in a study by Larson and his colleagues (1995), who showed that when high- and low-ability participants are given problems of comparable difficulty (that is, the problems are selected specifically to match the ability of each individual), the high- and low-ability people use comparable amounts of energy (that is, glucose consumption). Thus, one way of thinking about individual differences in cognitive ability is that higher-ability people process information with less effort (literally with less glucose consumption) than less-able people.

Many information-processing accounts of development include **executive functions**— the processes involved in planning and monitoring what we attend to and what we do with this input (Zelazo et al., 1997). Although it is tempting to view an executive as a little person (homunculus) residing in one's head making decisions based on stored knowledge and incoming perceptual information, such a view is not necessary. Aspects of planning and decision making that involve such executive function apparently involve the prefrontal cortex, in that damage to this area results in characteristic disorders in decision making (Fuster, 1989; Luria, 1973). Similarly, maturationally paced differences in the development of the prefrontal lobes have been associated with age-related changes in problem solving (Barkley, 1997; Dempster, 1993). Children's ability to solve many everyday problems involves establishing a goal, planning a course of action, executing

the desired strategies, and monitoring their progress toward their goal, all of which have been described as aspects of executive functioning.

We sometimes refer to such executive control processes as **metacognition**—knowledge of one's cognitive abilities and processes relating to thinking. Our executive functions are thought to be largely under voluntary control and are, in fact, what most clearly distinguish human information processors from computers. Unlike computers, we decide what to attend to; we select our own strategies for retaining and retrieving this input; we call up our own "programs" for solving problems; and, last but not least, we are often free to choose the very problems that we will attempt to solve. Clearly, we humans are rather versatile information processors indeed.

For every type of cognition (attention, memory) there is a corresponding type of metacognition (meta-attention, metamemory). For the most part, metacognition will be discussed with its corresponding cognition in this and later chapters in the book.[1]

Information-Processing Perspectives on Development

Given the brief framework just outlined, where should a psychologist with an information-processing point of view look for developmental differences in children's thinking? One place to look is semantic memory, or children's knowledge base in general. Many developmental psychologists have examined age differences in the structure of children's language concepts, and these differences will be discussed in Chapters 7 and 9. However, the benchmark of information-processing theories is the idea of limited mental capacity, and it is here that psychologists have searched for age differences that would explain developmental changes in children's thinking. There are apparently no capacity limitations to the long-term store. (Children's ability to store and subsequently retrieve information from the long-term store will be the focus of Chapter 8.) When looking for developmental differences in capacity, most researchers have limited their search to sensory registers and the short-term store of the multistore model described earlier and for differences in speed of processing.

In the sections to follow, I will discuss age differences in the short-term store and speed of processing. In comparison with these two topics, relatively little research has examined developmental differences in the sensory store, and I will summarize the conclusions of this research briefly here. Children from about the age of 5 years can register and hold relatively large amounts of visual information over a brief interval, about as much as older children and adults (Sheingold, 1973). However, young children are less able to get this information to the short-term store where they can make some sense of it. One factor certainly involved in age differences in getting information from the visual sensory store, or *iconic store*, to the short-term store is speed of processing. Research suggests that there are age differences in the speed with which sensory information is transmitted, as well as differences in the speed with which visual information is accumulated and extracted for interpretation from the iconic store (LeBlanc, Muise, & Blanchard, 1992). Because younger children process information slower than older children do, younger children lose more information before it can be encoded in memory.

The Short-Term Store

Traditionally, the capacity of the short-term store has been assessed by tests of **memory span** that measure the number of (usually) unrelated items that

can be recalled in exact order. Presentation of items is done rapidly (usually one per second), so there is minimal time for the application of strategies to aid recall. A child's memory span is considered a reflection of the size of the short-term store, or the capacity of working memory. Norms from the digit-span subtests of the Stanford-Binet and Wechsler IQ scales show a regular increase with age. Similar findings have been provided by Frank Dempster (1981), who reported, for example, that when digits are used, the memory span of 2-year-olds is about two items; of 5-year-olds, about four items; of 7-year-olds, about five items; and of 9-year-olds, about six items. The average memory span of adults is about seven items. Figure 5-3 shows the highly predictable growth of the memory span for digits (digit span) for children from age 2 years through adulthood (from Dempster, 1981).

Evidence for developmental differences in the capacity of the short-term store comes from a recent study by Nelson Cowan and his colleagues (in press) assessing *span of apprehension*, a term coined by Sperling (1960) to refer to the number of items that people can keep in mind at any one time, or the amount of information that people can attend to at a single time. Sperling found that the span of apprehension for adults was about four items. This is lower than the average adult memory span of seven items because factors such as focused attention, knowledge for the to-be-remembered information, and encoding strategies can affect memory span when items are presented more slowly (see later discussion). Does span of apprehension represent an absolute capacity of the short-term store, and does it increase with age? In the critical condition in the study by Cowan et al. (in press), first-grade and fourth-grade children and adults played a computer game. Over earphones they also heard series of digits that they were to ignore. Occasionally and unexpectedly, however, they were signaled to recall, in exact order, the most recently presented set of digits they had heard. Thus, participants were not explicitly attending to the digits, making it unlikely that they were using any encoding strategies to remember the series of digits. Thus, performance on this task seems to be a fair test of span of apprehension.

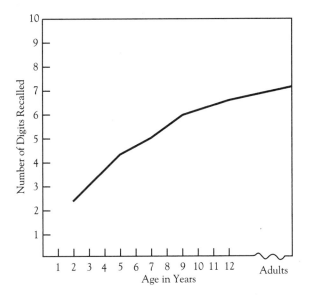

FIGURE 5-3   Children's memory span for digits (digit span) shows regular increases with age. SOURCE: "Memory Span: Sources of Individual and Development Differences," by F. N. Dempster, 1981, *Psychological Bulletin, 89,* 63–100. Copyright © 1981 American Psychological Association. Reprinted with permission.

Average span of apprehension was about 3.5 digits for adults, about 3 digits for fourth graders, and about 2.5 digits for first-grade children. Cowan and his colleagues interpreted these significant age differences as reflecting a true developmental difference in the capacity of the short-term store. According to Cowan et al., there seems to be an underlying difference in capacity, as reflected by differences in the span of apprehension, that serves as the foundation for age differences on memory span tasks.

Despite these impressive and robust findings, research has seriously questioned the idea that the capacity of the short-term is the only (or even most important) source of age differences on memory span tasks. For example, in one often-cited study, a group of graduate students at the University of Pittsburgh were given two simple memory tests. On one, they were read a series of numbers quickly (about one per second) and were asked to recall them immediately in exact order. On a second test, they

were briefly shown chess pieces on a chessboard in game-possible positions (again, about one chess piece per second) and then given the pieces and asked to place them at their previous positions on the board. Their performance on these tasks was compared with that of a group of 10-year-olds. In all fairness, these were not typical 10-year-olds—they were all chess experts, winners of local tournaments or members of chess clubs. When memory for the chess positions was tested, the children outperformed the adults. This finding is probably not surprising, given the expert status of the children. But the critical question is how they did when remembering the numbers. Does being a chess expert cause one's memory capabilities to improve overall, or was the children's remarkable performance limited to what they knew best? The results supported the latter interpretation. The adults, despite being outdone by the children when memory for chess positions was tested, were superior to the children when the test stimuli were numbers. The results of this experiment, conducted by Chi (1978), can be seen in Figure 5-4 (see also Schneider et al., 1993).

These findings indicate that having a detailed knowledge base in a particular domain facilitates memory for information from that domain but not necessarily for information from other areas. But how does being an expert in a subject such as chess result in improved memory span? Some researchers have proposed that age and individual differences in memory span may be caused by developmental differences in the use of *strategies* such as rehearsal (repeating the items to oneself) or chunking (recoding two or more items into a single memory unit). However, Frank Dempster (1981, 1985) and others have questioned both the capacity and strategy hypotheses regarding developmental changes in memory span. Concerning the role of strategies in memory span, Dempster (1981) concluded that "research offers little evidence that strategic variables are a source of span differences, even though several—rehearsal, chunking and retrieval strategies—appear to be sources of performance differences in other tasks" (pp. 78–79). Of ten strategic and nonstrategic variables investigated by Dempster, only one—ease of item identification—appeared to be a

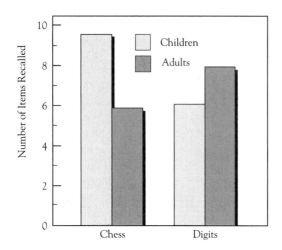

FIGURE 5-4   The average memory span for digits and chess arrays by chess-expert children and college-educated adults. SOURCE: Adapted from "Knowledge Structures and Memory Development," by M. T. H. Chi. In R. Siegler, (Ed.), *Children's Thinking: What Develops?* Copyright © 1978 Lawrence Erlbaum Associates, Inc. Reprinted with permission.

major source of developmental differences in memory span.

Ease of item identification relates to speed of processing: how quickly can a child identify an item? Speed of identification is an indication of processing efficiency; the faster an operation can be completed, the less mental effort it presumably requires for its execution. In work by Chi (1977), 5-year-olds required more time to identify photographs of faces than did adults and showed corresponding differences in memory span for the faces. When the amount of time that adults were permitted to view the faces was limited, however, Chi reported drastic reductions in age differences in memory span. Thus, although maturational differences in the capacity of the short-term store appear to be small (few psychologists would say nonexistent), maturational differences in speed of processing, which in turn affects memory span, are more substantial (Kail, 1993).

A distinction is often made between short-term memory and **working memory**, with the former involving only the storage of information held in the short-term system, whereas the latter involves storage capacity and the capacity to transform information held in the short-term system (Schneider & Pressley, 1997). Digit-span tasks described earlier assess the capacity of short-term memory. An example of a working-memory task can be found in the research of Siegel and Ryan (1989). They gave children sets of incomplete sentences, requiring them to supply the final word (for example, "In the summer it is very _____"). After being presented with several such sentences, children were asked to recall the final word in each sentence, in order. Such a test requires not only the short-term storage of information, but also some mental work dealing with the to-be-remembered information. Similar to the findings reported for digit span, reliable age differences in working memory are found, although working-memory span is usually about two items less than a child's short-term memory span (Case, 1985).

One popular account of working memory and its development has been presented by Baddeley and Hitch (Baddeley, 1986; Baddeley & Hitch, 1974). According to the Baddeley and Hitch model, age differences in verbal memory span (for example, recall of digits or words) are primarily caused by developmental differences in a phonological subsystem termed the **articulatory loop**. On verbal span tasks, phonological information is stored in the articulatory loop. These verbal representations (or memory traces) decay rapidly but can be maintained in working memory by verbal rehearsal. Although age differences in the rate that information decays in working memory have been reported (see Cowan, 1997), most researchers believe that age differences in rehearsal rate is the primary reason for developmental differences in memory span. The faster one rehearses, the more memory traces one can rehearse, the more information that can be kept active in working memory, the more one can remember. One factor that influences rehearsal rate is word length. Baddeley and Hitch assume that the articulatory loop involves a literal subvocalization process, with people saying the items to themselves. Longer words require more time to say, thus leaving less time to rehearse other words before they decay and are lost from working memory.

There is good evidence from the adult literature that such a process (or one very like it) actually occurs (see Baddeley, 1986, for an extensive review).

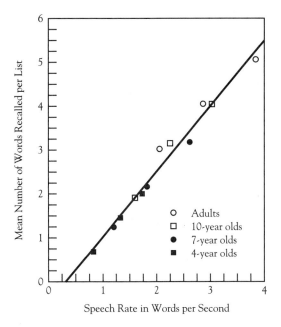

FIGURE 5-5 The relationship between word length, speech rate, and memory span as a function of age. As speech rate increases, more words are recalled, with both speech rate and words recalled increasing with age. SOURCE: "Speech Rate and the Development of Spoken Words: The Role of Rehearsal and Item Identification Processes," by C. Hulme, N. Thomson, C. Muir, and A. Lawrence, 1984, *Journal of Experimental Child Psychology*, 38, 241–253. Copyright © 1984 Academic Press. Reprinted with permission.

In the developmental literature, research has shown a relationship between the speed with which children can say words and memory span. With age, children are able to read or say words at a faster rate, and memory span increases accordingly (Hulme et al., 1984; Kail & Park, 1994). Figure 5-5 presents data from a study by Hulme and his colleagues (1984) showing a very regular, age-related relationship between speech rate (that is, how fast people can say the words) and the number of words recalled on a word-span task. Older children and adults have a faster rate of speech than younger children, and their memory spans vary accordingly.

It is interesting to note that differences in digit span have been found as a function of the language a person speaks. For example, Chinese speakers have considerably longer digit spans than English speakers do; this difference is apparent as early as age 4 and extends into adulthood (Chen & Stevenson, 1988; Geary et al., 1993). This cultural effect seems to be caused by differences in the rate with which number words (one, two, and so on) in the two languages are spoken. Languages such as Chinese with relatively short number words that can be articulated quickly enable longer digit spans than do languages such as English with relatively long number words that are articulated more slowly (Chen & Stevenson, 1988). In fact, in one study with bilingual children, children had longer digit spans in their second language (English) than their first (Welsh). This counterintuitive finding was because number words can be articulated more rapidly in English than in Welsh (Ellis & Hennelley, 1980). Thus, the greater digit spans of Chinese relative to American children, for example, seem not the result of some inherent cognitive or educational superiority for the Chinese children but, rather, the result of the language they speak.

What seems central to the various accounts of age differences in memory span is **speed of processing**. For example, Dempster's (1981) review of the literature concluded that the only factor influencing memory span is speed of item identification, and the research performed in the Baddeley and Hitch tradition similarly demonstrates that speed of speech articulation plays a central role in children's memory spans. Recent research has shown that both of these factors affect children's memory spans, but that neither factor alone adequately accounts for developmental differences in working memory (Henry & Millar, 1991; Hitch & Towse, 1995). Speed of processing must be considered along with other factors, such as children's familiarity with the to-be-remembered information. Nonetheless, age differences in speed of processing seem to be critically related to age differences in working memory and thus to cognitive development in general.

Speed of Processing

With respect to overall speed of processing, young children require more time, and thus presumably use more of their limited capacity, to execute most cognitive processes than do older children (Dempster,

1981). In a series of studies, Robert Kail (1991, 1997) has reported that the general developmental changes in processing speed are similar across different tasks. In Kail's studies, participants ranging in age from 6 to about 21 years were given a series of reaction-time tasks. For example, in some experiments participants were presented with a pair of letters in different orientations and were to determine as quickly as possible whether the two letters were identical or mirror images of each other. To do this, participants had to mentally rotate one letter into the same orientation as the other. In a name-retrieval task, the participants were shown pairs of pictures and asked to determine whether they were physically identical or had the same name (for instance, different examples of a banana, one peeled and one unpeeled). Patterns of responses over these two, and several other tasks were highly similar, with reaction times becoming faster with age (see also Hale, Fry, & Jessie, 1993; Miller & Vernon, 1997). Figure 5-6 presents the pattern of reaction times across age for a variety of tasks used in Kail's experiments. Note that despite substantial differences in the task requirements, all show essentially the same pattern of changes in reaction time across age. Recent research has even shown a similar (though not identical) age trend in reaction time over the first year of life (Canfield et al., 1997), and between 22- and 32-months of age (Zelazo, Kearsley, & Stack, 1995).

Kail interpreted these findings as reflecting age-related increases in the amount of processing resources available for the execution of cognitive operations. Kail acknowledged that knowledge (such as that possessed by a chess expert) influences speed of processing, and thus levels of performance on cognitive tasks, but he argued that maturationally based factors are primarily responsible for age-related differences in speed, and thus efficiency, of processing (see Kail & Salthouse, 1994).

Developmental and individual differences in knowledge cannot be dismissed as playing only a minor role in differences in speed of processing, though. The relationship between knowledge, speed, and cognitive performance has been demonstrated repeatedly (Chi, 1977). People process fa-

miliar information faster (and thus with less mental effort) than they do less familiar information, and children are relatively unfamiliar with much of what they encounter in their everyday world. With age, they become more experienced and in the process quicken their speed of responding. As Kail and Salthouse (1994) point out, however, although knowledge can substantially affect speed of performance on many tasks, the effects of knowledge appear to operate in a similar way for people of different ages. Thus, underlying individual and developmental differences in knowledge are maturationally based neurological differences, which, in combination, determine speed of processing and availability of mental capacity.

Speed of processing plays an important role not only on tasks where children are required to respond as quickly as they can, but also on tasks that do not demand rapid performance (see Kail, 1993). For example, in studies of memory, young children's performance can be improved merely by increasing the amount of time they have to study the to-be-remembered words (Douglas & Corsale, 1977; Naus, Ornstein, & Aivano, 1977). In one study examining children's use of a rehearsal memory strategy (repeating words to enhance memory), third-grade girls rehearsed more words and remembered more words when they were given more time between the presentation of successive words (from 5 to 10 seconds per word). The different rate of presentation made no difference to sixth-graders, nor to third-grade boys, but the added time apparently allowed the younger girls to compensate for their slower processing time, resulting in increased performance (Naus, Ornstein, & Aivano, 1977). Of course, for some tasks, providing children with all the time in the world will not change their performance. Several studies have given children extra time to study problems, such as determining what factors influence which way a balance scale will tilt (Siegler, 1976), but to no avail. Without explicit instructions or a greater understanding of the nature of the task, increased processing time seems to make no difference. Such patterns of results—with increased time enhancing young children's performance on some tasks but not others—caused Kail (1993) to

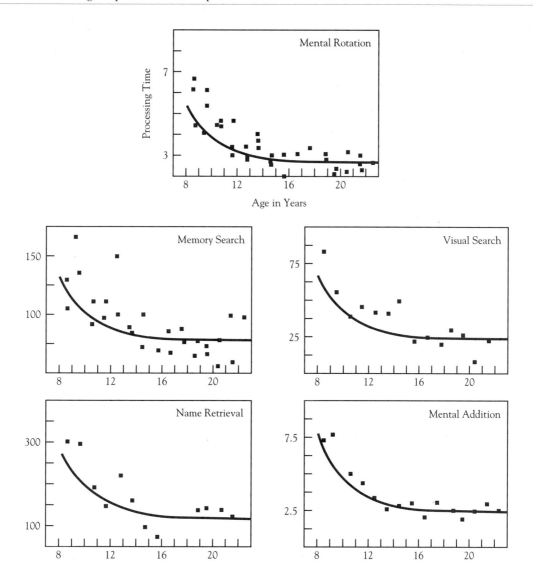

FIGURE 5-6 Developmental patterns of speed of processing for five cognitive tasks. SOURCE: "Development of Processing Speed in Childhood and Adolescence," by R. Kail. In H. W. Reese (Ed.), *Advances in Child Development and Behavior, 23*, 151–187. Copyright © 1991 Academic Press. Reprinted with permission.

conclude that "increased processing time may often be a necessary component of improved performance for younger children but it may not always be sufficient for improved performance" (p. 115).

What is the nature of those maturationally based changes that are proposed to underlie age-related

changes in speed of processing? They might involve the myelination of nerves in the associative ("thinking") area of the brain. As noted in Chapter 2, myelin is a fatty substance that surrounds nerves and facilitates transmission of nerve impulses. Whereas myelination of most sensory and motor areas of the brain is adultlike within the first several years of life, myelination of the associative area is not complete until the teen years and beyond.

Developmental Differences in the Efficiency of Processing

The findings of Dempster, Kail, and others reporting age-related changes in speed of processing concomitant with age-related changes in cognitive task performance are consistent with theories attributing changes in cognitive development to changes in general information-processing capacity (Halford, 1982; Pascual-Leone, 1970). Early "capacity models" of cognitive development took a neo-Piagetian perspective and essentially proposed that children's performance on tasks such as conservation could be accounted for by how much information they could hold in mind at a given time (Pascual-Leone, 1970; Stewart & Pascual-Leone, 1992). These theories proposed a domain-general set of cognitive resources that children allocated to various cognitive operations that increase with age. Such domain-general models have a difficult time explaining results such as those reported by Chi (1978), where chess-expert children had a greater memory span for chess positions than did adults, but not when digits served as stimuli. Some cognitive feats seem to be domain specific, with skills in one domain not generalizing to other domains. How can a theory that postulates a domain-general pool of resources account for such findings?

More contemporary theories propose age differences not so much in *absolute* capacity (although such differences may exist), but in the *efficiency* with which children use the mental capacity they have available to them (Bjorklund, Muir-Broaddus, & Schneider, 1990; Case, 1985; Kee, 1994). One influential theory of cognitive development that considers age differences in the efficiency with which information is processed is that of Robbie Case (Case, 1985, 1992a, 1998). (Aspects of Case's theory were discussed in the previous chapter when we examined neo-Piagetian approaches to cognitive development.) Case proposed age-related declines

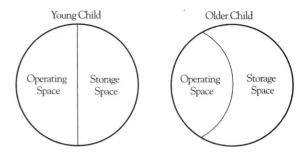

FIGURE 5-7   With age, children process information more efficiently, requiring less operating space and leaving more storage space.

in the amount of mental effort required to execute a cognitive process. Some of this improvement can be attributed to maturation. However, within each maturational stage children become increasingly adept at acquiring information and using strategies. This ability, in turn, fosters greater efficiency, resulting in heightened speed of processing.

Case distinguished between **storage space** and **operating space** when conceptualizing memory processes. Storage space is the mental space that an individual has available for storing information; operating space is the mental space that can be allocated to the execution of intellectual operations. Case also defined **total processing space** as the sum of storage and operating space.

Case proposed that there is a developmental decrease in the amount of operating space required for the execution of cognitive processes with a concomitant increase in operational efficiency. Simply put, as each new developmental skill is mastered and becomes practiced, the increase in processing efficiency frees attention (or processing space) for coordinating new strategies. Developmental changes in operating and storage space are displayed in Figure 5-7. Case's theory is illustrated in a study by Case and his colleagues (1982), who assessed the independent contributions of storage space and operating efficiency to memory performance. Storage space was measured by counting the number of items that children (ranging in age from 3 to 6 years) recalled under conditions that minimized the effects of memory strategies (for example, memory-span tasks). Operating efficiency was reflected by the speed with which a set of cognitive operations such as identifying items could be performed. Case and his associates predicted that there would be a relationship between operational efficiency (as reflected by speed of identification) and storage space (as reflected by how much was remembered). Children who were slow in identifying items (thus requiring substantial amounts of operating space) should realize lower levels of memory performance for those items. The data supported this prediction, showing a relationship between storage space and operating efficiency that was also related to age. Furthermore, when the processing speeds of college students were reduced by changing the task so that they no longer benefited from being able to say the words quickly (unfamiliar nonsense words were used), their level of memory performance was comparably reduced. The results of this study are graphically presented in Figure 5-8. As processing efficiency increased (as reflected by speed of processing), memory performance also increased. When adults were given a task reducing their processing efficiency to a level comparable to that of 6-year-olds, their memory performance was similarly modified. These results are similar to those reported by Hulme et al. (1984), who examined the relationship between word length, articulatory speed, and memory span (see Figure 5-5).

Few theorists today argue that there is a single set of resources that influence all aspects of cognition. Yet the possibility that a general-processing mechanism, in combination with more specific mechanisms, plays a substantial role in cognitive development is supported by much research and many theorists. Although capacity models are frequently expressed in terms of space, energy, or efficiency metaphors, they can also be expressed as a time metaphor. Older children require less time to process information than younger children do. This is reflected by age differences in speed of processing, discussed earlier. If we view speed of processing as a direct indication of capacity, we can avoid some definitional problems associated with resource theories

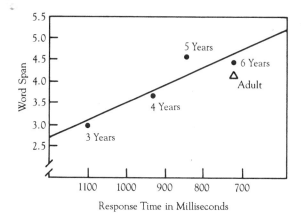

FIGURE 5-8   The relation between word span and speed of word repetition at age levels from 3 to 6 years and adulthood. Younger children were generally slower to identify words and had shorter word spans than older children. When the identification times of adults were slowed to levels comparable to those of 6-year-olds, they showed a corresponding deficit in word span. SOURCE: "Operational Efficiency and the Growth of Short-Term Memory Span," by R. Case, D. M. Kurland, and J. Goldberg, 1982, *Journal of Experimental Child Psychology, 23,* 386–404. Copyright © 1982 Academic Press. Reprinted with permission.

using metaphors of mental space or mental energy. Kail and Salthouse (1994) have proposed such a developmental theory; they suggest that a global processing-speed mechanism influences cognitive performance either directly (faster global processing results in enhanced performance) or indirectly by influencing the speed with which more domain-specific processing mechanisms (such as rehearsal) are executed. Each of these phenomena (global processing speed, specific processing speed, and cognitive performance) can be influenced by other factors associated with age (such as maturational changes in the brain or increased knowledge). Figure 5-9 illustrates the hypothetical relationship between these factors.

Based on evidence of regular age-related changes in speed of processing (discussed earlier), Kail and Salthouse (1994) proposed that speed of processing is a *cognitive primitive*, or a basic aspect of the human

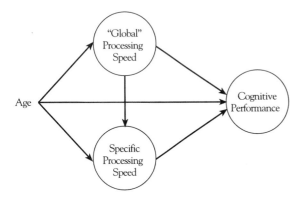

FIGURE 5-9   Model showing the possible relationships among age, global processing speed, specific processing speed, and cognitive performance. SOURCE: Adapted from "Processing Speed as a Mental Capacity," by R. V. Kail and T. A. Salthouse, 1994, *Acta Psychologica, 86*, 199–225. Copyright © 1994 by Elsevier Science Publishers BV. Adapted with permission.

cognitive architecture, much like the central processing unit of a computer is a basic part of the machine's hardware. Differences in this capacity change with age in regular ways and influence much cognitive functioning by limiting how much (or how quickly) information can be handled at any one time. Yet, age differences in speed of processing do not account for all age differences in cognitive performance. As Figure 5-9 shows, factors associated with age may directly influence cognitive functioning independent of processing speed, or age may affect task-specific processing speed. So although speed of processing is not everything, Kail and Salthouse (1994), like other capacity theorists, propose that it is perhaps the most important single factor underlying cognitive development.

The Role of Strategies in Cognitive Development

Given that children have some mental resources available to them, what do they do with these resources to "think"? In other words, from an information-processing perspective, how do they process information? Information must be encoded

or somehow represented in the cognitive system, and once it is in the mind/brain, something must be done with it. Perhaps the information—let's say the word *dog*—must be identified (a meaning must be found in memory for the visual stimulus), classified (as a small, four-legged, domestic mammal), compared with other stimuli or other items in memory (similar to cats; very different from sea slugs), or remembered for later on. Each of these operations (or set of operations) takes time and each requires experience to perform efficiently. Some may be executed automatically and unconsciously, whereas others may be executed only at the individual's discretion, with the mental operations and their results being available for conscious evaluation.

Much of the rest of this book will be concerned with developmental differences in these and other information-processing operations. In the present section, I would like to discuss a broad category of information-processing components—**strategies.** Strategies are goal-directed operations used to aid task performance. Strategies are usually viewed as being deliberately implemented, nonobligatory, and potentially available to consciousness (Harnishfeger & Bjorklund, 1990a; Pressley & Van Meter, 1993). And strategies develop.

Strategies are relevant to most aspects of cognitive development. For example, in memory development, commonly used strategies include rehearsing information or grouping to-be-remembered items by conceptual categories (for example, remembering all the outfielders on a baseball team in one group and all the pitchers in another). In mathematics, simple strategies of addition include counting on one's fingers or mental counting (for instance, for the problem 3 + 2 = ?, mentally starting with 3 and counting up two to arrive at 5). Strategies can be much more complicated and involve an evaluation component. For example, in reading, one must occasionally determine how well the recently read information is being understood. In all cases, the strategy is used to achieve some cognitive goal (remembering, adding, comprehending).

Although children often discover strategies on their own in the process of performing a task (Siegler & Jenkins, 1989), many important cognitive strategies are explicitly taught in school (Moely et al., 1992; Moely, Santulli, & Obach, 1995). In a classroom observational study, Barbara Moely and her colleagues (1992) reported that teachers in kindergarten through sixth grade taught a wide range of strategies that varied with the age of the child and the nature of the task. These included rote learning for simple repetitive tasks, elaboration, imagery, and self-checking, among others. Despite the diversity of strategies taught, Moely and her colleagues (1992) reported that the absolute frequency of strategy instruction was low. For example, specific strategy instruction was observed in an average of fewer than 3% of the teacher observations, with teachers providing some general instruction about how to deal with a task cognitively in 9.5% of the observations. In fact, 10% of the teachers observed in this study provided no strategy instruction at all. When focusing specifically on math instruction, however, second- and fifth-grade teachers were found to provide strategy or metacognitive instruction in nearly half of the observation intervals (Moely, Santulli, & Obach, 1995). Thus, strategy instruction in school varies with the teacher, the task, and the age of the children, with teachers generally providing children with instruction that is age-appropriate (that is, neither too simple nor too complicated for them to understand).

Mediational and Production Deficiencies

During the 1960s, it became obvious to cognitive developmental researchers that young children (usually preschoolers) typically do not generate and use the types of strategies that older children do. If strategies are so important to developmental differences in cognition, researchers reasoned, instructing a young child to use a strategy that is characteristic of an older child should result in changes in that child's cognitive performance.

Research using the logic of **training studies** flourished during the 1960s and 1970s and is still alive and well today. A three-step developmental progression of children's use of strategies was proposed. Early in development, children do not sponta-

neously generate a strategy to help them solve a task, and when children are shown a strategy, they are unable to use it effectively to guide their performance. This inability is called a **mediational deficiency** (Reese, 1962), meaning that a potentially effective strategy does not mediate task performance for young children. Presumably, these children do not have the mental apparatus to effectively use the strategy. For slightly older children (or for slightly simpler strategies), the imposition of a strategy results in improvement in task performance. In these cases, children do not *produce* the strategies spontaneously, but when shown what to do, they are able to follow instructions with corresponding improvements. Thus, they still have a **production deficiency** (Flavell, 1970); that is, they have the mental ability to use strategies but for some reason do not produce them without prompting. The stage of production deficiency is followed by a stage in which children produce strategies on their own without needing to have them imposed by an outsider.

Much cognitive developmental research through the 1970s focused on young children's production deficiencies (see Harnishfeger & Bjorklund, 1990a, for a brief history of research in strategy development). Many of the phenomena associated with concrete operations introduced by Piaget were examined from the viewpoint of production deficiencies. Demonstrations abounded, with researchers showing that 4-, 5-, and 6-year-olds could be taught to conserve (Gelman, 1969) and to take the visual perspective of another (Borke, 1975). Memory research used training studies extensively, demonstrating that under some conditions young children could be trained to use reasonably complex strategies such as rehearsal, organization, and imagery, although the effect of such training was often short-lived (see Schneider & Bjorklund, 1998; Schneider & Pressley, 1997; Chapter 8). It became clear that young children could be trained to use many of the strategies previously thought to be available only to older children. Tasks often had to be greatly simplified, and a trained 4-year-old rarely performed as well as an untrained 12-year-old, but younger children obviously had greater competence than psychologists had believed.

By showing that certain strategies could be taught to young children, researchers also illuminated something of the nature of what happens spontaneously in development. Thus, training studies were not done solely for their own sake (that is, to train children because they could be trained) but as a way of learning about the normal process of development.

What Are Production-Deficient Children Doing?

The emphasis on production deficiencies and their laboratory remediation resulted in a science that had a good deal to say about what older children do and about how to train younger children to resemble older children (at least in the laboratory). But it had little to say about what young children do spontaneously (Brown & DeLoache, 1978). If young children are not using strategies (unless we train them), what are they doing?

In recent years, developmental psychologists have concentrated on what production-deficient children do on their own. The answer is, basically, that they are also strategic. Preschool children, who do not spontaneously conserve liquid or organize sets of pictures according to familiar categories (such as animals, tools, and vegetables), nevertheless do things to help them perform tasks (see Wellman, 1988, for a review). These strategies often result in incorrect answers, but they are strategies nonetheless.

One simple but effective strategy used by 3- and 4-year-olds in trying to remember sets of pictures involves selectively attending to the pictures they want to remember (Baker-Ward, Ornstein, & Holden, 1984), including frequently re-attending to the stimuli, which reflects a form of visual rehearsal (Wellman, Ritter, & Flavell, 1975). Other early memory strategies include spontaneously labeling items presented for recall, a technique that is not very effective (Baker-Ward, Ornstein, & Holden, 1984), and using external memory cues. An example of the latter is found in the work of Heisel and Ritter (1981). Children were asked to hide an object in

one of 196 containers, arranged in a 14×14 grid, so that they could remember the location. Children 5 years and older chose distinctive positions for hiding the items (for example, the corners), demonstrating a memory strategy. Three-year-olds did not use such techniques, although some of them did use the strategy of attempting to hide the object in the same location on all trials. Because the locations were not distinctive, this strategy did not help memory performance, but it does reflect the intent to do something to aid memory.

Assessing memory strategies in naturalistic settings (for example, children's homes), DeLoache, Brown, and their colleagues have reported strategies for children as young as 18 months (DeLoache & Brown, 1983; DeLoache, Cassidy, & Brown, 1985). The procedure involves a hide-and-seek game, in which a toy (a stuffed animal, for example) is hidden in one of several locations in a child's home. Following delays of several minutes, the child is asked to retrieve the toy. DeLoache and Brown reported that young children engage in strategic behavior during the delay periods, including looking or pointing at the hiding location and repeating the name of the toy. In more recent research by Cohen (1996), 3- and 4-year-old children played a game of "store," in which they had to fill customers' vegetable orders. To complete these orders, children could use a variety of strategies including addition (add a tomato to an array), subtraction (take a tomato away from an array), and recognizing that no changes in an array had to be made to fill the order. These young children used a full range of the possible strategies and became more efficient (that is, made fewer moves to fill an order) with practice. These results make it clear that production deficiencies are relative. Even very young children use strategies; the strategies that they use tend to be simple and to increase in efficiency with age.

Following the findings of DeLoache, Brown, and others, it seems clear that preschool children engage in some planning that warrants being called a strategy. Still, their strategies lack the effectiveness of the procedures used by older children and often may not aid task performance at all. However, Wellman (1988) asserts that preschoolers' strategies are every

PHOTO 5-1   Apparatus used in studies of children's attentional strategies by Patricia Miller and her colleagues. (Courtesy of Patricia Miller.)

bit as goal-directed and performance-influencing as the strategies of older children are and that they are used in a wide range of situations. Recent findings support Wellman's interpretation, although we must be careful not to attribute too much in the way of strategic competence to the preschool child, for cognitive skills are clearly more effective and more easily observed in older children.

Utilization Deficiencies

Until recently, it was generally accepted that children progress from a mediational deficiency to a production deficiency and then finally are able to produce effective strategies on their own. But recent researchers have seriously questioned this progression and observed a phase in strategy development in which children use a strategy, sometimes as effectively as older children, but experience no benefit in performance. This phase in strategy development, first identified by Patricia Miller and her colleagues (Miller, 1990; Miller & Seier, 1994) has been referred to as a **utilization deficiency**. Most experiments performed by Miller and her colleagues involve children's use of a selective-attention strategy (DeMarie-Dreblow & Miller, 1988; Miller et al., 1986). Children (usually between the ages of 3 and

8 years) are shown a series of boxes with doors on top arranged into two rows of six columns (see Photo 5-1). On half of the doors are pictures of cages, meaning that those boxes contain pictures of animals. On the remaining doors are pictures of houses, meaning that those boxes contain pictures of household objects. Children are told to remember the location of one group of objects, either the animals or the household objects. They are also told that they can open any doors they wish during a study period. Children's attentional strategies can be examined by looking at the doors they choose to open during this study period.

The most efficient strategy, of course, is to open only those doors that have a drawing of the relevant category. In a series of experiments, Miller and her colleagues have found a developmental sequence in strategy development. In the first phase, preschoolers show no selective strategy, usually opening all the doors on the top first and then all the doors on the bottom, regardless of what picture is on the door. In the second phase, children use the selective strategy, but only partially: they still open many irrelevant doors. In the third phase, children use the strategy (that is, open mainly the relevant doors), but the strategy does not help them remember the locations of the items. This third phase constitutes a utilization deficiency. Not until the fourth phase, usually late in the preschool years, are children able to use the attentional strategy and also to benefit from its use.

Utilization deficiencies have since been documented in older children for more complex memory strategies, (Ackerman, 1996; Coyle & Bjorklund, 1996), reading (Gaultney, 1995), attention (Miller et al., 1991), and analogical reasoning (Muir-Broaddus, 1995), among others. Moreover, reviews of earlier research indicate that utilization deficiencies are very common, at least for memory strategies. For example, Miller and Seier (1994) reported strong or partial evidence of utilization deficiencies in more than 90% of all experiments examining children's spontaneous use of memory strategies. Similarly, utilization deficiencies have been found in more than 50% of memory training studies conducted over a 30-year period (Bjorklund et al., 1997). Earlier researchers typically dismissed their findings of young children using strategies but not benefiting from them, rarely discussing such results in their papers. It appears now, however, that such a finding is not a quirk or experimental error, but the typical pattern of strategy development.

The Cost of Strategy Use

One reason for researchers' reluctance to identify utilization deficiencies earlier is that in the prevailing theory, strategies, by definition, are implemented to facilitate task performance. Children's use of strategies in the absence of enhancements in task performance violated what everyone had come to believe was common knowledge. Why should young children who use a strategy not benefit from it? One speculation is that the execution of strategies requires substantial mental effort and that young children do not have enough information-processing resources to execute the strategy and still perform other aspects of the task as well (Bjorklund & Harnishfeger, 1987; Miller et al., 1991). That is, strategy use has a cost in mental effort, and young children exert so much of their limited resources executing the strategy that they do not retain suffi-

cient mental capacity to perform other aspects of the task efficiently.

This possibility was demonstrated in a dual-task memory experiment by Bjorklund and Harnishfeger (1987). Third- and seventh-grade children were instructed in an organizational memory strategy (remembering all the words from a category together). In addition, the children were required to tap an index finger on the space bar of a microcomputer as fast as they could. Their tapping rate during the memory training was compared with their rate during a baseline period when no memory task was given and during a free-recall memory task for which no training instructions had been provided. Decreases in tapping rate during the memory tasks were used as an indication of how much mental effort the children were expending on the tasks. The more slowly the children tapped (relative to when they were performing no memory task), the greater the mental effort required to perform the memory task was presumed to be. That is, the more mental effort required for the memory task, the more interference (measured in terms of decreased tapping rate) there should be on the secondary, tapping task.

Bjorklund and Harnishfeger reported that both the third- and seventh-graders showed increased interference as a result of the training, relative to the free-recall task. Furthermore, both groups later used the strategy that they had been shown during training. This use was indicated by increased clustering in recall, with children remembering words from the same category together. Only the seventh-grade children, however, showed a corresponding improvement in the number of words they recalled, relative to the free-recall task. The third-graders remembered no more words as a result of the training than they did when no memory instructions had been given, despite the fact that they used the strategy and expended greater amounts of mental effort. We interpreted these results as indicating that the third-graders used too much of their limited mental capacity in executing the strategy to have enough left over for other aspects of the memory task, such as retrieving specific words. Strategies are supposed to provide greater efficiency in processing, and had the third-grade children mastered the strategy to a greater degree, their memory performance would probably have improved. Nevertheless, under the conditions of this experiment, the memory performance did not improve. Similar findings and interpretations have been reported for other memory strategies (Guttentag, 1984), simpler attentional strategies (Miller et al., 1991), and a more complex elaboration memory strategy (Rohwer & Litrownik, 1983).

Strategies are effortful. Young children process information less efficiently than older children, making them less likely to use a strategy spontaneously and less likely to benefit from the imposition of a strategy. Cognitive processing becomes more efficient with age, allowing children to execute more strategies and to use them with greater effectiveness.

Siegler's Adaptive Strategy-Choice Model

The foregoing discussion might give the idea that for any given task, children use one strategy and perhaps with time and practice eventually begin using another, more efficient strategy. Such a perspective reflects how a good deal of strategy research during the past 25 years has been done, looking at changes in a single strategy over relatively brief periods of time. This perspective is an overly simplified one, however. Recent research has shown that children use a variety of different strategies to solve a single problem, sometimes several strategies at a single time. Evidence for multiple and variable strategy use has been found everywhere it has been looked for, including arithmetic (Alibali, 1999), scientific reasoning (Schauble, 1990), memory (Fletcher & Bray, 1997), spelling (Rittle-Johnson & Siegler, 1999), and conservation (Church & Goldin-Meadow, 1986), among others (see Siegler, 1996).

This perspective of multiple- and variable-strategy use is best exemplified by the **adaptive strategy choice model** of Robert Siegler (1996). I discussed Siegler's model briefly in Chapter 2 in the section on "Selectionist Theories of Cognitive and Brain Development." Basically, Siegler adopts the idea of natural selection from Darwin's theory of evolution and applies it to cognitive development. Stated most simply, Siegler proposes that, in cogni-

tive development, children generate a wide variety of strategies to solve problems and, depending on the nature of the task and the goals of the child, certain strategies are "selected" and used frequently, whereas others, that are less effective, are used less often and eventually decrease in frequency.

Siegler and his colleagues have demonstrated for a variety of strategies on a variety of tasks that children typically use multiple strategies, frequently switching from one strategy to another over repeated trials (Siegler, 1996; Siegler & Jenkins, 1989). The technique used by Siegler and his colleagues to assess children's multiple strategy use has been referred to as a **microgenetic method** and involves looking at developmental change within a single set of individuals over relatively brief periods of time — days or weeks, usually (see Miller & Coyle, 1999; Siegler & Crowley, 1991). For example, in learning to add, children frequently use a strategy that involves counting out loud both addends, called the sum strategy (for example, for $5 + 3 = ?$, saying "1, 2, 3, 4, 5 [pause], 6, 7, 8."). A more sophisticated strategy, called the min strategy, is to begin with the larger addend (in this case, 5) and count up from there (for example, saying "5 [pause], 6, 7, 8."). A still more sophisticated strategy, known as fact retrieval, is "just knowing" the answer — retrieving it directly from long-term memory without having to count at all (for example, simply saying "8" to the question "How much is $5 + 3$?"). When looking at group data, one gets the impression that children progress from using the sum strategy to using the min strategy to using fact retrieval. Yet closer examination reveals that individual children use a variety of these strategies at any one time: the frequencies with which these various strategies are used vary with age. (More will be said of children's arithmetic strategies in Chapter 12.)

Other examples of children's multiple-strategy use come from experiments assessing memory development. For example, in a study by McGilly and Siegler (1990), children in kindergarten, grade 2, and grade 4 were given a serial-recall task (to remember a list of digits in exact order). McGilly and Siegler observed the strategies the children used and later questioned them about their strategy use.

They reported that the children used a variety of different strategies on these tasks, with any given child using a combination of strategies over repeated trials. That is, multiple strategy use was the rule rather than the exception. In other research, Cox and his colleagues (Cox et al., 1989) demonstrated that third-grade children given instructions to sort words into groups by meaning not only improved their memory performance but also used more sophisticated rehearsal techniques. That is, improvements in one strategy (organization) led to improvements in another strategy (rehearsal), which in turn led to greater levels of memory performance. Moreover, children use a variety of different strategies on a single trial, often switching the combination of strategies they use from trial to trial (Coyle & Bjorklund, 1997).

Basically, Siegler sees multiple strategies existing within a child's cognitive repertoire at any one time, with these strategies competing with one another. Early in development or when a child is first learning a new task, relatively simple strategies will "win" most of the time. With practice and maturation, the child will use other, more effortful but more efficient strategies more frequently. Thus, Siegler believes that development does not occur in a steplike fashion but, rather, as a series of overlapping waves, with the distribution of those waves changing over time. Figure 5-10 presents Siegler's wave approach to cognitive development. Multiple strategies are available to children at every age, but which strategies are used most frequently changes with age.

More will be said about Siegler's account of strategy development later in this book, particularly in Chapter 12, examining age differences in arithmetic strategies. Siegler believes that age differences in how strategies are selected and used reflect an important way of viewing cognitive development that differs from conventional Piagetian and information-processing models. Perhaps the most important message from Siegler's work is that at any point in time and for any given task, children have a variety of strategies available to them. The issue facing cognitive developmental psychologists is not whether children are being strategic. Rather, we are seeking to discover what strategies and combination

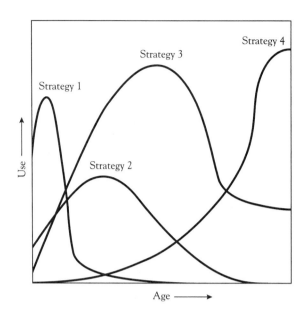

FIGURE 5-10   Siegler's adaptive strategy choice model of development. Change in strategy use is seen as a series of overlapping waves, with different strategies being used more frequently at different ages. SOURCE: Adapted from Siegler, R. S. (1996). *Emerging minds: The process of change in children's thinking.* New York: Oxford University Press.; thanks to Robert Siegler.

of strategies children of different ages use and how the simpler strategies used by young children develop into the more sophisticated and effective strategies used by older children and adults.

Implicit Strategy Use

Can strategies ever be implicit, out of our conscious awareness? We may not always be aware of the strategies we are using, but part of the definition of strategies I provided earlier made it explicit that strategies are at least *available* to consciousness. Recent research, however, has caused a reconsideration of this aspect of strategies, and this is illustrated by a recent experiment by Siegler and Stern (1998).

In their experiment, second-grade children were given a series of arithmetic problems of the following form: a + b − b = ?, for example, 37 + 16 − 16 = ? Most of you will recognize that there is a shortcut to solving such problems. Because the b term is both added to and then subtracted from the a term, they cancel each other out. Thus, the answer can be arrived at quite quickly, merely by stating the a term (37 in this example). The problem can also be solved by direct computation, of course (for example, $37 + 16 = 53$; $53 - 16 = 37$), which takes considerably longer.

Siegler and Stern tested a group of second-grade children during eight sessions on problems like these. Children's reaction times to solve each problem were recorded, and, after every trial, they were asked how they went about solving the problem. Although none of the children were using the shortcut strategy during the first session, most were using it, at least occasionally, by the end of the experiment. Siegler and Stern noted that latencies to solve the problems tended to be either very fast (4 seconds or less) or quite long (8 seconds or more). When children answered the problems quickly (under 4 seconds) they never showed evidence of computation, whereas they were almost always observed to compute the solution on problems when they had the longer latencies.

By recording both latencies to solve problems and explanations, Siegler and Stern were able to classify children's strategy use into several categories: (a) *computation*, in which children took a long time and were observed to compute (or said they computed) the solution; (b) *shortcut strategy*, in which children responded quickly and reported using the shortcut strategy; and (c) *unconscious shortcut strategy*, in which children responded quickly, showed no signs of computation, but claimed *not* to have used the shortcut procedure. Siegler and Stern reported that 88% of the children used the unconscious shortcut strategy before using the shortcut strategy. Nor was it the case that these children just lacked the verbal ability to express their ideas. Most of these children later used the shortcut strategy and provided adequate verbal descriptions of it. What these data suggest is that knowledge of the shortcut strategy was initially implicit (not available to consciousness), and only later became explicit.

Other evidence is consistent with Siegler and Stern's findings. For example, Goldin-Meadows and her colleagues (Church & Goldin-Meadows, 1986; Alibali & Goldin-Meadows, 1993) have shown that children often reveal more sophisticated strategies in their gestures than in their speech. For example, some children given a conservation of liquid task to solve referred to differences in height in their (erroneous) verbal explanations, but referred to differences in width with their hands. Children who made such mismatches were more likely to benefit from subsequent training than were those whose verbal explanations and gestures matched. These findings indicate that implicit processes, such as those hypothesized by Karmiloff-Smith (1992) and others (see discussion in Chapter 4) play an important role in the development of explicit processes such as strategies. Transitions from one strategy to another might not occur with a sudden burst of awareness (an "aha experience"), but first might be expressed only implicitly, before an explicit, and presumably more flexible, level of strategy use is realized.

Children's Knowledge Base and Cognitive Development

As traditionally conceived, information-processing accounts of cognition and development are domain general. Each person is seen as having a limited mental capacity to apply to a variety of problems, and processes or strategies that function in one context are expected to function well in other contexts. However, one of the consistent findings in cognitive development research over the past three decades has been the *domain specificity* of children's thinking. There are many examples in the literature and in everyday life of children performing one cognitive task like a champ while performing other seemingly similar tasks like a chump. The memory-span performance of chess-expert children reported by Chi (1978), discussed earlier in this chapter, is a perfect example.

How can such evidence of domain specificity be reconciled with the domain-general assumptions of the information-processing approach? A perspective that preserves the fundamental assumptions of information-processing approaches is to postulate that the amount of knowledge an individual already has in his or her mind/brain relating to the to-be-processed information affects how that information is processed. From this viewpoint, the amount of knowledge one possesses influences how new information is stored and integrated into one's previous knowledge and the speed and efficiency with which information is processed. Cognition, then, acts in a domain-specific fashion while operating with domain-general mechanisms.

Age differences in knowledge, or in one's **knowledge base,** have been given a central role by some researchers in cognitive development. For example, Susan Carey (1985) has written that "the acquisition and reorganization of strictly domain-specific knowledge . . . probably account for most of the cognitive differences between 3-year-olds and adults" (p. 512). Young children are novices at most tasks, having less knowledge than older children about the to-be-processed information and about what it is they are supposed to do on the task itself (Brown & DeLoache, 1978). To what extent are young children's less sophisticated cognitive skills a function of limits on their abilities to process information, on the one hand, or limits on their knowledge about information relevant to the task, on the other? Let me provide the general answer to this question at the start: Processing and knowledge cannot be understood independently of one another. How a person of any age processes information is a function of the prior knowledge that person possesses. Much like the relationship between structure and function, the relationship between processing and knowledge is bidirectional.

Experts and Novices

Although domain-specific cognitive processing and abilities can be found in people of any age, such differences are exaggerated when comparing experts and novices for some specific domains, such as chess, physics, or soccer. By studying differences in thinking, memory, or problem solving between experts and novices, we can get a clearer picture of how one's knowledge base affects cognition and its development (see Schneider, 1993).

One advantage experts have over novices seems to be in how easily they can group domain-relevant information. For example, research with children (Chi, 1978; Schneider et al., 1993) and adults (Chase & Simon, 1973) has found that chess experts process chess information faster than novices and also are able to recognize familiar grouping patterns, or "chunks," of chess pieces, whereas novices rely on remembering the position of individual pieces. This greater "chunking" ability effectively increases the memory span of the experts. Importantly, the memory-span advantage of chess experts for chess positions disappears (or becomes greatly reduced) when chess pieces are placed on the board in random, rather than in game-possible, positions (Chase & Simon, 1973; Schneider et al., 1993).

Related to experts' chunking ability is evidence that experts categorize facts related to their area of expertise in terms of higher-level concepts relative to novices (Chi, Feltovich, & Glaser, 1981; Johnson & Mervis, 1998). For example, Chi and her colleagues (1981) assessed the way adults who were either physics experts or novices classified physics problems. They reported that the experts classified problems with respect to underlying principles, whereas the novices were more apt to use superficial characteristics of the problems (the meanings of individual words or diagrams) as a basis for classification. Such higher-level classification for experts than for novices is not restricted to adults (Johnson & Mervis, 1994; McPherson & Thomas, 1989). For example, in a study by McPherson and Thomas (1989), 10- to 13-year-old expert and novice tennis players were evaluated for their performance and knowledge of tennis. As in the research with adults, child tennis experts focused on higher-level concepts and had more connections among concepts than novices, and this differential knowledge base affected actual tennis performance. According to McPherson and Thomas (1989), novices approach tennis problems in a general manner and as a result process tennis-related information more slowly and "must keep active in memory the features of the problem and the very general goal of finding a way to solve it" (p. 209). Just as knowledge of chess affects how experts and novices play the game, so too does knowledge of tennis affect how children make decisions during a match and how they execute their sport skill.

Despite the influence that knowledge has on developmental differences, however, it is likely that cognitive development is not equivalent to knowledge development. For example, in studies where knowledge is equated between younger and older children (Barnes, Dennis, & Haefele-Kalvaitis, 1996; DeMarie-Dreblow, 1991) age differences in performance are rarely eliminated. How knowledge is connected to other pieces of knowledge will affect how it is accessed and used to solve problems. Knowledge, however, is important. How much knowledge we have influences how we process information, including how we use strategies.

Knowledge and Strategies

Perhaps the relationship between knowledge and processing is most easily seen with respect to strategies. According to Daniel Kee (1994), "Most researchers acknowledge that strategic processing is dependent on the availability and accessibility of relevant knowledge" (see also Bjorklund et al., 1990; Rabinowitz & Kee, 1994). The primary reason hypothesized for this relationship is that having a detailed, or elaborated, knowledge base results in faster processing for domain-specific information, which in turn results in more efficient processing and greater availability of mental resources. The relationship between knowledge and strategy use has been demonstrated for a variety of different domains, including mathematics (Ashcraft, 1990), reading (Daneman & Green, 1986), text comprehension (Schneider, Körkel, & Weinert, 1989), problem solving (Chi, Feltovich, & Glaser, 1981), communication (Furman & Walden, 1990), memory (Ornstein, Baker-Ward, & Naus, 1988), and forming inferences (Barnes et al., 1996), among others.

One particularly straightforward demonstration of the interrelationship between knowledge, strategy use, mental effort, and cognitive performance was provided in a memory experiment by Kee and Davies (1990). These researchers used the dual-task procedure described earlier to assess the relationship between mental effort and knowledge base in the use of a memory strategy in 10- and 11-year-old children. Changes in rate of finger tapping as a function of strategy use and familiarity of the to-be-learned information were used as a measure of the mental effort required to perform the memory strategy. The children were given pairs of words and asked to form an association between them, so that when they were presented with the first word in a pair, they would be able to remember the second word (this is referred to as a **paired-associates task**). The children were instructed to use an **elaboration strategy** to help them learn the pairs. Elaboration consists of generating a relationship between paired items; for example, if the two words were arrow and glasses, an effective elaboration strategy might be to generate the image or statement "the arrow smashes the glasses" (see Kee, 1994; Pressley, 1982).

Kee and Davies (1990) generated two types of lists for the children to learn. One list consisted of "accessible" pairs (for example, stairs-tower, cowboy-ranch, pig-mud); these were pairs of items for which children would have substantial background knowledge, making it easy for them to generate elaborations. The other list consisted of "inaccessible" pairs (for example, ticket-knee, frog-chair, cake-valley); these were pairs of items for which children would have few pre-established associations, making the generation of elaborations more difficult (that is, more effortful).

The results indicated that the children remembered fewer of the inaccessible than the accessible pairs, showing that prior knowledge has an effect on how well one remembers. Moreover, the children expended more mental effort, as reflected by the reduction of tapping rate when performing the elaboration strategy, for the inaccessible than for the accessible pairs. Differences in memory performance and mental effort between the accessible and inaccessible lists were greatly reduced, however, when the children were provided with the elaborations (the provided condition), rather than having to generate them themselves (the generate condition). The difference in mental effort between the generate and provided conditions in this experiment is shown in Figure 5-11. The mental effort associated with having to generate elaborations for relatively unfamiliar pairs of items directly affected how children used the strategy and how much they remembered.

The relationship between knowledge, strategies, and cognitive task performance is a complicated one and an issue of central importance to cognitive development. More will be said of this relationship later in the book, particularly in Chapter 8. What is important to remember is that what and how much one knows influences how and how well one thinks. With age, children acquire more knowledge and, simply as a result of these quantitative increases, process information differently. Because knowledge impacts processing, children (and adults) think differently about topics on which they have detailed knowledge versus those on which they have less knowledge, thus accounting, in part, for the often-observed phenomenon of domain specificity.

Attention

One concept closely associated with information-processing approaches to cognition and development is that of attention. In everyday parlance, we use the term interchangeably with concentration. When we tell a child to "pay attention," we usually want that child to concentrate on the task at hand and not to let his or her mind wander to other things. Attention has been used similarly in the psychological literature. Psychologists who study attention are interested in how and why people attend to some objects and events in the environment and not to others. Developmental psychologists are interested in the development of various aspects of attention.

One assumption about attention is that it consumes limited mental resources. Thus, age differences in the ability to attend to, or to focus one's attention on, a particular stimulus or task have been presumed to reflect differences in the availability of and ability to allocate limited mental resources. Thus, attending to some task has often been seen as equivalent to allocating one's limited resources to

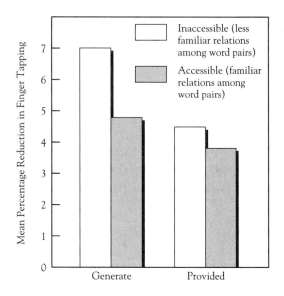

FIGURE 5-11   Mean percentage reduction in finger tapping as a function of accessibility for subjects in the dual-task memory experiment by Kee and Davies. SOURCE: "Mental Effort and Elaboration: Effects of Accessibility and Instruction," by D. W. Kee and L. Davies, 1990, *Journal of Experimental Child Psychology*, 49, 264–274. Copyright © 1990 Academic Press. Reprinted with permission.

that task. Yet attending means more than merely consuming limited resources. Developmental differences in attention have been examined for a variety of phenomena, including the extent to which children can sustain their focus on tasks, as well as their abilities to switch their focus between competing stimuli, to focus selectively on some stimuli to the exclusion of others, and to apply strategies for selective attention.

Sustaining Attention

One aspect of attention involves sustaining one's focus on a particular task—that is, paying attention. To some extent, we can measure this even in infancy, with some babies staying "on task" better than others. Some interesting evidence indicates that variations in attention in infants and toddlers (1- and 2-year-olds) are predictive of attention in early childhood (3.5 years) (Ruff et al., 1990). Such a finding suggests that some common factor may underlie individual differences in attentiveness, both in infancy and childhood, and might make possible the prediction of attention disorders from measurements in infancy.

The ability to sustain attention becomes increasingly important for children beyond infancy, and ample evidence indicates that children's attention span, the length of time for which they can sustain focused attention, increases with age. For example, Ruff and Lawson (1990) observed children between the ages of 1 and 4.5 years during free play. They noted a regular increase in focused attention during play over this time and attributed such increases, in part, to improved abilities to inhibit extraneous information. In other research, children between the ages of 30 and 54 months were given a series of tests of sustained visual attention, for example, attention during play, while watching television, and during a reaction-time task (Ruff, Capozzoli, & Weisberg, 1998). For each measure, attention increased with age, although it differed among the tasks, with attention during play and for television viewing developing earlier than attention during the reaction-time task. Also, there were only low to moderate correlations among the tasks, indicating that individual differences in attention were relatively domain specific in nature, tied to particular contexts.

One area where issues of sustained attention could have some social and educational implications concerns young children's attention to television shows. It is widely believed that children's comprehension of television is fragmented and passive, promoting a passive attitude toward thinking in general (Singer, 1980). However, there is evidence that young children can and do sustain attention to television shows, although the degree of attention varies with the comprehensibility of the program (Anderson & Lorch, 1983). For example, in a study by Lorch and Castle (1997), 5-year-old children watched special shows of *Sesame Street*. Some of the segments in the shows had been altered to make them less comprehensible by dubbing them in a foreign language, whereas others were intact (more comprehensible). Children were told to "watch and enjoy" the shows. However, they also were asked to press a button every time a loud buzzer went off, and to do this as fast as they could. This was a *secondary task* (viewing the TV show being the *primary task*), and reaction times to press the buzzer were used as an indication of how much attention they were showing to the TV program. The longer it took them to press the button, the more attention they were presumably paying to the television show.

Lorch and Castle reported that children paid more attention to the television show when more versus less comprehensible segments were showing, and that, when watching the shows, children devoted more attention to the more comprehensible segments. That is, they had slower reaction times to the secondary task when watching the more meaningful shows than the less meaningful shows, or when not looking at the TV at all. Also, the longer children sustained their attention to the meaningful segments (sustaining attention for 15 seconds or longer), the slower were their reaction times on the secondary task, implying that they were devoting more attention to the TV program. In general, children paid substantial attention to meaningful TV programs, implying active, rather than passive processing of the show's content, and they might become more actively involved (cognitively) the longer they continuously attend to the show.

Selective Attention

The term *attention* is frequently used as a synonym for *concentration*. When we concentrate, we focus our attention on some stimulus, ignoring others. **Selective attention** is the ability to concentrate only on chosen stimuli and not to be distracted by other "noise" in the environment. In general, selective-attention abilities increase with age, with young children giving a disproportionate amount of attention to information irrelevant to the task at hand and not enough attention to important information (Lane & Pearson, 1982).

Selective attention in children has been extensively studied using tests of **incidental learning.** In a typical experiment, children are shown pairs of

FIGURE 5-12   Stimulus materials used in central-incidental memory tasks. Children are instructed to attend to one stimulus class of pictures (the animals, for example) and are later tested for memory of both the central (animals) and incidental (household items) stimuli. SOURCE: "Strategies for Remembering," by J. W. Hagen. In S. Farnham-Diggory (Ed.), *Information Processing in Children*, p. 68. Copyright © 1972 Academic Press. Reprinted with permission.

pictures like those in Figure 5-12. One member of each pair is designated as central, and the children are told to remember it for later on. The other is designated as incidental and the children are told that they can ignore it (Hagen & Stanovich, 1977). Following stimulus presentation, the children are asked to recall the central stimuli, and, as would be expected, the older they are, the more they recall. Then, the children are asked to recall the incidental stimuli—the ones they were supposed to ignore.

Age differences are much smaller for the incidental recall. In fact, after about age 11, the amount of incidental information remembered actually decreases (Hagen & Stanovich, 1977). This means that when instructed to remember one set of items and ignore another, younger children have more difficulty with both. From results such as these, researchers have concluded that older children are better able to allocate attention in accordance with task demands and that they can store information more efficiently than younger children (Schiff & Knopf, 1985). Teachers and parents need to recognize the possibility that young children's seeming inability to learn prescribed lessons might be because they are filling their minds with incidental learning.

Other researchers have emphasized the role that age differences in the ability to exert inhibitory control plays in developmental differences in selective attention. For example, in research with 5- to 12-year-old children and adults (Ridderinkhof & van der Molen, 1995), participants were shown target arrays (central stimuli) with arrows pointing either to the left or the right. In each hand they held a bulb and were to squeeze the bulb in their right hand for a right facing arrow and the bulb in their left hand for a left-facing arrow. The target arrows were surrounded either by (1) incidental arrows (that children were told to ignore) that faced in the same direction as the target arrows, (2) incidental arrows that faced in the opposite direction, or (3) with diamonds, that served as a neutral stimulus. The length of time it took children to squeeze the bulb, depending on whether the distractor arrows were pointing in the same or opposite direction as the target arrows (all relative to the time it took to squeeze the bulb in the neutral "diamond" condition) was measured. The longer it took children to squeeze the bulb, relative to the neutral condition, the greater interference (and the poorer their selective attention) was proposed to be. Children's brain-wave patterns were also recorded. Ridderinkhof and van der Molen reported a reduction in interference effects with age, as measured both by patterns of hand squeezes and brain waves. Based on their findings, they concluded that age-related differences in inhibition account for much of the data and that this is related to developmental differences in the maturation of the frontal cortex (see also Ridderinkhof, van der Molen, & Band, 1997).

Attentional Strategies

When children must inspect something or make comparisons among objects, how do they allocate, or spend, their attention? Do children attend to some parts of a display more than to others? Do they

compare two objects carefully before declaring them the same or different? Are there age differences in what they do? Stated another way, what strategies of attention do children use when they must examine a stimulus or set of stimuli?

Classic work on developmental differences in children's attentional strategies was conducted by Vurpillot (1968; Vurpillot & Ball, 1979). In these studies, children were shown pictures of pairs of houses (see Figure 5-13). The children's task was to tell whether the windows in the two houses were the same or different. While they were making their decisions, their eye movements were recorded by a camera concealed behind the picture. It was found that preschool children rarely looked at all the windows before making a judgment. For example, when there were 12 windows in the two houses, 4- and 5-year-olds, on average, made a decision after looking at only 7 of the 12 windows. Children aged 6 to 8 years old, however, looked at between 10 and 12 of the windows, on average. Not surprisingly, the older children, who used a better strategy, were more apt to be correct in their judgments than the less strategic preschoolers (Vurpillot & Ball, 1979).

Research by Miller and her colleagues, discussed earlier with respect to utilization deficiencies, has similarly shown improved attentional strategies over the course of the preschool years. In this work, children are instructed to study and remember only a subset of items, hidden in clearly marked boxes (for example, they are asked to remember only the animals, which are hidden in boxes with cages marked on them). Most 3-year-olds open all boxes, both relevant (those with cages on them) and irrelevant (those with houses on them). Slightly older children begin to use a systematic strategy, but it is not typically until after 6 years of age that children consistently use a selective strategy on this task (DeMarie-Dreblow & Miller, 1988; Miller et al., 1986).

What Do Children Know about Attention?

Do young children know more about attentional processes than their behavior might indicate? That is, is their **meta-attention** greater than their

FIGURE 5-13   Stimulus materials used in research on attentional strategies. Children's eye movements are recorded as they determine whether the houses in each pair are the same or different. SOURCE: "The Development of Scanning Strategies and Their Relations to Visual Differentiation," by E. Vurpillot, 1968, *Journal of Experimental Child Psychology*, 6, 632–650. Copyright © 1968 Academic Press. Reprinted with permission.

attentional abilities? This often seems to be the case. Even though 4-year-olds generally cannot overcome distractions when performing "selective-attention" tasks, they are apparently aware that distractions are a problem, for they realize that two stories will be harder to understand if the storytellers speak simultaneously rather than taking turns (Pillow, 1988). By contrast, 3-year-olds would just as soon listen to stories told simultaneously as to have the storytellers take turns. In other research, Miller and Weiss (1982) asked 5-, 7-, and 9-year-olds to answer a series of questions about factors known to affect performance on an incidental-learning task (that is, a task like the "animals and objects" test described earlier). Although knowledge about attentional processes generally increased with age, even the 5-year-olds realized that one should at least *look first* at task-relevant stimuli and then *label* these objects as an aid to remembering them. The 7- and 10-year-olds further understood that one must *attend selectively* to task-relevant stimuli and *ignore* irrelevant information to do well on these problems.

However, at other times young children seem unaware that paying attention is something special. John Flavell and his colleagues (Flavell, Green, & Flavell, 1995a), asked 4-, 6-, and 8-year-old children a series of questions about attention. For example, if a woman is examining a set of decorative pins so that she can select one as a gift, what would be on her mind? Would she be focusing just on the pins, or might she have other things on her mind as well? Whereas almost all 8-year-olds and most 6-year-olds were aware that the woman would be thinking primarily about the pins and not likely thinking about other things, few 4-year-olds had this insight. It's as if they do not realize what is involved in selective attention. By 8 years of age, children's understanding of attentional focus was about as good as that of adults.

In sum, the development of attention is apparently a lengthy process in which children first learn to translate what they know into appropriate actions and then gradually come to rely on these strategies as they become more routinized and an effective means of gathering information to achieve their objectives.

New Approaches to Developmental Differences in Information Processing

I think it would be accurate to say that information-processing models, in one guise or another, remain the dominant perspective in cognitive development today. As with all psychological theories, however, information-processing conceptions of children's thought are constantly being tested, challenged, and modified. Some challenges to information-processing approaches come from the developing field of cognitive science. Psychologists are increasingly concerned with the biological basis of cognition and its development, including both neurological (proximate) and evolutionary (distal) causes. These have not been traditional concerns of information-processing approaches, and critics have argued convincingly that new theories must be developed that take the brain as seriously as the mind when describing and explaining cognition and its development (see Gibson & Petersen, 1991; Tooby & Cosmides, 1992).

But information-processing accounts of cognition and development have been sufficiently flexible to change with the times. Although few researchers today take the "mind as a computer" metaphor too seriously, most still believe that the mind/brain processes information (that is, encodes, represents, categorizes, retrieves). Thinking involves computation, done by bundles of nerve cells and not silicon chips. However, some of the basic assumptions of classical information-processing theory have slowly been eroding, such as the belief in a single set of generic resources or that all processing is serial in nature (that is, that we can only think of one thing at a time).

In the sections that follow, I discuss three new approaches within the general framework of information-processing theory: theories that posit developmental differences in inhibition and resistance to interference as the underlying cause of much of cognitive development; Charles Brainerd and Valerie Reyna's fuzzy-trace theory, which looks at age differences in basic processes, rather than higher-level, conscious processes, as the mechanisms for cognitive change; and connectionist models of cognitive development, which involve a particular type of computer simulations to achieve a better understanding of development.

Inhibition and Resistance to Interference

Inhibition and interference are old concepts in psychology. With the rise of information-processing theory, however, concepts of inhibition and interference fell out of grace, being seemingly incompatible with the computer metaphor of mind. As gaps in information-processing theory became apparent, theorists looking both at adult cognition and cognitive development re-examined the role that inhibition and **resistance to interference** might play in human thought. Although it is clearly important to activate knowledge or thought processes, it is equally important that we *don't* execute, or that we *inhibit*, processes at other times. A theory of cognition that examines only "activation" is going to have only part of the picture. And the role of inhibition might be especially important, or obvious, in children. Many of children's cognitive errors and their everyday "problem" behaviors come from things they do despite instructions otherwise (for example, "I didn't mean to trip Josh when he walked up the aisle, it just happened"). The basic idea at its simplest is that, with age, children are increasingly able to inhibit prepotent (primary) and often inappropriate mental or behavioral responses or to resist interference from both internal and external sources, and that these improved skills permit the more efficient execution of other cognitive operations.

Neurological Locus

Inhibitory and resistance-to-interference processes are seemingly related to the functioning of the frontal lobes of the neocortex (or the prefrontal cortex — see Chapter 2). The frontal lobes of the neocortex have many projections to other areas of the brain, including the limbic system, the "emotional" part of the brain. The prefrontal cortex is one of the last areas of the brain to reach full matu-

rity in ontogeny. Development of the frontal lobes in humans is rapid between birth and about 2 years of age. Another, less pronounced growth spurt occurs between about 4 and 7 years, with subsequent growth being slow and gradual into young adulthood (Luria, 1973).

Much evidence for the role of frontal lobes in inhibition in humans comes from cases of brain damage. Humans with frontal lobe damage have difficulty with planning and concentration. Frontal lobe dysfunction has been implicated in some psychiatric syndromes, such as obsessive-compulsive disorder (Malloy, 1987). One test that demonstrates the difficulty frontal lobe patients have with interference is the Wisconsin Card Sorting Test (WCST). The WCST consists of cards on which are depicted different objects (such as squares, stars, and circles) that vary in color and number (see Figure 5-14). The participants' task is to sort the cards into specified categories (that is, according to color, number, or shape), which is reinforced by the examiner. Without specifically informing the participant, the examiner then switches reinforcement to another category. For example, the initial category may be number, in which case participants would be reinforced for sorting all the target cards with four items on them under the cue card consisting of four circles, all the cards with three items on them under the cue card with the three crosses, and so on, regardless of the color or shape of the items on the cards. The examiner may then switch from number to shape, so that all target cards are now to be placed with the cue card consisting of the same shape (stars with stars, triangles with triangles, and so on), with color and number being irrelevant. Participants are corrected after a mistake, so they should presumably be able to learn a new classification scheme after only a few trials. Normal people do exactly this. However, patients with lesions in the frontal lobes do poorly on this task, often finding it difficult to make a new response (Milner, 1964). This reflects an inability to inhibit a previously acquired response. Based on these and related findings, it has become clear that the frontal lobes play a central role in the selection and regulation of behavior by

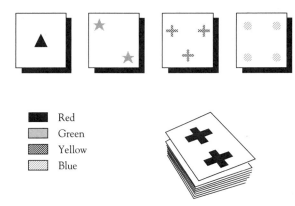

	Red
	Green
	Yellow
	Blue

FIGURE 5-14 The Wisconsin Card Sorting Test. SOURCE: "Some Effects of Frontal Lobotomy in Man," by B. Milner. In J. M. Warren & K. Akert (Eds.), *The Frontal Granular Cortex and Behavior*, McGraw-Hill, 1964.

inhibiting previous responses and fostering resistance to interference from extraneous stimuli (see Dempster, 1993; Diamond, 1991; Luria, 1973).

Developmental Differences in Inhibition and Resistance to Interference

Because we know the frontal lobes develop over infancy and childhood, we should expect corresponding changes in the ability to inhibit irrelevant information and to resist interference, and ample evidence demonstrates just that. Recall, for example, the research by Diamond (1985), discussed in Chapter 2, in which infants' performance on A-not-B object permanence tasks was related to development of the prefrontal lobes (see also Bell & Fox, 1992). Likewise, many of the tasks that adults with frontal lobe damage have difficulty performing also show improvements with development. For example, age differences are found in performance on the WCST, with young children performing much the way adults with frontal lesions perform (Chelune & Baer, 1986).

In a task that is essentially a simplified version of the WCST, children are given a set of cards with each card depicting one of two objects (a red boat or a blue rabbit, for example). Children first sort the pictures into groups on the basis of one dimension (shape, for example, boats versus rabbits), and then, after several trials, are told that the rules have changed and they must now sort the pictures on the basis of the other dimension (color, red versus blue) (Zelazo, Frye, & Rapus, 1996). Although 3-year-old children can easily sort the pictures into groups on the basis of either color or shape, they almost always fail on the "switch" trials, when the rules change from sorting on the basis of shape to color (or vice versa). Instead, they continue to sort the cards as they had previously, despite being able to articulate the rule. Zelazo and his colleagues attribute this failure to 3-year-olds' inability to reflect on their knowledge, something that develops between the ages of 3 and 5 years (Zelazo et al., 1997) (see further discussion of this and related tasks in Chapter 10). Zelazo might be correct about this, but it also seems clear that one of the difficulties these young children have is inhibiting the activation of the previously correct rule (boats go here, rabbits go there), despite seemingly knowing better.

Children's ability to regulate their behavior (which involves inhibiting undesired behavior as well as executing desired behavior) improves with age (see Kochanska et al., 1996; Luria, 1961). This includes using language to guide their behavior (see Luria, 1961; Vygotsky, 1962), with young children often displaying the same problems shown by adults with frontal lesions. For example, preschool children show the same difficulty in performing tasks in which verbal instructions contradict a more salient routine as do frontal lesion patients, such as the task in which participants are to tap once each time the examiner taps twice, and tap twice each time the examiner taps once (Diamond & Taylor, 1996). Young children's difficulties inhibiting their behavior to language can be seen even in simple games such as "Simon Says." Preschool and early school-age children make many inhibitory errors in this game, making responses to verbal commands even though Simon didn't say so; simplifying the game helps, but young children still make many more inhibitory errors than older children (LaVoie et al., 1981; Reed, Pien, & Rothbart, 1984).

Children also have a difficult time inhibiting their speech. For example, in research in which children were to name out loud only certain pictures on a page (for example, animals) but not say the names of distractor items (for example, people), kindergarten children showed no evidence of inhibiting their responses. They mentioned the distractor items as frequently on trials when they were told not to mention the distractor pictures as on trials when they were told to mention them (Kipp & Pope, 1997). (This reminds me of a verbally precocious 4-year-old who was telling a story to his parents about his day at school and then, in the middle of the story, suddenly started talking about a TV show he had recently seen. The child paused briefly and then said, "Oops, I just interrupted myself." He couldn't keep the distracting thought about the TV show from intruding on his story about his day at school.)

Changes in inhibitory processes over childhood have been related to a number of cognitive tasks. For example, children's ability to selectively forget information is affected by their ability to keep the to-be-forgotten information out of mind. Older children are better able to execute these inhibitory processes than younger children are (Harnishfeger & Pope, 1996; Lehman et al., 1997; see Wilson and Kipp, 1998). Age differences in selective attention (discussed earlier in this chapter) can be explained by young children's inability to ignore task-irrelevant stimuli. Although task instructions make it clear that they are to attend only to the central stimuli and ignore peripheral stimuli, they have a difficult time doing so (see Ridderinkhof et al., 1997). And young children's difficulty in inhibiting some behaviors (such as pointing to where an object is hidden) might impede their ability to deceive others in some situations (Carlson, Moses, & Hix, 1998).

Katherine Kipp Harnishfeger and I (Bjorklund & Harnishfeger, 1990; Harnishfeger, 1995; Harnishfeger & Bjorklund, 1994) proposed a model of inefficient inhibition in working memory to account for the influence of inhibition mechanisms on cognitive development. The central idea in this model is that differences in the ability to keep task-inappropriate information out of working memory influences task performance. Harnishfeger and Bjorklund suggested that young children not only have difficulty ignoring task-irrelevant stimuli in their environment, but they also have a difficult time keeping task-irrelevant "thoughts" out of working memory. They proposed that the greater amount of task-irrelevant information in working memory for young children results in greater "cognitive clutter," which effectively reduces functional working-memory space (see Lorsbach & Reimer, 1997).

Evidence for this comes from a study by Lorsbach, Katz, and Cupak (1998). They modified a procedure initially used to assess inhibition mechanisms during text processing in younger and older adults (Hamm & Hasher, 1992). Basically, third-grade, sixth-grade, and college students heard passages that initially led to a particular interpretation (for example, Mike and his mom were watching butterflies). During the second half of the passage, the story either continued as expected or the interpretation switched (they were actually watching birds). Participants were given memory tests to determine whether or not they still had the idea of butterflies (now disconfirmed) in their minds at the end of the story. Adults were able to "forget" about the initial, now disconfirmed, interpretation (that is, butterflies), keeping this irrelevant information out of working memory. Third- and sixth-grade-children were much less likely to do this. In other words, whereas adults were able to inhibit the irrelevant interpretation (butterflies) and focus only on the relevant interpretation (birds), the children had a more difficult time inhibiting the irrelevant information, resulting in cognitive clutter in their working memory.

Frank Dempster (1992, 1993) has focused on age differences in resistance to interference, such as reflected by children's performance on selective-attention tasks and the Wisconsin Card Sorting Test, both described earlier. Dempster sees resistance to interference as a basic-level process that is central to understanding cognitive development. However, this resistance to interference is not a unitary construct. Although Dempster believes that the frontal lobes are involved in most cases of resistance

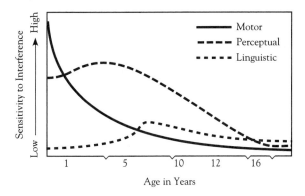

Figure 5-15 The hypothesized relationship between age and sensitivity to motor, perceptual, and linguistic interference. SOURCE: "Resistance to Interference: Developmental Changes in Basic Processing Mechanisms," by F. N. Dempster. In M. L. Howe & R. Pasnak (Eds.), *Emerging Themes in Cognitive Development, Vol. I: Foundations,* p. 19. Copyright ©1993 Springer-Verlag, New York, Inc. Reprinted with permission.

to interference, he contends that there are at least three separate types of interference phenomena, each with its own developmental course. The hypothesized relation between age and sensitivity to interference is shown in Figure 5-15 for the motor, perceptual, and verbal domains.

As can be seen from the figure, sensitivity to motor interference is greatest early in life. Such high sensitivity to motor interference would account for infants' behaviors on A-not-B object-permanence tasks (Diamond, 1985; see Chapter 2). Infants might know that an object was hidden at location B, but they cannot prevent themselves from reaching toward location A. Children's ability to inhibit responses increases over infancy and childhood, as reflected by the greater motor control children acquire during the elementary school years (which can be seen in playing a game of "Simon says," for example).

Sensitivity to perceptual interference shows a more gradual decline over late childhood and early adolescence. This, Dempster proposes, is reflected by young children's perception being stimulus bound, or, following Piaget, being perceptually centered. For example, in the conservation-of-liquid

task, preschool children cannot ignore the differences in height of the two containers. Their perception is centered on the most salient aspect of the perceptual array and they make their decisions on this aspect. According to Dempster, children during Piaget's preoperational period cannot easily resist perceptual sources of interference.

Dempster suggests that sensitivity to verbal interference remains relatively constant over development, peaking during early childhood, when language begins to play an increasingly important role in guiding problem solving (Vygotsky, 1962). This increase in sensitivity to verbal interference corresponds with the decrease seen in sensitivity to perceptual interference, suggesting a change in the underlying representational system.

Acknowledging that inhibitory processes play an important role in cognitive development seems to be an important step forward in helping us arrive at a better understanding of children's thinking. But such a perspective should be seen as supplementing information-processing views of development and not replacing them. Age changes in inhibition may *permit* certain other abilities to be expressed, but they do not seemingly *cause* them to develop. Improvements in inhibitory control may thus play a *permissive* role in cognitive development, with a certain level of inhibitory control being necessary before other specific abilities can develop.

Fuzzy-Trace Theory

Charles Brainerd and Valerie Reyna have suggested a new metaphor for cognitive development, proposing that the logical, structuralist approach of Piaget and the symbol-manipulation, "mind-like-a-computer" approach of information processing have each run their course. In their place, they suggest the metaphor of **intuitionism,** in which people prefer to think, reason, and remember by processing inexact, "fuzzy" memory representations rather than working logically from exact, verbatim representations. In a nutshell, according to Brainerd and Reyna, most cognition is intuitive, in that it is based on "fuzzy representations (senses, patterns, gists) in

CARTOON 5-1   Young children often have a difficult time not saying whatever is on their minds. SOURCE: Reprinted with special permission of King Features Syndicate.

combination with construction rules that operate on those representations" (Brainerd & Reyna, 1993, p. 50). Brainerd and Reyna refer to their approach as **fuzzy-trace theory** and have applied it to a wide range of cognitive contents (Brainerd & Reyna, 1992, 1993; Reyna & Brainerd, 1995).

Fuzzy-trace theory makes several basic assumptions about aspects of cognitive processing, as well as about how these aspects of processing vary with development. I will first mention each of the assumptions and then discuss how they relate to cognitive development. Table 5-1 outlines these assumptions.[2]

Assumptions of Fuzzy-Trace Theory

At the core of fuzzy-trace theory is the idea that memory representations (or memory traces) exist on a continuum from literal, verbatim representations to fuzzy, imprecise, gistlike traces. Take, for example, a transitive-inference problem in which children are shown a series of sticks varying in length. Stick A is 20 centimeters long, stick B is 20.5 centimeters long, and stick C is 21 centimeters long. The chil-

dren are shown each of two adjacent pairs of sticks (A and B; B and C) and asked to judge which item of each pair is longer. They then are asked to decide whether stick A or stick C is longer, without having seen these two particular sticks together and without being allowed to make a visual comparison of their lengths. Verbatim traces would correspond to the actual lengths of the sticks (expressed, perhaps, in the form of visual images). Fuzzy or gistlike traces would be of a less exact form, such as "C is long, B is not long and not short, A is short" or "The sticks get taller to my right." Either of these forms of representation can be used to solve the problem. Fuzzy-trace theory poses such questions as these: Which representation is cognitively easier? Which representations do people actually use? and, important for us, What develops?

An important assumption in fuzzy-trace theory is the idea that gist can exist at several different levels for the same information (for example, "A is short, C is long" and "The sticks get taller to my right"), and a single event will be represented in short-term memory by a variety of traces, from exact **verbatim**

TABLE 5.1 Some assumptions of fuzzy-trace theory and their relation to cognitive development[2]

---

1. Gist extraction and the fuzzy-to-verbatim continuua

Basic Assumption: People extract fuzzy, gist-like information from the stimuli and events they experience, following the *reduction to essence* rule. Traces for an event exist on a fuzzy-to-verbatim continuum. At one extreme are fuzzy traces that are vague, degenerated representations that maintain only the sense or pattern of recently encoded information. At the other extreme are verbatim traces, that are elaborated, exact representations of the recently encoded information.

Age Differences: Young children's memory is specialized for encoding and processing verbatim information; with age, their ability to extract gist improves.

2. Fuzzy-processing preference (intuition)

Basic Assumption: People prefer to reason, think, and remember intuitively, processing fuzzy rather than verbatim traces.

Age Differences: There is a shift in the reliance on verbatim and gist traces, sometime during the elementary school years, with children becoming increasing facile processing gist traces. Processing of verbatim traces declines in efficiency during adolescence.

3. Output interference

Basic Assumption: As people make responses, output interference occurs and interferes with subsequent processing.

Age Differences: Young children are more sensitive to the effects of output interference than older children or adults.

---

traces to a variety of inexact **fuzzy traces**. Moreover, these various traces are independent of one another. That is, gist traces are not simply the result of the deterioration of verbatim traces.

A central assumption of fuzzy-trace theory is that people of all ages prefer to use fuzzy traces when solving problems, although this preference does vary with age (see later). Brainerd and Reyna refer to this as the **reduction to essence rule.** Fuzzy traces cannot always be used to solve a problem, but, according to Brainerd and Reyna (1990), "it is a natural habit of mind to process traces that are as near to the fuzzy ends of fuzzy-to-verbatim continua as pos-

sible" (p. 9). In other words, there is a bias in human cognition toward thinking and solving problems intuitively rather than logically.

Fuzzy and verbatim traces differ in important ways. First of all, relative to verbatim traces, fuzzy traces are more easily accessed and generally require less effort to use. Also, verbatim traces are more susceptible to interference and forgetting than fuzzy traces. For example, when a shopper is comparing the prices of two sweaters at two stores, he or she will quickly forget the exact prices of the sweaters. More resistant to forgetting, however, will be the less-precise information that the sweater at Sears was cheaper than the comparable sweater at J.C. Penney. If your problem is to decide which sweater is the better buy, you can rely on the degraded, fuzzy knowledge of the relative prices of the two sweaters. If, however, you are required to write a check for one of the sweaters, you will need the verbatim information, and in that case it would be helpful if you wrote the price down, for it is unlikely that you will have remembered the exact price.

A final assumption of fuzzy-trace theory has to do with the role of **output interference** and how it varies with development. Brainerd and Reyna hold that the act of making responses produces output interference that hinders subsequent performance. This is similar to the theorizing of Dempster (1993) discussed with respect to inhibition and interference approaches to cognitive development. According to Brainerd and Reyna, output interference occurs in two forms: scheduling effects and feedback effects. Scheduling effects are caused by the serial nature of response systems. Although people can perform several different cognitive operations simultaneously (that is, in parallel), responses are made serially. This leads to a parallel-to-serial bottleneck at output, or response competition, with the various possible responses competing for priority of execution. Once a response is made, Brainerd and Reyna propose, irrelevant feedback is generated "that reverberates through the systems, degrading performance as it goes ... [and] introducing noise into working memory" (1990, p. 29). These researchers theorize that the "noise" in working memory competes with task-relevant information, reducing performance;

this is similar to what the inhibition theorists (Bjorklund & Harnishfeger, 1990; Hasher & Zacks, 1988) propose.

Developmental Differences

How does processing of fuzzy and verbatim traces vary with development? Fuzzy-trace theory makes specific predictions, some of which have been confirmed by research. First, there are age differences in gist extraction. Early in life, children are biased toward storing and retrieving verbatim traces. They do extract gist, of course, but relative to older children and adults, young children are biased toward the verbatim end of the continuum. A verbatim → gist shift occurs sometime during the early elementary school years, with children now showing a gist bias. Thus, the memory system for processing verbatim information should develop earlier than the system for processing fuzzy, gistlike information. Moreover, the memory system used for processing verbatim information should decline relatively early in development, likely during adolescence or young adulthood.

Evidence from a variety of sources supports the idea that preschool and early school-age children are more biased toward encoding and remembering verbatim traces, whereas older children, like adults, are more prone to encode and remember gist traces (Brainerd & Gordon, 1994; Marx & Henderson, 1996). For example, in research by Brainerd and Gordon (1994), preschool and second-grade children were given simple numerical problems. In one problem, children were given the following background information: "Farmer Brown owns many animals. He owns 3 dogs, 5 sheep, 7 chickens, 9 horses, and 11 cows." They were then asked a series of questions, some requiring verbatim knowledge for their correct answer, such as "How many cows does Farmer Brown own, 11 or 9?" and others requiring only gist information, such as "Which of Farmer Brown's animals are the most, cows or horses?" The results of this experiment are shown in Figure 5-16. They found that preschool children were better at remembering the verbatim numbers than the numerical gist, whereas the reverse was true for second-graders.

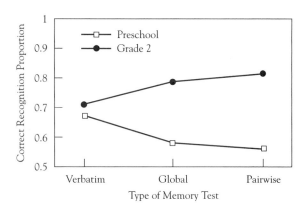

FIGURE 5-16   Proportion of correct recognition responses for verbatim, global, and pairwise problems for preschool and grade-2 children. SOURCE: Brainerd, C. J., & Gordon, L. L. (1994). Development of verbatim and gist memory for numbers. *Developmental Psychology, 30*, 163–177.

Consistent with the theorizing of the inhibition and resistance to interference theorists discussed earlier (Harnishfeger & Bjorklund, 1993; Dempster, 1993), age differences have been found in sensitivity to output interference, with younger children being more adversely affected than older children. Recent support for this contention has come from studies of selective attention (for example, Ridderinkhof et al., 1997), including tasks that have used developmental differences in evoked brain potentials on tasks involving interference (Ridderinkhof & van der Molen, 1995). One reason for young children's greater interference sensitivity is their reliance on verbatim traces, which are more susceptible to interference than fuzzy traces.

Fuzzy-trace theory has been useful in explaining some phenomena in the child developmental literature, among them the often inconsistent findings in research examining reasoning-remembering relationships and age differences in eyewitness testimony and suggestibility. These will each be discussed in later chapters. In addition, fuzzy trace theory has also predicted and discovered at least one new phenomenon. On free-recall tests with repeated trials, subjects tend to recall words with weaker memory representations (words that have not been recalled frequently before) before recalling words with stronger representations (words that have been recalled frequently before), and this effect varies with age. This pattern is opposite both to common sense and predictions made by standard information-processing theory, yet is explained by Brainerd and Reyna's *cognitive triage theory*, which is a subtheory within fuzzy-trace theory (Reyna & Brainerd, 1995; Brainerd et al., 1994; Harnishfeger & Brainerd, 1994). Without going into detail about the theory here, suffice it to say that cognitive triage explains this phenomenon chiefly by output interference effects in interaction with the strengths of the memory traces. The ability of a theory to predict new and often counterintuitive phenomena is often used as a yardstick of that theory's scientific merit, and although the phenomenon that cognitive triage explains might not be as pragmatically important as explaining age differences in eyewitness suggestibility, it certainly enhances the credibility of the theory.

Connectionist Perspective of Developmental Change

During the past two decades, psychologists have come increasingly to use computer simulations to test their theories. The use of computer simulations in cognitive psychology is not new. For a long time, it has been recognized that being able to simulate a phenomenon means that one must define quite precisely the various factors believed to be involved in any form of processing, resulting in a better (more detailed) model (see Elman et al., 1996; Klahr & MacWhinney, 1998). However, a particular type of modeling, which has implications for how we view the relation between innate and environmental factors in development, has emerged: **connectionist models**. Connectionist models, often referred to as *neural networks*, or *parallel distributed processing* (PDP) networks, attempt to simulate aspects of neural (that is, brain) processing. At their heart, connectionist models are *associationistic models*, with connections between individual units being the basis for computations (just as connections between

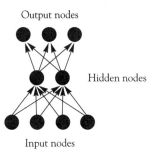

FIGURE 5-17 A simplified connectionist network with four input nodes, two "hidden" nodes, and three output nodes.

individual neurons are the basis of processing in the nervous system). Units (or nodes) in a connectionist network can be of different types. First, there are input nodes that receive information from some external source. Other nodes may receive input only from other nodes (just as interneurons receive input only from other neurons). Output nodes "produce a response." Connections between nodes can be excitatory (when node *a* activates node *b*, node *b* increases in its energy level) or inhibitory (when node *a* activates node *b*, node *b* decreases in its energy level). Different nodes can have different *weights*, such that more or less energy (activation from other nodes) is required for it to become active. These weights can change as a function of "experience" (that is, the history of patterns of activation that nodes receive). Figure 5-17 shows a very simple connectionist network. Unlike other computer simulations that involve symbol manipulation, processing is performed in parallel in connectionist networks, with many nodes being activated at any one time.

So how can a model that consists only of connections among simple nodes tell us anything about development and how nature and nurture interact in development? (For more detailed descriptions see, Elman et al., 1996 and Plunkett et al., 1997.) First, a connectionist model starts out with a certain *architecture*—a set of nodes, some inhibitory and some excitatory—that relate the input the model receives (that is, "experience") to the output the model produces (that is, a response to a certain task). This beginning architecture can be thought of as corresponding to what a child brings into the world (or brings to a particular task). It might, for example, be structured so that it responds to objects that move at a certain frequency, or to regularities observed when hearing a series of past-tense verbs (most, in English, have an "ed" added to the end of the root verb).

But if a connectionist system is only a specified architecture, there is no development. The architecture would dictate the relation between the input and output (perhaps with many different layers of intervening nodes), and that would be that. What is crucial in any connectionist network are *learning algorithms*. These learning algorithms change the architecture as a result of the experiences (the pattern of activation) the system receives. In other words, connectionist systems learn by changing the architecture (analogous to changing the brain). They have rules that dictate how changes in the input and the output are related. Connectionist systems are usually *trained*. That is, they are given some input, make some output, and then receive feedback about the correctness of their response. For example, if a connectionist system were to simulate performance on an A-not-B object permanence task, the system would get positive feedback if it "searched" in the B location on the critical B trial, but get negative feedback if its output was to search at the previous A location. A successful simulation will mirror how real children solve the problem. That is, the simulation should initially make perseverative errors on the A-not-B task, show the same pattern of errors infants make (for example, make different responses under different conditions of delay), and eventually make the correct response. To do this, the model must have one architecture at the beginning and a different one at the end that is like the mental architecture of the younger and older infant, respectively, and a learning algorithm that matches, at some level, the process of learning infants go through as they gradually come to solve the A-not-B problem. Of course, just because the computer programmer was smart enough to write a program that mimics how infants solve these problems doesn't mean that that's the way infants actually do it, but it's an impressive start.

One very important aspect of connectionist models is that they are a bit unpredictable. This is because the architecture and learning rules interact such that they produce *emergent properties*. Depending on the initial architecture, the learning rules, and the information the network receives, different architectures and different patterns of responses will emerge, just as individual differences in children's responses to any task will differ as a function of individual biological and experiential differences. Such emergent properties often take the form of what developmentalists have traditionally viewed as stage transitions, with relatively abrupt changes over a brief period of time. However, such changes can also be viewed as examples of *nonlinear change*, so that changes in a target behavior do not show gradual, incremental changes over time but, rather, demonstrate a rapid change in the target behavior over relatively brief periods (such as the rapid increase in children's vocabularies sometime during their second and third years).

What connectionist models do is avoid the idea of innate concepts or ideas (representational innateness). Rather, what is innate is the general architecture and some basic learning algorithms (architectural innateness), which might be, as the neo-nativists propose, domain specific, but not necessarily. But, unlike neo-nativists (for example, Spelke & Newport, 1998), they do not propose that children are born with specific concepts.

Connectionist models have been applied quite successfully to several areas of development (see Elman et al., 1996; Plunkett et al., 1997), but have been especially influential in the study of language development. Here, connectionist accounts of language development are contrasted with more "traditional" explanations offered by Chomsky and his followers, which take a decidedly nativist account (see discussion of these different approaches in Chapter 9). I provide no more than this brief sketch of connectionist models here, although the result of several connectionist models will be discussed later in Chapter 9 on language development. I introduce it here only to demonstrate a new and potentially valuable tool to assess developmental change, and one that purports to be able to "explain" some of the new evidence of symbolic sophistication in infants and young children (to be discussed in Chapters 6 and 7) without having to resort to the concept of representational innateness.

Summary

Information-processing approaches to the study of cognition emphasize the flow of information through processing systems; the system is seen as having a *limited capacity* for how much information children can hold and how quickly and elaborately children can process information. Cognitive operations are conceptualized as existing on a continuum with *automatic*, or effortless, *processes* at one extreme and strategic, or *effortful processes* at the other. Information-processing theories are concerned with the acquisition and manipulation of knowledge. *Declarative* knowledge, or memory, which includes *episodic* and *semantic memory*, is proposed to be available to consciousness (*explicit*), and is often contrasted with *nondeclarative*, or *procedural*, knowledge, or memory, which is unavailable to consciousness (*implicit*).

Minimal age differences in the actual capacity of the *sensory registers* and the *short-term store* have been found, although differences in the use of strategies, and especially in the *speed of processing*, have been found to account for much of the developmental difference in cognitive task performance.

Age differences in *efficiency of processing*, rather than absolute differences in capacity, have been proposed to account for developmental differences in children's thinking. Older children require less *operating space* for the execution of cognitive processes than younger children, leaving more *storage space* available or more space available for the execution of other cognitive operations.

Children's *strategies* have been extensively examined in *training studies*, in which young children who do not use a strategy spontaneously are instructed to use one. A three-stage sequence has been suggested. The earliest stage is represented by children who cannot benefit from strategic instruction; these children are said to illustrate a *mediational deficiency*. Slightly older children can benefit from a strategy when instructed but do not produce one spontaneously; they have a *production deficiency*. In the final stage, children generate a strategy spontaneously and use it to facilitate performance. More recent work has indicated that even production-deficient children use strategies spontaneously, although these strategies are not very sophisticated and might not facilitate performance. A new deficiency (a *utilization deficiency*) has recently been identified in children who use a strategy without experiencing any benefit from its use. Children actually use a variety of different strategies to solve any given problem, and such multiple- and variable-strategy use is explained by Siegler's *adaptive strategy choice model*.

It is becoming increasingly clear that what children know, or their *knowledge base*, plays an important role in how they process information. Recent data indicate that the child's domain-specific knowledge, acquired continuously throughout development, accounts for many of the adult/child differences observed in cognition.

Selective attention has most often been studied using *incidental learning* tasks. Older children are better able to ignore incidental information than are younger children, with this developmental trend reversing in old age. Developmental differences in *attentional strategies* have also been found, with young children being less systematic in their visual inspection of objects than older children.

Theories postulating age-related changes in *inhibition* and *resistance to interference* propose that infants' and children's inabilities to inhibit responses or to resist internal and external sources of interference contribute significantly to cognitive development. Neurological evidence suggests that development of the frontal lobes is important in the development of inhibition and resistance-to-interference. Several researchers have presented evidence of age-related changes in inhibition and resistance-to-interference and propose that these differences account for development on a wide range of cognitive tasks, including selective attention, memory, and verbal tasks.

Brainerd and Reyna's *fuzzy-trace theory* suggests *intuitionism* as a metaphor for cognition. Fuzzy-trace theory assumes that memory representations exist on a continuum from *verbatim* to *fuzzy*, or *gistlike traces*. People generally prefer to think with fuzzy as opposed to verbatim traces, but this develops, with young children showing more of a verbatim bias than older children. Processing of verbatim traces is relatively good in young children but declines in efficiency during adolescence. Fuzzy-trace theory assumes that *output interference*, resulting from scheduling effects and feedback effects, causes deterioration of performance and that younger children are more susceptible to the effects of output interference than older children or adults.

Connectionist models are computer models that simulate aspects of development through repeated activation of associated nodes. Connectionist models begin with learning algorithms and a certain architecture (meant to be analogous to brain structure) that is modified through "experience." These models have been successful in modeling certain aspects of development (particularly language development), and purport to be able to "explain" some of the new evidence of symbolic sophistication in infants and young children without having to resort to the concept of representational innateness.

Notes

1. The perspective that I've presented in this chapter could be considered to reflect the "soft-core" approach of information processing. It takes the "mind-as-a-computer" metaphor loosely and proposes that cognitive development involves changes in what and how (and how quickly) children process information. I have not taken a "hard-core" perspective of information processing, one that uses various types of computer simulations and formal models to describe and explain cognitive development (Klahr & MacWhinney, 1998). From my point of view, the formal modeling of cognitive development is an important tool, and developmental scientists who do such modeling make important contributions to our understanding of children's intellectual development. However, in a book that is already too long as far as my editor is concerned, I decided not to discuss these models here, with the exception of a short section on connectionist modeling at the end of the chapter.

The interested reader is referred to an excellent chapter by David Klahr and Brian MacWhinney (1998).

2. A fourth assumption of fuzzy trace theory is that short-term memory is reconstructive. However, because the theory predicts few developmental differences in reconstructive processes, this aspect of the theory will not be discussed here.

Key Terms and Concepts

limited capacity
multistore models
sensory registers
short-term store
long-term store
declarative memory
explicit memory
episodic memory
semantic memory
nondeclarative, or procedural memory
implicit memory
automatic processes
effortful processes
executive function
metacognition
memory span
working memory
articulatory loop
speed of processing
storage space
operating space
total processing space
strategies
training studies
mediational deficiency
production deficiency
utilization deficiency
adaptive strategy choice model
microgenetic method
knowledge base
paired-associates task
elaboration strategy
selective attention
incidental learning
meta-attention
inhibition
resistance to interference
fuzzy-trace theory
intuitionism
verbatim traces
fuzzy traces
reduction to essence rule
output interference
connectionist models

Suggested Readings

BJORKLUND, D. F., & MILLER, P. H. (Eds.) (1997). New themes in strategy development. Special Issue of *Developmental Review*, 17, December issue. This special edition of the journal *Developmental Review* contains state-of-the-art summaries of research in children's strategy development, including an article by Bjorklund, Miller, and colleagues looking at utilization deficiencies, one by Robert Siegler and colleagues presenting an updated version of his strategy choice model, and articles looking at longitudinal studies of strategy use, computer models of strategy use, and children's strategy use from a sociocultural perspective.

KEE, D. W. (1994). Developmental differences in associative memory: Strategy use, mental effort, and knowledge-access interactions. In H. W. Reese (Ed.), *Advances in Child Development and Behavior* (Vol. 25). San Diego: Academic Press. This chapter provides an excellent review of research looking at the interaction of knowledge, mental effort, and strategy use in development.

KAIL, R. V., & SALTHOUSE, T. A. (1994). Processing speed as a mental capacity. *Acta Psychologica*, 86, 199–225. This article presents research and theory relating to age differences in speed of processing, both over childhood and into old age, and the developmental relation between speed of processing and performance on a host of cognitive tasks.

HARNISHFEGER, K. K. (1995). The development of cognitive inhibition: Theories, definitions, and research evidence. In F. Dempster & C. Brainerd (Eds.), *New perspectives on interference and inhibition in cognition.* New York: Academic Press. Harnishfeger reviews theory and research dealing with age differences in inhibition and resistance to interference and how these processes relate to cognitive development.

REYNA, V. F., & BRAINERD, C. J. (1995). Fuzzy-trace theory: An interim synthesis. *Learning and Individual Differences*, 3, 27–59. This article presents a state-of-the art summary of fuzzy-trace theory by the theory's originators.

PLUNKETT, K., KARMILOFF-SMITH, A., BATES, E., ELMAN, J. L., & JOHNSON, M. H. (1997). Connectionism and developmental psychology. *Journal of Child Psychology and Psychiatry*, 38, 53–80. This article presents a relatively high-level introduction to connectionism and developmental psychology. For an expanded view, see Elman et al. (1996), *Rethinking Innateness*, in the recommended readings of Chapter 1.

Perception

All cognition begins in perception. Before we can make comparisons between two objects, categorize sets of items, retrieve a fact, or create an image, we must have the basic data from the external world with which to work. We can, of course, think about things without the need of actually perceiving the things we think about. We can create mental images of objects we've never seen (or that never existed) and auditory images of sounds we've never actually heard. Cognition is thus not a simple extension of perception. Nevertheless, most of what we think about consists of objects, words, or other messages that we received, in one form or another, through our senses.

Early developmental research in perception dealt with issues of basic sensory abilities (for example, whether babies can see and hear). Research questions have expanded during the past 40 years, however. How is it that infants learn to discriminate the sounds of their language? What perceptual biases, if any, are they born with that make the learning process easier? How do infants come to recognize their mothers and, eventually, other people? How do they categorize experience? These questions deal with perception during infancy, and although perceptual development over the course of childhood has not been ignored by developmental psychologists (see Gibson & Spelke, 1983), most research in the area has focused on the infant. Because of the wealth of information that has accumulated dealing with infant perception, the first and larger part of this chapter deals exclusively with perception during infancy, beginning with the neonate. The second part of the chapter examines perceptual development over the course of childhood. I will also examine developmental and gender differences in spatial cognition, a topic that perhaps more properly belongs in a chapter called "Cognition," but one, nonetheless, that is closely associated with visual perception.

Perceptual Development Through Infancy

Perceptual functioning in human infants is viewed today as an active process. Remember throughout this chapter that the infant is an active participant in the process of acquiring and interpreting perceptual information. Also keep in mind that infants are learning through their sensory perceptions. They are gaining knowledge, and this knowledge is being added to and is transforming their prior knowledge.

Basic Perceptual Abilities of Young Infants

For much of this century, many psychologists and physicians viewed young infants as passive nonperceivers, who were totally oblivious to their surroundings. In the past 30 years, we have learned much about the perceptual abilities of infants and realize that this view is greatly overstated. Newborns are far from mental giants, but they do enter the world able to perceive information with all their senses. Furthermore, babies have some perceptual biases. Some sights, sounds, and smells are innately more pleasing to them than others, and they learn to prefer other sensations in the first weeks of life.

Most research on infant perceptual development has been done on audition (hearing) and vision. This is due, in part, to the importance of these two senses for human information processing and to the fact that, vision in particular, shows substantial development over the first year of life. The chemical senses (olfaction and taste) and skin and body orientation senses tend to develop early, and, in fact, are quite well developed shortly after (and even before) birth. For example, babies can discriminate among a wide variety of odors early in life (Steiner, 1979), and they develop preferences for certain odors within the first week. In a study by Macfarlane (1975), for example, 6-day-old nursing babies were able to discriminate the odor of their mothers from those of other women. Mothers wore breast pads in their bras between nursings. Two breast pads—one from the baby's mother and the other from another woman—were placed on either side of an infant's head. Although there were no differences in infants' behaviors in this situation at 2 days of age, by day 6 babies were turning to their own mother's pad more often than to the pad of another woman. That is, not only can babies discriminate odors, they quickly learn to make associations with odors and to modify their behavior accordingly. In more recent work using a procedure similar to that of Macfarlane, researchers reported that infants develop a preference for the odor of milk versus amniotic fluid (which they had been living in for 9 months) by 4 days (Marlier, Schaal, & Soussignan, 1998), and that bottle-fed, 2-week-old infants preferred the breast odor of a lactating female to that of a nonlactating female (Makin & Porter, 1989).

Some Methodologies Used to Assess Infant Perception

How can a psychologist tell if an infant can see or hear something? That is, how can we determine if an infant can tell the difference between a bull's-eye and a checkerboard pattern, for example, or between her mother's voice and that of another woman? This basic problem hampered serious investigation of infants' perceptual and cognitive abilities for years, but the solution is really quite simple. What one must do is to find some behavior that an infant controls and use that behavior as an entry into what babies can perceive. For example, in the research just presented, researchers took advantage of babies' abilities to turn their heads in one direction or another to determine if they could discriminate and develop a preference for certain odors (Macfarlane, 1975).

The first and simplest technique to test infants' *visual* discrimination abilities was developed by Robert Fantz (1958, 1961). He placed alert babies in a looking chamber. Series of visual stimuli were placed in front of infants' eyes, and an observer peeking through a hole in the chamber above the infant recorded which stimuli the baby looked at the most. If groups of infants spend significantly more time gazing at one pattern than another, it can be assumed that they can differentiate between the two patterns and prefer to look at one relative to the other. If they couldn't tell the difference between the paired stimuli, there would be no difference in their looking behavior. Using this **visual preference paradigm,** Fantz was able to show that babies less than 1-week old can tell the difference between stimuli such as a schematic face, a bull's-eye pattern, and an unpatterned disk (see Figure 6-1).

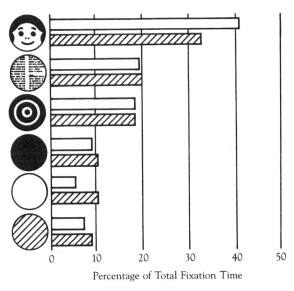

Percentage of Total Fixation Time

☐ Infants older than 3 months

▨ Infants 2 to 3 months old

FIGURE 6-1   Infants' visual attention to different patterns. SOURCE: "The Origin of Form Perception," by R. L. Fantz, 1961, *Scientific American, 204,* 66-72. Copyright © 1961 Scientific American, Inc. All rights reserved. Reprinted with permission.

Another behavior that very young infants can control is sucking. How might researchers use this behavior to tell if babies can discriminate between two different auditory signals? Anthony DeCasper and Melanie Spence (1986) used infants' ability to regulate their sucking to ask just this question, and whether infants were learning something about the outside world while still in utero. DeCasper and Spence asked pregnant women to read aloud one of three passages twice a day during the last six weeks of their pregnancies. Shortly after birth, the neonates were tested for which passages, if any, would have more reinforcing value. Headphones were placed over the babies' ears, and various passages were played to the infants. Nonnutritive sucking (that is, sucking on a pacifier) was assessed as a function of which passage was being played. First of all, a baseline sucking rate was determined for each baby (that is, how rapidly the infant sucked on a nipple when no passage was being played). The babies then heard a familiar passage (the one their mothers had read during pregnancy) or a novel passage (one their mothers had not read) as a function of changes in their sucking rate. For some infants, an increase in sucking rate was associated with the familiar passage, and a decrease in sucking rate was associated with the novel passage. The contingency was reversed for other infants. The general finding was that the familiar passage was more reinforcing than the novel passage. That is, infants were more likely to alter their sucking rate to hear the familiar passage than to hear the novel passage. Furthermore, the reinforcing value of the passage was independent of who recited it, an infant's mother or another woman. These results present unambiguous evidence of prenatal conditioning to auditory patterns. The infants were able to discern the auditory characteristics of these often-repeated passages, and the researchers were able to determine this by associating the various passages with changes in a behavior that infants could control themselves, that is, sucking rate.

A somewhat more complicated procedure is often used to evaluate infants' perception, memory, and concepts, and this is the *habituation/dishabituation* paradigm. **Habituation** refers to the decrease in response as a result of repeated presentation of a stimulus. The first day on the job in a noisy factory, for example, produces increased levels of physiological stress (heart rate, blood pressure). After a week in this environment, however, levels of stress decline, even though the noise remains. This is habituation. **Dishabituation** (sometimes referred to as release from habituation) occurs when, following habituation, a new stimulus is presented that increases our level of responding. If we switch from factory A to factory B, for instance, our levels of physiological stress rise, even though the new factory is no louder than the old one. The noises are different, causing an increase in responding, or a release from habituation.

How does this phenomenon relate to infant perception? The amount of time babies look at visual stimuli (or orient to auditory stimuli) is analogous to the worker's physiological reactions to loud noise. The longer infants are exposed to a visual stimulus, the less time they spend looking at it. Habituation is said to occur when an infant's looking time is signif-

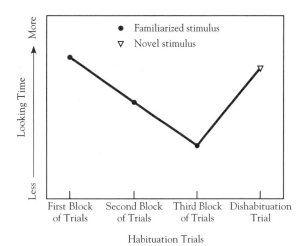

FIGURE 6-2   An example of results from a habituation/dishabituation experiment on infant visual attention. The amount of looking time decreases with repeated presentation of the same stimulus (habituation) but increases with the presentation of a new stimulus (dishabituation).

icantly less than it was initially (often defined as when visual fixation to the stimulus is 50% of what it was on the early trials). At that point, a new stimulus is presented. If attention (that is, looking time) increases from the level of immediately before, dishabituation is said to occur. A typical habituation/dishabituation curve is shown in Figure 6-2.

What does such a pattern mean? First, it demonstrates that infants can discriminate between the two stimuli. Babies might not have a preference for one over the other, but that they respond to the new stimulus with increased attention indicates that they can tell the difference between the two. This paradigm is very useful in determining infants' discrimination abilities when researchers are using stimuli for which babies might not have a decided preference.

Habituation and dishabituation also indicate memory. Infants are making a discrimination between one stimulus that is physically present and another that is present only in memory. They are not choosing between two stimuli that are before them but between one stimulus that is in front of their eyes and another that is only in their minds.

Using this procedure, evidence of habituation/dishabituation (and thus rudimentary memory) has been found for newborns (Friedman, 1972; Slater et al., 1985; Slater et al., 1991), and even in 32-week-old fetuses for vibroacoustic stimuli (Sandman et al., 1997). In one of the first studies to demonstrate this in newborns, Friedman (1972) habituated 1- to 3-day-old infants to one visual pattern and then, immediately after habituation, showed the babies a novel pattern. These neonates displayed the classic increase in responding to the new stimulus, indicative of memory (be it ever so brief).

One word of caution about Friedman's results is in order, however. Of 90 newborns initially tested, 50 were excluded for reasons such as crying and falling asleep. Of the 40 remaining, only 29 displayed dishabituation. Thus, only 32% of the original sample demonstrated the habituation/dishabituation phenomenon. Drop-out rates have been lower in some more recent studies (for example, of the 34 newborns tested by Slater et al. (1991), only 10 (29%) were excluded for fussiness and related problems). The high drop-out rate calls into question the generalizability of Friedman's (and others') findings. What Friedman's results indicate is that memory is within the capability of many human newborns, although the possibility exists that many infants do not possess such memory until several weeks after birth.

These are not the only methods used to assess infant perception. But these methodologies have been used for more than 30 years to evaluate what babies can perceive and what they know, and most of the research reviewed in this chapter, and much discussed in the next, used variants of these well-developed techniques.

Auditory Development

Homo sapiens, as other primates, is a visual species. However, we also depend on hearing for acquiring much information about our world. Although language can be transmitted through visual signs, the primary means of communication involves audition, and deaf children often experience significant retardation if they do not learn language through an alternate means (sign language) early in life (Sacks, 1989).

Auditory perception is well developed in the newborn. Sound is perceived in utero, and there is evidence that loud noises result in changes in the heart rates of 7-month-old fetuses (Bernard & Sontag, 1947). Infants appear to be more sensitive to high-frequency than to low-frequency tones (Trehub, Schneider, & Endman, 1980), and this might explain their seeming preference for the voices of women. As with smell, infants less than 1 week old have been shown to recognize their mothers on the basis of sound (DeCasper & Fifer, 1980; Spence & Freeman, 1996). For example, DeCasper and Fifer (1980) measured the rate at which 1- to 3-day-old infants sucked on a pacifier. Then they conditioned the babies to alter their sucking rate (faster for half of the babies and slower for the other half) to the tape-recorded voices of their mothers and of an unfamiliar woman. DeCasper and Fifer reported that these young infants varied their sucking rates to hear their mothers' voices, indicating that they not only could discriminate the voices of their mothers from that of another woman but also acquired a distinct preference for the voices of their mothers in a matter of days.

I noted in the preceding section that infants who heard stories being read to them by their mothers during the last six weeks of pregnancy were able to discriminate between that story and another, and preferred the one their mother had read to them (DeCasper & Spence, 1986). These findings indicate not only that the auditory system in newborns is working well but also that babies are learning some things about the outside world while still in utero. Moreover, more recent research following the same design as DeCasper and Spence used reported changes in heart rate to familiar and novel passages among third trimester fetuses, unambiguously indicating that learning occurs before birth (DeCasper et al., 1994).

Speech Perception

One particularly interesting aspect of infant auditory perception is the extent to which it is attuned to language. The basic units of speech are called **phonemes,** and evidence indicates that infants come into the world with the ability to perceive most, if not all, of the phonemes found in all human languages (see Aslin, Jusczyk, & Pisoni, 1998), suggesting substantial biological preparation for infants to learn language (but see Kuhl, 1987 for a counter interpretation).

Like colors, phonemes (such as "ba" and "pa") can be arranged on continuums, with gradual changes between them. For example, there is a range of sounds that we hear as "pa" and another range that we hear as "ba." Despite this continuum, we categorize phonemes into distinct groups. For example, we tend to hear either a "pa" sound or a "ba" sound, and not some hybrid of the two of them. And most of us agree on the point at which "ba" ends and "pa" begins, just like we agree on the division between orange and red. The gradual changes in phonemes (and in colors) are considered physical, and the dichotomies we perceive are considered perceptual.

Peter Eimas and his colleagues (1971) presented 1-month-old infants with one physical example of the "ba/pa" continuum until they had decreased the rate at which they sucked on a pacifier (habituation). The researchers then replaced the phoneme with another example along the "ba/pa" continuum. If the infants perceive the new sound as being from the same phonemic category as the previous sound (both "ba," for instance), they should continue to habituate (that is, decrease their sucking). This is because even though the sound is physically different from the one they heard before, it is just another example of the sound they had just heard repeatedly (that is, just another "ba"). If, however, they recognize this new sound as being from a different phonemic category (a "pa" rather than a "ba," for example), they should increase their sucking rate (dishabituation). Using this technique, Eimas and his colleagues found that very young infants, like their parents and older siblings who already possess language, can categorize phonemes. They hear either "ba" or "pa," and the dividing line they make between the two is the same as older members of their species make.

Other studies have used reinforcement techniques to assess infants' abilities to discriminate among phonemes. For example, Marean, Werner, and Kuhl (1992) reinforced 2-, 3-, and 6-month-old infants by the activation of a mechanical toy for turning their head when they heard a change from one vowel sound to another (either "A" to "I" or vice versa). This technique showed that even 2-month-olds were able to make the discrimination, despite changes in other auditory characteristics (that is, in the voice of the individual speaking). In related work, there is evidence that infants form *prototypes,* or "best examples," for sound categories. Infants identify vowel sounds representing a range of "good" examples of a vowel prototype while not identifying "less good" examples of the same vowels (Grieser & Kuhl, 1989).

If infants can discriminate basic phonemes shortly after birth, how is it they acquire the language sounds peculiar to their mother tongue? English-speaking adults have a difficult time discriminating phonetic contrasts that occur in Czech but that are not found in English. Yet, babies from English-speaking homes have little difficulty with these contrasts, suggesting that they were born with the ability (Trehub, 1976). Other studies have similarly shown that infants can make discriminations among speech sounds that are not found in their mother tongues and that their parents cannot make (Lasky, Syrdal-Lasky, & Klein, 1975; Werker et al., 1981). In other research, Eilers and her colleagues reported that 6- to 8-month-old infants from English-speaking homes were unable to discriminate some phonetic contrasts that are found in Spanish but not in English (Eilers, Gavin, & Wilson, 1979). Babies from homes where Spanish was spoken had no trouble with such contrasts. What these and other data suggest is that babies can make some sound discriminations that adult speakers of their language communities cannot make; with time, babies lose the ability to make these contrasts because they rarely hear them (see Colombo, 1986; Walley, Pisoni, & Aslin, 1981). Why should children lose this seemingly valuable ability? The flexibility to learn the sounds of any possible human language has a great adaptive advantage, of course, but keeping this flexibility, in our ancient past, likely was not. Once our ancestors learned one language, there was likely little need (or opportunity) to become proficient in another language. Thus, it makes more sense for the brain to dedicate neurons to processing the sounds it hears early in life. The alternative would give individuals more flexibility, but likely less proficiency in perceiving or producing any one language.

Speech perception is more than the ability to detect phonemes, of course, but involves the discrimination of individual words. And perhaps the word that young infants hear most frequently is their own name. Mandel, Jusczyk, and Pisoni (1995) asked "at what age can infants recognize the sound of their own name?" They used a reinforcement technique (infants turned their heads to hear a name spoken, either their own or one of three other names) to test this. Infants 4.5 months old spent more time listening to their own name than to other names, regardless of whether the other names had the same stress pattern as their own (for example, "Johnny" versus "Abby") or a different stress pattern (for example, "Johnny" versus "Elaine"). These findings indicate that infants are able to recognize frequently heard sound patterns at least by 4.5 months of age.

Music Perception

Although humans are especially prepared biologically to process language, we also seem to be well prepared to process music. For example, there is some evidence that young infants can imitate the pitch, loudness, melodic contour, and rhythm of their mothers' songs (see Gardner, 1983). Moreover, specific types of brain damage affect musical abilities, suggesting that the ability to perceive and produce music is rooted in evolution and biology (Gardner, 1983).

Many aspects of music perception appear to be adultlike very early in infancy. For example, babies seem to respond to changes in melody and rhythmic pattern much the same way adults do and seem to be able to distinguish "good" from "bad" melodies (see Trehub, Trainor, & Unyk, 1993). Examples of telling the difference between "good" (regular or

natural) musical patterns and "bad" (irregular or unnatural) musical patterns are particularly impressive, given the diversity of human musical systems. This was demonstrated in a study by Krumhansl and Jusczyk (1990), who had 4.5- and 6-month-old infants listen to segments of Mozart minuets. Some of the segments had pauses inserted at the end of each musical phrase (natural), whereas other segments had pauses inserted in the middle of phrases (unnatural). Infants learned to control which music they heard—natural or unnatural—by turning their heads in the direction of the speaker playing the music they preferred. Overall, infants spent more time listening to the natural than to the unnatural versions, with 22 of 24 6-month-olds and 20 of 24 4.5-month-olds showing this pattern. Other research has shown that infants as young as 6 months old prefer tones related by simple ratios (what most adults consider to be consonant, or pleasant sounding) over dissonant sounds (as is found in atonal music) (Schellenberg & Trehub, 1996). Given these infants' lack of musical experience, the results of these experiments suggest that music appreciation might not require a college class to attain but is a basic characteristic of the human nervous system.

Other research has shown that infants are prepared to hear more than just Western music; they are innately able to distinguish regular from irregular patterns in culturally different music systems. For example, in one study, infants and adults were played series of notes based on Western scales and Javanese pelog scales (Lynch et al., 1990). The formal description of these two musical systems is beyond the scope of this book (and my expertise); suffice it to say that the underlying scales differ considerably. Adults and 6.5-month-old infants heard well-tuned or out-of-tune patterns of both types of music and were asked to distinguish between the two. The infants, of course, weren't asked to "tell" the difference, but an operant-conditioning paradigm was used in which infants were rewarded for turning their heads to out-of-tune series. The adults, who merely raised their hands for an out-of-tune series, were better able to distinguish between in-tune and out-of-tune patterns in the Western music than in the Javanese music, reflecting the influence of experience on their musical perception. (The adults were American and all familiar with the Western but not the Javanese system.) The infants, however, were equally good at distinguishing the out-of-tune series for both the Western and Javanese patterns, "suggesting that infants may be born with an equipotentiality for the perception of scales from a variety of cultures" (Lynch et al., 1990, p. 275). That is, just as children are capable of and biologically prepared for acquiring any human language, they seem to be prepared for also acquiring any system of music.

The Development of Visual Perception

When can infants begin to make sense of their visual world? When can they discriminate between two visual stimuli or form visual concepts, for example? We, like our primate cousins, are a visual species. Survival during our prehistoric past would have been unlikely for a visually impaired child. Vision gives us information about both near and distant objects that touch and hearing cannot easily provide. Spatial cognition is an important "higher order" skill (see later discussion), and such thinking is based on vision. Perhaps because of the importance of vision to the species, or perhaps because we're better at thinking of ways of testing vision, visual perception has been the most studied sense in psychology, both in children and adults.

Vision in the Newborn

Newborns can perceive light, as demonstrated by the pupillary reflex (constriction of the pupil to bright light and dilation to low levels of illumination). However, **accommodation,** or focusing, of the lens is relatively poor at birth. Early research indicated that infants are born with a fixed lens, so that only stimuli approximately 20 centimeters away (about 8 inches) are in focus (Haynes, White, & Held, 1965), about the distance between an infant's eyes and his or her mother's face when nursing. More recent work by Banks (1980) indicated that

newborns likely do *not* have a fixed lens; however, accommodation is poor regardless of the distance an object is from an infant's eyes, and most of what newborns look at they see unclearly. But development of the muscles of the lens is rapid, and under favorable stimulus conditions, accommodation is adult-like by as early as 3 months of age.

Newborns will visually track a moving object, but their eyes will not necessarily move in harmony. **Convergence** refers to both eyes looking at the same object, an ability apparently not possessed by newborns (Wickelgren, 1967). Convergence and **coordination** (both eyes following a moving stimulus in a coordinated fashion) improve during the first months of life and are adult-like by 6 months (Aslin & Jackson, 1979).

Studies attempting to determine the *acuity* of infants, or the ability to see clearly, have yielded varied results, depending on the technique used. Acuity improves substantially during the first year of life, but is very poor at birth (Kellman & Banks, 1998). With normal acuity for adults being 20/20, estimates of newborn acuity range from 20/400 to 20/600, making the neonate legally blind in most states (Slater, 1995).

An important reason for newborns' poor vision is the underdeveloped state of their foveas, the area of the retina where there is the highest concentration of cones (color perceiving cells that provide the clearest vision). Although the fovea of a newborn is larger than that of an adult, individual cells are arranged differently, cells vary in size and shape, and the cones are more widely distributed in the fovea of newborns relative to adults. This makes the cones of newborns much less sensitive to light than those of an adult—by some estimates by a difference of 350 to 1 (Kellman & Banks, 1998).

Do newborns see the world in color, the way adults do? Although newborns might not be color blind, they apparently do not perceive much in they way of color. When differences in brightness are controlled for, infants can't discriminate between a wide range of colors until about 8 weeks of age (Allen, Banks, & Schefrin, 1988; Clavadetscher et al., 1988). Research has shown newborns can likely discriminate between the colors red and white, but cannot differentiate blue, green, and yellow from white (Adams, Courage, & Mercer, 1994). In general, newborns seem to process color information the same *way* adults do, but color vision itself is extremely poor (Adams & Courage, 1998).

Sensation in the newborn, in general, and vision in the newborn, in particular, should not be viewed as a passive process whereby stimuli randomly strike the sense organs. Rather, babies come into the world with dispositions to attend to certain classes of stimuli and with rules for acquiring information through their senses. These rules might change during infancy, but even newborns are prepared to operate on their perceptual worlds. Marshall Haith (1980) summed up his study of vision in neonates by postulating five rules that neonates use in acquiring and processing visual information:

Rule 1: If awake and alert and the light is not too bright, open your eyes.

Rule 2: If it is dark, keep looking, scanning the environment broadly.

Rule 3: If it is light and you see nothing, scan broadly, searching for edges.

Rule 4: If an edge is found, cease the broad scanning and stay in the general vicinity of the edge. Implement eye movements that cross the edge.

Rule 5: While in the proximity of edges, reduce the range of fixations perpendicular to the edges as the amount of contour in the area increases.

These rules for looking indicate that the newborn is well equipped for the task of seeing. Newborns might not display the flexibility in visual processing that older infants do, but their visual scanning is not random, and they do show some selectivity in the things they choose to look at.

Newborns have an impressive array of perceptual capabilities. They can see, hear, taste, and smell and can make subtle discriminations among stimuli in some modes. Their perception is not so acute as that of the toddler or even the 6-month-old, but research indicates that infants are able to make some sense of their world from the very beginning of life.

Discrimination and Attention

The research cited earlier indicated that newborns can discriminate differences in intensity of light and can track a moving object. But what really interests most cognitive psychologists is the question of what infants can see: Can they tell the difference, for example, between a checkerboard pattern and a bull's-eye? I described in the earlier section on Methodology a simple procedure developed by Fantz (1958) in which infants are shown two pictures and the time they look at the various stimuli is noted. If the stimuli chosen are sufficiently different, even very young infants will show a preference for one over the other, demonstrating by their differential looking time that they can tell the difference between the two stimuli. Because of the relatively poor acuity of young infants' vision, stimuli must be reasonably discrepant before discriminations can be made, but such discriminations are made by newborns (Slater, 1995).

Infants' visual discrimination abilities increase during the first several months. For example, 3-month-olds prefer their mothers' faces to the faces of strangers (Barrera & Maurer, 1981), indicating that they can identify their mothers on the basis of vision alone. By 5 to 7 months, infants can make relatively fine discriminations among stimuli, including that socially important class of visual stimuli, human faces (Cohen & Strauss, 1979).

There are some individual differences in the duration of infants' visual fixations, and they tend to be relatively stable over infancy, beginning as early as 2 weeks of age (Bronson, 1991; Colombo et al., 1991). Moreover, infants who are "short lookers"— that is, who spend less time per gaze before making an eye movement—tend to perform better on other tasks of perceptual/cognitive performance than do infants who are "long lookers" (Colombo, 1995; Colombo et al., 1991). Also, measures of looking time in infancy predict later childhood IQ (McCall & Carriger, 1993). This suggests that infant looking time is a reflection of the speed or efficiency of stimulus processing, which remains relatively stable during infancy and childhood (Colombo, 1995). Much more will be said about the relationship between measures of infant visual processing and later intelligence in Chapter 14.

Primary and Secondary Visual Systems

Babies come into the world prepared to see. But more important yet is that they are biologically prepared to look at some things more than others. The shift from attention based primarily on physical stimulus features to attention based on psychological characteristics reflects underlying changes in the organization of the visual nervous system. Gordon Bronson (1974) cited behavioral and anatomical evidence suggesting that babies' vision during the first month of life is controlled by the **secondary visual system.** This system, which mediates visually guided behavior in simple animals, appears to be better developed in human newborns than the more sophisticated but phylogenetically younger **primary visual system.** Bronson's interpretation is that vision during the first few months of life is qualitatively different from subsequent vision. The earliest visual processing (the secondary visual system) is under the control of subcortical portions of the brain, and it has different functions than does later visual processing, which is controlled chiefly by cortical brain structures (the primary visual system). These differences in brain control of vision account for developmental changes in visual preferences observed during the first 2 or 3 months of life.

According to Bronson, processing with the primary visual system is done by the fovea, the part of the retina where acuity is greatest, permitting the careful analysis of stimulus properties. With repeated exposure, infants can encode salient features of a stimulus, which serves as the basis for perceptual representations (or schemas). In other words, the primary visual system provides information concerning *what* a stimulus is. The secondary visual system operates mainly in the visual periphery (that is, nonfoveally) and orients the infant toward a stimulus, providing information concerning *where* a stimulus is.

Bronson proposed that the primary visual system begins influencing babies' vision at around 2 months, and as visual experiences accumulate, they increasingly affect what infants choose to look at. According to Bronson (1974),

> As memories accrue there is an increasing ability to utilize prior experience for the guidance of visual regard, and hence gaze no longer will be largely limited to the most salient aspects of a configuration. Around the third month babies are able to examine diverse aspects of a stimulus in a series of repeated refixations, and the development of this intentional scanning enables the infant to encode entire patterns where previously only isolated elements were recorded (for example, it is now a face that is smiled at, not just a pair of eyes). (p. 84)

Many parents can recognize this change. Babies during the first couple of months seem to stare at things, even if those things (such as eyes) happen to be located on a human face. By 3 or 4 months, however, many parents get the feeling that their baby is really looking at them. This feeling fits well with the research data.

More recent research has shown that Bronson's position is overstated. Although perhaps most of a newborn's visual processing is performed by subcortical brain areas, some limited cortical activity occurs in neonates. Changes in visual processing during the first several months of life appears *not* to be in the form of a relatively abrupt transition from the secondary to primary system, as Bronson proposed; rather, the changes are more gradual in nature (Johnson, 1998). Nevertheless, Bronson's (and others') description of the human newborn with an immature visual system is undisputed.

As I discussed in Chapter 2, the immaturity of the infant visual system might have an adaptive value. Recall the argument of Turkewitz and Kenny (1982), who suggested that the limited sensory abilities of young infants might protect them from sensory overload. Newborns must begin the process of constructing a coherent mental world, beginning with virtually no knowledge of the external world. Their sensory limitations might help them reduce the amount of information they have to deal with and thus aid them in constructing a simplified, comprehensible world.

The Development of Visual Preferences

What a baby, or anyone else for that matter, likes to look at depends on a variety of physical stimulus characteristics as well as psychological characteristics. Physical characteristics such as movement, amount of contour or contrast, complexity, symmetry, and curvature of the stimulus affect our looking behavior from a very early age. Familiarity and novelty, which determine the psychological significance of a stimulus for us, also affect the visual preferences of young infants, but these "psychological" factors increasingly influence infants' attention between 2 and 4 months; until this time, babies' visual attention is affected chiefly (but not exclusively) by physical stimulus features.

Physical stimulus characteristics. Movement is a potent stimulus characteristic influencing infants' visual attention. Everything else being equal, babies look more at a moving stimulus than at a comparable stimulus that is stationary. In an experiment by Haith (1966), newborns sucked on a nipple while watching a light display. On some trials, the light moved, tracing the outline of a triangle. Babies decreased their sucking on these trials, relative to those when the light did not move, indicating increased attention to movement.

Infants are also attracted to areas of high contrast, as reflected by the outline, or contour, of an object. In a pioneering study, Salapatek and Kessen (1966) assessed the visual scanning of newborns. Infants less than 1-week old were placed in a modified looking chamber with a white triangle painted on a black background situated before their eyes. The infants' eye movements were recorded and were contrasted with those when the triangle was not visible. Examples of the scanning patterns of the newborns when the triangle was present are shown in Figure 6-3. As can be seen, the infants' visual fixations were centered near the vertices of the triangles, the areas of most contrast. More recent research has indicated substantial individual variability in newborn scanning, with many infants during the first six weeks of life showing no systematic visual attention to stimulus contours; much of this variation has been attributed to differences in infant maturity at

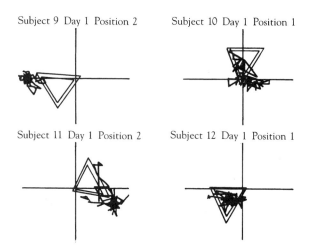

FIGURE 6-3   Examples of scanning patterns of newborns. SOURCE: "Visual Scanning of Triangles by the Human Newborn," by P. Salapatek and W. Kessen, 1966, *Journal of Experimental Child Psychology, 3,* 155–167. Copyright © 1966 Academic Press. Reprinted with permission.

birth (Bronson, 1990). By about 2 months, however, infants in the Bronson (1990) study were able to consistently direct their attention toward stimulus contours.

Work by Salapatek and his colleagues (Maurer & Salapatek, 1976; Salapatek, 1975) indicated that infants at 1 month of age direct their attention primarily to the outside of a figure and spend little time inspecting internal features. Salapatek referred to this tendency as the **externality effect.** By 2 months, however, most of infants' fixations are on internal stimulus features. An example of scanning patterns of 1- and 2-month-olds is shown in Figure 6-4.

Infants' preference for and processing of symmetrical forms have been shown for vertical stimuli. Although there seems to be no preference for *vertical symmetry* until the latter part of the first year, infants as young as 4 months process vertically symmetrical stimuli more efficiently than vertically asymmetrical or horizontal stimuli (Bornstein, Ferdinandsen, & Gross, 1981; Humphrey et al., 1986). Efficiency of visual processing in these studies was measured by rates of visual habituation, the decrease in attention as a result of repeated exposure to a stimulus. Four-

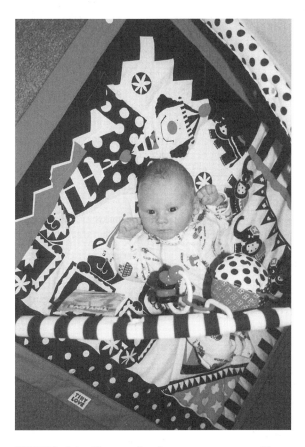

PHOTO 6-1 Young infants' attention is attracted by high contrast. (Photo by Barbara Bjorklund)

Scanning by a 1-month-old   Scanning by a 2-month-old

FIGURE 6-4 Examples of visual scanning of faces by 1- and 2-month-old infants. SOURCE: Adapted from Shaffer, D. R. (1993). *Social and personality development* (3rd ed.). Pacific Grove, CA: Brooks/Cole.

month-old infants acquired information about vertically symmetrical stimuli more effectively than about asymmetrical or horizontal information as reflected by their faster rates of habituation (that is, they looked at the symmetrical stimuli less on later trials than they looked at asymmetrical or horizontal stimuli). According to Marc Bornstein and his colleagues (1981), "The results . . . support the view that verticality has a special status in early perceptual development. . . . Whether innate, early maturing, or based on experience, the special quality of verticality generally may derive from the importance of the vertically symmetrical body and face" (p. 85).

Another physical stimulus feature of importance is that of curvature, or *curvilinearity*. Some of Fantz's original work demonstrated infants' preferences for curved stimuli, such as a bull's-eye, over linear (that is, straight-line) stimuli of comparable contour (Fantz, 1958). Ruff and Birch (1974) similarly observed a preference for curvilinear stimuli in 3- and 4-month-old infants, but they also found a preference for concentric stimuli, even if composed of straight lines (see Figure 6-5). This preference for curvature was reported even in a sample of newborns by Fantz and Miranda (1975), although only when the stimuli differed in their outer perimeter (recall the externality effect). Such preferences for curvature may help explain young infants' seeming preference to attend to the human face.

One somewhat surprising visual preference found in young infants is that for attractive female faces (Langlois et al., 1987). Judith Langlois and her colleagues asked college men and women to judge the attractiveness of adult Caucasian women from photographs. From these ratings, photographs of eight attractive and eight unattractive faces were selected, although the distribution of attractiveness was relatively normal (that is, there were no extremely attractive or unattractive faces). The photographs were selected so that all women had neutral expressions, had medium to dark hair, and did not wear glasses. In one part of the study, 2- to 3-month-old and 6- to 8-month-old infants were shown pairs of

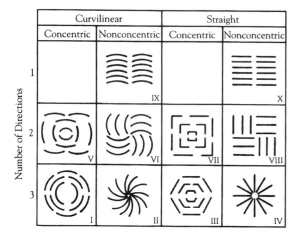

FIGURE 6-5 Examples of stimuli used to assess infants' preferences for curvature. SOURCE: "Infant Visual Fixation: The Effect of Concentricity, Curvilinearity, and Number of Directions," by H. A. Ruff and H. G. Birch, 1974, *Journal of Experimental Child Psychology, 17*, 460–473. Copyright © 1974 Academic Press. Reprinted with permission.

faces varying in attractiveness (one attractive and one unattractive face), and their looking time was measured. Both the younger and older infants spent significantly more time looking at the attractive faces than at the unattractive faces, with approximately two-thirds of the infants showing a preference for the more attractive faces. Furthermore, the preference for the more attractive faces was unrelated to how attractive an infant's mother was judged to be. More recent research has shown that this preference extends across sex, race, and age of the modeled face; 6-month-olds consistently showed a preference for attractive faces of both men and women, of both black and white adult females, and of 3-month-old infants, despite the fact that the infants had little or no experience with some of these classes of faces (Langlois et al., 1991).

In other research by Langlois and her colleagues, 12-month-old infants interacted with a stranger who wore a professionally constructed attractive or unattractive mask. The babies played more with the stranger wearing the attractive than the unattractive mask. In a second study, 12-month-old infants

spent more time playing with an attractive doll than an unattractive one (Langlois et al., 1990).

One possible explanation for these findings is that attractive faces might have more of the physical stimulus characteristics that attract infant attention than do unattractive faces. For example, attractive faces might be more curvilinear, concentric, and vertically symmetrical than unattractive faces. Another possibility is that infants might be born with a schema, or abstract representation, of a human face and that attractive faces match that schema better than unattractive ones. Some evidence indicates that attractive faces are those that reflect the "average" of a range of facial features (for example, average nose length, average distance between the eyes); that is, for both men and women, attractive faces are in essence average faces in terms of the features they possess (Langlois & Roggman, 1990; Rhodes & Tremewan, 1996). This would make sense from an evolutionary perspective. If attention to faces is important in forming social relations in early infancy, and thus to survival, the best bet would be to have an attentional bias toward "average" features (even if the combination of these "average" features results in an attractive, and thus "above average" face). Regardless of the reason, the data of Langlois and her colleagues indicate that what was once believed to be a learned preference (attractiveness) might have its basis in biology.

Attention to the Human Face

The work of Langlois and her colleagues suggests that by 2 months of age, infants are influenced by individual differences in the features of human faces. This work also implies that young infants know something about faces, with very little in the way of experience being necessary for them to express this knowledge.

In retrospect, such findings should not be surprising, for there is likely no single visual stimulus that is of greater importance to a human infant than that of the face of another member of his or her own species. Human infants are highly dependent on their parents for support and protection for a far longer time than other mammals, and their survival is made more likely by the strong social attachment they establish with their parents. Given this, it makes sense from an evolutionary perspective for infants to be oriented to the most social of stimuli, the human face.

Some of the earliest work in infant visual preferences revealed that babies of 4 months and older demonstrate a preference for the human face over other nonfacelike stimuli (Fantz, 1961). More recent research using more sensitive measures has shown that 2-month-old infants, but not 1-month-old infants, show a visual preference for facelike configurations (Maurer & Barrera, 1981). Such findings are consistent with evidence that the infant visual system becomes reorganized around 2 months of age (Bronson, 1974), with younger infants attending primarily to the external features of a stimulus (that is, the externality effect; Maurer & Salapatek, 1976) and being able to discern only the grossest features of a face.

Other research, however, has shown that newborns can distinguish between facelike and nonfacelike stimuli (Johnson et al., 1991; Morton & Johnson, 1991). These studies did not use a visual-preference paradigm, however. Rather, they showed infants different head-shaped stimuli, moving each stimulus across the babies' line of visual regard. Investigators measured the extent to which the infants followed each moving stimulus (1) with their eyes and (2) by turning their heads. Using these measures, studies have reported significantly greater eye or head movement to facelike stimuli than to nonfacelike stimuli for infants ranging in age from several minutes to 5 weeks old. Figure 6-6 presents the results of one such study (Johnson et al., 1991). Such evidence suggests that infants are born with some notion of "faceness" and will attend to such stimuli more than to others, at least when visual tracking is the dependent measure. Based on the results of their own studies plus those of others, Morton and Johnson (1991) concluded that "it can now be accepted with some degree of confidence that neonates find slowly moving faces with high-contrast definition particularly attractive stimuli" (p. 172). These researchers go on to caution that this does not mean that newborns understand the

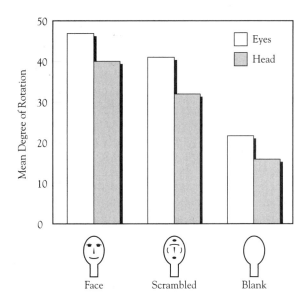

FIGURE 6-6 Newborn eye and head turns in following different stimuli. SOURCE: "Newborns' Preferential Tracking of Faces and Its Subsequent Decline," by M. H. Johnson, S. Dziurawiec, H. D. Ellis, and J. Morton, 1991, *Cognition, 40,* 1–19. Copyright © 1991 Elsevier Science Publishing Co., Inc. Reprinted with permission.

conceptual meaning of a face, merely that they prefer to visually track facelike rather than nonfacelike patterns.

Morton and Johnson (1991) developed a two-process theory for infant face preference. An initial process is accessed primarily through subcortical pathways, and this controls newborns' tracking of faces. This system is responsible for human newborns' preference for the human face, but because of limited sensory capabilities, infants are not able to learn about features of faces until about 8 weeks of age. Beginning about this time, this system loses its influence over infants' attention to faces, and the second process, which is under the control of cortical circuits, begins to take over. The functioning of this system depends on cortical maturation and experience with faces during the first two months of life, as infants begin to build a representation that enables them "to discriminate the human face from other stimuli and especially from faces of other species" (p. 178). Recent research by Quinn and Eimas (1996) has shown that 3- and 4-month-old infants are able to use cues from the faces of animals (dogs and cats, for example) to identify not only specific individuals, but which species an animal is. That is, they are able to acquire a category for "dogs" versus "cats" based on facial features, an ability that is consistent with Morton and Johnson's ideas.

Some evidence suggests, however, that even newborns might be able to make discriminations among faces, looking longer at faces of their mothers than of other women (Bushnell, Sai, & Mullin, 1989). In related research, Walton, Bower, and Bower (1992) reported that 12- to 36-hour-old infants would vary their rate of sucking more to see a picture of their mother's face than a picture of another woman's face. This suggests not only that newborns can tell the difference between faces and nonfaces, but also that they learn a preference for their mothers' faces within the first day of life (see also Walton & Bower, 1993).

The issue of young infants' abilities to attend to and recognize faces cannot be resolved at this time. But recent evidence makes it clear that even newborns are predisposed to be attentive to human faces. This makes sense from an evolutionary perspective; it is also consistent with the speculation of Fantz, who wrote nearly 40 years ago that infants' preferences for facelike patterns may "play an important role in the development of behavior by focusing attention to stimuli that will later have adaptive significance" (1961, p. 72).

Knowledge of Objects

One interesting aspect of form perception in infancy concerns the Gestalt concept of continuation. For example, Figure 6-7 shows a solid rectangle with two bars extending from its top and bottom. Adults infer that the rectangle is occluding a solid bar, although no solid bar is actually seen. Will infants make the same inference? How can one tell?

One way is by repeatedly showing infants the stimulus until their attention to it decreases (habituation), and then showing them a picture of a solid bar, in the same orientation as the partial bars in the

original stimulus. If they increase their attention to this stimulus, they would be treating it like a novel stimulus; this would be an indication that they had *not* inferred that the two partial bars in the original stimulus were connected. If, however, when shown the solid bar they show little interest in it (that is, they continue to habituate), they would be treating it like an "old" stimulus, one they've gotten tired of looking at. But it is not literally the "same old thing," but a different physical stimulus. If they treat it like an "old" stimulus, it would be because they have inferred that the rectangle in the original stimulus was occluding a solid bar.

When doing experiments like this, how do babies respond? Infants 4 months of age treat the solid bar as if it were an old stimulus (that is, they continue to habituate), but only for moving stimuli (as shown in by the arrows in Figure 6-7), not for stationary stimuli (Johnson & Aslin, 1996; Kellman & Spelke, 1983). Elizabeth Spelke (1985) speculated that this is an indication that infants are born with the notion of the persistence, coherence, and unity of objects. They "know," at some level, that objects are continuous in space. However, more recent research indicates that 2-month-old (Johnson & Aslin, 1995) and 4-month-old (Eizenman & Bertenthal, 1998) infants will show evidence of inferring object unity in some, but not other situations, and that newborns *increase* their attention to the solid bar (Slater et al., 1990), suggesting that babies are *not* born with this knowledge. Although infants are apparently not born with this knowledge, most, but not all, researchers agree that it is developed very early in life. Bogartz and Shinskey (1998), for example, propose that such results can be explained by simpler perceptual processes that do not require a conceptual "knowledge" of objects (that is, they do not require representational innateness). Rather, Bogartz and Shinskey note, some infants have a preference for familiarity and others for novelty, and mixing of data from these heterogeneous groups of infants actually produces the results seen in most of these "occlusion" experiments. Differences in preferences for familiarity versus novelty will be discussed later in this chapter, and Bogartz's ideas about *not* attributing conceptual knowledge to young

FIGURE 6-7   Example of Gestalt continuation

infants when their behavior can be explained by simpler perceptual processes will be discussed further in Chapter 7.

Psychological Stimulus Characteristics

Movement, contour, complexity, symmetry, curvature, and attractiveness continue to affect the attention of people throughout life. Beginning sometime around 2 to 4 months, however, the psychological characteristics of a stimulus—that is, the stimulus's familiarity or novelty—exert an increasing influence on whether and for how long it will be attended to. The fact that a stimulus's familiarity or novelty influences infants' attention implies some sort of memory for the stimulus event. For a stimulus to be regarded as familiar, it must be contrasted with some previous mental representation of that stimulus; that is, it must be contrasted with a stimulus that was previously known. Similarly, to be novel, a stimulus has to be slightly different from something that the perceiver already knows (Rheingold, 1985).

The increased importance of familiarity and novelty to infants' visual preference between 2 and 4 months of life is consistent with Bronson's (1974) theory of secondary and primary visual systems and Morton and Johnson's two-level system for attending to faces. That is, the nervous system goes through some changes (from primary subcortical to cortical control), permitting the retention of experiences and formation of long-term memories. Infants during the first two months of life are not functioning only at the subcortical level, of course. But their

visual cortices are immature, limiting intentional visual control and the retention of visual memories (Johnson, 1998).

Jerome Kagan (1971) proposed that beginning around 2 months, infants form **schemas,** or sensory representations, and that the similarity of a stimulus to previously formed schemas determines attention. A schema is not an exact copy of a stimulus but is "a representation of an event that preserves the temporal and spatial arrangement of its distinctive elements without necessarily being isomorphic with the event" (Kagan, 1971, p. 6). Kagan proposed the **discrepancy principle** to explain infants' attention to novel stimuli. Infants are most attentive to stimuli that are moderately discrepant from a schema. A stimulus that differs slightly from what a baby already knows (for example, a bearded face when the infant is familiar with nonbearded faces) is likely to maintain attention, whereas a highly familiar stimulus (a nonbearded face) or a highly discrepant one (a model of a face with its features scrambled) is likely to receive less of an infant's attention.

Support for the discrepancy principle has been provided by Robert McCall and his colleagues (McCall, Kennedy, & Appelbaum, 1977). In their experiments, infants between 2 and 4 months old were familiarized with stimuli and were later shown new stimuli that varied in their similarity to the originals. The researchers reported an inverted-U relationship between attention and similarity of the new stimulus to the standard (see Figure 6-8). Stimuli that were highly similar to the original and those that were highly discrepant received less attention than those that were moderately discrepant from the standard. This preference for novelty implies that some representation of the original stimulus (a schema) was retained and was used to guide subsequent visual processing.

Kagan's discrepancy principle, and much experimental data, such as those presented by McCall and his colleagues, suggest that once infants have the ability to form long-lasting visual memories, they use those memories, or schemas, as a standard and direct their attention to stimuli that are somewhat novel to them. However, it has long been known that, under some circumstances, infants actually

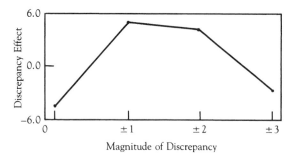

FIGURE 6-8   The relative amount of looking time (discrepancy effect) as a function of the magnitude of the discrepancy for 10-week-old infants. SOURCE: "Magnitude of Discrepancy and the Distribution of Attention in Infants," by R. B. McCall, C. B. Kennedy, and M. I. Appelbaum, 1977, *Child Development, 48,* 772–785. Copyright © 1977 The Society for Research in Child Development, Inc. Reprinted with permission.

prefer to attend to familiar, and not novel, stimuli (Hunter, Ames, & Koopman, 1983; Rose et al., 1982). In general, a preference for familiarity typifies the preference for younger infants, but also for older infants in the early phases of visual processing. For example, Rose and her colleagues (1982, Experiment 2) showed that groups of 3.5- and 6.5-month-old infants initially showed a preference for familiarity, followed by no preference, and eventually a preference for novelty (see also Courage & Howe, 1998 for similar results with 3-month-olds). In a similar vein, Richard Bogartz and his colleagues (Bogartz, Shinskey, & Speaker, 1997; Bogartz & Shinskey, 1998) have proposed that infants will prefer to look at familiar stimuli when processing is in its early stages. It takes time to create and store memory representations, so infants should have a preference for attending to familiar stimuli until memory representations are well developed. Once a stable memory representation has been formed, an infant's preference should switch to a novel stimulus. A similar model of infants' preference for familiar and novel stimuli was provided by Bahrick and Pickens (1995; Bahrick, Hernandez-Reif, & Pickens, 1997) and has been supported by evidence from the auditory mode (Spence, 1996), in addition to

the visual modality. Moreover, Bogartz and his colleagues propose that there are individual differences in infants' preferences for familiarity and novelty, and that experiments that rely on changes in infants' attention following habituation (such as the occlusion experiments discussed earlier) should take such individual differences into consideration. (Bogartz's ideas will be discussed further in Chapter 7 when examining representation in infancy.)

Depth Perception

One area of infant visual perception that has received considerable attention over the years is **depth perception.** At what age and under what conditions can infants discriminate visual patterns denoting depth? One reason for interest in the topic is that the ability to perceive depth appears to be innate for some species that are able to locomote shortly after birth, including chickens and goats (Walk & Gibson, 1961). Are human babies born with the ability to discriminate depth, or does the discrimination of depth require experience?

One factor that is important for the perception of depth concerns binocular cues. Because the two eyes are separated by several centimeters, the message one eye receives is slightly different from that received by its partner. This disparity produces information that is important for evaluating an object's distance from us. One ability critical to binocular depth perception is that of **bifoveal fixation,** the ability of the foveas of the two eyes to focus on the same object simultaneously. Richard Aslin (1977) tested bifoveal fixation in 1-, 2-, and 3-month-old infants. A target was moved past the infants' eyes at one of two constant speeds, and eye fixations were photographed. Aslin reported that the infants' eyes did not consistently converge on the targets until 2 months and did not do so without delay until 3 months. Thus, binocular cues to depth perception are not likely to be functioning well until the second or third month of life.

One reason for the interest in the development of depth cues is their importance in early locomotion. Many parents tell of their 8-month-old infants crawling off the side of the bed, sometimes to be caught by a watchful parent and sometimes not. What cues must infants attend to in order to avoid falling, and when and how do they develop? An apparatus designed to test these questions is the visual cliff (Walk & Gibson, 1961). The *visual cliff* consists of a glass-topped table with a board across its center. On one side of the board the infant sees a checkerboard pattern situated directly under the glass. This is referred to as the "shallow" side. On the other side the checkerboard pattern is several feet below the glass. This is referred to as the "deep" side (see Photo 6-2). Infants who can crawl (usually beginning around 7 or 8 months) are placed on the center board and called by their mothers from either side of the cliff. Will infants ignore the visual cues of depth on the "deep" side and crawl to their mothers, or will they fuss and refuse to traverse the "deep" side? Infants who crawl to their mothers on the "shallow" side but not on the "deep" side are said to be able to discriminate depth.

In general, early findings of Walk and Gibson indicated that babies rarely crawled to their mothers over the "deep" side. These findings suggest that once infants can crawl, they display fear, suggesting that little learning is necessary. However, more recent research by Bertenthal, Campos, and their colleagues found that the tendency to show fear on the visual cliff was related to the extent of previous locomotor experience (Bertenthal, Campos, & Barrett, 1984; Bertenthal, Campos, & Kermoian, 1994). Infants with more locomotor experience were more likely to show fear than their less experienced peers, suggesting that such experience is related to depth perception.

Self-produced movement and the development of vision.

In an interesting study of depth perception, the locomotive experience of one group of infants who did not yet crawl was enriched by letting them get around in walkers (Bertenthal et al., 1984). Unlike their noncrawling agemates who did not use walkers, the walker babies showed fear of heights (reflected by heart-rate acceleration when placed on the "deep" side of a visual cliff), indicating that the experience in the walkers accelerated the development of depth perception. These find-

PHOTO 6-2   An infant on a visual cliff. Infants who can perceive depth will crawl to their mothers across the "shallow" side but not across the "deep" side. (Topman/ The Image Works)

ings and others like them (Campos, Bertenthal, & Kermoian, 1992) suggest that there might be something about self-propelled movement that facilitates depth perception, or more specifically wariness of heights. This implies that perceptual systems do not develop in isolation but rather in coordination with motor systems. Bennett Bertenthal and his colleagues (1994) suggest that the "active control of locomotion, unlike passive locomotion, demands continuous updating of one's orientation relative to the spatial layout. This information is provided through multimodal sources, such as visual and vestibular coding of angular acceleration. With locomotor experience, changes in angular acceleration detected by the visual system are mapped onto analogous changes detected by the vestibular system. Fear or avoidance [on an apparatus such as the visual cliff] ensues when the expected mapping between visual and vestibular information is violated" (p. 142).

Perhaps the best known research dealing with self-propelled movement in perception is that of Held and Hein (1963) with kittens. In this classic study, kittens were raised in a darkened room and had visual experience only during training and testing. Pairs of kittens of the same age were used, one given normal visual-motor experience and the other given visual experience without associated motor experience. To do this, a special training apparatus was developed, shown in Figure 6–9. To train a pair of kittens, one (the active kitten) was harnessed to walk around the brightly decorated track and one (the passive kitten) was placed in a gondola to have identical visual experiences without the associated motor feedback. That is, although both kittens had the same visual experience, and both had motor experience in their darkened room, only the active kitten had visual experience concomitant with movement. After training, both kittens were tested on the visual cliff to determine if they showed a preference for sides. The passive kittens showed no preference for sides, indicating a lack of depth perception. By contrast, the active kittens consistently chose the "shallow" side, indicating that they could perceive depth.

In more recent research with human infants and toddlers, locomotive experience was related to aspects of visual/spatial cognition other than depth perception. For example, in a study by Kermoian and Campos (1988), 8.5-month-old infants were divided into three groups: (1) prelocomotive (that is, not yet crawling); (2) prelocomotive but with walker experience; and (3) locomotive (that is, crawling). The infants were then tested with a series of tasks in which they had to retrieve an object hidden under a cloth. Infants with locomotive experience, either by crawling or in a walker, showed more advanced performance on the object-retrieval task than the noncrawlers did. Moreover, there were no differences in performance between the crawlers and the walkers, suggesting that it is the locomotor experience and not maturation that is responsible for the advanced spatial memory. Other research has

FIGURE 6-9   The apparatus used in Held and Hein's study of the effects of locomotor experience on visual perception. The "active" kittens could locomote around the chamber, while the "passive" kittens could not, although they had comparable visual experiences. SOURCE: Adapted from "Movement-Produced Stimulation in the Development of Visually Guided Behavior," by R. Held & A. Hein, 1963, *Journal of Comparative and Physiological Psychology, 56,* 872–876, American Psychological Association.

similarly shown advantages in certain aspects of visual/spatial cognition associated with self-produced locomotion for infants, although these effects tend to be limited to specific abilities (Arterberry, Yonas, & Bensen, 1989; Bai & Bertenthal, 1992). For example, self-produced locomotion is associated with infants' ability to search for a hidden object after the infant is moved (that is, hiding the object in a container, then moving the infant 180 degrees before permitting him or her to search), but not after the container is moved (Bai & Bertenthal, 1992). These findings suggest that the effects on visual/spatial cognition of self-produced locomotion are domain specific rather than domain general.

The findings of Held and Hein with kittens and of Bertenthal, Campos, and their colleagues with children make it clear that visual perception does not simply develop as a result of maturation or visual experience but along with motor experience. This research points to the importance of studying the development of the whole child and not just looking at one system in isolation from other aspects of development.

Intermodal Integration

Although we often think of each sense as being distinct from all others, as adults we do a great deal of coordinating information between senses. We direct our vision to a loud noise, and we can identify our slippers by touch alone when we are awakened in the middle of the night by a barking dog outside our window. Recall that the effect of active locomotion on depth perception was attributed by Bertenthal and his colleagues (1994) to the coordination between visual and vestibular information. To what extent is such sensory integration available to infants, and how can we interpret such integration when we observe it?

At one level, **intermodal** (that is, between senses) **integration** is present at birth. Newborns move their heads and eyes in the direction of a sound, as if they wish to see what all the noise is about. In a series of experiments examining the effects of sound on visual scanning in newborns, Mendelson and Haith (1976) found that the presence of sound increased infants' visual attentiveness. The researchers suggested that this response to sound increases the likelihood that infants will discover something to look at.

An interesting demonstration of intermodal integration in young infants was provided by Elizabeth Spelke (1976). Spelke showed 4-month-old infants two films on side-by-side screens. On one screen was a film of a woman playing peekaboo; on the other screen was a hand holding a stick and striking a block of wood. A single sound track was played, corresponding either to the peekaboo or the drumming video. The babies somehow figured out which sound track went with which screen, devoting more looking time to the screen that matched the sound. That is, these 4-month-old infants realized that certain sound sequences go with certain visual displays and visually attended to those displays that provided such a match (see also Morrongiello & Fenwick, 1991).

In somewhat related work, Loraine Bahrick and John Watson (1985) investigated 5-month-olds' ability to integrate proprioceptive (relating to perception of body movements) and visual information. The babies were seated in infant seats equipped with a type of tray that prevented them from seeing their legs. Two video screens were placed in front of the infants. One screen displayed the infant's own legs; that is, the picture was transmitted live. On the other screen was a film of the legs of another infant (or in one experiment, the same infant's legs from a session recorded earlier). Thus, for one display (the contingent display), the movement of infants' legs was contemporaneous with their actual movement, whereas for the other display (the noncontingent display), the movement of legs was independent of the infants' current activity. Bahrick and Watson reasoned that if infants are able to integrate proprioception (as reflected by their own leg movements) and vision, they should be able to discriminate between the two films and spend more time looking at one than the other. This was their finding. In three experiments, 5-month-olds spent, on average, 67% of their time looking at the noncontingent display. Presumably, the lack of contingency between their leg movements and those seen on the video produced some discrepancy, and this resulted in increased attention to the noncontingent display. In a fourth experiment, Bahrick and Watson tested 3-month-olds and found no overall preference for either the contingent or the noncontingent display. They concluded that proprioceptive-visual integration is well established by 5 months and that the ability to detect the congruency between one's movements and their visual representation plays a fundamental role in an infant's perception of self, possibly underlying the development of visual self-recognition (discussed in Chapter 11). Other researchers, using a similar design that varied the spatial orientation of the images that infants saw, report that even 3-month-old infant can detect the congruence between their actual leg movements and a video image of those movements (Rochat & Morgan, 1995), suggesting that this might be an early developing ability.

A seemingly more complex intermodal feat concerns **intermodal** (or **cross-modal**) **matching.** In intermodal matching, a child must be able to recognize an object initially inspected in one modality (touch, for example) through another modality (vision, for example). Rose, Gottfried, and Bridger (1981) have shown that 6-month-old babies can perform visual-tactual integration. The infants were presented an object (either through touch alone or vision alone) for 60 seconds (familiarization phase) and were later presented a small set of objects through the alternative mode (transfer phase). The researchers reported that the infants spent more time exploring the novel objects (by manipulating or gazing at them) than the familiar ones during the transfer phase. That is, the babies showed dishabituation by examining the novel stimuli more than the familiar ones, even though familiarization was done in a different sensory modality. Other studies using similar methods have demonstrated intermodal matching for 4- to 6-month-old infants (Bushnell, 1981; Streri & Spelke, 1989).

In related research, Meltzoff and Borton (1979) reported visual-tactual integration in infants less than 1-month old. In their study, the infants were familiarized with one of two pacifiers (a sphere or a sphere with knobs, as shown in Figure 6-10) and later shown three-dimensional models of the two pacifiers. In two experiments, the infants looked significantly longer at the visual display that corresponded to the pacifier they had orally (but not visually) inspected seconds earlier. The findings of Meltzoff and Borton have been confirmed by some researchers (Gibson & Walker, 1984) but not by others (Rose & Ruff, 1987).

Although the results of research are not completely consistent, the prevailing interpretation is that infants, from early in life, can integrate information from two senses. Given that the perceptual information differs between the two modalities (sound and sight, or sight and touch), some system must integrate and permit comparison of such information. One form of cognition that requires intermodal integration is imitation, which was discussed briefly in Chapter 4 on Piaget's theory. We will look at the development of imitation again in Chapter 7

FIGURE 6-10   The shapes used in cross-modal matching study with 1-month-olds to assess tactual matching. SOURCE: "Intermodal Matching by Human Neonates," by A.N. Meltzoff and R. W. Borton, 1979, *Nature, 282,* 403–404. Copyright 1979 Macmillan Magazines Ltd. Reprinted with permission from *Nature.*

on infant representation, where such intermodal integration has been interpreted by some researchers as evidence of symbolic abilities in young infants (Meltzoff, 1995).

Categorization

Babies have distinct preferences for what they look at and display a rudimentary form of visual memory, as reflected by the effects that novelty and familiarity have on their preferences. As important as these basic processes are, our ability to deal effectively with new information would be hopelessly impaired if we did not form *categories*. By the process of categorization, one can treat objects that are perceptually different as being the same kind of thing. Uncle Joe, Aunt Mary, Mommy, Daddy, and the stranger on the street are all unique individuals, but at one level they're all the same: they're all people. Our ability to categorize allows us to reduce an enormous diversity of information into manageable units. A 6-month-old given a new stuffed animal, rattle, or bottle can identify each object and act toward it accordingly, even though he or she has never seen the object before. Each object is similar to something the child already knows, and the objects can be categorized and dealt with easily. The process of categorization is ubiquitous, permeating every aspect of our intellectual life, and the origins of categorization can be found in early infancy.

One technique that has been used to assess infants' perceptual categories is the habituation/dishabituation paradigm, discussed earlier in this chapter. How can this paradigm be used to assess infants' categories, or concepts? One way is by varying the stimuli that are presented during the habituation trials. Rather than habituating infants to a picture of a face of a single individual (Sally), for example, pictures of different individuals can be presented (Sally, Maria, Barbara, and Teresa). In both the single- and multiple-face cases, the amount of response declines with repeated exposure (that is, habituation). In the former case, infants are habituated to a specific stimulus (Sally), and in the latter case, to a category of stimuli (women's faces). After habituation has occurred, a new female face can be presented (Elizabeth). Infants who were habituated to a single face should recognize this new face as a novel stimulus and increase their attention to it (that is, show dishabituation). In contrast, infants who were habituated to women's faces in general should recognize it as just another example of a woman's face and continue to habituate. That is, even though they have never seen this face before, they should categorize it as familiar and direct relatively little of their attention to it.

The procedure and results just described are similar to those reported in an experiment by Cohen and Strauss (1979) for a group of 30-week-old infants. Cohen and Strauss interpreted their findings as evidence that such infants can abstract "appropriate conceptual categories regarding the human face" (p. 422). By continuing to habituate to the new stimulus, infants are, in effect, telling us that although the face is perceptually different from anything they have seen before, it is similar in general form to what they already know. They are telling us that they have acquired a category for female faces.

Research during the past 25 years has shown that infants as young as 3 months of age can organize objects into perceptual categories during relatively brief experimental sessions (Eimas & Quinn, 1994; Younger & Gottlieb, 1988). For example, in a series of experiments by Eimas and Quinn (1994), 3- and 4-month-old infants were habituated to a series of pictures of either horses or cats. Following habituation, the infants were shown a pair of new pictures, one from the habituated category (a "new" picture of a horse, for instance) and one from a different, but related category (a zebra or giraffe, for instance). Note that both pictures on these test trials were "new" to the infants, in that they had never been shown the specific picture of this horse before, nor of any giraffe or zebra. However, if they had formed a concept of "horse," they would recognize the new picture of a horse as "just another horse" and thus look longer at the giraffe (or zebra) than at the horse. This, in fact, is what Eimas and Quinn found. Infants formed categories of horses that were distinct from zebras, giraffes, and cats, and they formed categories of cats that were distinct from horses and tigers. However, these babies were not able to distinguish between cats and female lions, indicating that the perceptual similarity between cats and female lions is too great for infants of this age to form separate categories of them, at least with this little experience. But when 3- and 4-month-old infants were given more experience with cats before being tested for category formation, they were able to make the "cat versus female lion" categorical distinction (Eimas, Quinn, & Cowan, 1994; Quinn & Eimas, 1996), indicating that perceptual category formation for "natural" categories is quite well developed early in life.

In more recent research, Quinn and Eimas (1998) included humans as well as a potential category for 3- and 4-month-old infants. They found that when infants were familiarized with pictures of humans, they later included not only novel picture of humans as members of that category (that is, continued to habituate to pictures of humans), but also pictures of horses and fish, but not cars. That is, they treated horses and fish as if they were human. The reverse, however, did not hold, for when infants were familiarized with pictures of horses, they did not include humans in their categorizations (that is, they dishabituated to pictures of humans). What does this pattern mean? Quinn and Eimas suggested that babies already have experience interacting with humans, and that the "human" category serves as an anchor for interpreting other animals. After being familiarized with pictures of humans, other animals will share many of the same characteristics with humans, so that infants will initially classify nonhuman animals as human. Because they are less familiar before the experiment with nonhuman animals, the reverse is not true. Then, they learn the characteristics of "horses," for instance, but don't later mistake humans (or cats) for horses. They speculated that "the incorporation of nonhuman animal species into the categorical representation of humans may be the process that allows for the development of a representation of animals in general" (Quinn & Eimas, 1998, p. 171).

The Structure of Infants' Categories

When infants form categories, how do they do it? This question is not restricted to infant researchers but also concerns scientists interested in concept formation in adults (Posner & Keele, 1970; Rosch, 1975). One popular way of describing adult concepts is through category prototypes. A **prototype** is an abstract representation of a category. It reflects the central tendency, or "best example," of a category. Items that share many features in common with the prototype are said to be typical category exemplars (for instance, *robin* for the category *birds*), whereas items that share fewer features with the prototype are said to be atypical category exemplars (for instance, *ostrich* for the category *birds*) (see Rosch, 1975; Chapter 7).

Several researchers have demonstrated that infants form category prototypes much as adults do. The dot patterns in the first column of Figure 6-11 present the prototypes used in a study by Younger and Gotlieb (1988). The dot patterns to the right reflect examples of stimuli generated from the prototype. Some of these stimuli represent "low" distortion from the prototype (that is, they are very similar to the prototype), whereas others represent

"medium" and "high" distortion from the prototype. Three-, 5-, and 7-month-old infants were habituated to sets of dot patterns that varied in degree of distortion from the prototype (that is, either low, medium, or high levels of distortion). None of the infants ever saw the prototypes. After habituation, babies were shown pairs of stimuli. In one comparison, infants were shown one of the stimuli they had just been familiarized with (an "old" stimulus) and the prototype from which that "old" stimulus had been generated. Remember that infants had never seen the prototype before, only stimuli generated from it. What would babies look at longer? In general, babies looked at the "old" stimulus longer than the prototype. They acted as if the prototype was a familiar stimulus, even though they had never seen it before. This is a clear indication that infants as young as 3 months of age are forming categories based on prototypes, much as adults do. However, there was variation between infants of different ages. Three-month-olds only formed categories when they were familiarized with dot patterns that represented "good form," such as the cross (first row) in Figure 6-11. Five-month-olds formed categories for both "good" and "intermediate" forms (the middle row in Figure 6-11), but not "poor" forms (the bottom row in Figure 6-11), whereas 7-month-olds formed categories for all three types of stimuli. That is, it is easier for young infants to form categories for perceptual arrays with "good" form (highly regular with bilateral symmetry) than "poor" form, even though the rules of creating exemplars from the prototypes are the same for the various types of categories.

In related research with more "natural" categories, Roberts and Horowitz (1986; Roberts, 1988) showed that 9-month-old infants formed a category for the concept birds when habituated to highly typical exemplars of the category (for example, *sparrow*, *robin*, and *blue jay*). There was no evidence of concept formation, however, when atypical exemplars served as the habituation stimuli (for example, *turkey*, *ostrich*, and *chicken*). Like young children, infants are more apt to identify or form a category when provided with typical, as opposed to atypical, category exemplars (Anglin, 1977). The findings of these experiments are enlightening, suggesting that

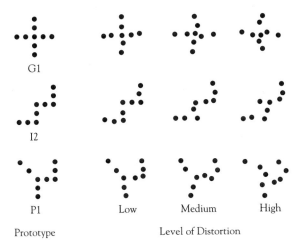

G1

I2

P1   Low   Medium   High

Prototype   Level of Distortion

FIGURE 6-11   Prototype dot patterns showing "poor"
(P), "intermediate" (I), and "good" (G) form. SOURCE:
Younger, B., & Gotlieb, S. (1988). Development of
categorization skills: Changes in the nature or structure
of infant form categories? *Developmental Psychology, 24,*
611–619.

the categorization process of infants is qualitatively
similar to that of older children and adults (see also
experiments by Younger, 1993).

Color Categories

Although languages vary greatly in the number of
terms they have to describe colors, people in all cultures seem to perceive colors similarly (Berlin & Kay,
1969). When people are given color chips to categorize into a specified number of groups, the outcomes
are highly similar regardless of whether the person
doing the sorting has 11 different basic color words
in his or her language or only 2 (Heider, 1972).

The interesting developmental question is "Do
infants categorize colors as adults do, or is there an
age-related progression in the categorization of
color?" I mentioned earlier that newborns seem to
possess the rudiments of color vision (Adams, Courage, & Mercer, 1994), but that such color vision is
limited to large stimuli and particular parts of the
color spectrum. Marc Bornstein and his colleagues
have investigated the question of color categorization using the habituation/dishabituation paradigm
with slightly older infants (Bornstein, Kessen, &

Weiskopf, 1976). Four-month-olds were habituated
to a color patch corresponding to a light wavelength
of 480 nanometers. Adults classify this color as blue.
After habituation, the infants were presented with
one of two different color patches, one corresponding to a wavelength 30 nanometers greater than the
habituated stimulus (510 nanometers) and one
corresponding to a wavelength 30 nanometers less
than the habituated stimulus (450 nanometers).
The two posthabituation stimuli were comparably
discrepant from the standard stimulus but in opposite directions. Adults classify the 450-nanometer
wavelength as blue, just as they classify the 480-
nanometer wavelength. But adults classify the 510-
nanometer wavelength as green. Thus, were adults
to be subjects in this experiment, they would show
dishabituation (increased visual attention) to the
510-nanometer wavelength because they classify it
as a color different from the standard blue. However,
they would continue to habituate to the 450-
nanometer wavelength of light because, although it
is comparably different in physical characteristics
from the standard, it is perceived only as a different
shade of the same color (both blue). How did the
babies respond? The 4-month-old infants showed
the same categorization responses as adults, habituating to the 450-nanometer stimulus and dishabit-
uating to the 510-nanometer stimulus. The researchers reported similar results for other color
boundaries. Although these findings do not prove
that the way humans categorize the color spectrum
is innate, they are strong evidence for that position.

Much has been learned about infant perception
during the past 30 years. Actually, this has been one
of the great success stories of developmental psychology. An amazing number of basic facts about
how infants perceive their world has been discovered. But this does not mean that we have learned
all there is to know, or that we have a proper understanding of these facts. Marshall Haith (1993), a
leading researcher in the field of infant perception,
cautions us not to become too complacent with our
newfound knowledge. For example, researchers
are all too likely to view infant perceptual skills as
all-or-none: Either babies can discriminate faces or
they can't; either they show a preference for novel

stimuli or they don't. This, Haith states, is too simplistic. Infants, like older children, show considerable variability in perceptual skills, behaving more
competently in some contexts than others. Rather
than asking when a particular ability is first seen in
development, it makes more sense to take a truly
developmental perspective, asking what the course
of development is for any particular ability and under what conditions an infant will display a particular skill.

This is related to a second issue. Simply describing a perceptual ability tells us nothing about what
the infant uses it for. Haith argues that we must take
a more functional view of perceptual skills in infancy, asking "how the baby applies his or her perceptual skills and knowledge in the real world" (p.
364). We know much about basic infant perceptual
abilities, and we will learn more when we examine
what impact those abilities have on an infant's life.

Finally, Haith discusses what he calls the "species
gap." The methods, theories, and concepts used for
assessing infant perception are totally different from
those used for assessing perception in childhood.
The result is that we treat infants as if they were
members of a different species. What we need are
methods and theories that take a wider view of perceptual development, integrating what we know
about infants' perception with what we know about
perception in children and adults.

Haith's comments are less criticisms of work that
has been done than they are suggestions for future
directions. One must start somewhere, and developmental psychologists have made a very good start,
indeed, in assessing the perceptual abilities of infants. But there is more to know, and future researchers must adopt slightly different ways of
thinking if scientific progress is to continue.

Perceptual Development
Beyond Infancy

Perceptual development is not complete at the end
of infancy. Although a 2-year-old's visual and auditory systems are very well developed, with age children are increasingly required to make more precise
discriminations among stimuli. In this section, we

FIGURE 6-12   An example of an ambiguous figure.
Young children have a difficult time seeing two inter-
pretations of a figure. SOURCE: Adapted from "The Role
of Frequency in Developing Perceptual Set," by B. R.
Bugelski and D. A. Alampay, 1961, *Canadian Journal of
Psychology, 15,* 205–208. Copyright © 1961 Canadian
Psychological Association. Reprinted with permission.

will look briefly at some aspects of perceptual development during childhood and examine age and gender differences in spatial cognition.

Interpreting Ambiguous Stimuli

Many things in the world are not what they appear
to be, at least not on first inspection. For example,
Figure 6-12 presents an example of an **ambiguous
figure.** This figure could be seen as a rat or as a man.
When presented with figures such as these, 3- and 4-
year-old children typically see only one thing or the
other. They will report the rat but if asked will deny
seeing the man, or vice versa. By 7 or 8 years of age,
however, most children are able to see both possibilities in the same figure, although not simultaneously. By 10 or 11 years of age, children report
seeing both interpretations at the same time
(Elkind, 1978). David Elkind (1978) proposed that
with age, children are able to reverse their perception from one image to another, much as Piaget proposed the concrete operational child could reverse
thought.

In related research, Gollin (1960) presented children with sets of drawings, with the members varying in the amount of detail they contained (see
Figure 6-13). When children 2.5 to 5 years of age

Set V

Set IV

Set III

Set II

Set I

FIGURE 6-13 Examples of stimuli varying in amount of detail. SOURCE: *Developmental Psychology: Childhood and Adolescence*, 4th edition, by David R. Shaffer, page 231. Copyright 1996 by Brooks/Cole Publishing Company. Adapted with permission of the author and publisher from "Factors Affecting the Visual Recognition of Incomplete Objects: A Comparative Investigation of Children and Adults," by E. S. Gollin, 1962. *Perceptual and Motor Skills, 15,* pp. 583–590. Copyright Southern Universities Press, 1962.

were asked to identify the pictures beginning with the least complete, the younger children needed to view the more complete pictures before making a proper identification (see also Elkind, 1978), suggesting that with age, children are increasingly able to regulate their perception.

Learning Distinctive Features

Eleanor Gibson (1969) proposed a theory of perceptual learning whereby children discover **distinctive features** of stimuli in their environment. That is,

with experience, children learn which characteristics of an object differentiate it from another. Perceptual learning is seldom explicitly taught to children, but through normal interaction with their environment, children learn which features are important for making discriminations, and, as would be expected, children from different environments and cultures learn slightly different things.

Of particular importance for children from technological societies is learning the distinctive features of letters. Our alphabet consists of letters that are not always easy to distinguish from one another. For example, 5-year-olds, even with preschool and *Sesame Street* experience, often confuse letters such as m and w, and b, d, and h (Chall, 1983). Research by Gibson and her colleagues using abstract stimuli similar to our alphabetic letters showed that 4- and 5-year-olds have more difficulty distinguishing between them than do older children (6- to 8-year-olds) (Gibson, Gibson, Pick, & Osser, 1962). From this and related research (see Gibson, 1969; Gibson & Levin, 1975), it is clear that the ability to make some of the perceptual discriminations necessary for reading is not available to many preschoolers. Given this, it is understandable that reading should not be part of the regular preschool curriculum.

Age differences in perceptual discrimination abilities are not limited to vision but are found in other modalities as well. For example, research by Jensen and Neff (1993) examined age differences in the ability to make basic auditory discriminations on the basis of sound intensity (loudness), frequency (pitch), and duration (timing). Subjects ranging in age from 4 years old to adults were presented with three auditory stimuli (tones) and were asked to determine which of the three tones was different from the other two. (This is an example of an oddity task, familiar to most young children from the *Sesame Street* game "One of These Things Is Not Like the Other.") Jensen and Neff reported that abilities to discriminate differences in intensity were adultlike by 4 years of age, whereas abilities to tell the difference between tones of different frequency and duration showed regular development over childhood, being relatively poor in many 4- and 5-year-old children. Jensen and Neff proposed that these basic auditory skills may be related to children's musical abilities, "as in the commonly observed difficulty of young children in staying 'on tune' or in rhythm" (1993, p. 106).

The very term perceptual learning implies that how a person perceives the world will vary as a function of his or her experience. The effects of experience on perception can most readily be seen by comparing people who have grown up in vastly different cultures. Research has demonstrated, for example, that how people interpret perspective in two-dimensional pictures, drawings, or photographs varies as a function of education and cultural experience (Hudson, 1960). Even young children in Western cultures use pictorial cues to infer three dimensions in photographs, whereas adults from some non-Western cultures rarely acknowledge three dimensions in interpreting drawings.

The effects of experience on perception are nicely illustrated in Turnbull's (1961) account of an African Pygmy's first trip out of the forest and his first experience with seeing a herd of buffalo crossing a wide plain in the distance:

> [When Kenge] saw the buffalo, still grazing lazily several miles away, far below . . . he said "What insects are those?" At first I hardly understood; then I realized that in the forest the range of vision is so limited that there is no great need to make an automatic allowance for distance when judging size. . . . When I told Kenge that the insects were buffalo, he roared with laughter and told me not to tell such stupid lies. . . . As we got closer, the "insects" must have seemed to get bigger and bigger. Kenge . . . kept his face glued to the window, which nothing would make him lower. . . . I was never able to discover just what he thought was happening—whether he thought that the insects were changing into buffalo, or that they were miniature buffalo growing rapidly as we approached. His only comment was that they were not real buffalo, and he was not going to get out of the car until we left the park. (pp. 252–253)

Developmental and Gender Differences in Spatial Cognition

Although all cognition is tied to perception, this connection seems especially apparent for **spatial**

cognition. Spatial cognition can be divided into three broad categories: **spatial orientation, spatial visualization,** and **object and location memory.** Spatial orientation is how people understand the placement of objects in space with themselves as the reference point. Spatial-orientation tasks include those in which participants are asked to distinguish geographic directions in an unfamiliar locale or to draw their way from point A to point B on a map. In contrast, spatial-visualization tasks involve visual operations, such as mentally rotating a figure or adjusting a tilted object to bring it to an upright position. Object and location memory is tested by having participants remember objects and their location from a spatial array. Both developmental and gender differences have been reported in each of these areas.

Spatial Orientation

Age differences in spatial orientation are found reliably on a variety of tasks. For example, Anooshian and Young (1981) asked three groups of children—first- and second-graders, fourth- and fifth-graders, and seventh- and eighth-graders—to point a telescope at landmarks surrounding their own neighborhoods. Even the youngest children performed well above chance on this task, indicating that they had formed a spatial representation of their neighborhood.

In other research, children are required to form "cognitive maps" to find their way around an area or to construct a model of an area. In one study by Herman and Siegel (1978), kindergarten, second-grade, and fifth-grade children walked repeatedly through a large model town consisting of buildings, streets, railroad tracks, and trees. Following the walks, the children were asked to re-create the layout from memory. Performance increased with age. Similar age-related improvements in the formation of cognitive maps have been found between 3- and 5.5-year-old children, although the spatial representations were poorly integrated for both the younger and older children (Herman, Shiraki, & Miller, 1985).

Some of these and other similar experiments have reported gender differences, with males per-

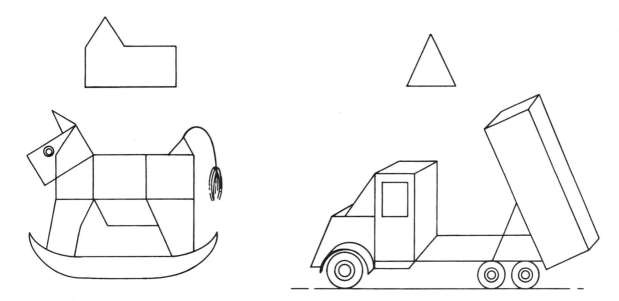

FIGURE 6-14 Items from the Children's Embedded Figures Test. Children are to locate the geometric form on top within the figure below. SOURCE: Modified and reproduced by special permission of the Publisher, Consulting Psychologists Press, Inc., Palo Alto, CA 94303 from *Children's Embedded Figures Test*, by S. A. Karp and N. Konstadt. Copyright © 1971 by Consulting Psychologists Press, Inc.

forming better than females (Anooshian & Young, 1981; Herman et al., 1985; Herman & Siegel, 1978). Gender differences are not always found at all ages, however, and other studies have failed to find any differences between males and females on spatial orientation tasks (Allen, Kirasic, & Beard, 1989; Hazen, 1982). One explanation for gender differences, when they are found, has to do with familiarity with the environment. For example, research by Hazen (1982) controlled for preschool children's experience with the environment and reported no gender differences in a spatial-orientation task. Thus, although age differences are robust on spatial-orientation tasks, gender differences are less so, but when gender differences are found, they invariably favor males.

Spatial Visualization

Age and gender differences have also been reported for spatial-visualization tasks. For example, tasks that purportedly assess **field dependence/field independence (FD/FI)** involve such analytic/spatial

skills. The concept of field dependence/field independence has its origins in adult perception. Herman Witkin and his associates (Witkin et al., 1962; Witkin et al., 1954) showed that some people have a difficult time perceiving component parts of a visual field separately from the whole. Witkin referred to such people as *field dependent*. In contrast, others could analyze the perceptual field into its discrete parts. Witkin referred to these people as *field independent*. An example of a task that assesses the FD/FI dimension is one in which a person must find a figure embedded in a larger picture. A couple of items from the Children's Embedded Figures Test are shown in Figure 6-14. Field-independent people discover the hidden object much more quickly than field-dependent people. In other words, the perception of field-dependent people is influenced by the entire perceptual field, so that they find it difficult to analyze any specific component within the field. Field-independent people are less affected by the global characteristics of a display and find it easier to discover the individual parts that make up the whole.

Correct answers: The first and second

FIGURE 6-15   Example of problem from the Vandenberg Test of Mental Rotation. Subject must select alternatives from the four on the right that is the same as the one on the left, only rotated [Correct answers: the first and second]. SOURCE: Vandenberg, S. G., & Kuse, A. R. Mental rotations, a group test of three-dimensional spatial visualization. *Perceptual and Motor Skills*, 1978, 47, 599–604. © Perceptual and Motor Skills 1978.

There is a general developmental trend toward increasing field independence—older children and adults take less time to identify objects in the Embedded Figures Test than younger children do (Witkin, Goodenough, & Karp, 1967). Witkin and his colleagues (1967) reported longitudinal results from a sample of males, followed from age 10 to 24 years. They found a steady change toward field independence from 10 to 17 years, with performance stabilizing at this point, showing no further improvement or change when subjects were tested at 24 years of age. Although people become more field independent with age, reflecting changes in developmental function, individual differences in FD/FI are relatively stable over time, with field-dependent children becoming field-dependent adults (Witkin et al., 1967).

Gender differences have been reported on tasks such as the Embedded Figures Test, with girls being more influenced by the background (that is, being more field dependent) than boys are (Harris, 1978; Witkin et al., 1967). A closer inspection of the studies included in Maccoby and Jacklin's (1974) classic review of gender differences, however, indicates that such differences were not detected universally. Of 77 research studies of spatial visualization, 30 found differences favoring males, 5 found differences favoring females, and 42 reported no significant gender differences. In short, although the "box score" tally of differences favors males, there are actually more studies failing to find reliable gender differences in spatial-visualization skills.

Gender differences, favoring males, have also been reliably found for *mental rotation tasks* (see Figure 6-15), in which a person must mentally rotate a visual stimulus to determine if it matches another stimulus (Casey et al., 1995), and block design tasks, in which sets of blocks are used to construct models (Livesey & Intili, 1996). Another relatively simple test of spatial visualization that has consistently yielded gender differences is Piaget and Inhelder's (1967) water-level problem (see Figure 6-16). In this problem, subjects are shown tipped bottles and asked to imagine the water level if the bottles were half-filled with water. The correct answer involves a knowledge of the horizontality of the water level; that is, the subjects should indicate (usually by drawing a line) that the level of the water would be horizontal across the bottle. In Piaget and Inhelder's

FIGURE 6-16   A water-level problem. Subjects are to draw the water line in each bottle to represent how it would look if it were half-filled with water.

work, preoperational children had difficulty with the task, often indicating that the water level would be parallel to the bottom of the bottle and not parallel to the ground.

Piaget and Inhelder's data suggested that knowledge of invariant horizontality (and verticality) develops in late childhood. Other researchers noted, however, that many adolescents and young adults have difficulty with the concept, with a disproportionate number of females experiencing such difficulties (see Kalichman, 1988; Vasta & Liben, 1996). Although early research attempting to train women to improve their performance on the water-level tasks were not successful (Thomas, Jamison, & Hummel, 1973), subsequent research by Liben and Golbeck (1980, 1984) demonstrated that female children and adults can improve their performance on horizontality problems when the task demands are modified or when they are given explicit information about the concepts dealt with in the tasks. These findings indicate that females have the ability to construct mature spatial representations and that some of the gender differences on these tasks "reflect males' and females' differential knowledge of the relevant physical phenomena" (Liben & Golbeck, 1984, p. 605).

A study that examined age and gender differences on the water-level task from a novel perspective was performed by Thomas and Turner (1991). Subjects ranged in age from 6.5 years to college age and were given a series of water-level tasks. Although the researchers obtained the typical age and gender differences in task performance, they found that children did not gradually become more competent at this task. Rather, at every age and for both males and females, there were two kinds of performers: those who solved the tasks correctly and those who did not. Thus, age differences were due not to children becoming increasingly accurate with age, but rather to age-related changes in the distribution of accurate versus inaccurate performers. That is, individual differences (for both sexes) in performing the water-level task were not a matter of degree, but rather could be better described as a dichotomy between accurate and inaccurate performers. At all age levels, there was a higher proportion of accurate

male performers than accurate female performers (see also Sholl & Liben, 1995; Thomas & Lohaus, 1993).

Although gender differences in spatial cognition have been consistently found, the absolute magnitude of those differences is small. One way of evaluating the size of such differences is to conduct a **meta-analysis**—a statistical technique that allows an investigator to evaluate the magnitude of a significant effect across a large number of studies. Janet Hyde (1981) performed such an analysis, reanalyzing the findings of spatial cognition studies reviewed by Maccoby and Jacklin (1974). Hyde reported that differences in visual/spatial ability attributed to the gender of the child accounted for less than 5% of the difference in performance. Other meta-analyses have reported similar findings. For example, Linn and Petersen (1985) reported that only between 1% and 5% of differences in spatial abilities can be attributed to gender, depending on the particular task. One exception noted by Linn and Petersen was mental rotation, in which males of all ages performed better than females did. Rosenthal and Rubin (1982) similarly reported small differences between the sexes in their meta-analysis, but also reported that the size of effect diminished across the years, with females showing a substantial gain in cognitive performance (relative to males) in recent years. One exception to this trend is mental rotation, which has shown no diminution in the gender difference over the years (Masters & Soares, 1993).

Object and Location Memory

Not all spatial ability tasks favor males. Females seem to be better at tasks that assess memory for location. In laboratory studies, females are better than males at remembering the locations of each item in an array of objects, with this ability increasing with age for both sexes (Cherney & Ryalls, 1998; Eals & Silverman, 1994; Silverman & Eals, 1992). For example, in a series of experiments with subjects ranging in age from 8.5 years to college adults, Silverman and Eals (1992) reported better memory for objects and for object location for females than for males. In several of their experiments, subjects were shown an

FIGURE 6-17   The initial stimulus array shown to subjects in a test of object and location memory. SOURCE: "Sex Differences in Spatial Abilities: Evolutionary Theory and Data," by I. Silverman and M. Eals. In H. Barkow, L. Cosmides, and J. Tooby (Eds.), *The Adapted Mind: Evolutionary Psychology and the Generation of Culture,* p. 537. Copyright 1992 by Oxford University Press. Used by permission of Oxford University Press, Inc.

FIGURE 6-18   The stimulus array with objects added. Subjects were to cross out all items not found in the original array. SOURCE: "Sex Differences in Spatial Abilities: Evolutionary Theory and Data," by I. Silverman and M. Eals. In H. Barkow, L. Cosmides, and J. Tooby (Eds.), *The Adapted Mind: Evolutionary Psychology and the Generation of Culture,* p. 538. Copyright 1992 by Oxford University Press. Used by permission of Oxford University Press, Inc.

array consisting of a variety of objects, as depicted in Figure 6-17. Sometime later, they were shown a larger array, as depicted in Figure 6-18, and were to cross out all items that were not in the original array. At all ages tested, females performed better than males. When asked about the correct location of items (for example, where in an array a particular item was originally located), females again performed better than males, although differences were not significant until adolescence (see also Kail & Siegel, 1977).

Explaining Gender Differences in Spatial Cognition

The "bent-twig" model.   How can these gender differences in spatial ability be explained? A myriad of factors have been proposed to explain these differences, including differential experience for males and females, genetics, prenatal hormones, and evolutionary accounts (see articles in Halpern, 1995). Not surprisingly, the most sophisticated explanations consider interactions of biological and experiential factors over the course of development. For

example, the **"bent-twig" model,** originally proposed by Sherman (1978), posits that males are biased from early in life toward activities involving spatial cognition, such as block building, carpentry, and activities involving throwing and catching objects. Because of these biases, they spend many more hours over childhood in these activities than girls. Thus, whatever gender differences in spatial abilities existed early in life attributable to biological factors, the differential experience of boys relative to girls in activities emphasizing spatial cognition increase this difference.

Research examining the "differential-experience" portion of the bent-twig hypothesis has shown that spatial abilities in women are related to personality measures of masculinity (Newcombe & Dubas, 1992; Signorella, Jamison, & Krupa, 1989). One reason for the relationship between masculine personality characteristics and spatial abilities might have to do with the types of activities girls engage in (Baenninger & Newcombe, 1995). For example, Nora Newcombe and her colleagues found that differences in spatial experience accounted for observed differences in spatial performance

(Newcombe, Bandura, & Taylor, 1983). They created a list of everyday activities that might occur in a population of high school and college students. In the first part of the study, college students were asked to classify the activities as masculine, feminine, or neutral. The raters typically selected those tasks judged to have high spatial content as masculine and as having more male participants:

Masculine	Neutral	Feminine
touch football	bowling	figure skating
baseball	softball	field hockey
basketball	advanced tennis	gymnastics
darts	table tennis	ballet
hunting	diving	disco dancing
skateboarding	drawing	embroidery
shooting pool	sculpting	knitting
car repair	photography	baton twirling
electrical	navigating	tailoring
circuitry	in a car	touch typing
sketching house	marching in a	
plans	band	

Subsequently, the researchers found small but significant gender differences among college students on a psychometric test with strong spatial components. Newcombe and her colleagues also reported a significant correlation between spatial activities and aptitude scores, particularly for females; that is, the more spatial activities one engages in, the greater one's spatial ability is likely to be (see also Newcombe & Dubas, 1992; Signorella et al., 1989).

Working with preschool children, Connor and Serbin (1977) similarly reported differences in visual/spatial play activities between boys and girls. These researchers further reported that the amount of boys' visual/spatial play correlated significantly with their performance on the Block Design subtest of the Wechsler Intelligence Scale for Children and the Preschool Embedded Figures Test, suggesting that gender differences in play activity are responsible in part for boys' generally greater spatial skills.

A very specific version of the bent-twig hypothesis was presented by M. Beth Casey (1996). Casey extended a model originally developed by Annett (1985), which proposed a genetic basis for handedness and brain laterality. According to Annett, most people inherit a "right-shift factor" that causes them to be right handed and to have the language center of the brain located in the left hemisphere. Evidence indicates that females show left-hemisphere dominance more than males do. This greater left-hemisphere dominance influences positively language abilities and negatively spatial abilities. People who inherit two dominant genes for this right-shift factor are said to be *homozygous* for this trait, whereas people who inherit one dominant and one recessive gene for this factor are said to by *heterozygous* for this trait. There is, for some traits, a *heterozygous advantage*; in this case, Annett proposed that people who inherit both the dominant and recessive genes for the right-shift factor (those who are heterozygous for the right-shift factor) should have an advantage in spatial abilities over those who inherit two dominant genes (those who are homozygous for the right-shift factor). How can one tell if one is hetero- or homozygous for this trait? There is no sure-fire way, but one good estimate is the number of close relatives one has who are right handers versus left handers or ambidextrous. People for whom all of their close relatives are right handed are likely homozygous for the right-shift trait and should thus have relatively good verbal skills and relatively poor spatial skills. People who have some close relatives who are not right handed are more likely to be heterozygous for the right-shift factor, and thus be better at spatial skills.

Casey's model takes Annett's "right-shift factor" hypothesis and proposes that this genetic predisposition interacts with environmental factors. Specifically, people who are heterozygous for the right-shift factor and who have extensive spatial experience, should have high spatial skills, whereas those who are homozygous for the right-shift factor or those who have minimal spatial experience, should have low spatial ability. She made these predictions specifically for right-handed females and tested her model (which is shown in Figure 6-19) in a series of studies.

In one study, Casey and Brabeck (1989) evaluated mental rotation performance in a group of college women (some with and some without nonright-handed close relatives) who were either math or science majors (and thus presumed to have substantial spatial experience) with college women

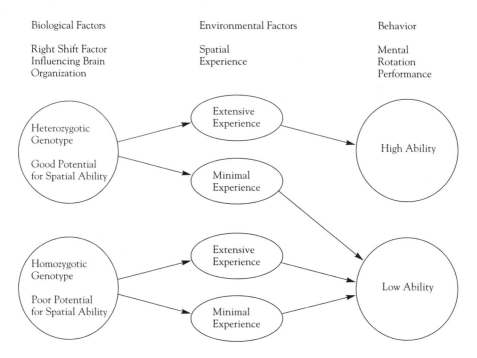

FIGURE 6-19   Casey's "bent-twig" model of individual differences on spatial cognition tasks for right-handed females. SOURCE: Casey, M. B. (1996). Understanding individual differences in spatial ability within females: A nature/nurture interactionist framework. *Developmental Review, 16,* 241–260. Used by permission of Academic Press.

who were not math or science majors (and thus presumed to have fewer spatial experiences). Their prediction was that heterozygous women with more spatial experience (math and science majors with some close relatives who were not right handed), would perform better on the mental rotation task than all other groups, and this was what they found. There was no difference in spatial abilities among the homozygous, heterozygous, or left-handed women who were not math or science majors; for the math and science majors, the left-handers and the homozygous right-handers performed comparably, and both did worse than the heterozygous, right-handed women did.

Casey's model is not without its critics (Halpern, 1996), but even her critics believe that the bent-twig model, in general form, is an appropriate one for investigating differences both between and within genders for spatial (and mathematical) differences.

An evolutionary hypothesis of gender differences in spatial cognition.   Although I am confident that some complex combination of biological and environment factors, such as those proposed by the bent-twig model, will account for most gender differences in spatial cognition, another level of analysis might prove useful: an evolutionary approach. One hypothesis is that the patterns of gender difference we find (better male performance on some tasks, better female performance on others) reflect our evolutionary history and the different demands placed on males and females during the past million years or so (Eals & Silverman, 1994; Geary, 1996; Silverman & Eals, 1992). In small groups of hunters and gatherers, men were likely responsible for hunting large game, requiring accurate throwing, eye-hand coordination, and long-distance travel, which required spatial orientation skills. Women most likely stayed near camp, where they tended to children and gathered food, the latter requiring fine-motor capabilities and the recognition of small perceptual differences (to distinguish between edible and poisonous berries, for example), which relate to object-location memory. The different evolutionary pressures led to different spatial skills that remain with us today (better spatial visualization abilities for males and better object and location memory for females).

Summary

From birth, infants actively use their perceptual systems to acquire information from their surroundings. By 1 week of age, babies can discriminate their mothers from other women by smell and by the sound of their voices. Newborns show a preference for high-pitched voices, and this preference might have its origins in the womb. Young infants can discriminate among *phonemes* and categorize language sounds much as adults do, and also appear to be biologically prepared to perceive music.

Vision is not well developed at birth, although the abilities of *convergence, coordination,* and *accommodation* of the lens improve rapidly during the first six months.

From birth, infants look longer at some stimuli than others, indicating that they can discriminate between the stimuli and have preferences. Among the physical characteristics of a stimulus that attracts infants' visual attention are movement, contour and contrast, certain levels of complexity, curvature, and facial attractiveness. Very young infants also seem to have a bias toward attending to the human face. Beginning around 2 months of age, infants' attention is increasingly influenced by psychological factors such as the familiarity or novelty of a stimulus. Kagan proposed the *discrepancy principle* to explain infants' preferences for novel stimuli, stating that stimuli that are moderately discrepant from a previously acquired schema are most likely to be attended to. Developmental differences in the organization of the visual nervous system have been proposed to account for changes in infants' visual preferences over the first several months of life. At birth, the phylogenetically older *secondary visual system* is functioning better than is the more sophisticated *primary visual system.*

Depth perception is affected by infants' ability to fixate both eyes on the same target (*bifoveal fixation*), which develops within the first three months. Research using the *visual cliff* demonstrates that crawling infants will not crawl onto the "deep" side, although the tendency to do so is related to the amount of crawling experience an infant has had. Other research has shown the importance of self-propelled movement in the development of visual perception in infancy.

Using the *habituation/dishabituation* paradigm, researchers have been able to demonstrate that infants can form visual categories. Habituation occurs when infants' looking time diminishes as a result of repeated presentation of a stimulus. Dishabituation occurs when looking time increases with the presentation of a new stimulus. Habituation and dishabituation to visual stimuli are found for newborns and reflect both discrimination and memory.

There are age-related differences in how children interpret ambiguous figures. Children learn the distinctive features of stimuli, with many 4- and 5-year-olds having difficulty distinguishing between letters such as *m* and *w.*

Both age and gender differences have been found on tasks of *spatial cognition,* with children improving with age and boys generally doing better than girls on most tasks involving *spatial orientation* and *spatial visualization.* Females perform better than males on tests of *object location and memory.* Gender differences have been explained by the *bent-twig model,* which explains gender differences as an interaction between biological and experiential factors. Explanations based on evolutionary psychology have also been proposed to account for some observed gender differences in spatial cognition.

Key Terms and Concepts

visual preference paradigm
habituation
dishabituation
phonemes
accommodation (of the lens)

convergence (of the eyes)
coordination (of the eyes)
secondary visual system
primary visual system
externality effect
schema
discrepancy principle
bifoveal fixation
depth perception
intermodal integration
intermodal (cross-modal) matching
category prototype
ambiguous figures
distinctive features
spatial cognition
spatial orientation
spatial visualization
object and location memory
field dependence/field independence (FD/FI)
meta-analysis
bent-twig model

Suggested Readings

MORTON, J., & JOHNSON, M. H. (1991). CONSPEC and CONLERN: A two-process theory of infant face recognition. *Psychological Review, 98,* 164–181. This paper reviews the small set of studies concerned with face recognition during the first few months after birth and provides a model proposing that infants are born with some innate information about faces as well as a "program" that guides them in learning about the facial features of others.

HAITH, M. M. (1993). Preparing for the 21st century: Some goals and challenges for studies of infant sensory and perceptual development. *Developmental Review, 13,* 354–371. Haith briefly reviews the state of the art in infant perceptual development and suggests directions for the future. These include taking a more continuous, developmental perspective of infant perception, integrating ideas about infant perception with those about older children, looking more at the brain basis of perceptual development, and increasing the emphasis on applying research findings to at-risk populations.

KELLMAN, P. H., & BANKS, M. S. (1998). Infant visual perception. In D. Kuhn & R. S. Siegler (Vol. Eds.), *Cognitive, language, and perceptual development,* Vol. 2 (pp. 103–146). In B. Damon (General Editor), *Handbook of child psychology.* New York: Wiley. This chapter reviews the basic research on infant visual perception. Written by two leaders in the field, it is an authoritative and often detailed account of how babies see.

SILVERMAN, I., & EALS, M. (1992). Sex differences in spatial abilities: Evolutionary theory and data. In J. H. Barkow, L. Cosmides, & J. Tooby (Eds.), *The Adapted Mind: Evolutionary Psychology and the Generation of Culture* (pp. 533–549). New York: Oxford University Press. This chapter presents experiments demonstrating male superiority on some tasks of spatial cognition and female superiority on others. What's highly unusual about this paper is that the authors interpret their findings in terms of evolutionary psychology, providing a model for research in this emerging field.

Representation

Mental Representation Through Infancy
Expressions of the Symbolic Function
What Do Infants Know? • *What Is Infant Cognition Made of?*

Learning to Use Symbols
Young Children's Interpretation of Pictures and Models
The Appearance/Reality Distinction
Distinguishing Between Imagined and Real Events • *Children's Theory of Mind*

Representational Changes over Childhood: Evidence from Classification
Classification • *The Development of Natural Language Categories*

Summary

Note

Key Terms and Concepts

Suggested Readings

One of the central issues in cognitive development concerns the nature of **representation.** How do children of different ages represent their world? Age differences in representation have been central to Piagetian and neo-Piagetian theories. For example, Piaget, Fischer, and Case each proposed developmental stages in representational abilities, progressing from sensorimotor, through symbolic, to abstract representation; and Karmiloff-Smith proposed developmental differences in the use of implicit and explicit representations, with the central mechanism of her theory being the redescription of representation. Information-processing approaches have traditionally been less concerned about stages of representation but have nonetheless held that how children represent information can influence subsequent processing. For example, Brainerd and Reyna's fuzzy-trace theory holds that information is represented along a verbatim-to-fuzzy continuum, and how any particular event is encoded will affect how it is remembered and used to solve problems.

In this chapter, I examine different aspects of children's developing abilities to symbolically represent their worlds. I begin with infancy, where there is much debate about when and to what extent infants can use symbols. The remainder of the chapter focuses on changes in representational abilities and preferences over childhood, with the focus being on the preschool child. This includes children's abilities to use external objects such as pictures and models as symbols, distinguishing between appearance and reality and between reality and fantasy, children's developing "theories of mind" (both of their own minds and of other people's), and differences in how children classify objects.

Mental Representation Through Infancy

The transition from the curious, hands-on-everything toddler to the contemplative, speaking child is a remarkable one indeed. Until very recently, few argued with Piaget's claim that infants represent information differently from older chil-

dren. According to Piaget, infants during their first 18 months or so represent objects and events by means of self-produced action (including perceptual "action"). They cannot mentally try out a behavior before executing it and cannot make mental contrasts between stimuli. Infants are not capable of symbolic representation until they are 18- to 24-months old. However, during the last two decades, considerable dissent has been forming concerning the symbolic abilities of infants, and I will explore some of this research in the sections to follow. But first, let's look at the changes in representation and behavior that Piaget and others observed beginning late in the second year of life.

Expressions of the Symbolic Function

According to Piaget, the **symbolic** (or, more properly, the **semiotic**) **function** has its origins in sensorimotor operations. This view is consistent with Piaget's epigenetic and constructivist positions, discussed in Chapter 4, which posit that every form of cognition is constructed from earlier, more primitive functioning. The symbolic function is expressed through a variety of mechanisms, including **deferred imitation, language, symbolic play,** and **mental imagery.**

Piaget's observations of *deferred imitation* were discussed in Chapter 4. Deferred imitation refers to observing a model and imitating the model's behavior after some significant period of time. To do this requires not only that children pay attention to a model but also that they store a mental representation of the target behavior and retrieve that representation from memory at the appropriate time. This, stated Piaget, requires the use of symbols, and this is not usually seen until about 18 months of life. More recent research on deferred imitation, suggesting a much earlier onset than proposed by Piaget, will be discussed later in this chapter.

Language is the most obvious form of the symbolic function. Although most children start uttering individual words by 10 to 12 months, not until 18 months or so do they put two words together into simple sentences. Piaget recognized language as a useful means by which people express their knowledge. But he was firm in his belief that we use language *because* we are symbolic, and not vice versa. In other words, language is a symptom of the symbolic function and not its cause. Language development and the developmental relation between language and thought will be discussed in Chapter 9.

Symbolic play is basically the game of pretending and was discussed in Chapter 3. The parents of most 2-year-olds can give examples of symbolic play. The 18-month-old who holds his mother's shoe to his ear and says "Hello" or the 2-year-old who feeds her doll imaginary cereal and scolds her for playing with her food, for example, are endearing to adults and reflect a child's increasingly sophisticated cognitive system.

Mental imagery is the internal representation of an external event. Although it is most easily thought of in terms of vision, Piaget used imagery to refer to mental representations of information from any sensory modality (for example, hearing or kinesthesia). According to Piaget, mental images are the result of internalized imitation. Imagery is not merely an exact copy of the perception of an object but is an active re-creation of a perception.

Piaget described two types of images: reproductive and anticipatory. **Reproductive images** are limited to evoking previously experienced sights and involve relatively static representations of objects. **Anticipatory images** allow the individual to envision transformations of an image, even if one has never experienced such transformations in the past. For instance, imagine your car rotated upward 90 degrees and suspended by its bumper from the branch of a tree. It is to be hoped that this is an event you have never actually experienced, but it is an image most adults can generate without much difficulty. Piaget contended that anticipatory images are not found until the concrete operational period, beginning around 7 years of age, with preschool children's use of images being limited to the reproductive type. This perspective was echoed by Jerome Bruner (1966), who described the preschool-age child's representations as *ikonic*, or perception-bound, and the school-age child's representations as *symbolic*, involving the use of language to symbolically represent events. This perspective implies that preschool children often attend to or reason about literal stimulus

features, whereas older children can represent problems in more abstract ways. This view is even shared by nonstage theorists such as Brainerd and Reyna (1990), who propose a gradual shift in encoding bias from mainly literal to mainly fuzzy traces between early and later childhood, as discussed in Chapter 5.

Few developmental psychologists would argue with the idea that children's cognition changes drastically toward the symbolic sometime between the ages of about 18 and 30 months of age. But a growing body of evidence suggests that infants and young children are far more sophisticated than Piaget proposed. What Piaget (and millions of parents) observed is real—no one is questioning his observations. But when one looks more carefully—designing experiments to better assess what infants and young children know, not just what they spontaneously show—there is evidence that Piaget greatly underestimated the knowledge and symbolic abilities of the sensorimotor child. To some (Fischer & Bidell, 1991), such evidence reflects only that Piaget had the timetable wrong; the order of stages is still the same, as are the processes underlying development. Others (Gelman & Williams, 1998; Spelke & Newport, 1998) see such evidence as indicating that the process of development is very different from that described by Piaget.

What Do Infants Know?

In this section, I examine some of the evidence for claims of greater knowledge/symbolic ability in infants and toddlers than recognized by Piaget. Infants' ability to imitate, their knowledge of objects, and their basic concept of number have all been studied and provide interesting and sometimes controversial evidence.

Neonatal Imitation

Research into **neonatal imitation** has generated perhaps more controversy about possible symbolic representation in early infancy than any other. Piaget (1962) initially noted that infants do not imitate "invisible gestures" such as facial expressions until about 12 months of age. This observation, and

Piaget's description of the development of imitation in general, went unchallenged until a 1977 report by Andrew Meltzoff and M. Keith Moore, demonstrating imitation of facial expressions by 6- to 21-day-old babies. Examples of the facial gestures modeled to infants in this experiment and responses by infants are shown in Photo 7-1. The number of tongue protrusions and mouth openings that infants made in response to an adult model were counted from video recordings of the sessions and contrasted with the number of each gesture made during baseline periods (that is, when no gestures were modeled). Meltzoff and Moore reported that infants made significantly more tongue protrusions to the tongue model than to the open-mouth model or during baseline. Similar patterns of results were found for mouth opening. Meltzoff and Moore interpreted these results as clear evidence for selective imitation of facial gestures during the first month of life. Other researchers have similarly reported imitation of tongue protrusions and other facial gestures in infants during the first two months of life (Legerstee, 1991; Meltzoff & Moore, 1992), with several researchers reporting imitation in newborns (Field et al., 1982; Vinter, 1986) (for a review, see Anisfeld, 1991).

The effect is somewhat elusive, however, and several experimenters have failed to replicate early imitation using procedures similar to those used by Meltzoff and Moore (Kaitz et al., 1988; Lewis & Sullivan, 1985; McKenzie & Over, 1983). Moreover, imitation of facial gestures actually declines during the first year of life. For the most-studied facial gesture of tongue protrusion, most investigators who have examined infants of different ages report a peak in imitation sometime during the first two months, followed by a decline within weeks to chance values (Abravanel & Sigafoos, 1984; Jacobson, 1979). This is indeed perplexing, in that we have what appears to be a sophisticated cognitive phenomenon that actually decreases in frequency over a very brief period of time. Sandra Jacobson (1979) has shown that tongue protrusions can also be elicited by a variety of tonguelike stimuli, such as a pen moved toward infants' faces. The only excep-

PHOTO 7-1   Photograph of 2- to 3-week-old infants imitating (a) tongue protrusion, (b) mouth opening, and (c) lip protrusion demonstrated by an adult experimenter. SOURCE: Meltzoff, A. N., & Moore, M. K. (1977). Imitation of facial and manual gestures by human neonates. *Science, 198,* 75–78.

tion to this decrease in facial imitation over time was reported by Meltzoff and Moore (1992), who assessed 2- and 3-month-old infants' responses over several trials. They, too, failed to find any evidence of facial imitation on the initial trial but did find imitation by these "older" infants on later trials.

How can neonatal imitation be explained? Meltzoff and Moore (1977, 1985) have suggested that modeling effects during early infancy could be attributed to (1) learning; (2) selective imitation, guided by the integration of information from one sensory modality (vision) with information from another (proprioception derived from self-initiated movements); or (3) an innate releasing mechanism, where reflexlike responses are elicited by a specific set of stimuli.

Meltzoff and Moore (1977, 1985) and others (Field et al., 1982; Jacobson, 1979) suggest that learning is an unlikely candidate to explain early imitation. The most compelling reason for rejecting a learning or reinforcement interpretation is that infants only hours old will match certain facial expressions to those of an adult (Field et al., 1982; Vinter, 1986). It is unlikely that such young infants would have had sufficient experience to "learn" these responses.

The second interpretation is the one favored by Meltzoff and Moore. They propose that the matching behavior observed in the early weeks of life is true imitation. Newborns are able to coordinate information from two senses. They can visually observe a stimulus, store an abstract representation of that stimulus, and compare it shortly thereafter with a proprioceptive representation (that is, their own movements). This position holds that newborns possess the ability to integrate information from two senses (that is, they possess intermodal integration, see Chapter 6). Meltzoff and Moore (1985) refer to this behavior as **active intermodal mapping.** If one accepts this interpretation, it advances the ability to coordinate two sensory modalities to a period many months earlier than that suggested by Piaget and others (Birch & Lefford, 1963). Such an interpretation is not without some additional empirical support. As discussed in Chapter 6, for example, research has demonstrated tactual-visual transfer of information in 4- to 6-month-olds (Bushnell, 1981; Streri & Spelke, 1989), and Meltzoff and Borton (1979) reported visual-tactual integration in infants less than 1 month old.

Yet, if the imitation observed in very young infants is selective and is accomplished by active intermodal mapping, why does it seemingly disappear only months after its appearance? The third alternative, that neonatal matching behavior is attributed to an innate releasing mechanism, attempts to account for the decline in imitation over the first six months (Abravanel & Sigafoos, 1984; Jacobson, 1979; Kaye, 1982). **Innate releasing mechanisms, or fixed-action patterns,** are inherited sets of behaviors elicited by specific sets of stimuli without prior environmental experience (Tinbergen, 1951).

The idea that neonatal imitation can best be explained as a fixed-action pattern is at odds not only with the theorizing of Meltzoff and Moore but also with Piagetian theory. Piaget's epigenetic approach holds that nothing comes from nothing, that every structure has its genesis in earlier structures. A corollary to this view is that every form of early intelligence serves as preparation for later forms of intelligence. Thus, early reflexes, although they may eventually drop out of the child's repertoire, serve as a basis for later, more advanced cognitive functioning. This is clearly seen in Piaget's description of imitative-like responses during the first three sensorimotor stages. The interpretation of early imitation as a fixed-action pattern is counter to Piaget's view, in that this reflexive matching behavior, which has the appearance of a legitimate cognitive function, need not lead to more advanced forms of imitation. Rather, the behavior disappears without specifically preparing the child for subsequent intellectual accomplishments.

What function might neonatal imitation play, then, if it is not preparation for later cognitive development? One interpretation is that such responses simply reflect "oral exploration" (babies stick their tongues out to interesting objects they wish to explore with their mouths) (Jones, 1996). Another interpretation is that such responses may play a specific role in survival for the infant at that time, and that time only, and that they disappear when they are no longer needed (Bjorklund, 1987b). Oppenheim (1981) has referred to such phenomena as **transient ontogenetic adaptations.** He argues that the young organism lives in a very different world from the adult, requiring different behavioral or neurological organization to cope with life. Such organization might not be the basis for later development but, rather, might be present only for survival at that time and in that specific environment. Jacobson (1979), for example, suggested that tongue protrusions might be functional in early nursing. Bjorklund (1987b) suggested that the apparent imitation by young infants might play a role in early social development. The matching of adult facial gestures by the infant might help maintain social interaction between the two, with these reflexes declining when infants are able to intentionally direct their gaze and control their head and mouth movements to social stimulation, somewhere between the second and fourth months of life (Cairns, 1979). In a similar vein, Legerstee (1991) suggested that early imitation serves as a form of prelinguistic communication. Tentative support for these positions has been provided by Heimann (1989), who found a relationship between imitation in newborns and mother-infant social interactions at 3 months of age; infants who showed high levels of neonatal imitation had more social interactions with their mothers three months later.

Meltzoff and Moore (1992) have a different but related idea. They propose that the decrease in facial imitation seen beginning around 2 months of age is caused by the increasing social orientation of infants. Beginning around this time, infants initially respond to people by playing social games. These games obfuscate imitation responses, making it appear that they disappear. However, when proper controls are used, as in Meltzoff and Moore's (1992) repeated-trials procedure, facial imitation is still found in 2- to 3-month-old infants. Meltzoff and Moore (1985) further argue against the view of neonatal imitation as a fixed-action pattern, writing that infants' imitative responses are not strongly stereotyped, as would be expected if they were governed by innate releasing mechanisms. Also, they note that infants have been shown to imitate a large number of different gestures and that it is not reasonable to propose a different reflex for each gesture.

The book is by no means closed on early infant imitation. However, with the evidence from other research demonstrating early, possibly innate, object knowledge (Spelke & Newport, 1998), Meltzoff and Moore's claim that neonatal imitation reflects active intermodal matching, and thus an early form of symbol use, is becoming increasingly plausible.

Deferred Imitation

Initial research by Piaget (1962), and later research by others (McCall, Parke, & Kavanaugh, 1977; Uzgiris & Hunt, 1975), demonstrated that infants are not able to display deferred imitation until they are about 18 months old. Piaget believed that deferred imitation is a reflection of the symbolic function.

Children must observe a model, store a representation of the model's behavior in memory, and retrieve that memory representation at some later time, attempting to reproduce the behavior. (Recall the example of Piaget's daughter who demonstrated deferred imitation of a temper tantrum at 16 months.) Given his theory, 18 to 24 months is the perfect time to see this behavior.

Evidence that deferred imitation might occur earlier surfaced in 1985, with the publication of papers by Meltzoff (1985) and by Abravanel and Gingold (1985). The basic procedure used in these, and later, studies involves showing infants some novel behavior, often with a new toy. For example, an infant may observe a model picking up a dumb-bell-shaped toy and taking one end off in a particular way (Meltzoff, 1988a). The infant, however, is not given an opportunity to play with the toy but only to watch a model use it. Sometime later, the infants are again shown the toy and their behavior is observed. If they show the novel behavior (in this case, taking apart the toy in a specific way) more than children who are given the toy for the first time, this is good evidence for deferred imitation. In other words, because other children who have never seen the toy before rarely take it apart, the fact that children who have seen it taken apart do so, implies that they learned this behavior from watching the model, rather than that taking the toy apart is just something that children normally do when playing with it.

The initial studies by Meltzoff (1985) and Abravanel and Gingold (1985) reported deferred imitation for 12- and 14-month-old infants over delays ranging from 10 minutes to 24 hours. Later research has extended these findings, reporting deferred imitation for 14-month-olds for novel behaviors after delays of two days (Hanna & Meltzoff, 1993) and one week (Meltzoff, 1988a), and after a five-week period for a sample of 9-month-olds (Carver & Bauer, 1999). More recent research has found evidence of deferred imitation in preverbal toddlers for periods of one to 12 months (Bauer & Wewerka, 1995; Mandler & McDonough, 1995; Meltzoff, 1995). Levels or quality of deferred imitation are typically greater for older than for younger infants (Abravenal & Gingold, 1985; Meltzoff, 1985), and few would claim that the imitation abilities of a 12-month-old infant are comparable with those of a 20- or 24-month-old child.

Moreover, toddlers will imitate not just adults but also other toddlers and televised models. One study reported deferred imitation (2 days) in 14-month-old children who watched the novel behavior of another 14-month-old, indicating the potential role of peers as models for very young children (Hanna & Meltzoff, 1993). Another study found deferred imitation (24 hours) in 14-month-olds for behaviors modeled by an adult on television (Meltzoff, 1988b). This latter finding indicates that young children can learn from two-dimensional displays and that toddlers can potentially acquire new behaviors from viewing television.

Is deferred imitation a type of explicit, or declarative memory? Recall from Chapter 5, *explicit* memory is contrasted with *implicit* memory. The former represents a deliberate attempt to remember and is potentially available to conscious awareness, whereas the latter is often referred to as "memory without awareness." Most researchers who have investigated deferred imitation in older infants believe it to be a form of nonverbal explicit memory (Bauer, 1996, 1997; Meltzoff, 1995). If so, this type of memory would be using the same type of representational system used by older children on verbal memory tasks (see Chapter 8 on memory).

How can one tell the difference between explicit and implicit memory in preverbal children? Perhaps one can't, but support for this argument comes from a study of adult amnesiacs. These people are unable to perform typical declarative memory tasks (memory with awareness) but do perform well on implicit memory tasks (memory without awareness). How do they perform on deferred imitation tasks? Just like they do on the declarative memory tasks—they fail them (McDonough et al., 1995). These findings suggest that deferred imitation tasks tap the same memory system as do declarative tasks used with older children (for example, "Tell me what you had for breakfast this morning"), and "that the neurolog-

ical systems underlying long-term recall are present, in at least rudimentary form, by the beginning of the second year of life" (Schneider & Bjorklund, 1998, p. 474).

Knowledge of Physical Objects

Perhaps the best documented evidence that infants are more sophisticated than Piaget proposed comes from studies examining **object permanence** and other aspects of infants' knowledge of physical objects. Such research does not necessarily reflect symbolic representation in early infancy but rather might indicate that infants have innate, or at least very early developing, knowledge of objects that requires only minimal environmental support and the maturation of infants' response systems to be expressed.

As you may recall from our discussion of Piaget's account of sensorimotor intelligence (Chapter 4), infants will not search for a hidden object until about 8 months and fail the A-not-B object-permanence task until about 12 months. Infants slightly younger than 8 months may retrieve a hidden object when they are in the process of reaching for it when it was covered, but this more likely reflects an inability to inhibit a prepotent response (Diamond, 1985) rather than demonstrating object permanence. Despite the robustness of these observations, growing evidence indicates that infants as young as 3.5 months have far more knowledge of objects than Piaget proposed, suggesting to some that this knowledge is innate (that is, representational innateness, Spelke & Newport, 1998).

The trick in demonstrating object knowledge in very young infants is to test behaviors appropriate to their developmental level. For example, it is impossible to assess object retrieval in 3- and 4-month-old infants because of their limited motor skills. Most researchers looking at early infant abilities have used variants of the habituation/dishabituation procedure, described with respect to infant perception and attention in Chapter 6. Basically, infants are shown an event repeatedly until their attention to it diminishes to a certain level (habituation). They are

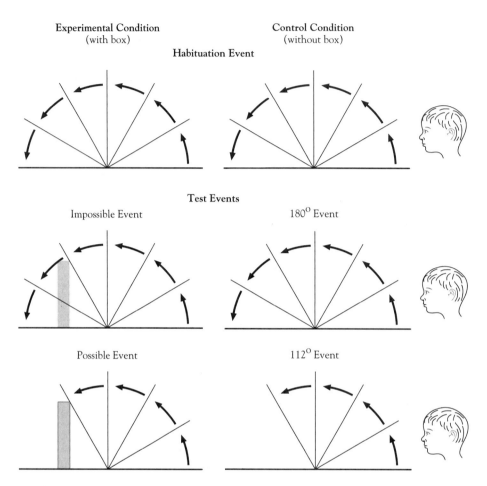

FIGURE 7-1   The habituation and test (dishabituation) events shown to infants in the experimental and control conditions in the object-permanence experiment by Baillargeon. SOURCE: From "Object Permanence in 3½- and 4½-month-old infants," by R. Baillargeon, 1987, *Developmental Psychology, 23*, 655–664. Copyright © 1987 American Psychological Association. Reprinted with permission.

then shown an alternative event, and changes in their level of attention are examined. As demonstrated in Chapter 6, following habituation, young infants will increase their attention (that is, show dishabituation) when a new stimulus is presented. The experimenter must be clever enough to take advantage of this characteristic of infant attention and to use it to infer knowledge of objects that previously went undetected.

Evidence of object permanence in very young infants is probably best exemplified by the work of

Renée Baillargeon (1987; Baillargeon & De Vos, 1991) using the **violation-of-expectation method.** In Baillargeon's experiment (1987), infants 3.5 and 4.5 months of age were habituated to a moving screen (see Figure 7-1). The screen was rotated 180 degrees, from being flat in a box with its leading edge facing the infant, rising continuously through an arc until it rested in the box with its leading edge farthest away from the infant. Once habituated to this event, infants in the experimental group were shown a colorful wooden block with a clown face painted on it, placed to the rear of the flat screen. In the "impossible event" condition, the screen was rotated upward (exactly as in the habituation trials), which, in the process, obscured the wooden block from the infant's sight. When the screen reached 90 degrees, the wooden block was removed, out of the view of the infant. The screen then continued its downward rotation until it lay flat. The screen was then rotated upward again and the wooden block was replaced, again unbeknownst to the infant, so that it reappeared once more when the screen was being rotated toward the infant. From the infant's perspective, such a series of events (the continuous movement of the screen, despite the presence of an obstacle) should have been impossible and violated their expectation of what should have happened. If the wooden object were real in space and time, the screen should have stopped when it reached it. This, in fact, is what infants did see on some trials (the "possible event"), with the screen stopping at the point at which it should have, given that there was an object on the other side. If the infants believed that the wooden block continued to exist, they should have shown surprise or increased looking time at the "impossible event" relative to the "possible event." Infants in the control condition saw the same sequence of screen movements but were never shown the wooden block. Thus, these infants had no reason to express surprise. Infants in all conditions received four test trials.

The results of this experiment for the 4.5-month-old infants are graphed in Figure 7-2. As can be seen, the infants in the experimental condition looked significantly longer at the "impossible event" than at the "possible event." For the experimental infants, there was apparently nothing surprising about the "possible event," but they knew that something was amiss when the screen failed to stop. No differences in looking time were found for the infants in the control condition. Similar findings were reported for 3.5-month-old infants (Baillargeon, 1987, Experiments 2 and 3; Baillargeon & De Vos, 1991).

The most straightforward interpretation of these results is that the infants believed that the block continued to exist even though it was out of their

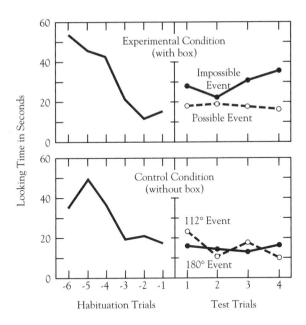

FIGURE 7-2 Looking times of infants in the experimental and control conditions during habituation and test trials in Baillargeon's experiment. Note the increased looking time for the infants in the experimental condition during the test trials for the impossible event. SOURCE: "Object Permanence in 3½- and 4½-month-old infants," by R. Baillargeon, 1987, *Developmental Psychology, 23,* 655–664. Copyright © 1987 American Psychological Association. Reprinted with permission.

sight, and they were surprised when the screen failed to stop. Their performance in the "impossible event" condition reflects not only a knowledge of the permanence of objects, but also a knowledge that one solid object cannot pass through another. Elizabeth Spelke (1991; Spelke et al., 1992) has similarly demonstrated in a series of experiments that infants as young as 2.5 months of age have a knowledge of the solidity and continuity of objects (the fact that a moving object continues on its path), and more recent research by Baillargeon and her colleagues has investigated young infants' understanding of support (an object must be supported or it falls), collisions (an object that is hit by another object moves) (Baillargeon, Kotovsky, & Needham, 1995), and containment (a larger object cannot fit into a smaller object) (Aguiar & Baillargeon, 1998).

Such knowledge is obvious to adults, but why should it be obvious to 3.5-month-old infants? One interpretation of these findings is that, counter to Piaget, such knowledge is not constructed from earlier knowledge but is part of the mental apparatus with which infants are born. That is, infants come into the world with substantive beliefs (representational innateness) about objects. This *neo-nativist* perspective was introduced when I described Karmiloff-Smith's theory in Chapter 4. Writing about young infants' knowledge of continuity and solidity, Spelke (1991) proposed that such knowledge "may derive from universal, early-developing capacities to represent and reason about the physical world. These capacities may emerge in all infants whose early growth and experience fall within some normal range. They may enable children to infer how any material body will move in any situation" (pp. 160–161). Spelke and her colleagues (Spelke, 1994; Spelke et al., 1992) have proposed that there are three core principles of innate knowledge about objects that infants possess: *cohesion,* the idea that objects have boundaries and that their components stay connected to one another; *continuity,* the idea that an object moves from one location to another in a continuous path and cannot be in the same place as another object; and *contact,* the idea that one object must contact another object to make it move. Infants' development of their ideas about cohesion, continuity, and contact develop with experience, but, according to Spelke, babies possess *core knowledge* (representational innateness) about these domains from birth.

A related idea is that infants do not possess innate beliefs about objects, but rather come into the world with highly constrained mechanisms for dealing with objects (architectural innateness). This perspective can still be considered one of neo-nativism, for it suggests specific constraints that make it easier for the infant to learn. But it is *processes* that are innate and not knowledge per se. This is a type of "starting-state" nativism as proposed by Gopnik and Meltzoff (1997) in their theory theory discussed in Chapter 4, and reflects

Baillargeon's perspective (Baillargeon, 1994; Baillargeon et al., 1995). According to Baillargeon, infants initially form a preliminary all-or-none concept about a phenomenon. Only later, with experience, does this concept get modified and result in an adult understanding.

Let me provide an example from Baillargeon's work on the development of infants' understanding of support. Using the violation-of-expectation method, much as was done in her work on object permanence, Baillargeon and her colleagues (1995) showed infants possible and impossible events reflecting the notion of support (see Figure 7-3). A gloved hand would push a box that sat atop a platform from left to right. In the possible event, the box stopped while firmly situated on the platform. In the impossible event, the box was pushed until only 15% of it rested on the platform. How did babies react to the impossible event? The youngest infants (3-month-olds) weren't surprised. As long as the box maintained some contact with the platform, they acted as if they expected it to remain on the platform and not to fall. Beginning around 4.5 months, the amount of contact between the box and the platform becomes important, and by 6.5 months, infants expect that the box will fall unless a significant portion of it is in contact with the platform.

How can one interpret these findings? According to Baillargeon, infants originally believe that any contact between two objects is enough for one to support the other. Only when there is no contact between two objects do they expect gravity to take over. Their concept gets progressively revised with experience, however, until they eventually arrive, quite early in life, at an adult-like concept of support. Baillargeon (1994; Baillargeon et al., 1995) provides evidence that other aspects of infants' knowledge of objects develop in a similar sequence from all-or-none to a progressively mature understanding of objects.

Does Baillargeon's work prove that infants' early knowledge of objects is based on innate *processing* (or architectural) constraints rather than innate *conceptual* (or representational) constraints? Not necessarily. In fact, although I generally tend to favor processing-constraint views over conceptual-

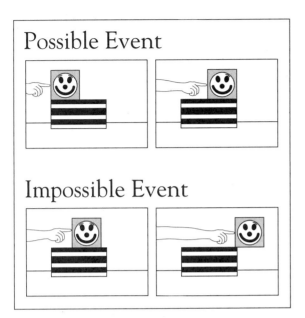

Possible Event

Impossible Event

FIGURE 7-3 Example of possible and impossible events for object support. SOURCE: Baillargeon, R. (1994). How do infants learn about the physical world? *Current Directions in Psychological Science, 3*, 133–140.

constraint views (such as those proposed by Spelke), a substantial database covering a host of infant motor, perceptual, and cognitive abilities can be interpreted by either perspective (Gelman & Williams, 1998; Spelke & Newport, 1998), and I would be surprised if infants were not born with both types of constraints. The bottom line seems to be that infants know more about the physical nature of objects and know it earlier than we once believed and that some innate constraints make the acquisition of such knowledge possible (Gelman & Williams, 1998).

Early Number Concepts

Perhaps one of the more surprising, and still controversial, claims made recently about infants' symbolic abilities is that 5-month-old infants can effectively add and subtract simple sets of numbers. It has been known for some time that very young infants can

detect differences in numerosity—that is, tell the difference between two arrays that differ in the number of objects they contain (Antell & Keating, 1983; van Loosbroek & Smitsman, 1990). But this is far removed from the claim that infants can perform simple addition and subtraction.

Evidence for this was reported in a study by Karen Wynn (1992), who used a variant of the violation-of-expectation method that has been so useful in assessing infants' cognitive abilities. The logic behind Wynn's procedure is similar to that used by Baillargeon (1987) discussed earlier, who showed infants "possible" and "impossible" events concerning the physical existence of objects and inferred infants' knowledge of object permanence based on their attention to the various events. In Wynn's experiment, 5-month-old infants were shown a sequence of events that involved the addition or subtraction of elements. Two of these sequences are shown in Figure 7-4. One sequence (the "possible outcome") led to the conclusion that 1 + 1 = 2; the other sequence (the "impossible outcome") led to the conclusion that 1 + 1 = 1. Infants sat in front of a stage and watched as one object was placed in it (step 1 in Figure 7-4). A screen was then raised, hiding the object (step 2 in Figure 7-4). The infant then watched as a second object was placed behind the screen (steps 3 and 4 in Figure 7-4). The screen was then lowered, revealing either two objects (the "possible outcome") or one object (the "impossible outcome"). If infants have some primitive concept of addition, they should be surprised and thus spend more time looking at the "impossible outcome." This was exactly what occurred, both for the addition problem shown in Figure 7-4 and for a simple subtraction problem (2 − 1 = 1). These findings have been replicated by others (Simon, Hespos, & Rochat, 1995).

How can these results best be interpreted? Infants seem not to be making only a perceptual discrimination between two arrays (that is, telling the difference between an array with one item in it and another with two). Rather, when they watch as one item is added to another behind a screen, they expect to see two items when the screen is dropped. This requires a certain level of object permanence

1. Object placed in case   2. Screen comes up   3. Second object added   4. Hand leaves empty

Then either: possible outcome   or: impossible outcome

5. Screen drops ...   ...revealing 2 objects   5. Screen drops ...   ...revealing 1 object

FIGURE 7–4   Sequence of events for the 1 + 1 = 2 (possible) outcome and the 1 + 1 = 1 (impossible) outcome from the experiment by Wynn (1992). SOURCE: "Addition and Subtraction by Human Infants," by K. Wynn, 1992, *Nature*, *358*, 749–750. Copyright © 1992 Macmillan Magazines Ltd. Reprinted with permission from *Nature*.

and memory, but also some rudimentary ideas about addition. They must infer that the second object was added to the first, without actually seeing that this was done (recall that the screen occluded their vision).

Of course, infants are not adding in the way young children add (even if they wanted to, they don't have sufficient motor coordination to count on their fingers). What infants seem to be doing is **subitizing,** which is quantifying small numbers of items without conscious counting. For example, when looking at playing cards, one immediately "knows" how many clubs, diamonds, hearts, or spades is on the card by looking at the configuration of objects (at least up to six). Direct counting is not necessary, nor is it necessary to actually read the number in the corner of the card. One can arrive at the correct number of items by subitizing. Based on Wynn's findings, 5-month-old infants seem to be able to do something similar, at least for the quantities of one and two. This line of work is provocative and suggests substantially greater quantitative (symbolic) knowledge in young infants than was previously believed, although it does not justify the conclusion that babies are born knowing basic arith-

metic or that infants and toddlers should be able to learn complicated mathematics given the proper instructions. Although the nature of their numerical competencies might not be fully known, it seems relatively certain that it is not the equivalent of the abilities found in children only a few years older.

What Is Infant Cognition Made Of?

The gospel according to Piaget held that infant cognition is sensorimotor in nature. Infants know their world through raw sensation and their direct actions on objects. Slowly, over the course of the first two years of life, cognition is changed, transformed (constructed) into symbol-based thought, permitting the child to conceptualize the world in a new way. There is little debate that cognition and behavior does change during the first two years of life. Brain growth is more rapid during the first two years than at any other time in postnatal life. Cognitive differences between the 10-month-old and the 2-year-old are dramatic, obvious to anyone who takes the time to look. Yet, there is increasing evidence that the huge changes in overt behavior that are apparent to all might be masking much smaller changes in underlying competencies. Infants seem to know a lot about their physical world from birth, or shortly thereafter, and are able to use simple symbol systems to remember events over extended periods of time and are possibly able to do simple computations.

Some of these skills are likely domain specific in nature. In Chapter 6, we saw that very young infants can recognize faces and perhaps are even born with a prototype for the human face (as reflected by their preference for "attractive" faces; see Langlois et al., 1987). Such skills are likely limited to face identification and recognition and do not generalize to other aspects of cognition. Similar arguments can be made for some of the cognitive abilities examined here. Infants' knowledge of the characteristics of objects might be restricted to certain classes of physical relations. For example, despite their substantial knowledge of the permanence, continuity, and solidity of objects, young infants apparently know nothing about inertia (Spelke, 1991). Similarly, knowledge of addition and subtraction might be domain specific, with the symbolic skills underlying simple computation being unavailable to other conceptual systems. Similar arguments have been made for neonatal imitation (Bjorklund, 1987b; Legerstee, 1991), which might function as a fixed-action pattern and serve a restricted role in early social development.

Other aspects of young infants' cognitions might be more domain general in nature. For example, the symbolic abilities underlying deferred imitation of novel events seem not to be restricted to any particular domain of knowledge. In a similar vein, Catherine Sophian (1997) has suggested that innate structures are more like tools that might be best suited for some contents (understanding objects, for example) but can also be used flexibly for other purposes (see also Gelman & Williams, 1998).

Do these new findings require a full-scale replacement of Piagetian ideas of sensorimotor development? Andrew Meltzoff (1990) apparently thinks so. In reviewing his and other people's research on cognitive development over infancy, Meltzoff concluded that "*in a very real sense, there may be no such thing as an exclusively 'sensorimotor period' in the nor-*

mal human infant" (p. 20, italics in the original). Jean Mandler (1992, 1998) takes a similar, though somewhat less drastic position. Mandler interprets the wealth of new information about infant cognition as requiring new theories. She has suggested a model similar to the one described in Chapter 4 by Karmiloff-Smith (1992), in which infants redescribe their perceptions (presumably including both the sensory and motor representations of the traditional sensorimotor stage) into conceptual form. Such conceptual knowledge can coexist with the type of knowledge Piaget described. It is not necessary to posit substantial amounts of innate knowledge, Mandler suggests. According to Mandler (1992), "We need only to grant that infants are born with a capacity to abstract certain kinds of information from perceptual displays that they will process, and to redescribe them into conceptual form. . . . I have suggested that this process is operative from at least a few months of age, which would allow concepts to develop in tandem with sensorimotor development, rather than having a later onset" (pp. 226–227).

Not everyone believes that the new research findings truly reflect advanced symbolic functioning or innate knowledge. For example, Kurt Fischer and Thomas Bidell (1991) argue that it is a great leap to infer that infants possess a concept of number or object permanence based on patterns of dishabituation. Any particular infant skill should not be viewed in isolation, but in the context of overall development. Rather than asking, for instance, when infants "really" have object permanence, Fischer and Bidell (1991) suggest that developmental researchers should ask more fruitful questions, including these: "What is the developmental sequence of object knowledge from earliest infancy through early childhood? How is the development of this sequence related to developments in other domains? How is it constrained by the nature of perceptual and sensorimotor processes, which are partly regulated by the genome, and by environmental inputs? How are such constraints evident at various points in developmental sequences?" (pp. 223–224). These are similar to the arguments made by Haith (1993) with respect to infant perceptual abilities (see Chapter 6). Similarly, Meltzoff and Moore (1998) have argued that studies using the violation-of-expectation methodology such as Baillargeon's do not necessarily reflect object permanence, although they do reflect *representational persistence*, or a memory of a particular event. This, Meltzoff and Moore claim, is only an initial step in representational knowledge. Yet, counter to the Piagetian perspective, they propose that the evidence from 30 years of infant research indicates that infants are representational from birth (that is, there is no purely sensorimotor period), although this ability develops gradually during the first two years of life.

On a more fundamental level, Richard Bogartz and his colleagues (Bogartz & Shinskey, 1998; Bogartz, Shinskey, & Speaker, 1997) have argued that it is not necessary to attribute innate knowledge of physical objects to account for the findings of studies that use infants' looking behavior as an indication of what they know. Bogartz and his colleagues (1997) "assume that young infants cannot reason, draw inferences, or have beliefs" (p. 411), and "that the infant does not enter the world with [knowledge of objects] nor does it acquire such knowledge of physical laws in the first 6 months of life" (p. 412). How, then, can one explain the data if there are no innate conceptual or processing constraints?

Bogartz and his colleagues suggest that young infants come into the world with a set of mechanisms for processing perceptual information, and that infants acquire knowledge of objects through perceptual experience (much as Piaget proposed). The nature of perceptual processing produces looking patterns that Baillargeon, Spelke, Wynn, and others interpret as "innate knowledge." According to Bogartz, Shinskey, and Speaker (1997), infants' perceptual processing "consists of analysis of the immediate representations of events, the construction in associative memory of the transformations of these immediate representations, abstraction of their forms, and the comparison of immediate perceptual representations to the representations stored in memory" (p. 411). All this processing takes time. In habituation/dishabituation tasks, infants look at familiar stimuli because it takes time to store memory representations. Novel events (that is, impossible

events in the studies described earlier) take even more time because initial encoding of the stimuli needs to be done. Infants show a preference for looking at the novel (impossible) over the familiar (habituated and possible) event simply because more processing is required to make sense of the former than the latter event. There is no need to postulate innate knowledge of physical laws, only laws about how infant perception and memory work. Similar arguments, based on characteristics of infants' perceptual and attentional mechanisms, have been made to account for 5-month-olds' apparent abilities to perform simple addition and subtraction as reported by Wynn (Haith & Benson, 1998; Simon, 1997) and for performance on object-permanence tasks as used by Baillargeon (Rivera, Wakeley, & Langer, 1999.

Who's right? That's a question that we can't answer yet, and perhaps one group doesn't have to be wrong for the other group to be right. Cognitive development does not follow a single course for all aspects of intelligence, and it is possible, and I believe likely, that infants' understanding of objects and the physical laws relating to them are multiply determined. Infants might possess some innate knowledge (representational constraints) as Spelke proposes, some innate processing mechanisms (architectural constraints) as suggested by Baillargeon, but at other times their behavior might be better explained by referring to more domain-general perceptual and memory mechanisms as proposed by Bogartz, rather than to highly constrained domain-specific processes. And most likely, infants' brains are structured so that domain-specific constraints (both representational and architectural) and domain-general mechanisms interact.

There is much excitement in infant research these days. Regardless of which interpretation one prefers, I think most researchers would agree that infants have far greater conceptual abilities than was previously believed, and every year we learn something else that infants know or can do. We should not lose sight, however, of what infants cannot do. There is no evidence, for example, that infants can be taught arithmetic, reading, or chemistry. Infancy is still a special time, and the infant mind remains far different from the mind that resides in the 3-year-old child. Remembering the limits of infant cognition is sometimes difficult when we look at all the things infants can do, but it is a thought we shouldn't lose.

Learning to Use Symbols

The term "symbol" as used in this and previous chapters has generally referred to some mental representation of a physical object or event. But in everyday parlance, symbol also refers to external referents for objects and events. For example, a picture or a photograph of an object is a stand-in for the real thing — it is a concrete, yet symbolic representation of an object that is not physically present. Likewise, scale models, such as a miniature representation of a room complete with doll-sized furniture, can serve as a symbolic representation of a larger, real room. Similarly, some things are not exactly what they seem. The ubiquitous refrigerator magnet attests to this. Cookies, candy bars, and many other "real" things are in actuality only magnets that look like something else. At a more abstract level, the letters and numbers so central to our technological culture are not what they seem to be but, rather, are symbols necessary for reading and computation. Judy DeLoache (1987; DeLoache & Marzolf, 1992) has referred to the knowledge that an entity can stand for something other than itself as **representational insight.** Representational insight extends beyond the abilities required for object permanence or deferred imitation. When can children understand and effectively use external forms of representation, such as pictures and models, and what does this tell us about their representational development?

In this section, I will examine three areas of research related to young children's use of external symbols. The first is the research of DeLoache and her colleagues looking at children's abilities to use pictures and scale models as representations for the real things. The second is research examining children's abilities to distinguish the differences between the appearance and reality of objects, and the third area examines young children's ability to distinguish imagining and experiencing.

Young Children's Interpretation of Pictures and Models

During the past several years, Judy DeLoache and her colleagues have been investigating preschool children's abilities to use models and pictures as symbols, and their studies have produced some interesting and, at first look, counterintuitive findings (DeLoache, 1995; DeLoache & Marzolf, 1992; DeLoache & Smith, 1999). In DeLoache's studies, 2- and 3-year-old children are asked to find a toy hidden in a room. Before searching for the object, they are shown a picture or scale model of the room, with the location of the hidden object made obvious in the picture or model. For example, children are shown a scale model of a room, with the experimenter hiding a miniature toy behind a chair in the model. The miniature toy and the model chair correspond to a large toy and a real chair in the adjoining real room. Children are then asked to find the toy in the room (retrieval 1). After searching for the toy in the room, they return to the model and are asked to find where the miniature toy was hidden (retrieval 2). If children cannot find the large toy in the room (retrieval 1) but can find the miniature toy in the scale model (retrieval 2), their failure to find the large toy cannot be because they forgot where the miniature toy was hidden. A better interpretation would be that the children cannot use the model in a symbolic fashion.

The results of one such experiment with 2.5- and 3-year-old children are graphed in Figure 7-5 (DeLoache, 1987). As can be seen, 3-year-olds performed comparably in both retrieval tasks, indicating that they remembered where the miniature toy was hidden and used the information from the scale model to find the large toy in the real room. The younger children showed good memory for where the miniature toy was hidden (retrieval 2 in the figure) but performed very poorly when trying to find the large toy in the real room (retrieval 1 in the

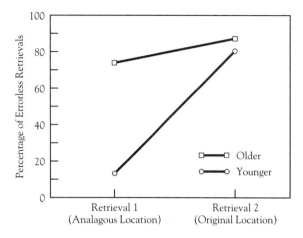

FIGURE 7-5   The number of errorless retrievals (correctly locating the hidden toy) for 2.5- (younger) and 3-year-olds (older) on a model task. Retrieval 1 involved locating the real toy in the real room; retrieval 2 involved locating the miniature toy in the model. SOURCE: "Rapid Change in the Symbolic Functioning of Very Young Children," by J. S. DeLoache, 1987, *Science, 238*, 1556–1557. Copyright © 1987 American Association for the Advancement of Science. Reprinted with permission.

Figure). This pattern of results suggests that 2.5-year-old children failed to recognize that the scale model was a symbolic representation of the large room. Recalling DeLoache's definition of representational insight as realizing that one entity can stand for another, it appears that on the scale-model task, 3-year-olds possess representational insight, whereas 2.5-year-old children do not.

A similar pattern of results was found when pictures of a room were used, with an experimenter pointing to the location in a picture where the toy was hidden (DeLoache, 1987, 1991). The primary difference between the picture and scale-model experiments was that the picture task was solved by 2.5-year-old children but not by 2-year-olds. Thus, when pictures are used as symbols, 2.5-year-olds demonstrate representational insight. Such competence is not achieved until 3 years of age, however, when a scale model is used (see also Dow & Pick, 1992).

Why should children perform more poorly using the scale model than the pictures? If I had been asked to make a prediction of which task would be the easier, my prediction would have been exactly the reverse. The model, being a more concrete stimulus, is more like the real room, and thus, it would seem, less symbolic sophistication would be required to use it to guide behavior. In fact, when young children are given toy objects versus pictures of objects to use in memory and simple problem-solving tasks, they usually perform better with the objects, not the pictures (Daehler, Lonardo, & Bukatko, 1979). Such was not the case with DeLoache's study, of course, and she proposed that one reason for the pattern of results was related to children's difficulty in thinking about an entity in two different ways at the same time, or what she refers to as **dual representation** (or **dual orientation**). A model, she argues, is an object worthy of attention all by itself. A picture, by contrast, is itself uninteresting, with its primary purpose being to represent something else. When models are made less interesting and less concrete, or when pictures are made more salient, performance should change.

This is exactly what DeLoache found. When models were viewed through a window, 2.5-year-olds' performance increased dramatically relative to the standard model task. Likewise, when 3-year-olds were allowed to play with the model before the hiding task, their performance significantly decreased. Making the model less salient for the 2.5-year-olds (by requiring that they view it through a window) enabled them to more easily represent the model as both an object and a model; making the model more salient for the 3-year-olds (by encouraging them to play with it) made it more difficult for them to treat it as a representation for something else, and their performance deteriorated. A similar result was found when pictures were made more salient. For example, rather than showing children a picture of the room, the experimenters showed them a picture of an object (a chair, for instance), with the miniature toy hidden behind the picture. This manipulation increased the saliency of the picture as an object and should have made it more difficult for young children to treat it as a symbol. This was precisely the case, with none of the 2.5-year-olds in this study successfully finding the large toy in the real room (DeLoache, 1991).

If dual representation is the key here, as De-Loache proposes, what would happen if young children had to use a model to find a hidden toy *without* dual representation? How can this be done? De-Loache, Miller, and Rosengren (1997) convinced children that a "shrinking machine" (an oscilloscope with flashing lights and computer-generated sounds) could actually shrink a room, something that the 2.5-year-old children easily believed. They were then given the "hiding" test as in previous research. First, a toy was hidden in the large room. Then the room was "shrunk" and the child searched for the toy in the miniaturized model. Their performance this time was exceptional. Whereas children who were given the standard (no shrinking room) instructions successfully found the toy on only 19% of all trials (about what one would expect by chance), children who searched in the shrunken (model) room were correct nearly 80% of the time. Why the difference? DeLoache and her colleagues reasoned that the children believed that *the miniaturized room was the same room as the larger room*; it was not a model, and thus not a symbol. In this case, as far as the children were concerned, dual representation was not necessary.

The ability to use one object to represent another is the essence of what we mean when we refer to symbol use. At a very basic level, we see this ability in very young children, most easily perhaps in symbolic play. For example, an 18-month-old might hold a shoe to her ear and pretend that it's a phone, or a 20-month-old child might place a napkin on his head and parade around the living room drawing attention to his "hat." In these cases, one object is being used as a symbol for another. But this is not quite what DeLoache means when she refers to representational insight. It is not enough to use an object as a symbol; one must know that the object can be both a symbol (for example, a representation of a room) and an object (for example, a model) at the same time. DeLoache and Marzolf (1992) make this point nicely, stating, "Young children are capable of responding to a single entity either concretely, as an

object itself, or abstractly, as a representation of something else. It is very difficult for them to do both at once, that is, to achieve dual representation" (p. 328).

Recent research has documented the development of dual representation for children's understanding of one common symbolic entity—pictures. DeLoache and her colleagues (1998) presented pictures of objects to children between the ages of 9 and 19 months in the United States and the Ivory Coast. The youngest children in both countries initially touched the pictures as if they were real objects, sometimes even trying to pick them off the page. By 19 months of age, children realized that the pictures represented something else: They now point at the depicted objects rather than try to manipulate them. DeLoache and her colleagues propose that infants' initial uncertainty about pictures causes them to explore them, which gradually results in their acquisition of the concept of "picture" and the understanding that they represent something else.

The Appearance/Reality Distinction

Adults know very well that things are not always what they appear to be. We realize that the appearance of an object does not necessarily correspond to its reality. This is not a knowledge we are born with but one that has a gradual developmental history. One problem that tests our ability to make this **appearance/reality distinction** is the conservation-of-liquid task used by Piaget. When water is poured from a short, stout glass into a tall, skinny one, the amount of water appears to have increased. We know, of course, that in reality the amount of water is the same. We also know that children much younger than 7 years are not cognizant of this fact.

As discussed in Chapter 4, conservation is the knowledge that quantitative relations between objects remain the same despite irrelevant perceptual transformations. A more basic form of the appearance/reality distinction concerns the knowledge that qualitative relations between objects remain the same despite some perceptual transformation. Quantitative properties have to do with amount, as in number, length, weight, or volume; in comparison, qualitative properties have to do with characteristics of type or form. For example, children would demonstrate qualitative constancy if they realized that their parents' car remained the same despite being painted. Piaget (1968) referred to such knowledge as reflecting **identity.** Identity and conservation are similar in that both involve a form of cognitive constancy, a realization that an entity remains unchanged despite changes in appearance. However, Piaget asserted that constancies involving qualitative properties do not require reversibility but merely a dissociation of the permanent and variable properties of an object. As such, qualitative constancies are developed during the preschool years. In fact, Piaget (1968) contended that object permanence is the first qualitative identity, being achieved between 18 and 24 months of age.

A pioneering study of qualitative identity was published by De Vries in 1969. In her study, children 3 to 6 years of age were familiarized with a trained cat named Maynard. In one condition, after the children petted Maynard, he was fitted with a realistic dog mask. Although the children did not actually see the mask being placed on Maynard, the cat's body and tail remained in full view of the children during the transformation. They were then asked questions concerning the identity of the animal. "What kind of animal is it now? Would this animal eat dog food or cat food? Does it bark or meow?" In general, 3-year-olds frequently believed that the mask had actually changed the identity of the animal, whereas most 5- and 6-year-olds believed that changes in the appearance of the animal had not altered its identity. De Vries referred to this type of qualitative constancy as *generic identity.*

In addition to her research involving changing the appearance of animals, De Vries also interviewed children about their beliefs about people wearing masks and about the constancy of gender as a result of certain irrelevant changes (for example, boys wearing dresses). Again, she reported that 3-year-olds tended to believe that changes in appearance result in changes in identity. This can account for young children's sometimes puzzling responses to costumes worn both by others and by themselves. For example, it is not uncommon at Halloween for

2- and 3-year-old children to be excited about wearing a costume, only to become distressed when the mask is placed over their faces or when they look at themselves in the mirror. Wearing a Darth Vader outfit is one thing, but wearing the mask is another story. Not all transformations of personal identity are so upsetting, however, as is evidenced by the number of scraped elbows and knees on children who wear their Batman underwear, tie a cape around their neck, and jump from tables and fences, convinced that they can fly. These children's behaviors are consistent with the belief that a significant change in appearance results in a change in identity.

Let me provide an anecdote to illustrate young children's thinking about how appearance can influence reality and their application of this thinking to solve problems. Three-year-old Nicholas sometimes spent the night with his grandparents, who would take him to preschool the following morning. Nicholas especially liked to ride with his grandfather because he drove a somewhat battered, stick-shift Chevy, which Nicholas called "Papa's car." Nicholas's grandmother, however, drove only cars with automatic transmissions, and thus she was unable to take Nicholas to school in Papa's car. One morning when Grandma was about to drive Nicholas to school, he said, "Grandma, dress up like a man this morning. Put on Papa's shirt and wear his hat." When asked why he wanted her to do that, he responded, "Then you can take me to school in Papa's car." Nicholas had a problem and attempted to solve it by changing his grandmother's appearance, which he believed would transform her temporarily into a man and give her the ability to drive a stick-shift car. More will be said concerning children's belief in the constancy of gender as a function of behavior or dress in Chapter 11.

In related research, John Flavell and his colleagues have extensively investigated young children's knowledge about the distinction between appearance and reality (Flavell, Green, & Flavell, 1986; Taylor & Flavell, 1984). In some experiments, children were presented with a realistic-looking fake rock made of sponge, or watched as white milk was poured into a red glass. The children were then asked two questions. The first concerned what the objects looked like, "how they look to your eyes right now." The second concerned the actual identity of the objects, "how they really and truly are." Somewhat surprisingly, Flavell and his colleagues reported that most 3-year-olds could not solve these seemingly simple problems. Their errors tended to be of two types: *phenomenism errors* and *intellectual realism errors*. Phenomenism errors typically occurred when appearance/reality tests involving color were used. Children stated, for example, that the milk looked red and "really and truly" was red. In contrast, intellectual realism errors were more likely to occur on tasks involving objects that looked like something they were not. For example, children would say that the fake rock was indeed a sponge and looked like a sponge. In general, when children erred, they did so by giving the same answer to both questions.

Before assuming that 3-year-olds cannot solve appearance/reality tasks, Flavell, Green, and Flavell (1986) simplified their problems. Children were acquainted with an experimenter, for example, and watched as she put on a soft plastic mask; then they were asked who the person in the mask "really and truly" was. For other tasks, they were asked questions about objects that had uncharacteristic sounds or smells (for example, socks that smelled like peanut butter). The 3-year-olds' performance on these simplified tasks was surprisingly poor, and in a subsequent study explicit training in making the appearance/reality distinction did little to improve their performance. More recent research has similarly failed to "teach" 3- and 4-year-olds the appearance/reality distinction, reflecting that young children's difficulty is not caused by a simple, easily remedied misunderstanding about the nature of the task (Flavell et al., 1987; Taylor & Hort, 1990). Given these findings, Flavell and his colleagues (1986) concluded that 3-year-olds "truly did not understand [the appearance/reality distinction], even minimally" (p. 23).

There is at least one exception to this pattern of failure, and that is when children are encouraged to participate in an act of deception. When 3-year-old children are induced to play a trick on someone (for example, "Let's trick Sally and make her think that this sponge really IS a rock, and not just a sponge that looks like one"), many are quite capable of doing so (Rice et al., 1997). These findings indicate that young children's knowledge of the appearance/reality distinction is not an all-or-none thing but develops over the preschool years.

Flavell and his colleagues (1986) speculated about the factors that can mediate children's development of the appearance/reality distinction. One likely candidate is **dual encoding.** Three-year-olds' inability to differentiate between the appearance of an object and its actual identity might stem, in part, from their difficulty in representing an object in more than one form at a time. That is, young children might focus on one aspect of a stimulus (its appearance or its actual identity) and give the same answer, based on either appearance or reality, regardless of the question asked. Thus, on the one hand, if the change in color is more salient to a child, the object looks red and is red (phenomenism error). If, on the other hand, the identity of the object is more salient, it is a sponge and looks like a sponge (intellectual realism error). Young children cannot act on multiple representations of an object simultaneously. With increasing age they become more adept at dual encoding, but not until later childhood or early adolescence can they "think about notions of 'looks like,' 'really and truly', 'looks different from the way it really and truly is', and so on in the abstract, metaconceptual way that older subjects can" (Flavell et al., 1986, p. 59).

The findings and interpretation of Flavell and his colleagues with respect to dual encoding are similar to those reported by DeLoache (1987, 1991; DeLoache & Marzolf, 1992) with respect to dual representation for pictures and models. Recall that DeLoache found that 2- and 2.5-year-old children had difficulty representing a model or a picture as both an object and a symbol simultaneously. DeLoache's findings support Flavell's contention that dual encoding/representation is an important step in preschool children's representational development. Together, the findings of Flavell and DeLoache suggest that there is not a single dual representational ability that emerges at a single time and affects thinking across all tasks. Rather, it appears as if this ability develops gradually over the years from ages 2 to 5, being found early (2.5 years) in some circumstances (using pictures as symbols), a bit later

(3 years) in others (using models as symbols), and later yet (4 to 5 years) in other situations (making the appearance/reality distinction).

Distinguishing Between Imagined and Real Events

Related to the appearance/reality distinction is children's ability to distinguish what they imagine and what they experience. In other words, do children realize that thinking or imagining something is distinct from actually doing or experiencing something? At one level, it is clear than even young children know the difference between imagining and doing. For example, although dreams can seem quite real to people of any age, apparently even 3- and 4-year-olds know the difference between dreams and reality, although many 3-year-olds seem to believe that the same dream is experienced by different people (Woolley & Wellman, 1992). Also, several researchers have shown that 4- and 6-year-olds can easily distinguish between real and pretend items (Golomb & Galasso, 1995; Harris et al., 1991). For example, when a pencil is placed on a table in front of a child, 4-year-olds can state that both they and a person sitting opposite them can see the pencil. When asked to close their eyes and imagine a pencil, however, they can state quite correctly that the person sitting across from them cannot see the imagined object.

But the ability to distinguish between an imagined and an experienced event seems to develop with age. For example, although 3-year-olds can often distinguish between seeing and imagining an object, this ability does improve with age (Woolley & Bruell, 1996), and many 3-year-olds believe that imagined events reflect reality (Woolley & Wellman, 1993). By age 4, children know very well the distinction between information gained from imagining (that is, without perceptual experience) and with perceptual experience.

Yet, the ability to make the distinction between imagined and experienced events is far from complete by age 4. For example, in research evaluating developmental differences in **source monitoring**—the awareness of the origins of one's memories, knowledge, or beliefs—children and adults are asked to perform certain actions (for instance, "touch your nose") or to imagine performing certain actions (for instance, "imagine touching your nose") (Foley & Ratner, 1998a; Foley, Santini, & Sopasakis, 1989). The ability to distinguish imagined from real actions improves over the preschool years (Welch-Ross, 1995), but even 6- and 7-year-olds have greater difficulty making such distinctions than older children or adults do (Foley & Ratner, 1998a; Parker, 1995). When children make errors they usually claim that they had performed an action they had actually only imagined. Thus, for young children, imagination can easily be remembered as reality. Interestingly, young children are often as good as adults at distinguishing something they said or did from something that someone else said or did (but not always; see Foley & Ratner, 1998a; Foley, Ratner, & Passalacqua, 1993, in Chapter 3 for counter example in collaborative learning). Their greatest difficulty comes from distinguishing between self-generated action and self-generated imagining.

Related to distinguishing real from imagined events is the distinction between fantasy and reality. Young children seem to have a difficult time differentiating between what is real and what is fantasy. Young children are more apt to believe in fantasy figures such as superheroes, monsters, Santa Claus, and the Tooth Fairy (the latter two of which adults heartily promote) than are older children and are prone to interpret events they don't understand as magic (Rosengren & Hickling, 1994). For example, Rosengren and Hickling (1994) asked 4- and 5-year-old children how certain objects could be changed (for example, "How can you make this piece of string look different?"), and most provided answers based on physical mechanisms ("Cut it in two."). Children were then shown some magic tricks (for example, putting two pieces of string together to make one piece), and asked for their explanations for the transformations. Whereas most 5-year-olds explained the changes as tricks that anyone could learn, many 4-year-olds explained them as magic that could only be performed by a magician.

Young children's tenuous grasp of the distinction between fantasy and reality is seen in experiments by Paul Harris and his colleagues (1991). As noted earlier, these researchers demonstrated that 4- and 6-year-olds could easily distinguish between real and imagined objects. For example, when asked to imagine that there was either a bunny or a monster in a box on a table in front of them, few children had any difficulty with the task; most stated quite clearly that the bunny or the monster was pretend and not real. But this knowledge was tenuous for many of the children. For example, after asking children to imagine a bunny or a monster in the box, the experimenter said she had to leave the room for a few minutes. Four of 12 4-year-olds who had imagined a monster in the box became frightened and wouldn't let the experimenter leave. No child asked to imagine a bunny became frightened. When the experimenter returned and questioned the children, nearly half of both the 4- and 6-years-olds admitted to wondering whether there was indeed a monster or a bunny in the box. Perhaps imagining made it so. That is, although nearly all of the children admitted that the bunny or the monster was make-believe at the beginning of the experiment, many had second thoughts at the end. Harris and his colleagues view this contradiction between children's beginning and final beliefs as a reflection of the uncertain state of young children's knowledge of fantasy versus reality. "Our general explanation is that when children imagine a creature such as a monster or rabbit in a box they start to wonder whether there is such a creature in the box, and they cannot completely discount that possibility. Thus, children's imagination increases the subjective likelihood that certain fantasy creatures might become encountered" (1991, p. 121). These results help explain why young children are often frightened by imagining bogey men in the closet or monsters under their beds. Although at one level they know the difference between imagined and real, at another level they possess a belief in magic, making the fantasy-reality distinction a tenuous one (but see Golomb & Galasso, 1995, for an alternate interpretation).

Let me provide an anecdote to illustrate young children's uncertainty about what is real and what is fantasy. Four-year-old Jeffrey was very impressed with the Disney movie *The Lion King*. He knew the cartoon was fiction, of course, and was quite aware that lions and hyenas can't actually talk. He was especially impressed with the character of Simba, the young lion cub and star of the movie. "Simba was so sad when his father died," he said. "Boy, what a good actor he is. He *really* looked sad." Jeffrey knew that this was fiction and that the characters were not real. But he still got confused. He was so impressed with the skills of the cartoon "actor" who played the role of Simba.

But how different are children from adults regarding magical thinking? Jaqueline Woolley (1997) thinks not too much. Children are more likely to attribute unfamiliar events to magic and to believe that "just wishing" can make something come true. But such thinking does not disappear at adolescence or adulthood. The belief systems of most cultures include supernatural beings who intervene in the physical world on a regular basis and who can be beseeched to intervene on people's behalf. Many adults are highly superstitious. They believe that blowing on dice before a roll will produce a good outcome, knocking on wood will prevent a bad outcome, and breaking a mirror will result in bad luck. Belief in the paranormal approaches 50% among American adults, including faith healing, demonic possession, and astrology. Thus, the tendency to provide a magical explanation for phenomenon for which we have no known physical explanation is not unique to children. One likely reason for children's greater tendency to believe in fantasy is knowledge. Older children and adults know more about how the physical world works and know the domains in their culture where belief in supernatural explanation is accepted (for example, religion) and where it is not (for example, David Copperfield's illusions).

Children's Theory of Mind

During the last two decades, the topic of children's **theory of mind** has become immensely popular. In fact, in 1998 Marc Bornstein, editor of the influential research journal *Child Development*, said, only half in jest, that "American cognitive development research has *become* theory-of-mind research" (January, 1998, personal communication). In general, the phrase "theory of mind" is used to refer to children's developing concepts of mental activity. A theory of mind is more than just a collection of concepts, however. Theory implies some coherent framework for organizing facts and making predictions (see the discussion of theory theories in Chapter 4). Having a theory of mind implies recognizing different categories of mind, such as dreams, memories, imagination, beliefs, and so on, and having some causal-explanatory framework to account for the actions of other people (that is, to explain why someone behaves as he or she does). For example, Henry Wellman (1990; Bartsch & Wellman, 1995) believes that adults' theory of mind is based on **belief-desire reasoning.** Basically, we explain and predict what people do based on what we understand their desires and beliefs to be—that is, by referring to their wants, wishes, hopes, and goals (their desires) and to their ideas, opinions, suppositions, and knowledge (their beliefs). Such belief-desire reasoning is depicted in Figure 7-6. Basically, this is what researchers typically mean when they talk about children developing a theory of mind. To what extent do they have a coherent explanatory "theory" to understand, predict, and explain behavior?

Developmental differences in theory of mind are reflections of developmental differences in how children represent the world—in this case, the mental world. In fact, most research examining children's ability to distinguish between appearance and reality (Flavell et al., 1986) or between imagining and experiencing (Harris et al., 1991) could properly be classified as theory-of-mind research (see Flavell & Miller, 1998).

This active research area can be divided into at least two major subtopics. The first, and the one that has spawned most of the research, concerns children's abilities to "read the minds" of others (Perner, 1991; Wellman, 1990). To what extent do young children understand that the perceptions, knowledge, and thoughts of others are different from their own? The second subtopic concerns children's developing knowledge of what it means to think and to perform other aspects of cognition, a topic related to metacognition as well as to representation.

Children's representation of others and of themselves as thinkers is vitally important to our species' way of life. Cooperation, competition, and social interaction in general as we know it would be radically different if we did not develop a theory of mind and the ability to "read" the minds of others. I believe that one reason for the popularity of this topic is its significance for understanding the human condition.

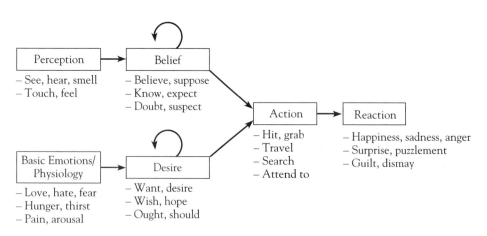

FIGURE 7-6 A simplified scheme depicting belief-desire reasoning. SOURCE: *The Child's Theory of Mind,* by H. M. Wellman. Copyright © 1990 Massachusetts Institute of Technology Press. Reprinted with permission.

"I KNOW WHAT I THINK, BUT WHAT'S IMPORTANT IS WHAT MY MOM THINKS I THINK!"

CARTOON 7-1 Knowing that someone else has thoughts and being able to infer those thoughts has important social and intellectual implications.
SOURCE: DENNIS THE MENACE® used by permission of Hank Ketcham and © 1990 by North America Syndicate.

Children as Mind Readers

When and how do children come to appreciate that other people have beliefs and desires, often different from their own, that motivate their behavior? To assess this question, researchers have developed tasks in which children must predict what another person will do or state, or what another person thinks, in an effort to determine what young children know about the minds of others.

False-belief tasks. The most frequently used tool to assess children's theory of mind is the **false-belief task,** first developed for use with chimpanzees

(Premack & Woodruff, 1978). In a standard false-belief task (first used with children by Wimmer & Perner, 1983), children watch as candy (or some other treat) is hidden in a special location (in a box, for example). Another person—for example, Maxi —is present when the treat is hidden but then leaves the room. While Maxi is out of the room, the treat is moved from the box to another container. When Maxi returns, will he know where the treat is hidden? The results of using variants of this standard task are relatively straightforward. Most 4-year-old children can solve the problem, stating that Maxi will look where the candy was originally hidden. Three-year-olds, in contrast, generally cannot solve the problem, stating that Maxi will look for the candy in the new hiding place, apparently not realizing that Maxi is not privy to the new information. This pattern is not confined to European and North American children but is apparently universal, being observed among the children of Baka pygmies living in the rain forests of Cameroon (Avis & Harris, 1991; but see Viden, 1996, for an exception and Lillard, 1998, for a discussion of cultural variations in theories of mind).

Some researchers have suggested that linguistic ambiguities (that is, how the questions are asked) contribute to 3-year-olds' poor performance on false-belief tasks (Lewis & Osborne, 1990). Yet, even when linguistic ambiguities are eliminated (Sullivan & Winner, 1993), young children continue to fail false-belief tasks. This pattern has led most scientists to agree that the research findings are not caused by some methodological flaw but by an underlying inability of young children to "read the minds" of others (Hogrefe, Wimmer, & Perner, 1986; Wellman, 1990). For example, Wellman and Bartsch (1988) assessed false belief by asking children questions about this seemingly straightforward story: "Jane wants to find her kitten. Jane's kitten is really in the playroom. Jane thinks her kitten is in the kitchen. Where will Jane look for her kitten? Where is the kitten really?" Most 3-year-olds (and even many 4-year-olds) stated that Jane would look in the playroom, consistent with the findings of others on more standard (and seemingly more challenging) false-belief tasks.

Why do 3-year-olds fail at the false-belief task? For one thing, they seem not to remember what they originally believed before any switch was made (Gopnik & Slaughter, 1991; Sullivan & Winner, 1993). For example, in a modification of the false-belief task, called the "Smarties" task, developed by Hogrefe, Wimmer, and Perner (1986), children are shown a box of "Smarties" (a type of candy in a distinctive box, with which British children are highly familiar) and asked what they think is in the box. Naturally, they say "Smarties." The box is then opened, revealing not candy but pencils. Children are then asked what they originally thought (that is, what they believed was in the box before being shown the contents), as well to predict what another child (who is not privy to the trick) will think is in the box. The first question assesses children's memory for their initial belief (referred to as **representational change**), whereas the second question assesses their ability to understand false belief. The correct answer to both of these questions, of course, is "Smarties," but most 3-year-olds say "pencils" to both questions; that is, they seem to forget their initial belief. Gopnik and Slaughter (1991) found that this memory deficit is not a general one but is specific to beliefs. Three-year-olds have little difficulty remembering their past images, perceptions, or pretenses. They have particular difficulty, however, remembering their past beliefs.

If young children's problem with false-belief tasks is not one of general memory, what can account for their poor performance? Josef Perner (1991, 1994), among others, has proposed that 3-year-old children lack the conceptual structures necessary to solve problems dealing with beliefs. In other words, they have a *representational deficit* and do not possess a true theory of mind (see also Gopnik & Astington, 1988; Flavell, 1988).

One possibility, originally proposed by Wimmer and Perner (1983), is that young children have difficulty with contradictory evidence. They cannot deal with two representations of a single object (the candy in location 1 and in location 2) simultaneously. This is similar to the *dual-encoding* (or *dual-representation*) hypothesis proposed by Flavell and his colleagues and DeLoache and her colleagues to ex-

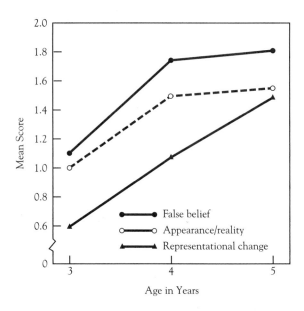

FIGURE 7-7 Average scores on false-belief, appearance-reality, and representational change questions for 3-, 4-, and 5-year-olds. Note the similar pattern of developmental change for each task. SOURCE: "Children's Understanding of the Representational Change and Its Relation to the Understanding of False Belief and the Appearance-Reality Distinction," by A. Gopnik & J. W. Astington, 1988, *Child Development, 59,* 26–37. Copyright © 1988 The Society for Research in Child Development. Reprinted with permission.

plain representational differences between younger and older preschoolers. Basically, this position argues that young children will fail in situations where they must consider two different beliefs or representations for one target.

Support for this position comes from a study by Gopnik and Astington (1988) in which they assessed 3-, 4-, and 5-year-old children's performance on a series of tasks, each requiring them to deal with contradictory evidence: false belief, appearance/reality distinction (Flavell et al., 1986), and representational change (remembering their past belief). The results of their study are graphed in Figure 7-7. As can be seen, performance on each of the three tasks varied with age, consistent with the idea that a single, domain-general mechanism underlies preschool children's representational abilities.

Other researchers have suggested that young children have the underlying representational abilities, but they lack some specific cognitive skills. For example, Frye, Zelazo, and Palfai (1995) proposed that young children cannot easily switch their perspectives from one focus to another. Three-year-old children have a difficult time changing their behavior on rule-governed tasks, such as the card-sorting tasks used by Frye, Zelazo, and Palfai (1995) and discussed earlier in Chapter 5. In these tasks, children are told to sort pictures into one of two piles on the basis of color, for instance ("All the red cards go in this pile, all the blue cards go in that pile"), and then, after several trials of this, they are told to now sort the cards by the objects depicted on them ("Now put the *boats* in this pile and the *cars* in that pile"). Despite being able to articulate the rule, most 3-year-olds continue to sort the cards by the previous dimension (color). They can state the rule, but have a tough time switching from one dimension to another. Frye and his colleagues believe that this is the deficit that young children have on false-belief tasks. Young children have a difficult time switching between their belief and that of another person. Related to this interpretation is the idea that young children have a difficult time inhibiting the more "cognitively salient" information. When their desire for an outcome is strong, they cannot easily inhibit acting on that desire (Moore et al., 1995). In a similar vein, young children might not have sufficient mental resources to hold the multiple interpretations in mind at the same time (Gordon & Olson, 1998).

Are there other factors that contribute to children's developing theory of mind? One interesting finding is that 3- and 4-year-old children's performance on false-belief tasks is related to family size (Perner, Ruffman, & Leekam, 1994; Jenkins & Astington, 1996). Children from larger families perform false-belief tasks better than children from smaller families. Why should there be a relation between family size and theory-of-mind reasoning? One explanation has to do with the role of siblings. The type of interaction provided by siblings facilitates developing a sophisticated theory of mind. Jenkins and Astington (1996) have shown that

family size is particularly important for children with low linguistic skills. Apparently, having siblings can compensate for delayed language development in influencing performance on false-belief tasks. More recent research indicates that it is only having *older*, not younger, siblings that has a facilitative effect on theory-of-mind reasoning (Ruffman et al., 1998). Ted Ruffman and colleagues believe that having older siblings stimulates pretend play, which helps younger children represent "counterfactual states of affairs," which is a necessary skill for solving false-belief tasks. Although siblings may be important, they are not necessarily more effective tutors than adults. Charlie Lewis and his colleagues (1996) administered a series of theory-of-mind tests to 3- and 4-year-old children and found that the number of adults that children interact with daily is the best single predictor of a child's performance on theory-of-mind tasks, with number of siblings and number of older children interacted with daily falling behind a child's age in importance.

Despite the impressive evidence that most 3-year-old children cannot solve false-belief tasks, there is evidence that 3-year-olds do solve other tasks that seemingly require an understanding of other minds, challenging the representational-deficit hypothesis. One particularly interesting study was performed by Clements and Perner (1994) and evaluated children's *implicit* understanding of false belief. In this study, children ranging in age from 2 years 5 months to 4 years 6 months were told a story about a mouse named Sam who had placed a piece of cheese in a specific location (Location A) so that he could get it later when he was hungry. While Sam was sleeping, Katie mouse found the cheese and moved it to another place (Location B). When Sam woke up, he said, "I feel very hungry now. I'll go get the cheese." Children were then asked "I wonder where he's going to look?" The answer most older children should give is Location A, where he originally hid it, while most younger children should say Location B, reflecting their lack of understanding of false belief. This is the standard, or explicit, false-belief task, and this was the pattern of results that Clements and Perner found. However, Clements and Perner also recorded where children *looked*, at

Location A or Location B. This is an *implicit task*, requiring no conscious awareness or verbal response. Now, all but the youngest children showed high levels of correct responding (that is, they looked at Location A). Figure 7-8 shows the average explicit and implicit understanding scores, based on children's performance on the tasks in this experiment. What these findings imply is that by about 3 years of age children have a well-developed *implicit* understanding of false belief that exceeds their explicit (verbalizable) knowledge. (A similar finding has been reported for infants' performance on A-not-B object-permanence tasks, with infants *looking* at the right location before *searching* at the right location [Ahmed & Ruffman, 1998].)

In other research, the first inkling of a theory of mind has been found in 18-month-old toddlers (Repacholi & Gopnik, 1997). In this study, 14- and 18-month-old infants were first tested for their preference for two types of food (Pepperidge Farm Goldfish and raw vegetables). They then watched as a woman tasted the two types of food. She expressed disgust for one type and happiness for the other. The woman then placed her hand, palm up, between the two bowls of food and said, "Can you give me some?" What did the infants do? The 14-month-olds gave the woman the type of food *they* liked, regardless of what food the woman liked. In contrast, the 18-month-olds were more likely to give the woman the food she had expressed a preference for, independent of whether it was what they liked best. That is, whereas the 14-month-olds responded egocentrically, the 18-month-olds did not, but recognized that their likes were different from those of another person.

One research area that has produced compelling evidence that young children have a knowledge of the beliefs of other people concerns *deception*. When young children play tricks on others, they sometimes seem to be aware of what the other person does and doesn't know.

Deception. Deception is an important skill in its own right. Deception is perhaps the consummate political skill, useful in love, war, and poker games. In fact, some theorists have speculated that early ho-

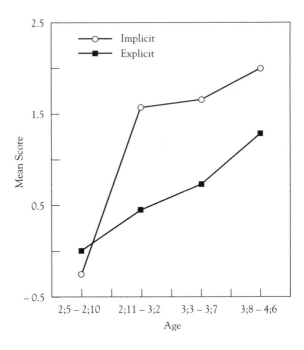

FIGURE 7-8 Average implicit and explicit understanding scores on false-belief task by age. SOURCE: Clements, W. A., & Perner, J. (1994). Implicit understanding of belief. *Cognitive Development, 9*, 377–395.

minids' abilities to deceive may have contributed significantly to the evolution of intelligence in our species (Bjorklund & Harnishfeger, 1995; Humphrey, 1976). But deception also reflects a knowledge of other minds. If children are so egocentric in perspective that they assume that if they know something (for example, where an apple is hidden) other people must know it, too, they will see trying to deceive as fruitless. Deception is only reasonable when a person (the deceiver) knows something that another person (the deceived) doesn't know; then attempts can be made to mislead or conceal information. Thus, deception is another indication that a child is able to "read" another's mind.

Observations by many parents would suggest that deception is frequently practiced (sometimes successfully, sometimes not) by 2- and 3-year-old children. For example, 3-year-old Carmen had gotten into her mother's make-up and spilled powder over the top of the bureau. She found a handkerchief and covered up the offending mess, acting as if nothing had ever happened. In this case, the ruse did not work. Sullivan and Winner (1991) relate an example of more successful deception by a 2-year-old. The child pretended to cry when his aunt said that she could not come over to play with him. When she relented, the child turned to his mother and said, "I tricked her. I made her think I was sad so she would come" (p. 160).

These observations have been supported by empirical science. For example, deception in hide-and-seek tasks was assessed in children ranging in age from 2.5 to 4 years by Chandler, Fritz, and Hala (1989; Hala, Chandler, & Fritz, 1991). In their studies, children were introduced to a hiding task involving several containers placed on a white surface made of a washable oil cloth material (see Figure 7-9). A puppet hid various pieces of "treasure," making footprints on the cloth from the start box to the container in which the treasure was hidden. A sponge was available that could be used to wipe up the puppet's footprints. After ensuring that the children understood the basics of the game, one of two experimenters (E1) left the room, and the remaining experimenter explained to the child that he or she should help the puppet hide the treasure so that E1 wouldn't be able to find it. The hide-and-seek game went on for several trials, with the sponge being taken away on later trials so that the puppet's footprints could not be wiped off. If children didn't think of it themselves on these later trials, they were shown how false tracks could be made (that is, tracks leading to the wrong container). The question of interest was the extent to which children would use a variety of deception strategies to make it difficult for E1 to find the treasure.

Several different types of deception were scored. The simplest involved withholding information—for example, by making sure that E1 was out of earshot before commenting on the hiding strategy they would use. Another involved destroying evidence by wiping away the tracks, leaving no sign of the path that the puppet took in hiding the treasure. A third involved openly lying—for example, telling E1 to look in an incorrect container. A fourth in-

FIGURE 7-9 Illustration of the hide-and-seek game used in research by Chandler and colleagues. The puppet would hide a "treasure" in one of the four containers, leaving footprints tracing her path. SOURCE: "Small-scale Deceit: Deception as a Marker of Two-, Three-, and Four-Year-Olds' Early Theories of Mind," by M. Chandler, A. S. Fritz and S. Hala, 1989, *Child Development, 60,* 1263–1277. Copyright © 1989 The Society for Research in Child Development. Reprinted with permission.

volved leaving a false trail of footprints leading to an incorrect container. The most sophisticated deceptive strategy involved a combination of both destroying the correct trail and laying a false trail.

Table 7-1 shows the proportion of 2-, 3-, and 4-year-olds who used the various deceptive strategies. As can be seen, children of all ages used deception, with no age differences between the three groups. Chandler and his colleagues concluded that these findings "leave little room for doubt that even children as young as 2.5 are already capable of engaging in a variety of well-crafted deceptive practices, best interpreted as strategies aimed at instilling false beliefs in others" (1989, p. 1274).

In a related study (Hala & Chandler, 1996), 3-year-olds were asked to play a trick on a person (Lisa) by moving some biscuits from their distinctive jar to a hiding place, so that Lisa would be fooled. When later asked where Lisa will look for the biscuits and where she will think the biscuits are, children who helped plan the deception performed quite well. In contrast, children who merely

TABLE 7-1   Percentage of 2-, 3-, and 4-year-olds using various deceptive strategies.

Deceptive strategy	Age years		
	2 (n = 10)	3 (n = 20)	4 (n = 20)
Withholding evidence	80	90	100
Destroying evidence	50	60	80
Lying	30	60	55
Producing false trails without destroying evidence	20	35	20
Destroying evidence and producing false trails	50	25	50

SOURCE: "Small-Scale Deceit: Deception as a Marker of Two-, Three-, and Four-Year Olds' Early Theories of Mind," by M. Chandler, A.S. Fritz and S. Hala, 1989, *Child Development*, 60, 1263–1277. Copyright 1989 The Society for Research in Child Development. Reprinted with permission.

observed the experimenter planning the deception or who planned a nondeception themselves, did not perform so well. Rather, they were more likely to answer this false-belief task erroneously, stating that Lisa would look for the biscuits in the biscuit jar. In other words, when they planned to deceive someone, they were later able to take the perspective of that person; when they were not actively involved in the deceit, however, they performed egocentrically, stating that the unsuspecting person would look for the biscuits where the children knew them to be.

In other research, Sullivan and Winner (1993) reported that 3-year-old children can solve the "Smarties" false-belief task (discussed earlier), but only when they are asked to actively trick another person. When the same task is used but without the "trick" instructions, 3-year-olds perform poorly. Sullivan and Winner (1993) interpreted these findings as indicating that 3-year-olds can understand false belief when it is embedded within a deceptive context. More recent research by Carlson, Moses, and Hix (1998) has similarly shown that 3-year-olds are able to use deception successfully under some situations.

Unfortunately, the picture is not as simple as the research by Chandler and his colleagues and Sullivan and Winner suggests, with more than a little room for doubt, at least according to some researchers. Most other studies report little evidence that children much under 4 years of age use deception in a way that reflects "mind reading" (Peskin, 1992, 1996; Sodian et al., 1991). For example, Beate Sodian and her colleagues (1991) reported that 3-year-olds were just as likely to use a deceptive strategy whether they were asked to mislead a competitor or help a collaborator (although Hala et al., 1991, report evidence that 3-year-olds can use a deceptive strategy selectively). Subtle differences in the way the deception tasks are performed seem to make a big difference in whether children younger than 4 years use deception selectively or not.

Researchers who fail to find evidence of deception in young children attribute the failure to conceptual deficiencies. Three-year-olds just do not understand about the beliefs and knowledge that others possess, consistent with their failure to solve false-belief tasks. Those who find evidence of deception, however, counter that young children indeed have the conceptual competency to deceive and thus have a theory of mind that involves the beliefs of others. The reason children perform better on the deception tasks may have to do with motivation, the more naturalistic nature of the deception tasks than the conventional false-belief tasks, and the fact that children are more actively involved in the deception tasks (Sullivan & Winner, 1993). Based on their findings using deception in a false-belief task, Sullivan and Winner (1993) state that 3-year-olds do not have a representational deficit as proposed by Perner and others, but that "3-year-olds' knowledge about mental states of others does not differ radically from that of 4-year-olds" (p. 147).

Do three-year-olds have a theory of mind? What can we make of the often-contradictory evidence concerning young children's theory of mind? There is actually much that the various researchers agree on. Three-year-olds seem to have a limited knowledge of other minds. In some circumstances, particularly involving deception or when implicit tasks are used, even 2.5-year-old children seem to be aware that they have knowledge not possessed by others. But young children's theory of mind, or belief-desire reasoning, is tenuous at best.

What kind of theory of mind do 3-year-olds have? Wellman (1990; Bartsch & Wellman, 1995) believes that it is actually quite similar to the theory possessed by adults. "I believe that it is undeniable that by age three children are engaged in the same everyday psychological enterprise as are adults—construing people as having minds and understanding action by the internal mental states of the actor" (1990, p. 188). If this is the case, why do 3-year-olds consistently fail standard false-belief tasks and many deception tasks? One explanation provided by Wellman and his colleagues (Bartsch & Wellman, 1989; Wellman, 1990) is that 3-year-olds place too much weight on desire relative to belief when making their decisions (Cassidy, 1998). It's not that 3-year-olds do not understand that other people have beliefs, but when there is a conflict between what someone wants (desire) and what someone knows (belief), they emphasize desire over belief. This is similar to an idea originally formulated by Piaget (1930) of **wishful thinking.** According to this concept, preschool children often do not differentiate between their wishes and their expectations. They believe that their desires are efficacious in and of themselves and therefore predict future events by how they want them to be. Several researchers have used this idea to explain why preschool children frequently overestimate their own abilities (Bjorklund & Green, 1992); following Wellman's ideas, wishful thinking might contribute to young children's poor performance on false-belief tasks. Such an explanation accounts for young children's elevated performance on deception tasks. In these situations, children want the other person to fail, making their wishes congruent with the correct response (see also research by Rice et al., 1997 on 3-year-olds' use of deception on appearance/reality tasks).

Yet, most would agree that the belief-desire reasoning of 3-year-olds is not identical to that of adults. Wellman (1990) makes it clear that in his view, 3-year-olds' theory of mind contains a mixture of both adultlike and nonadultlike features and that

we must be cautious and neither overestimate nor underestimate their thinking ability. Moreover, all researchers and theorists seem to concur that substantial changes in representational skills occur between the age of 3 and the early school years.

Theory of mind, evolved modules, and autism. Some theorists have proposed that theory of mind evolved over the course of human evolution and is the basis of our social intelligence (Baron-Cohen, 1995; Leslie, 1994). The social complexity of human groups demands attention to the actions of others, and having an idea of the beliefs and desires of others would provide a tremendous political advantage for anyone trying to predict the actions of other members of a group, or of rival groups. Consistent with the premises of evolutionary psychology (see Chapter 2), the cognitive and brain mechanisms underlying theory of mind have been proposed to be domain specific and modular in nature, rather than resulting from some domain-general ability. Thus, the theory goes, our ancestors developed specific skills relating to mindreading, and these skills are relatively independent of more general cognitive abilities.

One modular-type theory of theory of mind was presented by Simon Baron-Cohen (1995), who proposes four separate, interacting modules involved in mindreading that develop over infancy and early childhood. The earliest developing module is the *intentionality detector (ID)*, which interprets moving objects as having some volition or intention. For example, an object that is moving toward an individual might be perceived as an agent with some intention toward that individual (for instance, it wants to harm me, to be near me). This is a very primitive skill, likely possessed by all animals that have nervous systems. The second module is the *eye-direction detector (EDD)*, which has three related functions: It detects the presence of eyes or eye-like stimuli, determines whether the eyes are looking toward it or toward something else, and infers that if an organism's eyes are looking at something, then that organism sees that thing. In other words, this module is responsible for our belief that knowledge is gained through the eyes (both ours and the eyes of others). According to Baron-Cohen, these first two modules develop between birth and 9 months of age. The third module is the *shared-attention mechanisms (SAM)*. Whereas the ID and EDD involve only two objects/individuals (that is dyadic interactions/representations), the SAM involves triadic (three-way) interactions/representations. For example, if person A is looking at object B, and person C can see the eyes of person A and can see object B, person C can come to the conclusion that "You (person A) and I (person C) are looking at the same thing." This module develops between 9 and 18 months. Finally, the *theory of mind module (TOMM)* is roughly equivalent to the belief-desire reasoning described earlier, and is reflected by passing false-belief tasks. This develops between the ages of about 18 to 48 months.

I will not describe here the evidence Baron-Cohen provides for each of these modules, but refer the reader to Baron-Cohen's (1995) book. What evidence is there that these abilities are modular? Recall from Chapter 2 that modular abilities are domain-specific and relatively independent of other cognitive abilities (such as general intelligence). What evidence does Baron-Cohen have for this claim? His primary source of evidence is that the more advanced forms of mindreading (SAD and TOMM) are typically absent in one particular class of childhood psychiatric disorder, autism. Autism is a relatively rare (between 4 and 15 children per 10,000) but severe disorder characterized by social and communication disabilities. These children (and later adults) often seem to be in a world of their own and have a difficult time in most forms of social interaction. Baron-Cohen claims that the primary deficit of these children is an inability to read minds, or what he calls **mindblindness.** Evidence for this comes from studies in which autistic children are presented with false-belief and other theory-of-mind tasks and consistently fail them, despite performing well on other, nonsocial tasks. This is in contrast to children with mental retardation, such as Down Syndrome, who perform the theory-of-mind tasks easily, despite often doing poorly on other tasks that assess more general intelligence.

Most autistic children are able to perform well on the simpler tasks requiring the ID or EDD modules, but fail tasks involving the SAD and especially the TOMM modules. According to Baron-Cohen, autistic children are unable to understand other people's different beliefs, and as a result, the world consisting of other humans must be a confusing and frightening one, even for those children who are functioning at a relatively high intellectual level.

Although much research needs to be done to specify the different components involved in children's developing theories of mind, research with autistic children provides evidence that the ability is relatively independent of other cognitive skills and is consistent with the evolutionary psychological account that the skill is modular and evolved to solve the problems of dealing with other members of our own species in social settings.

Understanding Thinking

One characteristic of human beings is that we have a good deal of control over how we think and what we think about (or at least we *think* we do). How we direct our thought is a function, to a certain degree, of what we know about thinking. As cognition itself, this knowledge does not appear fully formed but must develop. Let me provide an anecdote to illustrate how an adult's idea about what it means to think can be very different from that of a young child.

Four-year-old Dexter had pushed his father's patience too far.

"Dexter," said his father, "I want you to go over to that corner and just *think* about all this for a while."

Instead of following his father's orders, Dexter stood where he was, not defiantly, but with a confused look and quivering lips, as if he were trying to say something but was afraid to.

"What's the matter now?" his father asked, his irritation still showing.

"But, Daddy," Dexter said, "I don't know *how* to think."

Obviously, 4-year-old Dexter did know how to think. He just didn't know that he did. The term "thinking" has associated with it specific meaning for most people. People think when they need to solve a difficult problem, whereas something that can be done easily and automatically is said to be done "without thinking." As adults, we know what we mean when we refer to thinking, but obviously, as the story illustrates, young children do not have the same understanding of mental processes as adults do.

Early research on children's understanding of thinking concentrated on preschool children's developing competencies, demonstrating, for example, that young children misunderstand mental verbs, such as "forget." For instance, when 4-year-olds are told a story about a person who fails to find an object, they say that that person "forgot" the whereabouts of the object, even if he or she didn't know its location ahead of time (Wellman & Johnson, 1979). In other research, preschoolers have been shown to be ignorant of the distinctions between remembering, knowing, and guessing (Johnson & Wellman, 1980). Yet preschool children are not totally out in left field when it comes to thinking about thought. For example, even 3-year-olds are able to distinguish real objects (such as chairs) from mental objects (such as wishes), and they also realize that mental activities can be about physically impossible things (such as a flying dog) (Wellman & Estes, 1986).

Children's understanding of mental activities continues to develop through childhood. For example, Flavell, Green, and Flavell (1998) asked 5-, 9-, and 13-year-old children and adults a series of questions related to mental uncontrollability. For instance, will a child who hears a strange noise automatically wonder what that noise is, even if he or she doesn't want to, and is it possible to go for three days without thinking about anything? Adults and older children understood that the mind "has a mind of its own" better than younger children. That is, they understood that the mind will sometimes "think" about things even if the person has no interest in thinking about it (the source of an unexpected

noise, for example), and that one cannot avoid thinking for an extended period of time. Although younger children sometimes understand these facts of mental life also, they are much less likely to make these claims than adolescents and adults.

Much of the work examining changes in children's understanding of mental concepts and activities beyond the preschool years has been done by Paula Schwanenflugel, William Fabricius, and their colleagues (Fabricius et al., 1989; Schwanenflugel, Fabricius, & Noyes, 1996; Schwanenflugel, Henderson, & Fabricius, 1998). In their studies, 8- and 10-year-old children and adults are read sentences involving different sets of adult-defined mental activities and asked to rate the similarity of the various activities. Each sentence is contrasted with every other sentence, with participants rating the similarity of the two mental activities on a seven-point scale (1 = exactly the same, 7 = completely different). Here are the stimulus sentences (with elaborations to children shown in brackets) used in one of their studies, illustrating five different types of mental activities (Fabricius et al., 1989, p. 1280)[1]:

List Memory

1. Making a list at home of all the kids in your new class without missing any. [It is soon after school starts in the year when you do it.]
2. Getting all the things at the store that your mother asked you to get. [She didn't give you a list. She just told you, and now you are at the store and you have to get them.]

Prospective Memory

3. Bringing back your permission slip for the field trip. [Nobody tells you. You have to bring it back yourself when you leave to go to school.]
4. Saying Happy Birthday on the right day to your friend who told you her birthday a long time ago.

Comprehension

5. Learning a new board game from the instructions on the box.
6. Reading your math book to be able to do the problems at the end of the lesson.

7. Feeling like you know how to get to your friend's house from the directions she is giving you. [You've never been to her house and she's telling you the directions.]

Attention

8. Trying to find the North Star in the sky on a starry night. [The North Star is a special bright star, and you know what it looks like, but there are lots of stars out.]
9. Listening to what your friend is saying to you in a noisy classroom.
10. Picking a yellow flower from a bunch of flowers of different colors.

Inference

11. Figuring out what your friend wants when he says, "Boy, that cookie looks good!"
12. Seeing a puddle on the ground and realizing it must have rained last night. [You didn't hear it rain last night. You just see the puddle in the morning.]
13. Knowing that your teacher likes the present you gave him by the look on his face.

The general findings from their studies reflect both some similarities and differences between 8- and 10-year-old children and adults in how they view mental activities. Adults distinguish several categories of mental activities (for example, memory, comprehension, attention, and inference). Like the adults, both 8- and 10-year-old children distinguish memory and inference as separate types of mental operations; but unlike the adults, they do not distinguish separate categories for comprehension and attention (see also Lovett & Flavell, 1990), nor are they as likely to distinguish among the various forms of memory (list, prospective, recall, recognition), although such discriminations are not totally absent in the children (Schwanenflugel, Fabricius, & Alexander, 1994). An awareness of the significance of the constructive processes (as reflected in such verbs as *estimate, guess, reason,* and *question*) in cognition increased with age, as did an understanding of the relation between memory- and comprehension-related verbs (Schwanenflugel et al., 1998).

Schwanenflugel and Fabricius propose that what is developing is a constructivist theory of mind, with adults viewing mental processes "as interactive, pervasive, and inherently interpretive" (Schwanenflugel et al., 1994, p. 39). Such a constructivist view is not fully shared by children, who focus more on inputs and outputs than on the similarities between the mental activities themselves. Schwanenflugel and her colleagues (1994) concluded that between the ages of 8 and 10 years, children become increasingly aware of a variety of different cognitive processes and of the important role of memory in cognitive task performance. Children also begin to distinguish between mental processes operating at retrieval, when performance is actually assessed, and at acquisition, when one is initially trying to "learn" something new. According to Schwanenflugel, and her colleagues (1994), "When children come to see that even information acquisition is influenced by selective and interpretive mental processes, they may be on the verge of their first generalized understanding of the constructive nature of mind" (pp. 41–42).

Representational Changes over Childhood: Evidence from Classification

At the center of the great and near-great stage theories of cognitive development is the idea of changes in the nature of mental representation between the preschool and school years. Piaget, Fischer, and Case all attest to the symbolic nature of thinking by the 2- and 3-year-old child, but all concur that thinking changes qualitatively sometime between 5 and 7 years of age. Piaget and the neo-Piagetians generally agree on the nature of the representational change. Piaget believed that preschool children's thinking is intuitive rather than logical in nature; moreover, their thinking is perceptually centered and based more on perceptual than abstract, or conceptual features.

Researchers have long been interested in the transition in representation that occurs during this time, and evidence from a variety of sources indicates changes in children's representation from (1) perceptual to conceptual properties of stimuli, and (2) schematic to conceptual/taxonomic categorical properties. The term **schematic** as used here refers to representing objects in terms of real or potential interactions with other items. Thus, a tractor may be thought about in terms of what it does (plows fields, pulls heavy equipment), who interacts with it (farmers), and where it is found (on farms, in barns), rather than in terms of its conceptual or taxonomic category (vehicle; similar to cars). Each form of representation reflects something important about an object, but which representation comes to mind first (perceptual, schematic, or conceptual) or which one we find easier to use in our thinking will influence how we think and what conclusions we're likely to reach when considering a problem.

In the remainder of this section, I will review research mainly from classification tasks that reflect some of these changes in representation over early and middle childhood. (Other research using classification tasks will be examined in Chapter 10 on problem solving.)

Classification

Classification refers to the grouping of objects on the basis of some set of characteristics. In many classification experiments, children are given a set of objects, pictures, or words and asked to group them so that items that are alike or go together in some way are grouped together. Following classification, children are usually asked to justify their groupings. By examining the composition of and justifications for their groupings, one can infer how children represent sets of items and the type of relations they use for categorizing diverse stimuli.

Although there are a variety of ways of describing age-related changes in classification, four general phases in classification can be identified. The earliest phase, typifying most 2- and some 3-year-olds, I have labeled **idiosyncratic classification** (also called fiat equivalence or random classification). Children group items together, usually in pairs, and either fail to provide a reason for their groupings or

provide one that is independent of any physical or conceptual characteristics of the stimuli (Denney & Acito, 1974; Inhelder & Piaget, 1964). For example, a child might sort pictures of a dog and an apple together and when asked why he or she made such a grouping, answer, "Because a dog barks and you can eat an apple." Alternatively, the child might simply label each object or state that "I like dogs and I like apples." This latter explanation may seem to reflect a grouping on the basis of likes and dislikes, but such a child will probably give the same justification for all pairings.

In a second phase, labeled here **perceptual classification,** children group items on the basis of perceptual characteristics. For example, table and chair go together because they both have four legs, or elephant and car go together because they're both big, or frog and tree go together because they're both green. Perceptual justifications are found mainly in the groupings of 3- and 4-year-old children but are also found in the classifications of older children.

Slightly older children tend to form their groupings on the basis of **complementary relations** (also called functional, schematic, or thematic classification). Denney (1974) described groupings based on complementary relations as those "composed of items that are different but share some interrelationship either in the subject's past experiences or in the experimental situation" (p. 41). For example, dog and apple go together because dogs can eat apples, or barn, tractor, and farmer go together because a farmer can drive a tractor into a barn. Complementary justifications increase in incidence over the preschool years and typically are replaced by conceptual justifications some time between the ages of 6 and 9 years.

Finally, children group items on the basis of **conceptual relations** (also called similarity, taxonomic, nominal, or categorical classification). I use this term to mean groupings based on similar category membership (for example, membership in categories such as animals, furniture, clothing) or shared function (for example, both birds and airplanes fly). Conceptual justifications can be found in the classifications of preschool children, but they increase in frequency between the ages of 6 and 10 years. The use of conceptual classification seems to be related to formal schooling (see Denney, 1974).

Evidence for Denney's "schooling" hypothesis is found in research examining the thinking of people from traditional cultures, where the shift from complementary to conceptual classification, as defined here, is typically not found (Cole & Scribner, 1977). The Soviet psychologist A. R. Luria (1976) studied the thinking styles of people from a remote area of Uzbekistan in the 1930s. Following are excerpts from Luria's study that reflect complementary classification similar to that shown by 5- and 6-year-olds from technologically more advanced cultures. In these examples, the subject was shown four pictures and was to choose the one that was different. This is known as an oddity problem.

Subject: Rakmat, age thirty-nine, illiterate peasant from an outlying district; . . . He is shown drawings of the following: *hammer-saw-log-hatchet.*

"They're all alike. I think all of them have to be here. See, if you're going to saw, you need a saw, and if you have to split something you need a hatchet. So they're all needed here."

We tried to explain the task by another, simpler example: "Look, here you have three adults and one child. Now clearly the child doesn't belong in this group."

"Oh, but the boy must stay with the others! All three of them are working, you see, and if they have to keep running out to fetch things, they'll never get the job done, but the boy can do the running for them. . . . The boy will learn; that'll be better, then they'll be able to work well together" [p. 55].

Subject is then shown drawing of: *bird-rifle-dagger-bullet.*

"The swallow doesn't fit here. . . . No . . . this is a rifle. It's loaded with a bullet and kills the swallow. Then you have to cut the bird up with the dagger, since there's no other way to do it. . . . What I said about the swallow before is wrong! All these things go together" [pp. 56–57].

The classification responses of this uneducated adult are reminiscent of the responses of 5-year-olds.

However, one must be cautious not to make value judgments concerning the thinking of people from traditional cultures. The thinking of the people described in Luria's study was well suited for their environment, and, in some ways, may be more advanced than our own. The demands of their world were different, requiring a different cognitive system. They did not have to worry about a monetary system of checks, automatic tellers, and credit cards, whereas we do. Human cognitive abilities are flexible. In fact, Luria noted that the thinking of these people became more conceptual as a result of formal education, reflecting the plasticity of human intelligence, even in adults.

Other research has shown that people from traditional cultures are able to classify objects according to conceptual criteria—they just don't think that it's a very intelligent way of doing things. For instance, in a study of Kpelle farmers from Liberia, adults consistently sorted objects into functional groups (for example, *knife* with *orange*; *potato* with *hoe*), rather than in terms of conceptual categories (for example, *potato* and *orange*; *hoe* and *knife*). This, many farmers stated, was the wise way to do it. When asked how a fool would do the task, the farmers classified the objects into neat conceptually based piles, exactly as Westerners do (Glick, 1975).

It should be noted that the developmental trend in classification described here is not stagelike. Although a preference for conceptual classification is usually observed in children 8 or 9 years of age, for example, some studies find this preference even in preschool-age children (Osborne & Calhoun, 1998), and complementary schemes continue to be used by older children and adults when the stimuli and task demands call for them (Greenfield & Scott, 1986; Rabinowitz & Mandler, 1983). Thus, people over a broad age range have available to them a variety of relations by which to classify objects. What changes in development seems to be the tendency for various forms of relations to be used, with conceptual relations being used in a wider range of contexts with increasing age. This is consistent with Siegler's (1996) observations that children use a variety of strategies on any cognitive task, with developmental changes being best described not as stage transitions but as changes in the frequency with which different strategies are used.

The use of alternative classification styles is not limited to older children and adults. Although one would not expect many conceptually based groupings in the sortings of 3-year-olds, children at least as young as 4 and 5 years use a variety of these classification schemes. Let me provide an example of a not-too-atypical 5-year-old who used an interesting mixture of styles in a single sorting task. The child was given 16 black-and-white line drawings of familiar objects that could, from an adult's perspective, be grouped into four categories (animals, clothes, food, and tools). He was told to put the drawings into groups so that "pictures that are alike or go together in some way are grouped together." He spontaneously provided justifications for his groupings as he sorted. This child grouped all items into pairs, although this was not a requirement of the task. His first pair was corn and banana, and they went together, he said, because they are both yellow (perceptual). Horse and pants go together because a cowboy needs pants to ride a horse (complementary); saw and shovel go together because they both have sharp points (perceptual); coat and shirt go together because you wear them (conceptual); pie and hat go together because they're both round (perceptual); hammer and screwdriver go together because they're both tools (conceptual); and rabbit and milk go together because they're both white (perceptual). This child had more perceptual justifications than is usual for a 5-year-old, but his mixture of justifications is typical for children of this age.

An example from another 5-year-old reflects the mixture of classification styles for children of this age, as well as their creativity and lack of planning. This child's first group consisted of the items shovel, saw, screwdriver, and hammer, and her justification was that they are all tools (conceptual). Next, she placed cat and milk together and said that a cat drinks milk (complementary); horse and corn go together because a horse eats corn (complementary); hat and coat go together because you wear them (conceptual); and squirrel and banana go together because a squirrel might eat a banana (complemen-

tary). The child was then left with three pictures, and rather than not including them in any group or rethinking some of her earlier categories, she paused and then placed pants, shirt, and pie together and said, "Well, you've got to get dressed to eat dessert." This last example shows children's tendencies to follow instructions to make groups even if it means being inventive. It also reflects young children's lack of planning. This child did not look at all the pictures first and then decide the best categorization plan. Rather, she noticed salient relations among items and formed her groups on an item-by-item basis. Older children, with more foresight, would not be left with squirrel and banana or shirt, pants, and pie.

The diversity of classification judgments made by the same child indicates that these styles reflect, for the most part, preferences on the part of the child. For example, children alter their sorting style as a function of changes in procedures or instructions. A clear example of the preference basis of children's classification styles is found in a study by Smiley and Brown (1979). Children were to choose which of two pictures went best with a standard picture. One of the alternatives was related to the standard on the basis of complementary relations (for example, for needle, thread), whereas the other alternative was related on the basis of conceptual relations (for example, for needle, pin). The majority of the selections of preschool and first-grade children reflected complementary relations. In contrast, fifth-grade and college students showed a marked preference for the conceptual relations. In a second experiment, kindergarten children were successfully trained to make selections based on conceptual relations. One day after training, however, the children were tested again, and their bias for complementary classification had returned. Thus, young children can easily be trained to use conceptual relations, but they revert to their preferred mode when given the opportunity to do so.

As the previous paragraphs indicate, preschool children's preferences for schematic over conceptual relations is far from perfect, and, depending on how one asks the question, sometimes no preferences at all are found (Waxman & Namy, 1997). One reason for this variability might have to do with individual differences in processing style. In a longitudinal study, Durham and Durham (1995) observed children and their mothers in play sessions at 13 and 24 months of age. Children were seen again at 36 months of age and administered a classification task in which they were given a target picture (for example, a *tennis shoe* or a *robin*) and asked to choose from three pictures (for *tennis shoe*: high-heeled shoe, foot, bed; for *robin*: duck, nest, envelope) "another one the same as this one" (p. 484). The most interesting result of this study was the relation between play behaviors at 13- and 24-month and children's classification responses at 36 months. Infants who pointed more at 13 months and who produced more nouns at 24 months were more likely to make conceptual (taxonomic) responses at 36 months (that is, select the high-heeled shoe and the duck in the examples above). In contrast, children who showed an interest in functional-relational play (defined as bringing together and integrating two objects in an appropriate way) at 13 months and who used more relational terms (such as "in," "on," "down") at 24 months, tended to classify pictures schematically at 36 months (that is, select the foot and the nest in the examples above). These findings suggest that there may be some potent individual differences in children's tendencies to classify their world either conceptually or schematically, and that this difference is found early in life and is relatively stable, at least over the preschool years.

There is other evidence of a schematic-to-conceptual shift in development, including research examining age differences in how children define words (Denney, 1974), word associations (Emerson & Gekowski, 1976), cued recall (Ackerman, 1986), errors in recognition memory (Scott, Serchuk, & Mundy, 1982), and children's specification of relations existing among a series of items (Anglin, 1970). For example, when preschool children are asked to define words, they typically describe a function for the word (for instance, "A hoe is for digging"), whereas older children more typically provide a category name (for instance, "A hoe is a type of garden tool") or a synonym (for instance, "A hoe is like a shovel") (Denney, 1974). Similarly, on word-association tasks, in which children are read a word and are to say the first word that comes into

their minds, older school-age children, like adults, usually provide a response word of the same conceptual class as the stimulus word (for example, *car: truck; dress: pants*). Preschool and early school-age children are more likely to provide a complementary response, stating a function of the stimulus word (for example, *car: drive*) or one that "goes with" the stimulus word (for example, *dress: girl*) (Emerson & Gekowski, 1976).

The Development of Natural Language Categories

Much of the work on children's classifications has been done with meaningful objects that can be classified into familiar language categories. Meaningful objects are related to other meaningful objects and can be referred to as belonging to one or more categories. All languages have terms to serve this function. **Natural language categories** refer to categorical terms that a language uses to describe and group a large number of words and concepts. Many natural language categories are hierarchical in nature. So, for example, *collie* is a language category term that includes all creatures of a particular canine breed. A more inclusive category term is *dog*, which includes all collies but also many other breeds that are not collies. From here our language provides us with terms of increasing inclusiveness, from *pets* or *canines* to *animals*. If one wanted to get technical about it, one could list the biological species, genus, family, class, and so on of which Fido is a member, with each step up the ladder being more inclusive than the one preceding it. Such language categories are obviously very important in communicating and classifying information. However, their development requires more than just learning the term; what children must learn is what characteristics an object must have to qualify for membership in a language category and when to use the term.

Two- and 3-year-old children obviously have some understanding of terms for broad, **superordinate categories** such as *animals, clothes,* or *food*. They use these words occasionally (for example, "Dresses are girls' clothes, not boys'"), and they seem to comprehend their meaning when used by an adult (for example, "Stop playing with your food!"). Yet, there are many superordinate category terms that young children typically do not use (most 3-year-olds do not speak of *vehicles*, *weapons*, or *tools*), and we must be careful not to attribute adult meaning to children's language categories. Young children may speak of food, clothes, and animals, but they may not give these words the same meanings that adults do (Nelson, 1996).

Basic-Level Categories

Eleanor Rosch, Carolyn Mervis, and their colleagues (Mervis & Rosch, 1981; Rosch et al., 1976) proposed that young children's early categories are not at the superordinate level but rather include objects that have similar overall configurations (for example, cars and chairs but not vehicles and furniture). As we saw in Chapter 6, infants can form primitive concepts for sets of objects that are perceptually similar (see Cohen & Younger, 1983; Reznick & Kagan, 1983). Rosch and her colleagues (1976) referred to such groupings as **basic-level categories.** In a series of experiments, they demonstrated that 3- and 4-year-old children were easily able to categorize sets of objects at the basic level, whereas few could organize items according to more superordinate categories. The children were shown sets of three pictures and asked to point to the two pictures "that are alike, that are the same kind of thing." In some triads, two of the pictures were examples from the same basic-level category (for example, two different types of cats or of cars). In other triads, the pictures were from different basic-level categories but from the same superordinate category (for example, a car and a train—both vehicles—or a cat and a dog—both animals). Both the 3- and 4-year-old children had no difficulty identifying the category membership of objects from the same basic-level categories. The 4-year-olds also performed well when matches were based on superordinate category relations; in contrast, the 3-year-olds' performance was at chance values for these latter problems. A similar developmental trend was observed in a more demanding sorting task, where children were to group pictures that went together or were alike in some way. Kindergarten and first-grade children easily grouped items according to basic-level categories, but only half of these children were able to sort items on the basis of superordinate category membership.

Perhaps even more impressive is evidence that children appear to be cognizant of basic-level categories well before their second birthday, before they have language terms for these concepts. For example, in some experiments, 15- to 18-month-old toddlers are presented with sets of objects that can be grouped into two basic-level categories. For instance, in studies by Gopnik and Meltzoff (1987, 1992), children were given four brightly colored human figures and four flat yellow rectangles. The children were then told simply to "play with these things" or "fix them up." At 15 months of age, children will serially touch all the items from one basic-level category and then touch all the items from the second category, termed "exhaustive sorting" by Mandler and Bauer (1988). At 18 months, many children will actually sort the two sets of items into discernible groups, picking up and moving objects so they are grouped with "their own kind" (Gopnik & Meltzoff, 1987, 1992; Sugarman, 1983). This, of course, occurs long before children can group items into superordinate categories, and reflects the fact that young children do have some basic categorical knowledge very early in life, before they have words for these concepts.

The Development of Category Prototypes

Other researchers have suggested that children acquire sets of features that characterize specific members of a category and gradually integrate these features to develop a higher-level, taxonomic concept. For instance, Jeremy Anglin (1977) proposed that children abstract the general features of a category and form a **category prototype.** As mentioned in Chapter 6, a category prototype is a mentalistic representation reflecting the most typical or best examples of that category. Forming such a prototype involves abstracting features possessed by most or all members of the category and ignoring features that are idiosyncratic to specific members and do not characterize the category as a whole. For example, one's prototype for *dog* probably includes four legs, fur, a tail, a certain shape of head, and a certain size. Your Chihuahua may be your favorite dog, but with its tiny size and lack of fur it is unlikely that it resembles your prototype for dog.

Anglin suggested that children's prototypes develop from their experiences with specific members of the category. In defining a category, Anglin suggested, young children often rely on visual imagery and their recollection of specific experiences with particular instances of the category. For instance, Sharon, at 4 years 7 months, described a dog as something that has "soggy ears that go, that hang down," that "goes 'ruff,'" and that "chases cats" (p. 205). Her definition of *dog* is based on specific experiences with them. Eventually, as children's experiences with the real world increase, their knowledge becomes broader and their categories more closely resemble those of adults.

Related to the idea of category prototypes is that of **category typicality.** Rosch and her colleagues (Mervis & Rosch, 1981; Rosch, 1975) proposed that some items are more representative of the prototype than others. Items that are highly typical of a category have more features in common with the category prototype than do less typical items. For example, both socks and shirt are appropriate examples of the category of clothing, but most adults would say that shirt is more typical of their idea of clothing than socks are. In other words, not all category members are created equal, with some items being more representative of our idea of a category than others. Adults show high intersubject agreement in their ratings of items in terms of typicality (Rosch, 1975), and differences in the typicality of category items influence adults' performance on a variety of cognitive tasks (Keller & Kellas, 1978). The questions of importance here are how children achieve an adult understanding of natural language categories and what role category typicality plays in this development.

In experiments where children are asked to select from a set of pictures or words all the examples of a specified category (for example, "Pick out all the pictures of clothes, things you can wear"), young children usually choose most of the items that adults judge to be highly typical of the category (for example, shirt and pants), but they often fail to include many items that adults judge to be less typical of the category (for example, gloves, hat, and tie) (Anglin, 1977; Bjorklund, Thompson, & Ornstein, 1983). Moreover, when children are asked to rate category items by typicality ("goodness of example"), children's ratings become progressively more adultlike with age (Bjorklund et al., 1983). Children are apparently sensitive to differences in category typicality at a very early age. In one set of experiments, toddlers as young as 13-months of age were more likely to group sets of prototypical items together (examples from both superordinate [for example, *animals*] and basic-level [for example, *dogs*] categories), than sets of items consisting of less typical items (Bauer, Dow, & Hertsgaard, 1995).

Other researchers, using a variety of cognitive tasks, have reported developmental differences in the semantic representation of category-typical and category-atypical items (Ackerman, 1986; Whitney & Kunen, 1983). In general, these researchers assert that age differences in how children process category information are due to the fact that with age, children reorganize their semantic concepts, realizing that some features are more important than others in defining items (see Bjorklund, 1985, for a review). Thus, although children's natural language categories can be described as prototypes much as adults' categories can, the nature of the prototypes changes. Children include fewer items as appropriate category members, with more typical exemplars being incorporated into children's category structures before less typical items. Furthermore, children's prototypes seem to be structured slightly differently from those of adults, with children emphasizing different features in defining natural language categories. Differences are most apparent during the preschool years and are greatly minimized (although not eliminated) by the time a child is 10 or 11 years of age (Bjorklund et al., 1983; Whitney & Kunen, 1983).

Summary

Representation is the way in which objects, events, and experiences are encoded or represented in the mind. Traditionally, representation during infancy has been referred to as sensorimotor, in that objects and events are known by action associated with those objects (either activity inherent in the object itself or the child's action on the object). Sensorimotor representation is replaced by mentalistic, symbolic representation (the *symbolic*, or *semiotic*, *function*) sometime around 18 to 24 months of age, as reflected by *symbolic play*, *deferred imitation*, *language*, and *mental imagery*.

Neonatal imitation has been observed, with Meltzoff and Moore attributing this phenomenon to *active-intermodal mapping* and thus seeing it as a reflection of symbolic functioning. Others observe that neonatal imitation typically disappears by about 2 months and suggest that neonatal imitation reflects a *fixed-action pattern* and a *transient ontogenetic adaptation*, serving a specific function at a particular time in development, rather than a reflection of symbolic ability. Evidence for *deferred imitation* has been found as early as 9 months of age, which has been interpreted as reflecting symbolic functioning. Evidence has been accumulating for early developing knowledge of objects and rudimentary symbolic representation during infancy. By using variations of the *violations-of-expectation method*, which is based on habituation/dishabituation procedures, researchers have demonstrated evidence of *object permanence*, and concepts of number (for example, *subitizing*) far earlier than Piaget had proposed.

The knowledge that an entity can stand for something other than itself has been referred to as *representational insight*. DeLoache and her colleagues have investigated the development of representational insight in children by examining how they deal with scale models and pictures. Whereas children as young as 2.5-years show representational insight when pictures are used, not until age 3 do children show representational insight with models. DeLoache proposes that *dual representation* (or *dual orientation*) is required before children can show representational insight.

Young children have a difficult time distinguishing between an object's appearance and its actual identity (*appearance/reality distinction*). Flavell and his colleagues speculated that children must be able to engage in *dual encoding* before this distinction can be made. Although 3- and 4-year-old children can distinguish between imagined and experienced

events, this distinction is tenuous, with preschoolers often thinking that make-believe objects can become real by imagining them as real. Young children also often show *source-monitoring errors*, confusing whether they had imagined or experienced an event.

Theory of mind refers to children's developing concepts of mental activity, both their own and others'. Concerning children as "mind readers," 3-year-olds usually fail *false-belief tasks*, although they seem to illustrate some semblance of *belief-desire reasoning*, especially on tasks that involve active deception or involve implicit, as opposed to explicit, understanding. Theory of mind has been proposed to be modular (domain-specific) in nature. Evidence of this comes from the general inability of children with autism to read minds, which has been referred to as *mindblindness*. Concerning children's understanding of thinking, preschoolers have a poor understanding of what is involved in mental activity; this ability improves during the early school years, and 8- and 10-year-olds show the beginning of a constructivist theory of mind.

The nature of children's symbolic representation varies over the course of childhood, with preschool children being especially attentive to *schematic relations* whereas older children are more attentive to conceptual relations. In *classification* experiments, children sort sets of objects so that items that are alike or go together in some way are grouped together. Four different phases in children's classification can be identified: (1) *idiosyncratic*, (2) *perceptual*, (3) *complementary* (*schematic*), and (4) *conceptual*. These classification phases do not have the quality of stages, and children can easily be trained to use a more advanced style than they use spontaneously. Even adults frequently use complementary schemes in certain situations.

Natural language categories comprise items that are related on the basis of some set of features and that can be referred to by a single language term (for example, dogs, pets, animals). Young children are able to categorize *basic-level* objects (for example, cars, chairs, dogs) and only later categorize on the basis of more *superordinate categories* (for example, vehicles, furniture, animals). One factor influencing the formation of superordinate natural language categories is that of *category typicality*. Some items are more representative of the *category prototype* than others. Children tend to learn the category membership of more-typical items before that of less-typical items, and their judgments of category typicality vary with age.

Note

1. From "Developing Theories of the Mind: Children's and Adults' Conceptions of Mental Activities," by W. V. Fabricius, P. J. Schwanenflugel, P. C. Kyllonen, C. R. Barclay, and S. M. Denton, 1989, *Child Development*, 60, 1278–1290. Copyright © 1989 The Society for Research in Child Development. Reprinted with permission.

Key Terms and Concepts

representation
symbolic (semiotic) function
deferred imitation
symbolic play
mental imagery
reproductive images
anticipatory images
neonatal imitation
active intermodal mapping
innate releasing mechanisms (fixed action patterns)
transient ontogenetic adaptations
object permanence
violation-of-expectation method
subitizing
representational insight
dual representation (dual encoding, dual orientation)
appearance/reality distinction
identity
source monitoring
theory of mind
belief-desire reasoning
false-belief task
representational change
wishful thinking
mindblindness
schematic representation
classification
idiosyncratic (fiat equivalence, random) classification
perceptual classification
complementary (functional, schematic, thematic) classification

conceptual (similarity, taxonomic, nominal, categorical) classification
natural language categories
superordinate categories
basic-level categories
category prototype
category typicality

Suggested Readings

MANDLER, J. (1998). Representation. In D. Kuhn & R. S. Siegler (Eds.), *Cognition, perception, and language*, Vol. 2 (pp. 255–308) of W. Damon (Gen. Ed.), *Handbook of child psychology*, New York: Wiley. Mandler provides an excellent review of research on representation in infancy and the debate concerning the nature of infants' representation. Another chapter in this volume that discusses infant representation is M. M. Haith & J. B. Benson, "Infant cognition" (pp. 199–254).

WELLMAN, H. M., & GELMAN, S. A. (1998). "Knowledge acquisition in foundational domains" (pp. 523–574). In D. Kuhn & R. S. Siegler (Eds.), *Cognition, perception, and language*, Vol. 2, of W. Damon (Gen. Ed.), *Handbook of child psychology*, New York: Wiley. In addition to discussing representation in infancy, this chapter also provides a good overview of children's early "psychological theories" (theories of mind), as well as their "biological theories" (theories about animate and inanimate things). Another chapter in this volume that discusses representation during childhood (theory of mind and appearance/reality distinction) is that of J. H. Flavell and P. H. Miller, "Social cognition" (pp. 851–898).

BARON-COHEN, S. (1995). *Mindblindness: An essay on autism and theory of mind*. Cambridge, MA: MIT Press. In this short and highly readable book, Baron-Cohen presents an evolutionary psychological account of theory of mind, and supports his idea that theory of mind is modular in nature with research on autistic children, whom, Baron-Cohen proposes, are "mindblind," in that they are not able to read the minds of other people, and thus find themselves in a social world they do not understand.

DELOACHE, J. S. (1995). Early understanding and use of symbols: The model model. *Current Directions in Psychological Science, 4*, 109–113. DeLoache provides a brief and easily comprehensible account of her research and theory about preschool children's developing understanding of symbols.

Memory Development

Memory Development in Infancy

Implicit Memory

Remembering Events

The Development of Event Memory • Children as Eyewitnesses
Infantile Amnesia and the Development of Autobiographical Memory

Piagetian Research on Reconstructive Memory

The Development of Memory Strategies

Rehearsal • Organization • Retrieval • Other Strategies
Gender Differences in Memory Performance and Strategy Use

Factors That Influence Children's Use of Memory Strategies

Encoding • Knowledge Base • Metamemory
Motivation • Culture and Memory Strategies

Consistency and Stability of Memory

Is "Memory" a Domain-General Faculty or a Set of Domain-Specific Abilities?
How Stable Is Memory Performance over Time?

Forgetting and Reminiscence

Summary

Key Terms and Concepts

Suggested Readings

A 4-month-old looks longer at a new picture than at one he has seen repeatedly; a 3-year-old recounts her class field trip to a bakery; a 7-year-old lists for her mother the names of all her classmates in preparing to send Valentine's Day cards; and a high school sophomore attempts to remember everything his father asked him to get at the corner store. Each of these diverse activities has at least one thing in common: memory. The 4-month-old can recognize a new stimulus only if he has some notion that it is different from a previously experienced but currently unseen stimulus. The memory requirements for the three older children are more demanding, but all involve retrieving from memory some previously stored information.

Memory is not a unitary phenomenon. Information must be encoded and possibly related with other information known to the individual. What knowledge already resides in memory influences the ease with which new information is stored and later retrieved. Furthermore, few acts of cognition do not involve memory. Classification, problem solving, and decision making all require the retrieval of previously stored information.

To make matters even more complex, memory can refer to the contents of one's mind (one's memories) or to the process of bringing that information to consciousness. The contents of memory can be *declarative*, or *explicit*, so that a person can consciously reflect on what he or she knows; or it can be *nondeclarative* (procedural), or *implicit*, unavailable to conscious evaluation. Moreover, there are two general types of declarative memory: *semantic memory*, which refers to the long-term repository of language terms, their definitions, and their relations to one another; and *episodic memory*, which refers to memories for events or episodes. For example, the definition for the word "avuncular" is part of my semantic memory, but my recollections of the events surrounding my learning the word (preparing for the Graduate Record Exam) are part of my episodic memory.[1] Most of this chapter will deal with ex-

plicit, episodic memory, although we will also look at research into implicit memory.

Concerning the process of remembering, researchers have specified different operations by which information in our minds can be retrieved. The most basic form of retrieval is **recognition,** in which a stimulus is presented to a person and he or she must merely signify whether that stimulus is new (not experienced previously) or old. Young children often show very high levels of recognition memory, and in some situations, age differences in recognition memory are quite small, causing some to assert that this ability changes little with development (see Perlmutter & Lange, 1978). However, recognition is not purely automatic, and developmental differences in children's application of what they know to the task at hand have also been reported for this form of memory (Dirks & Neisser, 1977).

More demanding in terms of self-activation is *recall*, in which some information is not currently perceived but must be retrieved from memory. Retrieval can be prompted by a specific environmental context or cue (**cued recall**), or the reminder might be general or be internally generated (**free recall**). An important developmental consideration in retrieving information in memory is the degree to which children will use information they have available to them. In general, recall (especially free recall) requires more in the way of self-initiation and the application of prior knowledge than recognition does.

The distinction between cued-recall and free-recall memory in young children can be appreciated when one attempts to get some information from a young child. Such a question as, "How was school today?," is apt to bring a response of "Fine." More detailed information can be forthcoming, however, if more specific questions are asked. For example, a 5-year-old boy who spent the afternoon with his grandparents seeing his first play, "Little Shop of Horrors," was asked by his mother, "Well, how was your afternoon?" The child replied, "OK." The mother persisted, "Well, did you have a good time?" The child said, "Yeah." However, when prompted by his grandmother ("Tell your mother about Audrey II, the plant"), he provided great details, telling how the plant ate some of the main characters,

---

1. *avuncular:* Of, pertaining to or resembling an uncle (*The American Heritage Dictionary of the English Language*).

talked, sang, and how it took three people underneath it to make it move. The child had a wealth of information, but it could only be accessed when specific cues were provided. Cues not only elicit additional accurate information but sometimes cause children to recall inaccurate information. This aspect of cued-recall memory will be discussed later in the chapter.

Most, if not all, aspects of children's memory development increase with age, but different types of memory follow slightly different developmental courses. For example, recognition seems to be better developed in children than recall. One possible reason for children's relatively good recognition memory performance, at least in some situations, might have to do with the nature of the stimuli. Several authors have proposed that memory for spatial location, or **location memory,** develops early, reducing or eliminating age differences in memory performance. This is a controversial claim, for most studies examining age differences in spatial memory find differences, although the magnitude of such differences are relatively small (Park & James, 1983; Schumann-Hengsteler, 1992). And some studies report no developmental differences. For instance, a study by Ellis, Katz, and Williams (1987) used recall and reconstruction tasks with people ranging in age from 3 years to elderly adults. Ellis and his colleagues reported no developmental improvements in memory for location, with the exception of *higher* performance for 3- and 4-year-old children in one condition. Other research has examined the performance of children and adults on the game *Concentration* (or *Memory*), where participants must find matches to cards placed face down on a table by turning over two cards on each turn (Baker-Ward & Ornstein, 1988; Schumann-Hengsteler, 1989). Children as young as 5 years of age performed as well as adults and sometimes better, at least on early trials when strategies were less important. Older children and adults eventually outperformed the younger children, but the location memories for young children were nonetheless impressive, and age differences were substantially less than those found on most other memory tasks (Schneider & Pressley, 1997).

Thus, we cannot say that location memory is *better* in younger than older children, nor that there are no development improvements in such memory. We can say, however, that young children have impressive memories for the location of objects and that this memory skill seems, at least, to undergo less development than other memory abilities.

Today's children use their memories in many of the same ways that children 100,000 years ago used their memories—for recognizing friendly and unfriendly people and situations, for recalling the sequence of actions they must make to achieve important goals (such as eating a meal), and for developing a personal sense of themselves (an autobiographical memory). In most of these situations, children do not deliberately "try" to commit this information to memory, but rather acquire it in the course of everyday activities, usually in social situations.

But today's children must use their memories in ways that our ancestors never could have dreamed of—to learn by rote the multiplication tables, to recall, in correct order, all the presidents of the United States or the monarchs of England, to learn the capital of every state, and to recognize by sight thousands of printed words. Such memorization is usually deliberate and requires much mental effort and the use of strategies. These tasks are typically learned in school. Children are expected to master these tasks without any reason other than "the teacher said to," and children from schooled cultures learn to do so with little questioning. This is often referred to as learning or memory "out of context," or **"context-independent" learning.** Of course children in information-age cultures have good reasons for learning such information, and context-independent learning is necessary for success in the modern world. But is it the same type of memory that is used when children remember their last birthday party? Might there be different courses of development for these different types of explicit memory?

In this chapter, research and theory dealing with the development of memory in children are examined. I will first examine briefly the memory development in infancy, followed by a brief look at children's implicit memory. This will be followed by a section on children's memories for events, specifically autobiographical memory. The next section will examine children's deliberate memory for school-type information in which strategies are so useful, followed by the topics of the consistency and stability of memory, and finally, the flip side of remembering, forgetting.

Memory Development in Infancy

Babies obviously remember things. The questions of interest are when and under what conditions infants demonstrate memory and how long these memories last. Research examining infants' search behavior, as reflected by object permanence tasks (see Chapters 4 and 7), indicates age changes in memory during the first year (Diamond, 1985). Recall Diamond's findings that the amount of delay necessary to yield the A-not-B error increased with each successive month between 7 and 12 months. Although Diamond proposed that developmental differences in the ability to inhibit a prepotent response were in part responsible for this effect, she also acknowledges that such results reflect age changes in memory over this six-month period (Diamond, Cruttenden, & Neiderman, 1994).

The bulk of research assessing infant memory has used variants of the habituation/dishabituation paradigm discussed in Chapter 6. To review, infants' attention to a stimulus declines as a result of repeated presentation of a stimulus (habituation) but returns to its previously high levels when a new stimulus is presented (dishabituation). Such a finding not only indicates that infants can discriminate between the two stimuli but also implicates memory, in that the discrimination is being made between one stimulus that is physically present and another that is present only in memory. In a related procedure, infants are familiarized with a stimulus and later shown two stimuli: the original, familiarized stimulus and a novel one. As in the habituation/dishabituation paradigm, preference for the novel stimulus is taken as evidence of memory for the original.

Using these **preference for novelty paradigms,** memory for visual stimuli has been found for some newborns. Research by Friedman (1972) illustrated that some newborns demonstrated dishabituation (discussed in Chapter 6), although other research suggests that this ability likely characterizes only the more maturationally advanced neonates. Nonetheless, basic visual memory is an early developing ability, certainly within the capacity of most infants within their first months of life.

Perhaps the most influential work demonstrating memory in infants by using the preference for novelty paradigm is that of Joseph Fagan (1973, 1974). One study showed that 5- and 6-month-old babies formed visual memories following brief exposures (5 to 10 seconds), and that these memories lasted as long as 2 weeks (Fagan, 1974). Fagan's procedures have been widely used by researchers, and recent work has suggested a relationship between individual differences in preference for novelty during infancy and childhood memory and intelligence. This research will be examined in Chapter 14. More recent research has shown that even 1-month-old infants demonstrate relatively long-lived memories. For example, in one study the mothers of 1- and 2-month-old infants read their babies one of two nursery rhymes over the course of two weeks. Infants were then brought into the laboratory and their preference for the familiar versus a novel nursery rhyme was tested. This was done by permitting infants to hear either the familiar or a novel nursery rhyme by modifying their sucking on a pacifier (for example, increase sucking rate to hear one rhyme, decrease to hear the other). After a 3-day delay between the time infants last heard their mothers read the familiar nursery rhyme and being tested in the lab, even 1-month-old babies showed a preference for the familiar rhyme, indicating memory for the auditory event (Spence, 1996).

Other research by Carolyn Rovee-Collier and her colleagues has used conditioning techniques, demonstrating retention over relatively long periods for very young infants (see Rovee-Collier, 1995; Rovee-Collier & Gerhardstein, 1997 for a review). In their procedure, a ribbon is tied to an infant's ankle and connected to a mobile that is suspended over the

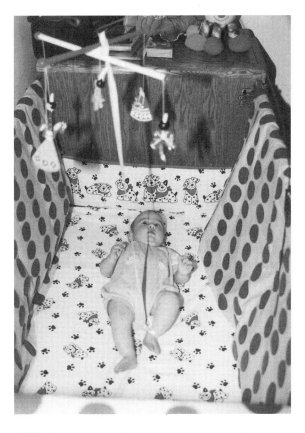

PHOTO 8-1   An infant connected to a mobile in an experiment to assess memory used by Carolyn Rovee-Collier and her colleagues. (Thanks to Carolyn Rovee-Collier)

crib. Infants quickly learn that when they kick their feet, the mobile moves, and they soon make repeated kicks, controlling the movement of the mobile overhead. In a typical experiment, for the first 3 minutes the ribbon is not connected to the mobile, so that kicks do not cause it to move (baseline nonreinforcement period). This period is followed by a 9-minute reinforcement period in which the ribbon and mobile are connected, and infants quickly learn to kick to make the mobile move. What will happen when the infants are hooked up to the apparatus hours or days later? Will they resume kicking (even when the ribbon is not connected to the mobile), or will their level of kicks be comparable to that observed during the 3-minute baseline? If the kicking

rate is high on these delayed trials, it reflects memory; if it is low, it reflects forgetting.

Rovee-Collier and her colleagues have used this procedure successfully with infants as young as 2 months of age. For example, Sullivan, Rovee-Collier, and Tynes (1979) varied the delayed-memory test between 48 hours and 336 hours (2 weeks) with 3-month-old infants. The researchers reported no forgetting by these young infants for as much as 8 days, and some babies displayed memory for the full 2-week interval. In related work, retention of conditioned responses during a 2-week period was obtained for infants as young as 8 weeks, although evidence of memory was obtained only under optimal conditions (distributing training over several sessions) (Vander Linde, Morrongiello, & Rovee-Collier, 1985). These results indicate that young infants can remember events over long intervals, although these skills do improve over the first several months of life.

More recent research by Rovee-Collier and her colleagues has focused on the role of context in infants' memories. How similar must the learning environment and testing environment be for babies to show retention? This was assessed in a study in which different aspects of the learning environment (in this case, the playpens in which the infants were tested) were changed between time of learning and time of testing (Rovee-Collier et al., 1992). Six-month-old infants were tested in the standard way, but the testing situation was made very distinctive. Infants sat in an infant seat that was placed in a playpen. The sides of the playpen were draped with a distinctive cloth (for example, yellow liner with green felt squares). Some infants were tested 24 hours later with the same cloth, whereas others were placed in the playpen that was draped with a blue liner and vertical red felt strips. The results of this experiment are presented in Figure 8-1 (expressed as kicking rate during testing relative to kicking rate during baseline). As can be seen, infants in the "No Change" condition demonstrated significantly better retention of the learned behavior than infants in the "Context Change" condition, indicating the important role that context plays in reinstating infants' memories.

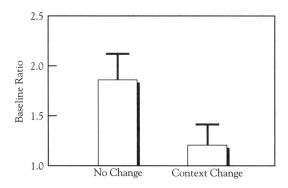

FIGURE 8-1   Mean baseline ratios for 6-month-old infants in a No Change (control) condition and a Context Change condition. The higher ratio for infants in the No Change condition reflects greater retention of the behaviors that were learned 24 hours earlier. SOURCE: Adapted from Rovee-Collier, C., Schechter, A., Shyi, C.-W. G., & Shields, P. (1992). Perceptual identification of contextual attributes and infant memory retrieval. *Developmental Psychology, 28,* 307–318.

Rovee-Collier et al. (1992) performed six other experiments, varying different aspects of the context. They concluded that infants do not respond to the context "as a whole," but rather seem to process individual components of a context. For instance, changes in visual patterns (for example, strips versus squares) or reversal of the foreground and background (for example, yellow liner with green squares versus green liner with yellow squares) disrupted memory, but changes in color did not (for other examples, see Bhatt, Rovee-Collier, & Shyi, 1994; Boller et al., 1996; Fagen et al., 1997). Rovee-Collier and Shyi (1992) speculated that infants' reliance on specific aspects of a context prevents them from retrieving memories in "inappropriate" situations. This may be especially important for infants with poor inhibitory abilities, who would be apt to retrieve previously acquired memories (actions) in a wide range of often inappropriate situations unless there were some potent constraints on the memory system (such as context specificity). The role of inhibitory factors in infant cognition has been addressed by several researchers, most notably Diamond, and this work was discussed in Chapter 2.

One interesting study by Rovee-Collier and her colleagues (Gulya et al., 1998) has demonstrated that 3-month-olds can remember arbitrary sequences, something that is seemingly important in learning language. In their study, infants were hooked up to a series of three mobiles, one at a time. Infants were seen again 24 hours later. Some infants were first cued with the first mobile they had seen and then hooked up to the second mobile (that is, these two mobiles were presented in the same serial order they had been presented the previous day). Other infants were first cued with the third mobile they had seen the day before followed by the second mobile (that is, the serial order of presentation was different than the previous day). Infants who received the mobiles in the same serial order on the two days demonstrated significantly more kicking when hooked up to the second mobile than those who received the mobiles in a different serial order than the day before. This is clear evidence that 3-month-old babies are able to remember over a 24-hour period a three-item arbitrary sequence. (Researchers using a very different paradigm have similarly shown that 8-month-olds can learn, very quickly, arbitrary patterns of syllables, again, critical for language acquisition [Aslin, Saffran, & Newport, 1998]).

The research of Rovee-Collier and her colleagues addresses memory early in infancy. Recent research has focused on memory in older infants and preverbal toddlers. This research has used **deferred imitation** tasks to measure memory (Bauer, 1997; Meltzoff, 1995). This research was discussed in Chapter 7 on representation, and so I will mention it only briefly again here. In most experiments, infants between about 10 and 20 months of age watch as an experimenter demonstrates some novel behavior with an unfamiliar toy. Infants do not play with the toy themselves, but only watch. At some later time, they are given the toy. If they display the novel behavior more so than a control group of infants who had not previously been shown the toy, it implies that they formed a long-term memory for the action they had only observed. The results of recent research are quite striking, showing that infants formed long-term memories for these novel actions that can last as long as one year (see Bauer,

1997; Meltzoff, 1995). These results suggest that preverbal infants and toddlers do in fact represent events in their long-term memories, and, under the right conditions, can access those memories months later.

Implicit Memory

The memory shown by infants in the preference for novelty task or in Rovee-Collier's conditioning experiments do not seem to require conscious awareness. That is, unlike most of the memory we will discuss in this chapter, it was not *explicit* — it did not involve children consciously retrieving information from their long-term stores. It is less clear whether the memory of older infants in the deferred imitation task was explicit or not. Many researchers believe it is (Bauer, 1997), but others think otherwise (Nelson, 1996). The alternative to explicit memory is **implicit memory,** or memory for some information without being consciously aware that one is remembering (see Schacter, 1992). This is "memory without awareness," and it is not limited to preverbal infants and toddlers but occurs also in older children and adults.

One test commonly used to assess implicit memory is the *word-stem task*. Here, participants are shown a series of words (perhaps for a recognition memory test), and some time later, after being tested for recognition, are given the first three letters of words and asked to complete each word stem with the first word that comes to mind (for example, cab___ for "cable"). Some of the word stems can be completed with "old" items (that is, words that were seen on the initial task), whereas others are "new" words. Implicit memory is demonstrated when participants complete more stem words that they had experienced earlier (or complete them faster) than for the new words, despite not recognizing these "old" words. That is, although they have no awareness of experiencing the words in the previous task, their performance is nonetheless influenced by the experience.

There has been relatively little developmental research on implicit memory, but what research has

been done presents a consistent picture. Although substantial age differences are found on tests of deliberate memorization (for instance, in the previous example, recognition of the words), few age differences are found when implicit memory is tested (Ausley & Guttentag, 1993; Naito, 1990; Perez, Peynircioglu, & Blaxton, 1998).

One procedure used to assess implicit memory in children involves the use of fragmented pictures of the type discussed in Chapter 6 (see Figure 6-13, page 183). Here, a fragmented picture is presented and children are asked to identify it. This is very difficult to do initially, but as more of the picture is completed, it becomes increasingly easier to identify the object. In experiments using this task, children are shown the series of degraded pictures and later given another task involving those pictures. Do children perform this second task better (faster or more accurately) for pictures they had previously seen, despite the fact that they might not remember seeing those pictures before? The answer is generally "yes," and, more important, there are few age differences in magnitude of the effects (Drummey & Newcombe, 1995; Hayes & Hennessy, 1996; Russo et al., 1995).

Let me provide an example of a study using this procedure. Hayes and Hennessy (1996) showed 4-, 5-, and 10-year-old children a series of pictures on one day and asked the children to identify the pictures (fragmented pictures) or to answer some questions about each item (for example, "What would you use an X for?"). Two days later the children were shown some of the previous pictures and some new ones to identify in a fragmented picture task. Children were also asked if they had remembered seeing each picture two days earlier. Although older children identified more pictures than the younger children, the *priming effect* (that is, the degree to which children identified "old" pictures sooner than "new" pictures) was equal for children of all ages. Also, there was no relation between how many pictures children of any age recognized (their explicit memory) and priming effects (their implicit memory). In other words, although children exhibited substantial differences in explicit memory, no developmental differences were found in implicit memory.

One interesting study of implicit memory involved showing 9- and 10-year olds pictures of preschool children, including some who had been their classmates 4 and 5 years earlier (Newcombe & Fox, 1994). Children were asked to determine whether or not each picture they were shown was that of a former classmate (an explicit recognition memory task); changes in the electrical conductance of their skin was also recorded. Greater changes in skin conductance for former classmates' pictures relative to pictures of unfamiliar children was used as a reflection of implicit recognition memory (that is, requiring no conscious awareness). Not surprisingly, children's performance was relatively poor on both the explicit and implicit tasks (although greater than expected by chance, indicating some memory of both the explicit and implicit types). However, there was no difference in skin conductance between children who performed well on the explicit task and those who performed poorly. This suggests that even the children whose performance on the explicit memory task was no greater than chance still "recognized" as many of their former classmates as those children who had performed better did. This pattern of data indicates that some children "remembered" (implicitly) more than they "knew" (explicitly). Similar results of greater implicit than explicit recognition of former classmates, using a different method of implicit memory, have been reported by Lie and Newcombe (1999).

These findings suggest that implicit memory is an early developing ability, perhaps more related to the development of semantic memory than to episodic memory (Tulving, 1987). Some theorists have speculated that implicit memory is under the control of automatic as opposed to effortful processes (Jacoby, 1991), and, following the theorizing of Hasher and Zacks (1979, see Chapter 5), that these processes show little development across childhood (Ausley & Guttentag, 1993). In fact, the procedures used to assess memory in infants (habituation/dishabituation and conditioning techniques) are likely more similar in nature to the tests used to assess implicit memory in older children than are the tests used to assess explicit memory. Recall from Chapter 6, Haith's (1993) comments of the need to bridge the gap between cognition in infancy and cognition in childhood by developing new research techniques and theories. Research using implicit memory techniques might be that bridge. In this spirit, Ausley and Guttentag (1993) suggested that "research using indirect [implicit] methods of memory assessment with children probably does provide a real avenue of continuity with infancy research, because these tests do not require an awareness of the previous occurrence of events for successful performance" (p. 254).

Remembering Events

Much of what we remember is for *events*, things that happen to us during the course of everyday life. Unlike implicit memory, **event memory** is explicit. We are aware that we are remembering. For most aspects of event memory, however, we did not specifically *try* to remember the event when we experienced it. In other words, for most event memories, the encoding of the event was unintentional. Because we had no intention of learning new information, our unintentional memory is not influenced by the use of deliberate encoding strategies, which accounts for much of the age differences observed on intentional memory tasks (see discussion of strategic memory later in this chapter). Rather, memory representations can be laid down involuntarily as part of ongoing activity, and several researchers have speculated that, in some cases, such "naturalistic learning" could actually produce higher levels of memory performance than more deliberate memorization attempts will, especially for young children (Istomina, 1975; Piaget & Inhelder, 1973).

The issue at hand is when and how it is that children remember the experiences of their everyday lives? How are these memories organized? How long do they last? And how is it that children come to acquire them?

The Development of Event Memory

A young child must master many aspects of memory if he or she is to remember important events. First, an event must be attended to and perceived. Then, the child must make some sense of that event so that it can be represented in his or her mind and recalled later on. If a child doesn't attend to the important aspects of an event or cannot make sense of what he or she experienced, there is really nothing to remember. One important thing to remember is that young children pay attention to different aspects of events than adults do and do not necessarily know what aspects of an event are important and which are trivial. For example, as adults, we know that the purpose of a baseball game is to watch the players on the field play ball. We automatically pay less attention to the field maintenance staff, the players on the bench, and most of the other spectators. However, young children don't always select the "right" things to pay attention to. At a baseball game they might spend more time watching the hot dog vendors, the bat boys, and the second base ump. What they remember of the game will thus be very different than what an older child or adult remembers.

Script-Based Memory

What is it that young children remember? One thing they tend to remember well is recurring events—what typically happens on a day-to-day basis. Katherine Nelson and her colleagues have demonstrated that preschool children tend to organize events in terms of **scripts,** which are a form of schematic organization with real-world events organized in terms of their causal and temporal characteristics (Nelson, 1993, 1996; Fivush, 1997). For example, a "fast-food restaurant" script might involve driving to the restaurant, entering the restaurant and standing in line, ordering, paying the cashier, taking the food to the table, eating, and then throwing away the trash before leaving. Scripts develop most readily for routine, repeated events. Children learn what "usually happens" in a situation, such as what happens at snack time at school, at a birthday party, or at a fast-food restaurant, and remember novel information in the context of these familiar events (Farrar & Goodman, 1992; Nelson & Gruendel, 1981).

Substantial research during the past decade or so demonstrates that even very young children organize information temporally in a script-like fashion (Bauer, 1997; Fivush, Kuebli, & Clubb, 1992), and

that such schematic organization for events doesn't change appreciably into adulthood (see Fivush & Hudson, 1990; Nelson, 1996 for reviews of this literature). Perhaps even more impressive is the evidence that even preverbal infants use temporal order to remember events. Research by Patricia Bauer and Jean Mandler (1989, 1992) tested infants ranging in age from 11.5 to 20 months on imitation tasks. The toddlers were shown a sequence of events (for example, putting a ball in a cup, inverting a smaller cup on top of the larger one, and shaking the cups) and later given the opportunity to interact with the materials again. Bauer and Mandler reported that the children re-enacted the sequence of events in the same temporal order they had been shown. This finding argues for the existence of a script-style memory organization long before children are able to talk.

Young children's tendencies to organize information following familiar scripts seems to result in their tendency *not* to remember much in the way of specific (that is, nonscript) information. For example, in a study by Robyn Fivush and Nina Hamond (1990), 2.5-year-old children were asked specific questions about recent special events, such as a trip to the beach, a camping trip, or a ride on an airplane. Rather than recalling the novel aspects of these special events, the children were more apt to focus on what adults would consider to be routine information. Take, for instance, the following conversation reported by Fivush and Hamond between an adult and child about a camping trip. The child first recalled sleeping out side, which is unusual, but then remembered very routine things:

> *Interviewer:* You slept outside in a tent? Wow, that sounds like a lot of fun.
> *Child:* And then we waked up and eat dinner. First we eat dinner, then go to bed, and then wake up and eat breakfast.
> *Interviewer:* What else did you do when you went camping? What did you do when you got up, after breakfast?
> *Child:* Umm, in the night, and went to sleep. (p. 231)

It seems strange that a child would talk about such routine tasks as waking up, eating, and going to bed when so many new and exciting things must have happened on the camping trip. But the younger the child, the more he or she might need to embed novel events into familiar routines. According to Fivush and Hamond, everything is new to 2-year olds, and they are in the process of learning about their surroundings.

Why should young children's memory be so tied to recurring events? One way to answer this question is to ask what the function of memory is for young children. Katherine Nelson (1996) has taken such a functional view (consistent with ideas from evolutionary psychology discussed in Chapter 2) and believes that memory has an adaptive value of permitting children to predict the likelihood of events in the future. Basically, by remembering the likelihood of an event's occurrence in the past, one can predict its likelihood of occurring in the future. From this perspective, some events (recurring ones) are more likely to be remembered than others (single events). According to Nelson (1996), "Memory for a single, one-time occurrence of some event, if the event were not traumatic or life-threatening, would not be especially useful, given its low probability. Thus, a memory system might be optimally designed to retain information about frequent and recurrent events—and to discard information about unrepeated events—and to integrate new information about variations in recurrent events into a general knowledge system" (p. 174). Nelson makes the point that memory for routine events makes it possible for infants to anticipate events and to take a part in, and possibly control of, these events. There is no such pay-off for a novel event, and thus it makes sense to forget it.

But children do eventually remember specific events, not just some generalized event memory. In fact, although 2- and 3-year-old children may rely heavily on scripts, they have been shown to remember specific information over extended periods of time (Fivush & Hamond, 1989; Hamond & Fivush, 1991). Before presenting research evidence for this, let me provide an anecdote. Two-and-one-half-year-old Kiesha, upon seeing an ice cube wrapped in a wash cloth, began a detailed account of a bee sting she received well over six months earlier, complete with time of day, where she and the bee had been

when the unfortunate incident occurred, and what Mom had done to soothe the pain. This is all the more remarkable, because Kiesha was only beginning to talk six months ago, and the accurate account she now gave was far more detailed than she could have given at the time of the sting. It must be noted that Kiesha's memory was prompted by the ice cube. Although all memory is prompted by some type of cue (Mandler, 1990), young children typically require very specific (and often repeated) cues before recalling information.

Research that demonstrates how long memories for specific events can last was presented by Hamond and Fivush (1991), who interviewed children 6 or 18 months after they had gone to Disney World. Children were either about 3 years old or 4 years old when they visited Disney World. All children recalled a great deal of information about their trip, even after 18 months. The older children recalled more details and required fewer prompts (cues) to generate recall than did the younger children. Nevertheless, recall for this single, special event was quite good, even though it did not fall nicely into a familiar routine.

The Role of Parents in "Teaching" Children to Remember

Hamond and Fivush also noted that children who talked more about the trip with their parents recalled more information about the trip. This suggests that parents can play an important role in children's early remembering, a point that has recently been made by several theorists (Fivush, 1997; Nelson, 1993) and consistent with the theorizing of Vygotsky (1978) and the sociocultural perspective discussed in Chapter 3 (Rogoff, 1998). For example, Judith Hudson (1990) has argued that children learn how to remember by interacting with their parents, that "remembering can be viewed as an activity that is at first jointly carried out by parent and child and then later performed by the child alone" (p. 172).

In most families, Hudson proposes, parents begin talking with young children about things that happened in the past. They ask questions such as, "Where did we go this morning?," "What did we see at the zoo?," "Who went with us?," "What else did we see?" From these interchanges, children learn that the important facts to remember about events are the whos, whats, whens, and wheres of their experiences. Through these conversations with their parents, they are learning to notice the important details of their experiences and to store their memories in an organized way that will be easily retrieved when needed.

In studying these interchanges between parents and preschoolers, Hudson found that parents do more than just ask the right questions. They also give the right answers when the child can't remember, showing children how the conversation should go. Young children generally show low levels of free recall, but can remember much more when specific cues are presented (Price & Goodman, 1990). In fact, Fivush and Hamond (1990) stated that "young children recall as much information as older children do, but they need more memory questions in order to do so" (p. 244). By asking repeated questions to children, adults are structuring the conversation, showing children how "remembering" is done. Moreover, by providing the missing information, children also learn that their parents will help them out when they can't seem to retrieve the information called for.

A good example of this was a conversation I overheard while riding on the Metro in Washington, D.C. A young mother and her 19-month-old daughter, Tanya, were returning home after a trip to the zoo.

> *Mother:* Tanya, what did we see at the zoo?
> *Tanya:* Elphunts.
> *Mother:* That's right! We saw elephants. What else?
> *Tanya:* (shrugs and looks at her mother)
> *Mother:* Panda bear? Did we see a panda bear?
> *Tanya:* (smiles and nods her head)
> *Mother:* Can you say "panda bear?"
> *Tanya:* Panda bear.
> *Mother:* Good! Elephants and panda bears. What else?
> *Tanya:* Elphunts.
> *Mother:* That's right, elephants. And also a gorilla.
> *Tanya:* Go-rilla!

The importance of these parent-child conversations is illustrated in research by Hilary Ratner (1984). She observed 2- and 3-year-old children interacting with their parents at home and recorded the number of times the mother asked the child about past events. She then tested the children's memory abilities. The children who showed better memory abilities at that time, and also a year later, were those whose mothers had asked them many questions about past events. Other research has shown that mothers who provide their preschool children with more evaluations of their memory performance and who use more elaborative language when talking about memory with their children, have children who remember past events better than do children with less elaborative mothers (Reese, Haden, & Fivush, 1993). That is, after making a statement about some previous event (for example, "Then we ate the cake"), elaborative mothers are more likely to provide comments that confirm or negate a child's statement (such as "That's right," "Yes," or "No") than less elaborative mothers.

The results of recent research point to the interactive role of parents and children in the process of "learning" how to remember. Thus, remembering becomes a cultural phenomenon, consistent with the ideas of Vygotsky and others who propose a sociocultural perspective of development (see Chapter 3). Parents teach children how to construct narratives (that is, create stories) in which to embed the important things that happen to them. This, in turn, allows them to share their experiences with others, a point we will return to later in this chapter. This is a practice characteristic of parents in postindustrial societies, such as ours, but it is not universal. For example, Mullen and Yi (1995) examined how frequently Korean and American mothers talked to their 3-year-old children about past events. They reported that the American mothers talked about the past with their young children nearly three times as often as the Korean mothers. This is consistent with reports that American children talk about past events more than Korean children (Han, Leichtman, & Wang, 1998), and that American adults report earlier childhood memories than Korean adults do (Mullen, 1994). This suggests that early language experience might contribute to the onset of autobiographical memory, a topic we will return to shortly.

It is also worth noting that there are differences in the event memories reported by girls and boys. When asked to remember information about earlier experienced events, girls tend to remember more information than boys (Haden & Reese, 1994; Reese, Haden, & Fivush, 1996; but not always, see Weber & Strube, 1999). For example, in a study by Haden and Reese (1994), children between the ages of 40 and 70 months participated in several sessions in which their mothers, fathers, or an experimenter asked them to recollect about salient events that had occurred in the recent past. Regardless of who interviewed the children (that is, their mothers, fathers, or the experimenter), girls remembered more details about past events than boys. These gender differences were related to ways in which parents converse with their sons and daughters about the past. Girls generally received more evaluations of their memory responses than boys. These findings suggest that the roots of females' greater event memory lie early in development and might be partly because of the way parents talk to boys and girls during attempts at remembering, with daughters being encouraged to embellish their memories more than sons are. Other research indicates that mothers talk to their male and female preschool children about different topics. For example, Flannagan, Baker-Ward, and Graham (1995) reported that in their conversations about school, mothers talked to their sons more about learning and instruction, whereas they tended to talk to their daughters more about social interactions. Thus, there are differences both in how parents talk to boys and girls about remembering events and what they are asked to remember, both of which seemingly affect what and how well children remember.

Children as Eyewitnesses

One topic in event memory that has attracted substantial research attention lately concerns the reliability of children as eyewitnesses. Not surprisingly, much of the recent interest has come about because of children's increasing participation in the legal system, either as victims of or as witnesses to purported crimes (Ceci & Bruck, 1993, 1995, 1998). Some of the issues of interest both to psychologists and to the legal profession are "How much do children of different ages remember of events they witnessed?," "How long do these memories last?," "How accurate are their memories?," and "How susceptible are children to suggestion?."

Age Differences in Children's Eyewitness Memories

Although there is much variability from study to study, most investigations of children's eyewitness memory begin by showing children a video of some event, having them observe some activity in their school, or involving them personally in an activity. Usually, children are not told that they will be asked to remember what they view. At some later time, often minutes after the event but in some cases days or weeks later, children are asked what they remembered (for example, "Tell me what happened in the video you saw" or "Tell me what happened in your classroom yesterday morning"). This is essentially a request for free recall. Typically, children will then be asked some more specific recall questions (for example, "What was the girl in the video wearing?" or "What did the man who came into your class yesterday morning do?"), which constitute cued recall. Often times, children will be asked some recognition memory questions (for example, "Was the girl wearing a white t-shirt?" or "Did the man play with the teddy bear?"). In some studies, the same or similar questions may be repeated, and in others questions are often intentionally suggestive, sometimes directing children to a "correct" answer ("Did the man play nicely with the teddy bear?") and sometimes leading to an "incorrect" answer ("Did the man rip the book?"). There are, of course, many variations, depending on the purpose of the study, but in most cases, children's memories for specific events are probed, often with the purpose of seeing how likely children are to change their answers or to be swayed by leading questions posed by an interviewer (see Ceci & Bruck, 1993, 1995, 1998; Qin et al., 1997 for reviews).

First, how much do children of different ages remember shortly after witnessing an event? When examining immediate (that is, within the same experimental session) free recall, substantial age differences are found (Ornstein, Gordon, & Larus, 1992; Poole & White, 1995). How much is remembered differs from study to study, but preschool children typically recall only a small proportion of information from an event to free-recall questions. Although young children recall very little information, what they do recall is highly accurate and central to the event (Goodman, Aman, & Hirschman, 1987; Poole & White, 1995). For example, in a video involving a boy and a girl in a park, with the boy stealing a bike, young children typically recall the bike theft, but are much less apt than older children or adults to mention in their free recall descriptions of the participants, characteristics of the bicycle, or things about the setting (Cassel & Bjorklund, 1995). Thus, young children's free recall is typically low, accurate, and about central aspects of an event. When children are provided general cues (for example, "Tell me what the girl looked like"), they recall more information, as you would expect. However, in addition to remembering more *correct* facts, they also tend to remember some *incorrect* "facts" as well, reducing the overall accuracy of their recall (Bjorklund et al., 1998; Goodman et al., 1994).

When children do falsely remember information to cues, does this actually change their memory representations? Will these children, when interviewed later, remember this misinformation again? The answer to this seems to depend on several factors, including the amount of time between the initial and later interviews. With delays of only several weeks or less, children seem *not* to recall their earlier false memories (Cassel & Bjorklund, 1995). But when delays are longer (Poole, 1995) or when children are merely asked to recognize, rather than recall, information (Brainerd & Reyna, 1996; Brainerd, Reyna, & Brandse, 1995), these false memories tend to persist, and might even be *more* resistant to forgetting than true memories (Brainerd & Mojardin, 1999).

These counterintuitive findings have been interpreted in terms of fuzzy-trace theory (Brainerd & Poole, 1997; Brainerd & Reyna, 1998; see Chapter 5). According to the theory, correct recognition is based on literal, or verbatim, memory traces, which are more susceptible to forgetting than are less-exact fuzzy, or gist, traces. In contrast, false recognition must be based on gist traces because there are no verbatim traces for false memories. Gist traces are more resistant to forgetting than verbatim traces, and thus the gist-based false memories become more likely to be remembered over long delays than the more easily forgettable verbatim-based true memories.

How long do these memories last? Although most studies have not assessed the long-term recollections of children, several have investigated children's memories of specific events for periods ranging from several weeks to two years (Flin et al., 1992; Salmon & Pipe, 1997). The results of these studies are not totally consistent, but a picture emerges of greater age differences in the accuracy of recall with increasing delays. Accuracy, as used here, does not refer to "how much" was remembered, but rather to the ratio of incorrect-to-correct information remembered. Children who recall very little, for example, but correctly recall that amount, have perfect accuracy. In contrast, a child who recalls a substantial amount of both correct (accurate) and incorrect (inaccurate) information, might demonstrate more recall, but less accuracy.

First, with delays of about one month or less, children of all ages and adults remember about the same proportion of accurate and inaccurate information as they did originally (Baker-Ward et al., 1993; Cassel & Bjorklund, 1995). Age differences in recall accuracy are found with longer delays, however. For example, Flin and his colleagues (1992) reported that both 6-year-olds and adults recalled as much inaccurate information after a 5-month delay as they had originally, but the 6-year-olds recalled *less accurate* information than the adults. Thus, the ratio of incorrect-to-correct recall became higher for the children than for the adults over the 5-month period (see also Poole & White, 1993). The conclusion from these studies is that age differences in accuracy are found, but only when memory is assessed after extended delays. Fuzzy-trace theory (Reyna & Brainerd, 1995, see Chapter 5) explains these findings by the greater rate of trace decay of verbatim (exact) relative to gist traces. Verbatim traces, favored by younger children, deteriorate more rapidly than the gist, or fuzzy traces favored by older children, resulting in greater loss of information over delays and corresponding increases in erroneous recall. These same arguments have been used to explain the phenomenon of infantile amnesia (see later). The verbatim traces favored by infants and young children are especially susceptible to deterioration, making it highly unlikely that these memories would be available years after their original encoding (Leichtman & Ceci, 1993).

Another factor that can influence children's recollection of an event is the number of times they are asked questions. It is very common in legal matters for witnesses to be asked the same or similar questions repeatedly. Does such questioning affect children's memory, or at least what they report to an interviewer?

Several researchers have reported that when young children are asked the same or similar questions in a single session, they are more likely to change their answers than older children are (Cassel, Roebers, & Bjorklund, 1996; Warren, Hulse-Trotter, & Tubbs, 1991). For example, in a study by Cassel, Roebers, and Bjorklund (1996), kindergarten, second-grade, and fourth-grade children and adults were asked questions about an event they had observed one week earlier. After recalling as much information about the event as they could (free recall), participants were asked a set of more specific questions (cued recall). Participants in one condition were asked a set of misleading questions, suggesting incorrect "facts" (for example, "The girl was wearing shorts, wasn't she?" when in fact she was wearing jeans). If participants rejected this alternative or provided no substantive answer to this question, they were asked a second misleading question again about the same topic (for example, "Don't you remember that the girl was wearing shorts?"). The percentage of correct, incorrect, and "don't know" responses to this second level of misleading questions is shown in Figure 8-2. As can be seen, the fourth-grade and adult participants rejected this second suggestion, very rarely agreeing with the inter-

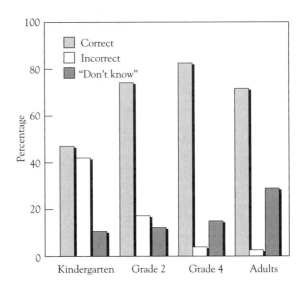

FIGURE 8-2 Percentage of various responses for participants given follow-up misleading questions, by grade. SOURCE: Adapted from data presented in Cassel, W. S., Roebers, C. E. M., & Bjorklund, D. F. (1996). Developmental patterns of eyewitness responses to increasingly suggestive questions. *Journal of Experimental Child Psychology, 61*, 116–133.

viewer, and the second-grade children weren't too different from these older participants. But the kindergarten children were just as likely to agree with this follow-up question as to disagree, even though just seconds previously most had correctly rejected the misleading question.

One reason for children's greater tendencies to change their answers is that they might interpret a repeated question as evidence that the interviewer was dissatisfied with their first answer and that another, different answer must be more correct. This is particularly likely in the Cassel et al. study discussed earlier, with the follow-up question coming immediately after a similarly posed question.

Asking the same or similar questions repeatedly does not always lead to greater "mind changing" and inaccurate recall. For example, Poole and White (1991) reported slightly lower levels of accurate recall as a result of repeated questioning in a single session for 4-, 6-, and 8-year-old children and adults (because of boredom, they speculated), but no corresponding increase in inaccurate information (which was low to begin with). Several other studies have reported *higher* levels of accurate recall when children are given repeated opportunities to remember events over different sessions (Baker-Ward, Hess, & Flannagan, 1990; Fivush & Hamond, 1989). This is a well-known phenomenon termed **hypernesia** (see Howe & Brainerd, 1989), in which the total amount remembered increases when people attempt to recall the target information repeatedly. In fact, Brainerd and Ornstein (1991) state, "Perhaps the most fundamental principle of memory is that repetition facilitates performance" (p. 15). Others, using similar experimental designs, report no appreciable changes in amount of accurate or inaccurate free recall (as opposed to cued recall) as a result of repeated questioning over different interviews (Cassel & Bjorklund, 1995).

Thus, repeated questioning can sometimes reduce accurate recall, can sometimes enhance it, and can sometimes make no difference. Obviously, several factors are responsible for the effects of repeated questioning on children, but, when the questions are *not* misleading (that is, they do not suggest a specific, inaccurate fact) and care is taken to ensure that children understand the nature of the questions, they can enhance amount remembered. This caused Poole and White (1995) to state that "Because repetition elicits additional information and is a relatively innocuous procedure when appropriate questions are used, sweeping recommendations to avoid repetition are not warranted" (p. 42).

Several factors are associated with children's eyewitness memory, including how children are interviewed (see Ceci, Bruck, & Battin, in press), their background knowledge for the event (Ornstein & Greenhoot, in press), and parent-children interaction style (Goodman et al., 1997). We saw in Chapter 5 that knowledge has a potent role in children's working memory and strategic memory, so we should not be surprised that it also plays an important role in eyewitness memory (Ornstein et al., 1997; Stein, Wade, & Liwag, 1997). For example, children's recollections of stressful and invasive medical procedures are related to their knowledge of the procedures; children who know more about the

procedure remember more accurate information (Clubb et al., 1993) and recall less inaccurate information (Goodman et al., 1994). Concerning style of parent-child interaction, Goodman and her colleagues (1994, 1997) reported that children who had emotionally supportive mothers who discussed the medical procedure with their children, recalled less inaccurate information about the procedure and were less suggestible than children with less sympathetic or talkative mothers.

Age Differences in Suggestibility

Perhaps the single most investigated area of eyewitness testimony, in both the adult and child literatures, concerns suggestibility (see Ceci & Bruck, 1993, 1995, 1998 for reviews). To what extent are children susceptible to suggestion? Research has shown that people of all ages report more inaccurate information when misleading questions are posed (that is, questions suggesting inaccurate information). The question for developmentalists, and for the legal profession, is "Are children more suggestible than adults?."

The general consensus to this question seems to be "yes." In an extensive review of the literature, Stephen Ceci and Maggie Bruck (1993) concluded that "there do appear to be significant age differences in suggestibility, with preschool children being disproportionately more vulnerable to suggestion than either school-age children or adults" (p. 431).

Most investigators looking for age differences in suggestibility have found it, although in varying degrees and only under certain circumstances (Ackil & Zaragoza, 1995; Bruck et al., 1995). The extent to which young children's reports of a witnessed event can be swayed is illustrated by a study performed by Allison Clarke-Stewart and her colleagues (Clarke-Stewart, Thompson, & Lepore, 1989; Goodman & Clarke-Stewart, 1991, Experiment 6). Preschool children watched a man posing as a janitor who either cleaned and arranged some toys, including a doll, or played with the toys in a somewhat rough and inappropriately suggestive manner. About an hour later, the janitor's "boss" interviewed the children about what they had seen. Of primary concern here is the situation in which children watched the janitor merely cleaning the toys although it was suggested to them that he had actually been playing with the toys improperly instead to doing his job. If a child in this situation initially did not agree with the interviewer's suggestion, subsequent leading questions were asked, with each question becoming increasingly stronger in its suggestion (that is, more explicitly suggesting misbehavior). Two-thirds of these children eventually followed the interviewers' suggestions, although it did not correspond to what they had seen. Moreover, when the children were questioned by their parents at the end of the session, all stuck with the story that they had given the interviewer. In sum, when suggestions and accusations were strong and persistent, young children were easily led and did not alter their newfound interpretations when later questioned by their parents.

In other research, Michelle Leichtman and Stephen Ceci (1995) assessed the effects of negative stereotyping and suggestion on preschool children's recollections of an event that happened at their school. An unfamiliar person, Sam Stone, came into children's classrooms, talked to the teacher, sat with the children during the reading of a story and made a comment about the story ("I know that story; it's one of my favorites!"), walked around the classroom, and finally left the room, waving good bye to the children. Children in the *stereotype* condition were given information about Sam Stone before his visit that depicted him as accident prone and irresponsible ("That Sam Stone is always getting into accidents and breaking things!"). Children in the *suggestion* condition were interviewed several times after Sam Stone's visit and given misinformation about the visit (Sam ripped a book and soiled a teddy bear when he visited). Children in the *stereotype-plus-suggestion* condition received both the negative stereotype before Sam Stone's visit and the misinformation afterwards, and children in the *control* condition received neither the stereotyped information nor the misinformation about Sam.

Ten weeks after the visit, the children were given an open-ended interview about what happened the day Sam Stone visited the classroom. Leichtman and Ceci (1995) reported that children who had

been given the stereotypes made a modest number of false statements about Sam in the interview (relative to children in the control condition), and that children in the suggestion condition made a substantial number of false reports. The highest levels of false reports about Sam's visit, however, came from children who received both the stereotyped information before and the misinformation after the visit; 46% of 3- and 4-year-old children and 30% of 5- and 6-year-old children said that Sam had either ripped a book or soiled a teddy bear, or both. The percentage of erroneous responses increased to 72% and 44% for the younger and older preschoolers, respectively, when children were asked specific follow-up questions concerning whether Sam had ripped a book or soiled a teddy bear.

Why are younger children often more susceptible to the effects of misinformation and suggestion than older children? One explanation comes from fuzzy-trace theory, as discussed earlier in this section (Brainerd & Poole, 1997; Reyna & Brainerd, 1995). According to fuzzy-trace theory, young children are more reliant on verbatim (exact) memory traces than older children. Because verbatim traces deteriorate rapidly, they may not be available when post-event information is provided or when suggestive questions are asked. Thus, the erroneous information has an excellent chance of being incorporated with "real" memories and becoming indistinguishable from them (Brainerd, Reyna, & Poole, in press; Ceci & Bruck, 1993). Similarly, it would seem that young children's elevated rates of erroneous information to unbiased cues (that is, questions that ask for more information but do not attempt to bias a child's answer one way or the other) might be the result of their greater reliance on verbatim traces.

Although children's memories can sometimes be changed as a result of misleading questions, in many cases, social factors, such as a desire to comply with adult requests, surely play a role in children's greater suggestibility (Bjorklund et al., 1998). Nonetheless, it seems as though that under certain circumstances children can come to believe their implanted memories and treat them as real.

One possible reason for young children's suggestibility has to do with their ability to know the source of their knowledge. For example, did a particular experience happen to them, a friend, or did they see it on TV? **Source monitoring** refers to being aware of the source of information one knows or remembers. This can be particularly important in cases of eyewitness testimony. "Was the information that the boy stole the bike something I saw, or something someone told me?" Research has shown that preschool and early school-age children often have difficulty monitoring the source of their memories (see discussion in Chapter 7). For example, children sometimes have difficulty determining whether they actually performed an act or just imagined it (Foley, Santini, & Sopasakis, 1989) and often incorrectly remember that an action carried out by another person during a joint activity was actually performed by them (Ackil & Zaragoza, 1995; Foley, Ratner, & Passalacqua, 1993; see discussion in Chapter 3). When young children make errors in such situations, they are much more likely to attribute an action to themselves that someone else actually did than vice versa. For example, in a study by Mary Ann Foley and her colleagues (1993), preschool children made a collage with an adult, taking turns putting objects on the collage. When later asked to tell who put each object on the collage, 4-year-old children were much more likely to say that they had put an object on the collage when they actually had not (an "I did it" error) than to say that the adult had put the object on when in fact they had (a "You did it" error). Findings such as these have caused some researchers to speculate that young children's increased susceptibility to suggestion might be caused largely by their difficulty in monitoring the source of what they know (Ceci & Bruck, 1995). Recent research backs up these speculations, showing that 6-year-old children who are poor at source monitoring are more prone to the effects of suggestion (Mazzoni, 1998).

Another reason contributing to young children's suggestibility might be their beliefs that their memory is invulnerable to suggestion. For example, O'Sullivan, Howe, and Marche (1996) interviewed preschool, first-grade, and third-grade children about factors that might influence their memory. Although children of all ages believed that central aspects of a story would be more likely to be remembered than peripheral details, only the third-grade children believed that their memories would be susceptible to suggestion. The preschool and first-grade children were confident that suggestion from a parent or sibling would not affect their recollection of an event.

False-Memory Creation

How easy is it to create a false memory in a person? Asking children misleading questions about an event they have seen can cause children to confuse the source of the information, thinking that the misinformation was actually something they experienced and not just something they heard someone else say (Ackil & Zaragoza, 1995). But how easy is it to actually get children, or adults, to believe an event happened to them that never really did?

This was first investigated by Elizabeth Loftus and her colleagues with adults (Loftus & Pickrell, 1995). College students were interviewed about four events that had supposedly happened to them in childhood (based on reports of parents and older siblings). One event, being lost in a mall at age 5, never actually occurred. The students were asked to write as much about each event as they could remember. They remembered, on average, 68% of the true events; they also "remembered" 25% of the false events, sometimes vividly (see also Hyman, Husband, & Billings, 1995; Oakes & Hyman, in press).

It seems that preschool children are even more susceptible to creating false memories than are adults. Stephen Ceci and his colleagues used a similar technique to that used by Loftus, and interviewed children over an 11-week period about events that might have happened to them (Ceci et al., 1994). For example, children were asked if they ever remember getting their finger caught in a mousetrap. Although few children admitted to experiencing these false events in the initial interviews, by the conclusion of the study, more than 50% of the preschool children and about 40% of 5- to 6-year-old children assented that these events did indeed happen and often provided substantial detail about the events. Moreover, many children continued to believe that these events actually happened even after being told by the interviewers and their parents that the events were just made up and never really happened. It seems that false memories of plausible but extraordinary events are relatively easy to put into young children's minds.

Plausibility is an important factor here. Even though getting one's finger caught in a mousetrap might be an event that few children have ever actually experienced, it is one that "could" happen in many households. Kathy Pezdek and Danelle Hodge (1999) demonstrated that about one-third of 5- to 7-year-old children "remembered" being lost in a mall (which they had not been), whereas only one of 19 children (about 5%) "remembered" being given an enema. Although most of these children knew what an enema was, the event was implausible. If such an embarrassing and invasive event had happened to them, they certainly would have remembered. Pezdek and Hodge also found that children reported more details for true memories than for false ones (see also Brown et al., 1998). Thus, although there is no "Pinocchio test" for determining whether a memory is true or not, on average, children's recollections of events that actually did happen to them tend to be clearer and more detailed than their recollections of planted, or false memories (see Pezdek & Taylor, 1999).

Infantile Amnesia and the Development of Autobiographical Memory

My wife and I received a letter from a woman several years ago who was worried because her 10-year-old son could remember very little from his preschool days. She said that she and her husband had always tried to be good parents but thought her son's inability to remember things from early childhood was an indication that either they hadn't done a very good job after all, or worse yet, they had done a truly terrible job and her son was repressing this painful period of his life. We wrote back to the woman, assuring her that her son's inability to remember events much before his fourth birthday is quite normal, and just because her child can't remember his experiences from this age doesn't mean that they didn't have an impact on him.

It is not just memories from infancy that escape us. For the most part, we are unable to remember much of anything before the age of 3.5 or 4 years, a phenomenon known as **infantile amnesia** (Cowan & Davidson, 1984; Pillemer & White, 1989). Moreover, most of us have a few memories for events that happened between the ages of about 3 and 6 years, but very few in comparison with what we can remember from after this time (Pillemer & White, 1989). Usher and Neisser (1993) studied this lack of memory for the early years by questioning college students about experiences they had had early in life — experiences such as the birth of a younger sibling, a stay in the hospital, a family move, or the death of a family member. To assess recall, a series of questions was asked about each event the person had experienced (for example, Who told you your mother was going to the hospital to give birth? What were you doing when she left? Where were you when you first saw the new baby?) The percentage of questions college students could answer increased substantially the older the person was when he or she had experienced the event. Usher and Neisser concluded that the earliest age of *any* meaningful recall was about age 2 for the birth of a sibling or a hospitalization, and age 3 for the death of a family member or a family move. What we lack specifically are **autobiographical memories,** which refer to personal and long-lasting memories, which are the basis for one's personal life history (Nelson, 1996).

Why Can't We Remember Events from Infancy and Early Childhood?

Sigmund Freud (1963) was the first to speculate on the reason for infantile amnesia, proposing that the events of infancy and early childhood are rife with sexual overtones toward one's mother and are just generally so traumatic that they are actively repressed. We protect our adult egos, claimed Freud, by preventing these disturbing memories from rising to consciousness.

Few scientists today agree with Freud's interpretation. Other, more cognitively based interpretations, proposed the possibility that (a) information is not stored for long-term retention before about 2 years of age and (b) that information is encoded differently by infants and toddlers than by older children and adults (see White & Pillemer, 1979). The first possibility seems unlikely. Research using the deferred-imitation procedure (Bauer, 1997; Meltzoff, 1995) discussed earlier in this chapter and in Chapter 7 has shown that infants between 9 and 16 months of age can encode and retain a simple experience for up to a period of one year. Other research has shown that events experienced in the first year of life are remembered as much as two years later (Myers, Clifton, & Clarkson, 1987; Perris, Myers, & Clifton, 1990). Children in these studies were tested as infants in auditory localization experiments, in which they reached for an object that made sounds. When they were brought back to the laboratory nearly two years later and put in the same situation, they were more likely to interact with the stimulus objects in appropriate ways than were control children who had no previous experience in the experimental situation. Thus, although the studies by Myers and Clifton might not reveal that children retain infantile memories they can tell others about, this research, along with the work by Nelson and her colleagues with older children (see Nelson, 1996), clearly indicates long-term retention is possible in infancy and young childhood. These do not qualify as autobiographical memories, of course, but they are long-term memories nonetheless.

The second alternative, that information is encoded differently during the early and later years of life, is consistent with observations made by Piaget and others that the nature of representation changes from infancy to early childhood (Bruner, 1966; Case, 1985) and then again (although less drastically) somewhere between the ages of 5 and 7 years. The minds that resided in our heads when we were infants are no longer there, replaced by minds that process symbols, especially verbal ones. In the process of reconstructing memories, we do so in terms of adult schemas and representations, which are not suitable for events encoded in infancy and early childhood.

Such an interpretation can account for our inability to retrieve memories from infancy, but 3- and 4-year-old children are clearly verbal and would presumably represent information in a similar symbolic form as adults. The fact that 3- and 4-year-old children can recount verbally events that happened many months or even years ago, suggests that this interpretation cannot be the entire answer (Fivush & Hamond, 1990; Nelson & Ross, 1980).

Several new explanations for infantile amnesia, based on recent research findings in memory and cognitive development, have been proposed. For example, several authors have suggested that for autobiographical memories to be laid down and later retrieved, there needs to be a sense of self (the "auto" in autobiographical) (Fivush, 1988; Howe & Courage, 1993; Welch-Ross, 1995). Research has shown that the sense of self develops gradually over the preschool years (see discussion of the development of self-concept in Chapter 11), and that, although young children have "memories," the experiences of early childhood occurred when the sense of self was poorly developed, thus providing no anchor for such events. Unless events can be related to the self, they cannot be retrieved at a later time.

Another alternative is that infantile amnesia is merely a consequence of the child's developing information-processing system (Leichtman & Ceci, 1993). Following the tenets of fuzzy-trace theory (Brainerd & Reyna, 1990; see discussion in Chapter 5 and earlier in this chapter), Leichtman and Ceci propose that there is a developmental shift in how events are represented, with young children encoding events primarily in terms of verbatim (precise) memory traces, whereas older children rely more on gist (less precise) traces. Verbatim traces are more susceptible to forgetting than gist traces. Thus, the heavy reliance on the highly forgettable verbatim traces makes memories from infancy and early childhood unavailable. Gist traces become increasingly available by the early school years, about the time when more memories can be retrieved. Leichtman and Ceci also note that children are becoming

CALVIN & HOBBES

increasingly facile with language at this time, using it not just for communication but as a representational system (Nelson, 1996; Vygotsky, 1962) and that these improved linguistic skills also likely contribute to improved autobiographical memory.

Changes in language and how language is used have been proposed for the phenomenon of infantile amnesia by other theorists (Fivush & Hamond, 1990; Nelson, 1993, 1996). Young children, in trying to understand and predict their world, are attentive to routines and embed novel events in terms of these routines (for example, what happens at breakfast; what happens on a trip to the grocery store). Such memories, ensconced as they are in routines, are not very distinctive and thus not easily retrievable later on. Even when events *are* distinctive, however, young children do not necessarily know how to organize the events in a memorable form. Recall from our earlier discussion of the development of event memory that children "learn" to remember through interactions with adults. Adults provide the cues and structure for children to form narratives—stories for embedding events and later for remembering them. Adults help children code the who, what, where, and when of events so that the important aspects of an experience can later be remembered. Only after being guided by adults can

children learn to code memories and realize that language can be used to share memories with others.

Katherine Nelson (1993) makes this point especially clear:

> The claim here is that the initial functional significance of autobiographical memory is that of sharing memory with other people, a function that language makes possible. Memories become valued in their own right—not because they predict the future and guide present action, but because they are shareable with others and thus serve a social solidarity function. I suggest that this is a universal human function, although one with variable, culturally specific rules. In this respect, it is analogous to human language itself, uniquely and universally human but culturally—and individually—variable. (p. 12)

Nelson's claim suggests that infantile amnesia might not be so significant in its own right, as Freud believed, but rather reflects an important transition in human cognition. This transition is based on everyday adult-child interaction and the developing language system and transforms the child into an individual who has a personal past that can be shared with others. This does not preclude the possibility that changes in the self-system (Howe & Courage, 1993) or in the information-processing system

(Leichtman & Ceci, 1993) do not also play an important role. My guess is that they do. The most recent theorizing of Nelson, Howe and Courage, and Leichtman and Ceci suggest that infantile amnesia reflects important changes occurring during early childhood—changes that permit autobiographical memory and that truly separates our species from all others.

Infantile Amnesia and Hypnotic Age Regression

But are memories from infancy and early childhood really gone, or are they just not retrievable by our conscious minds? What about hypnosis? Don't psychologists often use hypnosis to help people remember "forgotten" or "repressed" memories, and doesn't that sometimes include remembering events from one's early childhood? Yes, indeed, between 20% and 34% of psychotherapists report using hypnosis to help their patients "recall the unrecallable" (Lynn et al., 1997), and that sometimes includes memories from early childhood. But is it accurate and are these memories real? In general, people under hypnosis often do recall more details about an event than people not under hypnosis, but many of these details turn out to be false (Erdelyi, 1994).

In hypnotic age regression, adults are hypnotized and "brought back" to an earlier age. In doing so, will the adults now truly think like they did as children and will they remember events from their childhood better than nonhypnotized people? Nash (1987) reviewed more than 60 years of this literature, and his answer is a definitive "no." For example, in research in which adults are regressed to the preschool years and then given Piagetian tasks such as conservation (see Chapter 4), they act more like adults who are asked to *pretend* to solve the problem like a 4-year-old would than like an actual 4-year-old child. In one study, adults were age regressed to 3 years of age and asked to identify objects such as dolls, blankets, or teddy bears that were of particular importance and comfort to them at that time (Nash et al., 1986). The parents of both hypnotized and control participants were contacted to confirm the subjects' recollections. The hypnotized people were substantially *less* accurate in identifying favorite objects from their early childhoods than were the controls. The reports of the hypnotized participants matched those of their parents just 21% of the time, whereas the hit rate for the controls was 70%.

People who experience age regression might have the feeling of recalling a "real" memory. However, how confident one is in the veracity of a memory, unfortunately, does not always predict the truth of the memory. There is no evidence that hypnotic age regression can succeed in retrieving "repressed," or simply forgotten memories from childhood, despite many people's claims to the contrary.

Piagetian Research on Reconstructive Memory

Event memory, whether it involves recalling information using familiar scripts, remembering events under cross examination, or the establishment and retrieval of early autobiographical information, all have at least one thing in common: They are *constructive in nature*. Event memory does not involve the verbatim recall of a list of facts or the memorization of lines, like an actor in a play. Rather, we recall the gist of the message and in the process we transform what was actually said or done. That is, we interpret our experiences as a function of what we already know about the world, and our memory for events is colored by previous knowledge (Bartlett, 1932).

Although all event memory is said to be reconstructive, it should not be surprising that the longer the delay between experiencing an event and recalling it, the greater the distortion is apt to be. Memories from our childhood are good examples. Few of us have verifiable memories from our infancy, and many of the memories we do have are reconstructions, often based on events that transpired years after the event we are "recalling." I, for example, have a memory of being an infant (about 6 months) and having the croup (something like bronchitis). My memory of this event is vivid. I can feel the congestion in my chest, hear the vaporizer whir, smell the Vicks VapoRub, and see the living room of my grandparents' house while looking through the bars of my crib. My mistake was relating this vibrant and personally poignant memory to my mother. She listened carefully and then told me that I had never had the croup; it was my younger brother, Dick, who had the croup as an infant. I was about 4 years old at the time. My "memory" was a reconstruction—and of events I had only *observed*, not ones I had actually *experienced*. The type of error I made, thinking that an experience that had happened to my brother had actually happened to me, is called a *source monitoring error*, and was discussed previously in this chapter in the section on suggestibility.

Such a constructivist perspective is at the heart of Piaget's theory. Piaget believed that cognition is an act of construction, that children construct reality as a function of what is in the external world and their current cognitive structures (see Chapter 4). He viewed memory in a similar way, and this perspective is illustrated in a series of experiments by Piaget and Inhelder (1973). They reported that the stage of development of a child affects the retention of "operationally relevant" stimuli. For example, concrete operational children reconstruct seriated arrays (a series of sticks, each one longer than the preceding one) more accurately than preoperational children. In fact, Piaget and Inhelder reported that the performance of some preschool children who were shown seriated arrays was better 8 months later than it had been just 1 week after they saw the original stimulus! They proposed that children's memories become reorganized (reconstructed) over time, consistent with the reorganization of mental schemes from the preoperational to the concrete operational period. More recent research has seriously questioned that there is actually improvement in memory over time (Maurer et al., 1979). However, an alternate but related interpretation that has received research support is that preoperational and concrete operational children encode the stimuli differently, giving them slightly different memory representations to remember.

A study by Lynn Liben (1981) illustrates this position nicely. Children in grades one through five drew pictures of houses and trees on a hill, and their drawings were rated in terms of the concept of verticality. Figure 8-3 presents drawings reflecting immature (preoperative), transitional, and mature (operative) concepts of verticality. As can be seen, immature children draw objects so that they are perpendicular to the hill, whereas mature children draw objects so that they are perpendicular to the horizon. After being classified as immature, transitional, or mature, children were shown two drawings of a tree growing on a hill, one depicting an operationally advanced concept of verticality (the tree is perpendicular to the horizon, as in the mature drawing in Figure 8-3) and another depicting an operationally primitive concept of verticality (the tree is perpendicular to the hill, as in the immature drawing in Figure 8-3). The children were given a sheet of paper and asked to copy the pictures. They were also asked to reconstruct the picture from memory, with the delay between seeing the picture and reconstructing it being immediate in one experiment, 1 week in a second, and 5 months in a third.

The results of most interest for us concern the advanced stimulus (straight tree). The mature children reconstructed the stimulus more accurately than the less mature children for all three memory delays (mature → transitional → immature). What is especially interesting here, however, is that the results for copying mirrored those reported for recall. The children with the mature verticality concept copied the advanced stimulus more accurately than the transitional children, who were better than the children with the immature concept. There was virtually no difference between how the immature children drew the advanced stimulus when they were reconstructing it from memory (in some cases over 5 months) and how they drew it when they were copying it. In other words, the children with the immature concept of verticality distorted the advanced stimulus at encoding, making it conform to their preoperational level (that is, they copied it as being tipped). In reconstructing the image, they drew it as they had perceived it. Thus, their memory

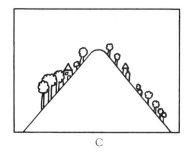

A   B   C

FIGURE 8-3   Children's drawings representing (a) immature, (b) transitional, and (c) mature concepts of verticality. SOURCE: Liben, L. S. (1981). Copying and reproducing pictures in relation to subjects' operative levels. *Developmental Psychology, 17,* 357–365.

was relatively accurate. What was inaccurate was their perception (encoding) of the stimulus.

The Development of Memory Strategies

From the inception of contemporary research on memory development in the late 1960s through the 1980s, most researchers focused on **memory strategies,** or **mnemonics.** As the research discussed so far in this chapter demonstrates, the field of memory development has broadened in the last decade to include many nonstrategic aspects of memory, although research into memory strategies continues (see Bjorklund & Douglas, 1997).

Although defined slightly differently by different people, memory strategies generally refer to deliberate plans adopted to enhance performance and subject to conscious evaluation (Harnishfeger & Bjorklund, 1990a). Three of the most investigated memory strategies in developmental psychology are *rehearsal,* in which a child repeats the target information; *organization,* in which the child combines different items into categories, themes, or other units; and *retrieval,* the process of accessing information and entering it into consciousness. The development of these and related strategies is examined briefly in the following sections. Although I discuss

research on memory strategies as if each strategy is independent of the others, when given the opportunity, children will actually use a combination of strategies on any single trial and change which strategies they use from trial to trial (Coyle & Bjorklund, 1997; Hock, Park, & Bjorklund, 1998). Thus, the picture of memory strategy development is a bit more complicated than the research I present in the following section makes it appear.

Rehearsal

The study most responsible for the interest in memory development was published in 1966 by John Flavell and his colleagues (Flavell, Beach, & Chinsky, 1966). Children in kindergarten and the second and fifth grades were shown a set of pictures that they were asked to remember. Following the presentation, there was a 15-second delay during which the children could prepare for the recall test. An experimenter, who was trained to identify lip movements corresponding to the words the children were trying to remember, watched the children's mouths. Flavell and his associates reported age-related increases in recall with corresponding increases in the amount of rehearsal. Eighty-five percent of the fifth graders displayed evidence of some spontaneous rehearsal, whereas only 10% of the kindergarten children did so. Furthermore, within a grade level, children who had rehearsed more recalled more, on average, than did children who had rehearsed less. These findings led the researchers to conclude that rehearsal is a powerful mnemonic that increases with age, with the frequency of rehearsal (the absolute number of times one rehearses) determining memory performance.

Later research by Ornstein, Naus, and Liberty (1975) questioned Flavell's frequency interpretation. These researchers used an *overt rehearsal procedure* with children in grades three, six, and eight. In this procedure, children are presented with a series of words to recall, with several seconds between each successive word. During this interval, the children are told they must repeat the most recently presented word at least once, and, if they wish, they may practice any other words they like. Thus, rehearsal is made obligatory (they must "rehearse" at least one word once during each interval), and the experimenters can determine exactly what the children are doing. Using this procedure, the researchers found no differences in the frequency of rehearsal across the three grade levels. Despite this equivalence in quantity of rehearsal, age differences in recall persisted, a perplexing finding given the interpretation of the earlier study by Flavell and his colleagues. However, Ornstein and his associates reported differences in the quality, or *style*, of rehearsal. Typical rehearsal protocols for a third- and an eighth-grade child are shown in Table 8-1. The number of words actually rehearsed is similar for the two children, but the style of rehearsing is very different. The younger child includes only one or, at best, two unique words per rehearsal set. (A rehearsal set refers to the words repeated during the interstimulus interval.) The researchers referred to this method as a **passive rehearsal** style. In contrast, the older child includes several different words per rehearsal set, a style labeled **active,** or **cumulative.** The child repeats the most recently presented word and then rehearses it with as many other different words as possible. From these and other data, Ornstein and his colleagues asserted that the important developmental changes are in style rather than frequency of rehearsal (see also Guttentag, Ornstein, & Siemens, 1987).

TABLE 8-1   Typical rehearsal protocols for an eighth- and third-grade child. Note the use of cumulative rehearsal by eighth graders and the more passive rehearsal style by third graders.

Word Presented	Rehearsal sets	
	Eighth-grade subject	Third-grade subject
1. Yard	Yard, yard, yard	Yard, yard, yard, yard, yard,
2. Cat	Cat, yard, yard, cat	Cat, cat, cat, cat, yard
3. Man	Man, cat, yard, man, yard, cat	Man, man, man, man, man
4. Desk	Desk, man, yard, cat, man, desk cat, yard	Desk, desk, desk, desk

SOURCE: Ornstein, P. A., Naus, M. J., & Liberty, C. (1975). Rehearsal and organizational processes in children's memory. *Child Development, 46,* 818–830. Copyright © The Society for Research in Child Development, Inc. Reprinted with permission.

A causal relationship between differences in the frequency and style of rehearsal and age differences in memory performance has been demonstrated in training studies. Preteenage children trained to use a cumulative rehearsal strategy display elevated levels of recall (Cox et al., 1989; Ornstein, Naus, & Stone, 1977). Thus, young children can be trained to use a rehearsal strategy, resulting in increases in memory performance (although age differences are rarely eliminated). What differs in development is children's inclination to implement a strategy, and not so much their ability to use it (that is, a *production deficiency,* see Chapter 5). This general pattern is not unique to rehearsal but, as will be seen, typifies other strategies as well.

Organization

One reason that active rehearsal benefits memory might be that conceptual relations are noticed among items that are rehearsed together (Ornstein & Naus, 1978). **Organization** in memory refers to the structure discovered or imposed on a set of items that is used to guide subsequent performance. In attempting to remember what groceries one must buy at the store, for example, we benefit by organizing the information by categories (dairy products, meats, vegetables) or meals (food necessary for pot roast, food necessary for Saturday's barbecue).

In a typical study of organization and recall, children are given a randomized list of items that can be divided into categories (several instances of FURNITURE, TOOLS, and OCCUPATIONS, for example). When the children recall the items, will they remember different ones from the same category together, even though they were not originally presented together? Recalling items from the same category together has been referred to as **clustering,** and adults who display high levels of clustering in their recall typically remember more than do adults displaying lower levels of clustering (Mandler, 1967). Developmentally, levels of recall and clustering usually increase with age, with preschool children's clustering often being at chance levels (see Schneider & Bjorklund, 1998).

Organization in memory can be measured more directly by giving children the opportunity to sort items into groups before recall (a **sort-recall** task). For example, Salatas and Flavell (1976) presented first graders with a set of 16 pictures, four each from four different categories (for example, ANIMALS, CLOTHING, TOYS, and TOOLS). The experimenter named each picture, identified the categories, and placed the pictures randomly on a table in front of the children. The children were told that they would be asked to remember the pictures later on and that they should put them together in a way that would help them recall the pictures. Following a 90-second study period, the children were asked to remember as many of the pictures as they could. Although the instructions would seem to bias children to organize (that is, physically sort) the items for recall, only 13 of 48 children (27%) organized the pictures according to categories to a significant degree. Other studies, requiring children to sort items before recall with instructions similar to those used by Salatas and Flavell ("Make groups that will help you remember"), report that children as old as 8 years often fail to organize items on the basis of meaning, but rather place items into groups randomly. Older children are more likely to group items on the basis of meaning and, as a result, realize higher levels of recall (Best & Ornstein, 1986; Hasselhorn, 1992). Yet, when the instructions are modified, stressing to children that they should make their groups on the basis of meaning, even preschoolers comply and demonstrate enhanced levels of memory performance (Lange & Jackson, 1974; Sodian, Schneider, & Perlmutter, 1986).

Other experiments, more explicitly training children to use an organizational strategy, have also yielded positive results. Young children, under certain instructional conditions, use an organizational strategy and display elevated levels of memory performance (Black & Rollins, 1982; Lange & Pierce, 1992). In other words, young children are capable of organizing information for recall, but they generally fail to do so spontaneously. As with rehearsal, training children to use an organizational strategy rarely eliminates age differences, and, under most conditions, young children fail to generalize the strategy to new situations or new sets of materials (Cox & Waters, 1986).

Young children will generalize a trained strategy if training is extensive enough (Carr & Schneider, 1991), but often the benefits of the strategy are reduced or lost. For example, in studies with both preschoolers and elementary school children (Bjorklund et al., 1994; Lange, Guttentag, & Nida, 1990; Lange & Pierce, 1992), children were trained to use a sorting, or clustering strategy (that is, grouping and remembering together items from the same category), and they used these strategies on subsequent generalization trials (that is, when they were given new sets of items to remember without any explicit instructions to use a strategy). Despite using the strategies, however, the children in these studies demonstrated little or no enhancement in memory performance. This is a demonstration of a *utilization deficiency,* discussed in Chapter 5 (Bjorklund et al., 1997; Miller, 1990), in which children use a strategy but gain little advantage in task performance. So using a strategy is only a first step. Once the mechanics of a strategy are learned, children must become sufficiently familiar with executing it before they can gain any benefit from it.

Retrieval

Once information has entered the memory system, something must be done to get it out. For recognition, the task is usually easy, with the original stimulus prompting the retrieval of the memory representation. For recall, however, it is not so simple.

Young children's retrieval deficits apparently have to do with their need to have the original encoding environment reinstated (recall the work of Rovee-Collier and her colleagues on context-specificity effects for infants' memories). For example, in research by Brian Ackerman (1985; 1997), children were given a set of cues associated with a target word at the time of presentation (for example, the cues *rose* and *tulip* for the target *lily*). Then they were re-presented with some or all of these cues at the time of retrieval, or possibly with an *extralist cue* that is associated with the target but was not paired with it at the time of presentation (for example, *flower* for *lily*). Children were to recall the target words associated with the cue words. Ackerman reported that 7-year-olds needed more of the original encoding environment reinstated to yield correct recall than did older children or adults. In other words, young children can recover the information, but they require more explicit reminders than older children before retrieval is successful. (Recall the anecdote presented earlier in the chapter about the preschool boy recalling his visit to the theater.)

An excellent study for demonstrating age differences in retrieval was done by Akira Kobasigawa (1974). Children in grades 1, 3, and 6 were presented with sets of pictures to remember. The pictures were grouped by categories, and the children were given cue cards that classified the objects. Pictures of animals went with a picture of a zoo, for example, and food pictures went with a card showing a grocery store. Using this method, Kobasigawa ensured that the children encoded the items according to common categories. Following presentation, the children were asked to recall as many of the

items as they could under one of three conditions. Children in the Free-Recall condition were asked to remember the items in any order that they liked. Children in the Available-Cue condition were shown the cue cards that had been paired with the items earlier (the zoo and grocery store) and were told that they could use these pictures to help them remember the other items. They were then asked to recall the items in any order they wished. Children in the Directive-Cue condition were shown each cue card, one at a time, were told how many items had been paired with it, and were asked to recall as many of those items as they could. Recall continued until children were tested on each of the cues.

The results of Kobasigawa's experiment are shown in Figure 8-4. Levels of memory performance increased with age for children in the Free-Recall condition, as would be expected. First- and third-grade children in the Available-Cue condition displayed no benefits relative to the children in the Free-Recall condition, but some advantage was observed for the oldest children. Few first-graders in this second condition made any use of the cues, apparently being unaware that using them would aid their memory. In contrast, approximately 75% of the third-graders used the cues in this condition, but, as can be seen from their level of performance, they used them poorly. Results were strikingly different in the Directive-Cue condition; under these conditions, developmental differences in the amount recalled was greatly minimized. These results indicate that the first- and third-graders had stored as much information about the to-be-remembered stimuli as the older children. Their problem was getting it out.

In general, young children benefit more from the imposition of retrieval cues than older children, presumably because older children spontaneously generate retrieval plans at the time of input, making the cues provided by the experimenter superfluous (Mistry & Lange, 1985; Schmidt & Schmidt, 1986). In general, research has confirmed age differences in the efficient use of retrieval cues and in children's knowledge of their effectiveness (Fabricius & Wellman, 1983), with young children being able to implement retrieval strategies when properly instructed.

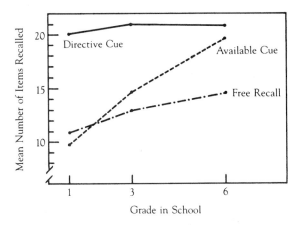

FIGURE 8-4 Children's mean levels of recall by grade and retrieval condition. SOURCE: Kobasigawa, A. (1974). Utilization of retrieval cues by children in recall. *Child Development, 45,* 127–134. Copyright © 1974 The Society for Research in Child Development, Inc. Reprinted with permission.

Other Strategies

Related to organization is the strategy of **elaboration.** Elaboration involves associating two or more items by creating a representation of them. (An elaboration study by Kee and Davies [1990] was discussed in Chapter 5.) If I needed to remember to buy a carton of milk on my way home from work, for example, I could generate an image of a cow sitting on the hood of my car or form a verbal elaboration, so that when I saw my "car" I would think of *carton.* In both cases, the sight of my car should elicit for me the thought of milk. Most research examining elaboration has used **paired-associate** procedures, in which children are given pairs of words and learn to recall one word when given its mate. Children tend not to use elaboration spontaneously until adolescence (Pressley & Levin, 1977; Rohwer et al., 1977), although as with other mnemonics, young children can be trained to use it (see Pressley, 1982).

Another memory strategy related to all of the others is children's *allocation of study time.* Rehearsal, organization, or elaboration can only be effective if children actually take the time to use them. In experiments examining developmental differences in the allocation of study time, children are given sets of items to remember and permitted to study them until they say they are ready for a memory test (Dufresne & Kobasigawa, 1989; O'Sullivan, 1993). A customary finding in these studies is that older children (typically 9- and 10-year-olds) are better at allocating their study time than younger children (preschoolers and early school-age children). Older children tend to study "harder" items more than "easier" items, whereas younger children are more likely to study both the "easy" and "hard" items equally (Dufresne & Kobasigawa, 1989).

Gender Differences in Memory Performance and Strategy Use

For the most part, researchers have not predicted gender differences in memory performance or strategy use and generally have not looked for them. Most of the memory strategies discussed can be described as highly "verbal" in nature, however, and females are generally believed to excel on verbal tasks relative to males (Maccoby & Jacklin, 1974; see Chapter 11). It might not be surprising, therefore, to find a female advantage for some of these memory strategies.

Cox and Waters (1986) reviewed research into memory development and concluded that reliable gender differences are found, favoring girls, in the use of organizational strategies in free recall. The strategy of organization would seem to be related to the structure of semantic memory, and to verbal processing in general. Cox and Waters pointed out that gender differences in organization and memory have generally not been analyzed by researchers, making the absolute number of studies investigating this issue small. Of those analyzing gender differences, about half report no significant differences in organization and memory between the sexes. For those studies reporting gender differences, all favor females, with differences being found over a broad age range (from 6-year-olds to adults). A more recent study by Waters and Schreiber (1991) reported gender differences (favoring females) for the more complicated (but highly verbal) strategy of elaboration. Gender differences were found in groups of eighth graders, tenth graders, and college students, although, for the oldest group, differences were most dramatic only under the most difficult condition (using low-frequency word pairs). The gender differences here are small and not found consistently. Nevertheless, based on past research (Maccoby & Jacklin, 1974), there is some reason to expect a small female advantage, and this is what is found in the research literature.

This review of memory strategy development might seem to present a picture of gradual change, with young children being essentially nonstrategic and older children learning to use increasingly sophisticated strategies with every passing year. From our earlier discussions in Chapter 5, we know that this is an overly simplistic view. Preschool children also use memory strategies, although they are usually very simple in nature and often ineffective (Wellman, 1988), and children of all ages use a variety of strategies, even on a single task (Siegler, 1996). Recent analyses from a 10-year longitudinal study demonstrated that the age-related pattern of changes in the strategies of rehearsal and organization are similar to those found in cross-sectional work; however, the study also reported much greater variability in strategy development than one might infer from cross-sectional studies (Schneider & Sodian, 1997). For example, although a minority of children showed a gradual increase in organization over the years (as reflected by clustering scores), others "jumped" from chance clustering to almost perfect organization over the course of successive interviews. Nonetheless, the strategies children use do, on average, become more sophisticated and more successful with age, as does their tendency to use them spontaneously in appropriate situations. In the next section, I will examine some of the factors that have been found to influence memory strategy development.

Factors That Influence Children's Use of Memory Strategies

Many factors influence children's strategic functioning, and some of them are examined in this section:

encoding, knowledge base, metamemory, and motivation. As you will see, these factors are interactive and can affect both strategic and nonstrategic aspects of children's memory. No single factor can be pointed to as the principal cause of strategy development. Depending on the strategy in question and the age of the child, some factors are more critical than others, but, in general, an understanding of memory development requires an understanding of the many interrelated cognitive changes that occur over development.

Encoding

What one remembers is a function of how one encoded, or represented, the information. Young children use fewer features than do older children in encoding individual words (Ackerman, 1985, 1997), which contributes to their lower overall levels of recall.

Making comparisons among semantic features when items are presented also varies with development and can affect the strategy of organization (Brainerd, Kingma, & Howe, 1986). Brainerd and his colleagues reported that although second- and sixth-grade children apparently encoded categorical features of words (for example, *animal* for the word *horse*), there was little spread of activation to other similarly encoded items at the time of presentation by either age group. This result is counter to findings for adults. In other words, the children encoded the individual items by category features but failed to identify categorical relations among the items they were asked to remember.

Such "item-by-item encoding" limits children's ability to use an organizational strategy. For example, it is well established that when information is organized at the time of learning, it will be retained for a longer period than unorganized information (Bartlett, 1932; Posner & Keele, 1970). Using this logic, Bjorklund and Hock (1982) tested the recall of 9- and 14-year-old children on sets of categorically related items under two conditions: immediately after presentation and after a 4-minute period in which the children were engaged in another task. In a series of experiments, Bjorklund and Hock found that 9-year-old children showed relatively high levels of memory performance when recall was tested immediately, but suffered a greater decrement in recall after a delay than did the older children. The greater memory loss as a result of delay for the younger children suggests that they had likely not organized the information according to categories at input, whereas the 14-year-old children had. This interpretation was supported by conditions that forced 9-year-old children to organize information. When biased to organize the items at input (by presenting all the items from the same category together) and provided with the proper prompts at the time of retrieval (for example, "Remember all the *tools* that were on the list"), the young children recalled at a level comparable to that of the 14-year-olds on both immediate and delayed testing. These findings indicate that preadolescent children typically do not encode categorical information in a way conducive to the use of an organizational strategy.

Knowledge Base

One important factor that has been shown to influence strategic memory is a child's **knowledge base** for the to-be-remembered information (Alexander & Schwanenflugel, 1994; Hasselhorn, 1995). Some data pertinent to this issue were presented in Chapter 5. Basically, when children are very knowledgeable about a particular domain, they process information from that domain rapidly and display enhanced levels of memory performance (recall Chi's [1978] chess-expert children).

The effects that differences in knowledge base have on children's memory probably stem from differences in the efficiency with which they expend their limited cognitive resources, as discussed in Chapter 5. Items that have many features associated with them require less in the way of mental effort to be activated than do less elaborately represented items, and memory strategies are likely to be used only when children have sufficient mental resources available to them after executing other task-related operations (such as identifying individual items). When extensive mental effort is required to process relatively unfamiliar information, strategies, when

used at all, are used inefficiently (Bjorklund, Muir-Broaddus, & Schneider, 1990; Kee, 1994).

With respect to recall, Bjorklund (1987a) proposed that age differences in knowledge base can affect memory in one of three general ways: (1) by increasing the accessibility of specific items (item-specific effects); (2) by the relatively effortless activation of relations among sets of items (nonstrategic organization); and (3) by facilitating the use of deliberate strategies. Research examining each of these alternatives is reviewed briefly next.

Item-Specific Effects

Item-specific effects are most easily observed when children are asked to recall sets of unrelated items (for example, *apple, army, clock, day, dress, flower, hammer, snow*). Recall typically improves with age, but there are no corresponding improvements in measures of organization (Ornstein, Hale, & Morgan, 1977). One interpretation of these findings is that individual items are more richly represented in the semantic memories of older children than in those of younger children, resulting in greater ease of retrieval. This interpretation is bolstered by studies using lists of unrelated items that are chosen because of their meaningfulness for children of different ages. In these studies, groups of children first evaluate words in terms of how meaningful each one is to them. From these ratings, recall lists are constructed that are balanced in meaningfulness over several ages, thus eliminating age differences in knowledge for the information to be remembered. Under these conditions, age differences for short lists of words are eliminated (Chechile & Richman, 1982; Ghatala, 1984).

Nonstrategic Organization

Concerning nonstrategic organization, Bjorklund has suggested that much of the improvement seen in children's recall of categorically related material over the school years can be attributed to age-related increases in the relatively automatic (effortless) activation of semantic memory relations (Bjorklund, 1987a; Bjorklund et al., 1990). For instance, highly associated words (for example, *dog* and *cat*, *hand* and *glove*, *mouse* and *cheese*) are processed faster and are more likely to be sorted together by 5- and 6-year-old children than are nonassociated words that are categorically related (for example, *dog* and *lion*, *cheese* and *milk*, *hand* and *head*). Older children show efficient processing for both highly associated and nonassociated categorically related words (Mc-Cauley, Weil, & Sperber, 1976). When highly associated words are used on memory tests, levels of recall and clustering are high for both younger and older children. When associative strength is low among categorically related words, however, only older children show elevated memory performance (Frankel & Rollins, 1985; Schneider, 1986). One reason proposed for this effect is that semantic relations between high associates are activated with relatively little expenditure of mental effort, resulting in retrieval that appears organized (all the high associates are recalled together) but does not require the use of a deliberate strategy.

In other studies, age differences in recall have been eliminated or greatly reduced when children have detailed knowledge about the information they are asked to remember (Bjorklund & Bjorklund, 1985; Bjorklund & Zeman, 1982; Lindberg 1980). For example, in a study by Bjorklund and Zeman (1982), children in grades 1, 3, and 5 were asked to recall the names of their classmates. Age differences in class recall were small and were significantly less than age differences found for lists of categorically related words (see Figure 8-5). Furthermore, children's recall of their classmates' names was not random but typically was highly organized (by seating arrangement, reading groups, sex, and so on). Yet, when queried about their use of strategies, most of the children in all grades were unaware of using any special technique to remember the names. Bjorklund and Zeman proposed that the classmates' names represented a well-established knowledge base, with relations among names being activated with relatively little effort. Thus, a strategy was not necessary for successful retrieval. In other words, although the outcome of the children's recall appeared to be strategic (highly organized retrieval), the processes underlying their performance were

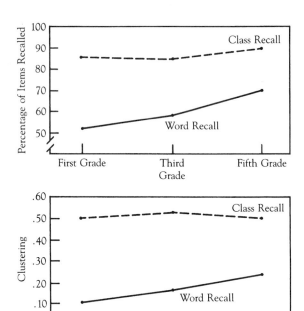

FIGURE 8-5   The average recall and clustering on class- and word-recall tasks by children in grades one, three, and five. SOURCE: Bjorklund, D. F., & Zeman, B. R. (1982). Children's organization and metamemory awareness in their recall of familiar information. *Child Development, 53,* 799–810. The Society for Research in Child Development, Inc.

not, but rather represented the relatively automatic activation and retrieval of relations among items in memory.

Facilitating Strategies

Another interpretation for the Bjorklund and Zeman findings is that the elaborated knowledge base that the children had for their classmates' names allowed them to use memory strategies efficiently. In fact, Bjorklund and Zeman proposed this possibility for the oldest children, who might have identified categorical relations in their recall while retrieving names on the basis of the relatively automatic activation of semantic memory relations and then continued to use this fortuitously discovered strategy for the remainder of their recall ("Hey, all those kids sit in the same row. I think I'll remember the rest of the kids by where they sit"). Peter Ornstein and his colleagues have championed this position, proposing that an elaborated knowledge base for sets of items allows the effective use of mnemonics (Folds et al., 1990; Ornstein, Baker-Ward, & Naus, 1988). The researchers propose that the use of memory strategies is facilitated by the automatic execution of certain parts of a task, even in very young children. Later in development, when children have a more sophisticated knowledge base and more experience, entire problem-solving routines can become automated. In support of this, several studies have demonstrated that children (and adults) more readily acquire strategies, both spontaneously and through training, and generalize a learned strategy to a new set of materials, when more familiar rather than less familiar stimulus items are use (Best, 1993; Bjorklund & Buchanan, 1989; Rabinowitz, Freeman, & Cohen, 1992).

The evidence is incontrovertible that age differences in knowledge base greatly influence age differences in memory performance. In research that specifically contrasts the role that various factors have on memory performance, such as intelligence and metamemory, knowledge base consistently accounts for more of the differences in memory performance than any other single factor (Alexander & Schwanenflugel, 1994; Hasselhorn, 1992).

Quantitative versus Qualitative Differences in Knowledge and Memory Performance

However, all knowledge is not created equal. Qualitative (rather than strictly quantitative) differences in how knowledge is structured will also influence how that knowledge is used (Ackerman, 1987; Muir-Broaddus & Bjorklund, 1990). Merely acquiring a set of "facts" about a topic does not provide the same cognitive advantage as when those "facts" are well integrated with each other and with related concepts. Research by Darlene DeMarie-Dreblow (1991) illustrates this position. In her study, second- through fifth-grade children were pretested on their knowledge of birds and their ability to remember

sets of birds. Children viewed five 10- to 15-minute videos about various species of birds during a one-week period. They were then tested again for their knowledge of birds and their ability to remember sets of birds. The training was successful, in that the children demonstrated significantly greater knowledge of birds than they had on the pretest. But their memory performance was no different than it had been initially. In this case, increased knowledge did *not* result in increased memory performance (see also Muir-Broaddus et al., 1995). There are several possible reasons for this pattern of results, including that greater exposure is needed before knowledge positively influences memory (possibly through increased speed of processing) and that knowledge must be appropriately structured before any benefits to cognition are observed. The latter interpretation suggests that *qualitative* differences in the structure of knowledge are as important as *quantitative* differences in determining the effect that knowledge has on children's thinking.

Metamemory

Metamemory refers to a knowledge of the workings of one's memory. If I were to ask you to recall your previous telephone number, for example, you would know that the information was there and that it was worth searching your memory for it. If I were to ask you for the telephone number of Bill Clinton, however, you would not bother to try to find it in the recesses of your mind. It is not there and never was, making any attempt at retrieving it ridiculous. This is an example of metamemory, knowing what you know, what you might know, and what you definitely do not know. Robert Kail (1990) described the process of remembering as occurring in a three-part sequence: diagnosis (deciding what needs to be done), treatment (executing the appropriate operations to do the job), and monitoring (checking how things are progressing). The use of strategies, discussed in earlier sections, falls within the realm of treatment. Diagnosis and monitoring are in the realm of metamemory. In general, the conclusion of research conducted over the past three decades is that metamemory knowledge increases with age, mirroring the increases typically reported for actual memory behavior (for reviews see Joyner & Kurtz-Costes, 1997; Schneider & Pressley, 1997).

How do we know what children know about their memories? One straightforward way of finding out is simply to ask them. This is essentially what was done in an interview study by Kreutzer, Leonard, and Flavell (1975). They asked children in kindergarten and the first, third, and fifth grades a series of questions about memory. For example, the children were asked if they ever forget things, if it would be easier to remember a phone number immediately after being told the number or after getting a drink of water, and if learning pairs of opposites (for example, boy/girl) would be easier or harder than learning pairs of unrelated words (for example, Mary/walk). Some kindergarten children asserted that they never forgot things, and fewer than 50% believed that phoning the friend immediately would yield more accurate recall. About half of the kindergarten and first-grade children believed that the arbitrary pairs would be easier to learn than the opposites or just as easy.

Young children's problems in evaluating task difficulty are illustrated in other situations also. For example, there are age-related improvements in making estimates of memory span (Yussen & Levy, 1975). There are similar improvements in knowing that it is easier to remember the gist of a story than to recall it verbatim (Kreutzer et al., 1975), that more study time should be apportioned to previously missed items than to previously recalled items (Masur et al., 1973), that the length of delay before testing should affect the amount of time one spends studying the target items (Rogoff, Newcombe, & Kagan, 1974), and that sets of categorized items are easier to recall than sets of noncategorized items (O'Sullivan, 1996).

In many situations, however, young children display metamnemonic competence. Even 3- and 4-year-olds realize that remembering many items is more difficult than remembering just a few (Yussen & Bird, 1979), and 4-year-olds pay more attention to the target information when they are given instructions to remember than when they are not (Baker-Ward , et al., 1984). One group of research-

ers reported that kindergarten and first-grade children understood reasonably well that re-learning something is faster than learning that same information for the first time and that the longer one studies something, the better one is likely to remember it (Kreutzer et al., 1975). When asked what they normally do to remember a phone number, even a majority of the kindergarten children mentioned writing it down, illustrating that they were aware of external devices for remembering information.

Children also show greater metamnemonic competence when they are in familiar surroundings. For instance, Ceci and Bronfenbrenner (1985) required 10- and 14-year-old children to perform a task in the near future (for example, take the cupcakes out of the oven) and observed their strategic time monitoring, the frequency with which they checked a clock during a waiting period. The children showed less strategic time monitoring when tested in a laboratory than in their homes, indicating to the authors that children might display greater metamemory competence in real-world versus contrived, laboratory settings (see also Wellman & Sommerville, 1980). Children might also have the metamemory knowledge but be unable to articulate it. For example, research by Cunningham and Weaver (1989) replicated preschool children's poor prediction of their memory spans when asked how many words they thought they could remember. Predictions were more accurate, however, when the children listened to a tape recording of words, stopping the tape when they had heard as many words as they thought they could recall.

One important aspect of metamemory knowledge concerns the role of strategies in facilitating memory performance. Young children are often unaware of strategies such as organization and rehearsal, or at least they are not conscious that these and related techniques can be useful when they are given a specific memory task (Justice, 1985). Children who are aware of the connection between strategic behavior and recall often remember more information than do children who do not posses such awareness (Justice et al., 1997). Furthermore, young children who have been taught a strategy are often unaware that using it facilitated their memory performance. This is illustrated in an experiment by

Ringel and Springer (1980). They trained first-, third-, and fifth-grade children to use an organizational strategy. The children were given pictures and instructed to sort them into groups on the basis of meaning and to use the groupings to help them remember the pictures. Each group of children showed improved memory performance as a result of training (relative to an earlier baseline phase). The children were then given a third memory task to assess transfer of training. After completing training but before beginning the transfer list, some of the children were provided with explicit feedback concerning their improved performance on the task, whereas others were not. The fifth-grade children transferred the organizational strategy to the new task under all conditions, whereas there was no evidence of significant transfer for any group of first graders. For the third-grade children, however, feedback made a difference. Those third graders who had received feedback concerning their memory performance transferred the organizational strategy to a new set of pictures. Third graders receiving no feedback did not, but, for the most part, reverted to a nonorganizational style characteristic of their pretraining behavior. In other words, knowing how well they were doing influenced the third-graders' generalization of a strtegy. The older children, apparently being better able to assess their own progress, did not require such feedback to transfer the strategy, and the younger children either were unable to transfer the strategy or at best needed more intensive instructions before generalization would take place. Other researchers have emphasized the role of metamemory in the effectiveness of strategy use and transfer, demonstrating that training in memory monitoring or other aspects of metamemory is responsible for the effectiveness and maintenance of strategy training (Ghatala et al., 1986; Leal, Crays, & Moely, 1985; Melot, 1998).

Given the impressive findings of the training studies, it seems reasonable that improvements in metamemory knowledge must be causally related to improvements in memory behavior, or metamemory knowledge → memory behavior. Yet, an argument can be made that metamemory knowledge grows out of memory behavior, or memory behavior → metamemory knowledge. That is, children perform memory strategies effectively and, as a result, acquire knowledge about strategies.

Research aimed at elucidating the relationship between metamemory knowledge and memory behavior in development was conducted by Cavanaugh and Borkowski (1980). They administered extensive memory and metamemory interviews to children in kindergarten and the first, third, and fifth grades. They reported that both metamemory knowledge and memory behavior increased with age but that, within a grade level, there was little significant relationship between the two factors. That is, knowing a child's level of metamemory knowledge did not predict well his or her level of memory performance when age was held constant.

Other research has shown that the relation one finds between metamemory and memory depends on the age of the child and the nature of the questions (Cantor, Andreassen, & Waters, 1985; Schneider, in press). For example, studies looking at metamemory/memory relations in categorization and elaboration tasks do not yield strong connections between the two factors until the elementary school years (Lange et al., 1990), and not consistently until about age 10 (Hasselhorn, 1992). However, when the task is simple and the metamemory questions are highly related to successful task performance, even preschool children show a significant relationship between metamemory knowledge and memory behavior. For example, in a study by Wolfgang Schneider and Beate Sodian (1988), 4- and 6-year-old children were asked to remember 10 objects that they placed in each of 10 play houses. Each house was associated with a picture of a person (for example, doctor, farmer, policeman, soccer player, sailor), and some of the items were related to the people (for example, syringe, tractor, police car, soccer ball, and ship), whereas others were not (for example, comb, letter, key, flower, and lamp). For both the 4- and 6-year-olds, children who were aware of the importance of associating the objects (syringe, tractor) with the people (doctor, farmer) performed better on the memory test. Thus, the relation between metamemory and memory is significant even for 4-year-olds when the task is sufficiently simplified and the metamemory questions are immediately pertinent to the memory behavior.

In general, the research evidence points to a bidirectional relationship between metamemory knowledge and memory behavior (Borkowski, Milstead, & Hale, 1988; Schneider & Bjorklund, 1998). Metamemory knowledge can result in improved memory performance, which, in turn, results in enhanced metamemory knowledge. Metamemory is obviously an important component in children's memory development. However, research findings suggest that metamemory competence is as much a consequence as it is a cause of competent memory behavior, the two being intimately entwined, and that this relationship varies as a function of age and task variables. Also, metamemory interacts with other factors. For example, as we noted earlier, children who are experts in a domain will remember more in that domain than will less-expert children. However, expert children's memory performance will be greatest when they also have substantial metamnemonic knowledge (Schneider, Schlagmüller, & Visé, 1998).

Motivation

Although every school teacher and most folks without Ph.D.s in cognitive psychology know that motivation is an important factor in learning and remembering, it is only recently that developmental psychologists have considered this in studies of memory development (Guttentag, 1995; Renninger, Hidi, & Krapp, 1992). Perhaps motivation was not seen as a "cognitive" factor and thus only indirectly related to "real" memory. This oversight has begun to be rectified in recent years, as researchers examine the role of motivation in children's memory performance.

Scott Paris (1988) outlined a model of memory based on **subjective expected utility,** which, in this context, basically refers to a person's beliefs about the usefulness of implementing any particular strategy. Paris notes that people of all ages often use memory strategies because they believe they will improve task performance (recall that strategies are defined as cognitive operations that are goal directed with the purpose of enhancing task performance). Moreover, young children often have misconceptions about the usefulness of strategies. That is, they

might be unaware that a particular strategy is or is not effective. As a result, task performance can be hindered until children acquire a better "feel" for the usefulness of a strategy. In some situations, however, children's faulty beliefs about the effectiveness of a strategy can be beneficial, such as in utilization deficiencies, in which children use a strategy without apparent benefit (Miller, 1990). In such situations, children might believe that the strategy is indeed helping them, which might cause them to continue using it, which in turn could eventually lead to more effective (and beneficial) strategy use (Bjorklund et al., 1997).

Several studies have looked at motivation by providing explicit rewards to children. For example, in an experiment by Anthony Cuvo (1974), children were given sets of words to rehearse and remember. Some words were identified as 10-cent items (that is, children would get a dime if they remembered them) whereas others were identified a 1-cent items. Fifth-grade children recalled more 10-cent words than 1-cent words, apparently because they rehearsed the former more than the latter. Similar findings have been reported for second-grade children, reflecting the fact that even 7- and 8-year-olds can modify their strategy use given the proper motivation (Kunzinger & Witryol, 1984).

In other research, children's study time has been influenced by the provision of specific incentives (Guttentag, 1995; O'Sullivan, 1993). For example, in a study by Julia O'Sullivan (1993), 4-year-old children used more sophisticated strategies and spent less time engaged in off-task behavior (that is, not paying attention) when the incentive for "good" memory performance was a highly valued toy (a box of crayons) versus a less-valued toy (a pencil). What is interesting is that the more sophisticated study behaviors did not result in enhanced memory performance, a finding similar to that reported by Robert Guttentag (1995) for third-grade children. Whether children in these experiments realized the limited effectiveness of their strategy use was not assessed, but these findings provide further evidence of children's poor metamemory concerning strategy use. However, they also provide support for the argument that strategy use is effortful and might not immediately improve task performance. Presumably, their continued use of the strategy would eventually lead to improved task performance. Thus, their poor metacognition, in this case, might be adaptive (Bjorklund, 1997a), in that were the children aware that their increased efforts were not leading to enhanced task performance, they might have resorted to an easier, but nonstrategic approach. Instead, their poor self-monitoring led to increased practice with the (currently) ineffective strategy, which, in time, should increase in effectiveness.

Closely related to the concept of motivation is that of *interest*. Children will presumably spend more time on tasks involving topics that are interesting to them. This might seem obvious, but until recently relatively little research has been done in this area. In general, there is evidence that working with interesting as opposed to uninteresting materials produces "deeper" cognitive processing (see Renninger et al., 1992; Tobias, 1994; but see O'Sullivan, 1997). More specifically, recent research has emphasized the importance of interest, particularly in instruction. According to Michael Pressley and his colleagues (1992), "many aspects of good strategies instruction are designed to increase interest in acquiring strategies" (p. 352). Interest breeds success, which in turn should increase children's interest in learning even more complex and effective strategies (see also Renninger, 1992).

Another factor that has been related to motivation is children's self-attributions of success and failure. That is, do children see their performance primarily as the result of effort, innate ability, or luck. Several researchers have demonstrated that children's attributions of success and failure influence their performance on a wide range of cognitive tasks, including memory (see Borkowski et al., 1988).

Culture and Memory Strategies

Cultures clearly differ in the extent to which they support and encourage particular memory strategies (Kurtz, 1990; Mistry, 1997). Rehearsal, organization, and elaboration, for example, are especially helpful to children from Western industrialized societies, whose school activities involve a great deal of rote memorization and list learning. Yet, these same strategies might not be so useful to unschooled children from nonindustrialized societies, whose most important memory tasks might involve recalling the location of objects (water; game animals) in a natural setting or remembering instructions passed along in the context of proverbs or stories.

For example, in list-learning experiments, Western children rely heavily on strategies acquired at school and clearly outperform their unschooled peers from nonindustrialized societies (Cole & Scribner, 1977; Rogoff & Waddell, 1982). The picture is much different, however, when the memory task is embedded in a meaningful and structured context. When tests are structured so that people must recall organized prose (as in a story) or items from spatially organized arrays (as in familiar scenes), few cultural differences in memory performance are found (see Rogoff, 1990).

A particularly clear demonstration of the importance of cultural context on memory performance is provided by a study by Rogoff and Waddell (1982). Previous research had shown that Guatemalan Mayan children's memory for lists of items was significantly worse than that of American children of the same age (Kagan et al., 1979). Rogoff and Waddell (1982) showed 9-year-old Guatemalan Mayan and U.S. children three-dimensional, culturally appropriate scenes of a model town. Twenty objects, such as animals, cars, people, and household items, were placed within the scene, and children were asked to remember the objects and their location. The 20 objects were then mixed into a pool of 80 objects, and, after a brief delay, the children were asked to reconstruct the scene. Counter to the earlier list-learning experiment, the Mayan children actually performed slightly *better* than the U.S. children did on the reconstruction task. These results clearly illustrate that the nonschooled, rural children's poor memory performance on the list-learning tasks was not caused by deficient memory abilities, but rather by the context in which memory was studied.

Greater performance for unschooled relative to schooled children have been found in other tasks as well. For example, unschooled Australian aboriginal children were better than their Anglo-Australian peers at remembering the location of objects in natural settings (Kearins, 1981), and African adolescents displayed better recall for orally transmitted stories than American adolescents (Dube, 1982). Indeed, Western children actually remember less if they try to rehearse or to organize information in these latter kinds of memory tasks (Rogoff, 1990).

These findings make perfectly good sense when viewed through the "lens" of Vygotsky's sociocultural theory (see Chapter 3): Cognitive development always occurs within a particular cultural context, which not only defines the kinds of problems that children must solve, but also dictates the strategies (or "tools of intellectual adaptation") that will enable them to master these challenges (Ellis, 1997).

Not all cultural differences in strategic memory functioning are between children in schooled and nonschooled societies. For example, studies have linked differences in American and German attitudes toward intellectual development to differences in memory strategy use (Carr et al., 1989; Kurtz et al., 1990). In these studies, second and third graders in Germany and the United States were trained to use a memory strategy (specifically, to recall related items together in clusters). Before training, children were given a battery of tests assessing their verbal and nonverbal intelligence, academic self-esteem, metamemory, spontaneous use of strategies, and attributional beliefs about learning (whether they attributed success and failure to luck, their own effort, or some inherent ability). Children's parents and teachers also answered questionnaires regarding their beliefs about children's academic success or failure and the extent of instruction in or encouragement of strategic thinking that occurred in the home and at school.

An initial finding was that the German children were significantly more strategic on their own than the American children were, although the American children did benefit from the memory training. Despite the German children's superiority on the memory task, however, the American children had more positive academic self-esteem and were more apt to attribute academic outcomes to effort (that is, hard work) than the German children were, something that has been associated with enhanced academic achievement (Borkowski & Turner, 1988; Dweck & Leggett, 1988). The German children, on the other hand, were more apt to believe that their success or failure in school-related tasks was due to ability (that is, inborn traits). Moreover, American children who believe in effort perform better than American children holding other views, and German children who believe in natural ability perform better than German children who hold other views (Kurtz, 1990). This shows that when studies of American children report that belief in effort is related to higher academic achievement, it is culturally dependent—holding only for that culture. Different patterns of performance are found for children from different cultures.

The source of this cultural difference in strategy use and attribution of success can be traced to the behaviors and attitudes of children's parents and teachers. German parents give children more direct strategy training, buy them more games that require strategic thinking, and check their homework more than do American parents. German teachers reported more direct strategy instruction than did American teachers (Carr et al., 1989; Kurtz et al., 1990). German parents and teachers were more likely to attribute children's academic performance to ability, whereas their American counterparts were more likely to attribute it to effort.

Consistency and Stability of Memory

With a chapter titled "Memory," your expectation may be that we are talking about a single cognitive skill. Memory can be tapped in different ways (recognition, recall), can occur in different situations (event memory, school- or laboratory-type tasks), and can involve deliberate strategies or be indirect and unintentional, but the implication is that there is a single, underlying "memory" ability. This, of course, is an empirical question, and there is every reason to believe that the phenomenon we call "memory" is not a domain-general skill but, rather, comprises different domain-specific abilities.

Is "Memory" a Domain-General Faculty or a Set of Domain-Specific Abilities?

The way to assess this question is to administer different memory tasks to children and note the intertask correlations. That is, do children who do well on one memory task perform well on others, and do children who perform poorly on one task perform poorly on others? Early developmental studies using this technique reported relatively high correlations among tasks, with the correlations increasing with age (Cavanaugh & Borkowski, 1980; Kail, 1979). These studies used strategic, laboratory tasks, and the results suggest that not only is there a general memory ability, but also a general strategy ability, at least for children 8 years of age and older. (Recall that young children show little spontaneous strategic behavior, at least on the tasks used in these investigations.)

Later research used a wider variety of tasks, including laboratory tasks such as digit-span and sort-recall, and "everyday" memory tasks, such as story recall (Kurtz-Costes, Schneider, & Rupp, 1995; Schneider & Weinert, 1995). These studies reported lower intertask correlations, suggesting that deliberate memory could better be thought of as a set of specific abilities rather than as a domain-general faculty. For example, Kurtz-Costes and colleagues (1995) administered a set of 12 memory tasks to 5-, 7-, and 9-year-old children, including several reflecting everyday activities (for example, remember to remind the interviewer of something at the end of the session; "shopping" for items at a store), school-related tasks (for example, remembering a geography "lesson"; recalling a story), and laboratory tasks (sort-recall and paired associates). The researchers reported little intertask consistency among the 12 tasks at any age, with only slightly more correlations reaching statistical significance than would be expected by chance. The average correlations among tasks did increase slightly with

age (average correlations = .07, .08, and .13 for 5-, 7-, and 9-year-olds, respectively), but, overall, little developmental differences were observed.

In related research, Schneider and Weinert (1995) expanded the type of tasks given to children, including a variety of memory-span tasks (word span, sentence span), sort-recall, and several story-recall tasks. As part of a longitudinal study, they assessed the intertask correlations in the same group of children at 4-, 6-, 8-, and 10-years old. Schneider and Weinert reported few developmental patterns. But they did find relatively high intertask correlations among the two span tasks and the two story-recall tasks. That is, consistency was high only when the parallel measures of story recall and word span were used. Like the results of Kurtz-Costes and her colleagues, these findings are consistent with the position that there is no unitary "memory" construct, nor little change in the relationship among memory tasks with development.

How Stable Is Memory Performance over Time?

One issue of interest to developmental psychologists is that of *stability*. In this case, stability refers to maintaining the same rank order with respect to ability over time. That is, will children who remember well at one age also remember well on a similar task several years later? Research investigating stability requires longitudinal assessment, and such expensive and laborious work has rarely focused on basic cognitive processes such as memory. One notable exception is the Munich Longitudinal Study on the Genesis of Individual Competencies (LOGIC) (Schneider & Sodian, 1997; Weinert & Schneider, 1986, 1992), which has followed children over a 10-year period and did extensive assessments of memory performance.

When looking at the stability of children's performance on a sort-recall task, Wolfgang Schneider and Franz Weinert (1995) reported relatively low long-term stability, with correlations of recall, sorting (the degree to which participants sort items into categories), and clustering never exceeding

TABLE 8-2   Stability of memory performance over time (long-term and short-term stability) obtained for strategy and recall measures for the sort-recall task from the Munich Longitudinal Project.

Variable	Two-year stability (4–6)	Two-year stability (6–8)	Two-year stability (8–10)	Four-year stability (4–8)	Six-year stability (4–10)	Short-term stability
Recall	.36	.29	.39	.20	.16	.68
Sorting	.17	.12	.07	.08	.02	.85
Clustering	.12	.16	.12	.08	.19	.64

SOURCE: Schneider, W., & Weinert, F. E. (1995). Memory development during early and middle childhood: Findings from the Munich longitudinal study (LOGIC). In F. E. Weinert & W. Schneider (Eds.), *Memory performance and competencies: Issues in growth and development.* Hillsdale, NJ: Erlbaum.

.20 over four-years time and .39 over a two-year period (Schneider & Sodian, 1991; Schneider & Weinert, 1995). Table 8-2 presents the pattern of correlations for different intervals and at different ages from the LOGIC sample. The column labeled "short-term stability" present correlations between tasks given to the same children within a two-week period. The high correlations here suggest that children's performance is stable when given over very brief intervals, suggesting that the tests themselves are reliable. What is not reliable is performance over longer periods.

Schneider and Weinert (1995) noted that long-term stability is higher for other memory tasks, however. For example, the correlations over a two-year period for sentence span, word span, and several measures of story recall were usually quite high (most in the .40 to .70 range), suggesting relatively high stability for these tasks. Schneider and Weinert suggested that the lower stabilities for the sort-recall tasks, in comparison with the memory-span and story-recall tasks, is related to the substantially greater strategic component required for the sort-recall tasks. That is, stability is relatively high for tasks involving relatively little in the way of deliberate strategic functioning (memory span and story recall), but lower when strategies play a crucial part in task performance.

Part of the problem with strategies is that they do not seem to develop in a gradual, step-by-step fashion, but rather change relatively abruptly. As part of the Munich Longitudinal Study, Sodian and

Schneider (1999) observed changes in strategy use over time by individual children. The researchers noted that only about 8% of the children showed a gradual improvement in the use of organizational memory strategies (sorting and clustering), with 81% "jumping" from chance sorting or clustering scores at one test interval to near perfect scores at the following measurement point. Thus, although cross-sectional data can give the impression of a gradual change in strategic functioning over childhood (with the implication of stability of individual differences), longitudinal data indicate that, for most children, the transition from astrategic to strategic, at least for organizational strategies, occurs relatively quickly, and at different ages for different children.

Forgetting and Reminiscence

All the information presented in this chapter to this point has dealt with remembering. But each of us is familiar with another side of memory—**forgetting.** Forgetting refers to failing to remember some information that one knew, or had previously remembered, some time earlier. Forgetting is not the same as never knowing. If a child is given 20 words to remember and recalls only 10 of them, the remaining 10 were not forgotten. They were never learned. Forgetting would occur when, some time following the initial test, the child was asked again to remember as many of the 20 words that he or she had seen earlier. If of the 10 words the child had originally remembered, only 5 were recalled again, we could say that the child forgot 5 words, or 50% of what he or she had remembered earlier.

In contrast to forgetting is **reminiscence.** Reminiscence refers to the recall of an item at some later time that was *not* remembered initially. For example, if our child who recalled 10 words originally (first test) later recalls 7 words (third test), 5 that he or she had remembered at the second session and 2 that had *not* been recalled earlier, those two words would be classified as reminiscence—words remembered on a third test that were not remembered on the second test.

Until recently, forgetting and reminiscence were not much studied by developmental psychologists. Forgetting was a relatively popular topic earlier in this century, but fell out of favor, partly because forgetting did not fit well with the computer metaphor of information processing models and because early studies reported few developmental differences in forgetting. It seemed that once something was learned, people of all ages were equally likely to remember (or forget) it (see Howe & Brainerd, 1989 for a review of the early research).

More recent research by Brainerd, Howe, and their colleagues has questioned this interpretation, stating that most earlier studies were methodologically flawed in one way or another (Brainerd, 1997; Howe & Brainerd, 1989; Howe & O'Sullivan, 1997). Some of the flaws included using measures that are not sensitive to developmental differences (for example, recognition rather than recall measures), ceiling effects in forgetting rates (that is, everyone forgot almost everything, making meaningful analyses impossible), ignoring reminiscence effects when evaluating forgetting effects, and a failure to control for differences in initial levels of learning (that is, older children learned more initially than younger children, giving them more to forget).

Brainerd, Howe, and their colleagues attempted to address these methodological problems by requiring that children of all ages learn the target information to a specified criterion (usually perfect recall). Once accomplished, children are tested again for the target material using recall measures, often days

and weeks later (Howe, 1991). Under these conditions, age differences in forgetting are found, with younger children forgetting at higher rates than older children and adults. Research using a variant of this paradigm has even been done with preverbal toddlers, with the finding that 12-month-olds show higher rates of forgetting than 18-month-olds did (Howe & Courage, 1997).

Although most forgetting experiments of the type described used lists of words, several have used stories as stimuli (Howe, 1991; Marche & Howe, 1995). For example, Mark Howe (1991) reported that second-grade children remembered more information than kindergartners did about a story after delays of both 2- and 9-days, illustrating greater forgetting for the younger relative to the older children (remember that all children learned the story to criterion).

Age differences in reminiscence appear to be less robust than those found for forgetting, at least for younger children. Age differences in reminiscence effects are often not found, and when they are, they are typically small (Cassel & Bjorklund, 1995; Poole & White, 1993). Analysis by Brainerd (1997) of data from earlier forgetting/reminiscence studies revealed interesting developmental differences, which are shown in Figure 8-6. As can be seen from the figure, the rate of reminiscence is constant from 4 to 8 years of age and then increases sharply to young adulthood. It is also interesting to note that reminiscence rate decreases again in the elderly.

In other research, Cassel and Bjorklund (1995) showed kindergarten, second grade, and college students a brief video and asked for their immediate recall of events in the video. After recalling all they could, participants were given a set of cues for items they had not remembered in free recall. Participants were tested for free-recall of the events in the video again one week and one month later. When considering only information people remembered initially in *free recall,* forgetting rates during the 1-week and 1-month sessions were comparable at all grades (about 50%). Forgetting rates were higher for information that was remembered originally to the cues, with the adults showing better retention (less forgetting) than the children. These results are consistent

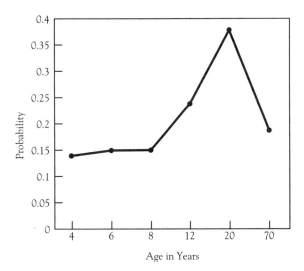

FIGURE 8-6 Developmental differences in reminiscence rates. The rate of reminiscence is stable from about 4 to 8 years of age and increases in young adulthood and declines in the elderly. (Thanks to Charles Brainerd for making this figure available.)

with the claims of Brainerd and Howe that developmental differences in degree of initial learning affect later forgetting. Information that adults and the children remembered in free recall was best (and equally) retained one week and one month later by all subjects. It was only for the less salient information that age differences were found; adults were better able to retain information they had retrieved only to the experimenter's cues than the children. Thus, age differences in forgetting are found for less salient information (Cassel & Bjorklund, 1995) and when all participants learn the to-be-remembered information perfectly (Brainerd, 1997), the latter being a situation that is rarely found in everyday life. Age differences in forgetting are less apt to be found, however, in some more "realistic" situations, when levels of initial memory vary with age. These results illustrate that answering the question of "Are there age differences in forgetting?" is not an easy one. To a large extent, it depends on where one looks.

One reason that has been proposed for age differences in forgetting (when they are found) has focused on developmental differences in how infor-

mation is encoded. This possibility was discussed earlier in this chapter in our discussion of children's eyewitness memories. Younger children are more likely to encode information in terms of literal, verbatim memory traces, whereas older children are more likely to encode information in terms of less-precise, gist memory traces (Brainerd & Reyna, 1990; Leichtman & Ceci, 1993). Verbatim traces, favored by the younger children, are less resistant to decay, thus producing higher forgetting rates for younger relative to older children. Age differences in verbatim and gist encoding are a central theme of fuzzy-trace theory (Brainerd & Reyna, 1990; Reyna & Brainerd, 1995), and were discussed in some detail in Chapter 5.

Summary

Memory is multifaceted, involving a host of other cognitive operations, and it is involved in all other complex forms of thinking. Memory can refer to the process of bringing information to consciousness or to the contents of memory. *Recognition* is generally good in young children, although age changes in recognition are found when the task demands become difficult or when children can apply their world knowledge to assist them in the recognition process. Young children's *location memory* is also good, showing little in the way of developmental differences. More substantial age differences are found for *free recall*. Children's recall is higher on *cued-recall* tasks, with younger children needing more specific cues before recalling information.

Infants display memory in habituation/dishabituation and *preference-for-novelty paradigms* shortly after birth. Conditioning techniques have been used to demonstrate memory in infants as young as 3 months for periods as long as 2 weeks, with infants' memories in these situations being greatly influenced by contextual effects. *Deferred-imitation* tasks have shown that older infants can retain information over relatively long periods of time.

In contrast to explicit, or intentional memory, few age differences are observed for *implicit memory*, when there is no conscious intention to remember something.

Young children's *event memory* is based on *scripts*, with memory first being for general routines and not for specific *autobiographical* experiences. Parents "teach" children how to remember by interacting with them and providing the structure for putting their experiences into narratives.

Recent research in event memory has focused on children as eyewitnesses. Age differences are found in the amount of information children remember, but what young children do recall tends to be accurate and for central components of an event. The accuracy of children's event memory is often adversely affected by repeated questioning, especially in a single session. Recent research has documented that young children are more susceptible to misleading questions (suggestions) and misinformation than older children and can easily be caused to form false memories.

Infantile amnesia refers to the inability to recall information from infancy and early childhood. Current theory about the reason for infantile amnesia focuses on the development of self-concept, developmental differences in how information is encoded, and changes in children's use of language to communicate their memories to others.

Piagetian research has stressed the constructive nature of memory, with recent research showing that children distort to-be-remembered information at time of encoding and not necessarily at time of retrieval.

The development of *memory strategies*, or *mnemonics*, has been found to be critically important to age changes in children's memory. In general, the use of strategies such as *rehearsal, organization, retrieval,* and *elaboration* increases with age. Young children who do not use a strategy spontaneously can be trained to use one, usually with corresponding improvements in memory performance. However, levels of performance are typically less than those shown by older children who use the strategy spontaneously, and children often do not transfer the strategy to new sets of materials.

Several factors influence developmental differences in children's use of strategies and memory per-

formance. Age differences in encoding are reflected by younger children using fewer semantic features to encode items than older children do and being less likely to make comparisons among features. Three types of influences of *knowledge base* on memory have been proposed: item-specific effects, nonstrategic organization, and facilitating strategies. Age differences in *metamemory*, what children know about the workings of their own memories, have been reported. Although even preschool children reveal metamemory knowledge in some situations, it increases throughout childhood. Research into the developmental relationship between metamemory knowledge and memory behavior has yielded mixed results, with the two apparently developing simultaneously and interactively. Differences in motivation have been found to affect children's memory performance. Cultural differences also play an important role in the use of memory strategies, with some cultures not using the relatively "*context-independent*" strategies taught in school to Western children.

Research has shown that memory is best conceptualized as a set of different, domain-specific skills rather than as a single mental faculty. There is relatively little stability of strategic memory, but greater short-term stability (2 years) for less obviously strategic tasks such as memory span and story recall.

Age differences in *forgetting* and *reminiscence* are typically found when researchers control for differences in levels of initial learning.

Key Terms and Concepts

recognition
cued recall
free recall
location memory
"context-independent" learning
preference-for-novelty paradigms
deferred imitation
implicit memory
event memory
scripts
hypermnesia
source monitoring
infantile amnesia
autobiographical memory
mnemonics

rehearsal
passive rehearsal
cumulative (active) rehearsal
organization
clustering
sort-recall
elaboration
paired-associates task
knowledge base
metamemory
subjective expected utility
forgetting
reminiscence

Suggested Readings

SCHNEIDER, W., & BJORKLUND, D. F. (1998). Memory. In D. Kuhn & R. S. Siegler (Vol. Eds.), *Cognitive, language, and perceptual development*, Vol. 2 (pp. 467–521). In B. Damon (General Editor), *Handbook of child psychology*. New York: Wiley. This article presents a concise, but more detailed, review of much of the research reviewed in this chapter.

SCHNEIDER, W., & PRESSLEY, M. (1997). *Memory development between 2 and 20* (2nd ed.). Mahwah, NJ: Erlbaum. This is a thorough review of memory development, from the beginning of psychology through the mid 1990s, written by two of the leading researchers in the field. This book is written for the professional researcher and advanced student.

PRESSLEY, M., & SCHNEIDER, W. (1997). *Introduction to memory development during childhood and adolescence.* Mahwah, NJ: Erlbaum. This is the beginner's version of the Schneider and Pressley book. It is written for an undergraduate audience and provides a good, easily understandable review of memory development in children.

COWAN, N. (Ed.) (1997). *The development of memory in childhood.* London: London University College Press. This book includes 12 chapters written by leading researchers and theorists on various topics of children's memory, including infant memory, strategies, event memory, metamemory, and children's eyewitness testimony, among others. The chapters were written with an undergraduate audience in mind.

CECI, S. J., & BRUCK, M. (1998). Children's testimony: Applied and basic issues. In I. E. Sigel & K. A. Renninger (Vol. Eds.), *Child psychology in practice* (Vol. 4) (pp. 713–774). In W. Damon (Gen. Ed.), *Handbook of child psychology.* New York: Wiley. This chapter presents an historical review and the latest research on children's eyewitness memory and suggestibility, including summaries of important legal cases in which children's testimony played a central role.

NELSON, K. (1996). *Language in cognitive development: The emergence of the mediated mind.* New York: Cambridge University Press. This book presents Katherine Nelson's theory on the role of language in cognitive development and in the process reviews research on the development of event and autobiographical memory.

Language Development

What Makes a Communication System a Language?

Describing Children's Language Development
A Brief Description of Early Language Development • Phonological Development
Morphological Development • Syntactic Development
Semantic Development • Pragmatics • Communicative Competence

Some Theoretical Perspectives of Language Development
Nativist Perspectives on Language Development
Social-Interactionist Perspectives of Language Development
Locke's Theory of Neurolinguistic Development
The Relation Between Lexical and Syntactic Development: Is a Grammar Module Necessary?

Gender Differences in Language Acquisition

Language and Thought
Nelson's Views of the Role of Language in Cognitive Development
The Self-Regulatory Function of Language • The Development of Inner Speech

Summary

Key Terms and Concepts

Suggested Readings

Human beings' use of language, more than any other single ability, is what most obviously distinguishes us from all other animals. Children around the globe acquire language without formal instruction. Language belongs to the class of abilities that are too important to be relegated to our conscious awareness and "free will" (Spelke & Newport, 1998). Some scientists believe that the evolution of language made human thought possible (Bickerton, 1990; Nelson, 1996). Despite the universality of language (that is, all groups of people possess it and develop it at about the same age), the language people learn depends on what is spoken around them. Language is thus strongly influenced both by humans' general biological inheritance and by the uniqueness of the environments in which they grow up.

This chapter is about the development of language and its interrelationship with cognition. Although a few nonhuman primates have shown simple language abilities (see Savage-Rumbaugh et al., 1993), none has approached the level found in all normal humans. Language does more than just permit people to communicate their current thoughts, perceptions, or emotions, but also plays an important role *within* an individual. The cognitive processes we possess that are uniquely human are made possible by our ability to use language. Through this ability, we gain wisdom from the mistakes of others and advance our culture anew with each generation instead of eternally reinventing ourselves. Our ability to use language has given us, for better or for worse, our dominance of the planet.

What Makes a Communication System a Language?

Humans are not the only species to have a complex communication system, but, by some definitions, we are the only species to have language. There are several features that most linguists, I think, would agree upon as typifying language, and these include **arbitrariness, productivity, semanticity, displacement,** and **duality** (Brown, 1973; Lyons, 1978).

1. *Arbitrariness.* Any pattern of sound (that is, any word) can refer to anything that the speakers of a language choose to have it refer to. A word is not inherently related to the concept it represents. For example, in English we refer to the bright yellow ball in the daytime sky as the "sun," and the "lesser light" of the evening as the "moon." The words themselves are arbitrary, having nothing to do with the objects themselves. If we wished to, we could agree to reserve the names, as some groups of people sometimes do (for instance, the word "bad," when used in the right context with the proper pronunciation, has a positive, not a negative, connotation to it). There are some exceptions, such as onomatopoeia words (for example, the "choo choo" sound resembles the sound that trains once made and thus conveys the meaning of a train).

2. *Productivity.* Languages are *creative*, or generative. Speakers of a language can produce an infinite number of sentences using only a finite set of words. A language does not consist of a specific set of sentences that are to be memorized. Rather, language has a system of rules (syntax, or grammar) that permits a speaker to produce and understand sentences that have never been before uttered.

3. *Semanticity.* Semanticity refers to the fact that language can represent objects, actions, events, and ideas symbolically.

4. *Displacement.* Language has the ability to displace the speaker and the listener from the here and now. People can talk about objects and events that are outside of their immediate context, both in time and space. Language permits us to talk about the past or the future and to know about events or objects that are miles away.

5. *Duality.* Duality refers to the fact that language is represented at two levels: *phonology*, the actual sound that a speaker produces, and the underlying abstract, meaning of language, reflected by the *syntax* (rules of putting words together) and *semantics* (meanings of those words and concepts).

Describing Children's Language Development

The concept of duality implies that there are at least two different *aspects* of language, but in fact there are at least five different aspects: phonology, morphology, syntax, semantics, and pragmatics, and they all develop.

In this section, I will first provide a very brief description of early language development, primarily to give readers some context in which to interpret what follows. I will then look at the five aspects of language just mentioned and provide a more indepth description of children's development for each aspect.

A Brief Description of Early Language Development

One of the traditional milestones of a child's life is the day she speaks her first word. This information is often recorded in the child's baby book and repeated again and again as an official milestone in the history of the family. When asked why this is such an important event, parents usually report something like this: "Well, he wasn't a baby anymore, he was a real person." Or they will say, "Suddenly we felt like we knew her as a person."

This "infant-to-human" transformation is not read by parents alone. Most psycholinguists and cognitive developmentalists consider the possession of language to be a key element of our humanness. It is the foundation of our unique form of intelligence — the ability to reflect on ourselves, to solve problems that have not yet happened, and to benefit from the experiences of others who lived generations before us or worlds away from us. And that it is done so well by virtually all preschoolers with minimal instruction from parents or other experts makes it even more amazing.

Infants' earliest vocalizations are cries, but they begin cooing and babbling between 2 and 4 months of age. Children typically say their first words late in their first year of life or shortly thereafter. Early

words are sometimes only recognized by family members and usually refer to people in the family ("Mama," "Dada"), or important objects. Most of the first 50 or so words that children acquire refer to familiar people, toys, and food (Nelson, 1974), and this is apparently true across different languages (Caselli et al., 1995).

At about 18 to 24 months, children know a few dozen words and begin putting them together, a few at a time, into short sentences or phrases. Again, the words they know are those that are important to them, such as actions (what happened and who did it), possession (what belongs to whom), location (where people and objects are), recurrence (requesting "more" or "again"), naming (familiar people and objects), and nonexistence ("all gone") (de Villiers & de Villiers, 1979).

Another way toddlers get the most meaning from their limited language abilities is by using gestures and intonations to supplement their sparse sentences. "MOMMY!" can be a clear cry of distress, whereas "Mommy?" can be the initiation of a light conversation. Add a little hand waving and an empty cup and "Mommy" becomes a request for a drink refill. And coming from behind a chairback, "Mommy" can be the beginning of a round of peek-a-boo. Take, for example, the toddler who gets his mother's attention by climbing up next to her on the sofa, putting one hand on each of her cheeks, and turning her face toward his as he finally says "Cookie?" And another 2-year-old who tells her parents that she doesn't want any more milk by giving a negative head shake as she says "More milk."

Although children at this age express limited words and ideas, they are capable of understanding much more. It is estimated that by the time children speak their first words, they understand approximately one hundred (Benedict, 1979). This brings us to the distinction between **productive language,** the language that children can actually produce, or speak, and **receptive language,** the language that children can understand. Receptive language exceeds productive language, with this distinction beginning early in infancy and persisting into adulthood (Hirsh-Pasek, Golinkoff, & Naigles, 1996).

For instance, in one study, 16- to 18-month-old toddlers were able to tell the difference between sentences such as "Where is Big Bird washing Cookie Monster?" and "Where is Cookie Monster washing Big Bird?," although most of the children were able to produce "sentences" only one word in length (Hirsh-Pasek & Golinkoff, 1991).

When children get beyond the two-word phase, they do so mostly by including only those words that convey the most meaning and omitting the "little" words that make language easy to understand but that are not absolutely necessary for understanding. For example, a child might say "Daddy give milk me" or "Amy me go Grandma's?" rather than "Give me the milk, Daddy," or "May Amy and I go to Grandma's?" When heard in context, the meaning of these abbreviated sentences are straightforward. Children are economical in their word choice, using only the concrete and high-information words that are most important in conveying meaning. Such speech has been described as **telegraphic,** in that it is accomplished much as telegrams were once written, including only the high-content words and leaving out all the ifs, ands, and buts.

During the three years from age 2 to age 5, children's language develops from baby talk to adultlike communication—surely an impressive feat to anyone who has tried to learn a second language during adulthood. Yet, children accomplish this with little formal instruction, only their day-to-day interactions with language-using adults and older children.

Children increase their vocabularies dramatically during these years, learning an average of a dozen new words a day. By school age, children know between 8,000 and 14,000 words (Carey, 1977). At the same time, they increase the length and content of their sentences.

Phonological Development

Phonology refers to the sounds of a language. Our unique anatomy permits us to make a wide range of sounds that can be combined into sequences of words. There are age-related changes in the tongue,

mouth, and position of larynx in the throat, and these physical differences mean that the sounds that infants and children are able to produce change over time (Stoel-Gammon & Menn, 1997).

Infants begin cooing and laughing between 2 to 4 months, and these vocalizations increase until 9 to 12 months, when they decline and one-word utterances begin (see Table 9-1). Sounds made during babbling vary widely, including both sounds heard in the baby's native language and sounds that are not. Babbling sounds change with age. All this caused some early theorists to conclude from diary studies that babbling served as an exotic smorgasbord of universal language sounds from which infants selected those they heard in the language being spoken around them, while gradually eliminating those they didn't hear (Jakobson, 1968). This popular theory is still cited today by some, but research findings have not supported it. Babbling does not contain all the sounds found in human language, only a small subset (Locke, 1983; Oller, 1980). The developmental changes in babbling reflect anatomic changes in the vocal apparatus more than approximations toward the sounds of one's native tongue (Ingram, 1989).

It has been suggested that babbling plays a more important role in language development than just a poor attempt at spoken words (Sachs, 1977). Babbling might serve as a way to relate socially with family members long before the cognitive system is able to appreciate the intricacies of language. In addition, there is evidence that although the *sounds* of babbling don't gradually come to approximate speech, the *intonation* of babbling does. Infants begin to "converse" in many ways that do not involve words, but rather the conventions of speech. They develop the ability to take turns (Snow & Ferguson, 1977), match the speaker's tone of voice, pause between strings of syllables, end phrases with upward or downward inflections (Tonkova-Yompol'skaya, 1969), and match the pitch of adults speaking to them—higher for mother, lower for father (Lieberman, 1967).

Children typically say their first words between 10 and 18 months, and their vocabulary increases,

TABLE 9-1 Developmental Stages of Infants' Babbling

Stage 1: *Reflexive crying and vegetative sounds (0 to 8 weeks)*

Infants in stage 1 cry as a reaction to a distressed state and make various vegetative sounds associated with feeding and breathing, such as burps, coughs, and sneezes. The vocal tract of these young infants closely resembles that of nonhuman primates; their tongue fills their oral cavity and their larynx is high in their neck (which permits them to breath and swallow simultaneously). This leaves little room for making different sounds. As the infant's head and neck grow, a greater variety of sounds become possible.

Stage 2: *Cooing and laughter (8 to 20 weeks)*

Infants at this age begin to make pleasant noises, especially during social interactions. These are mostly vowel sounds such as "oooh" and are termed cooing because they resemble the sounds made by pigeons. A few of the sounds will also contain some consonants such as *g* and *k*. Crying decreases and takes distinct forms that convey meaning to caregivers—discomfort, call, and request. Sustained laughter appears.

Stage 3: *Vocal play (16 to 30 weeks)*

This is a transition between cooing and true babbling. Infants begin to utter single syllables with prolonged vowel or consonant sounds.

Stage 4: *Reduplicated babbling (25 to 50 weeks)*

True babbling sounds appear, such as "bababa" and "nanana." Consonant-vowel patterns are repeated, and playful variations of pitch disappear. This type of vocalization is not just a response to caregiver's social interaction, but often occurs when no one is present. Deaf infants, although going through the first three stages, do not engage in true babbling at this time (Oller & Eilers, 1988).

Stage 5: *Jargon (9 to 18 months)*

Babbling consists of many nonrepeated consonant-vowel patterns. Jargon babbling is strings of sound filled with a variety of intonations and rhythms to sound like meaningful speech. Infants at this stage often sound as if they are carrying on their end of a conversation, with their intonations sometimes sounding as if they reflect questions or explanations, but their "words" are only babble sounds.

SOURCE: Stark, R. (1978). Features of infant sounds: The emergence of cooing. *Journal of Child Language, 5,* 1–12; and Stoel-Gammon, C., & Menn, L. (1997). Phonological development: Learning sounds and sound patterns. In J. Berko Gleason (Ed.), *The development of language* (4th ed.). Boston: Allyn & Bacon.

often quite rapidly, over the next year. Not surprisingly, many of these words are mispronounced, relative to adult speech, but an individual child's errors are often similar among groups of words. Furthermore, these errors in pronunciation seem to drift from one set of sounds to another, with children sometimes producing correct sounds at an early age and drifting to incorrect sounds in later months. For example, one child pronounced "turtle" correctly at 15 months and then as "kurkel" at 18 months (de Villiers & de Villiers, 1979).

Speech perception (as opposed to production) was discussed in Chapter 6. To reiterate briefly here, very young infants can perceive **phonemes,** the basic sound units of language, and they categorize them much as adults do. Young infants can also discriminate between the sounds of many different languages, something that their parents cannot do. Over time, however, infants lose the ability to tell the difference between sounds that are not found in their mother tongue. Thus, infant's auditory systems seem prepared to make sense of human speech, although their audition is modified over childhood as a function of what language sounds they hear.

Morphological Development

Morphology refers to the structure of something—in the case of language, the structure of words. Counter to what you might think, the word is *not* the smallest unit of meaning in a language. In English, for example, we add sounds to words to make them past tense (add an *ed*), to express the present progressive (add *ing*), or to make a word plural (add an *s*), and these word endings are also units of meaning. The smallest unit of meaning in a language is called a **morpheme,** and there are two types. **Free morphemes** can stand alone as words, such as "fire," "run," or "sad." In contrast, **bound morphemes** cannot stand alone but are attached to free morphemes. They convey meaning by changing the free morpheme they are attached to. These include the rules for making nouns plural (add an *s*), for making a verb past tense (add an *ed*), as well as prefixes (*un*likable) and suffixes (like*ness*). The average number of morphemes a child uses in a sentence, or the **mean length of utterance (MLU),** is a good measure of how far a child has developed linguistically. MLU is measured by recording a child's speech over a period of time and computing the average number of morphemes (both free and bound).

Roger Brown (1973) identified many of the morphemes used in children's early language and analyzed the speech of three unacquainted children (Adam, Eve, and Sarah) to determine the order in which these morphemes appear in development. He found 14 morphemes that occurred in almost the same order for the three children in his sample (see Table 9-2). Later research by Jill and Peter de Villiers (1973) extended these findings to 21 other preschoolers and found a high correlation between their sample and Brown's.

As can be seen from Table 9-2, many of the morphemes children learn are word endings. Once children learn these rules, they tend to apply them, even when it is not correct. For example, 2- and 3-year-olds learn that adding *-ed* to a verb makes it past tense and *-s* to a noun makes it plural. Al-

TABLE 9-2   Mean order of acquisition of 14 morphemes for three children

Morpheme	Example	MLU per child		
		Adam	Eve	Sarah
1. Present progressive	sing*ing*, walk*ing*	2.5	2.5	2.5
2. In, on & 3.		2.5	2.5	2.5
4. Plural, regular	apples, shoes	2.5	3.0	2.0
5. Past, irregular	*went, saw*	3.0	4.0	2.5
6. Possessive	Eve's, hers	3.5	2.5	2.5
7. Uncontractable copula	The dog *is* big.	3.0	4.0	3.0
8. Articles	a, the	3.5	4.0	3.0
9. Past, regular	talk*ed*, throw*ed*	4.0	3.0	4.0
10. Third person, regular	he run*s*, she swim*s*	4.0	4.0	3.5
11. Third person, irregular	he *does*, she *has*	3.5	4.0	4.0
12. Uncontractable	I *am* going.	4.0	4.0	4.0
13. Contractable copula	The dog's big.	4.0	4.0	4.0
14. Contractable auxiliary	I'm going.	4.0	4.0	4.0

SOURCE: Brown, R. (1973). *A first language: The early stages*, pp. 271, 274. Cambridge, MA: Harvard University Press. Copyright © 1973 by the President and Fellows of Harvard College. Reprinted by permission

though this may be generally true, there are many irregular verbs and nouns (especially in English), and although words such as *goed* (or *wented*), *drinked, runned, feets* (or *footes*), and *mices* follow the rules, they are incorrect. Children make these kinds of mistakes even when they have previously used the proper irregular word forms (for example, *went, drank, ran, feet,* and *mice*). This phenomenon is referred to as **overregularization** and usually begins around 20 months of age. Children often continue to overregularize words until about their third birthdays, when they are more likely to use the irregular forms of verbs and nouns properly (Marcus, 1995;

This is a wug.

Now there is another one.
There are two of them.
There are two _____.

This is a man who knows how to rick.
He is ricking. He did the same thing
yesterday. What did he do yesterday?
Yesterday he _____.

FIGURE 9-1 Two examples from the "wug" test. SOURCE: Berko, J. (1958). The child's learning of English morphology. *Word, 14,* 150–177.

Marcus et al., 1992). Children have learned a rule for regular words and generalize it to irregular words. Apparently, having a history of being understood is not as potent a motivator for using a certain form of language as is the acquisition of a rule and its generalization to all situations where it might apply. This phenomenon is not limited to children learning English, but has been found in a wide variety of languages, suggesting that children around the world approach the problem of language acquisition in a similar way (Slobin, 1970).

How can you know whether children understand the morphological rules of their language? One technique that has been quite successful is the "wug test" (Berko, 1958, see Figure 9-1). Children are shown a series of unfamiliar objects (for example, "This is a *wug*.") or pictures of people performing unfamiliar actions (for example, "This man knows how to rick.") For the "wug" example, children are then shown two of these creatures and told, "Now there are two of them, There are two _____." If children know the regular rules for making plurals, they will say "wugs." When shown a picture of a man who knows how "to rick," when asked what he did yesterday, children who know the rules will say

that "he ricked," and if they know the rules for the present progressive, they will say that currently "he is ricking" (Marcus et al., 1992).

Syntactic Development

Syntax is the knowledge of sentence structure, or grammatical rules—rules for how words are combined into sentences and how sentences are transformed into other sentences. Competent speakers of a language can use the same set of words to create very different meanings by applying basic grammatical rules. For example, the sentence, "The man drove the car," can be made negative ("The man didn't drive the car"), transformed to pose a question ("Did the man drive the car?"), or expressed in the passive voice ("The car was driven by the man"). If you followed these simple transformations of these English sentences, it means that you know the underlying structure, or syntax, of English. You might not be able to pass a freshman test of English grammar, but you implicitly know the rules. These rules might not be part of your explicit (declarative) knowledge. Few of us can actually state the rules used for transforming an active declarative sentence into a question or to the passive voice, but nonetheless, we are all linguistic experts when it comes to actual performance. Our syntactic expertise is so good that we can even recognize grammatical sentences that contain nonsense words. For example, the sentence "The golup was pudaded under his limnex" is meaningless because "golup," "pudaded," and "limnex" are all meaningless. But because you are an expert at English syntax, you know that the subject of the sentence is "golup" (and that it is animate and masculine), that "pudaded" is a verb, specifically an action that was done to the "golup," and a "limnex" is something (a noun) possessed by the "golup," possibly a body part. Not bad for nonsense.

The question central to language acquisition has been the acquisition of syntax. How is it that children make sense of the jumble of sounds that surround them to eventually discover the underlying rules of language? Although each of the world's 4,000 plus languages might have some unique features to them, they all also have some things in common with one another. That is, they all posses, at some "deep level" some common aspects of syntax (see Maratsos, 1998; Pinker, 1994). I will discuss some of these seemingly universal aspects of syntax later in this chapter.

One way of assessing syntactic development is to look at common grammatical forms and see how children of different ages use them. I will examine briefly young children's development of negatives, questions, passive sentences, and relating events in sentences.

Negatives

Early in the preschool years, children learn the power of negatives. In fact, many problems during the so-called "terrible twos" spring from children's new knowledge that they can have thoughts and wishes that don't necessarily reflect those of their parents, and that they can express them by using negatives. Early use of negatives involve tacking "n" words onto positive sentences, as in "No drink milk" or "Not bath, Mommy." They sometimes add the negative to the end of a sentence, as in "Drink milk no" (Bellugi, 1967).

Following this stage, the negative term is moved inside the sentence next to the main verb, for example, "I no do it" or "She no go." Eventually, children learn to use auxiliaries much as adults do and as reflected in sentences such as, "I don't want to do it," and "She can't have it." These later, more sophisticated negatives are also associated with longer sentences.

Questions

Questions develop from adding a raised intonation at the end of declarative sentences, such as "Aaron go outside, Mommy?" to more adultlike forms such as "Can I go outside, Mommy?" Sometime during the third year, the "wh" questions begin: "Where Daddy?" "What's this?" and the all-too-common, "Why?" (Brown, 1968).

More significant to developmentalists is the child's growing ability to answer "wh" questions. Different "wh" words refer to different parts of speech—*who, what,* and *where* refer to people, objects, and locations and are easily answered by young toddlers. For example, "Where's Mommy?" requires a simple response of "Outside" or "In the kitchen." In contrast, *when, which, how,* and *why,* require more difficult concepts and greater language ability. For example, asking a toddler "When did Daddy go to work?" or "Why did you leave the door open?" could result in great frustration for both adult and child (de Villiers & de Villiers, 1978).

Passive Sentences

Late in the preschool years, around age 5 or 6, children learn about passive sentences. With active sentences, the word order tells the story: "John hit the ball." Passive sentences take away that cue—"The ball was hit by John"—and young preschoolers get confused (Goodz, 1982). Interestingly, children first learn to interpret passive sentences when the verb refers to some observable event, such as "The horse was kicked by the cow." Later they learn passive sentences with less observable verbs, such as "Tommy was remembered by the teacher."

Relating Events in Sentences

Around the age of 3, children can relate two ideas by connecting them with *and*. They no longer have to string together short phrases such as "I went outside. I played on the swing." Now they can say, "I went outside and played on the swing." Later they can use other conjunctions such as *but, because,* and *while,* which gives them new ways to express more complex relationships between ideas than just tacking them together with "and" (de Villiers & de Villiers, 1978). There is quite a different meaning to "Mommy got mad and Daddy was late" and "Mommy got mad because Daddy was late."

Syntactic development does not stop at age 5, of course, but the differences between the grammar used by 6- and 7-year-olds and adults are subtle and minor. For instance, school-age children still must master subject-verb agreement (for example, "They were going" instead of "They was going") and the use of personal pronouns (for example, "He and she went" instead of "Him and her went"). But in general, the basic grammatical structure of school-age children's sentences varies little from that of adults.

How do children master this seemingly overly complicated task? The syntax of a language seems far more complex than young children's meager cognitive skills can handle. Yet, in the course of their first five years, most children become linguistic experts in their mother tongue. On top of all this, children learn language despite the fact that the speech that they hear is imperfect, or "degenerate," filled with errors, incomplete sentences, and mumbled words. Somehow, children take the imperfect language that surrounds them and weave a theory of language (that is, syntax) that corresponds to that which their parents speak. This, among other evidence, has caused many to propose that the learning of syntax has a strongly innate basis to it (see later section on Nativist Theories).

Semantic Development

Semantics refers to meaning, specifically the meaning of language terms. "Meaning" here, however, refers to more than just a simple definition. Words refer to concepts or objects, but are also related to other concepts or objects. For example, children must learn not only that "dog" refers to a four-legged family pet called Spot, but to other perceptually similar creatures, who themselves are members of the larger group of "mammals" and "animals." They must also learn that the word "dog" does not refer to horses, goats, or pigs, and that it might be related to other objects such as cats and fire hydrants, although not in the same way it is related to animals.

The Word Spurt

Perhaps the simplest indication of children's semantic development is the number of words they know. Children speak their first words at about 10 to 12 months of age and learn new words at a rate of about 8 to 11 per month. However, at about 18 months of age, or when children have about 50 words in their active vocabulary, the rate at which children learn new words increases substantially, to between 22 and 37 words per month (Benedict, 1979). This has been termed the **word spurt.** Most of the words children learn during this time are nouns, often labels for objects. (This is the time when children frequently ask "What's that?," as they point to every new object they see.) Although there has been some debate about whether all children display this word spurt (Goldfield & Reznick, 1990), the majority of children observed seemed to display such a spurt, although the age at which they show a spurt varies considerably (Mervis & Bertrand, 1994). Recent research indicates that infants in their second year of life spontaneously look at objects for familiar words. This ability increases in efficiency between 15- and 24-months of age, and the oldest children are about as fast as adults at doing this (Fernald et al., 1998). In other words, children in the latter part of their second year are getting faster at understanding the words they hear. Other research has shown that even children 12 to 17 months old are learning new words at a rapid rate, but for their *receptive* vocabulary (words they can recognize) rather than for their *productive* vocabularies (Schafer & Plunkett, 1998). This all indicates that toddlers' word spurt doesn't appear out of nowhere, but has its beginnings in pre-speaking processing.

What accounts for children's rapid acquisition of words, specifically nouns, during this time? Some have speculated that children have a set of specific language-processing constraints that kick in at this time to make word learning easy (Carey, 1978; Mervis & Bertrand, 1994). Carey (1978) labeled the process underlying the word spurt as **fast mapping.** Fast mapping refers to the ability to learn new words based on very little input (that is, few opportunities to learn the words), although children's understanding of words acquired through fast mapping are usually fragmented and incomplete. An experiment demonstrating fast mapping in children was conducted by Carolyn Mervis and Jacquelyn Bertrand (1994). In their study, children between the ages of 16 and 20 months were shown a set of objects, one of which was unfamiliar to them (for example, a garlic press). They were asked to pick out the items, one at a time, and were given a nonsense word for the unfamiliar item (for example, "May I have the dax?"). Only some of the children were able to learn new words for these unfamiliar items after only a few exposures (the "fast mappers"). These children were found to have larger vocabularies than the children who did not learn words for these novel items. This latter group of children was seen several months later, after they had gone through their word spurt, and now they, too, showed an ability to "fast map." These results indicate that the word spurt is associated with a special processing ability, reflected by fast mapping, in which children map novel words to novel objects for which they do not yet have a name.

Overextensions and Underextensions

Often, the errors children make in using words provides us with a good indication of their level of semantic development. Researchers who have analyzed these early errors find that one common pattern is to use **overextension**s — stretching a familiar word beyond its correct meaning (Thompson & Chapman, 1977). For example, children might use the word *doggie* to describe all four-legged creatures, even Daddy when he is on his hands and knees

(whether barking or not). Many developmental psychologists argue against the concept of error in children's early language use, pointing out that practices such as using overextensions result in having adults provide the correct words and can be very effective learning devices. For example, although children might use the word doggie to label a kitten or a horse, when given a set of pictures and asked to choose which one is a doggie, they usually perform well (Thompson & Chapman, 1977). By overextending the word "doggie," however, they usually get some expansion or clarification from adults (for example, "That's not a doggie, that's a kitty"), thus receiving more information about language than they would have gotten had they remained silent.

At other times, children will make **underextensions**—for example, claiming that only their pet Lucy Starbright is a "cat" and that other felines must go by another name. Underextensions indicate that children's boundary for a category is too restricted. During childhood, children learn to classify words and concepts as adults in their culture do. This process doesn't stop in childhood, however, but continues throughout life. It is likely that none of us has exactly the same meaning for all common concepts used in our native language (Nelson, 1996). That speakers of a language are able to make sense of what others say most of the time, however, suggests that most of us have very similar interpretations for the words we use. Both the number of words we know and our understanding of these words change during development. Children go from three or four words in their vocabularies at age 1 to about 10,000 words by age 6 (Smith, 1926; Carey, 1977). In fact, most changes in language development beyond the age of about 5 are not in syntax or phonology, but in semantics in the form of vocabulary growth. However, just because a child is able to use a word doesn't mean that he or she has the same understanding as an adult, and in the following section, we will look at the development of children's word meanings.

The Development of Word Meanings

The representation of the meanings of words has been referred to as *semantic memory*, the long-term repository of language terms, their definitions, and their interrelations with other entries in memory (see Chapter 5). (However, just how distinct this type of knowledge is from our general repository of world knowledge is currently under debate; see Schwanenflugel, 1991.)

We can think about word meaning in a variety of ways. One way of describing semantic memory is through **feature-list models.** Feature-list models of semantic memory hold that language concepts (or words) can be defined in terms of lists of characteristics or features they possess. Most feature-list theories of adult semantic memory hold that features are differentially weighted, with some being more important for the definition of a word than others (Rosch & Mervis, 1975; Smith, Shoben, & Rips, 1974). Thus, in development, children must learn to use features in the way adults do. Given that young children might emphasize different features of a word or concept than adults do (for example, perceptual, schematic), children must not only acquire new features for words but also reorganize the weights they give to words.

In a study in which children and adults were asked to rate the importance of features for defining a word (for example, how important to the concept *cheese* are the features "made with milk," "melts," "found near mice"), kindergarten and second-grade children made no differentiation among the various features, whereas fourth-grade children and adults did. That is, with age, children learn to give more weight to features that are more centrally associated with a given concept (Schwanenflugel, Guth, & Bjorklund, 1986).

Along these same lines, there is some evidence that preschool and early school-age children give too much emphasis to features that are only *characteristic* of a concept (for example, "tropical" for the concept *island*, or "ugly and mean" for the concept *burglar*) and less emphasis to features that are *defining* for a concept (for example, "surrounded by water" for island, or "steals something" for *burglar*). For instance, 5-year-old children in an experiment by Keil and Batterman (1984) were likely to say that a smelly, mean old man with a gun in his pocket who took one's television set was a robber, even though their parents did not want the set anymore and had

told the man he could have it. However, a friendly, cheerful woman who gave the children a hug was not declared to be a robber, even though she removed their toilet bowl and took it without permission. Other research suggests that it is not so much that children give more emphasis to characteristic than to defining features, but rather they give more weight to the many characteristic features in the description (Schwanenflugel et al., 1986). The more features there are, the more important, taken together, they become.

The Development of Scripts

Most research in semantic development has been concerned with how children define individual items and how those items are combined into language categories. (Research into the development of natural language categories was discussed in Chapter 7.) An alternative view of semantic development has been presented by Katherine Nelson and her colleagues, who have suggested that early language categories are based on functional, or schematic relations among words rather than conceptual, or taxonomic, relations (Nelson, 1996, 1986). More specifically, Nelson has suggested that children's early language categories are schematically organized, in that they are based on relations typifying real-world scenes, stories, and events (for example, what is involved in eating at a restaurant; objects and events dealing with sailing a ship) rather than more abstract conceptual categories (for example, fruits, vegetables, vehicles). Children's representations can be expressed in terms of **scripts** (Schank & Abelson, 1977). Scripts are a form of schematic organization, with real-world events "organized in terms of temporal and causal relations between component acts" (Nelson, 1983, p. 55). For example, a breakfast script might include setting the table, eating breakfast, and washing the dishes.

Nelson and her colleagues have argued that superordinate language categories such as *food, animals,* and *clothes* have their origins in earlier acquired, schematically based scripts (Lucariello, Kyratzis, & Nelson, 1992; Nelson, 1983). Certain items are more likely to be found in specific scripts than other items. So, for instance, a breakfast script is likely to include eating toast, cereal, or pancakes and drinking orange juice, milk, or cocoa. Much less likely to be found in a breakfast script would be French fries, ice cream, beer, or macaroni and cheese. Thus, in a particular script, several different items can be included, each of which would satisfy the conditions of the script. *Slot fillers* are items that could successfully complete the script (for example, juice and cocoa). Nelson has suggested that it is from these **slot-filler categories** that context-free, superordinate categories develop.

This hypothesis was tested in a memory experiment by Lucariello and Nelson (1985). Children's recall of sets of words was compared using lists consisting of items from different superordinate categories (animals, food, clothes) and lists consisting of items from script-derived categories, or slot-filler categories (zoo animals, lunch food, clothes you put on in the morning). Children remembered significantly more items from the slot-filler categories than from the superordinate categories. Based on these and other findings (Lucariello et al., 1992), Lucariello and Nelson asserted that children's early superordinate knowledge might be restricted to slot-filler categories, which have a more cohesive structure than superordinate categories. Lucariello and Nelson proposed that these schematically based groupings serve as the beginning for broader, context-free natural language categories.

Other researchers have failed to find such a difference between script-based, slot-filler categories and superordinate categories in preschool children, proposing, rather, that young children's semantic memories are organized in terms of both schematic and taxonomic relations very early in life (Blewitt & Krackow, 1992; Blewitt & Toppino, 1991). The results of Nelson and Lucariello's (1985) memory study is explained not by young children's bias to encode information in terms of slot-filler categories, but because items in most slot-filler categories are highly typical of their categories and are often highly associated with one another. When typicality and associativity are controlled for, the memory advantage afforded by slot-filler categories disappears (Krackow & Gordon, 1998, but see Lucariello, 1998, for different opinion of these findings). The position that young children's semantic memory is

organized along both schematic and taxonomic relations (and by typicality and associativity) seems to be an eminently reasonable one, given that even toddlers display knowledge of basic-level categories (see Chapter 7). However, as I noted in Chapter 7, young children's knowledge of superordinate categories goes through considerable development and their tendency to use superordinate category knowledge will be limited only to those categories for which they have an elaborated representation (Bjorklund, 1985). Thus, although schematic and superordinate category knowledge surely resides side by side in the minds of young children, much of their thinking, remembering, and reasoning is likely based on the more readily available schematic relationships, rather than on the more slowly developing superordinate category knowledge.

Pragmatics

How we actually use language in a social context, or the ability to use language to get things done in the world, is referred to as **pragmatics.** Pragmatics refers to knowledge about how language can be used and adjusted to fit different circumstances, such as using different tones when speaking to a teacher versus an agemate. Knowing the phonology, morphology, syntax, and semantics of language does one little good in communicating unless one can use language appropriately in a social context.

Children must learn a number of conversational principles to become effective communicators (Grice, 1975). Children must learn that messages need to have the right *quantity* of information, or be at the proper level of description. For example, a mother might request of her son that he "put the plates on the table." Such a message is likely at the proper level of abstraction to be properly understood. It would be unnecessary and inappropriate for the mother to say, "Open the kitchen cupboard door, remove a dish, using two hands, and take it into the dining room, and place it at the head of the table where your father usually sits. Repeat the procedure for the place where I usually sit, where your sister usually sits, and where you usually sit." At the other extreme, an instruction to "prepare the table for dinner" might not have enough information in it, especially if the job of putting out silverware usually fell to the boy's sister. Not surprisingly, children are more likely to provide too little rather than too much information. Good messages should have other characteristics, such as being truthful (except for jokes and sarcasm) and relevant to the present context. Also, speakers need to realize the importance of taking turns. Monologues do not make for good conversation.

Beginning early in life, children learn these various conversation principles. For example, toddlers know to watch their listener for signs that they are being understood (Wilcox & Webster, 1980); they know they must be close to their listener to be heard and that if they are not close to their listener they need to speak louder (Wellman & Lempers, 1977); and they know to clarify their speech when they are being misunderstood (Shwe & Markman, 1997). A responsive listener provides a speaker with nonverbal cues such as nods, gazes, and smiles, and he or she says "yes" and "uh-huh" at appropriate times to make it clear that the message is being understood. These skills increase with age, but even 2-year-olds use many of these tactics when listening to an adult (Miller, Lechner, & Rugs, 1985). Children also learn that, depending on the context, sometimes a question is not really a question. For example, when a father says, "How many times do I have to tell you to leave that alone?" and "Why do you insist on carrying that blanket everywhere?," children learn that the question is a rhetorical one and does not require a serious answer. Children learn from the speaker's tone of voice that these are really statements, because even young preschoolers seldom mistake them for real questions (de Villiers & de Villiers, 1978). And the reverse is also true: sometimes questions can be hidden in statements, such as asking a babysitter for a bedtime extension by stating, "Mommy always lets me watch 'The Simpsons'" (Reeder, 1981).

Speech Registers:
The Case of Black English

One aspect of pragmatics involves using different styles of speech in different situations. For example, children use one style of speech when at home or with their friends and another, more formal style when in school. These different styles are referred to as **speech registers** (Warren & McCloskey, 1997).

When the speech registers, or codes children use at home and the ones they are expected to use in school differ considerably, there is the potential for educational difficulties. Usually, children from middle-class families speak a "standard" version of the language that is similar to the more formal style used in school. In contrast, children from less affluent homes often speak a nonstandard version of the language that is often appreciably different from the one used in school (for example, Baugh, 1983; Bernstein, 1971). In the United States, this distinction between social (or home) language and school language among native speakers is often more obvious for children whose home language is described as **Black English** (or more recently as *Ebonics*).

Black English is familiar to most Americans. Although it is used mostly by African-Americans, not all African-Americans speak it, and many non-African-Americans do, so the term can be somewhat misleading. Black English has some special rules of pronunciation and syntax (see Table 9-3), the most obvious to many speakers of standard English being the use of the verb "to be." Unlike standard English, this verb is often not conjugated (for example, "We be" or "She be" as opposed to "We are" or "She is"), and sometimes is dropped from a sentence entirely. For instance, the verb "to be" can be left out if the sentence refers to a one-time or unusual occurrence of an event, as in the sentence, "He playing tennis" for a person who doesn't usually play tennis. But if the sentence refers to a recurrent event, the verb "to be" is included in the sentence. So for example, "He be playing tennis," describes a person who regularly plays tennis and is playing tennis at this moment (Warren & McCloskey, 1997). Black English is *not* a simplified or inferior linguistic form of standard English. For the most part, the two share common vocabulary and syntax, both are syntactically complex, and are used to express complicated ideas and emotions (Heath, 1989).

Despite the linguistic legitimacy and complexity of Black English, it is not the language of the schools, nor of the mainstream American marketplace. This means that teachers, who usually speak

TABLE 9-3   Sample Differences Between Standard English and Black English

Pronunciation and Word Forms		
Consonant Substitutions	/d/ for initial /th/	"Dey" for "They"
	/f/ or /t/ for final /th/	"toof" for "tooth"
	/v/ for medial /th/	"muvver" for "mother"
Consonant Deletions:	medial /r/	"doing" for "during"
	medial /l/	"hep" for "help"
	final consonants	"doe" for "door"
Syllable Contractions:		"spoze" for "suppose"
Stress on First Syllable in (some) Bisyllabic Words:		"Po'-lice" for "Police"
Hypercorrection:		"Pickted" for "picked"
		"2 childrens" for "2 children"

Sentence Structure	BE	SE
Multiple Negation:	"I ain't done nothing"	"I have not done anything"
Aspect:	"He be crazy"	"He's (usually) crazy"
	"He crazy"	"He's crazy (right now)"

Nonmarking or Nonmatching of Verb with Subject:		
	"She do all the work"	"She does all the work"
	"Two girl wearing hats"	"Two girls wearing hats"
Double Subjects:	"My daddy, he works . . ."	"My daddy works . . ."
Perfective *Done:*	"You done lost your mind"	"You have (already) lost your mind"

SOURCE: Warren, A. R., & McCloskey, L. A. Language in social contexts. In J. Berko Gleason (Ed.), *The development of language* (4th ed.). Copyright © 1997 by Allyn & Bacon. Reprinted by permission.

standard English, will often not understand children who speak Black English, and vice versa. Such children can have a difficult time reading text or comprehending directions expressed in standard English. As a result, they might be unjustly classified as less bright than children who speak standard English. For instance, the language abilities of children who speak Black English are often underestimated when they are tested using standard English (Adler, 1990; Wheldall & Joseph, 1986).

There has been substantial debate about how best to instruct children whose home language is Black English. Should they be taught using Black English, the dialect they know best, or should they be taught using standard English, the dialect, or register, of the marketplace? Most young speakers of Black English do learn some aspects of standard English and use it in school (DeStefano, 1972; Melmed, 1971). For example, in one study (DeStefano, 1972), the classroom speech of 8- to 11-year-old African-American children contained more components of standard English than their speech out of school, indicating that elementary school children are able to switch between social (Black

English) and school (standard English) registers. Yet, many African-American adolescents tend to *increase* their use of Black, compared with standard, English, as use of Black English becomes an important part of their social identity (Delpit, 1990).

The debate about how to educate children whose home language register is different from the language register used by teachers is a controversial one, involving social and political aspects, as well as linguistics and educational ones, and no simple answer can, or will, be offered here. But one important thing to remember is that Black English, or any other regional dialect, is not a linguistically inferior language relative to standard English, just as modern English is not inferior or superior to the Elizabethan English used by Shakespeare. One must also keep in mind that, despite Black English's linguistic equivalency to standard English, it's use can hinder educability and the opportunity to partake fully in the American economy. Black English is more than just a different language register, it is also a different dialect with some different syntactic and phonological rules compared with standard English. One's language also identifies it's user as a member of a social group, and children and adolescents might be reluctant to give up their language style merely for the sake of doing well in school. Ideally, children would master both dialects, just as children might ideally acquire a second language, and have the flexibility to switch between them as the situation demands. In such a situation, different dialects would then truly become different registers, to be used when and where appropriate.

Communicative Competence

Although children may have acquired the basic structure of language and know enough words to make most of their wants and feelings known by age 5 or 6, their ability to communicate effectively continues to increase with age. All types of language knowledge (phonology, morphology, syntax, semantics, and pragmatics) are combined in a package called **communicative competence** (Hymes, 1972). Generally, as children—or, indeed, adults—partic-

ipate in varied context, they become communicatively more competent.

Despite the seeming communicative sophistication of many preschoolers, effective communication between adult and child, or between child and child, is variable. Many messages within the grammatical competence of a child are simply not understood. Also, young children often have difficulty in conveying exactly the right message and are frequently unaware that their message was inadequate. To some extent, their difficulties in communicating effectively can be attributed to other aspects of their cognitive development, in particular to a tendency to assume that other people understand the world exactly as they do.

Communication and Egocentrism

For years, research and theory in communicative development followed the interpretation of Piaget (Flavell et al., 1968; Glucksberg, Krauss, & Weisberg, 1966). Piaget (1955) proposed that young children's speech is *egocentric* and *presocial*. In social situations, young children attempt to communicate with others, but their egocentric view of the world often results in speech that does not get the message across to a listener. This failure often does not bother preschool children, however, because in many cases they are unaware that the message is not being comprehended. Such egocentric speech can be observed in young children in a variety of contexts. Listen to the phone conversation of a 4-year-old. When the voice on the other end of the receiver asked Alese, "What are you wearing today?" Alese responded, "This," while looking down and pointing at her dress. This apparently is not an atypical phone conversation for a preschooler (see Warren & Tate, 1992 for other examples). The conversation of two 5-year-old boys playing together in a sandbox can be interesting. "I drive my truck over here, and then I drive beside your plane and I fill it up with stuff," says one child. In the meantime, the other is saying, "My plane's coming in for a landing. I drop bombs on your truck and crash into it. Boom!" Such a "conversation" would not be taking place if each child were alone. However, what one child says has little to do with the comments of the other. The two boys are talking "with" each other but not necessarily "to" each other. Piaget labeled such egocentric exchanges *collective monologues*.

Metacommunication

Research by Flavell and his associates (Beal & Flavell, 1982; Flavell et al., 1981) indicates that children 5 years of age and younger seem to recognize an inadequate or ambiguous message but seldom act on their uncertainty, behaving as if the message had been understood loud and clear. When kindergarten children were provided with ambiguous instructions for making a block building, for instance, they often looked puzzled and hesitated in selecting the appropriate block. Yet, when their building was completed, these children said that it was just like the model (which it was not) and that the instructions had been adequate for reproducing the model (which they had not). Beal and Flavell (1982) found that children's poor performance on these tasks could not be attributed to memory or attentional failures. Rather, their problems were a result of metacognitive deficits; they had "a poor understanding of message quality and its role in determining the success or failure of a communication" (p. 48).

Another **metacommunication** skill involves children's abilities to monitor their own speech. Are children aware of what they are saying and of the fact that they might not always be providing the listener with adequate information to be properly understood? Again, young children tend to display deficits in this area of metacommunication (for reviews see Shatz, 1983; Whitehurst & Sonnenschein, 1985). Young children's speech includes a greater incidence of omissions and ambiguities and requires greater contextual support to be comprehended than the speech of older children does.

One way of assessing children's self-monitoring abilities is to examine the frequency with which they correct their speech by repeating, by including new information, by telling the listener to forget the last thing that was said until later, and so forth.

Mary Ann Evans (1985) studied such *verbal repairs* in the speech of kindergarten and second-grade children during classroom "show and tell" sessions. Evans reported that the incidence of verbal repairs was significantly greater for the second-grade children than for the kindergartners, occurring for 19% of all the utterances for the older children compared with only 7% for the younger. The following is an example of a story by a second-grade girl that includes several verbal repairs:

> We went to—uh me and Don went to Aunt Judy's. And . . . and uh my brother came down on Fri—Friday night, Uh there was a acc—came on the train, And there was an accident. And they thought uh . . . that uh . . . the—there was an accident with a—a van, And they thought—there was pig's blood in it, And they thought there was somebody hurt. But it was the pig. (p. 370)

Evans proposed that the high incidence of self-repairs for the second-grade children relative to the kindergartners reflected an increased ability by the older children to monitor their speech. Evans suggested that as communication skills increase from this point through childhood, the ability to plan and organize one's thoughts improves, resulting in a reduction of verbal repairs into adolescence (Sabin et al., 1979). Thus, the incidence of verbal repairs is low in young children's speech because of poor self-monitoring skills, increases during middle childhood as children become increasingly aware of the effectiveness of their speech in conveying a message, and then decreases as other skills such as planning improve.

Preschoolers' communication competence. Despite the ample evidence of young children's poor communication skills, preschoolers' language is not as egocentric as Piaget and other early researchers believed. In the study of speech repairs by Evans (1985) just cited, for instance, many 5-year-olds displayed at least limited self-monitoring abilities. Young children's metacommunication skills can be poor in comparison with those of older children, but they are not nonexistent. In fact, several researchers have reported clearly nonegocentric use of language in the communication attempts of young children. Shatz and Gelman (1973) observed the speech of 4-year-old children when they talked to adults, to other 4-year-olds, or to 2-year-olds. They found that these children modified their speech to the 2-year-olds, using different tones of voice and shorter sentences, much as adults do.

Other research has demonstrated that preschool children show greater metacommunicative competence when the messages are embedded in familiar scripts, such as a trip to the grocery store (Furman & Walden, 1990).

Findings such as these, among others (Ackerman, 1993; Warren-Leubecker & Bohannon, 1989), suggest that young children have substantial metacommunication skills. As with many newly acquired skills, however, communication abilities seem to develop first in highly specific, familiar situations and are easily disrupted. With age, children display their communicative skills in increasingly diverse contexts, generalizing what they know to new and unfamiliar settings.

Some Theoretical Perspectives of Language Development

The question of how children learn to speak their mother tongue so readily has fascinated philosophers back at least to the time of the ancient Greeks. Yet, only in the latter half of this century has serious scientific study of language acquisition began. Here, I am referring to theories or perspectives on the acquisition of *syntax*, the underlying structure of language. Although there can still be considerable debate on how children come to learn the meaning of specific words, the most heated and complicated debates have arisen over how children come to learn the grammatical rules (that is, the syntax) of language. I in no way intend to cover in any detail the intricacies of theories of syntax development, but merely to describe some of the major points of the dominant perspectives so that the reader can get a general idea of how children approach the seemingly complicated task of learning to talk (see Berko

Gleason, 1997; Bloom, 1998; Bohannon & Bonvillian, 1997; Maratsos, 1998).

In very general terms, three major types of theories have been postulated to account for language acquisition: behavioral theories, nativist theories, and social interactionist theories. Behavioral theories were popular in the early and middle part of this century and proposed, basically, that children learn language like they learn any other complex behavior, through the principles of classical and operant conditioning (Skinner, 1957). Behaviorists emphasized the role of parents as models of and reinforcers for language. The behaviorists actually paid relatively little attention to children, who for generations had been producing perfectly understandable original sentences and phrases they could not have possibly learned through conditioning and imitation, such as "all-gone sticky" to announce that their hands have been washed.

Many claims of the behaviorists have not stood the test of time. For example, although words can be learned through conditioning principles in the laboratory, there is little evidence that such structured techniques are used by parents at home; yet almost all children are fluent in their native language before they reach school age. Other research has shown that parents seldom comment to children about the grammatical correctness of their spoken messages, only the meaningfulness of them (Brown & Hanlon, 1970), and although new words are obviously learned by imitation, new grammatical forms (such as plurals or the past tense) are typically not imitated until children are able to produce them spontaneously (Bloom, Hood, & Lightbown, 1974). All this makes it very unlikely that a behavioral theory of language development is adequate. Thus, one way in which children apparently do *not* learn the syntax of their mother tongue is through the conventional rules of classical and operant conditioning.

This does not mean that the environment in general and parents specifically do not play a role in children's language acquisition. Children are not born with the knowledge of a specific language, but learn to speak the language that is spoke around them, often *to* them. But traditional behavioral accounts are clearly not adequate. What are the alternatives? Nativist theorists propose that children are biologically prepared to learn language and do so with special, innate learning mechanisms, not through some domain-general set of learning devices as proposed by the behaviorists. Social interactionist theorists blend aspects of the behavioral and nativists perspectives together, granting that humans are specially prepared to acquire language, but that aspects of the environment, especially parents, also might be specially prepared to foster language acquisition, although not to the extent that Skinner and his behaviorist colleagues once believed.

In the following sections, I will outline some of the theory and data associated with nativist and social interactionist theories of language acquisition. This account is admittedly a cursory one, and readers who would like to pursue some of the ideas mentioned in this section, are encouraged to seek out some of the references listed in "Suggested Readings" at the end of the chapter.

Nativist Perspectives on Language Development

Contemporary nativist perspectives on language development can trace their beginnings to the work of Noam Chomsky (1957). Chomsky (1959) reviewed Skinner's (1957) book *Verbal Behavior* in the journal *Language* and wrote, "I can find no support whatsoever for the doctrine . . . that slow and careful shaping of verbal behavior through differential reinforcement is an absolute necessity" (1959, p. 42). Chomsky's ideas were as radical in one direction as Skinner's were in the other. Instead of viewing language as something taught, produced by the child's environment, Chomsky insisted that it is something innate, produced by the child's biology. Chomsky believed that language, as we commonly use the term, is only one part of this process—the **surface structure.** Infants hear this being spoken around them and end up being able to speak it themselves within a few years. However, no simple rules of learning or conditioning account adequately for this acquisition because the language children hear is too complicated and often too ambiguous for them

to discern the rules. Chomsky suggested that another mechanism is necessary to explain why children have the ability to sample the surface structure of the language being spoken around them and then produce it fully and fluently by the age of 3, even creating sentences that they could not have heard before.

Chomsky believed that a second structure of language exists, the **deep structure**—the underlying meaning of language. This is a more gut-level understanding of language, a "species-specific characteristic . . . latent in the nervous system until kindled by actual language use" (Sacks, 1989, p. 81). According to Chomsky, all human languages share this deep structure and it is an innate concept in humans, much like the concepts of time and space.

Because Chomsky believed this deep structure of language is inborn in all humans (a form of representational innateness), his theory is a biological one. He believed that humans possess a mental organ, much like a heart or liver, that is dedicated to language use and is located in the brain. This innate neural device (the **language acquisition device** or **LAD**) imposes order on incoming stimuli. This is not a totally novel concept. As Chomsky points out, a similar function has been found for the visual cortex; it orders incoming visual stimuli into meaningful patterns before passing them on to higher levels of the brain.

Chomsky's ideas about the innateness of language derive from linguistic theory. Other support for the nativism school of thought is less specifically linguistic in nature. For example, Lenneberg (1967) argued that language is a special human ability (that is, not just a result of "learning") that has a strong biological basis. Lenneberg noted several characteristics of language as support for this contention, among them:

1. *Language is species specific.* Humans are the only species to possess it. Apes can be taught simple sign language comparable with that of a 2-year-old child (Savage-Rumbaugh et al., 1993), and other species certainly do communicate complicated ideas (such as bees' ability to communicate the location of pollen-rich flowers), but, at

least as human linguists define it, only humans possess language.

2. *Language is species uniform.* All normal members of the species possess language. Moreover, the complexity of a language is not related to the complexity of a culture's technology. That is, the language of "primitive" people is no more nor no less complicated, on average, than is the language of people from information-age societies (Pinker, 1994).

3. *Language is difficult to retard.* Except for children raised in closets or in other severely deprived situations, nearly all children learn to speak. This is true for many severely retarded children, whose language is often far in excess of their more general intellectual abilities.

4. *Language develops in a regular sequence.* Children around the world acquire language in about the same way at about the same time. This is similar to the universal sequence of motor development.

5. *There are specific anatomical structures for language.* The structure of the mouth and throat are unique to our species and specially suited for the task of speaking. Equally critical, areas in the brain are dedicated to different aspects of language, and damage to specific areas of the brain can result in a very specific type of *aphasia,* or language disability.

6. *There are language disabilities that are genetically based.* Specific language disorders run in families, suggesting that there is a genetic basis for these disorders, with some apparently being controlled by a dominant gene (Gopnik & Crago, 1991).

All this is well and good, but how does this give us a better picture of how children actually acquire language? What it does is place language in the realm of important, species-uniform skills that was likely selected in human evolution for its survival value. But saying that language is based in biology, by itself, doesn't tell us a whole lot. We need to look at more specific theories and research to get a better picture of how it is that children acquire language. I will do this briefly in the next two sections. First, I will look at evidence for universal grammar that all

children begin life with and modify until it resembles the language spoken around them. I will then look at research suggesting that there is a critical period for language — a time when the child is biologically prepared to learn language.

Universal Grammar and Language Development

Following the nativist ideas of Chomsky, most linguistic theorists today believe that children over the world acquire language so easily because they posses at birth a "mental organ," specially designed to perform the job of learning language. In addition to this mental organ (the language acquisition device), infants also have at birth some primitive "knowledge" about the structure, or syntax of language. This is **universal grammar,** which consists of the basic grammatical rules that typify all languages. Having this "theory of syntax" in their heads from the beginning of life, children do not have to learn all the rules of their language. Rather, they have to examine the language that surrounds them, see how it fits with the universal grammar that resides in their brains, and make the appropriate modifications so that their innate theory of syntax comes to match the theory that people around them use.

Children, of course, don't actually "know" any language (universal or otherwise) at birth, but they have a set of *principles* and *parameters* that guide their interpretation of speech. Parameters, as used here, refers to aspects of a grammar that vary across languages. For example, although all languages have subjects, some languages require that proper sentences state the subject (as in the English, "I love you"), whereas in other languages the subject can be expressed as part of the verb, eliminating the necessity of stating the subject (as in the Spanish, "Te amo"). This is a parameter, and children must learn whether their language requires the subject explicitly stated (as in English) or not (as in Spanish). One piece of evidence for universal grammar is that English-speaking children's early sentences often resemble those of languages that don't require an explicit subject. This is reflected in children's statements such as "Helping Mommy" or "make a house" (Bloom, Lightbown, & Hood, 1975).

There are many similarities across languages that argue for a universal grammar. For example, all have extensive vocabularies divided into part-of-speech categories that include nouns and verbs; words are organized into phrases that follow a similar underlying rule system (called the X-bar system); all permit movement of grammatical categories, such as the subject-auxiliary inversion used to form declarative sentences in English into questions (for example, "You are going" transformed to "Are you going?"); and all use word prefixes or suffixes for verbs and nouns (for example, adding the "ed" to make a verb past tense) (Hoff-Ginsburg, 1997; Pinker, 1994). The similar way and rate that children acquire many of the same grammatical forms over the world is further evidence for a universal grammar.

One source of evidence that children will create a grammatical system based on some universal principles, comes from **pidgins** and **creoles** (Bickerton, 1990). When a group of people with a variety of native languages are taken from their homes and transported to a foreign land where they are not given the opportunity to participate in the majority culture or to learn the language of their new homeland, they develop a communication system termed a pidgin. Pidgins combine several languages at a rudimentary level and are used to convey necessary information within the group and between the group and its "hosts." Word order is often highly variable and there is little in the way of a grammatical system. (Bickerton proposed that pidgins might be similar in form to the protolanguage spoken by our ancient ancestors.)

But pidgins can quickly transform into true languages in the hands (or mouths) of children. Bickerton documented (based on historical evidence and his own studies of Hawaii Creole) how the children of pidgin speakers take the remnants of their parents' language and create a fully developed language in only one generation—a language termed a creole. Thus, rather than acquiring language in the typical sense, these children *create* a language. Although there might not be an easy interpretation of this phenomenon, the creation of a creole by chil-dren suggests that children posses an innate grammar and use it to "correct" the fragmented pidgin spoken by their parents and convert it into a true (and new) language.

Is There a Critical Period for Learning Language?

Almost without exception, adults learn things more easily than children do. This is hardly surprising. This truism is apparent in our school system. Children first starting school are not expected to master complicated material. In fact, some schools of thought argue that expecting too much in the way of intellectual mastery for young children is not only foolish but also emotionally harmful (Elkind, 1987). Young children just don't have the mental capacity to acquire and understand information that an older child or adult has.

But there is one major exception to this, and that is language development. Children are better than adults at acquiring both first and second languages. The cognitive system of the child is seemingly not less efficient in any respect than the adult's when it comes to language learning; rather, it is well suited to the demands, making immaturity highly adaptive for the important human ability of acquiring language. This has suggested to many that there is a *critical,* or *sensitive period* for learning language— that children must be exposed to language early in life if they are ever expected to master it.

Eric Lenneberg (1967) was the first vocal proponent of a critical period for language acquisition. Lenneberg proposed that language learning occurs exclusively or primarily in childhood. With age, the nervous system loses its flexibility, so that by puberty, the organization of the brain is fixed, making language learning difficult. In support of Lenneberg's claim, John Locke (1993) states that there are four types of evidence for a sensitive period for language acquisition. First, there are cases of people who were socially deprived or isolated during infancy and early childhood, who typically demonstrate only a tenuous mastery of language (particularly syntax) (Curtiss, 1977).

The second and largest body of evidence for a sensitive period comes from studies involving second-language learning, with eventual proficiency in the foreign tongue being related to the age of first exposure. For example, Johnson and Newport (1989) tested 46 native Chinese or Korean speakers who had emigrated to the United States and learned English as a second language. These people had arrived in the United States at ages ranging from 3 to 39 years and had lived in the United States between 3 and 26 years when they were tested (all were educated adults). Johnson and Newport reported that their subjects' proficiency in English was related to the age at which they arrived in the United States, not to the number of years they had been speaking the language nor to formal instruction. Figure 9-2 graphs average scores on a test of grammatical competency (having people determine whether or not a sentence is properly grammatical or not) as a function of age of arrival in the United States. As can be seen from the figure, people who learned their second language early in childhood showed greater proficiency as adults than did people who learned their second language later in childhood. In fact, people who arrived in the United States between the ages of 3 and 7 years had grammatical proficiency comparable with that of native speakers. Although it might not be surprising that one maintains an accent when the second language is not learned until the teen years, these data demonstrate that the same holds true for syntax.

A third source of evidence for a sensitive period comes from deaf children who are not exposed to any formal language, spoken or signed, until late in childhood or adolescence. For example, Elissa Newport (1990) has performed studies with such a population of deaf people, evaluating their proficiency in American Sign Language as a function of when they were first exposed to it. The logic here is similar to that in the Johnson and Newport study (1989), except in this study, American Sign Language is these people's first language, not their second. Newport reports results similar to those she found for second-language learning: Grammatical proficiency is related to age of first exposure to sign language and not to the number of years one has been using the language.

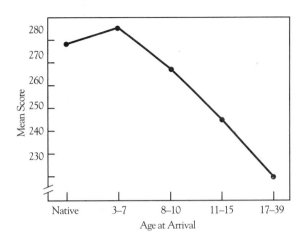

FIGURE 9-2 The relationship between age at arrival in the United States and total number of correct answers on a test of English grammar (data from Johnson & Newport, 1989, as reported in Newport, 1991). SOURCE: "Critical Period Effects in Second Language Learning: The Influence of Maturational State on the Acquisition of English as a Second Language," by J. S. Johnson and E. L. Newport, 1989. *Cognitive Psychology, 21,* 60–99. Copyright © 1989 Academic Press. Reprinted with permission.

The fourth type of evidence concerns recovery of language function after specific brain damage. Some of this research was discussed in Chapter 2. Basically, when the language areas of the left hemisphere are damaged early in life, much plasticity is observed, with other areas of the brain taking over the language function of the destroyed area. This plasticity is reduced with age (see Witelson, 1987).

Some interesting new research indicates differences in the organization of the brains between bilingual people who learned their second language in early childhood versus in adolescence or adulthood (Kim et al., 1997). In this study, brain images were taken of "early" and "late" bilinguals while they silently recited brief descriptions of events from the previous day. For people who had learned their second language in childhood, the same areas of their brains "lit up" regardless of whether they were using their first or second language. In contrast, different parts of the brains of the "late" bilinguals were activated when using their first versus second language.

Both the "early" and "late" bilinguals in this study reported comparable fluency in their second languages, so differences in language ability between these two groups is not likely the cause of this difference. Rather, these results suggest that different parts of the brain, and thus likely different cognitive processes, are involved when a second language is learned early in childhood rather than later.

Although there is still much to be learned about the nature of language acquisition, it is clear that the cognitive system of the young child is especially suited to language learning—both of a first and second language. This ability is gradually lost over childhood, and although adults are able to acquire a second language, they rarely attain the same proficiency that is achieved when language is acquired in childhood.

But why is language learning easier early in life than later? There has been much speculation over the years, with recent data providing researchers with evidence permitting them to go beyond interesting speculation to real (if still preliminary) theories.

The "Less Is More" Hypothesis

One hypothesis concerning why young children are better at language acquisition than older children and adults focuses not so much on their advanced cognitive abilities for processing language as on their cognitive limitations (Newport, 1991). For example, Newport (1991) has proposed that the cognitive limitations of infants and young children simplify the corpus (the body of language they process), thus making it easier to learn the complicated syntactical system of any human language. Newport's **"less is more" hypothesis** is based on the ideas of Turkewitz and Kenny (1982), who proposed that perceptual limitations in infancy are adaptive in that they allow one sensory system to develop (hearing, for example) without having to compete for neural resources with another, usually later-developing system (vision, for example). (Turkewitz and Kenny's ideas of the advantage of perceptual immaturity in infancy, along with some research examples, were discussed in Chapter 2.) The principal

application of these ideas to language acquisition is that children's limited information-processing abilities reduce the complexity of what they must master, resulting in easier initial acquisition. With success and time, maturationally paced abilities gradually increase, as does language learning.

Newport observes that children in early stages of language learning start out slowly, actually more slowly than adults learning a second language do. This is partly because children perceive and store only component parts of complex stimuli. Their speech starts with single morphemes (usually a single syllable), and they gradually increase the syntactic complexity and the number of units they can control. This is true not only in spontaneous speech but also in imitation. The result is that they are able to extract only limited pieces of the speech stream. But, claims Newport, because of their limited cognitive abilities, the simplified language that they deal with makes the job of learning language easier. Adults, in contrast, begin learning a second language faster than children, producing more complex words and sentences. This is because they more readily perceive and remember the whole complex stimulus. But the advantage is short lived. They extract more of the language input but are then faced with a more difficult problem of analyzing everything all at once. As a result, adult learners often fail to analyze aspects of language they have acquired in a rotelike fashion, limiting the eventual proficiency they are apt to attain.

Newport (1991) presents the result of a computer simulation, in which a computer program was given aspects of language to "learn." The "language-learning" mechanism of the computer program was constant, but the size of the input filter was varied, which effectively limited how much the computer program could keep in memory at any one time. This is essentially equivalent to varying the size of a child's short-term store. In the simulation, the input filter became less restricted over repeated trials, similar to the effect that maturation has on the size of the short-term store in developing children (Dempster, 1981). Newport reports that the restricted filter did result in the loss of data for morphology (the smallest units of word meanings, including word endings that denote pluralization and verb tense), making initial learning worse than when a less restricted input filter was used. However, there was greater loss at the whole-word level than at the morphology level (indicating that prefixes and suffixes were often retained). Importantly, the restricted filter resulted in an improvement in the signal-to-noise ratio (that is, the ratio of relevant linguistic information to irrelevant background information). There was also greater loss of data from accidental co-occurrences than from systematic co-occurrences of form and meaning. This means that with the less restricted filter (reflecting a larger short-term store), many language-irrelevant associations were retained, which impeded rather than facilitated language learning. Newport (1991) concluded that "overall, then, a learning mechanism with a restricted input filter more successfully acquired a morphology; the same learning mechanism with a less restricted filter, or with no filter at all, entertains too many alternative analyses and cannot uniquely determine which is the better one" (p. 127). A similar conclusion was reached by Jeffrey Elman (1994), using a very different connectionist type of computer simulation. Elman ued the metaphor "the importance of starting small" to describe his findings and suggested that the critical period for language acquisition involves the developmental delay of certain abilities rather than the loss of some language-specific capabilities.

There seems to be little debate that children are especially prepared to learn language. In other words, most people who have thought deeply about the issue believe that the nativist perspective has something going for it. However, there is considerable debate about the role that the social environment plays in language acquisition in interaction with children's innate disposition. Clearly, language is acquired in the social context of a mother-child relationship, with infants being oriented to people and the sounds that people make. Language is used to soothe and orient infants, serving as an effective communication system long before any words can be understood (Fernald, 1992; Locke, 1993). What role does the social environment play? Is it enough for children just to hear adult language that surrounds them for them to acquire language, or is more social input required (or at least beneficial)? In the following section, I will examine some claims of people who advocate a social-interactionist perspective of language acquisition, believing that social factors cannot be separated from biological ones in explaining the development of this uniquely human ability.

Social-Interactionist Perspectives of Language Development

Most contemporary theorists who adhere to a social-interactionist perspective believe that the nativists have most of the story right. There is an overwhelming (though not unanimous) belief that humans are specially prepared to acquire language, that something akin to universal grammar exists, and that there is a critical period for language. Despite this near consensus, some theorists see the social environment as playing a more important role than some of the more vocal proponents of the nativist camp believe. This interactive perspective is well illustrated in the theorizing of Jerome Bruner (1983). He rejected the idea that language is encountered willy-nilly by the child and that the innate language acquisition device abstracts rules from this shower of spoken language. Instead, Bruner believes that language is carefully presented to children by the people around them. Not only is the content selected for the child's current abilities, but the presentation is executed to provide the best possible chance of learning.

In the following section, I will review research on the role of child-directed speech and how the way adults talk to infants and young children might contribute to language acquisition. I will then examine one specific theory of neurolinguistic development that takes an explicitly social-interactionist perspective.

Child-Directed Speech

Anyone who has listened to adults, especially mothers, talking to babies, knows that it is a special type of speech that is *not* used when talking to other adults. In everyday parlance, this is termed "baby talk" ("Hi big girl! How is my baby today? Huh? How is Mama's little angel? Did we just go for a walk? Did you and mommy just walk around the block? We did, didn't we? Did you see the kitty? Huh? Did we see the little kitty?").

The speech that mothers, and others, use with infants and young children is special. It is simpler and more redundant than the speech they use with their older children. Such speech was originally termed *motherese* (Snow, 1972), and subsequent research has revealed additional properties, showing that mothers typically talk to their young children using high-pitched tones, exaggerated modulations, simplified forms of adult words, many questions, and many repetitions (see Hoff-Ginsburg, 1997). When "motherese" was found to be used by fathers and 4-year-old children (Sachs & Devin, 1976), the new term became **child-directed speech,** or **infant-directed speech** when directed specifically to infants, and it was suggested that this special form of speech is connected with some innate language-transmittal mechanism found in adults—the counterpart to Chomsky's language acquisition device. (Bruner [1983] suggested that adults have a device in their brains that responds to infants and young children by automatically altering speech to a more understandable form, and he even suggested an appropriate name, **language acquisition support system** or **LASS.**)

Prosodic features of child-directed speech. Beginning in the late 1970s and early 1980s, a new phase of research focused on the prosodic features of speech, or **prosody,** the ups and downs of the tones and the rhythms of the sounds we make. Instead of counting repetitions or comparing words used in infant-directed (I-D) speech versus adult-directed (A-D) speech, researchers used instruments to measure the acoustic features of different types of speech. I-D speech, compared with A-D speech, was found to have a higher mean frequency, a wider range of frequencies, and a greater incidence of rising frequency contours. In other words, when mothers talk to infants, they use higher tones of voice in general, more high and low tones, and more tones that move from low to high (Fernald & Mazzie, 1991).

Using this acoustic comparison method, mothers in other cultures were studied as they interacted with their infants, and these same general prosodic features were found for Latvian, Comanche, Mandarin Chinese, Japanese, Sinhala, Russian, and Swedish mothers (see Fernald, 1992; Fisher & Tokura, 1996; Kuhl et al., 1997). In a study of French, Italian, German, Japanese, British, and American families, Anne Fernald and her colleagues (1989) demonstrated typical I-D speech versus A-D speech differences for both mothers and fathers. Not all cultures use the same exaggerated style of I-D speech as American mothers (and fathers) frequently do, but as the list of cultures mentioned suggests, some aspects of infant-directed speech might be universal (Fernald, 1992; Kuhl et al., 1997).

Why do people use I-D speech when talking to babies? One reason seems to be because this is the way babies "want" to be spoken to. They are more attentive to adults who speak to them using I-D rather than to A-D speech. For example, 4-month-old infants who have been conditioned to turn their heads to one side or the other to select which of two tapes they will listen to, will turn their heads to hear I-D speech over A-D speech. There is even evidence that 1-month-old infants show a preference for I-D speech (Cooper & Aslin, 1990, 1994).

One interesting study examined mothers of deaf infants signing to their babies and to their deaf friends (Masataka, 1996). Similar to the findings for spoken language, the mothers signed more slowly, used more repetitions, and greater exaggerations of movements to their deaf infants than to their deaf adult friends. Moreover, like hearing babies, the deaf infants paid greater attention and made more affective responses to infant-directed signing than to adult-directed signing. In a follow-up study, Nobuo Masataka (1998) demonstrated that *hearing* babies, who had never been exposed to sign language, were also more responsive to the greater exaggerations found in infant-directed sign language than to adult-directed sign language, suggesting that this effect is not modality specific.

Other studies have shown that when I-D speech styles are used, young infants can discriminate between words that have very slight differences in sounds (Moore, Spence, & Katz, 1997). For example, research has shown that 1- to 4-month-old infants can discriminate among three-syllable sequences (such as "mar*ana*" versus "ma*lana*") if the words are spoken using the exaggerated style of I-D speech (Karzon, 1985). For instance, in the examples above, the middle syllables would be accented ("ma-**ra**-na" and "ma-**la**-na") in I-D speech, which would not be the case in normal adult-to-adult speech (see Trehub, Trainor, & Unyk, 1993). Babies this age cannot tell the difference between the two words when they are spoken in normal A-D speech. In related work by Stern and his colleagues (Stern, Spieker, & MacKain, 1982), mothers of 2-, 4-, and 6-month-old babies were found to use rising intonations when they wished to get a baby's attention and down-up-down phrasing (as in the "malana" example above) when wishing to maintain an infant's attention. The results of these and other studies suggest that babies are born ready to process certain types of language, and it is no coincidence that the singsongy type of speech babies best understand is the same kind of speech that adults and children seem compelled to produce in the presence of an infant.

The role of child-directed speech.   Earlier theories about child-directed speech centered on mothers' roles as teachers of language for their children (Hoff-Ginsburg, 1985; Moerk, 1986). Individual differences in how mothers converse with their 1- and 2-year-old children have been found to be related to early aspects of language development (see Hoff-Ginsberg, in press). For example, the use of *expansions* (expanding a statement that a child made), repetitions, and questions, all frequent in child-directed speech, has been shown to be related to children's language development. The relation between mothers' speech and children's language development is not straightforward, however, with different aspects of mothers' speech influencing different aspects of their children's language development at different times. Nevertheless, it seems clear that mothers are indeed "teaching" their children something important about the syntactic properties of language, even if that "something" cannot be easily specified.

Infant-directed speech seems also to serve other types of development at much earlier ages. A study by Daniel Stern and his colleagues (1983) showed that the prosodic features of mothers' I-D speech peak when the infant is 4 months old, almost half a year before the infant shows any sign of understanding specific words. This has led to the alternative interpretation that I-D speech plays a role not only in syntactic development but also in the emotional relationship between infant and caregiver. Fernald (1992) has suggested that by using specific tones, the mother regulates the infant's emotions, behavior, and attention and also conveys her own emotional state to her infant. Fernald divides I-D speech into four different acoustical patterns, all of which are used by British, American, German, French, and Italian mothers when talking to their 12-month-old infants. These patterns are used to convey the mother's approval, express prohibition, ask for attention, and provide comfort to the infant. Such nonverbal communication is important in developing secure mother-infant attachment, and, according to Locke (1994), "Spoken language piggybacks on this open channel, taking advantage of mother-infant attachment by embedding new information in the same stream of cues" (p. 441). Although a secure attachment is not necessary for children to develop language, there is evidence that maltreated toddlers have significant delays in language acquisition (Cicchetti, 1989).

In the previous section examining the critical period for language acquisition, the importance of "starting small" was emphasized. Children's limited information processing abilities might limit the amount of information they can process, which might make the task of acquiring language easier. But if young children acquire language best by "starting small," this is apparently accomplished not only because of their limited cognitive abilities but also with the help of adults (Bjorklund & Schwartz, 1996). Adults around the world talk to children using highly repetitive and greatly simplified child-directed speech. As children's language competencies increase, so too does the complexity of language addressed to them. Thus, in the early phases of language acquisition, children receive a highly simplified language corpus. According to

David Bjorklund and Richard Schwartz (1996), "Such modified language, accompanied with young children's limited information-processing abilities, results in children receiving a much reduced body of linguistic evidence from which to extract the phonological, syntactic, and semantic rules of their mother tongue" (p. 26).

The significance of using simplified child-directed speech for language acquisition is illustrated by anecdotal evidence that simply being exposed to adult-directed speech is not sufficient to learn a first or second language. For example, a hearing child of deaf parents, who was confined to his home because of poor health, learned sign language from his parents but could neither speak nor understand spoken English by the age of 3, despite frequently watching television (Moskowitz, 1978). In another example, Dutch children who regularly watched (and frequently preferred) German television, often failed to understand the programs and did not achieve appreciable control of German (reported in Snow et al., 1976). Not only does watching and listening to television provide no opportunity for social (and language) give and take, but the language heard on television consists almost totally of adult-directed speech and not the modified (and simplified) child-directed speech that children typically receive from adults.

Research examining the role that child-directed speech plays in development makes it clear that although infants might be biologically prepared to acquire their mother tongue, language development is embedded within the social-emotional context of the family. Language development cannot be properly understood unless it is viewed as part of the broader human developmental perspective (see Locke, 1993).

Locke's Theory of Neurolinguistic Development

John Locke (1997) has formulated a neurolinguistic theory of language acquisition that emphasizes the interplay of biologically paced and experiential factors. Locke has proposed that there are four neurologically based phases of language acquisition, with the initial phase beginning before birth and the final phase beginning at about 3 years of age and extending into the years beyond. These phases overlap one another to a significant degree (that is, they are not stages, with one stage replacing the preceding one), and children are receptive to different types of linguistic information and perform different types of linguistic operations at different phases (see Table 9-4).

Locke calls the first phase *vocal learning*. While still in utero, infants are aware of and react to the prosody (that is, the rhythmic characteristics) of their mothers' voices. DeCasper, Spence, and their colleagues (DeCasper & Spence, 1986; Spence & Freeman, 1996) have demonstrated that infants are "learning" something about the language that their mothers speak during the last several weeks (or more) before birth. Moreover, infants show a preference (apparently present at birth; Mehler et al., 1988) for listening to their mother tongue over foreign languages and are responsive to the emotional tone of language (see Fernald, 1992; Locke, 1993). During this phase, infants are predisposed by their biology to orient to people who are talking and to respond to such behavior. Thus, this early phase is actually one of social cognition that sets the stage for later language development.

While the child is still learning about prosody, the second phase, which Locke refers to as *utterance acquisition*, begins at 5 to 7 months of age. Included during this phase are not only children's first words but also short phrases that sometimes sound like simple sentences ("Time to go to bed"). Although the young child using such phrases sound grammatically sophisticated, Locke considers the phrases to be *formulaic*, in that they were acquired by rote memorization and do not involve any grammatical analysis. During this phase, children are acquiring words and simple phrases from listening to others. This represents the acquisitive, or storage, phase of language development. Children have a set of "starter" utterances that they can use in restricted contexts, effectively increasing the quality (if not quantity) of their interactions with adults.

Beginning about 20 months is the *analysis and computation* (or *utterance analysis*) phase. This is the

TABLE 9-4 Phases and Processing Systems, and Neural Cognitive Mechanisms Associated with the Development of Linguistic Capacity, along with the corresponding Areas of Language in Locke's Neurolinguistic Theory

Age of onset	Developmental phases and systems	Neurocognitive mechanisms	Linguistic domains
Prenatal	Vocal learning	Specialization in social cognition	Prosody and sound segments
5–7 months	Utterance acquisition	Specialization in social cognition	Stereotyped utterances
20–37 months	Analysis and computation	Grammatical analysis mechanism	Morphology Syntax Phonology
3+ years	Integration and elaboration	Social cognition and grammatical analysis	Expanded lexicon, automatized operations

SOURCE: Locke, J. L. (1997). A theory of neurolinguistic development. *Brain and Language, 58*, p. 268.

first grammatical phase, in that an internal (that is, neurologically based) system acts on the language information stored during phase 2 and imposes some (syntactic) structure on it. Although the mechanisms involved in this third phase are seemingly innate (akin to the mechanisms of Chomsky's language acquisition device), they can only operate on information already in long-term memory. Thus, if for some reason a child has not acquired a sufficient body of language utterances, there will be nothing to analyze. According to Locke (1997), "The structure analysis system locates recurring elements within and across utterances, and thereby learns the rules by which utterances are to be synthesized and parsed" (p. 273). Perhaps the clearest evidence of this phase is found in the overregularization of irregular verbs and noun plurals, discussed earlier in this chapter (for example, "runned," "goed," "mouses").

Locke proposes that it is the rapidly expanding lexicon, acquired during phase 2, that prompts the grammatical processes during this third phase to come into operation. Evidence for this comes from research demonstrating a positive relationship between total vocabulary and grammatical sophistication in a group of 20-month-old toddlers (Bates, Bretherton, & Snyder, 1988; see discussion of the

relation between vocabulary growth and syntactic complexity below). Not surprisingly, this reflects a bidirectional relationship between structure and function, with what one knows influencing how (and perhaps whether) one processes information.

Locke refers to the final phase as *integration and elaboration*, beginning about 3 years of age. Now, as a result of the child's acquiring some basic grammatical rules, new information can be readily organized, making it easier to acquire new words (thus effectively extending the efficiency of utterance acquisition). This is similar to the facilitative effects that an elaborated knowledge base has on subsequent learning and memory, discussed in Chapter 8. Because children now have rules for classifying language terms and forms, new information can be readily acquired, resulting in the creation of larger and larger vocabularies.

But how does Locke's theory help explain the fact that young children are better at learning language than older children and adults are? Figure 9-3 shows age-related changes in the efficiency of utterance acquisition (phase 2) and utterance analysis (phase 3). The shaded area in the figure reflects a critical period in which a certain level of utterances have to be acquired for the analysis and computation mechanisms to work efficiently.

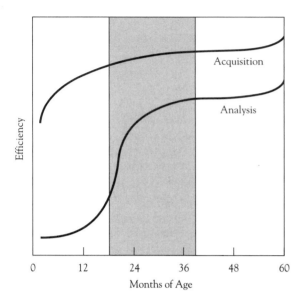

FIGURE 9-3   Age changes in the acquisition and analysis phases in Locke's neurolinguistic theory. The shaded area is a critical period in which utterance-acquisition must reach a certain level of efficiency in order to fully activate and stabilize an utterance-analytic mechanism that is intrinsically "ready" to respond to experience. SOURCE: Locke, J. L. (1997). A theory of neurolinguistic development. *Brain and Language, 58,* 280.

According to Locke, if children have not acquired a sufficiently large body of language utterances by the time the analysis-and-computation phase kicks in, language learning will be hampered. The efficiency of utterance acquisition is in high gear by 12 months and continues to be high through the preschool years. In contrast, the efficiency of utterance analysis begins low, and begins to peak at about 20 months, only after a high level of acquisition efficiency is attained (that is, after children have acquired a relatively large number of words). This figure shows what is proposed to happen in normal development. The two systems (utterance acquisition and utterance analysis) are functioning at high levels of efficiency together for nearly a two-year period. This results in the acquisition of basic grammatical forms, which serve as the foundation

for the integration-and-elaboration phase, which leads to mature language use.

But what happens if a child is not exposed to a sufficiently large body of language utterances or if the utterance acquisition system is not operating at peak efficiency early in development? This alternative is shown in Figure 9-4. Now, when the utterance analysis system is ready to kick in, there is little in the way of stored information to operate on. As a result, little in the way of analysis and computation is done during this critical period, and efficient analysis actually decreases following this critical period of language development (reflected by the shaded area in Figure 9-4). According to Locke (1997), "the critical phase for grammatical analysis, timed by unidentified endogenous factors, expires soon. When the lexically delayed [children] finally have enough words, neurodevelopmental conditions no longer favor instatement of grammatical capability. A child who has not realized a sizable lexical increase by about 24 months is therefore at developmental risk, for his analytic-computational capability may not turn all the way on" (p. 288).

By extending the logic of Locke's model, one can see why people who are not exposed to a language until later in life are apt to have difficulty in acquiring the syntax (Curtiss, 1977). Their utterance analysis system is no longer functioning at peak efficiency. Thus, although individual vocabulary items can still be acquired, using these utterances as a basis for grammar is less easily done, because the period of highest efficiency for the utterance analysis system has long since passed.

Locke provides evidence from a variety of sources, including language-delayed children, cases of brain damage, neurological organization for language, and cross-species comparisons, to support his theory. He emphasizes that early language development is supported by biologically based dispositions in infants to orient to language and the people who speak it. He is explicit that language development involves the bidirectional relation between biologically paced changes and the social environment: "All phases in the induction of linguistic capacity are affected by interactions between neuromaturational events and social stimulation" (1997, p. 279).

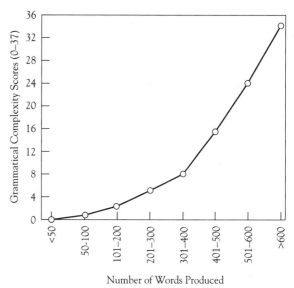

FIGURE 9-4 Changes in the acquisition and analysis for the lexically-delayed child. Because the utterance-acquisition phase is behind schedule, by the time there are enough utterances to enable the utterance-analysis mechanisms to produce grammar, the optimal time has passed. SOURCE: Locke, J. L. (1997). A theory of neurolinguistic development. *Brain and Language, 58,* 289.

FIGURE 9-5 Grammatical complexity increases as a function of the size of children's vocabularies. SOURCE: Bates, E. (1999). On the nature of language. In R. Levi-Montalcini, D. Baltimore, R. Dulbecco. & F. Jacob (Series Ed.) & E. Bizzi, P. Calissano, & V. Volterra (Vol. Ed.), *Frontiere della biologia [Frontiers of biology], The brain of homo sapiens.* Rome: Giovanni Trecanni.

He recognizes that language is an inherently social phenomenon and that its beginnings can be found as much in social and emotional responding as in perceptual and cognitive abilities.

The Relation Between Lexical and Syntactic Development: Is a Grammar Module Necessary?

Locke's theory addresses the relation between lexical and syntactic development, proposing that a certain level of utterance acquisition (that is, a certain vocabulary size) needs to be achieved before utterance analysis can begin. In other words, children have to know a certain number of words before their "grammar module" kicks in.

Related to Locke's hypothesis is the observation of the close relation of vocabulary size and gram-matical complexity during the preschool years (Bates, 1999; Bates & Goodman, 1997), which is illustrated in Figure 9-5 (from Bates, 1999). Elizabeth Bates and her colleagues have demonstrated this relation in longitudinal and cross-sectional studies, in late talkers and early talkers, in children with Down Syndrome and Williams Syndrome, in children with language disorders, in people with brain damage, and for a variety of languages (see Bates, 1999; Bates & Goodman, 1997). The relation between vocabulary size and syntactic complexity is stronger than the relation between age and syntactic complexity, making it unlikely that age alone is the common underlying factor (see also Robinson & Mervis, 1998).

Do these data support Locke's hypothesis? Yes, in a general way I believe they do, but they also suggest that the connection between vocabulary size and syntactic complexity might be more direct than what Locke proposes. According to Locke, children must attain a certain number of lexical items before their utterance-analysis module can function properly. Thus, the theory is still based on the idea of children having a domain-specific grammatical organ (something like Chomsky's language-acquisition device), consistent with nativists' viewpoints. Bates and her colleagues argue that the strong relation between vocabulary and syntactic development argues against the need for a "grammar module" (that is, against representational innateness). Rather, as vocabulary increases, grammar emerges from a need to organize the growing corpus. According to Bates and her colleagues, words and grammar are two sides of the same coin, developing together, with changes in one affecting changes in the other. It is not necessary to hypothesize separate innate modules, á la Chomsky, to account for the data. Rather, they propose a connectionist approach (see Chapter 5), in which grammar emerges out the acquisition and analysis of individual words (Elman et al., 1996). Such an approach still hypothesizes that there are innate constraints that influence how language items are processed (architectural constraints), but it avoids the idea of a specific grammar module that has a ready-made theory of syntax that children will discover just by being exposed to language. Instead, through adjustments that children make as they acquire words (changing weights in the connectionist model, see Chapter 5), grammar emerges without the need of specific, innate structures. I will not attempt to elaborate on this model here, but mention it only to demonstrate that there are other reasonable alternatives to the nativist view of language acquisition, in which there are innate constraints on how language is processed (architectural contraints) without having to resort to the idea of innate modules (representational constraints).

But is there really that much of a difference between the approach that Bates and her colleagues are proposing and that of, say John Locke? At one level, no, but at another level, yes. Both models view language as different from other forms of cognition and suggest that children are prepared to learn language—that is, they are born with some language-specific constraints. However, nativist perspectives propose that different aspects of language

development are relatively independent. Even Locke, who proposes that a certain level of lexical development is necessary for the grammar module to work properly, sees children as being born with a domain-specific syntactic device. The perspective taken by Bates and her colleagues differs in that they see language acquisition as emerging gradually without the need of a highly specific grammar module but through the interaction between a brain with innate processing constraints and a language-speaking world.

The difference is how one defines innateness (Elman et al., 1996; see Chapter 1). The perspective of the nativists is consistent with the view that infants are born with innate knowledge in some domains, such as object knowledge (Spelke & Newport, 1998), and that language acquisition is truly special, needing special innate mechanisms to explain its development. The view of Bates and her colleagues is more consistent with the developmental-systems perspective, introduced in the first two chapters of this book, and with the viewpoint that much of the "symbolic" behavior seen in infancy can be best explained in terms of perceptual processing (see Chapter 7, Bogartz, Shinskey, & Speaker, 1997). Which perspective is right, or at least closer to the truth? I have my biases, but don't claim to have *the* answer; I do know that there will be some lively debates on this issue, at least in some academic circles, during the next decade.

Gender Differences in Language Acquisition

There is a persistent belief that females are better than males at language and language-related skills. For example, girls and women are believed to be better readers than boys and men, with this difference appearing early and lasting into adulthood. Research pertinent to this question will be examined in Chapter 12. Here, I will review research concerning possible gender differences in the acquisition of a first language.

Gender differences in the rate of language acquisition have been found (Bornstein & Haynes, 1998; Clarke-Stewart, 1973), although other studies have failed to observe any significant gender differences (McCarthy, 1954), and some find a difference favoring young girls for spontaneous speech but not on standardized tests (Morisset, Barnard, & Booth, 1995). In related research, Michael Lewis and his colleagues reported greater vocalization by infant girls than by boys. For example, 3-month-old girls were found to vocalize more than boys in response to their mother's invitation to "talk" (Lewis & Freedle, 1973), and infant girls between the ages of 3 and 13 months vocalized more to facial stimuli than did boys of the same age (Lewis, 1969). In a meta-analysis summarizing the effects in over 30 studies that looked at differences in how mothers talked with their sons and their daughters, Leaper, Anderson, and Sanders (1998) reported moderate gender differences, with mothers talking more and using more supportive speech with their daughters than with their sons. Other research has shown that mothers talk about different things with their sons versus their daughters. For example, examining the emotion talk of women to their 2-, 3-, and 4-year-old children, mothers were more apt to explain emotions to boys rather than just to label them, but they showed no difference in the use of explanations and labels with their daughters (Cervantes & Callanan, 1998). Of equal interest, even the youngest girls in this study talked about emotions quite frequently and as often as older girls. In contrast, emotion talk was less frequent for the youngest boys and increased with age.

Others have proposed that the gender differences sometimes found in language acquisition are related to cultural factors. For example, there is evidence that in Greece, where boys are valued more than girls, boys rather than girls are more vocally responsive (Roe et al., 1985). Perhaps the gender differences favoring girls found in the United States can be attributed to different ways in which girls and boys are spoken to rather than to endogenous factors. Recall from Chapter 8 on memory development that parents use a more elaborative conversation style with their daughters than with their sons when prompting them to remember past events (Haden & Reese, 1994). Such differences are related to gender differences in event memory (girls' better than boys') and are consistent with the hypothesis provided by Roe et al. that differences in cultural practices are responsible, in part, for gender differences in rate of language acquisition.

However, some gender differences in early language are found that are *not* related to differences in how parents talk to boys and girls. Haden, Haine, and Fivush (1997) reported that girls between 40 and 70 months of age produced longer and more structured narratives than did boys of the same age; however, unlike other aspects of language presented to boys and girls, there were no differences in how parents used narratives to talk about past experiences with their sons and daughters. These results indicate that girls are more advanced in their narrative production than boys and that a simple socialization explanation cannot adequately account for these differences.

As of this writing, the question of gender differences in language acquisition is up in the air. Research suggests that girls might be more vocal than boys early in infancy and that this difference leads to a subsequent advantage in learning a first language. However, other research suggests that whatever small advantage in language acquisition girls do hold is a function of cultural practices, with boys in some cultures displaying the typical "feminine" pattern of faster language acquisition we've come to expect in our culture.

Language and Thought

Although most laypeople would concur that language is not only a system of communication but an important vehicle for thought, most theorists of language would likely disagree. Language is used to *express* thought, both to others and to ourselves, but it is not thought itself (Pinker, 1994). Some developmental psychologists have taken a different perspective. For example, theorists such as Jerome Bruner (1966) argued that the ability to use language as a conceptual tool transforms a child's thinking during early childhood. Moreover, the use of language in social situations facilitates this transformation. Knowledge of the physical world is imbedded in the social world, and language is a universal mechanism for communicating and thus structuring knowledge. Perhaps more to the point, language is used to communicate ideas and thoughts (that is, mental representations) between people, and language structures these mental representations. This perspective is probably best represented by the work of Katherine Nelson (1993, 1996). Along similar lines, the Soviet psychologists Alexander Luria (1961) and Lev Vygotsky (1962) proposed that language directs much of children's intelligent behavior, with the relationship between language and thought changing developmentally.

Nelson's Views of the Role of Language in Cognitive Development

Earlier in this chapter, Katherine Nelson's ideas about how children come to represent events through *scripts* was discussed. In the previous chapter, I reviewed research indicating how parents use language to "teach" their children how to remember, and how such social interactions might be the basis for the beginnings of autobiographical memory. Nelson (1993, 1996) has used these, and other research findings to support her idea of the central role that language plays in early cognitive development.

Her basic claim is that children's early language, and the language spoken to them, organizes their mental world. Language is used not only to communicate but to think. Nelson attributes many of the changes that occur around the age of 4 (theory of mind, for instance) to children's ability to use language both as a system of communication and as a means of representing experience. Nelson does not equate language and thought. Language is a form of mental representation, but not the only one. Her claim is "that it is human language and its potential for different ways of formulating thought that has driven and continues to drive human cognitive development on both the evolutionary and the individual scale" (1996, p. 87).

I will not discuss Nelson's theory in detail here. Many of the basic findings she uses to support her theory have been discussed elsewhere in this and other chapters. What is important about Nelson's work is the demonstration that language *and* thought develop together in a social context and that to ignore the role that language plays in cogni-

tive development, as most contemporary theorists do, is to miss an important part of the picture.

The Self-Regulatory Function of Language

Luria (1961) proposed three stages in children's ability to use language to regulate their behavior. In the first stage, occurring between approximately 18 months and 3 years, the language of others can initiate motor action, but language does not inhibit an ongoing activity. For example, giving a 2-year-old a rubber ball and saying "Squeeze" might result in the child's squeezing the ball, but simple statements such as "Stop" or "That's enough" will not be sufficient to inhibit the motor action. (Exceptions to this would be toddlers' well-learned reactions to parental commands such as "No!" or "Don't touch that!") In the second stage, occurring from approximately 3 to 4.5 years of age, speech has an impulsive role in regulating behavior, in that children respond not to the conceptual message of a language command but to its physical characteristics. A 3-year-old told to press a ball twice in response to a light, for example, will customarily press many times, being unable to inhibit excitation from tactual sources. But if the child is instructed to say "Go! Go!" to a flash of light and to accompany her verbalizations with two presses, she will easily learn the task. Finally, in stage 3, from approximately 4.5 to 5.5 years of age, children are able to use the meaning of speech to regulate their behavior. According to Luria (1961), "The regulatory function is steadily transferred from the impulsive side of speech to the analytic system of elective significative connections which are produced by speech" (p. 92).

Although early attempts to replicate the Soviet work by Western scientists met with mixed results (see Fuson, 1979; Wozniak, 1972), the results of several more recent, well-designed American studies have provided support for Luria's position (Diamond & Taylor, 1996; Saltz, Campbell, & Skotko, 1983). In the study by Eli Saltz and his colleagues (1983), it was hypothesized, following Luria, that young children should have increasing difficulty inhibiting motor action as the intensity of the verbal command increases. The louder the command, the greater the tendency to make impulsive responses.

Preschool children were given a set of positive instructions to follow (for example, "Clap your hands") and a set of negative instructions (for example, "Don't touch your toes"). The instructions were given in one of three different intensities, ranging from soft, which was slightly below normal speaking intensity, to loud, which was a shout. For the younger children (average age 4 years 1 month), the number of impulsive errors (that is, responding when instructed not to respond) increased with the intensity of the command. The reverse was true for older children (average age 5 years 6 months), with the loudest commands producing the fewest impulsive errors. These results are consistent with Luria's position that children under 5 years of age respond to the physical energy of spoken words, with word meaning playing a lesser role in the inhibition of an ongoing activity.

The Development of Inner Speech

Luria's work represents extensions of a theory originally proposed by Vygotsky (1962), who believed that thought and speech have different roots in development, with the two initially being independent; that is, thought is prelinguistic, and speech is preintellectual. In development, however, thought and speech merge, with thought becoming verbal and speech rational. This developmental relationship between language and thought, particularly during the stages where the two cross, has attracted the interest of psychologists.

Vygotsky was particularly interested in the role of **egocentric speech** in affecting children's thought. Egocentric speech, or **private speech,** as it is commonly referred to, can be thought of as speech-for-self. It is overt language that is carried out with apparent satisfaction even though it does not function to communicate. Private speech can be observed both when children are alone and in social settings.

Vygotsky believed that private speech plays a specific role in affecting children's thought and problem solving. Language can serve to guide children's behavior (and thus their thought), but young children cannot yet use language covertly, "in their heads." To benefit from the self-regulatory function

of language, young children must essentially talk to themselves, using their speech to guide thought and behavior. With development, the self-regulatory function of language changes so that children can direct their behavior using **inner speech.** In other words, private speech serves as a **cognitive self-guidance system** and then goes "underground" as covert verbal thought. (Vygotsky contrasted his position with that of Piaget [1955], who believed that private speech plays no functional role in cognitive development but is merely symptomatic of ongoing mental activity.)

Several studies have assessed aspects of Vygotsky's theory of private speech, and most generally find support for his ideas. For example, Laura Berk (1986) observed first- and third-grade children during daily math periods for four months. Various forms of private speech were recorded (for example, task-irrelevant, self-stimulating speech; task-relevant, externalized speech; and task-relevant, external manifestations of inner speech such as lip movements), as well as other aspects of their overt behavior (movement, pointing to objects to help them add) and measures of their task performance (daily math papers and achievement and IQ tests). Berk reported high levels of private speech in this sample of children that changed with age. The self-guidance function of private speech varied with age and eventually gave way to covert, inner speech. Most of the children's task-relevant externalized speech was used to guide their problem solving, with third-graders using more internalized forms of speech (for example, inaudible mutterings, lip and tongue movements) to facilitate their performance. The total amount of private speech was positively related to intelligence at grade 1 but not at grade 3, an indication that brighter children begin to use private speech to guide their problem solving earlier than less bright children and also stop sooner, as thought goes "underground" as inner speech (see also Berk & Landau, 1993; Kohlberg, Yaeger, & Hjertholm, 1968).

Also consistent with Vygotsky's claims, children rely more heavily on private speech when facing difficult rather than easy tasks, when deciding how to proceed after making errors (Berk, 1992), and their performance often improves after turning to

DENNIS THE MENACE

"I'M GONNA HAVE TO STOP THINKIN' OUT LOUD."

CARTOON 9-1 Young children often have a difficult time keeping their thoughts to themselves. SOURCE: Dennis the Menace, used by permission of Hank Ketcham and © 1986 by North America Syndicate.

self-instruction (Behrend, Rosengren & Perlmutter, 1989; Berk & Spuhl, 1995). Moreover, private speech does eventually go "underground," progressing from words and phrases, to whispers and mutterings, to inner speech (Bivens & Berk, 1990).

In addition to the developmental trend in private speech, there is evidence that young children might not even believe that inner speech is possible. Instead, they believe that a person cannot "talk to herself" and think at the same time. When preschool children are prompted to use inner speech (for example, "Silently think about how your name sounds"), they are just as likely to say that they had a *picture* of their name in their head while thinking as to say that they said their name in their head (Flavell, Green, Flavell, & Grossman, 1997).

In general, although some discrepancies from Vygotsky's theory have been reported, the conclusion of the existing research seems to be that there is indeed a developmental relationship between language and thought, along the lines that Vygotsky and his colleagues hypothesized.

Summary

Several features typify language, including *arbitrariness* (any word can be used to express any concept), *productivity* (language is "creative"), *semanticity* (language can represent objects, actions, events, and ideas symbolically), *displacement* (ability to displace speaker from the here and now), and *duality* (language is represented at two levels: phonology and syntax).

Children usually speak their first words around 10 months. Their *receptive language* (what they can comprehend) is greater than their *productive language* (what they can speak), and early sentences are *telegraphic,* including only the high-content words.

Children's language development can be described on several dimensions, including *phonology, morphology, semantic, syntax,* and *pragmatics.*

Infant babbling goes through a series of stages, related to changes in the child's anatomy.

Morphemes (both *free* and *bound*) are the smallest unit of meaning in a language. Children learn rules and *overregularize* irregular words to fit these rules (forming words such as "goed" and "mouses"). The average number of morphemes used in a sentence, or the *mean length of utterance (MLU),* is a good indication of the language complexity of a preschool child.

Syntactic development progresses quickly over the preschool years and is reflected in regular age-related changes in forming negatives, asking questions, using the passive voice, and relating events in sentences.

Semantic development refers to the development of word meaning. Around 18 months of age, children experience a *word spurt,* in which the rate of new word learning (mostly nouns) increases rapidly. This has been attributed to *fast mapping,* in which children are able to learn novel words with minimal input. Early in development, children often make *overextensions*, applying a word beyond its correct meaning (calling all four-legged animals "dog"), but sometimes make *underextensions*, incorrectly restricting the use of a term (believing that only their pet, Fido, deserves the label "dog"). Semantic memory can be described using *feature-list models*, with the number and type of features children use to define words changing with age. Aspects of children's semantic memories seem to be schematically organized on the basis of *scripts*. Nelson has proposed that broad-based superordinates (such as food) have their basis in context-specific, script-related, *slot-filler categories* (such as things you eat at breakfast).

Pragmatics refers to knowledge about how language can be used and adjusted to fit different circumstances. Even young children are aware of some basic aspects of pragmatics, although there are also substantial improvements with age. *Speech registers* refer to a distinct style of speaking which is used only in specific contexts (for example, when talking to children, when talking in school). In the United States, the distinction between social (or home) language and school language among native speakers is often more obvious for children whose home language is described as *Black English*—a dialect of American English used mostly (but not exclusively) by members of the African-American community—which is characterized by some special rules of pronunciation and syntax.

Communicative competence refers to the various types of language knowledge (phonology, morphology, syntax, semantics, and pragmatics) that are combined in a package to yield effective communication. Preschool children often display poor communication and *metacommunication* skills, being less aware of factors that influence comprehension of messages than older children.

Behavioral theories of language (syntax) acquisition have generally been discredited and replaced by nativist and social-interactionist theories. Nativist theories follow the theorizing of Noam Chomsky, who proposed language has both a *surface* and a *deep structure*, that children are born with a *language ac-*

quisition device (LAD), and all that is needed for language acquisition is exposure to speech. Nativists propose there is an innate *universal grammar* that contains the basic syntactic structure of all human languages. Both a first and second language are learned more easily by younger than older children, suggesting a critical period for language learning. Newport's *"less is more" hypothesis* suggests that young children's cognitive limitations actually make it easier for them to acquire a first or second language than for older children or adults to do so.

Social-interactionist theorists examine the interplay between language, cognitive, and social development. Young infants are responsive to human speech and are especially responsive to *infant-directed* (or *child-directed*) *speech*. Locke proposed a theory of neurolinguistic development involving four overlapping and interactive stages: vocal learning, utterance acquisition, analysis and computation, and integration and elaboration. Differences in the timing of peak efficiency of these stages accounts for the performance of some language-delayed children. Bates and her colleagues similarly proposed that there is a direct relation between a child's vocabulary size and syntactic complexity, and that one need not postulate a "grammar module" (representational innateness) to account for the acquisition of grammar.

Gender differences in language acquisition favoring girls have occasionally been found, but there is evidence that different cultural practices regarding how boys and girls are treated play an important role in possible gender differences in language acquisition.

Nelson proposed that language structures the thought of young children and that many of the cognitive changes that occur around the age of 4 years (for example, theory of mind) are largely the result of children's use of language. The Soviet psychologists Luria and Vygotsky proposed that language directs much intelligent behavior in children. Luria proposed that speech cannot inhibit the motor action of young children, with slightly older children's responses to speech being impulsive, in that they respond to the physical and not the conceptual features of language in directing their behavior. By 5 years of age, children are able to use the conceptual features of speech (that is, its meaning) to guide their behavior. Vygotsky proposed that *egocentric*, or *private*, *speech* has a special role in guiding children's thinking and behavior. Young children's private speech serves as a *cognitive self-guidance system* and is eventually replaced by covert verbal thought. Recent research provides support for Vygotsky's theory.

Key Terms and Concepts

arbitrariness
productivity
semanticity
displacement
duality
productive language
receptive language
telegraphic speech
phonology
phonemes
morphology
morphemes
free morphemes
bound morphemes
mean length of utterance (MLU)
overregularization
syntax
semantics
word spurt
fast mapping
overextensions
underextensions
feature-list models (of semantic memory)
scripts
slot-filler categories
pragmatics
speech register
Black English
communicative competence
metacommunication
surface structure
deep structure
language acquisition device (LAD)
universal grammar

pidgins
creoles
"less is more" hypothesis
child-directed speech
infant-directed speech
language acquisition support system (LASS)
prosody
private (egocentric) speech
inner speech
cognitive self-guidance system

Suggested Readings

LOCKE, J. L. (1993). *The child's path to spoken language*. Cambridge, MA: Harvard University Press. This book provides the reader with an up-to-date account of language development in a readable, straightforward manner. Locke looks at the interplay of biological, social, cognitive, and emotional factors in language development. Readers who find it easy to get lost in the complicated linguistic analyses so common in the area of child language will find this book refreshing.

BERKO GLEASON, J. (ED.) (1997). *The development of language* (4th ed.). Boston, MA: Allyn & Bacon. This book consists of 11 chapters, each written by experts in the field on various topics of language development, including phonology, morphology, semantics, syntax, and pragmatics. The chapters are up-to-date and provide more detailed accounts of the various areas of language development than afforded here.

HOFF-GINSBERG, E. (1997). *Language development*. Pacific Grove, CA: Brooks/Cole. This is a recent textbook that presents an overview of all aspects of language development, from linguistic theory to brain development.

BATES, E., & GOODMAN, J. C. (1997). On the inseparability of grammar and the lexicon: Evidence from acquisition, aphasia and real-time processing. In G. Altman (Ed.), Special issue on the lexicon, *Language and Cognitive Processes, 12*, 507–586. This article presents the position that the development of grammar and vocabulary cannot be viewed as separate phenomena, and suggests an alternative account of the development of grammar, one that does not require a universal grammar as proposed by Chomsky and his followers.

Problem Solving and Reasoning

Problem Solving
The Development of Problem Solving
Problem Solving as Inducing and Using Rules

Planning

Reasoning
Analogical Reasoning • *Formal Reasoning*
Scientific Reasoning • *Reasoning-Remembering Relationships*

Summary

Note

Key Terms and Concepts

Suggested Readings

Life is full of problems that we seek to solve. Problems and their attempted solutions start early. Infants will strive to retrieve a fallen toy, overcoming obstacles along the way. The problems we face, and their solutions, become more complicated as we get older, but they all have certain things in common. We say that someone is solving a problem when there is a specific goal in mind that cannot be attained immediately because of the presence of one or more obstacles. We solve problems by learning rules or by using (sometimes discovering) one or more strategies. Sometimes a problem takes several attempts before it is solved, and we must be able to evaluate our progress toward the goal, if for no other reason, to know when the problem has been solved. Thus, the four basic requirements of problem solving are goals, obstacles, strategies for overcoming the obstacles, and an evaluation of the results (DeLoache, Miller, & Pierroutsakos, 1998).

Much of what we have covered in this book to this point can be considered to be in the realm of problem solving. The classic tasks of conservation and classification, for example, are problem-solving tasks. Arithmetic problems, which will be discussed in Chapter 12, are clearly problem-solving tasks. To some extent, many tasks assessing memory are problem-solving tasks, with the goal being to remember as much as one possibly can. In this chapter, I will describe children's general problem-solving abilities, beginning in infancy. This will be followed by a brief section on planning. The remaining part of the chapter will be devoted to a special type of problem solving, reasoning.

Problem Solving

The Development of Problem Solving

When do children first solve problems? Based on our definition of what constitutes **problem solving** (having a goal, obstacles to that goal, strategies, and evaluation of results), infants cannot be said to solve problems until they demonstrate some sense of **goal-directed behavior.** Recall from our discussion of Piaget's theory of sensorimotor development, goal-directed behavior requires that "need precede

action." That is, infants do not discover an interesting outcome fortuitously (for example, hitting a mobile with their arm), but rather first seek to achieve a specific goal (move a mobile) and then act accordingly. This is also the beginning of cause and effect (means-end) thinking. Infants must realize that they must do something quite specific (make physical contact with the mobile) before the mobile will move.

Piaget proposed that not until about 8 months of age, during the substage of coordination of secondary circular reactions, are infants able to accomplish this. At this time, they can use one behavior *strategically* in the service of another (for example, push aside a cloth to retrieve a toy hidden underneath). Thus, following from Piaget's classic work, we can say that problem solving begins at least during the latter part of the first year of life.

But must infants wait that long to solve simple problems? Infants younger than 8-months can clearly learn to control aspects of their environments to make interesting things happen (Rovee-Collier & Gerhardstein, 1997; Lewis, Alessandri, & Sullivan, 1990). For example, infants 2 to 8 months of age learned to pull a lever to see a color picture of a baby's face and to hear an accompanying song (Lewis et al., 1990). Even the youngest infants learned to pull the lever to get the reinforcement and became angry when the lever pulls no longer produced the interesting outcome. But the study by Lewis et al., although it had a specific goal to be achieved, does not have all the classic aspects of problem solving. The only obstacle was infants learning the association between their behavior and the outcome, and there seems to be no explicit strategy involved. True problem solving, involving means-end action sequences, seems not to be found until about the time Piaget originally proposed (the latter half of the first year).

Peter Willatts (1990) has performed some interesting experiments demonstrating means-end problem solving in infants. In one study, 6-, 7-, and 8-month-old infants were placed on a table. In front of the infants was a long cloth with a toy placed on the cloth, out of the infants' reach. Here's a goal (get that toy) and an obstacle (it is out of reach). The solution is to strategically use one behavior (pull the cloth toward them) to achieve their goal (get the toy). How did the infants do? The 6-month-olds often retrieved the toy, but their behavior was not always intentional. Instead of pulling the cloth to them and fixing their attention on the toy, these youngest infants often simply played with the cloth, looked away from the toy, and, after a while, the toy finally was in their reach. By 8-months of age, infants were much less apt to play with the cloth. They grabbed the cloth and immediately began pulling it to bring the toy closer to them. They kept their fixation on the toy and quickly and efficiently brought the toy within their grasp, often holding out a hand in anticipation of the toy's arrival. The 7-month-olds fell between the 6- and 8-month-olds.

Although means-end problem-solving might be within the capacity of infants as young as 7- and 8-months of age, it does not mean that children will display such behavior on more complicated tasks. This is illustrated by an interesting study performed by Bullock and Lütkenhaus (1988). In their study, children between the ages of 15- and 35-months were asked to perform one of several tasks, for example, to stack blocks to copy a house built by an adult. The youngest children (average age, 17-months) showed little specific goal-directed behavior. They did play with the blocks and build "something," but there was little evidence that they kept the goal of building a house in mind during their activities. In contrast, most 2-year-olds were able to keep the goal in mind and build the house. These children also did a good job at monitoring their performance (evaluating the results of their behavior). Almost all these children made at least one correction, and 85% of the 2-year-olds stacked all the blocks correctly on at least one trial. The reactions of the children to their problem-solving attempts also reveals their evaluations of their behavior toward achieving their goal. Only about a third (36%) of the 17-month-olds showed some clear sign of emotion to their performance (smiling or frowning), whereas 90% of the older children (32-month-olds) did so.

The tasks children need to solve get more complicated as they get older, and so their problem-solving abilities must also improve. One factor that has been found to have a significant impact on prob-

lem solving is knowledge. The more one knows about a particular topic or the more familiar one is with the context, the more sophisticated problem solving will be.

Let me provide an example for learning the rules behind a computer game. Stephen Ceci (1996) has proposed that context influences how people approach and solve problems. Ceci defines context as the way in which a problem in represented in long-term memory; that is, it consists of what a person knows about a task, including the reason for performing it. Ceci (1996) reports an experiment in which 10-year-old children were asked to predict where, on a computer screen, an object would land by using a joystick to mark on the screen the next position of the object. The object varied in size (big or small), color (dark or light), and shape (square, circle, or triangle), producing 12 combinations of features (two sizes × two colors × three shapes). A simple algorithm was written so that (1) squares would move upward and circles downward, and triangles would stay on the horizontal; (2) dark figures would move to the right and light figures to the left; and (3) large objects would move diagonally from lower left to upper right, whereas small objects would move in the opposite direction. So, for example, a large, light square would move upward, leftward, and from the lower left to the upper right.

Figuring out how the object would move (that is, where it would be on the next trial) seems like it would be a difficult task for children (as well as for adults), and it was. The children were given 15 sessions with the task, with 50 trials per session. Some children were simply asked to predict where the object would move on each trial. Other children were told that this was a video game, the purpose of which was to capture flying animals. The three shapes were changed to a butterfly, a bee, and a bird. These children were told to use the joystick to place the "butterfly net" so that they could "capture the prey" on each trial. The algorithm (that is, the rule by which the target moved on each trial) was identical in both conditions.

The results of this study are graphed in Figure 10-1. As can be seen, the two groups started out similarly, performing relatively poorly over the first five sessions. However, the children in the video-game

FIGURE 10-1   Children's mean proportion of accurate predictions of the position of a moving object in a video game versus laboratory context. SOURCE: From Stephen J. Ceci, *On intelligence . . . more or less: A bioecological treatise on intellectual development,* ©1990, p. 39. Reprinted by permission of Prentice-Hall, Englewood Cliffs, New Jersey.

context then took off, performing at levels approaching 90% by the ninth session. In comparison, the children given the laboratory context continued to perform poorly, never really improving on the task over the 15 sessions. Discovering the algorithm depended on the mental context in which the problem was presented. The rules were the same for all children, but the context, a form of knowledge, influenced greatly children's problem-solving performance (see also Oyen & Bebko, 1996 for a similar example of different memory strategy use when "instruction" is done via a computer game versus formal instruction).

Problem Solving as Inducing and Using Rules

One way of thinking about children's problem solving is considering their acquisition and use of *rules*. Rules specify relations between two or more variables, and are usually thought of in terms of "if . . . then" statements ("If condition A exists, make response X; if condition B exists, make response Y")

(Zelazo & Jacques, 1997). One tradition in developmental psychology has focused on children's acquisition of the rules of formal logic ("If *p* then *q*," and so on), which will be discussed in a separate section later in this chapter. The second concerns children inducing, or discovering, a rule as a result of experience and using these rules to solve problems (DeLoache et al., 1998).

When Can Children Induce Rules?

When can children induce rules for solving a problem from experience? One simple task that requires the discovery of a rule is an *oddity problem*. This will be familiar to any readers who grew up watching *Sesame Street* and the game "One of these things is not like the other." In this game, and in oddity problems in general, people must figure out which object is different, or odd, relative to the others in the set. These problems can be very simple, based on perceptual similarity (for example, § § ¥), or more complex, based on conceptual similarity (for example, tiger, elephant, blue jay; or Brainerd, Gopnik, Karmiloff-Smith).

Oddity tasks can even be administered to preverbal children and animals. In these cases, subjects are shown a series of problems and receive a food reward when they select the correct (odd) item. William Overman and his colleagues (1996) used such an oddity task, showing toddlers from 16 months of age through adults series of three objects, two of which were the same (Experiment 1). When subjects selected the odd object they received a food reward. This was a difficult task for toddlers (16 to 31 months of age), even more difficult for the preschoolers (32 to 60 months of age), but relatively trivial for participants 6 years of age and older. Yet, most of the toddlers (16- to 31-month-olds) did eventually learn the task, although it took them several hundred trials, and most children of all ages quickly solved the problems when given verbal instructions (Experiment 2).

It is interesting that the lack of verbal instructions (that is, performing the task using nonverbal procedures as is done when testing animals) was particularly detrimental for children between the ages of about 2.5 and 5 years of age. Similar findings have been reported by other researchers (Inhelder & Piaget, 1964), and they have been interpreted as indicating that younger children approach oddity problems differently than older children (see Overman et al., 1996). Obviously, the approach the 2.5- to 5-year-old children used to solve the oddity problems was ineffective. It appears that these preschool children's reliance on language made inducing a rule based solely on behavior very difficult, whereas the problem was simple enough for older children and adults to figure out without being told explicitly what to do. But the fact that these children were able to solve the problem easily as soon as they were told the rule ("Pick the one that's different"), indicates that they can apply this rule across different problems, but just have a difficult time inducing a rule based on behavior alone.

Rule-Assessment Approach

Much of cognitive development can be viewed as a process of inducing rules to solve problems. Many problems can share many of the same underlying features, and thus require the application of very similar rule systems. For example, many of the problems developed by Piaget involved children learning about the physical world and, according to Piaget, require children to learn a set of logical rules for their solution. Although each problem would have something unique about it, a universal set of cognitive structures develops to handle these problems.

Robert Siegler (1976, 1981) developed a rule-based model of cognitive development to explain many of the concepts that children acquire over childhood initially described by Piaget and others. In his **rule-assessment approach,** cognitive development is characterized by the acquisition of increasingly powerful rules for solving problems. Let me provide a description of the rule-assessment approach for the balance-scale problem (Siegler, 1976, 1981). For this problem, children are shown a balance scale, similar to that shown in Figure 10-2. Weights are then placed on the two sides of the scale, and children must predict which side of the scale will fall (if either). Children must consider not

FIGURE 10-2   Example of a balance scale task. The scale would be locked and weights would be placed on the two sides and children were to predict which side, if either, would fall.

only the number of weights on the two sides, but also their distance from the midpoint. Weights farther away from the midpoint will have a greater impact on the movement of the scale than weights closer to the midpoint. Siegler discerned four rules children used on this task. Children using Rule 1 consider only a single dimension: the amount (number) of weights on each side. Thus, children who use Rule 1 should say that the side with the most weights should fall, regardless of where those weights are placed. This will lead to some correct predictions, but also to some incorrect predictions. Children using Rule 2 similarly predict that the side with the most weights will drop, but when the number of weights is equal on both sides, they then consider the distance from the scale's midpoint. With Rule 3, children use both the weight and the distance dimensions; they predict that the side with either more weights or greater distance from the center will go down. If one side has more weights and the other side has greater distance, they muddle through the problem. Finally, children using Rule 4 make the appropriate computations of weight and distance, thus deriving the correct answer regardless of how the weights are distributed across the scale.

Siegler (1976) reported that 88% of children 5- to 17-years of age consistently applied one (or several) of these four rules in solving balance-scale problems. Most 5-year-olds used Rule 1, whereas 9-year-olds most often used Rules 2 or 3. Adolescents (13 to 17 years of age) usually used Rule 3, with very few children ever using the most sophisticated Rule 4. Perhaps somewhat surprisingly, most college students also rely on Rule 3, with only a minority of them using the most sophisticated Rule 4 (and the only one that will consistently produce a correct answer) (Siegler, 1981). This use of systematic rules breaks down on the balance-scale problem when younger children are tested. Siegler (1981) reported that none of the 3-year-olds he tested, and about half of the 4-year-olds, used any discernible rule. The problem was apparently beyond their comprehension, and they were unable to generate even the simplest rule (more weights win) to solve these problems. Other studies have confirmed this sequence (Amsel et al., 1996; McFadden, Dufresne, & Kobasigawa, 1986), and Siegler (1981) reports similar sequences following similar rules for a variety of tasks (for example, probability judgment, conservation, judging the projection of shadows).

Siegler (1996) has since modified his view of children's problem solving, proposing that, instead of a stage-like progression, children have a variety of strategies available to them to solve problems at any one time, and that these strategies "compete" for use. Siegler's *adaptive strategy-choice model* was discussed in some detail in Chapter 5. There is much evidence in the recent problem-solving literature to suggest that Siegler is right. Rather than presenting that evidence here, however, I will postpone a discussion of the adaptive strategy-choice model in greater detail for the development of arithmetic strategies in Chapter 12.

Learning to Follow Rules

Philip Zelazo and his colleagues have focused on preschool children's ability to follow simple sets of rules and propose that following relatively arbitrary sets of rules is a reflection of consciousness and cognitive self-control (Zelazo & Jacques, 1997; Zelazo et al., 1997). In an early experiment, Zelazo and Reznick (1991) gave children between the ages of 31 and 36 months of age a sorting task to complete. Children were shown sets of pictures and given two rules to follow: "If it's something found *inside* the house, then it goes in this box. If it's something found *outside* the house, then it goes in that box." Pictures included a variety of objects, some of which were obviously "inside" things (bed, TV), and others that were obviously "outside" things (snowman, plane). Children were also given a "knowledge"

task. Now, instead of having to sort each object into one of two boxes, they were shown each card and simply asked "Is this something found inside the house or is it found outside?" All children performed well on the knowledge task (that is, they answered correctly when asked if an object belonged "inside" or "outside"). However, only the oldest children (36-months) could put this knowledge into action, sorting the cards correctly into boxes. The younger groups of children (31- and 33.5-month-olds) did not sort items correctly, despite "knowing" to which category each item belonged. Later research indicated that 32-month-old children similarly failed the sorting task (and passed the knowledge task) despite having each item labeled ("This is a bed, where does it go?"), being reminded of the rules ("Remember, if it goes inside, then you put it here, and if it goes outside you put it here"), and receiving feedback and rewards for correct responding (Zelazo, Reznick, & Piñon, 1995).

These findings indicate that 36-month-old children can follow an arbitrary rule system, whereas younger children have a difficult time doing so, despite *knowing* the rules. However, 3-year-old children's ability to follow and coordinate rules is far from fully developed. This is indicated by experiments using the *dimensional card sorting task*, discussed briefly in Chapter 5 (Zelazo, Frye, & Rapus, 1996). In this task, children are shown sets of cards that vary on two dimensions. Figure 10-3 provides an example of the cards used in these experiments. Children are shown two target cards, a yellow car and a green flower, for instance. When playing the color game, they are told that all the yellow cards go here (with the yellow car) and all the green cards go there (with the green flower). Children then are given a series of test cards (for instance, yellow flowers and green cars), and are asked to sort them by color. This most children do easily. Then children are told they are going to play a new game, the shape game. (For half the children the shape game is played first, and for the other half, the color game is played first.) In the shape game, children are to place cars in this box (with the yellow car) and flowers in that box (with the green flower). These are called *switch trials*, because the rules have been

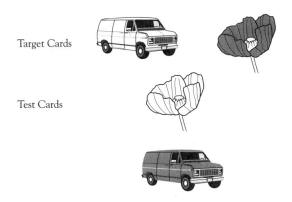

Target Cards

Test Cards

FIGURE 10-3   Dimensional card-sorting task.
Children are to sort cards initially by one dimension
(color) and later by a second dimension (shape).
SOURCE: Zelazo, P. D., Frye, D., & Rapus, T. (1996).
An age-related dissociation between knowing rules and
using them. *Cognitive Development, 11,* 37–63.

switched (from sorting on the basis of color to
shape, or vice versa). Now, most 3-year-old children
fail, continuing to sort the cards according to the
original dimension. Yet, when asked what the new
rule is, most can easily and correctly tell the experimenter. That is, like the 32-month-olds for the simpler task (Zelazo & Reznick, 1991), 3-year-olds can
verbalize the rule but cannot execute the problem.
By 4 years of age, most children do fine on both
tasks.

Why do children have difficulties on these tasks,
and what develops so that by 4 and 5 years of age
most children can follow simple rule systems relatively easily? One thing to look at on these tasks is
the type of errors children make. Children tend to
persist making responses they had learned earlier,
termed *perseverative errors* (Zelazo, Reznick, &
Piñon, 1995; Zelazo et al., 1996), and this suggests
that one source of their problem is poor inhibitory
control (Harnishfeger & Bjorklund, 1993). That is,
children have learned a response in this context and
have a difficult time not making that response (sort
by color) when the rules change (now sort by
shape). Although I'm convinced that children's developing inhibitory abilities play a role in their use
of rules, it cannot be the entire answer. For example,

Zelazo and his colleagues (1996, Experiment 2) reported that 3-year-olds made perseverative errors on
the dimensional card sorting task after only one trial
on the original dimension. That is, it was not necessary for children to acquire a well-learned response
for them to make errors on the switch trials.

What, then, accounts for the development of
rule use over the preschool years? According to
Zelazo and his colleagues, children gain increasing
conscious control over their problem solving, and
this is captured by the **cognitive complexity and
control (CCC)** theory (Zelazo & Frye, 1997). Much
like the distinction between implicit and different
levels of explicit representation in Karmiloff-Smith's
(1992) theory (see Chapter 4), Zelazo and Frye propose that there are age-related changes in the complexity of rule systems that children can represent.
According to Zelazo et al., (1997), developmental
differences in *reflection* give children increased control over their behavior and cognition. "Reflection is
defined as a recursive process whereby the contents
of consciousness become an object of consciousness
so that they can be operated on and modified . . .
[H]igher order rules mediate reflective awareness of
lower order rules and make possible the deliberate
selection of lower order rules for use. In the absence
of a higher order rule, children will perseverate on
whichever lower order rules are most compelling"
(p. 21). In other words, children acquire rules early
on and can follow them in certain situations. But
coordinating rules requires greater conscious reflection, and this develops over the preschool years. It is
interesting to see the parallel in development between rule use reported by Zelazo and his colleagues
and theory of mind research discussed in Chapter 7.
Although speculative, it appears that a single representational system might be underlying cognition in
these seemingly different areas.

Planning

An important part of problem solving is *planning*. In
many complicated problems, several steps must be
executed in order before a goal can be reached.
There is little planning involved for an 8-month-old,

whose goal is to get a toy by pulling on a cloth. But as the problems get more complicated, so does the need for planning. For example, in the study by Bullock and Lütkenhaus (1988) discussed earlier, children had to plan ahead as to which blocks they would select first and which needed to be used only later. There were several aspects to the problem, and, although a trial-and-error procedure might have eventually produced a correct answer, it rarely did for the youngest children in the Bullock and Lütkenhaus study.

Planning is difficult for young children, and they rarely do it, or at least rarely do it well. There are many reasons for this, associated with children's limited cognitive abilities. Ellis and Siegler (1997) have listed several reasons for young children's generally poor planning abilities:

1. Planning often requires inhibition of currently active behavior. As you may recall from our discussion of the development of inhibition/ resistance from interference in Chapter 5, these abilities increase with age, with preschool children often having difficulty inhibiting an ongoing activity (Harnishfeger & Bjorklund, 1993).

2. Planning takes time, and children often prefer to do a task quickly than to do it accurately. This, in part, might be facilitated by adults' reactions to children's problem-solving attempts. Adults often praise children for the attempt, telling them that they have performed better than they actually have. Related to this, children's goals in solving a problem might not be identical to that of an adult, and they might not have the metacognitive ability to evaluate how successfully they achieved their goal, tending to overestimate their performance (Bjorklund, 1997a).

3. Planning is often viewed as difficult, time-consuming, and subjectively unpleasant. This is true not only for children but also for adults. Planning is a special type of strategy (or metastrategy), and strategies are used when people cannot solve a problem using less effortful procedures. If you have reason to believe that the solution to a problem will "just come to you" as you fiddle with the components (such as putting your new barbecue grill together without reading the instructions), then why spend the time planning? A plan (as many strategies) should be used only when solving the problem can't be done without one.

4. When children do generate a plan, they are not always successful. Why spend the time and effort when the outcome is uncertain?

5. It might be more fun to "wing it." Problem solving can present novel activities for children, and the implementation of a plan might make the process less enjoyable.

Such a description makes it seem as if young children approach problems in a willy-nilly fashion, and if they're lucky, eventually bump into the right solution. There is a bit of trial-and-error learning in most problem solving, but rarely are children's approaches to a problem totally random. They tend to select problem-solving strategies that are appropriate (if not always optimal) for the task at hand, and often modify their strategies as they progress through the problem (Siegler, 1996). However, young children rarely demonstrate the forward-looking approach that older children and adults often do when solving a complicated problem.

Preschool children do show signs of some planning in some situations, of course. For example, several studies have asked preschoolers to "plan" a trip to a grocery store (Gauvain & Rogoff, 1989; Hudson, Shapiro, & Sosa, 1995). In one study, children were asked to get several items from a model grocery store (Gauvain & Rogoff, 1989). Most 5-year-olds did an efficient item-by-item search, but older children were more likely to display signs of explicit planning by looking through the entire store and then searching for specific objects based on where they believed they would be located. The result was a more effective search. In other research, Judith Hudson and her colleagues (1995) asked 3-, 4-, and 5-year-olds to plan a trip to a grocery store (or to the beach). Children were also told of potential mishaps that could occur (you forgot to bring your shopping list) and asked how they might remedy or prevent the situation. They reported that recognizable plans were relatively rare for the 3- and 4-year-olds, but quite common for the 5-year-old children. Age differences were also found both in children's responses

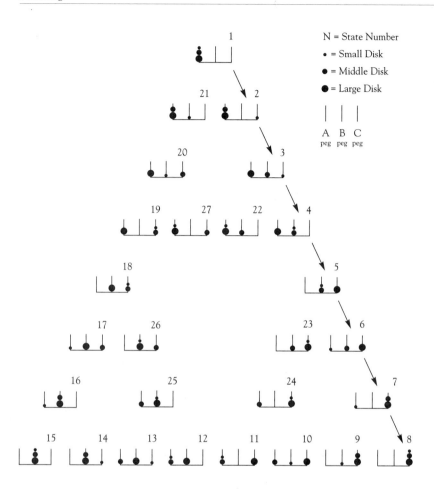

N = State Number
• = Small Disk
● = Middle Disk
● = Large Disk

A   B   C
peg peg peg

FIGURE 10-4 Possible legal moves on a three-disk Tower of Hanoi problem. The most efficient solution path is shown by the arrows on the far right. SOURCE: Fireman, G. (1996). Developing a plan for solving a problem: A representational shift. *Cognitive Development, 11,* 107–122.

to remedy and prevent a mishap. Children of all ages were able to suggest some remedy to a potential problem (although the number of plans to remedy mishaps did increase with age), but very few 3- and 4-year-old children suggested plans to prevent a mishap. Only the 5-year-old children made a substantial number of prevention plans.

In other research, 4- and 5-year-old children were asked to plan a route through a large space to retrieve a set of objects as quickly as possible (Fabricius, 1988). Children were familiarized with the space and then asked to retrieve the objects "the quick way." Fabricius concluded that the 5-year-old children engaged in *forward search,* in which a person envisions a series of moves that will achieve a partial solution. In other words, 5-year-olds had a plan that permitted them to foresee the conse-

quences of their moves and thus made relatively few "backtracking" moves during their search. The 4-year-olds were less apt to do this, and when they did engage in forward search, they did so inconsistently.

One example of a problem where planning is important is the Tower of Hanoi problem. The three-disk version of this problem is illustrated in Figure 10-4. Children are shown a structure with three pegs, with three different sized disks on one peg (the one to the far left, for instance). The task is to get all the disks to the peg on the opposite side by moving only one peg at a time and obeying the rule that a larger peg cannot be placed on a smaller peg. This task can be solved in seven moves, which are indicated by the arrows in Figure 10-4. It would seem that planning is important in solving this problem. Having an idea in mind ahead of time (or figuring one out soon after the task begins) would seem to be associated with the likelihood of finding the right solution quickly.

Several researchers have emphasized that the first move children make on the Tower of Hanoi task is important and reflects and influences their planning on the task (Klahr & Robinson, 1981). However, a study by Gary Fireman (1996) with first- and second-grade children on the three-disk problem failed to find any relation between making the optimal first move (move number 2 in Figure 10-4) and later success on the problem. Children who never solved the problem were just as likely to make a correct first move as were children who eventually solved the problem within the 3-minute time limit. Does this mean that planning is actually *not* important in the Tower of Hanoi problem? Not at all. This is a difficult task for children of this age, and most of the planning on this task seems to come after a few moves are made as children become familiar with the problem and the range of strategies they have available to them to solve the problem. Before planning could occur, children needed to learn, in a hands-on way, the constraints associated with the problem. According to Fireman (1996), at the start of the task "children were not concerned with the strategy of reducing the problem depth or attaining a subgoal. Instead, children's initial actions explored the range of legal and illegal moves. Apparently, the children had to experience the instructions in action, despite their initial, spontaneous declaration that they understood the goal of the problem" (p. 120). Planning for these children came only after getting acquainted with the problem.

Rudiments of planning may be found in early childhood, but even older children and adults are often reluctant to engage in planning (Chalmers & Lawrence, 1993). In general, planning is a late developing ability and many of us, adults as well as children, approach many problems with as little planning as possible.

Reasoning

Reasoning is a special type of problem solving. Reasoning usually requires that one make an *inference*.

That is, to reason, one must go beyond the information given. It is not enough to figure out the rules associated with some game. That's problem solving, but not necessarily reasoning. In reasoning, one must take the evidence presented and arrive at a new conclusion based on that evidence. The result is often new knowledge (DeLoache et al., 1998).

We use some forms of reasoning in our everyday lives, and we are so accustomed to thinking this way that we are often unaware of it. Other types of reasoning are highly formalized (in fact, termed formal reasoning), which most of us do not engage in regularly, and when we do we are certainly conscious of it. In the following sections, I will discuss three types of reasoning: analogical reasoning, formal reasoning, and scientific reasoning, and conclude with a discussion of the relation between reasoning and memory.

Analogical Reasoning

Perhaps the type of reasoning that most people are familiar with is **analogical reasoning.** Analogical reasoning involves using something you already know to help you understand something you don't know yet. Analogical reasoning involves **relational mapping**—the application of what one knows about one set of elements (the relation of A to B) to relations about different elements (the relation of C to D). Classic analogical reasoning problems are stated A:B :: C: ? For example, *dog* is to *puppy* as *cat* is to ?. The answer here, of course, is *kitten*. By knowing the relation between the first two elements in the problem (a *puppy* is a baby *dog*), one can use that knowledge to complete the analogy for a new item (*cat*). Analogies are thus based on *similarity relations*. One must understand the similarity between dogs and cats and puppies and kittens if one is to solve the above analogy.

How basic is analogical reasoning to cognitive development? Is it an early or late developing ability? How well adults are able to solve analogies is related to general intelligence as measured by IQ tests (Sternberg, 1985), and one advantage gifted children have over nongifted children is in their ability to solve analogies (Muir-Broaddus, 1995). Individual differences in analogical reasoning are found over the life span and are predictive of intelligence. This suggests that it is a complex skill that is influenced by a variety of other cognitive abilities and does not peak early in life. According to Piagetian theory (Inhelder & Piaget, 1958), analogical reasoning is a sophisticated ability that is not seen until adolescence. Others, however, have proposed that analogical thinking serves as the basis for other reasoning and problem-solving tasks (Halford, 1993), and might be present at birth (Goswami, 1996).

How can there be such divergence of opinion about when analogical reasoning is first seen in development? Part of the problem lies in the nature of the problems children are asked to solve. In cases when successful problem solving is not seen until late childhood or adolescence, the problems often involve objects or concepts with which children are unfamiliar. Perhaps more than any other factor, knowledge for the objects and relations among objects in analogical reasoning problems is paramount in determining whether a child will solve or fail to solve a problem. Other factors also contribute to a child's success on analogical-reasoning problems, including memory for the premises, availability of mental resources, representation of the relations, and metacognitive knowledge (see DeLoache et al., 1998; Gentner, 1989). In the following section, I will review children's ability to solve analogical-reasoning problems and look at some of the factors that contribute to this developmental progression.

Analogical Reasoning in Young Children

Counter to the traditional Piagetian account of analogical reasoning, several theorists have proposed that very young children are capable of such reasoning, and in fact use analogical reasoning to solve a host of problems (Goswami, 1996; Halford, 1993). Children can use what they know about solving one problem to solve a related problem. One would expect this ability to increase with age, as knowledge, mental capacity, memory, and other factors increase with age, but there is no a priori reason that this ability should not be present in infancy. In fact,

Usha Goswami (1996) has proposed the **relational primacy hypothesis,** proposing that analogical reasoning is available early in infancy.

In one of the few experiments to assess analogical reasoning in infants, Chen, Sanchez, and Campbell (1997) tested 1-year-old infants (Experiment 1). The basic task involved placing a desirable toy out of reach of the infant, with a barrier between the baby and the toy. Two strings, one attached to the toy and one not, were also out of the infant's reach, but each string was on a cloth that *was* within reach. To get the toy, the infants had to pull the cloth toward them and then pull the string attached to the toy. (This is similar to the task described earlier by Willatts, [1990]). There were three similar tasks, although the toy, the barrier, and the color of the cloth varied among the three tasks. These are illustrated in Figure 10-5. If infants did not solve the problem after 100 seconds, their parents modeled the correct solution for them. The primary research question concerned whether, after solving an initial problem, either with or without parental modeling, would the infants see the similarity with the later problems and be more apt to solve them? That is, would infants use analogical reasoning to solve the subsequent problems?

Few children solved the first problem spontaneously (most required help from a parent). However, the percentage of infants solving the problems increased from 29% for the first problem, to 43% for the second, and 67% for the third (Experiment 1). Infants' problem solving was also rated for "efficiency," with higher scores reflecting a greater goal-directed approach, as opposed to a trial-and-error approach to the problem. As can be seen in Figure 10-6, efficiency increased steadily over the three problems.

The research by Chen and her colleagues (1997) reveals that 1-year-olds are able to use the similarity between tasks analogically to solve problems. However, this is very different from the classic problems used in research. The first study to demonstrate analogical reasoning in young children using a more traditional task was performed by Holyoak, Junn, and Billman (1984). In their study, preschool and kindergarten children had to move some gumballs in

FIGURE 10-5   The configuration of the three problems 1-year-old infants solved. SOURCE: Chen, Z., Sanchez, R. P., & Campbell, T. (1997). From beyond to within their grasp: The rudiments of analogical problem solving in 10- and 13-month-olds. *Developmental Psychology, 33,* 790–801. Copyright © 1997 by the American Psychological Association. Reprinted with permission.

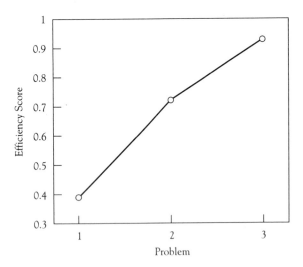

FIGURE 10-6   Infants' problem-solving efficiency scores. SOURCE: Chen, Z., Sanchez, R. P., & Campbell, T. (1997). From beyond to within their grasp: The rudiments of analogical problem solving in 10- and 13-month-olds. *Developmental Psychology, 33,* 790–801. Copyright © 1997 by the American Psychological Association. Reprinted with permission.

one bowl on a table to another, out-of-reach bowl, without leaving their chair. They had various objects available to them that they could use to solve the problem, including scissors, an aluminum cane, tape, string, and a sheet of paper. Before solving the problem, children heard a story about a genie who had a similar problem. The genie's problem was to move some jewels from one bottle within his reach to another bottle, out of his reach. One way in which he solved this problem was to roll his magic carpet into a tube and pass the jewels down the tube into the second bottle. Another solution that other children heard was to use his magic staff to pull the second bottle closer to him. After hearing the stories, children were told to think of as many ways that they could to solve *their* problem—to get the gumballs from one bowl to another. About half of the preschool and kindergarten children solved the "magic staff" problem, and the remainder did so after a hint. That is, these 4.5- to 6-year-old children were able to reason by analogy. However, they were less successful with the "magic carpet" analogy,

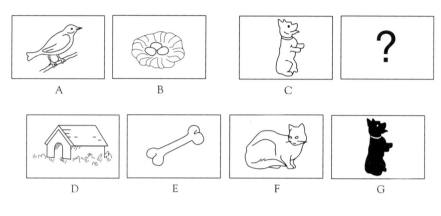

FIGURE 10-7 Example of problem used in Goswami & Brown. Children must select from set of pictures in bottom row (pictures D through G) the one that best completes the visual analogy on the top row. (The correct answer is D). SOURCE: Goswami, U., & Brown, A. L. (1990). Higher-order structure and relational reasoning: Contrasting analogical and thematic relations. *Cognition* 36, 207–226. Reprinted with permission of Elsevier Science.

suggesting that young children's performance on analogical reasoning tasks is highly dependent on the similarity between objects. The "magic staff" and the aluminum cane were more perceptually similar to one another, Holyoak and his colleagues argued, than were the "magic carpet" and the sheet of paper, making the former analogy easier to use for these young children than the latter. But the basic finding that preschool children could use the similarity in one story to solve a similar (analogous) problem, suggests that such reasoning is well within the capability of these children, counter to the traditional Piagetian position.

Not all similarity is perceptual, however. Sometimes the similarity between objects is *relational.* This is illustrated in a study by Goswami and Brown (1990), who showed 4-, 5-, and 9-year-old children sets of pictures of the A:B :: C: ? type. Children were given four alternatives and had to choose which of the four best completed the analogy. An example of a problem used in this study is shown in Figure 10-7. In this problem, children must discover the relation between bird and nest (a bird lives in a nest) and find the proper match for dog (here, dog house). Chance performance on this task would be 25%, and children of all ages performed greater than expected by chance (59%, 66%, and 94% correct for the 4-, 5-, and 9-year-olds, respectively). Note that children are not solving the problem based on *perceptual similarity.* The bird and dog look nothing

alike, nor do the nest and the dog house. To solve this problem, they must do so on the basis of *relational similarity*—the relation between the A and B terms (bird and nest) is used to find the best match for the C term (dog). This is clearly a more advanced form of analogical reason than that demonstrated by the 1-year-old infants in the Chen et al. (1997) study.

However, children might have not been using analogical reasoning to solve this problem. Maybe they were simply selecting the item that "went best with" the dog. This apparently was not the case, however. Children in a control group were asked exactly this question: pick the one that "goes best" with the C term (in this case, dog). When asked to do this, children were no more likely to select the analogical choice (here, dog house) as they were a high associate (here, bone). Thus, children's performance on the analogical-reasoning task cannot be attributed to responding on the basis of strictly associative or thematic relations, but rather reflects the use of true analogical reasoning.

The fact that at least some young children were solving these problems using true analogical reasoning was reflected by the type of errors they made. For example, Goswami (1996) reports a 4-year-old child, Lucas, who, after seeing the *bird : nest :: dog : ?* problem, figured out what the answer should be without seeing the alternatives. However, what he figured was wrong. "Lucas first told us that the correct solution was *puppy*. He argued, quite logically, 'Bird lays eggs in her nest . . . dog—dogs lay babies, and the babies are—umm—and the name of the babies is puppy'" (p. 102). Lucas quickly changed his mind when he saw that a puppy was not among the alternatives, rethought the problem and identified the "lives in" relation. However, his first idea was also relational. He had simply identified a type of relation (*type of offspring*) different than that identified by the experimenters. Successful analogical reasoning requires identifying the "right" relation, but there can be many different relations existing between sets of items, and, outside of the laboratory or classroom, there might not be clearcut "right" and "wrong" answers.

Factors Affecting Children's Analogical Reasoning

According to Goswami's (1996) analogical primacy view, the ability to reason by analogy is present in infancy. Even if we accept such a position, however, many factors influence children's success on any given analogical-reasoning task. For example, Graeme Halford (1993) has proposed that analogical reasoning develops in a stage-like fashion reminiscent of Piaget, based on the availability of mental resources. A child's ability to symbolically represent concepts and relations will also affect whether and how a child will use analogical reasoning (see DeLoache et al., 1998).

Analogical reasoning and relational shift. Related to how a child represents a problem are the types of relations children identify and base their reasoning on. For example, although the research of Goswami and Brown (1990) indicates that young children *can* use analogies based on relational similarity, it does not mean that they do so easily, especially when they can form analogies based on perceptual similarity. Dedre Gentner (1989) has argued that a **relational shift** occurs in the development of analogical reasoning, in which young children are more likely to focus on perceptual similarity, whereas older children and adults focus more

on relational similarity in solving problems. (Compare this with the "shift" between perceptual and conceptual basis of classification discussed in Chapter 7.) For example, infants and young children are more influenced by the surface similarity of objects, such as an object's shape. Older children, on the other hand, are more tuned to the underlying relation between sets of objects. For example, the better performance of the preschool children in the Holyoak (1984) study for the "magic staff" than the "magic carpet" analogy was attributed to the greater perceptual similarity between the magic staff and the aluminum cane available to solve the "gumball" problem, than between the magic carpet and the sheet of paper (for other examples, see Daehler & Chen, 1993; Pierce & Gholson, 1994). When there is a conflict between object similarity and relational similarity, young children's ability to use relational similarity is hindered (see Goswami, 1996).

Knowledge. One factor that affects whether children will use relational similarity to solve an analogical-reasoning problem is knowledge, or familiarity. How familiar are children with the underlying relations used to make the analogy? Remember, the function of analogical reasoning is to use something you know to help you understand something you don't know. From this perspective, analogical reasoning can only make sense if a child is familiar with the base relation. You might get a better understanding of the human nervous system, for example, if you see it as analogous to electrical circuits. But if you know nothing about electrical circuits, it won't help you understand the nervous system at all, no matter how well developed your analogical reasoning abilities are. I think it is fair to say that all major theorists acknowledge the importance of knowledge and familiarity on the development of analogical reasoning, although they might disagree on the exact role that knowledge plays in such development (see DeLoache et al., 1998; Goswami, 1996).

The role of familiarity is illustrated in a study by Goswami (1995) that used a familiar children's story, *Goldilocks and the Three Bears,* as the basis for analogical reasoning. Goswami (1995) used the familiar story of the three bears ("The Daddy Bear has all the big things, the Mummy Bear has all the medium-sized things, and the Baby Bear has all the tiny things") to help children make *transitive mappings*. A transitive relation involves at least three objects, such as the length of objects. If object A is longer than object B, and object B is longer than object C, then object A must be longer than object C (that is, A → B → C). Can young children use the transitive relation on one dimension as a basis for mapping transitive relations on another dimension? Or, stated somewhat differently, can children map the transitive relation from one dimension (the Daddy, Mummy, and Baby bear) to another (size, for instance)?

In Goswami's (1995) study, 3- and 4-year-old children were asked to use the relation in the Goldilocks story (Daddy Bear → Mummy Bear → Baby Bear) to classify objects that differed in quantity (a lot versus a medium amount versus a little pizza, candy, or lemonade), or to rank order (three levels) certain phenomena on the basis of loudness (footsteps), pitch (of voices), temperature (of porridge), saltiness (of porridge), width (of beds), or height (of mirrors). Four-year-olds generally performed well on all these tasks, using the Three Bears analogy to map onto other dimensions. Three-year-olds did less well, although they performed above chance levels on most tasks, indicating that they, too, could use the familiar (perhaps less familiar to them than to the 4-year-olds) story as a basis for making analogical relations.

Metacognition. To what extent is explicit awareness of the relations between entities on analogical reasoning tasks important in solving problems? Can children think analogically but be unable to articulate what they are doing? Might such knowledge be *implicit*, and unavailable to consciousness? It certainly appears that the knowledge that the infants in the Chen et al. (1997) study had was implicit. These preverbal children's metacognitive understanding of the problem and their solutions to them was likely nonexistent. How important is metacognitive knowledge for analogical reasoning during childhood?

That analogical relations can be explicit to young children was illustrated by the example of 4-year-old Lucas discussed earlier, who generated an analogical relation (albeit an incorrect one) for the bird:nest :: dog: ? problem before seeing the alternatives. Successful training of analogical reasoning is often best accomplished when children receive explicit instruction about the rationale behind the training (Brown & Kane, 1988; Chen & Daehler, 1993), much as has been found in the training of memory strategies (see Chapter 8). This suggests, not at all surprisingly, that knowing what one is doing (that is, having metacognitive knowledge) facilitates analogical reasoning.

One set of studies relevant to metacognitive knowledge was done by Brown, Kane, and their colleagues (Brown & Kane, 1988; Brown, Kane, & Long, 1989), who assessed children's **learning to learn** on a series of analogical reasoning tasks. Learning to learn refers to improvements in performance on new tasks as a result of performance on earlier tasks, during which time children learn a general rule or approach to problems. That is, participants learn a general set of rules that they can apply to new tasks, so that performance on later tasks is enhanced relative to performance on earlier tasks.

In Brown and Kane's studies, preschool children were given a series of problems similar to the "magic carpet" story used by Holyoak and his colleagues (1984). For example, some children were first given the genie problem. If they did not solve it, they were told about how rolling the "carpet" could be used to transport the jewels. They were then given a similar problem (the Easter Bunny needing to transport eggs by using a rolled up blanket), and then a third (a farmer transporting cherries using a rolled-up rug). Children receiving this series of problems, and who were given the solution to a problem when they failed, showed a large learning-to-learn effect. For the "rolling" solution, 46% of the children used analogical reasoning to solve the second problem, and 98% of the children did so for the third task.

This compares with a control group, who received the three sets of "rolling" problems but who did not receive the hints. They showed only 20% transfer after the first problem and 39% after the second.

Does a learning-to-learn effect have to involve metacognition? Not necessarily. But some of the children's comments suggested that their improved performance on the later problems was the result of their awareness of analogical reasoning strategies. For example, one 4-year-old child in the Brown and Kane (1988) study, after solving two "rolling" problems, commented at the beginning of the third problem: "And all you need to do is get this thing rolled up? I betcha!" (p. 517). Brown and Kane (1988) commented that children had developed a mind-set to look for analogies, expecting to extract some general rule to solve problems and to be able to use knowledge they acquired in one context elsewhere.

Formal Reasoning

To this point, we have examined children's informal reasoning, or the type of reasoning children might use in their everyday lives (even if the problems are invented by a psychologist). Informal reasoning is contrasted with formal reasoning. According to De-Loache, Miller, and Pierroutsakos (1998), "In **formal reasoning,** the *form* of an argument, not its semantic content, is crucial. Logical, not empirical, truth matter: The internal consistency of a set of premises and the conclusion drawn from them is all that counts, not whether or how they map onto the real world" (p. 804). Why should such decontextualized reasoning be of interest to developmental psychologists, who are ostensibly concerned about children's intellectual development in the real world? The answer is that formal-reasoning ability has long been viewed as a hallmark of adult, and especially scientific, thinking. This is seen clearly in Piaget's account of adolescent thinking (Inhelder & Piaget, 1958). It is no accident that Piaget called this final stage of cognitive development formal operations (see Moshman, 1998).

Piaget proposed that not until 11 or 12 years of age is formal reasoning first seen and that the thinking of adults (and older adolescents) corresponds to

a certain type of logical operation—specifically, **propositional logic.** Propositional logic is a form of symbolic logic that involves two or more factors (conventionally, P and Q), with each factor having two possible values (for instance, true or false). Take, for example, two coins, a penny and a dime. Each coin has two and only two possible values, heads and tails. In flipping these coins we have four possible combinations: both the penny and the dime are heads (P and Q); the penny is heads and the dime is tails (P and not Q); the penny is tails and the dime is heads (not P and Q); and both the penny and the dime are tails (not P and not Q).

These four alternatives can themselves be combined, resulting in 16 outcomes that are referred to as the 16 binary operations.[1] Piaget proposed that these 16 binary operations correspond to mental operations characteristic of formal operational thought. One of these operations, implication, is found frequently in human discourse and is expressed as "P implies Q." This means that Q is true if P is true, or P implies Q "if and only if no interpretation makes [P] true and [Q] false" (Quine, 1972, p. 40). In everyday language, implication is expressed in "if . . . then" statements. Tests of implication usually take the following form:

1. If there is a P, then there is a Q.
2. There is a P.
3. There is a Q.

Subjects are to determine the validity of the third statement, which in this example is true. Conversely, there is the invalid form of implication, and tests of this are usually expressed as follows:

1. If there is a P, then there is a Q.
2. There is no P.
3. There is no Q.

In this case, the third statement is not necessarily true, for although P implies Q, the initial premise does not require that "not P implies not Q." For example, "If John passes calculus, then he will take his girlfriend out to dinner." Given this statement, the girlfriend can expect dinner if John passes calculus. Should John fail, however, dinner is not necessarily out of the question.

Based on observations from a variety of experimental tasks and the verbal reports of their participants, Inhelder and Piaget concluded that concrete operational children are unable to use the 16 binary operations to solve problems, whereas formal operational thinkers can use each of the 16 operations as the tasks demand.

A substantial amount of research has generally supported Piaget's view that formal, logical reasoning is not observed for most preadolescent children (Markovits & Vachon, 1989; Overton et al., 1987). But what about adults? Do *we* really think this way? Apparently not, at least not most of the time. For example, Paris (1973) assessed the ability of children and adults to comprehend statements of propositional logic, including "if . . . then" implication statements. Paris reported that even 7-year-olds could answer correctly valid implications, for instance, "If there is a P, then there is a Q. There is a P. There is a Q" (true or false?). However, both 7-year-olds and adults performed poorly on the invalid implications, for example, "If there is a P, then there is a Q. There is no P. There is no Q" (true or false?). That is, not only can concrete operational children not solve invalid forms of implication, but neither can college students. Rather, like children, adults tend to interpret the reasonableness of the problem ("John didn't say anything about taking his girlfriend out to dinner if he fails.)

Yet, as Paris (1973) demonstrated, even young children can reason logically for some problems in some situations. An interesting example of this is provided in a study by Hawkins, Pea, Glick, and Scribner (1984), who presented verbal syllogisms to 4- and 5-year-old children. Syllogisms are problems that require deductive reasoning (a characteristic of formal reasoning) and are of the form:

1. Socrates was a man.
2. All men are mortal.
3. Socrates was mortal.

On such problems, participants are to discern the truth of the third statement given the first two. Note that the truth value of the third statement is based solely on the content of the first two, not on the basis of what one knows to be true of the real world. Piaget proposed that to solve syllogisms, the conclusions drawn from the premises "must be held to be true only by reason of the premises and quite independently of the empirical truth of these premises" (Piaget, 1969b, p. 32). Hawkins and his colleagues presented preschool children with syllogisms of three types: (1) *fantasy*, involving imaginary characters of which the children had no knowledge (for example, "Every banga is purple"); (2) *congruent*, in which the premises were consistent with children's world knowledge (for example, "Bears have big teeth"); and (3) *incongruent*, in which the premises were in contradiction to the children's knowledge (for example, "Glasses bounce when they fall"). Here are examples of a fantasy, congruent, and incongruent syllogism:

Fantasy Syllogism
>Every banga is purple.
>Purple animals sneeze at people.
>Do bangas sneeze at people?

Congruent Syllogism
>Bears have big teeth.
>Animals with big teeth can't read books.
>Can bears read books?

Incongruent Syllogism
>Glasses bounce when they fall.
>Everything that bounces is made of rubber.
>Are glasses made of rubber?

The children were given eight problems of each type, with some children being presented the set of fantasy problems first and others being presented the fantasy problems second or third.

In keeping with Piaget's observations, children consistently failed the incongruent problems (13% correct). They were not able to ignore what they know about the world in answering these questions. In other words, they were not able to think "formally," using only the *form* of the problem to generate an answer. Children's performance was excellent, however, for the congruent problems (94%). But such performance does not require any reasoning at all. Children could have used their world knowledge to answer the question ("Do bears read books? Of course not!"). In fact, when children's justifications of their answers to the congruent problems were examined, most of them (81%) were described as *empirical*, with reference being made to their practical world knowledge. Very few of their justifications were classified as *theoretical* (10%), in which reference was made only to the information presented in the problem.

But what about the fantasy questions? Here, performance is independent of children's past knowledge. They posed questions about hypothetical characters, requiring, it would seem, formal reasoning. Children's performance on the fantasy problems was very high, particularly when these problems were presented first (94% correct). The percentage of correct answers was lower on these problems when the congruent or incongruent problems preceded them (66% correct). Furthermore, children's justifications on the fantasy problems were likely to be classified as theoretical when the fantasy problems were presented first (58%), although nontheoretical explanations predominated when the fantasy problems were presented later in the session (92% nontheoretical explanations).

One interpretation of these findings is that 4- and 5-year-old children possess rudiments for formal reasoning. However, this study also reveals the tenuous nature of such reasoning in young children. They consistently failed the incongruous problems. When their real-world knowledge conflicted with the *form* of the problem, they almost always went with what they know (generally not a bad strategy to follow). Yet when imaginary characters were used, young children's responses and their justifications were indicative of formal reasoning (see also Markovits & Vachon, 1989). Nevertheless, children were easily biased away from such deductions when the fantasy problems were preceded by the congruent or incongruent problems. Obviously, formal reasoning is not well-established in young children and is displayed only under optimal conditions (compare with Fischer's skill theory, discussed in Chapter 4).

Scientific Reasoning

Not all logical reasoning is decontextualized. Logic comes in handy frequently in everyday life, especially if you happen to make your living being a scientist. I discussed scientific reasoning briefly in Piaget's model of formal operations (Chapter 4). **Scientific reasoning** involves generating hypotheses about how something in the world works and then systematically testing those hypotheses. Basically, one uses scientific reasoning by identifying the factors that can affect a particular phenomenon (the rate at which a pendulum oscillates, as in the example provided in the Piaget chapter, for instance), and exhaustively varying one factor at a time while holding the other factors constant. As you will recall, Piaget proposed that scientific reasoning is not found until adolescence (Inhelder & Piaget, 1958). Subsequent research has not always supported Piaget's theories, but it is generally agreed that scientific reasoning is a late-developing ability that is not easily demonstrated by many adults (Kuhn, Amsel, & O'Loughlin, 1988). (Recall, however, that "theory theory" accounts of development propose that something akin to theory testing, and thus scientific reasoning, characterizes even infants and young children [Gopnik & Meltzoff, 1997].)

Let me provide an example from research by Kuhn and her colleagues. Deanna Kuhn and her colleagues (1988) presented hypothetical information about the relation between certain foods and the likelihood of catching colds to sixth- and ninth-grade students and to adults of varying educational backgrounds. Participants were first interviewed to determine which foods they thought might be associated with colds. Then, over several trials, they were given a series of foods (for example, oranges, baked potatoes, cereal, Coca-Cola), each associated with an outcome (cold or no cold). Some foods were always associated with getting a cold (baked potatoes, for instance), some were always associated with not getting colds (cereal, for instance), and others were independent of getting colds (that is, sometimes they were associated with getting colds, and sometimes not). At least one outcome was consistent with a participant's initial opinion about the "healthiness" of a food, and one inconsistent with it.

Scientific reasoning involves hypotheses, but what is most crucial about the scientific method is that it involves *evidence*. Maybe you have grown up believing that eating chicken soup will make you healthy, but science requires that *evidence*, when available, be used to provide an answer. Initial responses on these questions were usually based on prior beliefs, but as more evidence accumulated, most adults increased their decisions based on that evidence. The adolescents, however, were much less apt to consider evidence in their decisions, but instead relied more frequently on extra-experimental beliefs (for example, "The juice makes a difference because my mother says orange juice is better for you"). In fact, 30% of the sixth graders never made a single spontaneous evidenced-based response. Yet, when asked how they knew one food did or didn't have an effect, most participants of all ages were able to provide an evidenced-based answer, although children were still less likely to do so than adults. This indicates that reasoning from evidence is something that sixth graders can do, but that they choose not to do spontaneously. It's also worth noting that the adults did not fare perfectly on these problems either. Only the most highly educated adults (philosophy graduate students) consistently solved these problems using the evidence that was presented.

Scientific reasoning can improve with practice. Several researchers have given participants of varying ages sets of scientific problems to solve over repeated testing sessions (Kuhn et al., 1995; Schauble, 1996). In these studies, participants' performance improved over sessions and generalized to different scientific problems (for example, from determining what factors affect the speed of a car to determine what factors influence school achievement). However, although participants of all ages showed improvements over sessions, preadolescent children showed fewer gains than adults. Elementary school children can be trained to use scientific reasoning with explicit instruction, but transfer of such trained strategies is limited to older preadolescent children only (Chen & Klahr, in press).

Why do children, adolescents, and many adults perform so poorly on scientific reasoning problems? Kuhn and her colleagues (1988) argued that scientific reasoning involves thinking *about* theories rather than just working with them. In other words, scientific reasoning requires a high level of metacognition. Scientific reasoning requires integrating theories (or hypotheses) with data (or evidence). When the two agree, there is little problem. Problems occur when hypotheses and evidence are in

conflict. Kuhn (1989) has speculated that children (and many adults) take one of two extreme approaches to theory-data conflicts: *Theory-bound children* distort the data to fit the theory, whereas *data-bound children* focus not on the global theory to explain their results but, rather, on isolated patterns of results (to avoid conflict with the theory).

Although poor metacognition might be the overarching reason for peoples' difficulties with scientific reasoning, it is not the only one. Children and adolescents often do not conduct effective experiments; they frequently fail to vary one factor systematically, or they come to a decision before all possible factors have been tested. Children, and to a lesser extent adults, have a positive-results bias. They put more weight on results that produce good outcomes (for example, good academic performance, good health) than on results that yield negative outcomes (see DeLoache et al., 1998). Adolescents' preexisting beliefs also strongly influence their scientific reasoning. Outcomes that are consistent with their prior beliefs are quickly and uncritically accepted, whereas evidence counter to their beliefs are regarded more critically (Klaczynski, 1997; Klaczynski & Narasimham, 1998).

In general, the "big" picture of scientific reasoning painted by Inhelder and Piaget (1958) more than 40 years ago has not been drastically changed. Scientific reasoning is rarely found in children. What the new research indicates, however, is that scientific reasoning is only occasionally found in adolescents and adults without specific training. Given these findings, it makes good sense for university-level psychology students to have a course in research methods, where the logic of experimental design is made explicit. College students are clearly capable of such thinking, but we should not be surprised that it does not come spontaneously or easily to them.

Reasoning-Remembering Relationships

Most reasoning tasks are examples of "higher-order" cognition, in that they involve more than the basic-level processes of encoding, categorizing, and short-term memory. Yet, these basic-level processes clearly influence a child's ability to perform reasoning problems. That is, like other forms of complex thinking, reasoning is supported by a host of lower-level forms of cognition.

One basic-level process that has been proposed to be involved in most, if not all forms of reasoning is memory. Children need to remember the premises of a problem to solve it. One popular explanation for young children's poor reasoning abilities is that they forget the premises on which their reasoning is based. This has been illustrated for *transitive-inference* problems. Transitive inference is the process of inferring the relation between two concepts or objects from a knowledge of their relation to other concepts or objects. For instance, in a series of sticks arranged in increasing length (for example, A, B, C, D, and E), there is an implicit knowledge that any given stick is both larger than the one immediately preceding it (for example, $C \rightarrow B$) and smaller than the one immediately following it (for example, $C \leftarrow D$). However, children do not necessarily know the relation between two items that have not been specifically compared. For example, if D is longer than C, and C is longer than B, what is the relation between B and D? Although it is obvious to adults, it is not always apparent to children.

Tom Trabasso and his colleagues argued that it is not young children's lack of reasoning ability, per se, that prevents them from solving transitive inference problems but, rather, their poor memories. They forget the premises ($C \rightarrow B$; $C \leftarrow D$; and so on.), making it difficult if not impossible for them to come up with the right answer. To support their position, Bryant and Trabasso (1971) showed that young children can solve transitive-inference problems when given extensive training on all the premises. Sticks of different colors were used, and children were presented with successive pairs of sticks and asked to judge which was the longer (for example, A or B; B or C; C or D; D or E). The children were later tested for their retention of the premises (for example, their memory that the red stick A was longer than the yellow stick B). The children were then asked to make judgments concerning pairs of sticks that had not been presented together before (in our example, they might be asked which is longer: the yellow

stick B or the blue stick D). Counter to the findings of Piaget and others, children as young as 4 years in these experiments were able to answer the critical transitive-inference question correctly, indicating that young children have the competence to solve such problems but that limitations of memory prevent them from displaying this competence under some circumstances.

Such results seem clear-cut and appear to reflect a significant relationship between reasoning and remembering. However, research by Brainerd and Kingma (1984) demonstrated that the relationship is more apparent than real. They modified the standard transitive-inference paradigm, inserting occasional memory probes for adjacent relations (for example, "Which is longer, A or B?"). In a series of experiments, they found that memory for the premises was independent of reasoning performance. In other words, one was not able to predict reasoning performance based on memory for the premises.

Reyna and Brainerd have investigated more thoroughly the relation between reasoning and memory and have interpreted these relations in terms of **fuzzy-trace theory** (Reyna, 1992; Reyna & Brainerd, 1995; see Chapter 5). As you may recall from our earlier discussion of fuzzy-trace theory, people of all ages have a bias toward reasoning using the more readily available and inexact fuzzy (gist) traces. Thus, when a reasoning task can be accomplished with fuzzy traces, performance can progress without the child's remembering the specifics of the background information (that is, without using verbatim information). Verbatim information deteriorates more rapidly than gist information, so that it should not be surprising that children forget the details (that is, the specific premises) but still retain enough of the fuzzy traces from the representation to solve the problem. Younger children will fail the transitive-inference task (and others) not because they forget the premise, but because of faulty reasoning. In addition, young children's greater tendency to encode and reason with verbatim traces provides them with another handicap. Such traces are more prone to being forgotten and are more difficult (mentally effortful) to use in solving many reasoning problems. Older children will solve the transitive-inference problem because of their efficient processing of fuzzy traces (that is, proper reasoning with gistlike traces), independent of whether they remember the verbatim information or not.

In other situations, fuzzy-trace theory predicts that there will be a significant relationship between memory for background facts and reasoning. For example, in mental arithmetic problems, correct answers can only be obtained by processing verbatim information. If children forget the premise (for example, 8 + 9 = ?), they cannot rely on fuzzy traces to arrive at the correct answer. In these cases, dependencies between memory and reasoning are indeed found (Brainerd & Reyna, 1988).

Although different reasoning requires different types of information, Reyna and Brainerd propose that most everyday reasoning involves primarily gist traces, often supported by verbatim sources, such as dictionaries, reference books, and lists (Reyna, 1992). For example, as I write this section, I rely on my gistlike understanding of fuzzy-trace theory, frequently checking one of Brainerd and Reyna's many papers on the topic to confirm my interpretation and to obtain the details of experiments. Thus, although I could not write this section on fuzzy-trace theory without substantial verbatim information, my decisions about how to organize the section, what, in general, to include, and what to emphasize are based on the gistlike traces I have established from reading papers on fuzzy-trace theory and discussions I've had with colleagues and students on the topic over the last several years.

Summary

Problem solving involves having a goal, obstacles to that goal, strategies for overcoming the obstacles, and an evaluation of the results. Infants have shown signs of true *goal-directed behavior* and problem solving in the latter part of the first year. Problem solving improves over the preschool years and is influenced by how much knowledge the problem solver has about the task to be solved or the context in which the task is embedded.

Some forms of problem solving involve the discovery or induction of rules. Rules for simple oddity problems can be learned by preverbal toddlers, especially when accompanied by language instructions. In the *rule-assessment approach*, cognitive development is characterized by the acquisition of increasingly powerful rules for solving problems. Although the rule-assessment approach describes reasonably well the development of many tasks (for example, balance-scale problem, conservation), children typically use a variety of strategies for any particular problem, as exemplified by Siegler's adaptive strategy-choice model. Zelazo and his colleagues have focused on children's developing ability to follow rules and report that young children often fail to use a rule even though they can demonstrate knowledge of the rule. This is especially apparent when the rules governing a task change (for example, from sorting cards by color to sorting cards by shape). *Cognitive complexity and control (CCC) theory* proposes that there are age-related changes in the complexity of rule systems that children can represent and that developmental differences in conscious awareness give children increased control over their behavior and cognition.

Planning is an important aspect of problem solving, but is a relatively late-developing phenomenon. Some reasons for young children's frequent failure to plan include poor inhibition abilities, a bias toward speed over accuracy, planning is difficult and time consuming and does not always improve task performance, and that it may be more fun to solve novel problems without planning. Planning improves over the preschool years, and most 5-year-olds display planning for simple tasks.

Reasoning is a special type of problem solving that requires that one make an inference. *Analogical reasoning* involves *relational mapping*—the application of what one knows about one set of elements to relations about different elements. The *relational primacy hypothesis* proposes that analogical reasoning is available early in infancy. Although there is some evidence for this, preschool children have difficulty with more traditional analogy problems, although they are able to solve them in some situations. Similarity (perceptual and relational) between different aspects of a problem plays an important role in solving analogies. There appears to be a *relational shift* in the development of analogical reasoning, in which young children are more likely to focus on perceptual similarity, whereas older children and adults focus more on relational similarity in solving problems. Other factors that influence children's success at analogical reasoning are knowledge for the relations on which the analogy is based, and metacognition, or a conscious awareness of the basis on which one is solving a problem.

In *formal reasoning* the *form* of an argument, not its semantic content, is crucial. Piaget proposed that formal reasoning is the hallmark of adult cognition and was reflected by adolescents' and adults' use of *propositional logic*, a form of symbolic logic that involves two or more factors (conventionally, P and Q), with each factor having two possible values (for instance, true or false). Counter to Piaget's theory, propositional logic is frequently not shown by adults. Other forms of formal reasoning, such as syllogisms, can be demonstrated by preschool children under certain situations when statements in a problem do not contradict their world knowledge.

Scientific reasoning involves generating hypotheses about how something in the world works and then systematically testing those hypotheses. Scientific reasoning is also a late-developing ability, in part because of the metacognitive difficulty involved in reasoning *about* theories.

Reasoning and memory for the premises of a problem have been proposed to be related. However, in many cases, depending on the nature of the problem, they are not. Reyna and Brainerd applied *fuzzy-trace theory* to reasoning-remembering relations to account for the inconsistent pattern found in the research literature.

Note

1. The sixteen binary operations of propositional logic following Inhelder and Piaget (1958) are: (1) Affirmation: All combinations are possible, for example, P and Q, P and not Q, not P and Q, and not P and not Q are all possible; (2) Negation: No combinations are possible; (3) Conjunction: P is true and Q is

true; (4) Incompatibility: P is never true if Q is true, and vice versa; (5) Disjunction: P is true or Q is true (or both are true); (6) Conjunctive Negation: P is false and Q is false; (7) Implication: P implies Q; (8) Nonimplication: P does not imply Q; (9) Reciprocal Implication: Q implies P; (10) Negation of Reciprocal Implication: Q does not imply P; (11) Equivalence: The effect of P is equal to the effect of Q; (12) Reciprocal Equivalence: The effect of P is not equal to the effect of Q; (13) Affirmation of P: P is true independent of Q; (14) Negation of P: P is false independent of Q; (15) Affirmation of Q: Q is true independent of P; (16) Negation of Q: Q is false independent of P.

Key Terms and Concepts

problem solving
goal-directed behavior
cognitive complexity and control (CCC) theory
rule-assessment approach
reasoning
analogical reasoning
relational mapping
relational primacy hypothesis
relational shift
learning to learn
formal reasoning
propositional logic
scientific reasoning
fuzzy-trace theory

Suggested Readings

DeLoache, J. S., Miller, K. F., & Pierroutsakos, S. L. (1998). Reasoning and problem solving. In D. Kuhn & R. S. Siegler (Vol. Eds.), *Cognitive, language, and perceptual development*, Vol. 2 (pp. 801–850). In B. Damon (General Editor), *Handbook of child psychology*. New York: Wiley. This chapter presents an up-to-date, comprehensive review of the developmental literature of problem solving and reasoning, extending beyond the topics covered in this textbook.

Goswami, U. (1996). Analogical reasoning and cognitive development. In H. W. Reese (Ed.), *Advances in child development and behavior* (Vol. 26) (pp. 92–138). San Diego: Academic Press. This chapter provides an excellent review of research examining analogical reasoning in children. Much of the review focuses on Goswami's own research, which is substantial, influential, and interesting.

ZELAZO, P. D., & JACQUES, S. (1997). Children's rule use: Representation, reflection and cognitive control. *Annals of Child Development, 12* (pp. 119–176). London: Jessica Kingsley Press. This chapter provides a review of children's rule-following, beginning with classic Soviet work by Luria and his colleagues, and concluding with the contemporary research of Zelazo and his colleagues.

KUHN, D., AMSEL, E., & O'LOUGHLIN, M. (1988). *The development of scientific thinking skills.* San Diego: Academic. This book provides an excellent overview of research on the development of scientific reasoning, as well as presenting the authors' own innovative work.

REYNA, V. F. (1992). Reasoning, remembering, and their relationship: Social, cognitive, and developmental issues (pp. 103–132). In M. L. Howe, C. J. Brainerd, & V. F. Reyna (Eds.), *Development of long-term retention.* New York: Springer-Verlag. This chapter provides a clear presentation of fuzzy-trace theory as it relates to reasoning-remembering relations.

11

Social Cognition

As a cognitive psychologist, I tend to believe that most aspects of human behavior are a function, to some significant degree, of one's cognitions. I find this especially easy to believe of the social behavior of children. A child can be only as social as his or her level of cognitive functioning will permit. One cannot expect a child to behave in a socially appropriate way if that child cannot understand the social relationships among individuals and the ramifications of behaving in one way as opposed to another. **Social cognition** refers to cognition about social relationships and social phenomena. Nonsocial cognition deals with words, numbers, maps, images, and inanimate objects in general; such "hard," or "cold," cognition can be contrasted with the "soft," or "warm," cognition that involves thinking about people and their relationships with one another.

Many of a child's day-to-day activities involve interactions with people. These interactions require thought. Children must make evaluations of social situations and must understand their relationships with other people in a particular context. This requires an appreciation of who they are as social beings and who their fellow interactants are. It involves anticipating the thoughts and feelings of others and the execution of social "strategies." These strategies can be aimed at facilitating the formation of relationships, such as mother-infant attachment or playground friendships, or the successful completion of some cooperative task, such as jumping rope or playing baseball.

It could be argued, I believe, that social cognition is actually the purest type of cognition because of its importance to everyday functioning. Many have argued that competing and cooperating with conspecifics (fellow members of our own species) might have been the single most powerful force in the evolution of human intelligence (Alexander, 1989; Humphrey, 1976). In other words, the most important type of cognition for our species is social cognition. I would argue that understanding ourselves and others is just as important today as it was in our evolutionary past. Although we can employ our intellect today to figure out how to use computers, automatic teller machines, and VCRs, we remain a social species, and our social "thinking" likely still has the greatest impact on us on a day-to-day basis.

There are few narrow topics in cognitive development. Research into memory, perception, and language involves many subtopics, with numerous facets to each. The number of topics subsumed under the rubric of social cognition, however, is even greater. Any thinking involved in any social setting or about any social phenomenon is a potential area of inquiry. And there is not necessarily a hard line drawn between social and nonsocial cognition. For example, much of the research I reviewed on theory of mind in Chapter 7 could have just as easily been included in a chapter on social cognition (see Flavell & Miller, 1998).

I will not attempt to provide a representative review of the topics in developmental social cognition. Rather, I have selected six topics to review, in varying degrees of detail, hoping to provide you with a flavor of developmental social cognition, how the research is done, and how it is relates to nonsocial cognitive development. In the sections to follow, I first outline two broad theories of developmental social cognition: Bandura's social cognitive theory and Dodge's social information processing model. I then review research on the development of self, children's perspective taking, children's humor, and the cognitive bases of gender identification.

Social Cognitive Theory

One of the most influential theories in developmental psychology during the past 35 years has been Albert Bandura's **social learning theory**, recently renamed **social cognitive theory** by Bandura to reflect a more mentalistic approach. Initial formulations of social learning theory (Bandura & Walters, 1963; Miller & Dollard, 1941) were based on extensions of models of classical and operant conditioning, popular throughout most of this century in American psychology. It became apparent, however, that explicit reinforcement was not necessary for children (and adults) to learn about their social world. Rather, people learn much about their world simply by watching. As the field of cognitive psychology developed over the 1960s and 1970s, Bandura incorporated many cognitive principles, transforming his theory into a cognitive one in which children learn about important social relationships by watching (Bandura, 1986, 1989).

Despite the social learning origins of social cognitive theory, there are many similarities between the ideas expressed in social cognitive theory and those expressed by Piaget (as discussed in Chapter 4). For example, unlike earlier social learning theory, social cognitive theory proposes that children play an active role in interacting with their environment. As Piaget did, Bandura believes that children affect their environment as much as their environment affects them. Bandura refers to this interaction between children and their environment as **reciprocal determinism**, with children determining how others respond toward them as much as they are influenced by others. Bandura proposes that there are complex interactions between children's thoughts, feelings, and behaviors and the external environment. How children feel or think about something will affect their behavior. Likewise, their behavior in certain situations will influence their thought. Each of us tries to make sense of our behavior and often we change our thinking and beliefs to be in line with our actions (Gazzaniga, 1985). Children's behavior will influence how other people in the environment perceive and act toward them, which will, of course, affect their thinking and behavior. Thus, Bandura proposes a process of causation that gives serious attention to the internal states of children (their thoughts and emotions), their observable behaviors, and the perceptions and actions of others.

Bandura proposed five capabilities that contribute to children's learning about their social world and their place in it, each of which develops: (1) symbolization, (2) forethought, (3) self-regulation, (4) self-reflection, and (5) vicarious learning. The first capability, that of **symbolization**, means that we can think about our social behavior in words and images. This is necessary for us to be aware of various aspects of our actions. The capability of **forethought** means that we are able to anticipate the consequences of our actions and the actions of others. This future-time perspective motivates behavior.

Self-regulation involves adopting standards of acceptable behavior for ourselves. These include aspirational standards (hoped-for levels of accomplishment) as well as social and moral standards. A capacity for **self-reflection** allows us to analyze our thoughts and actions.

The final capability, that of **vicarious learning**, is the cornerstone of social cognitive theory. Children need not receive specific reinforcement for their behavior to learn; rather, they learn much social behavior merely by observing others. This places **observational learning** at the center of Bandura's theory. Bandura proposed four subprocesses that govern observational learning: attentional processes, retention processes, production processes, and motivational processes. Information must be attended to, coded in memory, stored, and retrieved, and the behavior must be performed at the appropriate time. Each of these processes changes with age, and a failure in any one process (retention, for example) rules out successful observational learning.

Children do not need to physically imitate a model to have learned from observing the model. Children might have learned all they need to know from observing but never have the motivation to produce the behavior. For instance, Money and Ehrhardt (1972) proposed that both boys and girls learn appropriate male and female sex roles but typically imitate only same-sex behavior. Learning the opposite-sex role is important in development, for it informs a child what behaviors should complement his or hers. But although opposite-sex roles are learned, they are coded negatively and are not to be imitated, whereas same-sex roles are coded positively and are incorporated into a child's behavior.

Although imitation is not necessary for observational learning to occur, imitation is an important component of observational learning and child development. It is the clearest indication that children have learned through watching and the primary means by which children acquire new behaviors.

The Development of Imitation

Although there is substantial debate about when and to what extent infants can imitate novel behaviors (as discussed in Chapter 7), imitation clearly takes on a symbolic character by late in the first year of life, when toddlers can observe a model and defer imitation of that behavior until a later time. This is where Bandura's account of observational learning begins.

Imitation during childhood has important implications for development. On the one hand, imitation serves as a means for children to acquire new behaviors, important in mastering their intellectual and physical worlds. Children can learn to walk, run, and throw merely by exercising their innately endowed abilities, but they learn to use a fork, to slide into second base, and to tap dance largely through imitation. On the other hand, imitation also plays an important role in social development. It functions as a method of communication between children and their parents and generally serves to sustain social interactions (Grusec & Abramovitch, 1982). An abundance of research shows that many socially important phenomena are acquired through observation without direct instruction (see Shaffer, 1993).

Following Bandura's theory, after children have attended to a model and formed a mental representation of the behavior, they must convert that representation to action. Yet, there are some things that children observe that they do not have the motoric ability to reproduce. For example, although a 5-year-old boy may have watched and mentally practiced the behaviors involved in driving a car, because of his short arms and legs (among other things), he is physically unable to produce the behaviors he has observed. Despite such obvious shortcomings, young children frequently overestimate their imitative abilities. They have watched a behavior being performed and believe that "seeing is knowing." (More than one parent has been shocked to see his or her young child behind the wheel of a moving car.) In a study in which mothers recorded the imitative attempts of their preschoolers, children overestimated their imitative abilities 55.5% of the time—stating that they were capable of imitating a behavior when they were not. Cases of underestimation were rare, occurring on only 4.7% of the observations (Bjorklund, Gaultney, & Green, 1993). Young children have great confidence in their own abilities. To improve observational learning, children must learn to

monitor and compare their actions to their symbolic representations and to correct mismatches. As these production processes improve with age, the difference between what children know and what they can produce declines (Bandura, 1989).

People have a tendency to think of imitation as a lesser cognitive skill—imitation is something unimaginative adults, small children, and even animals do. This might be true of unimaginative adults and small children, but it is not true of animals (Whiten & Ham, 1992). Very little in the way of object imitation (important in tool use) is observed even in our close relatives the chimpanzees (Tomasello et al., 1987). Given the substantial cognitive abilities of chimpanzees, this is somewhat surprising. Tomasello, Savage-Rumbaugh, and Kruger (1993) have speculated that one reason for chimps' failure to imitate readily is that "unlike human children, they do not develop in a social environment in which adult conspecifics are constantly encouraging their attention to objects, intentionally teaching them how to use objects as tools, and rewarding them for imitating actions on objects" (p. 1689). In other words, human children's imitation of actions on objects is fostered by their social environment, whereas the different structure of chimpanzee social environments is not conducive to imitation. Such an interpretation makes imitation not only an important cognitive tool for social learning but also a cognitive ability that emerges from a uniquely human social context.

Michael Tomasello and his colleagues (1993) evaluated their idea by testing mother-reared chimpanzees (that is, chimpanzees reared by their own chimpanzee mothers), human-reared (enculturated) chimpanzees, and 18- and 30-month-old human children on a series of object-imitation tasks. The social experiences of the enculturated chimps were similar to those of the children; Tomasello and his associates hypothesized that such experiences should foster imitation. They reported that the mother-reared chimpanzees were much poorer at immediate imitation than either the enculturated chimps or the human children, who did not differ from one another. Somewhat surprisingly, the enculturated chimpanzees actually showed greater deferred imitation (two days after observing the actions) than the children (see also Bering et al., 1998). These find-ings indicate that chimpanzees possess the rudimen-tary cognitive skills for object imitation but rarely express it in species-typical situations. When pro-vided with a human-typical rearing environment, however, the abilities appear, comparable to those observed for 30-month-old children. Such experi-ence does not (nor ever could) make a chimpanzee think like a human, but the rearing conditions of these animals did change substantially their cognitions.

These findings are consistent with the develop-mental systems approach discussed in Chapter 2 (Gottlieb, Wahlsten, & Lickliter, 1998), in that species-atypical environments can produce species-atypical behaviors, in this case humanlike imitation in chimpanzees. For human cognitive development, these results point to the necessity of considering the role of the social environment when examining the development of a cognitive ability.

The Development of Self-Efficacy

The concept of **self-efficacy**, the extent to which a person views himself or herself as an effective indi-vidual, plays a central role in Bandura's theory. Self-efficacy develops through experience. Children evaluate the effectiveness of their own actions, com-pare it with the actions of others, and are told by others how their behavior meets certain standards. Children who believe they are competent (even if they are not) develop feelings of positive self-efficacy. Conversely, when self-efficacy is poor, peo-ple tend to behave ineffectually, regardless of their actual abilities (Bandura, 1997). Developing feelings of positive self-efficacy has important consequences for children's social, emotional, and intellectual de-velopment (Bandura et al., 1996). One should not think of self-efficacy as a general characteristic of a child. Rather, self-efficacy (and the related concept of self-worth) is specific to a domain and a task (Harter, Waters, & Whitesell, 1998). A child can have a positive sense of self-efficacy for playing base-ball, for example, but a poor sense of self-efficacy for doing long division.

The development of self-efficacy begins early, as infants learn that they can exert some control over their environment. Beginning around 3 or 4 months, babies learn that their actions have conse-quences—that if they kick their feet, the mobile over the crib will move and if they smile and coo their parents will smile and talk back to them. In-fants who have experienced some control over their environments are better able to learn new behaviors (Finkelstein & Ramey, 1977). Mary Ainsworth and her colleagues have proposed that parents' respon-siveness to their infants' attempts to communicate their needs gives the infants some sense of control over their parents and is related to later social and cognitive development (Ainsworth et al., 1978).

With the development of language and other symbols, children are able to reflect on their new so-cial and intellectual abilities and evaluate what oth-ers tell them about their skills. Initially, the family provides children with feedback on their effective-ness. As children approach school age, their peer group becomes a valuable source of information, and school itself is a potent agent in forming chil-dren's self-efficacy. Children learn through daily ex-perience with teachers and peers that they are good at some tasks and not so good at others (Bandura, 1997).

Although children learn self-efficacy through ex-perience, developing a positive sense of self-efficacy is facilitated by a generally optimistic (and unrealis-tic) opinion of their own abilities. Preschool chil-dren think that they can remember more items, communicate more effectively, perform tasks better, and imitate a model more accurately than they actu-ally can (Bjorklund et al., 1993; Plumert, 1995; Schneider, 1998). Young children's beliefs that they know more than they actually do and can do more than they actually can provides them with positive perceptions of their own skills. This positive sense of self-efficacy might encourage children to attempt things that they would not try if they had a more re-alistic idea of their abilities. In other words, their cognitive immaturity, as reflected by their unrealis-tic assessments of their abilities, can actually facili-tate development rather than hinder it (Bjorklund, 1997a; Bjorklund & Green, 1992). (However, it also poses some problems. For example, Plumert (1995) reports that 6-year-olds who consistently overestimate their physical abilities are more accident prone than less optimistic children.)

This point is made by Deborah Stipek and her colleagues (Stipek, 1984; Stipek & Daniels, 1988), who found that young children can make relatively accurate predictions of how other children are likely to perform on schoollike tasks but are overly optimistic in predicting their own future performance. Stipek suggested that this overly optimistic self-perception is due to **wishful thinking,** a concept originally introduced by Piaget (1930): Children wish for A's on their report card; therefore, they expect A's (see also Schneider, 1998). By the third or fourth grade, children's assessments of their own abilities move closer to reality, and they are able to tell the difference between what they wish would happen and what they can reasonably expect to happen.

Stipek believes that this tendency to overestimate their own abilities enhances children's self-efficacy and gives them the confidence to attempt things they would not otherwise try. There is some preliminary evidence that brighter 3-year-olds overestimate their abilities (on an imitation task) more than less-bright 3-year-olds, suggesting an adaptive value of overestimation in young children (Bjork-lund et al., 1993). Stipek (1984) proposed that rather than trying to make young children's self-assessments more accurate, we should "try harder to design educational environments which maintain their optimism and eagerness" (p. 53). The positive consequences of overestimation are not limited to the preschool years. Recent research has shown, for example, that 8- to 11-year-old children who overestimated their capabilities had better school performance than less optimistic children (Lopez et al., 1998).

This does not mean, however, that young children are incapable of judging their performance. Research evidence indicates that children are aware of adults' expectations and know when they have not met them by as young as 2 years of age, at least when simple tasks with definite criteria of success are used (Stipek, Recchia, & McClintic, 1992). For example,

in a study by Stipek and her colleagues (1992), preschool children were given simple puzzles to solve (some of which had oversized pieces, making success impossible). Many children, some as young as 2 years of age, responded to failure on these tasks by turning their head or body away from the experimenter and otherwise generally avoiding social contact. They seemingly thought that their performance was not what it should have been and anticipated some negative response from the adult. Likewise, when young children succeeded on these tasks, they sought adult attention, anticipating approval. Thus, even very young children are sometimes aware of their successes and failures and are responsive to reactions (or anticipated reactions) from others to their performances.

Although we become better able to assess our physical and cognitive abilities with age, individual differences become apparent, with some children retaining a more optimistic perspective of their abilities than others. For example, Carol Dweck and her colleagues (Dweck & Leggett, 1988; Dweck & Reppucci, 1973) have found in some children a maladaptive pattern of achievement behavior that they describe as **helplessness**. These children avoid challenge, do not persist in the face of difficulty, and tend to attribute their failure on tasks to a lack of ability rather than to a lack of effort or an inappropriate strategy. Other children display an adaptive pattern termed **mastery orientation**: They enjoy and seek challenge, persist in the face of obstacles, and tend to view their failings as caused by lack of effort or strategy use rather than by a lack of ability. Not surprisingly, mastery-oriented children have a better-developed sense of self-efficacy and, at least in the United States, are more likely to be successful on a wide range of tasks than children showing the helpless pattern.

Bandura's ideas have been applied to many different contents, the majority of which are more social in character than cognitive. As a cognitive psychologist, however, I believe that knowledge, be it of inanimate objects, of other people, or of one's self, is mentally represented and operated on by a set of cognitive mechanisms. Bandura's approach to development acknowledges this, blurring the

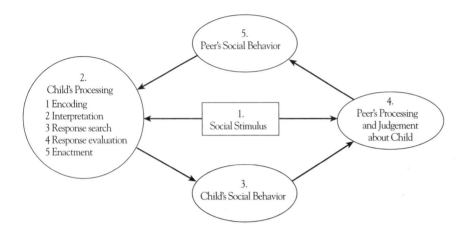

FIGURE 11-1   Dodge's model of social exchange in children. SOURCE: From "Social Competence in Children," by Dodge et al., 1986, *Monographs of the Society for Research in Child Development, 51*, (Serial No. 213). Copyright © 1986 The Society for Research in Child Development, Inc. Reprinted with permission.

distinction between what is social and what is cognitive, recognizing that it is all governed by the same nervous system.

Social Information Processing

Social cognitive theorists have adopted many of the tenets of information processing. Social information must be encoded, compared with other pertinent information, and retrieved so that social interactions run smoothly. The more skillfully social information is processed, the more socially competent a child is seen to be. Kenneth Dodge and his colleagues have postulated a theory that describes the mental processes involved in evaluating social information (Crick & Dodge, 1994; Dodge, 1986; Dodge et al., 1986; see also Rubin & Krasnor, 1986). Dodge's original model of social exchange in children is shown in Figure 11-1.

As can be seen in the model, there are five major units of social interaction. The first is the social stimulus, or cue. This is the information that a child must process. For example, a shove by another child, a smile, a scowl, a pout, and an invitation to join a game are all social signals that must be interpreted. The second unit of the model is a child's social information processing of these cues. A child must make sense of the social cues and decide how to respond. More will be said of this unit shortly. Once a child evaluates the information, he or she

must emit some social behavior. Does the 6-year-old enter the play group by jumping in the middle of an ongoing game, ask if she can play, too, or just stand to the side, waiting to be asked? This behavior serves as a social stimulus for a child's peers, who make some judgment of the child. (The model has been reformulated to include a sixth stage between the representation and search processes in which children clarify their goals in the situation [Crick & Dodge, 1994]. The reformulated model refines the theory but does not substantially change it. The basic model has been quite successful in accounting for a wide range of children's social behaviors.)

Of major concern here is the part of Dodge's theory dealing with **social information processing**. How do children make sense of social information to select a proper social response? Dodge postulated five sequential steps of information processing that are necessary for competent social functioning:

1. *Encoding.* The child must first encode the social stimulus. This requires that the child be properly attentive and adequately perceive the social signal. The child must know what cues are important to encode. For a child entering an already established group, for example, whether he is greeted by a smile or a frown is an important social cue. Less critical are things such as what the other children are wearing or that Kevin needs a haircut.

2. *Interpretation.* Once encoded, the social information must be interpreted. What does this infor-

mation mean? To determine meaning, children must compare this information with what they already know. What does it mean if the child is greeted by smiles? This will depend on what this child knows about the smiles of others in similar situations. "When I approach a group of kids I know who are already playing a game, smiles are usually a sign of welcome. But when Marvin smiles at me, it usually means he's going to trip me the first chance he gets." Children develop rules for interpreting social signals. These rules are probably not conscious and are executed in a matter of microseconds.

3. *Response search.* Once an interpretation has been made, children must decide what their next move is. They must generate a variety of response alternatives. Do they join the group? If so, by what means? Do they approach the playground bully, walk around him, think of something clever to say, or run away? With age, children have a greater number of more sophisticated options from which to choose, which should contribute greatly to behaving in a socially competent fashion.

4. *Response evaluation.* Once responses have been generated, they must be evaluated. Does it make sense to approach the bully, hitting him before he hits me, or might one of the other options be wiser? To what extent can children anticipate the consequences of their behavior, selecting the response alternative that will be most successful in the current situation?

5. *Enactment.* Finally, the child must execute the chosen response.

Dodge proposed that these steps are executed in order. However, steps of processing can be skipped. When they are, it is likely that socially incompetent behavior will result. The first response a child comes up with might not be the ideal response for the situation. If this response is not evaluated and found wanting, the resulting behavior will probably not ingratiate the child to his or her peers. Similarly, a child might make a decision based on misinterpreted information. The quiet manner of a peer while studying may have been interpreted as an invitation to horse around, or the smile of the well-known bully may have been construed erroneously as a peace offering. Also, as mentioned earlier, the wrong information might be encoded. The cues may have been there, but they may have been ignored or missed because the child was attentive to other more salient environmental or internal cues.

Dodge and his colleagues tested this model with respect to the social skill of peer-group entry—that is, entering an established group of other children (Dodge et al., 1986). Children in kindergarten and the first and second grades were shown videotapes of two children playing a game and were asked a series of questions related to peer-group entry. The questions were selected so that each of the five aspects of Dodge's model of social information processing could be evaluated. After viewing the video, for example, the children were asked to imagine that they wanted to join the group. They were then asked how much the child on the left and then the child on the right from the video would like to play with them. Answers to these questions reflected the children's interpretation of social cues, step 2 of the model. The children were then asked the reasons for their decisions. Answers to this question indicated the children's use of specific cues from the videotapes in making their decisions, step 1 of the model (encoding). The children were then asked to think of as many ways as possible to join the group, step 3 of the model (response search). After this, the children viewed five scenarios consisting of the original video of two children playing followed by the arrival of a third child who attempted to join the group. The new arrival displayed one of five strategies for joining the group (competent, aggressive, self-centered, passive, or authority intervention). The children were then asked a series of questions concerning the potential effectiveness of each of the five strategies, to assess step 4 of the model (response evaluation). Finally, the children were asked to pretend that they wished to play with the experimenter and were told to "show me how you would ask me if you could play with me." This corresponded to step 5 of the model (enactment).

In a separate session, conducted one to two weeks later, each child was brought into a room in which two other children were already playing and was told to play with these children. Based on videotapes of these sessions and interviews with the children, each child's actual peer-group entry was evaluated.

The most important aspect of the results of this study concerns the prediction of children's peer-group entry (their actual social behavior) as a function of their skills at social information processing. In general, children who scored higher on the assessment of social information processing were rated as more successful at actual peer-group entry. Children who used presented cues (step 1), who generated competent and nonaggressive strategies in response to a hypothetical entry situation (step 3), who evaluated incompetent responses negatively (step 4), and who demonstrated high skill in enactment of responses (step 5) were relatively likely to perform competently and successfully in actual group entry (Dodge et al., 1986). Furthermore, Dodge and his colleagues reported that these skills were relatively independent of one another, suggesting that each contributes something unique to social judgment and behavior rather than reflecting different aspects of a single social intelligence. Other researchers have tested the relation between children's competence for each of the five areas of social information processing and subsequent social behavior, and as Dodge et al. (1986), report modest relations (Dodge & Price, 1994; Slaby & Guerra, 1988).

The area in which social information processing theory has been most frequently applied is aggressive behavior (Coie & Dodge, 1998; Crick & Dodge, 1996). Research has found characteristic ways in which—at least some—aggressive children encode, interpret, search, evaluate, and enact social behavior. For example, highly aggressive children have been found to be less likely to recall relevant social cues from a videotape (Dodge et al., 1995) and to be more attentive to potentially aggressive cues (Gouze, 1987) than less aggressive children. Concerning interpretation, highly aggressive children are more likely to interpret an ambiguous situation (for example, a peer spills water on you) as having an aggressive, rather than accidental, intent (Graham & Hudley, 1994) and also interpret events with clearly benign intentions as hostile (Dodge et al., 1986) than less aggressive children are. Con-

cerning response search, aggressive children tend to generate more atypical and socially inappropriate responses than less aggressive children (see Coie & Dodge, 1998) and have a difficult time inhibiting aggressive responses (Perry, Perry, & Rasmussen, 1986). Aggressive children perceive aggressive responses as socially appropriate and normative (Guerra, Huesmann, & Hanish, 1995), and believe that they can engage in aggression relatively easily (Perry et al., 1986). Although such a pattern does not reduce in any way the effect of other, more traditionally "social" factors, on aggression, it does point to the conclusion that how children process social information with respect to aggression is related to their own level of aggressive behavior.

The work of Dodge and his colleagues clearly points to the cognitive basis of social behavior. Complex social situations must be evaluated and thought about just as strictly intellectual situations must be contemplated. Theories of nonsocial information processing have specified routines (such as encoding and retrieval) and structures (such as the short-term store and semantic memory) with relative precision. Although there is still much debate concerning the particulars of nonsocial information processing, there is also much consensus. The field of social information processing is less advanced because it is more complicated. How can one specify the features of a social stimulus? How is social information represented in long-term memory? How is it retrieved? Can the concepts of the short-term store, schemas, and strategies, so useful for explaining nonsocial cognition, be successfully applied to social cognition? Social information processing is in its infancy. However, the work of Dodge and others (Rubin & Krasnor, 1986) represents an exciting beginning to research that will surely lead to a better understanding of the development of children's social lives.

The Development of a Concept of Self

Few mental concepts are more important to us than the personal sense of self. By **self-concept,** I mean the way a person defines himself or herself. Some theorists have speculated that a conscious awareness of oneself greatly influences cognitive development, particularly the use of goal-directed strategies (Bullock & Lütkenhaus, 1988). Others have stressed the significance of a sense of self for social and emotional development (Brooks-Gunn & Lewis, 1984; Gallup, 1979). Many believe that it is our well-developed sense of self that makes humans unique as a species. In fact, some people have speculated that it was the development of self-awareness that vaulted our hominid ancestors to full human cognition and social organization (Alexander, 1989). The significance of the concept of self for the developing person and for the species cannot be overstated.

How can we know if young children have a concept of self? If they are too young to talk, we cannot ask them and must infer self-awareness from their behavior. Piaget (1952), among others, proposed that infants only gradually come to recognize themselves as distinct from the objects around them, with the distinction becoming fully developed sometime around 18 to 24 months of age (see Chapter 4).

Perhaps one of the earliest indications of a self-concept is infants' ability to differentiate themselves from other people and objects. Infants during the first several months of life should be receiving various forms of proprioceptive, visual, and acoustic feedback from their behavior. This should give them some sense of "who they are," at least with respect to other people.

How can one determine this? One technique is to show infants pictures or videos of themselves along with pictures of videos of other infants or objects and assess their looking time (Bahrick, Moss, & Fadil, 1996; Legerstee, Anderson, & Schaffer, 1998). If infants "recognize" themselves, they should pay less attention (a novelty effect), or possibly more attention (a familiarity effect) to these other stimuli than to images of themselves (see the discussion of preference for novelty/familiarity effects in Chapter 6). If they can't tell the difference between images of themselves and those of other people or objects, there should be no differential attention to any of the stimuli. In experiments using variants of this technique, infants as young as 3 months of age were able to discriminate between images of themselves and same-aged infants (Bahrick et al., 1996; Legerstee et al., 1998), suggesting a primitive form of self-recognition early in infancy. How do infants this young know what they look like? The most likely source of this self-knowledge is mirrors; infants as young as 2-months-old often have daily exposure to their image from mirrors (Bahrick, 1995), and so by 3 months of age, they recognize themselves as a familiar sight.

Still, the ability to differentiate one's self from the environment is a far cry from what we typically mean by a sense of self. In fact, theorists have proposed that two types of self-concept develop in the first two years of life. The first type, that typifies infants from birth to about 15–18 months old, has been referred to as the I-self (Lewis, 1991) or the implicit self (Case, 1991). The I-self or implicit self reflects what Lewis (1991) termed the "machinery of the self." There is no self-awareness of the I-self. There is a distinction between the self and others and a realization that "I can cause things to happen." This is contrasted with the me-self (Lewis, 1991) or explicit self (Case, 1991). The me-self requires a conscious (explicit) awareness of the self, or, as Lewis has stated, the "idea of me."

How can one tell if an infant has an explicit self as opposed to an implicit self? One technique that some people think captures the idea of an explicit self (or the me-self) is visual self-recognition. Children prove that they have a sense of self by recognizing themselves in a mirror. The procedure involves placing a mark on a child's nose or forehead and then seeing the child's reaction to his or her image in the mirror. Children's behavior in the marked condition is then compared to their behavior when there are no marks on their faces or to the behavior of other unmarked children.

Children show the first signs of self-recognition beginning around 15 months by touching the mark on their face rather than touching the mirror (Lewis & Brooks-Gunn, 1979). Not all studies report mark-directed behavior this early (Schulman & Kaplowitz, 1977), but by 18 to 24 months this form of self-recognition is found in about 75% of all children tested. It is also found in the great apes—chimpanzees and orangutans (Gallup, 1979)—but their level of self-awareness does not advance beyond the basic self-recognition shown by 2-year-old children.

Our culture provides more ways than mirrors for children to identify themselves. For example, when do children show a sense of self in pictures or videos? Povinelli and his colleagues (Povinelli, Landau, & Perilloux, 1996; Povinelli & Simon, 1998) took Polaroid photos or video taped preschool children while playing. Without the children knowing it, the experimenters placed large stickers on the children. How would children react when they saw themselves in the photos or on the video with stickers on their heads? Most 2- and younger 3-year-old children did not reach for the sticker on their heads, whereas most older preschoolers did. All children, however, removed the sticker when they looked at themselves in a mirror (Povinelli et al., 1996). These results suggest that children's developing sense of self develops gradually over the preschool years, as their ability to deal with different modes of representation (mirrors, photos, videos) develops.

The development of a sense of self, as reflected by self-recognition, has important consequences for emotional, social, and cognitive development. Brooks-Gunn and Lewis (1984) make this clear: "The acquisition of the self by the end of the second year not only facilitates the acquisition of social knowledge, but underlies social competence, peer relations, gender identity, and empathy" (p. 234). The change from a helpless newborn, who seemingly cannot distinguish where he or she ends and the world begins, to a self-conscious child is a remarkable and important change indeed.

Mirror recognition is not the only sign of self-awareness that develops late in the second year. In one study, the ability to recognize oneself in a mirror was associated with the tendency to become embarrassed in certain situations, suggesting that both are related to the emergence of a child's concept of self (Lewis et al., 1989). But perhaps the most important indication of a sense of self can be gleaned from children's use of language. Late in the second year or early in the third year, many children begin using the personal pronouns I, me, my, and mine, thereby indicating a distinction between themselves and others (Lewis & Brooks-Gunn, 1979; see also Stipek, Gralinski, & Kopp, 1990).

As was noted in Chapter 8 on memory, the development of a sense of self during the second and third years of life has been proposed as one reason for infantile amnesia—our inability to remember information from infancy and early childhood. What we fail to remember is autobiographical memory, and there can be no such memory (no "auto") unless there is a sense of self (see Howe & Courage, 1993).

Once children realize they are distinct from other people and objects, how can we determine how they think about themselves? One way of gaining some insight into children's self-concepts is simply to ask them to describe themselves. Preschool children generally describe themselves in terms of physical characteristics ("I'm strong," "I have brown hair," "I have blue eyes"), by their actions ("I run real fast," "I play baseball," "I walk my dog"), where they live, and who's in their family (Keller, Ford, & Meachum, 1978; Livesley & Bromley, 1973). Rarely do preschool children provide psychological descriptions of themselves (for example, "I'm happy," "I'm smart," "I'm friendly"). This self-definition in terms of physical characteristics is consistent with the Piagetian idea that children's thinking is concrete and tied to specific experiences. This picture does not change substantially during the early school years. As children approach adolescence, their thinking becomes more abstract, and so does the way they view themselves. Children are now more likely to define themselves in terms of psychological qualities—things they like and personality characteristics (Montemayor & Eisen, 1977). (For a more in depth discussion of the development of self-concept over childhood, see Harter, 1998.)

Taking the Perspective of Another

Having a well-developed sense of self requires a knowledge that who one is and what one thinks is independent, to some important extent, of other people and their thoughts. The flip side of a sense of self, then, is an awareness that other people can have different thoughts, beliefs, and motivations than you have. They might see the world differently than you do and have different wants and goals in any particular situation. This ability to take the perspective of others is what some people have referred to as having a theory of mind, discussed in some detail in Chapter 7. Theory of mind, as it is usually defined, seems to be well developed by the age of 4 in most children. But the ability to take the perspective of others in social situations develops more gradually over childhood, as was suggested by Piaget (see Chapter 4). Piaget proposed that children much younger than 7 or 8 years of age are egocentric, in that they see the world from their own perspective and have a difficult time understanding that other people have points of view different from their own. According to Piaget, this egocentric attitude permeates children's entire cognitive lives, including their understanding of social relations.

To reiterate briefly our previous discussions of egocentricity, preschool children's visual perspectives and communicative skills are more self-centered than those of older children. However, perspective-taking abilities in both vision and communication develop gradually over the preschool and school years and do not show abrupt changes around the age of 7, as Piaget hypothesized. So, for example, children as young as 18 months point out interesting objects to their parents, apparently aware that they are seeing something that their parents are not (Rheingold, Hay, & West, 1976). Four-year-olds adapt their speech as a function of whom they are speaking to, realizing that people of different ages require that they use different tones of voice, different words, and different sentence structures to be properly understood (Shatz & Gelman, 1973). Yet, when the tasks get more complex, children's performance deteriorates, illustrating their egocentric perspective.

As can be seen, **perspective-taking** abilities develop gradually over early childhood, with the range of situations in which children can accurately take the perspective of another increasing with age. Sometimes, the same child displays aspects of both egocentric and nonegocentric perspectives in the

same behavior. For example, 3-year-old Joey saw his mother crying, upset about something that he did not quite understand. Joey ran and got his teddy bear and gave it to his mother, telling her that she could hold it for a while until she felt better. Joey was showing empathy for his mother, illustrating that he could recognize an emotion in someone else. This clearly requires a nonegocentric perspective of the world. However, Joey's solution to his mother's problem was to give her his teddy bear. It made him feel better when he was upset, so surely it would relieve his mother's distress. Although the teddy bear might actually have cheered his mother up, it was not for the reason that Joey inferred. His limited knowledge of adult concerns and his own history with feelings of sadness resulted in an egocentric solution, despite his being nonegocentric enough to identify a familiar emotion in another person.

Selman's Theory of Social Role Taking

One neo-Piagetian theory that deals specifically with developmental differences in children's ability to take the perspective (or role) of another is that of Robert Selman (1976). Selman presented children ranging from preschool-age to adolescence with various dilemmas. One story dealt with a little girl named Holly, who was the best tree climber in the whole neighborhood. Worried about her safety, however, her father made Holly promise not to climb trees anymore. Later, a friend asked Holly to climb a tree to rescue a kitten that was stuck in the branches. Holly was the only person in the neighborhood who could climb well enough to save the kitten. Yet, she had promised her father not to climb trees. After hearing this story, the children were asked what Holly should do, and why. From their answers to these and other dilemmas, Selman was able to infer their perspective-taking ability.

Selman proposed five levels of perspective taking in children (see Table 11-1). Children's perspective-taking ability improves gradually with age, and children progress through these stages in order (Selman, 1980). During the earliest stage (Stage 0: approximate ages 3 to 6 years) children know that other people are different from them and that they have

TABLE 11-1   Selman's levels of role taking

Stage	Approximate age	Description
0. Egocentric role taking	3 to 6 years	Children cannot take the perspective of others; can understand their own feelings, but not that others may interpret social actions differently.
1. Social informational role taking	6 to 8 years	Children understand that people can have different views of events and different motivations but have difficulty keeping both perspectives in mind simultaneously.
2. Self-reflective role taking	8 to 10 years	Children realize that other people evaluate their actions and that others may have legitimate views; can reflect on their own thoughts from another perspective, but cannot reflect on their own perspective and that of another person at the same time.
3. Mutual role taking	10 to 12 years	Children can take two points of view at the same time and realize that other people can do the same.
4. Social and conventional system role taking	12 to 15 years	Adolescents can take a detached view of a relationship and see it from the perspective of a third party; can interpret their behavior and that of others from a societal perspective.

SOURCE: Selman, R. (1976). Social-cognitive understanding: A guide to educational and clinical practice. In T. Lickona (Ed.), *Moral development and behavior*. New York: Holt, Rinehart, & Winston. Copyright © 1976 T. Likona. Reprinted with permission.

thoughts and feelings. As Piaget had suggested, however, Selman concluded that Stage 0 children believe that other people's thoughts and feelings are nearly identical to their own. In the story about Holly, for example, a child might say that Holly's father would be pleased if Holly saved the kitten. Holly sees the importance of it, so surely her father would, too. At this stage, children understand the thoughts and emotions of others by projecting their own past experiences onto others. "A teddy bear makes me happy when I'm sad, so it will also make Mom happy." Selman referred to this period as the stage of *egocentric role taking*.

Stage 1, that of *social information role taking*, covers children from the ages of about 6 to 8 years. During this stage, children realize that two different people can have different perspectives of things that can lead them to different actions. Despite this ability, children have great difficulty keeping both viewpoints in mind at once, and they are likely to focus on one perspective at the expense of another. In the story about Holly, children might concentrate on her promise to her father or on the importance of

saving the kitten. They are capable of noticing the conflict, but it is not salient to them. Children at this stage begin to think of the intention behind actions and realize that other people also take intent into consideration when behaving or when evaluating someone else's behavior.

In the next stage (Stage 2: *self-reflective role taking*), characterizing children from the ages of about 8 to 10 years, children begin to realize that other people can evaluate their actions. They understand that their own perspective is not the only valid one, and they can begin to judge themselves by how others view them. However, children of this age cannot simultaneously coordinate their own perspective with that of another person. A child in Stage 2 might know her own desires and those of her brother but be unable to coordinate the two to yield a successful compromise.

In Stage 3 (*mutual role taking*: approximately 10 to 12 years) children are able to take two points of view simultaneously. They realize, furthermore, that other people can take their perspective. In the story about Holly, Stage 3 children realize that Holly's father might not agree with her about her climbing the tree to rescue the kitten; however, they believe that Holly's father would be able to understand if she did save the kitten. Her motives could be expressed and could be understood by her father.

In the final stage, that of *social and conventional system role taking* (Stage 4: 12 to 15 years and older), the adolescent is able to take a detached view of a dyadic relationship and view it from the perspective of a third person. This third person could be a peer, a parent or teacher, or society. Children begin to compare their own views with those of society at large, and they realize that the social system in which they operate is a product of the shared views of the members of society.

Selman's theory has generally received support from the research literature (Gove & Keating, 1979; Selman et al., 1983; Urberg & Docherty, 1976).

Perspective Taking and Cultural Learning

Perspective-taking skills are critical for normal human functioning, and they develop gradually over childhood. The greater a child's ability to understand and take the perspective of another, the greater is his or her potential involvement in everyday human social interaction. One recent theory has taken this perspective to its logical extreme, proposing that human perspective-taking abilities are responsible for our unique intelligence and that developmental differences in such skills are associated with other landmarks of human cognitive development (Tomasello, Kruger, & Ratner, 1993).

Michael Tomasello and his colleagues argue that what sets humans apart from other species is **cultural learning**—the transmission of acquired information and behavior both within and across generations with a high degree of fidelity. Although it can be argued whether other species, such as chimpanzees, have something akin to human culture (Boesch, 1993), no other species communicates the lessons of one generation to another, thus passing on the ways and traditions of the group, as effectively as do humans. Tomasello and his colleagues argue that at the center of humans' impressive cultural-learning abilities is perspective taking.

According to Tomasello and his colleagues (1993), "In cultural learning, learners do not just direct their attention to the location of another individual's activity; rather, they actually attempt to see a situation the way the other sees it—from inside the other's perspective, as it were" (p. 496). They do not just learn from others but through others.

Tomasello et al. propose that there are three stagelike levels of learning in humans, which develop over childhood, so that each more advanced form is based on a more sophisticated type of perspective taking: imitative learning, instructed learning, and collaborative learning. Together, these three forms of learning constitute cultural learning. Not all human learning, of course, fits into one of these three categories. Much of what a person or animal learns is not "cultural" in nature. What is unique about cultural learning is that it requires the learner to be able to take the perspective of another.

Imitative learning occurs when the learner internalizes something of the model's behavioral strategies and intentions for executing the behavior. This requires perspective taking. What is the goal of a particular behavior? Why is the model engaging in these actions? For any act of modeling to be considered imitative learning, it is not enough for a child simply to mimic a behavior displayed by another; one must also appreciate the purpose or intention of that behavior. For example, if an infant observes a person opening a jar and then proceeds to make similar hand motions, this may not be imitative learning. Does the infant realize that the purpose of the behavior is to open the jar? If not, the infant might make the twisting motions without applying adequate pressure to remove the lid. According to the theory, imitative learning occurs only if the learner has an understanding of the purpose of the behavior.

Although we've seen earlier that even neonates will imitate facial gestures (Meltzoff & Moore, 1985), nothing new is learned in these situations and infants certainly do not need to have an understanding of the intentional state of the model (that is, why the model is engaging is such behavior). According to Tomasello and his colleagues, imitative learning is first seen during the latter part of the first year, when infants begin to imitate language sounds and actions with objects (Abravanel & Gingold, 1985).

If imitative learning were the only form of cultural learning, human culture and cognition would be much less complex than we know it to be. A more sophisticated form of cultural learning, requiring more sophisticated perspective taking, is **instructed learning**. Here, teaching is involved, with a more accomplished person instructing a less accomplished person. But not all cases of instruction qualify for instructed learning in the framework proposed by Tomasello and his associates. Instructed learning requires that "children learn about the adult, specifically, about the adult's understanding of the task and how that compares with their own understanding" (p. 499). What distinguishes instructed learning from other aspects of "learning from instruction" is that in the former, children will reproduce the instructed behavior in the appropriate context to regulate their own behavior. That is, as in imitative learning, children must understand the purpose of the behavior—the adult's purpose when he or she initially taught the behavior. Children must internalize the adult's instruction, not just repeat a behavior on demand. Thus, a child who is taught to bounce a ball off the wall and into the wastebasket has learned a complicated trick. But it is a trick that can be acquired by a monkey and is not the same as learning that putting a ball in a basket in certain situations is a goal to a game. Each is learning through instruction, but only the latter is instructed learning.

According to Tomasello and his colleagues, self-regulation is the best evidence of instructed learning. Self-regulation refers, basically, to self-control—a person's ability to purposefully direct his or her own behavior in the pursuit of some goal. Effective self-regulation requires the monitoring of one's actions and progress toward the goal (forms of metacognition). It is also reflected in children's self-regulated speech—their use of self-produced language to direct their problem-solving behavior (see Chapter 9). Tomasello and his colleagues proposed that such self-regulation and the associated metacognitive competence are not present until about

the age of 4 (Luria, 1961). Moreover, this age is when, according to some, children first demonstrate a theory of mind (Perner, 1991; see Chapter 7), in that they can solve the false-belief task, demonstrating that they realize that other people can have different knowledge and a different perspective from their own. This last point is critical, for true instructed learning requires that the learner appreciate the perspective of the teacher. According to Tomasello and his associates (1993), "To learn from an instructor culturally—to understand the instruction from something resembling the instructor's point of view—requires that children be able to understand a mental perspective that differs from their own, and then to relate that point of view to their own in an explicit fashion" (p. 500).

In both imitative and instructed learning, an adult or more accomplished person passes on information to a child or less accomplished person. Although in instructed learning the teacher might modify his or her behavior in accordance with the behavior of the student, the direction of effect clearly moves from the teacher to the student. This is not the case in the third form of cultural learning, **collaborative learning**. Collaborative learning involves two (or more) individuals, with neither being an authority or expert. Rather, collaborative learning occurs in the process of peer interaction, when two people work together to solve a common problem (see further discussion of collaborative, or cooperative, learning in Chapter 3). Tomasello and his colleagues point out that collaborative learning is different from imitative and instructional learning in that it is a process of cultural creation rather than cultural transmission.

What type of perspective taking is required for collaborative learning to occur? According to Tomasello and associates, collaborative learning requires that a child be able to represent his or her peer as a reflective agent, capable of reflecting on his or her own thoughts and the thoughts of fellow interactants. An example of reflective, or recursive, representation is when a child understands not only that another person can have a different point of view from his or hers, but also that the other person can think about other people's perspectives. For

TABLE 11-2   Major characteristics of three types of cultural learning

Cultural learning process	Social-cognitive ability	Concept of person	Cognitive representation
Imitative (9 months)	Perspective taking (e.g., joint attention, social referencing)	Intentional agent (0 order)	Simple (other's perspective)
Instructed (4 years)	Intersubjectivity (e.g., false-belief task, intentional deception)	Mental agent (1st order)	Alternating/coordinated (other's and own perspective)
Collaborative (6 years)	Recursive intersubjectivity (e.g., embedded mental-state language)	Reflective agent (2nd order)	Integrated (dyad's intersubjectivity)

SOURCE: Tomasello, M., Kruger, A. C., & Ratner, H.H. (1993). Cultural learning. *Behavioral and Brain Sciences, 16,* 495–511. Copyright © 1993 Cambridge University Press. Reprinted with the permission of Cambridge University Press.

example, "Tom thinks that I think Jessie is a jerk" is a form of recursive thinking. This is necessary for collaborative learning, which often occurs in the midst of disagreement and conflict. For example, children must be able to evaluate and comment on another child's criticism of their previous suggestion if collaborative learning and the creation of a new joint perspective is to take place. Each participant needs to be able to think of the other participant as being a reflective thinker—as being able to reflect back on his or her past arguments and the arguments made by other participants—if a single solution to a problem is to be reached. According to Tomasello and his colleagues, this is first achieved during the early school years, between 6 and 7 years of age.

Table 11-2 summarizes the major features of each of the three types of cultural learning according to Tomasello, Kruger, and Ratner.

The ideas of Tomasello and his colleagues have much in common with those of Perner, Wellman, and others who have examined young children's representations of other minds (discussed in Chapter 7). The degree to which children can "read the minds" of other people—understand their beliefs, intentions, and mental states—varies developmentally and serves as the cognitive basis for effective social interaction. Tomasello and his colleagues take this perspective a bit further, integrating it with a Vygotskian sociocultural perspective, in proposing that how children conceive of people with whom

they interact "is an integral component of the basic learning process" (p. 502).

Although there is some lively debate concerning whether we are the only species to possess the perspective-taking skills necessary to display cultural learning as Tomasello and his colleagues suggest (Boesch, 1993), I think it is fair to say that no other species is in the same ballpark as *Homo sapiens* when it comes to cultural learning. What Tomasello, Kruger, and Ratner's theory does is place human cognition and its development within the realm of social cognition. Our unmatched behavioral and intellectual flexibility finds its origins not so much in tool use, spatial ability, abstract mathematical reasoning, or even language, but in social cognition. Many contemporary theorists of human evolution propose that our unique intelligence evolved because of the need to cooperate, compete, and understand other members of our own species. The theory of Tomasello and his associates regarding the ontogeny of cultural learning takes this point seriously, arguing that what is unique about human intelligence is to be found in social cognition.

Children's Humor

Developmental differences in the appreciation of humor have been hypothesized to be a function of children's level of cognitive development—specifically, their ability to deal with symbols. Most developmental researchers have proposed that humor is reflected in the child's ability to perceive *incongruity*, noticing (or creating) a discrepancy between what is usual or expected and what is experienced (McGhee, 1979; Pien & Rothbart, 1980; Shultz & Robillard, 1980). Of course, incongruity can be defined only by what a child already knows, both in terms of world knowledge and in terms of general cognitive capabilities. As such, what is incongruous, and thus funny, to a 2-year-old (for example, calling the family cat "doggie"), will be perceived as babyish and just plain stupid to an older child. Likewise, because of older children's greater knowledge base and increased abilities to process information, things they find funny (such as "knock-knock" jokes) will go over the heads of most preschool children.

Humor and Mental Effort

According to Paul McGhee (1976, 1979), incongruity is most likely to be perceived as humorous when the discrepancy is of some intermediate magnitude (compare with Kagan's [1971] discrepancy principle, discussed in Chapter 6). In other words, there is an inverted-U relationship between magnitude of cognitive incongruity and appreciation of humor. McGhee proposed that children (and adults, for that matter) gain the greatest satisfaction in resolving problems of some moderate degree of difficulty. Creating or comprehending humor is perceived as being an intellectual challenge, with "pleasure in mastery" being intrinsically rewarding. The funniest jokes, for both adults and children, are those that take a little mental effort to figure out. Too easy, and they are boring; too difficult, and they are not worth the effort.

McGhee (1976) tested this theory by assessing children's appreciation of jokes as a function of their level of cognitive development. In one experiment, McGhee tested children in grades 1, 2, and 5 and college students. Within the first and second grades, half of the children were classified as conservers on conservation-of-weight tasks, and half were classified as nonconservers. All the fifth-grade and college students were conservers. The participants were read

jokes requiring a knowledge of conservation for their appreciation. (For example: "Mr. Jones went into a restaurant and ordered a whole pizza for dinner. When the waiter asked if he wanted it cut into six or eight pieces, Mr. Jones said: 'Oh, you'd better make it six. I could never eat eight!'") After reading each joke, the experimenter asked each person to rate the joke on a five-point scale for how funny it was.

McGhee evaluated the children's appreciation of the jokes as a function of their level of cognitive development (that is, conservers or nonconservers) and grade level. The children who found the jokes funniest were the first- and second-grade conservers. Nonconservers generally did not find the humor in the jokes, nor did the older children, though for different reasons. For the nonconservers, there was nothing to laugh about. The response given by Mr. Jones in the example joke is one they might have given themselves. In contrast, the joke was trivial for the fifth-graders, taking little in the way of mental effort. Only for the young conservers was the joke funny. These children had only recently mastered conservation, making the challenge of interpreting the joke greatest for them.

Humor and Cognitive Development

According to McGhee (1979), incongruity alone is not enough to create humor. Of course, a playful attitude and atmosphere will increase the likelihood that any incongruous event will be perceived as funny. The same incongruous episode can be viewed as interesting or even fearful in one situation and humorous in another as a function of the cues available in the environment. Most critical for humor, according to McGhee, is the ability to represent objects and events symbolically. McGhee proposed that humor requires comparing some event with a similar event in memory, and he believes that children do not develop this ability sufficiently well until sometime between their first and second birthdays. He sees humor as a type of intellectual play that requires symbols. Symbols allow children to engage in fantasy and make-believe, and these "pretend" activities serve as an introduction to the world of humor. Preschoolers play with make-believe friends and slay make-believe monsters right out in the open. Make-believe, of course, is not always humorous, but it allows children to craft incongruous and thus funny situations that do not exist in reality, such as pretending that their dog is a horse or that their playmate has purple hair.

McGhee proposed four stages of humor development, beginning when the capacity for fantasy and make-believe develops, sometime late in the second year. In stage 1, typifying children between 18 and 24 months, children substitute one object for another in a playful game of pretending. For example, Piaget (1962) observed his daughter Jacqueline at 15 months clutching a cloth that vaguely resembled her pillow. She held it in her hand, sucked her thumb, and lay down, closing her eyes. But while she was pretending to sleep, she was laughing hard. To this toddler, pretending the cloth was her pillow was funny.

Children's first verbal jokes occur in stage 2. The simplest of these jokes involves calling something by its wrong name. A 2-year-old finds great mirth in calling the family dog a cow, in labeling a hamburger macaroni and cheese, or in pointing to her eye and calling it a nose. Such humor might not seem all that sophisticated, but it requires greater abstraction than the object-dependent humor of stage 1. Children no longer need a physical prop to make a joke. The word is enough.

Soon, however, children's humor becomes more complex, usually beginning around age 3. Now, it is not enough merely to call a dog a cat. Because of 3-year-olds' increasing knowledge of things in their environment, distortions must be more drastic for something to be funny. So, for example, a cow that says "oink oink" and has a curlicue tail is funny, whether that cow is seen in a picture or is just imagined.

What is humorous to a stage-3 child is often a function of how absurd something looks. Preschool children's attention is often drawn to perceptual or literal stimulus features. This overreliance on appearance affects children's humor. A picture of an elephant sitting in a tree is funny to a 3-year-old, as is a picture of a fish swimming inside a car filled with water. These pictures are funny to 3-year-olds not because they defy logic but just because they are unusual. The incongruity is visual, not logical.

Beginning around 6 or 7 years of age, children's humor makes a more drastic change and starts to resemble the humor of adults. According to McGhee, the ability to understand double meanings of words and sentences is the hallmark of stage 4 and much of adult humor. A sentence with a serious (and obvious) meaning taken one way can be funny if viewed differently. A favorite of my daughter Heidi at 6 years involved a woman mailing three socks to her son away in the army. Why did she mail three socks? Because he had written saying he had "grown another foot." Appreciation of the joke requires an understanding of the double meaning of "grown another foot." Most 7-year-olds have the ability to represent two meanings of a single word or phrase simultaneously, and from this time on, humor takes a distinctly adult form, although most adults are still likely to groan at jokes that have an 8-year-old rolling on the floor with laughter. (Such as this joke that 8-year-old Jeffrey thought was hilarious and apparently had made up himself: "Why did the brave chicken cross the road? 'Cause he wanted to prove that he wasn't chicken. Get it?")

An interesting case study, looking at spontaneous humor based on analysis of daily diary entries for a boy between the ages of 15 and 30 months, provides partial support for the developmental model offered by McGhee, at least for the transition between stages 2 and 3 (Johnson & Mervis, 1997). This child's humor showed the same type of changes as has been found in cross-sectional studies; however, he did not show the stage-like changes that McGhee proposed. Rather, even after he was able to appreciate and make jokes based on more sophisticated bases, this child frequently resorted to less mature forms of humor. This is reminiscent of the pattern of strategy development suggested by Siegler (1996; see Chapter 5), with cognitive development involving the coexistence and competition of different strategies at different levels of sophistication.

Fortunately, children's humor develops beyond simple jokes as their knowledge bases and cognitive abilities increase over the elementary school years. Such changes are especially apparent in children's appreciation of verbal jokes and riddles, which has been studied extensively by Thomas Shultz and his colleagues (Shultz & Horibe, 1974; Shultz & Pilon, 1973). In their experiments, children were told jokes and were asked to rate them on a five-point scale for how funny they were. The children were later asked to explain the jokes and were asked whether they could have a second meaning. The extent to which the children smiled or laughed at the jokes was also measured.

Most jokes and riddles revolve around the discovery of ambiguities, although some ambiguities require more in the way of cognitive abilities to discover than others. The earliest ambiguities that children can appreciate involve two words that sound alike, termed *phonological ambiguity*. For example:

"Waiter, what's this?"

"That's bean soup, ma'am."

"I'm not interested in what it's been, I'm asking what it is now."

The joke centers on the different meanings of the similar sounding words "bean" and "been." Many "knock-knock" jokes rely on this type of ambiguity for their humor. For example:

"Knock, knock."

"Who's there?"

"Freeze."

"Freeze who?"

"Freeze a jolly good fellow!"

Although 6- and 7-year-old children can appreciate the two meanings of two words that sound alike, their appreciation is limited by their attentiveness to literal (here acoustic) perceptual features.

Following close behind in appreciation are jokes based on the dual meaning of a single word, termed *lexical ambiguity*. For example:

"Order! Order in the court!"

"Ham and cheese on rye, Your Honor."

Here the humor does not derive from a confusion of two different words but revolves around two differ-

ent meanings of the same word. Here is one more example of lexical ambiguity:

"How do you keep a skunk from smelling?"

"Hold its nose."

Most of the verbal jokes and riddles of elementary school children are based on phonological or lexical ambiguity. There are more complex forms of jokes, of course, involving ambiguities not of a single word but of the entire structure of the sentence. For example:

"I saw a man eating shark in the aquarium."

"That's nothing. I saw a man eating herring in the restaurant."

or

"I would like to buy a pair of alligator shoes. "

"Certainly. What size does your alligator wear?"

In these two cases, the jokes do not hinge on the interpretation of a single word but on how the whole sentence is interpreted. Is it a shark who eats men, or a man who is eating shark? Are the shoes made of alligator hide, or are the shoes made to fit your pet alligator's feet? The humor is based on two different syntactical relations among words within a sentence. Shultz referred to these jokes as being based on *surface-structure ambiguity*.

More complex yet are jokes based on *deep-structure ambiguity*. For example:

"Call me a cab."

"OK, you're a cab."

Deep-structure ambiguity results when two different underlying meanings (or deep structures) are projected onto a single sentence structure (or surface structure). Appreciation of the humor based on surface- and deep-structure ambiguities is not usually attained until 11 or 12 years of age, reflecting changes in representational abilities associated with the onset of adolescence.

Shultz and Horibe (1974) further proposed that there are two steps in interpreting most jokes: first, an appreciation of the incongruity, and second, an appreciation of the resolution of the joke. Shultz and

Horibe presented jokes to children between the ages of 6 and 12 years. The original form of the jokes had incongruity and resolution, as in the "Order in the court" joke provided earlier. The response ("Ham and cheese on rye, Your Honor") is both incongruous and presents a resolution to the incongruity. Other forms of the jokes maintained the incongruity but eliminated the resolution. For example:

"Silence! Silence in the court!"

"Ham and cheese on rye, Your Honor."

There is incongruity here. Ordering lunch to a judge's request for silence is not expected. But the joke loses its punch when the ambiguous word "order" is replaced by the nonambiguous word "silence." The third form of the joke removed the incongruity. For example:

"Order! Order in the court!"

"I only want the truth to be told, Your Honor."

There is no incongruity in this version and, thus, no chance of humor.

Children of all ages concurred that the form of the joke in which the incongruity was removed ("I only want the truth to be told, Your Honor") was not funny. However, the 6-year-olds tended to view both the original jokes and the forms with the resolution removed ("Silence in the court!") as equally funny. Older children found the original jokes funnier than those with the resolution removed, and this difference increased with age. Shultz and Horibe proposed a two-step developmental process: Young children find humor in pure incongruity, and older children appreciate the resolution of the incongruity.

Research has clearly demonstrated that a child's understanding and appreciation of humor varies as a function of his or her level of cognitive development. Other factors, of course, affect humor. Some topics (aggression, sex) are more likely to be a source of humor than others, and humor plays an important role in greasing the gears of social interaction. Yet, the core of humor is cognitive. Simple visual jokes can be comprehended by 3-year-olds. But as the basis of jokes becomes more abstract and less dependent on visual cues, it becomes increas-ingly difficult for children to identify and resolve the conflict. Children's abilities to represent events, both real and unreal, and to view multiple meanings of a single situation determine what they find funny.

Cognitive Bases of Gender Identity

Being male or female is a matter of biology, plain and simple. But behaving in a fashion consistent with societal views of masculinity and femininity and identifying oneself with males or females encompasses more than biology. This process of incorporating the roles and values of one's sex is referred to as **gender identification**. Our identification of ourselves as male or female has implications far beyond reproduction. Unlike other demarcations of social standing such as age, occupation, or marital status, our gender is one characteristic that remains constant throughout development. All societies make distinctions between the sexes, although outside of reproduction there are few if any universal roles or behaviors delineating the sexes. What is universal is the significance that gender has in defining who an individual is in society and the striving of children around the world to acquire an appropriate gender role.

Many factors contribute to children's gender identification. One important factor is their ability to understand gender as a concept and that gender remains stable over time and is consistent over situations. Whether a boy decides to identify with his father is related to what he understands about his gender, that of his father, and the continuity of his own gender over time. Children should not be expected to behave as if gender is important if they are not yet aware that differences among males and females exist and that their own gender is constant. Another important factor is children's knowledge of gender stereotypes. What information do they have about how boys and men and girls and women behave, and what consequences does this knowledge have for their own actions and attitudes? Most research during the past decade concerning gender knowledge has examined gender schemas. In the following sections, I review research on the development of gender constancy and gender schemas and how these cognitive factors relate to the societally important process of gender identification.

The Development of Gender Constancy

One of the first people to postulate a cognitive basis for gender identification was Lawrence Kohlberg (1966). He proposed that children's understanding of gender develops in the same way as their understanding of the physical world. According to Kohlberg, knowledge of gender follows Piaget's model of cognitive development, with children not having a mature notion of gender until the advent of concrete operations, beginning about 7 years of age.

Kohlberg proposed that a key cognitive accomplishment in the understanding of gender is that of **gender constancy**—the knowledge that gender remains the same despite changes in physical appearance. One of the first studies to test this aspect of Kohlberg's theory was conducted by Rheta De Vries (1969) as part of a larger study of the appearance/reality distinction, discussed in Chapter 7. De Vries reported that 3-year-olds believed that a person temporarily changes his or her sex when engaging in opposite-sex behavior or when wearing opposite-sex clothing. That is, boys who wear girls' clothes or play girls' games are, for the time being, girls.

The significance of dress in determining gender for young children is illustrated by an observation reported by Stone and Church (1973). A new family had moved into the neighborhood with a baby. When a 4-year-old girl was asked whether the baby was a boy or a girl, she responded, "I don't know. It's so hard to tell at that age, especially with their clothes off" (p. 297). Another demonstration of gender being determined by dress came from my daughter, Heidi, when she was about 3. She declared that I could not wear a pink shirt because if I did, I would be a girl. The major difference between boys and girls, she said, is that girls wear pink and boys do not. Always fashion conscious, she added that both boys and girls could wear blue and yellow. Pink, it seemed, is the critical color.

Following De Vries's study, several researchers investigated the development of gender constancy in greater detail (Ruble, Balaban, & Cooper, 1981; Slaby & Frey, 1975). In a study by Slaby and Frey (1975), children aged 2 to 5.5 years were interviewed about their belief in the constancy of gender. In agreement with Kohlberg's theory, Slaby and Frey reported three components in the development of gender constancy: gender identity, gender stability, and gender consistency. Slaby and Frey defined **gender identity** as the ability to identify oneself as male or female and to accurately identify the gender of others. **Gender stability** refers to the knowledge that gender remains stable over time. Thus, little boys at some point come to believe that they will become fathers when they grow up, and little girls believe that they will become mothers. The questions the researchers asked made it clear that the children were expressing not just a preference but a necessity; for example, they asked boys: "Could you ever be a mommy when you grow up?" **Gender consistency** refers to the knowledge that gender remains the same despite changes in behavior or dress. The researchers tested this knowledge with questions such as: "If you wore boys' clothes, would you be a girl or a boy?" and "If you played girls' games, would you be a boy or a girl?" These questions might seem trivial to an adult, but answers by preschool children can be quite revealing (for example, "I can't wear girls' clothes, 'cause then I'd be a girl!").

Slaby and Frey reported an age-related developmental sequence, such that gender identity was acquired before gender stability and gender stability was acquired before gender consistency (that is, identity → stability → consistency). Other researchers have confirmed this three-stage sequence, with gender identity being achieved, on average, by 2.5 years, gender stability by 4 or 5 years, and gender consistency by 6 or 7 years (Eaton & Von Bargen, 1981; Ruble et al., 1981). This sequence of development is not confined to North America or to industrialized countries but has also been found in traditional communities in Belize, Kenya, Nepal, and American Samoa (Munroe, Shimmin, & Munroe, 1984).

As with many other aspects of cognition in young children, performance can be helped or hindered by subtle changes in the task. For example, Eaton and Von Bargen (1981) asked preschool children gender-constancy questions pertaining to (1) themselves, (2) a same-sex child, and (3) an opposite-sex child. The children answered the questions relating to themselves at a more advanced level than they did the questions relating to a same-sex child; these latter questions were answered at a more advanced level than the questions relating to an opposite-sex child (see also Gouze & Nadelman, 1980). In other words, young children become confident of the stability and consistency of their own gender before that of the gender of other children, particularly children of the opposite sex. These, and other research findings (Beal & Lockhart, 1989) indicate that seemingly subtle differences in how the gender-constancy task is administered can result in dramatic changes in children's responses. These findings indicate that beliefs about the constancy of gender are not well established until middle childhood. However, they also indicate that even preschoolers sometimes believe that gender is constant over time and situations. The range of situations in which they believe this, however, is limited and expands with age.

Consequences of Gender Constancy for Gender Identification

Why should knowing that gender is constant over time and over situations affect children's gender identification? For one thing, it makes little sense to learn the behaviors and roles of one gender if you are not certain that your own gender will remain the same.

Several researchers have compared attention to same-sex models for children who score high on tests of gender constancy (knowing that gender is stable or consistent over time), with children who seem unaware of either the consistency or stability of gender. In an early study, by Slaby and Frey (1975), preschool children were shown a 5.5-minute silent video depicting a man and a woman engaging in simple, separate activities. The man was on one side of the screen, and the woman on the other. As children watched the film, an observer recorded the amount of time they spent attending to the male and female models. Slaby and Frey reported that the high-gender-constancy children spent more time looking at the same-sex model than did the low-gender-constancy children, and this effect was stronger in boys than in girls. That is, the high-gender-constancy boys looked at the male model longer than did the other boys (108.2 seconds versus 63.0 seconds), and the high-gender-constancy girls looked more at the female model than did the other girls (86.8 seconds versus 63.8 seconds).

Other researchers have reported findings similar to those of Slaby and Frey. For example, in one study, 5-year-old boys who scored high on gender constancy spent more time viewing TV programs featuring a greater percentage of men than did boys who scored lower on a test of gender constancy; no such effect, however, was found for girls (Luecke-Aleksa et al., 1995). In other research, Ruble, Balaban, and Cooper (1981) showed high- and low-gender-constancy children cartoons, complete with commercials of same-sex or opposite-sex children playing with a gender-neutral toy (a movie viewer). Children were later given the opportunity to play with the movie viewer, along with many other toys not shown in the commercial. The results of this study are shown in Figure 11-2. As can be seen, there was little difference between the high- and low-gender-constancy children when viewing a same-sex model. Differences were dramatic, however, when the children had viewed an opposite-sex model playing with the toy. The low-gender-constancy children showed no differentiation. They actually played with the movie viewer slightly more when they had seen an opposite-sex child in the commercial. Not so for the high-gender-constancy children: these children knew that gender remains constant over time and that there are certain things that boys do and other different things that girls do. When these young children thought that a toy was appropriate for an opposite-sex child (as reflected by the commercial), they avoided it. The important

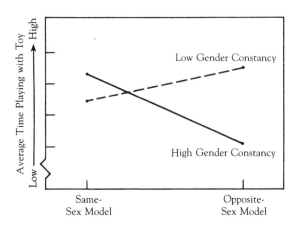

FIGURE 11-2   Average amount of time spent playing with a toy as a function of stage of gender constancy (high versus low) and sex of model in the commercial (same-sex versus opposite-sex). SOURCE: Adapted from "Gender Constancy and the Effects of Sex-Typed Television Toy Commercials," by Ruble, D. N., Balabon, T., & Cooper J., 1981, *Child Development, 52,* 667–673. Copyright © 1981 The Society for Research in Child Development, Inc. Adapted with permission.

point here is that this distinction is not made until children have acquired the cognitive sophistication to know that gender is a stable characteristic.

Despite the impressive effects of some of these studies, other aspects of gender behavior seem not to be related to a child's level of gender constancy. For example, although several studies have found that gender constancy is related to a child's sex-type preferences (that is, whether children choose or value same- versus opposite-sex toys or activities) (Kuhn, Nash, & Brucken, 1978; Smetana & Letourneau, 1984), more studies have found no such relationship (Bussey & Bandura, 1992; Lobel & Menashri, 1993). Moreover, children's level of gender constancy apparently is not related to their knowledge of gender stereotypes (Levy & Carter, 1989; Martin & Little, 1990). And perhaps most telling is that children start displaying sex-stereotyped behavior for toy preferences before 2 years of age, long before they demonstrate a high degree of gender constancy (Caldera, Huston, & O'Brien, 1989; Perry, White, & Perry, 1984).

Certainly there is more to the process of gender identification than strictly cognitive factors, but it is very likely that cognitive factors other than gender constancy might be involved in the process (see Ruble & Martin, 1998). In recent years, researchers have emphasized the role of knowledge of gender stereotypes as an important factor, with gender schemas playing a central role as the organizing mechanisms underlying children's gender knowledge.

Gender Schemas

Contemporary cognitive theories of gender identification have been based on the tenets of information processing, particularly the concept of schemas (Bem, 1981; Levy & Fivush, 1993; Martin, 1993; Martin & Halverson, 1981). I discussed the concept of schemas in Chapter 6. A schema is a mentalistic structure consisting of a set of expectations and associations that guide processing with respect to a particular content. A **gender schema** influences how children process information about gender and serves as a way for them to organize information about sex. According to Martin and Halverson (1981), schemas develop primarily from observation. Sex is a salient characteristic in children's worlds, relating both to themselves and to others. It is thus used to organize information in place of other more subtle characteristics of a person or event that might be used by older and more knowledgeable children. Children use their developing gender schemas to evaluate the appropriateness of some behavior. When children can answer questions such as "Is this OK for boys to do?" positively, they attempt to acquire more information about the activity ("What are the rules of football? How do you throw a pass?").

Not surprisingly, children's knowledge of gender stereotypes increases with age. For example, when children are asked to determine whether a toy (a doll or a gun) or an activity (ironing shirts or driving a truck) is more appropriate for males or females, older children show a greater understanding of the cultural stereotypes than younger children (see

Signorella, Bigler, & Liben, 1993, for a review). Also, when children are given the option that an activity or toy might be appropriate for both males and females, elementary school girls are more apt to choose such an activity or toy than boys, reflecting greater flexibility regarding sex stereotypes in girls than in boys (see Ruble & Martin, 1998 for review).

In most studies assessing children's knowledge of gender stereotypes, concrete objects (for example, hammer, doll) or specific activities (for example, playing football, jumping rope) are used as stimuli. In addition to these objects and activities, however, genders come to have *metaphoric* meanings. Some objects or characteristics, which have no concrete association with either males of females, are nonetheless associated with one gender or the other. For example, most people would tend to associate "bear," "dog," and "angry" with males and "heart," "pink," and "flower" with females. When do children make such associations? Leinbach, Hort, and Fagot (1997) developed a test to assess children's knowledge of metaphorical sex stereotypes. They tested children between the ages of 3 and 7 years and reported that children as young as 4 years of age consistently classified metaphorical items according to their "appropriate" gender stereotype, although this tendency increased with age. Three-year-olds, in contrast, rarely made such classifications. Also, they reported that 4-year-old children who were high in gender constancy were more likely to classify sex-stereotyped metaphorical items "appropriately" than 4-year-olds who scored low on a gender-constancy test.

A particular type of gender schema is the **gender script,** which is a temporally organized event sequence related to gender. Knowledge of such scripts should increase with age, with children presumably becoming more familiar with same-sex than with opposite-sex gender scripts. This was investigated in a study by Boston and Levy (1991). Preschool children were given a series of scrambled pictures that when placed in order would make a coherent event. Some of these events were stereotypically feminine (for example, doing laundry, preparing dinner in the kitchen), and others were stereotypically masculine (for example, building a birdhouse, barbecuing).

Children were shown the pictures one set at a time and told to "put these in the order the way they would happen" (p. 424).

First, older preschoolers were better able to sequence the pictures than were younger preschoolers, demonstrating an age-related increase in gender-script knowledge, although even the youngest children (3.5 to 4 years old) performed quite well at sequencing the pictures. Following the researchers' predictions, boys were more accurate at sequencing masculine activities than feminine activities. Contrary to predictions, girls showed no difference in the accuracy of sequencing the feminine and masculine activities.

One primary function of schemas is to organize information, making it more accessible in memory. Several researchers have demonstrated that children better remember information that is consistent with their sex stereotypes than inconsistent information (Bauer, 1993; Liben & Signorella, 1993; Welch-Ross & Schmidt, 1996). Perhaps the most impressive demonstration of this is a study by Patricia Bauer (1993) with a group of 25-month-old toddlers. In her study, children were shown a series of six activities: two stereotypically masculine activities (for example, building a house), two stereotypically feminine activities (for example, putting a diaper on a baby), and two neutral activities (for example, having a birthday party). Children were then encouraged to imitate each activity, both immediately and following a two-week delay. The results were similar both for immediate and delayed imitation: Although there was no difference in successful imitation among the three types of activities for the girls, the boys showed greater imitation of the masculine and neutral activities than of the feminine activities. Moreover, the boys spent more time interacting with the props for the masculine and neutral activities than for the feminine activities. These results suggest that, at least for boys, gender schemas are operating as early as 2 years of age, with boys avoiding traditionally feminine activities.

Although both boys and girls show a decided preference for same-sex toys and activities, and both boys and girls seem to remember and understand same-sex stereotypes better than opposite-sex stereotypes (Liben & Signorella, 1993; Martin, Wood, & Little, 1990), these effects generally appear earlier (as in the Bauer, 1993, study) and are more extreme (as in the Boston and Levy, 1991, study) in boys than in girls. Consistent with these observations, boys show sex-stereotyped toy preferences earlier than girls (O'Brien & Huston, 1985) and avoid opposite-sex toys more than girls (Fagot, Leinbach, & Hagan, 1986). One interpretation of these findings is that young boys are more strongly sex-stereotyped than young girls (Bauer, 1993).

A developmental assessment of gender schemas and their relations to sex-stereotypic behavior was done by Serbin and Sprafkin (1986). Because sex is a highly salient dimension, Serbin and Sprafkin hypothesized that young children would use gender to classify people and activities to a greater extent than older children would. Older children, whose knowledge of sex roles is greater and whose gender schemas are thus more elaborated, were expected to be more flexible in their classifications, relying less on gender and more on other characteristics of behavior. To assess this hypothesis, 3- to 7-year-old children were administered a gender classification task. In this task, the children were shown photographs of adults engaging in some routine activities. For example, one picture was of a man stirring a pot. The children were then shown three other pictures and were asked to choose the one that "went best" with the standard. One picture was of a man reading (same sex, different activity); children who chose this picture as going with the standard would be making a classification based on gender. A second picture was of a woman rolling dough (different sex, similar activity); children choosing this picture would be making their classification on the basis of type of activity. A third picture was of a woman sweeping (different sex, different activity); this was a control picture, and children who chose this alternative would presumably be responding randomly. The children were also administered tests of sex typing. For example, they were shown pictures of objects typically associated with males (hammer, shovel, baseball) and others typically associated with females (iron, needle and thread, baby bottle) and were asked who would use each object—boys,

girls, or both. When children said that the object could be used by either boys or girls, they were later asked which sex would use it most. The extent to which children made sex-stereotypic responses was used as an indication of their knowledge of sex-stereotypes.

Following the researchers' predictions, children's classifications of activities on the basis of gender declined with age. Three-year-olds chose the same-sex/different-activity picture 57% of the time. This percentage decreased to 20% for the 7-year-olds. Furthermore, children's gender classifications were significantly related to their knowledge of sex roles. Children who knew more about sex roles tended to make *fewer* classifications on the basis of gender. In other words, as children's knowledge of sex roles expands, so do their gender schemas. The better established children's gender schemas are, the more flexible they become in interpreting gender differences, and the more tolerant they become of people engaging in cross-sex activities (Stoddart & Turiel, 1985). Thus, whereas a 4-year-old might be aghast that his sister's teenage boyfriend wears a dangling earring, the 7-year-old codes it only as an exception to the rule and realizes that it does not alter the "maleness" of the person.

There are many levels of gender identification, however, and even young children who have mastered only the rudiments of gender differences can behave in a more sex-typed fashion than less knowledgeable children. For example, Fagot, Leinbach, and Hagan (1986) assessed the relationship between the ability of young children to identify pictures of males and females and their adoption of sex-typed behaviors. Children between the ages of 21 and 40 months were shown pairs of pictures (one of a male and one of a female) and were asked to identify the boys and girls (or men and women). The children were also observed in their preschool classroom to obtain measures of sex-typed behaviors. Differences in aggression, interaction with same-sex peers, and play with sex-stereotyped toys (for example, blocks, trucks, and carpentry tools for boys) were measured. The researchers reasoned that 2- and 3-year-old children with greater knowledge of gender differences (as reflected by their ability to identify males and females) should show greater sex-typed behavior.

The results generally supported the researchers' hypothesis of a relationship between gender knowledge and sex-stereotypic behavior in young children. Children who could correctly apply gender labels to the pictures were more likely to play with same-sex peers, and girls who performed well on this task showed almost no aggression in the classroom. Aggression is more associated with males than with females, so preschool girls who showed low levels of aggression were assumed to be displaying more sex-appropriate behavior than girls who showed more aggression.

Unlike the other measures of sex typing in this study, toy preference (that is, which toys the children played with during school) was not related to the ability to identify males and females. Rather, boys and girls generally displayed a preference for sex-typed toys regardless of their level of gender knowledge. This finding is similar to one reported by Perry, White, and Perry (1984), who found no relationship between young children's toy preferences and their knowledge of sex stereotypes for toys. Rather, children (particularly boys) showed a preference for same-sex toys before showing a knowledge of which toys are usually for girls and which are usually for boys. These results suggest that early toy and play preferences are not related to children's understanding of gender. Instead, these patterns might be the result of biological differences in activity and interactional styles between the sexes or to differences in the type of toys and activities adults introduce to children.

Support for a biological rather than environmental basis for early toy preference comes from studies examining the relation between prenatal exposure to the male hormone androgen and later toy preference (Berenbaum & Hines, 1992; Berenbaum & Snyder, 1995). Children who had been exposed to high levels of androgen before birth (because of overproduction of androgen in the fetus's adrenal glands) were seen when they were between the ages of 3 and 8 years and contrasted for their toy preference with groups of nonaffected boys and girls (Berenbaum & Hines, 1992). (In a nice method-

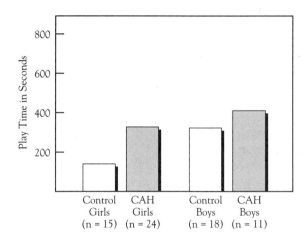

FIGURE 11-3 Average time spent playing with boys' toys for androgenized (CAH) and control boys and girls. SOURCE: Adapted from "Early Androgens are Related to Childhood Sex-Typed Toy Preferences," by S.A. Berenbaum & M. Hines, 1992, *Psychological Science, 3,* p. 205. Copyright © 1992 Cambridge University Press.

ological touch, the control children were sisters, brothers, or cousins of the affected children.) Children were brought into a playroom where stereotypically masculine, feminine, and neutral toys were available. As expected, for the control children, boys played more often with the masculine toys and girls played more often with the feminine toys. For the androgenized boys, there was no difference in their toy preferences from the control boys, although the affected boys spent somewhat greater time playing with the masculine toys than did the control boys (see Figure 11-3). In contrast, the androgenized girls demonstrated a strong masculine toy preference. As can be seen in Figure 11-3, the androgenized girls spent much more time playing with the masculine toys than did control girls, such that masculine toy preferences were comparable with those of the boys. This pattern of toy preference was replicated in later research (Berenbaum & Snyder, 1995).

These results, coupled with the findings that young children's toy preferences are not related to their knowledge of gender stereotypes, suggest that early toy preference is influenced more by biological than by cognitive factors. Berenbaum's studies suggest that exposure to prenatal androgen has a de-feminizing effect on toy preferences, although extra androgen is apparently not necessary for boys to show this defeminizing effect. This does not mean, however, that androgen has a direct effect on toy preference. (I seriously doubt that there is a part of the brain that causes us to find toy guns attractive and toy dolls unattractive.) One possibility is that the androgen influences activity level, tempera-ment, or motor skills, which leads to a preference for more stereotypically masculine toys (Halverson & Waldrop, 1973; O'Brien & Huston, 1985).

These findings in no way imply that children's gender-related behavior is biologically "fixed." Chil-dren around the world are exposed to a wide variety of culturally "appropriate" male and females models, and the social setting, more than anything else, de-termines what behaviors children will adopt for their own. But it should not be surprising that biol-ogy can predispose male and female children toward certain general types of behavior (boys more to ma-nipulation of objects and large-muscle activity, per-haps, and females to social relations). And it is interesting that boys tend to be more sex-typed (that is, approach and attend to male and avoid fe-male activities/models) than females. Might this also reflect a biological influence? Biology is not des-tiny, and, as has been made clear throughout this book, there are no pure biological or environmental factors on development. But acknowledging that some aspects of gender behavior are influenced by biological dispositions in interaction with a child's social environment, can help us better understand the developmental process of gender identification.

Gender Knowledge, Sex-Stereotypic Behavior, and Intelligence

From a cognitive developmental viewpoint, gender is a concept that children acquire sometime by the early school years. Accordingly, bright children should acquire the concept of gender (that is, what gender-appropriate behavior is) earlier than others. Several researchers have examined this possibility. For example, in a study by Gouze and Nadelman

(1980), children between the ages of 3.5 and 7 years were given versions of Slaby and Frey's gender-constancy task described previously. Children were also administered the vocabulary subtest from the Wechsler Preschool and Primary Scale of Intelli-gence (WPPSI) (see Chapter 13). This subtest is highly correlated with the WPPSI full-scale IQ test. There were positive correlations between gender-constancy scores and scores on the vocabulary test, suggesting that within this age range, more intelli-gent children acquire notions of gender constancy before less intelligent children do.

Similar conclusions that brighter children ac-quire gender-related knowledge before less bright children comes from a meta-analysis examining age, sex, and IQ effects in nearly 200 studies on chil-dren's gender schema knowledge (Signorella et al., 1993). The studies examined in this analysis in-cluded those that asked children to determine whether objects or activities were masculine or fem-inine (or both). Margaret Signorella and her col-leagues found that children with higher IQ scores were more likely to make sex-stereotypic selections than children with lower IQ scores. (They also re-ported children who watched more television made more sex-stereotypic selections, suggesting that chil-dren learn gender stereotypes as much from TV as from live people.)

Following these results, if knowledge of gender roles varies as a function of one's level of cognitive development, brighter children should behave in a sex-stereotyped way earlier than do average or below-average children. This possibility was investi-gated by Connor and Serbin (1977), who observed 35 play activities of preschool children. Some of these activities had been evaluated by a sample of adults as being "traditionally masculine" (for exam-ple, playing with balls and trucks), others as being "traditionally feminine" (playing with dolls and kitchen utensils), and others as being neutral (play-ing with a blackboard and puzzles). The amount of time each child spent playing in each activity was recorded and children were assigned a score for sex-stereotypic activity. Boys who engaged mainly in masculine-rated activities, for example, would have high sex-stereotypic scores, whereas boys who engaged mainly in neutral or feminine-rated activities would have lower sex-stereotypic scores. Similar scores were computed for girls. In addition, the children were administered the vocabulary subtest of the WPPSI. The results of this study indicated a strong relationship between preschool children's scores for sex-stereotypic activities and their scores on the vocabulary test. When controlling for the effect of age, the researchers found a correlation between sex-stereotypic play activities and vocabulary of .88 for boys and .81 for girls. In other words, preschool children who engaged in sex-stereotypic activities had higher vocabulary scores than less sex-stereotypic children did. These results are consistent with the position that brighter preschool children learn about gender and its significance before less bright children do (Gouze & Nadelman, 1980) and behave accordingly.

Children's Theories of Gender

The process of gender identification is a complex one, involving biological dispositions and culture-appropriate experiences. However, it also seems clear that cognitive differences among children contribute substantially to their developing identification with members of their own sex. Controversy does exist concerning how important cognitive factors are in gender identification (in comparison with environmental and biological factors), as well as which aspects of cognitive development are most important. Moreover, once cognitive factors are given their due, there is the question of how gender knowledge in its various forms influences children's sex roles and behaviors. But there is little question that children's knowledge of gender roles and their understanding of the concept of gender are important for development.

Children realize early that gender is an important dimension and formulate theories concerning exactly what it is that differentiates the sexes. Many of these theories are wrong. For example, a 6-year-old boy noticing that my infant daughter had brown hair, just like his, asked if that meant "she will be a boy when she gets older." A 4-year-old eating at an Italian restaurant with his parents and another cou-

ple noticed that his father and the other gentleman had ordered pizza, whereas his mother had ordered lasagna. In the car on the way home, the child announced that he had figured it out: "Men eat pizza and women don't."

Once a child starts mingling with peers, what other children do determines to a large extent what is viewed as appropriate male and female behavior, often independent of the wishes of that child's parents. For example, friends of mine refused to buy guns for their 3-year-old son and restricted the number of aggressive programs he watched on television. Nevertheless, the boy learned from his preschool peers that gun play is boys' stuff: he ran around the house pointing sticks, spoons, or fingers at people and saying "bang," despite constant reprimands from his parents. He had learned from other 3-year-olds one special thing that boys do and, over his parents' objections, was making it something that he did as well.

Children continually gain knowledge about what differentiates males and females in society, and with this knowledge they continually devise and test theories about sex differences. Their early theories are simplistic, based on the grossest of characteristics (clothing, for example), and often not even tangentially related to societal sex stereotypes. However, much like the scientist delving into a new field of inquiry, they discard old theories, try new ones, and eventually acquire the meaning of gender that is implicitly agreed upon by members of their society.

How "Special" Is Social Cognition?

Should social cognition be covered at all in a textbook on cognitive development, or does it more properly belong in books about social development? My opinion is that social cognition is merely a subset of cognition, but it is an important one. People use the same brains they use to solve analogical-reasoning problems or to compute the cost per ounce of laundry detergent to figure out what other people are thinking and how they themselves should best behave. Whereas people with faulty mathematical or scientific reasoning abilities will likely get along all right in the world, someone who lacks a well-developed sense of self, an ability to take the perspective of another, or who is ineffective at social information processing, is in for a tough time.

I mentioned in the introduction to this chapter that some people believe that human intelligence evolved in the form that it has chiefly to deal with other members of our species (Alexander, 1989). We are far more intelligent than necessary to eke out an existence on the African savannas. In fact, so are chimpanzees. Nicholas Humphrey (1976) has suggested that most of humans' technological genius is absent from our daily lives. If alien anthropologists had observed Albert Einstein during a typical day, they would likely infer that that he had a "humdrum mind." But we do use our superior intelligence everyday when dealing with other people. We became the intelligent species not so much to cope with the demands of a hostile physical world, but to meet the demands of hostile members of our own species.

But this form of cognition, like all others, develops. Children are born prepared by evolution for a social world, but they do not have the requisite skills necessary to function effectively in that world. Their social intelligence unfolds, in part following a universal time line, much as Piaget proposed, but also varying as a function of the particular society they are born into. There is much variability among cultures, and children must have the cognitive skills to adapt to the particular environment in which they live. But what is common to all children across the globe is that they are part of a social species, and they develop the requisite intellectual skills necessary to live in such a world.

Summary

Social cognition is cognition about social relations and social phenomena. Many topics can be subsumed under the heading of social cognition. Albert Bandura's *social cognitive theory* is an extension of earlier *social learning theory* and is mainly a theory of how children operate cognitively on their social experiences. Bandura postulated five capabilities that

contribute to development, all of which change with age: *symbolization, forethought, self-regulation, self-reflection,* and *vicarious learning*. Bandura believes that children affect their environment as much as their environment affects them and referred to such interaction as *reciprocal determinism*. Following social cognitive theory, *observational learning* involves four subprocesses, each of which changes with development: attentional processes, retention processes, production processes, and motivational processes. *Self-efficacy* is the sense of control people have over their lives, beginning in infancy and developing over the course of childhood. Children who feel they have little or no control over things that happen to them show *helplessness*, whereas children with a positive sense of self-efficacy are said to have a *mastery orientation*.

Dodge proposed a model that adopts many of the tenets of contemporary information-processing approaches to explain children's social functioning. Dodge proposed five sequential steps of *social information processing* that are necessary for competent social behavior: (1) encoding of the social stimulus, (2) interpretation of the social information, (3) response search, in which children generate possible response alternatives, (4) response evaluation, in which children evaluate the potential effectiveness of the various alternatives, and (5) enactment, in which children execute the chosen response. Research by Dodge and his colleagues has shown a relationship between the efficacy of children's social information processing and their social behavior, suggesting that how children process social information plays a significant role in their social competence.

A child's *self-concept* begins to develop in infancy, with mirror recognition being observed as early as 15 months for some children. Children's self-concept changes over childhood and is reflected in how they describe themselves.

Selman proposed a five-stage model, describing the social role-taking abilities of children from about 4 years of age through adolescence. With age, children are increasingly able to take the perspective of another and are able to coordinate different perspectives. Tomasello and his colleagues proposed three types of *cultural learning* (*imitative learning*, *instructed learning*, and *collaborative learning*), each based on underlying *perspective-taking* abilities that develop over childhood.

Children's humor develops through a series of stages, based on their level of cognitive development. Humor is based on the identification of incongruity, and incongruity is most likely to be perceived when the discrepancy is of some intermediate magnitude. Humor changes over the school years, with the type of verbal jokes children appreciate becoming more sophisticated into adolescence.

Children's knowledge of *gender constancy* develops over the preschool years, with *gender identity* preceding *gender stability*, which precedes *gender consistency*. Level of gender constancy has been associated with children's attention to same-sex models, although most studies have not found a relationship between gender constancy and children's knowledge of sex stereotypes or toy preferences. *Gender schemas* are mentalistic structures consisting of a set of associations and expectations related to gender. These schemas influence how children process information related to gender and are related to their knowledge of sex stereotypes and gender-related behavior. As children's knowledge of gender expands, their schemas change, resulting in a more sophisticated use of gender in classifying people and behavior. During the preschool years, intellectually more advanced children tend to know more about sex stereotypes than less bright children do.

Key Terms and Concepts

social cognition
social learning theory
social cognitive theory
reciprocal determinism
symbolization
forethought
self-regulation
self-reflection
vicarious learning
observational learning
self-efficacy
wishful thinking
helplessness
mastery orientation
social information processing
self-concept
perspective taking
cultural learning
imitative learning
instructed learning
collaborative learning
gender identification
gender constancy
gender identity
gender stability
gender consistency
gender schema
gender script

Suggested Readings

BANDURA, A. (1989). Social cognitive theory. In R. Vasta (Ed.), *Annals of child development* (pp. 1–60). Greenwich, CT: JAI. This paper concisely presents the most recent formulation of Bandura's social cognitive theory. It deals with the central concepts of social cognitive theory (for example, symbolizing capacity, vicarious learning, and observational learning) and devotes several pages to the issue of self-efficacy.

DODGE, K. A., PETTIT, G. S., McCLASKEY, C. L., & BROWN, M. M. (1986). Social competence in children. *Monographs of the Society for Research in Child Development, 51* (Serial No. 213). This monograph presents Dodge's social information processing theory, along with the results of experiments testing the theory. Despite its being nearly 15 years old, I think it's the best source for getting the "big picture" of social information processing.

HARTER, S. (1998). The development of self-representation. In N. Eisenberg (Vol. Ed.), *Social, emotional, and personality development*, Vol. 3 (pp. 553–617), of W. Damon (Gen. Ed.), *Handbook of child psychology*. New York: Wiley. Harter presents a thorough review of research and theory on the development of self-concept from infancy through adolescence, including research on self-evaluation.

RUBLE, D. N., & MARTIN, C.L. (1998). Gender development. In N. Eisenberg (Vol. Ed.), *Social, emotional, and personality development*, Vol. 3 (pp. 933–1016), of W. Damon (Gen. Ed.), *Handbook of child psychology*. New York: Wiley. Ruble and Martin provide an up-to-date review of gender development, not only from a cognitive perspective, but also from social and biological perspectives. It is likely the best single source for a comprehensive review of issues, theory, and research on gender development.

12

Schooling and Cognition

In the previous chapters, we have examined the development of basic cognitive abilities. These abilities, including perceptual discrimination, selective attention, memory, and language, are each modified by the contexts in which we develop. Yet some cognitive abilities seem to develop only in certain contexts, particularly school. Reading is perhaps the best example of this. Children learn to read using the basic cognitive skills that characterize them as members of our species, but it is unheard of for an unschooled child in an illiterate culture ever to learn to read. We as a species did not evolve to read. Unlike language, reading is rarely acquired "spontaneously." Reading is understandably classified in educational circles as a language skill, but it is a very different language skill, acquired in a very different way, from a child's mother tongue. Although all normal children learn to be proficient speakers of their native language, not all learn to be proficient readers, even with instruction.

Reading is perhaps the single most important technological skill in postindustrial cultures. Although one may be regarded as intelligent despite being illiterate, it is difficult to think of an illiterate person becoming educated in modern society. Not only does educational success depend on reading proficiency but so does occupational success. One can sustain life and even support a family legally in our culture while being illiterate, but it is difficult, and few of the rewards of contemporary culture go to those who cannot read. And poor reading among American adults is not a rarity. It has been estimated that nearly one-quarter of American adults—between 35 to 50 million people—cannot read much beyond a third-grade level (see Adams, Treiman, & Pressley, 1998).

If reading is the number one technological skill in modern society, mathematical abilities must come in second. Verbal and quantitative skills constitute the two major subtests of the Scholastic Assessment Test (SAT), the Graduate Record Exam (GRE), and even most IQ tests (see Gardner, 1983). Although there is more to verbal and quantitative abilities than reading and mathematics, these are

the core abilities. (As far as I know, there are no provisions to administer the SAT or GRE to illiterate people.)

Unlike reading, basic mathematical skills can be acquired without formal schooling. Beginning in preschool, children in postindustrial societies receive instruction in simple number concepts and arithmetic, and math constitutes one of the primary subject areas in schools.

In this chapter, I will review the development of reading and mathematical abilities. Both topics have been investigated mainly through information-processing theory, although Piaget had much to say about children's early number concepts. Individual and gender differences in these topics have been of great interest to educators and the public at large, and I will devote considerable space to these issues. I will also examine the connection between reading and knowledge ("Does reading make you smarter?") and look at cultural differences in mathematics ability. Although the distinction in the attainments of basic arithmetic abilities between children in schooled and unschooled cultures is of great theoretical importance, differences in mathematical attainment between children in different information-age cultures is of great practical importance and of interest to American educators, and I will briefly examine some of these differences.

In the latter part of the chapter I will look at several issues directly related to cognitive development and schooling. I selected these issues from the many topics that I could have included in this chapter primarily because I believe they are related to issues that we have already dealt with in this book or will deal with in the final two chapters. First, how does the effect of schooling influence cognitive development in comparison with the effect of age? Second, what is the effect of schooling on IQ? And finally, what are the costs and benefits of academic preschools for children from middle-class homes? Issues related to preschool education for children judged to be "at risk for mental retardation" will be discussed in Chapter 14.

The Development of Reading Skills

A Brief Overview of Learning to Read

Learning to read involves the acquisition of a set of skills, each built on the preceding skills. Jeanne Chall (1979) proposed five stages in the development of proficient reading, ranging from the pre-reading skills of the preschool child to the highly skilled reading of the adult.

In stage 0, covering the years before a child enters first grade, children must master the prerequisites of reading, most notably learning to discriminate the letters of the alphabet. By the time children enter school, many can already "read" some words, such as "Pepsi," "McDonalds," and "Pizza Hut." Their ability to recognize these popular symbols, flashed at them from the television and seen repeatedly on the roadside or the dinner table, indicates that children can tell the difference between patterns of letters, even if they are unable to sound out the words. Children's knowledge of letters and single words is generally better than it was several generations ago, partly because of the influence of children's television shows such as "Sesame Street."

Stage 1 covers children's first year of formal reading instruction. In first grade, children learn phonological recoding skills, the skills used to translate written symbols into sounds and thus words (more will be said about phonological recoding skills later). This is followed in the second and third grades by stage 2, in which children learn to read fluently. By the end of the third grade, most school children have mastered the letter-to-sound correspondence and can read most words and simple sentences they are given. But reading is effortful for these children, in that the process of identifying individual words requires so much of their limited mental resources that they often do not comprehend much of what they read. They are still concentrating on what individual sets of letters mean and are not very skilled at putting the words together to abstract the broader meaning of the text.

The change from "learning to read" to "reading to learn" begins in stage 3, spanning grades 4 through 8. Children can now more readily acquire information from written material, and this is reflected by the school curriculum. Children in these grades are expected to learn from the books they read. If children have not mastered the "how to's" of reading by fourth grade, progress in school can be difficult.

Stage 4, beginning in the high school years, reflects truly proficient reading, with children becoming increasingly able to comprehend a variety of written material and to draw inferences from what they read.

Based on this brief description, it would appear that reading does not develop hand in hand with language development. Rather, reading is built on a well-established language system and develops alongside general cognitive development.

Emergent Literacy

Although most children learn to read in school, most learn *about* reading in the home. They learn that arbitrary written symbols correspond to spoken language and convey meaning. They learn that language is used to communicate with others, as a memory reminder (writing down a phone number to call later), and for pleasure (Bialystok, 1996). In the United States and many other literate cultures in the world, books are written just for adults to read to children. Parents who share story books with their preschool children are teaching them much about reading and are preparing their children for success in a literate culture (see discussion in Chapter 3 on sociocultural nature of early language and reading).

But most preschool children do not read—not really. They might be able to identify Coca-Cola, Burger King, or Fruit Loops signs when they see them, but this is not really reading. Nevertheless, what children are learning during story times with a parent and in a household where reading is done frequently are skills that set the stage for true reading. The idea that there is a developmental continuum of reading skills, from those of the preschooler to those of the proficient reader, is referred to as **emergent literacy**. According to Whitehurst and Lonigan

(1998), emergent literacy "consists of the skills, knowledge and attitudes that are presumed to be developmental precursors to conventional forms of reading and writing . . . and the environments that support these developments (for example, shared book reading . . .) (p. 849). Whitehurst and Lonigan (1998) list nine components of emergent literacy, which I will discuss briefly here.

1. *Language*: Reading is obviously a language skill, and children need to be versatile with their spoken language before they can be expected to read it. However, skilled (and even early) reading requires more than just proficiency with spoken language. Reading does *not* seem to be simply a reflection of spoken language, with children with advanced language skills becoming children with advanced reading skills. For example, Crain-Thoreson and Dale (1992) examined a group of early-talkers over several years and found virtually no relation between spoken language skills and literacy knowledge at age 4.5 years. Later reading, however, that involves "reading to learn," might be more sensitive to children's background knowledge, their vocabulary, and familiarity with complex grammar (Mason, 1992).

2. *Conventions of print*: Children exposed to reading in the home know the conventions of print. For example, in English, children learn that reading is done left-to-right, top-to-bottom, and front-to-back.

3. *Knowledge of letters*: Most children can recite their ABCs before entering school and can identify individual letters of the alphabet (although some children think "elemeno" is the name of the letter between "k" and "p"). Knowledge of letters is critical for reading. For example, research has shown that kindergarten children's ability to name letters predicts their later reading achievement scores (Näslund & Schneider, 1996; Schneider & Näslund, 1999).

4. *Linguistic awareness*: Children must learn to identify not only letters but also linguistic units, such as phonemes, syllables, and words. Perhaps

the most important set of linguistic abilities for reading deals with phonological processing, or the discrimination and making sense of the various sounds of a language. More will be said about phonological processing in the following sections.

5. *Phoneme-grapheme correspondence*: Once children have figured out how to segment and discriminate the various sounds of a language, they must learn how these sounds correspond to written letters. Most begin this process during the preschool years, with letter knowledge and phonological sensitivity developing simultaneously and reciprocally (Burgess & Lonigan, 1998).

6. *Emergent reading*: Many children pretend to read. They will take a familiar story book and "read" one page after another, often "just like Daddy does," or will take an unfamiliar book and pretend to read, making up a narrative to go along with the pictures on the pages.

7. *Emergent writing*: Similar to pretend reading, children often pretend to write, making squiggles on a page to "write" their name or a story, or stringing together real letters to produce something they think corresponds to a story, a shopping list, or a note to Mom.

8. *Print motivation*: How interested are children in reading and writing? How important is it for them to figure out what the secret code is that permits adults to make sense of a series of marks on a page? Some evidence indicates that young children who are interested in print and reading have greater emergent literacy skills than less motivated children (Crain-Thoreson & Dale, 1992). Children who are interested in reading and writing are more likely to notice print, ask questions about print, encourage adults to read to them, and spend more time reading once they are able.

9. *Other cognitive skills*: There are a host of individual cognitive skills, in addition to those associated with language and linguistic awareness, that influence a child's reading ability. Various aspects of memory are very important, and some of these will be discussed.

Many studies have related aspects of emergent literacy to later reading ability, some of which will be discussed in the sections to follow. Relations between any specific component of emergent literacy and later reading are sometimes difficult to establish. However, it is clear that families that provide "the whole package" of emergent literacy skills to their children have children who are better readers, both early in school and later, than families that provide less of the package (Bialystok, 1996; Whitehurst & Lonigan, 1998).

As in other aspects of school performance, differences in reading are frequently found as a function of socioeconomic status (SES). Children from poverty homes are much more likely to encounter reading problems in school than are children from middle-income homes. The point I want to make here is that these SES differences do not begin in school, but in the home in the years before children begin formal reading instructions. Parents from lower-SES families are much less likely to read to their children, have fewer books in the house, and generally do not foster the emergent literacy skills that are so important in learning to read. Reading may be a highly technological skill, but its origins are in everyday family interactions. Does this mean that children's literacy skills are determined before they enter school? No, but their experiences at home do establish a foundation on which school instruction is based. And home environments tend to be stable. Children who receive intellectual support for literacy early in life can expect similar support later on (see Chapter 14 for a discussion of the stability of intelligence). This implies that children from homes in which emergent literacy is *not* fostered, will likely not receive the kind of support during the elementary school years that is associated with proficient reading. However, it also suggests that if the amount or quality of support in the environment (both home and school) changes for the better, so, too, may children's reading abilities. Reading is a skill that involves a host of developing cognitive skills that children must learn to coordinate to become proficient. But it is also a cultural invention—it is not part of our evolutionary heritage—and, perhaps more than any other complex cognitive skill, is as much a product of a child's social environment as it is of his or her developing brain.

Cognitive Development and Reading

Early Reading Skills

One early skill that predicts good reading in later years is **phonemic awareness**. Phonemic awareness is the knowledge that words consist of separable sounds. Such awareness is generally not available to preschool children. In one study, 4- and 5-year-olds were taught to tap once for each sound in a short word (Liberman et al., 1974). For instance, children would tap twice for "at" and three times for "cat." Although the children presumably understood the task, their performance was poor, with none of the 4-year olds (and only a few of the 5-year-olds) performing it accurately. Although this task might seem trivial, it predicts children's early reading achievement quite well (Liberman & Shankweiler, 1977). Other aspects of phonological awareness (such as children's abilities to detect rhymes) also develop slowly over the preschool and early school years and predict remarkably well children's early reading skills (Gottardo, Stanovich, & Siegel, 1996; Wagner et al., 1997). This is also true in other languages besides English (Lundberg, Frost, & Petersen, 1988; Schneider & Näslund, 1999), including Chinese, which includes a phonetic component in its characters (Ho & Bryant, 1997).

Recent research has shown that children's sensitivity to rhymes leads to awareness of phonemes, which in turn affects reading and also presumably makes it easier for children to recognize written words that both sound and look alike (for example, *cat* and *hat*) (Bryant et al., 1990). Other research has suggested that it is not children's sensitivity to rhymes, per se, that is the critical component to literacy, but rather the ability to segment phonemes (Muter et al., 1998). Muter and her colleagues tested a group of preschool children (average age, 4 years, 3 months) on rhyming and phonemic segmentation abilities. Tests of rhyming included asking children to identify pictures and then to pick out those that rhyme, and to produce words that rhymed with each of two words ("day" and "bell"). For one test of phonemic segmentation, children were shown a picture of an object (a cat, for instance), the interviewer provided the first two phonemes ("ca"), and children were asked to finish the word (in this case, say "t"). In another test, children were shown a picture and asked to say the word without the first phoneme (for example, "Bus without the /b/ says. . . . ," with the correct response being "us"). The researchers reported that reading ability at the end of first grade was significantly related to preschool phonemic segmentation ability but not to rhyming ability.

Not surprisingly, instruction in phonemic awareness relates to later reading ability. For example, kindergarten and first-grade children who are given explicit instruction in phonemic awareness display better early reading ability than children not given such instruction (Cunningham, 1990; Schneider et al., 1997). Cunningham states that the results from her training study argue against the idea that phonemic awareness is a consequence of learning to read. Rather, she proposes, as have others (Bryant et al., 1990), phonemic awareness is causally related to reading achievement, even in the early stage of learning to read.

The Role of Phonological Processing in Identifying Words

Phonological recoding. The reason that phonological awareness is such a good predictor of early reading, of course, is that early reading generally involves sounding out words. This process of **phonological recoding** is the basis of the majority of reading instruction programs in the United States today (the **phonics** method). Children are taught the sound of each letter and how to combine these sounds, blending them into words.

Truly proficient reading is not done by sounding out each letter but rather by directly retrieving the meaning of the whole word from memory (wholeword or visually based retrieval). Think for a while about how you read. Very few college students sound

words out, letter by letter, but rather simply know the meaning of a word when they see it. Adults and older children who read phonetically are not good readers. The amount of mental effort it takes to process a single word by this method is tremendous, making it unlikely that much meaning will be obtained from what is read. Yet without phonological recoding skills, we would be unable to read novel words (such as *defenestration*, defined as the act of throwing something out of a window); we would be limited to reading only words we have learned before. So it seems that phonological skills are necessary if one's reading ability is to advance.

The key to proficient reading is the process of *automatization*, the effortless retrieval of word meaning. Being able to access the meaning of words, expending little or none of one's limited resources in the process, is critical for skilled reading. When too many mental resources are used just getting the meaning of individual words, too few resources are left to piece the words together and understand the greater meaning of the text (recall the discussion in Chapter 5 of the limited nature of mental resources). Robert Siegler (1988, 1996) has developed the **adaptive strategy-choice model** to describe how children read words. (Siegler has also applied his model to memory and arithmetic strategies, as discussed in Chapter 5 and later in this chapter.) According to Siegler, children's first choice of a strategy for word identification is that of visually based retrieval (or **fact retrieval**), done automatically (or nearly so). If children are not sufficiently familiar with the word to retrieve its meaning directly from long-term memory, they fall back to more effortful strategies, in this case, phonological recoding. As children become more experienced with the words they read and better able in general to automatize processing, reading becomes more proficient.

Phonological processing and reading disabilities. There is substantial evidence that perhaps the principal cognitive factor underlying reading disability, often referred to as **dyslexia,** is faulty phonological processing (Adams et al., 1998; Shankweiler et al., 1995; Vellutino, Scanlon, & Spearing, 1995). Children are said to have a reading disability if they have great difficulty in learning to read despite an average intelligence. Stated another way, if a child's reading ability is substantially worse than his or her general intellectual ability would predict, that child is said to be reading disabled, or dyslexic.

Keith Stanovich (1988) proposed that phonological processing is a relatively modular function, little influenced by "higher," conscious cognitive structures. Thus, according to Stanovich's model, phonological processes should be independent of other, more general aspects of cognition, including IQ. There is evidence that this is the case. For example, Linda Siegel (1988) reports that reading-disabled children from a range of IQ levels have equal difficulty on phonological processing tasks. For instance, pseudoword reading requires children to read a sequence of pronounceable letters that do not make up an English word (for example, *joak, kake*). Related to pseudoword reading, phonological-lexical tasks require children to determine which of two pseudowords sounds like a real word (for example, *kake, dake*). In Siegel's study, performance of reading-disabled children was poor on these tasks and did not differ among children as a function of IQ level.

Reading-disabled children's phonological-processing abilities improve with age, but they typically start school with poorer phonological skills than good readers and usually stay behind. For example, research by Siegel and her colleagues (Siegel, 1993; Siegel & Ryan, 1988) compared the phonological processing of groups of reading-disabled and nondisabled children between the ages of 7 and 14 years. As one test of phonological processing, children were asked to read pseudowords. The results are shown in Figure 12-1. As can be seen, older disabled readers were better at pseudoword reading than younger disabled readers, demonstrating that these skills were developing in these children. However, the performance of 13- and 14-year-old disabled readers was comparable to that of 7- and 8-year-old nondisabled readers, reflecting significant retardation of this skill. Moreover, recent longitudinal research suggests that phonological-processing abilities remain relatively stable over childhood (Wagner, Torgesen, & Rashotte, 1994; Wagner et al., 1997), making early intervention all the more important.

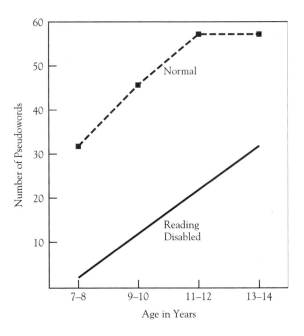

FIGURE 12-1   Accuracy of pseudoword reading as a function of age for normal and reading-disabled children. SOURCE: "The Cognitive Basis of Dyslexia," by L. S. Siegel. In R. Pasnak and M. L. Howe (Eds.), *Emerging Themes in Cognitive Development*, Vol. II: *Competencies*. Copyright © 1993 Springer-Verlag New York, Inc. Reprinted with permission.

Recent research using brain imaging techniques has supported the interpretation that phonological problems are at the core of many reading disabilities. In a study by Sally Shaywitz and her colleagues (1998), adults with developmental reading disabilities (dyslexia) and non-reading-disabled adults were given a series of reading-related tasks that varied in the amount of phonological processing required to perform each task. Brain activation patterns, as measured by functional MRI (see Chapter 2), were observed between the normal and dyslexic readers. Shaywitz and her colleagues reported different brain-wave patterns for the normal and dyslexic readers, especially when the tasks required substantial phonological processing. Compared with the normal readers, the dyslexic readers showed underactivation in some portions of the brain (mainly posterior regions) and overactivation in others (mainly anterior regions). Underactive parts of the brain included those areas typically associated with phonological processing and cross-modal integration. In reading, cross-modal integration (see discussion of cross-modal integration in infancy in Chapter 6) involves the translation of symbols in one modality (in this case vision, as in the letters and words on a page) into another modality (in this case audition, as in the sounds of letters and words). Shaywitz and her colleagues (1998) concluded that the patterns of brain activity of dyslexic readers "provide evidence of an imperfectly functioning system for segmenting words into their phonological constituents . . . and adds neurobiological support for previous cognitive/behavioral data pointing to the critical role of phonological analysis and its impairment in dyslexia" (p. 2640).

Comprehension

But reading involves more than just identifying words. Reading involves understanding language, including stories, instructions for assembling a VCR, and cognitive development textbooks, among other things. Children must relate the meaning of individual words and sentences to abstract the broader meaning that a written text intends. Such a process is referred to as **reading comprehension**.

The role of working memory in reading comprehension. Reading comprehension is not a single process but a set of processes that all must be integrated to function smoothly. Individual words must be identified, of course, and related to other words in the sentence. One factor that limits children's comprehension is the amount of information they can hold in working memory at any one time. Meredyth Daneman and her colleagues have proposed that it is necessary for information to be retained in working memory for as long as possible so that each newly read word in a passage can be integrated with the words and concepts that preceded it. Younger or less-proficient readers have less available mental capacity to store and maintain information in working memory because it is necessary for them

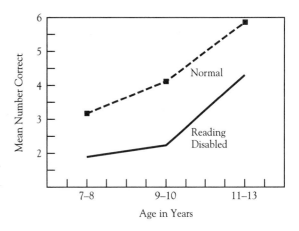

FIGURE 12-2 Performance on a working-memory task as a function of age for normal and reading-disabled children. SOURCE: "The Cognitive Basis of Dyslexia," by L. S. Siegel. In R. Pasnak and M. L. Howe (Eds.), *Emerging Themes in Cognitive Development*, Vol. II: *Competencies*. Copyright © 1993 Springer-Verlag New York, Inc. Reprinted with permission.

to devote considerable capacity to the processes involved in identifying words and comprehension. Daneman and her colleagues showed that listening span, defined as the number of successive short sentences that can be recalled verbatim, correlates significantly with comprehension for people ranging from preschoolers to college students (Daneman & Blennerhassett, 1984; Daneman & Green, 1986).

As with phonological coding, differences in working-memory capacity differentiate disabled from nondisabled readers (de Jong, 1998; Siegel & Ryan, 1989; Swanson, Ashbaker, & Lee, 1996). For example, Siegel and Ryan (1989) gave normal and reading-disabled children, ranging in age from 7 to 13 years, a series of incomplete sentences, requiring them to supply the final word of each sentence. Sentences they used included the following: "In the summer it is very _____. People go to see monkeys in a _____. With dinner we sometimes eat bread and _____." After being presented two, three, four, or five such sentences, children were asked to repeat the final words, in order, that they had generated for each sentence. The results of the study are graphed in Figure 12-2. As can be seen, working memory improved for both the disabled and normal readers with age, but the disabled readers had shorter memory spans than the normal readers at each age level.

Individual differences in working memory are not only related to reading comprehension, but also to writing ability. Swanson and Berninger (1996) reported that working memory performance was a significant predictor of both reading comprehension and writing ability in groups of fourth-, fifth-, and sixth-grade children. However, Swanson and Berninger proposed that writing skills are related to a domain-specific set of working-memory operations, whereas reading comprehension is related to a more general set of processing resources.

The role of knowledge in reading comprehension. Another critical factor in reading comprehension is the knowledge an individual has of the material being read. As discussed in Chapter 5, having detailed knowledge of a topic permits one to process information about that topic more efficiently (Bjorklund, Muir-Broaddus, & Schneider, 1990). This is especially true in reading comprehension.

Richard Anderson and his colleagues (Anderson et al., 1984) defined reading as "a process in which information from the text and the knowledge possessed by the readers act together to produce meaning" (p. 8). In other words, "reading is a constructive process" (p. 9), in which the background knowledge that one brings to a text interacts with what is written on the page to produce understanding. Anderson and his associates cite considerable evidence from the research literature to support these claims. In one study, for example, second-graders who were equated in reading skill were tested for their knowledge of spiders and then given a passage about spiders to read (Pearson, Hansen, & Gordon, 1979). The children who knew more about spiders at the outset were better at answering subsequent questions about the passage, especially those questions that involved reasoning. Instructional efforts aimed at increasing background knowledge have also been found to enhance reading comprehension (Hansen & Pearson, 1983; Omanson et al., 1984). The relation between background knowledge and text comprehension will be explored further in Chapter 14.

In other research, the ease with which children could think of a sentence containing a word (referred to as *context availability*) predicted several aspects of word processing (word identification, determining whether a set of letters was a word or not) for second-, third-, and fifth-grade children, and for high- and low-ability readers in each grade (Schwanenflugel & Noyes, 1996). However, the effect of context availability was greater for younger and low-ability readers than for older and high-ability readers. Schwanenflugel and Noyes suggested that young and low-ability readers have difficulty connecting low-context available words to their meanings, and the result is many reading errors. Although context availability might not be equivalent to "knowledge" as defined by Anderson and his colleagues (1984), it is, I argue, a function of word knowledge, and this research demonstrates the importance of background knowledge not only for reading comprehension, but also for reading individual words.

The role of monitoring on reading comprehension. Another factor related to reading comprehension is the ability to monitor one's understanding of a text and to adjust reading strategies accordingly (Brown & Smiley, 1978; Paris & Oka, 1986). Good readers easily recognize when they don't comprehend something they are reading. They then take the necessary action to rectify the situation. This can involve rereading a sentence, reading more slowly, checking back a few lines to see if some important information might have been missed, or perhaps consulting a dictionary. These are ideal skills; children do not approach them until the high-school years, and many people never develop them fully. In general, comprehension-monitoring skills improve with age and experience (Baker, 1985; Garner, 1990), and, importantly, they can be improved with instruction (Palincsar & Brown, 1984).

How to Instruct Children How to Read

The focus of this chapter is on children's developing cognitive abilities as they relate to important tasks, here reading. As such, I have chosen not to get involved in the often-heated debate of how best to teach children how to read. However, the topic should not be totally neglected, and I will here briefly outline the two major approaches to reading instruction and comment on how the research evidence weighs in on this topic.

Basically (and simplistically), reading instruction can be thought of as either (1) a *bottom-up process*, with children learning the individual components of reading (identifying letters, letter-sound correspondence) and putting them together to achieve meaning; or (2) a *top-down process*, with children's goals, background knowledge, and expectations determining what information they select from text (see Adams et al., 1998). This latter is a constructivist perspective, reminiscent of Piaget's ideas. Surely, skilled reading involves both bottom-up and top-down processes, making any dichotomy artificial. However, reading instruction, particularly in the early grades, often emphasizes one over the other, and thus the dichotomy has some basis in reality.

Curricula that emphasize bottom-up processes are exemplified by the phonics method, discussed earlier. Here, children are taught specific letter-sound correspondence, often independent of any "meaningful" context. Curricula that emphasize top-down processes are exemplified by the **whole-language approach**. According to Marilyn Adams and her colleagues (1998), "the whole language approach holds that learning is anchored on and motivated by meaning. Further, since meaning and meaningfulness are necessarily defined internally and never by pronouncement, learning can be effective only to the extent that it is cognitively controlled by the learner" (p. 277). Thus, whole-language curricula emphasize reading interesting and meaningful text from the very beginning. Classrooms where whole language is taught are more apt to be student—rather than teacher—centered, have an integration of reading and writing within the overall curriculum, have an avoidance of drill, and are less likely to have rigid abilities groupings. All this sounds quite inviting, actually. However, many proponents of the whole language approach "have steadfastly, adamantly, and sometimes vitriolically denied the value and rejected the practice of skills instruction, including phonics, and this has been a point of heated contention" (Adams et al., 1998, p. 277).

The research evidence reviewed earlier in this chapter should make clear the importance of basic-level (bottom-up) processing in learning to read. Phonological skills are the single best predictor of reading ability (and disability). These abilities do not develop spontaneously, but are acquired only with practice, and usually explicit instruction. Curricula that ignore phonics, regardless of how "meaningful" they make the experience of reading, are risking the literacy of many of their students. This is not to argue for a curriculum that has children reading only stories about "Dick, Jane, and their dog Spot." But it does argue for including some aspects of phonics in any reading instruction.

Does Reading Make You Smarter?

Reading is a skill that is rarely acquired "spontaneously" but must be taught, usually in school. Thus, it seems plausible that literacy is one of the factors responsible for cognitive differences between schooled and nonschooled cultures. Moreover, it also seems plausible that within a literate society, people who read more become smarter or more knowledgeable than people who read less.

These are reasonable hypotheses that have been examined by several researchers over the years. First, let's consider the general effect of literacy. Are people who learn to read cognitively different from people who do not? Proposals that they are have been referred to as *Great Divide* theories (Olson & Torrance, 1991; Scribner & Cole, 1981). Researchers such as Patricia Greenfield (1972) have proposed that experience with written language helps to develop a set of cognitive operations that are more elaborate and effective in dealing with abstract concepts than those afforded by spoken language only. Moreover, Greenfield believed that the effect of literacy on cognition is not an all-or-none thing but a continuum. The more people read, the more sophisticated their cognitive abilities become.

This position was seriously challenged by results of a study of the Vai people of Africa by Scribner and Cole (1981). The Vai people use three types of written scripts, each for a different purpose: English is learned in school and used in formal settings (writing letters to the government); Arabic is used for reading the Koran; and a native Vai script is used for personal communications and some business transactions. At the time of the study, some Vai knew all three scripts, and some knew only one or two. Moreover, some Vai knew one or two of the scripts but had never attended school, thus making it possible to separate the effects of literacy from the effects of schooling. Scribner and Cole reported no effect of nonschooled literacy on the Vai people's cognitive performance. That is, people who could read and write but had never attended school showed patterns of cognitive performance similar to those of illiterate, nonschooled people. The conclusion from these results is that it is formal schooling, and not reading per se, that contributes to differences in cognitive performance.

Recently, researchers have begun to examine again the issue of literacy and cognition, some proposing that Scribner and Cole's test with the Vai was not a fair one. The literacy Scriber and Cole investigated (for example, letter writing in the Vai script) might not have been at a sufficiently high level to produce the types of cognitive effects that reading and writing can produce in a more widely literate society. Keith Stanovich and his colleagues (Stanovich, 1993; Stanovich, West, & Harrison, 1995) have done a series of studies investigating this issue, some of which I will describe.

In one set of studies, Stanovich and his colleagues asked fifth-graders to keep diaries over a three-week period of their out-of-school activities, including the amount of time they spent reading, as well as the type of material they read. They reported a moderate correlation between book reading time and vocabulary knowledge (.39), suggesting that the more children read, the more vocabulary words they know. Supporting this conclusion, Schwanenflugel, Stahl, and McFalls (1997) demonstrated that fourth-grade children learn the meaning of unknown and partially known words as a result of reading stories containing those words.

In another study, fifth-grade children were given lists of children's books and authors and asked to check the ones they recognized. This served as a measure of print exposure (Cipielewski & Stanovich, 1992). Cipielewski and Stanovich reasoned

that children who read more would identify more of the books and authors. The researchers then related performance on the print exposure measures to children's reading comprehension test scores. They reported that performance on the print exposure measures predicted fifth-grade reading ability, even after taking into consideration the children's third-grade reading skills. That is, it was not simply the case that better third-grade readers read more and became better fifth-grade readers. Rather, after reading ability in third grade had been controlled for, the amount of print exposure contributed significantly to children's reading ability.

In other research, reading ability in grade 1 was related to print exposure and reading ability in grade 11 (Cunningham & Stanovich, 1997). First-grade reading ability predicted reading ability in the 11th grade, even after controlling for differences in cognitive ability. Also, first-grade reading ability was significantly related to exposure to print 10 years later, even after controlling for grade 11 reading-comprehension ability. Cunningham and Stanovich reasoned that children who learn to read early may develop a habit of reading that will stay with them throughout their lives.

Stanovich and his colleagues performed one study outside of the laboratory, with groups of adults waiting in Washington's National Airport lounge (West, Stanovich, & Mitchell, 1993). They unobtrusively observed people sitting by themselves waiting for planes. People who did not read anything during a 10-minute period were classified as nonreaders, whereas people who did read something during the 10-minute period were classified as readers. The people were then approached by an experimenter and asked if they wished to participate in a brief study. Approximately 90% of the people approached agreed to participate (111 readers and 106 nonreaders).

The people were then given a series of tests assessing their print exposure (author recognition test, magazine recognition test, newspaper recognition test), vocabulary, cultural literacy recognition (a measure of general cultural knowledge), and TV and film recognition. The average scores of the readers and the nonreaders are shown in Table 12-1.

TABLE 12-1 Contrast of readers and nonreaders on a variety of measures

Variable	Average score for nonreaders	Average score for readers
Author recognition test	.401	.635
Magazine recognition test	.598	.751
Newspaper recognition test	.370	.529
Television recognition test	.426	.468
Film recognition test	.292	.320
Vocabulary checklist	.516	.731
Cultural literacy recognition	.600	.770
Age	35.3	41.4
Education	15.2	16.5

SOURCE: Data from R. F. West, K. E. Stanovich, and H. Mitchell, 1993; table from "Does Reading Make You Smarter? Literacy and the Development of Verbal Intelligence," by K.E. Stanovich, 1993, *Advances in Child Development and Behavior, 24*. Copyright © 1993 Academic Press. Reprinted with permission.

As can be seen, the readers scored higher on the author, magazine, and newspaper recognition tests, validating that the people classified as readers did indeed have significantly greater print exposure. The readers and nonreaders were comparable in terms of television and film knowledge, but the readers scored higher than the nonreaders on the vocabulary checklist and on the test of cultural literacy. The readers were also older than the nonreaders and had more education. Further analyses indicated that the differences in print exposure between the readers and the nonreaders remained significant even after differences in age and education were statistically controlled for (see also Stanovich et al., 1995).

The studies by Stanovich and his colleagues did not involve literate versus illiterate people, but children and adults who had had different amounts of exposure to print. Children and adults who read more have better reading comprehension, larger vocabularies, and greater general knowledge than children and adults who read less. Reading might not change all aspects of cognition. Nevertheless, I don't think it would be too much of an overstate-

ment to conclude that reading makes you smarter, or at least more knowledgeable.

Gender Differences in Reading and Verbal Abilities

"Female superiority on verbal tasks has been one of the more solidly established generalizations in the field of gender differences," wrote Maccoby and Jacklin (1974, p. 75) in introducing their section on gender differences in verbal ability in their seminal book that set the stage for contemporary investigations of gender differences. Despite this strong opening statement, Maccoby and Jacklin followed with the observation that the magnitude of such differences is small and often insignificant, but when differences do appear in the data, they usually favor females.

The definition of verbal tasks can be quite broad. It typically includes tests of vocabulary, spelling, and reading comprehension, all topics closely associated with reading. As we saw in Chapter 9, gender differences in rate of language acquisition favoring girls are sometimes found (and sometimes not) but are small in magnitude. Gender differences in verbal tasks have been found more frequently, again favoring females, but, as we'll see, the differences are not always robust and they seem to be getting smaller over the years.

In this section, I examine research evidence concerning possible gender differences in reading and other verbal tasks. Are females really more verbal than males, and if so, what is the nature of this difference? One concern of most researchers interested in gender differences is their source. Is it possible to determine whether differences, when found, have a primarily biologic origin or can be traced primarily to environmental causes?

Gender Differences in Reading Ability

In reviewing research on gender differences, Diane Halpern (1997) concluded that females, on average, perform better than males on "tasks that require rapid access to and use of phonological and semantic information in long-term memory, [and] production and comprehension of complex prose" (p. 1091). There is no single reason for these gender differences, but the preponderance of boys who are classified as reading disabled is strong evidence for a biological basis for gender differences in reading ability. Boys are far more likely than girls to be in special education classes for reading, and it is likely that most of the studies that have assessed gender differences in verbal abilities (including reading) have excluded reading-disabled children (Hyde & Linn, 1988). Thus, perhaps gender differences in general reading ability would be found to be greater were more low-scoring boys included in the testings. But, more to the point, the fact that many aspects of reading disabilities can be traced to basic cognitive abilities that are found early and tend to be stable over childhood, suggests that there is a substantial biological component to reading disabilities.

Despite this evidence, what do gender differences in reading disabilities tell us about the nature of possible gender differences in the general population? Can we generalize our findings of gender differences from research with the learning disabled to normal populations, or are dyslexic children a qualitatively distinct subgroup? I don't have an answer to this question, but the fact that gender differences are so small in the normal population and that boys are so overrepresented in reading-disabled classes suggests that we must be cautious in making generalizations from the dyslexic to the general population concerning the nature of gender differences.

Reading and the expression of feelings (both verbal tasks) are viewed as stereotypically female activities and might contribute to girls' superior verbal skills. Also, many of the stories in children's reading books are not inherently interesting to children (Blom, Waite, & Zimet, 1968), and there is evidence that boys are particularly motivated by the interest level of the reading material. For example, Asher and Markel (1974) reported that fifth-grade boys displayed better comprehension for stories of high interest than for those of low interest. This difference in reading level was much smaller for fifth-grade girls. Gender differences in reading ability were small and insignificant for high-interest stories (the boys' average reading score was 9.33, the girls'

10.71) but large and significant in favor of girls for low-interest stories (the boys' average score was 5.57, compared with the girls' score of 9.32). Similar findings of a greater influence of topic interest on reading and academic performance for boys than for girls have been reported by several other researchers (Renninger, 1992; Schiefele, Krapp, & Winteler, 1992).

Meta-Analytic Studies of Gender Differences in Reading and Verbal Abilities

Maccoby and Jacklin's 1974 review of gender differences was primarily descriptive. That is, they reviewed the literature for studies that examined gender differences and computed a "box score" of the results, finding girls to be the "winners" more frequently than the boys. This does not give us an idea of the magnitude of the effects, however. In the past 20 years or so, a new method has been developed that permits researchers to get a better appreciation of the magnitude of gender differences across a large number of studies, termed **meta-analysis**. Meta-analysis is a statistical technique that allows an investigator to evaluate the magnitude of a significant effect across numerous studies. Meta-analysis provides an estimate of *effect size*, which is expressed in terms of how large the average differences between males and females are across the various studies, taking into consideration the overall amount of variability. An effect size of 1.0 would mean that the average male-female difference was one standard deviation in magnitude. If this were for IQ, for example, it would be equivalent to saying that the average difference between the sexes was about 15 points, which would be quite substantial. The statistic of effect size is used because it would be meaningless to compute mean performance across the many different studies, which used different measurements and often assessed different verbal tasks. By using the effect size statistic, differences in performance among different studies can be meaningfully combined.

The first meta-analysis of verbal gender differences was reported by Janet Hyde (1981), who examined 27 studies of verbal ability included in the original Maccoby and Jacklin review. Hyde reported an effect size of .24 (about one-quarter of a standard deviation, favoring females) and concluded that the gender of the child alone accounted for approximately 1% of the variance in verbal performance. In other words, these findings mean that the differences, although statistically significant, are small in absolute magnitude. To give an idea of the magnitude of these differences, the idealized distribution of verbal skills for males and females is graphed in Figure 12-3 (expressed as standard scores, from Hyde, 1981). As can be seen, there is substantial overlap of performance between the genders, and the absolute difference in the means are small.

Since the publication of Hyde's report, several other meta-analytic studies of gender differences in verbal ability have been published, and they generally point to the same conclusion: Although gender differences in verbal abilities favoring females continue to be found, the effect size is small in an absolute sense, and, perhaps surprisingly, getting smaller over the decades (Feingold, 1988; Hyde & Linn, 1988; Marsh, 1989, but for a different interpretation of the data, see Hedges & Nowell, 1995). For example, Hyde and Linn (1988) reviewed 165 different studies, involving 1,418,899 participants, and reported that the effect size, again favoring females, for studies published after 1973 was .10, or one-tenth of a standard deviation (compared with .23 for pre-1973 studies). In fact, since 1972, performance on the Scholastic Assessment Test (SAT)-Verbal has actually slightly favored males (mean scores = 437 for males and 425 for females, effect size = −.1086). This seems particularly anomalous, given the general belief among college students that females perform better on the SAT-Verbal than males do (Feingold, 1988).

What might be the reason for the decline in gender differences in verbal abilities between the sexes during the past 20 years, and for the actual reversal on the SAT-Verbal? One possibility, suggested by Hyde and Linn (1988), is that there has been an increase in the flexibility of gender roles beginning in the 1970s, with boys being encouraged to engage in activities previously reserved for girls. Another possibility is that test publishers during the past 20 years have been attempting to minimize gender

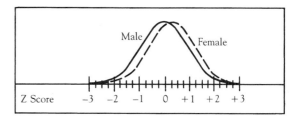

FIGURE 12-3 The idealized distribution of verbal ability for males and females. SOURCE: "How Large are Cognitive Gender Differences? A Meta-Analysis Using w^2 and d," by J. S. Hyde, 1981, *American Psychologist, 36,* 892–901. Copyright © 1981 American Psychological Association. Reprinted with permission.

differences in their tests, possibly accounting for the diminished gender differences in performance (Stanley et al., 1992). Although this interpretation is questioned by others (Feingold, 1988), it seems that changes in test construction are at least partly responsible for the small male superiority now found on the SAT-Verbal. The verbal portion of the SAT includes more technical and science-related topics than previously, and males likely have a better knowledge base for such material (Halpern, 1992; Hyde & Linn, 1988).

Based on the most recent meta-analyses, what can be concluded about gender differences in verbal skills? First, they do seem to exist but are so small on average that knowing the gender of a person would not help one predict how verbal he or she would be. Even if these differences are based in biology, the two sexes are biologically more alike in verbal abilities than they are different.

Children's Number and Arithmetic Concepts

Although the quintessential symbols of human cognition are probably found in language, a good case can be made for the primacy of number. Our tendency to quantify objects and events in our world is ubiquitous. The bulk of the technological advancements made during the past three centuries, and particularly in this century, can be attributed to our species' quantitative skills. Although children develop a basic sense of number and mathematical relations without explicit instruction, most people's mathematical abilities are acquired through formal instruction. This is true even of simple arithmetic as well as more complicated mathematics.

In the following sections, I review aspects of children's earliest concepts of number and then take a brief look at the development of basic arithmetic skills. Although mathematical reasoning, in our culture, develops beyond arithmetic, most developmentally oriented research has focused on children's acquisition of arithmetic concepts, and I review this literature here. I then look briefly at characteristics of math-disabled children, followed by a look at cross-cultural differences in mathematical achievement. At the conclusion of this section, I examine the controversial topic of gender differences in mathematical ability. Do such differences exist? If so, how big are they, and what difference do they make?

Conservation of Number

Piaget (1965) believed that the concept of number is reflected in conservation. **Conservation-of-number** tasks follow the same basic procedures as all of Piaget's conservation problems. Children are first shown a set of items—black jelly beans, for instance. The children are then asked to take white jelly beans from a container so that there are an equal number of black and white beans. Once the appropriate number of white beans has been selected (with assistance from the experimenter, if necessary), the beans are arranged in two rows, one black and one white (see Figure 12-4). While the children are watching, the experimenter spreads out the white jelly beans so that the line of white beans extends beyond the line of black beans. The children are then asked if the two rows still have the same number of jelly beans. If they answer no, they are asked which row has more, and why.

As with conservation in general, Piaget proposed three stages in the acquisition of the conservation

"Select from the jar the same number of white jelly beans as there are black jelly beans."

"Are there the same number of black jelly beans as there are white jelly beans?"

The row of white jelly beans is extended while the child watches.

"Are there the same number of white jelly beans as there are black jelly beans now? Which has more? Why?"

FIGURE 12-4   A conservation-of-number task.

of number. In stage 1, children are unable to consistently establish a one-to-one correspondence between the two sets of items. So, for example, stage-1 children select too few or too many white jelly beans or fail to arrange them in a one-to-one relationship with the black beans. When two equal sets of beans are established and one is modified, children say that the longer, less-dense row now has more beans in it, being unable to ignore the perceptual differences between the two rows. During stage 2, children can establish an "intuitive one-to-one correspondence" (Piaget, 1965) between the items in the two sets, but judgments of equivalence between the sets do not last long. Once the beans in one row are extended, the children say that there are more in the longer row. Only the stage-3 child (concrete operations) realizes that the number of beans does not change when one of the rows is elongated, but that changes in spatial extension of elements are compensated for by equivalent changes in the density of the elements.

Non-Piagetian research, using variants of Piaget's original task, has generally replicated his observations, illustrating that (1) children are able to form a one-to-one correspondence before they can conserve; (2) young children make their evaluations on the basis of relative length, independent of other factors; (3) slightly older children sometimes consider density but do not coordinate the dimensions of length and density, thus failing to conserve in many situations; and (4) not until 7 or 8 years of age do children consistently pass conservation-of-number tasks (see Brainerd, 1978a).

Young Children's Knowledge of Number

Although most children do not display conservation of number before 7 years of age, anyone who has been around preschoolers for any length of time knows that they obviously have some concept of number, but adults watching a 2- or 3-year-old use numbers might wonder exactly what that sense is. The 18-month-old might respond with a loud and definitive "Two!" when asked how many cookies he wants, and the 3-year-old might point at her dolls, saying "One, two, three, seven, nine, twelve-teen, three-teen, seventeen." Each is displaying some knowledge of number, yet neither is using numbers with the same consistency and meaning that a 7- or 8-year-old child is capable of. Primitive notions of number (or at least quantity) can be found very early in development: Newborns can discriminate between arrays differing in only one element (Antell & Keating, 1983), and remember from Chapter 7 the proposal by Karen Wynn (1992) that 5-month-old infants have some grasp of addition and subtraction, revealed by patterns of attention when objects are surreptitiously added or subtracted from arrays. Although whatever babies are doing in these situations is more than what we thought—not all that long ago—they could do, it is not, I believe, qualitatively similar to the simple arithmetic that children do just a few years later. A full understanding of the number concept is not obvious until the early school years, and possibly beyond.

Rochel Gelman and C. R. Gallistel (1978) emphasized what knowledge of numbers preschool children possess rather than stressing what they do not know and concluded that young children have a rather sophisticated, though limited, knowledge of numbers.

How do children's conceptions of numbers develop? One popular non-Piagetian candidate for the precursor of number conservation is counting. Gelman and Gallistel (1978) have extensively investigated children's early counting and have proposed five principles of counting:

1. The one-one principle: Each item in an array is associated with one and only one number name (such as "two").
2. The stable-order principle: Number names must be in a stable, repeatable order.
3. The cardinal principle: The final number in a series represents the quantity of the set.
4. The abstraction principle: The first three principles can be applied to any array or collection of entities, physical (for example, chairs, jelly beans) or nonphysical (for example, minds in a room, ideas).
5. The order-irrelevant principle: The order in which things are counted is irrelevant.

Gelman and Gallistel referred to the first three principles as the "how-to" principles of counting and proposed that children as young as 2.5 years demonstrate knowledge of them under some circumstances. For example, in a counting experiment where 3-, 4-, and 5-year-old children were asked to discern the number of objects in a series of arrays, all groups of children used the one-one principle (that is, one unique number name per object), although performance deteriorated for the youngest children for arrays of six or greater. Gelman and Gallistel also reported that children who counted items in arrays used the stable-order principle; more than 90% of the 4- and 5-year-olds and 80% of the 3-year-olds used the same list of number words in the same order on all of their trials. The children sometimes used an idiosyncratic list of number words (for example, "one, two, six"), but they used this list consistently across arrays of varying size.

Children seem to have mastered the cardinal principle by age 4. For example, Karen Fuson and her colleagues demonstrated that after counting arrays of objects ranging in number from 2 to 19, 3- and 4-year-old children generally gave the last counting word they had spoken in response to the question "How many things are there?" (Fuson et al., 1985). This was true even for children who counted incorrectly, implying that accurate counting is not a requirement for attainment of the cardinal principle (see also Gelman, Meck, & Merkin, 1986). However, many 2- and 3-year olds seem to have only a tenuous grasp of the cardinality principle (Bermejo, 1996). For example, children might correctly count a set of objects, "One, two, three, four, five," but, when asked how many objects are in the set, instead of stating the last number they counted ("five"), they often count again (Fuson, 1988). It's as if the purpose of the first count was independent of determining "how many" objects were in the set. Most of these children can come up with the correct answer, but that they seemed to think that a second count was necessary suggests that this knowledge is not well established.

In related research, Briars and Siegler (1984) investigated children's knowledge of the counting principles. These researchers asserted that children must induce which features of counting are critical and which are merely optional in enumerating an array, and they speculated that some children might believe that more is required for successful counting than is actually the case. In their experiment, 3-, 4-, and 5-year-old children watched a puppet counting and were asked to determine whether the puppet had counted properly. The puppet demonstrated (sometimes accurately and sometimes inaccurately) five features of counting, one of which was necessary for counting and four of which were optional. The necessary feature was that of word-object correspondence, which encompasses the first two principles of Gelman and Gallistel (one-one correspondence and stable order). The four optional features were that (1) adjacent objects were counted consecutively, (2) counting started from the end rather than the middle, (3) counting progressed from left to right, and

(4) each object in an array was pointed to exactly once. Children's knowledge that word-object correspondence was critical in counting increased with age (30%, 90%, and 100% for the 3-, 4-, and 5-year-olds, respectively). However, 60% of the 5-year-olds also viewed other features, such as beginning to count at an end rather than in the middle and pointing to each object only once, as essential. In other words, young children learn the critical features of counting by 4 years of age but infer, from watching others, additional features that are characteristic of, but not necessary for, proper counting.

The relation between children's counting and conservation of number has been explored in several experiments. For instance, Fuson, Secada, and Hall (1983) reported significantly higher levels of number conservation (69%) by 4- and 5-year-old children who were required to count the elements in both sets before judging which set, if either, was larger, than by children given a standard conservation-of-number task (14%).

In another experiment, Geoffrey Saxe (1979) administered a series of counting and conservation tasks to 4-, 5-, and 6-year-old children. On the counting tasks the children were required to assess the equivalence of two rows of dots differing in length and, later, to select the same number of beads from a container as there were dots on a card. In each case, the task was constructed so that counting was necessary to yield the correct answer. The conservation tasks were similar to those used by Piaget, with beads in one row compressed on one trial and elongated on another. Saxe classified each child as conserving or not conserving on the conservation-of-number tasks and as prequantitative or quantitative on the counting tasks. The children were classified as prequantitative if they counted items in the arrays but did not use the results of counting to solve the problem. They were classified as quantitative counters if they used counting to aid their performance, although they might not have used exactly the same number words or order as adults conventionally do. Saxe found that no child who was prequantitative with respect to counting was also a conserver; in contrast, 22 children displayed

TABLE 12-2   Number of children classified jointly according to understanding of number concept (conservers versus nonconservers) and counting ability (prequantitative versus quantitative)

Counting ability	Number concept	
	Nonconservers	Conservers
Prequantitative	12	0
Quantitative	22	20

SOURCE: Adapted from "Developmental Relations Between Notational Counting and Number Conservation," by G. Saxe, 1979, *Child Development, 50,* 189–197. Copyright © 1979 The Society for Research in Child Development, Inc. Adapted with permission.

sophisticated counting skills but were still unable to conserve (see Table 12-2). In related research, Catherine Sophian (1995) reports that children under 6 years of age do not conserve number when they are prevented from counting the arrays. These findings are consistent with the view that quantitative counting skills are a necessary but not sufficient condition for the attainment of conservation of number.

In summary, young children do possess a limited knowledge of numbers and relations among numbers, but they are restricted to dealing with small quantities. As children's knowledge of numbers expands, they refine their number concept, discriminating between what is necessary and what is optional in dealing with numbers; and importantly, their ability to deal with large quantities increases and their belief in the invariance of number is applied more consistently across a wider range of tasks.

Children's Arithmetic Concepts

Clearly young children have some concept of number. They can count and can determine which of two quantities is the larger. But when can children perform tasks of basic arithmetic such as addition and subtraction? These skills are not formally taught until the first grade in many schools, and from a Piagetian perspective, they require concrete-operational ability.

Piaget's Perspective on Children's Early Arithmetic

Piaget (1965) proposed that addition and subtraction require inversion reversibility, something that is not achieved (according to Piaget) until about 7 years of age. For example, if 5 + 3 = 8, then, by the logical rule of inversion, 8–3 must equal 5.

In one experiment by Piaget (1965), children were shown an array of eight objects. The array was then modified; for example, it was divided into two equal sets of four objects and was then divided a second time into unequal sets (seven and one, for instance). Do children recognize the equivalence of these two groupings? In other words, do they know that 4 + 4 is the same as 7 + 1? As with conservation of number, Piaget reported three stages in children's early arithmetic abilities. In stage 1, characterizing 5- and 6-year-olds, the children typically relied on the spatial arrangement of the objects, erroneously asserting that there were different numbers of elements in the two combinations. In stage 2, the children could correctly solve the task, but only after counting the objects or establishing a spatial one-to-one correspondence between the items. The stage-3 children (7-year-olds) solved the problem without resorting to physical counting techniques. Without this understanding, according to Piaget, children cannot have a true comprehension of addition, although they can be taught to memorize certain formulas (for example, 2 + 3 = 5, but will they know what 3 + 2 equals?).

More recent research has questioned some of Piaget's interpretations and has demonstrated that even preschool children are able to handle simple addition and subtraction problems. Their approaches to addition and subtraction usually involve counting out loud, often with use of fingers or other objects. Perhaps the simplest strategy consists of counting from 1 to the first addend (in 3 + 5 = ?, the first addend is 3), then counting the second, then counting the two together (for example, "1, 2, 3 . . . 1, 2, 3, 4, 5 . . . 1, 2, 3 . . . 4, 5, 6, 7, 8"; or a bit more efficiently, "1, 2, 3 . . . 4, 5, 6, 7, 8"). This has been referred to as the **sum strategy,** and although it usually produces the correct answer, it takes a considerable amount of time to execute and is not very effective when large addends are involved (such as 23 + 16 = ?) (Baroody & Ginsburg, 1986).

Young children can use more economical counting strategies for adding small numbers. For example, given the problem 3 + 2 = ?, a 5- or 6-year-old might start with the cardinal value of the first number ("3") and continue counting from there ("4, 5"). This has been referred to as the **min strategy**; children start with the larger addend and then count up from it the number corresponding to the smaller addend—that is, the *minimum* number of counts. This strategy is taught during the early school years.

Preschoolers use a variety of such rules to arrive at correct answers to simple addition and subtraction problems. These rules, however, almost always involve forward counting by ones of concrete objects, including fingers (Carpenter & Moser, 1982). Such addition and subtraction by counting can be successful for unpracticed combinations such as 14 + 1 = ? and 15–1 = ?, which is in violation of Piaget's tenet that true addition cannot be achieved by simple counting (Starkey & Gelman, 1982).

The Development of Mental Arithmetic

Sometime during the early school years, children's solutions to simple arithmetic problems become covert. They no longer rely on counting objects or their fingers but perform the calculations in their heads. At this point, knowing precisely what children are doing becomes more difficult, because the only evidence of the mental processes underlying performance is the answers they give. However, children's arithmetic strategies can be inferred from how quickly they solve the problems. For example, if children are using the min strategy, their reaction times to solve problems will vary as a function of the second, smaller addend.

In fact, based on patterns of reaction times to solve simple addition problems, it has been demonstrated that children in the early elementary school years frequently use the min strategy (Groen & Resnick, 1977). In the min model (the mathematical model used to describe children's use of the min strategy), a mental counter is set to the first addend (in the problem 5 + 3 + ?, the counter would be set to 5). The counter is then increased by increments of one until enough have been added (here, 3). Children's reaction times to solve problems vary as a function of the second, smaller addend. Thus, for any individual child, arriving at an answer for 5 + 4 (thinking "5 . . . 6, 7, 8, 9") takes longer than arriving at an answer for 5 + 2 (thinking "5 . . . 6, 7") because the mental counter must tick off four times for the former problem but only two times for the latter. In other words, reaction times are proportional to the smaller or minimum number being added.

Some time during the elementary school years, children begin to use fact retrieval to answer simple arithmetic problems (see Ashcraft, 1990). When adults are given the problem 7 + 5 = ?, for example, they need not start at 7 and mentally increase this by 5 to arrive at the answer. Rather, the knowledge that 7 + 5 = 12 resides in long-term memory, and this fact can be retrieved just like any other fact in memory.

This shift in development from procedural (that is, counting) to retrieval-based techniques for solving simple arithmetic problems reflects changes in the efficiency of information processing. With age, children solve problems more quickly. This increased speed can be attributed to the fact that processes are becoming more automatic, requiring less of one's limited mental capacity for successful execution. First-graders' use of counting strategies is highly conscious and laborious in contrast with the fact retrieval of older children. However, even 5- and 6-year-olds apparently store and retrieve some arithmetic facts. For small whole-number problems (for example, 2 + 2 = ?), young children's performance is relatively rapid, indicating fact retrieval (Hamann & Ashcraft, 1985; Siegler & Shrager, 1984). With age and experience, more arithmetic facts become stored and can be retrieved with increasing ease, without the need of laborious counting procedures. Although children learn how to multiply later than they learn how to add, much of even third-grade children's multiplication seems to be based on fact retrieval (Koshmider & Ashcraft, 1991), likely as a result of memorizing the multiplication tables.

Arithmetic becomes more complex, of course, and as it does, children must rely again on procedural knowledge. When subtraction involves "borrowing" (as in 92–59 = ?) or addition involves "carrying" (as in 92 + 59 = ?), procedures are at first slow and difficult, but with practice they become more efficient. In general, the development of arithmetic competence can be described as involving an increase in the efficiency of both procedural knowledge and, most important, information retrieval (Ashcraft, 1990; Kaye, 1986). Older children know more facts, can retrieve those facts more easily, and, when necessary, can use arithmetic procedures more efficiently than younger children.

One factor that appears to be important in successful mental arithmetic is working memory. To arrive at a correct answer to a simple problem such as 7 + 5 = ?, children must hold the two addends in mind and execute the addition operation (either by retrieving the "fact," or through some counting method). Adams and Hitch (1997) have shown for groups of both English- and German-speaking children (ranging in age from about 7.5 to 11.5 years) that differences in memory span play a critical role in computation. They also found a relation between the speed of adding the digits and both age and memory span, confirming the role of speed of processing in memory span discussed in Chapter 5.

Another factor related to children's successful use of arithmetic strategies is metacognition, as reflected by children's knowledge of the effectiveness and appropriateness of different strategies. For example, Carr and Jessup (1995) presented second-grade children with sets of arithmetic problems and metacognitive assessment in April and tested them again two months later in June. Children were asked about the effectiveness of the strategies they used (for example, "Why did you use that way for this problem?"), and other questions about the appropriateness of the strategy (for example, "When do you use that way to get the answer?" and "Is there any time it's not a good idea to use that way?"). Carr and Jessup looked at changes in children's use of the min strategy, fact retrieval, and decomposition and the relation between changes in strategy use and metacognition. **Decomposition** consists of transforming the original problem into two or more simpler problems. If the problem were 13 + 3 = ?, for example, a child might say, "13 is 10 and 3; 3 and 3 are 6; 10 and 6 are 16; so the answer is 16."

Children's use of the decomposition and fact retrieval strategies increased over the two-month period (although the accuracy of fact retrieval did not increase over this same time), and the use of the min strategy decreased over time. How did children's metacognitive knowledge in April predict their strategy use in June? Quite well for the decomposition strategy, but not well at all for the use of fact retrieval. Carr and Jessup reasoned that metacognition is important when strategy use is both effortful and in the early stages of being acquired, something that described the decomposition strategy well. It is less important, however, for highly automated and less effortful strategies, such as fact retrieval.

Is Children's Acquisition of Arithmetic Strategies Stagelike?

The impression one might get from this research is of a steady improvement in arithmetic strategy use, with children moving from the sum to the min to the fact-retrieval strategy in a regular, stagelike progression. Such a view is not entirely accurate, however. At any given age, children use a variety of strategies to solve arithmetic problems, although the average sophistication of their strategies increases with age (Ashcraft, 1990; Bisanz & LeFevre, 1990).

This has been demonstrated in several studies by Robert Siegler and his colleagues (Siegler, 1987; Siegler & Jenkins, 1989; Siegler & Shrager, 1984). In one study, Siegler (1987) assessed the techniques used by kindergarten and first- and second-grade children in solving a variety of addition problems. The children's reaction times to solve the problems were obtained from a video recording of the sessions. Following completion of each problem, the children were asked what they had done to "figure out the answer to that problem." The problems were selected so that different patterns of reaction times among the problems were predicted by various models (for example, the min model, the fact-retrieval model, and a counting model). Rather than analyzing performance collapsed over all trials, Siegler conducted separate analyses for different strategies.

Based on analyses of reaction times, errors, and verbal reports, Siegler discerned five general approaches to solving the addition problems. Four of these were the sum strategy, the min strategy, decomposition, and the fact-retrieval technique, as discussed previously. A fifth strategy was guessing. Most children used a variety of these strategies on the problems; 62% reported using three or more across the various problems. The min strategy was used most frequently, but even it was used on no more than 40% of the trials at any age. The older children were more likely to use the fact-retrieval and decomposition strategies than were the kindergarten children.

In general, the children showed little homogeneity of strategy use in these addition problems. Similar findings were reported by Siegler and Shrager (1984) for 4- and 5-year-olds. In their study, the use of strategies varied as a function of the difficulty of the problem. The harder the problem, the more likely the children were to use overt strategies such as counting on their fingers, rather than covert strategies such as fact retrieval. Comparable results were found in a study by Kristina Rosenblum and her colleagues (1996), who assessed 4- to 6-year-old children's strategy use when computing moves on a board game ("Chutes and Ladders") from a pair of dice. It seems that children use a variety of arithmetic strategies not only in "school-type" tasks, but also in social (game) situations.

Siegler and Jenkins (1989) looked at the acquisition of the min strategy using a short-term longitudinal study (or a microgenetic approach, see Chapter 3). In this study, Siegler and Jenkins examined the development of arithmetic strategies in eight children over an 11-week period. Four- and 5-year-old children were selected who (1) could perform simple addition using counting methods but (2) never used the min strategy. Over 11 weeks, these children were given a series of addition problems to solve.

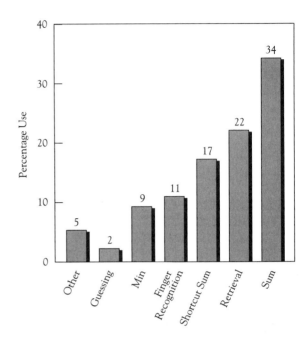

FIGURE 12-5   Percent use for each arithmetic strategy. SOURCE: Adapted from Siegler, R. S., & Jenkins. E. (1989) *How children discover strategies.* Hillsdale, NJ: Erlbaum.

Siegler and Jenkins reported that all the children used multiple strategies. These included the sum, min, fact retrieval, and decomposition strategies discussed earlier, plus strategies such as finger recognition (putting up two fingers on one hand and three on the other and saying "five"), shortcut sum (similar to the sum) counting from the first addend (similar to min, but counting the larger addend), and guessing. The percentage of the most frequently used strategies can be seen in Figure 12-5. As can be seen, there was great variety in strategy use. Moreover, different children used different combinations of the strategies, so that any particular child used a unique mixture of the strategies in his or her solutions. Also, over the course of the 11 weeks, the children's strategies tended to become more sophisticated, so that the children who started mainly by guessing or using the sum strategy progressed to using the min or fact-retrieval strategy more frequently.

One major aspect of the Siegler and Jenkins study was children's "discovery" of the min strategy.

Remember that none of the children were using the min strategy at the beginning of the study. By the 11th week, seven of the eight children were using the min strategy, and six of these children were able to describe how they used it.

It is interesting to note that the first time the children used the min strategy, and also on the problem immediately before it, they took much longer than average to arrive at a solution. Siegler and Jenkins speculated that the longer times spent on these problems indicated that the children were experiencing conflict, or interference from alternative strategies and that new strategies require more mental effort than previously established ones. Thus the children required more time and did some hemming and hawing before arriving at an answer.

Siegler's adaptive strategy-choice model, discussed earlier in this chapter with regard to reading and in Chapter 5, applies here as well. The model proposes that, in general, the various strategies that children know compete with one another (Siegler, 1996). Sometimes one strategy will win the mental competition (the min strategy, for example) and sometimes another strategy will win (fact retrieval, for example). With age, experience, and improved information-processing abilities, more sophisticated strategies are apt to win, so that min, on average, replaces sum, and later on, fact retrieval replaces min. But for new problems or problems with which children are less familiar, the older, more familiar, or fallback strategies often come up as the winners. Thus, from Siegler's perspective, strategy development is not a simple matter of replacing older, less sophisticated strategies with newer, more powerful ones. Rather, multiple strategies reside side by side in one's mind and compete with one another for the chance to solve problems. There are age changes in which newer strategies are likely to win the competition, but old strategies never die, they just lie in wait for the chance to be used in cases where the newer strategy doesn't quite fit or fails to produce the correct answer.

Math Disabilities

When discussing the development of reading earlier in this chapter, I found it useful to examine cogni-tive differences in normal versus reading-disabled children, in part because reading is such an important technological skill that reading disabilities are important in their own right, but also to provide additional support for the mechanisms that underlie "normal" development. One way of inferring that a process is important to development is to look at processing in children who show some disabilities. The same logic holds true for math disabilities.

Math-disabled children can be identified early (in kindergarten) and their progress in arithmetic followed. David Geary and his colleagues have taken this longitudinal approach and report that math-disabled children display two types of difficulties (Geary, 1990, 1993; Geary, Bow-Thomas, & Yao, 1992; Geary, Brown, & Samaranayake, 1991). First, these children show poor procedural skills, in that they use a more immature mix of arithmetic strategies than normal children do. Also, first-grade math-disabled children show poorer knowledge of the rules of counting. Using a procedure similar to the one described earlier by Briars and Siegler (1984) in which a puppet counts arrays either correctly or incorrectly, Geary and his associates found that math-disabled children demonstrated an immature understanding of counting. For example, many believed that adjacent items in an array had to be counted consecutively for the count to be correct. However, Geary and his colleagues note that the procedural skills of many kindergarten and first-grade math-disabled children approach those of their normal peers by the end of second grade. That is, with respect to using procedures, they catch up, suggesting that their deficit was a developmental delay.

The second source of difficulties for math-disabled children is a memory-retrieval deficit. Math-disabled children retrieve fewer facts from long-term memory (that is, they use fact retrieval less often), and when they do, they are often wrong. Moreover, simple practice at fact retrieval alone does not appreciably improve performance, and, unlike procedural difficulties, these deficits tend not to improve to the level of their agemates with time (see Geary, 1993).

One possible reason for these children's persistent problems with fact retrieval has to do with working-memory capacity. For example, Geary and his colleagues (1991) reported that the digit spans for math-disabled children were about one word less than for normal children (for forward digit span, 4.2 words versus 5.3 words for the math-disabled and normal children, respectively). This deficit might be the result of faster decay of information (that is, the memory representations might disappear more quickly in working memory for math-disabled children), to slower counting speed (recall from Chapter 5 that digit span is related to articulation rate), or to a slower domain-general speed-of-processing capacity (Bull & Johnston, 1997). Because these children make computation errors, they arrive at many incorrect answers, and these answers can become part of their long-term memory representations of arithmetic facts. Unfortunately, they are wrong.

The deficits shown by many math-disabled children are similar to those shown by many reading-disabled children. In fact, there is considerable overlap between the two populations. In a large-scale study of math disabilities, N. A. Badian (1983) reported that 43% of math-disabled children were also classified as reading disabled, and that 56% of reading-disabled children were similarly classified as math disabled. Both math and reading disabilities seem to share a common problem—the inability to retrieve information efficiently from long-term memory. Math facts are thought to be represented in a semantic network system, much as word definitions are. Geary (1993) proposed that a single deficit underlies many math and reading disabilities. "At the cognitive level, this deficit manifests itself as difficulties in the representation and retrieval of semantic information from long-term memory. This would include fact-retrieval problems in simple arithmetic and, for instance, word-recognition and phonological awareness in reading" (p. 356).

Yet, many children read just fine but have great difficulty in math, and vice versa. It appears that there is no single cause of math disability (or of reading disability, for that matter), and that some of these disabilities are domain specific in nature. However, the substantial overlap between the reading- and math-disabled populations suggests that there

are some domain-general abilities involved in these important technological skills, namely working-memory capacity and efficiency of retrieval from semantic memory.

Cultural Differences in Mathematics

Mathematics is truly the universal language (although many would give that distinction to love, I suppose). Regardless of one's mother tongue, the rules of mathematics are the same all over the globe. However, most forms of mathematics beyond arithmetic are explicitly taught, at least in our culture. Yet, people from traditional cultures still have a need for basic arithmetic and other forms of mathematical problem solving. How do people from nonschooled societies acquire mathematics? How is it similar and how is it different from what happens in cultures such as ours where formal schooling is universal?

There are also differences in mathematical attainment between different information-age cultures. In recent years, this has been brought to the public's attention by reports of substantial differences in mathematics performance between American children and college students and those from other information-age cultures, particularly those in East Asia. How different are Americans from East Asians in mathematical attainment, when do those differences appear, and what factors contribute to them? These issues will be discussed in the next section, following a brief examination of arithmetic in unschooled cultures.

Arithmetic in Unschooled Cultures

Kpelle children from Liberia have a particular problem mastering mathematics in Western-style schools. Specific "perceptual deficits" linked to their home environments were hypothesized to account for their difficulties. Kpelle children do not discriminate geometric forms well, and such problems were attributed to a lack of perceptual stimulation (see Laboratory of Comparative Human Cognition, 1983). Gay and Cole (1967), however, stated that

Kpelle children are not lacking in perceptual experiences but merely have different ones from American children. These researchers thought that by examining the daily lives of the Kpelle, they could discern mathematically relevant experiences and possibly use them to improve instruction in Western-style mathematics.

Gay and Cole (1967) assessed the concept of measurement among the Kpelle and found that there was no single form of measurement that was used for a variety of commodities. The Kpelle, however, did have a consistent way of measuring rice, a commodity that was very important for their existence. Rice was the only cash crop for Kpelle farmers, and the buying and selling of rice constituted an important part of Kpelle life. Gay and Cole evaluated Kpelle farmers' ability to estimate the amount of rice in bowls of varying size and contrasted their performance with that of Americans. The Kpelle were consistently more accurate in this task than were the Americans, reflecting a mathematical competence not apparent by previous tests.

More recently, research has examined the arithmetic ability of nonschooled Brazilian children and has shown that these children possess a high level of computational skill, but only when the problems are tied to real-life situations (Guberman, 1996). For example, Carraher, Carraher, and Schliemann (1985) examined 9- and 15-year-old unschooled street vendors and gave them a series of arithmetic problems to solve. Problems that were imbedded in real-life contexts (for example, "If a large coconut costs 76 cruzeiros, and a small one costs 50, how much do the two cost together?") were solved at a much higher rate than the same problem presented out of context (for example, "How much is 76 + 50?"). Carraher and associates reported that the children answered the context-appropriate questions correctly 98% of the time; in contrast, the out-of-context questions were answered correctly only 37% of the time. Reviewing their research on schooled versus nonschooled Brazilian children's mathematical reasoning, A. D. Schliemann (1992) stated that these children use mathematics to solve everyday problems, where mistakes have real consequences. This is contrasted with school learning, in which children are taught standardized procedures with little or no application. Schliemann (1992) concluded that unschooled street vendors (and unschooled people from other professions, such as brick layers and lottery bookies) develop a flexible arithmetic system and apply it appropriately within their work context, and that "unschooled people develop at work not only fixed procedures to solve specific problems but a conceptual and flexible understanding of the mathematical models applied to solve problems" (p. 2).

In other research, Steven Guberman (1996) has shown that Brazilian shantytown children frequently use their knowledge of currency to help them to solve school-type arithmetic problems. Also, interviews with children's parents indicated that parents adjusted the complexity of the purchases they asked their children to make depending on the perceived skill of the child. As children grew older and more arithmetically competent, parents presented them with more difficult real-world problems to solve (purchases to make). This is consistent with "working within the zone of proximal development," a concept developed by Vygotsky (1978) and discussed in some detail in Chapter 3.

Academic Performance by American and Asian Schoolchildren

Recently, evidence has been accumulating that American school children lag behind children from other industrialized countries in their academic knowledge, including mathematics (Baker, 1992; Mullis & Jenkins, 1990; Stevenson & Lee, 1990). Figure 12-6 graphs mathematics test scores of first- and fifth-grade children from the United States (Minneapolis), Japan (Sendai), and Taiwan (Taipei) (Stevenson & Lee, 1990). As can be seen, the children from the United States performed more poorly than the children from the two Asian cultures, with the differences being quite substantial as early as the first grade. The magnitude of the differences suggests that the Chinese and Japanese children are getting a better mathematics education than the American children, but that this gap is found so early points to differences in the home.

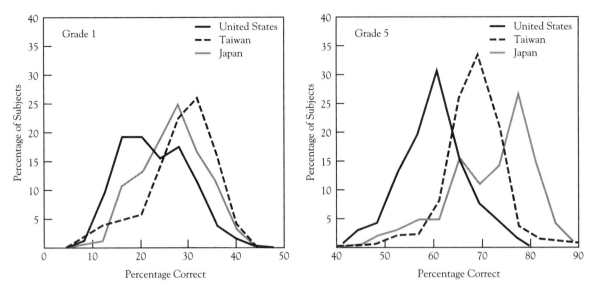

FIGURE 12-6   Frequency distributions of mathematics scores for first- and fifth-grade children in the United States, Japan, and Taiwan. SOURCE: "Context of Achievement," by H. W. Stevenson & S. Y. Lee, 1990, *Monographs of the Society for Research in Child Development*, 55, (Serial No. 221). Copyright © 1990 The Society for Research in Child Development, Inc. Reprinted with permission.

One possible reason for the early difference might be the greater digit spans for many East Asian relative to American children, because of differences in the rate at which the number words can be articulated in the different languages (Geary et al., 1993; see discussion of this in Chapter 5). But there are also early differences in the use of arithmetic strategies. Geary and his colleagues have examined differences in the arithmetic strategies used by Chinese and American first graders (Geary et al., 1996; Geary, Fan, & Bow-Thomas, 1992). The researchers reported that Chinese first-grade children used a more sophisticated mix of strategies, including decomposition. The Chinese children were also faster at retrieving an answer directly from long-term memory (that is, at fact retrieval) than the American children were. However, this speed advantage was apparently limited to retrieval of arithmetic facts and did not reflect an overall greater speed-of-processing advantage, for the Chinese and American children were equally fast at counting (although recall our discussion in Chapter 3 that Chinese preschool children are able to count to 20 before American children, Miller et al., 1995). Other re-

search has shown that this advantage in the use of arithmetic strategies for Chinese relative to American children is present even before the start of formal schooling (Geary et al., 1993).

One might ask, "So what?" We're talking about the most basic of arithmetic abilities which American children clearly master by the end of elementary school. But children's early arithmetical accomplishments set the stage for later achievements. Geary and his colleagues (1992) argue that "if the mastery of basic skills facilitates the acquisition of more complex mathematical concepts and procedures, then the results of the current study suggest that Chinese children will have a consistent 3- to 4-year advantage over their American peers in the development of mathematical cognition" (p. 184).

What is the origin of these differences? One source of the difference is likely practice. Children who practice elementary computation more frequently are able to retrieve math facts more quickly from long-term memory and have greater opportunities to develop arithmetic strategies than children who practice them less often (Geary et al., 1992). Harold Stevenson and his colleagues report that

Chinese and Japanese children do indeed spend more time on mathematics, both in and out of the classroom (Fuligni & Stevenson, 1995; Stevenson & Lee, 1990). Thus, we have the very commonsense finding of practice makes perfect (or at least makes for enhanced performance), with children who practice arithmetic more frequently (Chinese and Japanese children) performing better than children who practice it less frequently (American children).

But what causes this cultural difference in time invested in mathematics and the overall greater academic performance? Again, the answer is quite commonsensical: parents' attitudes and behavior regarding education and child rearing. Although American parents tend to believe that their children's academic performance is due to effort, this tendency to emphasize effort and hard work is even more obvious in Japanese and Chinese parents. Japanese mothers, for instance, are more likely to believe that their children's academic performance can be improved than are American mothers. These Japanese women also take personal pride in the success of their children (and shame in their failure) and require their children to establish regular study habits. They are less likely to be satisfied with their children's academic performance, and they set higher academic standards for their children than American mothers. In addition, the Buddhist, Confucian, and Shintoistic traditions of Japan, which value order, intellectual growth, and social good, might contribute to a cultural setting that is geared for success in school.

Because of Japan's cultural traditions, children also spend more time in school and devote a higher percentage of their school time to academic material than do American children. For example, whereas the average school year in Minneapolis is 174 days, it is 230 in Taipei and 243 in Sendai (Stevenson & Lee, 1990). Recent research has shown that American kindergarten (Frazier, 1993) and first-grade children (Frazier & Morrison, 1998) show greater improvements in academic subjects as a result of attending an extended-year schooling program (210–230 days) rather than a school program of conventional length (180 days).

It's worth noting that American children of recent Asian descent perform better in school, on average, than white or black native-born Americans do (Chen & Stevenson, 1995). A major reason for this difference is the attitudes that Chinese- and Japanese-American parents have toward education. For example, a study by Lin and Fu (1990) compared the child-rearing practices of Caucasian-American parents with those of Chinese parents from Taiwan and immigrant-Chinese parents living in the United States. They reported that both the immigrant-Chinese and the Taiwanese parents rated higher on parental control, encouragement of independence, and emphasis on achievement than Caucasian-American parents did. In other research Chinese-American 7- and 8-year-old children spent more time doing homework and taking music lessons, spent less time playing organized sports, and had less free time than comparable European-American children (Huntsinger, Jose, & Larson, 1998). The Chinese-American parents also used more formal teaching methods for math and reading than did the European-American parents. From these findings, it can be seen how cultural attitudes of Chinese-American parents exert an influence on their children's educational attainment, which is likely responsible for the academic edge these children have in American schools.

One recent finding of note is that the Chinese-American differences in arithmetic ability are a recent phenomenon. Geary and his colleagues (1996) administered a series of arithmetic tests to younger and older Chinese and American adults. For the young adults (college students), there was a significant difference favoring the Chinese over the Americans. There was no such cultural difference, however, for the older adults (most over 60 years old)—the older Americans performed as well in arithmetic as the older Chinese did. In fact, although the younger Chinese outperformed the older Chinese adults on arithmetic, the reverse was true for the American sample. Here, the older adults actually performed better then the younger adults. This suggests that whatever the factors are that are responsible for the cultural differences in arithmetic, they are of recent origin.

After looking at the Japanese and Chinese educational systems, it is tempting to think that American children can easily catch up merely by increasing the number of days they spend in school. Stevenson and Lee (1990) caution that a simple extension of the school day or school year is not the answer. Chinese and Japanese children may spend more days and more hours in school than American children do, but their school day is structured differently, providing them more physical exercise as well as more academic experiences. For example, first- and fifth-grade children in both Japan and Taiwan have more breaks and recesses than American children do. In both countries, the school day is highly structured, with 40–45 minute classes followed by 10–15 minute breaks. A common observation by Westerners in Asian schools is how attentive the children are. Such intense concentration is attributed partly to the frequent opportunities children have for vigorous play provided by between-class breaks (Pellegrini & Bjorklund, 1997; Pellegrini & Davis, 1993). Stevenson and Lee reported that children in the Minneapolis schools had no more than two recesses per day, whereas first-graders in the two Asian schools had four, and fifth graders had between five and eight. It's worth noting that although the Chinese and Japanese fifth-graders spent more hours per week in school than the American children, the school day for first-graders in both Taipei (4 hours) and Sendai (5 hours) was shorter than in Minneapolis (6 hours), reflecting an awareness of the attentional limitations of these young children.

Before immediately assuming that the Japanese or Taiwanese educational system is superior to that of the United States, we must remember that the educational systems in each country have evolved within different cultures. The system that works for the Japanese cannot likely be transported to the United States and be expected to work here. The creativity that is permitted (and often encouraged) within many American schools, for example, and the young intellectual maverick so valued in American universities would be lost in a Japanese system that emphasizes conformity and respect for the past. This is not to say that the poor performance of American children in mathematics (or geography and the sciences) relative to children in other developed countries is inevitable or acceptable. What it does mean is that solutions to educational problems in a country must be solved within that coun-

try's culture and cannot be solved simply by importing a system that evolved elsewhere.

Gender Differences in Mathematical Ability

When most people think of gender differences in academic abilities, perhaps the first area to come to mind is mathematics, with males generally being better than females. (The other area is verbal abilities, with the common wisdom being that females are generally more verbal than males, as discussed earlier in this chapter.) Such observations date back in the scientific literature to at least 1894, with Havelock Ellis's comments on male superiority on a host of cognitive tasks, and continue to be much studied today. What is the nature of gender differences in mathematical abilities? When, in development, are they observed? Are they a reflection primarily of inherited biology or of educational opportunities?

Perhaps the best place to start looking for answers to some of these questions is the 1974 review of gender differences by Maccoby and Jacklin. Maccoby and Jacklin reviewed the findings of 27 studies in which gender differences in quantitative (mathematical) ability had been assessed. Of the studies reporting significant differences between the sexes, the vast majority favored boys. Studies with preadolescent children, however, found either no gender differences in mathematics or small but significant differences favoring girls. Boys did not achieve quantitative superiority until 10 to 12 years of age, and after midadolescence, no findings were reported in which girls outscored boys.

Meta-Analysis of Gender Differences in Mathematics

Similar to what has been done evaluating gender differences in verbal abilities, researchers have used meta-analysis to evaluate the many studies looking at gender differences in mathematical ability. To reiterate, meta-analysis is a statistical technique that allows an investigator to evaluate the magnitude of a significant effect across a large number of studies. Differences between the sexes across studies is expressed in terms of effect size, with 1.0 corresponding to a difference equivalent to one standard deviation. The first meta-analysis of gender differences in mathematical ability was reported by Hyde (1981), but more recent and extensive studies have since been published, each reporting similar results (Feingold, 1988; Hedges & Nowell, 1995; Hyde, Fennema, & Lamon, 1990; Marsh, 1989).

Take, for example, the meta-analysis reported by Hyde and her colleagues (1990). It included 100 studies and the data of 3,175,188 participants. Contrasts were made between elementary school children for simple arithmetic computation, high-school students, college students, and adults. Several main conclusions can be stated:

1. Similar to the Maccoby and Jacklin (1974) findings, gender differences are small and often nonsignificant for arithmetic computation in elementary school, and what effect there is favors girls.
2. Significant differences in mathematics favoring males are first seen in high school, with this difference increasing some in college and adulthood (effect sizes = .29, .41, and .59 for high school, college, and adult samples, respectively).
3. The magnitude of the gender differences between males and females has declined over the past several decades (effect sizes: pre-1973 = .31; post-1973 = .14).
4. Sex differences are greater at the highest ability levels, with males much more likely than females to be represented among the top percentiles of mathematics ability.

Related to this last point are the results of meta-analyses by Feingold (1992) and Hedges and Nowell (1995) looking at gender differences in variability. Both Feingold (1992) and Hedges and Nowell (1995) report that males are much more variable than females in their performance. This greater male variability has long been noted (Ellis, 1894; Hollingworth, 1918) and is not limited to mathematics (Hedges & Nowell, 1995). These results suggest that for the great majority of the population, there is much overlap and little real difference in mathematical abilities between males and females. Differences are most apparent at the extremes, par-

ticularly at the upper levels of performance. This finding is similar to that reported by Thomas and Turner (1991) for gender differences in spatial abilities (see Chapter 6).

Gender Differences at the Extremes

Differential representation of males and females in the top 5% of mathematics ability has been demonstrated most dramatically by Camilla Benbow and Julian Stanley (1980). These researchers examined the verbal and mathematics SAT scores of a group of seventh- and eighth-grade children selected to participate in a study of mathematically skilled youth conducted at Johns Hopkins University. The students were selected in a series of talent searches conducted between 1972 and 1979 and scored in the top 5% of students taking the exam. The data revealed consistent gender differences favoring boys. Further, the students were essentially equivalent in verbal SAT scores and in math-course background. Benbow and Stanley (1983) reported similar findings in a second investigation with a much larger number of students (nearly 40,000). In this second study, they found that the disparity between the sexes was greater at the higher ability levels. For example, the ratio of boys to girls scoring 420 or more on the SAT-Math was 1.5:1. In contrast, this boy-to-girl ratio was 4.1:1 for students scoring 600 or more, and 13:1 for the small number of students scoring 700 or more.

Source of Gender Differences in Mathematics

Benbow and Stanley's participants were selected in advance for exceptional math ability. It is possible that comparisons of scores in their sample have limited generalizability to the remaining 95% of the population. Moreover, their data reveal nothing about the sources of the observed gender differences in SAT scores. There is also no compelling reason to conclude that SAT scores reflect innate differences in aptitude or capacity. In fact, Fox (1976) underscored the fact that teachers, parents, and peers all have negative feelings about mathematically talented girls. Likewise, children's books, magazines, and the popular media often present females in stereotypic ways that militate against stronger interest in mathematics.

Another alternative to explain gender differences on the SAT is that males and females differ in their background knowledge, including mathematics problem-solving strategies, and that differences in cognitive processing are responsible for the gender differences in test performance. This possibility was assessed in a study by Byrnes and Takahira (1993), who gave 11th- and 12th-grade students SAT math problems to solve, a strategy questionnaire, and a test of background mathematical knowledge. The strategy questionnaire presented students with an SAT problem and several alternative strategies, from which they were to select the one they used to solve the problem. Table 12-3 shows one example. The knowledge test assessed knowledge of the concepts needed to solve SAT problems—for example, knowledge of what a tangent is. Byrnes and Takahira reported that males performed better than females on the SAT problems and that they also scored higher on the strategy and background knowledge tests. In fact, these two measures accounted for 50% of the variance in the SAT scores, and when participants' performances on the strategy questionnaire and the knowledge test were controlled for statistically, gender differences were no longer significant.

It is unclear why the males showed greater strategy and background knowledge than the females did. The number of high-school math courses taken and the grade-point average in those courses was comparable for the males and females in this study (although no information was obtained concerning the level of math courses taken). Byrnes and Takahira propose that the most likely reason for gender differences on the SAT involves a multitude of factors, including socialization, physiological, and cognitive factors. The researchers note, for example, that socialization factors play an important role in fostering an interest in mathematics, with interest, in turn, influencing cognitive arousal and selective attention (Renninger, Hidi, & Krapp, 1992).

This alternative was investigated by Raymond and Benbow (1986) in a study that assessed the relationship between parental attitudes, gender typing,

TABLE 12-3   An example of a problem and the strategies listed for it. Subjects are to choose which alternative they used for solving the problem.

Midpoint problem:

(1) On the number line above, which of the following is the coordinate of the midpoint of the segment PQ?

(a) $\frac{x}{2}$ (d) $2(x+1)$

(b) $\frac{x+1}{2}$ (e) $\frac{x(x+1)}{2}$

(c) $x + \frac{1}{2}$

Problem/strategy	Percentage of subjects
1. I added the two points (x and $x+1$) together and divided by 2.	56*
2. I multiplied the two points (x and $x+1$) together and divided by 2.	17
3. I figured to get $x+1$ and divided by 2.	6
4. I knew the answer had to be between x and $x+1$. So, I substituted a number for x. I used each of these numbers to get the answers.	13
5. I just guessed.	6
6. Other (please explain).	2

*Successful strategy.

SOURCE: "Explaining Gender Differences on SAT-Math Items," by J. P. Byrnes and S. Takahira, 1993 *Developmental Psychology, 29*, 805–810. Copyright © 1993 American Psychological Association. Adapted with permission. (Original problem from November 1987 SAT exam, Educational Testing Service.)

and mathematical ability for groups of adolescents scoring high on the quantitative and verbal portions of the SAT. Raymond and Benbow reported that mathematically talented students received greater parental encouragement in mathematics than did verbally talented students and that this pattern did not differ with sex. Related to this, the amount of encouragement in mathematics that children received was comparable for boys and girls, regardless of their area or level of talent (that is, high verbal or high math). Finally, mathematically talented girls were no more sex typed as masculine than were verbally talented girls, and there was no relationship between sex typing and SAT scores. Raymond and Benbow concluded that parental socialization practices during adolescence could not account for mathematical ability in this group of mathematically talented children.

One fascinating and educationally important finding in the new set of studies is the steady reduction of gender differences in mathematics ability since the 1960s. Why are gender differences in mathematics ability decreasing over time? The answer favored by many is that attitudes and curricula are changing, gender roles are being viewed more flexibly (Hyde & Linn, 1988), and that girls are taking more mathematics courses than before (Marsh, 1989). There is some evidence that this is true. In Herbert Marsh's (1989) assessment of math performance of 14,825 students in the High School and Beyond project, much smaller gender differences in performance were found than in previous studies. This was associated with evidence that the boys and the girls in the study had taken, on average, equal numbers of mathematics courses in high school. However, as noted earlier in this chapter in discussing the diminishing gender differences in verbal abilities, there is also evidence that test publishers over the past 20 years have been attempting to minimize gender differences in their tests, possibly accounting for the diminished gender differences in performance (Stanley et al., 1992), although this interpretation is questioned by others (Feingold, 1988). Whatever the reason, gender differences favoring males in high-school mathematics and beyond are still found, but they are relatively small in magnitude and getting smaller. The only exception to this statement concerns performance at the highest levels, where males are disproportionately represented.

What do mathematically gifted females do? It is perhaps worth looking at the exceptions to this phenomenon, the minority of females who fall within the top 5% in mathematics ability. What are these people like? Lubinski and Benbow (1992; Lubinski,

Benbow, & Sander, 1993) have followed a sample of mathematically gifted females (top 1%) from identification in seventh grade to young adulthood. Compared with equally mathematically gifted males, the females tended to select different areas of study in college: The males were two to three times more likely to choose careers in engineering or the physical sciences than the females, who were more likely to pursue careers in biology, the social sciences, or the humanities.

Why this difference? One possibility is that there are still educational or occupational roadblocks for women in these traditionally male-dominated fields. However, Lubinski and Benbow proposed an alternative interpretation. They found that these mathematically gifted women are different from the mathematically gifted men in some noncognitive ways that could influence their choice of careers. For instance, in an assessment of values, gifted males gave higher ratings to theoretical issues than gifted females did. The reverse was true for ratings of social issues. Lubinski and Benbow (1992) reported that having strong theoretical values was positively associated with an interest in the physical sciences, whereas an interest in social values was negatively associated with interest in physical sciences. Basically, Lubinski and Benbow are proposing that other gender differences—possibly rooted in biology, possibly in socialization—contribute significantly to career choice, in addition to cognitive abilities. People choose a career not only because they think they will be good at it (that is, that they have the requisite intellectual abilities), but also because it fits their values and interests. This position is consistent with Scarr and McCartney's genotype → environment model, suggesting that people select environments in which they feel comfortable.

The relation between spatial and mathematical abilities. It's worth examining the relation between spatial and mathematical abilities. Males show a consistent advantage on certain types of spatial cognition (but not other types; see discussion in Chapter 6), and these spatial abilities are related to mathematical performance. For example, M. Beth Casey and her colleagues (1995) assessed spatial ability (using a mental-rotation task, see Figure 6-15 in Chapter 6) in groups of adolescents. They also obtained scores on the SAT-Math scores, reporting that males outperformed females on the mental-rotation task and on the SAT-Math for all but the lowest ability level. Moreover, performance on the mental-rotation task predicted SAT-Math scores for both males and females. And when participants' spatial performance was statistically controlled for, the gender difference on the SAT-Math was eliminated. That is, differences in spatial ability were responsible (at least in a statistical sense) for gender differences on mathematical performance.

David Geary (1995, 1996) has similarly noted the relations between sex, spatial ability, and mathematical performance, and has proposed an evolutionary account for gender differences in math performance. Basically, Geary proposes that, over evolutionary time, there has been selection pressure on human males to develop spatial abilities, primarily for the purpose of navigation (see similar arguments by Silverman & Eals, 1992 in Chapter 6). In development, gender differences in hormones and experiences (particularly in the types of play boys and girls engage in, see also Bjorklund & Brown, 1998) foster differences in boys' and girls' abilities to process 3-dimensional space, which are related to certain types of mathematical abilities.

Geary's proposal in no way implies that females are not capable of advanced mathematics. But his proposal does suggest that boys and girls could benefit from different types of educational curricula when it comes to mathematics (Geary, 1996) and reinforces the idea that individual and gender differences in spatial abilities could be the root of individual and gender differences in mathematics.

Schooling and Cognitive Development

There should be little question that schooling makes a difference in how a child thinks. In our day-to-day experience, children who attend school are brighter than children who don't, and children in more advanced grades are smarter than children in lower grades. But children in higher grades not only have had more school experience than children in lower grades, they are also older. Does attending

school actually make a difference in cognitive development above and beyond the effect of age?

Schooling versus Age Effects on Intelligence

The question of how schooling versus age influences intelligence has been addressed by examining the effects of years of education on intellectual performance while statistically controlling for age (Cahan & Cohen, 1989) or, more frequently, by using the *cut-off method*, in which children who just missed the cut-off date for entering school are compared with children who are close to their age but just made the cut-off date. Thus, the two groups of children are nearly identical in age but differ in that the former group has had one more year of education than the latter group (Morrison, Griffith, & Frazier, 1996). For example, Cahan and Cohen compared intelligence test scores and school achievement of fourth-, fifth-, and sixth-grade children (Cahan & Cohen, 1989). They reported significant effects of schooling; children in the higher grade scored better than children their same age in the lower grade. These findings clearly show that IQ and related cognitive skills are strongly associated with schooling. In this study, effects of both age and schooling were reported (that is, older children did better than younger children, and children with one more year of school did better than children without the extra year), but the effect of schooling was two to three times greater than the effect of age (Bentin, Hammer, & Cahan, 1991; Cahan & Cohen, 1989). In related research, kindergarten and first-grade children showed greater gains on tests of cognitive skills over periods when there was more academic information presented during school (between October and April) than for comparable time periods when less academic information was provided (from April to October) (Huttenlocher, Levine, & Vevea, 1998).

The results of this line of research may not be surprising. After all, we expect education to produce smarter children. But these findings force us to question the concept of intelligence as measured by IQ tests. IQ tests are age-based. The norms change as a function of age, not grade. (The construction of the logic behind IQ tests will be discussed in Chapter

13.) The results of the research cited here indicate that not only should age be considered in computing an IQ score, but so should school experience. Moreover, the idea that some intelligence tests can be "culture fair" (that is, used in any culture without yielding biased results) must be questioned. One of the tests used by Cahan and Cohen (1989) was the Ravens' Progressive Matrices Test, a test that has been proposed to produce "an index of intellectual capacity whatever [a person's] nationality or education" (Raven, Court, & Raven, 1975, p. 1). The effects of one year's schooling were found to be twice as large as the effects of one year of age on the Ravens' test, seriously challenging the fairness of such a test when assessing children from cultures where there is no formal education.

Other researchers, notably Frederick Morrison and his colleagues, have looked at age versus schooling effects for specific cognitive and educational abilities for children just beginning formal education. In Morrison's research, "old kindergarten" children, who just missed the school-entry cut-off date, are compared with "young first-grade" children, with contrasts typically being made at the beginning and end of the school year. Morrison and his colleagues report both schooling and age effects, depending on the particular skill that is being assessed. For example, one year of schooling has a greater effect than one year of age on (1) phonological awareness (Bentin et al., 1991; Morrison et al., 1996); (2) free-recall memory, including simple strategy use (Morrison, Smith, & Dow-Ehrensberger, 1995; Morrison et al., 1996); (3) accuracy in mental arithmetic (Bisanz, Morrison, & Dunn, 1995); (4) the ability to understand complex sentences with longer subjects (Ferreira & Morrison, 1994); (5) knowledge of the alphabet (Morrison et al., 1996); and (6) the ability to use causal structure (that is, connections between different pieces in a story) in recalling stories (Varnhagen, Morrison, & Everall, 1994). However, significant *age* effects have also been found for (1) subsyllabic segmentation (the ability to differentiate between sounds within one-syllable words; for example, for the word "grasp," being able to segment "gr" from "asp") (Morrison et al., 1996); (2) conservation of number (Bisanz et al., 1995); (3) the use of simple arithmetic strategies, such as fact retrieval and vari-

ous counting methods (Bisanz et al., 1995); (4) gist recall of stories (Varnhagen et al., 1994); (5) the ability to understand the use of pronouns in sentences (Ferreira & Morrison, 1994); and (6) vocabulary, cultural knowledge, and general narrative skills (Morrison et al., 1996). Of course, for most academic abilities, significant effects are found for both school experience and age (Morrison, Griffith, & Alberts, 1997).

The conclusion to draw from this research is that changes in different cognitive skills follow different developmental paths, reflecting a large degree of domain specificity. Some skills, such as phonemic awareness, free-recall memory, accuracy of mental arithmetic, and the abilities that underlie IQ test performance, are greatly affected by schooling experiences. Presumably, the experiences children have in school have a direct impact on these skills (for example, reading instruction affects phonemic awareness). However, other seemingly closely related skills, such as story recall, use of arithmetic strategies, and vocabulary, are more influenced by the presumably maturational and general (versus schooling-specific) experiences associated with age. According to Morrison and his colleagues (1996), this pattern reflects a substantial degree of specificity in the timing, magnitude, and nature of changes in cognitive abilities.

The Effect of Schooling on IQ

The research contrasting the effects of one year of schooling versus one year of age demonstrates that schooling, indeed, plays a role in cognitive development, at least for some important skills. I suppose that this should not be surprising, given the evidence presented earlier in this and in previous chapters demonstrating substantial differences in mathematics, memory, and classification abilities for children from schooled versus nonschooled cultures. But the question of a relationship between schooling and intellectual functioning is not a trivial one. For example, to what extent does schooling affect IQ? Cahan and Cohen (1989) found that one year of schooling has a substantial effect on IQ, twice the size associated with one year of age. That schooling affects IQ indicates that an IQ score is greatly influenced by experiential factors and is not solely under the influence of genetic or other biological factors that are relatively impervious to societal-level effects. The effects of schooling on IQ have been studied for a number of years, and Stephen Ceci (1991, 1996; Ceci & Williams, 1997) has organized and reviewed this literature, making the point that schooling indeed has a powerful impact on IQ.

In addition to citing Cahan and Cohen's (1989) data as evidence for the influence of schooling on IQ, Ceci examined several additional areas of research pertinent to the schooling-IQ question, some of which I will mention here.

1. Perhaps the most obvious approach to the question would be to compute correlations between years of education and IQ. When this is done, the correlations tend to be very high, usually higher than .60 and often in excess of .80. The effects remain large even after controlling for differences in socioeconomic status.

2. There is a small but statistically significant drop in children's IQ over summer vacation. This drop is larger among children from low-income homes, probably because their summer activities have less resemblance to school activities than those of children from more affluent homes.

3. Children who attend school intermittently, being frequently absent, have lower IQs than children who attend school regularly. What is typically found in samples of frequently truant children is that IQ scores get lower with age. That is, children lose IQ points as they get older, associated in part with the fact that they increasingly fall behind in school. This reflects a cumulative deficit, with the result that the intellectual deficits increase with age. Similar cumulative deficit effects have been reported for children of parents in the lower versus middle socioeconomic stratum, in that the difference in IQ between the two groups becomes greater with age.

4. Children who enter school late show an IQ decrement relative to children who start school on time. In one study, children experienced, on average, a five-point IQ deficit for each year that their schooling was delayed.

5. Just as people who start school late have lower IQs, so, too, do people who drop out of school early. In one study of Swedish males, Harnquist (1968) reported a loss of 1.8 IQ points for each year of school not finished.

6. There is evidence that the quality and not just the quantity of schooling is important for IQ effects. For example, a study of American blacks who migrated from segregated and poor school systems in Georgia to better quality systems in Philadelphia between World Wars I and II showed that children gained about one-half an IQ point for each year they were enrolled in the Philadelphia schools (Lee, 1951). However, it is difficult to measure quality of schooling, and other investigators question the connection between quality of school and IQ (Bouchard & Segal, 1985).

Taken together, the evidence is impressive that attending school influences one's IQ. Again, perhaps this should not be too surprising, in part because IQ tests, although purporting not to assess specific aptitudes, do tap general cultural knowledge (the information and vocabulary subtests on the Wechsler scales, for example, do this), much of which is learned in school. What seems inarguable is that whatever IQ tests measure, it is influenced greatly by the school experience.

The Costs and Benefits of Academic Preschools

The evidence presented in the preceding sections clearly shows that schooling has a powerful impact on cognitive development. People in schooled cultures think differently from people in nonschooled cultures; one year of schooling has a greater impact on cognition than one year of age; schooling influences IQ; and reading, perhaps the quintessential school-taught skill, makes you smarter. All this, along with evidence that a longer school year likely produces cognitive gains, makes a compelling argument for extended education, at least in postindustrial societies. In fact, some people have looked at the evidence and concluded that intellectual gains could be even greater if formal education were to begin even earlier (Doman, 1984). If starting school at 5 is good, surely starting school at 4, 3, or even 2 is better.

This is an argument made by many educators and parents in the United States. Many families in the United States have a tendency to push their young children. Many preschool programs have academic curricula, preparing 3- and 4-year-old children for the rigors of school. These parents believe that if children can be taught the important skills used in reading and arithmetic in preschool, they will have an intellectual advantage when they enter kindergarten or first grade.

The logic follows from the evidence of the relation between schooling and cognition in older children and adults, but does it make sense for preschool children? Is there a single relation between the amount of formal education and intelligence for all ages? Or might the effects of formal schooling vary with the age of the child? For example, recall that although older Japanese and Chinese schoolchildren spend more time in school per day than their American counterparts, first-grade children in these countries actually spend fewer hours in school than American children. Also, Japanese and Chinese elementary school children in all grades have more recesses than American children do. This seems to be a recognition of the limited attention span of younger children and an acknowledgment that one must take the developmental abilities of children into consideration when constructing a curriculum (Pellegrini & Bjorklund, 1997).

Evidence indicates that children who attend high quality child-care programs during the preschool years score higher on measures of cognitive ability during elementary school than do matched groups of children who do not attend preschool programs (Broberg et al., 1997). But quality child care does not necessarily mean academically oriented child care. In fact, several researchers and educators have seriously questioned the idea of academic instruction for preschoolers (Elkind, 1987; Sigel, 1987). David Elkind (1987), for example, states that

academic programs for preschoolers amount to *miseducation*. Young children do not have the cognitive capacity to adequately master the academic skills of these programs, and the overall result is unnecessary stress with no long-term benefits.

Despite the importance of this issue, there has been surprisingly little research on it. Research by Hyson, Hirsh-Pasek, and Rescorla (1990; Rescorla, Hyson, & Hirsh-Pasek, 1991) is a notable exception. In their study, 4-year-old children attending prekindergarten programs were assessed. Children were given tests of academic skills, creativity, social competence, and emotional well-being at the end of their prekindergarten program and again toward the end of their kindergarten year. Parents were also interviewed concerning their attitudes about education and their expectations for their children's academic achievement. The preschool programs were classified as high academic or low academic. High-academic programs stressed adult-directed instruction, whereas low academic programs did not but instead followed a "developmentally appropriate" curriculum (Bredekamp & Copple, 1997). Not surprisingly, parents who believed in adult-directed education tended to put their children in the more academically oriented preschools.

Table 12-4 presents children's scores on each of nine measures. The Academic Schools Test assessed school-related cognitive skills and was given at the end of the prekindergarten year; the PASS is also a test of academic skills that was given at the end of the kindergarten year; the Ravens' Matrices is a nonverbal test of intelligence; the Harter and Pike scales are tests of self-concept; the MYCATS (Measurement of Young Children's Attitudes Toward School) assesses children's general feelings about school, their teachers, and their perceived difficulty and enjoyment of school; the purposes of creativity and test anxiety tests are self-evident. The Ravens' Matrices test and the creativity test were given only once, during the summer before children entered kindergarten. The MYCATS was given only at the conclusion of kindergarten.

As can be seen from the table, there were no significant differences in academic ability between the children who attended the high-academic and

TABLE 12-4   Comparison for Child Outcome Variables for children who attended academic versus nonacademic preschools. The Academic Schools and PASS tests assessed school-related cognitive skills; the Ravens' Matrices is a nonverbal test of intelligence; the Harter and Pike scales assess self-concept. The Ravens' Matrices and Creativity/Originality tests were given only once before children entered kindergarten. The MYCATS was given only at the end of kindergarten.

Variable	High-academic mean score (n = 46)	Low-academic mean score (n = 44)
Academic Schools (Preschool)	45.61	43.84
PASS (Kindergarten)	7.91	8.60
Ravens' Matrices	63.70	63.27
Creativity/Originality	1.21	1.25
Harter & Pike (Preschool)	3.35	3.27
Harter & Pike (Kindergarten)	3.08	3.01
Test Anxiety (Preschool)	5.10	5.61
Test Anxiety (Kindergarten)	5.56	5.87
MYCATS (school attitudes)	13.15	14.00

SOURCE: Adapted from "Academic Environments in Preschool: Challenge or Pressure?" by M.C. Hyson, K. Hirsh-Pasek, and L. Rescorla, 1990, *Early Education and Development, 1,* 401–423, Wide Range, Inc.

low-academic programs. Performance on the cognitive skills tests both at the end of preschool (Academic Schools) and at the end of kindergarten (PASS) was comparable, as was performance on the Ravens' Matrices test of intelligence. A small difference was found for test anxiety at the end of preschool, with children attending the academically oriented preschools showing greater test anxiety than children attending the developmentally appropriate programs.

Further correlational analyses showed some other small but interesting relationships. For example, the extent to which mothers endorsed adult-directed in-

struction for preschool children did predict academic skills during preschool, with mothers who favored formal instruction having children who performed better on the Academic Schools Test than preschoolers who had mothers who did not endorse adult-directed instruction. There was no significant relation between mothers' endorsement of adult-directed instruction and academic skills in kindergarten, but this factor did correlate negatively with preschool measures of creativity. Thus, mothers scoring high on the adult-instruction scale tended to have children rated as lower in creativity. Also, the degree to which the preschools endorsed adult-directed practices was negatively related to children's test anxiety at the end of kindergarten (the greater the emphasis on adult-directed practices, the higher was children's anxiety). Finally, children who attended the developmentally appropriate schools were more likely to have a positive attitude toward school than were children who attended the high-academic programs.

Hyson and her associates cautioned that most of these effects, although statistically significant, are small in magnitude. Nevertheless, the pattern is clear. In general, there were no long-term benefits of an academically oriented preschool program, and some evidence indicates that such programs might actually be detrimental. The researchers proposed two alternative interpretations of the data. The first points to the small differences between the schools, so that from a practical perspective the academic orientation of a school likely makes little difference in the long run. The second, stronger, interpretation of their data holds that an academic orientation provides no advantage and actually has some small negative consequences. Hyson and colleagues concluded that whichever interpretation is adopted, there seems to be no defensible reason for encouraging formal academic instruction during the preschool years. Rather, for most children from middle-class homes, cognitive development and creativity can best be fostered in a developmentally appropriate preschool program that considers children's limitations as well as their abilities. In the opinion of these researchers, "it may be developmentally prudent to let children explore the world at their own pace rather than to impose our adult timetables and anxieties on them" (p. 421).

Although few studies have assessed the effects of a preschool program's academic structure on later performance, the study by Hyson and her associates is not alone. For example, reviewing the long-term consequences of various preschool programs for disadvantaged children, Weikart and Schweinhart (1991) reported that 15-year-old children who had teacher-directed preschool instruction felt considerable alienation from school, home, and society relative to 15-year-olds who had attended a child-centered preschool program. Although there were no differences between the children in IQ or academic achievement, those who had attended the direct-instruction programs engaged in twice the number of delinquent acts, participated less in sports, and had lower educational expectations than did those who had attended the developmentally appropriate programs.

Although the results of these studies must be viewed as tentative, they are consistent with the perspective that cognitive development during the early years of life is best accomplished outside a formal, teacher-directed environment. Young children's cognitive system is immature, and because of this, learning and development might take place best in unstructured settings. The skills of young children are different from the skills of older children and might be ideally suited for the learning they need to do at this time in their lives (Bjorklund, 1997a; Bjorklund & Green, 1992). These findings argue that children ought not be hurried through a childhood that has purposes in and of itself.

Summary

Reading is perhaps the most critical technological skill for people in postindustrial societies. Chall has proposed five stages of learning to read: (1) the pre-reading skill of letter identification, (2) phonological recoding in the first grade, (3) fluent but effortful reading in grades 2 and 3, (4) "reading to learn" in grades 4 through 8, and (5) proficient reading in high school and beyond.

Emergent literacy refers to the skills, knowledge and attitudes that are presumed to be developmental precursors to conventional forms of reading and writing and the environments that support these developments. There are at least nine components to emergent literacy, including language, knowledge of the conventions of print (for example, reading is done left-to-right), knowledge of letters, linguistic awareness, phoneme-grapheme correspondence, emergent reading, emergent writing, print motivation, and other cognitive abilities, such as memory.

Phonemic awareness and *phonological recoding* are important skills for both beginning and later reading, with dyslexic, or reading-disabled, children generally having delayed phonological processing skills. *Reading comprehension* involves working memory and is influenced by one's knowledge base and monitoring skills, each of which develops over childhood. Research has shown that reading-disabled children show deficits in working-memory capacity.

Two broadly defined types of reading instruction have been used, *phonics*, which is a bottom-up system that emphasizes learning letter-sound correspondence, and the *whole-language approach*, which is a top-down system that emphasizes a reader's construction of meaning. Although reading surely involves both top-down and bottom-up processes, research evidence makes it clear that any reading program should include some instruction in phonics.

Research by Stanovich and his colleagues has shown that the more children and adults read, the higher their scores on tests of vocabulary, reading comprehension, and cultural knowledge are.

More boys than girls are classified as reading disabled, or *dyslexic*, but differences in reading ability beyond dyslexic children are small, with boys being more influenced by text interest than girls are. *Meta-analyses* have found that females show an overall advantage in verbal abilities relative to males, although the magnitude of this gender difference has diminished during the last several decades.

Children's concept of number has been studied in terms of *conservation of number*, following Piaget. Children cannot conserve number until approximately 6 or 7 years of age. However, more recent research indicates that children as young as 2 years have some notion of number. Some researchers have focused on counting as a precursor to conservation of number. Children appear to acquire a knowledge of counting gradually during the preschool years, and this knowledge precedes that necessary for conservation of number.

Research on children's arithmetic has concentrated primarily on the strategies children use to solve problems. Early arithmetic is done out loud, often on fingers. Children's early strategies include the *sum strategy*, with children counting all numbers, and the *min strategy*, with children beginning with the larger addend and counting up from there. More sophisticated strategies include retrieving addition and subtraction facts directly from long-term memory (*fact retrieval*) and *decomposition*, in which a problem is decomposed into simpler problems. One way of assessing mental arithmetic is by evaluating reaction times. Researchers have proposed that children first apply effort-consuming counting procedures in doing mental arithmetic and use fact retrieval later. Siegler has proposed the adoptive *strategy choice model* showing that children actually use a variety of arithmetic strategies, making it inappropriate to classify children as users of a single approach to solve arithmetic problems.

Math-disabled children typically display procedural deficits early but often catch up to their peers by second grade. Difficulties in storing and retrieving math facts from long-term memory persist, however, with deficits in working-memory capacity being a likely contributor to math disability.

Gender differences in mathematics favoring males are not typically found until high school, then increase slightly into college and adulthood. The absolute magnitude of these differences is small, however, and has been decreasing during the past 30 years. The largest gender differences are found among the most mathematically gifted, with boys being disproportionately represented.

The mathematics performance of people from traditional cultures, although usually much poorer than that of people from technological societies, is improved when their familiarity with the test materials and the context of testing are considered.

Patterns of cognitive abilities vary as a function of culture even in those societies that require formal education, with different values and educational practices affecting children's academic performance. Differences in educational practices between countries (Japan and the United States, for example) are a function of differences in culture, and educational reform cannot be done simply by importing a system evolved elsewhere.

Attending school enhances development of many cognitive skills above and beyond the effects of age, although age has a greater impact on development of other cognitive abilities. Evidence from a variety of sources suggests that schooling influences IQ. Children who attend preschool programs that stress academics, demonstrate no long-term gains and have a less positive attitude about school than children who attend nonacademic preschool programs.

Key Terms and Concepts

emergent literacy
phonemic awareness
phonological recoding
phonics
adaptive strategy choice model
fact retrieval
dyslexia
reading comprehension
whole-language approach
meta-analysis
conservation of number
sum strategy
min strategy
decomposition

Suggested Readings

ADAMS, M. J., TREIMAN, R., & PRESSLEY, M. (1998). Reading, writing, and literacy. In I. E. Sigel & K. A. Renninger (Vol. Eds.), *Child psychology in practice* (Vol. 4) (pp. 275–355). In W. Damon (Gen. Ed.), *Handbook of child psychology*. New York: Wiley. This chapter provides an up-to-date review of the development of children's reading. The authors also examine the development of other educational topics, such as spelling and writing.

SIEGEL, L. S. (1993). The cognitive basis of dyslexia. In R. Pasnak & M. L. Howe (Eds.), *Emerging Themes in Cognitive Development*: Vol. 2. *Competencies* (pp. 33–52). New York: Springer-Verlag. In this short article, Siegel reviews research from her lab and others' concerning cognitive abilities in reading-disabled children. The presentation is clear, and the reader is left with an appreciation of how reading-disabled and nondisabled children differ in basic cognitive abilities.

GINSBURG, H. P., KLEIN, A., & STARKEY, P. (1998). The development of children's mathematical thinking: Connecting research with practice. In I. E. Sigel & K. A. Renninger (Vol. Eds.), *Child psychology in practice* (Vol. 4) (pp. 401–476). In W. Damon (Gen. Ed.), *Handbook of child psychology*. New York: Wiley. This chapter reviews research and theory on children's developing mathematical abilities, covering topics of more advanced math as well as the basic number concepts and arithmetic discussed in this chapter. Ginsburg and his colleagues devote about half of their chapter to mathematical education, making this an excellent book for those interested in instruction.

HYDE, J. S., FENNEMA, E., & LAMON, S. J. (1990). Gender differences in mathematics performance: A meta-analysis. *Psychological Bulletin, 107,* 139–155. This is the most recent of the several meta-analyses of gender differences in mathematical ability. The discussion of the findings is clear, so the article is easily understood even by the mathematically challenged of either gender.

CECI, S. J. (1991). How much does schooling influence general intelligence and its cognitive components? A reassessment of the evidence. *Developmental Psychology, 27,* 703–722. In this paper, Ceci provides a thorough review of the research examining the relationship between quantity and quality of schooling and intellectual functioning.

RESCORLA, L., HYSON, M. C., & HIRSH-PASEK, K. (Eds.). (1991). *Academic instruction in early childhood: Challenge or pressure?* San Francisco: Jossey-Bass. This short edited volume (less than 100 pages long) presents a detailed description of the study by Hirsh-Pasek and colleagues of the effects of early academic instruction on children's development, along with five other papers on this topic written by others.

13

Approaches to the Study of Intelligence

L ook at the fingers of your right hand. No two are alike. That's the way children are." This homily, attributed to a retired elementary school teacher, reflects the individuality of children. To this point, my primary focus has been on developmental function, the form that cognition takes in the species over time. Theories and research on developmental function are concerned with cognition in the typical child at any given age or stage and the general processes that influence transitions from lower levels of cognitive functioning to more advanced levels. I have not ignored individual differences in the previous chapters, in fact, much of the research in the previous chapter on schooling dealt with individual differences. But individual differences take center stage in the last two chapters of this book, which concentrate on the origins and stability of individual differences in children's thinking. At any given age, some children function better than others do. Differences in rate of development are partly responsible. Johnny attains concrete operations a year ahead of Joey, but Joey will eventually catch up. Yet, within any given developmental level, some children solve most problems more efficiently than other children do despite the qualitatively similar form of their cognitions. How can such differences be conceptualized? How and why do these individual differences come about? Are they stable over time? What are the origins of these differences?

This brings us to the concept of **intelligence.** If you were to ask a psychologist her specialty and she stated "the study of intelligence," she would probably be referring to individual differences in how people process information, or think. The term intelligence itself need not be used solely to reflect the nature of individual differences in thought. As the term is used today, however, investigations of intelligence are almost always concerned with the magnitude, pattern, origins, or stability of individual differences in mental functioning.

Intelligence is an elusive concept. Most broadly, it refers to acting or thinking in ways that are goal-directed and adaptive (Sternberg & Slater, 1982). This definition covers a lot of ground, allowing much leeway for theorists to sculpt their own meanings of the concept while still being understood by others. Although what is viewed to be important in determining intelligence varies from theorist to theorist, professional researchers and laypeople alike generally agree about the common characteristics of intelligence. Based on interviews conducted both with the "man (and woman) on the street" and psychologists who study intelligence, Robert Sternberg and his colleagues (1981) reported that people believe that intelligence involves three main sets of skills:

1. *Practical problem-solving ability*: These skills include getting to the heart of a problem, interpreting information accurately, seeing all aspects of a problem, and reasoning logically.
2. *Verbal ability*: These skills include speaking and writing clearly and articulately, dealing effectively with people, having detailed knowledge about a particular field, reading widely and with good comprehension, and having a good vocabulary.
3. *Social competence*: These skills include displaying curiosity, being sensitive to the needs and desires of others, being on time for appointments, having a social conscience, and making carefully considered and fair judgments.

Sternberg and his colleagues (1981) referred to such conceptions as *implicit* theories of intelligence and contrasted them with the *explicit* theories that psychologists and educators construct when generating their formal models and measures of mental functioning. In the greater part of this chapter, I examine some explicit theories of intelligence. Although much of the chapter concentrates on the theory and practice of IQ testing, which is certainly the most used and best known method for evaluating intelligence, even more total space is given to alternatives to the testing approach to intelligence. In the next chapter, I continue the discussion of intelligence, focusing on the extent to which intelligence is biologically and environmentally influenced, and the stability of intelligence over time.

The Psychometric Approach to the Study of Intelligence

The major approach to the study of individual differences in intelligence since the turn of the century has been the **psychometric** (or **differential**) **approach**. Psychometric theories of intelligence have as their basis a belief that intelligence can be described in terms of mental **factors** and that tests can be constructed that reveal individual differences in the factors that underlie mental performance. Factors are related mental skills that (presumably) affect thinking in a wide range of situations. For example, a verbal factor can be tapped by tests assessing a variety of more specific verbal skills such as vocabulary and reading comprehension. An individual may possess a general facility with words and language concepts that influences his or her performance on most tasks involving the processing of language terms and concepts.

Factors of Intelligence

What constitutes a factor is determined by a statistical procedure known as **factor analysis**. In factor analysis, numerous test items are administered to people, and the resulting data are examined to see which items fit together well. Tests might show, for example, that the pattern of individual differences among people is very similar on vocabulary, reading comprehension, story completion, and verbal analogies. That is, people who score high on one of these tests usually score high on all of them, whereas people who score low on one usually score low on all of them. In contrast, performance on these test items might not correlate as highly with performance on items that involve rotating three-dimensional figures, solving maze problems, or quickly placing geometric forms in a form board, although these three tests might all correlate highly with one another. What do the first tests (vocabulary, reading comprehension, story completion, and verbal analogies) have in common? It is not difficult to conclude that all involve some aspect of verbal thinking, whereas the second set (3-D rotation, maze learning, and

form-board performance) are all basically nonverbal and involve some form of spatial thinking. Accordingly, based on the results of the statistical analysis, an investigator can assume that two factors that account for individual differences among people are verbal ability and spatial thinking.

Patterns of performance are not always clear-cut, however. The extent to which sets of test items correlate with one another is a matter of degree. Only in textbooks do we find perfect data that can be interpreted in only one way. Thus, how one defines mental factors is influenced not only by the data but also by one's theoretical and statistical perspective.

Determining the number and makeup of factors is a function of the items included on a test (you could not very well have a verbal component if no verbal items were included in your test) and the particular way you perform statistical analyses. Based on variants of the same form of analysis, the number of factors that have been proposed to account for human intelligence has varied considerably. On the one hand, Charles Spearman (1927) proposed that intelligence consists of only two kinds of factors. He viewed the most critical kind of factor as a general one, labeled **g,** that influences performance on all intellectual tasks. He saw the other kind of factors as specific ones that are not generalizable and that are each pertinent to only a single task. As such, these highly specific abilities are of little interest to psychologists trying to construct theories to explain individual differences among people. In other words, from Spearman's point of view, intelligence exists on a single dimension and is not some multifaceted phenomenon (that is, there is actually only one factor of intelligence, g). Intellectual functioning is relatively homogeneous, or even, across different tasks performed by a single person. Smart people are smart all the time (or most of the time, anyway), and dumb people are consistently dumb. (I will have more to say about the concept of g later in this and in the following chapter).

At the other extreme, J. P. **Guilford's** (1988) **structure-of-the-intellect theory** includes 180 unique intellectual factors organized along three dimensions. One dimension includes six forms of mental operations, a second includes five contents on which the operations function, and a third includes six possible products that result from applying a given operation to a particular content. Figure 13-1 illustrates Guilford's model.

Between the extremes of Spearman and Guilford lie theories such as L. L. Thurstone's (1938), which names seven "primary mental abilities":

1. *Verbal comprehension*, which includes vocabulary and reading comprehension.
2. *Verbal fluency*, as measured by tests that require rapid production of words ("Tell me as many names of animals that you can as quickly as you can").
3. *Number*, as reflected by arithmetic word problems.
4. *Spatial visualization*, measured by the mental manipulation of symbols or geometric forms.
5. *Memory*, evaluated by tests of recall for lists of words or of the ability to associate names with pictures of people.
6. *Reasoning*, as exemplified in analogies (for example, "Doctor is to hospital as teacher is to _____?").
7. *Perceptual speed*, involving the rapid recognition of symbols, such as crossing out all the 3s that are embedded in a string of numbers.

Also falling between the extremes is Raymond Cattell's (1971) theory, which recognizes both a general intellectual factor similar to Spearman's *g* and two second-order factors that he called **fluid abilities** and **crystallized abilities**. Basically, Cattell proposed that fluid intelligence is biologically determined and is reflected in tests of memory span and most tests of spatial thinking. In contrast, crystallized intelligence is best reflected in tests of verbal comprehension or social relations, skills that depend more highly on cultural context and experience.

Despite this plurality of theories, the diverse models are not as discrepant as they appear on first examination. In fact, whether there is only a single factor or there are many factors that make up intelligence is a matter of interpretation even within a given psychometric theory. Toward the end of his career, for example, Spearman acknowledged that group factors (such as verbal abilities) do exist along

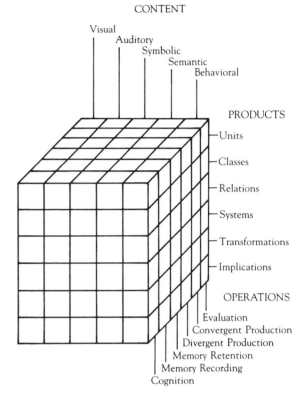

FIGURE 13-1 Guilford's structure-of-the-intellect model. Guilford (1988) specified 180 unique cognitive factors varying as a function of (1) the type of mental operation, (2) the type of content, and (3) the product that results from applying a given operation to a particular content. SOURCE:: "Some Changes in the Structure of the Intellect Model," by J. P. Guilford, 1988, *Educational and Psychological Measurement*, 48, Vol. 1. Reprinted with permission of Ruth B. Guilford.

with a more general intellectual factor. Similarly, Thurstone conceded that his primary mental abilities typically do correlate with one another, suggesting a general factor of intelligence. Thus, despite their diversity, most psychometricians would agree that there is a general factor of intelligence but that there are also "lower-level" factors, reflective of more specific skills (Daniel, 1997). Differences among the various theorists seem to concentrate on the extent to which intelligence can be described by *g* or by other sets of lower-level factors.

The best evidence for the existence of *g* is what has been termed the **positive manifold**, the frequent finding of high correlations among scores on sets of cognitive tests that have little in common with one another in content or types of strategies used (see Daniel, 1997; Jensen, 1998). This is exactly what Spearman proposed earlier in the 20th century, and the finding is still with us today.

Research has produced at least one interesting caveat to the positive manifold. Detterman and Daniel (1989) found much higher correlations among scores on a variety of cognitive and intelligence tasks for low-IQ people than for high-IQ people. For example, in one study, adults with mental retardation (mean IQ = 67.5) and college students (mean IQ = 115.5) were given a battery of nine cognitive tasks and an IQ test. Detterman and Daniel correlated performance on the cognitive tasks with IQ and then examined the correlations of the scores on the nine cognitive tasks with each other. The correlations were considerably higher for the low-IQ group (.60 for IQ scores and .44 for the cognitive tasks) than for the high-IQ group (.26 for IQ scores and .23 for the cognitive tasks), which basically means that the cognitions of high-IQ people (in this case, college students) are more varied than the cognitions of low-IQ people are. Although there is no single interpretation of this finding, Douglas Detterman (1987) proposed that intelligence is made up of several independent processes, although each of these is influenced by central (domain-general) processes. According to Detterman (1987), mental retardation is caused by a deficit in central processes, which in turn affects all other components in the cognitive system, producing relative homogeneity of cognitive function. When there is no central deficit, however, variability is more apt to be found in different components of intelligence, thus producing lower correlations. In other words, a certain level of domain-general central processing resources must exist for individual components of intelligence to operate adequately. Once that level is achieved, there will be substantial variability in cognitive task performance within a given person. However, if that level is not achieved, as is the case for the people with mental

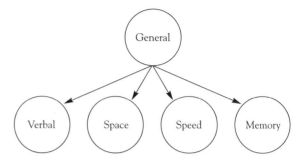

FIGURE 13-2   Hierarchical model of cognitive abilities. Intelligence is composed of specific cognitive abilities (for example, verbal, spatial, speed of processing, memory) that are intercorrelated and influenced by a higher-order general intellectual factor, *g*.

retardation, no individual component will receive enough in the way of processing resources to function well, resulting in relative homogeneity of cognitive functioning, and thus high correlations.

Most psychometricians today adhere to some form of the **hierarchical model of cognitive abilities** (Carrol, 1993). Basically, this model postulates a series of relatively specific cognitive abilities, such as verbal, spatial, speed of processing, and memory, as shown in Figure 13-2. These abilities, however, are correlated with one another (recall the positive manifold), and are influenced by a second-order general factor, or *g*. Thus, this model suggests that, depending on how one looks at the data, one can find evidence for either domain generality (*g*) or domain specificity (separate verbal and spatial modules, for example), and both could be correct (Petrill, 1997).

Psychometric theories have affected research and practice in psychology significantly over the course of this century. For example, many of the achievement tests (designed to assess specific achievement in a topic, such as reading or mathematics, rather than general intelligence) administered regularly in American schools are based on extensions of Thurstone's multifactor theory. And researchers from a variety of theoretical perspectives continue to search for a general intellectual factor (Jensen, 1998) or to argue that the quest for *g* is fruitless (Ceci, 1996).

IQ Tests

Although mental testing has had a profound influence on psychologists' attempts to conceptualize the nature of intelligence, the greatest impact of mental testing has been IQ tests. Intelligence testing is so widespread in our society that it is virtually impossible for a child to graduate from high school without having been administered at least one IQ test and more than a dozen tests assessing more specific academic aptitudes.

IQ tests are less the result of psychometric theorizing than they are the instruments that produce the raw data for theory construction. IQ tests were developed at the turn of the century in France by Alfred Binet and Theodore Simon. The original tests—and to a large extent even modern versions—were not based on explicit theory. Rather, they were constructed to assess school-related abilities and to differentiate among those children who could benefit from standard school instruction and those who would require special education. It would be inappropriate, however, to classify IQ tests as atheoretical. As will be seen later, modern IQ tests are based on certain concepts of what intelligence is. Nevertheless, pragmatic considerations of which items best differentiate children of a given age are critical in the construction of IQ tests, causing some to question their contribution to understanding the underlying mechanisms of intelligence (Sternberg, 1985).

An abundance of IQ-type tests are available today. Many are pencil-and-paper tests that can be administered to a group. The standard tests by which most are judged include the Stanford-Binet and the three intelligence scales developed by David Wechsler: the Wechsler Preschool and Primary Scale of Intelligence (WPPSI), the Wechsler Intelligence Scale for Children (WISC), and the Wechsler Adult Intelligence Scale (WAIS). These tests have been standardized on large samples and are individually administered by trained examiners using standardized procedures.

The **Stanford-Binet** was developed in 1916 by Lewis Terman, who made extensive revisions of Binet's original scale. The test has gone through revisions from time to time, the most recent one being in 1986 (Thorndike, Hagen, & Sattler, 1986). The current version consists of 15 subtests, organized in a three-level hierarchical model of the structure of intelligence. A general reasoning factor (g) is the most inclusive (see Table 13-1). The authors admit that the exact nature of this general ability is unclear but maintain that g reflects the type of intelligence that a person uses to solve problems that he or she has not been previously taught to solve.

There are three second-level factors: crystallized abilities, fluid-analytic abilities, and short-term memory. Crystallized abilities reflect cognitive skills used for solving verbal and quantitative problems. These abilities are greatly influenced by the environment, particularly school. Fluid-analytic abilities

TABLE 13-1   Three-level hierarchical model of Stanford-Binet

g			
Crystallized abilities		Fluid-analytic abilities	Short-term memory
Verbal reasoning	Quantitative reasoning	Abstract/visual reasoning	
Vocabulary	Quantitative	Pattern analysis	Bead memory
Comprehension	Number series	Copying	Memory for sentences
Absurdities	Equation building	Matrices	Memory for digits
Verbal relations		Paper folding and cutting	Memory for objects

SOURCE: Adapted from *The Stanford-Binet Intelligence Scale: (4th Edition) Guide for Administering and Scoring,* by R. L. Thorndike, E. P. Hagen, and J.M. Sattler. Copyright 1986 The Riverside Publishing Company. Reprinted with permission.

represent cognitive skills necessary for solving novel problems involving nonverbal stimuli; the knowledge necessary to solve such problems is not influenced substantially by academic experience. The short-term memory factor involves people's ability to retain newly perceived information for a brief time and to hold information retrieved from long-term store that is used in an ongoing task.

Three factors exist at the third level: verbal reasoning, quantitative reasoning, and abstract/visual reasoning. These factors are more specific and dependent on content than the first- or second-level factors are.

The **Wechsler scales** have similarly been revised periodically since their inception in the 1940s. The three scales are similar in that each consists of a series of subtests that are organized according to two larger factors: verbal and performance abilities. Following is a description of the verbal and performance subtests of the WISC (3rd edition) (Wechsler, 1991), with examples of the types of items included in each subtest. The examples provided here are *not* items from the WISC-III but are similar in form to items found on it.

Verbal IQ

Information: Children are asked questions assessing their general world knowledge, similar to the following: "How many pennies make a dime?" "What do the lungs do?" "What is the capital of Italy?"

Similarities: Children are read two words in pairs similar to the following and are to tell how they are alike: pear-peach; inch-ounce; snow-sand.

Arithmetic: Children are given arithmetic problems. The easiest involve counting and addition and subtraction using physical reminders. A child might be shown a picture of nine trees and asked to cover up all but five. More complex problems are read aloud; for example, "Joyce had six dolls and lost two. How many dolls did she have left?" "Three girls had 48 cookies. They divided them equally among themselves. How many cookies did each girl get?"

Vocabulary: Children are read words and are to tell what each word means.

Comprehension: Children are asked questions assessing their knowledge of societal conventions and of appropriate behavior in a variety of situations: "What are some reasons we need soldiers?" "What are you supposed to do if you find someone's watch in school?" "Why is it important to have speed limits on roads?"

Digit Span: Children are read digits at a rate of one per second and are to repeat them back in exact order. This is followed by a test in which children must repeat the numbers in the reverse order in which the examiner spoke them. This is an optional test.

Performance IQ

Picture Completion: Children are shown black-and-white pictures and are to determine what important part of each picture is missing.

Coding: Children are shown a key associating simple geometric figures (for instance, a triangle, a square, and a circle) with other symbols (a cross, a vertical line, and so on). Children are to mark the associated symbol below a set of randomly arranged figures as quickly as possible without skipping any. Bonus points are given for fast response times.

Picture Arrangement: Children are given a series of pictures in a mixed order and are to arrange them so that they tell a sensible story.

Block Design: Children are given nine cubes, colored red on two sides, white on two sides, and red and white on two sides. They are shown designs and are to reproduce them using the nine blocks. Bonus points are given for fast response times.

Object Assembly: Children are given pieces of a familiar object in a scrambled order. They are to put the pieces together to make the object. Bonus points are given for fast response times.

Symbol Search: Children are shown a target symbol (for example, ≠) and beside it a series of three symbols (for example, $\partial \infty ¥$, or $¥ \partial ≠$). Children must determine if the first (target) symbol is contained in the second (search) set of symbols. This is an optional test.

TABLE 13-2 Examples of items on the Bayley Scales of Infant Development

Items typifying infants between 1 and 3 months	Items typifying infants between 5 and 7 months	Items typifying infants between 9 and 12 months	Items typifying infants between 14 and 17 months
Responds to sound of bell.	Smiles at mirror image	Responds to verbal requests. (Can child perform some act upon request, such as waving in response to "bye-bye" or clapping hands in response to "pat-a-cake"?	Scribbles spontaneously (Will child attempt to scribble before it is demonstrated by examiner?)
Regards red ring. (Does infant attend to a red ring suspended by string 8 inches from infant's eye?)	Turns head after fallen spoon. (Does infant turn head in direction of a spoon that falls to the floor and makes a noise?)	Puts cube in cup on demand. (Will infant place a cube in a cup when asked to do so?)	Says two words. (Does child say two recognizable words during the interview?)
Vocalizes once or twice. (Does infant coo, gurgle, squeal during examination period?)	Shows interest in sound production. (Does infant intentionally use objects to make noise?)	Stirs with spoon in imitation. (Will infant imitate the examiner who makes a stirring motion in a cup?)	Shows shoes or other clothing. (Will child point to his or her shoes in response to question "Where are your shoes?")
Demonstrates circular eye coordination: red ring. (Does infant follow circular path of red ring moved above infant's eyes?)	Picks up cube deftly and directly. (Does child pick up small cube?)	Attempts to scribble. (After examiner demonstrates scribbling on a piece of paper, will infant attempt to scribble when given the chance?)	Builds a tower of three cubes.
Displays social smile. (Does infant smile or laugh in response to smile from examiner?)	Vocalizes four different syllables.	Turns pages of book.	Attains toy with stick. (When small toy is placed out of reach of child, will child use stick to attempt to attain it?)

SOURCE: Adapted from *Manual of the Bayley Scales of Infant Development* , by N. Bayley, 1969. Copyright 1969 The Psychological Corporation. Adapted with permission.

Mazes: Children are shown mazes drawn on paper and are to draw their way out of the maze with a pencil. This is an optional test.

Wechsler (1974) noted that the verbal/performance dichotomy reflects "two principal modes by which human abilities express themselves" (p. 9), while acknowledging that mental abilities could also be classified in other ways. In fact, in the 1991 revision of the WISC, scores for four factors can be derived: Verbal Comprehension (Information, Similarities, Vocabulary, Comprehension), Perceptual Organization (Picture Completion, Picture Arrangement, Block Design, Object Assembly), Freedom from Distractibility (Arithmetic, Digit Span), and Processing Speed (Coding, Symbol Search).

Although the youngest children who can be assessed using the Wechsler or Stanford-Binet scales are early preschoolers, psychometricians have not forgotten infants. Tests to assess infant intelligence have been developed with the same psychometric properties as IQ tests and yield a **developmental quotient (DQ)**. Tests such as the Bayley Scales of Infant Development (Bayley, 1969), the Gesell Developmental Schedules (Gesell & Amatruda, 1954), the Neonatal Behavioral Assessment Scale (Brazelton, 1973), and their precursors are based on evaluations of individual differences in sensory and motor abilities. These tests have been well standardized, are reliable (that is, there is high test-retest and intertester agreement), and describe important differences among infants (McCall, Hogarty, & Hurlburt, 1972). Table 13-2 presents examples of items on the Bayley Scales of Infant Development (Bayley, 1969, 1st edition). I say more about DQ tests in Chapter 14.

Basically, IQ tests (and DQ tests) are standardized on large samples of people, and items that differentiate among people of a given age are retained, whereas items that do not (those that are too easy or too difficult) are eliminated. For each age assessed, the number of test items the average child passes is determined. For example, the number of items passed by 50 percent of the 8-year-olds in the standardization sample would reflect the number of items an average 8-year-old should be able to pass.

Historically, the relationship between the number of items passed and the age of the child was expressed as a quotient of one's **mental age** to one's chronological age (thus the term *intelligence quotient*, or IQ). A child's mental age corresponds to the number of items he or she passes. If a child passes the number of items equal to the number passed by an average 12-year-old, the child's mental age is 12 years. The child's mental age is then divided by his or her chronological age, and the result is multiplied by 100. Thus, a 10-year-old child with a mental age of 10 years has an IQ of 100 (10/10 × 100). A 10-year-old with the mental age of 9.5 years has an IQ of 95 (9.5/10 × 100), and a 10-year old with a mental age of 12 has an IQ of 120 (12/10 × 100).

The concept of mental age has received substantial criticism (see Wechsler, 1974). One criticism of the concept is that a 7-year-old with a mental age of 10 and a 10-year-old with the same mental age are not, in reality, of comparable intelligence. They may have the same mental age with respect to test performance, but they do not have the same kind of mind. Also, a 5-year-old with a mental age of 6 has an IQ of 120; a 10-year-old with a comparable IQ has a mental age of 12. In the first case, the child's mental age is one year ahead of his chronological age; in the second case, there is a difference of two years.

These and other problems led test developers to abandon the concept of mental age and develop instead a **deviation IQ**. Children's performance is compared with that of children of their own age and not with the performance of older or younger children. Thus, tests can be constructed so that the statistical characteristics of IQ are the same at each age level. Modern tests are constructed so that IQ scores

FIGURE 13-3   Theoretical distribution of WISC-III scores. The test is constructed so that 50% of all people at a given age will have IQ scores of 100 and below, and 50% will have scores of 100 and above.

are distributed according to a normal distribution with specified statistical properties. The theoretical distribution of IQ scores for the WISC is shown in Figure 13-3. As can be seen, children with scores of 100 have IQs equal to or greater than 50% of the population. Children with scores of 115 have IQs equal to or greater than approximately 84% of the population. Thus, by knowing a child's IQ score, one knows where he or she stands with respect to intelligence relative to his or her agemates.

The renouncement of the concept of mental age and the use of the deviation IQ enable a more accurate comparison among children of a specified age. However, the use of the deviation IQ to express intelligence makes developmental contrasts difficult. IQ tests are not constructed to be a mechanism for understanding the development of intelligence. By using the deviation IQ, in fact, we hold developmental differences constant, so that we can make comparisons among agemates in the same way for children of all ages. As I noted earlier, this procedure has obvious advantages for making comparisons of children's intelligence. For the developmentalist, however, the difficulties arise when changes in intelligence over time are of interest.

There is nothing magic about the IQ test itself. It does not necessarily measure innate intelligence, nor does it necessarily reflect a constant value that will typify an individual throughout life. In fact, although IQ does correlate significantly with academic success and occupational status (Brody, 1997), many argue that it is limited in the type of mental functioning it measures and that to view an IQ score as an indication of a child's total intelligence is misleading (see especially the discussions of Gardner's and Ceci's theories later in this chapter).

Some Issues Regarding Standardized Tests

The remainder of this chapter deals with alternative approaches to the study of intelligence—basically, approaches that don't see IQ tests as the only or the best (or perhaps even a good) measure of intelligence. I think few people would argue that IQ tests are the last word in intelligence—that a score on a test accurately reflects one's true intelligence. But I think that most educators and scientists (but not all) who have given the subject serious thought would concur that IQ tests measure some aspect of intelligence, particularly as it relates to academic performance. I put myself in this large camp. But even in the area of predicting academic performance, IQ tests are far from perfect. For example, there has been much controversy about IQ testing of minority children, with critics arguing that the tests and the testing situation do not serve as a fair assessment for such children. In a different but related vein, recent evidence indicates that some of the standardized achievement tests used in making college admission decisions, such as the SAT and the ACT, might not be tapping the skills they purport to tap. I will look briefly at these two issues here.

IQ Tests and Minority Children

Minority children in the United States consistently score lower on IQ tests than white, middle-class children. In one respect, this should be expected, because IQ tests do their best job predicting school success, and minority children often perform more poorly in school than their majority counterparts. But does this mean that minority children are less intelligent than children from the majority? Posing this question requires one to evaluate what is meant

by intelligence and the extent to which IQ tests assess it.

IQ testing has had many critics, especially when it comes to evaluation of minority children's intelligence. The tests, state many critics, are based on skills and knowledge deemed important by the majority culture. Children from minority homes might not share the same values or have access to the same knowledge that middle-class children do, making the test culturally biased. There is a strong movement today pushing the idea that intelligence can only be meaningfully assessed within the culture in which a child lives (Laboratory of Comparative Human Cognition, 1983; Miller-Jones, 1989). Thus, although IQ tests measure accurately some aspects of intelligence for children from the majority culture, they do not assess intelligence adequately for minority children. Moreover, the rigorously standardized nature of IQ tests might be a detriment to minority children because the tests must be administered in a constant format. The examiner cannot provide feedback to a child and usually cannot probe a child's answers to determine if he or she has more knowledge than reflected by an initial response. Minority children might have different expectations of what type of answers the examiner is looking for, and children's competencies will be masked by the requirements of standard test administration (Miller-Jones, 1989).

Dalton Miller-Jones (1989) provides several examples of how a 5-year-old black child's performance on an IQ test could be underestimated because of the standardized nature of the test:

> Tester: "How are wood and coal alike? How are they the same?"
> Child: "They're hard."
> Tester: "An apple and a peach?"
> Child: "They taste good."
> Tester: "A ship and an automobile?"
> Child: "They're hard."
> Tester: "Iron and silver?"
> Child: "They're hard." (p. 362)

These answers all earn a score of zero, but does this mean that the child does not know the conceptual relation between iron and silver or between an apple and a peach? By the rules of the test, no feedback can be provided, and the child must guess what type of answer the examiner wants. There is nothing incorrect about the child's answers to these questions, but they do not fit the test makers' conceptions. They also do not likely exhaust this child's knowledge of the relations between these objects, but the test format precludes finding this out.

Other aspects of test administration also influence minority children's performance on IQ tests. The testing situation, for example, with a child sitting quietly across the table from an adult and answering a series of questions, might be more familiar and comfortable to a middle-class child than to a lower-class or minority child. Also, in most testing situations, the examiner is a member of a different ethnic and social class than the minority child, adding further to the discomfort and novelty of the testing situation.

Not all agree that there is bias against minority children in mental testing, of course (Jensen, 1998). Despite all the criticism, the tests are cost efficient and widely accepted (though not universally) by both educational professionals and the public. Yet most would argue that we could do a better job in assessing minority children's intelligence and achievement, and Miller-Jones (1989) makes five recommendations for improving minority assessment:

1. When assessing any area of intelligence, it is important to specify the cognitive processes that might be involved in the task or elicited by the stimuli.
2. Multiple tasks with different materials should be used with the same individual.
3. Tests must be appropriate for the culture from which the child comes.
4. The connection must be validated between the cognitive operations assessed by a test and the attainment of school-related concepts such as arithmetic and reading.
5. Procedures must be developed that permit an examiner to probe for the reasoning behind a child's answers.

Miller-Jones's advice is sound and applies to nonminority as well as to minority children.

Achievement Tests and Reading Comprehension

Although IQ tests are the crowning glory of the psychometric approach, achievement tests such as the Scholastic Assessment Test (SAT) and the American College Testing Assessment (ACT) have become a staple of the American educational system. The SAT and the ACT are taken by hundreds of thousands of college-bound students annually and consist of two major sections—the verbal and the mathematical—each assessing a variety of language and mathematical skills predictive of success in college.

One section of the verbal portion of both the SAT and the ACT is a reading comprehension test. On this test, students read short texts and then answer multiple-choice questions about them. These tests are designed to measure students' ability to read and understand English prose passages. But do they? In a series of experiments, college students were given the multiple-choice questions from reading comprehension sections of the SAT or the ACT and asked to guess the right answer without reading the text (Katz & Lautenschlager, 1994; Katz et al., 1990). Their performance was compared with that of a group of students who read the corresponding text before answering the questions and was related to their own performance on the entire verbal portion of the SAT.

The researchers reported that students not given the passages to read performed far better than expected by chance, and often nearly as well as students who actually read the passages. This was true for the ACT, an old version of the SAT, and a newer version (not yet in general use) of the SAT. For example, in the study by Katz and Lautenschlager (1994), correct performance of students who read the passages of the new SAT before answering the questions was 74.9%. Performance of students who answered the questions without reading the passages was 42.9%. Chance performance on this task is 20%. Similarly, for students taking the ACT reading comprehension test without reading the passages, correct performance was 48.9%. Students who read the passages scored 69.5%, with chance again being 20%. Students performed better when they read the passages, but "good guesses" resulted in performance substantially greater than expected by chance. Reading comprehension performance on both the SAT and ACT was related to how well students did on the overall verbal subtest of the SAT.

These findings suggest that performance on the reading comprehension sections of the SAT and ACT is not tapping reading ability, per se, but rather some other general verbal abilities. It's worth noting that students performed much closer to chance (20%) when they answered reading comprehension questions without reading the passages on the Graduate Record Exam (GRE) (percentage correct = 27.1%) (Katz & Lautenschlager, 1994).

Information-Processing Approaches to the Study of Intelligence

One criticism of the psychometric approach, and IQ tests specifically, is that test construction is based primarily on pragmatic considerations—which items discriminate reliably among children—and not on theoretical considerations (Sternberg, 1985). The factors that constitute intelligence are determined by statistical analyses and not on the basis of any a priori model of intelligence. As I noted earlier, however, it would be unfair to say that IQ tests are atheoretical. Nevertheless, pragmatic considerations of selecting items that discriminate among children of a given age are still of extreme importance in choosing which items will be included on the tests. Thus, although IQ tests can assess individual differences in intelligence well, they are less successful at providing insight into the nature of the intelligence that underlies test performance. This is critical not just from the point of view of theory, but also for practice. For instance, Detterman and Thompson (1997) propose that the key to improving education (particularly special education) is an understanding of the basic cognitive abilities that underlie individual differences in intelligence. With such an understanding, educational interventions can be individualized, and only through such practices will children, especially those who's style of learning differs from the majority, reap the benefit of educational research.

Individual differences in cognitive abilities have been extensively studied from the information-processing perspective. In a sense, the same mechanisms used to describe developmental function from an information-processing perspective can be used to describe individual differences. Thus, for example, differences in how information is encoded, speed of processing, how easily information is categorized, and metacognition can all be sources of individual (as well as developmental) differences in thinking and intelligence.

When cognitive psychologists examine individual differences in children's thinking, they often make contrasts between groups known to vary on the basis of IQ (for example, normal children and children with mental retardation or gifted and nongifted children) or between children matched in IQ who differ on the basis of some academic ability (for example, good and poor readers or learning-disabled and nondisabled children). In such studies, researchers attempt to discover the underlying processes responsible for group differences in IQ, task performance, or academic skill. No attempt will be made here to assess the origins of mental retardation, learning and reading disabilities, or giftedness. The etiologies of these intellectual exceptionalities are interesting and important but would require separate chapters (or books) to investigate properly (although Chapter 12 discussed possible origins of reading and math disabilities). Rather, I will examine differences in cognitive processing between exceptional and normal children to elucidate the nature of cognition in general and to discover educationally important differences in thinking among these groups of children.

Strategies

Research contrasting children with and without mental retardation has indicated that the tendency to use memory and problem-solving strategies is a major cognitive difference between the two groups. Strategies allow people to plan the course of their cognitive operations, to anticipate the consequences of their acts and the acts of others. Given this view of strategies, it is not surprising that many researchers have proposed that strategies are a central aspect of intelligence (Bray, Fletcher, & Turner, 1996; Das, 1984). For example, J. P. Das (1984) has written that "what qualifies as intelligence may be the ability to plan or structure one's behavior with an end in view. The more efficient and parsimonious the plan is, the more intelligent the resulting behavior" (p. 116).

A common finding on memory and learning tasks is that normal children are more likely than children with mental retardation to use strategies to aid their performance (Bray & Turner, 1986; Brooks, Sperber, & McCauley, 1984). For example, in memory studies where normal children and children with mental retardation are given the opportunity to rehearse information before testing, children with mental retardation are less likely to rehearse in preparation for recall than are normal children of the same age. Similarly, when children are required to rehearse (as in the overt-rehearsal procedure described in Chapter 8; see Ornstein, Naus, & Liberty, 1975), qualitative differences in rehearsal are found. Children and adolescents with retardation are more likely to rehearse one or two unique items each time they rehearse than they are to rehearse several different items together (cumulative rehearsal). Such a simple repetition strategy is similar to that observed for younger normal children (see Bray & Turner, 1986). In other words, children with mental retardation show deficient rehearsal strategies, both in the amount they rehearse and the style of rehearsal, which are directly related to their levels of recall. This hypothesis of strategy deficiency is not limited to free recall and the strategy of rehearsal but has also been proposed for a variety of problem-solving tasks and strategies (see Brooks et al., 1984).

Children with retardation, like young children, can be trained to use memory and learning strategies, with corresponding improvements in performance. Similarly, they are also likely to switch back to a nonstrategic style on subsequent tasks (Belmont, Ferretti, & Mitchel, 1982; Campione et al., 1985). For example, Joseph Campione and his colleagues (1985) trained adolescents with mild retardation and normal children (matched in mental age) to solve matrix problems selected from the Raven's Progressive Matrices Test. Figure 13-4 presents two examples of these problems. To solve the matrices, children must select from six alternatives the one that best completes the matrix. For the first matrix, they must realize that the pattern has been rotated. The correct response for this problem is a circle with the filled quadrant oriented in the proper direction (about 5 o'clock). In the second example, the children must learn a subtraction strategy, realizing that the alternative on the far right is the same as the object on the far left with the smaller, inside object deleted. The correct response for this problem would be an empty diamond. Both the younger normal children and the adolescents with mental retardation learned how to solve the various matrix problems. When the children were presented with new problems, however, differences between the groups were found. The normal children were able to transfer their newly learned strategies to other problems much more effectively than the adolescents with mental retardation were. This was true both of problems similar to those on which they had been trained and of problems that were slightly novel. The researchers argued that their results point to an important difference in cognitive functioning between children with and without mental retardation and provide support for the significance of transfer mechanisms to theories of intelligence.

Similar differences in strategy implementation have been hypothesized to explain the difference in task performance between good and poor readers, between learning-disabled and nondisabled children, and between gifted and nongifted children (Bauer, 1979; Bauer & Newman, 1991). For example, Bauer (1979) gave 9- and 10-year-old learning disabled (LD) and non-learning disabled (non-LD) children a series of free-recall tasks. No group differences were found for the last several items on the

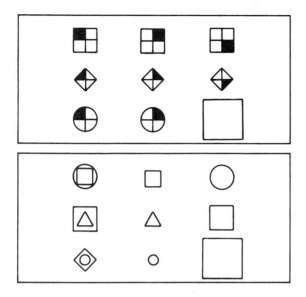

FIGURE 13-4 Examples of matrices used in a training study. Children must select an alternative that will complete the pattern in each matrix. For the first problem, the correct answer would be a circle with a black lower right-hand quadrant; for the second problem, the correct answer would be a diamond shape. SOURCE: "Breakdown of Flexible Use of Information: Intelligence-Related Differences in Transfer Following Equivalent Learning Performance," by J. C. Campione, A. L. Brown, R. A. Ferrara, R. S. Jones, and E. Steinberg, 1985, *Intelligence*, 9, 297–315. Copyright © 1985 Ablex Publishing Corporation. Reprinted by permission.

lists. Recall for these last items was characteristically high and was attributed to children's emptying the contents of their short-term store, without the need of any specific strategy. In contrast, large group differences were noted in the recall of items from the beginning of the list. Recall of items from the beginning of a list has usually been interpreted as reflecting the use of strategies. In other words, the LD children differed from the nondisabled children in strategy use but not in nonstrategic functioning. This interpretation was bolstered by the results of two subsequent experiments in which Bauer observed lower levels of categorical clustering (an indication of the memory strategy of organization; see Chapter 8) for the LD children. Similar observa-

tions have been made for poor readers, who likewise show lower levels of memory performance than do good readers of equal IQ (Dallago & Moely, 1980; Goldstein, Hasher, & Stein, 1983).

In other research, Jane Gaultney (1998) statistically equated the amount of strategy use on memory tasks between third-, fourth-, and fifth-grade LD and non-LD children and found that non-LD children benefited more from comparable strategy use than LD children. That is, even when LD children were strategic (sometimes as strategic as non-LD children), they didn't reap the benefits of the strategy in memory performance compared with the non-LD children. This is an indication of a utilization deficiency, and Gaultney proposed that the LD children exerted more mental effort executing the memory strategies than the non-LD children did, and as a result had less mental capacity available for holding items in working memory.

Differences in strategy use are sometimes found to be a source of differences in task performance between gifted and nongifted children (Gaultney, Bjorklund, & Goldstein, 1996; Geary & Brown, 1991). For example, in a series of free recall experiments, Gaultney and her colleagues (1996) contrasted gifted and nongifted middle-school children for their use of memory strategies and found that gifted children consistently were more likely to be strategic than their nongifted peers. One interesting finding of their study was that, despite the greater use of strategies by gifted than nongifted children, it was more important to task performance for the nongifted children to be strategic than for the gifted children. This is illustrated by looking at the average performance of children classified as strategic compared with those classified as nonstrategic for the gifted and nongifted children in this study. Figure 13-5 presents the mean difference in recall between the strategic children and nonstrategic children over five trials, separately for the gifted and nongifted children. The higher the score, the greater advantage to recall there was for being strategic. The first thing to note is that all the scores are positive (from a little over 1 word to about 3.5 words remembered per trial). This means that, on

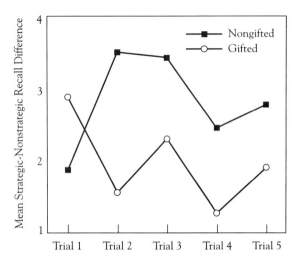

FIGURE 13-5 Mean strategic minus nonstrategic difference in recall for gifted and nongifted children at each trial. The higher the score, the greater the advantage for being strategic. SOURCE: Gaultney, J. F., Bjorklund, D. F., & Goldstein, D. (1996). To be young, gifted, and strategic: Advantages for memory performance. *Journal of Experimental Child Psychology, 61,* p. 51.

average, it was always to a child's advantage to be strategic. But look at the difference between the gifted and nongifted children. Except for the first trial, it made a greater difference in amount recalled for the nongifted children to be strategic than it did for the gifted children. That is, the difference between nongifted children who used a memory strategy and those who did not was quite large. This difference was much smaller for the gifted children.

Why should being strategic be more important for nongifted than gifted children? Gaultney and her colleagues proposed that many gifted children did not need strategies to perform reasonably well on this task. When nonstrategic gifted and nongifted children were compared, the gifted children did significantly better. Thus, Gaultney and her colleagues proposed that much of the superior performance of the gifted children was mediated by nonstrategic factors, including, perhaps, faster speed of processing and a more elaborated knowledge base.

Interestingly, the tendency of many gifted children to "just know" an answer, could sometimes have a negative side effect. For example, Harnishfeger and Bjorklund (1990b) speculated that some gifted children have not needed to use deliberate learning and memory strategies during the elementary school years because they have been able to apprehend course material in a relatively automatic fashion. When the cognitive demands become more challenging in middle- or high-school, these children might be at a disadvantage relative to their lower-IQ but more strategic peers, accounting, in part, for some of the academic difficulties some gifted teenagers encounter. I have seen similar difficulties in some bright students making the transition from high school to college or from junior college to university.

In other research, Geary and Brown (1991) assessed gifted, nongifted, and mathematically disabled third- and fourth-grade children's selection and use of strategies in solving a series of addition problems. All the children used some combination of strategies to solve the problems, but the gifted children used the most mature mix of strategies, followed by the normal children and finally the mathematically disabled children. Geary and Brown concluded that the principal reason for the group differences in strategy use in this experiment was in children's long-term memory organization of basic addition facts. The gifted third- and fourth-grade children knew their basic math facts (9 + 7 = 16; 6 + 8 = 14) better than the other two groups of children, permitting them to use more efficient strategies. In other words, one of the reasons for gifted children's more effective use of strategies was their greater knowledge base.

Knowledge Base

Just as developmental differences can be explained, in part, by differences in knowledge base (see Chapters 5, 8, and 10), so can individual differences. Concerning memory differences between good and poor readers, for example, some researchers have suggested that they are more likely to stem from differences in knowledge base than from differences in strategy use. The semantic memories of poor readers are not as well developed as the semantic memories of good readers are, resulting in the inefficient retrieval of word meaning from long-term store and, thus, less effective processing of verbal information (Bjorklund & Bernholtz, 1986; Vellutino & Scanlon, 1985). This possibility was illustrated in a study by Bjorklund and Bernholtz (1986). Good and poor junior high school readers (average age = 13 years), matched for IQ, were given a series of concept and memory tasks. In a first session, children were asked to select examples from specified natural language categories (for example, birds, clothes, tools) and to rate each item in terms of how typical it was of its category. (Category typicality was discussed in Chapter 7.) In general, differences in judged typicality affect the performance of both children and adults on a variety of tasks, and children's judgments become more adultlike with age. Bjorklund and Bernholtz reported that the judgments of the 13-year-old poor readers resembled those of normal 9-year-olds and were less adultlike than were the ratings of the good readers. In other words, differences in the semantic memory organization of good and poor 13-year-old readers were found with respect to category typicality.

In later experiments, children were given sets of 12 typical and 12 atypical items to recall in any order they wanted. In one experiment, the typicality of the items was based on norms generated by adults (adult-generated lists). In another experiment, the typicality of the items was based on each child's self-generated norms, obtained from the earlier session (self-generated lists). Significant differences in memory performance were observed only for the adult-generated lists. Recall was comparable between the good and poor readers when typical and atypical category items were selected based on each child's own judgments. Furthermore, measures of strategy use in these experiments (based on amount of clustering and latencies between the recall of words) indicated that the good readers were no more strategic than the poor readers were. Rather, their superior memory performance could best be attributed to differences in knowledge base. These results do not mean that there are no strategic differences between good and poor readers. Rather, the results indicate that differences in knowledge

base contribute significantly to performance differences observed between these two groups of children and might be partly responsible for any apparent differences noted in strategy use.

In related research, Scott, Greenfield, and Sterental (1986) reported differences in knowledge of familiar words between groups of 6- to 8-year-old LD and non-LD students. Children were presented with a series of four pictures from a single superordinate category (for example, banana, apple, strawberries, orange: fruit). Twelve superordinate categories were studied in all. The children were asked a series of questions concerning how the items were alike and different from one another. LD and non-LD children differed considerably on the number of responses they provided to these questions, revealing a difference in knowledge of familiar superordinate categories. That is, as in the study by Bjorklund and Bernholtz (1986) of 13-year-old good and poor readers, a major difference between the LD and non-LD children was in their knowledge base for familiar language concepts.

One study that demonstrates the importance of knowledge base in learning and memory and its relation to IQ is that of Schneider, Körkel, and Weinert (1989). German children in grades 3, 5, and 7 were evaluated for their knowledge of soccer and were classified as soccer experts or soccer novices. The children were also administered a series of intelligence tests, and these results, along with their school grades in math and German, were used to classify them as successful or unsuccessful learners. The children were then presented with a well-organized narrative text about soccer and were later asked to recall it. Amount remembered was computed by number of idea units the children recalled about the story. Patterns of results with respect to expertise and IQ were similar for the children at each of the three grade levels and are summarized (averaged over grade) in Figure 13-6. As would be expected, memory performance was better for the soccer experts than for the soccer novices. However, the researchers reported no difference in performance between the academically successful learners and the unsuccessful ones. That is, being a good learner (and having a high IQ) did not result in

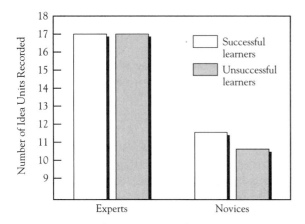

FIGURE 13-6 Number of idea units remembered about a soccer story for high- and low-aptitude soccer experts and soccer novices. In this case, being an expert eliminated any effect of academic aptitude (IQ) on performance. SOURCE: Adapted from data presented in Schneider, W., Körkel, J., & Weinert, F. E. (1989). Domain-specific knowledge and memory performance: A comparison of high- and low-aptitude children. *Journal of Educational Psychology, 81*, 306–312.

better performance by either the expert or the novice children. Having a detailed knowledge of the subject matter was enough to yield high levels of memory performance. Similarly, having an impoverished knowledge of the subject matter was enough to yield low levels of performance, regardless of a child's level of IQ (see also Recht & Leslie, 1988; Walker, 1987). Although IQ might be related to academic performance, such as reading comprehension, what seems especially important for intelligent performance is knowledge. Children with substantial knowledge of a subject act smart when dealing with matter from that subject area, independent of their level of IQ.

This situation is admittedly not typical. In most contexts, successful learners do, of course, perform better than unsuccessful learners do. One important reason why this is so, however, is that successful learners generally know more about the things they are dealing with than unsuccessful learners do. Successful learners acquire information more readily and thus have a more elaborated knowledge base on which to base future learning. The more children

know, the more easily they are able to learn and remember new information.

A detailed knowledge base does not always eliminate IQ effects, however. In studies by Wolfgang Schneider and David Bjorklund (1992; Schneider, Bjorklund & Maier-Brückner, 1996), high- and low-IQ second- and fourth-grade children were classified as soccer experts and novices and given two sort-recall memory tasks. Children were given sets of written words to remember, which they could sort into categories before recalling them (see Chapter 8). On one task, sets of soccer-related words in one of four categories (soccer plays, equipment, players, parts of the field) were used as stimuli; in the second task, sets of words from familiar language categories were used (tools, fruits, mammals, vehicles—the nonsoccer list). As in the study by Schneider and his colleagues (1989) that examined story recall, experts remembered more than novices from the soccer-related list (but not, of course, from the nonsoccer-related list). However, the effect of IQ was not eliminated in these studies, with high-IQ children remembering more than low-IQ children on both the soccer and nonsoccer lists, regardless of level of expertise. Schneider and Bjorklund (1992) argued that intelligence played a greater role here than in the story-recall experiment because of the more deliberate encoding strategies used on sort-recall tasks. Expertise can reduce or eliminate the impact of intelligence (as measured by IQ) in some situations, but IQ will have a residual effect when explicit strategies, such as those used in sort-recall tasks, are called for.

Speed of Information Processing

Older children perform most, if not all, aspects of information processing faster than younger children do (see Kail, 1991). Moreover, both children and adults show similar patterns of reaction times across a large variety of tasks (Kail & Salthouse, 1994). Similar differences in speed of retrieval between gifted and nongifted children (Saccuzzo, Johnson, & Guertin, 1994) and between LD and non-LD children (Ceci, 1983) have also been observed. It is possible that the differences in memory performance between LD and non-LD children and between good and poor readers attributed to strategy use or knowledge base can be mediated by differences in speed of processing. Some children might require more time to activate relevant concepts used on these memory and problem-solving tasks than other children do, which in turn requires greater expenditure of mental effort. The increased effort associated with the slower retrieval of language terms, for example, might be indirectly responsible for the less strategic approach of these children to the task and, thus, for their overall lower levels of performance.

In addition to distinguishing LD from non-LD children and good readers from poor ones, the efficiency of retrieval from long-term memory has been hypothesized to be an important component in individual differences in intelligence in the general population (Jensen, 1998). Most forms of intelligence require retrieving information in memory and acting on that information. Several researchers have reasoned that people who retrieve information quickly and efficiently will display an advantage on cognitive tasks, particularly verbal ones. Hunt and his colleagues provided support for this position using a variety of experimental tasks. In one study, Hunt, Davidson, and Lansman (1981) asked adults to verify category statements such as "A dog is an animal." They found that the time needed to confirm such statements correlated significantly with verbal ability.

Although not all studies examining the relationship between speed of processing and intelligence have found high correlations (List, Keating, & Merriman, 1985), most, looking at both children and adults, do (Hutton, Wilding, & Hudson, 1997; Keating & Bobbitt, 1979). Moreover, speed of information processing correlates significantly both with performance on timed tests, when speed is important, and on nontimed tests, when fast responding is irrelevant (Vernon & Kantor, 1986). Several reviews of the literature have found moderate correlations (between about −.30 and −.50) between speed of responding and intelligence, with faster responding (and thus presumably faster information processing) being associated with higher IQs (Jensen, 1998). The suggestion from this pattern of results, along with the evidence from the developmental lit-

erature indicating the role of speed of processing in cognitive development (Kail, 1991), suggests that speed of processing is an important component of individual differences in intelligence.

Individual differences in speed of processing are reliable but often small, and they point to important differences in intelligence at a microscopic level. Differences are often in milliseconds, and it may be wondered what the significance of a 50-millisecond (1/20th of a second) difference might be with respect to intelligence. Although such differences are small, they can be important indeed. Perhaps one of the most important cognitive skills for people in technological societies is reading. Small differences in rate of retrieving the meaning of a word or in integrating letters to form words can, over a very short time, result in substantial differences in reading rate and reading comprehension.

Working Memory

There seems little debate that speed of processing is an important component to general intelligence. But might there be other basic-level mechanisms that are equally or more important? Linda Miller and Philip Vernon (1996) proposed that working memory is a good candidate for a basic-level process that plays an important role in intelligence beyond the impact of speed of processing.

Miller and Vernon (1996) tested children between 4 and 6 years of age. Children were administered the WISC and batteries of reaction-time and working-memory tasks. Not surprisingly, children became faster with age and working-memory span increased with age. Also, when general reaction time and memory factors were computed, the two were found to correlate significantly (−.44; the shorter the reaction time, the greater working memory tended to be). This is consistent with research reported in Chapter 5 on the relation between speed of item identification and memory span (Hulme et al., 1984). Reaction time was also significantly correlated with IQ at each age (overall correlation = −.42), as would be expected from the research reviewed earlier. The correlation between IQ and working memory, however, was even greater (.82), and remained significant even after the effects of reaction time and age were taken into consideration. This led Miller and Vernon to the conclusion that, for children between the ages of 4 and 6 years, "memory accounts for significant variability in intelligence" (p. 184). Reaction time, in contrast, has a smaller role in intelligence, at least once individual differences in working memory are taken into consideration.

Metacognition

Speed of processing and working memory are clearly important components of intelligence. Yet, other more macro processes vary among people and probably contribute to individual differences in intelligence. Strategies such as rehearsal have already been mentioned. A related phenomenon that has been postulated as being significant to individual differences in intelligence is metacognition, a person's understanding of his or her own cognitive abilities (Brown, 1978; Sternberg, 1985). Basically, the brighter individuals of any age are those who possess the executive functions to monitor their task performance and to apply the techniques they possess to solve a problem. John Borkowski and his colleagues have suggested that differences in metacognition are a major cause of differences in strategy use and training effectiveness between children with and without mental retardation (Borkowski, Reid, & Kurtz, 1984), between reflective and impulsive children (Borkowski et al., 1983), between gifted and nongifted children (Borkowski & Peck, 1986), and between children within the normal range of intelligence (Carr, Borkowski, & Maxwell, 1991).

In a study by Borkowski and Peck (1986), gifted and nongifted 7- and 8-year-olds were instructed to use an elaboration strategy or a simpler clustering strategy on a memory task. They were later tested for transfer of the strategy to other memory problems. Elaboration involves creating a relationship between two items, so that the presentation of one item will elicit the recall of the other. For example, if I wanted to remember the pair of words *banana-coat*, I might form an image of a bunch of bananas hanging in a closet where I usually find my coat. Or I might think that a banana peel covers a banana in

a way similar to how a coat covers my body. Although forming such relations may seem like a lot of work, the memory performance of both children and adults is facilitated by the use of an elaboration strategy (see Pressley, 1982; Chapter 8). For the children who received the clustering instructions (for example, "Try to remember words from the same category together"), training was less explicit than it was for the children who were trained to use the elaboration strategy. Would both the gifted and nongifted children be able to benefit from the training, and would the extent of training affect the transfer of the strategy differently for the two groups of children?

Both the gifted and the nongifted children who were trained in the elaboration strategy learned it. Differences between the groups for this strategy became apparent during a generalization task, when the children were given different sets of problems to learn. The gifted children were more likely to generalize the strategy they had learned than were the nongifted children, with the extent of generalization being significantly related to scores on a battery of metamemory questions. For the clustering strategy, differences in training as well as transfer between the two groups of children were noted. The gifted children benefited more from the minimal training than did the nongifted children. This difference was extended to the transfer trials. That is, gifted children required less explicit prompting before they would learn a strategy and generalize it to new situations. According to Borkowski and Peck (1986), because of their greater metamemory awareness, "gifted children realized the effectiveness of the strategy and applied it appropriately even without the aid of complete and explicit instructions" (p. 193). Although gifted children apparently do not always show greater metacognitive awareness relative to nongifted children (see Alexander & Schwanenflugel, 1996; Alexander, Schwanenflugel, & Carr, 1995), when task performance is challenging, gifted children typically show greater metacognitive knowledge than their nongifted peers (Kurtz & Weinert, 1989).

Although the picture is obviously complex, information-processing models provide researchers with specific aspects of cognition to investigate as the source of intellectual differences among people and experimental methods to facilitate the search. Although my bias is certainly showing here, I believe that models that examine developmental changes in information processing are likely to lead the field in the years to come in producing important and exciting insights into individual differences in human intelligence (see Bjorklund & Schneider, 1996).

Piagetian Approaches to the Study of Intelligence

Information-processing approaches to individual differences in children's thinking have the advantage of reasonably well-developed theories and methods that can be applied for understanding intelligence. As with psychometric approaches, however, there is nothing inherently developmental about information-processing theories. One theory that is explicitly developmental in its orientation is Piaget's. Although Piaget himself did not apply his theory to individual differences, others have, and some of this research is now examined briefly.

Several researchers have demonstrated that individual differences on Piagetian tasks (for example, conservation, classification) predict academic ability. For instance, performance on batteries of Piagetian tasks has been shown to predict early (first- and second-grade) academic skills as well as or even better than standardized IQ tests (Kingma, 1984; Lunzar, Dolan, & Wilkinson, 1976). In related research, Byrd and Gholson (1985) reported that degree of operativity (evidenced by performance on a series of conservation and classification tasks) was significantly related to the reading ability of second- and fourth-grade children. In fact, operativity was related to a variety of reading-related measures, including memory, metamemory, and metareading (knowledge about reading), although these other measures correlated only slightly with one another. These findings led Byrd and Gholson to conclude that developmental and individual differences in reading strategies are not mediated by memory skills

or knowledge about memory strategies as much as they are by operative (that is, logical) abilities.

In other research, Deanna Kuhn (1976), testing middle-class children from the first through the seventh grades, failed to find a significant correspondence between Piagetian task performance and IQ for her older groups of children. All the children were administered the WISC and a series of Piagetian tasks. The Piagetian tasks for the younger children (first through third grade) included class inclusion, seriation, conservation of amount, and multiple classification. The older children were given three tests of formal operational ability (Inhelder & Piaget, 1958), including the pendulum problem that was discussed in Chapter 4. Kuhn reported a significant relation between scores on the battery of Piagetian tasks and IQ for 6- to 8-year-olds (correlation = .69) but not for children approaching formal operations (correlation = .22). Kuhn suggested that the environmental factors causing children to excel on IQ tests are not the same as those affecting the rate of progress through Piagetian stages. Such environmental influences increase over time, Kuhn proposed, resulting in reduced correspondence between Piagetian and psychometric tests with advancing age.

Wolfgang Schneider and his colleagues (1999) observed an opposite pattern of correlations between Piagetian and psychometric tests. In their longitudinal study, correlations between preschool tests of cognitive ability (for example, conservation of number) and psychometric tests were low (average correlation = .24), whereas the relation between formal reasoning tests given in grades 4 through 6 and psychometric tests was higher (median correlation = .48). An additional and impressive finding in this study was the high correlations between psychometric tests given at ages 7 and 9 and formal and scientific reasoning tests given at ages 11 and 12 (median correlation = .51). In other words, psychometric and Piagetian-type tasks not only correlated significantly with one another when they were administered at the same point in time, but psychometric tests given during the elementary school years predicted logical reasoning abilities five years later.

Why the contradiction between the findings of the Schneider group and Kuhn? The tasks used by Schneider and his colleagues to assess preschool cognition reflect some of the earliest acquired cognitive accomplishments during this time (number conservation is typically the first conservation task children master), whereas those used by Kuhn reflect abilities usually acquired during the elementary school years (for example, class inclusion, multiple classification). One interpretation of these findings is that tasks that assess the transition from pre- to concrete operations, as used by Kuhn, tap similar underlying cognitive abilities as do psychometric tests, whereas tasks that assess earlier-developing skills, such as those used by Schneider and his colleagues, tap cognitive abilities that are qualitatively different from those tapped by psychometric tests (Bjorklund, 1999). That is, the nature of early intelligence is more homogenous during the preschool years than it is by age 6 or 7 years.

In other research, Lloyd Humphreys and his colleagues have examined the relationship between a battery of Piagetian tasks, Wechsler IQ tests, and academic ability for children of varying intellectual aptitudes (normal children and children with mental retardation) and ages (6 to 18 years) (Humphreys, 1980; Humphreys & Parsons, 1979; Humphreys, Rich, & Davey, 1985). Humphreys and his colleagues administered 27 different Piagetian tasks to the children. The tasks ranged from those that assessed early concrete operational abilities to those that evaluated formal operational skills. Correlations between the children's performance on Piagetian tasks and on Wechsler IQ tests were in excess of .80. Comparable results were reported when a subset of only 13 Piagetian tasks was selected. Humphreys also reported significant correlations between sets of Piagetian tasks and measures of academic achievement (correlations in excess of .70), only slightly lower than those found with verbal IQ. Furthermore, correlations between performance on these tasks and a general intelligence factor (g) were also high for most tasks, indicating to Humphreys that the battery of Piagetian tasks measures the same aspect of general intelligence as do psychometric tests. In general, there was a great deal of over-

lap among the Piagetian tasks, the Wechsler IQ scales, and measures of academic achievement. However, there were some differences between the tasks in the intellectual skills they assessed. Humphreys was not able to specify the nature of these differences, but he asserted that given the current data, each measure is a valid index of intelligence (Humphreys et al., 1985).

In comparison with researchers adhering to the psychometric and information-processing approaches, Piagetian researchers have done comparatively little work on individual differences in children's thinking. This is understandable given Piaget's emphasis on developmental function. What has been done, however, is encouraging. For example, the data of Kuhn (1976) and Schneider and his colleagues (1999) suggest that the relationship between the intelligence assessed by Piagetian measures and psychometrically measured intelligence can vary as a function of developmental level— that is, that the nature of intelligence changes with age, influencing patterns of individual differences. And Humphreys's work demonstrates that statistical analyses typically used with psychometric data can be applied successfully to Piagetian tests of intelligence. Piaget's theory has been a favorite of many educators for years, and standardized variants of Piagetian tasks, should they be developed, may be well received and used in the future.

Sternberg's Triarchic Theory of Intelligence

A theory of intelligence that has received substantial attention is Robert Sternberg's (1985) **triarchic theory**. The model includes three subtheories—the contextual, the experiential, and the componential—each of which is examined briefly.

The Contextual Subtheory

The **contextual subtheory** holds that intelligence must be viewed in the context in which it occurs. Intelligent behaviors for the middle-class American schoolchild might not be considered intelligent for the ghetto dropout or the unschooled Guatemalan farm boy. Sternberg (1997) defines intelligence as "the mental activities necessary for adaptation to, as well as shaping and selection of, any environmental context. According to this definition, intelligence is not just reactive to the environment but also active in forming it. It offers people an opportunity to respond flexibly to challenging situations" (p. 1030). By defining intelligence in terms of real-world environments, he stresses the importance of the external as well as the internal world to intelligence. Such a definition also avoids the circularity of theories that basically define intelligence as a score on an IQ test (or a test of information processing).

From this definition, Sternberg proposes three processes of intelligence: *adaptation, selection,* and *shaping.* Adaptation is adjustment of one's behavior to achieve a good fit with one's environment. When adaptation is not possible or not desirable, a person can select an alternative environment in which he or she can adapt well. Failing to adapt to the whims of a new supervisor, for example, a person can choose to quit her job and select another. Or a child might find it difficult to get along with children in the neighborhood and instead become friendly with other children from school who do not live as close by. If for some reason a new environment cannot be selected, however, a person can attempt to shape the environment. The employee can try to convince her supervisor to change his ways or may go over his head to bring changes from above. The child can try to alter the behavior of his neighborhood peers by placating them with his mother's cookies or by inviting one child at a time over to play instead of inviting the entire group.

Although these three processes typify intelligence universally, what is required for adaptation, selection, and shaping will vary among different groups of people, so that a single set of behaviors cannot be specified as intelligent for all individuals. Also, what is deemed to be intelligent at one point in life might not be so judged later. For example, because children have less freedom than adults to select new environments and are often powerless to shape significantly certain aspects of these environ-

ments, adapting to their uncomfortable surroundings might be the most intelligent option they have. Thus, whereas the school-phobic adult will select nonacademic environments, the 10-year-old child typically cannot, making adaptation the most intelligent choice.

Basically, the contextual subtheory is one of **cultural relativism**. Intellectual skills that are critical for survival in one culture might not be as important in another. Likewise, important intellectual skills within a culture can undergo some change from one generation to another. For example, arithmetic computation has unquestionably been a vital skill for people in technological societies. The significance of arithmetic to intelligence was noted by Wechsler in the construction of the WISC and WAIS and their subsequent revisions: each has an arithmetic subtest. Yet, with the widespread use of calculators, being able to add and subtract numbers quickly and accurately becomes a little less critical to everyday functioning. Although I would not care to say that arithmetic computation will become unimportant, in the generations ahead it will probably be viewed as much less critical to intelligence than it is today and, certainly, than it was a generation ago.

Sternberg is not the only person to propose a theory of intelligence that is culturally relative (see, for example, Laboratory of Comparative Human Cognition, 1983). Such theories have rightly been criticized, however, for preventing any general conclusions about the universal nature of human intellectual functioning. According to such theories, everything is relative, and thus intelligence can be studied only from the perspective of a particular culture or subculture. Sternberg avoids this problem by combining his contextual subtheory with the experiential and componential subtheories, which propose aspects of intelligence that are universal.

The Experiential Subtheory

The **experiential subtheory** is concerned with how prior knowledge influences performance on certain cognitive tasks. More specifically, the subtheory examines the ability to deal with novelty and the degree to which processing is automatized (that is, made to involve relatively little mental effort). Both skills are highly dependent upon experience. A stimulus is novel only to the extent that it differs in some way from what is already familiar (Rheingold, 1985). Similarly, newly acquired processing skills are rarely executed effortlessly but require substantial expenditure of one's limited mental effort for their deployment. Only when a skill has been exercised frequently does it become automatized (Shiffrin & Schneider, 1977). Sternberg proposes that how people respond to novelty and the ease with which they can automatize information processing are important and universal aspects of intelligence.

The importance of such skills is apparent in any occupation. Good scientists must be able to apprehend quickly the relevant factors that are influencing whatever phenomenon they are concerned with. If scientists are to make major contributions to their field, however, they must also be able to devise clever ways of testing their hypotheses and to appreciate the significance of an unexpected result. These factors are important not only in the ivory tower but also in more worldly occupations. This importance was made apparent to me by an electrician who installed three ceiling fans in my home after two other electricians had failed. He quickly discerned what approach to take, and after nine hours of running into more obstacles than I knew existed in my walls and above my ceilings, he finished the task. After I expressed my appreciation for a job well done, the electrician commented: "Any yahoo can lay wire in a straight line. It only takes brains when things don't go as you planned."

The experiential subtheory suggests what tasks are good indicators of intelligence—namely, those that involve dealing with novelty or automatic processing for their successful completion. Many of the laboratory tasks of modern cognitive psychology are good candidates for assessing intelligence because they stress speed of responding, which is a good indicator of the extent to which processing has become automatized. For example, simple letter-identification tasks, in which people must respond as rapidly as possible to signal the presence of a specified letter, measure the degree to which processing

for this overlearned code (the alphabet) is automatized. Similarly, word-identification tasks (deciding whether a letter string is a word or not) and category-identification tasks (deciding whether a word is a member of a specified category or not) also test automatic processing. More complex laboratory tasks such as solving analogies or syllogisms probably assess aspects of both automatic processing and response to novelty. Similarly, many items on psychometric batteries test the same processes as do lab tasks and, Sternberg asserts, are probably better estimators of intelligence. That is because these items are usually more difficult than the lab tasks, involving, on the average, greater degrees of novelty. Examples of psychometric test items that would fit Sternberg's experiential subtheory include picture arrangement ("Put these pictures together so that they make a story"), similarities ("How are television and education alike?"), and comprehension ("Why might it be important that Supreme Court judges be appointed and not elected?").

The Componential Subtheory

The **componential subtheory** is Sternberg's information-processing model of cognition. Sternberg (1997) argues that intelligence has a common core of mental processes that can be used in any environmental context or culture. These include recognizing the existence and defining the nature of a problem; representing information about the problem; devising a strategy for solving the problem; allocating sufficient mental resources to solve the problem; and monitoring and evaluating one's solution to the problem. How does one go about doing all these things? Basically, they require different aspects of information processing.

Briefly, Sternberg proposed three general types of information-processing components: metacomponents, performance components, and knowledge-acquisition components. *Metacomponents* are metacognitive abilities, involving the monitoring of task performance and the allocation of attentional resources. *Performance components* include encoding, mental comparison, and retrieval of information.

And *knowledge-acquisition components* are the processes involved in gaining new knowledge and selectively acting on recently encoded information and information in one's long-term store. These three components interact so that deficits in any one component can result in deficits in any of the other components. Individual differences in any of these components reflect differences in how people process information and, thus, important differences in intelligence.

Following Sternberg's componential subtheory, why should intelligence increase with age? The major reason is a growth in knowledge base. The knowledge-acquisition components provide a mechanism for a steadily increasing knowledge base. As the knowledge base increases, more sophisticated forms of knowledge acquisition are possible, which, in turn, further increase the knowledge base. The components lead to increases in knowledge, which lead to more effective use of the components, and so on. Similarly, feedback from the knowledge-acquisition and performance components to the metacomponents can result in improved metacognition. This leads to increased self-monitoring, which, in turn, results in the increased efficacy of the metacomponents. Again, feedback loops among the components lead to increased efficiency and, thus, a smarter individual. In general, the mechanisms that explain how intelligence develops in children are basically the same mechanisms that explain how a person becomes more effective at a particular task with increased experience.

Although the triarchic theory has three distinct parts, Sternberg stresses that they work together in an integrated fashion. Figure 13-7 (from Sternberg, 1988) illustrates this interaction. Starting with the bottom of the figure, we must first look at the information-processing components of intelligence and their interactions. We must realize, however, that these components can be applied to a broad range of situations, including those in which we are highly familiar (for which automatization is likely) to those in which we are highly unfamiliar, or novel. Finally, we must evaluate how these aspects of intelligence affect the external world, and how we adapt, select, or shape the contexts in which we live.

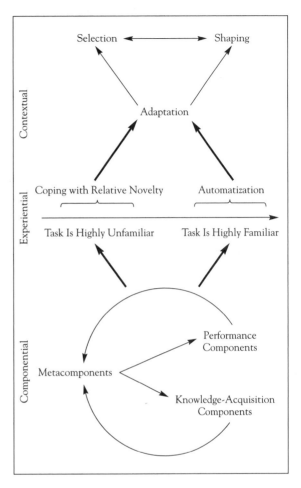

FIGURE 13-7   Relationships among the various aspects of the triarchic theory of intelligence. SOURCE: Sternberg, R. J. (1988). *The triarchic mind: A new theory of human intelligence.* New York: Viking.

The Triarchic Theory Applied to Education

Each of the three subtheories of Sternberg's triarchic theory has a corresponding style of thinking associated with it. People strong with respect to the contextual subtheory are skilled at *practical thinking* (using and applying information); people strong with respect to the experiential subtheory excel at *creative thinking* (discovering, creating, and inventing); and people strong with respect to the componential subtheory perform well at *analytical thinking* (analyzing, evaluating, critiquing). Sternberg also proposed that each of these three thinking abilities is relatively independent. That is, they are not hierarchically related to a factor of general intelligence (*g*).

If people do indeed have different intellectual patterns based around these three thinking styles, people who receive instruction that matches their preferred style should learn more easily than people who receive instruction that does not match their preferred style. To assess this hypothesis, one must first generate a test to assess thinking style, then develop a curriculum tailored to each style of thinking, and finally adequately assess how much was learned as a result of matched versus mismatched instruction. Sternberg and his colleagues (1996) did just that in a study with 199 gifted high-school students.

Gifted high-school students attended an intense, four-week summer college-level course in introductory psychology. Students' thinking style was evaluated as either practical, creative, analytic, or balanced (see later). All students were assigned the same textbook and attended the same morning lecture series. Instruction varied, however, during afternoon sessions, with students receiving instruction that either matched their preferred style (for example, analytic style-analytic instruction) or not (for example, creative style-analytic instruction). Examples of the type of tasks that would exemplify each of the three types of thinking style are shown in Table 13-3. Course performance was assessed by multiple-choice exams, homework assignments that evaluated practical, creative, or analytic thinking, and essay exams that asked for either practical, creative, or analytic responses.

Children were administered an abbreviated version of the *Sternberg Triarchic Abilities Test* (STAT). This test assessed the three basic types of thinking styles (practical, creative, analytic) for three types of content (verbal, quantitative, and figural), resulting in nine subtests. Examples for each thinking style for the verbal content are (from Sternberg et al., 1996, p. 131):

TABLE 13-3   Examples of the instruction and assessment method based on the triarchic theory that might be used in a course in cognitive development

Practical (contextual subtheory)
  What are the implications of the fact of infantile amnesia for your life? For the legal system?

Creative (experiential subtheory)
  Design an experiment to test a theory of infantile amnesia.

Analytical (componential subtheory)
  Compare Freud's theory of infantile amnesia with Katherine Nelson's theory.

Practical-Verbal: Students were presented with some everyday problems in the life of an adolescent and asked to come up with a solution (for example, what would you do about a friend who has a substance-abuse problem?).

Creative-Verbal: Students were given verbal analogies preceded by false premises (for example, money falls off trees). They had to solve the analogies as if the false premises were true.

Analytic-Verbal: Students had to figure out the meaning of artificial words from natural context. Students would see a novel word used in a paragraph and would have to infer the meaning of the word from the context.

Sternberg and his colleagues reported that the three subsections of the STAT (practical, creative, and analytic) were low- to moderately correlated with one another. When factor-analytic techniques were applied to the data, nine factors emerged (one for each thinking-style × content combination). According to Sternberg and his colleagues (1996), these findings indicate that "clearly, the STAT is not just another measure of Spearman's (1927) *g* (general ability)" (p. 134). The reason that most psychometric tests load heavily on *g* is likely because of the relatively narrow range of abilities tested—and not because it underlies *all* intellectual functioning.

Sternberg and his colleagues next correlated children's STAT scores with their performance in the course and found moderate but significant correlations between scores on each of the three subtests and course performance (correlations ranged from .24 to .42). More critical, however, was the performance of students whose thinking style matched the instruction they received. The results here were quite consistent: Students who received instruction matched to their thinking style performed significantly better than mismatched students did. Moreover, the same pattern of results was found not just for the homework and essay assessments (some of which would have matched children's thinking style), but also for the multiple-choice items.

In later research, Sternberg, Torff, and Grigorenko (1998) designed a social studies curriculum based on the triarchic theory for third-grade children (Study 1) and an introductory psychology curriculum for advanced eighth-grade children (Study 2). Unlike their earlier research (Sternberg et al., 1996), the curriculum involved all three aspects of thinking for all students. Course performance was contrasted among students who had the triarchic instructions, those who had special instruction in critical thinking, and those who received a "traditional" curriculum. The results of the research were consistent across the two studies: Students who received the triarchic instruction performed better, on a variety of dependent measures, than did children who received either the critical thinking or traditional curricula (although those receiving the critical thinking curriculum usually performed better than those receiving the traditional one). And to top it off, third-grade children given the triarchic instruction enjoyed the course more than the other students did.

Sternberg's theory has been a popular one with psychologists and educators since its inception in the mid 1980s. The theory is based on solid experimental work (aspects of the componential and experiential subtheories have been well documented), and the latest research on the application of the three subtheories (or three thinking styles) to instruction will do nothing but make the theory more popular. In sum, I believe that Sternberg's triarchic theory, or other multifaceted theories like it, will

lead research on the nature of human intelligence in the decades ahead.

Gardner's Theory of Multiple Intelligences

Howard Gardner (1983, 1993, 1999) has proposed the theory that intelligence is composed of separate components, or modules, much like the concept of factors used by the psychometric approach. Gardner's **theory of multiple intelligences** is different, however, because it relies heavily on neuropsychological evidence for the existence of relatively independent "frames of mind." Gardner originally proposed seven such abilities, but has added one more and speculated about a ninth (Gardner, 1999): (1) linguistic, (2) logical-mathematical, (3) musical, (4) spatial, (5) bodily-kinesthetic, (6) interpersonal, (7) intrapersonal, (8) naturalist, and (possibly) (9) spirituality/existential. Linguistic and logical-mathematical intelligences are highly valued in technological societies such as ours, and people high in these types of intelligence are generally viewed as smart. Musical intelligence is usually associated with the composition or performance of music, and spatial intelligence involves the ability to perceive form, solve visual problems, and get around effectively in one's environment. Bodily-kinesthetic intelligence is reflected in control of one's body as epitomized by athletes of exceptional ability. The two forms of personal intelligence involve knowing how to deal with others (interpersonal) and knowledge of one's self (intrapersonal). Naturalistic intelligence concerns knowledge of the natural world (fauna and flora), and spiritual/existential intelligence deals with issues related to the meaning of life (and death), and other aspects of the "ultimate" human condition.

Gardner's claim is not that these are eight (or nine) different components of a single intelligence, but rather that these represent eight distinct intelligences, each being independent of the others. And there may be more. Gardner's proposal is for different, domain-specific forms of intelligence, the antithesis of *g*-based theories. For Gardner, each form of intelligence represents a modular, brain-based capacity.

Gardner asserts that these various forms of intelligence are of different degrees of importance in different cultures and at different times in history. For example, in a hunting society, physical dexterity, an ability to locomote effectively, and an understanding of one's natural surroundings are more important than numerical computation skills. In medieval Europe's apprenticeship system, emphasis was placed on bodily, spatial, and interpersonal abilities, whereas in today's Western society, 400 years later, the emphasis is on linguistic and logical-mathematical skills (Gardner, 1984a). Thus, Gardner views the cultural aspects of intelligence to be of utmost importance: different cultures value different types of intelligence. Moreover, Gardner argues that our society's reliance on IQ tests to classify children in terms of intelligence does a great disservice to many of them and to society itself. Because these tests emphasize linguistic and mathematical abilities, children gifted in other areas, such as working with their hands, are often "thrown on society's scrap heap" (Gardner, 1984a, p. 76), instead of receiving the education that could enhance their special abilities.

Criteria of an Intelligence

On what basis did Gardner select his list of intelligences? He lists a set of criteria that must be met for an ability to be considered an intelligence (although every criterion need not be met by an ability for it to be considered an intelligence).

Potential isolation by brain damage. Ample evidence indicates that damage to specified areas of the brain can selectively impair language production or comprehension. Similar evidence abounds for mathematical, musical, and spatial abilities. There is even evidence that damage of the frontal lobes of the neocortex can leave general intellectual functioning unimpaired but produce a socially tactless individual, affecting interpersonal intelligence. The frontal cortex plays an important role in the inhibi-

tion of task-irrelevant and inappropriate responses (see Chapters 2 and 5), and many of those inappropriate responses that are no longer inhibited occur in social situations (Fuster, 1989).

The existence of savants and prodigies. An intelligence is reflected by exceptionalities, and thus can be exhibited by savants and prodigies. *Savants* (sometimes called idiot savants) are people who are mentally retarded but possess an exceptional talent in a single domain. Savants have been identified for a number of skills, most notably in mathematics and music. In the movie *The Rain Man*, an autistic man was able to discern the number of toothpicks that had fallen out of a box after a mere glance and could keep accurate track of the card counts in a game of blackjack. Other mathematical savants have an extraordinary facility with the calendar, being able to provide quickly the day of the week for any date in history (for example, September 14, 1522). Savants are perhaps most impressive when it comes to musical ability. There have been numerous newspaper articles and television stories about people with severe mental retardation who can play Beethoven piano sonatas after hearing them only once. Although these are impressive abilities, what is customarily lacking in savants is creativity. To my knowledge, there have been no musical savants who compose great music or who are great improvisers, only those with an outstanding ability to play back accurately what they have heard.

The *prodigy* is on the other side of the coin from the savant. A prodigy is a child with generally normal abilities in all but a small number of areas (usually one). Similar to savants, prodigies are most frequently found in the areas of mathematics and music. Wolfgang Amadeus Mozart was the quintessential musical prodigy. Raised in a musical family, he was playing instruments and composing music, while still a preschooler, at a level few humans ever attain. He was touring the great capitals of Europe by age 8, but aside from his musical prowess, Wolfgang was a normal boy. This is shown in an observation made in 1764 by Daines Barrington (cited in Gould, 1992), who was impressed by the 8-year-old Mozart's musical skill but also noted that music seemed to be the only area in which Mozart was exceptional:

> I must own that I could not help suspecting his father imposed with regard to the real age of the boy, though he had not only a most childish appearance, but likewise had all the actions of that stage of life. For example, whilst he was playing to me, a favorite cat came in, upon which he immediately left his harpsichord, nor could we bring him back for a considerable time. He would also sometimes run about the room with a stick between his legs by way of horse. (p. 10)

Why do savants and prodigies indicate multiple intelligences? Gardner believes that such exceptionalities reflect modular, brain-based skills, and that such skills surely exist in the general population. The savant and the prodigy are only extreme examples of unevenness in abilities, but their existence suggests that the special skills they possess are domain-specific and can be found in lesser degrees of development in the vast normal range of the human population.

An identifiable core operation or set of operations. Consistent with modern cognitive science, Gardner believes that each intelligence should have associated with it one or more basic information-processing operations, specialized to deal with a particular type of input (language, music, and so on). For example, sensitivity to pitch relations would be a core operation for musical intelligence and the ability to imitate movements made by others would be central to bodily intelligence.

A distinctive developmental history, along with a definable set of expert end-state performances. An intelligence must develop. Any skill that is present fully formed when it first appears does not qualify as a type of intelligence. Also, it must have an identifiable end-state—that is, a level of performance attainable by mature experts. We can certainly specify a developmental course and an expert end-state for most, if not all, of Gardner's intelligences. The gifted writer or speaker serves as the expert for verbal intelligence, as does the mathematician for mathematical intelligence, the professional athlete

or dancer for bodily intelligence, the composer or musician for musical intelligence, the visual artist or trail guide for spatial intelligence, perhaps the skilled politician or therapist for interpersonal intelligence, the philosopher for intrapersonal intelligence, the biologist, or possibly the hunter or farmer, for naturalist intelligence, and religious leaders for spiritual/existential intelligence. Some of these intelligences can have different developmental courses leading to slightly different expert end-states, with developmental milestones along the way from immature to mature performance.

An evolutionary history and evolutionary plausibility. Why do humans possess these intelligences? Human intelligence is not an insignificant part of the human condition and likely played an important role in the evolution of our species. As such, there should be some evolutionary history of an intelligence (and perhaps evidence of antecedents of these abilities in other species), and a plausible evolutionary explanation of how these intelligences may have been selected. We clearly share social skills and social organization with our primate cousins (see Byrne & Whiten, 1988), and spatial and bodily intelligence with most large mammals. Even abilities that might be unique to humans, such as music (although this is debated), have an evolutionary plausibility. Music is an important part of contemporary humans' lives. We fall in love to music, praise God to music, and go to war to music. (I loved the line from a Woody Allen movie, directly related to this last point: "Every time I hear Wagner, I get the urge to invade Poland.") Although I find it hard to find phylogenetic antecedents to music (my guess is that it grew out of general language ability), it is easy to see how once the ability evolved, those who had control of music could have an important social advantage relative to others.

Support from experimental psychological tasks and from psychometric findings. Psychologists from both the cognitive-experimental and psychometric approaches have been studying tasks that assess at least some of the eight intelligences, and findings from these literatures should reveal important individual differences. Psychologists have most often studied tasks assessing language, spatial, and mathematical abilities.

Susceptibility to encoding in a system. One of the hallmarks of human cognitive functioning is that it is based on symbols. Ideally, an intelligence should have its own symbol system. This seems to be true for language, mathematics, and music, and perhaps for spatial and bodily intelligence.

As I noted earlier, each of these criteria does not have to be met for an ability to be classified as an intelligence. But these are the criteria that Gardner (1983) lists "by which each candidate intelligence can be judged" (p. 66).

Multiple Intelligences and Education

Gardner argues for the exclusion of intelligence and aptitude tests from our schools because, as currently practiced, they measure only two types of intelligence and ignore other equally important types. Gardner is not opposed to intellectual assessment in general, however. He advocates the development of measures that would evaluate all types of intelligence. He believes that such assessments should be done early so that intellectual strengths can be discovered and developed through education. Although Gardner believes that each form of intelligence has its origins in biology, he also believes that they are flexible and can be enhanced by education.

Gardner and his colleagues have implemented some of these ideas in a preschool program called Project Spectrum (Gardner & Hatch, 1989; Wexler-Sherman, Gardner, & Feldman, 1988). The curriculum for 4- and 5-year-old children is based on the various domains of intelligence in Gardner's theory. Assessment of children's abilities in each of these domains extends naturally from the curriculum, making the assessment ecologically valid for children. Children are given substantial freedom to explore within the preschool environment, being encouraged, but never forced, to experience all the content areas. Based on observations in the preschool, 15 different subskill areas have been identi-

fied within the framework of Gardner's theory (see Table 13-4). Clear distinctions are noted among children in each of these areas, bolstering the claim that each represents a distinct form of intelligence (Wexler-Sherman et al., 1988).

Although there has not yet been a rigorous experimental test of Gardner's theory, preliminary results are available. Gardner and Hatch (1989) report two small-scale assessments of the theory—one with a group of 20 preschool children and another with a group of 15 kindergarten and first-grade children. An assessment procedure was developed to evaluate each of seven intelligences (the naturalist and spirituality intelligences had not been identified at the time of this assessment). For the preschoolers, Gardner and Hatch reported that children did not perform at the same level on the various tasks but showed distinct intellectual profiles, as predicted by the theory. Similar findings were reported for the kindergarten children. Among the first-grade children, however, the five first-grade girls showed no intellectual weaknesses and many strengths (only two first-grade boys were tested, too small a sample to warrant comment). Given the small sample sizes, no definitive conclusions can be reached, but the data, at least from the younger children, are consistent with Gardner's theory and indicate that an assessment measure can be constructed and that the theory is testable.

Gardner's theory has attracted a lot of attention since its inception in 1983. I find that of all the theories of intelligence I mention in class, Gardner's is usually my students' favorite. But the merits of a theory are not determined by popular vote. How does Gardner's account of intelligence stack up against other, more conventional accounts, or to Sternberg's triarchic theory?

First, Gardner (1984b) complains that Sternberg's account of intelligence is not sufficiently different from the psychometric account in that it leaves room for a general intellectual factor, not too dissimilar from Spearman's *g*. Sternberg (1984) countered that it is too early to compare the two theories because there have been no experimental tests of Gardner's theory itself. Is Gardner's theory,

TABLE 13-4 Types of intelligences and examples of tasks used in Project Spectrum

Type of intelligence	Tasks	Examples
Music	Production	Singing familiar and novel songs
	Perception	Identifying patterns of bell chimes
Language	Narrative	Telling a story from pictures on a storyboard
	Descriptive	Reporting a sequence of events
Numbers	Counting	Counting moves in a board game
	Calculating	Creating a notational system, performing mental calculations, and organizing number information in the context of a game
Visual arts	Drawing	Making pictures
	3-D	Working with clay
Movement	Dance	Responding to rhythm and performing expressive dance movements
	Athletic	Maneuvering through an obstacle course
Science	Logical inference	Playing treasure hunt games
	Mechanical	Using household gadgets
	Naturalistic	Observing, appreciating, and understanding natural phenomena in classroom "Discovery Area"
Social	Social analysis	Playing with scale model of classroom
	Social roles	Interacting with peers

SOURCE: Adapted with permission from Wexler-Sherman, C., Gardner, H., & Feldman, D. H. (1988). A pluralistic view of early assessment: The Project Spectrum approach. *Theory Into Practice, 27,* 77–83. Copyright © 1988 Ohio State University.

in fact, testable? Perhaps not easily. Gardner presents a framework about what is and what is not an intelligence. But even here, there is room for debate. For example, chess performance would fit many of the criteria set by Gardner to qualify as a candidate for an intelligence. There are chess prodigies, chess has a developmental history with an expert end-state, and chess ability perhaps meets other criteria (symbol systems, core set of operations). It does not have a plausible evolutionary explanation, however, and rightly seems not to be an intelligence. Also, Gardner's theory includes abilities that most people have not traditionally considered to be in the realm of intelligence. Musical talent has always been recognized as something special but usually as something distinct from intelligence. And although athletic ability and bodily control are certainly important human characteristics, they are not typically considered to be mental operations in the

way that mathematical computation and verbal comprehension, which have been at the center of the definition of intelligence, are.

In many ways, Gardner's theory is an extension of the domain-specific theories of psychometricians such as Guilford. Gardner's considerable contribution has been getting people to look for evidence beyond psychometric testing, placing intelligence in the realm of both biology and culture, where it belongs. Gardner's ideas have been very influential, particularly in educational circles. Gardner might indeed find greater independence of intellectual abilities than *g* theorists typically find. But one reason for this might be that Gardner includes a broader range of intelligences than do conventional psychometric theorists. Thus, part of Gardner's appeal is his broader definition of intelligence. This may also be part of the difficulty in evaluating his theory.

Ceci's Bioecological Theory of Intelligence

The most recent addition to new theories of intelligence that takes a developmental perspective is Stephen Ceci's **bioecological theory of intelligence** (Ceci, 1993, 1996). Ceci believes that biological factors play a critical role in the development of intelligence, with some aspects of intellectual functioning being influenced by critical periods. Moreover, Ceci acknowledges that there is impressive evidence demonstrating the relationship between basic processes, such as speed of information processing, and psychometric intelligence, and he further acknowledges that performance on a variety of intellectual tasks tends to be highly correlated within individuals (that is, the positive manifold). However, Ceci does not believe that these facts reflect a single, underlying intellectual factor such as *g*, nor that human intelligence is highly heritable. In introducing his theory, Ceci (1996) writes, "I shall argue against the view that there exists a singular, biologically based resource pool *g* that underpins macrolevel measures of intelligence (IQ) via constraining the microlevel processes (e.g., encoding) that it is presumed to be built upon. Further, I shall take issue with the claim that individual differences in intelligence, as indexed by IQ scores, *explain* individual differences in real-world success" (p. 8).

What Ceci does believe, like Gardner, is that intelligence is a multifaceted set of abilities. *Context* is at the center of Ceci's theory. Context greatly influences how (and what) abilities are acquired and how those abilities are expressed. Ceci's perspective is one of domain specificity. He argues that the motivation, expectations, and, importantly, the background knowledge that an individual has will greatly influence how intelligently he or she behaves.

The Role of Context

Ceci defines four types of context: physical, social, mental, and historical. The physical context consists of external stimuli that can influence the course of development or the expression of intelligence (for example, the presence of chemicals or language sounds during prenatal development). The social context consists of the knowledge people possess concerning the social appropriateness of certain activities. For example, older children are more apt to play with a toy if they think that toy is appropriate for their own gender (Ruble, Balaban, & Cooper, 1981). (I know one young man who, some years ago, refused to eat quiche, believing the popular book out at the time that *Real Men Don't Eat Quiche*. Some years later, a bit more secure in his masculinity, he found it quite tasty indeed and now even cooks it.) The mental context consists of the way in which a problem is represented in long-term memory; that is, it consists of what a person knows about a task, including the reason for performing it. Finally, the historical context is the period in history in which a person lives and the influences on development that are peculiar to that time. For example, children growing up in war-torn Bosnia in the early 1990s will have a very different view of the world than Bosnians of the previous generation (and hopefully the next) do. Likewise, the experiences of people who were children during the Great Depression and then went through World War II influenced their cognitions in ways that were clearly different from earlier and later generations. (I'm sure being a teenager in the 1960s had a particular impact on me and my peers, quite different from that on people who were teenagers in the 1980s or 1990s.)

In Chapter 10 on problem solving, I presented an experiment by Ceci (1996) that reflects context. In that experiment, 10-year-old children learned a complex algorithm for anticipating the movement of a figure on a computer screen much faster when the context was that of a game (catching butterflies) than that of a laboratory task. In fact, even after 750 trials, most children never learned the algorithm in the context of a laboratory task, whereas children in the game context were right an average of about 90% of the time.

Another set of studies that demonstrates the importance of context for intellectual-task performance was performed by Ceci and Liker (1986, 1988), who examined the intellectual profiles of expert racetrack handicappers. Ceci and Liker identified two groups of men who attended the racetrack nearly every day. One group was classified as experts, who were especially skilled at predicting the odds for any given horse when the race begins. The nonexperts were far from amateurs but were not as accurate as the experts at predicting odds. The men were administered IQ tests and were asked to handicap both real and imaginary races. Through statistical analyses of subjects' solutions, Ceci and Liker identified a seven-way interactive model that experts used to predict how fast a horse would run the final quarter mile. None of the men could verbally describe this model, but the statistical analyses demonstrated quite clearly that the experts were using the model to arrive at their estimates. The specifics of these algorithms are beyond the scope of this book (and my expertise at handicapping races), but the message is that they were complex.

Ceci and Liker generated a score reflecting how well the experts used this model and correlated it with IQ. The result was a correlation of –.07, which basically means that there was no systematic relationship between IQ and skill on this complex task. IQ was useless in predicting how well the men would do on this task.

Ceci (1993) extended these results by contrasting a low-IQ (IQ = 81) expert who had a fifth-grade education with a high-IQ (IQ = 121) expert who had a master's degree in mathematics education on a simulated task that required the men to predict the price of stocks and bonds. The algorithm used for computing prices on this task was the same one that the experts used in handicapping races (although they weren't told this). Ceci reports that the performance of the two men gradually became better than chance over 600 trials, but that there was no difference between the high-IQ and the low-IQ expert. That is, having a high IQ yielded no advantage when the men had to generalize their skill to another context.

Knowledge and Cognitive Complexity

What makes someone intelligent, then? Ceci obviously believes that intelligence varies as a function of what one is doing. There are no intelligent people, only people who behave intelligently on various tasks (and not so intelligently on others). But what is it that produces intelligent performance on a task? Ceci's short answer is knowledge. People who know more about a certain topic deal with information from that topic more efficiently. The longer answer involves what Ceci has called **cognitive complexity**. According to Ceci (1996), cognitive complexity "refers to the degree to which one's [cognitive] processes are able to operate on one's knowledge structures in a complex, efficient, and flexible manner. Cognitive complexity is limited by the efficiency of cognitive processes, which in turn are involved in the acquisition of knowledge and its structure" (p. 16). Thus, individual differences in how the expert handicappers used the seven-way model in computing odds is a measure of cognitive complexity.

Ceci argues that cognitive complexity is independent of IQ, or g. Cognitive complexity is dependent upon basic cognitive operations, but only as they relate to a specified knowledge base. Cognitive operations, such as a reasoning algorithm or a memory strategy, are domain specific. They are usually acquired on specific tasks with particular sets of stimuli, and the same operations that are used skillfully in one domain will often be used poorly (or not at all) in another domain. This is reflected in the evidence that both children and adults do a poor job at transferring strategies across domains. As the strategy user gets older, some strategies do become more context independent, in that an operation in one domain (such as figuring how to decrease a quiche recipe by a factor of 3) can be used in a different domain (such as figuring how much milk and how many eggs to buy so that one can prepare a quiche recipe reduced by a third). However, even adults are generally not very good at transferring techniques learned in one domain to another (Detterman, 1992). We may get better at transferring knowledge and strategies with age (that is, more context independent), but few of us ever get truly good at it.

More than any other factor, knowledge—both in terms of quantity and organization—influences cognitive complexity and thus intelligence. The important role of knowledge in developmental and individual differences in cognition is well documented. We have seen theory and data demonstrating this with respect to general information-processing abilities (Chapter 5), memory (Chapter 8), problem solving (Chapter 10), and text processing (Schneider et al., 1989, this chapter), among other topics. Developmental and individual differences in knowledge acquisition play a significant role in Sternberg's componential and experiential subtheories. But of all major intelligence theorists, Ceci places the greatest emphasis on knowledge. Ceci conceptualizes knowledge as including not only facts but also procedures and strategies for solving problems. For Ceci, knowledge is the engine that runs intelligence.

Is knowledge equivalent to intelligence, then? Not quite. It is not sufficient merely to have a large quantity of knowledge; knowledge must be integrated and elaborated in such a way that information from that domain can be retrieved, encoded, classified, and otherwise processed in an efficient manner (that is, treated in a cognitively complex way) (DeMarie-Dreblow, 1991; Muir-Broaddus & Bjorklund, 1990). But Ceci believes the single factor that is most central to cognitive complexity (and thus to intelligence) is knowledge. This makes intelligence a domain-specific phenomenon, in that no person has comparable knowledge across all domains.

Yet Ceci's theory provides more room for domain-general abilities than does Gardner's. Figure 13-8 presents Ceci's model of cognitive complexity. In this model, domains are represented by Roman numerals (these can reflect abilities used in handicapping races, playing a certain class of video games, writing prose, playing chess, and so on). Note that each cognitive process is tied to a specific domain. Ceci believes that this is true at least for the acquisition of that process. With practice, however, a process can become increasingly transdomainal, in that it might appear in another domain (note, for example, that rehearsal is found in four domains in Figure 13-8) and this can lead a child to recognize the context-independent utility of such a process and apply it in other domains. This model predicts that there will be low correlations between use of a process, such as rehearsal, across the various domains, because a cognitive operation will likely be differen-

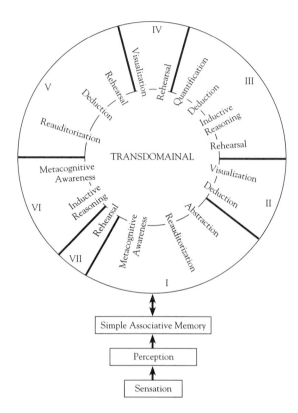

FIGURE 13-8 Ceci's model of cognitive complexity. Domains of knowledge are represented by Roman numerals. Cognitive operations are initially tied to a specific domain but can become transdomainal. SOURCE: "Contextual Trends in Intellectual Development," by S. J. Ceci, 1993, *Developmental Review, 13*, 403–435. Copyright © 1993 Academic Press, Inc. Reprinted with permission.

tially successful in different contexts. Yet, Ceci opens the door for some limited domain-general characteristics of intelligence.

The book is not closed on the nature of intelligence. Sternberg, Gardner, and Ceci make it clear that intelligence is a many-splendored thing—that any theorist who proposes that intelligence is a single phenomenon that influences all aspects of intellectual functioning equally is just not looking at the data. Yet, the evidence of the positive manifold and the fact that basic processes do predict IQ test performance relatively well, for example, argue that there might be some general, cross-domain mechanisms that influence, to various degrees, most if not all cognitive task performance. I do not plan to provide here my own theory of intelligence. However, from the evidence presented in this chapter and from evidence that I present in the following chapter, I am willing to take a stand that falls somewhere between my reading of Sternberg and Ceci. Intelligence, I believe, is multifaceted, with intellectual functioning varying considerably as a function of a person's knowledge and the context in which the cognitive operations were acquired and are assessed. Yet, certain aspects of information processing also appear to be domain general and will influence task performance to a significant degree in a variety of contexts. Factors such as motivation and practice are critically important, and, even at their best, measures of basic processing cannot account for all, or even most, of the variance in intellectual development. The most tenable position from my point of view is that some aspects of human intelligence are domain general in nature, whereas others are domain specific in nature. Even if I am right about this, there is much room for speculation about how much of intelligence is domain general and how much is domain specific.

Summary

Intelligence is generally understood to reflect goal-directed and adaptive functioning, involving sets of problem solving, verbal, and social skills.

The primary approach to the study of individual differences in intelligence has been the *psychometric approach*. Intelligence is described in terms of *factors*, or sets of related abilities that can be discerned on tests by the statistical technique of *factor analysis*. The number of factors that has been proposed to constitute intelligence has varied considerably from one (Spearman's general *g* factor) to 180 in *Guilford's structure-of-the-intellect model*. The best evidence for the existence of *g* is the *positive manifold*, the fact that a person's performances on a variety of different cognitive tasks tend to be similar. The impact of the psychometric approach has been most strongly expressed in *IQ tests*. IQ tests assess intellectual abilities relative to a normative population. Many researchers and theorists have argued that IQ tests are not theory based, they are limited in the type of mental functioning they assess, and they are culturally biased, with minority children often misinterpreting the testing situation.

Information-processing approaches to intelligence provide researchers with well-developed theories and methods for assessing individual differences in intelligence. Differences in rate of processing, strategy use, working memory, knowledge base, metacognition, and other information-processing components have been suggested as the basis for individual differences in children's thinking. Developmental psychologists often use information-processing paradigms to explain differences in the thinking of children of different IQ levels (normal versus children with mental retardation) and children of comparable IQ but differential academic abilities (learning disabled versus nondisabled).

Several researchers have correlated children's performance on Piagetian tasks with academic performance and IQ and have generally found significant relations. The research seems to indicate that both Piagetian and psychometric tests assess the same general form of intelligence but that each also measures aspects of intelligence not measured by the other.

Sternberg's *triarchic theory* consists of three subtheories: *contextual*, *experiential*, and *componential*, each with a characteristic thinking style (practical, creative, and analytic). The contextual subtheory states that intelligence must be evaluated in the environment in which the individual lives. The experiential subtheory proposes that how people deal with novelty and the extent to which they can automatize cognitive functioning are important aspects of intelligence. The componential subtheory describes the three universal information processing mechanisms by which knowledge is acquired and manipulated. The theory is an attempt to go beyond earlier approaches by viewing intelligence from a wider scope.

Gardner's *theory of multiple intelligences* relies heavily on neuropsychological evidence and postulates eight distinct forms of intelligence: linguistic, logical-mathematical, musical, spatial, bodily-kinesthetic, interpersonal, intrapersonal, and naturalistic. Gardner lists several criteria of an intelligence, including potential isolation by brain damage, the existence of savants and prodigies, an identifiable set of operations, developmental history, an evolutionary history and plausibility, support from experimental and psychometric tasks, and susceptibility to an encoding system.

Ceci's *bioecological theory* stresses the importance of context in determining intelligent behavior. Ceci emphasizes the role of knowledge in intelligence, operating through *cognitive complexity*, the degree to which mental processes can operate efficiently on knowledge structures.

Key Terms and Concepts

intelligence
psychometric (differential) approach
factors
factor analysis
g (Spearman's g, general intelligence)
Guilford's structure-of-the-intellect model
fluid abilities
crystallized abilities
positive manifold
hierarchical model of cognitive abilities
IQ (intelligence quotient) tests
Stanford-Binet
Wechsler scales
DQ (development quotient) tests
mental age
deviation IQ
triarchic theory
contextual subtheory
cultural relativism
experiential subtheory
componential subtheory
theory of multiple intelligences
bioecological theory of intelligence
cognitive complexity

Suggested Readings

GOULD, S. J. (1981).*The Mismeasure of Man.* New York: Norton. This very readable book provides a history of the research, theory, and politics of intelligence assess-

ment. In addition to pointing out skeletons in the closets associated with IQ testing, Gould provides a good critique of the history and methods of the psychometric approach. Gould doesn't shy away from controversy and shows how science and politics can never be fully separated.

JENSEN, A. R. (1998). *The g factor: The science of mental ability.* Westport, CT: Praeger. Everything you always wanted to know about *g* but didn't know who to ask, from the most ardent contemporary advocate of *g*. This book provides a thorough examination of research and theory about general intelligence, although there is little discussion of developmental issues.

STERNBERG, R. J. (1985). *Beyond IQ: A Triarchic Theory of Human Intelligence.* Cambridge: Cambridge University Press. This is the long version of Sternberg's triarchic theory. I am recommending it because it covers all the bases, beginning with an introductory chapter that provides a critique of the standard psychometric approach and why a new theory of intelligence is needed in the first place.

GARDNER, H. (ED.). (1993). *Multiple Intelligences: The Theory in Practice.* New York: Basic. This book consists of a series of chapters, most of which were published earlier, presenting and assessing the theory of multiple intelligences. The first four chapters introduce the theory, and the remaining chapters deal with the theory's application (real and potential) to education.

CECI, S. J. (1993). Contextual trends in intellectual development. *Developmental Review* 13, 403–435. This paper presents the short version of Ceci's bioecological theory of intelligence, stressing the importance of context on intelligent behavior. The interested reader will want to look at Ceci's 1996 book *On intelligence: A bioecological treatise on intellectual development* (2nd edition). Cambridge, MA: Harvard University Press.

BJORKLUND, D. F., & SCHNEIDER, W. (1996). The interaction of knowledge, aptitudes, and strategies in children's memory performance. In H. W. Reese (Ed.), *Advances in child development and behavior*, Vol. 25 (pp. 59–89). San Diego: Academic. As the title indicates, this article reviews research looking at the interaction of knowledge, aptitude, and strategies on children's memory performance, and the authors conclude by stating that although domain-specific knowledge might be the single most important factor in intelligence, other domain-general and *g*-like mechanisms (possibly speed of processing and metacognition) also play a critical role in children's intelligent behavior.

Origins, Modification, and Stability of Intellectual Differences

In the previous chapter, we looked at a variety of theories of intelligence. If I had to summarize the major issue that differentiates the various theories, I believe it would have to be the extent to which intelligence is viewed as a unitary phenomenon versus a multifaceted one. Essentially, this is the issue of whether intelligence is domain general or domain specific in nature.

This relatively esoteric issue has historically been tied to another issue that has considerable real-world application and that has provoked considerable controversy: the extent to which intelligence is inherited, determined primarily by one's genes, rather than being a matter of experience.

People who believe that intelligence is best represented by a unitary factor tend to believe that single factor is highly heritable—that is, that people are born smart or not so smart, that this is a stable characteristic across the life span, and that this single factor permeates all aspects of one's intellectual life (Jensen, 1998). People who believe that intelligence is not a unitary factor but varies with the type of problems one encounters and with the context tend to believe that environmental factors determine the bulk of individual differences in intelligence—that is, that our environments make us smart or not so smart, that we can increase (or decrease) our intelligence through experience, and that intelligence is not even stable across situations, let alone years (Ceci, 1996). These are socially and educationally important issues. How we view intelligence in terms of its origins (What are the seeds of intelligence?) and its modifiability (Can intelligence be enhanced through education, and if so, how much?) affects real-world decisions, particularly as they relate to education and one's occupation.

Given what's at stake, it's not surprising that people take strong, often emotional stands on the issue. But science should not be in the business of supporting or refuting a theory because it stirs strong emotions or is politically correct (or incorrect). Science is part of society and cannot be divorced from contemporary political and social forces; but the crux of science is objectivity, and, to the extent that we can, we must let the data speak for themselves, while being mindful of the social ramifications our results might have.

That being said, to what extent are individual differences in intelligence a function of nature versus nurture? As I mentioned in Chapter 1, the proper question here is not *how much* of intelligence is attributable to nature (genes, biology) and *how much* to nurture (experience, environment), but rather *how do nature and nurture interact to produce a particular pattern of development or of intelligence*. This can best be accomplished by using models that take seriously the transaction between biological and environmental factors. I introduced two of those models in Chapter 2 (the developmental systems approach and Scarr and McCartney's genotype → environment theory). Basically, these models propose that there is a bidirectional interaction between organismic factors (for example, genes, hormones) and environmental factors (for example, physical and social environment), and that the two are intricately entwined, making it impossible to evaluate one without considering the other (that is, a contextualist perspective). Yet even within these transactional models, there is considerable latitude for interpretation of which factors (genotype versus social environment, for example) play the major role in shaping development and intellect.

In this chapter, I examine some of the research relating to these issues. I first introduce a transactional approach to intelligence, similar to the developmental systems approach discussed in Chapter 2. I then look at recent work in behavioral genetics that argues for a strong role of genetics in intelligence. I follow this with research focusing on the role of environmental factors in influencing intelligence—in the establishment as well as the modification and maintenance of intelligence. Finally, I include a section on the stability of intelligence from infancy to young adulthood. There is no definitive conclusion at the end of this chapterr—no bold statement saying what intelligence is and is not. But I hope the chapter will provide enough of both theory and data for students to appreciate better what is perhaps the most magnificent quality of our species—our intelligence.

A Transactional Approach to the Study of Intelligence

In Chapters 1 and 2, a general approach to studying development was introduced. This approach emphasized the bidirectionality of structure and function. Bidirectionality can be studied at many levels, of course, from the function of a firing neuron affecting its subsequent growth, to the actions of a child influencing how significant others respond to him or her. I want to focus on this latter level now, examining the transaction between a child and people in his or her immediate environment, and how this transaction might affect a developing intellect.

It has long been recognized that children play a critical role in their own development. Piaget clearly recognized this, placing the child's mental and physical actions at the center of his theory. Yet throughout most of this century, theorists who looked at the development of intelligence tended to view children as passive beings who are either constrained by their biology to develop in a certain way or shaped and molded by their environment (usually early environment). Little emphasis was given by theorists in either extreme camp to children themselves. This began to change in the 1960s, with Richard Bell (1968) emphasizing the idea that parent and child have equal abilities to contribute to a social exchange and that each affects the other. This viewpoint holds that cognitive influences are transactional (Sameroff & Chandler, 1975; Sameroff & Suomi, 1996), for not only do parents act to produce behavior in their children, but children also modify their parents' behaviors.

The **transactional model** as proposed by Arnold Sameroff views the child's biological constitution (genotype in Figure 14-1) as having an organizing effect on the development of the child (phenotype in Figure 14-1). However, the child's environment (environtype in Figure 14-1) also has an organizing effect on the child. What is critical in the transactional model is the *bidirectional* effects between the multiple levels of organization (compare with the developmental systems approach described in Chapter 2 and Figure 2-1). The environment and child have reciprocating effects, which influence that child's biology, and so forth, and these factors continue to transact over the course of development. From this viewpoint, then, *development is seen as the continuous and bidirectional interaction between an active organism with a unique biological constitution and a changing environment.* Although Sameroff initially used the transactional model primarily to explain the long-term effects of biological impairments during early infancy in different environments, the model, in general form, can be applied to explain parent-child interactions in a wide range of contexts.

The transactional model has been used to understand the nature of differences in intelligence among children as a function of socioeconomic status. Socioeconomic status (SES) is customarily defined in terms of level of family income, parents' occupational status, and years of parental education. Research has consistently shown that a significant portion of the differences in IQ and academic achievement among children can be attributed to SES factors (see Ceci, 1996); children from disadvantaged homes fare worse than children from more advantaged homes do.

Variables such as SES do not influence children independently of other factors. Thus, there is a high

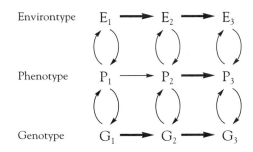

FIGURE 14-1 The transactional model of development, reflecting the continuous interaction of the child's constitution and the environment over time. SOURCE: Sameroff, A. J., & Suomi, S. J. (1996). Primates and persons: A comparative developmental understanding of social organization (pp. 97–120). In R. B. Cairns, G. H. Elder, Jr., & E. J. Costello (Eds.), *Developmental Science.* New York: Cambridge University Press. Reprinted with the permission of Cambridge University Press.

correlation between SES and home environment, friend selection, neighborhood, academic expectation, and academic opportunities, among other factors. Arnold Sameroff and Michael Chandler (1975) proposed that some caretaking environments (middle-income homes) are more likely to produce intellectually and socially competent children than others (lower-income homes). Furthermore, children who experience perinatal trauma (trauma at or around the time of birth) were proposed to be especially susceptible to nonsupportive caretaking, so that the negative consequences of early biological impairment are exacerbated in such environments. That is, Sameroff and Chandler proposed a transaction between infants' biological constitution and their environment, as reflected by differences in SES.

Support for Sameroff and Chandler's model was provided by an examination of the outcomes of children experiencing stress at birth (oxygen deprivation, or anoxia) as a function of their SES level. Although differences in developmental level between normal and biologically impaired infants are obvious at birth in both lower- and middle-income groups, these differences are diminished and often eliminated by age 6 or 7 years in middle-income homes. In contrast, these differences are maintained or increase with age in lower-income homes. Sameroff and Chandler speculated that distressed infants, characterized by more aversive cries, slower attainment of social-developmental milestones such as smiling and vocalization, and a sickly appearance, receive different types of treatment in different environments. In reasonably affluent and well-educated families, these distressed children might receive lavish attention and stimulation, facilitating the amelioration of their impaired condition. In deprived, stressed, and poorly educated families, these same infant characteristics result in a pattern of reduced attention and stimulation and, thus, continued cognitive and social deficits. That is, there is a transaction between parent and child, with the particular characteristics of the child interacting with the particular characteristics of the parents, yielding distinct patterns of development.

The effects of different caretaking environments as a function of infants' biological status were assessed experimentally in a series of studies by P. Sandford Zeskind and Craig Ramey (1978, 1981). Infants from poor, rural environments who had been classified as at high risk for mental retardation were assigned to one of two care-giving environments. Infants in one group received medical care and nutritional supplements and participated in an educationally oriented day-care program beginning at approximately 3 months of age (experimental group). Infants in a control group received the medical care and nutritional supplements but did not participate in the day-care program. Within each group, approximately half of the infants were classified as fetally malnourished at birth, whereas the remaining infants were described as biologically normal. Fetal malnourishment typically produces infants who are developmentally delayed and lethargic and who have aversive cries.

At 3 months of age, fetally malnourished infants in both the control and experimental groups had lower developmental scores on the Bayley Mental Developmental Index than the nonmalnourished (normal) infants did. However, Stanford-Binet IQ scores at 24 and 36 months demonstrated (1) overall higher IQ scores for the experimental than for the control children, (2) no difference in IQ scores between the normal and fetally malnourished infants in the experimental group, and (3) higher IQ scores for the normal than for the fetally malnourished infants in the control group. IQ scores at 36 months are shown for the four groups of this experiment in Table 14-1. In general, the pattern of IQ change observed in this experiment is similar to that observed by Sameroff and Chandler (1975), with the effects of a nonsupportive environment (the control group) being especially deleterious for the biologically distressed children.

Zeskind and Ramey also measured the degree of mother-child interaction in the home. They reported that in the experimental group there was no difference in the amount of maternal attention received by fetally malnourished and normal infants. In the control group, however, fetally malnourished

TABLE 14-1 Mean Stanford-Binet scores at 36 months for children in the Zeskind and Ramey study

	Biologically normal	Fetally malnourished
Experimental (day-care) group	98.1	96.4
Control group	84.7	70.6

SOURCE: Adapted from Zeskind, P. S., & Ramey, C. T. (1981). Sequelae of fetal malnutrition: A longitudinal, transactional, and synergistic approach. *Child Development, 52,* 213–218. Copyright © 1981 The Society for Research in Child Development, Inc., Adapted with permission.

infants were receiving less maternal attention by 24 months than the normal children. Consistent with Sameroff's transactional interpretation, the researchers proposed that the increased responsivity of fetally malnourished infants receiving the educational day care resulted in increased attention from their mothers and a generally positive developmental outcome. In contrast, the withdrawn and sickly behavior of the fetally malnourished infants in the control group resulted in less maternal attention, exaggerating the injurious effects of their biological impairment.

Although the patterns reported here, while children were still participating in the enrichment program, are impressive and demonstrate the transaction of children's biology and environment in development, they do not mean that the effects of fetal malnutrition have necessarily disappeared. When environments change (as when children leave the enrichment program) patterns of interaction can also change and the residual effects of fetal malnutrition might return (Zeskind, 1996). But the pattern demonstrated by Zeskind and Ramey provides an elegant demonstration of the dynamic relation between children's biology and their environment over time and indicates that any simple interpretations of "biological causes" or "environmental causes" are likely wrong.

Most of the research we will examine in the remainder of this chapter does not fit as many of the pieces of the puzzle together as nicely as did the

Zeskind and Ramey study. Some examine genetic factors and others examine detailed characteristics of the home environment, but it is the unusual study that carefully measures biological and environmental characteristics and has good experimental controls while assessing intelligence in natural contexts. Nonetheless, all the research presented here can be viewed from the perspective of the transactional model. Although the next several sections are roughly divided into accounts of genetic factors and environmental factors, never lose sight of the fact that intelligence (or any other aspect of cognitive development) is always a transaction between an active organism with its own biological dispositions, and a changing environment.

Behavioral Genetics and the Heritability of Intelligence

In this section, I examine the role of genetics in influencing intelligence, exploring studies that have (1) assessed the relationship between basic-level (and thus presumably "biologically determined") cognitive abilities and IQ, and (2) compared the IQs of people as a function of genetic relationship (for example, identical twins, siblings, and unrelated individuals). Although environmental effects can be assessed in such studies, they are usually only done so at a global level. For example, adoptive siblings are assumed to share the same environment but to have different genes, whereas monozygotic (identical) twins separated early in life are proposed to have identical genetic endowments but different environments. Despite the nonspecific way environments are usually defined in these investigations, such studies, particularly in combination with investigations providing detailed analyses of children's surroundings, yield important insights into the nature of individual differences in intelligence.

The Concept of Heritability

Some explanation concerning what is meant by the term **heritability** is appropriate here. Heritability is the extent to which differences in any trait within a population can be attributed to inheritance. Heritability is expressed as a statistic that ranges from 0 (none of the differences in a trait are attributed to inheritance) to 1.0 (100% of the differences in a trait are attributed to inheritance). It reflects the proportion of variance in an observed trait that is due to genetic variability.

Heritability is a population statistic, in that it describes average differences among people within a population. It does not refer to how much of any one person's intelligence (or height or personality characteristics) can be attributed to genetic factors, only what percentage of the difference in a trait within a specific population can be attributed to inheritance, on average.

For the purpose of illustration, assume that individual differences in height are due to only two factors: inheritance and diet. On an isolated island, every person receives 100% of his or her nutritional needs (no one receives less or more). The average height of men on the island is 6 feet. If you were to meet two men from this island, one being 6 feet 1 inch tall and the other being 5 feet 11 inches tall, 100% of the 2-inch difference in their height would be attributable to inheritance—in other words, heritability would be 1.0. The reason for this is that their environments (diets in this case) are homogeneous: no differences in environments exist. Thus, any difference in height between people must be attributable to inheritance.

What would happen if a famine hit the island, changing the diet of the people and thus the average height (from 6 feet to 5 feet 10 inches, say)? If the change were uniform (if, for example, everyone were getting 75% of his or her nutritional needs), the heritability would still be 1.0. Although the environment would have changed drastically, it would have changed equally for everyone. Thus, because everyone's environment would have changed equally, 100% of the differences in height would still be attributable to inheritance. If the effects of the famine were not uniform, however, the heritability picture would change. If some people still received 100% of their nutritional needs, others 75%, and others only 50%, now when you met two men from

the island who differed by 2 inches in height you would know that, on average, some proportion of this difference must be attributable to differences in diet; that is, heritability in this latter case would be something less than 1.0. The more heterogeneous the environments are, the lower the heritability will be. Heritability is thus relative, varying with the environmental conditions in which people within the population live.

The concept of heritability is the same regardless of whether we are studying height or intelligence. One difference between concepts such as height and intelligence, however, is that of measurement. When we express height in inches or meters, we can be confident that the measure accurately reflects the underlying concept. There is less confidence with intelligence. In most studies examining the heritability of intelligence, IQ or other psychometric tests are used to measure intelligence. Thus, the findings of these studies more accurately pertain to the heritability of IQ (and usually g), with IQ being one (popular) index of intelligence.

Most of the research in behavioral genetics (and in the studies to follow examining the effects of home environment) are not experimental in nature but correlational. Given the reliance on correlations for interpreting the findings of these studies, let me say a few words about correlations as they are used in the remainder of this chapter. Correlations measure the degree to which two factors vary. Correlations range from 1.0 (a perfect positive relation) to −1.0 (a perfect negative relation), with 0 being chance (no systematic relation). For example, we would expect a positive correlation between height and weight. Taller people, on average, are heavier than shorter people. There are many exceptions, so the correlation will not be perfect, but we would expect a correlation in the magnitude of .60 or .70. The correlation between weight and some measure of intelligence, however, should be close to zero. Among a group of adults, we would not expect heavy people to be more or less smart, on average, than light people.

In familial studies of intelligence, the IQs (or speed of processing) of people of a known genetic relationship are correlated. For example, the IQs of sets of monozygotic twins might be obtained, and the score of each twin paired with his or her mate's. These scores can be contrasted with the IQs of randomly chosen, genetically unrelated people. In the latter case, the IQ of one person is paired at random with the IQ of another, and the correlation is computed. In the former case, a high correlation is expected, because the twins are genetically identical and grew up in the same home at the same time. In fact, the strong genetic position would predict a correlation of 1.0 even for monozygotic twins reared apart. In the case of the unrelated people, the correlation should be 0; knowing the IQ of one unrelated person does not help predict the IQ of another randomly selected person. Thus, the higher the correlation, the greater the relationship. These statistics are then used to infer the degree to which a characteristic is heritable (see later).

The statistical models underlying heritability are complicated and beyond the scope of this chapter (see Appendix B of Plomin, DeFries et al., 1997 for a discussion of the statistical models underlying estimates of heritability). Although, as traditionally conceived, these models assume that environmental and genetic effects are independent, more current models include effects assessing the interaction of genetic and environmental effects (G × E). For example, a certain characteristic might be more strongly expressed in one environment than another. These models also take into consideration the covariation of genetic and environmental effects, or genotype-environment correlations. In fact, the genotype → environment model of Scarr and McCartney (1983) discussed in Chapter 2 reflects such correlations. Thus, although it is not trivial to interpret results from behavioral-genetic research in terms of the transactional model discussed in an earlier section (and patterns of correlations might not tell the entire story of genetic and environmental effects), most contemporary behavioral geneticists would agree, I think, with the basic tenets of the transactional model presented earlier. This is not to say that behavioral geneticists view the developing nature of intelligence the same way as people such as Sameroff or Zeskind and Ramey do, discussed in the previous section. However,

both groups of scientists see intelligence as developing as a dynamical relationship between one's biological constitution and a changing environment and that this relation varies over the course of development.

Elementary Cognitive Tasks and Intelligence

Elementary cognitive tasks (ECTs) are simple laboratory tests designed to measure peoples' response times as they make presumably simple decisions. These include short-term memory scanning, retrieval of familiar words from the long-term store, and simple categorization tasks (Jensen, 1998). Some of these tasks were described in Chapter 13 in the discussion of information-processing approaches to individual differences (Hunt, Davidson, & Lansman, 1981). The basic processes measured by ECTs are presumed to be closely related to physiological functioning and thus primarily under the influence of endogenous (and inherited) factors.

Arthur Jensen and his colleagues, among others, have presented evidence that response times for several ECTs are significantly related to g-factor scores obtained from conventional psychometric tests (see Jensen, 1993, 1998). As was noted in Chapter 13, significant relations have been found between efficiency of retrieval from the long-term memory store and verbal ability for both adults (Hunt et al., 1981) and children (Keating & Bobbitt, 1979). Following Jensen's argument, variations in these basic cognitive processes are probably inherited and are the basis for individual differences in intelligence. To bolster this contention, several researchers have demonstrated significant relationships between aspects of evoked brain potentials measured via electroencephalograph (EEG) apparatus and psychometrically measured intelligence (see Jensen, 1998).

One study that attempted to assess the genetic basis of performance on ECTs was done by Petrill, Thompson, and Detterman (1995). They administered a series of timed cognitive tasks (see Chapter 13) to 287 monozygotic (genetically identical) and dizygotic (genetically nonidentical) twin pairs between 6 and 13 years of age.

The correlation between decision times on the information-processing tasks and psychometrically measured intelligence had previously been found to be significant (correlation = −.42). Decision times also proved to be highly heritable. The correlation of decision times for the identical twins was .61, but was only .39 for the nonidentical twins. This resulted in a heritability of about 45 percent (see also McGue et al., 1984). Heritability for other cognitive tasks was lower, with the heritability of simple reaction times being zero. Nevertheless, the findings clearly reflect a strong genetic basis for overall speed of processing (decision time) on experimental cognitive tasks, and this speed component was strongly related to a general intellectual factor.

Even if speed of information processing is highly heritable, why should it correlate so highly with psychometric measures of intelligence? Jensen (1993) states the dilemma: "It seems almost incredible that individual differences in reaction time (RT) in simple tasks that involve no intellectual content and are so easy as to be performed by most persons in less than 1 second should be correlated with scores on nonspeeded, complex tests of reasoning ability, vocabulary, and general knowledge—the kinds of content that compose IQ tests" (p. 53). Jensen (1993) proposed three possible brain-based reasons for the high correlations of reaction times with measures of g. First, speed of information processing might reflect speed of nerve transmission. Speed is important because of the brain's limited capacity to process information. Only so much can be done at once; faster processing will permit more to be done, and this will be true across domains. Second, there is evidence that people whose reaction times are more variable over trials have lower psychometrically measured intelligence (Eysenck, 1987). Third, the longer neurally encoded information can be maintained in immediate consciousness, the more efficient cognition will be. Thus, more durable memory traces, with information being retained longer in short-term memory, result in more effective information processing. Jensen acknowledges that the neurological aspects of his theory are still speculative but states that the theory is consistent with the empirical evidence showing a strong relation between speed of information processing and g.

Although the findings and theories regarding ECTs are intriguing and applauded by many, not all researchers are ready to accept them as conclusive or as representative of functioning on higher-level cognitive tasks. For example, Stephen Ceci (1996) argues that other important cognitive skills, such as strategic and metacognitive processes, are ignored in this research. Also, it is well established that response times on simple cognitive tasks can vary greatly as a function of a person's knowledge base. Response times are fast when decisions are made concerning very familiar information but slow when dealing with less familiar information (Case, Kurland, & Goldberg, 1982; Chi, 1977). Differences in knowledge base might be indirectly responsible for many of the group and individual differences observed in some of these experiments, and such differences might well be more a function of education and general experience than they are of genetics (see Ceci, 1996, Chapter 13, for a compelling argument of this). As with most of the issues surrounding intelligence, the controversy continues, and clarification of these provocative ideas awaits future research.

Familial Studies of Intelligence

Most researchers in behavioral genetics take the position that the primary influence of genes on intelligence is indirect. Genes do not necessarily make someone intelligent but, rather, influence behavior and the experiences an individual will have. For example, the genes of a child's parents influence how those parents behave toward the child, affecting a substantial part of that child's experiences, especially early in life. And children's own genotypes determine which situations they find comfortable and pleasing, which causes them to seek out some environments and to avoid others (Bouchard et al., 1990; Scarr, 1993). Thus, although genes surely influence things such as the rate of neural transmission or the durability of memory traces, which might have a direct effect on cognitive functioning

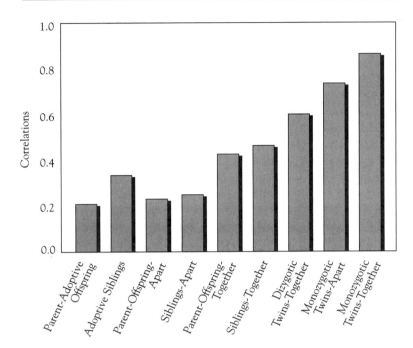

FIGURE 14-2 Average correlations of familial studies of intelligence. SOURCE: Adapted from data published by Bouchard, T. J., Jr., & McGue, M. (1981). Familial studies of intelligence: A review. *Science, 212,* 1055–1059.

(Jensen, 1998), their *indirect* effect, through the behavior of parents and of the children themselves, can have even greater consequences for the development of intellect. (Review Scarr and McCartney's genotype → environment theory in Chapter 2.)

The preponderance of research examining the heritability of intelligence has dealt with comparisons of IQ scores among people of varying genetic relationships (or **familial studies of intelligence**). If one holds a genetic theory of intelligence, the greater the genetic similarity between two groups of individuals, the higher the correlations of their IQs should be. One of two general approaches has usually been taken: adoption studies, in which the parents who rear the children are genetically unrelated to them (Plomin, Fulker et al., 1997; Weinberg, Scarr, & Waldman, 1992) and twin studies, in which monozygotic twins separated early in life are contrasted with dizygotic (nonidentical) twins and people of varying genetic relationships (Bouchard et al., 1990; Wilson, 1983).

Familial studies of intelligence have been conducted since the early part of this century. However,

evidence of falsification of data by Sir Cyril Burt, a prominent British psychologist and an important contributor to this literature, had caused many to question the reliability of the early findings. But several large-scale and tightly controlled adoption and twin studies have been conducted since the Burt fraud, and their findings are relatively consistent. Bouchard and McGue (1981) reviewed 111 familial studies of intelligence, eliminating the studies by Burt and others that did not meet their methodological and statistical criteria. A summary of some of the average correlations from this investigation is given in Figure 14-2. The results of several dozen additional studies over the past two decades has not altered the patterns shown in this figure (Plomin & Petrill, 1997).

Generally, the correlations increase as genetic similarity increases, implying a significant role for genetics in patterns of individual differences in intelligence. From these correlations, heritability estimates are derived. The easiest way to compute a heritability coefficient (H) is by using data from twin studies. The correlation (denoted as r) based on data from nonidentical twins is subtracted from the correlation based on data from identical twins, and the difference is doubled, or,

$$H = (r \text{ identical twins } - r \text{ nonidentical twins}) \times 2$$

If you take the correlations the IQs of identical twins reared together shown in Figure 14-2 (.86) and those of nonidentical twins reared together (.60), the resulting computation is

$$H = (.86 - .60) \times 2 = .52$$

This means that the heritability of intelligence (at least based on this data set) is .52, or that 52% of the differences in intelligence between people is attributed to genetics.

Based on the dozens of studies that have been conducted during the past 25 years or so, there is some variability in heritability estimates, ranging from a low of about .30 to a high of slightly more than .70 (Bouchard et al., 1990; Plomin & Petrill, 1997). A somewhat conservative conclusion based on the available data would be that the heritability of IQ is approximately .50, meaning that, on average, 50% of the difference in intelligence between people in a population can be attributed to genetics (Plomin & Petrill, 1997). However, recall that heritability is a relative population statistic, meaning that it is subject to change over time and populations. So, for example, research has indicated that IQ has a higher heritability in adulthood than in childhood, is higher in North American whites than in North American blacks, and is higher in whites living in Great Britain than in whites living in America (see Ceci, 1993).

Developmental Differences in Heritability

Let's look at the relation between age and heritability of IQ, and let's start in infancy. Research by Petrill and his colleagues looked at the heritability of intelligence for infants who scored low on infant psychometric (g-loaded) tests (10th percentile or below, low-g infants) (Petrill et al., 1997), as well as those who scored high on psychometric tests (90th percentile or above, high-g infants) (Petrill et al., 1998) from the McArthur Longitudinal Twin Study.

Infants were first tested at 14 months of age using the Bayley Scale of Infant Development, and again at 20, 24, and 36 months (with the Stanford-Binet being administered at the 36-month testing). For both groups of extreme infants, the correlations of IQs (or DQs) were higher for monozygotic (identical) than for dizygotic (nonidentical) twins, reflecting the influence of inheritance, although this pattern varied with age. The difference between the correlations between the two twin groups was small and nonsignificant at 14 months for both the high- and low-g children. This reflects a small, nonsignificant genetic effect on infant intelligence at 14 months of age. The difference in the correlations between the monozygotic and dizygotic groups was larger and significant at the 24- and 36-month tests for the high-g group and at 20 and 24 months for the low-g group, however, indicating significant genetic effects on intelligence. These findings indicate that both high- and low-levels of g (as reflected by extreme scores on psychometric tests) are significantly influenced by genetics late in infancy, with the genetic effect generally increasing into early childhood.

In other research using the adoption-study method, Plomin, Fulker, Corley, and DeFries (1997) used longitudinal data to assess the similarity in IQ between adopted children and both their biological and adoptive parents at different ages. They administered sets of cognitive tasks to children and to their adoptive and biological parents. Children were tested at 1, 2, 3, 4, 7, 12, and 16 years of age. The researchers contrasted the correlations between a general cognitive ability measure (derived from the set of cognitive tasks) between children and their adoptive and biological parents at the different ages tested. A control group of children who was raised by their biological parents was also included. The results of their study are shown in Figure 14-3. As can be seen, the correlations of cognitive ability between the children and their adoptive parents starts out low and declines over childhood, increasing a bit between the 14- and 16-year assessment. In contrast, the pattern of correlations between the children and their biological parents is very similar to that found for the control group (biological parents

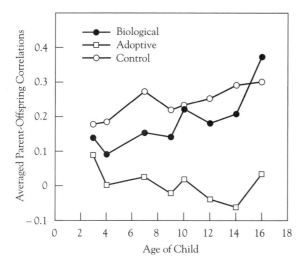

FIGURE 14-3 Age changes in parent-offspring correlations of cognitive abilities for adoptive children and the (a) biological parents, (b) their adoptive parents, and (c) a control group of parents and their biological offspring. SOURCE: Plomin, R., Fulker, D. W., Corley, R., & DeFries, J. C. (1997). Nature, nurture, and cognitive development from 1 to 6 years: A parent-offspring adoption study. *Psychological Science, 8,* 442–447.

living with their offspring). The correlations increase steadily over the elementary school years, peaking in adolescence. Similar patterns were found for specific cognitive abilities (spatial ability, speed of processing, and recognition memory). This pattern reflects an increasing genetic influence on cognitive abilities as children move from childhood to their teen years.

The Role of the Environment in Behavioral Genetic Analyses

If we accept the .50 heritability figure, this means that about 50% of the differences in IQ between people are attributable to nongenetic effects, namely environment (Plomin & Petrill, 1997). In family comparisons, behavioral geneticists typically consider the environmental effects of shared and nonshared environments. A **nonshared environment** is an environment unique to an individual, not shared by a sibling, for instance. A **shared envi-**

ronment is a home environment shared by different family members. Thus, twins, for example, growing up in the same home at the same time would share the same family environment. Nontwin siblings growing up in the same family at different times would not share the same environment to the extent that twins do. As noted in Chapter 2, research has consistently shown that siblings become less alike the older they get and that this reflects the contribution of nonshared environments (McCartney, Harris, & Bernieri, 1990). Following the arguments of Scarr and McCartney (1983; Scarr, 1992, 1993), with increasing age, children's genotypes influence them to select their own environments, and the experiences they have in those environments affect their intelligence. Thus, some portion of the nonshared-environmental effects can likely be attributed to indirect genetic effects (active genotype → environment effects in Scarr and McCartney's model).

After reading the preceding paragraphs on the direct and indirect effects of genetic relatedness on intelligence, you might be tempted to wonder if the environment has any meaningful effect on intelligence. The data on adoptive versus biological parents seems especially telling. Children are more like their biological parents than like their adoptive parents and become increasing that way as they get older. It seems that the environment has no influence on intelligence. Such a conclusion, though tempting to make given the evidence from behavioral genetics, is flat out wrong.

The behavioral genetics research I've reported here looks at correlations of IQs (or other tests of cognitive ability) as a function of degree of genetic similarity, and the conclusion is clear—the more similar two groups of people are genetically, the higher the correlation. But remember that correlations are independent of means, in this case, average levels of IQ scores. When looking at average levels of IQ, environment (as reflected, for example, by the average level of IQ in the parental home) can have a greater effect than biology. How can this be? How can there be such an overpowering genetic relation when looking at correlations and there be a strong environmental effect when looking at means?

The combined impact of environment and genetics on intelligence is illustrated in the transracial adoption study of Sandra Scarr and Richard Weinberg (1976; Weinberg et al., 1992). Black children born primarily of parents from lower-income homes were adopted by white, primarily upper-middle-class parents. The average IQ of the adopted children who were placed in middle-income homes as infants was found to be 110, 20 points higher than the average IQ of comparable children being reared in the local black community and comparable with the estimated IQs of their adopted parents. This effect demonstrates the potent influence of environment on IQ. However, the correlation between the children's IQs and their biological mothers' educational level (IQ scores were not available for the biological mothers) was significantly higher (.43) than a similar correlation with the children's adoptive parents' educational level (.29).

The findings of this study appear paradoxical at first. How could the level of the children's IQ be more similar to that of their adopted parents, yet the correlation of their IQs be higher with the educational level of their biological mothers? To help understand this difference, keep in mind that correlations in this type of research reflect the degree to which knowing a parent's IQ (or equivalent) score will predict where a child's IQ will fall relative to other children in his or her particular group. Correlations are independent of level of IQ; that is, correlations predict rank order and not level of IQ. In fact, the 20-point IQ difference between the children and their biological mothers could, theoretically, have been accompanied by a perfect correlation (1.0). In such a hypothetical situation, the child with the highest IQ of all the children (125, let's say) would have the biological mother with the highest IQ of all the mothers (105, let's say); the child with the next highest IQ (119) would have the biological mother with the next highest IQ (101), and so on until the child with the lowest IQ (82), who would have the biological mother with the lowest IQ (65). The correlation would be perfect, yet there would be, on average, a 20-point IQ difference between the children and their biological mothers (see Table 14-2).

TABLE 14-2   IQ data from a hypothetical set of mothers and their children demonstrating a perfect correlation

	Mother's IQ	Child's IQ
Mother-child pair 1	105	125
Mother-child pair 2	101	119
Mother-child pair 3	98	117
Mother-child pair 4	94	115
Mother-child pair 5	91	113
Mother-child pair 6	88	108
Mother-child pair 7	82	100
Mother-child pair 8	77	99
Mother-child pair 9	69	92
Mother-child pair 10	65	82
Mean IQ	87	107
Correlation = 1.0		

In the Scarr and Weinberg study, the adopted children had all been placed in intellectually stimulating home environments and had received similar treatment at the hands of their academically accelerating adoptive parents. Such stimulation was responsible for their relatively high levels of IQ in comparison with their biological mothers. Furthermore, given the similar patterns of experience that these children had, individual differences among the children were best predicted by genetics. When environmental conditions are relatively homogeneous, as they presumably were for the adopted children in the Scarr and Weinberg study, the best predictor of individual differences in intelligence is genetics. Prediction here refers to knowing a child's relative rank in a specified group of children (that is, where the child stands compared with his or her peers) and not to the actual level of IQ. When environments vary considerably (that is, are heterogeneous), differences in environments will play a more substantial role in affecting individual differences in intelligence (see later discussion). Thus, had the environments of the adopted families been more varied, chances are the correlations between the IQs of the children and their adoptive parents would have been greater. In other words, the heritability of intelligence is not constant but varies as a function of the similarity of environments among the people under study. As I noted earlier, however, nonshared-environmental factors increase in influence as children get older, which serve, essentially, to make the environments experienced by children more dissimilar to one another. Because these nonshared environments are influenced by their genetics (active genotype → environment effects), one would still expect the correlations of children's IQs with their biological parents to be high relative to those of adoptive parents during adolescence.

A recent study has explicitly assessed the interaction of genetics and environment on IQ using patterns of correlations derived from sets of siblings. Rowe, Jacobson, and van der Oord (in press) obtained verbal IQ scores (from the Peabody Picture Vocabulary Test) from 3,139 sibling pairs, including sets of monozygotic and dizygotic twins, and adopted siblings. The siblings, all adolescents, were White, African American, and Hispanic, and came from economically diverse backgrounds. Of particular interest to Rowe and his colleagues was the relation between education level of the children's parents and the heritability of IQ. The range of education of the parents was from no school to graduate or professional training. Rowe and his colleagues first computed correlations between siblings as a function of genetic relationship and found, similar to other research, that correlations increased as degree of genetic similarity increased. For example, the correlation of the monozygotic twins was .73, the correlation of full siblings was .39, and the correlation of unrelated siblings was .07. They next used forms of regression analyses to obtain estimates of heritability and shared-environmental effects as a function of parental education.

For the overall sample, the researchers reported that a heritability of .57 and an effect of shared environment of .13, which is similar to results reported by others. The patterns differed, however, when education level of the parents was considered. For adolescents in the low-education group (high school education or less), Rowe and his colleagues reported a heritability of .26 and an effect of shared environ-

ment of .23. In other words, both genetics and shared environment accounted for about one-quarter of the variability of differences in verbal IQ for the low-education group. In contrast, for the high-education group (greater than high-school education), the researchers reported a heritability of .74 and an effect of shared environment of 0. That is, heritability increased from about 25% for offspring of parents with less than a high-school education to about 75% for offspring of children with greater than a high-school education, with a corresponding decrease in the effects of shared environment (from about 25% to about 0%).

These findings indicate, consistent with the theorizing of others (Bronfenbrenner & Ceci, 1994; Scarr, 1992), that heritability increases with improved environmental conditions, here as reflected by level of parental education. This is because harmful environments might have a particularly strong influence on the development of certain traits, whereas, according to Sandra Scarr (1992), average or above average environments will have little impact beyond that contributed by genetics (recall Scarr's "good enough parents" from Chapter 2). Although we need not adopt Scarr's ideas of "good enough parents" to make sense of these data, the findings of Rowe and his colleagues indicate that environment and genetics do indeed interact and that these interactions can be found by using the methods of behavioral genetics.

It's worth noting that heritability for actual school performance is less than heritability for IQ scores and more under the influence of family environment (Duyme, 1988; Teasdale & Owen, 1984). For example, in an adoption study done in France by Michel Duyme (1988), adopted children's school success (for example, grade retention, assignment to special education classes) was correlated with the socioeconomic status of their adopted and biological parents. These correlations were greater between children and their adoptive parents (correlation = .37) than between the children and their biological parents (correlation = .10 for biological father and .16 for biological mother). Other research evaluated genetic and shared-environmental (family) factors on specific cognitive abilities and school success in sets of identical and nonidentical twins (Thompson, Detterman, & Plomin, 1991). Thompson and her colleagues reported that specific cognitive abilities (verbal, spatial, perceptual speed, and memory) showed a greater genetic influence (about 57%) than shared-environmental influence (about 5%). The pattern was reversed, however, for school achievement, with genetic influence being about 21% and the shared-environment influence being about 68%.

Why should specific cognitive abilities (like general cognitive abilities) be more influenced by genetic factors, whereas school achievement, which is related to general IQ and to specific cognitive abilities, be more influenced by shared environment? One reason for this pattern is that school success is influenced by noncognitive factors such as level of aspiration and family attitudes toward education. This brings to mind the debates discussed in Chapter 13 about what IQ tests really measure. If we're looking for intelligent behavior, perhaps school success is the better measure than the out-of-context IQ test (Ceci, 1996). However, if a strictly cognitive measure of intelligence is more important, then perhaps the IQ score is the better index.

Most behavioral genetic studies of intelligence (or school success) do not actually measure the environment but simply assume that children reared together share a common environment and children not reared together experience different environments, or that environmental conditions can be captured by categorizing families according to social class. This, of course, is an overly simplistic definition of environment, and behavioral genetics can be justly criticized for not better defining what constitutes an environment. Some recent behavioral genetics studies have done a better job of measuring the environment, using techniques developed by researchers looking for environmental correlates of intelligence. For example, the HOME scale developed by Bradley, Caldwell, and Elardo (1977) provides a detailed analysis of parental behavior (for example, responsivity of the mother, style of discipline) and characteristics of the home environment (for example, provision of play materials, books) that are hypothesized to be associated with intelli-

gence. (I will discuss the HOME scale and studies using it in some detail in the next section.) The HOME scale was used in a study by Hilary Coon and her colleagues (1990) to evaluate genetic and environmental effects in a group of adopted children from the Colorado Adoption Project. Coon and her colleagues reported, as have previous studies (to be discussed later), that characteristics of the home environment had some direct effects on 7-year-old children's cognitive abilities, particularly individual differences in the organization of the home environment. Children from more organized homes fared better than children from disorganized homes. However, Coon and associates reported that the principal environment-development effects were mediated by indirect genetic effects, as discussed earlier in this chapter. In other words, genetic characteristics of the parents influenced the type of environments they constructed for their children, which in turn contributed to individual differences in children's cognitive performance.

Genes for Intelligence

Despite the evidence that psychometric intelligence, specifically *g*, is highly heritable (about 50% of the variance in *g* is due to genetic influence), until recently it was still impossible to point to a single gene for *g*. That changed with a report published in 1998 by M. J. Chorney and colleagues that identified a form of a gene on chromosome 6 that occurs more frequently in high-*g* children than in children average in *g*. Chorney and colleagues (1998) proposed that the genetic contribution to *g* (and thus to psychometric intelligence) is controlled by many different genes, and thus the impact on *g* of any single gene would be small. The researchers selected children ranging from 6 to 15 years of age who had been given a WISC IQ test. The high-*g* sample had an average IQ of 136, whereas the control group had an average IQ of 103. Additional samples of high-*g* (who had scored in the top 3% on SAT tests) and control adolescents were also tested, to serve as a replication group for the original sample. Using modern DNA assessment techniques, the frequencies of certain genes (or *alleles*, different versions of the same gene, such as a gene for blue eyes versus a gene for brown eyes) were identified, and the frequencies of these genes noted between the high-*g* and control groups.

Chorney and colleagues reported that one allele of a specific gene (insulin-like growth factor-2 receptor) occurred about twice as often in the high-*g* group as in the control group. In other words, this particular variant of the gene was associated with high-*g* ability. Is this a gene for genius? Hardly. Although the allele occurred more frequently in the high-*g* group than in the control group, only about a third of the high-*g* children had the allele, as did about 16% of children in the control group, despite having average IQs. Overall, Chorney and colleagues proposed that this allele accounts for about 2% of the variance of *g*, equivalent to about 4 IQ points. Given that about 50% of the variance for *g* is genetic, if other genes have about the same effect on *g* as this one does, we could expect to find another 24 genes that influence *g*.

The discovery of a gene associated with intelligence tells us nothing about how that gene works. Does it influence speed of processing? Is it related to metacognition? Might it have different effects at different times in development? Moreover, the gene might influence intelligence only indirectly, possibly through interactions with other genes or with certain environments. This research represents an exciting first step in the interface of molecular biology and the behavioral genetics of intelligence. But it is only a first step, although it may well be a revolutionary one (see Plomin & Rutter, 1998).

How Seriously Should We Take Heritability Studies of IQ?

At one level, the behavioral genetics of intelligence is a highly esoteric topic, steeped in statistical models that most people don't even bother to try to understand. At a second level, however, it is the study of down-to-earth issues that most people have some opinions about and that affect social, economic, and educational policies. How much of one's intelligence is "in the genes"? And if the answer to that question is "quite a lot," what does it mean about

educability and the modification of intelligence over the course of development?

From time to time, the highly statistical analyses of behavioral genetics get translated to the public at large and invariably a controversy ensues. In 1994 Richard Herrnstein and Charles Murray published *The Bell Curve*, in which they presented detailed analysis of a large longitudinal data base assessing the relation of IQ with occupation level, income, job disability, criminality, and welfare dependency, as well as ethnic and racial differences in IQ and what all this means for society. Their conclusion was that IQ is highly heritable, has a greater impact on the previously listed factors than any other single variable, and that social policy should be made with these "facts" in mind. Not surprisingly, there was an uproar from the academic, educational, and political communities against Herrnstein and Murray's claims (see Jacoby & Glauberman, 1995). Many critics claimed, not so much that the data they reported were flawed, but that they erroneously equated IQ with intelligence (see discussions in Chapter 13) and confused correlation with causality (does low IQ cause one to have less education and lower income, or the reverse?).

I will not examine Herrnstein and Murray's claims here, nor attempt to support or refute them. The purpose of this chapter and the previous one is to provide a look at what intelligence is, its origins, and how it changes (or remains stable) over time. An important part of that picture comes from studies of the heritability of IQ. I am convinced that IQ tests assess something important for people from information-age societies, that the .50 heritability of IQ reported by behavioral geneticists is real, and that this tells us something important about intelligence. However, I also believe that this is only part of the "intelligence" picture. Intelligence is a multifaceted thing, and I believe that a highly heritable general factor (*g*) can coexist with other aspects of intelligence (a position not all theorists of intelligence would agree with). Recall our earlier discussion of the transactional model. Biologically based abilities (or disabilities) will transact with the environment over time, yielding patterns of behavior and development that cannot be neatly described as

"50% of the variance can be attributed to genetics." The main point I want to make here is that having an understanding of the various perspectives of the nature of intelligence is a good thing, not just for academics or students trying to pass a test, but for citizens of a modern democracy.

Experience and Intelligence[1]

Undoubtedly, one's intellect is greatly influenced by experience. Even proponents of a strong genetic perspective such as Scarr (1993) argue that one's genotype has its greatest influence in terms of which environments a child explores and experiences. Others, however, argue that the environments in which children are reared and the experiences they have during childhood mold intellect, far more than do genetic influences (see Ceci, 1996).

In discussing experience and intelligence, it is useful to distinguish among the establishment, modification, and maintenance of intelligence. What factors are responsible for establishing intellectual competence? Once a certain level of intellectual functioning has been achieved, what is necessary to maintain that level? Finally, to what extent can an established level of intelligence be modified, either positively or negatively? Factors that influence the establishment of intelligence most certainly also exert an influence on its maintenance and modification. But it is important to recognize that these three aspects of the intelligence-experience relationship can be distinct. Once intellectual competence is established, the child will not necessarily maintain that same relative level of intelligence independent of his or her surroundings. That is, establishing some level of intellectual ability does not guarantee that that level will be maintained or that it cannot be modified.

Establishing Intellectual Competence

Extremes in environments can have drastic effects on intelligence. Studies with laboratory animals clearly show that social, emotional, and intellectual functioning is greatly impaired when animals are raised in restricted environments (Greenough, Black, & Wallace, 1987). Although these lab experiments cannot be done with children, some naturalistic studies have been done in institutions and homes, assessing the consequences of growing up in impoverished environments.

Institutionalization Studies

Several **institutionalization studies** examined the effects of maternal deprivation, where infants had been separated from their mothers and raised in overcrowded and understaffed institutions (Dennis, 1973; Spitz, 1945). The results of such early living conditions were increased susceptibility to illness; retarded physical, mental, and social development (Provence & Lipton, 1962; Skeels, 1966); and, in some cases, death (Spitz, 1945).

For example, Wayne Dennis (1973) contrasted the outcomes of children reared in an orphanage in Beirut, Lebanon, called the Crèche, with those of infants placed in adoptive homes. The Crèche was a charity-run institution for illegitimate children. Infants received little direct stimulation in the form of play or other social interactions. The infants spent much of their day in small cribs without toys and with sheets covering the sides, limiting substantially what they could see. Life was more varied for older children, but opportunities for intellectual stimulation and the development of normal patterns of adult-child interaction were minimal. Furthermore, many of the primary caretakers were "graduates" of the Crèche themselves and were characterized by low IQ scores and a general unresponsiveness toward their young wards. Dennis reported that infants who remained institutionalized displayed signs of severe retardation within their first year and that their average IQs by age 16 ranged between 50 and 80. In contrast, infants leaving the Crèche for adoptive homes before the age of 2 years regained normal intellectual functioning, having average IQ scores of about 100. Children adopted following their second birthday also demonstrated gains in intellectual performance, but they typically performed several years below their age level on all subsequent testings.

The effects of social deprivation appear early, within the first two or three months of life, reflected in infants' responses to simply being held. For example, Provence and Lipton (1962) describe 2- and 3-month-old institutionalized infants as feeling "something like sawdust dolls; they moved, they bent easily at the proper joints, but they felt stiff or wooden" (p. 56). Signs of retardation and inappropriate social reactions to adults increased during the first two years, although these signs decreased some as children became able to move around on their own and were removed from nurseries to wards for older children (Provence & Lipton, 1962; Skeels, 1966).

The influence of spending their early years in institutions persisted years after children were removed from the foundling homes and placed in adoptive or foster homes. For example, Provence and Lipton (1962) followed, into the preschool years, a small group of institutionalized infants who had been placed in foster homes, most between 18 and 24 months of age. Provence and Lipton commented on the considerable resilience and capacity for improvement that these children showed, while noting that early institutionalization still caused long-term problems. These children, although relating to other toddlers, did not form strong personal attachments, either to other children or to adults. Their emotional behavior was described as "increasingly impoverished and predominantly bland. . . . One gained the impression on watching them that they had largely given up on their efforts to initiate a contact with the adult" (p. 145). These children continued to improve, socially and intellectually, over the preschool years, so that many looked, on causal observation, like normal children. But closer examination revealed problems in forming emotional relationships, control of impulses, language development, and flexible problem solving. In testing situations with adults, the children rarely sought assistance from their mothers, nor did they frequently turn to their mothers for comfort when distressed.

Research by Dennis, Provence and Lipton, and others like them are natural experiments and demonstrate how extremes in early environment can affect children's intellectual development. But such studies, although informative, lack the experimental rigor that psychologists like. (For example, there was no random assignment of children to an orphanage or to adoption.) Furthermore, such early deprived environments probably represent an extreme of child rearing and might not be applicable to the vast majority of parent-child interaction styles.

The Home Environment: Naturalistic Studies of Parent-Child Interaction

Beginning in the late 1960s, researchers began evaluating parent-child interaction patterns in the homes of young children. One of the more impressive longitudinal projects evaluating the quality of parent-child interactions and later intelligence is that conducted by Betty Caldwell, Richard Bradley, and their colleagues. They developed an inventory for assessing the quality of the home environment, called the Home Observation for Measurement of the Environment (HOME) scale (Caldwell & Bradley, 1978; Bradley et al., 1977). The **HOME scale** is divided into six subscales and is used to code aspects of a child's home environment that relate to intellectual development. Following are some sample items from the six subscales.

1. *Emotional and Verbal Responsivity of the Mother*
   a. Mother spontaneously vocalizes to child at least twice during visit (excluding scolding).
   b. Mother responds to child's vocalizations with a vocal or verbal response.
   c. Mother caresses or kisses child at least once during visit.
2. *Avoidance of Restriction and Punishment*
   a. Mother does not shout at child during visit.
   b. Mother neither slaps nor spanks child during visit.
   c. Mother does not interfere with child's actions or restrict child's movement more than three times during visit.

3. *Organization of the Physical and Temporal Environment*
   a. Someone takes the child to the grocery store at least once a week.
   b. When Mother is away, care is provided by one of three regular substitutes.
   c. The child's environment appears safe and free of hazards.
4. *Provision of Appropriate Play Materials*
   a. Child has a pull or push toy.
   b. Mother provides toys or interesting activities for child during interview.
   c. Mother provides toys for literature and music (books, records).
5. *Maternal Involvement with the Child*
   a. Mother tends to keep child within visual range and to look at him or her often.
   b. Mother "talks" to child while doing her work.
   c. Mother structures child's play period.
6. *Opportunities for Variety in Daily Stimulation*
   a. Father provides some care giving every day.
   b. Mother reads stories to child at least three times weekly.
   c. Child has at least three or more books of his or her own.

Subsequent studies revealed moderate correlations (.30 – .60) between HOME scores and IQ measures (Bradley & Caldwell, 1976; Bradley et al., 1989). More specifically, mothers who were emotionally and verbally more responsive to their infants, who provided more play materials for their children, and who were generally more involved with their children during observations when their infants were 6 and 24 months of age, had children with higher Stanford-Binet IQ scores at 54 months of age than did mothers who provided less stimulation for their youngsters (Bradley & Caldwell, 1976). Table 14-3 presents the correlations between 6- and 24-month HOME scores and 54-month IQ scores for children in this study.

More recent research using the HOME scale has demonstrated that descriptions of the home environment during the first two years of life predict academic performance at age 11 reasonably well (Bradley, 1989). However, the picture is compli-

TABLE 14-3   Correlations between 54-month Stanford-Binet performance and scores on the HOME scale at 6 and 24 months

HOME subscale	Correlations	
	6 months	24 months
1. Emotional and Verbal Responsibility of Mother	.27	.50**
2. Avoidance of Restriction and Punishment	.10	.28*
3. Organization of Physical and Temporal Environment	.31*	.33*
4. Provision of Appropriate Play Materials	.44**	.56**
5. Maternal Involvement with Child	.28*	.55**
6. Opportunities for Variety in Daily Stimulation	.30*	.39**
Total score	.44**	.57**
Multiple correlation[a]	.50*	.63**

[a]This represents the correlation of all HOME subscales with Binet scores.
*p < .05
**p < .01

SOURCE: Adapted from "The relation of infants' home environment to mental test performance at fifty-four months: A follow-up study," by R. H. Bradley and B. M. Caldwell, 1976, *Child Development, 47,* 1172–1174. Copyright © 1976 The Society for Research in Child Development, Inc. Adapted with permission.

cated. A beneficial early environment, for example, is not apt to have long-term consequences if later environments are less supportive. That is, when the childhood environment is stable, patterns of development are usually stable; when the childhood environment is constantly changing, patterns of intellectual development are also apt to change (Bradley, 1989). Thus, not only is a beneficial early environment important for sound intellectual development, but so is its stability—the beneficial environment also needs to be continuous.

This point was made explicit in a longitudinal study by Sameroff and his colleagues (Sameroff et al., 1993). Children from mainly lower-SES homes were administered IQ tests at 4 and 13 years of age. Children's home environments were also evaluated for risk factors (for example, family size, father absence, maternal education, maternal stress, maternal anxiety). First, Sameroff and his colleagues reported that a composite score of risk factors associated with each child's home life accounted for 34% of the variance in IQ scores at 4 years of age and 37% at 13 years of age. (This percentage increased to 50% at both ages when researchers used a more liberal measure of risk factors.) Thus, environmental risk contributed significantly to children's IQ; this remained true even after SES and mothers' IQ scores were taken into consideration. Second, the researchers reported that children's IQ scores at age 4 were significantly related with their IQ scores at age 13 (correlation = .72). However, environmental-risk scores were also highly correlated between age 4 and 13 years (correlation = .76). Thus, children living in nonsupportive and high-risk environments at age 4 were likely to be living in similar environments at age 13. It is exactly under such conditions that high correlations in IQs over time are expected to be found.

More recent research has used the HOME scales, or measures like it, to examine further the connection between parenting behaviors and later intellectual development for a variety of populations. For example, there has been an increase in the United States in recent years of teenagers giving birth. Research has demonstrated that many of the children of adolescent mothers have major delays in their intellectual, language, and social development (C. Miller et al., 1996). Why should this be the case? Is just being a young mother enough to have negative consequences for one's offspring? Research indicates that it is not youth, per se, but knowledge of child development and "readiness" to be a parent that make a difference (Benasich & Brooks-Gunn, 1996; C. Miller et al., 1996). For example, C. Miller and her colleagues (1996) interviewed pregnant adolescents about their knowledge of child development and their attitudes about parenting. Mother-child interaction style was later evaluated when the infants were 6 months old, and children's intellectual, language, and behavioral development were assessed at 3 years of age. Miller and her colleagues found that adolescent mothers' lack of knowledge about child development and their unrealistic attitudes

about parenting influenced their perceptions of their children which, in turn, affected their behavior toward their children. Mothers who were better prepared for childrearing had children with fewer behavioral problems and better cognitive performance than less-well prepared young women did. A similar pattern of results was reported by Benasich and Brooks-Gunn (1996), who found that adolescent mothers' knowledge of child development and concepts of child rearing when their infants were 12 months of age predicted the quality of the home environment, frequency of behavior problems, and IQ at 36 months of age.

Other studies have looked at the effect of the home environment for children with various degrees of biological and environmental risk. For example, Margret Caughy (1996), examined the relation between several biological risk factors (low birth weight, length of hospitalization, rehospitalization during first year), environmental risk factors (low income, low maternal education, quality of the home environment as measured by a version of HOME Scale), and tests of mathematical and reading readiness in a group of 867 5- and 6-year-old children. Caughy reported a strong relation between maternal education and HOME scores with both reading and mathematics performance. Not surprisingly, children from more intellectually supportive homes performed better on these tests. Also, biological risks (for example, low birth weight) adversely affected children's academic scores, although the impact of biological risk was not as great overall as that of environmental risk. And importantly, the children who were most adversely affected were those who experienced early health problems *and* who lived in impoverished environments as reflected primarily by low HOME scores. For example, children who were rehospitalized during their first year of life and came from homes with low HOME scores (indicating a nonsupportive intellectual environment) had significantly lower mathematics scores than did children who came from similar homes (that is, also having low HOME scores) but who were not rehospitalized. In contrast, rehospitalization did not affect academic scores for those children who came from homes with higher HOME scores (that is, a supportive intellectual environment). These findings are consistent with the transactional model described earlier and indicate that children living in nonsupportive homes are especially affected by biological risk.

Another study that illustrates the interaction between maternal behaviors and children's biological risks was performed by Susan Landry and her colleagues (1997). In this study, 187 very low birth weight (VLBW) infants (less than 1600 grams at birth) and 112 full-term infants, all from Lower SES homes, were followed longitudinally to 40 months of age. All these VLBW infants were at least three weeks "early" (that is, a gestational age of 36 weeks or less), and all had medical problems. Seventy-three of the VLBW infants were described as having high medical risk (high-risk group), whereas the remaining 114 were described as having low medical risk (low-risk group). Several maternal behaviors were coded at 6 and 12 months of age, and children were administered a test of language abilities, the Bayley Scale of Mental Development, and, at 36 months, the Stanford-Binet.

As would be expected, several aspects of maternal behavior predicted children's level of intellectual development. For example, mothers who frequently tried to maintain their child's interest or behavior in an ongoing activity had children with higher cognitive and language scores than did mothers who used maintaining strategies less often. Also, mothers who were restrictive, who used physical or verbal attempts to stop what their children were doing or saying, had children with lower cognitive and language scores. With respect to restrictiveness, the authors stated that "these results suggest that children whose early experiences are frequently interrupted with requests to stop doing something are not able to assume independence in their learning at a normal rate" (pp. 1049–1050). Although the effect of restrictiveness was found for all groups of children, it was especially pronounced for the high-risk group. This restrictiveness style might send the message to children that they are not capable of controlling their own behavior or taking the initiative, and such a style seems to be particularly detrimental for high-risk children, who,

because of their medical problems, are often more developmentally delayed than other VLBW children are.

Naturalistic studies are generally consistent in their findings. Children who grow up in emotionally supportive homes and receive cognitively rich experiences tend to have higher IQs than do children growing up in high-risk homes who receive less intellectual stimulation. But the type of experiences children receive and later intellectual performance is also related to characteristics of the children. The adverse effects of a nonstimulating environment are often exaggerated for high-risk children in particular (children with early health problems).

There are a number of possible explanations for this latter fact. It might be that high-risk infants and children do not have the intellectual wherewithal to benefit from stimulating experiences. Alternatively, their biological impairment might result in different interaction patterns between themselves and their mothers, and this interaction pattern, with the children themselves contributing significantly to the transaction, produces a developmental course that is less than conducive to good intellectual functioning (recall the Zeskind and Ramey study). I think that it is relatively easy to see how high-risk children can contribute to their own intellectual development in this way. It might be less obvious, however, to see how "normal" children also play a role in their own development.

The Role of Children in Affecting Their Own Development

One criticism of the observational studies just reviewed is that they are correlational in nature, making any definitive statement about cause and effect impossible. For example, Burton White (1978) reported that placing children behind barriers, such as in a playpen, for long periods is not conducive to good intellectual development. Given these findings, it is tempting to conclude that restricting a child's exploration by extensive use of a playpen causes lower levels of intellectual functioning at a later time. Although this might be true, the role of the child must also be considered. Some children are easier to keep in a playpen than others. Some children are content sitting and playing with a few favorite toys and rarely complain about their confinement. Others make it very difficult for their parents to make frequent use of the playpen, letting the parents know in no uncertain terms that life behind bars is not for them. The end result might be the same: The child given more freedom to explore develops a sharper intellect than does the child who spends more time in the playpen. However, factors inherent in the child (that is, tolerance for confinement) might be just as critical as the parents' behavior in affecting the course of development. Again, parent-child interaction must be viewed as transaction, and we should not lose track of the child's role in influencing the structure of his or her own environment.

A home observational study that considered the possible role of children in influencing their own development was conducted by Jean Carew (1980). Carew observed the behaviors of mothers and their children in their homes when the children were between the ages of 12 and 33 months and related her observations to children's IQ scores at 36 months. Carew reported that mothers' behaviors (for example, providing highly intellectual stimulation) when their children were between 12 and 27 months of age best predicted IQ level at 36 months. However, mothers' behaviors toward their children during the 30- to 33-month observation period were less predictive of IQ. During this time, solitary, child-initiated activities accounted for more of the individual differences in IQ level at 36 months than did mothers' behaviors. Similarly, in a Swedish longitudinal study, quality of the home environment predicted children's verbal abilities at age 40 months of age but not when children were tested at 101 months of age (second grade) (Broberg et al., 1997). These findings suggest that the direct influence of parents on children's behavior diminishes with age, as children take an increasingly active role in guiding their own development (see Scarr & McCartney, 1983). This is also consistent with the findings discussed earlier that the heritability of intelligence increases with age, as specific parental-

environmental influences decline and genetic influences increase.

This decline, of course, in no way implies that how parents behave toward their children does not affect them after 30 (or 100) months of age. What must be kept in mind, however, is that children play a crucial role in influencing their own development at an early age and that parental influences must be evaluated as a continuous transaction between children and their parents, both of whom are changed as a result of the interactions.

The Effects of Experience on Establishing Intellectual Competence from a Developmental Perspective

The results of research, both from behavioral genetics and from those measuring carefully the home environment, suggest that the contributions of environment to individual differences in children's intelligence vary at different times in development. That is, there is not a constant relation between environment and intelligence but, rather, a dynamic one, changing over time. Along similar lines, the possibility that genetic and environmental factors influence children's intellects differently at different ages was investigated in a longitudinal study by Keith Yeates and his colleagues (1983). They examined the intellectual development of children from low SES homes classified as at high risk for mental retardation. Children were given Stanford-Binet IQ tests at ages 24, 36, and 48 months. Their mothers were also administered an IQ test, and the investigators assessed the quality of the home environment and mother-child interactions at various points over the course of the study, using the HOME scale.

Using maternal IQ level as a measure of genetic influence on children's intelligence, Yeates and his colleagues reported that at 24 months, measures of maternal IQ and of home environment combined accounted for only 11% of the differences in children's IQ scores. The picture changed, however, by 48 months. At this time, the combined effects of maternal IQ level and home environment accounted for nearly three times as much of the differences in children's Stanford-Binet scores (29%) as was the case at 24 months, with maternal IQ level and the HOME measure contributing equally to individual differences.

Following a theory proposed by Robert McCall (1981), Yeates and his associates suggested that neither genetic nor environmental differences have much effect on children's mental development during the first two years. McCall asserted that infant development is highly *canalized*, meaning that it follows a species-typical pattern in all but the most limited environments. For instance, nearly all children babble (even deaf babies), walk, and acquire object permanence sometime before their second birthday. These patterns of development are relatively unaffected by all but the most adverse effects of genetics and environment. With the advent of symbolic functioning, the quality of cognition changes, and, according to McCall, children's intellects are more affected by variations in both genetics and environment.

Given this insight, we must interpret carefully the connection between early experience and later intellectual development. For example, in a longitudinal study, Burton White (1978) reported that behaviors of parents when their children are between 10- and 18-months of age predict their children's IQ at age 5. However, his study did not take into consideration children's environments much beyond this 10- to 18-month period. Supportive and nurturing parents of toddlers are likely to be similarly supportive when their children are 3, 4, and 5 years old. Thus, the significant correlations between parental behaviors during the second year of life and IQ at age 5 cannot be easily interpreted. Although environmental causes are clearly indicated, the exact nature of the relationship is not apparent. Competent parenting when the child is older might be equally as important as, or even more important than, good parenting early in a child's life. Alternatively, the supportive behaviors of mothers when their children are 15 months old might produce competent 3-year-olds, and the self-directed behavior of children from this point on might be mainly responsible for high IQs at age 5.

Although the overall picture is somewhat murky, it is apparent that experiences during the preschool years set the stage for later intellectual accomplishments. Supportive and responsive environments tend to produce intelligent and competent children. It is impossible at this time to specify when, during childhood, these experiences are most important or to be precise concerning the role children have in affecting their own development. Rather, from the available literature one can conclude that early experience is important, but so is later experience. Also, from infancy, children play an important role in their own development, helping to shape their own intellects. From a transactional perspective, we cannot put any numbers or percentages on how much of intellectual growth is influenced by nature versus nurture or how much is child-initiated or parent-initiated. From the current perspective, in fact, *how much* is the wrong question. The better question concerns how nature and nurture interact to yield a particular pattern of development, always keeping in mind that the child plays an active role in shaping his or her own life course.

Modification and Maintenance of Intellectual Functioning

It seems clear from the preceding discussion that individual differences in intelligence can be influenced by a child's early environment. A related series of questions concerns the modification of intelligence. Will the elevated or depressed IQ levels that are found in some populations still be present decades later, or can people's level of intellectual functioning be modified by subsequent experiences?

In the section to follow, the modification and maintenance of intellectual functioning are considered for two related sets of conditions. First, to what extent are the intellectual deficits resulting from an impoverished early environment permanent? Can the deleterious effects of deprivation be ameliorated? And second, to what extent are the intellectual benefits resulting from enriched early environments permanent? Are intellectual skills that have been acquired during the preschool years maintained into later childhood?

Modification of Retardation Caused by Early Experience

As noted previously in this chapter, an early impoverished environment often results in reduced mental functioning. Based on the results of institutionalization studies of the type described earlier (Dennis, 1973; Spitz, 1945), it was once assumed that the deleterious effects of stimulus and social deprivation are permanent. Nevertheless, evidence suggesting the reversibility of the negative consequences of early deprivation has surfaced from time to time. Observations of children reared in relative isolation, for example, have indicated some plasticity of intellectual functioning with rehabilitation. One of the best-documented studies of the mental growth of isolated children is that of Koluchova (1976). A set of monozygotic twins who were physically and psychologically normal at 11 months experienced abuse, neglect, and malnutrition until discovered at 7 years 2 months. The children had no language and had an estimated mental age of about 3 years. They were placed in foster care and provided an educational program in the hope that they would attain some semblance of intellectual normalcy. The program was far more successful than originally expected; the twins had WISC scores of 93 and 95 by 11 years of age and of 101 and 100 by 14 years. Several other studies have similarly reported normal intellectual or language functioning following educational intervention for children initially classified as retarded because of neglect or isolation over the preschool years (see Clarke & Clarke, 1976). Related to these findings are reports of drastic changes in the intellectual performance of children from war-torn Southeast Asia in the 1970s adopted into American homes (Clark & Hanisee, 1982; Winick, Meyer, & Harris, 1975), which I discussed briefly in Chapter 2. It must be noted, however, that these are exceptions. Not all children

who experience severe deprivation early in life show such reversibility as a result of later education (Curtiss, 1977).

One controversial study concerning the reversibility of the negative effects of early experience was reported by Harold Skeels (1966). Skeels studied infants who were inmates of an orphanage. The orphanage was similar to many other Depression-era institutions, overcrowded and understaffed, and it was the type of institution that had been associated with reduced mental functioning by as early as 4 months of age (Spitz, 1945).

During the course of several years, 13 children (10 girls and 3 boys) from the orphanage were transferred to a school for the mentally retarded and placed on the wards of the brighter women inmates. These infants all showed signs of retardation at time of placement. Their IQ scores ranged from 35 to 89, with an average of 64.3. The average age at placement was 19 months, with a range from 7 to 36 months. These 13 children made up the experimental group. A contrast group was chosen from children who remained in the orphanage until at least the age of 4, 8 boys and 4 girls. The mean IQ score of the children in this group was 86.7 when first tested (mean age at first test = 16 months), with a range from 50 to 101.

The children in the experimental group received loving attention from the mentally retarded women. There was competition between wards to see who would have the first baby to walk or to talk. The attendants also spent much time with the youngsters. In almost every case, a single adult (inmate or attendant) became closely attached to a child, resulting in an intense one-to-one relationship that was supplemented by other adults.

The experimental children remained in the institution for an average of 19 months and were then returned to the orphanage, with most being subsequently placed in adoptive homes.

On their removal from the school for the mentally retarded, each child was administered an IQ test; the average score was 91.8, an increase of 27.5 points. The children in the contrast group were tested at approximately 4 years of age and had an

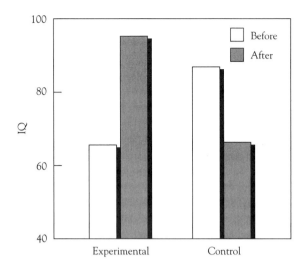

FIGURE 14-4 Average IQ scores before placement and two-and-one-half years after completion of program for children in the experimental and control groups. SOURCE: Adapted from data presented in Skeels, H. M. (1966). Adult status of children with contrasting early life experiences. *Monographs of the Society for Research in Child Development, 31* (Serial No. 105).

average IQ score of 60.5 points, a decline of 26.2 points. The children were retested approximately 2.5 years later, with the experimental group having an average score of 95.9 and the contrast group an average of 66.1 (see Figure 14-4).

The results of this study are very impressive and demonstrate that toddlers characterized as severely retarded can realize significant gains in intelligence when placed in certain environments. Skeels extended his study, following these people into adulthood when they were between 25 and 35 years old. IQ tests were not given, but information was obtained concerning the occupational and educational levels of the subjects, as well as information pertaining to their social adjustment. All 13 people in the experimental group had married, whereas only 2 of the 11 surviving members of the contrast group had married. The median number of years of formal education completed by the experimental group was 12 (that is, high school education), whereas the contrast group had completed a median of only 2.75 years. Most experimental subjects or their spouses

were employed in skilled or semiskilled jobs. The range of socioeconomic status, based on income and occupation, was comparable with regional norms. In contrast, with one exception, people in the contrast group were in the lowest two socioeconomic levels. Four of the people in the contrast group remained institutional inmates, 5 held menial jobs such as dishwashers or cafeteria help, and only 1 had a skilled occupation (compositor and typesetter). IQ scores were available for some of the 28 children of the experimental subjects and ranged from 86 to 125, with an average of 103.9. In general, people in the experimental group, who started life with a severe disadvantage, were normal by a variety of intellectual, occupational, and social standards.

The Skeels study demonstrates the potential plasticity of human intelligence. However, the study is not without its detractors. As an experiment, it leaves much to be desired. Skeels took advantage of a naturally occurring situation and assessed the effects of early environments within the constraints imposed on him by ethical and institutional considerations. As a result, there is much to fault with the methodology of the study, and although the study has been widely praised, its serious shortcomings have also been noted (see Longstreth, 1981).

One interpretation of the Skeel's study consistent with the transactional view of development popular today is that the intellectual immaturity of the retarded women might actually have facilitated social interaction with the orphans, providing them with stimulation they would not normally have received in the orphanage. In most situations, the characteristics of the severely retarded children in the experimental group would not produce lavish attention from adults. Most well-intending adults who direct their attention to a child expect some response in return. Children who are nonresponsive and generally lethargic tend not to elicit continued stimulation from adults, particularly adults from highly stressed homes (Sameroff & Chandler, 1975). This presumably would be especially true of overburdened members of an institution's staff. Because of the limited mental capacity of the inmates, however, their attention might have been repeatedly directed to the children even in the absence of appropriate responses. After prolonged stimulation, the children might have become more responsive and begun the climb back to normal intellectual functioning. That is, it is possible that the intellectual immaturity of the institutionalized women in the Skeels study matched the needs of the children. Of course, highly responsive women of normal or above-normal intelligence could also have served as appropriate "therapists" for these children, as was apparently the case in the Asian adoption studies cited earlier (Clark & Hanisee, 1982). But this is not the type of experience that these children could have expected from the orphanage staff. Moreover, had the children remained in the institution for the mentally retarded for considerably longer, their intellectual gains would surely have been lost. As their intelligence increased, so would their needs for intellectual stimulation, quickly exceeding the boundaries of what the mentally retarded women could have provided.

In more recent times, after the fall of Ceausescu in communist Romania in 1989, hundreds of infants and young children were discovered in overcrowded and understaffed institutions, under conditions of nutritional and social deprivation at least as horrendous as those that existed in institutions during the early part of this century (Kaler & Freedman, 1994). Many of these malnourished infants were adopted into advantaged homes across the globe. Some were adopted very early in life (0 to 6 months), whereas others were not adopted until after 2 or 3 years of age (O'Connor et al., in press; Morison, Ames, & Chisholm, 1995; Rutter et al., 1998). What happened to these children, all of whom were suffering from the effects of malnutrition and emotional neglect when adopted? Were they able to catch up, and, if so, by how much? What effect did age of adoption (or, stated another way, time spent institutionalized) have on their eventual recovery?

Research examining the course of development for Romanian children adopted in United Kingdom (UK) provides some preliminary answers to these questions (O'Connor et al., in press; Rutter et al., 1998). Romanian children left their institutions for adoptive homes at ages ranging from a few months old to 42 months of age. For comparison purposes,

TABLE 14-4 Scores on the General Cognitive Index (GCI) at age 6 for UK and Romanian children by the age they were adopted. SOURCE: Adapted from O'Connor, T. G., Rutter, M., Beckett, C., Keaveney, L., & Kreppner, J. M., and the English and Romanian Adoptees Study Team. (in press) *Child Development*.

Nation	Age	GCI Scores
UK	0–8 mos	117
Romanian	0–6 mos	114
Romanian	7–24 mos	101
Romanian	24–42 mos	90

they were classified into one of three groups: those adopted between 0 and 6 months, 7 and 24 months, and 25 and 42 months. These children were compared with a group of infants born in the UK and adopted by other UK parents. All of the UK-born children were adopted between 0 and 6 months of age. All children were administered the McCarthy scale at 6 years of age. This scale produces a Global Cognitive Index (GCI) that has a population mean of 100 (like an IQ test).

The researchers reported remarkable recovery of cognitive abilities in all groups of Romanian adoptees. Despite the substantial developmental delay that all the Romanian adopted children had demonstrated when first arriving to the UK, each group had mean GCI scores within the normal range (see Table 14-4). The average GCI score of the 0–6-month adopted Romania children was no different from that of the UK-adopted children. However, the scores did vary as a function of how long children had been institutionalized; children who had been institutionalized for 2 years or longer before being adopted had the lowest overall scores, and children who had been institutionalized for 6 months or less had the highest overall scores.

These findings indicate the remarkable resiliency of children to the effects of early deprivation, but also the long-term consequences of prolonged nutritional, social, and emotional neglect. One should not be surprised that children who experienced more than two years of extreme privation demonstrated some long-term effects. However, that many of these children were functioning above normal at

6 years of age is impressive, and we must wait for future research before we know if this group will show any subsequent gains.

In other research, changes in the intellectual functioning of children from an isolated Guatemalan farming village were assessed by Jerome Kagan, Robert Klein, and their associates (1973; Kagan et al., 1979). During the first year of life, infants were tightly bundled and restricted to the inside of a windowless hut. The babies were frequently ill, and some suffered from malnutrition. There were very few toys or objects with which to play, and adults were minimally interactive with the infants, spending most of their waking hours working outside and away from the hut. The children remained restricted to the hut until they were able to locomote well, usually between 13 and 16 months. Similar to institutionalized children (Spitz, 1945), these infants displayed retarded intellectual and social development during their first two years.

However, once children were able to walk, they encountered a complex world of people, domestic animals, and other children. They were assigned adult tasks at an early age, so that 8-year olds were responsible for cooking meals, helping their fathers in the fields, cleaning, or taking care of infants.

Despite their early confinement, when these children were evaluated on a series of memory and perceptual tests, they performed as well as middle-class American children (Kagan & Klein, 1973). However, when these children were tested on more complex cognitive tasks that included classifying objects into conceptual categories and conservation of liquid and matter, the Guatemalan children performed significantly worse than their American counterparts (Kagan et al., 1979). Kagan and Klein interpreted these findings as indicating that the intellectually harmful results of early experience can be reversed when children encounter more stimulating and challenging environments beginning in their second year. Special intervention is not necessary, as long as the environment is sufficiently stimulating to permit the development of the cognitive skills that are the basis for successful functioning in all human societies. The poorer performance of children on the more complex tasks was probably not

the result of experiences in infancy but, rather, a lack of schooling. Educational opportunities for these children were minimal, and performance on the type of cognitive tests used in this study has been shown to be greatly influenced by formal schooling (Rogoff, 1990). In general, the major difference in the interpretation of the two Guatemalan studies is one of degree. The deleterious consequences of restricted infant experience can be modified by adequate postinfancy stimulation. What is adequate depends on what particular cognitive skills one is dealing with. The more complex the skills, the more intense the experiential intervention must be.

Along these lines, the short-term effectiveness of **compensatory education programs** has been well documented by several projects designed to provide preschool children from low-income homes with the intellectual skills necessary to do well in school (Klaus & Gray, 1968; Ramey, Campbell, & Finkelstein, 1984). Such programs have raised the IQ scores of high-risk children by 10 to 15 points during the course of the program. These experimental programs, most of which were begun in the 1960s, varied considerably in the organization of their curricula, ranging from programs based on Piagetian theory to those using behavior modification techniques as advocated by B. F. Skinner and other behaviorists. What most programs did have in common was an emphasis on language and problem-solving skills and a low student-teacher ratio, allowing substantial individual attention to children. Generally, the greatest gains were demonstrated by children in the more rigorous, highly structured programs. In some studies, large gains in IQ level were noted relative to control subjects and to the children's performance before they entered the programs (see Barnett, 1995). In others, intervention began shortly after birth, with children demonstrating high IQ scores relative to control children at every age tested, thus never needing compensation for below-average intellectual achievement (Garber, 1988; Ramey, Campbell, & Finkelstein, 1989). More will be said about the long-term effects of such intervention programs in the following section.

But before we move on, let us consider a final question relating to the reversibility of deleterious effects of early experience: At what age is plasticity lost? Unfortunately, we are not able to answer this question. We do know from animal research that plasticity is reduced with age (Scott, 1968) and that we are most malleable as infants. Human development has been proposed to be highly canalized during the first 18 or 24 months of life, meaning that all children follow the species-typical path "under a wide range of diverse environments and exhibit strong self-righting tendencies following exposure to severely atypical environments" (McCall, 1981, p. 5). In other words, although infants might be adversely affected by early maladaptive environments, there is a strong tendency to return to a course of normalcy, given an appropriate environment. This plasticity is progressively reduced later in life, beginning as early as 18 or 24 months of age. In general, the earlier intervention is begun, the greater its chance of reversing an established behavior pattern, if for no other reason than older children and adults are more reluctant than younger children to accept the imposition of a drastically changed environment.

Maintenance of the Beneficial Effects of Early Experience on Intelligence

If the effects of a negative early environment can be reversed, what about the effects of a beneficial early environment? If intelligence can be modified for the better by experiences later in childhood, can a later-childhood environment also modify a child's intellectual functioning for the worse?

For the most part, evidence of the long-term effects of positive early environments comes from follow-up studies of preschool compensatory education programs. Although the initial reports of these programs were favorable, doubts concerning their long-term effectiveness began to surface shortly thereafter. The initial gains in IQ and academic performance shown by program graduates were slowly lost, and by the end of the fourth grade, levels of intellectual attainment were comparable between children who had participated in the programs and those who had not (Klaus & Gray, 1968). Figure 14-5

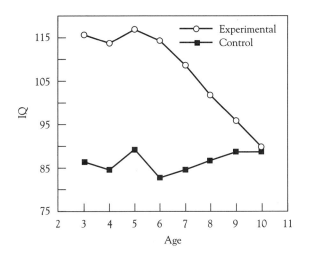

FIGURE 14-5 Typical pattern of IQ changes for experimental and control children during preschool program (2 to 6 years) and after.

shows the typical pattern of IQ changes for graduates of preschool intervention programs.

Despite these findings, researchers were not ready to dismiss the influence of early compensatory education on the later intellectual functioning of high-risk children, and several investigators inquired into the long-term (from middle school and beyond) consequences of the preschool experience. Two of the more comprehensive investigations of the long-term effects of preschool compensatory education programs were reported by Irving Lazar and his colleagues (1982), who evaluated the effects of 11 experimental programs, and W. Steven Barnett (1995), who examined the effects of 36 model demonstration projects and large-scale public programs. The findings of the two studies were similar. Compensatory preschool programs had minimal long-term effects on IQ and academic achievement. Although the programs had an initial impact on children's IQ scores, few reliable differences were found between experimental and control subjects by 10 years of age. Preschool graduates did score higher on some achievement tests than control children did, but this effect was not widespread.

More encouraging findings were found for school competence. For example, Lazar and his colleagues

(1982) reported the median rate of assignment to special education classes was 13.8% for children who had participated in preschool programs and 28.6% for control children. Although less dramatic, there were also significant group differences in the percentage of children who were held back in grade. The median grade-retention rate was 30.5% for children in the control group and 25.8% for children who had participated in the preschool programs (Lazar et al., 1982). Differences were also found in children's attitudes toward achievement. Program graduates were more likely to give achievement-related reasons for being proud of themselves, and the mothers of the experimental children felt more positively about their children and their likelihood of success than did the mothers of the control subjects.

There have been some exceptions to this general pattern, including the North Carolina Abecedarian Program (Campbell & Ramey, 1994). Children from rural North Carolina, identified as at-risk for mental retardation, attended an educationally oriented daycare program beginning shortly after birth and continuing until they entered first grade. When tested at age 12, children who had attended the preschool program had significantly higher IQ scores (94) than control children (88) did. Also, children in the preschool group scored consistently higher on a battery of academic tests (Woodcock-Johnson Psychoeducational Battery, see Figure 14-6). Similar effects of greater sixth-grade reading and math achievement for high-risk children who attended an urban preschool program relative to control children have also been reported (Reynolds et al., 1996).

The findings of the long-term benefits of preschool intervention are somewhat mixed. On the one hand, most (but not all) studies found that the intellectual benefits realized during the preschool years were lost when the program responsible for the gains was discontinued. Once intellectual competence is attained, it must be maintained. Apparently, the intellectual environment for most of the low-income children after leaving the program was not sufficiently supportive to maintain the level of intelligence established during the preschool years. On the other hand, several studies have reported long-term intellectual effects, and, taken together,

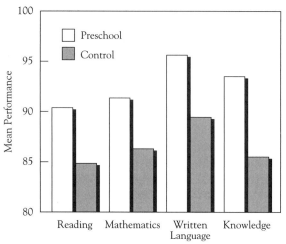

FIGURE 14-6 Mean scores on Woodcock-Johnson Psychoeducational Battery at age 12 for children who participated in the Abecedarian preschool program and control children. SOURCE:: Adapted from data presented in Campbell, F. A., & Ramey, C. T. (1994). Effects of early intervention on intellectual and academic achievement: A follow-up study of children from low-income families. *Child Development, 65*, 684–698.

there are several significant and important noncognitive benefits of compensatory education. The difference in assignment to special education classes alone represents a significant savings in tax dollars, justifying the cost of the preschool programs (Karoly et al., 1998). Furthermore, differences in grade retention (and presumably the probability of completing high school) and in personal and maternal attitudes suggest that program graduates will be more likely to succeed economically in the years to come than will children in the control conditions.

If long-term cognitive effects of preschool compensatory education are only occasionally found, how can we explain the long-term school-related benefits that are consistently produced? Doris Entwisle (1995) suggested four reasons: (a) *easing transition to first grade*. The initial higher IQs and achievement made by high-risk children who attend these programs makes the work load of first grade easier to handle; (b) *preventing placement in low tracks*. Children who start first grade at a higher

TABLE 14-5 Mean percentile ranks for children in Project Follow Through for subtests of the WRAT and the MAT.

Time of test	WRAT reading	MAT reading	MAT math	MAT spelling
Last year of Follow Through:				
Grade 3	63rd	38th	62nd	47th
After completion of Follow Through:				
Grade 5	53rd	22nd	29th	37th
Grade 6	38th	20th	27th	37th

SOURCE: Adapted with permission from "A Follow-up of Follow-Through: The Later Effects of the Direct Instruction Model on Children in Fifth and Sixth Grades," by W. C. Becker and R. Gersten, 1982, *American Educational Research Journal, 19,* 75–92. Copyright © 1982 American Educational Research Association.

level are less apt to get placed in lower reading and math tracks and are thus more likely to progress throughout the year and beyond. This can result in a reduced likelihood of being retained and assigned to special educational classes; (c) *rising expectations held by significant others.* Parents, grandparents, and older siblings might increase their expectations for a child's success based on the child's increased performance in preschool. In one study, high-risk children who attended preschool had parents who were more involved in their education in first grade than did children who did not attend preschool (Reynolds et al., 1996); and (d) *providing the support of peers.* Children who have more preschool experience show better cooperative play, are more sociable, and better liked than are children without the experience. Much of what children learn in school is social, or derived from social experience, and getting off to a good start in first grade, because of their preschool experience, can have its benefits.

What if the compensatory preschool program had been extended into the early elementary school years? Might there then have been long-term effects of early education? This question was evaluated by Wesley Becker and Russell Gersten (1982). They examined the academic performance of fifth- and sixth-grade children who had participated in Project Follow Through, a program designed to take over where the federally funded preschool Project Head Start left off. In Project Follow Through, low-income children are provided with compensatory education through the third grade. Becker and Gersten evaluated the effectiveness of five different Follow Through programs, comparing children's

performance with that of control groups and with national norms on a series of achievement tests.

Children in the study had been administered portions of the Wide Range Achievement Test (WRAT) or the Metropolitan Achievement Test (MAT). Significant differences were found between the Follow Through and control children in both the fifth and sixth grades. Most striking were differences in reading level on the WRAT and differences on the spelling and math-problem-solving subscales of the MAT, all in favor of the Follow Through children. Of 180 statistical comparisons made between the control and the Follow Through children from the five different programs, 76 (42%) favored the Follow Through children, whereas only 2 (1%) favored the control subjects. Thus, compensatory education programs that are continued beyond the preschool years have beneficial effects on academic achievement.

Becker and Gersten also compared the performance of the Follow Through children on the WRAT and MAT with national norms. Mean percentile ranks for the Follow Through children for tests given in the third, fifth, and sixth grades are presented in Table 14-5. The percentiles are based on national averages for the WRAT and the MAT, with a score of 50 representing average performance. Tests given in the third grade reflect the children's performance while they were still participating in Project Follow Through, whereas scores in the fifth and sixth grades reflect performance two and three years after termination of the program.

The most striking aspect of these data is the steady decline in percentile standing as a function of grade. These high-risk children were performing close to or above the national average on three of these four tests in the third grade (the exception being MAT reading, 38th percentile). Two years after they had left Follow Through, only their WRAT reading scores were comparable to the national average, and by the sixth grade they had declined to the 38th percentile. These results indicate that although the Follow Through children maintained an academic advantage relative to matched sets of control children, they showed a decrement relative to national averages after leaving the program. Again, the social and educational benefits of the program are significant. However, as with the findings of Lazar and his associates (1982) and Barnett (1995), intellectual gains diminished once the children left the program.

How Modifiable Is Human Intelligence?

In general, the results of the studies reviewed in the previous sections indicate that the negative effects of early experience can be reversed and the beneficial effects of an early stimulating environment can be altered by experiences that follow it. Human intelligence is modifiable in both positive and negative directions. Intelligence is not something that once gotten is necessarily kept. Intelligence, as measured by IQ tests, is a reflection of a person's intellectual functioning at a given time. Once established, intelligence (or any other complex behavior, for that matter) must be maintained. If the environmental supports responsible for establishing cognitive competence are removed, we should not be surprised that intelligence suffers.

The results of these studies reflect a flexible cognitive system that over the course of childhood can be greatly modified by changes in the environment. However, the research cited can be criticized for not being representative of the way the world is structured for most children. Fortunately, few children spend their early years restricted to closets, and most children who are provided stimulating environments as preschoolers can expect comparably stimulating environments in the years to come. These studies indicate what *can* happen to levels of intelli-

gence over childhood and not necessarily what actually *does* happen.

Maintenance of a certain level of intelligence is most likely to be found when a child's environment remains stable. However, the environments in which children find themselves change over time. One such change is the shift from home to school. Another related shift is from a family-centered life-style to a peer-centered life-style. Such a shift does not occur all at once, but with increasing age, children become more independent of their families' influence and more dependent on their peers or their own inherent traits in determining the type of activities they choose (Scarr & McCartney, 1983). To the extent that these changes in environments do not represent major shifts in intellectual emphasis, levels of intelligence can be expected to be maintained. The more diverse the changing environments, the greater the change in level of intelligence that can be expected.

The Stability of Intelligence

We like to believe that the world we live in is relatively stable and predictable. This predilection includes some implicit beliefs concerning the stability of mental functioning. We have looked at the issue of stability briefly in earlier chapters in this book. For example, certain aspects of memory performance remain stable over time, whereas other aspects do not. But the primary arena for the study of stability of mental functioning has been the topic of intelligence. To what extent is intellectual functioning, as measured by IQ or other general assessments of intelligence, stable over time? Will a bright 5-year-old turn out to be an intelligent teenager, or is prediction of adolescent and adult intelligence from early childhood no more reliable than tossing a coin? And what about infancy? Is there any way that we can predict what level of intellectual functioning a child will attain from assessments in infancy?

Traditionally, developmental psychologists have tended to believe in the stability of cognitive ability. One reason for this perspective is that our profession specializes in investigating conditions in early life that predict later behavior or prepare the child for subsequent accomplishments. Despite our common-sense assumptions of the stability of intelligence and our professional biases that cause us to look for stability over time, what is the evidence? To what extent are individual differences in intellectual functioning stable over infancy and childhood?

Defining Stability

Before looking at any evidence, let me define again what is meant by **stability.** Obviously, stability does not mean that intelligence stays the same over time. Of course children get smarter as they get older. Rather, stability refers to the relative constancy of individual differences — the extent to which different children maintain their rank order over time in comparison with their peers. Is the valedictorian of her kindergarten class likely to be among the top students when her high school class graduates? Is the highly attentive 4-month-old likely to be a better reader than his less attentive peer?

Stability in this sense is measured by correlations of rank order. If a group of children is given IQ tests at age 5, for example, they can be ranked in IQ score from highest to lowest. If that same group is tested again at age 10, we can compare the rankings of the children's IQ scores at the two ages. If the rankings are similar, the correlation will be positive and high. If there is no stability of individual differences in IQ scores between ages 5 and 10, the correlation will be close to 0. It is also possible, although seemingly unlikely, that the brightest children at age 5 will be, on the average, the least bright children at age 10, resulting in a negative correlation. Note that the correlations used to assess stability are unrelated to the actual level of performance. Correlations may be high, implying stability, although the average level of performance might have systematically increased (or decreased) for most members of the sample.

In the following sections, the stability of individual differences in intelligence over time is examined. For the most part, IQ data are used as a measure of intellectual functioning, although several studies are reported that used other measures of cognition. In addition to investigating stability of intelligence via cross-age correlations, I also examine patterns of change. That is, although there might be high correlations between measures of intelligence at two ages, that does not mean that intelligence has not changed over that period. In other words, the relationship between developmental function — patterns of change that characterize the species — and the stability of individual differences will be evaluated.

Predicting Later Intelligence from Tests in Infancy

One hot research topic in cognitive development over the past decade or so has been that of predicting childhood IQ from measures taken in infancy. Before presenting this new research, let me provide a little necessary history.

Developmental psychologists and psychometricians have generally believed that intelligence is stable over time, including from infancy into childhood. In part, this prediction is based on the assumption that human intelligence can best be described as a unitary construct that varies in a continuous fashion over time. From a psychometric perspective, this is best described as a single general factor of intelligence, *g*. When developmental function is continuous and quantitative in nature, there is every reason to expect that individual differences will be stable (**continuity with stability**).

Testing such an hypothesis is relatively straightforward. Tests given in infancy are correlated with IQ tests given in childhood. The problem, of course, is developing tests that assess intelligence in infancy. Such tests have been around for nearly 60 years in the form of infant psychometric scales that produce a developmental quotient (DQ) with the same psychometric properties as IQ tests. Examples from one of these tests, the first edition of the Bayley Scale, were presented in Chapter 13. However, when babies who were given the Bayley and other scales are later administered IQ tests in early childhood, the correlations are disappointingly low. Prediction is only slightly greater for high-risk infants. Table 14-6 summarizes the results

TABLE 14-6   Median correlations between DQ test scores and later IQ test scores for normal and high-risk samples

| | Normal sample | | | | High-risk sample | | | |
| | Age at follow-up test (years) | | | | Age at follow-up test (years) | | | |
Infant test (months)	3	4–5	6+	Mean	3	4–5	6+	Mean
3–4	.04 (4)*	.06 (2)	.07 (3)	.06	.14 (2)	.08 (4)	.07 (2)	.10
5–7	.25 (14)	.20 (5)	.06 (6)	.15	.27 (5)	.24 (13)	.28 (3)	.26
8–11	.20 (8)	.23 (5)	.21 (3)	.21	.29 (6)	.23 (10)	.29 (6)	.27
Mean	.16	.16	.11		.23	.18	.21	

*Numbers in parentheses represent number of studies in each median correlation.

SOURCE: Fagan, J. F., III, & Singer, J. T. (1983). Infant recognition memory as a measure of intelligence. In L. P. Lipsitt & C. K. Rovee-Collier (Eds.), *Advances in infancy research* (Vol. 2). Norwood, NJ: Ablex.

of studies examining the relationship between sensorimotor tests of development and later IQ scores for both normal and high-risk samples as a function of age of testing (both in infancy and in childhood). As can be seen, the correlations are uniformly low; the average correlation between infant tests and IQ scores at age 6 years is only .11 for normal infants. Prediction is often considerably higher for infants scoring very low on the tests (for example, below 80), suggesting some power of these tests to predict pathology in limited situations (see McCall, Hogarty, & Hurlburt, 1972).

This should be very discouraging for people who believe the continuity-with-stability theory of intelligence, yet there is always the argument that the infant DQ tests are not sensitive enough, and new tests will eventually find the relationship. Yet, others have looked at these data and are not surprised. The reason for the low correlations is that development varies in a discontinuous way between infancy and childhood, with qualitative differences in the nature of intelligence. When developmental function is discontinuous (that is, relatively abrupt and qualitative in nature), there is no reason to expect stability. The bright sensorimotor child might become a bright preoperational child, for example, but because of the substantial difference in the nature of

cognition between the infant and preschool child, such stability should not be expected.

This **discontinuity-with-instability** position was best articulated by Robert McCall and his colleagues (McCall, Eichorn, & Hogarty, 1977), who demonstrated using longitudinal data that there is little stability of individual differences in cognitive performance even across different stages in infancy, to say nothing of between infancy and later childhood. For example, McCall and his associates were able to identify five stages in cognitive development between birth and 3 years of age: birth to 2 months; 2 to 8 months; 8 to 13 months; 13 to 21 months; and 21 to 31–36 months. These correspond roughly to Piaget's stages of sensorimotor development, as outlined in Chapter 4. McCall and his colleagues found that there was substantial stability of individual differences (that is, high cross-age correlations) when comparing performance *within* a stage (for example, between 8 and 12 months), but much less stability (that is, low cross-age correlations) when comparisons were made *between* stages (for example, between 10 and 14 months). These data very nicely demonstrate continuity with stability for contrasts *within* a cognitive stage and discontinuity with instability for contrasts *between* cognitive stages.

This, basically, is where the argument stood until the 1980s, when new research was reported providing evidence of stability of intelligence from infancy to childhood. The evidence came from what to many was an unlikely source—measures of infant memory and attention. Recall from our discussions of infant perception and attention in Chapter 6 the habituation/dishabituation paradigm. Infants are presented a stimulus (a picture, for example) and their attention to that stimulus is noted (in this case, looking time). The same stimulus is presented repeatedly, with the typical finding that infant attention to the stimulus decreases. When attention to the stimulus decreases sufficiently (usually to 50% of what it was on the initial trials), the infant is said to have habituated to the stimulus.

This same technique has been used to assess recognition memory. Some time after habituation (minutes, hours, or even days), the infant is shown two stimuli, usually simultaneously. One of the stimuli is the same picture the infant had been habituated to earlier. The other stimulus is a new one. Memory is indicated if infants look at the novel stimulus more than at the habituated stimulus. They still remember the old stimulus and are still tired of looking at it. This *preference-for-novelty* measure has been used extensively and has revealed much about infant memory capacity.

Psychologists began to look for relationships between individual differences in measures of infant attention/memory and childhood IQ. Joseph Fagan was the first person to systematically examine this relationship, which is fitting, given that he was a pioneer of the preference-for-novelty technique in assessing infant recognition memory.

In an early review, Fagan and Singer (1983) examined the results of previously published experiments concerning the prediction of childhood intelligence from infants' preferences for novelty by means of visual recognition, and they also reported the results of their own longitudinal study. The ages of infants assessed ranged from 3 to 7 months and assessments of childhood IQ for 12 sets of data ranged from 2 to 7.5 years. The range of correlations between infants' preferences for novelty and later

IQ was .33 to .66, with a mean value of .44. That is, the stronger an infants' preference for novelty was (the more they looked at the novel versus the familiar stimulus), the higher their IQ during early childhood was apt to be. Compare this with the values given in Table 14-6, where average correlations between sensorimotor tests and IQ scores for normal infants ranged from .16 (for IQ tests given between the ages of 3 and 5 years) to .11 (for IQ tests given at age 6 and beyond). Similar results were later reported using habituation measures, with infants who habituate faster having higher childhood IQs (see Bornstein, 1989; Bornstein & Sigman, 1986).

Habituation and preference-for-novelty tasks have been used with hearing and touch as well as vision, and researchers have reported comparable correlations with childhood IQ when infants are tested in these other modalities (hearing—O'Connor, Cohen, & Parmelee, 1984; touch—Rose, Feldman, Wallace, & McCarton, 1991). Results are found both for full-term (Rose, Feldman, & Wallace, 1992; Slater, Cooper et al., 1989) and preterm (Rose et al., 1989; Sigman et al., 1986) infants. Two more recent reviews of the literature have demonstrated the reliability of these findings. Bornstein (1989) reports a median correlation between infant measures of habituation and childhood IQ of .49; the median correlation between preference for novelty and childhood IQ was .46. McCall and Carriger (1993) reviewed a total of 27 different studies and reported median correlations between infant measures and childhood IQ of .41 for habituation and .37 for preference for novelty. There have been nearly a dozen recently published research papers that were not reviewed in the McCall and Carriger paper, and in each case significant correlations between infant cognitive measures and later IQ are reported (Dougherty & Haith, 1997; Thompson, Fagan, & Fulker, 1991).

The evidence just cited indicates that there is a moderate degree of continuity of developmental function and stability of individual differences from infancy to early childhood. Given these findings, how might continuity of developmental function be interpreted? Bornstein and Sigman (1986)

examined several possibilities and concluded that the high correlations can best be explained by the continuity of an underlying process. This model proposes that there is a constant process that underlies individual differences in both the allocation of infant attention and later performance on tests of intelligence. The question is, what might that process be?

Most researchers have assumed that habituation and preference for novelty involve information-processing mechanisms and that such mechanisms are stable in form over infancy and into childhood (Bornstein & Sigman, 1986; Fagan, 1992; McCall & Carriger, 1993). For example, habituation and recognition memory involve encoding of a stimulus, storing it, categorizing it, comparing a present stimulus with a memory representation, and discriminating the old from the new stimulus. McCall and Carriger (1993) further suggest that the information-processing mechanisms underlying performance might be "the disposition to inhibit responding to familiar stimuli and to stimuli of minor prominence (e.g., low energy, static, etc.)" (p. 77). Such a position is consistent with evidence presented in Chapter 5 of age-related differences in sensitivity to interference and the ability to inhibit prepotent responses. Such basic inhibitory abilities can play an important role not only in cognitive development (Bjorklund & Harnishfeger, 1990; Dempster, 1993) but also in individual differences in cognitive functioning (Harnishfeger & Bjorklund, 1994).

Another related aspect of information processing that might underlie both infant and childhood measures is the ability to process novelty. Particularly, the preference-for-novelty paradigm used for assessing recognition memory involves the handling of novel information. Unlike many of the sensorimotor skills assessed on infant scales of intelligence, these abilities are also characteristic of cognition in later life and, thus, might serve as a basis for the continuity of intelligence.

Along similar lines, Robert Sternberg (1985) has argued that response to novelty is a major element of individual differences in intelligence that is constant across the life span (recall Sternberg's theory from Chapter 13). He proposes that how people react to novel situations is central to most definitions of intelligence. Even what Piaget called assimilation and accommodation, for example, are essentially means for dealing with novel environmental events. In a similar vein, Harriet Rheingold (1985) has stressed the importance of novelty in development. She asserts that the development of behavior, including mental processes, can be viewed as a process of becoming familiar with our world (both internal and external). The child's task in development is "to render the novel familiar." Thus, like Sternberg, Rheingold sees the process of acquiring new knowledge—of rendering the novel familiar—to be a central aspect of development that is continuous throughout life.

Related to the preference-for-novelty interpretation is Marc Bornstein and Marian Sigman's (1986) suggestion that motivation to explore new environments underlies the stability of cognitive functioning during infancy and early childhood. Infants high in such motivation would tire quickly from repeated presentation of a single stimulus and thus display a rapid rate of habituation. Similarly, such infants should be eager to inspect a new stimulus when one is presented, displaying strong preferences for novelty.

Let us return to an issue introduced earlier in this chapter. Does this new evidence of continuity with stability from infancy to childhood mean that there is a general factor of intelligence, or *g*? The data certainly seem to point in that direction. Joseph Fagan (1992) believes that the origins of intelligence can be found in the infant's ability to process information, and that such processing is tapped by habituation and recognition memory procedures. These basic-level information-processing abilities have a high heritability. This all suggests that there is a strong biological (genetic and possibly prenatal) basis for individual differences in intelligence. Fagan (1992) suggests that what underlies intelligence is best thought of as information-processing mechanisms and not a mental factor; nevertheless, the relatively high prediction of later intelligence from infant measures is consistent with the continuity-with-stability position advocated by *g* theorists.

Recent evidence supports the idea of the stability of information-processing mechanisms that underlie tests both in infancy and childhood. For example, Rose and Feldman (1995) reported that visual recognition memory tests given at 7 months correlated significantly at age 11 years not only with IQ scores (correlation = .41) but also with perceptual speed (correlation = .38). In other work, Dougherty and Haith (1997) found infant visual reaction time (the time it took infants to begin an eye movement toward a picture after it appeared) taken at 3.5 months of age correlated significantly both with childhood IQ (correlation = .44) and with childhood visual reaction times (measured similarly as they were in infancy; correlation = .51) at age 4. These studies argue for cognitive continuity from infancy through childhood and that speed of processing is the likely component that underlies intellectual performance and is responsible, at least in part, for the stability observed.

But the correlations, although substantially higher than found with infant DQ tests, are far from perfect, and Fagan and others point out that individual differences in infant information processing do not constitute the whole picture. For example, reliable differences in IQ scores are found between children of different races and different parental educational backgrounds in the United States. Yet, no differences have been found between children of different races or with different parental educational backgrounds on measures of recognition memory (Fagan, 1984). This suggests that experiential factors play a separate role in the establishment of intelligence.

The combined influence of basic information-processing abilities and environmental factors is nicely illustrated in research by Catherine Tamis-LeMonda and Marc Bornstein (Bornstein, 1989; Tamis-LeMonda & Bornstein, 1989). They demonstrated that the quality of mother-child interaction predicted childhood intelligence at age 4 independent of infant habituation rates. In other words, how parents interact with their babies has an important influence on their children's intelligence beyond that measured by habituation rate. This means that intelligence is a multifaceted thing, and we

must interpret any global pronouncements concerning its development very cautiously.

Intelligence is not a single, well-defined dimension. If a g factor does exist, it reflects only part of the picture. The work of Fagan, Bornstein, and others suggests that at least some aspects of intelligence vary continuously over infancy and childhood and are stable over time. Yet the earlier claim by McCall and his colleagues (McCall, Eichorn, & Hogarty, 1977) that intelligence during infancy changes in a discontinuous manner and is unstable over time is also likely true. The difference is that the various investigators are measuring different aspects of infant intelligence, with some aspects changing continuously and showing stability and others changing discontinuously and showing instability.

The Stability of IQ Scores over Childhood

Prediction of Adult IQ from Childhood Data

Although infant psychometric measures do not predict later IQ scores well, the stability of individual differences in intelligence as measured by IQ tests increases dramatically by age 2. Table 14-7 summarizes the findings of longitudinal studies by Bayley (1949) and Honzik, MacFarlane, and Allen (1948), and it presents the correlations between scores on intelligence tests given at various times during childhood and IQ scores as young adults (17 or 18 years of age). Whereas the correlations between intelligence tests given at 12 months and at 18 years are approximately 0, the correlations rise quickly by the beginning of the third year. The correlations with adult IQ scores rise rapidly until early childhood and are relatively stable from age 8 or so on. Kopp and McCall (1982) have stated that "following age 5, IQ is perhaps the most stable, important behavioral characteristic yet measured" (p. 39).

Why should there be such a high degree of stability in IQ scores over the course of childhood, especially when predictions from infant psychometric tests are so poor? In all likelihood, the reason for the increased stability of IQ scores beginning around age 2 is the increasing similarity of the test items and of the nature of intelligence for children 2 years

TABLE 14-7 Cross-age correlations between IQ tests given in childhood and adult IQ scores

Age of testing	Honzik, MacFarlane, and Allen (1948)	Bayley (1949)
1 year	—	−.14
2–3 years	.33	.40
4–5 years	.42	.52
6–7 years	.67	.68
8–9 years	.71	.80
10–11 years	.73	.87
12–13 years	.79	—
14–15 years	.76	.84

of age and beyond. Following Piaget, there is a qualitative change in intelligence occurring sometime between 18 and 30 months of age. Children become symbol users and will remain symbol users throughout their lives. IQ tests are constructed to reflect meaningful dimensions of intelligence for people of a given age, and, accordingly, the ability to retrieve and manipulate symbols is a central aspect of most if not all intelligence tests from the 2-year level onward. There is thus a continuity of developmental function, to the extent that symbolic functioning is involved in measuring intelligence at all ages. Although continuity of developmental function does not necessitate stability of individual differences, it can be seen from the earlier discussion of IQ prediction from infancy data that such a relationship probably exists.

Patterns of IQ Change During Childhood

Despite the impressive stability of the rank order of IQ scores from the early school years, there is still room for change, particularly change in the level of IQ. Recall that correlations of rank order are statistically independent of average values. So, for example, the average level of IQ scores could vary substantially for a particular sample of children and affect the correlations of rank order only minimally.

McCall, Appelbaum, and Hogarty (1973) extensively examined patterns of IQ change over childhood. They analyzed IQ data from the Fels Longitudinal Study. In their study, the data of 80 people (38 males, 42 females) who had been administered a Stanford-Binet IQ test at 17 points in development (ages 2.5, 3, 3.5, 4, 4.5, 5, 5.5, 6, 7, 8, 9, 10, 11, 12, 14, 15, and 17 years) were examined for changes in level and pattern of IQ scores over time.

First, how much change, in terms of IQ points, was observed? The range of IQ scores for a given child was obtained, and the difference between a child's highest score during the 17 testing sessions and his or her lowest score was computed. Note that this is not the difference between a child's IQ score at 17 years and his or her score at 2.5 years, but the difference between the highest and lowest scores a child received, independent of age. The average shift in IQ score for children in this sample was 28.5 points. The range for 21% of the children in this sample was 20 points or less, and 43% shifted between 21 and 30 points sometime between 2.5 and 17 years of age. Slightly more than one-third of the sample (36%) showed shifts of more than 30 points, with one child displaying an amazing increase of 74 points! Although such a drastic change is rare, shifts of more than 50 points have been reported by other researchers (Honzik et al., 1948; Moore, 1967). In general, it's fair to say that, on average, IQ scores changed substantially during the 15-year period.

One potential problem with longitudinal studies is that children can become "test wise" as a result of repeated testings. It is possible that the large shifts in IQ scores observed in this study were due to practice effects, with the children getting better at taking the tests with experience, and that this resulted in elevated levels of performance as they grew older. This explanation, although reasonable, was not supported by the data. McCall and his colleagues subjected the IQ scores to cluster analysis, a statistical technique that discerns common patterns among sets of data. Thus, children showing similar patterns of IQ change over time would be grouped together in a single cluster. The cluster analysis yielded five distinct patterns of IQ change, graphed in Figure 14-7.

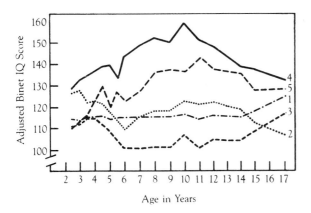

FIGURE 14-7 Mean IQ scores over time for five clusters of children. SOURCE:: "Developmental Changes in Mental Performance," by R. B. McCall, M. I. Appelbaum, and P. S. Hogarty, 1973, *Monographs of the Society for Child Development, 38,* (Serial No. 150). Copyright © 1973 The Society for Research in Child Development, Inc. Reprinted with permission.

The first thing to note is that the general trend is not consistently increasing IQ scores with each subsequent testing, making unlikely the hypothesis that the large IQ shifts observed for this sample were caused by practice effects.

The largest cluster was cluster 1 (45% of the sample), with children displaying minimal systematic variation from a slightly rising pattern over childhood. Cluster 2 (11%) showed a sharp decline in IQ between the ages of 4 and 6 years, with a slight recovery in middle childhood, followed by a decrease in adolescence. Cluster 3 (13%) also showed a decline in IQ scores during the preschool years, followed by relatively stable performance from 6 to 14 years and an increase to age 17. Cluster 4 (9%) demonstrated a rapid rise in IQ scores, peaking between 8 and 10 years, followed by a comparably sharp decline. Cluster 5 (6%) showed a steady rise in IQ scores until age 8 or 10 years, much like the pattern for children in cluster 4, but displayed less of a subsequent drop in scores. The data for 16% of the sample followed no consistent pattern.

Note in Figure 14-7 that the children having the highest IQ scores (Cluster 4) also displayed the greatest amount of IQ change. This result is consistent with the findings of other investigators, who have similarly reported that very bright children tend to change more in test scores over time than children with lower scores do (Terman & Merrill, 1937). Along these same lines, it is interesting to observe that for the two groups of children showing the overall highest levels of IQ (clusters 4 and 5), scores increased until 8 or 10 years of age and then declined. Although speculative, one interpretation of this pattern is that at 8 to 10 years there is a transition in cognitive functioning (concrete to formal operations, for example) and that bright concrete operational thinkers, although making the transition to formal operations sooner than less bright children, do not maintain their high level of performance for this qualitatively different style of thought. A possibility suggested by McCall and his colleagues is that children's intellectual performance during the early school years is under the direct influence of their parents, who emphasize acquiring basic skills in math and reading. As children grow older and develop interests outside the home, parents' influence on their intellectual functioning wanes, and IQ scores drop accordingly (compare with Scarr & McCartney, 1983).

Some support for this latter position was obtained by McCall and his colleagues. As part of the Fels Longitudinal Study, children and their parents were evaluated on a variety of behavioral and attitudinal factors during the course of the project. McCall and his associates examined aspects of parents' child rearing, including their attitudes toward discipline and academic achievement. The children having the highest overall IQ scores and showing the most change in test scores over childhood (clusters 4 and 5) were characterized by having parents who were classified as accelerating, in that they strove to increase their children's mental or motor development. These parents also tended to have clear household policies, were rewarding, and had medium to severe penalties for children's transgressions. The researchers described these parents as providing an encouraging and rewarding environment with some structure and enforcement of the rules. These findings are consistent with the researchers' view that the children's increase in IQ scores during the early school years was due to the influence of their academically oriented parents.

Children in the two clusters showing decreasing preschool IQ scores (clusters 2 and 3) tended to have parents who were minimally accelerating. Cluster-2 children were the least severely penalized, whereas cluster-3 children were the most severely punished of any group. The parents of children in cluster 1 showed a wide range of attitudes and behaviors.

The study by McCall and his colleagues (1973) indicates that substantial changes in IQ scores occur over the course of childhood for some children, with the average shift being 28.5 points. These findings should be considered relative to the very high stability of individual differences reported in the literature. How can rank order of individual differences be so high, yet actual levels of IQ vary so drastically for some children? One clue to this paradox can be found by again examining Figure 14-7. Note that the lines depicting IQ change for the five clusters remain relatively distinct over the 15-year period. After age 7, there are only two points at which any line crosses another. Thus, despite the substantial variability in IQ scores that these lines reflect, the rank order of the various clusters remained essentially unchanged for most testings. Moreover, recall again that the children who showed the greatest amount of change were high-IQ children. Because of the way IQ tests are constructed, a change in IQ score from 130 to 160 is not the same as a 30-point shift from 75 to 105. In the former case, a child's relative rank order changes from approximately the 97th to the 99th+ percentile. In both cases, a child would be brighter than all but a small minority of his agemates. In contrast, a change in IQ from 75 to 105 represents a change in relative rank order from about the 5th to the 63rd percentile, a change from borderline mentally retarded to slightly above normal! As the data indicate, changes of the former type are more common than are changes of the latter type, leaving the impression, both statistically and intuitively, that intelligence is relatively stable over time (McCall et al., 1973).

One way of looking at the interaction between developmental function and individual differences is to examine the stability of IQ over time for high- versus low-IQ children. Might children with low IQs, for instance, show greater (or perhaps less) stability over time than groups of average or high-IQ children do? A study by Ramey, Yeates, and Short (1984) investigated this possibility.

These researchers examined IQ data from a longitudinal project that was designed to provide compensatory education to a group of preschool children from low-income homes. Children in the control group were provided with nutritional supplements and received regular medical attention commencing shortly after birth. In addition to the nutritional and medical aid, children in the experimental group were enrolled in an academically oriented preschool program beginning by 3 months of age. Children in both groups were given infant psychometric tests at 6, 12, and 18 months and the Stanford-Binet at 24, 36, and 48 months.

By 18 months of age, children in the experimental group had higher IQs than children in the control group did. For example, Stanford-Binet scores for the experimental group at 36 and 48 months were 102 and 103, respectively; in contrast, comparable scores for the control group were 84 and 89. These data indicate that an academically oriented preschool program can have a substantial effect on the intellectual functioning of a group of high-risk children, altering the level of developmental function relative to children in a control condition.

But will these two groups show the same pattern of stability over four years of testing? That is, would the cross-age correlations be similar between the low- and the average-IQ groups? These correlations are shown in Table 14-8. As can be seen, the pattern of correlations was highly similar between the two groups, despite the fact that their average IQ scores differed significantly. Very similar results were reported for a larger group of children by Ramey, Lee, and Burchinal (1989), who concluded that although early intervention can raise overall level of intellectual functioning, it does not change the "spread or scatter or predictability of these scores over time" (p. 226).

TABLE 14-8 Cross-age correlations with Stanford-Binet at 48 months for experimental and control children

Age of testing	Experimental group (mean 48-month IQ = 102.7)	Control group (mean 48-month IQ = 89)
6 months	.25	.33
12 months	.31	.21
18 months	.46	.52
24 months	.65	.66
36 months	.75	.78

SOURCE: Adapted with permission from Ramey, C. T., Yeates, K. O., & Short, E. J. (1984). The plasticity of intellectual development: Insights from preventive intervention. *Child Development, 55,* 1913–1925. Copyright © 1984 The Society for Research in Child Development, Inc.

The data indicate that level of intellectual functioning can be modified substantially by educational intervention without influencing the pattern of individual differences within a group. In other words, given a group of children, the rank order will remain relatively constant if all the children within that group experience basically the same environment. If the environment is relatively impoverished (as was the case for children in the control group), the overall level of IQ will be low. If the environment is relatively enriched (as was the case for children in the experimental group), the overall level of IQ will be high. Thus, although developmental function (relative to IQ scores, anyway) can be influenced by specific experiences, these same experiences seem not to influence the stability of individual differences.

Has Intelligence Changed During This Century?

In discussing the stability and consistency of IQ scores over time, I have necessarily made use of longitudinal data, in which the same people are tested at different points in their development. But a related question about changes in IQ over time can be asked: Has the absolute level of intelligence, as measured by IQ, changed during the century? If so, are we getting smarter or dumber? As I mentioned in Chapter 13, IQ tests are routinely restandardized. One reason for this is to keep the tests relevant for contemporary populations. Questions that might have been appropriate for people in 1930 can be meaningless for people in the year 2000. But, perhaps more critically, tests are restandardized so that the average remains at or about 100. If people start scoring higher or lower, on average, than 100, the test loses some of its statistical properties that makes it so valuable as an assessment tool.

There are several ways of evaluating whether average IQ scores have changed over historical time. One is to examine the scores of many people who take the same test at different times (for example, in 1960 versus in 1980). Another is to give people today versions of earlier IQ tests, standardized on samples decades before.

What prediction would you make? On the one hand, scores on standardized tests such as the SAT have been reported to decline over the past 40 years, and there has been much lament in the popular press about the "dumbing of America." Perhaps, then, IQ scores have gone down over the decades. On the other hand, more people are receiving both primary and secondary education than in decades past, and public health has improved considerably since the early years of the 20th century, so perhaps we're getting smarter.

The answer is that we're getting smarter, and that this phenomenon is not limited to the United States but is worldwide. The average increase in IQ is about 3 points per decade, which corresponds to more than a full standard deviation since 1940. This phenomenon has been termed the **Flynn effect,** after James Flynn (1987), the first person to describe the phenomenon systematically.

How can this be explained? One explanation concerns more education for more people, which surely is a contributor to the change. However, the largest changes in performance are for *fluid abilities,* which are supposedly less influenced by education and cultural differences (see Chapter 13). That is, the type of cognitions that have changed the most are those *least* influenced by education and culture. Another explanation relates to better nutrition and health care. More people are healthy, thus fewer people score very low on IQ tests. A third speculation is that life has gotten more complex. We are constantly being bombarded with visual messages from television, but also from photographs and billboards. (These and other possible explanations of the Flynn effect are discussed in Neisser, 1998.)

If these gains reflect true increases in intelligence, they would reflect cultural changes of enormous magnitude. Flynn (1987) thinks otherwise. Surely some aspects of intellectual functioning have changed. But the absurdity of a 30 point IQ increase since 1900 must cause one to ponder what the IQ test is actually measuring. The IQ test is a good measure of intelligence and permits us to know where a person stands relative to other people in his or her cohort. But the fact that IQ can change so substantially over historical time emphasizes the relative nature of the measure. This does not diminish its usefulness, but it does suggest that an IQ score is not "the" measure of a permanent and stable intelligence.

Summary

Issues concerning the heritability of intelligence are related to perspectives on whether intelligence is domain general or domain specific in nature, with domain-general (g) theorists typically believing that intelligence is primarily biologically based and stable over time. Most current theorists adopt some variant of a *transactional approach* to studying the development of intelligence, emphasizing the interactive and bidirectional relations of children and their environments.

Heritability is a statistic that refers to the extent to which differences in a trait within a population are the result of inheritance. One approach to the heritability of intelligence has been to examine *elementary-cognitive tasks (ECTs)*. Research has shown that response times on ECTs are related to psychometrically measured g, suggesting to some that these simple, and presumably inherited, cognitive operations are the basis for higher-order intelligence.

Familial studies of intelligence, comparing the IQs of people of varying degrees of genetic relations (monozygotic twins, adopted siblings), have been a major tool for assessing the heritability of intelligence. Studies show that the correlations of IQ between groups of people increase as genetic similarity increases. The current estimate of the heritability of IQ is about .50, meaning that, on average, 50% of the difference in IQ scores among people in a population can be attributed to inheritance. The heritability of IQ increases with age, attributed in part to a lessening of the effect of *shared environment* and a greater impact of *nonshared environment* on intelligence.

Early approaches to assessing the effects of experience on intelligence used human *institutionalization studies*, demonstrating that intellectual functioning can be seriously impaired under conditions of physical and social deprivation. Naturalistic studies of parent-child interaction, often assessing the quality of the environment using the *HOME scale*, generally find that mothers who provide their children with a variety of objects to play with and who are responsive have brighter children than do mothers who provide less intellectual stimulation. The effects of a nonstimulating environment tend to be especially detrimental for children with early medical problems. The role of the child in affecting the parent-child relation must also be investigated, with more competent children possibly eliciting more competent parenting. Because of age-related changes in children's abilities, the role of environmental factors in intellectual development is likely to be different at different times in development.

Early environmentally induced retardation can be reversed under certain conditions. Similarly, children from intellectually impoverished, low-income homes who receive cognitively enriched early experience through intensive *compensatory education* display immediate gains in IQ scores. However, follow-up data indicate that many of the gains manifested by these children are lost after the program ends. Once intellectual accomplishments are established, they must be maintained by subsequent environments. If the contexts of early, middle, and later childhood are highly similar, the relative level of intelligence is likely to be comparable across these years. Modifications in environment and experience, however, can foster modifications in intellectual attainments, for better or for worse.

Stability of intelligence is the degree to which the rank order of individual differences remains constant over time. Stability is evaluated by cross-age correlations, with high correlations reflecting stability of individual differences. Evidence from the psychometric literature indicates that the correlation between scores on sensorimotor tests given in infancy and IQ scores later in childhood is low. However, other research has shown significant correlations between measures of infants' preference for novelty and rate of habituation and later IQ scores. The findings suggest that infant intelligence is multifaceted, with some aspects presumably developing in a discontinuous fashion (*discontinuity-with-instability*) and others developing in a continuous fashion (*continuity with stability*).

Stability of individual differences in intelligence over the course of childhood increases with age. These increases are attributed to age-related increases in the similarity of cognitive functioning between children and adults. Despite the high cross-age correlations, however, there are significant changes in level and pattern of IQ over age. Other research indicates that groups of children who differ considerably in level of intelligence show comparable patterns relative to the stability of individual differences.

The *Flynn effect* refers to the systematic increase in IQ scores over the 20th century. Although speculative, changes in nutrition, health, education, and to a generally more complex environment have been hypothesized to account for this effect.

Note

1. In discussing the relation between experience and intelligence, I am referring only to *postnatal social experience*. Prenatal and postnatal physical experience also can have a profound effect on intelligence. Such experiences include nutrition, disease, prenatal and postnatal drug exposure, environmental poisoning, and prenatal, perinatal, or postnatal physical trauma. These are all examples of experiential (rather than genetic) influences on intelligence and should be considered when evaluating the effect of experience on intelligence. However, because psychologists have tended to emphasize the influence of social experience on intelligence and because of space limitations, with a few exceptions, I will not discuss these effects in this chapter.

Key Terms and Concepts

transactional model
heritability
elementary cognitive tasks (ECTs)
familial studies of intelligence
shared environment
nonshared environment
institutionalization studies
HOME scale
compensatory education programs
stability
continuity with stability
discontinuity with instability
Flynn effect

Suggested Readings

NEISSER, U., BOODOO, G., BOUCHARD, T. J., BOYKIN, A. W., BRODY, N., CECI, S. J., HALPERN, D. F., LOEHLIN, J. C., PERLOFF, R., STERNBERG, R. J., & URBINA, S. (1996). Intelligence: Knowns and unknowns. *American Psychologist, 51,* 77–101. The authors of this article present the consensus of a task force of the American Psychological Association about what we know and don't know about intelligence. The task force and this paper were in response to the controversy following the publication of *The Bell Curve* by Herrnstein and Murray in 1994. The report provides a brief, even-handed view of many aspects of intelligence, including its definition, heritability, the influence of environment, and group differences.

PLOMIN, R., & PETRILL, S. A. (1997). Genetics and intelligence: What's new? *Intelligence, 24,* 53–77. Plomin and Petrill present a concise, up-to-date account of "what's new" in the behavioral genetics of intelligence. They take a decidedly developmental perspective, making this article particularly relevant.

SAMEROFF, A. J., SEIFER, R., BALDWIN, A., & BALDWIN, C. (1993). Stability of intelligence from preschool to adolescence: The influence of social risk factors. *Child Development, 64,* 80–97. This longitudinal study demonstrates the influence that various risk factors have on children's intelligence and the stability of both intelligence and risk factors over time.

BARNETT, W. S. (1995). Long-term effects of early childhood programs on cognitive and school outcomes. *The Future of Children, 5* (No. 3, Winter). This article presents the most recent examination of the long-term effects of preschool compensatory educational programs and provides suggestions for future research and intervention.

McCALL, R. B., & CARRIGER, M. S. (1993). A meta-analysis of infant habituation and recognition memory performance as predictors of later IQ. *Child Development, 64,* 57–79. McCall and Carriger present an overview of research and theory relating to the prediction of childhood intelligence from infant measures of information processing (habituation and preference for novelty). McCall and Carriger's perspective emphasizes both possible biological as well as environmental factors in the prediction of childhood IQ from infancy.

Epilogue
Cognitive Development: What Changes and How?

Seven "Truths" about Cognitive Development

Diversity of Opinions, but a Single Science

This has been a long book, covering many different topics from a variety of perspectives. Are there any general "truths" about cognitive development that can be succinctly stated, as in "Everything you wanted to know about cognitive development in 25 words or less"? Well, 25 words or less would be a bit too brief, but I will try, in 10 pages or less, to list several general "truths" of cognitive development as I see them, based on the information presented in this book. These "truths" are not self-evident, but have been derived from research and substantial thought over the course of this century. Although I've tried to be objective in presenting research and theory throughout the book (often accompanied with my own interpretations), I will present here *my* perspective of cognitive development and not the "average opinion" of the field.

Seven "Truths" about Cognitive Development

I have identified seven "truths" that I think can be abstracted from reading the preceding 14 chapters. They are actually generalizations that I think are true about cognitive development, and I make no pretense that they have the authority of scientific law. Because the evidence for these "truths" has been presented throughout this book, I have provided little or no empirical support for them here. Each of these issues was raised, directly or indirectly, in Chapter 1 and can be viewed as the general themes that ran throughout the book.

When reading the research-packed chapters of a book like this, it is easy to get lost in the details and miss the general themes, or "truths," that the details convey. And, quite honestly, I realize that general themes presented in an introductory chapter often do not have the organizing effect for students they are intended to have. The purpose of this epilogue is to re-introduce those themes, hoping that, after reading the book, they will make more sense and help the reader see cognitive development as a dynamic field tied together by some general "truths" that tell a coherent, but sill developing, story.

1. *Cognitive development proceeds through the dynamical and reciprocal transaction of a child's biological constitution (including genetics) and his or her physical and social environment (including culture).*

This, to my mind, is the core assumption underlying development—all development. This is seen in the developmental-systems approach described in Chapter 2 on the "Biological Bases of Cognitive Development" and in the transactional model of development, as described in Chapter 14 when I explained how to think about the origins, maintenance, and modification of individual differences in intelligence. And this assumption has been emphasized throughout the book whenever I discussed the origins of developmental or individual differences in some cognitive ability.

This reflects the contemporary view of how nature and nurture interact to yield a particular pattern of development. From this perspective, children come into the world prepared by biology (and evolution) to make sense of the world. This biology, as reflected primarily by the organization of a child's brain, does not simply blossom but, rather, develops as a function of experience. For many phenomena, the brain has evolved to "expect" certain species-typical experiences and will develop in the same way at about the same time for children the world over, in all but extreme circumstances. However, equally important are specific aspects of children's physical and social environments that cause them to develop skills unique to them (or to that culture). Experience does not so much mold the mind as it interacts with genetic predisposition to move a child's thinking in one direction or another.

There are real biological constraints on cognitive development, although the strength of these constraints vary among different cognitive abilities. Some aspects of cognitive development, such as language and theory of mind, are based on cognitive skills fashioned by hundreds of thousands of years of evolution and seem to need only a "normal" human environment to be acquired. Others, such as reading and mathematics beyond simple addition and subtraction, are cultural inventions. We make use of cognitive skills that evolved for other purposes to learn to read and to do algebra, but this is only done in a highly supportive environment.

Despite the differences between cognitive skills such as language and reading (what David Geary referred to as biologically primary and biologically sec-

ondary abilities, respectively), all cognitive abilities develop through the continuous and bidirectional interaction between multiple levels of organization, from the genetic, through the nervous system, to the physical and social environment. The direction of causation is not one way. Biology (genetics) does not *cause* someone to acquire language or to excel on algebra word problems; neither does "environment" *cause* someone to understand that others have beliefs and desires different from one's own or to become a proficient reader. The only way to understand cognitive development is to look at the multiple levels of organization and the reciprocal interactions among them. This is why the emphasis on the biological bases of cognitive development, as exemplified by research in behavioral genetics (Chapter 14) and developmental cognitive neuroscience (Chapter 2) is compatible with sociocultural perspectives of development (Chapter 3). Each alone provides only a part of the story. But the story only makes sense when the two parts are integrated, not put side by side, but viewed in continuous interaction with one another.

Central to the issue of the transaction of biological and social factors in development is the concept of *innateness*. As I mentioned in the Introduction, many developmental psychologists would just as soon see this term never used, for it only makes people think of the false dichotomy of "nature versus nurture." But the concept will not go away, and in Chapter 1 I introduced three ways in which something can be "innate": representational innateness, architectural innateness, and chronotopic innateness. In each case, genetics provides some *constraints* on cognitive processing, making it easier to process certain classes of information (such as language), while limiting how the brain can process other information. Such constraints narrow the range of stimuli and situations we can make sense of, but in the process make the job of learning about a human world easier for infants and children.

But what is the nature of these constraints? I presented research and theory throughout this book (but especially in Chapter 7 on "Representation") contrasting representational and architectural constraints (or innateness). Representational constraints refer to representations that are hard-wired into the brain so that some types of "knowledge" are innate. Some have proposed that many accomplishments in infancy, such as knowledge of the physical properties of objects, reflect representational constraints. Interaction with the physical environment is necessary for development to occur, but little in the way of "learning," as traditionally conceived, is done. Researchers from the Chomskian tradition have proposed that language acquisition is governed by representational constraints of this nature (universal grammar). In contrast, architectural constraints refer to ways in which the architecture of the brain is organized at birth. For instance, some neurons are excitatory, other inhibitory; different neurons require different amounts of activation to fire; and they may have many or few connections to other sets of neurons, both within and outside their immediate area. Such constraints limit the way in which information can be processed, not because children are born with innate representations (for example, what a grammar is), but because certain neurons/areas of the brain are only able to process certain types of information and pass it along to certain other areas of the brain. At this level of innateness, the brain is "prepared" to process certain types of information, but subsequent structuring of the brain depends more on the specific experiences that children have than is the case with representational constraints.

From the research I reviewed throughout this book, I am convinced that both representational and architectural constraints (and chronotopic constraints, referring to the timing of development) exist. As of this writing, however, I believe that the constraints for most higher-order forms of cognition are likely of the architectural kind. Much of human cognition and development is universal, confirming a common human nature and possibly representational constraints. But the latest research in infant perception and representation seems to favor the prevalence of architectural constraints (see Chapters 6 and 7), and there is a lively debate among the various camps of psycholinguists about exactly this controversy (see Chapter 9). Not long ago, the debate over the nature of language acquisition seemed to have been settled, and the Chomskians (representational nativists) had won. Today, the arguments have been refined and a vigorous debate is on again.

2. Cognitive development is a constructive process, with children playing an active role in the constructions of their own minds.

This is a truth that we can trace back to Piaget, and, in some form or another, it is a truth that all cognitive developmentalists believe. Children are not passive creatures, waiting to be shaped by their environments; nor are they "victims" of their genetics, with cognitive abilities simply unfolding. Rather, children act on their environments, making sense of the world as they do. This "sense making" is a constructive process, in that children interpret objects and events in their world in terms of what they already know and thus *create* knowledge as much as they record it. This constructivist perspective is seen explicitly in a variety of theories, including Piaget's, the neo-Piagetian theories of Robbie Case and Kurt Fischer (Chapter 4); theory theories of cognitive development, including Annette Karmiloff-Smith's theory of representational redescription (Chapter 4) and theory of mind (Chapter 7); fuzzy-trace theory (Chapter 5); Katherine Nelson's account of autobiographical memory (Chapter 8); and reading comprehension (Chapter 12), among others. Children use their basic-level abilities to encode, categorize, and retrieve information, but actively organize that information to make sense of it. We are a "sense making" species, and this process is an inherently constructive one.

This does not mean, however that we must take some postmodernist view that there is no objective reality, that every child constructs a reality that is unique to only him or her, or that it is fruitless to try to understand how another person thinks. There is a real world out there, and our sense organs evolved to perceive that world. Children learn to perceive (construct) the physical world in pretty much the same way regardless of where they are born. Again, our species-typical genome interacts with our species-typical environment to develop a prototypical human mind.

Yet, one's mind is also structured by the particular social environment in which we live. A child, in interaction with the social environment, will construct a mind that is well-suited to the specific cultural context in which he or she lives. For example, children in middle-class America (and elsewhere) "learn" to remember in a narrative style by the prompts their parents give them when recalling recent events (Chapter 8). Other cultures will provide other types of cognitive supports to their children (see Chapter 3), meaning that other types of cognition will develop.

There is much "structure" in cognitive development, from the constraints on what information the brain can process and how that processing can be done, to the organization of the physical and social environment that surrounds children from birth. Children actively construct a mental world within the bounds of these constraints. From this perspective, the child should not be viewed simply as the product of the interaction of genetic and environmental forces, but as an active biological and social agent who, by trying to make sense of the world, shapes his or her own cognitive development.

3. Cognition is multifaceted, and different cognitive skills show different patterns of developmental function and stability of individual differences.

Children get smarter as they get older. But *how* do they get smarter? What is the pattern of change over infancy and childhood, and do all cognitive abilities show essentially the same pattern? Developmental psychologists have spilled much ink debating this issue. Piaget, for example, proposed that development proceeds in a stagelike manner, with qualitative changes in thinking occurring relatively abruptly between stages. Other contemporary theorists, such as Robbie Case and Kurt Fischer, though loosening considerably the criteria for what constitutes a stage, also find qualitative, discontinuous changes in cognitive development. For example, these theorists, and many others, have observed a reorganization in thought between infancy and early childhood, another change between the ages of 5 to 7 years, and again at adolescence. I think the data and interpre-

tations of these and other theorists are compelling, and I have little reason to doubt that cognition, as they measure it, develops in a stagelike fashion. However, cognition is not a single, monolithic phenomenon. Rather, there are multiple aspects and types of cognition, each of which develops. And whereas some display patterns of discontinuities, where new skills and abilities emerge from the accretion or reorganization of earlier skills, others change in a more continuous and quantitative fashion. Children's information processing gets faster, their spans of apprehension increase, they acquire more knowledge, they can keep more irrelevant information out of working memory, and they have a greater number of problem-solving strategies to select from. Many of these abilities can be described as "basic-level processes," and from these simple, often unconscious processes, significant differences in cognitive functioning emerge.

There is not one developmental function for cognitive development, but many. An important point to remember is that these various types of cognitions can develop independently of one another. That is, although different types of cognitive processing clearly interact, they often show different patterns of developmental function, with some developing in a gradual and continuous nature and others developing in a more abrupt, discontinuous way. And some skills might develop very early whereas related skills are slow to emerge. For example, in Chapter 8, "Memory," we saw how implicit memory (memory without awareness) is quite good in young children and shows relatively little development in comparison with explicit memory (memory with awareness). Both memory skills can be used by the same child on a single task, and yet these skills can be at very different levels of proficiency. This is not a contradiction, but merely an indication that cognition is not a single "thing" that develops uniformly within a given child, but a collection of abilities, each having its own developmental schedule.

And the developmental schedule of a cognitive ability will influence patterns of individual differences, specifically the stability of individual differences over time. When should a child's cognitive ability, in comparison with that of his or her peers, remain stable over time, and when should we expect instability? By stability, I am referring to maintaining the same rank order in a cognitive ability over time. The answer one gets to this question depends on the pattern of developmental differences one observes. As we saw in Chapter 14 on intelligence, when the particular type of cognition under study changes in a qualitative way (such as representation from infancy to early childhood), there is little stability. Infants who score high on tests that can be described in Piagetian terms might or might not become high-IQ 3- and 4-year-olds. The reason is that the nature of intelligence measured by these tests changes in a qualitative way over time, and when there is discontinuity of developmental function (as one gets with qualitative, stagelike changes), there is instability of individual differences. However, when what underlies the cognitive tests change in a quantitative way, such as speed or efficiency of processing, then stability of individual differences can be expected. When we have continuous developmental function (as we typically do when we have quantitative changes) we can expect stability of individual differences.

We thus should expect stability (and perhaps consistency) of cognitive ability when the underlying cognitive abilities are qualitatively the same from one time to another. In a similar way, when the environment that is "responsible" for establishing intellectual competence remains stable over time, one should expect stability of individual differences. Parents who provide an intellectually supportive (or nonsupportive) environment for their toddlers will likely provide similar support as their children get older. In other words, the kind of changes we see in children's thinking over time will vary both as a function of how the underlying (endogenous) cognitive ability changes and as a function of how the social and physical (exogenous) environment changes over time.

4. *Cognitive development involves changes in both domain-general and domain-specific mechanisms.*

Consistent with the observation that different cognitive skills go though different patterns of change

over time, some of those skills cut across a large number of domains and contents (domain general), whereas others are much more specific in nature (domain specific). But how can the two reside side by side? Either there are domain-general skills that permeate all cognitive tasks or there are not. Not necessarily. Some aspects of cognitive development, such as speed of processing or capacity of working memory, influence most complex cognitive tasks. This is seen in Piaget's stages, in Robbie Case's idea of central conceptual structure (Chapter 4), in resource theories of cognitive development (Chapter 5), and in the concept of g in individual differences in intelligence (Chapter 13). Yet, when we are able to measure these domain-general skills and relate them to cognitive task performance, we find that they account for only a portion of the variance (although often a major portion). The remaining portion of developmental or individual differences can sometimes be attributed to domain-specific abilities. Rather than seeing the two concepts as being antagonistic to one another, they can be seen as interacting. For example, I am convinced that there are domain-specific abilities (modules, if you like) for language acquisition. However, I also think that it's quite likely that language acquisition is facilitated by children's general level of information-processing abilities, for example, by how much information they can hold in working memory at any one time (see Chapter 9).

A domain-general ability does not have to account for everything to be real. And it doesn't have to influence *all* "higher-order" cognitive abilities. It is sufficient that a single cognitive phenomenon (such as speed of processing, for example) has comparable effects on multiple tasks for us to postulate that it is a domain-general ability. This does not negate the very real possibility of multiple cognitive abilities that are relatively independent of one another. In fact, it is clear that there is no single, domain-general ability that subsumes all others. But it is also clear (to me, at least) that to postulate that the human mind consists of only a set of independent and "cognitively impenetrable" modules also misses the point. Multiple intelligences exist (whether of the type proposed by Howard Gardner in Chapter 13 or of some other classifications); but they coexist with one or more domain-general abilities. It is difficult at this time to specify the exact nature of this domain-general skill or skills, but patterns of results from studies examining a diverse range of abilities make it clear that it (or they) exists.

5. *Cognitive development involves changes in the way information is represented, although children of every age possess a range of ways in which to represent experiences.*

What changes in cognitive development? To return to the issues raised in Chapter 1, one aspect of change has to be the way in which children represent their experiences. What are the differences in how children represent the world? We have seen many different perspectives on this. Piaget, and others, proposed that infants lack symbols, such as found in language and apparently used in deferred imitation. Instead, they represent the world as raw sensation and action. Others, however, point to evidence of simple symbolic functioning in even very young infants, as reflected by imitation of facial gestures by newborns and deferred imitation by infants in their first year of life.

But is this truly symbolic reasoning? Do results such as these mean that there are no qualitative changes in symbolic ability from infancy onward? I think not. Actually, it is often impossible to say when an infant or child "has" a specific skill. This is because children will sometimes display an ability when the task is highly simplified and they are provided with substantial support (hints, limited range of choices, social praise and guidance, and so on). What does it mean when we do experiments and find that 4-month-olds demonstrate some behavior consistent with a knowledge of the permanence of objects or that 4-year-olds solve syllogisms when nonsense terms are used ("Every banga is purple")? Do 4-month-olds really "have" a concept of object permanence comparable with that of 18-month-olds and do 4-year-olds understand logical reasoning in the same way that adolescents do? No, I don't think so. But experiments like these do indicate that the development of many of these complex skills is not an all-or-nothing phenomenon. We should not be looking simply at "when" children can perform certain tasks but, rather, when they can perform them under certain conditions and what this says about the nature of the underlying representations and the mechanisms for their development.

This is illustrated not only in research in infancy, but also in research looking at representation in young children. Judy DeLoache's research on young children's understanding of models and pictures shows this "now they have it, now they don't" phenomenon, depending on how the task is constructed. Children's understanding of pretense, the appearance/reality distinction, deception, and theory of mind, go through similar changes over the preschool years. These are important changes that affect how children behave in the real world on a daily basis. But the research also shows that how sophisticatedly children behave depends on where we look. For example, a finding I found particularly telling was that of Clements and Perner (1994) who demonstrated that 3-year-old children failed the false-belief task when explicit knowledge was required (verbalizing the answer), but "passed" the task when only implicit knowledge was used as a measure (spontaneous looking behavior), much as is done in infancy research. So, can 3-year-olds solve false-beliefs tasks or can't they? Based on this research, there is obviously not a straightforward answer to the question, and this is true for most similar questions. What does seem apparent, however, is that the modal representational skills (those that children use most of the time) increase in sophistication with age and are used in an increasing number of contexts.

Figure E-1 presents the hypothetical relation between age and general cognitive abilities that I think captures the typical pattern of development for many (but certainly not all) types of cognition, including representation. Most of children's cognitive abilities occur within a relatively narrow range that increase with age. This is reflected by the hatch-marked areas in the figure. Yet, in a minority of situations, children perform at somewhat higher or somewhat lower levels, depending on the characteristics of the task, their motivation, and the amount of support they receive when performing

Range within which minority of cognitive functioning of individual child occurs

 Range within which majority of cognitive functioning of individual child occurs

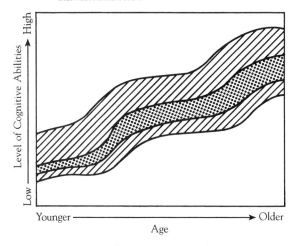

FIGURE E-1 Hypothetical relation between age and range of cognitive abilities. The majority of a child's cognitive functioning occurs within a relatively narrow range. However, a minority of children's cognitive functioning occurs within a substantially broader range. The absolute level of a child's cognitive functioning increases with age.

the task. This perspective is consistent with a sociocultural viewpoint that proposes that there is a zone of proximal development within which instruction from a more experienced partner will benefit children's performance (Chapter 3). But you need not be a Vygotskian to note this developmental pattern. It is found not only in laboratory tasks but also in children's everyday lives.

6. Background knowledge, or knowledge base, has a significant influence on how children think.

One important component of "support" for children when solving almost any cognitive task is the background knowledge they have about the task. Knowledge is represented in children's minds, and the way that knowledge is represented might change in some qualitative ways with age. But strictly *quantitative* changes in knowledge play a substantial role in cognitive development. In fact, some have proposed

that, for most cognitive tasks, knowledge is what differentiates younger from older children. What a child knows affects greatly how a child thinks.

I believe that this latter statement is indisputable. Knowledge cannot be separated from processing, and the amount of knowledge a child possesses, how that knowledge is organized, and its ability to be accessed, will determine, to a large extent, how well a child will solve a problem. From this perspective, children get smarter as they get older because they become more knowledgeable. We have seen the effects of background knowledge repeatedly throughout this book—on speed of processing, memory span, strategies (Chapter 5), event and strategic memory (Chapter 8), language acquisition (Chapter 9), problem solving (Chapter 10), gender identification (Chapter 11), and reading and mathematics (Chapter 12). Increasing knowledge is one of the single most important factors in cognitive development.

However, knowledge itself is not enough. How a child organizes the knowledge he or she has is important to how that knowledge will be used, and although the amount of knowledge a child possesses will affect related cognitive processes, such as memory span and speed of processing, these basic-level abilities will also affect how an elaborated knowledge base is used. Again, we must always be cognizant of the interaction between different levels of organization.

How much a child knows has also been shown to be important in individual differences in cognition, or intelligence (Chapter 13). This is seen most clearly in Sternberg's and Ceci's theories of intelligence, but also in information-processing approaches. When children have detailed knowledge in some domain, their performance on tasks using that knowledge is often high regardless of their level of psychometric intelligence (that is, IQ). On other tasks, however, particularly those in which strategic functioning plays a critical role, knowledge can significantly facilitate performance, but it seems not to eliminate IQ-related differences.

I think the picture of the role of knowledge—long-term memory representations of events and "facts"—is relatively clear for both developmental function and individual differences. Differences in knowledge base account for much of the variance of performance on many cognitive tasks, with older and more intelligent children typically having more knowledge than younger and less intelligent children do. How much children know about a topic will influence how they process information about that topic and how readily they can acquire new information in that domain. But knowledge is not everything, and the effects of knowledge on task performance will vary with the nature of the task. Moreover, one cannot ignore that there are developmental and individual differences in the processes by which knowledge is acquired. These processes, and how they interact with the knowledge that a child possesses, must also be understood to get the full picture of cognitive development.

7. Children's problem solving becomes increasingly strategic with age; children have a broader selection of strategies to choose from, and they become more effective in their selection and monitoring of problem-solving strategies.

In one sense, this final "truth" of cognitive development is not very surprising. Quite obviously, children become better problem solvers with age. But what is important here is the *way* in which they become better problem solvers.

The core idea here, presented in Chapter 1, is that children gain greater intentional control over their problem solving as they get older. They become more strategic, in that they use a variety of different cognitive operations in the service of attaining a specific goal. These are "optional" operations, in that they are not required for performing the task, but they are executed presumably to enhance task performance. Even infants show goal-directed, strategic behaviors, although the complexity and effectiveness of these strategies increase with age.

Strategies are influenced by basic-level processes such as speed of processing and working memory, but they are also influenced by higher-order processes, such as metacognition. With age, children not only become more cognizant of the strategies they use but also of their effectiveness. Good meta-cognition is not always necessary for good cognition, but when problem solving is governed by the use of goal-directed strategies, knowing how well one is doing (that is, monitoring task performance) and assessing which strategies will be most effective and when, enhances considerably task performance. Such metacognitive abilities increase with age and are better developed in high-ability (gifted) children than in children of average or below-average intelligence.

Several points about strategic development are worthy of mention here. First, strategies are effortful. They deplete a child's limited mental resources for any given task (regardless of whether those resources are domain general or domain specific in nature). As such, there is a cost to using strategies. Sometimes that cost is expressed in an actual decline (or failure to enhance) task performance, a phenomenon known as a utilization deficiency. Similarly, when young children are taught strategies, which improve their performance, they often resort to their nonstrategic ways when given the opportunity to do so. The extra effort they put into the task is not worth the improved performance they get out of it. So strategies should not be used when they don't need to be, and children seem to realize this when, for example, they have detailed knowledge for a task that make strategies unnecessary.

Second, strategies do not develop in stagelike fashion. Rather, children seem to have multiple strategies available to them for any given task at any given time. This is best exemplified by Robert Siegler's adaptive strategy choice model, discussed in several chapters in this book (especially Chapters 5 and 12). The number of strategies available to a child increases with age, as does the effectiveness of the modal strategy that is used on any particular task.

Third, and closely related to the second point, there is much variability in strategy use. On some tasks, children will use several different strategies simultaneously (or successively), and on others will switch between different strategies on consecutive trials. This variability is important in development and is not just "noise" or "measurement error." For too long, psychologists have looked at only "average" patterns of performance and ignored within-child variability. Differences *between* individual children were often seen as important or interesting, but differences in cognitive functioning *within* a given child over brief periods of time were rarely seen as anything of great import. These differences are important, however. Qualitative changes, or at least changes in modal strategies, can occur during times of high instability (high within-child variability), and less drastic changes might be influenced by the diversity of responses children make on a given task over repeated opportunities. Variability of responses creates novelty, and through novel responses to old problems new, and sometimes more effective, solutions are found.

Diversity of Opinions, but a Single Science

There is almost as much diversity among cognitive developmentalists as there is in children's cognitive development. The topics studied by cognitive developmentalists range from microprocesses such as speed of processing and memory span, to macroprocesses such as metacognition and theory of mind. Too often researchers who study one type of cognition (microprocesses) share little interest with those who study others (macroprocesses), and vice versa. For many who study microprocesses, looking at "the big picture" might be philosophically appealing, but scientifically fruitless. For example, although asking questions about metacognition and self-awareness can provide interesting descriptions of consciousness and its development, it leaves us with the feeling that the "ghost in the machine" is still in charge. In contrast, for many who study macroprocesses, to reduce cognitive development much below the level of conscious awareness or "meaning" results in an overabundance of details about children's performance on trivial tasks in unreal situations. Why bother? Similar disagreements exist among developmentalists who view a child's developing intellect to be a function primarily of his or her genetic inheritance with those who view the social environment as playing the predominant role in cognitive development. Disagreement among scientists in a field, particularly a field that still has a long way to go before becoming a mature science, is not a bad thing. In fact, it is a good thing, for disagreement stimulates theory construction and experimentation. What is bad, however, is if the proponents of different viewpoints of cognitive development talk past one another or, worse, ignore one another.

I think there are many "truths" about cognitive development. Both microprocesses and macroprocesses are worthy of study, as are the biological and social origins of development. Realizing that cognitive development occurs on multiple, interacting levels of analysis and that the reality of macroprocesses such as self-awareness does not reduce the significance of microprocesses such as speed of processing (and vice versa), goes a long way to producing an integrated view of a child's developing mind. It is not just that "all these things are interesting and thus should be studied." Rather, cognitive development happens at a variety of levels, and cognitive developmentalists need to be cognizant of this and the interactions among the various levels to develop a true developmental science.

Glossary

accommodation   In Piaget's theory, the process of changing a mental structure to incorporate new information; contrast with assimilation. (Chapter 4)

accommodation (of the lens)   In vision, the process of adjusting the lens of the eye to focus on objects at different distances. (Chapter 6)

active intermodal mapping   In Meltzoff and Moore's account of neonatal cognitive abilities, the ability to integrate information from two senses. (Chapter 7)

active rehearsal   See cumulative rehearsal.

adaptation   In Piaget's theory, the process of adjusting one's cognitive structures to meet environmental demands; includes the complementary processes of assimilation and accommodation. (Chapter 4)

adaptive strategy choice model   Siegler's model to describe how strategies change over time; the view that multiple strategies exist within a child's cognitive repertoire at any one time, with these strategies competing with one another for use. (Chapters 5, 12)

ambiguous figures   Drawings or pictures that can be interpreted in several different ways. (Chapter 6)

analogical reasoning   Reasoning that involves using something one already knows to help reason about something not known yet. (Chapter 10)

anticipatory images   In Piaget's theory, mental images that allow the individual to envision transformations of an image, even if one has never experienced such transformations in the past; contrast with reproductive images. (Chapter 7)

appearance/reality distinction   The knowledge that the appearance of an object does not necessarily correspond to its reality. (Chapter 7)

arbitrariness   The fact that a word is not inherently related to the concept it represents. (Chapter 9)

architectural constraints (or architectural innateness)   Ways in which the architecture of the brain is organized at birth; the type and manner in which information can be processed by the brain. (Chapter 1)

articulatory loop   In Baddeley and Hitch's model of the short-term store, a phonological system that stores phonological information. (Chapter 5)

assimilation   In Piaget's theory, the process of incorporating information into already existing cognitive structures; contrast with accommodation. (Chapter 4)

autobiographical memory   Personal and long-lasting memories that are the basis for one's personal life history. (Chapter 8)

automatic processes   Cognitive processes that require no mental effort (or mental space) for their execution, and are hypothesized (1) to occur without intention and without conscious awareness, (2) not to interfere with the execution of other processes, (3) not to improve with practice, and (4) not to be influenced by individual differences in intelligence, motivation, or education. Contrast with effortful processes. (Chapter 5)

axon   The long fiber of a neuron that carries messages from that cell to another. (Chapter 2)

basic-level categories   Categories composed of objects that are perceptually similar; contrast with superordinate categories. (Chapter 7)

basic reflexes   In Piaget's theory, the first substage of sensorimotor development, in which infants know the world only in terms of their inherited action patterns. (Chapter 4)

behavioral genetics The study of genetic effects on behavior and on complex psychological characteristics such as intelligence and personality. (Chapter 2)

belief-desire reasoning The process whereby we explain and predict what people do based on what we understand their desires and beliefs to be. (Chapter 7)

bent-twig model Proposal that biological differences between males and females bias males to have different experiences than females and these differential experiences account for gender differences in spatial abilities. (Chapter 6)

bidirectionality of structure and function (structure ↔ function) The reciprocal interaction of structure and function to produce a pattern of development. (Chapter 1)

bifoveal fixation The ability of the foveas of the two eyes to focus on the same object simultaneously, critical to binocular depth perception. (Chapter 6)

bioecological theory of intelligence Ceci's theory that intelligence is a multifaceted set of domain-specific abilities influenced by biological and environmental factors, and that intellectual abilities are highly influenced by the context in which they were acquired and in which they are expressed. (Chapter 13)

biologically primary abilities Cognitive abilities that have been selected for in evolution, are acquired universally, and children typically have high motivation to perform tasks involving them, such as language. (Chapter 2)

biologically secondary abilities Cognitive abilities that build upon biologically primary abilities but are principally cultural inventions, and often tedious repetition and external motivation are necessary for their mastery, such as reading. (Chapter 2)

Black English A dialect of American English used mostly (but not exclusively) by members of the African-American community, which is characterized by some special rules of pronunciation and syntax. (Chapter 9)

bound morphemes Morphemes that cannot stand alone but are attached to free morphemes, such as the word endings "ed" and "ing" in English. (Chapter 9)

category prototype An abstract representation of a category, reflecting the central tendency, or "best example," of a category. (Chapters 6, 7)

category typicality The idea that some items are more representative of the category prototype than others. Items that are highly typical of a category have more features in common with the category prototype than do less typical items. (Chapter 7)

Ceci's bioecological theory of intelligence See bioecological theory of intelligence.

central conceptual structure In Case's theory, a network of semantic nodes and relations that plays a central role in mediating children's performances across a broad range of tasks. (Chapter 4)

centration In Piaget's theory, the tendency of preoperational children to attend to one aspect of a situation to the exclusion of others; contrast with decentration. (Chapter 4)

cerebral cortex See neocortex.

cerebral lateralization Functional specialization of the two hemispheres of the brain. (Chapter 2)

child-directed speech The specialized register of speech adults and older children use when talking to infants and young children. (Chapter 9)

chronotopic constraints (or chronotopic innateness) Neural limitations on the developmental timing of events. (Chapter 1)

classification The grouping of objects on the basis of some set of characteristics. (Chapter 7)

class inclusion In Piaget's theory, the knowledge that a subordinate class (for example, dogs) must always be smaller than the superordinate class in which it is contained (for example, animals). (Chapter 4)

clustering In memory tasks, recalling items from the same category together. (Chapter 8)

cognition The processes or faculties by which knowledge is acquired and manipulated. (Chapter 1)

cognitive complexity In Ceci's bioecological theory, the degree to which one's cognitive processes can operate on one's knowledge structures in a complex, efficient, and flexible manner; cognitive complexity is limited by the efficiency of cognitive processes, which in turn are involved in the acquisition of knowledge and its structure. (Chapter 13)

cognitive complexity and control (CCC) theory Proposal that there are age-related changes in the complexity of rule systems that children can represent, and that developmental differences in conscious awareness give children increased control over their behavior and cognition. (Chapter 10)

cognitive self-guidance system In Vygotsky's theory, the use of private speech to guide problem-solving behavior. (Chapter 9)

collaborative learning   In the theory of cultural learning of Tomasello et al., the third stage of cultural learning, which involves two (or more) individuals, with neither being an authority or expert, and occurs in the process of peer interaction when two people work together to solve a common problem; contrast with imitative learning, instructed learning; see also cultural learning. (Chapter 11)

communicative competence   Mastery of five aspects of language: semantics, syntax, morphology, phonology, and pragmatics. (Chapter 9)

compensation (reciprocity)   In Piaget's theory, a form of reversibility so there exists for any operation another operation that compensates for the effects of the first. (Chapter 4)

compensatory education programs   Programs designed to provide preschool children from low-income homes with the intellectual skills necessary to do well in school. (Chapter 14)

complementary (functional, schematic, thematic) classification   In classification tasks, the grouping together of items from conceptually different categories based on interrelationships in a person's past experiences or in the present situation; contrast with idiosyncratic, perceptual, and conceptual classification. (Chapter 7)

componential subtheory   In Sternberg's triarchic theory, an information-processing model of intelligence that includes three types of components: knowledge acquisition, performance, and metacomponents. (Chapter 13)

conceptual (similarity, taxonomic, nominal, categorical) classification   In classification tasks, the grouping together of items based on similar category membership or shared function; contrast with idiosyncratic, perceptual, and complementary classification. (Chapter 7)

concrete operations   In Piaget's theory, the third major stage of cognitive development, in which children can decenter their perception, are less egocentric, and can think logically about concrete objects. (Chapter 4)

connectionist models   Computer models that simulate aspects of development through repeated activation of associated nodes. (Chapter 5)

conservation   In Piaget's theory, the knowledge that the quantity of a substance remains the same despite changes in its form. (Chapter 4)

conservation of number   In Piaget's theory, the knowledge that the number of items in an array remains the same despite changes in the form of the array. (Chapter 12)

constructivism   The position, central to Piaget's theory, that people interpret objects and events that surround them in terms of what they already know, so that one's current state of knowledge guides processing, substantially influencing how (and what) new information is acquired. (Chapter 4)

"context-independent" learning   Learning of a skill or strategy independent of a specific situation in which the skill will be applied. (Chapter 8)

contextual subtheory   In Sternberg's triarchic theory, the idea that intelligence must be viewed in terms of the context in which it occurs. (Chapter 13)

continuity versus discontinuity of development   The scientific debate over whether developmental change is gradual (continuous) or relatively abrupt (discontinuous). (Chapter 1)

continuity with stability   The expectation and research finding that there is stability of individual differences in cognitive performance over time when the developmental function underlying performance is continuous and quantitative in nature; see also continuity versus discontinuity of development; stability; contrast with discontinuity with instability. (Chapter 14)

convergence (of the eyes)   Both eyes looking at the same object. (Chapter 6)

cooperative learning   Exercises in which students are encouraged to assist each other so that the less competent members of the team are likely to benefit from the instruction they receive from their more skillful peers, who also benefit by playing the role of teacher. (Chapter 3)

coordination (of the eyes)   Both eyes following a moving stimulus in a coordinated fashion. (Chapter 6)

coordination of secondary circular reactions   In Piaget's theory, the fourth substage of sensorimotor development, in which infants are able to coordinate two or more behavior patterns to achieve a goal. (Chapter 4)

corpus callosum   A thick mass of nerves that connects the right and left hemispheres of the neocortex. (Chapter 2)

creoles   Languages that develop when children transform the pidgin language of their parents to a grammatically more complex "true" language. (Chapter 9)

critical (sensitive) period   The time in development (usually early in life) when a certain skill or ability is most easily acquired. (Chapter 2)

cross-modal matching   See intermodal matching.

crystallized abilities   In Cattell's theory of intelligence, intellectual abilities that develop from cultural context and learning experience; contrast with fluid abilities. (Chapter 13)

cued recall In memory research, a task in which a subject recalls information after being given prompts or cues. (Chapter 8)

cultural learning The transmission of acquired information and behavior both within and across generations with a high degree of fidelity. The theory of Tomasello and colleagues proposes three stagelike levels of cultural learning, with each more advanced form being based on a more sophisticated type of perspective taking: imitative learning, instructed learning, and collaborative learning. (Chapter 11)

cultural relativism The idea that intellectual skills critical for survival in one's culture may not be important in another. (Chapter 13)

cumulative (active) rehearsal In memory research, type of rehearsal in which a person repeats the most recently presented word and then rehearses it with as many other different words as possible. (Chapter 8)

Darwinian algorithms Domain-specific cognitive programs that evolved to accomplish specific adaptive functions. (Chapter 2)

decentration In Piaget's theory, the ability of concrete operational children to consider multiple aspects of a stimulus or situation; contrast with centration. (Chapter 4)

declarative memory Facts and events stored in the long-term memory, which come in two types: episodic and semantic memory; see also explicit memory; contrast with nondeclarative memory. (Chapter 5)

decomposition An arithmetic strategy in which children transform the original problem into two or more simpler problems. (Chapter 12)

deep structure In Chomsky's theory, the grammatical organization and meaning that underlies all language; contrast with surface structure. (Chapter 9)

deferred imitation Imitation of a modeled act sometime after viewing the behavior. (Chapters 4, 7, 8)

dendrites The numerous fibers of a neuron that receive messages from other neurons. (Chapter 2)

depth perception The ability to discriminate visual patterns denoting depth; see also bifoveal fixation, visual cliff. (Chapter 6)

development Predictable changes that occur in structure or function over the life span. (Chapter 1)

developmental cognitive neuroscience The perspective that takes data from a variety of sources—molecular biology, cell biology, artificial intelligence, evolutionary theory, as well as conventional cognitive development—to create a picture of how the mind/brain develops. (Chapter 2)

developmental contextual model See developmental systems approach.

developmental function The form that development takes over time. (Chapter 1)

developmental invariance Developmental pattern such that a cognitive skill does not improve steadily over childhood but reaches adult competence early in life and remains stable thereafter. (Chapter 1)

developmental systems approach (developmental contextual model) Perspective that views development as the result of bidirectional interaction between all levels of biological and experiential variables. (Chapters 1, 2)

deviation IQ Method of constructing IQ scores that compares a child's performance to that of other children the same age; contrast with mental age. (Chapter 13)

differential approach See psychometric approach.

differentiation (of neurons) The final stage of neuronal development, in which neurons gain in size, produce more dendrites, and extend their axons farther away from the cell body. (Chapter 2)

discontinuity of development See continuity versus discontinuity of development.

discontinuity with instability The expectation and research finding that there is instability of individual differences in cognitive performance over time when the developmental function underlying performance is discontinuous and qualitative in nature; see also continuity versus discontinuity of development; stability; contrast with continuity with stability. (Chapter 14)

discrepancy principle The idea that infants are most attentive to slightly novel stimuli. (Chapter 6)

dishabituation The tendency to show renewed interest in a stimulus when some features of it have been changed; contrast with habituation. (Chapter 6)

displacement The fact that what one speaks about need not be limited to the immediate context. (Chapter 9)

distinctive features The characteristics of an object that differentiate it from other objects. (Chapter 6)

domain-general abilities General, underlying cognitive abilities that influence performance over a wide range of situations (or domains); contrast with domain-specific abilities. (Chapter 1)

domain-specific abilities Cognitive abilities specific to one cognitive domain under control of a specific mind/brain function; contrast with domain-general abilities. (Chapter 1)

DQ (development quotient) tests A test of infant abilities, such as the Bayley Scales of Infant Development. (Chapter 13)

dual encoding See dual representation.

duality Refers to the fact that language is represented at two levels: *phonology*, the actual sound that a speaker produces, and the underlying abstract, meaning of language, reflected by the *syntax* (rules of putting words together) as well as *semantics* (meaning of those words and concepts). (Chapter 9)

dual orientation See dual representation.

dual representation (dual encoding, dual orientation) The ability to represent an object simultaneously as the object itself and as a representation of something else. (Chapter 7)

dyslexia Reading disability, such that a person has difficulty in learning to read despite an average intelligence. (Chapter 12)

effortful processes Cognitive processes that consume some of the information-processing system's limited capacity and are hypothesized to (1) be available to conscious awareness, (2) interfere with the execution of other processes, (3) improve with practice, and (4) be influenced by individual differences in intelligence, motivation, or education; contrast with automatic processes. (Chapter 5)

egocentricity In Piaget's theory, the tendency to interpret objects and events from one's own perspective. (Chapter 4)

egocentric speech See private speech.

elaboration A memory strategy that involves creating associations between two or more unrelated items. (Chapters 5, 8)

elementary cognitive tasks (ECTs) Simple laboratory tests designed to measure subjects' response times as they make presumably simple decisions; the low-level, or basic, processes measured by ECTs are presumed to be closely related to physiological functioning and thus primarily under the influence of endogenous (and inherited) factors. (Chapter 14)

emergent literacy The skills, knowledge, and attitudes that are presumed to be developmental precursors to conventional forms of reading and writing and the environments that support these developments. (Chapter 12)

empiricism Philosophical perspective that nature provides only species-general learning mechanisms, with cognition arising as a result of experience. (Chapter 1)

epigenesis The emergence of new structures and functions during the course of development. (Chapter 2)

episodic memory Long-term memory of events or episodes; contrast with semantic memory; see also autobiographical memory; event memory. (Chapter 5)

equilibration In Piaget's theory, the process by which balance is restored to the cognitive structures through assimilation and accommodation. (Chapter 4)

event memory Memory for everyday events, a form of episodic memory. (Chapter 8)

evolution The process of change in gene frequencies in populations over many generations that in time produces new species. (Chapter 2)

executive control structures In Case's theory, mental structures that involve a representation of the problem situation, a representation of the objectives of the task, and a representation of the particular strategy or procedures for solving the problem. (Chapter 4)

executive function The processes involved in regulating attention and in determining what to do with information just gathered or retrieved from long-term memory. (Chapter 5)

experience-dependent processes (or experience-dependent synaptogenesis) Processes whereby synapses are formed and maintained as a result of the unique experiences of an individual; contrast with experience-expectant processes. (Chapter 2)

experience-expectant processes (or experience-expectant synaptogenesis) Processes whereby synapses are formed and maintained when an organism has species-typical experiences; as a result, functions (such as vision) will develop for all members of a species, given a species-typical environment; contrast with experience-dependent processes. (Chapter 2)

experiential subtheory In Sternberg's triarchic theory, the subtheory concerned with how prior knowledge influences performance, specifically with the individual's ability to deal with novelty and the degree to which processing is automatized. (Chapter 13)

explicit memory Memories that are available to conscious awareness and can be directly assessed by tests of recall or recognition memory; see also declarative memory; contrast with implicit memory. (Chapter 5)

externality effect The tendency of young infants (1-month-olds) to direct their attention primarily to the outside of a figure and to spend little time inspecting internal features. (Chapter 6)

fact retrieval   In information-processing approaches to cognition, the retrieval of a fact directly from long-term memory without using effortful procedures. (Chapter 12)

factor analysis   A statistical technique used to define mental factors by analyzing results from intelligence tests. (Chapter 13)

factors   In psychometric approaches to intelligence, a set of related mental skills (such as verbal or spatial skills) that underlies intellectual functioning. (Chapter 13)

false-belief task   A type of task used in theory-of-mind studies, in which the child must infer that another person does not possess knowledge that he or she possesses (that is, that other person holds a belief that is false). (Chapter 7)

familial studies of intelligence   Studies in which some measure or measures of intelligence among people of a known genetic relationship are correlated; the extent to which performance varies as a function of genetic similarity is used as an indication of the heritability of that measure; see also heritability. (Chapter 14)

fast mapping   The ability to learn new words based on very little input. (Chapter 9)

feature-list models (of semantic memory)   Models of semantic memory that hold that language concepts (or words) can be defined in terms of lists of the characteristics or features they possess. (Chapter 7)

field dependence/field independence (FD/FI)   Thinking styles defined by the degree to which a person can perceive parts of a visual field separately from the whole. (Chapter 6)

fixed-action patterns   See innate releasing mechanisms.

fluid abilities   In Cattell's theory of intelligence, intellectual abilities that are biologically determined and reflected in tests of memory span and spatial thinking; contrast with crystallized abilities. (Chapter 13)

Flynn effect   The systematic increase in IQ scores (about 3 points per decade) observed over the 20th century. (Chapter 14)

forethought   In Bandura's social cognitive theory, the ability to anticipate the consequences of one's actions and the actions of others. (Chapter 11)

forgetting   The failure to retrieve information that one had retrieved on a previous attempt. (Chapter 8)

formal operations   In Piaget's theory, the final stage of cognitive development, in which children are able to apply abstract logical rules. (Chapter 4)

formal reasoning   The type of reasoning in which the *form* of an argument, not its semantic content, is crucial. (Chapter 10).

free morphemes   Morphemes that can stand alone as a word, such as "dog," "chase," or "happy." (Chapter 9)

free recall   In memory research, a task in which a subject recalls information without specific cues or prompts. (Chapter 8)

function   In developmental psychology, action related to a structure, such as movement of a muscle, firing of a nerve, or activation of a mental representation; contrast with structure; see also bidirectionality of structure and function. (Chapter 1)

functional invariants   In Piaget's theory, the processes of organization and adaptation that characterize all biological systems and operate throughout the life span. (Chapter 4)

fuzzy traces   In fuzzy-trace theory, imprecise memory representations that are more easily accessed, generally require less effort to use, and are less susceptible to interference and forgetting than verbatim traces. (Chapters 5, 10)

fuzzy-trace theory   Brainerd and Reyna's theory that proposes that information is encoded on a continuum from verbatim to fuzzy, gistlike traces, and that developmental differences in many aspects of cognition can be attributed to age differences in encoding and in differences in sensitivity to output interference. (Chapters 5, 10)

g (Spearman's g, general intelligence)   In psychometric theory, the idea that intelligence can be expressed in terms of a single factor, general intelligence or *g*, first formulated by Spearman in the early 1900s. (Chapter 13)

Gardner's theory of multiple intelligences   See theory of multiple intelligences.

gender consistency   The concept that gender remains the same despite changes in behavior. (Chapter 11)

gender constancy   The concept that gender remains the same despite changes in physical appearance, time, and behavior; includes gender identity, gender stability, and gender consistency. (Chapter 11)

gender identification   The process of identifying oneself as male or female and adopting the roles and values of that gender. (Chapter 11)

gender identity   The ability of children to identify themselves as either boys or girls. (Chapter 11)

gender schema   A mentalistic structure consisting of a set of expectations and associations that guide processing with respect to gender. (Chapter 11)

gender script   A particular type of gender schema that is a temporally organized event sequence related to gender. (Chapter 11)

gender stability   The concept that gender remains the same over time. (Chapter 11)

general genetic law of cultural development   The idea that cognition occurs on two planes, first the social, between individuals, and later the psychological, as it is internalized by the child. (Chapter 3)

general intelligence   See *g*.

genetic epistemology   The experimental study of the development of knowledge, originated by Piaget. (Chapter 4)

genotype → environment effects   In Scarr and McCartney's theory, the proposal that one's genotype (genetic constitution) influences which environments one encounters and the type of experiences one has, or that genes drive experience. Three types of genotype → environment effects are proposed: passive, evocative, and active. (Chapter 2)

goal-directed behavior   Means-end problem solving, seen first in the latter part of the first year. (Chapters 4, 10)

"good enough" parents   The controversial proposal by Scarr that individual differences in parenting have little consequence for children's development and that "good enough" parents are adequate for proper development. (Chapter 2)

guided participation   Adult-child interactions, not only during explicit instruction but also during the more routine activities and communication of everyday life; the process and system of involvement of individuals with others as they communicate and engage in shared activities; contrast with zone of proximal development; see also sociocultural perspective. (Chapter 3)

Guilford's structure-of-the-intellect model   A theory of intelligence derived from factor analysis, postulating 180 factors. (Chapter 13)

habituation   The tendency to decrease responding to a stimulus that has been presented repeatedly; contrast with dishabituation. (Chapter 6)

helplessness   A maladaptive pattern of achievement behavior in which children avoid challenge, do not persist in the face of difficulty, and tend to attribute their failure on tasks to a lack of ability rather than a lack of effort or an inappropriate strategy. (Chapter 11)

hemispheres   The two approximately equal halves of the neocortex. (Chapter 2)

heritability   The extent to which differences in any trait within a population can be attributed to inheritance. (Chapter 14)

hierarchical model of cognitive abilities   The model that proposes that intelligence is composed of specific cognitive abilities (for example, verbal, spatial, speed of processing, memory) that are intercorrelated and influenced by a higher-order general intellectual factor, *g*. (Chapter 13)

hierarchization   In Piaget's theory, the fact that each current structure can be traced to earlier, more primitive structures, which were necessary for the attainment of the more advanced structure. (Chapter 4)

HOME scale   The Home Observation for Measurement of the Environment scale, a scale developed by Bradley, Caldwell, and Elardo that provides a detailed analysis of parental behavior and characteristics of the home environment that are hypothesized to be associated with intelligence. (Chapter 14)

homogeneity of cognitive function   Assumption in stage theories that a child's cognition is relatively homogeneous, or even, across different tasks and contexts. (Chapter 1)

hypermnesia   In memory research, the net increase in recall over repeated trials. (Chapter 8)

hypothetico-deductive reasoning   In Piaget's theory, a formal operational ability to think hypothetically. (Chapter 4)

identity   In Piaget's theory, realizing that qualitative properties of an object can change without changing the nature of that object (for example, realizing that a car remains the same despite being painted); contrast with conservation. (Chapter 7)

idiosyncratic (fiat equivalence, random) classification   In classification tasks, the grouping together of items without justification related to any physical or conceptual characteristics of the stimuli; contrast with perceptual, complementary, and conceptual classification. (Chapter 7)

imagery   See mental imagery.

imaginary audience   Expression of adolescent egocentrism, with adolescents feeling that they are constantly "on stage," or playing to an imaginary audience. (Chapter 4)

imitative learning In the theory of cultural learning of Tomasello et al., the first stage of cultural learning, which occurs when the learner internalizes something of the model's behavioral strategies and intentions for executing the behavior; contrast with instructed learning, collaborative learning; see also cultural learning. (Chapter 11)

implicit memory Memory without awareness; implicit memory can be assessed only indirectly; (Chapters 5, 8)

incidental learning Acquiring knowledge about noncentral aspects of a task or situation; see also unintentional memory. (Chapter 5)

individual differences Differences in patterns of intellectual aptitudes among people of a given age. (Chapter 1)

inductive reasoning The type of thinking that goes from specific observations to broad generalizations and, in Piaget's theory, is characteristic of formal operational thought. (Chapter 4)

infant-directed speech The specialized register of speech adults and older children use when talking specifically to infants. (Chapter 9)

infantile amnesia The inability to remember events from infancy and early childhood. (Chapter 8)

inhibition The ability to prevent from making some cognitive or behavioral response. (Chapter 5)

innate releasing mechanisms Inherited sets of behaviors elicited by specific sets of stimuli without the need of prior environmental experience. (Chapter 7)

inner speech In Vygotsky's theory, the covert language used to guide thought. (Chapter 9)

institutionalization studies Studies of the effects of minimal human contact on children reared in institutions. (Chapter 14)

instructed learning In the theory of cultural learning of Tomasello et al., the second stage of cultural learning, involving a more accomplished person instructing a less accomplished person; instructed learning requires that children learn about the adult, specifically about the adult's understanding of the task and how that compares with their own understanding; contrast with imitative learning, collaborative learning; see also cultural learning. (Chapter 11)

intelligence Acting or thinking in ways that are goal-directed and adaptive. (Chapter 13)

intermodal integration The coordination or integration of information from two or more senses. (Chapter 6)

intermodal (cross-modal) matching The ability to recognize an object initially inspected in one modality (touch, for example) via another modality (vision, for example). (Chapter 6)

intrinsic activity In Piaget's theory, the assumption that babies are born ready to make contact with their environment and that cognitive structures, by their very nature, seek to be active. (Chapter 4)

intuitionism In fuzzy-trace theory, the tendency of people to prefer to think, reason, and remember by processing inexact, "fuzzy" memory representations rather than working logically from exact, verbatim representations. (Chapter 5)

inversion See negation.

IQ (intelligence quotient) tests Aptitude tests, such as the Stanford-Binet and Wechsler scales, that are intended to measure aspects of intellectual functioning. (Chapter 13)

knowledge base The general background knowledge a person possesses, which influences most cognitive task performance. (Chapters 5, 8)

language acquisition device (LAD) In Chomsky's theory, the hypothetical construct possessed by all humans at birth enabling them to acquire language. (Chapter 9)

language acquisition support system (LASS) The idea proposed by Bruner that adults and older children have learning devices that interact with children's language acquisition devices (LAD). (Chapter 9)

lateralization See cerebral lateralization.

learning to learn Performance on later tasks is enhanced as a result of performance on earlier tasks, in which a general set of rules or approaches to a problem is acquired. (Chapter 10)

"less is more" hypothesis Newport's hypothesis that the cognitive limitations of infants and young children may serve to simplify the body of language they process, thus making it easier to learn the complicated syntactical system of any human language. (Chapter 9)

limited capacity The concept that one's information-processing ability is restricted (that people can only do so many things at any single time). Metaphors for capacity include mental space, mental energy or effort, and time. (Chapter 5)

location memory See object and location memory.

long-term store In information-processing approaches to cognition, the large and presumably permanent repository of information in the brain. (Chapter 5)

mastery orientation An adaptive pattern of achievement behavior in which children enjoy and seek challenge, persist in the face of obstacles, and tend to view their failings as due to lack of effort or strategy use rather than to a lack of ability. (Chapter 11)

mean length of utterance (MLU) A measure of language development defined by the average number of meaningful language units (root words and endings) a child uses at any one time. (Chapter 9)

mediational deficiency The inability of young children to use a strategy even if it is taught to them; contrast with production deficiency and utilization deficiency. (Chapter 5)

memory span The number of items a person can hold in the short-term store, assessed by testing the number of (usually) unrelated items that can be recalled in exact order. (Chapter 5)

memory strategies See mnemonics.

mental age Level of mental functioning (in years) as measured by the number of items passed on an intelligence test, formerly used in determining IQ scores; contrast with deviation IQ. (Chapter 13)

mental combinations In Piaget's theory, the final substage of sensorimotor development, a transition between the action-oriented world of the infant and the symbol-oriented world of the child. (Chapter 4)

mental imagery The internal representation of an external event; see anticipatory images and reproductive images. (Chapter 7)

meta-analysis A statistical technique that allows an investigator to evaluate the magnitude of a significant effect across a large number of studies, by providing an estimate of effect size, expressed in terms of how large average differences between targeted groups are across the various studies, taking into consideration the overall amount of variability. (Chapters 6, 12)

meta-attention Knowledge of factors that influence one's attention. (Chapter 5)

metacognition Knowledge about one's own thoughts and the factors that influence thinking. (Chapter 5)

metacommunication Knowledge of the adequacy of one's own communication abilities. (Chapter 9)

metamemory Knowledge of one's own memory abilities and the factors that influence memory. (Chapter 8)

microgenetic development In Vygotsky's sociocultural theory, changes that occur over relatively brief periods of time, in seconds, minutes, or days, as opposed to larger-scale changes, as conventionally studied in ontogenetic development. (Chapter 3)

microgenetic method A research methodology that looks at developmental change within a single set of individuals over relatively brief periods of time (days or weeks, usually). (Chapter 5)

migration (of neurons) The movement of neurons to their permanent positions in the brain, most of which is completed during the prenatal period. (Chapter 2)

mindblindness A deficit in theory of mind, characteristic of people with autism, in which a person cannot read the minds of others. (Chapter 7)

min strategy An arithmetic strategy in which children faced with an addition problem start with the largest addend and count up from there. (Chapter 12)

mnemonics (memory strategies) Effortful techniques used to improve memory, including rehearsal, organization, and elaboration. (Chapter 8)

modularity Concept that certain areas of the brain are dedicated to performing specific cognitive tasks. (Chapter 1)

morphemes Meaningful language units. (Chapter 9)

morphology In the study of language development, the knowledge of word formation. (Chapter 9)

motherese See child-directed speech.

multiple intelligences See theory of multiple intelligences.

multistore models Information-processing models proposing that information is processed serially through a sequence of memory stores (sensory register, short-term store, long-term store). (Chapter 5)

myelin A sheet of fatty substance that develops around the neurons to promote faster transmission of electrical signals through the nervous system. (Chapter 2)

myelination The development of myelin around neurons, which proceeds at different rates in different areas of the brain. (Chapter 2)

nativism Philosophical perspective that human intellectual abilities are innate. (Chapter 1)

natural language categories Language terms that include a wide range of exemplars; most natural language categories are hierarchical in nature (for example, animal; canine; dog). (Chapter 7)

natural selection In Darwin's theory of evolution, the idea that more individuals are produced in a generation than can usually survive, and that variations in individuals make some members of a species more fit than others and thus more likely to survive to reproduce; according to Darwin, natural selection is the primary mechanism for evolution. (Chapter 2)

negation (inversion)   A form of Piagetian reversibility such that any operation can always be negated, or inverted. (Chapter 4)

neocortex   The outer layer of the brain, which gives humans their highly developed intelligence. (Chapter 2)

neonatal imitation   The ability of newborns to reproduce some behavior, such as a facial expression, that they have seen in others. (Chapter 7)

neo-nativism (structural constraint theory)   The idea that much cognitive knowledge, such as object concept and certain aspects of language, is innate, requiring little in the way of specific experiences to be expressed, and that there are biological constraints, in that the mind/brain is designed to process certain types of information in certain ways. (Chapter 4)

neural constructivism   The theory that brain development, and thus cognitive development, proceeds as a dynamic interaction between the development of the neural substrate and the environment. (Chapter 2)

neural Darwinism   Edelman's theory that groups of neurons are in constant competition with one another, each attempting to recruit adjacent neurons to their group and thus perform a particular function. (Chapter 2)

neuroimaging techniques   New technologies that permit imaging of brain activities, including high-density event-related potentials, positron emission tomography (PET), and functional magnetic resonance imaging (f MRI). (Chapter 2)

neuron   Nervous system cell through which electrical and chemical signals are transmitted. (Chapter 2)

neurotransmitters   Chemicals in synapses that serve to transmit electrical impulses between neurons. (Chapter 2)

nondeclarative, (or procedural) memory   Knowledge in the long-term store of procedures that are unconscious; see also implicit memory; contrast with declarative memory. (Chapter 5)

nonshared environment   A home environment that is unique to an individual, not shared by a sibling, for instance. (Chapter 14)

object and location memory   A form of spatial cognition that involves locating and remembering objects in arrays. Unlike other forms of spatial cognition, object and location memory tends to be better in females than in males and shows relatively little improvement over development. (Chapters 6, 8)

object permanence   The knowledge that objects have an existence in time and space independent of one's own perception or action on those objects. (Chapters 4, 7)

observational learning   The ability to learn about the world simply by watching, central to Bandura's social cognitive theory; according to Bandura, observational learning includes four subprocesses: attentional processes, retention processes, production processes, and motivational processes. (Chapter 11)

ontogenetic development   Development of the individual over his or her lifetime. (Chapter 3)

operating space   In Case's theory of working memory, the mental space that can be allocated to the execution of intellectual operations. (Chapter 5)

operations   In Piaget's theory, particular types of cognitive schemes that are mental (that is, require symbols), derive from action, exist in organized systems (structures of the whole), and follow a set of logical rules, most importantly that of reversibility. (Chapter 4)

optimal level   In Fischer's theory, the maximum level of complexity of a skill that the individual can control. (Chapter 4)

organization (in memory research)   The structure discovered or imposed upon a set of items that is used to guide memory performance. (Chapter 8)

organization (in Piaget's theory)   The idea that every intellectual operation is related to all other acts of intelligence. (Chapter 4)

output interference   In fuzzy-trace theory, response competition in the form of scheduling effects and feedback effects, produced by the act of making responses. (Chapter 5)

overextensions   In the study of language development, the stretching of a familiar word beyond its correct meaning; for example, calling all four-legged mammals "doggie." (Chapter 9)

overregularization   In the study of language development, the tendency to apply rules to words when they are not appropriate, for example, runned, foots, mices. (Chapter 9)

paired-associates task   A task in which subjects are given pairs of words to study and later are presented with one word of a pair and asked to recall the word previously paired with it. (Chapters 5, 8)

passive rehearsal   Style of rehearsing in which a person includes few (usually one) unique items per rehearsal set; contrast with cumulative rehearsal. (Chapter 8)

perceptual centration   See centration.

perceptual classification   In classification tasks, the grouping together of items on the basis of perceptual characteristics; contrast with idiosyncratic, complementary, and conceptual classification. (Chapter 7)

perceptual decentration   See decentration.

personal fable   A belief in one's uniqueness and invulnerability, which is an expression of adolescent egocentrism. (Chapter 4)

perspective taking   The ability to understand the perspective of others, which is particularly important in social development. (Chapter 11)

phonemes   Individual sounds that are used to make up words. (Chapters 6, 9)

phonemic awareness   The knowledge that words consist of separable sounds; contrast with phonological recoding. (Chapter 12)

phonics   Reading instruction method based on learning letter-sound correspondence; see also phonological recoding. (Chapter 12)

phonological recoding   Reading skills used to translate written symbols into sounds and words; contrast with phonemic awareness. (Chapter 12)

phonology   In language acquisition, the knowledge of how words are pronounced. (Chapter 9)

phylogenetic development   Development over evolutionary time. (Chapter 3)

pidgins   Structurally simple communication systems that arise when people who share no common language come into constant contact. (Chapter 9)

plasticity (of cognition and behavior)   The extent to which behavior can be changed. (Chapter 1)

positive manifold   In psychometric approaches to intelligence, the high correlations among scores on sets of cognitive tests that have little in common with one another in terms of content or types of strategies used. (Chapter 13)

pragmatics   In the study of language development, knowledge about how language can be adjusted to fit different circumstances. (Chapter 9)

preference for novelty paradigms   Tasks in which an infant's preference, usually measured in looking time, for a novel as opposed to a familiar stimulus is used as an indication of memory for the familiar stimulus. (Chapter 8)

preoperations   In Piaget's theory, the second major stage of cognitive development (approximately ages 2 to 7), characterized by prelogical, intuitive thought. (Chapter 4)

primary circular reactions   In Piaget's theory, the second substage of sensorimotor development, in which infants extend their reflexes to acquire new patterns of behavior that were not present at birth. (Chapter 4)

primary visual system   The phylogenetically more recent visual system, functioning poorly in newborns; processing of visual information is done by the fovea, permitting careful analysis of stimulus properties; contrast with secondary visual system. (Chapter 6)

private (egocentric) speech   Children's speech apparently for self and not directed to others. (Chapter 9)

problem solving   Process in which someone has a specific goal in mind that cannot be attained immediately because of the presence of one or more obstacles; problem solving involves a goal, obstacles to that goal, strategies for overcoming the obstacles, and an evaluation of the results. (Chapter 10)

production deficiency   Children's tendency not to use spontaneously a strategy that they are capable of using when instructed; contrast with mediational deficiency and utilization deficiency. (Chapters 5)

productive language   The language a child can actually produce, or speak; contrast with receptive language. (Chapter 9)

productivity   The fact that speakers can combine a finite set of words to produce an infinite set of sentences. (Chapter 9)

proliferation (of neurons)   The process of nerve-cell division by mitosis. (Chapter 2)

propositional logic   A form of symbolic logic that involves two or more factors (conventionally, P and Q), with each factor having two possible values (for instance, true or false), used by Piaget and Inhelder to describe formal operational thought. (Chapter 4)

prosody   The intonational and stress pattern and the tempo of an utterance. (Chapter 9)

psychometric (differential) approach   The theory that intelligence can be described in terms of mental factors and that tests can be constructed that reveal individual differences in the factors underlying mental performance. (Chapter 13)

qualitative versus quantitative differences   The degree to which cognitive development reflects changes in type or kind (qualitative) versus amount or rate (quantitative). (Chapter 1)

reading comprehension The ability to relate the meaning of individual words and sentences to abstract the broader meaning of a written text. (Chapter 12)

reasoning A particular type of problem solving that involves making inferences. (Chapter 10)

receptive language The language that a child can understand; contrast with productive language. (Chapter 9)

reciprocal determinism In Bandura's theory, the belief that children have as much of an effect on their environment as their environment has on them. (Chapter 11)

reciprocity See compensation.

recognition Process in which a person remembers a familiar stimulus upon being presented with it again; contrast with free recall. (Chapter 8)

reduction to essence rule In fuzzy-trace theory, the assumption that people of all ages are biased to extract the gist from a message. (Chapter 5)

reflective abstraction In Piaget's theory, the ability to reflect upon knowledge one already possesses, and without the need of additional information from the external environment, to arrive at new knowledge; characteristic of adolescent thought. (Chapter 4)

rehearsal A memory strategy in which target information is repeated; see also cumulative rehearsal. (Chapter 8)

relational mapping The application of what one knows about one set of elements (the relation of A to B) to relations about different elements (the relation of C to D). (Chapter 10)

relational primacy hypothesis The hypothesis that analogical reasoning is available early in infancy. (Chapter 10)

relational shift In analogical reasoning, the proposal that there is in development a shift from focusing on perceptual similarity to relational similarity to solve problems. (Chapter 10)

reminiscence In memory research, the recall of specific items on later trials that were not recalled on earlier trials. (Chapter 8)

representation The mental encoding of information. (Chapters 1, 7)

representational change In false-belief tasks, children's false memory for their initial belief. (Chapter 7)

representational constraints (or representational innateness) Representations that are hard-wired into the brain so that some types of "knowledge" are innate. (Chapter 1)

representational insight The knowledge that an entity can stand for something other than itself. (Chapter 7)

representational redescription In Karmiloff-Smith's theory, processes whereby the mind redescribes (re-represents) its own representations. (Chapter 4)

reproductive images In Piaget's theory, mental images that are limited to evoking previously experienced sights and involve relatively static representations of objects; contrast with anticipatory images. (Chapter 7)

resistance to interference The ability to ignore irrelevant information so that it does not impede task performance; its inverse is interference sensitivity. (Chapter 5)

reversibility In Piaget's theory, the knowledge that an operation can be reversed, characteristic of the concrete operational period; see also compensation, negation. (Chapter 4)

rule-assessment approach An approach that explains cognitive development in terms of the acquisition of increasingly powerful rules for solving problems. (Chapter 10).

scaffolding An expert, when instructing a novice, responding contingently to the novice's responses in a learning situation, so that the novice gradually increases his or her understanding of a problem. (Chapter 3)

schema An abstract representation of an object or event. (Chapter 6)

schematic representation The representation of objects in terms of real or potential interactions with other objects. (Chapter 7)

schemes See structures.

scientific reasoning A type of reasoning that involves the generation of hypotheses and the systematic testing of those hypotheses. (Chapter 10)

scripts A form of schematic organization, with real-world events organized in terms of temporal and causal relations between component acts. (Chapters 8, 9)

secondary circular reactions In Piaget's theory, the third substage of sensorimotor development, in which infants first learn to control events in the external world. (Chapter 4)

secondary visual system The phylogenetically older visual system, functioning relatively well in the newborn; processing is done primarily in the visual periphery (that is, nonfoveally), and orients the infant toward a stimulus, providing information concerning where a stimulus is; contrast with primary visual system. (Chapter 6)

selectionist theories   Any theory that proposes that a large number of brain cells/cognitive operations/behaviors are generated and only those "successful" ones are selected by the immediate environment and survive; whereas, nonselected cells/cognitive operations/behaviors decrease infrequency or die. (Chapter 2)

selective attention   Concentration on chosen stimuli without distraction by nontarget stimuli. (Chapter 5)

selective cell death   Early developmental process in which neurons that are not activated by sensory and motor experience die. (Chapter 2)

self-concept   The way a person defines himself or herself. (Chapter 11)

self-efficacy   The belief that one can influence one's own thoughts and behavior. (Chapter 11)

self-reflection   In Bandura's social cognitive theory, the ability to analyze one's thoughts and actions. (Chapter 11)

self-regulation   The process of adopting standards of acceptable behavior, including aspirational standards (hoped-for levels of accomplishment) as well as social and moral standards. (Chapter 11)

semanticity   The fact that language can represent events, ideas, actions, and objects symbolically. (Chapter 9)

semantic memory   Long-term memory representation of definitions and relations among language terms; contrast with episodic memory. (Chapter 5)

semantics   In language acquisition, knowledge of the meaning of words and sentences. (Chapter 9)

semiotic function   See symbolic function.

sensorimotor stage   In Piaget's (and Case's) theory, the first major stage of cognitive development (birth to approximately 2 years), in which children understand their world through sensory and motor experiences. (Chapter 4)

sensory registers   Memory stores for each sensory modality (touch, vision, hearing) that presumably can hold large quantities of information but only for very brief periods of time (milliseconds). (Chapter 5)

shared environment   A home environment shared by different family members. (Chapter 14)

short-term store (primary memory, contents of consciousness)   Memory store that can hold a limited amount of information for a matter of seconds; cognitive operations are executed in the short-term store and in-

formation can be maintained indefinitely in the short-term store through operations such as rehearsal; see also working memory. (Chapter 5)

slot-filler categories   Groups of items that could successfully complete a script (for example, juice and cocoa for a breakfast script). (Chapter 9)

social cognitive theory   Bandura's theory of how individuals operate cognitively on their social experiences and how these cognitive operations influence behavior and development. (Chapter 11)

social information processing   As exemplified by Dodge's theory, the view that social information must be encoded, compared with other pertinent information, and retrieved so that social interactions run smoothly. (Chapter 11)

social learning theory   An earlier version of Bandura's social cognitive theory. (Chapter 10)

sociocultural perspective   A perspective of cognitive development that emphasizes that development is guided by adults interacting with children, with the cultural context determining to a large extent how, where, and when these interactions take place; see also guided participation; zone of proximal development. (Chapter 3)

sociohistorical development   Changes that have occurred in one's culture and the values, norms, and technologies such a history has generated (Chapter 3)

sort-recall task   In memory research, a task in which children have the opportunity to sort items into groups before recall. (Chapter 8)

source monitoring   The awareness of the origins of one's memories, knowledge, or beliefs. (Chapters 3, 7, 8)

spatial cognition   The type of cognition that involves processing visual information in terms of spatial relationships, including spatial orientation, spatial visualization, and object and location memory. (Chapter 6)

spatial orientation   How people understand the placement of objects in space with themselves as the reference point. (Chapter 6)

spatial visualization   An aspect of spatial cognition that involves the mental manipulations of visual stimuli, such as performing mental rotation or solving embedded-figures problems. (Chapter 6)

Spearman's g   See g (general intelligence).

speech register   A distinct style of speaking, which is used only is specific contexts (for example, when talking to children; when talking in school). (Chapter 9)

speed of processing How quickly any cognitive operation can be executed; hypothesized to be a measure of limited capacity and related to performance on many cognitive tasks. (Chapter 5)

stability In developmental psychology, the degree to which a person maintains over time the same rank order in comparison with peers for a particular characteristic. (Chapters 1, 14)

stages Relatively discrete periods of time in which functioning is qualitatively different from functioning at other periods. (Chapter 1)

Stanford-Binet An individually administered IQ test. (Chapter 13)

states versus transformations In Piaget's theory, the proposal that preoperational children center their attention on specific states and ignore the transformations between states; whereas, the reverse is true for concrete operational children. (Chapter 4)

Sternberg's triarchic theory See triarchic theory.

storage space In Case's theory of working memory, the mental space that an individual has available for storing information. (Chapter 5)

strategies Goal-directed and deliberately implemented mental operations used to facilitate task performance; see also mnemonics. (Chapters 1, 5)

structural constraint theory See neo-nativism.

structure In developmental psychology, a substrate of the organism that develops, such as muscle, nervous tissue, or mental knowledge; contrast with function; see bidirectionality of structure and function. (Chapter 1)

structure of the intellect See Guilford's structure-of-the-intellect model.

structures (schemes) In Piaget's theory, the enduring knowledge base by which children interpret their world. (Chapter 4)

structures of the whole (structures d'ensemble) In Piaget's theory, the proposal that operations exist in an organized system, with all operations being integrated with all others. (Chapter 4)

subitizing Quantifying small numbers of items without conscious counting. (Chapter 7)

subjective expected utility A person's beliefs about the usefulness of any behavior; in memory research, a person's belief about the usefulness of implementing any particular strategy. (Chapter 8)

sum strategy A simple addition strategy used by young children that involves counting together the two addends of a problem. (Chapter 12)

superordinate categories Broad, higher-level categories, such as animals, clothing, or food; contrast with basic-level categories. (Chapter 7)

surface structure In Chomsky's theory, the actual words of a sentence, derived from the deep structure. (Chapter 9)

symbolic (semiotic) function In Piaget's theory, the underlying symbolic nature of cognition, occurring toward the end of the sensorimotor period and expressed via deferred imitation, language, symbolic play, and mental imagery. (Chapter 7)

symbolic play Pretending; in Piaget's theory, an expression of the symbolic function. (Chapters 3, 7)

symbolization In Bandura's social cognitive theory, the ability to think about one's social behavior in terms of words and images. (Chapter 11)

synapse The tiny space between the dendrite of one neuron and the axon of another through which chemical messages are passed. (Chapter 2)

synaptogenesis The process of synapse formation. (Chapter 2)

syntax In language acquisition, the knowledge of how words are put together to form grammatical sentences. (Chapter 9)

telegraphic speech Children's economical use of words, including only high-information words that are most important in conveying meaning. (Chapter 9)

tertiary circular reactions In Piaget's theory, the fifth substage of sensorimotor development, in which infants invent slightly new behaviors to achieve their goals. (Chapter 4)

theory of mind A person's concepts of mental activity; used to refer to how children conceptualize mental activity and how they attribute intention to and predict the behavior of others; see also belief-desire reasoning. (Chapter 7)

theory of multiple intelligences Gardner's theory postulating eight components, or modules, of intelligence (1) linguistic, (2) logical-mathematical, (3) musical, (4) spatial, (5) bodily-kinesthetic, (6) interpersonal, (7) intrapersonal, and (8) naturalistic. (Chapter 13)

theory theories Theories of cognitive development that combine neo-nativism and constructivism, proposing that cognitive development progresses by children generating, testing, and changing theories about the physical and social world. (Chapter 4)

tools of intellectual adaptation   Vygotsky's term for methods of thinking and problem-solving strategies that children internalize from their interactions with more competent members of society. (Chapter 3)

total processing space   In Case's theory of working memory, the sum of storage and operating space, or the total mental space in working memory a person has available for the execution of a task. (Chapter 5)

training studies   Experiments in which children's cognitive task performance is assessed after they are instructed in the use of a strategy; used to assess mediational and production deficiencies. (Chapter 5)

transactional model   A framework that views development as the continuous and bidirectional interchange between an active organism with a unique biological constitution, and a changing environment. (Chapter 14)

transient ontogenetic adaptations   Behaviors that play a specific role in survival for an individual at one time only and then disappear when they are no longer needed. (Chapter 7)

triarchic theory   Sternberg's theory that describes intelligence in terms of three subtheories: contextual, experiential, and componential. (Chapter 13)

underextensions   Incorrectly restricting the use of a term (for example, believing that only one's pet, Fido, deserves the label "dog"). (Chapter 9)

universal grammar   In nativist theories of language acquisition, the innate grammar that characterizes all human languages. (Chapter 9)

utilization deficiency   The inability of children to benefit from strategies they are able to implement; contrast with mediational deficiency and production deficiency. (Chapter 5)

verbatim traces   In fuzzy-trace theory, precise, literal memory representations that are less easily accessed, generally require more effort to use, and are more susceptible to interference and forgetting than fuzzy traces. (Chapter 5)

vicarious learning   In Bandura's social cognitive theory, learning without the need to receive specific reinforcement for one's behavior; rather, learning by observing others. (Chapter 10)

violation-of-expectation method   Based on habituation/dishabituation procedures, techniques in which increases in infants' looking time are interpreted as reflecting a violation of an expected outcome. (Chapter 7)

visual cliff   An apparatus designed to test infants for depth perception. (Chapter 6)

visual preference paradigm   In research with infants, observing the amount of time infants spend looking at different visual stimuli to determine which one they prefer (that is, look at more often); such preferences indicate an ability to discriminate between stimuli. (Chapter 6)

Wechsler scales   Individually administered IQ tests, including the WPPSI-R, the WISC-R, the WISC-III, and the WAIS-R. (Chapter 13)

whole-language approach   A top-down approach to teaching reading that emphasizes the readers' active construction of meaning; often excludes the use of phonics. (Chapter 12)

wishful thinking   A characteristic of preschool thought such that children often do not differentiate between their wishes and their expectations. (Chapter 7)

word spurt   The rapid increase in word (mostly noun) learning, occurring at about 18 months of age. (Chapter 9)

working memory   The capacity to store and transform information being held in the short-term system. See short-term store. (Chapter 5)

zone of proximal development   In Vygotsky's theory, the difference between a child's actual level of ability and the level of ability that he or she can achieve when working under the guidance of an instructor; contrast with guided participation; see sociocultural perspective. (Chapter 3)

References

ABRAVANEL, E., & GINGOLD, H. (1985). Learning via observation during the second year of life. *Developmental Psychology, 21,* 614–623.

ABRAVANEL, E., & SIGAFOOS, A. D. (1984). Explaining the presence of imitation during early infancy. *Child Development, 55,* 381–392.

ACKERMAN, B. P. (1985). Children's retrieval deficit. In C. J. Brainerd & M. Pressley (Eds.), *Basic processes in memory development: Progress in cognitive development research.* New York: Springer-Verlag.

ACKERMAN, B. P. (1986). Retrieval search for category and thematic information in memory by children and adults. *Journal of Experimental Child Psychology, 42,* 355–377.

ACKERMAN, B. P. (1987). Descriptions: A model of nonstrategic memory development. In H. W Reese (Ed.), *Advances in child development and behavior* (Vol. 20). Orlando, FL: Academic.

ACKERMAN, B. P. (1993). Children's understanding of the speaker's meaning in referential communication. *Journal of Experimental Child Psychology, 55,* 56–86.

ACKERMAN, B. P. (1996). Induction of a memory retrieval strategy by young children. *Journal of Experimental Child Psychology, 62,* 243–271.

ACKERMAN, B. P. (1997). The role of setting information in children's memory retrieval. *Journal of Experimental Child Psychology, 65,* 238–260.

ACKIL, J. K., & ZARAGOZA, M. S. (1995). Developmental differences in eyewitness suggestibility and memory for source. *Journal of Experimental Child Psychology, 60,* 57–83.

ADAMS, G. R., & JONES, R. M. (1981). Imaginary audience behavior: A validation study. *Journal of Early Adolescence, 1,* 1–10.

ADAMS, J. W., & HITCH, G. J. (1997). Working memory and children's mental addition. *Journal of Experimental Child Psychology, 67,* 21–38.

ADAMS, M. J., TREIMAN, R., & PRESSLEY, M. (1998). Reading, writing, and literacy. In I. E. Sigel & K. A. Renninger (Vol. Eds.) *Child psychology in practice* (Vol. 4). In W. Damon (Gen. Ed.), *Handbook of child psychology.* New York: Wiley.

ADAMS, R. J., & COURAGE, M. L. (1998). Human newborn color vision: Measurement with chromatic stimuli varying in excitation purity. *Journal of Experimental Child Psychology, 68,* 22–34.

ADAMS, R. J., COURAGE, M. L., & MERCER, M. E. (1994). Systematic measurement of human neonatal color vision. *Vision Research, 34,* 1691–1701.

ADEY, P. S., & SHAYER, M. (1992). Accelerating the development of formal thinking in middle and high school students: II. Postproject effects on science achievement. *Journal of Research in Science Teaching, 29,* 81–92.

ADLER, S. (1990). Multicultural clients: Implications for the SLP. *Language, Speech, and Hearing in the Schools, 21,* 135–139.

AGUIAR, A., & BAILLARGEON, R. (1998). Eight-and-a-half-month-old infants' reasoning about containment events. *Child Development, 69,* 636–653.

AHMED, A., & RUFFMAN, T. (1998). Why do infants make A not B errors in a search task, yet show memory for the location of hidden objects in a nonsearch task? *Developmental Psychology, 34,* 441–453.

AINSWORTH, M. D. S., BLEHAR, M. C., WATERS, E., & WALL, S. (1978). *Patterns of attachment: A psychological study of the Strange Situation.* Hillsdale, NJ: Erlbaum.

ALEXANDER, J. M., & SCHWANENFLUGEL, P. J. (1994). Strategy regulation: The role of intelligence, metacognitive attributes, and knowledge base. *Developmental Psychology, 30,* 709–723.

ALEXANDER, J. M., & SCHWANENFLUGEL, P. J. (1996). Development of metacognitive concepts about thinking in gifted and nongifted children: Recent research. *Learning and Individual Differences, 8,* 305–325.

ALEXANDER, J. M., SCHWANENFLUGEL, P. J., & CARR, M. (1995). Development of metacognition in gifted children: Directions for future research. *Developmental Review, 15,* 1–37.

ALEXANDER, R. D. (1989). Evolution of the human psyche. In P. Mellers & C. Stringer (Eds.), *The human revolution: Behavioural and biological perspectives on the origins of modern humans.* Princeton, NJ: Princeton University Press.

ALIBALI, M. W. (1999). How children change their minds: Strategy change can be gradual or abrupt. *Developmental Psychology, 35,* 127-145.

ALIBALI, M. W., & GOLDIN-MEADOWS, S. (1993). Gesture-speech mismatch and mechanisms of learning: What the hands reveal about a child's state of mind. *Cognitive Psychology, 25,* 468–573.

ALLEN, D., BANKS, M. S., & SCHEFRIN, B. (1988). Chromatic discrimination in human infants. *Investigative Ophthalmology and Visual Science, 29* (Suppl.), 25.

ALLEN, G. L., KIRASIC, K. C., & BEARD, R. L. (1989) Children's expression of spatial knowledge. *Journal of Experimental Child Psychology, 48,* 114–130.

ALS, H. (1995). The preterm infant: A model for the study of fetal brain expectation. In J-P. Lecanuet, W. Fifer, N. Krasnegor, & W. Smotherman, (Eds.), *Fetal development: A psychobiological perspective.* Hillsdale, NJ: Erlbaum.

AMSEL, E., GOODMAN, G., SAVOIE, D., & CLARK, M. (1996). The development of reasoning about causal and noncausal influence on levers. *Child Development, 67,* 1624–1646.

ANDERSON, D. R., & LORCH, E. P. (1983). Looking at television: Action or reaction? In J. Bryant & D. R. Anderson (Eds.), *Children's understanding of television: Research on attention and comprehension.* New York: Academic.

ANDERSON, R. C., HIEBERT, E. H., SCOTT, J. A., & WILKINSON, I. A. G. (1984). *Becoming a nation of readers: The report of the Commission on Reading.* Washington, DC: U. S. Department of Education.

ANGLIN, J. M. (1970). *The growth of word meaning.* Cambridge, MA: MIT Press.

ANGLIN, J. M. (1977). *Word, object, and conceptual development.* New York: Norton.

ANISFELD, M. (1991). Neonatal imitation: A review. *Developmental Review, 11,* 60–97.

ANNETT, M. (1973). Laterality of childhood hemiplegia and the growth of speech and intelligence. *Cortex, 9,* 4–33.

ANNETT, M. (1985). *Left, right, hand, and brain: The right shift theory.* London: Erlbaum.

ANOOSHIAN, L. J., & YOUNG, D. (1981). Developmental changes in cognitive maps of a familiar neighborhood. *Child Development, 52,* 341–348.

ANTELL, S. E., & KEATING, D. P. (1983). Perception of numerical invariance in neonates. *Child Development, 54,* 695–701.

ANTINUCCI, F. (ED.). (1989). *Cognitive structure and development in nonhuman primates.* Hillsdale, NJ: Erlbaum.

ARNETT, J. (1992). Reckless behavior in adolescence: A developmental perspective. *Developmental Review, 12,* 339–373.

ARTERBERRY, M., YONAS, A., & BENSEN, A. S. (1989). Self-produced locomotion and the development of responsiveness to linear perspective and texture gradients. *Developmental Psychology, 25,* 976–982.

ASHCRAFT, M. H. (1990). Strategic processing in children's mental arithmetic: A review and proposal. In D. F. Bjorklund (Ed.), *Children's strategies: Contemporary views of cognitive development.* Hillsdale, NJ: Erlbaum.

ASHER, S. R., & MARKEL, R. A. (1974). Sex differences in comprehension of high- and low-interest reading material. *Journal of Educational Psychology, 66,* 680–687.

ASLIN, R. N. (1977). Development of binocular fixation in human infants. *Journal of Experimental Child Psychology, 23,* 133–156.

ASLIN, R. N., & JACKSON, R. W. (1979). Accommodative-convergence in young infants: Development of a synergistic sensory-motor system. *Canadian Journal of Psychology, 33,* 222–231.

ASLIN, R. N., JUSCZYK, P. W., & PISONI, D. B. (1998). Speech and auditory processing during infancy. In D. Kuhn & R. S. Siegler (Eds.), *Cognitive, language, and perceptual development,* Vol. 2, In W. Damon (Gen. Ed.), *Handbook of child psychology.* New York: Wiley.

ASLIN, R. N., SAFFRAN, J. R., & NEWPORT, E. L. (1998). Computation of conditional probability statistics by 8-month-old infants. *Psychological Science, 9,* 321–324.

ASTINGTON, J. W., & GOPNIK, A. (1988). Knowing you've changed your mind: Children's understanding of representational change. In J. W. Astington, P. L. Harris, & D. R. Olson (Eds.), *Developing theories of mind.* Cambridge: Cambridge University Press.

ASTINGTON, J. W., & JENKINS, J. M. (1995). Theory of mind development and social understanding. *Cognition and Emotion, 9*, 151–165.

ATKINSON, R. C., & SHIFFRIN, R. M. (1968). Human memory: A proposed system and its control processes. In K. W. Spence & J. T. Spence (Eds.), *The psychology of learning and motivation: Advances in research and theory* (Vol. 2). New York: Academic.

AUSLEY, J. A., & GUTTENTAG, R. E. (1993). Direct and indirect assessments of memory: Implications for the study of memory development. In M. L. Howe & R. Pasnak (Eds.), *Emerging themes in cognitive development: Vol. 1. Foundations.* New York: Springer-Verlag.

AVIS, J., & HARRIS, P. L. (1991). Belief-desire reasoning among Baka children: Evidence for a universal conception of mind. *Child Development, 62*, 460–467.

AZMITIA, M. (1992). Expertise, private speech, and the development of self-regulation. In R. M. Diaz & L. E. Berk (Eds.), *Private speech: From social interaction to self-regulation.* Hillsdale, NJ: Erlbaum.

BADDELEY, A. D. (1986). *Working memory.* Oxford: Clarendon.

BADDELEY, A. D., & HITCH, G. J. (1974). Working memory. In G. Bower (Ed.), *The psychology of learning and motivation: Advances in research and theory* (Vol. 8). New York: Academic.

BADIAN, N. A. (1983). Dyscalculia and nonverbal disorders of learning. In H. R. Myklebust (Ed.), *Progress in learning disabilities.* New York: Stratton.

BAENNINGER, M., & NEWCOMBE, N. (1995). Environmental input to the development of sex-related differences in spatial and mathematical ability. *Learning and Individual Differences, 7*, 363–379.

BAHRICK, L. E. (1995). Intermodal origins of self-perception. In P. Rochat (Ed.), *The self in infancy: Theory and research.* New York: Elsevier Science.

BAHRICK, L. E., HERNANDEZ-REIF, M., & PICKENS, J. N. (1997). The effect of retrieval cues on visual preferences and memory in infancy: Evidence for a four-phase attention function. *Journal of Experimental Child Psychology, 67*, 1–20.

BAHRICK, L. E., MOSS, L., & FADIL, C. (1996). The development of self recognition in infancy. *Ecological Psychology, 8*, 189–208.

BAHRICK, L. E., & PICKENS, J. N. (1995). Infant memory for object motion across a period of three months: Implications for a four-phase attention function. *Journal of Experimental Child Psychology, 59*, 343–371.

BAHRICK, L. E., & WATSON, J. S. (1985). Detection of intermodal proprioceptive-visual contingency as a po-

tential basis of self-perception in infancy. *Developmental Psychology, 21*, 963–973.

BAI, D. L., & BERTENTHAL, B. I. (1992). Locomotor status and the development of spatial skills. *Child Development, 63*, 215–226.

BAILLARGEON, R. (1987). Object permanence in 3 1/2- and 4 1/2-month-old infants. *Developmental Psychology, 23*, 655–664.

BAILLARGEON, R. (1994). How do infants learn about the physical world? *Current Directions in Psychological Science, 3*, 133–140.

BAILLARGEON, R., & DE VOS, J. (1991). Object permanence in young infants: Further evidence. *Child Development, 62*, 1227–1246.

BAILLARGEON, R., KOTOVSKY, L., & NEEDHAM, A. (1995). The acquisition of physical knowledge in infancy. In G. Lewis, D. Premack, & D. Sperber (Eds.), *Casual understandings in cognition and culture.* Oxford: Oxford University Press.

BAKER, D. P. (1992). Compared to Japan the U. S. is a low achiever—really. *Educational Research, 22*, 18–20.

BAKER, L. (1985). How do we know when we don't understand? Standards for evaluating text comprehension. In D. L. Forrest-Pressley, G. E. MacKinnon, & T. G. Waller (Eds.), *Metacognition, cognition, and human performance* (Vol. 1). Orlando, FL: Academic.

BAKER-WARD, L., GORDON, B. N., ORNSTEIN, P. A., LARUS, D. M., & CLUBB, P. A. (1993). Young children's long-term retention of a pediatric visit. *Child Development, 64*, 1519–1533.

BAKER-WARD, L., HESS, T. M., & FLANNAGAN, D. A. (1990). The effect of involvement on children's memory for events. *Cognitive Development, 5*, 55–69.

BAKER-WARD, L., & ORNSTEIN, P. A. (1988). Age differences in visual-spatial memory performance: Do children really out-perform adults when playing Concentration? *Bulletin of the Psychonomic Society, 26*, 331–332.

BAKER-WARD, L., ORNSTEIN, P. A., & HOLDEN, D. J. (1984). The expression of memorization in early childhood. *Journal of Experimental Child Psychology, 37*, 555–575.

BALABAN, M. T., ANDERSON, L. M., & WISNIEWSKI, A. B. (1998). Lateral asymmetries in infant melody perception. *Developmental Psychology, 34*, 39–48.

BALDWIN, J. M. (1895). *Mental development in the child and the race.* New York: Macmillan.

BANDURA, A. (1986). *Social foundations of thought and action: A social cognitive theory.* Englewood Cliffs, NJ: Prentice-Hall.

BANDURA, A. (1989). Social cognitive theory. In R. Vasta (Ed.), *Annals of child development*. Greenwich, CT: JAI.

BANDURA, A. (1997). *Self-efficacy: The exercise of control*. New York: Freeman.

BANDURA, A., BARBARANELLI, C., CAPRARA, G. V., & PASTORELLI, C. (1996). Multifaceted impact of self-efficacy beliefs on academic functioning. *Child Development, 67*, 1206–1222.

BANDURA, A., & WALTERS, R. H. (1963). *Social learning theory and personality development*. New York: Holt, Rinehart & Winston.

BANKS, M. S. (1980). The development of visual accommodation during early infancy. *Child Development, 51*, 646–666.

BARKLEY, R. A. (1997). Behavioral inhibition, sustained attention, and executive functions. Constructing a unifying theory of ADHD. *Psychological Bulletin, 121*, 65–94.

BARKOW, J. H., COSMIDES, L., & TOOBY, J. (EDS.) (1992). *The adapted mind: Evolutionary psychology and the generation of culture*. New York: Oxford University Press.

BARNES, M. A., DENNIS, M., & HAEFELE-KALVAITIS, J. (1996). The effects of knowledge availability and knowledge accessibility on coherence and elaborative inferencing in children six to fifteen years of age. *Journal of Experimental Child Psychology, 61*, 216–241.

BARNETT, W. S. (1995). Long-term effects of early childhood programs on cognitive and school outcomes. *The Future of Children, 5* (No. 3, Winter).

BARON-COHEN, S. (1995). *Mindblindness: An essay on autism and theory of mind*. Cambridge, MA: MIT Press.

BAROODY, A. J., & GINSBURG, H. P. (1986). The relationship between initial meaningful and mechanical knowledge of arithmetic. In J. Hiebert (Ed.), *Conceptual and procedural knowledge: The case of mathematics*. Hillsdale, NJ: Erlbaum.

BARRERA, M. E., & MAURER, D. (1981). Recognition of mother's photographed face by the three-month-old infant. *Child Development, 52*, 714–716.

BARTLETT, F. C. (1932). *Remembering: A study in experimental and social psychology*. Cambridge: Cambridge University Press.

BARTSCH, K., & WELLMAN, H. M. (1989). Young children's attributions of action to beliefs and desires. *Child Development, 60*, 946–964.

BARTSCH, K., & WELLMAN, H. M. (1995). *Children talk about the mind*. New York: Oxford University Press.

BATES, E. (1999). On the nature of language. In R. Levi-Montalcini, D. Baltimore, R. Dulbecco. & F. Jacob (Series Ed.) & E. Bizzi, P. Calissano, & V. Volterra (Vol. Ed.), *Frontiere della biologia [Frontiers of biology]*, *The brain of homo sapiens*. Rome: Giovanni Trecanni.

BATES, E., BRETHERTON, I. M., & SNYDER, L. (1988). *From first words to grammar: Individual differences and dissociable mechanisms*. New York: Cambridge University Press.

BATES, E., & GOODMAN, J. C. (1997). On the inseparability of grammar and the lexicon: Evidence from acquisition, aphasia and real-time processing. In G. Altman (Ed.), Special issue on the lexicon. *Language and Cognitive Processes, 12*, 507–586.

BAUER, P. J. (1993). Memory for gender-consistent and gender-inconsistent event sequences by twenty-five-month-old children. *Child Development, 64*, 285–297.

BAUER, P. J. (1997). Development of memory in early childhood. In N. Cowan (Ed.) *The development of memory in childhood*. Hove East Essex, UK: Psychology Press.

BAUER, P. J., Dow, G. A., & HERTSGAARD, L. A. (1995). Effects of prototypicality on categorization in 1- to 2-year-olds: Getting down to basics. *Cognitive Development, 10*, 43–68.

BAUER, P. J., & MANDLER, J. M. (1989). One thing follows another: Effects of temporal structure on 1- to 2-year-olds' recall of events. *Developmental Psychology, 25*, 197–206.

BAUER, P. J., & MANDLER, J. M. (1992). Putting the horse before the cart: The use of temporal order in recall of events by one-year-old children. *Developmental Psychology, 28*, 441–452.

BAUER, P. J., & WEWERKA, S. S. (1995). One- and two-year olds recall events: Factors facilitating immediate and long-term memory of 13.5 and 16.5-month-old children. *Child Development, 64*, 1204–1223.

BAUER, R. H. (1979). Memory, acquisition, and category clustering in learning-disabled children. *Journal of Experimental Child Psychology, 27*, 365–383.

BAUER, R. H., & NEWMAN, D. R. (1991). Allocation of study time and recall by learning-disabled and nondisabled children of different ages. *Journal of Experimental Child Psychology, 52*, 11–21.

BAUGH, J. (1983). *Black street speech: Its history, structure, and survival*. New York: Academic.

BAUMRIND, D. (1993). The average expectable environment is not good enough: A response to Scarr. *Child Development, 64*, 1299–1317.

BAYLEY, N. (1949). Consistency and variability in the growth of intelligence from birth to eighteen years. *Journal of Genetic Psychology, 75*, 165–196.

BAYLEY, N. (1969). *The Bayley Scales of Infant Development*. New York: Psychological Corporation.

BEAL, C. R., & FLAVELL, J. H. (1982). Effects of increasing salience of message ambiguities on kindergarteners' evaluations of communicative success and message adequacy. *Developmental Psychology, 10,* 43–48.

BEAL, C. R., & LOCKHART, M. E. (1989). The effect of proper name and appearance change on children's reasoning about gender constancy. *International Journal of Behavioral Development, 12,* 195–205.

BECKER, W. C., & GERSTEN, R. (1982). A follow-up of Follow Through: The later effects of the direct instruction model for children in fifth and sixth grades. *American Educational Research Journal, 19,* 75–92.

BEHREND, D. A., ROSENGREN, K., & PERLMUTTER, M. (1989). A new look at children's private speech: The effects of age, task difficulty, and parent presence. *International Journal of Behavioral Development, 12,* 305–320.

BEILIN, H. (1992). Piaget's enduring contribution to developmental psychology. *Developmental Psychology, 28,* 191–204.

BELL, M. A., & FOX, N. A. (1992). The relations between frontal brain electrical activity and cognitive development during infancy. *Child Development, 63,* 1142–1163.

BELL, R. Q. (1968). A reinterpretation of the direction of effects in studies of socialization. *Psychological Review, 75,* 81–95.

BELLUGI, U. (1967). *The acquisition of negation.* Unpublished doctoral dissertation, Harvard University.

BELMONT, J. M., FERRETTI, R. P., & MITCHEL, D. W. (1982). Memorizing: A test of untrained mildly retarded children's problem solving. *American Journal of Mental Deficiency, 87,* 197–210.

BEM, S. (1981). Gender schema theory: A cognitive account of sex-typing. *Psychological Review, 88,* 354–364.

BENASICH, A. A., & BROOKS-GUNN, J. (1996). Maternal attitudes and knowledge of child-rearing: Associations with family and child outcomes. *Child Development, 67,* 1186–2105.

BENBOW, C. P., & STANLEY, J. C. (1980). Sex differences in mathematical ability: Fact or artifact? *Science, 210,* 1262–1264.

BENBOW, C. P., & STANLEY J. C. (1983). Sex differences in mathematical reasoning: More facts. *Science, 222,* 1029–1031.

BENEDICT, H. (1979). Early lexical development: Comprehension and production. *Journal of Child Language, 6,* 183–200.

BENTIN, S., HAMMER, R., & CAHAN, S. (1991). The effects of aging and first-grade schooling on the development of phonological awareness. *Psychological Science, 2,* 271–274.

BERENBAUM, S. A., & HINES, M. (1992). Early androgens are related to childhood sex-typed toy preferences. *Psychological Science, 3,* 203–206.

BERENBAUM, S. A., & SNYDER, E. (1995). Early hormonal influences on childhood sex-types activity and playmate preferences: Implications for the development of sexual orientation. *Developmental Psychology, 31,* 31–42.

BERING, J., BJORKLUND, D. F., RAGAN, P., & DAHMS, B. (March, 1998). *Deferred imitation of object-related actions in enculturated, juvenile great apes.* Paper presented at Conference on Human Development, Mobile, AL.

BERK, L. E. (1986). Relationship of elementary school children's private speech to behavioral accompaniment to task, attention, and task performance. *Developmental Psychology, 22,* 671–680.

BERK, L. E. (1992). Children's private speech: An overview of theory and the status of research. In R. M. Diaz & L. E. Berk (Eds.), *Private speech: From social interaction to self-regulation.* Hillsdale, NJ: Erlbaum.

BERK, L. E., & LANDAU, S. (1993). Private speech of learning disabled and normally achieving children in classroom academic and laboratory contexts. *Child Development, 64,* 556–571.

BERK, L. E., & SPUHL, S. T. (1995). Maternal intervention, private speech, and task performance in preschool children. *Early Childhood Research Quarterly, 10,* 145–169.

BERKO, J. (1958). The child's learning of English morphology. *Word, 14,* 150–177.

BERKO GLEASON, J. (ED.) (1997). *The development of language* (4th edition). Boston, MA: Allyn & Bacon.

BERLIN, B., & KAY, P. (1969). *Basic color terms: Their universality and evolution.* Berkeley: University of California Press.

BERMEJO, V. (1996). Cardinality development and counting. *Developmental Psychology, 32,* 263–268.

BERNARD, J., & SONTAG, L. W. (1947). Fetal reactivity to tonal stimulation: A preliminary report. *Journal of Genetic Psychology, 70,* 205–210.

BERNINGER, V. W., & CORINA, D. (1998). Making cognitive neuroscience educationally relevant: Creating bidirectional collaborations between educational psychology and cognitive neuroscience. *Educational Psychology Review, 10,* 343-354.

BERNSTEIN, B. (1971). *Class codes and control,* Vol. 1. London: Routledge & Kegan Paul.

BERTENTHAL, B. I., & CAMPOS, J. J. (1987). New directions in the study of early experience. *Child Development, 58,* 560–567.

BERTENTHAL, B. I., CAMPOS, J., & BARRETT, L. (1984). Self-produced locomotion: An organizer of emotional, cognitive, and social development in infancy. In R. Emde & R. Harmon (Eds.), *Continuities and discontinuities in development.* New York: Plenum.

Bertenthal, B. I., Campos, J. J., & Kermoian, R. (1994). An epigenetic perspective on the development of self-produced locomotion and its consequences. *Current Directions in Psychological Science, 3,* 140–145.

Best, D. L. (1993). Inducing children to generate mnemonic organizational strategies: An examination of long-term retention and materials. *Developmental Psychology, 29,* 324–336.

Best, D. L., & Ornstein, P. A. (1986). Children's generation and communication of mnemonic organizational strategies. *Developmental Psychology, 22,* 845–853.

Bhatt, R. S., Rovee-Collier, C., & Shyi, C.-W. G. (1994). Perception and 24-hour retention of feature relations in infancy. *Developmental Psychology, 30,* 142–150.

Bialystok, E. (1996). Preparing to read: The foundations of literacy. In H. W. Reese (Ed.), *Advances in child development and behavior,* Vol. 26. San Diego: Academic.

Bickerton, D. (1990). *Language and species.* Chicago: University of Chicago Press.

Birch, H. G., & Lefford, A. (1963). Intersensory development in children. *Monographs of the Society for Research in Child Development, 32* (Serial No. 110).

Bisanz, J., & LeFevre, J. (1990). Strategic and nonstrategic processing in the development of mathematical cognition. In D. F. Bjorklund (Ed.), *Children's strategies: Contemporary views of cognitive development.* Hillsdale, NJ: Erlbaum.

Bisanz, J., Morrison, F. J., & Dunn, M. (1995). The effects of age and schooling on the acquisition of elementary quantitative skills. *Developmental Psychology, 31,* 221–236.

Bivens, J. A., & Berk, L. E. (1990). A longitudinal study of the development of elementary school children's private speech. *Merrill-Palmer Quarterly, 36,* 443–463.

Bjorklund, D. F. (1985). The role of conceptual knowledge in the development of organization in children's memory. In C. J. Brainerd & M. Pressley (Eds.), *Basic processes in memory development: Progress in cognitive development research.* New York: Springer-Verlag.

Bjorklund, D. F. (1987a). How age changes in knowledge base contribute to the development of children's memory: An interpretive review. *Developmental Review, 7,* 93–130.

Bjorklund, D. F. (1987b). A note on neonatal imitation. *Developmental Review, 7,* 86–92.

Bjorklund, D. F. (1997a). The role of immaturity in human development. *Psychological Bulletin, 122,* 153–169.

Bjorklund, D. F. (1997b). In search of a metatheory for cognitive development (or, Piaget's dead and I don't feel so good myself). *Child Development, 68,* 142–146.

Bjorklund, D. F. (1999). What individual differences can teach us about developmental function and vice versa. In F. E. Weinert & W. Schneider (Eds.), *The Munich Longitudinal Study on the Genesis of Individual Competencies (LOGIC).* Cambridge: Cambridge University Press.

Bjorklund, D. F., & Bernholtz, J. F. (1986). The role of knowledge base in the memory performance of good and poor readers. *Journal of Experimental Child Psychology, 41,* 367–373.

Bjorklund, D. F. & Bjorklund, B. R. (1985). Organization versus item effects of an elaborated knowledge base on children's memory. *Developmental Psychology, 21,* 1120–1131.

Bjorklund, D. F., Bjorklund, B. R., Douglas, R. B., & Cassel, W. S. (1998). Children's susceptibility to repeated questions: How misinformation changes children's answers and their minds. *Applied Developmental Science, 2,* 101–113.

Bjorklund, D. F., & Brown, R. D. (1998). Physical play and cognitive development: Integrating activity, cognition, and education. *Child Development, 69,* 604–606.

Bjorklund, D. F., & Buchanan, J. J. (1989). Developmental and knowledge base differences in the acquisition and extension of a memory strategy. *Journal of Experimental Child Psychology, 48,* 451–471.

Bjorklund, D. F., & Douglas, R N. (1997). The development of memory strategies. In N. Cowan (Ed.), *The development of memory in childhood.* Hove East Sussex, UK: Psychology Press.

Bjorklund, D. F., Gaultney, J. F., & Green, B. L. (1993). "I watch, therefore I can do": The development of meta-imitation during the preschool years and the advantage of optimism about one's imitative skills. In M. L. Howe & R. Pasnak (Eds.), *Emerging themes in cognitive development:* Vol. 2., *Competencies.* New York: Springer-Verlag.

Bjorklund, D. F., & Green, B. L. (1992). The adaptive nature of cognitive immaturity. *American Psychologist, 47,* 46–54.

Bjorklund, D. F., & Harnishfeger, K. K. (1987). Developmental differences in the mental effort requirements for the use of an organizational strategy in free recall. *Journal of Experimental Child Psychology, 44,* 109–125.

BJORKLUND, D. F., & HARNISHFEGER, K. K. (1990). Children's strategies: Their definition and origins. In D. F. Bjorklund (Ed.), *Children's strategies: Contemporary views of cognitive development.* Hillsdale, NJ: Erlbaum.

BJORKLUND, D. F., & HARNISHFEGER, K. K. (1995). The role of inhibition mechanisms in the evolution of human cognition. In F. Dempster & C. Brainerd (Eds.), *New perspectives on interference and inhibition in cognition.* New York: Academic .

BJORKLUND, D. F., & HOCK, H. S. (1982). Age differences in the temporal locus of memory organization in children's recall. *Journal of Experimental Child Psychology, 32,* 347–362.

BJORKLUND, D. F., & KIPP, K. (1996). Parental investment theory and gender differences in the evolution of inhibition mechanisms. *Psychological Bulletin, 120,* 163–188.

BJORKLUND, D. F., MILLER, P. H., COYLE, T. R., & SLAWINSKI, J. L. (1997). Instructing children to use memory strategies: Evidence of utilization deficiencies in memory training studies. *Developmental Review, 17,* 411–442.

BJORKLUND, D. F., MUIR-BROADDUS, J. E., & SCHNEIDER, W. (1990). The role of knowledge in the development of strategies. In D. F. Bjorklund (Ed.), *Children's strategies: Contemporary views of cognitive development.* Hillsdale, NJ: Erlbaum.

BJORKLUND, D. F., & SCHNEIDER, W. (1996). The interaction of knowledge, aptitudes, and strategies in children's memory performance. In H. W. Reese (Ed.), *Advances in child development and behavior,* Vol. 26. San Diego: Academic.

BJORKLUND, D. F., SCHNEIDER, W., CASSEL, W. S., & ASHLEY, E. (1994). Training and extension of a memory strategy: Evidence for utilization deficiencies in the acquisition of an organizational strategy in high- and low-IQ children. *Child Development, 65,* 951-965.

BJORKLUND, D. F., & SCHWARTZ, R. (1996). The adaptive nature of developmental immaturity: Implications for language acquisition and language disabilities. In M. Smith & J. Damico (Eds.), *Childhood language disorders.* New York: Thieme Medical.

BJORKLUND, D. F., THOMPSON, B. E., & ORNSTEIN, P. A. (1983). Developmental trends in children's typicality judgments. *Behavior Research Methods and Instrumentation, 15,* 350–356.

BJORKLUND, D. F., & ZEMAN, B. R. (1982). Children's organization and metamemory awareness in their re-call of familiar information. *Child Development, 53,* 799–810.

BLACK, M. M., & ROLLINS, H. A. (1982). The effects of instructional variables on young children's organization and free recall. *Journal of Experimental Child Psychology, 31,* 1–19.

BLAKEMORE, C., & VAN SLUYTERS, R. C. (1975). Innate and environmental factors in the development of the kitten's visual cortex. *Journal of Physiology, 248,* 663–716.

BLASI, C. H. (1996). Vygotsky y la escuela sociohistórica. In R. A. Clemente & C. H. Blasi (Eds.), *Contextos de desarrollo psicoilógico y educación.* Mâlaga, Spain: Aljibe.

BLEWITT, P., & KRACKOW, E. (1992). Acquiring taxonomic relations in lexical memory: The role of superordinate category labels. *Journal of Experimental Child Psychology, 54,* 37–56.

BLEWITT, P., & TOPPINO, T. C. (1991). The development of taxonomic structure in lexical memory. *Journal of Experimental Child Psychology, 51,* 296–319.

BLOM, G. E., WAITE, R. R., & ZIMET, S. (1968). Content of first-grade reading books. *The Reading Teacher, 21,* 317–323.

BLOOM, L. (1998). Language acquisition in developmental contexts. In D. Kuhn & R. S. Siegler (Eds.), *Cognitive, language, and perceptual development,* Vol. 2. In W. Damon (Gen. Ed.), *Handbook of child psychology.* New York: Wiley.

BLOOM, L., HOOD, L., & LIGHTBOWN, P. (1974). Imitation in language development: If, when and why. *Cognitive Psychology, 6,* 380–420.

BLOOM, L., LIGHTBOWN, P., & HOOD, L. (1975). Structure and variation in child language. *Monographs of the Society for Research in Child Development, 40* (Serial No. 160).

BOESCH, C. (1993). Toward a new image of culture in wild chimpanzees? *Behavioral and Brain Sciences, 16,* 514–515.

BOGARTZ, R. S., & SHINSKEY, J. L. (1998). On perception of a partially occluded object in 6-months olds. *Cognitive Development, 13,* 141–163.

BOGARTZ, R. S., SHINSKEY, J. L., & SPEAKER, C. (1997). Interpreting infant looking: The event set x event set design. *Developmental Psychology, 33,* 408–422.

BOHANNON, J. N., & BONVILLIAN, J. D. (1997). Theoretical approaches to language acquisition. In J. Berko Gleason (Ed.), *The development of language* (4th edition). Boston, MA: Allyn & Bacon.

BOLLER, K., ROVEE-COLLIER, C., GULYA, M., & PRETE, K. (1996). Infants' memory for context: Timing effects of postevent information. *Journal of Experimental Child Psychology, 63,* 583–602.

BORKE, H. (1975). Piaget's mountains revisited: Changes in the egocentric landscape. *Developmental Psychology, 11,* 240–243.

BORKOWSKI, J. G., MILSTEAD, M., & HALE, C. (1988). Components of children's metamemory: Implications for strategy generalization. In F. E. Weinert & M. Perlmutter (Eds.), *Memory development: Universal changes and individual differences.* Hillsdale, NJ: Erlbaum.

BORKOWSKI, J. G., & PECK, V. A. (1986). Causes and consequences of metamemory in gifted children. In R. J. Sternberg and J. C. Davidson (Eds.), *Conceptions of giftedness.* Cambridge: Cambridge University Press.

BORKOWSKI, J. G., PECK, V., REID, M. K., & KURTZ, B. (1983). Impulsivity and strategy transfer: Metamemory as mediator. *Child Development, 54,* 459–473.

BORKOWSKI, J. G., REID, M. K., & KURTZ, B. E. (1984). Metacognition and retardation: Pragmatic, theoretical and applied perspectives. In P. H. Brooks, R. Sperber, & C. McCauley (Eds.), *Learning and cognition in the mentally retarded.* Hillsdale, NJ: Erlbaum.

BORKOWSKI, J. G., & TURNER, L. A. (1988). Transitational characteristics of metacognition. In W. Schneider & F. E. Weinert (Eds.), *Interactions among aptitudes, strategies, and knowledge in cognitive performance.* Hillsdale, NJ: Erlbaum.

BORNSTEIN, M. H. (1989). Stability in early mental development: From attention and information processing in infancy to language and cognition in childhood. In M. H. Bornstein & N. A. Krasnegor (Eds.), *Stability and continuity in mental development: Behavioral and biological perspectives.* Hillsdale, NJ: Erlbaum.

BORNSTEIN, M. H., FERDINANDSEN, K., & GROSS, C. G. (1981). Perception of symmetry in infancy. *Developmental Psychology, 17,* 82–86.

BORNSTEIN, M. H., & HAYNES, O. M. (1998). Vocabulary competence in early childhood: Measurement, latent construct, and predictive validity. *Child Development, 69,* 654–671.

BORNSTEIN, M. H., HAYNES, O. M., O'REILLY, A. W., & PAINTER, K. M. (1996). Solitary and collaborative pretense play in early childhood: Sources of individual variation in the development of representational competence. *Child Development, 67,* 2910–2929.

BORNSTEIN, M. H., KESSEN, W., & WEISKOPF, S. (1976). Color vision and hue categorization in young infants. *Journal of Experimental Psychology: Human Perception and Performance, 2,* 115–129.

BORNSTEIN, M. H., & SIGMAN, M. D. (1986). Continuity in mental development from infancy. *Child Development, 57,* 251–274.

BOSTON, M. B., & LEVY, G. D. (1991). Changes and differences in preschoolers' understanding of gender scripts. *Cognitive Development, 6,* 417–432.

BOUCHARD, T. J., JR., LYKKEN, D. T., MCGUE, M., SEGAL, N. L., & TELLEGEN, A. (1990). Sources of human psychological differences: The Minnesota study of twins reared apart. *Science, 250,* 223–228.

BOUCHARD, T. J., JR., & MCGUE, M. (1981). Familial studies of intelligence: A review. *Science, 212,* 1055–1059.

BOUCHARD, T. J., JR., & SEGAL, N. (1985). Environment and IQ. In B. Wolman (Ed.), *Handbook of intelligence.* New York: Wiley.

BRADLEY, R. H. (1989). The use of the HOME inventory in longitudinal studies of child development. In M. H. Bornstein & N. A. Krasnegor (Eds.), *Stability and continuity in mental development: Behavioral and biological perspectives.* Hillsdale, NJ: Erlbaum.

BRADLEY, R. H., & CALDWELL, B. M. (1976). The relation of infants' home environment to mental test performance at fifty-four months: A follow-up study. *Child Development, 47,* 1172-1174.

BRADLEY, R. H., CALDWELL, B. M., & ELARDO, R. (1977). Home environment, social status, and mental test performance. *Journal of Educational Psychology, 69,* 697–701.

BRADLEY, R. H., CALDWELL, B. M., ROCK, S. L., RAMEY, C. T., BARNARD, K. E., GRAY C., HAMMOND, M. A., MITCHELL, S., GOTTFRIED, A. W., SIEGEL, L., & JOHNSON, D. L. (1989). Home environments and cognitive development in the first 3 years of life: A collaborative study including six sites and three ethnic groups in North America. *Developmental Psychology, 25,* 217–235.

BRAINERD, C. J. (1978a). *Piaget's theory of intelligence.* Englewood Cliffs, NJ: Prentice-Hall.

BRAINERD, C. J. (1978b). The stage question in cognitive-developmental theory. *The Behavioral and Brain Sciences, 2,* 173–213.

BRAINERD, C. F. (1996). Piaget: A centennial celebration. *Psychological Science, 7,* 191–195.

BRAINERD, C. J. (1997). Children's forgetting, with implications for memory suggestibility. In N. L. Stein, P. A. Ornstein, B. Tversky, & C. J. Brainerd (Eds.), *Memory for everyday and emotional events.* Hillsdale, NJ: Erlbaum.

BRAINERD, C. J., & ALLEN, T. W. (1971). Training and generalization of density conservation: Effects of feedback and consecutive similar stimuli. *Child Development, 42,* 693–704.

BRAINERD, C. J., & BRAINERD, S. H. (1972). Order of acquisition of number and liquid quantity conservation. *Child Development, 43*, 1401–1405.

BRAINERD, C. J., & GORDON, L. L. (1994). Development of verbatim and gist memory for numbers. *Developmental Psychology, 30*, 163–177.

BRAINERD, C. J., & KASZOR, P. (1974). An analysis of two proposed sources of children's class inclusion errors. *Developmental Psychology, 10*, 633–643.

BRAINERD, C. J., & KINGMA, J. (1984). Do children have to remember to reason? A fuzzy-trace theory of transitivity development. *Developmental Review, 4*, 311–377.

BRAINERD, C. J., KINGMA, J., & HOWE, M. L. (1986). Spread of encoding and the development of organization in memory. *Canadian Journal of Psychology, 40*, 203–223.

BRAINERD, C. J., & MOJARDIN, A. H. (1999). Children's and adults' spontaneous false memories for sentences: Long-term persistence and mere-testing effects. *Child Development.*

BRAINERD, C. J., & ORNSTEIN, P. A. (1991). Children's memory for witnessed events: The developmental backdrop. In J. Doris (Ed.), *The suggestibility of children's memory.* Washington, DC: American Psychological Association.

BRAINERD, C. J., & POOLE, D. A. (1997). Long-term survival of children's false memories: A review. *Learning and Individual Differences, 9*, 125–152.

BRAINERD, C. J., & REYNA, V. F. (1988). Generic resources, reconstructive processing, and children's mental arithmetic. *Developmental Psychology, 24*, 324–334.

BRAINERD, C. J., & REYNA, V. F. (1990). Gist is the grist: Fuzzy-trace theory and the new intuitionism. *Developmental Review, 10*, 3–47.

BRAINERD, C. J., & REYNA, V. F. (1992). The memory independence effect: What do the data show? What do the theories claim? *Developmental Review, 12*, 164–186.

BRAINERD, C. J., & REYNA, V. F. (1993). Domains of fuzzy trace theory. In M. L. Howe & R. Pasnak (Eds.), *Emerging themes in cognitive development: Vol 1., Foundations.* New York: Springer-Verlag.

BRAINERD, C. J., & REYNA, V. F. (1996). Mere memory testing creates false memories in children. *Developmental Psychology, 32*, 467–478.

BRAINERD, C. J., & REYNA, V. F. (1998). Fuzzy-trace theory and children's false memories. *Journal of Experimental Child Psychology, 71*, 81-129.

BRAINERD, C. J., REYNA, V. F., & BRANDSE, E. (1995). Are children's false memories more persistent than their true memories? *Psychological Science, 6*, 359–364.

BRAINERD, C. J., REYNA, V. F., HARNISHFEGER, K. K., & HOWE, M. L. (1994). Is retrievability grouping good for recall? *Journal of Experimental Psychology: General, 122*, 249–268.

BRAINERD, C. J., REYNA, V. F., & POOLE, D. A. (in press). Fuzzy-trace theory and false memory: Memory theory in the courtroom. In D. F. Bjorklund (Ed.), *False memory creation in children and adults: Theory, research, and implications.* Mahwah, NJ: Erlbaum.

BRAY, N. W., FLETCHER, K. L., & TURNER, L. A. (1996). Cognitive competencies and strategy use in individuals with mild retardation. In W. E. MacLean Jr. (Ed.) *Handbook of mental deficiency, psychological theory and research,* (3rd edition). Hillsdale, NJ: Lawrence Erlbaum.

BRAY, N. W., & TURNER, L. A. (1986). The rehearsal deficit hypothesis. In N. R. Ellis & N. W. Bray (Eds.), *International review of research in mental retardation* (Vol. 14). New York: Academic.

BRAZELTON, T. B. (1973). *Neonatal Behavioral Assessment Scale.* Clinics in Developmental Medicine, No. 50. Philadelphia, PA: Lippincott.

BREDEKAMP, S., & COPPLE, C. (EDS.) (1997). *Developmentally appropriate practice in early childhood programs* (rev. edition). Washington, DC: National Association for the Educational of Young Children.

BRIARS, D., & SIEGLER, R. S. (1984). A featural analysis of preschoolers' counting knowledge. *Developmental Psychology, 20*, 607–618.

BROBERG, A. G., WESSELS, H., LAMB, M. E., & HWANG, C. P. (1997). Effects of day care on the development of cognitive abilities in 8-year-olds: A longitudinal study. *Developmental Psychology, 33*, 62–69.

BRODY, N. (1997). Intelligence, schooling, and society. *American Psychologist, 52*, 1046–1050.

BRONFENBRENNER, U., & CECI, S. J. (1994). Nature-nurture reconceptualized in developmental perspective: A bioecological model. *Psychological Review, 101*, 568–586.

BRONSON, G. (1974). The postnatal growth of visual capacity. *Child Development, 45*, 873–890.

BRONSON, G. W. (1990). Changes in infants' visual scanning across the 2–14-week age period. *Journal of Experimental Child Psychology, 49*, 101–125.

BRONSON, G. W. (1991). Infant differences in rate of visual encoding. *Child Development, 62*, 44–54.

BROOKS, P. H., SPERBER, R., & McCAULEY, C. (EDS.). (1984). *Learning and cognition in the mentally retarded.* Hillsdale, NJ: Erlbaum.

BROOKS-GUNN, J., & LEWIS, M. (1984). The development of early self-recognition. *Developmental Review, 4*, 215–239.

BROWN, A. L. (1978). Knowing when, where, and how to remember: A problem of metacognition. In R. Glasser (Ed.), *Advances in instructional psychology*. New York: Halstead.

BROWN, A. L., & DELOACHE, J. S. (1978). Skills, plans and self-regulation. In R. S. Siegler (Ed.), *Children's thinking: What develops?* Hillsdale, NJ: Erlbaum.

BROWN, A. L., & KANE, M. J. (1988). Preschool children can learn to transfer: Learning to learn and learning by example. *Cognitive Psychology, 20*, 493-523.

BROWN, A. L., KANE, M. J., & LONG, C. (1989). Analogical transfer in young children: Analogies as tools for communication and exposition. *Applied Cognitive Psychology, 3*, 275–293.

BROWN, A. L. & SMILEY, S. S. (1978). The development of strategies for studying texts. *Child Development, 49*, 1076–1088.

BROWN, R. (1968). The development of WH questions in child speech. *Journal of Verbal Learning and Verbal Behavior, 7*, 279–290.

BROWN, R. (1973). *A first language: The early stages*. Cambridge, MA: Harvard University Press.

BROWN, R., & HANLON, C. (1970). Derivational complexity and the order of acquisition in child speech. In R. Brown (Ed.), *Psycholinguistics*. New York: Free Press.

BROWN, R. D., BARMAN, N., HONS, S., & BJORKLUND, D. F. (March, 1998). *Fiction or truth: Children's memories for events as a function of the involvement of physical harm*. Poster presented at 12th Annual Florida Conference on Cognition, Perception, Sensation, Language, and Action, Miami, FL.

BROWN, R. D., & BJORKLUND, D. F. (1998). The biologizing of cognition, development, and education: Approach with cautious enthusiasm. *Educational Psychology Review, 10*, 355-373.

BRUCK, M., CECI, S. K., FRANCOEUR, E., & BARR, R. (1995). "I hardly cried when I got my shot!" Influencing children's reports about a visit to their pediatrician. *Child Development, 66*, 193–208.

BRUNER, J. S. (1966). On cognitive growth. In J. S. Bruner, R. R. Olver, & P. M. Greenfield (Eds.), *Studies in cognitive growth*. New York: Wiley.

BRUNER, J. S. (1983). *Child's talk: Learning to use language*. New York: Norton.

BRYANT, P. E., MacLEAN, M., BRADLEY, L. L., & CROSSLAND, J. (1990). Rhyme and alliteration, phoneme detection, and learning to read. *Developmental Psychology, 26*, 429–438.

BRYANT, P. E., & TRABASSO, T. (1971). Transitive inference and memory in young children. *Nature, 232*, 456–458.

BULL, R., & JOHNSTON, R. S. (1997). Children's arithmetical difficulties: Contributions from processing speed, item identification, and short-term memory. *Journal of Experimental Child Psychology, 65*, 1–24.

BULLOCK, M., & LÜTKENHAUS, P. (1988). The development of volitional behavior in the toddler years. *Child Development, 59*, 664–674.

BURGESS, S. R., & LONIGAN, C. J. (1998). Bidirectional relations of phonological sensitivity and prereading abilities: Evidence from a preschool sample. *Journal of Experimental Child Psychology, 70*, 114–141.

BUSHNELL, E. W. (1981). The ontogeny of intermodal relations: Vision and touch in infancy. In R. D. Walk & H. L. Pick, Jr. (Eds.), *Intersensory perception and sensory integration*. New York: Plenum.

BUSHNELL, I. W. R., SAI, F., & MULLIN, J. T. (1989). Neonatal recognition of the mother's face. *British Journal of Developmental Psychology, 7*, 3–15.

BUSS, D. M. (1995). Evolutionary psychology. *Psychological Inquiry, 6*, 1–30.

BUSSEY, K., & BANDURA, A. (1992). Self-regulatory mechanisms governing gender development. *Child Development, 63*, 1236–1250.

BYRD, D. M., & GHOLSON, B. (1985). Reading, memory, and metacognition. *Journal of Educational Psychology, 77*, 428–436.

BYRNE, R., & WHITEN, A. (EDS.) (1988). *Machiavellian intelligence: Social expertise and the evolution of intellect in monkeys, apes, and humans*. Oxford: Clarendon.

BYRNES, J. P., & FOX, N. A. (1998). The educational relevance of research in cognitive neuroscience. *Educational Psychology Review, 10*, 297-342.

BYRNES, J. P., & TAKAHIRA, S. (1993). Explaining gender differences on SAT-Math items. *Developmental Psychology, 29*, 805–810.

CAHAN, S., & COHEN, N. (1989). Age versus schooling effects on intelligence development. *Child Development, 60*, 1239–1249.

CAIRNS, R. B. (1979). *Social development: The origins and plasticity of interchanges*. San Francisco: W. H. Freeman.

CALDERA, Y. M., HUSTON, A. C., & O'BRIEN, M. (1989). Social interactions and play patterns of parents and toddlers with feminine, masculine, and neutral toys. *Child Development, 60*, 70–76.

CALDWELL, B. M., & BRADLEY, R. H. (1978). *Home observation for measurement of the environment*. Little Rock, AR: University of Arkansas at Little Rock.

CAMPBELL, F. A., & RAMEY, C. T. (1994). Effects of early intervention on intellectual and academic achievement: A follow-up study of children from low-income families. *Child Development, 65*, 684–698.

CAMPIONE, J. C., BROWN, A. L., FERRARA, R. A., JONES, R. S., & STEINBERG, E. (1985). Breakdowns in flexible use of information: Intelligence-related differences in transfer following equivalent learning performance. *Intelligence*, 9, 297–315.

CAMPOS, J. J., BERTENTHAL, B. I., & KERMONIAN, R. (1992). Early experience and emotional development: The emergence of wariness of heights. *Psychological Science*, 3, 61–64.

CANFIELD, R. L., SMITH, E. G., BREZSNYAK, M. P., & SNOW, K. L. (1997). Information processing through the first year of life. *Monographs of the Society for Research in Child Development*, 62, (Serial No. 250).

CANTOR, D. S., ANDREASSEN, C., & WATERS, H. S. (1985). Organization in visual episodic memory: Relationships between verbalized knowledge, strategy use, and performance. *Journal of Experimental Child Psychology*, 40, 218–232.

CAPON, N., & KUHN, D. (1979). Logical reasoning in the supermarket: Adult females' use of a proportional reasoning strategy in an everyday context. *Developmental Psychology*, 15, 450–452.

CAREW, J. V. (1980). Experience and the development of intelligence in young children at home and in day care. *Monographs of the Society for Research in Child Development*, 45 (Serial No. 187).

CAREY, S. (1977). The child as a word learner. In M. Halle, J. Bresnan, & G. A. Miller (Eds.), *Linguistic theory and psychological reality*. Cambridge, MA: MIT Press.

CAREY, S. (1985). Are children fundamentally different kinds of thinkers and learners than adults? In S. F. Chapman, J. W. Segal, & R. Glaser (Eds.), *Thinking and learning skills*, Vol. 2. Hillsdale, NJ: Erlbaum.

CARLSON, S. M., MOSES, L. J., & HIX, H. R. (1998). The role of inhibitory processes in young children's difficulties with deception and false belief. *Child Development*, 69, 672–691.

CARPENTER, T. P., & MOSER, J. M. (1982). The development of addition and subtraction problem-solving skills. In T. P. Carpenter, J. M. Moser, & T. A. Romberg (Eds.), *Addition and subtraction: A cognitive perspective*. Hillsdale, NJ: Erlbaum.

CARR, M., BORKOWSKI, J. G., & MAXWELL, S. E. (1991). Motivational components of underachievement. *Developmental Psychology*, 27, 108–118.

CARR, M., & JESSUP, D. L. (1995). Cognitive and metacognitive predictors of mathematics strategy use. *Learning and Individual Differences*, 7, 235–247.

CARR, M., KURTZ, B. E., SCHNEIDER, W., TURNER, L. A., & BORKOWSKI, J. G. (1989). Strategy acquisition and transfer among American and German children: Environmental influences on metacognitive development. *Developmental Psychology*, 25, 765–771.

CARR, M., & SCHNEIDER, W. (1991). Long-term maintenance of organizational strategies in kindergarten children. *Contemporary Educational Psychology*, 16, 61–72.

CARRAHER, T. N., CARRAHER, D., & SCHLIEMANN, A. D. (1985). Mathematics in the streets and in the schools. *British Journal of Developmental Psychology*, 3, 21–29.

CARROL, J. B. (1993). *Human cognitive abilities*. New York: Cambridge University Press.

CARSON, M. T., & ABRAHAMSON, A. (1976). Some members are more equal than others: The effect of semantic typicality on class-inclusion performance. *Child Development*, 47, 1186–1190.

CARVER, L. J., & BAUER, P. J. (1999). When the event is more than the sum of its parts: Individual differences in 9-month-olds long-term ordered recall. *Memory*, 2, 147–174.

CASE, R. (1974). Mental strategies, mental capacity and instruction: A neo-Piagetian investigation. *Journal of Experimental Child Psychology*, 18, 382–397.

CASE, R. (1985). *Intellectual development: Birth to adulthood*. New York: Academic.

CASE, R. (1991). Stages in the development of the young child's first sense of self. *Developmental Review*, 11, 210–230.

CASE, R. (1992a). *The mind's staircase: Exploring the conceptual underpinnings of children's thought and knowledge*. Hillsdale, NJ: Erlbaum.

CASE, R. (1992b). The role of the frontal lobes in the regulation of cognitive development. *Brain and Cognition*, 20, 51–73.

CASE, R. (1998). The development of conceptual structures. In D. Kuhn & R. S. Siegler (Vol. Eds.), *Cognition, perception, and language* (Vol. 2), in W. Damon (Gen. Ed.), *Handbook of child psychology*. New York: Wiley.

CASE, R., KURLAND, M., & GOLDBERG, J. (1982). Operational efficiency and the growth of short-term memory span. *Journal of Experimental Child Psychology*, 33, 386–404.

CASE, R., & OKAMOTO, Y. (1996). The role of central conceptual structures in the development of children's thought. *Monographs of the Society for Research in Child Development*, 61 (Serial No. 246).

CASELLI, M. C., BATES, E., CASADIO, P., FENSON, J., FENSON, L., SANDERL, L., & WEIR, J. (1995). A cross-linguistic study of early lexical development. *Cognitive Development*, 10, 159–199.

CASEY, M. B. (1996). Understanding individual differences in spatial ability within females: A nature/nurture interactionist framework. *Developmental Review, 16,* 241–260.

CASEY, M. B., & BRABECK, M. M. (1989). Exceptions to male advantage on a spatial task: Family handedness and college major as a factor identifying women who excel. *Neuropsychologia, 27,* 689–696.

CASEY, M. B., NUTTALL, R., PEZARIS, E., & BENBOW, C. P. (1995). The influence of spatial ability on gender differences in mathematics college entrance test scores across diverse samples. *Developmental Psychology, 31,* 697–705.

CASSEL, W. S., & BJORKLUND, D. F. (1995). Developmental patterns of eyewitness memory and suggestibility: An ecologically based short-term longitudinal study. *Law & Human Behavior, 19,* 507–532.

CASSEL, W. S., ROEBERS, C. E. M., & BJORKLUND, D. F. (1996). Developmental patterns of eyewitness responses to increasingly suggestive questions. *Journal of Experimental Child Psychology, 61,* 116–133.

CASSIDY, K. W. (1998). Preschools' use of desires to solve theory of mind problems in a pretense context. *Developmental Psychology, 34,* 503–511.

CATTELL, R. B. (1971). *Abilities: Their structure, growth and action.* Boston: Houghton Mifflin.

CAUGHY, M. O. (1996). Health and environmental effects on the academic readiness of school-age children. *Developmental Psychology, 32,* 515–522.

CAVANAUGH, J. C., & BORKOWSKI, J. G. (1980). Searching for metamemory-memory connections: A developmental study. *Developmental Psychology, 16,* 441–453.

CECI, S. J. (1983). Automatic and purposive semantic processing characteristics of normal and language/learning disabled (L/LD) children. *Developmental Psychology, 19,* 427–439.

CECI, S. J. (1991). How much does schooling influence general intelligence and its cognitive components? A reassessment of the evidence. *Developmental Psychology, 27,* 703–722.

CECI, S. J. (1993). Contextual trends in intellectual development. *Developmental Review, 13,* 403–435.

CECI, S. J. (1996). *On intelligence: A bio-ecological treatise on intellectual development* (2nd edition). Cambridge, MA: Harvard University Press.

CECI, S. J., & BRONFENBRENNER, U. (1985). "Don't forget to take the cupcakes out of the oven": Prospective memory, strategic time-monitoring, and context. *Child Development, 56,* 152–164.

CECI, S. J., & BRUCK, M. (1993). Suggestibility of the child witness: A historical review and synthesis. *Psychological Bulletin, 113,* 403–439.

CECI, S. J., & BRUCK, M. (1995). *Jeopardy in the courtroom: A scientific analysis of children's testimony.* Washington, DC: American Psychological Association.

CECI, S. J., & BRUCK, M. (1998). Children's testimony: Applied and basic issues. In I. E. Sigel & K. A. Renninger (Vol. Eds.) *Child psychology in practice* (Vol. 4). In W. Damon (Gen. Ed.), *Handbook of child psychology.* New York: Wiley.

CECI, S. J., BRUCK, M., & BATTIN, D. (in press). The suggestibility of children's testimony. In D. F. Bjorklund (Ed.), *False-memory creation in children and adults: Theory, research, and implications.* Mahwah, NJ: Erlbaum

CECI, S. J., & LIKER, J. (1986). A day at the races: A study of IQ, expertise, and cognitive complexity. *Journal of Experimental Psychology: General, 115,* 255–266.

CECI, S. J., & LIKER, J. (1988). Stalking the IQ-expertise relation: When the critics go fishing. *Journal of Experimental Psychology: General, 117,* 96–100.

CECI, S. J., LOFTUS, E. F., LEICHTMAN, M., & BRUCK, M. (1994). The role of source misattributions in the creation of false beliefs among preschoolers. *International Journal of Clinical and Experimental Hypnosis, 62,* 304–320.

CECI, S. J., & WILLIAMS, W. M. (1997). Schooling, intelligence, and income. *American Psychologist, 52,* 1051–158.

CERVANTES, C. A., & CALLANAN, M. A. (1998). Labels and explanations in mother-child emotion talk: Age and gender differentiation. *Developmental Psychology, 34,* 88–98.

CHALL, J. S. (1979). The great debate: Ten years later, with a modest proposal for reading stages. In L. B. Resnick & P. A. Weaver (Eds.), *Theory and practice of early reading.* Hillsdale, NJ: Erlbaum.

CHALL, J. S. (1983). *Stages of reading development.* New York: McGraw-Hill.

CHALMERS, D., & LAWRENCE, J. A. (1993). Investigating the effects of planning aids on adults' and adolescents' organization of a complex task. *International Journal of Behavioral Development, 16,* 191–214.

CHANDLER, M., FRITZ, A. S., & HALA, S. (1989). Small-scale deceit: Deception as a marker of two-, three-, and four-year-olds' early theories of mind. *Child Development, 60,* 1263–1277.

CHANGEUX, J. P., & DEHAENE, S. (1989). Neural models of cognitive function. *Cognition, 33,* 63–109.

CHASE, W. G., & SIMON, H. A. (1973). Perception in chess. *Cognitive Psychology, 4,* 55–81.

CHECHILE, R. A., & RICHMAN, C. L. (1982). The interaction of semantic memory with storage and retrieval processes. *Developmental Review, 2,* 237–250.

CHELUNE, G. J., & BAER, R. A. (1986). Developmental norms for the Wisconsin Card Sorting Test. *Journal of Clinical and Experimental Neuropsychology, 8*, 219–228.

CHEN, C., & STEVENSON, H. W. (1988). Cross-linguistic differences in digit span of preschool children. *Journal of Experimental Child Psychology, 46*, 150–158.

CHEN, C., & STEVENSON, H. W. (1995). Motivation and mathematics achievement: A comparative study of Asian-American, Caucasian-American, and East Asian high school students. *Child Development, 66*, 1215–1234.

CHEN, Z., & DAEHLER, M. (1989). Positive and negative transfer in analogical reasoning problem-solving. *Cognitive Development, 4*, 327–344.

CHEN, Z., & KLAHR, D. (in press). All other things being equal: Acquisition and transfer of the control of variables strategy. *Child Development.*

CHEN, Z., SANCHEZ, R. P., & CAMPBELL, T. (1997). From beyond to within their grasp: The rudiments of analogical problem solving in 10- and 13-month olds. *Developmental Psychology, 33*, 790–801

CHERNEY, I. D., & RYALLS, B. O. (March, 1998). *Incidental memory as a function of gender and development.* Paper presented at Conference on Human Development, Mobile, AL

CHI, M. T. H. (1977). Age differences in memory span. *Journal of Experimental Child Psychology, 23*, 266–281.

CHI, M. T. H. (1978). Knowledge structure and memory development. In R. Siegler (Ed.), *Children's thinking: What develops?* Hillsdale, NJ: Erlbaum.

CHI, M. T. H., FELTOVICH, P. J., & GLASER, R. (1981). Categorization and representation of physics problems by experts and novices. *Cognitive Science, 5*, 121–152.

CHOMSKY, N. (1959). A review of Skinner's *Verbal Behavior. Language, 35*, 26-58.

CHOMSKY, N. (1957). *Syntactic structures.* The Hague: Mouton.

CHORNEY, M. J., CHORNEY, K., SEESE, N., OWEN, M. J., DANIELS, J., MCGUFFIN, P., THOMPSON, L. A., DETTERMAN, D. K., BENBOW, C., LUBINSKI, D., ELEY, T., & PLOMIN, R. (1998). A qualitative trait locus associated with cognitive ability in children. *Psychological Science, 9*, 159–166.

CHUGANI, H. T., PHELPS, M. E., & MAZZIOTTA, J. C. (1987). Positron emission tomography study of human brain functional development. *Annals of Neurology, 22*, 487–497.

CHURCH, R. B., & GOLDIN-MEADOW, S. (1986). The mismatch between gesture and speech as an index of transitional knowledge. *Cognition, 23*, 43–71.

CICCHETTI, D. (1989). How research on child maltreatment has informed the study of child development: Perspectives from developmental psychopathology. In D. Cicchetti & V. Carlson (Eds.), *Child maltreatment: Theory and research on causes and consequences of child abuse and neglect.* New York: Cambridge University Press.

CIPIELEWSKI, J., & STANOVICH, K. E. (1992). Predicting growth in reading ability from children's exposure to print. *Journal of Experimental Child Psychology, 54*, 74–89.

CLARK, E. A., & HANISEE, J. (1982). Intellectual and adaptive performance of Asian children in adoptive American settings. *Developmental Psychology, 18*, 595–599.

CLARKE, A. D. B., & CLARKE, A. M. (1976). Formerly isolated children. In A. M. Clarke, & A. D. B. Clarke (Eds.), *Early experience: Myth and evidence.* London: Open Books.

CLARKE-STEWART, A. K. (1973). Interactions between mothers and their young children: Characteristics and consequences. *Monographs of the Society for Research in Child Development, 38* (Serial No. 153).

CLARKE-STEWART, A., THOMPSON, W., & LEPORE, S. (1989, April). *Manipulating children's testimony through interrogation.* Paper presented at the meeting of the Society for Research in Child Development, Kansas City, MO.

CLAVADETSCHER, J. E., BROWN, A. M., ANKRUM, C., & TELLER, D. Y. (1988). Spectral sensitivity and chromatic discrimination in 3- and 7-week-old infants. *Journal of the Optical Society of America, 5*, 2093–2105.

CLEMENTS, W. A., & PERNER, J. (1994). Implicit understanding of belief. *Cognitive Development, 9*, 377–395.

CLUBB, P. A., NIDA, R. E., MERRITT, K., & ORNSTEIN, P. A. (1993). Visiting the doctor: Children's knowledge and memory. *Cognitive Development, 8*, 361–372.

COHEN, L. B., & STRAUSS, M. S. (1979). Concept acquisition in the human infant. *Child Development, 50*, 419–424.

COHEN, L. B., & YOUNGER, B. A. (1983). Perceptual categorization in the infant. In E. K. Scholnick (Ed.), *New trends in conceptual representations: Challenges to Piaget's theory?* Hillsdale, NJ: Erlbaum.

COHEN, M. (1996). Preschooler's practical thinking and problem solving: The acquisition of an optimal solution. *Cognitive Development, 11*, 357–373.

COIE, J. D., & DODGE, K. A. (1998). Aggression and antisocial behavior. In N. Eisenberg (Vol. Ed), *Social, emotional, and personality development*, Vol. 3. In W. Damon (Gen. Ed.), *Handbook of child psychology.* New York: Wiley.

COLE, M. (1990). Cognitive development and formal schooling: The evidence from cross-cultural research.

In L. C. Moll (Ed.), *Vygotsky and education*. New York: Cambridge University Press.

Cole, M., & Scribner, S. (1977). Cross-cultural studies of memory and cognition. In R. V. Kail, Jr., & J. W. Hagen (Eds.), *Perspectives on the development of memory and cognition*. Hillsdale, NJ: Erlbaum.

Colombo, J. (1986). Recent studies in early auditory development. In G. J. Whitehurst (Ed.), *Annals of child development* (Vol. 3). Greenwich, CT: JAI.

Colombo, J. (1995). On the neural mechanisms underlying developmental and individual differences in visual fixation in infancy: Two hypotheses. *Developmental Review, 15*, 97–135.

Colombo, J., Mitchell, D. W., Coldren, J. T., & Freeseman, L. J. (1991). Individual differences in infant visual attention: Are short lookers faster processors or feature processors? *Child Development, 62*, 1247–1257.

Connor, J. M., & Serbin, L. A. (1977). Behaviorally based masculine and feminine-activity-preference scales for preschoolers: Correlates with other classroom behaviors and cognitive tests. *Child Development, 48*, 1411–1416.

Coon, H., Fulker, D. W., DeFries, J., & Plomin, R. (1990). Home environment and cognitive ability of 7-year-old children in the Colorado Adoption Project: Genetic and environmental etiologies. *Developmental Psychology, 26*, 459–468.

Cooper R. P., & Aslin, R. N. (1990). Preference for infant-directed speech in the first month after birth. *Child Development, 61*, 1584–1595.

Cooper, R. P. & Aslin, R. N. (1994). Developmental differences in infant attention to the spectral properties of infant-directed speech. *Child Development, 65*, 1663–1677.

Corballis, M. C. (1990). *The lopsided ape: Evolution of the generative mind*. New York: Oxford University Press.

Cosmides, L., & Tooby, J. (1987). From evolution to behavior: Evolutionary psychology as the missing link. In J. Dupre (Ed.), *The latest and the best essays on evolution and optimality*. Cambridge, MA: MIT Press.

Cosmides, L., Tooby, J., & Barkow, J. H. (1992). Introduction: Evolutionary psychology and conceptual integration. In J. H. Barkow, L. Cosmides, & J. Tooby (Eds.), *The adapted mind: Evolutionary psychology and the generation of culture*. New York: Oxford University Press.

Courage, M. L., & Howe, M. L. (1998). The ebb and flow of infant attentional preferences: Evidence for long-term recognition memory in 3-month-olds. *Journal of Experimental Child Psychology, 70*, 26–53.

Cowan, N. (1997). The development of working memory. In N. Cowan (Ed.), *The development of memory in childhood*. Hove East Sussex, UK: Psychology Press.

Cowan, N., & Davidson, G. (1984). Salient childhood memories. *Journal of Genetic Psychology, 145*, 101–107.

Cowan, N., Nugent, L. D., Elliott, E. M., Ponomarev, I., & Saults, J. S. (in press). The role of attention in the development of short-term memory: Age differences in the verbal span of apprehension. *Child Development*.

Cox, B. C., Ornstein, P. A., Naus, M. J., Maxfield, D., & Zimler, J. (1989). Children's concurrent use of rehearsal and organizational strategies. *Developmental Psychology, 25*, 619–627.

Cox, D., & Waters, H. S. (1986). Sex differences in the use of organization strategies: A developmental analysis. *Journal of Experimental Child Psychology, 41*, 18–37.

Coyle, T. R., & Bjorklund, D. F. (1996). The development of strategic memory: A modified microgenetic assessment of utilization deficiencies. *Cognitive Development, 11*, 295–314.

Coyle, T. R., & Bjorklund, D. F. (1997). Age differences in, and consequences of, multiple- and variable strategy use on a multitrial sort-recall task. *Developmental Psychology, 33*, 372–380.

Crabtree, J. W., & Riesen, A. H. (1979). Effects of the duration of dark rearing on visually guided behavior in the kitten. *Developmental Psychobiology, 12*, 291–303.

Crain-Thoreson, C., & Dale, P. S. (1992). Do early talkers become early readers? Linguistic precocity, preschool language, and emergent literacy. *Developmental Psychology, 28*, 421–429.

Crick, N. R., & Dodge, K. A. (1994). A review and reformulation of social information-processing mechanisms in children's social adjustment. *Psychological Bulletin, 115*, 74–101.

Crick, N. R., & Dodge, K. A. (1996). Social information-processing mechanisms in reactive and proactive aggression. *Child Development, 67*, 993–1002.

Cronbach, L. J. (1957). The two disciplines of scientific psychology. *American Psychologist, 12*, 671–684.

Cunningham, A. E. (1990). Explicit versus implicit instruction in phonemic awareness. *Journal of Experimental Child Psychology, 50*, 429–444.

Cunningham, A. E., & Stanovich, K. E. (1997). Early reading acquisition and its relation to reading experience and ability 10 years later. *Developmental Psychology, 33*, 934–945.

Cunningham, J. G., & Weaver, S. L. (1989). Young children's knowledge and their memory span: Effects of task and experience. *Journal of Experimental Child Psychology, 48*, 32–44.

CURTISS, S. (1977). *Genie: A psycholinguistic study of a modern day "wild child."* New York: Academic.

CUVO, A. J. (1974). Incentive level influence on overt rehearsal and free recall as a function of age. *Journal of Experimental Child Psychology, 18*, 167–181.

CYNADER, M., BERMAN, N. M., & HEIN, A. (1976). Recovery of function in cat visual cortex following prolonged deprivation. *Experimental Brain Research, 25*, 139–156.

CZIKO, G. (1995). *Without miracles: Universal selection theory and the second Darwinian revolution.* Cambridge, MA: MIT Press.

DAEHLER, M. & CHEN, Z. (1993). Protagonist, theme and goal objects: Effects of surface features on analogical transfer. *Cognitive Development, 8*, 211–229.

DAEHLER, M. W., LONARDO, R., & BUKATKO, D. (1979). Matching and equivalence judgments in very young children. *Child Development, 50*, 170–179.

DALLAGO, M. L. P., & MOELY, B. E. (1980). Free recall in boys of normal and poor reading levels as a function of task manipulations. *Journal of Experimental Child Psychology, 30*, 62–78.

DAMAST, A. M., TAMIS-LEMONDA, C. S., & BORNSTEIN, M. H. (1996). Mother-child play: Sequential interactions and the relation between maternal beliefs and behaviors. *Child Development, 67*, 1752–1766.

DANEMAN, M., & BLENNERHASSETT, A. (1984). How to assess the listening comprehension skills of prereaders. *Journal of Educational Psychology, 76*, 1372–1381.

DANEMAN, M., & GREEN, I. (1986). Individual differences in comprehending and producing words in context. *Journal of Memory and Language, 25*, 1–18.

DANIEL, M. H. (1997). Intelligence testing: Status and trends. *American Psychologist, 52*, 1038–1045.

DANNER, F. W., & DAY, M. C. (1977). Eliciting formal operations. *Child Development, 48*, 1600–1606.

DARWIN, C. (1859). *The origin of species.* New York: Modern Library.

DAS, J. P. (1984). Cognitive deficits in mental retardation. A process approach. In P. H. Brooks, R. Sperber, & C. McCauley (Eds.), *Learning and cognition in the mentally retarded.* Hillsdale, NJ: Erlbaum.

DAS, J. P., KIRBY, J., & JARMAN, R. F. (1975). Simultaneous and successive syntheses: An alternative model for cognitive abilities. *Psychological Bulletin, 82*, 87–103.

DAS, J. P., & MOLLOY, G. N. (1975). Varieties of simultaneous and successive processing in children. *Journal of Educational Psychology, 67*, 213–220.

DASEN, P. R. (ED.). (1977). *Piagetian psychology: Cross-cultural contributions.* New York: Gardner.

DAWKINS, R. (1982). *The blind watchmaker.* Essex, England: Longman.

DECASPER, A. J., & FIFER, W. P. (1980). Of human bonding: Newborns prefer their mother's voice. *Science, 208*, 1174–1176.

DECASPER, A. J., LECANUET, J.-P., BUSNEL, M.-C., GRANIER-DEFERRE, C., & MAUGEAIS, R. (1994). Fetal reactions to recurrent maternal speech. *Infant Behavior and Development, 17*, 159–164.

DECASPER, A. J., & SPENCE, M. J. (1986). Prenatal maternal speech influences newborns' perception of speech sounds. *Infant Behavior and Development, 9*, 133–150.

DE JONG, P. F. (1998). Working memory deficits of reading disabled children. *Journal of Experimental Child Psychology, 70*, 75-96.

DELOACHE, J. S. (1987). Rapid change in the symbolic functioning of very young children. *Science, 238*, 1556–1557.

DELOACHE, J. S. (1991). Symbolic functioning in very young children: Understanding of pictures and models. *Child Development, 62*, 736–752.

DELOACHE, J. S. (1995). Early understanding and use of symbols: The model model. *Current Directions in Psychological Science, 4*, 109–113.

DELOACHE, J. S., & BROWN, A. L. (1983). Very young children's memory for the location of objects in a large scale environment. *Child Development, 54*, 888–897.

DELOACHE, J. S., CASSIDY, D. J., & BROWN, A. L. (1985). Precursors of mnemonic strategies in very young children's memory for the location of hidden objects. *Child Development, 56*, 125–137.

DELOACHE, J. S., & MARZOLF, D. P. (1992). When a picture is not worth a thousand words: Young children's understanding of pictures and models. *Cognitive Development, 7*, 317–329.

DELOACHE, J. S., MILLER, K. F., & PIERROUTSAKOS, S. L. (1998). Reasoning and problem solving. In D. Kuhn & R. S. Siegler (Vol. Eds.), *Cognitive, language, and perceptual development*, Vol. 2, In W. Damon (Gen. Ed.), *Handbook of child psychology.* New York: Wiley.

DELOACHE, J. S., MILLER, K. F., & ROSENGREN, K. S. (1997). The credible shrinking room: Very young children's performance with symbolic and nonsymbolic relations. *Psychological Science, 8*, 308–313.

DELOACHE, J. S., PIERROUTSAKOS, S. L., UTTAL, D. H., ROSENGREN, K. S., & GOTTLIEB, A. (1998). Grasping the nature of pictures. *Psychological Science, 9*, 205–210.

DeLoache, J. S., & Smith, C. S. (1999). Early symbolic representation. In I. Sigel (Ed.), *Theoretical perspectives in the concept of representation*. Mahwah, NJ: Erlbaum.

Delpit, L. D. (1990). Language diversity and learning. In S. Hynds & D. L. Rubin (Eds.), *Perspectives on talk and learning*. Urbana, IL: National Council of Teachers of English.

DeMarie-Dreblow, D. (1991). Relation between knowledge and memory: A reminder that correlation does not imply causality. *Child Development, 62*, 484–498.

DeMarie-Dreblow, D., & Miller, P. H. (1988). The development of children's strategies for selective attention: Evidence for a transitional period. *Child Development, 59*, 1504–1513.

Dempster, F. N. (1981). Memory span: Sources of individual and developmental differences. *Psychological Bulletin, 89*, 63–100.

Dempster, F. N. (1985). Short-term memory development in childhood and adolescence. In C. J. Brainerd & M. Pressley (Eds.), *Basic processes in memory development: Progress in cognitive development research*. New York: Springer.

Dempster, F. N. (1992). The rise and fall of the inhibitory mechanism: Toward a unified theory of cognitive development and aging. *Developmental Review, 12*, 45–75.

Dempster, F. N. (1993). Resistance to interference: Developmental changes in a basic processing mechanism. In M. L. Howe & R. Pasnak (Eds.), *Emerging themes in cognitive development*. Vol. 1: *Foundations*. New York: Springer-Verlag.

Denney, N. (1974). Evidence for developmental changes in categorization criteria for children and adults. *Human Development, 17*, 41–53.

Denney, N. W., & Acito, M. A. (1974). Classification training in two- and three-year-old children. *Journal of Experimental Child Psychology, 17*, 37–48.

Dennis, W. (1973). *Children of the Crèche*. New York: Appleton-Century-Crofts.

DeStefano, J. (1972). Social variation in language: Implications for teaching reading to Black ghetto children. In J. A. Figurel (Ed.). *Better reading in urban schools*. Newark, DE: International Reading Association.

Detterman, D. K. (1987). What does reaction time tell us about intelligence? In P. E. Vernon (Ed.), *Speed of information processing and intelligence*. Norwood, NJ: Ablex.

Detterman, D. K. (1992). Transfer on trial: The case for the prosecution. In D. K. Detterman & R. J. Sternberg (Eds.), *Transfer on trial: Intelligence, cognition, and instruction*. Norwood, NJ: Ablex.

Detterman, D. K., & Daniel, M. H. (1989). Correlations of mental tests with each other and with cognitive variables are highest for low IQ groups. *Intelligence, 13*, 340–359.

Detterman, D. K., & Thompson, L. A. (1997). What is so special about special education? *American Psychologist, 52*, 1082–1090.

de Villiers, J. G., & de Villiers, P. A. (1973). A cross-sectional study of the acquisition of grammatical morphemes in child speech. *Journal of Psycholinguistic Research, 2*, 267–278.

de Villiers, J. G., & de Villiers, P. A. (1978). *Language acquisition*. Cambridge, MA: Harvard University Press.

de Villiers, P. A., & de Villiers, J. G. (1979). *Early language*. Cambridge, MA: Harvard University Press.

De Vries, R. (1969). Constancy of generic identity in the years three to six. *Monographs of the Society for Research in Child Development, 34* (Serial No. 127).

Diamond, A. (1985). Development of the ability to use recall to guide action as indicated by infants' performance on AB. *Child Development, 56*, 868–883.

Diamond, A. (1991). Frontal lobe involvement in cognitive changes during the first year of life. In K. R. Gibson & A. C. Petersen (Eds.), *Brain maturation and cognitive development: Comparative and cross-cultural perspectives*. New York: Aldine de Gruyter.

Diamond, A., Cruttenden, L., & Neiderman, D. (1994). AB with multiple wells: 1. Why are multiple wells sometimes easier than two wells? 2. Memory or memory + inhibition? *Developmental Psychology, 30*, 192–205.

Diamond, A., & Taylor, C. (1996). Development of an aspect of executive control: Development of the abilities to remember what I said and to "Do as I say, not as I do." *Developmental Psychobiology, 29*, 315–324.

Diaz, R. M., Neal, C. J., & Vachio, A. (1991). Maternal teaching in the zone of proximal development: A comparison of low- and high-risk dyads. *Merrill-Palmer Quarterly, 37*, 83–108.

Dirks, J., & Neisser, U. (1977). Memory for objects in real scenes: The development of recognition and recall. *Journal of Experimental Child Psychology, 23*, 315–328.

Dodge, K. A. (1986). A social information processing model of social competence in children. In M. Perlmutter (Ed.), *Minnesota symposium on child psychology* (Vol. 18). Hillsdale, NJ: Erlbaum.

Dodge, K. A., Petit, G. S., Bates, J. E., & Valente, E. (1995). Social information processing patterns partially mediate the effect of early physical abuse on later conduct problems. *Journal of Abnormal Psychology, 104*, 632–643.

DODGE, K. A., PETTIT, G. S., MCCLASKEY, C. L., & BROWN, M. M. (1986). Social competence in children. *Monographs of the Society for Research in Child Development, 51* (Serial No. 213).

DODGE, K. A., & PRICE, J. M. (1994). On the relation between social information processing and socially competent behavior in early school-age children. *Child Development, 65*, 1385–1397.

DOMAN, G. (1984). *How to multiply your baby's intelligence.* Garden City, NY: Doubleday.

DOUGHERTY, T. M., & HAITH, M. M. (1997). Infant expectations and reaction time as predictors of childhood speed of processing and IQ. *Developmental Psychology, 33*, 146–155.

DOUGLAS, J. D., & CORSALE, K. (1977). The effects of mode and rate of presentation on evaluative encoding in children's memory. *Child Development, 48*, 46–50.

DOW, G. A., & PICK, H. L. (1992). Young children's use of models and photographs as spatial representations. *Cognitive Development, 7*, 351–363.

DRACHMAN, D. B., & COULOMBRE, A. J. (1962). Experimental clubfoot and arthrogryposis multiplex congenita. *Lancet*, 523–526.

DRUMMEY, A. B., & NEWCOMBE, N. (1995). Remembering versus knowing the past: Children's explicit and implicit memory. *Journal of Experimental Child Psychology, 59*, 549–565.

DUBE, E. F. (1982). Literacy, cultural familiarity, and "intelligence" as determinants of story recall. In U. Neisser (Ed.), *Memory observed: Remembering in natural contexts.* San Francisco: W. H. Freeman.

DUFRESNE, A., & KOBASIGAWA, A. (1989). Children's spontaneous allocation of study time: Differential and sufficient aspects. *Journal of Experimental Child Psychology, 47*, 274–296.

DURHAM, P., & DURHAM, F. (1995). Developmental antecedents of taxonomic and thematic strategies at 3 years of age. *Developmental Psychology, 31*, 483–493.

DUYME, M. (1988). School success and social class: An adoption study. *Developmental Psychology, 24*, 203–209.

DWECK, C. S., & LEGGETT, E. L. (1988). A social-cognitive approach to motivation and personality. *Psychological Review, 95*, 256–273.

DWECK, C. S., & REPPUCCI, N. D. (1973). Learned helplessness and reinforcement responsibility in children. *Journal of Personality and Social Psychology, 25*, 109–116.

EALS, M., & SILVERMAN, I. (1994). The hunter-gatherer theory of spatial sex differences: Proximate factors mediating the female advantage in recall of object arrays. *Ethology and Sociobiology, 15*, 95–105.

EATON, W. O., & VON BARGEN D. (1981). Asynchronous development of gender understanding in preschool children. *Child Development, 52*, 1020–1027.

EDELMAN, G. M. (1987). *Neural Darwinism: The theory of neuronal group selection.* New York: Basic Books.

EILERS, R. W., GAVIN, W. J., & WILSON, W. R. (1979). Linguistic experience and phonemic perception in infancy: A cross-linguistic study. *Child Development, 50*, 14–18.

EIMAS, P. D., & QUINN, P. C. (1994). Studies on the formation of perceptually based basic-level categories in young infants. *Child Development, 65*, 903–917.

EIMAS, P. D., QUINN, P. C., & COWAN, P. (1994). Development of exclusivity in perceptual based categories of young infants. *Journal of Experimental Child Psychology, 58*, 418–431.

EIMAS, P. D., SIQUELAND, E. R., JUSCZYK, P., & VIGORITO, J. (1971). Speech perception in infants. *Science, 71*, 303–306.

EIZENMAN, D. R., & BERTENTHAL, B. I. (1998). Infants' perception of object unity in translating and rotating displays. *Developmental Psychology, 34*, 426–434.

ELKIND, D. (1967). Egocentrism in adolescence. *Child Development, 38*, 1025–1033.

ELKIND, D. (1978). *The child's reality: Three developmental theories.* Hillsdale, NJ: Erlbaum.

ELKIND, D. (1987). *Miseducation: Preschoolers at risk.* New York: Knopf.

ELKIND, D. (1996). Inhelder and Piaget on Adolescence and adulthood: A postmodern appraisal. *Psychological Science, 7*, 216–220.

ELKIND, D., & BOWEN, R. (1979). Imaginary audience behavior in children and adolescents. *Developmental Psychology, 15*, 38–44.

ELLIS, H. (1894). *Man and woman: A study of human secondary sexual characters.* London: Walter Scott.

ELLIS, N. C., & HENNELLEY, R. A. (1980). A bilingual word-length effect: Implications for intelligence testing and the relative ease of mental calculation in Welsh and English. *British Journal of Psychology, 71*, 43–52.

ELLIS, N. R., KATZ, E., & WILLIAMS, J. E. (1987). Developmental aspects of memory for spatial location. *Journal of Experimental Child Psychology, 44*, 401–412.

ELLIS, S. (1997). Strategy choice in sociocultural context. *Developmental Review, 17*, 490–524.

ELLIS, S., & ROGOFF, B. (1986). Problem solving in children's management of instruction. In E. Mueller & C. Cooper (Eds.), *Process and outcome in peer relationships*. Orlando, FL: Academic.

ELLIS, S., & SIEGLER, R. S. (1997). Planning and strategy choice, or why don't children plan when they should? In S. L. Friedman & E. K. Scholnick (Eds.), *Why, how, and when do we plan: The developmental psychology of planning*. Hillsdale, NJ: Erlbaum.

ELMAN, J. (1994). Implicit learning in neural networks: The importance of starting small. In C. Umilta & M. Moscovitch (Eds.), *Attention and performance XV: Conscious and nonconscious information processing*. Cambridge, MA: MIT Press.

ELMAN, J. L., BATES, E. A., JOHNSON, M. H., KARMILOFF-SMITH, A., PARISI, D., & PLUNKET, K. (1996). *Rethinking innateness: A connectionist perspective on development*. Cambridge, MA: MIT Press.

EMERSON, H. F., & GEKOWSKI, W. L. (1976). Interactive and categorical grouping strategies and the syntagmatic-paradigmatic shift. *Child Development, 47*, 1116–1121.

ENTUS, A. K. (1977). Hemispheric asymmetry in processing of dichotically presented speech and non-speech stimuli by infants. In S. J. Segalowitz & F. A. Gruber (Eds.), *Language development and neurological theory*. New York: Academic.

ENTWISLE, D. R. (1995). The role of schools in sustaining early childhood program benefits. *The Future of Children, 5* (No. 3, Winter).

ERDELYI, M. (1994). Hypnotic hypermnesia: The empty set of hypermnesia. *International Journal of Clinical and Experimental Hypnosis, 42*, 379–390.

EVANS, M. A. (1985). Self-initiated speech repairs: A reflection of communicative monitoring in young children. *Developmental Psychology, 21*, 365–371.

EYSENCK, H. J. (1987). Speed of information processing, reaction time, and the theory of intelligence. In P. E. Vernon (Ed.), *Speed of information processing and intelligence*. Norwood, NJ: Ablex.

FABRICIUS, W. V. (1988). The development of forward search planning in preschoolers. *Child Development, 59*, 1473–1488.

FABRICIUS, W. V., SCHWANENFLUGEL, P. J., KYLLONEN, P. C., BARCLAY, C. R., & DENTON, S. M. (1989). Developing theories of the mind: Children's and adults' conceptions of mental activities. *Child Development, 60*, 1278–1290.

FABRICIUS, W. V., & WELLMAN, H. M. (1983). Children's understanding of retrieval cue utilization. *Developmental Psychology, 19*, 15–21.

FAGAN, J. F., III. (1973). Infants' delayed recognition memory and forgetting. *Journal of Experimental Child Psychology, 16*, 424–450.

FAGAN, J. F., III. (1974). Infant recognition memory: The effects of length of familiarization and type of discrimination task. *Child Development, 45*, 351–356.

FAGAN, J. F., III. (1984). The relationship of novelty preferences during infancy to later intelligence and recognition memory. *Intelligence, 8*, 339–346.

FAGAN, J. F., III. (1992). Intelligence: A theoretical viewpoint. *Current Directions in Psychological Science, 1*, 82–86.

FAGAN, J. F., III, & SINGER, J. T. (1983). Infant recognition memory as a measure of intelligence. In L. P. Lipsitt & C. K. Rovee-Collier (Eds.), *Advances in infancy research* (Vol. 2). Norwood, NJ: Ablex.

FAGEN, J., PRIGOT, J., CARROLL, M., PIOLI, L., STEIN, A., & FRANCO, A. (1997). Auditory context and memory retrieval in young infants. *Developmental Psychology, 68*, 1057–1066.

FAGOT, B. I., LEINBACH, M. D., & HAGAN, R. (1986). Gender labeling and the adoption of sex-typed behaviors. *Developmental Psychology, 22*, 440-443.

FANTZ, R. L. (1958). Pattern vision in young infants. *Psychological Record, 8*, 43–47.

FANTZ, R. L. (1961). The origin of form perception. *Scientific American, 204*, 66–72.

FANTZ, R. L., & MIRANDA, S. B. (1975). Newborn attention to form of contour. *Child Development, 46*, 224–228.

FARRAR, M. J., & GOODMAN, G. S. (1992). Developmental changes in event memory. *Child Development, 63*, 173–187.

FEINGOLD, A. (1988). Cognitive gender differences are disappearing. *American Psychologist, 43*, 95–103.

FEINGOLD, A. (1992). Sex differences in variability in intellectual abilities: A new look at an old controversy. *Review of Educational Research, 62*, 61–84.

FERNALD, A. (1992). Human maternal vocalizations to infants as biologically relevant signals: An evolutionary perspective. In J. H. Barkow, L. Cosmides, & J. Tooby (Eds.), *The adaptive mind: Evolutionary psychology and the generation of culture*. New York: Oxford University Press.

FERNALD, A., & MAZZIE, C. (1991). Prosody and focus in speech to infants and adults. *Developmental Psychology, 27*, 209–221.

FERNALD, A., PINTO, J. P., SWINGLEY, D., WEINBERG, A., & McROBERTS, G. W. (1998). Rapid gains in speed of verbal processing by infants in the 2nd year. *Psychological Science, 9*, 228–231.

FERNALD, A., TAESCHNER, T., DUNN, J., PAPOUSEK, M., FUKUI, I, AND BOYSSON-BARDIES, B. DE. (1989). A cross-language study of prosodic modifications in mothers' and fathers' speech to infants. *Journal of Child Language, 16,* 477–501.

FERREIRA, F., & MORRISON, F. J. (1994). Children's knowledge of syntactic constituents: Effects of age and schooling. *Developmental Psychology, 30,* 663–678.

FIELD, D. (1987). A review of preschool conservation training: An analysis of analyses. *Developmental Review, 7,* 210–251.

FIELD, T. M., WOODSON, R., GREENBERG, R., & COHEN, D. (1982). Discrimination and imitation of facial expression by neonates. *Science, 218,* 179–181.

FINKELSTEIN, N. W., & RAMEY, C. T. (1977) Learning to control the environment in infancy. *Child Development, 48,* 806–819.

FIREMAN, G. (1996). Developing a plan for solving a problem: A representational shift. *Cognitive Development, 11,* 107–122.

FISHBEIN, H. D. (1976). *Evolution, development, and children's learning.* Pacific Palisades, CA: Goodyear.

FISCHER, K. W. (1980). A theory of cognitive development: The control and construction of hierarchies of skills. *Psychological Review, 87,* 477–531.

FISCHER, K. W., & BIDELL, T. (1991). Constraining nativist inferences about cognitive capacities. In S. Carey & R. Gelman (Eds.), *The epigenesis of mind: Essays on biology and cognition.* Hillsdale, NJ: Erlbaum.

FISCHER, K. W., & BIDELL, T. (1998). Dynamic development of psychological structures in action and thought. In R. M. Lerner (Vol. Ed.), *Theoretical models of human development,* Vol. 1, of W. Damon (Gen. Ed.), *Handbook of child psychology.* New York: Wiley.

FISCHER, K. W., & HENCKE, R. W. (1996). Infants' construction of actions in context: Piaget's contribution to research on early development. *Psychological Science, 7,* 204–211.

FISCHER, K. W., & ROSE, S. P. (1996). Dynamic growth cycles of brain and cognitive development. In R. W. Thatcher, G. R. Lyon, J. Rumsey, & N. Krasnegor (Eds.) *Developmental neuroimaging: Mapping the development of brain and behavior.* San Diego: Academic.

FISHER, C., & TOKURO, H. (1996). Acoustic cues to grammatical structure in infant-directed speech: Cross-linguistic evidence. *Child Development, 67,* 3192–3218.

FIVUSH, R. (1988). The functions of event memory: Some comments on Nelson and Barsalou. In U. Neisser & E. Winograd (Eds.), *Remembering reconsidered: Ecological and traditional approaches to the study of memory.* New York: Cambridge University Press.

FIVUSH, R. (1997). Event memory in early childhood. In N. Cowan (Ed.), *The development of memory in childhood.* Hove East Sussex, UK: Psychology Press.

FIVUSH, R., & HAMOND, N. R. (1989). Time and again: Effects of repetition and retention interval on 2-year-olds' event recall. *Journal of Experimental Child Psychology, 47,* 259–273.

FIVUSH, R., & HAMOND, N. R. (1990). Autobiographical memory across the preschool years: Toward reconceptualizing childhood amnesia. In R. Fivush & J. A. Hudson (Eds.), *Knowing and remembering in young children.* Cambridge: Cambridge University Press.

FIVUSH, R., & HUDSON, J. A. (EDS.). (1990). *Knowing and remembering in young children.* Cambridge: Cambridge University Press.

FIVUSH, R., KUEBLI, J., & CLUBB, P. A. (1992). The structure of events and event representations: A developmental analysis. *Child Development, 63,* 188–201.

FLANNAGAN, D., BAKER-WARD, L., & GRAHAM, L. (1995). Talk about preschool: Patterns of topic discussion and elaboration related to gender and ethnicity. *Sex Roles, 32,* 1–15.

FLAVELL, J. H. (1963). *The developmental psychology of Jean Piaget.* Princeton, NJ: Van Nostrand.

FLAVELL, J. H. (1970). Developmental studies of mediated memory. In H. W. Reese & L. P. Lipsitt (Eds.), *Advances in child development and child behavior* (Vol. 5). New York: Academic.

FLAVELL, J. H. (1971). Stage-related properties of cognitive development. *Cognitive Psychology, 2,* 421–453.

FLAVELL, J. H. (1978). Developmental stage: Explanans or explanandum? *Behavioral and Brain Sciences, 2,* 187.

FLAVELL, J. H. (1982). On cognitive development. *Child Development, 53,* 1–10.

FLAVELL, J. H. (1988). The development of children's knowledge about mind: From cognitive connections to mental representations. In J. W. Astington, P. L. Harris, & D. R. Olson (Eds.), *Developing theories of mind.* Cambridge: Cambridge University Press.

FLAVELL, J. H. (1996). Piaget's legacy. *Psychological Science, 7,* 200–203.

FLAVELL, J. H., BEACH, D. R., & CHINSKY, J. H. (1966). Spontaneous verbal rehearsal in a memory task as a function of age. *Child Development, 37,* 283–299.

FLAVELL, J. H., BOTKIN, P. T., FRY, C. L., WRIGHT, J. W., & JARVIS, P. E. (1968). *The development of role-taking and communication skills in children.* New York: Wiley.

FLAVELL, J. H., EVERETT, B. A., CROFT, K., & FLAVELL, E. (1981). Young children's knowledge about visual perception: Further evidence for level 1-level 2 distinction. *Developmental Psychology, 17,* 99–107.

FLAVELL, J. H., GREEN, F. L., & FLAVELL, E. R. (1986). Development of knowledge about the appearance-reality distinction. *Monographs of the Society for Research in Child Development, 51* (Serial No. 212).

FLAVELL, J. H., GREEN, F. L., & FLAVELL, R. R. (1995a). The development of children's knowledge about attentional focus. *Developmental Psychology, 31,* 706–712.

FLAVELL, J. H., GREEN, F. L., & FLAVELL, E. R. (1995b). Young children's knowledge about thinking. *Monographs of the Society for Research in Child Development,* 60 (1, Serial No. 243).

FLAVELL, J. H., GREEN, F. L., & FLAVELL, E. R. (1998). The mind has a mind of its own: Developing knowledge about mental uncontrollability. *Cognitive Development, 13,* 127–138.

FLAVELL, J. H., GREEN, F. L., FLAVELL, E. R., & GROSSMAN, J. B. (1997). The development of children's knowledge about inner speech. *Developmental Psychology, 68,* 39–47.

FLAVELL, J. H., GREEN, F. R., WAHL, K. E., & FLAVELL, E. R. (1987). The effects of question clarification and memory aids on young children's performance on appearance-reality tasks. *Cognitive Development, 2,* 127–144.

FLAVELL, J. H., & MILLER, P. H. (1998). Social cognition. In D. Kuhn & R. S. Siegler (Vol. Eds.), *Cognition, perception, and language (Vol. 2),* in W. Damon (Gen. Ed.), *Handbook of child psychology.* New York: Wiley.

FLAVELL, J. H., SPEER, J. R., GREEN, F. L., & AUGUST, D. L. (1981). The development of comprehension monitoring and knowledge about communication. *Monographs of the Society for Research in Child Development,* 46 (Serial No. 192).

FLAVELL, J. H., & WOHLWILL, J. F. (1969). Formal and functional aspects of cognitive development. In D. Elkind & J. H. Flavell (Eds.). *Studies in cognitive development.* London: Oxford University Press.

FLETCHER, K. L., & BRAY, N. W. (1997). Instructional and contextual effects on external memory strategy use in young children. *Journal of Experimental Child Psychology, 67,* 204–222.

FLIN, R., BOON, J., KNOX, A., & BULL, R. (1992). The effect of a five-month delay on children's and adult's eyewitness memory. *British Journal of Psychology, 83,* 323–336.

FLYNN, J. R. (1987). Massive IQ gains in 14 nations: What IQ tests really measure. *Psychological Bulletin, 101,* 171–191.

FODOR, J. A. (1983). *The modularity of mind.* Cambridge, MA: MIT Press.

FOLDS, T. H., FOOTO, M., GUTTENTAG, R. E., & ORNSTEIN, P. A. (1990). When children mean to remember: Issues of context specificity, strategy effectiveness, and intentionality in the development of memory. In D. F. Bjorklund (Ed.), *Children's strategies: Contemporary views of cognitive development.* Hillsdale, NJ: Erlbaum.

FOLEY, M. A., & RATNER, H. H. (1998a). Distinguishing between memories for thoughts and deeds: The role of prospective processing in children's source monitoring. *British Journal of Developmental Psychology, 16,* 465–484.

FOLEY, M. A., & RATNER, H. H. (1998b). Children's recoding in memory for collaboration: A way of learning from others. *Cognitive Development, 13,* 91–108.

FOLEY, M. A., RATNER, H. H., & PASSALACQUA, C. (1993). Appropriating the actions of another: Implications for children's memory and learning. *Cognitive Development, 8,* 373–401.

FOLEY, M. A., SANTINI, C., & SOPASAKIS, M. (1989). Discriminating between memories: Evidence for children's spontaneous elaborations. *Journal of Experimental Child Psychology, 48,* 146–169.

FOX, L. H. (1976). Sex differences in mathematical precocity: Bridging the gap. In D. P. Keating (Ed.), *Intellectual talent: Research and development.* Baltimore: Johns Hopkins University Press.

FRANKEL, M. T., & ROLLINS, H. S. (1985). Associative and categorical hypotheses of organization in the free recall of adults and children. *Journal of Experimental Child Psychology, 40,* 304–318.

FRAZIER, J. A. (March, 1993). *Influences of extended-year of schooling on academic achievement and cognitive development.* Paper presented at meeting of the Society for Research in Child Development, New Orleans, LA.

FRAZIER, J. A., & MORRISON, F. J. (1998). The influence of extended-year schooling on growth of achievement and perceived competence in early elementary school. *Child Development, 69,* 495–517.

FREUD, S. (1963). Three essays on the theory of sexuality. In J. Strachey (Ed. and Trans.), *The standard edition of the complete psychological works of Sigmund Freud* (Vol. 7). London: Hogarth.

FREUND, L. S. (1990). Maternal regulation of children's problem-solving behavior and its impact on children's performance. *Child Development, 61,* 113–126.

FRIEDMAN, S. (1972). Habituation and recovery of visual response in the alert human newborn. *Journal of Experimental Child Psychology, 13,* 339–349.

FRYE, D., ZELAZO, P. D., & PALFAI, T. (1995). Theory of mind and rule-based reasoning. *Cognitive Development, 10,* 483–527.

FULIGNI, A. J., & STEVENSON, H. W. (1995). Time use and mathematics achievement among American, Chinese, and Japanese high school students. *Child Development, 66*, 830–842.

FURMAN, L. N., & WALDEN, T. A. (1990). Effects of script knowledge on preschool children's communicative interactions. *Developmental Psychology, 26*, 227–233.

FURTH, H. G. (1969). *Piaget and knowledge: Theoretical foundations.* Englewood Cliffs, NJ: Prentice-Hall.

FUSON, K. C. (1979). The development of self-regulating aspects of speech: A review. In G. Zivin (Ed.), *The development of self-regulation through private speech.* New York: Wiley.

FUSON, K. C. (1988). *Children's counting and concepts of number.* New York: Springer-Verlag.

FUSON, K. C., PERGAMENT, G. G., LYONS, B. G., & HALL, J. W. (1985). Children's conformity to the cardinality rule as a function of set size and counting accuracy. *Child Development, 56*, 1429–1436.

FUSON, K. C., SECADA, W. G., & HALL, J. T. (1983). Matching, counting, and conservation of numerical equivalence. *Child Development, 54*, 91–97.

FUSTER, J. M. (1989). *The prefrontal cortex: Anatomy, physiology, and neuropsychology of the frontal lobe.* New York: Raven.

GALLUP, G. G., JR. (1979). Self-recognition in chimpanzees and man: A developmental and comparative perspective. In M. Lewis & L. A. Rosenblum (Eds.), *Genesis of behavior: Vol. 2. The child and its family.* New York: Plenum.

GARBER, H. L. (1988). *The Milwaukee Project: Preventing mental retardation in children at risk.* Washington, DC: American Association on Mental Retardation.

GARDINER, M. F., FOX, A., KNOWLES, F., & JEFFREY, D. (1996). Learning improved by arts training. *Nature, 381*, 284.

GARDNER, H. (1983). *Frames of mind: The theory of multiple intelligences.* New York: Basic.

GARDNER, H. (1984a, March 19). Human intelligence isn't what we think. *U.S. News and World Report,* pp. 75–78.

GARDNER, H. (1984b). Assessing intelligence: A comment on "Testing intelligence without IQ tests." *Phi Delta Kappan, 65*, 699–700.

GARDNER, H. (ED.). (1993). *Multiple intelligences: The theory in practice.* New York: Basic.

GARDNER, H. (1999). Are there additional intelligences? The case for naturalist, spiritual, and existential intelligences. In J. Kane (Ed.), *Education,* *information and transformation.* Englewood Cliffs, NJ: Prentice-Hall.

GARDNER H., & HATCH, T. (1989). Multiple intelligences go to school: Educational implications of the theory of multiple intelligences. *Educational Researcher, 18* (No. 8), 4–10.

GARNER, R. (1990). Children's use of strategies in reading. In D. F. Bjorklund (Ed.), *Children's strategies: Contemporary views of cognitive development.* Hillsdale, NJ: Erlbaum.

GAULTNEY, J. F. (1995). The effect of prior knowledge and metacognition on the acquisition of a reading comprehension strategy. *Journal of Experimental Child Psychology, 59*, 142–163.

GAULTNEY, J. F. (1998). Utilization deficiencies among children with learning disabilities. *Learning and Individual Differences, 10*, 13–28.

GAULTNEY, J. F., BJORKLUND, D. F., & GOLDSTEIN, D. (1996). To be young, gifted, and strategic: Advantages for memory performance. *Journal of Experimental Child Psychology, 61*, 43–66.

GAUVAIN, M., & ROGOFF, B. (1989). Collaborative problem solving and children's planning skills. *Developmental Psychology, 25*, 139–151.

GAY, J., & COLE, M. (1967). *The new mathematics and an old culture.* New York: Holt, Rinehart & Winston.

GAZZANIGA, M. S. (1985). *The social brain: Discovering the networks of the mind.* New York: Basic.

GEARY, D. C. (1990). A componential analysis of an early learning deficit in mathematics. *Journal of Experimental Child Psychology, 49*, 363–383.

GEARY, D. C. (1993). Mathematical disabilities: Cognitive, neuropsychological, and genetic components. *Psychological Bulletin, 114*, 345–362.

GEARY, D. C. (1995). Reflections of evolution and culture in children's cognition: Implications for mathematical development and instruction. *American Psychologist, 50*, 24–37.

GEARY, D. C. (1996). Sexual selection and sex differences in mathematical abilities. *Behavioral and Brain Sciences, 19*, 229–284.

GEARY, D. C., BOW-THOMAS, C. C., FAN, L., & SIEGLER, R. S. (1993). Even before formal instructions. Chinese children outperform American children in mental arithmetic. *Cognitive Development, 8*, 517–529.

GEARY, D. C., BOW-THOMAS, C. C., LIU, F., & SIEGLER, R. S. (1996). Development of arithmetic competencies in Chinese and American children: Influence of age, language, and schooling. *Child Development, 67*, 2022–2044.

GEARY, D. C., BOW-THOMAS, C. C., & YAO, Y. (1992). Counting knowledge and skill in cognitive addition:

A comparison of normal and mathematically disabled children. *Journal of Experimental Child Psychology, 54*, 372–391.

GEARY, D. C., & BROWN, S. C. (1991). Cognitive addition: Strategy choice and speed-of-processing differences in gifted, normal and mathematically disabled children. *Developmental Psychology, 27*, 398–406.

GEARY, D. C., BROWN, S. C., & SAMARANAYAKE, V. A. (1991). Cognitive addition: A short longitudinal study of strategy choice and speed of processing differences in normal and mathematically disabled children. *Developmental Psychology, 27*, 787–797.

GEARY, D. C., FAN, L., & BOW-THOMAS, C. C. (1992). Numerical cognition: Loci of ability differences comparing children from China and the United States. *Psychological Science, 3*, 180–185.

GEARY, D. C., SALTHOUSE, T. A., CHEN, G-P., & FAN, L. (1996). Are East Asian versus American differences in arithmetical ability a recent phenomenon? *Developmental Psychology, 32*, 254–262.

GELMAN, R. (1969). Conservation acquisition: A problem of learning to attend to relevant attributes. *Journal of Experimental Child Psychology, 7*, 167–187.

GELMAN, R., & GALLISTEL, R. (1978). *The child's understanding of number.* Cambridge, MA: Harvard University Press.

GELMAN, R., MECK, E., & MERKIN, S. (1986). Young children's numerical competence. *Cognitive Development, 1*, 1–30.

GELMAN, R., & WILLIAMS, E. M. (1998). Enabling constraints for cognitive development and learning: Domain-specificity and epigenesis. In D. Kuhn & R. S. Siegler (Vol. Eds.), *Cognition, perception, and language,* Vol. 2, of W. Damon (Gen. Ed.), *Handbook of child psychology,* New York: Wiley.

GENTNER, D. (1989). The mechanisms of analogical learning. In S. Vosniadou & A. Ortony (Eds). *Similarity and analogical reasoning.* London: Cambridge University Press.

GESELL, A., & AMATRUDA, C. (1954). *Developmental diagnosis.* New York: Paul B. Holber.

GHATALA, E. S. (1984). Developmental changes in incidental memory as a function of meaningfulness and encoding condition. *Developmental Psychology, 20*, 208–211.

GHATALA, E. S., LEVIN, J. R., PRESSLEY, M., & GOODWIN, D. (1986). A componential analysis of the effects of derived and supplied strategy-utility information on children's strategy selections. *Journal of Experimental Child Psychology, 41*, 76–92.

GIBSON, E. J. (1969). *Principles of perceptual learning and development.* New York: Appleton-Century-Crofts.

GIBSON, E. J., GIBSON, J. J., PICK, A. D., & OSSER, H. (1962). A developmental study of the discrimination of letter-like forms. *Journal of Comparative and Physiological Psychology, 55*, 897–906.

GIBSON, E. J., & SPELKE, E. S. (1983). The development of perception. In J. H. Flavell, & E. M. Markman (Eds.), *Cognitive development.* Vol. 3 of P. H. Mussen (Gen. Ed.), *Handbook of child psychology.* New York: Wiley.

GIBSON, E. J., & WALKER, A. S. (1984). Development of knowledge of visual-tactual affordances of substance. *Child Development, 55*, 453–460.

GIBSON, K. R. (1991). Myelination and behavioral development: A comparative perspective on questions of neoteny, altriciality and intelligence. In K. R Gibson & A. C. Petersen (Eds.), *Brain maturation and cognitive development: Comparative and cross-cultural perspectives.* New York: Aldine de Gruyter.

GIBSON, K. R., & PETERSEN, A. C. (EDS.). (1991). *Brain maturation and cognitive development: Comparative and cross-cultural perspectives.* New York: Aldine de Gruyter.

GLICK, J. (1975). Cognitive development in cross-cultural perspective. In F. Horowitz (Ed.), *Review of child development research* (Vol. 4). Chicago: University of Chicago Press.

GLUCKSBERG, S., KRAUSS, R. M., & WEISBERG, R. (1966). Referential communication in nursery school children: Method and some preliminary findings. *Journal of Experimental Child Psychology, 3*, 333–342.

GOLDFIELD, B. A., & REZNICK, J. S. (1990). Early lexical acquisition: Rate, content, and the vocabulary spurt. *Journal of Child Language, 17*, 171–184.

GOLDSTEIN, D., HASHER, L., & STEIN, D. K. (1983). Processing of occurrence-rate and item information by children of different ages and abilities. *American Journal of Psychology, 96*, 220–241.

GOLLIN, E. S. (1960). Developmental studies of visual recognition of incomplete objects. *Perceptual and Motor Skills, 11*, 289–298.

GOLOMB, C., & GALASSO, L. (1995). Make believe and reality: Explorations of the imaginary realm. *Developmental Psychology, 31*, 800–810.

GOODMAN, G. S., AMAN, C. J., & HIRSCHMAN, J. (1987). Child sexual and physical abuse: Children's testimony. In C. J. Ceci, M. P. Toglia, & D. F. Ross (Eds.), *Children's eyewitness memory.* New York: Springer-Verlag.

GOODMAN, G. S., & CLARKE-STEWART, A. (1991). Suggestibility in children's testimony: Implications for sexual abuse investigations. In J. Doris (Ed.), *The suggestibility of children's recollections: Implications for eye-*

witness testimony. Washington, DC: American Psychological Association.

GOODMAN, G. S., QUAS, J. A., BATTERMAN-FAUNCE, J. M., RIDDLESBERGER, M. M., & KUHN, J. (1997). Children's reactions to and memory for a stressful event: Influences of age, anatomical dolls, knowledge, and parental attachment. *Applied Developmental Science, 1,* 54–75.

GOODMAN, G. S., QUAS, J. A., BATTERMAN-FAUNCE, J. M., RIDDLESBERGER, & KUHN, J. (1994). Predictors of accurate and inaccurate memories of traumatic events experienced in childhood. *Consciousness and Cognition, 3,* 269–294.

GOODMAN, J. F. (1992). *When slow is fast enough: Educating the delayed preschool child.* New York: Guilford.

GOODZ, N. S. (1982). Is before really easier to understand than after? *Child Development, 53,* 822–825.

GOPNIK, A. (1996). The post-Piaget era. *Psychological Science, 7,* 221–225.

GOPNIK, A., & ASTINGTON, J. W. (1988). Children's understanding of representational change and its relation to the understanding of false belief and the appearance-reality distinction. *Child Development, 59,* 26–37.

GOPNIK, A., & CRAGO, M. D. (1991). Familial aggregation of a developmental language disorder. *Cognition, 39,* 1–50.

GOPNIK, A., & MELTZOFF, A. (1987). The development of categorization in the second year and its relation to other cognitive and linguistic developments. *Child Development, 58,* 1523–1531.

GOPNIK, A., & MELTZOFF, A. N. (1992). Categorization and naming: Basic-level sorting in eighteen-month-olds and its relation to language. *Child Development, 63,* 1091–1103.

GOPNIK, A., & MELTZOFF, A. N. (1997). *Words, thoughts, and theories.* Cambridge, MA: MIT Press.

GOPNIK, A., & SLAUGHTER, V. (1991). Young children's understanding of changes in their mental states. *Child Development, 62,* 98–110.

GORDON, A. C. L., & OLSON, D. R. (1998). The relation between acquisition of a theory of mind and the capacity to hold in mind. *Journal of Experimental Child Psychology, 68,* 70–83.

GOSWAMI, U. (1995). Transitive relational mapping in three- and four-year-olds: The analogy of Goldilocks and the Three Bears. *Child Development, 66,* 877–892.

GOSWAMI, U. (1996). Analogical reasoning and cognitive development. In H. W. Reese (Ed.), *Advances in child development and behavior* (Vol. 26). San Diego: Academic.

GOSWAMI, U., & BROWN, A. L. (1990). Higher-order structure and relational reasoning: Contrasting analogical and thematic relations. *Cognition, 36,* 207–226.

GOTTARDO, A., STANOVICH, K. E., & SIEGEL, L. S. (1996). The relationships between phonological sensitivity, syntactic processing, and verbal working memory in the reading performance of third-grade children. *Journal of Experimental Child Psychology, 63,* 563–582.

GOTTLIEB, G. (1971). Ontogenesis of sensory functioning in birds and mammals. In E. Tobach, L. R. Aronson, & E. Shaw (Eds.), *The biopsychology of development.* New York: Academic.

GOTTLIEB, G. (1991a). Experiential canalization of behavioral development: Theory. *Developmental Psychology, 27,* 4–13.

GOTTLIEB, G. (1991b). Experiential canalization of behavioral development: Results. *Developmental Psychology, 27,* 35–39.

GOTTLIEB, G., WAHLSTEN, D., & LICKLITER, R. (1998). The significance of biology for human development: A developmental psychobiological systems view. In R. M. Lerner (Vol. Ed.), *Theoretical models of human development,* Vol. 1, in W. Damon (Gen. Ed.), *Handbook of child psychology.* New York: Wiley.

GOULD, S. J. (1992, February). Mozart and modularity. *Natural History 101,* 8–14.

GOUZE, K. R. (1987). Attention and social problem solving as correlates of aggression in preschool males. *Journal of Abnormal Child Psychology, 15,* 181–197.

GOUZE, K. R., & NADELMAN, L. (1980). Constancy of gender identity for self and others in children between the ages of three and seven. *Child Development, 51,* 275–278.

GOVE, F. L., & KEATING, D. P. (1979). Emphatic role-taking precursors. *Developmental Psychology, 15,* 594–600.

GRAHAM, S., & HUDLEY, C. (1994). Attributions of aggressive and nonaggressive African-American male early adolescents: A study of construct accessibility. *Developmental Psychology, 30,* 365–373.

GRAY, W. M., & HUDSON, L. M. (1984). Formal operations and the imaginary audience. *Developmental Psychology, 20,* 619–627.

GREENE, T. R. (1991). Text manipulations influence children's understandings of class inclusion hierarchies. *Journal of Experimental Child Psychology, 52,* 354–374.

GREENFIELD, D. B., & SCOTT, M. S. (1986). Young children's preferences for complementary pairs: Evidence against a shift to a taxonomic preference. *Developmental Psychology, 22,* 19–21.

GREENFIELD, P. (1972). Oral or written language: The consequences for cognitive development in Africa, the United States, and England. *Language and Speech, 15*, 169–178.

GREENOUGH, W. T., BLACK, J. E., & WALLACE, C. S. (1987). Experience and brain development. *Child Development, 58*, 539–559.

GREENOUGH, W. T., MCDONALD, J., PARNISARI, R., & CAMEL, J. E. (1986). Environmental conditions modulate degeneration and new dendrite growth in cerebellum of senescent rats. *Brain Research, 380*, 136–143.

GRICE, H. P. (1975). Logic and conversation. In P. Cole & J. Morgan (Eds.), *Speech acts: Syntax and semantics*, Vol. 3, New York: Academic.

GRIESER, D., & KUHL, P. K. (1989). Categorization of speech by infants: Support for speech-sound prototypes. *Developmental Psychology, 25*, 577–588.

GROEN, G. J., & RESNICK, L. B. (1977). Can preschool children invent addition algorithms? *Journal of Educational Psychology, 69*, 645–652.

GRUSEC, J. E., & ABRAMOVITCH, R. (1982). Imitation of peers and adults in a natural setting: A functional analysis. *Child Development, 53*, 233–240.

GUBERMAN, S. R. (1996). The development of everyday mathematics in Brazilian children with limited formal education. *Child Development, 67*, 1609–1623.

GUERRA, N. G., HUESMANN, L. R., & HANISH, L. (1995). The role of normative beliefs in children's social behavior. In N. Eisenberg (Ed.), *Review of personality and social psychology, development, and social psychology: The interface.* Thousand Oaks, CA: Sage.

GUILFORD, J. P. (1988). Some changes in the structure-of-the-intellect model. *Educational and Psychological Measurement, 48*, 1–4.

GULYA, M., ROVEE-COLLIER, C., GALLUCCIO, L., & WILK, A. (1998). Memory processing of a serial list by young infants. *Psychological Science, 9*, 303–307.

GUTTENTAG, R. E. (1984). The mental effort requirement of cumulative rehearsal: A developmental study. *Journal of Experimental Child Psychology, 37*, 92–106.

GUTTENTAG, R. E. (1995). Mental effort and motivation: Influences on children's memory strategy use. In F. E. Weinert & W. Schneider (Eds.), *Memory performance and competencies: Issues in growth and development.* Hillsdale, NJ: Erlbaum.

GUTTENTAG, R. E., ORNSTEIN, P. A., & SEIMENS, L. (1987). Children's spontaneous rehearsal: Transitions in strategy acquisition. *Cognitive Development, 2*, 307–326.

HADEN, C. A., & REESE, E. (1994, April). *Gender differences in development of autobiographical memory.* Paper presented at the Conference on Human Development, Pittsburgh, PA.

HADEN, C. A., HAINE, R. A., & FIVUSH, R. (1997). Developing narrative structure in parent-child reminiscing across the preschool years. *Developmental Psychology, 33*, 295–307.

HAGEN, J. W. (1972). Strategies for remembering. In S. Farnham-Diggory (Ed.), *Information processing in children.* New York: Academic.

HAGEN, J. W., & STANOVICH, K. G. (1977). Memory: Strategies of acquisition. In R. V. Kail, Jr., & H. W. Hagen (Eds.), *Perspectives on the development of memory and cognition.* Hillsdale, NJ: Erlbaum.

HAIER, R. J., SIEGEL, B. V., NUECHTERLEIN, K. H., HAZLETT, E., WU, J. C., PAEK, J., BROWNING, H. L., & BUCHSBAUM, M. S. (1988). Cortical glucose metabolic rate correlates of abstract reasoning and attention studies with positron emission tomography. *Intelligence, 12*, 199–217.

HAIER, R. J., SIEGEL, B. V., TANG, C., ABEL, L., & BUCHSBAUM, M. S. (1992). Intelligence and changes in regional cerebral glucose metabolic rate following learning. *Intelligence, 16*, 415–426.

HAITH, M. M. (1966). The response of the human newborn to visual movement. *Journal of Experimental Child Psychology, 3*, 235–243.

HAITH, M. M. (1980). *Rules that babies look by: The organization of newborn visual activity.* Hillsdale, NJ: Erlbaum.

HAITH, M. M. (1993). Preparing for the 21st century: Some goals and challenges for studies of infant sensory and perceptual development. *Developmental Review, 13*, 354–371.

HAITH, M. M., & BENSON, J. B. (1998). Infant cognition. In D. Kuhn & R. S. Siegler (Vol. Eds.), *Cognitive, language, and perceptual development*, Vol. 2. In W. Damon (General Editor), *Handbook of child psychology.* New York: Wiley.

HALA, S., & CHANDLER, M. (1996). The role of strategic planning in accessing false-belief understanding. *Child Development, 67*, 2948–2966.

HALA, S., CHANDLER, M., & FRITZ, A. S. (1991). Fledgling theories of mind: Deception as a marker of three-year-olds' understanding of false belief. *Child Development, 62*, 83–97.

HALE, S., FRY, A. F., & JESSIE, K. A. (1993). Effects of practice on speed of information processing in children and adults: Age sensitivity and age invariants. *Developmental Psychology, 29*, 880–892.

HALFORD, G. S. (1982). *The development of thought.* Hillsdale, NJ: Erlbaum.

HALFORD, G. S. (1993). *Children's understanding: The development of mental models.* Hillsdale, NJ: Erlbaum.

HALPERN, D. F. (1992). *Sex difference in cognitive abilities* (2nd ed.). Hillsdale, NJ: Erlbaum.

HALPERN, D. F. (ED.) (1995). Special issue: Psychological and psychobiological perspectives on sex differences in cognition. I. Theory and research. *Learning and Individual Differences, 7.*

HALPERN, D. F. (1996). Sex, brains, and spatial cognition. *Developmental Review, 16,* 261–270.

HALPERN, D. F. (1997). Sex differences in intelligence. *American Psychologist, 52,* 1091–1102.

HALVERSON, C. F., & WALDROP, M. F. (1973). The relations of mechanically recorded activity level to varieties of preschool play behavior. *Child Development, 44,* 678–681.

HAMANN, M. S., & ASHCRAFT, M. H. (1985). Simple and complex mental addition across development. *Journal of Experimental Child Psychology, 40,* 49–72.

HAMM, V. P., & HASHER, L. (1992). Age and the availability of inferences. *Psychology and Aging, 7,* 56–64.

HAMOND, N. R., & FIVUSH, R. (1991). Memories of Mickey Mouse: Young children recount their trip to Disneyworld. *Cognitive Development, 6,* 433–448.

HAN, J. J., LEITCHMAN, M. D., & WANG, Q. (1998). Autobiographical memory in Korean, Chinese, and American children. *Developmental Psychology, 34,* 701–713.

HANNA, E., & MELTZOFF, A. N. (1993). Peer imitation by toddlers in laboratory, home, and day care contexts: Implications for social learning and memory. *Developmental Psychology, 29,* 701–710.

HANSEN, J., & PEARSON, P. D. (1983). An instructional study: Improving the inferential comprehension of good and poor readers. *Journal of Educational Psychology, 75,* 821–829.

HARLOW, H. (1959, December). The development of learning in the Rhesus monkey. *American Scientist,* 459–479.

HARLOW, H. F., DODSWORTH, R. O., & HARLOW, M. K. (1965). Total isolation in monkeys. *Proceedings of the National Academy of Science, 54,* 90–97.

HARNISHFEGER, K. K. (1995). The development of cognitive inhibition: Theories, definitions, and research evidence. In F. Dempster & C. Brainerd (Eds.), *New perspectives on interference and inhibition in cognition.* New York: Academic.

HARNISHFEGER, K. K., & BJORKLUND, D. F. (1990a). Children's strategies: A brief history. In D. F. Bjorklund (Ed.), *Children's strategies: Contemporary views of cognitive development.* Hillsdale, NJ: Erlbaum.

HARNISHFEGER, K. K., & BJORKLUND, D. F. (1990b). Memory functioning of gifted and nongifted middle school children. *Contemporary Educational Psychology, 15,* 346–363.

HARNISHFEGER, K. K., & BJORKLUND, D. F. (1993). The ontogeny of inhibition mechanisms: A renewed approach to cognitive development. In M. L. Howe & R. Pasnak (Eds.), *Emerging themes in cognitive development: Vol. 1. Foundations.* New York: Springer-Verlag.

HARNISHFEGER, K. K., & BJORKLUND, D. F. (1994). Individual differences in inhibition: Implications for children's cognitive development. *Learning and Individual Differences, 6,* 331–355.

HARNISHFEGER, K. K., & BRAINERD, C. J. (1994). Nonstrategic facilitation of children's recall: Evidence of triage with semantically related information. *Journal of Experimental Child Psychology, 57,* 259–280.

HARNISHFEGER, K. K., & POPE, R. S. (1996). Intending to forget: The development of cognitive inhibition in directed forgetting. *Journal of Experimental Child Psychology, 62,* 292–315.

HARNQUIST, K. (1968). Relative changes in intelligence from 13 to 18. *Scandinavian Journal of Psychology, 9,* 50–64.

HARRIS, L. J. (1978). Sex differences in spatial ability: Possible environmental, genetic and neurological factors. In M. Kinsborne (Ed.), *Asymmetrical function of the brain.* New York: Cambridge University Press.

HARRIS, P. L., BROWN, E., MARRIOTT, C., WHITTALL, S., & HARMER, S. (1991). Monsters, ghosts and witches: Testing the limits of fantasy-reality distinction in young children. *British Journal of Developmental Psychology, 9,* 105–123.

HARTER, S. (1998). The development of self-representation. In N. Eisenberg (Vol. Ed), *Social, emotional, and personality development,* Vol. 3, of W. Damon (Gen. Ed.), *Handbook of child psychology.* New York: Wiley.

HARTER, S., WATERS, P., & WHITESELL, N. R. (1998). Relational self-worth: Differences in perceived worth as a person across interpersonal contexts among adolescents. *Child Development, 69,* 756–766.

HASHER, L., & ZACKS, R. T. (1979). Automatic and effortful processes in memory. *Journal of Experimental Psychology: General, 108,* 356–388.

HASHER, L., & ZACKS, R. T. (1988). Working memory, comprehension, and aging: A review and a new view. In G. H. Bower (Ed.), *The psychology of learning and motivation: Advances in research and theory* (Vol. 22). San Diego: Academic.

Hasselhorn, M. (1992). Task dependency and the role of category typicality and metamemory in the development of an organizational strategy. *Child Development, 63*, 202–214.

Hasselhorn, M. (1995). Beyond production deficiency and utilization inefficiency: Mechanisms of the emergence of strategic categorization in episodic memory tasks. In F. E. Weinert & W. Schneider (Eds.), *Memory performance and competencies: Issues in growth and development*. Hillsdale, NJ: Erlbaum.

Hawkins, J., Pea, R. D., Glick, J., & Scribner, S. (1984). "Merds that laugh don't like mushrooms": Evidence for deductive reasoning by preschoolers. *Developmental Psychology, 20*, 584–594.

Hayes, B. K., & Hennessy, R. (1996). The nature and development of nonverbal implicit memory. *Journal of Experimental Child Psychology, 63*, 22–43.

Haynes, H., White, B. L., & Held, R. (1965). Visual accommodation in human infants. *Science, 148*, 528–530.

Hazen, N. L. (1982). Spatial exploration and spatial knowledge: Individual and developmental differences in very young children. *Child Development, 53*, 826–833.

Heath, S. B. (1989). Oral and literate traditions among Black Americans living in poverty. *American Psychologist, 44*, 367–373.

Hebb, D. O. (1949). *The organization of behavior*. New York: Wiley.

Hedges, L. V., & Nowell, A. (1995). Sex differences in mental test scores, variability, and numbers of high-scoring individuals. *Science, 269* (July 7), 41–45.

Heider, E. R. (1972). Universals in color naming and memory. *Journal of Experimental Psychology, 93*, 10–20.

Heimann, M. (1989). Neonatal imitation gaze aversion and mother-infant interaction. *Infant Behavior and Development, 12*, 495–505.

Heisel, B. E., & Ritter, K. (1981). Young children's storage behavior in a memory for location task. *Journal of Experimental Child Psychology, 31*, 350–364.

Held, R., & Hein, A. (1963). Movement-produced stimulation in the development of visually guided behavior. *Journal of Comparative and Physiological Psychology, 56*, 872–876.

Hellige, J. B. (1993). Unity of thought and action: Varieties of interaction between the left and right cerebral hemispheres. *Current Directions in Psychological Science, 2*, 21–25.

Hendler, M., & Weisberg, P. (1992). Conservation acquisition, maintenance, and generalization by mentally retarded children using equality-rule training. *Journal of Experimental Child Psychology, 54*, 258–276.

Henry, L. A., & Millar, S. (1991). Memory span increases with age: A test of two hypotheses. *Journal of Experimental Child Psychology, 51*, 459–484.

Herman, J. F., Shiraki, J. H., & Miller, B. S. (1985). Young children's ability to infer spatial relationships: Evidence from a large, familiar environment. *Child Development, 36*, 1195–1203.

Herman, J. F., & Siegel, A. W. (1978). The development of cognitive mapping of the large-scale environment. *Journal of Experimental Child Psychology, 26*, 389–406.

Herrnstein, R. J., & Murray, C. (1994). *The bell curve: Intelligence and class structure in American life*. New York: Simon & Schuster.

Hirsh-Pasek, K., & Golinkoff, R. M. (1991). Language comprehension: A new look at some old themes. In N. A. Krasnegor, D. R. Rumbaugh, R. L. Schiefelbusch, & M. Studdert-Kennedy (Eds.), *Biological and behavioral determinants of language development*. Hillsdale, NJ: Erlbaum.

Hirsh-Pasek, K., Golinkoff, R. M., & Naigles, L. (1996). Young children's use of syntactic frames to derive meaning. In K. Hirsh-Pasek & R. M. Golinkoff (Eds.), *The origins of grammar: Evidence from early language comprehension*. Cambridge, MA: MIT Press.

Hiscock, M., & Kinsbourne, M. (1980). Asymmetries of selective listening and attention switching in children. *Developmental Psychology, 16*, 70–82.

Hitch, G. J., & Towse, J. (1995). Working memory: What develops? In F. E. Weinert & W. Schneider (Eds.), *Memory performance and competencies: Issues in growth and development*. Hillsdale, NJ: Erlbaum.

Ho, C. S-K., & Bryant, P. (1997). Phonological skills are important in learning to read Chinese. *Developmental Psychology, 33*, 946–951.

Hock, H. S., Park, C. L., & Bjorklund, D. F. (1998). Temporal organization in children's strategy formation. *Journal of Experimental Child Psychology, 70*, 187–206.

Hoff-Ginsburg, E. (1985). Some contributions of mothers' speech to their children's syntactic growth. *Journal of Child Language, 12*, 367–385.

Hoff-Ginsberg, E. (1997). *Language development*. Pacific Grove, CA: Brooks/Cole.

Hoff-Ginsberg, E. (in press). The social environment and language learning. In H. Grimm (Ed.), *Encyclopedia, Vol 3: Language Development*. Hogrefe-Verlag: Gottingen.

Hoffman, M. L. (1975). Developmental synthesis of affect and cognition and its implications for altruistic motivation. *Developmental Psychology, 11*, 607–622.

Hogrefe, G.-J., Wimmer, H., & Perner, J. (1986). Ignorance versus false belief: A developmental lag in attribution of epistemic states. *Child Development, 57,* 567–582.

Hollingsworth, L. (1918). Comparison of the sexes in mental traits. *Psychological Bulletin, 25,* 427–432.

Holyoak, K. J., Junn, E. N., & Billman, D. O. (1984). Development of analogical problem-solving skills. *Child Development, 55,* 2042–2055.

Honzik, M. P., MacFarlane, J. W. & Allen, L. (1948). Stability of mental test performance between 2 and 18 years. *Journal of Experimental Education, 17,* 309–324.

Howe, M. L. (1991). Misleading children's story recall: Forgetting and reminiscence of the facts. *Developmental Psychology, 27,* 746–762.

Howe, M. L., & Brainerd, C. J. (1989). Development of long-term retention. *Developmental Review, 9,* 302–340.

Howe, M. L., & Courage, M. L. (1993). On resolving the enigma of infantile amnesia. *Psychological Bulletin, 113,* 305–326.

Howe, M. L., & Courage, M. L. (1997). Independent paths in the development of infant learning and forgetting. *Journal of Experimental Child Psychology, 67,* 131–163.

Howe, M. L., & O'Sullivan, J. T. (1997). What children's memories tell us about recalling our childhoods: A review of storage and retrieval processes in the development of long-term retention. *Developmental Review, 17,* 148–204.

Hudson, J. A. (1990). The emergence of autobiographical memory in mother-child conversation. In R. Fivush & J. A. Hudson (Eds.), *Knowing and remembering in young children.* Cambridge: Cambridge University Press.

Hudson, J. A., Shapiro, L. R., & Sosa, B. B. (1995). Planning in the real world: Preschool children's scripts and plans for familiar events. *Child Development, 66,* 984–998.

Hudson, W. (1960). Pictorial depth perception in subcultural Africa. *Journal of Social Psychology, 52,* 183–208.

Hulme, C., Thomson, N., Muir, C., & Lawrence, A. (1984). Speech rate and the development of spoken words: The role of rehearsal and item identification processes. *Journal of Experimental Child Psychology, 38,* 241–253.

Humphrey, G. K., Humphrey, D. E., Muir, D. W., & Dodwell, P. C. (1986). Pattern perception in infants: Effects of structure and transformation. *Journal of Experimental Child Psychology, 41,* 128–148.

Humphrey, N. K. (1976). The social function of intellect. In P. P. G. Bateson & R. A. Hinde (Eds.), *Growing points in ethology.* Cambridge: Cambridge University Press.

Humphreys, L. G. (1980). Me thinks they do protest too much. *Intelligence, 4,* 179–183.

Humphreys, L. G., & Parsons, C. K. (1979). Piagetian tasks measure intelligence and intelligence tests assess cognitive development. *Intelligence, 3,* 369–382.

Humphreys, L. G., Rich, S. A., & Davey, T. C. (1985). A Piagetian test of general intelligence. *Developmental Psychology, 21,* 872–877.

Hunt, E., Davidson, J., & Lansman, M. (1981). Individual difference in long-term memory access. *Memory and Cognition, 9,* 599–608.

Hunter, M., Ames, E., & Koopman, R. (1983). Effects of stimulus complexity and familiarization time on infant preferences for novel and familiar stimuli. *Developmental Psychology, 19,* 352–383.

Huntsinger, C. S., Jose, P. E., & Larson, S. L. (1998). Do parent practices to encourage academic competence influence the social adjustment of young European American and Chinese American children? *Developmental Psychology, 34,* 747–756.

Huttenlocher, J., Levine, S., & Vevea, J. (1998). Environmental input and cognitive growth: A study using time-period comparisons. *Child Development, 69,* 1012-1029.

Huttenlocher, P. R. (1994). Synaptogenesis, synapse elimination, and neural plasticity in human cerebral cortex. In C. A. Nelson (Ed.), Threats to optimal development. *The Minnesota symposium on child psychology,* Vol. 27. Hillsdale, NJ: Erlbaum.

Hutton, U., Wilding, J., & Hudson, R. (1997). The role of attention in the relationship between inspection time and IQ in children. *Intelligence, 24,* 445–460.

Hyde, J. S. (1981). How large are cognitive gender differences? A meta-analysis using ω^2 and d. *American Psychologist, 36,* 892–901.

Hyde, J. S., Fennema, E., & Lamon, S. J. (1990). Gender differences in mathematics performance: A meta-analysis. *Psychological Bulletin, 107,* 139–155.

Hyde, J. S., & Linn, M. C. (1988). Gender differences in verbal ability: A meta-analysis. *Psychological Bulletin, 194,* 53–69.

Hyman, I. E., Husband, T. H., & Billings, F. J. (1995). False memories of childhood experiences. *Applied Cognitive Psychology, 9,* 181–197.

Hymes, D. (1972). On communicative competence. In J. B. Pride & J. Holmes (Eds.), *Sociolinguistics.* Harmondsworth, England: Penguin.

HYMOVITCH, B. (1952). The effects of experimental variations on problem solving in the rat. *Journal of Comparative and Physiological Psychology, 45,* 313–321.

HYSON, M. C., HIRSH-PASEK, K., & RESCORLA, L. (1990). Academic environments in preschool: Challenge or pressure? *Early Education and Development, 1,* 401–423.

INGRAM, D. (1989). *First language acquisition: Method, description, and explanation.* London: Cambridge University Press.

INHELDER, B., & PIAGET, J. (1958). *The growth of logical thinking from childhood to adolescence.* New York: Basic.

INHELDER, B., & PIAGET, J. (1964). *The early growth of logic in the child.* New York: Norton.

ISTOMINA, Z. M. (1975). The development of voluntary memory in preschool-age children. *Soviet Psychology, 13,* 5–64.

JACKSON, J. F. (1993). Human behavioral genetics: Scarr's theory, and her views on intervention: A critical review and commentary on their implications for African American children. *Child Development, 64,* 1318–1332.

JACOBSON, S. W. (1979). Matching behavior in the young infant. *Child Development, 50,* 425–430.

JACOBY, L. L. (1991). A process dissociation framework: Separating automatic from intentional uses of memory. *Journal of Memory and Language, 30,* 513–541.

JACOBY, R., & GLAUBERMAN, N. (EDS.) (1995). *The Bell Curve debate: History, documents, opinions.* New York: Times.

JAKOBSON, R. (1968). *Child language, aphasia, and phonological universals.* The Hague: Mouton.

JENKINS, J. M., & ASTINGTON, J. W. (1996). Cognitive factors and family structure associated with theory of mind development in young children. *Developmental Psychology, 32,* 70–78.

JENSEN, A. R. (1993). Why is reaction time correlated with psychometric g? *Current Directions in Psychological Science, 2,* 53–56.

JENSEN, A. R. (1998). *The g factor: The science of mental ability.* Westport, CT: Praeger

JENSEN, J. K., & NEFF, D. L. (1993). Development of basic auditory discrimination in preschool children. *Psychological Science, 2,* 53–56.

JOHNSON, C. N., & WELLMAN, H. M. (1980). Children's developing understanding of mental verbs: Remember, know, and guess. *Child Development, 51,* 1095–1102.

JOHNSON, D. W., & JOHNSON, R. T. (1987). *Learning together and alone: Cooperative, competitive, and individualistic learning* (2nd edition). Englewood Cliffs, NJ: Prentice Hall.

JOHNSON, D. W., & JOHNSON, R. T. (1989). *Cooperation and competition: Theory and research.* Edina, MN: Interaction.

JOHNSON, J. S., & NEWPORT, E. L. (1989). Critical period effects in second language learning: The influence of instructional state on the acquisition of English as a second language. *Cognitive Psychology, 21,* 60–99.

JOHNSON, K. E., & MERVIS, C. B. (1994). A microgenetic analysis of first steps in children's acquisition of expertise on shorebirds. *Developmental Psychology, 30,* 418–435.

JOHNSON, K. E., & MERVIS, C. B. (1997). The first steps in emergence of verbal humor: A case study. *Infant Behavior and Development, 20,* 187–196.

Johnson, K. E., & Mervis, C. B. (1998). Impact of intuitive theories on feature recruitment throughout the continuum of expertise. *Memory & Cognition, 26,* 383–401.

JOHNSON, M. H. (1998). The neural basis of cognitive development. In D. Kuhn & R. S. Siegler (Vol. Eds.), *Cognition, perception, and language* (Vol. 2). In W. Damon (Gen. Ed.), *Handbook of child psychology* (5th edition). New York: Wiley.

JOHNSON, M. H., DZIURAWIEC, S., ELLIS, H. D., & MORTON, J. (1991). Newborns' preferential tracking of faces and its subsequent decline. *Cognition, 40,* 1–19.

JOHNSON, S. P., & ASLIN, R. N. (1995). Perception of object unity in 2-month-old infants. *Developmental Psychology, 31,* 739–745.

JOHNSON, S. P., & ASLIN, R. N. (1996). Perception of object unity in young infants: The roles of motion, depth, and orientation. *Cognitive Development, 11,* 161–180.

JONES, S. S. (1996). Imitation or exploration? Young infants' matching of adults' oral gestures. *Child Development, 67,* 1952–1969.

JOYNER, M. H., & KURTZ-COSTES, B. (1997). Metamemory development. In N. Cowan (Ed.), *The development of memory in childhood.* Hove East Sussex, UK: Psychology Press.

JUSTICE, E. M. (1985). Categorization as a preferred memory strategy: Developmental changes during elementary school. *Developmental Psychology, 21,* 1105–1110.

JUSTICE, E. M., BAKER-WARD, L., GUPTA, S., & JANNINGS, L. R. (1997). Means to the goal of remembering: Developmental changes in awareness of strategy use-performance relations. *Journal of Experimental Child Psychology, 65,* 293–314.

KAGAN, J. (1971). *Change and continuity in infancy.* New York: Wiley.

KAGAN, J. (1976). New views on cognitive development. *Journal of Youth and Adolescence, 5,* 113–129.

KAGAN, J., & KLEIN, R. E. (1973). Cross-cultural perspectives on early development. *American Psychologist, 28,* 947–961.

KAGAN, J., KLEIN, R. E., FINLEY, G. E., ROGOFF, B., & NOLAN E. (1979). A cross-cultural study of cognitive development. *Monographs of the Society for Research in Child Development, 44* (Serial No. 180).

KAIL, R. V., JR. (1979). Use of strategies and individual differences in children's memory. *Developmental Psychology, 15,* 251–255.

KAIL, R. (1990). *The development of memory in children* (3rd ed.). New York: W. H. Freeman.

KAIL, R. (1991). Development of processing speed in childhood and adolescence. In H. W. Reese (Ed.), *Advances in child development and behavior* (Vol. 23). San Diego: Academic.

KAIL, R. (1993). The role of a global mechanism in developmental change in speed of processing. In M. L. Howe & R. Pasnak (Eds.), *Emerging themes in cognitive development: Vol. 1. Foundations.* New York: Springer-Verlag.

KAIL, R. (1997). Processing time, imagery, and spatial memory. *Journal of Experimental Child Psychology, 64,* 67–78.

KAIL, R. V., & LEVINE, L. E. (1976). Encoding processes and sex-role preferences. *Journal of Experimental Child Psychology, 21,* 256–263.

KAIL, R., & PARK, Y-S. (1994). Processing time, articulation time, and memory span. *Journal of Experimental Child Psychology, 57,* 281–291.

KAIL, R. V., & SALTHOUSE, T. A. (1994). Processing speed as a mental capacity. *Acta Psychologica, 86,* 199–225.

KAIL, R. V., JR., & SIEGEL, A. W. (1977). Sex differences in retention of verbal and spatial characteristics of stimuli. *Journal of Experimental Child Psychology, 23,* 341–347.

KAITZ, M., MESCHULACH-SARFATY, O., AUERBACH, J., & EIDELMAN, A. (1988). A reexamination of newborns' ability to imitate facial expressions. *Developmental Psychology, 24,* 3–7.

KALER, S. R., & FREEDMAN, B. J. (1994). Analysis of environmental deprivation: Cognitive and social development in Romanian orphans. *Journal of Child Psychology and Psychiatry, 35,* 769–781

KALICHMAN, S. C. (1988). Individual differences in water-level task performance: A component-skill analysis. *Developmental Review, 8,* 273–295.

KARMILOFF-SMITH, A. (1979). *A functional approach to language.* Cambridge: Cambridge University Press.

KARMILOFF-SMITH, A. (1991). Beyond modularity: Innate constraints and developmental change. In S. Carey & R. Gelman (Eds.), *The epigenesis of mind: Essays on biology and cognition.* Hillsdale, NJ: Erlbaum.

KARMILOFF-SMITH, A. (1992). *Beyond modularity: A developmental perspective on cognitive science.* Cambridge, MA: MIT Press.

KAROLY, L. A., GREENWOOD, P. W., EVERINGHAM, S. S., HOUBÉ, J., KILBURN, M. R., RYDELL, C. P., SANDERS, M., & CHIESA, J. (1998). *Investing in our children: What we know and don't know about the costs and benefits of early childhood interventions.* RAND Distribution Services.

KARP, S. A., & KONSTADT, N. (1971). *Children's Embedded Figures Test.* Palo Alto, CA: Consulting Psychologists.

KARZON, R. G. (1985). Discrimination of polysyllabic sequences by one- to four-month-old infants. *Journal of Experimental Child Psychology, 39,* 326–342.

KATZ, S., & LAUTENSCHLAGER, G. J. (1994). Answering reading comprehension items without passages on the SAT-I, the ACT, and the GRE. *Educational Assessment, 2,* 295-308.

KATZ, S., LAUTENSCHLAGER, G. J., BLACKBURN, A. B., & HARRIS, F. (1990). Answering reading comprehension items without passages on the SAT. *Psychological Science, 1,* 122–127.

KAUFMAN, A. S., & KAUFMAN, N. L. (1983). *Kaufman Assessment Battery for Children (K-ABC).* Circle Pines, MN: American Guidance Service.

KAYE, D. B. (1986). The development of mathematical cognition. *Cognitive Development, 1,* 157–170.

KAYE, K. (1982). *The mental and social life of babies: How parents create persons.* Chicago: University of Chicago Press.

KAYE, K., & MARCUS, J. (1981). Infant imitation: The sensory-motor agenda. *Developmental Psychology, 17,* 258–265.

KEARINS, J. M. (1981). Visual-spatial memory in Australian aboriginal children of desert regions. *Cognitive Psychology, 13,* 434–460.

KEATING, D. P., & BOBBITT, B. L. (1979). Individual differences in cognitive processing: Components of mental ability. *Child Development, 49,* 155–167.

KEE, D. W. (1994). Developmental differences in associative memory: Strategy use, mental effort, and knowledge-access interactions. In H. W. Reese (Ed.), *Advances in child development and behavior* (Vol. 25). New York: Academic.

KEE, D. W., & DAVIES, L. (1990). Mental effort and elaboration: Effects of accessibility and instruction. *Journal of Experimental Child Psychology, 49*, 264–274.

KEIL, F. C. (1998). Cognitive science and the origins of thought and knowledge. In R. M. Lerner (Vol. Ed.), *Theoretical models of human development*, Vol. 1, of W. Damon (Gen. Ed.), *Handbook of child psychology*. New York: Wiley.

KEIL, F. C., & BATTERMAN, N. (1984). A characteristic-to-defining shift in the development of word meaning. *Journal of Verbal Learning and Verbal Behavior, 23*, 221–236.

KELLER, A., FORD, L. H., JR., & MEACHUM, J. A. (1978). Dimensions of self-concept in preschool children. *Developmental Psychology, 14*, 483–489.

KELLER, D., & KELLAS, G. (1978). Typicality as a dimension of encoding. *Journal of Experimental Psychology: Human Learning and Memory, 4*, 78–85.

KELLMAN, P. H., & BANKS, M. S. (1998). Infant visual perception. In D. Kuhn & R. S. Siegler (Vol. Eds.), *Cognitive, language, and perceptual development*, Vol. 2. In W. Damon (Gen. Ed.), *Handbook of child psychology*. New York: Wiley.

KELLMAN, P. J., & SPELKE, E. S. (1983). Perception of partly occluded objects in infancy. *Cognitive Development, 15*, 483–524.

KERMOIAN, R., & CAMPOS, J. J. (1988). Locomotor experience: A facilitator of spatial cognitive development. *Child Development, 59*, 908–917.

KESSEN, W. (1996). American psychology just before Piaget. *Psychological Science, 7*, 196–199.

KIM, K. H. S., RELKIN, N. R., LEE, K-M., & HIRSCH, J. ET AL. (1997). Distinct cortical areas associated with native and second languages. *Nature, 388* (July 12), 171–174.

KINGMA, J. (1984). Traditional intelligence, Piagetian tasks, and initial arithmetic in kindergarten and primary school grade one. *Journal of Genetic Psychology, 145*, 49–60.

KIPP, K., & POPE, S. (1997). The development of cognitive inhibition in stream-of-consciousness and directed speech. *Cognitive Development, 12*, 239–260.

KLACZYNSKI, P. A. (1997). Bias in adolescents' everyday reasoning and its relationship with intellectual ability, personal theories, and self-serving motivation. *Developmental Psychology, 33*, 273–283.

KLACZYNSKI, P. A., & NARASIMHAM, G. (1998). Development of scientific reasoning biases: Cognitive versus ego-protective explanations. *Developmental Psychology, 34*, 175–187.

KLAHR, D., & MACWHINNEY, B. (1998). Information processing. In D. Kuhn & R. S. Siegler (Vol. Eds.), *Cognitive, language, and perceptual development*, Vol. 2. In W. Damon (Gen. Ed.), *Handbook of child psychology*. New York: Wiley.

KLAHR, D., & ROBINSON, M. (1981). Formal assessment of problem solving and planning processes in preschool children. *Cognitive Psychology, 13*, 113–148.

KLAUS, R. A., & GRAY S. (1968). The early training project for disadvantaged children: A report after five years. *Monographs of the Society for Research in Child Development, 33* (Serial No. 120).

KOBASIGAWA, A. (1974). Utilization of retrieval cues by children in recall. *Child Development, 45*, 127–134.

KOCHANSKA, G., MURRAY, K., JACQUES, T. Y., KOENIG, A. L., & VANDEGEEST, K. A. (1996). Inhibitory control in young children and its role in emerging internalization. *Child Development, 67*, 490–507.

KOHLBERG, L. (1966). A cognitive-developmental analysis of children's sex-role concepts and attitudes. In E. E. Maccoby (Ed.), *The development of sex differences*. Stanford, CA: Stanford University Press.

KOHLBERG, L., YAEGER, J., & HJERTHOLM, E. (1968). Private speech: Four studies and a review of theories. *Child Development, 39*, 691–736.

KOLB, B., & WHISHAW, I. Q. (1981). Neonatal frontal lesions in the rat: Sparing of learned but not species-typical behavior in the presence of reduced brain weight and critical thickness. *Journal of Comparative and Physiological Psychology, 95*, 235–276.

KOLB, B., & WHISHAW, I. Q. (1990). *Fundamentals of human neuropsychology* (3rd edition). San Francisco: W. H. Freeman.

KOLUCHOVA, J. (1976). A report on the further development of twins after severe and prolonged deprivation. In A. M. Clarke and A. D. B. Clarke (Eds.), *Early experience: Myth and evidence*. London: Open Books.

KOPP, C. B., & McCALL, R. B. (1982). Predicting later mental performance for normal, at-risk, and handicapped infants. In P. B. Baltes & O. G. Brim (Eds.), *Life-span development and behavior* (Vol. 4). New York: Academic.

KOPP, C. B., SIGMAN, M., & PARMELEE, A. H. (1974). Longitudinal study of sensorimotor development. *Developmental Psychology, 10*, 687–695.

KORNER, M. (1991). Universals of behavioral development in relation to brain myelination. In K. R. Gibson & A. C. Petersen (Eds.), *Brain maturation and cognitive development: Comparative and cross-cultural perspectives*. New York: Aldine de Gruyter.

KORNHUBER, H. H., BECHINGER, D., JUNG, H., & SAUER, E. (1985). A quantitative relationship between the extent of localized cerebral lesions and the intellectual and behavioral deficiency in children. *European*

Archives of Psychiatry and Neurological Science, 235, 125–133.

KOSHMIDER, J. W., & ASHCRAFT, M. H. (1991). The development of children's mental multiplication skills. *Journal of Experimental Child Psychology, 51,* 53–89.

KRACKOW, E., & GORDON, P. (1998). Are lions and tigers substitutes or associates? Evidence against slot filler accounts of children's early categorization. *Child Development, 69,* 347–354.

KRATOCHWILL, T. R., & GOLDMAN, J. A. (1973). Developmental changes in children's judgments of age. *Developmental Psychology, 9,* 358–362.

KREUTZER, M. A., LEONARD, C., & FLAVELL, J. H. (1975). An interview study of children's knowledge about memory. *Monographs of the Society for Research in Child Development, 40* (Serial No. 159).

KRUMHANSL, C. L., & JUSCZYK, P. W. (1990). Infants' perception of phrase structure in music. *Psychological Science, 1,* 70–73.

KUHL, P. K. (1987). Perception of speech and sound in early infancy. In P. Salapatek & L. Cohen (Eds.), *Handbook of infant perception.* New York: Academic.

KUHL, P. K. (1992). Speech prototypes: Studies on the nature, function, ontogeny and phylogeny of the "centers" of speech categories. In Y. Tohkura, E. Vatikiotis-Bateson, & Y. Sagiska (Eds.), *Speech perception, production and linguistic structure.* Tokyo: Ohmsha.

KUHL, P. K., ANDRUSKI, J. E., CHRISTOVICH, I. A., CHRISTOVICH, L. A., KOZHEVNIKOVA, E. V., RYSKINA, V. L., STOLYAROVA, E. I., SUNDBERG, U., & LACERDA, F. (1997). Cross-language analysis of phonetic units in language addressed to infants. *Science, 277* (1 August), 684–686.

KUHN, D. (1976). Relation of two Piagetian stage transitions to IQ. *Developmental Psychology, 12,* 157–161.

KUHN, D. (1989). Children and adults as intuitive scientists. *Psychological Review, 96,* 674–689.

KUHN, D., AMSEL, E., & O'LOUGHLIN, M. (1988). *The development of scientific thinking skills.* San Diego: Academic.

KUHN, D., & BRANNOCK, J. (1977). Development of the isolation of variable scheme in experimental and "natural experiment" contexts. *Developmental Psychology, 13,* 9–14.

KUHN, D., GARCIA-MILA, M., ZOHAR, A., & ANDERSEN, C. (1995). Strategies of knowledge acquisition. *Monographs of the Society for Research in Child Development, 60* (Serial No. 245).

KUHN, D., LANGER, J., KOHLBERG, L., & HAAN, N. S. (1977). The development of formal operations in logical and moral judgment. *Genetic Psychology Monographs, 95,* 97–188.

KUHN, D., NASH, S. C., & BRUCKEN, L. (1978). Sex role concepts of two- and three-year-olds. *Child Development, 49,* 445–451.

KUNZINGER, E. L., & WITRYOL, S. L. (1984). The effects of differential incentives in second-grade rehearsal and free recall. *Journal of Genetic Psychology, 144,* 19–30.

KURTZ, B. E. (1990). Cultural differences in children's cognitive and metacognitive development. In W. Schneider & F. E. Weinert (Eds.), *Interactions among aptitudes, strategies, and knowledge in cognitive performance.* New York: Springer-Verlag.

KURTZ, B. E., SCHNEIDER, W., CARR, M., BORKOWSKI, J. G., & RELLINGER, E. (1990). Strategy instruction and attributional beliefs in West Germany and the United States: Do teachers foster metacognitive development? *Contemporary Educational Psychology, 15,* 268–283.

KURTZ, B. E., & WEINERT, F. E. (1989). Metamemory, memory performance, and causal attributions in gifted and average children. *Journal of Experimental Child Psychology, 48,* 45–61.

KURTZ-COSTES, B., SCHNEIDER, W., & RUPP, S. (1995). Is there evidence for intraindividual consistency in performance across memory tasks? New evidence on an old question. In F. E. Weinert & W. Schneider (Eds.), *Memory performance and competencies: Issues in growth and development.* Hillsdale, NJ: Erlbaum.

LABORATORY OF COMPARATIVE HUMAN COGNITION. (1983). Culture and cognitive development. In W. Kessen (Ed.), *History, theory, and methods.* Vol. 1 of P. H. Mussen (Gen. Ed.), *Handbook of child psychology.* New York: Wiley.

LANDRY, S. H., SMITH, K. E., MILLER-LONCAR, C. L., & SWANK, P. R. (1997). Predicting cognitive-language and social growth curves from early maternal behaviors in children at varying degrees of biological risk. *Developmental Psychology, 33,* 1040–1053.

LANE, D. M., & PEARSON, D. A. (1982). The development of selective attention. *Merrill-Palmer Quarterly, 28,* 317–337.

LANE, M. K., & HODKIN, B. (1985). Role of atypical exemplars of social and nonsocial superordinate categories within the class inclusion paradigm. *Developmental Psychology, 21,* 909–915.

LANGE, G., GUTTENTAG, R. E., & NIDA, R. E. (1990). Relationships between study organization, retrieval organization, and general strategy-specific memory knowledge in young children. *Journal of Experimental Child Psychology, 49,* 126–146.

LANGE, G., & JACKSON, P. (1974). Personal organization in children's free recall. *Child Development, 45,* 1060–1067.

LANGE, G., & PIERCE, S. H. (1992). Memory-strategy learning and maintenance in preschool children. *Developmental Psychology, 28,* 453–462.

LANGLOIS, J. H., RITTER, J. M., ROGGMAN, L. A., & VAUGHN, L. S. (1991). Facial diversity and infant preferences for attractive faces. *Developmental Psychology, 27,* 79–84.

LANGLOIS, J. H., & ROGGMAN, L. A. (1990). Attractive faces are only average. *Psychological Science, 1,* 115–121.

LANGLOIS, J. H., ROGGMAN, L. A., CASEY, R. J., RITTER, J. M., RIESER-DANNER, L. A., & JENKINS, V. Y. (1987). Infant preferences for attractive faces: Rudiments of a stereotype? *Developmental Psychology, 23,* 363–369.

LANGLOIS, J. H., ROGGMAN, L. A., & RIESER-DANNER, L. A. (1990). Infants' differential social responses to attractive and unattractive faces. *Developmental Psychology, 26,* 153–159.

LARSON, G. E., HAIER, R. J., LaCASSE, L., & HAZEN, K. (1995). Evaluation of a "mental effort" hypothesis for correlations between cortical metabolism and intelligence. *Intelligence, 21,* 267–278.

LASKY, R. E., SYRDAL-LASKY, A., & KLEIN, R. E. (1975). VOT discrimination by four- to six-and-a-half-month-old infants from Spanish environments. *Journal of Experimental Child Psychology, 20,* 215–225.

LaVOIE, J. C., ANDERSON, K., FRAZE, B., & JOHNSON, K. (1981). Modeling, tuition, and sanction effects on self-control at different ages. *Journal of Experimental Child Psychology, 31,* 446–455.

LAZAR, I., DARLINGTON, R., MURRAY, H., ROYCE, J., & SNIPPER, A. (1982). Lasting effects of early education: A report from the Consortium for Longitudinal Studies. *Monographs of the Society for Research in Child Development, 47* (Serial No. 195).

LEAL, L., CRAYS, N., & MOELY, B. E. (1985). Training children to use a self-monitoring study strategy in preparation for recall: Maintenance and generalization effects. *Child Development, 56,* 643–653.

LEAPER, C., ANDERSON, K. J., & SANDERS, P. (1998). Moderators of gender effects on parents' talk to their children: A meta-analysis. *Developmental Psychology, 34,* 3–27.

LeBLANC, R. S., MUISE, J. G., & BLANCHARD, L. (1992). Backward masking in children and adolescents: Sensory transmission, accrual rate and asymptotic performance. *Journal of Experimental Child Psychology, 53,* 105–114.

LECOURS, A. R. (1975). Myelogenetic correlates of the development of speech and language. In E. H. Lenneberg & E. Lenneberg (Eds.), *Foundations of language development: A multidisciplinary approach.* New York: Academic.

LEE, E. S. (1951). Migration: A Philadelphia test of the Klineberg hypothesis. *American Journal of Sociology, 16,* 227–232.

LEGERSTEE, M. (1991). The role of person and object in eliciting early imitation. *Journal of Experimental Child Psychology, 51,* 423–433.

LEGERSTEE, M., ANDERSON, D., & SCHAFFER, A. (1998). Five- and eight-month-old infants recognize their faces and voices as familiar social stimuli. *Child Development, 69,* 37–50.

LEHMAN, E. B., McKINLEY-PACE, M. J., WILSON, J. A., SAVSKY, M. D., & WOODSON, M. E. (1997). Direct and indirect measures of intentional forgetting in children and adults: Evidence for retrieval inhibition and reinstatement. *Journal of Experimental Child Psychology, 64,* 295–316.

LEICHTMAN, M. D., & CECI, S. J. (1993). The problem of infantile amnesia: Lessons from fuzzy-trace theory. In M. L. Howe & R. Pasnak (Eds.), *Emerging themes in cognitive development: Vol. 1. Foundations.* New York: Springer-Verlag.

LEICHTMAN, M. D., & CECI, S. J. (1995). The effect of stereotypes and suggestion on preschoolers reports. *Developmental Psychology, 31,* 568–578.

LEINBACH, M. D., HORT, B. E., & FAGOT, B. I. (1997). Bears are for boys: Metaphorical associations in young children's gender stereotypes. *Cognitive Development, 12,* 107–130.

LENG, X., & SHAW, G. L. (1991). Toward a neural theory of higher brain function using music as a window. *Concepts in Neuroscience, 2,* 229–258.

LENNEBERG, E. H. (1967). *Biological foundations of language.* New York: Wiley.

LERNER, R. M. (1991). Changing organism-context relations as the basic process of development: A developmental contextual perspective. *Developmental Psychology, 27,* 27–32.

LESLIE, A. (1994). ToMM, ToBy, and agency: Core architecture and domain specificity. In L. Hirschfeld & S. Gelman (eds.), *Mapping the mind: Domain specificity in cognition and culture.* Cambridge: Cambridge University Press.

LEVIN, I., & DRUYAN, S. (1993). When sociocognitive transaction among peers fails: The case of misconceptions in science. *Child Development, 64,* 1571–1591.

LEVINE, S. C. (1993). Effects of early unilateral lesions: Changes over the course of development. In G. Turkewitz & D. A. Devenny (Eds.), *Developmental time and timing*. Hillsdale, NJ: Erlbaum.

LEVY, G. D., & CARTER, D. B. (1989). Gender schema, gender constancy, and gender-role knowledge: The roles of cognitive factors in preschoolers' gender-role stereotype attributions. *Developmental Psychology, 25,* 444–449.

LEVY, G. D., & FIVUSH, R. (1993). Scripts and gender: A new approach for examining gender-role development. *Developmental Review, 13,* 126–146.

LEWIS, C., FREEMAN, N. H., KYRIAKIDOU, C., MARIDAKI-KASSOTAKI, K., & BERRIDGE, D. M. (1996). Social influence on false belief access: Specific sibling influences or general apprenticeship? *Child Development, 67,* 2930–2947.

LEWIS, C., & OSBORNE, A. (1990). Three-year-olds' problems with false belief: Conceptual deficits of linguistic artifact. *Child Development, 61,* 1514–1519.

LEWIS, M. (1969). Infants' responses to facial stimuli during the first year of life. *Developmental Psychology, 1,* 75–86.

LEWIS, M. (1991). Ways of knowing: Objective self-awareness of consciousness? *Developmental Review, 11,* 231–243.

LEWIS, M., ALESSANDRI, S. M., & SULLIVAN, M. W. (1990). Violation of expectancy, loss of control and anger expression in young infants. *Developmental Psychology, 63,* 630–638.

LEWIS, M., & BROOKS-GUNN, J. (1979). *Social cognition and the acquisition of self.* New York: Plenum.

LEWIS, M., & FREEDLE, R. O. (1973). Mother-infant dyad: The cradle of meaning. In P. Pilner, L. Krames, & T. Alloway (Eds.), *Communication and affect: Language and thought.* New York: Academic.

LEWIS, M., & SULLIVAN, M. W. (1985). Imitation in the first month of life. *Merrill-Palmer Quarterly, 31,* 315–333.

LEWIS, M., SULLIVAN, M. W., STANGER, C., & WEISS, M. (1989). Self development and self-conscious emotions. *Child Development, 60,* 146–156.

LIBEN, L. S. (1981). Copying and reproducing pictures in relation to subjects' operative levels. *Developmental Psychology, 17,* 357–365.

LIBEN, L. S., & GOLBECK, S. L. (1980). Sex differences in performance on Piagetian spatial tasks: Differences in competence or performance? *Child Development, 51,* 594–597.

LIBEN, L. S., & GOLBECK, S. L. (1984). Performance on Piagetian horizontality and verticality tasks: Sex-related differences in knowledge of relevant physical phenomena. *Developmental Psychology, 20,* 595–606.

LIBEN, L. S., & SIGNORELLA, M. L. (1993). Gender-schematic processing in children: The role of initial interpretations of stimuli. *Developmental Psychology, 29,* 141–149.

LIBERMAN, I. Y., & SHANKWEILER, D. (1977). Speech, the alphabet, and teaching to read. In L. B. Resnick & P. A. Weaver (Eds.), *Theory and practice of early reading.* Hillsdale, NJ: Erlbaum.

LIBERMAN, I. Y., SHANKWEILER, D., FISCHER, R. N., & CARTER, B. (1974). Explicit syllable and phoneme segmentation in the young child. *Journal of Experimental Child Psychology, 18,* 201–212.

LICKLITER, R. (1990). Premature visual stimulation accelerates intersensory functioning in bobwhite quail neonates. *Developmental Psychobiology, 23,* 15–27.

LIE, E., & NEWCOMBE, N. S. (1999). Elementary school children's explicit and implicit memory for faces of preschool classmates. *Developmental Psychology, 35,* 102-112.

LIEBERMAN P. (1967). *Intonations, perception, and language.* Cambridge, MA: MIT Press.

LILLARD, A. (1998). Ethnopsychologies: Cultural variations in theories of mind. *Psychological Bulletin,123,* 3–32.

LIN, C.-Y. C., & FU, V. R. (1990). A comparison of child-rearing practices among Chinese, immigrant Chinese, and Caucasian-American parents. *Child Development, 61,* 429–433.

LINDBERG, M. (1980). The role of knowledge structures in the ontogeny of learning. *Journal of Experimental Child Psychology, 30,* 401–410.

LINN, M. C., & PETERSEN, A. C. (1985). Emergence and characterization of sex differences in spatial ability: A meta-analysis. *Child Development, 56,* 1479–1498.

LIST, J. A., KEATING, D. P., & MERRIMAN, W. E. (1985). Differences in memory retrieval: A construct validity investigation. *Child Development, 56,* 138–151.

LIVESLEY, W., & BROMLEY, D. (1973). *Person perception in childhood and adolescence.* New York: Wiley.

LIVESEY, D. J., & INTILI, D. (1996). A gender difference in visual-spatial ability in 4-year-old children: Effects on performance of a kinesthetic acuity task. *Journal of Experimental Child Psychology, 63,* 436–446.

LOBEL, T. E., & MENASHRI, J. (1993). Relations of conceptions of gender-role transgressions and gender constancy to gender-typed toy preferences. *Developmental Psychology, 29,* 150–155.

LOCKE, J. L. (1983). *Phonological acquisition and change.* New York: Academic.

LOCKE, J. L. (1993). *The child's path to spoken language.* Cambridge, MA: Harvard University Press.

LOCKE, J. L. (1994). Phases in the child's development of language. *American Scientist, 82,* 436–445.

LOCKE, J. L. (1997). A theory of neurolinguistic development. *Brain and Language, 58,* 265–326.

LOFTUS, E. F. (1992). When a lie becomes memory's truth: Memory distortion after exposure to misinformation. *Current Directions in Psychological Science, 1,* 121–123.

LOFTUS, E. F., & PICKRELL, J. E. (1995). The formation of false memories. *Psychiatric Annals, 25,* 720–725.

LONGSTRETH, L. E. (1981). Revisiting Skeels' final study: A critique. *Developmental Psychology, 17,* 620–625.

LOPEZ, D. F., LITTLE, T. D., OETTINGEN, & BALTES, P. B. (1998). Self-regulation and school performance: Is there optimal level of action-control? *Journal of Experimental Child Psychology, 70,* 54–74.

LORCH, E. P., & CASTLE, V. J. (1997). Preschool children's attention to television: Visual attention and probed response times. *Journal of Experimental Child Psychology, 66,* 111–127.

LORSBACH, T. C., KATZ, G. A., & CUPAK, A. J. (1998). Developmental differences in the ability to inhibit the initial misinterpretation of garden path passages. *Journal of Experimental Child Psychology, 71,* 275-296.

LORSBACH, T. C., & REIMER, J. F. (1997). Developmental changes in the inhibition of previously relevant information. *Journal of Experimental Child Psychology, 64,* 317–342.

LOVELL, K. (1961). A follow-up study of Inhelder and Piaget's "The growth of logical thinking." *British Journal of Psychology, 52,* 143–153.

LOVETT, S. B., & FLAVELL, J. H. (1990). Understanding and remembering: Children's knowledge about the differential effects of strategy and task variables on comprehension and memorization. *Child Development, 61,* 1842–1858.

LUBINSKI, D., & BENBOW, C. P. (1992). Gender differences in abilities and preferences among the gifted: Implications for the math-science pipeline. *Current Directions in Psychological Science, 1,* 61–66.

LUBINSKI, D., BENBOW, C. P., & SANDER, C. (1993). Reconceptualizing gender differences in achievement among the gifted. In K. A. Keller, F. J. Monks, & A. H. Passow (Eds.), *International handbook of research on and development of giftedness and talent.* New York: Pergamon.

LUCARIELLO, J. (1998). Together wherever we go: The ethnographic child and the developmentalists. *Child Development, 69,* 355–358.

LUCARIELLO, J., KYRATZIS, & NELSON, K. (1992). Taxonomic knowledge: What kind and when? *Child Development, 63,* 978–998.

LUCARIELLO, J., & NELSON, K. (1985). Slot-filler categories as memory organizers for young children. *Developmental Psychology, 21,* 272–282.

LUECKE-ALESKA, D., ANDERSON, D. R., COLLINS, P. A., & SCHMITT, K. L. (1995). Gender constancy and television viewing. *Developmental Psychology, 31,* 773–780.

LUNDBERG, I., FROST, J., & PETERSON, O.-P. (1988). Effects of an extensive programme for stimulating phonological awareness in pre-school children. *Reading Research Quarterly, 23,* 264-284.

LUNZAR, F. A., DOLAN, T., & WILKINSON, J. E. (1976). The effectiveness of measures of operativity, language, and short-term memory in the prediction of reading and mathematical understanding. *British Journal of Educational Psychology, 46,* 295–305.

LURIA, A. R. (1961). *The role of speech in the regulation of normal and abnormal behavior.* New York: Liveright.

LURIA, A. R. (1973). *The working brain.* New York: Basic Books.

LURIA, A. R. (1976). *Cognitive development: Its cultural and social foundations.* Cambridge, MA: Harvard University Press.

LYNCH, M. P., EILERS, R. E., OLLER, K., & URBANO, R. C. (1990). Innateness, experience, and music perception. *Psychological Science, 1,* 272–276.

LYNN, S. J., LOCK, T. G., MYERS, B., & PAYNE, D. G. (1997). Recalling the unrecallable: Should hypnosis be used to recover memories in psychotherapy? *Current Directions in Psychological Science, 6,* 79–83.

LYONS, J. (1978). *Semantics,* Vol. 1. New York: Cambridge University Press.

MACCOBY, E. E., & JACKLIN, C. N. (1974). *The psychology of sex differences.* Stanford, CA: Stanford University Press.

MACFARLANE, A. (1975). Olfaction in the development of social preferences in the humane neonate. *CIBA Foundation Symposium 33: Parent-infant interaction.* Amsterdam, The Netherlands: Elsevier.

MACLEAN, P. D. (1990). *The triune brain in evolution: Role in paleocerebral functions.* New York: Plenum.

MAGNUSSON, D., & CAIRNS, R. B. (1996). Developmental science: Toward a unified framework. In R. B. Cairns, G. H. Elder, Jr., & E. J. Costello (Eds.), *Developmental Science.* New York: Cambridge University Press.

MAKIN, J. W., & PORTER, R. H. (1989). Attractiveness of lactating females' breast odors to neonates. *Child Development, 60,* 803–810.

MALLOY, P. (1987). Frontal lobe dysfunction in obsessive-compulsive disorder. In E. Perecman (Ed.), *The frontal lobes revisited*. New York: IRBN.

MANDEL, D. R., JUSCZYK, P. W., & PISONI, D. B. (1995). Infants' recognition of sound patterns of their own names. *Psychological Science, 5*, 314–317.

MANDLER, G. (1967). Organization and memory. In K. W. Spence & J. T. Spence (Eds.), *The psychology of learning and motivation* (Vol. 1). New York: Academic.

MANDLER, J. M. (1990). Recall and its verbal expression. In R. Fivush & J. Hudson (Eds.), *Knowing and remembering in young children*. Cambridge: Cambridge University Press.

MANDLER, J. M. (1992). How to build a baby: II. Conceptual primitives. *Psychological Review, 99*, 587–604.

MANDLER, J. (1998). Representation. In D. Kuhn & R. S. Siegler (Eds.), *Cognition, perception, and language*, Vol. 2, of W. Damon (Gen. Ed.), *Handbook of child psychology*. New York: Wiley.

MANDLER, J. M., & BAUER, P. J. (1988). The cradle of categorization: Is the basic level basic? *Cognitive Development, 12*, 247–264.

MANDLER, J. & MCDONOUGH, L. (1995). Long-term recall of event sequences in infancy. *Journal of Experimental Child Psychology, 59*, 457–474.

MANION, V., & ALEXANDER, J. M. (1997). The benefits of peer collaboration on strategy use, metacognitive causal attribution, and recall. *Journal of Experimental Child Psychology, 67*, 268–289.

MARATSOS, M. (1998). The acquisition of grammar. In D. Kuhn & R. S. Siegler (Eds.), *Cognitive, language, and perceptual development*, Vol. 2. In W. Damon (General Editor), *Handbook of child psychology*. New York: Wiley.

MARCHE, T. A., & HOWE, M. L. (1995). Preschoolers report misinformation despite accurate memory. *Developmental Psychology, 31*, 554–567.

MARCUS, G. F. (1995). Children's overregularization of English plurals: A quantitative analysis. *Journal of Child Language, 22*, 447–460.

MARCUS, G. F., PINKER, S., ULLMAN, M., HOLLANDER, M., ROSEN, T. J., & XU, F. (1992). Overregularization in language acquisition. *Monographs of the Society for Research in Child Development, 57* (Serial No. 228).

MAREAN, G. C., WERNER, L. A., & KUHL, P. K. (1992). Vowel categorization by very young infants. *Developmental Psychology, 28*, 396–405.

MARKOVITS, H., & VACHON, R. (1989). Reasoning with contrary-to-fact propositions. *Journal of Experimental Child Psychology, 47*, 398–412.

MARLIER, L., SCHAAL, B., & SOUSSIGNAN, R. (1998). Neonatal responsiveness to the odor of amniotic and lacteal fluids: A test of perinatal chemosensory continuity. *Child Development, 69*, 611–623.

MARSH, H. W. (1989). Sex differences in the development of verbal and mathematics constructs: The High School and Beyond Study. *American Educational Research Journal, 26*, 191–225.

MARTIN, C. L. (1993). New directions for investigating children's gender knowledge. *Developmental Review, 13*, 184–204.

MARTIN, C. L., & HALVERSON, C. F. (1981). A schematic processing model of sex-typing and stereotyping in children. *Child Development, 49*, 1119–1134.

MARTIN, C. L., & LITTLE, J. K. (1990). The relation of gender understanding to children's sex-typed preferences and gender stereotypes. *Child Development, 61*, 1427–1439.

MARTIN, C. L., WOOD, C. H., & LITTLE, J. K. (1990). The development of gender stereotype components. *Child Development, 61*, 1891–1904.

MARX, M. H., & HENDERSON, B. (1996). A fuzzy trace analysis of categorical inferences and instantial associations as a function of retention interval. *Cognitive Development, 11*, 551–569.

MASANGKAY, Z. S., MCCLUSKEY, K. A., MCINTYRE, C. W., SIMS-KNIGHT, J., VAUGHN, B. E., & FLAVELL, J. H. (1974). The early development of inferences about the visual precepts of others. *Child Development, 45*, 357–366.

MASATAKA, N. (1996). Perception of motherese in a signed language by 6-month-old deaf infants. *Developmental Psychology, 32*, 874–879.

MASATAKA, N. (1998). Perception of motherese in Japanese sign language by 6-month-old hearing infants. *Developmental Psychology, 34*, 241–246.

MASON, J. M. (1992). Reading stories to preliterate children: A proposed connection to reading. In P. B. Gough, L. C. Ehri, & R. Treiman (Eds.), *Reading acquisition*. Hillsdale, NJ: Erlbaum.

MASTEN, A. S., & COATSWORTH, J. D. (1998). The development of competence in favorable and unfavorable environments. *American Psychologist, 53*, 205–220.

MASTERS, S., & SOARES, M. (1993). Is the gender difference in mental rotation disappearing? *Behavioral Genetics, 23*, 337–341.

MASUR, E. I., MCINTYRE, C. W., & FLAVELL, J. H. (1973). Developmental changes in apportionment of study time among items in a multitrial free recall task. *Journal of Experimental Child Psychology, 15*, 237–246.

MATHENY, A. P., JR., WILSON, R. S., DOLAN, A. B., & KRANTZ, J. Z. (1981). Behavioral contrasts in twinships: Stability and patterns of differences in childhood. *Child Development, 52*, 579–598.

MAURER, D. & BARRERA, M. (1981). Infants' perception of natural and distorted arrangements of a schematic face. *Child Development, 52*, 196–202.

MAURER, D., & SALAPATEK, P. (1976). Developmental changes in the scanning of faces by young infants. *Child Development, 47*, 523–527.

MAURER, D., SIEGEL, L. S., LEWIS, T. L., KRISTOFFERSON, M. W., BARNES, R. A., & LEVY, B. (1979). Long-term memory improvement? *Child Development, 50*, 106–118.

MAYR, E. (1982). *The growth of biological thought: Diversity, evolution, and inheritance.* Cambridge, MA: Belknap.

MAZZONI, G. (1998). Memory suggestibility and metacognition in child eyewitness testimony: The roles of source monitoring and self-efficacy. *European Journal of Psychology of Education, 13*, 43–60.

MCCABE, A. E., SIEGEL, L. S., SPENCE, I., & WILKINSON, A. (1982). Class-inclusion reasoning: Patterns of performance from three to eight years. *Child Development, 53*, 780–785.

MCCALL, R. B. (1981). Nature-nurture and the two realms of development: A proposed integration with respect to mental development. *Child Development, 52*, 1–12.

MCCALL, R. B., APPELBAUM, M. I., & HOGARTY, P. S. (1973). Developmental changes in mental performance. *Monographs of the Society for Research in Child Development, 38* (Serial No. 150).

MCCALL, R. B., & CARRIGER, M. S. (1993). A meta-analysis of infant habituation and recognition memory performance as predictors of later IQ. *Child Development, 64*, 57–79.

MCCALL, R. B., EICHORN, D. H., & HOGARTY, P. S. (1977). Transitions in early mental development. *Monographs of the Society for Research in Child Development, 42* (Serial No. 171).

MCCALL, R. B., HOGARTY, P. S., & HURLBURT, N. (1972). Transitions in infant sensori-motor development and the prediction of childhood IQ. *American Psychologist, 27*, 728–748.

MCCALL, R. B., KENNEDY, C. B., & APPELBAUM, M. I. (1977). Magnitude of discrepancy and the distribution of attention in infants. *Child Development, 48*, 772–785.

MCCALL, R. B., PARKE, R. D., & KAVANAUGH, R. D. (1977). Imitation of live and televised models by children one to three years of age. *Monographs of the Society for Research in Child Development, 42* (Serial No. 173).

MCCARTHY, D. (1954). Language development in children. In L. Carmichael (Ed.), *A manual of child psychology* (2nd ed.). New York: Wiley.

MCCARTNEY, K., HARRIS, M. J., & BERNIERI, F. (1990). Growing up and growing apart: A development meta-analysis of twin studies. *Psychological Bulletin, 107*, 226–237.

MCCAULEY, C., WEIL, C. M., & SPERBER, R. D. (1976). The development of memory structure as reflected by semantic-priming effects. *Journal of Experimental Child Psychology, 22*, 511–518.

MCDONOUGH, L., MANDLER, J. M., MCKEE, R. D., & SQUIRE, L. R. (1995). The deferred imitation task as a nonverbal measure of declarative memory. *Proceedings of the National Academy of Sciences, 92*, 7580–7584.

MCFADDEN, G. T., DUFRESNE, A., & KOBASIGAWA, A. (1986). Young children's knowledge of balance scale problems. *Journal of Genetic Psychology, 148*, 79–94.

MCGHEE, P. E. (1976). Children's appreciation of humor: A test of the cognitive congruency principle. *Child Development, 47*, 420–426.

MCGHEE, P. E. (1979). *Humor: Its origins and development.* San Francisco: W. H. Freeman.

MCGILLY, K., & SIEGLER, R. S. (1990). The influence of encoding strategic knowledge on children's choices among serial recall strategies. *Developmental Psychology, 26*, 931–941.

MCGUE, M., BOUCHARD, T. J., JR., LYKKEN, D. T., & FEUER, D. (1984). Information processing abilities in twins reared apart. *Intelligence, 8*, 239–258.

MCKENZIE, B., & OVER, R. (1983). Young infants fail to imitate facial and manual gestures. *Infant Behavior and Development, 6*, 85–96.

MCPHERSON, S. L., & THOMAS, J., R. (1989). Relation of knowledge and performance in boys' tennis: Age and expertise. *Journal of Experimental Child Psychology, 48*, 190–211.

MEHLER, J., JUSCZYK, P., LAMBERTZ, G., HALSTED, N., BERTONCINI, J., & AMIEL-TISON, C. (1988). A precursor of language acquisition in young infants. *Cognition 29*, 143–178.

MELMED, P. J. (1971). Black English phonology: The question of reading interference. *Monographs of the Language-Behavior Research Laboratory, 1*.

MELOT, A-M. (1998). The relationship between metacognitive knowledge and metacognitive experiences: Acquisition and re-elaboration. *European Journal of Psychology of Education, 13*, 75–89.

MELTZOFF, A. N. (1985). Immediate and deferred imitation in fourteen- and twenty-four-month-old infants. *Child Development, 56*, 62–72.

MELTZOFF, A. N. (1988a). Infant imitation after a 1-week delay: Long-term memory for novel acts and multiple stimuli. *Developmental Psychology*, *24*, 470–476.

MELTZOFF, A. N. (1988b). Imitation of televised models by infants. *Child Development, 59*, 1221–1229.

MELTZOFF, A. N. (1990). Towards a developmental cognitive science: The implications of cross-modal matching and imitation for the development of memory in infancy. A. Diamond (Ed.), *The development and neural bases of higher cognitive functions*, Vol. 608, *Annals of the New York Academy of Sciences* (pp. 1–31).

MELTZOFF, A. N. (1995). What infant memory tells us about infantile amnesia: Long-term recall and deferred imitation. *Journal of Experimental Child Psychology, 59*, 497–515.

MELTZOFF, A. N., & BORTON, R. W. (1979). Intermodal matching by human neonates. *Nature, 282*, 403–404.

MELTZOFF, A. N., & MOORE, M. K. (1977). Imitation of facial and manual gestures by human neonates. *Science, 198*, 75–78.

MELTZOFF, A. N., & MOORE, M. K. (1985). Cognitive foundations and social functions of imitation and intermodal representation in infancy. In J. Mehler & R. Fox (Eds.), *Neonate cognition: Beyond the booming buzzing confusion*. Hillsdale, NJ: Erlbaum.

MELTZOFF, A. N., & MOORE, M. K. (1992). Early imitation within a functional framework: The importance of person identity, movement, and development. *Infant Behavior and Development, 15*, 479–505.

MELTZOFF, A. N., & MOORE, M. K. (1998). Object representation, identity, and the paradox of early permanence: Steps toward a new framework. *Infant Behavior and Development, 21*, 201–235.

MENDELSON, M. J., & HAITH, M. M. (1976). The relation between audition and vision in the human newborn. *Monographs of the Society for Research in Child Development, 41* (Serial No. 167).

MEROLA, J. L., & LIEDERMAN, J. (1985). Developmental changes in hemispheric independence. *Child Development, 56*, 1184–1194.

MERVIS, C. B., & BERTRAND, J. (1994). Acquisition of the novel name-nameless category (N3C) principle. *Child Development, 65*, 1646–1662.

MERVIS, C. B., & ROSCH, E. (1981). Categorization of natural objects. *Annual Review of Psychology, 32*, 89–115.

MEULEMANS, T., VAN DER LINDEN, M., & PERRUCHET, P. (1998). Implicit sequence learning in children. *Journal of Experimental Child Psychology, 69*, 199–221.

Miami Herald, January 18, 1998. "Georgia governor thinks music will educate newborns classically."

MILLER, C. L., MICELI, P. J., WHITMAN, T. L., & BORKOWSKI, J. G. (1996). Cognitive readiness to parent and intellectual-emotional development in children of adolescent mothers. *Developmental Psychology, 32*, 533–541.

MILLER, K. F., SMITH, C. M., ZHU, J., & ZHANG, H. (1995). Preschool origins of cross-national differences in mathematical competence. *Psychological Science, 6*, 56–60.

MILLER, L. C., LECHNER, R. E., & RUGS, D. (1985). Development of conversational responsiveness: Preschoolers' use of responsive listener cues and relevant comments. *Developmental Psychology, 21*, 473–480.

MILLER, L. T., & VERNON, P. A. (1996). Intelligence, reaction time, and working memory in 4- to 6-year-old children. *Intelligence, 22*, 155–190.

MILLER, L. T., & VERNON, P. A. (1997). Developmental changes in speed of information processing in young children. *Developmental Psychology, 33*, 549–554.

MILLER, N. E., & DOLLARD, J. (1941). *Social learning and imitation*. New Haven, CT: Yale University Press.

MILLER, P. H. (1990). The development of strategies of selective attention. In D. F. Bjorklund (Ed.), *Children's strategies: Contemporary views of cognitive development*. Hillsdale, NJ: Erlbaum.

MILLER, P. H., & COYLE, T. R. (1999). Developmental changes: Lessons from microgenesis. In E. K. Scholnick, K. Nelson, S. A. Gelman, & P. H. Miller (Eds.), *Conceptual development: Piaget's legacy*. Mahwah, NJ: Erlbaum.

MILLER, P. H., HAYNES, V. F., DEMARIE-DREBLOW, D., & WOODY-RAMSEY, J. (1986). Children's strategies for gathering information in three tasks. *Child Development, 57*, 1429–1439.

MILLER, P. H., & SEIER, W. L. (1994). Strategy utilization deficiencies in children: When, where, and why. In H. W. Reese (Ed.), *Advances in child development and behavior* (Vol. 25). New York: Academic.

MILLER, P. H., SEIER, W. L., PROBERT, J. S., & ALOISE, P. A. (1991). Age differences in the capacity demands of a strategy among spontaneously strategic children. *Journal of Experimental Child Psychology, 52*, 149–165.

MILLER, P. H., & WEISS, M. G. (1982). Children's and adults knowledge about what variables affect selective attention. *Child Development, 53*, 543–549.

MILLER-JONES, D. (1989). Culture and testing. *American Psychologist, 44*, 360–366.

MILNER, B. (1964). Some effects of frontal lobectomy in man. In J. M. Warren & K. Akert (Eds.), *The frontal granular cortex and behavior*. New York: McGraw-Hill.

MISTRY, J. (1997). The development of remembering in cultural context. In N. Cowan (Ed.), *The development of memory in childhood*. Hove East Sussex, UK: Psychology Press.

MISTRY, J. J., & LANGE, G. W. (1985). Children's organization and recall of information in scripted narratives. *Child Development, 56*, 953–961.

MITHEN, S. (1996). *The prehistory of the mind: The cognitive origins of art, religion and science*. London: Thames and Hudson.

MOELY, B. E., HART, S. S., LEAL, L., SANTULLI, K. A., RAO, N., JOHNSON, T., & HAMILTON, L. B. (1992). The teacher's role in facilitating memory and study strategy development in the elementary school classroom. *Child Development, 63*, 653–672.

MOELY, B. E., SANTULLI, K. A., & OBACH, M. S. (1995). Strategy instruction, metacognition, and motivation in the elementary school classroom. In F. Weinert & W. Schneider (Eds.), *Memory performance and competencies: Issues in growth and development*. Hillsdale, NJ: Erlbaum.

MOERK, E. L. (1986). Environmental factors in early language acquisition. In G. J. Whitehurst (Ed.), *Annals of child development* (Vol. 3). Greenwich, CT: JAI.

MOLFESE, D. L., & MOLFESE, V. J. (1980). Cortical responses of preterm infants to phonetic and nonphonetic speech stimuli. *Developmental Psychology, 16*, 574–581.

MONEY, J. (1988). *Gay, straight, and in-between: The sexology of erotic orientation*. New York: Oxford University Press.

MONEY, J., & EHRHARDT, A. A. (1972). *Man and woman, boy and girl*. Baltimore: Johns Hopkins University Press.

MONTEMAYOR, R., & EISEN, M. (1977). The development of self-conceptions from childhood to adolescence. *Developmental Psychology, 13*, 314–319.

MONTEPARE, J. M., & McARTHUR, L. B. (1986). The influence of facial characteristics on children's age perceptions. *Journal of Experimental Child Psychology, 42*, 303–314.

MOOD, D. W. (1979). Sentence comprehension in preschool children: Testing an adaptive egocentrism hypothesis. *Child Development, 50*, 247–250.

MOORE, C., JARROLD, C., RUSSELL, J., LUMB, A., SAPP, F., & MacCALLUM, F. (1995). Conflicting desire and the child's theory of mind. *Cognitive Development, 10*, 467–482.

MOORE, D. S., SPENCE, M. J., & KATZ, G. S. (1997). Six-month-olds' categorization of natural infant-directed utterances. *Developmental Psychology, 33*, 980–989.

MOORE, T. (1967). Language and intelligence: A longitudinal study of the first eight years. Part I. Patterns of development in boys and girls. *Human Development, 10*, 88–106.

MORISON, S., AMES, E. W., & CHISHOLM, K. (1995). The development of children adopted from Romanian orphanages. *Merrill-Palmer Quarterly, 41*, 411–430.

MORISSET, C. E., BARNARD, K. E., & BOOTH, C. L. (1995). Toddlers' language development: Sex differences within social risk. *Developmental Psychology, 31*, 851–865.

MORRISON, F. J., GRIFFITH, E. M., & ALBERTS, D. M. (1997). Nature-nurture in the classroom: Entrance age, school readiness, and learning in children. *Developmental Psychology, 33*, 254–262.

MORRISON, F. J., GRIFFITH, E. M., & FRAZIER, J. A. (1996). Schooling and the 5–7 shift: A natural experiment. In A. Sameroff & M. M. Haith (Eds.), *Reason and responsibility: The passage through childhood*. Chicago: University of Chicago Press.

MORRISON, F. J., SMITH, L., & DOW-EHRENSBERGER, M. (1995). Education and cognitive development: A natural experiment. *Developmental Psychology, 31*, 789–799.

MORRONGIELLO, B. A., & FENWICK, K. D. (1991). Infants' coordination of auditory and visual depth information. *Journal of Experimental Child Psychology, 52*, 277–296.

MORTON, J., & JOHNSON, M. H. (1991). CONSPEC and CONLERN: A two-process theory of infant face recognition. *Psychological Review, 98*, 164–181.

MOSHMAN, D. (1998). Cognitive development beyond childhood. In D. Kuhn & R. S. Siegler (Vol. Eds.), *Cognitive, language, and perceptual development*, Vol. 2. In W. Damon (General Editor), *Handbook of child psychology*. New York: Wiley.

MOSKOWITZ, B. A. (1978, November). The acquisition of language. *Scientific American*, 92–108.

MUIR-BROADDUS, J. E. (1995). Gifted underachievers: Insights from the characteristics of strategic functioning associated with giftedness and achievement. *Learning and Individual Differences, 7*, 189–206.

MUIR-BROADDUS, J. E., & BJORKLUND, D. F. (1990). Developmental and individual differences in children's memory strategies: The role of knowledge. In W. Schneider & F. E. Weinert (Eds.), *Aptitudes, strategies and knowledge in cognitive performance*. New York: Springer-Verlag.

MUIR-BROADDUS, J. E., RORER, E., BRADEN, T., AND GEORGE, C. (1995). The effects of a knowledge base manipulation on individual differences in processing speed and recall. *Contemporary Educational Psychology, 20,* 403-409.

MULLEN, M. K. (1994). Earliest recollections of childhood: A demographic analysis. *Cognition, 52,* 55–79.

MULLEN, M. K., & YI, S. (1995). The cultural context of talk about the past: Implications for the development of autobiographical memory. *Cognitive Development, 10,* 407–419.

MULLIS, I. V. S., & JENKINS, L. B. (1990). *The reading report card, 1971–88: Trends from the nation's report card.* Princeton, NJ: Educational Testing Service.

MUNROE, R. H., SHIMMIN, H. S., & MUNROE, R. L. (1984). Gender understanding and sex role preference in four cultures. *Developmental Psychology, 20,* 673–682.

MUTER, V., HULME, C., SNOWLING, M., & TAYLOR, S. (1998). Segmentation, not rhyming, predicts early progress in learning to read. *Journal of Experimental Child Psychology, 71,* 3-27.

MYERS, N. A., CLIFTON, R. K., & CLARKSON, M. G. (1987). When they were very young: Almost-threes remember two years ago. *Infant Behavior and Development, 10,* 123–132.

NAITO, M. (1990). Repetition priming in children and adults: Age-related dissociation between implicit and explicit memory. *Journal of Experimental Child Psychology, 50,* 462–484.

NASH, M. R. (1987). What, if anything, is age regressed about hypnotic age regression? A review of the empirical literature. *Psychological Bulletin, 102,* 42–52.

NASH, M. R., DRAKE, M., WILEY, R., KHALSA, S., & LYNN, S. J. (1986). The accuracy of recall of hypnotically age regressed subjects. *Journal of Abnormal Psychology, 95,* 298–300.

NÜSLUND, J. C., & SCHNEIDER, W. (1996). Kindergarten letter knowledge, phonological skills, and memory processes: Relative effects on early literacy. *Journal of Experimental Child Psychology, 62,* 30–59.

NAUS, M. J., ORNSTEIN, P. A., & AIVANO, S. (1977). Developmental changes in memory: The effects of processing time and rehearsal instructions. *Journal of Experimental Child Psychology, 23,* 237–251.

NEISSER, U. (ED.) (1998). *The rising curve: Long-term gains in IQ and related measures.* Washington, DC: American Psychological Association.

NELSON, C. A., & BLOOM, F. E. (1997). Child development and neuroscience. *Child Development, 68,* 970–987.

NELSON, K. (1974). Variations in children's concepts by age and category. *Child Development, 45,* 577–584.

NELSON, K. (1983). The derivation of concepts and categories from event representatives. In E. K. Skolnick (Ed.), *New trends in conceptual representation: Challenges to Piaget's theory?* Hillsdale, NJ: Erlbaum.

NELSON, K. (1986). *Event knowledge: Structure and function in development.* Hillsdale, NJ: Erlbaum.

NELSON, K. (1993). The psychological and social origins of autobiographical memory. *Psychological Science, 4,* 7–14.

NELSON, K. (1996). *Language in cognitive development: The emergence of the mediated mind.* New York: Cambridge University Press.

NELSON, K., & GRUENDEL, J. (1981). Generalized event representations: Basic building blocks of cognitive development. In M. Lamb & A. Brown (Eds.), *Advances in developmental psychology,* Vol. 1. Hillsdale, NJ: Erlbaum.

NELSON, K., & ROSS, G. (1980). The generalities and specifics of long-term memory in infants and young children. In M. Perlmutter (Ed.), *New directions for child development: Children's memory.* San Francisco, CA: Jossey-Bass.

NESSE, R. M., & WILLIAMS, G. C. (1994). *Why we get sick: The new science of Darwinian medicine.* New York: Times Books.

NEWCOMBE, N., BANDURA, M. M., & TAYLOR, D. C. (1983). Sex differences in spatial ability and spatial activities. *Sex Roles, 9,* 377–386.

NEWCOMBE, N., & DUBAS, J. S. (1992). A longitudinal study of predictors of spatial ability in adolescent females. *Child Development, 63,* 37–46.

NEWCOMBE, N., & FOX, N. A. (1994). Infantile amnesia: Through a glass darkly. *Child Development, 65,* 31–40.

NEWCOMBE, N., & HUTTENLOCHER, J. (1992). Children's early ability to solve perspective-taking problems. *Developmental Psychology, 28,* 635–643.

NEWPORT, E. L. (1990). Maturational constraints on language learning. *Cognitive Science, 14,* 11–28.

NEWPORT, E. L. (1991). Contrasting concepts of the critical period for language. In S. Carey & R. Gelman (Eds.), *Epigenesis of mind: Essays in biology and knowledge.* Hillsdale, NJ: Erlbaum

NOWAKOWSKI, R. S. (1987). Basic concepts of CNS development. *Child Development, 58,* 568–595.

NYITI, R. M. (1982). The validity of "cultural differences explanation" in the rate of Piagetian cognitive development. In D. A. Wagner & H. W. Stevenson (Eds.), *Cultural perspectives on child development.* San Francisco: W. H. Freeman.

OAKES, M. A. & HYMAN, I. E., JR. (in press). The changing face of memory and self. In D. F. Bjorklund (Ed.), *False-memory creation in children and adults: Theory, research, and implications.* Mahwah, NJ: Erlbaum.

O'BRIEN, M., & HUSTON, A. C. (1985). Development of sex-typed play behavior in toddlers. *Developmental Psychology, 21,* 866–871.

O'CONNOR, J. J., COHEN, S., & PARMELEE, A. H. (1984). Infant auditory discrimination in preterm and full-term infants as a predictor of 5 year intelligence. The effects of global severe privation on cognitive competence: Extension and longitudinal follow-up. *Developmental Psychology, 20,* 159–165.

O'CONNOR, T. G., RUTTER, M., BECKETT, C., KEAVENEY, L., & KREPPNER, J. M., AND THE ENGLISH AND RO-MANIAN ADOPTEES STUDY TEAM. (in press) *Child Development.*

OLLER, D. K. (1980). The emergence of the sounds of speech in infancy. In G. Yeni-Komshian, J. F. Kavanaugh, & C. A. Ferguson (Eds.), *Child phonology:* Vol. 1. *Productions.* New York: Academic.

OLLER, D. K., & EILERS, R. (1988). The role of audition in babbling. *Child Development, 59,* 441–449.

OLSON, D. R., & TORRANCE, N. (EDS.), (1991). *Literacy and orality.* Cambridge: Cambridge University Press.

OMANSON, R. C., BECK, I. L., VOSS, J. F., & MCKEOWN, M. G. (1984). The effects of reading lessons on comprehension: A processing description. *Cognition and Instruction, 1,* 45–67.

OPPENHEIM, R. W. (1981). Ontogenetic adaptations and retrogressive processes in the development of the nervous system and behavior. In K. J. Connolly & H. F. R. Prechtl (Eds.), *Maturation and development: Biological and psychological perspectives.* Philadelphia: International Medical Publications.

ORNSTEIN, P. A., BAKER-WARD, L., & NAUS, M. J. (1988). The development of mnemonic skill. In M. Weinert & M. Perlmutter (Eds.), *Memory development.* Hillsdale, NJ: Erlbaum.

ORNSTEIN, P. A., GORDON, B. N., & LARUS, D. M. (1992). Children's memory for a personally experienced event: Implications for testimony. *Applied Developmental Psychology, 6,* 49–60.

ORNSTEIN, P. A., & GREENHOOT, A. F. (in press). Remembering the distant past: Implications of research on children's memory for the recovered memory debate. In D. F. Bjorklund (Ed.), *False-memory creation in children and adults: Theory, research, and implications.* Mahwah, NJ: Erlbaum.

ORNSTEIN, P. A., HALE, G. A., & MORGAN, J. S. (1977). Developmental differences in recall and output organization. *Bulletin of the Psychonomic Society, 9,* 29–32.

ORNSTEIN, P. A., & NAUS, M. J. (1978). Rehearsal processes in children's memory. In P. A. Ornstein (Ed.), *Memory development in children.* Hillsdale, NJ: Erlbaum.

ORNSTEIN, P. A., NAUS, M. J., & LIBERTY, C. (1975). Rehearsal and organizational processes in children's memory. *Child Development, 46,* 818–830.

ORNSTEIN, P. A., NAUS, M. J., & STONE, B. P. (1977). Rehearsal training and developmental differences in memory. *Development Psychology, 13,* 15–24.

ORNSTEIN, P. A., SHAPIRO, L. R., CLUBB, P. A., FOLLMER, A., & BAKER-WARD, L. (1997). The influence of prior knowledge on children's memory for salient medical experiences. In N. L. Stein, P. A. Ornstein, B. Tversky, & C. Brainerd (Eds.), *Memory for everyday and emotional events.* Mahwah, NJ: Lawrence Erlbaum.

OSBORNE, J. G., & CALHOUN, D. O. (1998). Themes, taxons, and trial types in children's matching to sample: Methodological considerations. *Journal of Experimental Child Psychology, 68,* 35–50.

O'SULLIVAN, J. T. (1993). Preschoolers' beliefs about effort, incentives, and recall. *Journal of Experimental Child Psychology, 55,* 396–414.

O'SULLIVAN, J. T. (1996). Children's metamemory about the influence of conceptual relations on recall. *Journal of Experimental Child Psychology, 62,* 1–29.

O'SULLIVAN, J. T. (1997). Effort, interest, and recall: Beliefs and behaviors of preschoolers. *Journal of Experimental Child Psychology, 65,* 43–67.

O'SULLIVAN, J. T., HOWE, M. L., & MARCHE, T. A. (1996). Children's beliefs about long-term retention. *Child Development, 67,* 2989–3009.

OVERMAN, W., BACHEVALIER, J., MILLER, M., & MOORE, K. (1996). Children's performance on "animal tests" of oddity: Implications for cognitive processes required for tests of oddity and delayed nonmatch to sample. *Journal of Experimental Child Psychology, 62,* 223–242.

OVERTON, W. F., WARD, S. L., NOVECK, I. A., BLACK, J., & O'BRIEN, D. P. (1987). Form and content in the development of deductive reasoning. *Developmental Psychology, 23,* 22–30.

OYEN, A.-S., & BEBKO, J. M. (1996). The effects of computer games and lesson contexts on children's mnemonic strategies. *Journal of Experimental Child Psychology, 62,* 173–189.

PALINCSAR, A. S., & BROWN, A. L. (1984). Reciprocal teaching of comprehension-monitoring activities. *Cognition and Instruction, 1,* 117–175.

PALINCSAR, A. S., BROWN, A. L., & CAMPIONE, J. C. (1993). First-grade dialogues for knowledge acquisition and use. In E. A. Forman, N. Minilk, & C. A.

Stone (Eds.), *Contexts for learning.* New York: Oxford University Press

PAPOUSEK, H. (1977). The development of learning ability in infancy (Entwicklung der Lernfähigkeit im Säuglingsalter). In G. Nissen (Ed.) *Intelligence, learning, and learning disabilities (Intelligenz, Lernen und Lernstörungen).* Berlin: Springer-Verlag.

PARIS, S. G. (1973). Comprehension of language connectives and propositional logical relationships. *Journal of Experimental Child Psychology, 16,* 278–291.

PARIS, S. G. (1988). Motivated remembering. In F. E. Weinert & M. Perlmutter (Eds.), *Memory development: Universal changes and individual differences.* Hillsdale, NJ: Erlbaum.

PARIS, S. G., & OKA, E. R. (1986). Children's reading strategies, metacognition, and motivation. *Developmental Review, 6,* 25–56.

PARK, D., & JAMES, Q. J. (1983). Effects of encoding instructions on children's spatial and color memory: Is there evidence for automaticity? *Child Development, 54,* 61–68.

PARKER, J. F. (1995). Age differences in source monitoring of performed and imagined actions on immediate and delayed tests. *Journal of Experimental Child Psychology, 60,* 84–101.

PARKIN, A. J. (1997). The development of procedural and declarative memory. In N. Cowan (Ed.), *The development of memory in childhood.* Hove East Sussex, UK: Psychology Press.

PASCUAL-LEONE, J. (1970). A mathematical model for the transition rule in Piaget's developmental stages. *Acta Psychologia, 32,* 301–345.

PEARSON, P. D., HANSEN, J., & GORDON, C. (1979). The effect of background knowledge on young children's comprehension of explicit and implicit information. *Journal of Reading Behavior, 11,* 201–209.

PELLEGRINI, A. D., & BJORKLUND, D. F. (1997). The role of recess in children's cognitive performance. *Educational Psychologist, 32,* 35–40.

PELLEGRINI, A. D., & DAVIS, P. (1993). Confinement effects on playground and classroom behavior. *British Journal of Educational Psychology, 63,* 88–95.

PEREZ, L. A., PEYNIRCIOGLU, Z. F., & BLAXTON, T. A. (1998). Developmental differences in implicit and explicit memory performance. *Journal of Experimental Child Psychology, 70,* 167–185.

PERLMUTTER, M., & LANGE, G. (1978). A developmental analysis of recall-recognition distinctions. In P. A. Ornstein (Ed.), *Memory development in children.* Hillsdale, NJ: Erlbaum.

PERNER, J. (1991). *Understanding the representational mind.* Cambridge, MA: MIT Press.

PERNER, J. (1994). The many faces of belief: Reflections on Fodor's and the child's theory of mind. *Cognition.*

PERNER, J., RUFFMAN, T., & LEEKAM, S. R. (1994). Theory of mind is contagious: You catch it from your sibs. *Child Development, 67,* 1228–1238.

PERRIS, E. E., MYERS, N. A., & CLIFTON, R. K. (1990). Long-term memory for a single infancy experience. *Child Development, 61,* 1796–1807.

PERRY, D. G., PERRY, L. C. & RASMUSSEN, P. (1986). Cognitive social learning mediators of aggression. *Child Development, 57,* 700–711.

PERRY, D. G., WHITE, A. J., & PERRY, L. C. (1984). Does early sex typing result from children's attempts to match their behavior to sex role stereotypes? *Child Development, 55,* 2114–2121.

PESKIN, J. (1992). Ruse and representations: On children's ability to conceal information. *Developmental Psychology, 28,* 84–89.

PESKIN, J. (1996). Guise and guile: Children's understanding of narratives in which the purpose of pretense is deception. *Child Development, 67,* 1735–1751.

PETRILL, S. A. (1997). Molarity versus modularity of cognitive functioning? A behavioral genetic perspective. *Current Directions in Psychological Science, 6,* 96–99.

PETRILL, S. A., SAUDINO, K., CHERNY, S. S., EMDE, R. N., FULKER, D. W., HEWITT, J. K., & PLOMIN, R. (1997). Exploring the genetic etiology of low general cognitive ability from 14 to 36 months. *Developmental Psychology, 33,* 544–548.

PETRILL, S. A., SAUDINO, K., CHERNY, S. S., EMDE, R. N., FULKER, D. W., HEWITT, J. K., & PLOMIN, R. (1998). Exploring the genetic and environmental etiology of high general cognitive ability in fourteen- to thirty-six-month-old twins. *Child Development, 69,* 68–74.

PETRILL, S. A., THOMPSON, L. A., & DETTERMAN, D. K. (1995). The genetic and environmental variance underlying elementary cognitive tasks. *Behavioral Genetics, 25,* 199–209.

PEZDEK, K., & HODGE, D. (1999). Planting false childhood memories in children. The role of event plausibility. *Child Development.*

PEZDEK, K., & TAYLOR, J. (in press). Discriminating between accounts of true and false events. In D. F. Bjorklund (Ed.), *False-memory creation in children and adults: Theory, research, and implications.* Mahwah, NJ: Erlbaum.

PHILLIPS, S., KING, S., & DUBOIS, L. C. (1978). Spontaneous activity of female versus male newborns. *Child Development, 49,* 590–597.

PIAGET, J. (1930). *The child's conception of physical causality.* London: Routledge & Kegan Paul.

PIAGET, J. (1952). *The origins of intelligence in children.* New York: Norton.

PIAGET, J. (1954). *The construction of reality in the child.* New York: Basic.

PIAGET, J. (1955). *The language and thought of the child.* New York: World.

PIAGET, J. (1962). *Play, dreams, and imitation in childhood.* New York: Norton.

PIAGET, J. (1965). *The child's conception of number.* New York: Norton.

PIAGET, J. (1967). Genesis and structure in the psychology of intelligence. In J. Piaget, *Six psychological studies.* New York: Vintage.

PIAGET, J. (1968). *On the development of memory and identity.* Worcester, MA: Clark University Press.

PIAGET, J. (1969a). *The child's conception of the world.* Totowa, NJ: Littlefield & Adams.

PIAGET, J. (1969b). *Judgment and reasoning in the child.* London: Routledge.

PIAGET, J. (1971). *Biology and knowledge.* Chicago: University of Chicago Press.

PIAGET, J. (1972). *Play and development.* Maria W. Piers (Ed.). Norton: New York.

PIAGET, J., & INHELDER, B. (1967). *The child's conception of space.* New York: Norton.

PIAGET, J., & INHELDER, B. (1969). *The psychology of the child.* New York: Basic.

PIAGET, J., & INHELDER, B. (1973). *Memory and intelligence.* New York: Basic.

PIEN, D., & ROTHBART, M. K. (1980). Incongruity, humor, play, and self-regulation of arousal in young children. In P. E. McGhee & A. J. Chapman (Eds.), *Children's humor.* Chichester, England: Wiley.

PIERCE, K. A., & GHOLSON, B. (1994). Surface similarity and relational similarity in the development of analogical problem solving: Isomorphic and nonisomorphic transfer. *Developmental Psychology, 30,* 724–737.

PILLEMER, D. B., & WHITE, S. H. (1989). Childhood events recalled by children and adults. In H. W. Reese (Ed.), *Advances in child development and behavior* (Vol. 21). New York: Academic.

PILLOW, B. H. (1988). Young children's understanding of attentional limits. *Child Development, 59,* 31–46.

PINE, K. J., & MESSER, D. J. (1998). Group collaboration effects and the explicitness of children's knowledge. *Cognitive Development, 13,* 109–126.

PINKER, S. (1994). *The language instinct: How the mind creates language.* New York: Morrow.

PINKER, S. (1997). *How the mind works.* New York: Norton.

PLOMIN, R., DEFRIES, J. C., MCCLEARN, G. E., & RUTTER, M. (1997). *Behavioral genetics* (3rd edition). New York: Freeman.

PLOMIN, R., FULKER, D. W., CORLEY, R., & DEFRIES, J. C. (1997). Nature, nurture, and cognitive development from 1 to 6 years: A parent-offspring adoption study. *Psychological Science, 8,* 442–447.

PLOMIN, R., & PETRILL, S. A. (1997). Genetics and intelligence: What's new? *Intelligence, 24,* 53–77.

PLOMIN, R., & RUTTER, M. (1998). Child development, molecular genetics, and what to do with genes once they are found. *Child Development, 69,* 1221–1240.

PLUMERT, J. M. (1995). Relation between children's overestimation of their physical abilities and accident proneness. *Developmental Psychology, 31,* 866–876.

PLUMERT, J. M., & NICHOLS-WHITEHEAD, P. (1996). Parental scaffolding of young children's spatial communication. *Developmental Psychology, 32,* 523–532.

PLUNKETT, K., KARMILOFF-SMITH, A., BATES, E., ELMAN, J. L., & JOHNSON, M. H. (1997). Connectionism and developmental psychology. *Journal of Child Psychology and Psychiatry, 38,* 53–80.

POIRIER, F. E., & SMITH, E. O. (1974). Socializing functions of primate play. *American Zoologist, 14,* 275–287.

POOLE, D. A. (1995). Strolling fuzzy-trace theory through eyewitness testimony (or vice versa). *Learning and Individual Differences, 7,* 87–93.

POOLE, D. A., & WHITE, L. T. (1991). Effects of question repetition on the eyewitness testimony of children and adults. *Developmental Psychology, 27,* 975–986.

POOLE, D. A., & WHITE, L. T. (1993). Two years later. Effects of question repetition and retention interval on the eyewitness testimony of children and adults. *Developmental Psychology, 29,* 844–853.

POOLE, D., & WHITE, L. (1995). Tell me again and again: Stability and change in the repeated testimonies of children and adults. In M. S. Zaragoza, J. R. Graham, C. N. Gordon, R. Hirschman, & Y. S. Ben Porath (Eds.), *Memory and testimony in the child witness.* Newbury Park, CA: Sage.

POSNER, M. I., & KEELE, S. W. (1970). Retention of abstract ideas. *Journal of Experimental Psychology, 83,* 304–308.

POVINELLI, D. J., LANDAU, K. R., & PERILLOUX, H. K. (1996). Self-recognition in young children using delayed versus live feedback: Evidence of a developmental asynchrony. *Child Development, 67,* 1540–1554.

POVINELLI, D. J., & SIMON, B. B. (1998). Young children's understanding of briefly versus extremely delayed images of the self: Emergence of the autobiographical stance. *Developmental Psychology, 34,* 188–194.

PREMACK, D., & WOODRUFF, G. (1978). Does the chimpanzee have a theory of mind? *Behavioral and Brain Sciences, 1,* 515–526.

PRESSLEY, M. (1982). Elaboration and memory development. *Child Development, 53,* 296–309.

PRESSLEY, M., EL-DINARY, P. B., MARKS, M. B., BROWN, R., & STEIN, S. (1992). Good strategy instruction is motivating and interesting. In K. A. Renninger, S. Hidi, & A. Krapp (Eds.), *The role of interest in learning and development.* Hillsdale, NJ: Erlbaum.

PRESSLEY, M., & LEVIN J. R. (1977). Task parameters affecting the efficacy of a visual imagery learning strategy in younger and older children. *Journal of Experimental Child Psychology, 24,* 53–59.

PRESSLEY, M., & VAN METER, P. (1993). Memory strategies: Natural development and use following instruction. In R. Pasnak & M. L. Howe (Eds.), *Emerging themes in cognitive development*: Vol. 2. *Competencies.* New York: Springer-Verlag.

PRICE, D. W. W., & GOODMAN, G. S. (1990). Visiting the wizard: Children's memory for a recurring event. *Child Development, 61,* 664–680.

PROVENCE, S., & LIPTON, R. C. (1962). *Infants in institutions: A comparison of their development with family-reared infants during the first year of life.* New York: International Universities Press.

PYLYSHYN, Z. (1980). Computation and cognition: Issues in the foundations of cognitive science. *Behavioral and Brain Sciences, 3,* 111–132.

QIN, J. M., QUAS, J. A., REDLICH, A. D., & GOODMAN, G. S. (1997). Children's eyewitness testimony: Memory development in the legal context. In N. Cowan (Ed.), *The development of memory in childhood.* Hove East Sussex, UK: Psychology Press.

QUARTZ, S. R., & SEJNOWSKI, T. J. (1997). The neural basis of cognitive development: A constructivist manifesto. *Behavioral and Brain Sciences, 20,* 537–596.

QUINE, W. V. (1972). *Methods of logic.* New York: Holt, Rinehart & Winston.

QUINN, P. C., & EIMAS, P. D. (1996). Perceptual cues that permit categorical differentiation of animal species by infants. *Journal of Experimental Child Psychology, 63,* 189–211.

QUINN, P. C., & EIMAS, P. D. (1998). Evidence for a global categorical representation of humans by young infants. *Journal of Experimental Child Psychology, 69,* 151–174.

RABINOWITZ, M., FREEMAN, K., & COHEN, S. (1992). Use and maintenance of strategies: The influence of accessibility to knowledge. *Journal of Educational Psychology, 84,* 211–218.

RABINOWITZ, M., & KEE, D. (1994). A framework for understanding individual differences in memory: Strategy-knowledge interactions. In P. A. Vernon (Ed.), *Handbook of the neuropsychology of individual differences.* New York: Academic.

RABINOWITZ, M., & MANDLER, J. M. (1983). Organization and information retrieval. *Journal of Experimental Psychology: Learning, Memory and Cognition, 9,* 430–439.

RAMEY, C. T., CAMPBELL, F. A., & FINKELSTEIN, N. W. (1984). Course and structure of intellectual development in children at risk for developmental retardation. In P. H. Brooks, R. Sperber, & C. McCauley (Eds.), *Learning and cognition in the mentally retarded.* Hillsdale, NJ: Erlbaum.

RAMEY, C. T., LEE, M. W., & BURCHINAL, M. R. (1989). Developmental plasticity and predictability: Consequences of ecological change. In M. H. Bornstein & N. A. Krasnegor (Eds.), *Stability and continuity in mental development: Behavioral and biological perspectives.* Hillsdale, NJ: Erlbaum.

RAMEY, C. T., YEATES, K. O., & SHORT, E. J. (1984). The plasticity of intellectual development: Insights from preventive intervention. *Child Development, 55,* 1913–1925.

RAMSAY, D. S., & WEBER, S. L. (1986). Infants' hand preferences in a task involving complementary roles for the two hands. *Child Development, 57,* 300–307.

RATNER, H. H. (1984). Memory demands and the development of young children's memory. *Child Development, 55,* 2173–2191.

RATNER, H. H., & FOLEY, M. A. (1997). *Children's collaborative learning: Reconstruction of the other in the self.* Paper presented at meeting of the Society for Research in Child Development, Washington, DC.

RAUSCHER, F. H., ROBINSON, K. D., & JENS, J. J. (1998). Improved maze learning through early music exposure in rats. *Neurological Research, 20,* 427–432. .

RAUSCHER, F. H., SHAW, G. L., & KY, K. N. (1993). Music and spatial task performance. *Nature, 365,* 611.

RAUSCHER, F. H. SHAW, G. L., LEVINE, L. J., & KY, K. N. (August, 1994). *Music and spatial task performance: A causal relationship.* Paper presented at meeting of the American Psychological Association, Los Angeles.

RAUSCHER, F. H., SHAW, G. L., LEVINE, L. J., WRIGHT, E. L., DENNIS, W. R., & NEWCOMB, R. L. (1997). Music training causes long-term enhancement of preschool children's spatial-temporal reasoning. *Neurological Research, 19,* 2–8.

RAVEN, J. C., COURT, J. H., & RAVEN, J. (1975). *Manual for Raven's Progressive Matrices and Vocabulary Scales.* London: Lewis.

RAYMOND, C. L., & BENBOW, C. P. (1986). Gender differences in mathematics: A function of parental support and student sex typing? *Development Psychology, 22,* 808–819.

RECHT, D. R., & LESLIE, L. (1988). Effect of prior knowledge on good and poor readers' memory of text. *Journal of Educational Psychology, 80,* 16–20.

REED, M. A., PIEN, D. L., & ROTHBART, M. K. (1984). Inhibitory self-control in preschool children. *Merrill-Palmer Quarterly, 30,* 131–147.

REEDER, K. (1981). How young children learn to do things with words. In P. S. Dale & D. Ingram (Eds.), *Child language—An international perspective.* Baltimore: University Park.

REESE, E. (1995). Predicting children's literacy from mother-child conversations. *Cognitive Development, 10,* 381–405.

REESE, E., HADEN, C., & FIVUSH, R. (1993). Mother-child conversations about the past: Relationships of style and memory over time. *Cognitive Development, 8,* 403–430.

REESE, E., HADEN, C. A., & FIVUSH, R. (1996). Mothers, fathers, daughters, sons: Gender differences in autobiographical reminiscing. *Research on Language and Social Interaction, 29,* 27–56.

REESE, H. W. (1962). Verbal mediation as a function of age level. *Psychological Bulletin, 59,* 502–509.

RENNINGER, K. A. (1992). Individual interest and development: Implications for theory and practice. In K. A. Renninger, S. Hidi, & A. Krapp (Eds.), *The role of interest in learning and development.* Hillsdale, NJ: Erlbaum.

RENNINGER, K. A., HIDI, S., & KRAPP, A. (eds.) (1992). *The role of interest in learning and development.* Hillsdale, NJ: Erlbaum.

REPACHOLI, B. M., & GOPNIK, A. (1997). Early reasoning about desires: Evidence from 14- and 18-month-olds. *Developmental Psychology, 33,* 12–21.

RESCORLA, L., HYSON, M. C., & HIRSH-PASEK, K. (EDS.). (1991). *Academic instruction in early childhood: Challenge or pressure?* San Francisco: Jossey-Bass.

REUBENS, A, HUBERTZ, M., SULLIVAN, J., & BJORKLUND, D. F. (March, 1998). *The role of mothers in the development of young children's arithmetic strategies in the context of a game.* Poster presented at Conference on Human Development, Mobile, AL.

REYNA, V. F. (1992). Reasoning, remembering, and their relationship: Social, cognitive, and developmental issues. In M. L. Howe, C. J. Brainerd, & V. F. Reyna (Eds.), *Development of long-term retention.* New York: Springer-Verlag.

REYNA, V. F., & BRAINERD, C. J. (1995). Fuzzy-trace theory: An interim analysis. *Learning and Individual Differences, 7,* 1–75.

REYNOLDS, A. J., MAVROGENES, N. A., BEZUCZKO, N., & HAGEMANN, M. (1996). Cognitive and family-support mediators of preschool effectiveness: A confirmatory analysis. *Child Development, 67,* 1119–1140.

REZNICK, J. S., FUESER, J. J., & BOSQUET, M. (1998). Self-corrected reaching in a three-location delayed-response search task. *Psychological Science, 9,* 66–70.

REZNICK, J. S., & KAGAN, J. (1983). Category detection in infancy. In L. P. Lipsitt & C. K. Rovee-Collier (Eds.), *Advances in infancy research* (Vol. 2). Norwood, NJ: Ablex.

RHEINGOLD, H. L. (1985). Development as the acquisition of familiarity. *Annual Review of Psychology, 36,* 1–17.

RHEINGOLD, H. L., HAY, D. F., & WEST, M. J. (1976). Sharing in the second year of life. *Child Development, 47,* 1148–1158.

RHODES, G., & TREMEWAN, T. (1996). Averageness, exaggeration, and facial attractiveness. *Psychological Science, 7,* 105–110.

RICE, C., KOINIS, D., SULLIVAN, K., TAGER-FLUSBERG, & WINNER, E. (1997). When 3-year olds pass the appearance-reality test. *Developmental Psychology, 33,* 54–61.

RIDDERINKHOF, K. R., & VAN DER MOLEN, M. (1995). A psychophysiological analysis of developmental differences in the ability to resist interference. *Child Development, 66,* 1040–1056.

RIDDERINKHOF, K. R., & VAN DER MOLEN, M. & BAND, G. P. H. (1997). Sources of interference from irrelevant information: A developmental study. *Journal of Experimental Child Psychology, 65,* 315–341.

RINGEL, B. A., & SPRINGER, C. J. (1980). On knowing how well one is remembering: The persistence of strategy use during transfer. *Journal of Experimental Child Psychology, 29,* 322–333.

RITTLE-JOHNSON, B., & SIEGLER, R. S. (1999). Learning to spell: Variability, choice, and change in children's strategy use. *Child Development, 70,* 304–316.

RIVA, D., & CAZZANIGA, L. (1986). Late effects of unilateral brain lesions sustained before and after age one. *Neuropsychology, 24,* 423–428.

RIVERA, S. M., WAKELEY, A., & LANGER, J. (1999). The drawbridge phenomenon: Representational reasoning or perceptual preference? *Developmental Psychology. 35,* 427–435.

ROBERTS, K. (1988). Retrieval of a basic-level category in prelinguistic children. *Developmental Psychology, 24,* 21–27.

ROBERTS, K., & HOROWITZ, F. D. (1986). Basic level categorization in seven- and nine-month-old infants. *Journal of Child Language, 13,* 191–206.

ROBINSON, B. F., & MERVIS, C. B. (1998). Disentangling early language development: Modeling lexical and grammatical acquisition using an extension of case-study methodology. *Developmental Psychology, 34,* 363–375.

ROCHAT, P., & MORGAN, R. (1995). Spatial determinants in the perception of self-produced leg movements by 3- to 5-month-old infants. *Developmental Psychology, 31,* 626–636.

ROE, K. V., DRIVAS, A., KARAGELLIS, A., & ROE, A. (1985). Sex differences in vocal interaction with mother and stranger in Greek infants: Some cognitive implications. *Developmental Psychology, 21,* 372–377.

ROGOFF, B. (1990). *Apprenticeship in thinking: Cognitive development in social context.* New York: Oxford University Press.

ROGOFF, B. (1998). Cognition as a collaborative process. In D. Kuhn & R. S. Siegler (Vol. Eds.), *Cognition language, and perceptual development,* Vol. 2. In W. Damon (Gen. Ed), *Handbook of child psychology.* New York: Wiley.

ROGOFF, B., MISTRY, J., GÖNCÜ, & MOSIER, C. (1993). Guided participation in cultural activity by toddlers and caregivers. *Monographs of the Society for Research in Child Development, 58* (Serial No. 236).

ROGOFF, B., NEWCOMBE, N., & KAGAN, J. (1974). Planfulness and recognition memory. *Child Development, 45,* 972–977.

ROGOFF, B., & WADDELL, K. J. (1982). Memory for information organized in a scene by children from two cultures. *Child Development, 53,* 1224–1228.

ROHWER, W. D., JR., & LITROWNIK, J. (1983). Age and individual differences in the learning of a memorization procedure. *Journal of Educational Psychology, 75,* 799–810.

ROHWER, W. D., JR., RAINES, J. M., EOFF, J., & WAGNER, M. (1977). The development of elaborative propensity during adolescence. *Journal of Experimental Child Psychology, 23,* 472–492.

ROSCH, E. (1975). Cognitive representations of semantic categories. *Journal of Experimental Psychology: General, 7,* 192–233.

ROSCH, E., & MERVIS, C. B. (1975). Family resemblances: Studies in the internal structure of categories. *Cognitive Psychology, 7,* 573–605.

ROSCH, E., MERVIS, C. B., GRAY, W. D., JOHNSON, D. M., & BOYES-BRAEM, P. (1976). Basic objects in natural categories. *Cognitive Psychology, 8,* 382–439.

ROSE, S. A. (1990). Cross-modal transfer in human infants: What is being transferred? *Annals of the New York Academy of Sciences, 608.*

ROSE, S. A., & FELDMAN, J. F. (1995). Prediction of IQ and specific cognitive abilities at 11 years from infancy measures. *Developmental Psychology, 31,* 685–696.

ROSE, S. A., FELDMAN, J. F., & WALLACE, I. F. (1992). Infant information processing in relation to six-year cognitive outcomes. *Child Development, 63,* 1126–1141.

ROSE, S. A., FELDMAN, J. F., WALLACE, I. F., & McCARTON, C. (1989). Infant visual attention: Relation to birth status and developmental outcome during the first 5 years. *Developmental Psychology, 25,* 560–576.

ROSE, S. A., FELDMAN, J. F., WALLACE, I. F., & McCARTON, C. (1991). Information processing at 1 year: Relation to birth status and developmental outcome during the first 5 years. *Developmental Psychology, 27,* 723–737.

ROSE, S. A., GOTTFRIED, A. W., & BRIDGER, W. H. (1981). Cross-modal transfer in 6-month-old infants. *Developmental Psychology, 17,* 661–669.

ROSE, S., GOTTFRIED, A. W., MELLOY-CARMINAR, P., & BRIDGER, W. H. (1982). Familiarity and novelty preferences in infant recognition memory: Implications for information processing. *Developmental Psychology, 18,* 704–713.

ROSE, S. A., & RUFF, H. A. (1987). Cross-modal abilities in human infants. In J. S. Osofsky (Ed.), *Handbook of infant development* (2nd edition). New York: Wiley.

ROSENBLUM, K., KENNEDY, E. C., PEREZ, E. E., & BJORKLUND, D. F. (March, 1996). *Developmental differences in young children's number strategies in a game context.* Paper presented at Conference on Human Development, Birmingham, AL.

ROSENGREN, K. S., & HICKLING, A. K. (1994). Seeing is believing: Children's explanations of commonplace, magical, and extraordinary transformations. *Child Development, 65,* 1605–1626.

ROSENTHAL, R., & RUBIN, D. B. (1982). Further meta-analytic procedures for assessing cognitive gender differences. *Journal of Educational Psychology, 74,* 708–712.

ROVEE-COLLIER, C. (1995). Time windows in cognitive development. *Developmental Psychology, 51,* 1–23.

Rovee-Collier, C., & Gerhardstein, P. (1997). The development of infant memory. In N. Cowan (Ed.) *The development of memory in childhood.* Hove East Sussex UK: Psychology Press.

Rovee-Collier, C., Schechter, A., Shyi, C.-W. G., & Shields, P. (1992). Perceptual identification of contextual attributes and infant memory retrieval. *Developmental Psychology, 28,* 307–318.

Rovee-Collier, C., & Shyi, C.-W. G. (1992). A functional and cognitive analysis of infant long-term retention. In M. L. Howe, C. J. Brainerd, & V. F. Reyna (Eds.), *Development of long-term retention.* New York: Springer-Verlag.

Rowe, D. C., Jacobson, K. C., & van der Oord, E. J. C. G. (in press). Genetic and environmental influences on vocabulary IQ: Parental education level as a moderator. *Child Development.*

Rubin, K. H., & Krasnor, L. R. (1986). Social cognitive and social behavior perspectives on problem solving. In M. Perlmutter (Ed.), *Minnesota Symposium on Child Psychology* (Vol. 18). Hillsdale, NJ: Erlbaum.

Ruble, D. N., Balaban, T., & Cooper, J. (1981). Gender constancy and the effects of sex-typed televised toy commercials. *Child Development, 52,* 667–673.

Ruble, D. N., & Martin, C. L. (1998). Gender development. In N. Eisenberg (Vol. Ed), *Social, emotional, and personality development,* (Vol. 3). In W. Damon (Gen. Ed.), *Handbook of child psychology.* New York: Wiley.

Ruff, H. A., & Birch, H. G. (1974). Infant visual fixation: The effect of concentricity, curvilinearity, and number of directions. *Journal of Experimental Child Psychology, 17,* 460–473.

Ruff, H. A., Capozzoli, M., & Weisberg, R. (1998). Age, individuality, and context as factors in sustained visual attention during the preschool years. *Developmental Psychology, 34,* 454–464.

Ruff, H. A., & Lawson, K. R. (1990). Development of sustained, focused attention in young children during free play. *Developmental Psychology, 26,* 85–93.

Ruff, H. A., Lawson, K. R., Parrinello, R., & Weissberg, R. (1990). Long-term stability of individual differences in sustained attention in the early years. *Child Development, 61,* 60–75.

Ruffman, T., Perner, J., Naito, M., Parkin, L., & Clements, W. A. (1998). Older (but not younger) siblings facilitate false belief understanding. *Developmental Psychology, 34,* 161–174.

Russo, R. Nichelli, P., Gibertoni, M., & Cornia, C. (1995). Developmental trends in implicit and explicit memory: A picture completion study. *Journal of Experimental Child Psychology, 59,* 566–578.

Rutter, M., & the English and Romanian Adoptees study team. (1998). Developmental catch-up, and delay, following adoption after severe global early privation. *Journal of Child Psychology and Psychiatry, 39,* 465–476.

Sabin, E. J., Clemmer, E. J., O'Connell, D. C., & Kowal, S. (1979). A pausological approach to speech development. In A. W. Siegman & S. Feldstein (Eds.), *Of speech and time: Temporal speech patterns in interpersonal contexts.* Hillsdale, NJ: Erlbaum.

Saccuzzo, D. P., Johnson, N. E., & Guertin, T. L. (1994). Information processing in gifted versus nongifted African American, Latino, Filipino, and white children: Speeded versus nonspeeded paradigms. *Intelligence, 19,* 219–243.

Sachs, J. (1977). The adaptive significance of linguistic input to prelinguistic infants. In C. E. Snow & C. A. Ferguson (Eds.), *Talking to children: Language input and acquisition.* Cambridge: Cambridge University Press.

Sachs, J., & Devin, J. (1976). Young children's use of age-appropriate speech styles in social interaction and role-playing. *Journal of Child Language, 3,* 81–98.

Sacks, O. (1989). *Seeing voices: A journey into the word of the deaf.* New York: Harper Perennial.

Salapatek, P. (1975). Pattern perception in early infancy. In L. B. Cohen & P. Salapatek (Eds.), *Infant perception: From sensation to cognition* (Vol. 1). New York: Academic.

Salapatek, P., & Kessen, W. (1966). Visual scanning of triangles by the human newborn. *Journal of Experimental Child Psychology, 3,* 155–167.

Salatas, H., & Flavell, J. H. (1976). Behavioral and metamnemonic indicators of strategic behavior under remember instructions in first grade. *Child Development, 47,* 81–89.

Salmon, K., & Pipe, M-E. (1997). Props and children's event reports: The impact of a 1-year delay. *Journal of Experimental Child Psychology, 65,* 261–292.

Saltz, E., Campbell, S., & Skotko, D. (1983). Verbal control of behavior: The effects of shouting. *Developmental Psychology, 19,* 461–464.

Sameroff, A. J., & Chandler, M. J. (1975). Reproductive risk and the continuum of caretaking causality. In F. D. Horowitz (Ed.), *Review of child development research* (Vol. 4). Chicago: University of Chicago Press.

Sameroff, A. J., Seifer, R., Baldwin, A., & Baldwin, C. (1993). Stability of intelligence from preschool to adolescence: The influence of social risk factors. *Child Development, 64,* 80–97.

Sameroff, A. J., & Suomi, S. J. (1996). Primates and persons: A comparative developmental understanding of social organization. In R. B. Cairns, G. H. Elder, Jr., & E. J. Costello (Eds.), *Developmental Science*. New York: Cambridge University Press.

SANDMAN, C. A., WASHWA, P., HETRICK, W., PORTO, M., & PEEKE, H. V. S. (1997). Human fetal heart rate dishabituation between thirty and thirty-two weeks gestation. *Developmental Psychology, 68,* 1031–1040.

SAVAGE-RUMBAUGH, E. S., MURPHY, J., SEVCIK, R. A., BRAKKE, K. E., WILLIAMS, S. L., & RUMBAUGH, D. M. (1993). Language comprehension in ape and child. *Monographs of the Society for Research in Child Development, 58* (Serial No. 233).

SAXE, G. B. (1979). Developmental relations between notational counting and number conservation. *Child Development, 50,* 180–187.

SAXE, G. B., GUBERMAN, S. R., & GEARHART, M. (1987). Social processes in early number development. *Monographs of the Society for Research in Child Development, 52* (Serial No. 216).

SCARR, S. (1992). Developmental theories for the 1990s: Development and individual differences. *Child Development, 63,* 1–19.

SCARR, S. (1993). Biological and cultural diversity: The legacy of Darwin for development. *Child Development, 64,* 1333–1353.

SCARR, S., & MCCARTNEY, K. (1983). How people make their own environments: A theory of genotype → environment effects. *Child Development, 54,* 424–435.

SCARR, S., & WEINBERG, R. A. (1976). IQ test performance of black children adopted by white families. *American Psychologist, 31,* 726–739.

SCARR, S., & WEINBERG, R. A. (1978). The influence of "family background" on intellectual attainment. *American Sociological Review, 43,* 674–692.

SCHACTER, D. L. (1992). Understanding implicit memory. *American Psychologist, 47,* 559–569.

SCHAFER, G., & PLUNKETT, K. (1998). Rapid word learning by fifteen-month-olds under tightly controlled conditions. *Child Development, 69,* 309–320.

SCHANK, R. C., & ABELSON, R. P. (1977). *Scripts, plans, goals and understanding.* Hillsdale, NJ: Erlbaum.

SCHAUBLE, L. (1990). Belief revision in children: The role of prior knowledge and strategies for generating evidence. *Journal of Experimental Child Psychology, 49,* 31–57.

SCHAUBLE. L. (1996). The development of scientific reasoning in knowledge-rich context. *Developmental Psychology, 32,* 102–119.

SCHELLENBERG, E. G., & TREHUB, S. E. (1996). Natural musical intervals: Evidence from infant listeners. *Psychological Science, 5,* 272–277.

SCHIEFELE, U., KRAPP, A., & WINTELER, A. (1992). Interest as a predictor of academic achievement: A meta-analysis of research. In K. A. Renninger, S. Hidi, & A. Krapp (Eds.), *The role of interest in learning and development.* Hillsdale, NJ: Erlbaum.

SCHIFF, A. R., & KNOPF, I. J. (1985). The effect of task demands on attention allocation in children of different ages. *Child Development, 56,* 621–630.

SCHLIEMANN, A. D. (1992). Mathematical concepts in and out of school in Brazil: From developmental psychology to better teaching. *Newsletter of the International Society for the Study of Behavioural Development* (Serial No. 22, No. 2), 1–3.

SCHMIDT, C. R., & SCHMIDT, S. R. (1986). The use of themes as retrieval cues in children's memory for stories. *Journal of Experimental Child Psychology, 42,* 237–255.

SCHNEIDER, W. (1986). The role of conceptual knowledge and metamemory in the development of organizational processes in memory. *Journal of Experimental Child Psychology, 42,* 218–236.

SCHNEIDER, W. (1993). Domain-specific knowledge and memory performance in children. *Educational Psychology Review, 5,* 257-273.

SCHNEIDER, W. (1998). Performance prediction in young children: Effects of skill, metacognition and wishful thinking. *Developmental Science, 1,* 291–297.

SCHNEIDER, W. (in press). The development of metamemory in children. In D. Gopher & A. Koriat (Eds.). *Attention and performance XII: Cognitive regulation of performance-Interaction of theory and application.* Cambridge, MA: MIT Press.

SCHNEIDER, W., & BJORKLUND, D. F. (1992). Expertise, aptitude, and strategic remembering. *Child Development, 63,* 461–473.

SCHNEIDER, W., & BJORKLUND, D. F. (1998). Memory. In D. Kuhn & R. S. Siegler (Vol. Eds.), *Cognitive, language, and perceptual development,* Vol. 2. In W. Damon (Gen. Ed.), *Handbook of child psychology.* New York: Wiley.

SCHNEIDER, W., BJORKLUND, D. F., & MAIER-BRÜCKNER, W. (1996). The effects of expertise and IQ on children's memory: When knowledge is, and when it is not enough. *International Journal of Behavioral Development, 19,* 773–796.

SCHNEIDER, W., GRUBER, H., GOLD, A., & OPWIS, K. (1993). Chess expertise and memory for chess positions in children and adults. *Journal of Experimental Child Psychology, 56,* 328–349.

SCHNEIDER, W., KÖRKEL, J., & WEINERT, F. E. (1989). Domain-specific knowledge and memory performance:

A comparison of high- and low-aptitude children. *Journal of Educational Psychology, 81,* 306–312.

SCHNEIDER, W., KÜSPERT, P., ROTH, E., & VISÉ, M. (1997). Short- and long-term effects of training phonological awareness in kindergarten: Evidence from two German studies. *Journal of Experimental Child Psychology, 66,* 311–340.

SCHNEIDER, W., & NÄSLUND, J. C. (1999). The impact of early phonological processing skills on reading and spelling in school: Evidence from the Munich Longitudinal Study. In F. E. Weinert & W. Schneider (Eds.), *The Munich Longitudinal Study on the Genesis of Individual Competencies (LOGIC).* Cambridge: Cambridge University Press.

SCHNEIDER, W., PERNER, J., BULLOCK, M., STEFANEK, J., & ZIEGLER, A. (1999). The development of intelligence and thinking. In F. E. Weinert & W. Schneider (Eds.), *The Munich Longitudinal Study on the Genesis of Individual Competencies (LOGIC).* Cambridge: Cambridge University Press.

SCHNEIDER, W., & PRESSLEY, M. (1997). *Memory development between 2 and 20* (second edition). Mahwah, NJ: Erlbaum.

SCHNEIDER, W., SCHLAGMÜLLER, M., & VISÉ, M. (1998). The impact of metamemory and domain-specific knowledge on memory performance. *European Journal of Psychology of Education, 13,* 91–103.

SCHNEIDER, W., & SODIAN, B. (1988). Metamemory-memory behavior relationship in young children: Evidence from a memory-for-location task. *Journal of Experimental Child Psychology, 45,* 209–233.

SCHNEIDER, W., & SODIAN, B. (1991). A longitudinal study of young children's memory behavior and performance in a sort-recall task. *Journal of Experimental Child Psychology, 51,* 14–29.

SCHNEIDER, W., & SODIAN, B. (1997). Memory strategy development: Lessons from longitudinal research. *Developmental Review, 17,* 442–461.

SCHNEIDER, W., & WEINERT, F. E. (1995). Memory development during early and middle childhood: Findings from the Munich longitudinal study (LOGIC). In F. E. Weinert & W. Schneider (Eds.), *Memory performance and competencies: Issues in growth and development.* Hillsdale, NJ: Erlbaum.

SCHULMAN, A. H., & KAPLOWITZ, C. (1977). Mirror-image response during the first two years of life. *Developmental Psychobiology, 10,* 133–142.

SCHUMANN-HENGSTELER, R. (1989, July). *Memory development: The analysis of a popular picture game.* Paper presented at the Tenth Biennial Meeting of the International Society for the Study of Behavioral Development, Jyvaskyla, Finland.

SCHUMANN-HENGSTELER, R. (1992). The development of visuo-spatial memory: How to remember location. *International Journal of Behavioral Development, 15,* 445–471.

SCHWANENFLUGEL, P. J. (1991). An introduction to the psychology of word meaning. In P. J. Schwanenflugel (Ed.), *The psychology of word meanings.* Hillsdale, NJ: Erlbaum.

SCHWANENFLUGEL, P. J., FABRICIUS, W. V., & ALEXANDER, J. (1994). Developing theories of mind: Understanding concepts and relations between mental activities. *Child Development, 65.*

SCHWANENFLUGEL, P. J., FABRICIUS, W. V., & NOYES, C. R. (1996). Developing organization of mental verbs: Evidence for the development of a constructivist theory of mind in middle school. *Cognitive Development, 11,* 265–294.

SCHWANENFLUGEL, P. J., GUTH, M. E., & BJORKLUND, D. F. (1986). A developmental trend in the understanding of concept attribute importance. *Child Development, 57,* 421–430.

SCHWANENFLUGEL, P. J., HENDERSON, R. L., & FABRICIUS, W. V. (1998). Developing organization of mental verbs and theory of mind in middle childhood: Evidence from extension. *Developmental Psychology, 34,* 512–524.

SCHWANENFLUGEL, P. J., & NOYES, C. R. (1996). Context availability and the development of word reading skills. *Journal of Literary Research, 28,* 35–54.

SCHWANENFLUGEL, P. J., STAHL, S. A., & McFALLS, E. L. (1997). Partial word knowledge and vocabulary growth during reading comprehension. *Journal of Literary Research, 29,* 531–553.

SCOTT, J. P. (1968). *Early experience and the organization of behavior.* Belmont, CA: Brooks/Cole.

SCOTT, M. S., GREENFIELD, D. B., & STERENTAL, E. (1986). Abstract categorization ability as a predictor of learning disability classification. *Intelligence, 10,* 377–387.

SCOTT, M. S., SERCHUK, R., & MUNDY, P. (1982). Taxonomic and complementary picture pairs: Ability in two- to five-year olds. *International Journal of Behavioral Development, 5,* 243-256.

SCRIBNER, S., & COLE, M. (1981). *The psychology of literacy.* Cambridge, MA: Harvard University Press.

SEARLE, J. R. (1992). *The rediscovery of the mind.* Cambridge, MA: MIT Press.

SELMAN, R. (1976). Social-cognitive understanding: A guide to educational and clinical practice. In T. Lickona (Ed.), *Moral development and behavior.* New York: Holt, Rinehart, & Winston.

SELMAN, R. (1980). *The growth of interpersonal understanding*. New York: Academic.

SELMAN, R. L., SCHORIN, M. Z., STONE, C. R., & PHELPS, E. (1983). A naturalistic study of children's social understanding. *Developmental Psychology, 19*, 82–102.

SENDEN, M. VON (1960). *Space and sight: The perception of space and shape in the congenitally blind before and after operation*. Glencoe, IL: Free Press.

SERBIN, L. A., & SPRAFKIN, C. (1986). The saliency of gender and the process of sex typing in three- to seven-year-old children. *Child Development, 57*, 1188–1199.

SHAFFER, D. R. (1993). *Social and personality development* (3rd edition). Pacific Grove, CA: Brooks/Cole.

SHANKWEILER, D., CRAIN, S., KATZ, L., FOWLER, L., LIBERMAN, A. M., BRADY, S. A., THORNTON, R., LUNQUIST, E., DREYER, L., FLETCHER, J. M., STUEBING, K. K., SHAYWITZ, S. E., & SHAYWITZ, B. A. (1995). Cognitive profiles of reading-disabled children: Comparison of language skills in phonology, morphology, and syntax. *Psychological Science, 6*, 149–156.

SHATZ, M. (1983). Communication. In J. H. Flavell & E. M. Markman (Eds.), *Cognitive development*. Vol. 3 of P. H. Mussen (Gen. Ed.), *Handbook of child psychology*. New York: Wiley.

SHATZ, M., & GELMAN, R. (1973). The development of communication skills. *Monographs of the Society for Research in Child Development, 38* (Serial No. 152).

SHAYWITZ, S. E., SHAYWITZ, B. A., PUGH, K. R., FULBRIGHT, R. K., CONSTABLE, R. T., MENCL, W. E., SHANKWEILER, D. P., LIBERMAN, A. M., SKUDLARSKI, P., FLETCHER, J. M., KATZ, L., MARCHIONE, K. E., LACADIE, C., GATENBY, C., & GORE, J. C. (1998). Functional disruption in the organization of the brain for reading in dyslexia. *Proceedings of the National Academy of Science USA, 95*, 2636–2641.

SHEINGOLD, K. (1973). Developmental differences in intake and storage of visual information. *Journal of Experimental Child Psychology, 16*, 1–11.

SHERMAN, J. A. (1978). *Sex-related cognitive differences: An essay on theory and evidence*. Springfield, IL: Charles C. Thomas.

SHIFFRIN, R. M., & SCHNEIDER, W. (1977). Controlled and automatic human information processing: II. Perceptual learning, automatic attending, and a general theory. *Psychological Review, 84*, 127–190.

SHOLL, M. J., & LIBEN, L. S. (1995). Illusory tilt and Euclidean schemes as factors in performance on the water-level task. *Journal of Experimental Psychology: Learning, Memory, and Cognition, 15*, 110–125,

SHUCARD, J. L., & SHUCARD, D. W. (1990). Auditory evoked potentials and hand preference in 6-month-old infants: Possible gender-related differences in cerebral organization. *Developmental Psychology, 26*, 923–930.

SHULTZ, T. R., & HORIBE, F. (1974). Development of the appreciation of verbal jokes. *Developmental Psychology, 10*, 13–20.

SHULTZ, T. R., & PILON, R. (1973). Development of the ability to detect linguistic ambiguity. *Child Development, 44*, 728–733.

SHULTZ, T. R., & ROBILLARD, J. (1980). The development of linguistic humor in children: Incongruity through rule violation. In P. E. McGhee & A. J. Chapman (Eds.), *Children's humor*. Chichester, England: Wiley.

SHWE, H. I., & MARKMAN, E. M. (1997). Young children's appreciation of the mental impact of their communicative signals. *Developmental Psychology, 33*, 630–636.

SIEGEL, L. S. (1988). Evidence that IQ scores are irrelevant to the definition and analysis of reading disabilities. *Canadian Journal of Psychology, 42*, 201–215.

SIEGEL, L. S. (1993). The cognitive basis of dyslexia. In R. Pasnak & M. L. Howe (Eds.), *Emerging themes in cognitive development: Vol. 2, Competencies*. New York: Springer-Verlag.

SIEGEL, L. S., McCABE, A. E., BRAND, A. E., & MATHEWS, J. (1978). Evidence for the understanding of class inclusion in preschool children: Linguistic factors and training effects. *Child Development, 49*, 688–693.

SIEGEL, L. S., & RYAN, E. B. (1988). Development of grammatical-sensitivity, phonological, and short-term memory skills in normally achieving and learning disabled children. *Developmental Psychology, 24*, 28–37.

SIEGEL, L. S., & RYAN, E. B. (1989). The development of working memory in normally achieving and subtypes of learning disabled children. *Child Development, 60*, 973–980.

SIEGLER, R. S. (1976). Three aspects of cognitive development. *Cognitive Psychology, 8*, 481–520.

SIEGLER, R. S. (1981). Developmental sequences within and between concepts. *Monographs of the Society for Research in Child Development, 46* (Serial No. 189).

SIEGLER, R. S. (1987). The perils of averaging data over strategies: An example from children's addition. *Journal of Experimental Psychology: General, 116*, 250–264.

SIEGLER, R. S. (1988). Individual differences in strategy choices: Good students, not-so-good students, and perfectionists. *Child Development, 59*, 833–851.

SIEGLER, R. S. (1996). *Emerging minds: The process of change in children's thinking*. New York: Oxford University Press.

Siegler, R. S., & Crowley, K. (1991). The microgenetic method: A direct means for studying cognitive development. *American Psychologist, 46,* 606–620.

Siegler, R. S., & Ellis, S. (1996). Piaget on childhood. *Psychological Science, 7,* 211–215.

Siegler, R. S., & Jenkins, E. (1989). *How children discover strategies.* Hillsdale, NJ: Erlbaum.

Siegler, R. S., & Shrager, J. (1984). Strategy choices in addition and subtraction: How do children know what to do? In C. Sophian (Ed.), *Origins of cognitive skills.* Hillsdale, NJ: Erlbaum.

Sielger, R. S., & Stern, E. (1998). Conscious and unconscious strategy discoveries: A microgenetic analysis. *Journal of Experimental Psychology: General, 127,* 377-397.

Sigel, I. E. (1987). Does hothousing rob children of their childhood? *Early Childhood Research Quarterly 2,* 211–225.

Sigman, M., Cohen, S. E., Beckwith, L., & Parmelee, A. H. (1986). Infant attention in relation to intellectual abilities in childhood. *Developmental Psychology, 22,* 788–792.

Signorella, M. L., Bigler, R. S., & Liben, L. S. (1993). Developmental differences in children's gender schemata about others: A meta-analytic review. *Developmental Review, 13,* 147–183.

Signorella, M. L., Jamison, W., & Krupa, M. H. (1989). Predicting spatial performance from gender stereotyping in activity preferences and in self-concept. *Developmental Psychology, 25,* 89–95.

Silverman, I., & Eals, M. (1992). Sex differences in spatial abilities: Evolutionary theory and data. In J. H. Barkow, L. Cosmides, & J. Tooby (Eds.), *The adapted mind: Evolutionary psychology and the generation of culture.* New York: Oxford University Press.

Simon, T. J. (1997). Reconceptualizing the origins of number knowledge: A "non-numerical" account. *Cognitive Development, 12,* 349–372.

Simon, T. J., Hespos, S. J., & Rochat, P. (1995). Do infants understand simple arithmetic? A replication of Wynn (1992). *Cognitive Development, 10,* 253–269.

Singer, J. L. (1980). The power and limitations of television: A cognitive affective analysis. In P. H. Tannenbaum & R. Abeles (Eds.), *The entertainment functions of television.* London: Academic.

Skeels, H. M. (1966). Adult status of children with contrasting early life experiences. *Monographs of the Society for Research in Child Development, 31* (Serial No. 105).

Skinner, B. F. (1957). *Verbal behavior.* New York: Appleton-Century-Crofts.

Skinner, B. F. (1974). *About behaviorism.* New York: Knopf.

Slaby, R. G., & Frey, K. S. (1975). Development of gender constancy and selective attention to same-sex models. *Child Development, 46,* 849–856.

Slaby, R. G., & Guerra, N. G. (1988). Cognitive mediators of aggression in adolescent offenders: 1. Assessment. *Developmental Psychology, 24,* 580–588.

Slater, A. (1995). Visual perception and memory at birth. In C. Rovee-Collier & L. P. Lipsitt (Eds.), *Advances in infancy research,* Vol. 9. Norwood, NJ: Ablex.

Slater, A., Cooper, R., Rose, D., & Morison, V. (1989). Prediction of cognitive performance from infancy to early childhood. *Human Development, 32,* 137–147.

Slater, A., Earle, D. C., Morison, V., & Rose, D. (1985). Pattern preferences at birth and their interaction with habituation-induced novelty preferences. *Journal of Experimental Child Psychology, 39,* 37–54.

Slater, A., Mattock, A., Brown, E., & Bremner, G. J. (1991). Form perception at birth: Cohen and Younger (1984) revisited. *Journal of Experimental Child Psychology, 51,* 395–406.

Slater, A. M., Morison, V., Somers, M., Mattock, A., Brown, E., & Taylor, D. (1990). Newborn and older infants' perception of partly occluded objects. *Infant Behavior and Development, 13,* 33–49.

Slater, A. M., & Kingston, D. J. (1981). Competence and performance variables in the assessment of formal operational skills. *British Journal of Educational Psychology, 51,* 163–169.

Slobin, D. I. (1970). Universals of grammatical development in children. In G. B. Flores, J. Arcais, & W. J. M. Levelt (Eds.), *Advances in psycholinguistics.* Amsterdam, The Netherlands: North-Holland.

Smetana, J. G., & Letourneau, K. J. (1984). Development of gender constancy and children's sex-typed free play behavior. *Developmental Psychology, 20,* 691–695.

Smiley, S. S., & Brown, A. L. (1979). Conceptual preference for thematic or taxonomic relations: A nonmonotonic age trend from preschool to old age. *Journal of Experimental Child Psychology, 28,* 249–257.

Smith, E., Shoben, E., & Rips, L. (1974). Structure and process in semantic memory: A featural model for semantic decisions. *Psychological Review, 81,* 214–241.

Smith, M. (1926). An investigation of the development of the sentence and the extent of vocabulary in young children. *University of Iowa Studies in Child Welfare, 3* (5).

Snow, C. (1972). Mother's speech to children learning language. *Child Development, 43,* 549–565.

Snow, C. E., Arlman-Rupp, A., Hassing, Y., Jobse, J., Joosten, J., & Vorster, J. (1976). Mothers' speech in three social classes. *Journal of Psycholinguistic Research, 5*, 1–20.

Snow C. E., & Ferguson C. A. (Eds.). (1977). *Talking to children: Language input and acquisition.* Cambridge: Cambridge University Press.

Socha, T. J., & Socha, D, M. (1994). Children's task-group communication. In L. R. Frey (Ed.), *Group communication in context: Studies of natural groups.* Hillsdale, NJ: Erlbaum.

Sodian, B., & Schneider, W. (1999). Memory strategy development: Gradual increase, sudden insight, or roller coaster? In F. E. Weinert & W. Schneider (Eds.), *The Munich Longitudinal Study on the Genesis of Individual Competencies (LOGIC).* Cambridge: Cambridge University Press.

Sodian, B., Schneider, W., & Perlmutter, M. (1986). Recall, clustering, and metamemory in young children. *Journal of Experimental Child Psychology, 41*, 395–410.

Sodian, B., Taylor, C., Harris, P. L., & Perner, J. (1991). Early deception and the child's theory of mind: False trails and genuine markers. *Child Development, 62*, 468–483.

Sophian, C. (1995). Representation and reasoning in early numerical development: Counting, conservation, and comparison between sets. *Child Development, 66*, 559–577.

Sophian, C. (1997). Beyond competence: The significance of performance for conceptual development. *Cognitive Development, 12*, 281–303.

Spearman, C. (1927). *The abilities of man.* New York: Macmillan.

Spelke, E. S. (1976). Infants' intermodal perception of events. *Cognitive Psychology, 5*, 553–560.

Spelke, E. S. (1985). Perception of unity, persistence and identity: Thoughts on infants' conceptions of objects. In J. Mehler & R. Fox (Eds.), *Neonate cognition.* Hillsdale, NJ: Erlbaum.

Spelke, E. S. (1991). Physical knowledge in infancy: Reflections on Piaget's theory. In S. Carey & R. Gelman (Eds.), *Epigenesis of mind: Essays in biology and knowledge.* Hillsdale, NJ: Erlbaum.

Spelke, E. S. (1994). Initial knowledge: Six suggestions. *Cognition, 50*, 431–455.

Spelke, E. S., Breinlinger, K., Macomber, J., & Jacobson, K. (1992). Origins of knowledge. *Psychological Review, 99*, 605–632.

Spelke, E. S., & Newport, E. L. (1998). Nativism, empiricism, and the development of knowledge. In R. Learner (Vol. Ed.), *Theories of Theoretical models of human development,* Vol. 1 of W. Damon (Gen. Ed.), *Handbook of child psychology,* New York: Wiley.

Spence, M. J. (1996). Young infants' long-term auditory memory: Evidence for changes in preference as a function of delay. *Developmental Psychobiology, 29*, 685–695.

Spence, M. J., & Freeman, M. S. (1996). Newborn infants prefer the maternal low-pass filtered voice, but not the maternal whispered voice. *Infant Behavior and Development, 19*, 199–212.

Sperling, G. (1960). The information available in brief visual presentations. *Psychological Monographs, 74* (No. 11).

Sperry, R. W. (1993). The impact of the promise of the cognitive revolution. *American Psychologist, 48*, 878–885.

Spitz, R. (1945). Hospitalism: An inquiry into the genesis of psychiatric conditions in early childhood. *Psychoanalytic Study of the Child, 1*, 53–74.

Spreen, O., Tupper, D., Risser, A., Tuokko, H., & Edgell, D. (1984). *Human developmental neuropsychiatry.* New York: Oxford University Press.

Stanley, J. C., Benbow, C. P., Brody, L. E., Dauber, S., & Lupkowski, A. E. (1992). Gender differences on eighty-six nationally standardized aptitude and achievement tests. In N. Coangelo, S. G. Assouline, & D. L. Ambroson (Eds.), *Talent development.* Unionville, NY: Trillium.

Stanovich, K. E. (1988). Explaining the differences between the dyslexic and garden variety poor reader: The phonological-core variance-difference model. *Journal of Learning Disabilities, 21*, 590–604, 612.

Stanovich, K. E. (1993). Does reading make you smarter? Literacy and the development of verbal intelligence. In H. W. Reese (Ed.), *Advances in child development and behavior* (Vol. 24). Orlando, FL: Academic.

Stanovich, K. E., West, R. F., & Harrison, M. R. (1995). Knowledge growth and maintenance across the life span: The role of print exposure. *Developmental Psychology. 31*, 811–826.

Stark, R. (1978). Features of infant sounds: The emergence of cooing. *Journal of Child Language, 5*, 1–12.

Starkey, P., & Gelman, R. (1982). The development of addition and subtraction abilities prior to formal schooling in arithmetic. In T. P. Carpenter, J. M. Moser, & T. A. Romberg (Eds.), *Addition and subtraction: A cognitive perspective.* Hillsdale, NJ: Erlbaum.

Stein, N. L., Wade, E., & Liwag, M. D. (1997). A theoretical approach to understanding and remembering emotional events. In N. L. Stein, P. A. Ornstein, B. Tversky, & C. J. Brainerd (Eds.), *Memory for everyday and emotional events.* Hillsdale, NJ: Erlbaum.

STEINER, J. E. (1979). Human facial expressions in response to taste and smell stimulation. In H. W. Reese & L. P. Lipsitt (Eds.), *Advances in child development and behavior* (Vol. 13). New York: Academic.

STERN, D. N., SPIEKER, S., BARNETT, R. K., & MACKAIN, K. (1983). The prosody of maternal speech: Infant age and context related changes. *Journal of Child Language, 10*, 1–15.

STERN, D. N., SPIEKER, S., & MACKAIN, K. (1982). Intonation contours as signals in maternal speech to prelinguistic infants. *Developmental Psychology, 18*, 727–735.

STERNBERG, R. J. (1984). Fighting butter battles: A reply. *Phi Delta Kappan, 65*, 700.

STERNBERG, R. J. (1985). *Beyond IQ: A triarchic theory of human intelligence.* Cambridge: Cambridge University Press.

STERNBERG, R. J. (1988). *The triarchic mind: A new theory of human intelligence.* New York: Viking.

STERNBERG, R. J. (1997). The concept of intelligence and its role in lifelong learning and success. *American Psychologist, 52*, 1030–1037.

STERNBERG, R. J., CONWAY, B. E., KETRON J. L., & BERNSTEIN, M. (1981). People's conceptions of intelligence. *Journal of Personality and Social Psychology, 41*, 37–55.

STERNBERG, R. J., FERRARI, M., & CLINKENBEARD, P. (1996). Identification, instruction, and assessment of gifted children: A construct validation of a triarchic model. *Gifted Child Quarterly, 40*, 129–137.

STERNBERG, R. J., & SLATER, W. (1982). Conceptions of intelligence. In R. J. Sternberg (Ed.), *Handbook of human intelligence.* Cambridge: Cambridge University Press.

STERNBERG, R. J., TORFF, B., & GRIGORENKO, E. L. (1999). Teaching triachically improves school achievement. *Journal of Educational Psychology, 90*, 374-384.

STERNBERG, S. (1969). High-speed scanning in human memory. *Science, 153*, 652–654.

STEVENSON, H. W., & LEE, S. Y. (1990). Context of achievement. *Monographs of the Society for Research in Child Development, 55* (Serial No. 221).

STEVENSON, J., & FREDMAN, G. (1990). The social environmental correlates of reading ability. *Journal of Child Psychology and Psychiatry, 31*, 681–698.

STEWART, L., & PASCUAL-LEONE, J. (1992). Mental capacity constraints and the development of moral reasoning. *Journal of Experimental Child Psychology, 54*, 251–287.

STIPEK, D. (1984). Young children's performance expectations: Logical analysis or wishful thinking? In J. G. Nicholls (Ed.), *Advances in motivation and achievement: Vol 3. The development of achievement motivation.* Greenwich, CT: JAI.

STIPEK, D., & DANIELS, D. (1988). Declining perceptions of competence: A consequence of changes in the child or the educational environment? *Journal of Educational Psychology, 80*, 352–356.

STIPEK, D. J., GRALINSKI, J. H., & KOPP, C. B. (1990). Self-concept development in the toddler years. *Developmental Psychology, 26*, 972–977.

STIPEK, D. J., RECCHIA, S., & McCLINTIC, S. (1992). Self-evaluation in young children. *Monographs of the Society for Research in Child Development, 57* (Serial No. 226).

STODDART, T., & TURIEL, E. (1985). Children's concepts of cross-gender activities. *Child Development, 56*, 1241–1252.

STOEL-GAMMON, C., & MENN, L. (1997). Phonological development: Learning sounds and sound patterns. In J. Berko Gleason (Ed.), *The development of language* (4th edition). Boston, MA: Allyn & Bacon.

STONE, C. A., & DAY, M. C. (1978). Levels of availability of a formal operational strategy. *Child Development, 49*, 1054–1065.

STONE, L. J., & CHURCH, J. (1973). *Childhood and adolescence: A psychology of the growing person.* New York: Random House.

STRERI, A., & SPELKE, E. S. (1989). Effects of motion and figural goodness on haptic object perception in infancy. *Child Development, 60*, 1111–1125.

SUGARMAN, S. (1983). *Children's early thought: Development in classification.* Cambridge: Cambridge University Press.

SULLIVAN, K., & WINNER, E. (1991). When 3-year-olds understand ignorance, false belief and representational change. *British Journal of Developmental Psychology, 9*, 159–171.

SULLIVAN, K., & WINNER, E. (1993). Three-year-olds' understanding of mental states: The influence of trickery. *Journal of Experimental Child Psychology, 56*, 135–148.

SULLIVAN, M. W., ROVEE-COLLIER, C. K., & TYNES, D. M. (1979). A conditioning analysis of infant long-term memory. *Child Development, 50*, 152–162.

Sun-Sentinel (Fort Lauderdale, FL), Friday, May 22, 1998. "Classical music for preschoolers among new laws."

SUOMI, S., & HARLOW, H. (1972). Social rehabilitation of isolate-reared monkeys. *Developmental Psychology, 6*, 487–496.

SWANSON, H. L., ASHBAKER, M. H., & LEE, C. (1996). Learning-disabled readers' working memory as a function of processing demands. *Journal of Experimental Child Psychology, 61,* 242–275.

SWANSON, H. L., & BERNINGER, V. W. (1996). Individual differences in children's working memory and writing skills. *Journal of Experimental Child Psychology, 63,* 358–385.

TAMIS-LEMONDA, C. S., & BORNSTEIN, M. H. (1989). Habituation and maternal encouragement of attention in infancy as predictors of toddler language, play, and representational competence. *Child Development, 60,* 738–751.

TANNER, J. M. (1978). *Fetus into man: Physical growth from conception to maturity.* Cambridge, MA: Harvard University Press.

TAYLOR, M., & FLAVELL, J. H. (1984). Seeing and believing: Children's understanding of the distinction between appearance and reality. *Child Development, 55,* 1710–1720.

TAYLOR, M., & HORT, B. (1990). Can children be trained in making the distinction between appearance and reality? *Cognitive Development, 5,* 89–99.

TEASDALE, T. W., & OWEN, D. R. (1984). Heredity and familial environment in intelligence and educational level: A sibling study. *Nature, 309,* 620–622.

TEASLEY, S. D. (1995). The role of talk in children's peer collaborations. *Developmental Psychology, 31,* 207–220.

TERMAN, L. M., & MERRILL, M. A. (1937). *Measuring intelligence.* Boston: Houghton Mifflin.

THATCHER, R. W. (1992). Cyclical cortical reorganization during childhood. *Brain and Cognition, 20,* 24–50.

THATCHER, R. W. (1996). Neuroimaging of cyclic cortical reorganization during human development. In R. W. Thatcher, G. R. Lyon, J. Rumsey, & N. Krasnegor (Eds.) *Developmental neuroimaging: Mapping the development of brain and behavior.* San Diego: Academic.

THATCHER, R. W., LYON, G. R., RUMSEY, J., & KRASNEGOR, N. (EDS.) (1996). *Developmental neuroimaging: Mapping the development of brain and behavior.* San Diego: Academic.

THELEN, E., & SMITH, L. B. (1998). Dynamic systems theories. In R. M. Lerner (Vol. Ed.), *Theoretical models of human development,* Vol. 1 of W. Damon (Gen. Ed.), *Handbook of child psychology.* New York: Wiley.

THOMAS, H., JAMISON, W., & HUMMEL, D. D. (1973). Observation is insufficient for discovering that the surface of still water is invariantly horizontal. *Science, 101,* 173–174.

THOMAS, H., & LOHAUS, A. (1993). Modeling growth and individual differences in spatial tasks. *Monographs of the Society for Research in Child Development, 58* (Serial No. 237).

THOMAS, H., & TURNER, G. F. (1991). Individual difference and development in water-level task performance. *Journal of Experimental Child Psychology, 51,* 171–194.

THOMPSON, J. R., & CHAPMAN, R. S. (1977). Who is "Daddy" revisited? The status of two-year-olds' overextended words in use and comprehension. *Journal of Child Language, 4,* 359–375.

THOMPSON, L. A., DETTERMAN, D. K., & PLOMIN, R. (1991). Associations between cognitive abilities and scholastic achievement: Genetic overlap but environmental differences. *Psychological Science, 2,* 158–165.

THOMPSON, L. A., FAGAN, J. F., & FULKER, D. W. (1991). Longitudinal prediction of specific cognitive abilities from infant novelty preference. *Child Development, 62,* 530–538.

THORNDIKE, R. L., HAGEN, E. P., & SATTLER, J. M. (1986). *The Stanford-Binet Intelligence Scale (4th edition): Guide for administering and scoring.* Chicago: Riverside.

THURSTONE, L. L. (1938). *Primary mental abilities.* Chicago: University of Chicago Press.

TIMNEY, B., MITCHELL, D. E., & CYNADER, M. (1980). Behavioral evidence for prolonged sensitivity to effects of monocular deprivation in dark-reared cats. *Journal of Neurophysiology, 43,* 1041–1054.

TINBERGEN, N. (1951). *The study of instinct.* New York: Oxford University Press.

TOBIAS, S. (1994). Interest, prior knowledge, and learning. *Review of Educational Research, 64,* 37–54.

TOMASELLO, M., DAVIS-DASILVA, M., CAMAK, L., & BARD, K. (1987). Observational learning of tool use by young chimpanzees. *Human Evolution 2,* 175–183.

TOMASELLO, M., KRUGER, A. C., & RATNER, H. H. (1993). Cultural learning. *Behavioral and Brain Sciences, 16,* 495–511.

TOMASELLO, M., SAVAGE-RUMBAUGH, S., & KRUGER, A. C. (1993). Imitative learning of actions and objects by children, chimpanzees, and enculturated chimpanzees. *Child Development, 64,* 1688–1705.

TONKOVA-YOMPOL'SKAYA, R. V. (1969). Development of speech intonation in infants during the first two years of life. *Soviet Psychology, 7,* 48–54.

TOOBY, J., & COSMIDES, L. (1992). The psychological foundations of culture. In J. H. Barkow, L. Cosmides, & J. Tooby (Eds.), *The adapted mind: Evolutionary psychology and the generation of culture.* New York: Oxford University Press.

TREHUB, S. E. (1976). The discrimination of foreign speech contrasts by infants and adults. *Child Development, 47,* 466–472.

TREHUB, S. E., SCHNEIDER, B. A., & ENDMAN, M. (1980). Developmental changes in infants' sensitivity to octave-band noises. *Journal of Experimental Child Psychology, 29,* 282–293.

TREHUB, S. E., TRAINOR, L. J., & UNYK, A. M. (1993). Music and speech processing in the first year of life. In H. W. Reese (Ed.), *Advances in child development and behavior* (Vol. 24). San Diego: Academic.

TUDGE, J. R. H. (1992). Processes and consequences of peer collaboration: A Vygotskian analysis. *Child Development, 63,* 1364–1379.

TUDGE, J., PUTNAM, S., & VALSINER, J. (1996). Culture and cognition in developmental perspective. In R. B. Cairns, G. H. Elder, Jr., & E. J. Costello (Eds.), *Developmental Science.* New York: Cambridge University Press.

TUDGE, J. R. H., WINTERHOFF, P. A., & HOGAN, D. M. (1996). The cognitive consequences of collaborative problem solving with and without feedback. *Child Development, 67,* 2892–2909.

TULKIN, S. R., & KONNER, M. J. (1973). Alternative conceptions of intellectual functioning. *Human Development, 16,* 33–52.

TULVING, E. (1985). Memory and consciousness. *Canadian Psychology, 26,* 1–12.

TULVING, E. (1987). Multiple memory systems and consciousness. *Human Neurobiology, 6,* 67–80.

TURKEWITZ, G. (1993). The influence of timing on the nature of cognition. In G. Turkewitz & D. A. Devenny (Eds.), *Developmental time and timing.* Hillsdale, NJ: Erlbaum.

TURKEWITZ, G., & DEVENNY, D. A. (EDS.). (1993). *Developmental time and timing.* Hillsdale, NJ: Erlbaum.

TURKEWITZ, G., & KENNY, P. (1982). Limitations on input as a basis for neural organization and perceptual development: A preliminary theoretical statement. *Developmental Psychobiology, 15,* 357–368.

TURNBULL, C. M. (1961). *The forest people.* New York: Simon & Schuster.

TURNER, A. M., & GREENOUGH, W. T. (1985). Differential rearing effects on rat visual cortex synapses. I. Synaptic and neuronal density and synapses per neuron. *Brain Research, 329,* 195–203.

URBERG, K. A., & DOCHERTY, E. M. (1976). Development of role-taking skills in young children. *Developmental Psychology, 12,* 198–203.

USHER, J. A., & NEISSER, U. (1993). Childhood amnesia and the beginnings of memory for four early life events. *Journal of Experimental Psychology: General, 122,* 155–165.

UZGIRIS, I. C. (1964). Situational generality of conservation. *Child Development, 35,* 831–841.

UZGIRIS, I. C. (1983). Organization of sensorimotor intelligence. In M. Lewis (Ed.), *Origins of intelligence: Infancy and early childhood* (2nd edition). New York: Plenum.

UZGIRIS, I. C., & HUNT, J. McV. (1975). *Assessment in infancy: Ordinal scales of psychological development.* Urbana, IL: University of Illinois Press.

VALDEZ-MENCHACA, M. C., & WHITEHURST, G. J. (1992). Accelerating language development through picture book reading: A systematic extension to Mexican day care. *Developmental Psychology, 28,* 1106–1114.

VANDER LINDE, E., MORRONGIELLO, B. A., & ROVEE-COLLIER, C. (1985). Determinants of retention in 8-week-old infants. *Developmental Psychology, 21,* 601–613.

van LOOSBROEK, E., & SMITSMAN, A. W. (1990). Visual perception of numerosity in infancy. *Developmental Psychology, 26,* 916–922.

VARNHAGEN, C. K., MORRISON, F. J., & EVERALL, R. (1994). Age and schooling effects in story recall and story production. *Developmental Psychology, 30,* 969–979.

VASTA, R., & LIBEN, L. S. (1996). The water-level task: An intriguing puzzle. *Current Directions in Psychological Science, 5,* 171–177.

VELLUTINO, F. R., & SCANLON, D. M. (1985). Free recall of concrete and abstract words in poor and normal readers. *Journal of Experimental Child Psychology, 39,* 363–380.

VELLUTINO, F. R., SCANLON, D. M., & SPEARING, D. (1995). Semantic and phonological coding in poor and normal readers. *Journal of Experimental Child Psychology, 59,* 76–123.

VERNON, P. E., & KANTOR, L. (1986). Reaction time correlations with intelligence test scores obtained under either timed or untimed conditions. *Intelligence, 10,* 315–330.

VIDEN, P. G. (1996). Junín Quechua children's understanding of mind. *Child Development, 67,* 1707–1716.

VINTER, A. (1986). The role of movement in eliciting early imitations. *Child Development, 57,* 66–71.

VURPILLOT, E. (1968). The development of scanning strategies and their relation to visual differentiation. *Journal of Experimental Child Psychology, 6,* 632–650.

VURPILLOT, E., & BALL, W. A. (1979). The concept of identity and children's selective attention. In G. Hale and M. Lewis (Eds.), *Attention and cognitive development.* New York: Plenum.

VYGOTSKY, L. S. (1962). *Thought and language.* Cambridge, MA: MIT Press.

VYGOTSKY, L. S. (1978). *The mind in society: The development of higher psychological processes.* Cambridge, MA: Harvard University Press.

VYGOTSKY, L. S. (1981). The genesis of higher mental functions. In J. V. Wertsch (Ed.), *The concept of activity in Soviet psychology.* Armonk, NY: Sharpe.

WABER, D. P., CARLSON, D., MANN, M., MEROLA, J., & MOYLAN, P. (1984). SES-related aspects of neuropsychological performance. *Child Development, 55,* 1878–1886.

WAGNER, R. K., TORGESEN, J. K., & RASHOTTE, C. A. (1994). Development of reading-related phonological processing abilities: New evidence of bidirectional causality from a latent variable longitudinal study. *Developmental Psychology, 30,* 73–87.

WAGNER, R. K., TORGESEN, J. K., RASHOTTE, C. A., HECHT, S. A., BARKER, T. A., BURGESS, S. R., DONAHUE, J., & GARON, T. (1997). Changing relations between phonological processing abilities and word-level reading as children develop from beginning to skilled readers: A 5-year longitudinal study. *Developmental Psychology, 33,* 468–479.

WALK, R. D., & GIBSON, E. J. (1961). A comparative and analytical study of visual depth perception. *Psychological Monographs, 75* (No. 519).

WALKER, C. H. (1987). Relative importance of domain knowledge and overall aptitude on acquisition of domain-related information. *Cognition and Instruction, 2,* 25–42.

WALLEY, A. C., PISONI, D. B., & ASLIN, R. N. (1981). The role of early experience in the development of speech perception. In R. N. Aslin, J. R. Alberts, & M. R. Petersen (Eds.), *Development of perception: Psychobiological perspectives:* Vol. 1. *Audition, somatic perception, and chemical senses.* New York: Academic.

WALTON, G. E., BOWER, N. J. A., & BOWER, T. G. R. (1992). Recognition of familiar faces by newborns. *Infant Behavior and Development, 15,* 265–269.

WALTON, G. E., & BOWER, T. G. R. (1993). Newborns form prototypes in less than 1 minute. *Psychological Science, 4,* 203–205.

WARREN, A., HULSE-TROTTER, K., & TUBBS, E. C. (1991). Inducting resistance to suggestibility in children. *Law and Human Behavior, 15,* 273–285.

WARREN, A. R., & MCCLOSKEY, L. A. (1997). Language in social contexts. In J. Berko Gleason (Ed.), *The development of language* (4th edition). Boston, MA: Allyn & Bacon.

WARREN, A. R., & TATE, C. S. (1992). Egocentrism in children's telephone conversations: Recent evidence regarding Piaget's position. In R. Diaz & L. Berk (Eds.), *From social interaction to self-regulation.* Hillsdale, NJ: Erlbaum.

WARREN-LEUBECKER, A., & BOHANNON, J. N. (1989). Pragmatics: Language in social context. In J. B. Berko Gleason (Ed.), *The development of language* (2nd edition). Columbus, OH: Charles E. Merrill.

WATERS, H. S., & SCHREIBER, L. L. (1991). Sex differences in elaborative strategies: A developmental analysis. *Journal of Experimental Child Psychology, 52,* 319–335.

WAXMAN, S., & GELMAN, R. (1986). Preschoolers' use of superordinate relations in classification and language. *Cognitive Development, 1,* 139–156.

WAXMAN, S. R., & NAMY, L. L. (1997). Challenging the notion of a thematic preference in young children. *Developmental Psychology, 33,* 555–567.

WEBER, A., & STRUBE, G. (1999). Memory for events experienced and events observed. In F. E. Weinert & W. Schneider (Eds.), *The Munich Longitudinal Study on the Genesis of Individual Competencies (LOGIC).* Cambridge: Cambridge University Press.

WECHSLER, D. (1974). *Manual for the Wechsler Intelligence Scale for Children–Revised.* New York: Psychological Corporation.

WECHSLER, D. (1991). *Wechsler Intelligence Scale for Children* (3rd edition). San Antonio, TX: Psychological Corporation.

WEIKART, D. P., & SCHWEINHART, L. J. (1991). Disadvantaged children and curriculum effects. In L. Rescorla, M. C. Hyson, & K. Hirsh-Pasek (Eds.), *Academic instruction in early childhood: Challenge or pressure?* San Francisco: Jossey-Bass.

WEINBERG, R. A., SCARR, S., & WALDMAN, I. D. (1992). The Minnesota Transracial Adoption Study: A follow-up of IQ test performance at adolescence. *Intelligence, 16,* 117–135.

WEINERT, F. E., & SCHNEIDER, W. (1986). *The Munich Longitudinal Study on the Genesis of Individual Competencies (LOGIC).* Munich, Germany: Max Planck Institute for Psychological Research.

WEINERT, F. E., & SCHNEIDER, W. (1992). *The Munich Longitudinal Study on the Genesis of Individual Competencies (LOGIC).* Munich, Germany: Max Planck Institute for Psychological Research.

WELCH-ROSS, M. K. (1995). An integrative model of the development of autobiographical memory. *Developmental Review, 15,* 338–365.

WELCH-ROSS, M. K., & SCHMIDT, C. R. (1996). Gender-schema development and children's constructive story memory: Evidence for a developmental model. *Child Development, 67,* 820–835.

WELLMAN, H. M. (1988). The early development of memory strategies. In F. Weinert & M. Perlmutter (Eds.), *Memory development: Universal changes and individual differences.* Hillsdale, NJ: Erlbaum.

WELLMAN, H. M. (1990). *The child's theory of mind.* Cambridge, MA: MIT Press.

WELLMAN, H. M., & BARTSCH, K. (1988). Young children's reasoning about beliefs. *Cognition, 30,* 239–277.

WELLMAN, H. M., & ESTES, D. (1986). Early understanding of mental entities: A reexamination of childhood realism. *Child Development, 57,* 910–923.

WELLMAN, H. M., & GELMAN, S. A. (1998). Knowledge acquisition in foundational domains. In D. Kuhn & R. S. Siegler (Vol. Eds.), *Cognitive, language, and perceptual development,* Vol. 2. In W. Damon (Gen. Ed.), *Handbook of child psychology.* New York: Wiley.

WELLMAN, H. M., & JOHNSON, C. N. (1979). Understanding mental processes: A developmental study of remember and forget. *Child Development, 50,* 79–88.

WELLMAN, H. M., & LEMPERS, J. D. (1977). The naturalistic communicative and organismic points of view. In D. B. Harris (Ed.), *The concept of development.* Minneapolis: University of Minnesota Press.

WELLMAN, H. M., RITTER, K., & FLAVELL, J. H. (1975). Deliberate memory behavior in the delayed reactions of very young children. *Developmental Psychology, 11,* 780–787.

WELLMAN, H. M., & SOMERVILLE, S. C. (1980). Quasi-naturalistic tasks in the study of cognition: The memory-related skills of toddlers. In M. Perlmutter (Ed.), *Naturalistic approaches to children's memory.* San Francisco: Jossey-Bass

WERKER, J. F., GILBERT, J. H. V., HUMPHREY, K., & TEES, R. C. (1981). Developmental aspects of cross-language speech perception. *Child Development, 52,* 349–355.

WERTSCH, J. V., & TULVISTE, P. (1992). L. S. Vygotsky and contemporary developmental psychology. *Developmental Psychology, 28,* 548–557.

WEST, R. F., STANOVICH, K. E., & MITCHELL, H. (1993). Reading in the real world and its correlates. *Reading Research Quarterly, 28,* 34–50.

WEXLER-SHERMAN, C., GARDNER, H., & FELDMAN, D. H. (1988). A pluralistic view of early assessment: The Project Spectrum approach. *Theory Into Practice, 27,* 77–83.

WHELDALL, K., & JOSEPH, R. (1986). Young black children's sentence comprehension skills: A comparison of performance in standard English and Jamaican Creole. *First Language, 6,* 149–154.

WHITE, B. L. (1978). *Experience and environment: Major influences on the development of the young child* (Vol. 2). Englewood Cliffs, NJ: Prentice-Hall.

WHITE, S. H., & PILLEMER, D. B. (1979). Childhood amnesia and the development of a socially accessible memory system. In J. F. Kihlstrom & F. J. Evans (Eds.), *Functional disorders of memory.* Hillsdale, NJ: Erlbaum.

WHITEHURST, G. J., FALCO, F., LONIGAN, C. J., FISCHAL, J. E., DEBARYSHE, B. D., VALDEZ-MANCHACA, M. C., & CAUFIELD, M. (1988). Accelerating language development through picture book reading. *Developmental Psychology, 24,* 552–559.

WHITEHURST, G. J., & LONIGAN, C. J. (1998). Child development and emergent literacy. *Child Development, 69,* 848–872.

WHITEHURST, G. J., & SONNENSCHEIN, S. (1985). The development of communication: A functional analysis. In G. J. Whitehurst (Ed.), *Annals of child development* (Vol. 2). Greenwich, CT: JAI.

WHITEN, A., & HAM, R. (1992). On the nature and evolution of imitation in the animal kingdom: Reappraisal of a century of research. In P. Slater, J. Rosenblatt, C. Beer, & M. Milinski (Eds.), *Advances in the study of behavior* (Vol. 21). New York: Academic.

WHITNEY, P., & KUNEN, S. (1983). Development of hierarchical conceptual relationships in children's semantic memories. *Journal of Experimental Child Psychology, 35,* 278–293.

WICKELGREN, L. (1967). Convergence in the human newborn. *Journal of Experimental Child Psychology, 5,* 74–85.

WILCOX, J., & WEBSTER, E. (1980). Early discourse behavior: An analysis of children's responses to listener feedback. *Child Development, 51,* 1120–1125.

WILKINSON, A. (1976). Counting strategies and semantic analysis as applied to class inclusion. *Cognitive Psychology, 8,* 64–85.

WILLATTS, P. (1990). Development of problem-solving strategies in infancy. In D. F. Bjorklund (Ed.), *Children's strategies: Contemporary views of cognitive development.* Hillsdale, NJ: Erlbaum.

WILSON, R. S. (1983). The Louisville Twin Study: Developmental synchronies in behavior. *Child Development, 54,* 298–316.

WILSON, S. P., & KIPP, K. (1998). The development of efficient inhibition: Evidence from directed-forgetting tasks. *Developmental Review, 18,* 86-123.

WIMMER, H., & PERNER, J. (1983). Beliefs about beliefs: Representation and constraining function of wrong beliefs in young children's understanding of deception. *Cognition, 13,* 103–128.

WINER, G. A. (1980). Class-inclusion reasoning in children: A review of the empirical literature. *Child Development, 51,* 309–328.

WINICK, M., MEYER, K. K., & HARRIS, R. C. (1975). Malnutrition and environmental enrichment by early adoption. *Science, 190,* 1173–1175.

WITELSON, S. F. (1985). On hemisphere specialization and cerebral plasticity from birth; Mark II. In C. Best (Ed.), *Hemispheric function and collaboration in the child.* New York: Academic.

WITELSON, S. F. (1987). Neurobiological aspects of language in children. *Child Development, 58,* 653–688.

WITKIN, H. A., DYK, R. B., FATERSON, H. F., GOODENOUGH, D. R., & KARP, S. A. (1962). *Psychological differentiation.* New York: Wiley.

WITKIN, H. A., GOODENOUGH, D. R., & KARP, S. A. (1967). Stability of cognitive style from childhood to young adulthood. *Journal of Personality and Social Psychology, 7,* 291–300.

WITKIN, H. A., LEWIS, H. B., HERTZMAN, M., MACHOVER, K., MEISSNER, P., & WAPNER, S. (1954). *Personality through perception.* New York: Harper.

WOOD, D., BRUNER, J. S., & ROSS, G. (1976). The role of tutoring in problem-solving. *Journal of Child Psychology and Psychiatry, 17,* 89–100.

WOODS, B. T., & CAREY, S. (1979). Language deficits after apparent clinical recovery from childhood aphasia. *Annals of Neurology, 6,* 405–409.

WOOLLEY, J. D. (1997). Thinking about fantasy: Are children fundamentally different thinkers and believers from adults? *Child Development, 68,* 991–1011.

WOOLLEY, J. D., & BRUELL, M. J. (1996). Young children's awareness of the origins of their mental representations. *Developmental Psychology, 32,* 335–346.

WOOLLEY, J. D., & WELLMAN, H. M. (1992). Children's conceptions of dreams. *Cognitive Development, 7,* 365–380.

WOOLLEY, J. D., & WELLMAN, H. M. (1993). Origin and truth: Young children's understanding of imaginary mental representations. *Child Development, 64,* 1–17.

WOZNIAK, R. H. (1972). Verbal regulation of motor behavior: Soviet research and non-Soviet replications. *Human Development, 15,* 13–57.

WYNN, K. (1992). Addition and subtraction by human infants. *Nature, 358,* 749–750.

YAKOVLEV, P. I., & LECOURS, A. R. (1967). The myelenogenetic cycles of regional maturation of the brain.

In A. Minkowski (Ed.), *Regional development of the brain in early life.* Oxford: Blackwell.

YEATES, K. O., MACPHEE, D., CAMPBELL, F. A., & RAMEY, C. T. (1983). Maternal IQ and home environment as determinants of early childhood intellectual competence: A developmental analysis. *Developmental Psychology, 19,* 731–739.

YOUNGBLOOD, L. M., & DUNN, J. (1995). Individual differences in young children's pretend play with mother and sibling: Links to relationships and understanding of other people's feelings and beliefs. *Child Development, 66,* 1472–1492.

YOUNGER, B. (1993). Understanding category members as "the same sort of thing": Explicit categorization in ten-month infants. *Child Development, 64,* 309–320.

YOUNGER, B., & GOTLIEB, S. (1988). Development of categorization skills: Changes in the nature or structure of infant form categories? *Developmental Psychology, 24,* 611–619.

YUSSEN, S. R., & BIRD, J. E. (1979). The development of metacognitive awareness in memory, communication, and attention. *Journal of Experimental Child Psychology, 28,* 300–313.

YUSSEN, S. R., & LEVY, V. M., JR. (1975). Developmental changes in predicting one's own span of short-term memory. *Journal of Experimental Child Psychology, 19,* 502–508.

ZELAZO, P. D., CARTER, A., REZNICK, J. S., & FRYE, D. (1997). Early development of executive function: A problem-solving framework. *Review of General Psychology, 1,* 198–226.

ZELAZO, P. D., & FRYE, D. (1997). Cognitive complexity and control: A theory of the development of deliberate reasoning and intentional action. In M. Stamenov (Ed.), *Language Structure, Discourse, and the Access to Consciousness.* Amsterdam & Philadelphia: John Benjamins.

ZELAZO, P. D., FRYE, D., & RAPUS, T. (1996). An age-related dissociation between knowing rules and using them. *Cognitive Development, 11,* 37–63.

ZELAZO, P. D., & JACQUES, S. (1997). Children's rule use: Representation, reflection and cognitive control. *Annals of Child Development, 12.* London: Jessica Kingsley.

ZELAZO, P. D., KEARSLEY, R. B., & STACK, D. M. (1995). Mental representation for visual sequences: Increased speed of central processing from 22 to 32 months. *Intelligence, 20,* 41–63.

Zelazo, P. D., & Reznick, J. S. (1991). Age-related asynchrony of knowledge and action. *Child Development, 62,* 719–735.

Zelazo, P. D., Reznick, J. S., & Piñon, D. E. (1995). Response control and the execution of rules. *Developmental Psychology, 31,* 508–517.

Zeskind, P. S. (1996, April). Infant crying: A biobehavioral synchrony between infants and caregivers. Paper presented at the Conference on Human Development, Birmingham, AL.

Zeskind, P. S., & Ramey, C. T. (1978). Fetal malnutrition: An experimental study of its consequences on infant development in two caregiver environments. *Child Development, 49,* 1155–1162.

Zeskind, P. S., & Ramey, C. T. (1981). Sequelae of fetal malnutrition: A longitudinal, transactional, and synergistic approach. *Child Development, 52,* 213–218.

Author Index

Abelson, R. P., 285
Abrahamson, A., 95
Abramovitch, R., 337
Abravanel, E., 196, 197, 198, 199, 348
Acito, M. A., 225
Ackerman, B. P., 134, 228, 230, 258, 260, 263, 291
Ackil, J. K., 247, 249
Adams, G. R., 98
Adams, M. J., 64, 365, 369, 373, 383, 400
Adams, R. J., 166, 181
Adey, P. S., 101
Adler, S., 288
Aguiar, A. 200
Ahmed, A., 218
Ainsworth, M. D. S., 338
Aivano, S., 126
Alampay, D. A., 182
Alberts, D. M., 395
Alexander, J. M., 69, 224, 261, 263, 420
Alexander, R. D., 335, 343, 362
Allen, D., 165
Allen, L., 471
Allen, T. W., 100
Alessandri, S. M., 312
Alibali, M. W., 135, 137
Als, H., 32
Aman, C. J., 245
Amatruda, C., 409
Ames, E., 174
Ames, E. W., 461
Amsel, E., 316, 328, 332
Anderson, D., 343
Anderson, D. R., 141

Anderson, K. J., 305
Anderson, L. M., 46
Anderson, R. C., 372
Andreassen, C., 265
Anglin, J. M., 180, 228, 229, 230
Anisfeld, M., 196
Annett, M., 49, 189
Anooshian, L. J., 184, 185
Antell, S. E., 203, 379
Antinucci, F., 87
Applebaum, M. I., 173, 174, 472, 473
Arnett, J., 98
Arterberry, M., 176
Ashbaker, M. H., 371
Ashcraft, M. H., 139, 382, 383
Asher, S. R., 376
Aslin, R. N., 163, 165, 172, 174, 238, 298
Astington, J. W., 66, 216, 217
Atkinson, R. C., 119
Ault, R. L., 124
Ausley, J. A., 239, 240
Avis, J., 215
Azmitia, M., 69

Baddeley, A. D., 124
Badian, N. A., 386
Baenninger, M., 188
Baer, R. A., 147
Bahrick, L. E., 174, 177, 343
Bai, D. L., 176
Baillargeon, R., 87, 109, 200, 201, 202, 203, 206
Baker, D. P., 387
Baker, L., 372
Baker-Ward, L., 132, 139, 235, 244, 245, 247, 263, 264

Balaban, M. T., 46
Balaban, T., 354, 355, 356, 432
Baldwin, A., 477
Baldwin, C., 477
Ball, W. A., 143
Band, G. P. H., 143
Bandura, A., 188, 335, 336, 337, 338, 356, 363
Banks, M. S., 165, 192
Barclay, C. R., 232
Barkley, R. A., 121
Barkow, J. H., 23, 25, 56
Barnard, K. E., 305
Barnes, M. A., 139
Barnett, W. S., 462, 463, 466, 478
Baron-Cohen, S., 221, 222, 232
Baroody, A. J., 382
Barrera, M. E., 166
Bartlett, F. C., 76, 253, 260
Bartsch, K., 215, 215, 221
Bates, E. A., 21, 157, 301, 303, 310
Batterman, N., 285
Battin, D., 247
Bauer, P. J., 198, 199, 229, 230, 238, 239, 241, 251, 357, 358
Bauer, R. H., 414
Baugh, J., 287
Baumrind, D., 36
Bayley, N., 409, 410
Beach, D. R., 255
Beal, C. R., 290, 355
Bebko, J. M., 314
Becker, W. C., 456
Beckett, C., 461
Behrend, D. A., 308
Beilin, H., 99
Bell, M. A., 45, 147

Subject Index

Abstract dimensional stage, in Case's neo-Piagetian theory, 106
Abstract tier, in Fischer's skill theory, 104, 105
Abstraction principle, 379
Academic preschools, costs and benefits of, 396–399. *See also* Compensatory education
Accommodation, in Piaget's theory, 77–78, 79, 80, 83, 104
defined, 77
and imitation, 85–87
Accommodation, of the eye lens, 165
Achievement tests. *See* Graduate Record Exam; Scholastic Aptitude Test
Active genotype → environment effects, in Scarr and McCartney's theory, 35–36, 447, 449
Active intermodal mapping, 197, 198
Active rehearsal. *See* Cumulative rehearsal
Activity. *See* Intrinsic activity
Acuity, visual, 165
Adaptation. *See also* Accommodation; Assimilation, in Piaget's theory
defined, 76
in Piaget's theory, 76–77, 81
in triarchic theory, 423
Adaptive nature of immaturity. *See* Immaturity
Adaptive strategy choice model, 27, 135, 136, 316, 369, 385

Addition. *See* Mathematics
in infancy, 203–205
Adoption studies, 35, 36, 445, 446, 448
Age vs. schooling, effects on intelligence, 394, 395
Allocation of study time, 259
Altruism, influence of genetics, 34
Ambiguity
perceptual, 182, 183
role in humor, 352
Ambiguous figures, interpretation of, 182, 183
American College Testing Assessment (ACT), 412, 413
American Sign Language, 295
Analogical reasoning, 320–326
role of knowledge, 324, 325
role of metacognition, 325, 326
in Piaget's theory, 321
Analysis and computation phases, in Locke's neurolinguistic theory of language development, 300–303
Analytical thinking, 426
Androgen, in sex-stereotypic activities, 359, 360
prenatal, gender differences in thinking, 53
A-not-B object permanence task, 85, 87, 218
and neocortical development, 45
and inhibition, 147, 149
and memory, 236
Anoxia, 440
Anticipatory images, 195

Appearance/reality distinction, 209–212
Apprenticeship in thinking, 63
Arbitrariness, in language, 276
Architectural constraints (innateness), 13, 40, 41, 110, 154, 202, 206, 304, 480, 481
Arithmetic. *See* Mathematics
Articulation rate, 124, 125
Articulatory loop, 124
Assimilation, in Piaget's theory, 77–81, 86, 104
defined, 77
Attention, 140–145
capacity, 140
and incidental learning, 141
in infancy, 141, 142, 166, 167
and inhibition, 143
selective, 141–143, 145, 355
strategies of, 143
to television, 141
understanding of, 143, 145, 224
Attention processes, in Bandura's social cognitive theory, 336
Attention span, 141
Attractiveness, in infant attention, 169, 170
Attributions, of success and failure
cultural differences in, 268
and metacognition, 267
and strategy use, 268
Audition (hearing)
in childhood, 183
and developmental timing, 31, 32
in infancy, 160–165
Autism, and theory of mind, 221, 222